African American National Biography

African American National Biography

SECOND EDITION

HENRY LOUIS GATES JR.

EVELYN BROOKS HIGGINBOTHAM

Editors in Chief

VOLUME 3: CHANDLER, DANA C., JR. – DICKINSON, CASTOR

OXFORD
UNIVERSITY PRESS

OXFORD
UNIVERSITY PRESS

Oxford University Press is a department of the University of Oxford.
It furthers the University's objective of excellence in research, scholarship,
and education by publishing worldwide.

Oxford   New York
Auckland   Cape Town   Dar es Salaam   Hong Kong   Karachi
Kuala Lumpur   Madrid   Melbourne   Mexico City   Nairobi
New Delhi   Shanghai   Taipei   Toronto

With offices in

Argentina   Austria   Brazil   Chile   Czech Republic   France   Greece
Guatemala   Hungary   Italy   Japan   Poland   Portugal   Singapore
South Korea   Switzerland   Thailand   Turkey   Ukraine   Vietnam

Oxford is a registered trademark of Oxford University Press in the UK and certain other countries.

Published in the United States of America by
Oxford University Press
198 Madison Avenue, New York, NY 10016

Library of Congress Cataloging-in-Publication Data
African American national biography / editors in chief Henry Louis Gates Jr., Evelyn Brooks Higginbotham. – 2nd ed.
p. cm.
Includes bibliographical references and index.
ISBN 978-0-19-999036-8 (volume 1; hdbk.); ISBN 978-0-19-999037-5 (volume 2; hdbk.); ISBN 978-0-19-999038-2 (volume 3; hdbk.);
ISBN 978-0-19-999039-9 (volume 4; hdbk.); ISBN 978-0-19-999040-5 (volume 5; hdbk.); ISBN 978-0-19-999041-2 (volume 6; hdbk.);
ISBN 978-0-19-999042-9 (volume 7; hdbk.); ISBN 978-0-19-999043-6 (volume 8; hdbk.); ISBN 978-0-19-999044-3 (volume 9; hdbk.);
ISBN 978-0-19-999045-0 (volume 10; hdbk.); ISBN 978-0-19-999046-7 (volume 11; hdbk.); ISBN 978-0-19-999047-4 (volume 12;
hdbk.); ISBN 978-0-19-992077-8 (12-volume set; hdbk.)
1. African Americans – Biography – Encyclopedias.   2. African Americans – History – Encyclopedias.
I. Gates, Henry Louis.   II. Higginbotham, Evelyn Brooks, 1945-
E185.96.A4466 2012
920'.009296073 – dc23
[B]
2011043281

1 3 5 7 9 8 6 4 2
Printed in the United States of America
on acid-free paper

African American National Biography

C CONTINUED

Chandler, Dana C., Jr. (7 Apr. 1941–), visual artist, educator, and activist, was born in Lynn, Massachusetts, the second of seven children of Dana C. Chandler Sr., a longshoreman, and Ruth Chandler. At age five Dana Chandler Jr. and his family moved to Roxbury, Massachusetts, a predominantly African American community. Chandler's parents, who had not attended school beyond the ninth and eleventh grades, raised their children to recognize the importance of completing high school and earning a college degree. Chandler grew up in a poor, working-class family and attended Boston's public schools throughout childhood and adolescence. He received primary and elementary education at the Asa Gray and Sherwin schools. After a six-month hospital stay to treat rheumatic fever, he transferred from Boston Latin School to J.P. Timility Junior High School. At Boston Technical High School his art teachers Ralph Rosenthal and Gunnar Munnick inspired him to become an artist. In 1959 Chandler graduated from Boston Technical and received the school's first annual art award. After graduation he remained at Boston Technical for two years serving as a student assistant.

In 1962 Chandler got married (his wife's name is unknown) and was accepted into the Massachusetts College of Art in Boston. In 1963 he helped found the Boston Artists Association, and he and his wife had a daughter before filing for divorce. In college Chandler worked full-time for the Jamaica Plain Area Planning Action Council (APAC). Chandler and fellow residents of the Jamaica Plain housing project established APAC to address the needs of African American communities affected by Lyndon Johnson's poverty program.

After graduating from the Massachusetts College of Art in 1967 with a B.S. in Education, Chandler witnessed a riot that strengthened his commitment to militant black nationalism. In June 1967 police brutally beat many of his friends for protesting inequity in the welfare system at Grove Hall in Dorchester, Massachusetts. As one of many urban insurrections in America during the 1960s, the riot compelled Chandler to combine visual art and social and political activism. From this time on he used his paintbrush as a weapon to retaliate against antiblack racism in America.

By 1968 Chandler was engaged in struggles against racism in American political, social, educational, and art institutions. Chandler worked briefly as a researcher for the Brandeis-Lindbergh Center for the Study of Violence, hired to interview black Americans to determine why they committed violent acts. Perceiving this research as reinforcement of racist oppression, Chandler interviewed violent white Americans instead. Shortly thereafter he became director of the African Arts curriculum project for the Educational Development Center in Newton, Massachusetts, a white upper-middle-class suburb. He also served as youth organizer for the Model Cities program and worked briefly with Elma Lewis at Lewis's National Center for Afro-American Art. In 1969 Chandler challenged centuries of racism and Eurocentrism in American art as curator of *Twelve Black Artists from Boston*, an exhibition at the Rose Art Museum in Waltham, Massachusetts. Presented by the Afro-American Organization, a group of black artists in Boston, and displayed from 20 July to 31 August, the exhibition showcased the long-neglected brilliance of black visual artists; among the artists included in the show were CALVIN BURNETT, Gary Rickson, Richard Yarde, and Alfred J. Smith Jr. In 1970, on behalf of all African Americans, Chandler presented a proposal to the Boston Museum of Fine Arts and local newspapers requesting millions of dollars in government reparations for enduring centuries of institutional racism. In response, the museum hosted the exhibition *Afro-American Artists, New York and Boston*.

In retaliation against Chandler's antiracist verbal and artistic statements during a time of heightened racial tensions in America, vandals destroyed and set fire to his art studio in 1971. He obtained a new studio space at Northeastern University in exchange for teaching a course there in African American art history. Also in 1971 Dr. William Holmes, the president of Simmons College in Boston, arranged for Chandler to be hired as an assistant professor of art and art history in the college's art department. During the early 1970s Chandler was a cultural critic for the Massachusetts periodical the *Bay State Banner*.

From 8 March to 2 April 1976 Chandler's exhibition *If the Shoe Fits, Hear It! Paintings and Drawings, 1967–1976* was displayed at the Northeastern University art gallery. In 1977 he created the African American Master Artists-in-Residence Program (AAMARP) in the division of fine arts at Northeastern University to provide Boston's black artists opportunities to interact with one another. Chandler directed the program for several years and was one of its resident artists.

By 1986 Chandler had given lectures, participated in exhibits, and been a visiting professor at hundreds of colleges and universities and had created several thousand works. He had also married his second wife, Deborah Dancy, with whom he had five children. On 4 March 1987 the exhibition *Dana Chandler Retrospective 1967–1987* opened at the Massachusetts College of Art and Huntington Avenue Gallery. In 1997 Chandler's exhibition *KKKrimes against Womanity* was displayed in the Trustman Art Gallery at Simmons College, at which time Chandler served as the college's interim director of African American studies. In 2004 he contributed paintings to the exhibition *AAMARP the Legacy*, celebrating the program's twenty-fifth anniversary, and his murals were featured in the exhibition *Walls of Heritage, Walls of Pride* at the Cambridge Arts Council gallery.

Uncompromising in his assessment of racism, sexism, and racial violence in America, Dana C. Chandler Jr. has made significant contributions to African American and American art, history, and culture. Chandler's works are in the collections of prestigious museums and galleries in America and are represented in the art history slide collections of more than a hundred colleges and universities. His posters, drawings, paintings, murals, and collages balance aesthetic form and the function of political messages. Chandler's art encourages black women to practice self-defense, challenges stereotypes regarding black sexuality, protests genocide, and emphasizes the threat that drugs pose to black liberation. He also celebrates African American culture through positive images of black neighborhoods and families, such as his series *Black on Black by Black for Black Drawings*. Chandler's life and works embody the ways in which art, intellect, and activism together can communicate antiracist messages.

FURTHER READING

Dana Chandler's papers are housed at the Smithsonian Institution's Archives of American Art in Washington, D.C. The *Dana Chandler Interviews*, conducted by Robert Brown from 11 March to 5 May 1993, are also housed at the Smithsonian's Archives of American Art.

Chandler, Dana. *Dana Chandler Retrospective, 1967–1987* (1987).

Chandler, Dana. *If the Shoe Fits, Hear It!: Paintings and Drawings, 1967–1976* (1976).

Fax, Elton. "Dana Chandler," in *Black Artists of the New Generation* (1977).

KIMBERLY CURTIS

Chaney, James Earl (30 May 1943–21 June 1964), plasterer and civil rights activist, was born in Meridian, Mississippi, to Ben Chaney, at that time a worker in an ice cream factory, and Fannie Lee (Roberth) Chaney, a cook and domestic. Like many of their black neighbors in Meridian, the Chaneys struggled to provide for their five children, of whom James, or J. E., as he was known, was the second born and the eldest son. When J. E. was seven Ben Chaney found steady work as a plasterer, one of the better-paying trades open to African Americans in Mississippi. His work required frequent travel, however, leaving J. E. as the eldest male in the house, a role he took seriously, ensuring that his younger siblings performed their chores. J. E. was protective of his mother, who took in laundry and worked in a white school to supplement her husband's wages, but had an uneasy relationship with his father, who kept a girlfriend in Laurel, Mississippi. Ben Chaney, a taciturn man, taught his children to be polite and respectful to white people, but never to trust them completely.

That advice was born of family history. Both Ben's cousin and Fannie Lee Chaney's stepgrandfather had "come up missing" for defying white supremacy and for refusing to stay in the place required of them by Jim Crow etiquette.

Hoping to provide her children with the education that she had been denied, Fannie Lee Chaney sent her five children to St. Joseph's Academy in Meridian, a private Roman Catholic school. When J. E. was in his early teens, however, his mother was forced to give up her various jobs to look after her own mother, who was sick. Her children were transferred to Meridian's segregated public schools. In 1959 when J. E. was sixteen, he entered Meridian's Harris Junior College and befriended the sons of C. R. Darden, the president of the Mississippi NAACP. He also participated in his first civil rights protest—wearing self-made paper NAACP buttons to class. When the college principal demanded that Chaney remove the buttons, he refused and was suspended for a week. Chaney was expelled from the college in 1960 for fighting, and he attempted to enlist in the army. He passed the aptitude test but, as an asthmatic, failed his physical. J. E. then hitchhiked with a friend to Wichita Falls, Texas, where he worked for several months hauling hay before returning to Meridian. Although still ill at ease around his father, he began working with him as a plasterer, joined

James Earl Chaney, civil rights worker who, along with two other men, was abducted, killed, and buried an earthen dam near Philadelphia, Mississippi, 21 June 1964. (AP Images.)

the union, and began serving his apprenticeship in early 1961. Chaney's hours were long and required travel throughout the state, where he witnessed a number of the civil rights protests that had gotten under way that year in the South's most resistant segregationist state. He may have taken part in some of these protests, but formally began his civil rights career in October 1963, when Sue Brown, a Harris student who was youth council president of the Meridian NAACP, asked him to meet with Matt Suarez, a full-time civil rights organizer for the Congress on Racial Equality (CORE). Street-savvy, and somewhat restless, Chaney was exactly the type of volunteer Suarez had been looking for: someone who knew whom to trust in Meridian's black community, and whom to fear and avoid in the white community. Having driven throughout the state in search of plastering jobs, J. E. proved invaluable in ferrying Suarez to clandestine night-time meetings with other organizers. In early 1964 he also befriended and worked with Mickey and Rita Schwerner, white CORE activists from New York City, to build a community center in Meridian for black teenagers. The community center became the hub of civil rights activity in Meridian, offering a library and classes in black history as well as advice on voter registration. In Meridian, as in most of Mississippi, only a handful of African Americans were allowed to vote.

In April 1964 Chaney became a full-time organizer for CORE. Among other activities he helped organize the picketing of a Woolworth's in downtown Meridian, CORE's most direct challenge to segregation in Mississippi's second largest city up to that time. The black community was almost unanimous in its support for the boycott, though the only black citizen to cross the picket line was Chaney's own aunt, who was determined to get her shopping done that Saturday, whatever her nephew said. In mid-May CORE organized another round of picketing of the Meridian Woolworth's, which led to the arrests of eleven protestors, including J. E.'s eleven-year-old brother, Ben Jr.

Chaney also began working with Schwerner and other activists in voter registration efforts in nearby Clarke and Neshoba counties in preparation for that year's Mississippi Summer Project, also known as Freedom Summer. Organized by ROBERT P. MOSES and a coalition of Mississippi civil rights groups, Freedom Summer would bring more than a thousand northern civil rights volunteers into Mississippi in an effort to force a confrontation with the state and local authorities. Moses, Chaney, and their fellow activists hoped that such a confrontation would finally force the federal government to pass a civil rights law to end segregation and secure black voting rights. Chaney and Schwerner's central role in organizing Meridian and Neshoba County brought them to the attention of local white supremacists. When the police arrested Schwerner during the Meridian Woolworth's protests that May, Billy Birdsong, a leading member of the city's Ku Klux Klan, attacked him in the police station. The police officers present did nothing to intervene.

On 20 June 1964 Chaney and Schwerner returned to Meridian following a week-long training session for Freedom Summer volunteers in Oxford, Ohio. During that meeting Bob Moses and others reminded the volunteers of the strong likelihood that they could be beaten, jailed, or killed. The following morning the two men drove off for Longdale in Neshoba County to investigate a recent attack by Klansmen on the black Mount Zion Methodist Church, which Chaney and Schwerner had addressed three weeks earlier as part of their voter registration efforts. The two had hoped to use the church as a Freedom School during the Mississippi Summer Project. Accompanied by Andrew Goodman, a white anthropology major from Queens College in New York City whom they had met at Oxford, Chaney and Schwerner arrived in Longdale to find that Klansmen had razed the church building and had badly beaten several members of the congregation. The three civil rights workers also learned that the same men responsible for that attack had vowed to kill Schwerner, a goateed, Jewish left-wing New Yorker who seemed to embody for these white supremacists everything that was to be despised about "outside agitator" civil rights activists.

At 3 o'clock that afternoon, while driving back to Meridian, Chaney, Schwerner, and Goodman were flagged down by Neshoba County Deputy Sheriff Cecil Ray Price, an ally of the Klansmen. Price arrested the men, ostensibly because Chaney had been speeding and his station wagon had a flat tire, and held them in the Neshoba County jail in Philadelphia until 10:30 P.M., when Sheriff Lawrence Rainey ordered the men released.

Ten miles south of town Chaney's station wagon was stopped again by Deputy Price, this time accompanied by three carloads of members of the Ku Klux Klan, whom either he or Sheriff Rainey had alerted, as Price and Rainey were both Klan members. The three civil rights workers were then bundled into Price's car. Chaney resisted and was clubbed by Price's leather blackjack. The three men were then driven off the main road into the woods.

The Klansmen shot Schwerner through the heart and Goodman through the chest, both at point blank range, killing them instantly. One account of the executions suggests that Chaney pleaded for his life with one of the men, whom he knew from Meridian, but to no avail. Chaney was then shot through the abdomen by one of the assailants, then shot in the lower back by another, who also fired a third, fatal, shot through the black man's head. The bodies of the three men were then buried under an earthen dam being constructed in an isolated part of Neshoba County.

Two days later Chaney's station wagon was found, torched. Despite the entreaties of the three civil rights workers' families and fellow activists, who searched in vain for their comrades, the FBI moved slowly to investigate the disappearance and to provide protection for the organizers arriving for Freedom Summer. The bodies were unearthed six weeks later, though it would take another four months before federal authorities charged eighteen white men with conspiracy to deny the civil rights of James Chaney, Michael Schwerner, and Andrew Goodman. After a series of delays eight men, including Deputy Price, were found guilty of conspiracy by an all-white jury in November 1967. None of the seven men served more than six years in prison. In 2003 Mississippi Congressman BENNIE THOMPSON began lobbying the U.S. Justice Department to reopen the case and to try the surviving conspirators for the murders of Chaney, Goodman, and Schwerner. In January 2005, Edgar Ray Killen, a preacher and recruiter for the Klan in Neshoba County in the 1960s, was arrested for the murders of Chaney, Goodman, and Schwerner. Killen had been among those arrested for the murders in 1967, but had been set free when one of the twelve jurors had refused to convict a minister. In June 2005 a racially integrated jury found Killen not guilty of murder of the three men, but guilty of manslaughter for his role in recruiting the mob that carried out the killings. Killen, then eighty years of age, was sentenced to the maximum sentence of sixty years in prison.

Historians have noted several legacies of the June 1964 murders in Neshoba County. Although the deaths of their comrades haunted Mississippi activists, the Mississippi Summer volunteers were also inspired to build on the work of Chaney, Goodman, and Schwerner, even though they continued to face violence and intimidation. At least three activists were killed and scores injured, seventy buildings were bombed or burned, and more than one thousand civil rights activists were arrested in Mississippi that summer. Pressured by international outrage at the killings, the federal government, too, stepped up its efforts to enforce the rule of law in Mississippi, until the 1965 Voting Rights Act finally brought democracy to that troubled state. The most significant consequence of the murders was perhaps more prosaic, and more personal. Rita Schwerner lost her husband. Robert and Carolyn Goodman lost their son. And one week before the murders, and while he was in Ohio, Chaney's girlfriend, Mary Nan McCoy, gave birth to his daughter, Angela. James Chaney would never see, and never hold, his daughter.

FURTHER READING

Cagin, Seth, and Philip Dray. *We Are Not Afraid: The Story of Goodman, Schwerner, and Chaney and the Civil Rights Campaign for Mississippi* (1988).

Dittmer, John. *Local People: The Struggle for Rights in Mississippi* (1995).

Fireside, Harvey. *The Mississippi Burning Civil Rights Murder Conspiracy Trial* (2002).

Huie, William Bradford. *Three Lives for Mississippi* (1965; 2000).

STEVEN J. NIVEN

Chaney, John (21 Jan. 1932–), basketball coach and educator, was born in Jacksonville, Florida, to Earley Chaney (whose maiden name is not now known) and a father he never knew. The oldest of three children, Chaney grew up in a poor section of Jacksonville called Black Bottom. Chaney's mother was a domestic worker for a white lawyer's family in the Riverside section of the city. Although Chaney never met his biological father, his stepfather, Sylvester Chaney, was a major influence in his life. Chaney's experience of childhood poverty would play a major role in his lifelong commitment to improving the lives of the student athletes under his charge.

Chaney moved to Philadelphia, Pennsylvania, at the age of fourteen when his stepfather got a job at the Veteran's Hospital. Chaney emerged as a basketball star at Ben Franklin High School in Philadelphia. Despite being named the MVP of the Philadelphia Public League in 1951, he received no scholarship offers from the local college basketball programs but was recruited by Bethune-Cookman College in Daytona, Florida, and received a basketball scholarship. At Bethune-Cookman he was named a National Association of Intercollegiate Athletes (NAIA) All-American and was selected as MVP of the NAIA tournament in 1953. Beyond the basketball court, Chaney learned valuable lessons from the school's founder MARY MCLEOD

BETHUNE. Indeed, Chaney never forgot the message of the revered civil rights leader that those who rise, must lift. Chaney met his wife Jeanne at Bethune-Cookman and they were married in Philadelphia in 1955. The couple had three children.

In the early 1950s African Americans had a difficult time breaking into the NBA, as many teams still had unofficial quotas on the number of black players on each team. Therefore Chaney was forced to continue his playing career in the less prestigious, though not less competitive, Eastern Basketball League. Chaney played for Sunbury from 1955 until 1963 and then served as a player-coach for Williamsport from 1963 to 1966. Individual success abounded for Chaney in the Eastern League as he was named a league All-Star seven times, including two season MVP awards. In addition, he was named MVP of the league's All-Star game in 1959 and 1960.

The Eastern League played most of its games on weekends, which allowed players to hold other jobs. Chaney began teaching in the Philadelphia public schools while playing in the Eastern League. He held several different positions until he started fulltime teaching and coaching at Sayre Junior High School in Philadelphia in 1963. After a serious car accident ended his professional playing days, Chaney took an assistant coaching position at Simon Gratz High School in Philadelphia in 1966. While at Simon Gratz, Chaney developed his trademark care and concern for his students. Chaney often cooked breakfast in the morning in the school's cafeteria for students who otherwise might not have eaten. Moreover, he would often call the students on his team at night to check and make sure that their homework was done.

Chaney's collegiate coaching career began in 1972 at Cheney State University, a small National Collegiate Athletic Association (NCAA) Division II school in Pennsylvania. He quickly turned Cheney State into one of the best Division II programs in the country. In a ten-year coaching career at the school he led the Wolves to eight NCAA tournament berths, winning the national championship in 1978. A tenured professor in the school's department of health, physical education, and recreation, he received the State of Pennsylvania Distinguished Faculty Award in 1979. Chaney received a master's degree in Urban Education from Antioch College in Ohio in 1979.

When Temple University named Peter Liacouras as the new president in 1982, one of the first steps Liacouras took was to hire John Chaney as the men's head basketball coach. Liacouras was looking to revitalize the struggling school in North Philadelphia and hiring Chaney was a key aspect of this project. It did not take long for Chaney to prove Liacouras right. In just his second season, in 1984, Chaney led the Owls to their first NCAA tournament win since 1958. During the 1987–1988 season Chaney's team finished 32–2 and was ranked number one in the country before losing to Duke in the NCAA tournament. Chaney was named coach of the year by several major publications at the conclusion of the season.

Chaney's success as a coach and educator could be attributed to the discipline that he instilled in his players both on and off the court. Chaney designed a schedule that included 5:30 A.M. practice, to maximize time for his players to attend class and study. He monitored the class attendance of his players and he established a strict dress code for players for game days. On the court Chaney's trademark matchup zone forced his players to play a tough, disciplined style of defense that often frustrated opponents.

Throughout his career Chaney was a consistent voice for reform of collegiate athletics. When the NCAA imposed stricter academic standards on college athletes through Proposition 48 in 1986, Chaney was one of the most vocal opponents of the measure, appearing on television programs, including *Nightline* where he debated ARTHUR ASHE, and writing articles in major publications against the NCAA measures. Chaney's major argument against Proposition 48 and its counterpart, Proposition 42, was that it placed too much emphasis on the Scholastic Aptitude Test (SAT), a test that Chaney believed to be racially biased. Chaney felt that admissions decisions should be left up to the universities themselves and not the NCAA. Chaney proudly pointed to Temple alumni and NBA stars Eddie Jones and Aaron McKie as evidence that the SAT was not an accurate predictor of college success. Jones and McKie were forced to sit out a year under Proposition 48 rules, yet both graduated from Temple and went on to establish a scholarship fund at their alma mater in Chaney's name.

Chaney's passionate nature, however, led to some highly publicized incidents that threatened his career. In 1994 he rushed into a post-game press conference and threatened University of Massachusetts head coach John Calipari after he objected to Calipari's handling of game officials. Chaney apologized but was suspended by Temple from coaching for one game. During a game against crosstown rival St. Joseph's University in 2005, Chaney sent in one of his players to intentionally foul several Hawk players. The incident turned ugly when St. Joseph's senior John Bryant broke his arm after falling awkwardly as a result of a hard foul by a Temple player. Chaney again apologized, but Temple nonetheless suspended Chaney from coaching duties for the five remaining games of the regular season.

The hallmark of Chaney's coaching career was his desire to give opportunities to players from disadvantaged backgrounds, a passion stemming from his own experience of poverty in Black Bottom. When he was inducted into the Naismith Memorial Basketball Hall of Fame in Springfield, Massachusetts, in 2001, Chaney talked about a picture in his office. Called "Dreams," the painting showed an African American boy, living in obvious poverty, lying on a bed clutching a football. As he later said to a reporter, "There's always something that's eating inside of me when I think about youngsters. All he wants to do, this kid, is get up out of that bed, out of abject poverty, and just go out and play. It's so simple, a life, yet we find ourselves very often ignoring dreams of young people. And that's why I put that piece up there, because that's what I feel so strongly about" (*Washington Post*, 11 Nov. 2005).

Chaney retired as Temple's basketball coach in March 2006, after twenty-four seasons during which he led his team to NCAA tournaments seventeen times and five NCAA regional finals. He was twice named national coach of the year.

FURTHER READING

Hunt, Donald. *Chaney: Playing for a Legend* (2003).
Wartenberg, Donald. *Winning Is an Attitude: A Season in the Life of John Chaney and the Temple Owls* (1991).

THOMAS A. MOGAN

Chanticleer, Raven (13 Sept. 1928–31 Mar. 2002), curator, fashion designer, dancer, and artist, was born James Watson in rural Woodruff, South Carolina, to sharecropper parents whose names are unknown. Little information about his early years is available except that he attended the Fashion Institute of New York and studied at the Sorbonne in Paris before moving to New York in the 1960s.

As Chanticleer established himself as a fashion designer in New York City he also began to propagate the biographical embellishments and falsehoods that would be repeated until his death: that he was born in Harlem to a Barbadian concert pianist and a Haitian high school principal; that he completed a master's degree at the Sorbonne; that as a five-year-old he designed a prize-winning folding chair for a competition at the 1940 World's Fair.

Whether or not he grew up in Harlem, Chanticleer identified so strongly with its place at the center of black history and culture that in 1989 he created the Harlem African American Wax and History Museum, a collection of around twenty life-size figures, including HARRIET TUBMAN, MALCOLM X, and MAGIC JOHNSON, as well as numerous paintings, in a brownstone at 316 W 115 Street. As curator of the wax museum Chanticleer often drew on his imaginary Harlem childhood, telling a reporter in 1998, for example, that the wax figures of LANGSTON HUGHES and RICHARD WRIGHT were suggested by their visits to his family's home in the Sugar Hill section of Harlem in the 1930s. He also "recalled" seeing DUKE ELLINGTON, COUNT BASIE, and BILLIE HOLIDAY at the Apollo Theater. Though he larded his stories with appearances by some of the best-known names in African American history, Chanticleer also dug deeper, honoring Hale House founder CLARA HALE, the inventor MADAME C. J. WALKER, and the educator MARY MCLEOD BETHUNE.

In the 1960s Chanticleer founded the Raven Chanticleer Dancers, which performed in Manhattan nightclubs wearing costumes of his own design. He was one of the first blacks to design for the Bergdorf Goodman department store. In step with the rapid changes of 1960s fashion, Chanticleer fabricated clothing of plastic and other transparent materials, including garbage bags, and became known for what he called "beautiful clothes for stout, voluptuous women" (*New York Times*, 8 Apr. 2002).

Chanticleer personified entrepreneurship, craftsmanship, and civic pride. He purchased and renovated his Harlem townhouse in 1985, long before MAGIC JOHNSON, former U.S. president Bill Clinton, and the Starbucks chain of coffee houses moved into the neighborhood. He invested about five thousand dollars of his own savings in each wax sculpture, first researching photographs and other images of the subject, then building a papier maché and plaster frame, covering it in wax, and designing and making the costume. He spent hundreds of hours giving tours to schoolchildren, reporters, and anyone else curious enough to make an appointment and a monetary donation.

As embellished or outright fictitious as they were, Chanticleer's stories conveyed an immense and aesthetically polished pride in Africa and in African Americans. Though educated at highly regarded schools in New York and Paris he concocted an additional credential from the University of Ghana. As the museum's sole curator, fabricator, fund-raiser, and docent he spoke often not just of his flamboyant career in fashion and entertainment but also of his wish to "give back for what my place of birth has given to me" (*Los Angeles Sentinel*, 1994). Significantly the first four figures he completed for inclusion in his museum were Malcolm X, Nelson Mandela, the civil rights pioneer FANNIE LOU HAMER, and himself.

Chanticleer's quirky neighborhood project eventually attracted corporate attention. In 1996 a black history month art exhibit sponsored by Merrill Lynch included a series of portraits painted by Chanticleer. The portraits included iconic African Americans, such as BETTY SHABAZZ, RUBY DEE, and LEONTYNE PRICE, and were loaned from a Merrill Lynch employee's personal collection.

Chanticleer often spoke of buying a bigger building and expanding his exhibits. Yet his singular vision and methods confined his museum to a two-hundred-square-foot basement space that accommodated up to a couple of hundred visitors a month, by telephone appointment only. By contrast the educators Elmer and Joanne Martin, the founders of Baltimore's Great Blacks in Wax Museum, received a $100,000 state grant to develop their storefront museum, put together a board of trustees, raised nearly half a million dollars in two years, and expanded into thirty thousand square feet of exhibition and office space. While the Great Blacks in Wax exhibitions may have been more traditionally coherent, the Martins did not greet visitors at the door dressed in handmade African-inspired dress.

"It's my life, my mistress, my everything," Chanticleer told a reporter in 2000. "Even as a child, from the age of 5, I wanted to work with wax and take it to the max" (*American Visions*, 2000). Raven Chanticleer never married. His survivors include three nieces and three nephews, who did not carry on his work.

FURTHER READING
Bell, Bell. "Wax Museum Leaves an Impression," [New York] *Daily News*, 24 Nov. 1997.
Rasbury, Angeli. "Blacks in Wax: Great Blacks in Wax Museum," *American Visions* (Oct./Nov. 2000).
Thomas, Don. "In the Village of Harlem, USA: The African American Wax & History Museum of Harlem," *New York Beacon*, 28 Feb. 2001.
"Wax Museum Brings Famous African Americans to Life," *Los Angeles Sentinel*, 6 Jan. 1994.
Obituary: *New York Times*, 8 Apr. 2002.

INGRID SCHORR

Chappell, Edward Carter, Jr. (1750–26 Feb. 1826), a Revolutionary War soldier, was born Edward Carter in Colchester, Connecticut, to Edward (Ned) and Jenny Carter. Edward had six siblings, Aaron, Jacob, Asher, Esau, Sally, and an unidentified child who died in 1763. Ned, Jenny, and Edward were documented slaves of Mr. Jonathan Kellogg of Colchester, as were three of Edward's six siblings. Some of the remaining siblings may also have been slaves. Edward's father served in the armed forces at Crown Point during the campaign of 1755 in the French and Indian War, earning his emancipation as a result. It is possible that Ned Carter served on the behalf of Mr. Kellogg, a common practice at the time, but there are no records stating that this was so. The children were not all owned by Jonathan Kellogg, but divided among his sons. Ned also served during the American Revolution from 1777 to 1783. On 25 July 1766 Edward's mother Jenny died. His father then remarried a woman named Sybil, and they had two more children. Around 1794 Sybil died, and Edward's father was forced to seek financial assistance from the town of Colchester. The town in turn threatened to sue Jonathan Kellogg's children for support. This action by the town authorities may suggests that at least some of the Carter children continued to be owned by some of the Kellogg family as late as 1794. The case was dropped after Ned died in 1797.

In the spring of 1773 Edward married Eunice Williams at the local congregational church in Chatham, Massachusetts. The couple remained married until Edward's death in 1826 and had eleven children. No marriage record exists. In the words of Eunice, she and Edward were "poor and illiterate." It may have been the family's poverty that caused their son William to commit a burglary. He was convicted for theft and served eight months in Newgate Prison.

Edward, like his father, served time in the army and fought in the American Revolution. He first served in Colonel John Penfield's 23rd militia regiment for nine months and participated in the battle of White Plains before enlisting in the spring of 1777, after which time he served another three years in the 6th Company of the Third Regiment of the Connecticut line under Captain Simon Spalding, and Lieutenant Andrew Fitch. As a result of his service, Edward and his family were emancipated, and moved briefly to Willington, Connecticut, where he leased a plot of land and built a house. He chose this area because there were fewer blacks and hoped that it would be easier to find work as a result. The selectmen of Willington, however, did not wish to have more black residents and ordered him and his family to move out. Carter then moved to Colchester before settling finally in Ellington, Connecticut, where he purchased land near the Tolland line. At this time, he began using his full name, Edward Carter Chappell. He had enlisted into the army under an alias, Ned Carter. He died in February of 1826, at the age of seventy-six. His wife remained in Ellington for the remainder of her days and was able to collect the pension of her late husband.

FURTHER READING

Brown, Barbara W., and James M. Rose. *Black Roots in Southeastern Connecticut, 1650–1900* (1980).

Connecticut Historical Society. *Collections of the Connecticut Historical Society, Volume 8* (1903).

Johnston, Henry P. *The Record of Connecticut Men in the Military and Naval Service during the War of the Revolution, 1775–1783* (1997).

TIMOTHY NICHOLSON

Chappelle, Dave (24 Aug. 1973–), comedian, producer, and actor, was born David Khari Webber Chappelle in Washington, D.C., the youngest of three children. His parents, William David Chappelle and Yvonne Seon, were both educators. His father was a professor of the arts at Antioch College in

Dave Chappelle. The comedian performs at the Laugh Factory in New York City, April 2004. (AP Images.)

Yellow Springs, Ohio, and his mother, who earned an M.A. in Divinity Studies and a Ph.D. in African American Studies, founded the world's first African American Studies Program at Ohio's Central State University in 1974. She also worked closely with Patrice Lumumba, the first legally elected Prime Minister of the Democratic Republic of the Congo, during the early days of civil unrest in the African country. Chappelle's parents separated when he was two years old. He divided his time between living with his mother in Washington, D.C., and spending summers with his father in Yellow Springs.

Despite his parents' professions, Chappelle was not an enthusiastic student, though he was enthralled with media. He spent hours in front of the television, collecting ideas and role models. Because of his preoccupation with media and entertainment, Chappelle's mother, no doubt seeking to provide positive inspiration for her son, gave him the 28 September 1987 issue of *Time* with BILL COSBY on the cover to read. Chappelle felt an immediate connection with the veteran comic and decided that comedy was his calling. At his mother's urging, Chappelle frequented local comedy clubs, observing the delivery style and demeanor of other performers. In a conversation with one of the comics and the owner of the club, Chappelle was encouraged to take acting classes. Consequently, he transferred from Eastern High School to the Duke Ellington School of the Arts, where he studied theatre, learning skills of improvisation, the classics, creative writing, and other acting techniques. At fourteen Chappelle fearfully made his debut at the comedy club with his mother and grandmother in the audience. However, his fear soon subsided when he received positive response from the audience. Heartened by his initial success, Chappelle sought a similar outcome in New York City at the legendary Apollo Theatre. However, he was heckled tremendously and ushered off stage. Having deemed his appearance at the Apollo to be a learning experience, Chappelle later recaptured his earlier success in different comedy clubs around New York City, solidifying his reputation among his peers and colleagues.

Chappelle graduated from high school in June 1991. Soon after, at age nineteen, he moved to Hollywood. He received his first television development deal, creating a show entitled *I'm the Man*, which failed to generate any interest beyond its pilot episode. He also appeared in films, making his debut as Ahchoo in Mel Brooks's spoof *Robin Hood: Men in Tights* (1993), and as Ozzie in Herbert Ross's *Undercover Blues* (1993). He received major recognition as the stand-up comedian Reggie Warrington (an apparent homage to the filmmakers Reginald

and Warrington Hudlin), who cruelly takes EDDIE MURPHY's overweight professor Sherman Klump to task in the box-office hit remake of *The Nutty Professor* (1996). While making this film, Chappelle was urged by his idol Murphy to write his own material, which would further his stake in show business.

Taking Murphy's advice, Chappelle and his writing partner Neal Brennan created *Half Baked* (1998), a satire that extolled the virtues of smoking marijuana. The film performed modestly with audiences, earning just over $17 million at the box office. Soon after, Chappelle's father died after a lengthy illness, and this, coupled with another failed venture with television, resulted in his disillusionment with the entertainment business. Despite this, he appeared in a variety of small roles, in films such as *Woo* (1998), *You've Got Mail* (1998), with fellow comedian Martin Lawrence in *Blue Streak* (1999), and *Undercover Brother* (2002). He also made a well-received special for HBO television of his stand-up act, entitled *Dave Chappelle: Killin' Them Softly* (2000).

Yet nothing Chappelle had done previously would match the comic and political genius found in his variety series *Chappelle's Show*, which aired on Comedy Central between 2003 and 2006. Inspired by a lack of variety programming on television, Chappelle lampooned race, class, politics, and drug abuse with keen insight and acerbic intelligence reminiscent of RICHARD PRYOR. Chappelle also poked fun at celebrity culture, commenting on topics from R&B singer R. Kelly's alleged underage sexual abuse case to actor SAMUEL L. JACKSON's aggressive line delivery. These renderings and many others made *Chappelle's Show* "must see" television viewing. The Comedy Central network saw a tremendous increase in ratings and the first season of the show became the biggest selling "TV-to-DVD" set of all time. The massive success of the show moved Comedy Central to offer Chappelle $50 million for ensuing seasons.

Despite his enormous success, Chappelle walked away from the deal and retreated to Africa in an effort to reclaim his sense of self and peace of mind. Accused of drug addiction and mental instability, Chappelle decided that his well-being was not worth succumbing to the combative and controlling nature of Hollywood. After his return from Africa, he retreated to the farm he purchased in Yellow Springs and reassessed his life. He turned his attention back to stand-up and focused on other projects he cared about, such as his concert-comedy film *Dave Chappelle's Block Party* (2005).

Directed by Michel Gondry and reminiscent of the concert film *Wattstax* (1973), the film blended Chappelle's comedy with the musicianship of Erykah Badu, Mos Def, Talib Kweli, Dead Prez, Jill Scott, Kanye West, and the reunited hip-hop group The Fugees.

Chappelle married Elaine Mendoza Erfe in 2001. The couple had two children. Over a short but prolific career he made an indelible mark on the American comedic tradition. More impressively, he did so on his own terms and in a manner that allowed him to more than live up to Richard Pryor's declaration that he had passed the baton to Chappelle's capable hands.

FURTHER READING

Cobb, William Jelani. *The Devil and Dave Chappelle* (2007).

Watkins, Mel, ed. *African American Humor: The Best Black Comedy from Slavery to Today* (2002).

Watkins, Mel. *On the Real Side: A History of African American Comedy* (1999).

MARK D. CUNNINGHAM

Charles, Ezzard Mack (7 July 1921–28 May 1975), boxer and former light heavyweight and heavyweight champion of the world, was born in Lawrenceville, Georgia, the son of William and Alberta Charles. His father was a truck driver; little is known about his mother. According to Charles, his unusual first name came from the doctor who delivered him, W. P. Ezzard. His early life before his boxing career is somewhat vague. What is known is that at about the age of nine, he moved from Georgia to live with his grandmother and great-grandmother in Cincinnati, Ohio, following the divorce of his parents.

He took up amateur boxing as a teenager, and while still in high school won the Amateur Athletic Union's national middleweight title. In 1940, just nineteen years old, Charles turned professional and over the next three years fought thirty-six times, with thirty-four wins, one loss, and one draw. Charles did not shy away from the toughest middleweights and light heavyweights of his day, beating two future International Boxing Hall of Fame fighters, Charley Burley and Joey Maxim, twice in 1942. He had a rocky start to 1943, with a decision loss to another future hall of famer, Jimmy Bivins, and his first knockout loss to Lloyd Marshall. During 1944 and 1945 Charles served in the U.S. Army during World War II.

Upon his return Charles wreaked havoc on the light heavyweight division. From 1946 to 1948 he defeated nearly every outstanding fighter in the division. He beat ARCHIE MOORE three times, including once by knockout. Charles also avenged his two 1943 losses by beating Bivins three times, and knocking Marshall out in their next two fights. Despite these accomplishments Charles was unable to secure a shot at the world light heavyweight title. Nevertheless his absolute domination of the division during much of the 1940s led to his being named the greatest light heavyweight fighter ever by numerous sports writers and boxing magazines.

In 1949, in search of a championship fight and bigger paydays, Charles began to campaign as a heavyweight. It did not take him long to make his presence known. After just a few tune-up and exhibition fights, on 22 June 1949, Charles challenged JERSEY JOE WALCOTT for the vacant National Boxing Association heavyweight championship. The fight is generally remembered as one of the most lackluster heavyweight championship bouts of all time, but at the end of fifteen dull rounds Charles was declared the winner and new champion. Over the course of the next two years Charles defended the title just three times.

Despite his obvious boxing skills and accomplishments Charles never managed to capture the imagination of sporting fans or writers. He was pleasant, well mannered, and always generous in praising his opponents, yet he could also retreat into periods of long silences and moodiness. He carefully kept information about his personal life from fans and journalists alike. In fact, until 1951 and the birth of his first daughter, only his closest relatives and friends even knew that he had married longtime girlfriend Gladys Gartrell in December 1949. Perhaps more than his personality, however, Charles had to struggle against the awesome presence of JOE LOUIS. Officially the legendary Louis had retired in 1949 after a dozen years as the undisputed heavyweight champion of the world. Unofficially, however, the American public still considered Louis to be the real champion. In that light, Charles was viewed as just another pretender to the throne. In 1950, however, Louis returned to the ring. Financial need, not pride, drove him in his comeback. On 27 September of that year he faced Charles for the world heavyweight championship. For Charles the experience was little short of torture. As a young man he had idolized Louis, but the man he faced in 1950 was just a shell of the once-great champion. At thirty-six, with nearly sixteen years of tough fights behind him, Louis was too old and too slow to keep up with the quicker, younger Charles. Charles won a lopsided decision, but even in victory he was criticized for not finishing off Louis.

Charles's reign as the world heavyweight champion was brief. He fought and defeated some good fighters in defending his title in 1951, including Lee Oma and two old foes, Maxim and Walcott. In July 1951, however, Walcott shocked Charles with a seventh round knockout. One year later the two men fought again, with Walcott winning by decision. Charles continued to campaign over the next two years, beating some fringe contenders, but losing important bouts against Nino Valdes and Harold Johnson in late 1953. With his career suddenly in doubt Charles managed to summon up two good performances, knocking out COLEY WALLACE in December 1953 and then destroying hard-hitting Bob Satterfield in just two rounds a month later. By this time a new heavyweight champion had emerged, setting the stage for one of the best heavyweight bouts of the 1950s.

Rocky Marciano had taken the title in 1953, knocking out Walcott, and then knocking him out again in a rematch. On 17 June 1954 Marciano and Charles met in New York City. Charles dominated the early rounds, bloodying Marciano's nose and opening up a dangerous cut over the champion's eye. Marciano's strength carried him through the danger, and during the latter stages of the fight he landed crushing blows that somehow failed to knock Charles to the canvas. Marciano retained the title through unanimous decision. The fight had been so entertaining, however, that an immediate rematch was set up for the following September. In this return match Marciano seemed headed for an easy victory when in the sixth round the champion broke from a clinch bearing one of the most horrific cuts ever seen in a championship fight, this one through his left nostril. The blood flowed in spurts over the next two rounds, but despite Charles's valiant efforts, Marciano finally wore him down and knocked him out in the eighth round.

For all intents and purposes the two fights with Marciano in 1954 effectively ended Charles's days as a top fighter. He fought on until 1959, losing thirteen of his last twenty-three fights. Charles was at last inducted into the International Boxing Hall of Fame in 1990, fifteen years after his death from amyotrophic lateral sclerosis.

FURTHER READING

Horstman, Barry M. "Ezzard Charles: Sensitive Champ Fought His Way to Top," *Cincinnati Post*, 1 Mar. 1999.

Sullivan, Russell. *Rocky Marciano: The Rock of His Times* (2002).

MICHAEL L. KRENN

Charles, Ray (23 Sept. 1930–10 June 2004), singer, bandleader, and entrepreneur, was born Ray Charles Robinson in Albany, Georgia, the son of Bailey Robinson, a day worker, and Aretha (maiden name unknown). Charles's younger brother and only sibling drowned at age four. By the age of seven Charles had lost his sight to glaucoma and was sent to the State School for the Blind and Deaf in St. Augustine, Florida, where he remained until his mother's death when he was fifteen. It was during his time at the school for the blind, which was segregated by race, that he received formal piano lessons and learned to read braille. After his mother's death, he set out on his own, traveling and working as a musician around Jacksonville, Florida.

Charles's earliest influences as a musician were the jazz and blues pianist Charles Brown and the pianist and singer NAT KING COLE. His ability to learn the styles of both musicians allowed him to gain work in clubs where audiences were familiar with their music. Sensing the need to branch out beyond Florida, Charles moved to Seattle, Washington, at the age of eighteen. In Seattle, Charles formed a band, the McSon trio, and made his first recording, his own composition, "Confession Blues," on the Swing Time label owned by Jack Lauderdale, who encouraged Charles to move to Los Angeles in 1950. In Los Angeles, Charles recorded two more singles for Swing Time before he began to tour nationally with the guitarist LOWELL FULSON.

Ray Charles crossed musical boundaries and entertained generations of fans. Photographed in 1960. (Library of Congress.)

Charles eventually became Fulson's musical director. In 1952 Charles signed with the Shaw Agency and began to tour nationally as a solo artist. On the strength of his second single, "Baby Let Me Hold Your Hand," Charles was signed to a recording contract by Ahmet Ertugen, the founder of Atlantic Records. Charles's first release for the label was "It Should Have Been Me" (1952).

Charles's early recordings with the Atlantic label favored the styles of Charles Brown and Nat Cole—styles that had earned him a minor reputation as a rhythm-and-blues artist. But it was with the single "I've Got a Woman," backed by "Come Back Baby," that Charles began to exhibit the innovative style that would become the foundation of soul music. At the core of Charles's innovation was his use of chords and rhythms drawn from black gospel music to write and record music that had distinctly secular themes. "I've Got a Woman," for example, was based on "Let's Talk about Jesus," a gospel hit for the Bells of Joy in 1951. Follow-up recordings by Charles, like "A Fool for You" (1955) and "Drown in My Own Tears" (1955), also adhered to Charles's "soul" strategy, but "Hallelujah, I Love Her So" in May 1956 became his first crossover hit. As Charles's new style became popular, he began to face criticism from black ministers and gospel audiences. The genius of his burgeoning style was his intuitive understanding that the "Saturday night sinner" and the "Sunday morning saved" were often one and the same. The addition of doo-wop girls called the Raeletts accentuated a feeling of call and response, the verbal interaction common between a black minister and his choir. By the time Charles scored with the gospel-frenzied "What'd I Say," a top-ten pop single in 1959, he had inspired legions of followers, many of whom, like SAM COOKE and ARETHA FRANKLIN, went directly from the black church to the pop charts.

Much of Charles's early success was rooted in his ability to master many musical genres, most notably jazz, rhythm and blues, and soul. After Charles and his band made a successful appearance at the 1958 Newport Jazz Festival, Atlantic capitalized on his growing popularity with the recording *The Genius of Ray Charles* (1959), which included the pop standards "Don't Let the Sun Catch You Crying," "Come Rain or Shine," "It Had To Be You," and the big-band romp "Let the Good Times Roll." The album was the last that Charles recorded for the label, though there were subsequent releases of previously recorded music. In November 1959 Charles signed with ABC-Paramount, which offered a larger advance on future royalties, a higher rate of royalties, and ownership of his own master recordings.

Charles had mixed success with his first two singles for ABC-Paramount, but with the third release he achieved his biggest hit ever.

Hoagy Carmichael's "Georgia on My Mind" (1960) was an old ballad that sentimentally recalls the American South. Charles infused the song with his unique soulful style and in the process made it one of his signature tunes. The song went to number three on the pop charts and earned Charles the first two of twelve Grammy Awards from the National Academy for the Recording Arts and Sciences. The following year Charles achieved his first number-one pop song and another Grammy with PERCY MAYFIELD's "Hit the Road Jack."

The success of "Georgia on My Mind" signaled a new direction in Charles's recording career. Always fascinated by country-and-western musicians, Charles finally recorded a full-fledged country song, Hank Snow's "I'm Moving On," toward the end of his tenure at Atlantic. This was followed by Charles's groundbreaking *Modern Sounds in Country and Western Music* in April 1962. Though ABC-Paramount was fearful that Charles would lose his core fan base, Charles scored his second number-one pop single with "I Can't Stop Loving You." Despite the label's initial concerns, the song also topped the R&B charts for sixteen weeks. So successful was *Modern Sounds in Country and Western Music* that Charles released a follow-up in late 1962. *Modern Sounds in Country and Western Music 2* included versions of Hank Williams's "Your Cheating Heart" and the popular standby "You Are My Sunshine."

When Charles released *Ingredients in a Recipe for Soul* in 1963, it was clear that he had so successfully integrated so many genres into his repertoire that it was no longer possible to label his music simply jazz, soul, or country and western. Ray Charles was becoming widely known as a song stylist, as evidenced by the success of his renditions of tracks like "That Lucky Old Sun" and "Ol' Man River," both from *Ingredients in a Recipe for Soul*, and the singles "Without Love (There Is Nothing)" and "Busted," a top-five single on both the pop and R&B charts. In 1964 Charles was arrested for drug possession in Boston. He received a five-year suspended sentence, kicked his twenty-year heroin addiction, and miraculously continued his music career unabated. Although taste in popular music changed during the 1960s, with the appearance of Motown and British groups like the Rolling Stones and the Beatles, Charles continued to make quality recordings in his own style. He even covered "Yesterday" and "Eleanor Rigby" by the Beatles on his recordings *Listen* (1967) and *A Portrait of Ray* (1968). Charles also began to record themes for Hollywood films, the best known being "The Cincinnati Kid" (1965) and "In the Heat of the Night," the latter from the 1967 film starring SIDNEY POITIER. The film's soundtrack was arranged by Charles's old friend QUINCY JONES, whom he had met when he moved to Seattle in 1948. Charles's "Here We Go Again," released in 1967, was his last major crossover recording until the late 1980s.

Although Charles largely remained on the periphery of the civil rights movement as a recording artist, preferring to provide financial assistance privately, he did offer his political vision on *A Message from the People* (1972). This album includes versions of STEVIE WONDER's "Heaven Help Us All," JAMES WELDON JOHNSON's "Lift Every Voice and Sing" (often referred to as the "Negro National Anthem"), and Dick Holler's "Abraham, Martin and John." The recording also features a stirring version of "America the Beautiful" that was rereleased as a single in 1976 to coincide with the U.S. bicentennial celebration. Charles also earned a Grammy Award in 1975 for his rendition of Wonder's politically charged "Living for the City."

Charles recorded regularly with little fanfare throughout the late 1970s and early 1980s, though he was feted with awards and acknowledgements. In 1981 he was awarded a star on the Hollywood Boulevard "Walk of Fame." He was among the first inductees into the Rock Hall of Fame in 1986, and in 1979 the state of Georgia declared his version of "Georgia on My Mind" the official state song. Charles released his autobiography *Brother Ray*, written with David Ritz, in 1978. He had a bit of a renaissance in the mid-1980s, making popular recordings with the country artists Willie Nelson ("Seven Spanish Angels"), George Jones ("We Didn't See a Thing"), and Hank Williams Jr. ("Two Old Cats like Us"). In 1989 he teamed again with Quincy Jones to record "I'll Be Good to You," with Chaka Khan. The song reached number one on the R&B charts. Charles earned his twelfth Grammy Award in 1993 for "A Song for You." Popular cameos on *Sesame Street* and commercial endorsements for Pepsi Cola kept his music and image firmly embedded in the minds of generations of Americans.

Ray Charles was married twice and had nine children, but his music always took precedence over all other activities. He died of liver disease on 10 June 2004 and was buried in Inglewood Cemetery, Inglewood, California. Throughout his career Charles maintained an intense touring schedule, not simply for the economic benefit but also to bring various styles of black music to audiences that may have otherwise remained unfamiliar with them. Charles's influence on American popular music has perhaps been rivaled only by figures like DUKE ELLINGTON, B. B. KING, and JAMES BROWN, all of whom toured well into their sixties and seventies, each holding up the banner for the particular brand of popular music he is best known for. Charles's remarkable ability to draw from many styles of popular music made it possible for him to cross—and thereby diminish—musical, racial, political, and geographical barriers.

FURTHER READING
Charles, Ray, with David Ritz. *Brother Ray* (1978).
Lydon, Michael. *Ray Charles: Man and Music* (1998)
Wexler, Jerry, and David Ritz. *Rhythm and Blues: A Life in American Music* (1993).

MARK ANTHONY NEAL

Charles, Robert (1865?–27 July 1900), emigrationist and militant, was born near Pine Bluffs in Copiah County, Mississippi, the fourth of ten children of Jasper Charles and Mariah (maiden name unknown), sharecroppers. Though Robert never lived under slavery, the exigencies of the crop-lien system ensured that his family remained heavily in debt to their landlord and to the local furnishing merchant. Thus Jasper Charles could neither expand his holdings nor leave them. The family supplemented its meager earnings by fishing and by hunting the bountiful small game to be found in the nearby pine forests. Although we know few details of Robert Charles's early life, it seems probable that he gained his proficiency with a rifle in the piney groves of Copiah County.

The adolescent Charles witnessed the erosion of African American citizenship rights that had been established during Reconstruction. His father was a loyal Republican and even sat on local juries throughout the 1870s. In 1883, however, when Charles was seventeen, a mob of white night riders burned a nearby church that had hosted a black political gathering. White Democrats also assassinated an independent white candidate who had been trying to build a coalition between black sharecroppers and economically pressed white farmers. On the eve of that year's elections the Charles family hid out in the woods, fearing that they too would be attacked.

His opportunities for gainful employment and self-determination rapidly diminishing in Pine Bluffs, Robert traveled thirty miles to Vicksburg in 1887, finding work as a laborer, first on the city's modernized water system and then as a section hand on the Louisville, New Orleans, and Texas Railroad. Modernity was coming to Vicksburg, the region's largest town, but it was to be built on the backs of men like Robert Charles. The records of the LNO&T suggest that he was a model employee who was never fired nor even formally reprimanded. He frequented the bars and brothels of Levee Street, Vicksburg's unpaved red-light district, but drank only in moderation. He was never arrested, no mean feat given the brutal and often arbitrary policing of Levee Street by its white constables. The ever-present danger of violence—and the presence in Vicksburg of marauding packs of rabid dogs—convinced Charles to protect himself with a rifle, as did most men, black and white. Charles also purchased, illegally, a pistol.

It was during an attempt to retrieve his pistol from its hiding spot on a freight train on 23 May 1892 that Robert and his brother Henry engaged in a gun battle with white guards, just as the train was pulling away from Rolling Fork station, forty miles north of Vicksburg. Recognizing that he could not avoid capture for long, Charles changed his name to Curtis Robertson and returned to Copiah County. Two years later, after being convicted of selling moonshine, he left again, this time for New Orleans.

As in Vicksburg, Charles had little difficulty finding work in the Crescent City—on the docks, as a street cleaner, as a boiler man in a city hotel, in lumber mills, and on nearby sugar plantations. Again his employers praised his work ethic. One wrote a letter of recommendation declaring, "Any person in need of a good man will find [R. Charles] a good, honest, and reliable man" (Hair, 95). Hyman Levy, one of his few white acquaintances, would later recall that he found Charles to be stylish, intelligent, and well educated. Neighbors believed him to be a "scholar" of some sort.

In spite of his general reticence Charles was vocal about the need of blacks to defend themselves against lynching, which was becoming more frequent. He also resented the racist vituperation to be found in New Orleans, most popular newspaper, *States*. Its editor, Henry Hearsey, an unreconstructed Confederate major, urged a "final solution" to the race problem and believed that a coming race war would result in the "extermination" of the black race (Hair, 91). By all accounts, however, Charles did not advocate violent reprisals against whites, and police records indicate that he was never arrested during his six years in New Orleans. His own favored solution remained one that would have pleased Henry

Hearsey: emigration to Africa. In May 1896 Charles joined the International Migration Society (IMS), but the organization collapsed before he could fulfill his dream of emigrating to Liberia. He nonetheless continued to correspond with the president of the IMS and traveled throughout Louisiana and Mississippi distributing emigrationist pamphlets.

Two developments hardened Charles's hatred of white supremacy and his determination to emigrate to Africa. The first was the passage in 1898 of racially prejudicial legislation, including a poll tax that removed more than 125,000 black Louisianans from the electoral rolls. The second was the particularly gruesome lynching in 1899 in Newnan, Georgia, of SAM HOSE, a black man accused of rape and murder. Special trains of "spectators" arrived from Atlanta to watch as Hose was tortured, burned, and mutilated. Body parts were later sold as souvenirs. Upon reading of this outrage the normally taciturn Charles was "beside himself with fury," one witness noted (Williamson, 205). Charles's immediate response to these developments was not violent. Rather he wrote to Bishop HENRY M. TURNER and volunteered to become a subscription agent for Turner's emigrationist magazine, the *Voice of Missions*. In 1899 and 1900 Charles traveled throughout New Orleans selling Turner's magazine and advocating its black nationalist and emigrationist philosophy.

The life of Robert Charles up to that point, then, was relatively unremarkable. Yet his reactions to an otherwise routine police stop on Monday, 23 July 1900, suggest that something inside Charles snapped; he could no longer suffer the daily indignities of racism in silence. That evening at 11:00 P.M. a police sergeant saw Charles and his roommate, Lenard Pierce, waiting outside the home of a black woman, who may have been Charles's former partner. Though the neighborhood was integrated, the white patrolmen demanded to know what their business was at that time of night. Although accounts differ as to who fired the first shot, a fracas broke out that resulted in Charles's shooting a patrolman before escaping into the night. Pierce was arrested.

Charles must have known that his chances of escape were slim, that he would never make it to Liberia, and that he would probably be lynched. He returned to his home to retrieve his Winchester, rapid-firing rifle, but as he attempted to leave he discovered that there were three policemen waiting for him. Charles immediately threw open his door and shot Captain John T. Day, one of the New Orleans Police Department's most decorated officers, straight through the heart, killing him instantly. He then threatened to kill the other officers and shot one of them through his eye. After a tense two-hour standoff in the dark, during which Charles goaded and swore at the police officers, he escaped.

Charles's brazen attack on white police officers provoked thousands of whites to roam throughout the city, indiscriminately attacking and shooting at black bystanders. A mob of three thousand whites tried, unsuccessfully, to lynch Lenard Pierce, who was being held in jail. The police also thwarted the mob's attempt to burn down the Storyville red-light district. On Friday 27 July the police learned that Charles was hiding in the New Orleans home of fellow migrants from Copiah County. Charles, no doubt aware of the impossibility of escape or survival, decided to make a final, though ultimately futile, last stand. He shot and killed two of the four policemen who came to apprehend him, and then began firing into the crowd of more than a thousand spectators that had gathered to witness his arrest and probable death. Within an hour between ten and twenty thousand armed police officers, state militia, and others had surrounded the building. Estimates suggest that five thousand bullets struck the building, which the police set on fire. Charles killed three more men, injured nineteen others, and was shot at least forty times before a volunteer policeman finally killed him.

The Charles affair reflected the frenzied, racial climate of the turn-of-the-century South, a climate largely tolerated by the rest of the nation. The federal courts accepted the southern states' disfranchisement plans and devoted no resources to investigating atrocities like the Sam Hose lynching or the Wilmington riot of 1898, during which a white mob burned down the newspaper offices of ALEXANDER MANLY and precipitated a coup d'etat in North Carolina's largest city. To respond to such violence with violence as Robert Charles did was undoubtedly counterproductive. By killing seven white policemen and others he also brought about the deaths of at least twelve African Americans who were killed by rampaging white mobs. It is not surprising that many of the city's African American residents condemned Charles for putting their lives and property in danger, as well as for breaking a biblical commandment.

Others were able to contextualize, if not justify, Charles's actions. The antilynching campaigner IDA B. WELLS-BARNETT investigated the New Orleans riot and concluded that Charles was no "desperado," but rather acted out of self-defense in a desperate situation. There was even a folk song about Charles that drew on the legends of STAGOLEE and JOHN HENRY. The jazz musician JELLY ROLL MORTON once claimed that he had known the song, but "found out that it was best for me to forget it ... in order to go along with the world on the peaceful side" (cited in Hair, 179).

FURTHER READING
Hair, William Ivy. *Carnival of Fury: Robert Charles and the New Orleans Race Riot of 1900* (1976).
Williamson, Joel. *The Crucible of Race: Black White Relations in the American South since Emancipation* (1984)

STEVEN J. NIVEN

Charleston, Oscar McKinley (12 Oct. 1896–6 Oct. 1954), baseball player and manager, was born in Indianapolis, Indiana, to Tom Charleston, a construction worker, and Mary Thomas. The seventh of eleven children, he served as a batboy for a local professional team before enlisting in the army at age fifteen. While stationed in the Philippines with the black Twenty-Fourth Infantry, Charleston honed his athletic skills in track and baseball, becoming the only African American player in the Manila baseball league in 1914. Following his army discharge a year later, he joined the Indianapolis ABCs at a salary of $50 per month. The American Brewing Company sponsored the ABCs, but C. I. TAYLOR, Negro League pioneer, directed day-to-day operations.

Charleston, nicknamed Charlie, was a five foot eleven inch, 185-pound center fielder who batted and threw left-handed. Described as barrelchested, he would have difficulty maintaining his weight as his career progressed. He played a very shallow center field in his fielding heyday and counted on his speed to reach balls hit over his head. During his first year with the ABCs, he married Helen Grubbs from Indianapolis, but the marriage soon ended in divorce. Although described by his peers as basically a quiet man off the field, he displayed a fiery competitive temper as a player. He fought umpires, opponents, and fans, contesting calls, sliding hard into bases, and battling spectators for balls hit into the stands. Likened to his contemporary Ty Cobb for his baseball skills and competitiveness, Charleston, for some sportswriters, was not the "black Ty Cobb," but rather Cobb was the "white Oscar Charleston."

After three years with the ABCs, Charleston in 1919 joined the Chicago American Giants run by the Negro National League entrepreneur RUBE FOSTER. At a time when white ballplayers were often bound to restrictive contracts, it was common "blackball" practice for players, lured by better money offers, to change teams relatively often. Contracts were either poorly written or ignored, and barnstorming teams often made the most money. In 1921 Charleston moved to the St. Louis Giants and gained superstar status, reportedly batting .434 in the sixty-game season, including fourteen doubles and league-leading eleven triples, fifteen home runs, and thirty-four stolen bases. Although box score statistics for the Negro Leagues are fragmentary, available numbers give Charleston a career hitting average of .350 in the Negro Leagues from 1919 through 1937, .365 in Cuban League winter ball, which he played annually from 1919 through 1928, and .318 versus white major leaguers in fifty-three exhibition games from 1915 through 1936.

Charleston began the 1922 season in St. Louis but returned mid-year to Indianapolis, earning $325 per month, $125 above any teammate and one of the highest salaries in black baseball. In 1924 he jumped to the Harrisburg Giants of the Eastern Colored League for four years as player-manager, batting .391 in 1924, .418 in 1925 with a league-leading fifteen doubles and sixteen home runs, and .335 in 1927 with eighteen doubles and twelve home runs. In Harrisburg he married Jane Blaylock, the daughter of a Methodist bishop. The couple had no children and divorced after about twenty years. In 1928 and 1929 Charleston was on the roster of the Philadelphia Hilldales and hit .360 and .339, respectively.

As the Depression made the financial life of teams in the Negro Leagues especially precarious, independent, barnstorming clubs raided their ranks. The Homestead Grays of Pittsburgh, owned by CUM POSEY, signed Charleston and other top players from failing franchises for the 1930 season. Because added weight had reduced his outstanding skills as a center fielder, Charleston moved to first base. Yet during the 1930 and 1931 seasons he hit a combined .371. In time, Posey and his successor, GUS GREENLEE, who bought out Posey in 1932 to stock up his Pittsburgh Crawfords, accumulated the best black team in history, including the future Hall of Famers SATCHEL PAIGE, JOSH GIBSON, JAMES "COOL PAPA" BELL, JUDY JOHNSON, and Charleston, who was player-manager for the "Craws" from 1932 through 1937. As his skills began to diminish, Charleston batted .376 in 1933, .333 in 1934, and .288 in 1935. When the Dominican Republic Summer League in 1937 enticed many of the Crawford stars to move south, the team collapsed. Charleston moved to the Toledo Crawfords in 1938, but that franchise folded in mid-season 1939; the manager-first baseman joined the Philadelphia Stars, remaining for five seasons.

During World War II Charleston worked at the Philadelphia quartermaster depot. In 1945 he managed the Brooklyn Brown Dodgers, Branch Rickey's cover team set up to scout JACKIE ROBINSON and other African American players. As the Negro Leagues faded away, Charleston's career ended with managing stints with the Philadelphia Stars (1946) and the Indianapolis Clowns (1947–1948). In 1949 he retired and worked in the baggage department of Philadelphia's Pennsylvania Railway Station. He died in Philadelphia following a heart attack and stroke. Charleston's election in 1976 to the Baseball Hall of Fame in Cooperstown, New York, as the second Negro league player after Josh Gibson, finally brought recognition to his career and supported the sportswriter Grantland Rice's earlier observation, "It's impossible for anyone to be a better ball player than Oscar Charleston."

FURTHER READING

Appel, Martin, and Burt Goldblatt. *Baseball's Best: The Hall of Fame Gallery* (1977).
Bankes, James. *The Pittsburgh Crawfords* (1991).
Holway, John. *Blackball Stars: Negro League Pioneers* (1988).
Obituary: *Pittsburgh Courier*, 16 Oct. 1954.
This entry is taken from the *American National Biography* and is published here with the permission of the American Council of Learned Societies.

DAVID BERNSTEIN

Charlton, Cornelius H. (24 July 1929–2 June 1951), Korean War veteran and Congressional Medal of Honor winner, was born in Eastgulf, Raleigh County, West Virginia, the son of Van Charlton and Clara Thompson. In 1944, at the age of fifteen, Cornelius, called "Connie" by his friends, moved with his family to New York, taking up residence in the Bronx. There he graduated from Monroe High School in 1946. Charlton soon thereafter joined the U.S. Army, serving in an engineering outfit and stationed in Germany as part of the post–World War II occupation forces. Deciding to make a career for himself in the army, Charlton reenlisted in 1950 and was sent overseas to serve in the Korean War.

Charlton's service in the Korean War serves to highlight the black experience in this often forgotten conflict whose combatants seldom receive their proper due. The valuable service of black soldiers and sailors in World War II as well as rising political pressure persuaded President Harry Truman to desegregate the military as a whole in 1947 with the issuance of Executive Order 9981. However, despite the valiant World War II service of such all-black army units as the Ninety-Second and Ninety-Third Divisions in Italy and the Pacific, which produced a number of men such as JOHN FOX and Edward Carter who belatedly received the Medal of Honor, segregated regiments were usually the subject of harsh postwar criticism for their so-called overall poor performance. Significantly this criticism usually emanated from white officers who chose to deride the service of black soldiers as a whole while failing to recognize any weak leadership exhibited by white officers. By the time the Korean War began in 1950, integration in the army, despite the increased number of black soldiers, had changed little. Although blacks were assigned to combat units at nearly the same ratio as whites, most still served in segregated units that had too many men because the army's segregation policies did not allow them to be assigned to combat units with white soldiers. With black enlistment in the army exceeding 12 percent and far outdistancing that of the other service branches, change was inevitable. The unit in which Charlton fought would play a role, somewhat paradoxically, in bringing true integration to the U.S. Army.

Following his arrival in Korea, Charlton was assigned with his engineering regiment to a non-combat area behind the American front lines. However, Sergeant Charlton wanted to take part in the fighting and requested transfer to a combat unit; he was assigned to Company C of the Twenty-fourth Infantry Regiment, Twenty-fifth Division, Eighth Army. This was a segregated unit that was famous for its service in the Pacific during World War II. As squad leader, Charlton was stationed with his men in the vicinity of Seoul, South Korea, at Chipo-Ri. On 2 June 1951 the Korean position on Hill 543 was attacked by the men of the Twenty-fourth Regiment. With his leader wounded and subsequently evacuated, Charlton led the assault amid heavy fire and was severely wounded. Nevertheless, he continued alone and, despite being hit by a grenade, successfully routed the enemy. Following this determined and heroic action, Charlton (later known as "the Hero of Hill 543") succumbed to his wounds at a field hospital. For his "indomitable courage, superb leadership, and gallant self sacrifice," Charlton was posthumously awarded the Congressional Medal of Honor on 24 January 1952. His remains were eventually returned to West Virginia for burial in a family plot in Pocahontas Cemetery near Bramwell.

Despite Charlton's heroism as well that of another Medal of Honor winner, Private William Thompson, the Twenty-fourth Infantry Regiment came under a different kind of fire from within the army itself. Although individual men of the regiment were noted for their heroism, the unit as a whole was said to have "performed poorly," and was considered a "weak link" in the Twenty-fifth Division's line. Some officers claimed that the men of the Twenty-fourth were malingerers or "prone to panic," but still others asserted that the unit's problems lay not with its men but with the leadership of the white officers and their discrimination against its black officers. In reality the situation was almost the same as the one that existed in World War II and revealed the truly demoralizing effect segregation and discrimination continued to exert over the U.S. Army's black soldiers. Fortunately the one difference that helped resolve the situation was the fact that many combat officers were in favor of integration and made no attempt to question the combat ability of black troops, as was widely done after World War II. As a result of the army's integration efforts, just a month after Charlton's death the Twenty-fourth Infantry Regiment was deactivated on 1 October 1951 and its men transferred to fully integrated infantry units. Ironically, the phasing out of his regiment may be viewed as one of the lasting legacies of Charlton's achievement.

Charlton lay forgotten for many years in an abandoned cemetery. In 1990 he was reburied in the American Legion Military Cemetery in Beckley, West Virginia, with full military honors and was given a headstone reflecting his status as a Medal of Honor winner.

FURTHER READING

MacGregor, Morris J., Jr. *Integration of the Armed Forces 1940–1965* (1981).

West Virginia Division of Culture and History. "Cornelius Charlton: A Forgotten Hero," *Bramwell Aristocrat* (Feb. 1990), http://www.wvculture.org/History/military/charltoncornelius03.html.

GLENN ALLEN KNOBLOCK

Charlton, Dimmock (1799–?), also known as Tallen and John Bull, was enslaved in Africa, shipped to America, freed by the interception of a British vessel, made prisoner of war while serving in the British navy, then tricked into slavery in Savannah, Georgia; he earned and purchased his freedom three times over, being defrauded the first two times.

From accounts he gave later in life, it is believed he was born among the Kissi, a people ethnologically related to the Malinke, in what is now Guinea, on a tributary of the Niandan River. His given name was Tallen. Captured in a local war at age 12, and brought to the coast for sale as a slave, he was being transported across the Atlantic when the ship carrying him was intercepted by a British vessel, probably in 1811. The exact circumstances remain a matter of controversy. By his own account, recorded in 1857, the slave ship was Spanish. The historian John Blassingame observes (327) that this is unlikely, because Spain was at that time an ally of Great Britain. However, during the Peninsular War of 1808–1813, Spanish guerrillas fighting against Napoleon were allies of Britain, while Napoleon's brother Joseph Bonaparte had been formally installed as King of Spain, so a given Spanish ship off the African coast might have been either ally, enemy, or without allegiance. However, the young man later named Dimmock did not understand European languages at the time, so identification is not certain.

He may have been taken to England, or put ashore on the island of Demerrara, formerly Dutch, but recently occupied by British forces. At some point in the next year, he became a cabin boy on the H.M.S. *Peacock*, was known by the name of John Bull, and served in the British navy during the War of 1812. When the *Peacock* was sunk by the U.S.S. *Hornet*, 24 February 1813, most of the crew were rescued and made prisoners of war. The *Hornet* arrived in New York the following April.

He was left in the charge of a Lieutenant William H. Harrison of Virginia—not the future U.S. president William Henry Harrison—who took him to Savannah, Georgia. The historical record does not explain why a prisoner of war was separated from the other prisoners taken on the same ship and transported hundreds of miles away. Harrison left him at the home of Judge Thomas Usher Pulaski Charlton, who proposed that the lieutenant should leave the young man in his care as a permanent placement. The lieutenant said he had no authority to do so—although collusion in precisely that objective cannot be ruled out. When Harrison sent for the prisoner to be returned, the judge wrote back that the boy had died of a fever. According to accounts later provided by the judge's slaves, he called them together and instructed that from now on the boy's name was Dimmock Charlton.

As Dimmock Charlton he was sold to a series of men in rapid succession. First, the judge sold him to a tailor named John P. Setz to settle a debt owed by Judge Charlton for a suit of clothes. In response to Charlton's protests that he was not a slave but a British sailor and a prisoner of war, Setz took him to Augusta and sold him a year later to a steamboat captain named DuBois. After two years, he was sold to a Captain Davidson, then to William Robinson in Savannah. A common way for an enslaved person to secure freedom was to hire their own time from an agreeable master, find work on their own, and save money to purchase themselves, over and above what they owed each week for essentially renting their own time and labor. Charlton made such an arrangement with Robinson, and, after working as a stevedore, paid Robinson $800. Robinson promptly had Charlton sent to jail, found a new buyer, and sold him. In early seventeenth-century Virginia, a contract for purchase of freedom might have been enforceable at law, but in nineteenth-century Georgia, it relied totally on the good faith of the owner.

The new purchaser, James Kerr, vaguely agreed that Dimmock could purchase his freedom for the money Kerr had paid Robinson. Dimmock assumed that this amount was $700, which he paid, although it was $250 above the purchase price. Kerr also agreed to purchase the wife and children Dimmock had married and fathered in the meantime, accepting over $1500 from Dimmock to secure their freedom, while buying them for $600. Eventually, Kerr sold each of them, separately. At this point, Dimmock despaired of fair dealing in purchasing his freedom and reasserted his claim to be a British subject, falsely enslaved in the first place. Sold and resold in short order, by men who thought his claims might be credible and their investment at risk, he ended up with a man named Benjamin Garman, who allowed him to purchase his freedom, again, and actually kept the bargain. The man known as Dimmock Charlton resumed the name of John Bull, which he had used in the British navy.

This account was first written down in 1857 or 1858 and published in the *National Anti-Slavery Standard* in New York, when Charlton sought help in New York securing the freedom of his granddaughter, Ellen, who was in the care of two sisters of James Kerr, residing in that state. Louisa Kerr, testifying in response to a writ of habeas corpus, acknowledged she had heard that Charlton was at one time a sailor on the *Peacock*, and she believed it. The journals of the abolitionist CHARLOTTE FORTEN GRIMKÉ record a visit from Charlton on Sunday 21 November 1858. After securing his granddaughter's freedom and placing her with a family in Canada, John Bull arranged to go to England, where he secured a statement from a pensioner in Greenwich Hospital, Thomas Trethowan, who confirmed he was the same person who had served on board the *Peacock*.

Old and unable to work, John Bull had an uncertain claim on the British government based on his naval service and having been a prisoner of war. Antislavery activists in Britain made an appeal for funds to defray the costs of emigration to Canada. There is no established historical record of the outcome, nor of the events or duration of his final years.

FURTHER READING

Blassingame, John W. *Slave Testimony: Two Centuries of Letters, Speeches, Interviews, and Autobiographie,* (1977).

Cox, Mary L., and Susan H. Cox. *Narrative of Dimmock Charlton* (1859).

CHARLES ROSENBERG

Charlton, Samuel (1760–1843), slave and soldier in the Continental army, is a person about whom little early information is available. Nothing is known of his parents, childhood, or young life. What is known is that Charlton served as a teamster, a fairly common assignment for African American soldiers. States tended to use African American troops, particularly in the early years of the war, as unarmed privates to serve the functions of orderlies, servants, or regimental musicians or else consigned them to logistical functions. Charlton, however, despite being a teamster, often found himself in combat situations.

The Continental army raised by the Continental Congress was multiracial, but soon after George Washington took command in the spring of 1775 he ordered recruiting officers not to enlist African Americans. In a council of war on 8 October 1775 Washington and other prominent officers decided unanimously to bar all slaves and, by a wide majority, all African Americans from enlisting in the Continental army. Confronted with a shortage of soldiers, however, Washington soon reversed this decision. By the end of the war African American soldiers had usually served longer terms than had their white counterparts. As the war went on, states increasingly turned to African Americans to deal with manpower shortages in their regiments, and many Continental army officers began to appreciate the competence of African American soldiers.

New Jersey faced difficulties from the beginning in supplying the troops requested by the Continental Congress. Many citizens of the state would have preferred to keep troops at home because of British and Loyalist activity within New Jersey. The state legislature in 1775 and again in 1779 forbade slaves from serving in state forces. The war had unleashed new social forces, however, and manumission was considered in some quarters. Governor William Livingston requested a manumission law in 1778 from the legislature, but the body failed to act and the matter was dropped soon thereafter. Eventually, however, the legislature manumitted the slaves of Loyalist masters who served in the American armed forces. Despite the formal illegality of slaves serving in the New Jersey militia or the Continental line, they did indeed do just that. Thus Charlton continued to serve, albeit illegally. This apparently was not uncommon as there were numerous slaves in New Jersey regiments, and no one appears to have been overly concerned with the matter so long as the master's permission had been granted.

Charlton saw action at Brandywine, Germantown, Monmouth, and other locations. The battle of Monmouth on 28 June 1778 was a result of an American effort to engage the British as they evacuated Philadelphia. The British under General Henry Clinton were met by an American force under the command of General Washington near Monmouth. The original American plan was to attack the British column while it was vulnerable on the road. Major General Charles Lee advanced on the British rear guard, but believing that he was about to be enveloped, he ordered a retreat. The retreat was made in poor order, and Washington had to rally the force. The harsh words exchanged between Lee and Washington and the dispute over Lee's conduct at the battle eventually resulted in a court-martial for Lee. Washington placed his troops in a defensive position to repel the British. The American artillery proved central to the American victory that day. Charlton, though a teamster during this battle, was placed among the artillery. Some accounts have him near Mary Ludwig Hays McCauley or Molly Pitcher when she took her husband's place at a cannon. Some accounts also have Washington praising Charlton for his actions during the battle, though this may merely be legend.

Despite his Revolutionary War service, however, Charlton remained in slavery at the conclusion of the conflict and lived in New Jersey with his maser. Many masters manumitted their slaves after Revolutionary War service in New Jersey, and the state legislature manumitted Loyalist slaves who were captured or fled and served in the Continental army. But Charlton was subject to a master who failed to reward him for the patriotic duties he had performed. He was freed only upon his master's death, along with the rest of his master's slaves. Once he was freed, Charlton moved with his wife to New York City, where he lived until his death in 1843. Charlton later appeared as an example of black heroism and patriotic service in the writings of the black abolitionist and historian WILLIAM C. NELL as he argued for African American equality.

FURTHER READING

Greene, Robert Ewell. *Black Courage 1775–1783: Documentation of Black Participation in the American Revolution* (1984).

Johnson, Edward A. *A School History of the Negro Race in America from 1619 to 1890* (1911).

National Society Daughters of the American Revolution. *Minority Revolutionary War Service: Delaware, Maryland, New Jersey, 1775–1783* (1998).

Nell, William C. *Services of Colored Americans in the Wars of 1776 and 1812* (1851).

Walling, Richard S. *Men of Color at the Battle of Monmouth, June 28, 1778* (1994).

M. KELLY BEAUCHAMP

Chase, Leah (6 Jan. 1923–), chef and the "Queen of Creole cooking," was born Leah Lange in New Orleans, Louisiana, to Charles Robert Lange, a caulker in a Madisonville shipyard, and Hortensia (Raymond) Lange. She was the eldest girl in a family of fourteen children, eleven of whom lived to adulthood. She was raised in the small rural fishing town of Madisonville, about thirty miles north of New Orleans. The family was poor, living mainly on vegetables from her father's garden. Her mother had only a sixth-grade education. In a 2003 interview Chase said that poverty, not segregation, was the most difficult experience of her childhood.

Chase's parents instilled in her a deep religious faith as well as the importance of family and service to the community. They were strict and believed strongly in education. She started school at age four. Her father did not want her to associate with non-Catholics, so Chase was sent to New Orleans in 1937, where she lived with an aunt and attended the all-black St. Mary's Academy. Her parents supplied fresh produce to the nuns, and Chase sewed for other students to earn money for board. She graduated at age sixteen and returned to Madisonville.

When she was eighteen Chase returned to New Orleans for her first job, at the Oriental Laundry in the French Quarter. After a week she took a job in the Colonial Restaurant on Chartres Street, also in the French Quarter. It was her first experience inside a restaurant. The Colonial closed, reopening as the Coffee Pot restaurant on Royal Street, serving only breakfast and hamburgers for lunch. Chase, along with two coworkers, asked the owner if they could add Creole wieners and spaghetti, which they sold for sixty cents. She also briefly managed two amateur boxers and worked in a betting establishment posting numbers on a board.

Late in 1945 Chase met Edgar "Dooky" Chase II, a trumpet player with his own jazz orchestra. On 8 July 1946, they married. Three daughters and a son were born between 1946 and 1953. Chase earned money by taking in sewing, despite her distaste for the work. When her children reached school age, she began working in her father-in-law's restaurant three days a week.

Edgar "Dooky" Chase Sr. had opened the Globe Sandwich Shop in the historic Treme neighborhood in 1939. The restaurant started as a po' boy stand, selling the famous New Orleans sandwich (hot meat or fried seafood on hollowed-out French bread) and lottery tickets. As a result of the success of Dooky Sr.'s wife Emily's cooking, the family had stopped selling lottery tickets and expanded the restaurant to their living quarters. Chase expected to be a made a hostess and waitress but instead ended up in the kitchen.

Chase wanted to create a restaurant with table service, something unusual for black patrons who were, as she wrote, usually "given a fork and knife" and seated (Chase, 13). There were few true "sit-down" restaurants at which blacks could eat. Chase made changes in the kitchen, eventually transforming the menu to Creole de Couleur food. She changed the décor after Dooky Sr. died in 1957, sewing curtains herself and modeling the fancy chairs after other restaurants in the Quarter.

Dooky's was even a place for black teenagers with few other options to gather. According to Chase, you either went to church or to Dooky's to meet people in the black community. Upstairs at Dooky Chase, civil rights leaders held strategy meetings as early as the 1940s, and voter registration meetings in the 1960s. Although interracial meetings were illegal in Louisiana until 1961, Dooky Sr.'s popularity precluded the local police from breaking them up, and the restaurant was a meeting place for all races. Chase closed the restaurant on Mardi Gras 1961 in support of a black boycott of the biggest event in New Orleans, and the busiest day of the year. The restaurant fed Freedom Riders, and it was often the only place where black entertainers were welcome. The clientele included prominent African American writers such as JAMES BALDWIN and ERNEST J. GAINES and musicians such as DUKE ELLINGTON, COUNT BASIE, SARAH VAUGHAN, LENA HORNE, and the Jackson 5. RAY CHARLES named the restaurant in his recording of the 1900 Hickman-Jordan-Bartley song "Early in the Morning" on his 1989 album, *The Genius Sings the Blues*. Politicians and civil rights leaders from THURGOOD MARSHALL, MARTIN LUTHER KING JR., and John F. Kennedy to JESSE LOUIS JACKSON SR. patronized Dooky's. In 1965, when Hurricane Betsy flooded the restaurant, Chase cooked the food so it would not spoil, and with a police escort distributed it to people who had lost their electricity as a result of the storm. She published *The Dooky Chase Cookbook* (1990) and *And Still I Cook* (2003).

Chase served on the boards of the New Orleans Museum of Art and the New Orleans Arts Council. A patron and collector of African American art, her restaurant became known for its fine art collection, including paintings by JACOB ARMSTEAD LAWRENCE, and drawings by Clifton Webb, DAVID CLYDE DRISKELL, and MEL EDWARDS.

In 1984 Chase received a Candace Award for outstanding black role models from the National Coalition of 100 Black Women (NCBW). In 1997 she became the first black woman to receive the Loving Cup Award for unselfish service to the community from the *Times-Picayune* newspaper of New Orleans, which she once described as her most cherished award. In 2003 she was selected by the National Visionary Leadership Project (NVLP) and interviewed as an inspirational role model. Along with several awards form the NAACP, Chase received the Weiss Award from the National Conference of Christians and Jews, Outstanding Woman from the National Council of Negro Women, and numerous other tributes.

In 2005 the restaurant was again flooded, this time by Hurricane Katrina. Chase and her family evacuated the city but eventually returned to live in a Federal Emergency Management Agency (FEMA) trailer across the street from the restaurant, determined to reopen it in its original location on Orleans Avenue, despite being surrounded by poverty and projects, for the sake of the still-abandoned neighborhood. Her grandson, a firefighter, saved the art collection. Chase said, in her 2003 NVLP interview, that "can't is not in the dictionary," a lesson she learned from her mother. Despite losing her own restaurant Chase participated in fund-raisers for local communities devastated by the 2005 hurricanes. In order to raise money to reopen Dooky Chase, she made the famous Gumbo z'herbes on Holy Thursday 2006, the last day to eat meat before Easter Sunday. The gumbo consists of a variety of greens, always an odd number, along with sausage, chicken, and other meats. As late as early 2007 the restaurant had still not been restored, and Leah and Dooky Chase continued to live in a trailer.

Despite her lack of formal training, Chase turned Dooky Chase into an institution. A woman of hard work and strong faith, Chase overcame poverty, segregation, and hurricanes to become a community leader and a role model, always giving to family and community.

FURTHER READING

The 2003 National Visionary Leadership Project (NVLP) interview provides details of Chase's life and insight into her personality.

Allen, Carol. *Leah Chase: Listen, I Say Like This* (2002).

Chase, Leah. *The Dooky Chase Cookbook* (1990).

Chase, Leah. *And Still I Cook* (2003).

JANE BRODSKY FITZPATRICK

Chase, William Calvin (22 Feb. 1854–3 Jan. 1921), journalist, was born in Washington, D.C., the son of William H. Chase, a blacksmith, and Lucinda Seaton. He attended schools in Washington, and at the age of ten, upon the death of his father, he went to work selling newspapers and later doing odd jobs around newspaper offices. Completing the preparatory department at Howard University, he took a position in the government printing office. He was later appointed by FREDERICK DOUGLASS to a position in the office of the recorder of deeds, a post once held by Douglass, then moved on to become a clerk in the War Department. In 1886 he married Arabella V. McCabe; they had two children.

Despite his government appointments, Chase early in his life showed a keen interest in journalism. Even as he held government posts, he wrote for and even served as the editor of newspapers serving Washington's black community. In 1882, by means that cannot be determined, he founded a newspaper of his own, the *Washington Bee*. Although he later took law courses at Howard, gaining admission to the bar in 1889 and beginning a practice he never abandoned, the *Bee* became his life's work; he died at his desk.

Although it never achieved the national prominence of some other papers, the *Bee*, published continuously from its founding until early 1922, about a year after Chase's death, was among the longest lived of the many African American newspapers established in the nineteenth century. Washington's black community was quite influential during the years Chase was active and he used the *Bee* to make himself a major force in that community's life.

Like many African American editors of the time, Chase created in the *Bee* a newspaper that was combative, Republican, and deeply involved in the racial questions of its day. He was especially concerned about discrimination in the nation's capital, which increased notably during the first two decades of the *Bee*'s existence. After the turn of the century, he published articles that exposed discrimination in federal employment, a growing problem during the administrations of Theodore Roosevelt and William Howard Taft. Later he made the *Bee* a major voice in protesting the Wilson administration's onslaught, after 1913, against African American federal workers.

Chase also became a notable figure in African American politics. Throughout his career, he was a champion of racial solidarity and self-help, politically, economically, and socially. Indeed, despite an unceasing militancy in opposition to discriminatory laws and practices, he argued against agitation for integrated education, citing chiefly the positive role autonomous schools could play for African American teachers and students alike, especially in encouraging racial pride. "Mixed schools," he wrote in 1883, "will do more to impress our children that they must forever be flunkies and servants than anything else."

At the same time, he tended to take a somewhat erratic course in dealing with other prominent black leaders. From the beginning he engaged in running battles, usually quite personalized but focusing particularly on questions of political partisanship, with such emerging, influential African American leaders as T. THOMAS FORTUNE, an editor of a newspaper in New York. He also entered into erratic alliances with the various major organizations, from Fortune's Afro-American Council in the late nineteenth century to the subsequent National Association for the Advancement of Colored People—an organization he sometimes praised but also sometimes vilified as the "National Association for the Advancement of Certain People," mainly because of personal tensions with its major figures.

From 1895 until 1915 both Chase and the *Bee* figured in the politics surrounding BOOKER T. WASHINGTON's leadership, the central defining issue of the age. Financial considerations were not entirely absent from Chase's role. Until about 1905 Chase was generally opposed to Washington, despite his own tendency to favor strategies based on self-help and racial solidarity—strategies at the heart of Washington's program. He generally sided with those who focused on Washington's accommodationism, condemning Washington's apparent willingness to compromise on issues of political and social rights to gain economic improvement. After that time, Washington, always aware of the influence of the African American press, began to financially support the publication of the *Bee*. Chase, while remaining militant on issues of racial justice, responded by making the newspaper one of Washington's most consistent supporters.

Despite his activities in national affairs, and despite the real crises he confronted as an African American in Jim Crow America, Chase achieved his greatest influence through his role in an area of controversy that was almost entirely local: leadership of the District of Columbia's schools for black children. It was not a minor issue. These schools provided a major source of employment for Washington's educated African American community and served as the institutional focus for that community as well. Even before becoming editor of the *Bee*, Chase had attacked what he saw as corruption and favoritism on the part of school officials, and he continued to do so throughout his career.

After about 1910 Chase gradually emerged as the chief spokesman for members of the District's African American community dissatisfied with the management of the schools. Attacking the leadership of Roscoe Conkling Bruce, assistant superintendent for black schools and onetime protégé of Booker T. Washington, Chase made what he continued to see as corruption in the schools a central theme in the pages of the *Bee*. He also became the moving spirit in a "Parents' League," formed to exert pressure on the District's board of education to bring about, particularly, Bruce's ouster. Through his efforts, Chase did much to produce a 1920 congressional investigation of the schools and of Bruce's administration, resulting in the assistant superintendent's departure, at the urging of the board, a few months later.

Fully living up to the motto he himself gave the *Bee*, "Honey for friends, stings for enemies," Chase was a significant voice in turn-of-the-century African American life.

FURTHER READING

Meier, August. *Negro Thought in America* (1963).

Simmons, William. *Men of Mark* (1887).

This entry is taken from the *American National Biography* and is published here with the permission of the American Council of Learned Societies.

DICKSON D. BRUCE

Chase-Riboud, Barbara (26 June 1939–), sculptor, poet, novelist, and painter, was born Barbara Chase in Philadelphia, Pennsylvania, the only daughter of Charles Edward Chase, a contractor, and Vivian May West, a medical technician. Chase grew up in a nurturing middle-class environment and took dance lessons at the age of five, piano lessons at six, and art lessons at seven. In 1946 she enrolled at the Fletcher Memorial Art School in Philadelphia, where she received her first art prize for creating a small Greek vase. She flourished intellectually and was admitted to the Philadelphia Museum School of Art, where she studied dance with MARION CUYJET, a master ballet teacher. She also attended Philadelphia's Academy of Music. At eleven years old, she began writing poetry and enrolled at the Philadelphia High School for Girls. In 1954 she won the National Scholastic Art Contest. For the first time, she exhibited her prints at the ACA (American Contemporary Artists) Gallery in New York City, and her woodcut print *Reba* was purchased by the Museum of Modern Art, New York. She graduated from the Philadelphia High School for Girls summa cum laude. In 1954 she enrolled at Tyler School of Fine Arts in Elkins Park, Pennsylvania (affiliated with Temple University), and graduated in 1957. That same year she was the first African American woman to win *Mademoiselle* magazine's Guest Editorship Award.

One year later she studied at the American Academy in Rome. Chase's stay in Italy gave her the opportunity to participate in the mainstream of Western art. During her time in Rome she decided to spend three months traveling and studying art in Egypt, where she became familiar with Egyptian art. Her trip to Egypt was a pivotal experience and influenced her artistic view. In fact, it was the ancient Egyptian ruins that had a major impact

on her change of artistic perspective. In 1959 Chase returned to the United States to attend Yale University, where she studied design and architecture with Joseph Albers, Vincent Scully, Philip Johnson, Louis Kahn, and Alvin Eisenman. The following year she received her master's degree from Yale and moved to London, where she stayed for a year. In 1961 she left London for Paris, where she started working for the *New York Times* as a promotional artist director. There she met and married Marc Riboud, a French photographer. The wedding took place in Mexico at the ranch of Sheila Hicks, the internationally known fiber artist.

In 1962 Chase-Riboud visited France, Greece, Morocco, and Spain, where she met the artist Salvador Dali and the writers JAMES BALDWIN, Henry Miller, and Jean Chalon. She traveled the following year to the Soviet Union, where she spent some time with dissident painters and discovered the poet Anna Akhmatova. During the same year she bought La Chenillère, an eighteenth-century farmhouse at Pontlevoy, in the Loire Valley, France, where she set up her atelier. She then worked in Verona, Italy, where she perfected the technique of making direct cut and folded models from sheet wax. This greatly aided in her skills and style as a sculptor. Her first son, David Charles, was born in 1964, and she had a second son, Alexis Karol, in 1967.

In 1965 Chase-Riboud visited the People's Republic of China, where she met Chou En-lai, had a state dinner with Mao Tse-Tung, and wrote the "Chinese" poems. In 1966 she had her first exhibition in Paris at the Cadran Solaire art gallery. She also exhibited in Dakar, Senegal, at the First African Festival of Arts, where she met President Léopold Senghor. While in Africa she attended the Pan-African Festival in Algiers, where she met ELDRIDGE CLEAVER and other Black Panthers.

Chase-Riboud's travels to Africa and Asia influenced not only her literary career but also her works of art. Her sculptures are a combination of geometric bronze forms and braided silk fibers. Her best-known 1970s sculptures also reflect African masks. For example, her 1972 freestanding sculpture *Confessions for Myself* was made of black bronze and black wool. The hanging braids and fibrous stands allude to the supernatural, the rites and magic of Africa, and other non-Western realities. In parallel, during the same year, she wrote the poem "Soledad." She exhibited aluminum sculptures at Air France Gallery in New York. Throughout the 1970s her art pieces won several awards, and she exhibited them in museums in the United States and Europe. She subsequently received international recognition for the organic bronze sculptures, made of wax, organic woven fiber, and metal, that she created using a propane torch, a hot plate, and carving tools.

Chase-Riboud began her literary career in 1974 with a book of poetry, edited by TONI MORRISON, called *From Memphis to Peking*. Chase-Riboud was the first African American woman to visit China after the revolution, and these poems reflect her previous visit to China as well as her visit to Egypt. She insisted that her writing was not secondary to her sculpture, but more like a parallel vocation. In an interview about her careers as an artist and a writer, she remarked: "There's something terribly healthy about sculpture. It's very fundamental. You build something. You look at it. It's finished. But a book is never finished" (*Los Angeles Times*, May 1990). Her next literary work was the novel *Sally Hemings* (1979), a book that established her as an important writer. The idea for the novel stemmed from Chase-Riboud's longtime fascination with the story of the slave SALLY HEMINGS, who had a sexual relationship with Thomas Jefferson. The novel expressed Chase-Riboud's concerns about the arbitrary racial divisions in American society. Though the book engendered controversy among many whites, who saw the novel as defaming the name of a founding father, it was critically acclaimed. Riboud received the Janet Heidinger Kafka Prize for best historical novel. Thus she started a distinguished career as a prominent and influential African American writer.

Chase-Riboud and her husband, Marc Riboud, divorced in 1981, and in the same year she met and married Sergio Tosi, an Italian publisher, art expert, and historian, in Paris. In 1986 she published her second novel, *Valide: A Novel of the Harem*, about the kidnapping and enslavement of an American Creole girl by Algerian pirates in 1802. It is a historical representation of the condition of slave women in the harem during the Ottoman Empire. Chase-Riboud won the Carl Sandburg Prize in 1988 for a book of poetry called *Portrait of a Nude Woman as Cleopatra*. By using Plutarch's description of Cleopatra and the events in her life, she created a poem that she called the melologue. A melologue, a recitation with musical accompaniment, is supposed to be spoken by one person imitating both male and female voices. In the poem Chase-Riboud describes Cleopatra as an ordinary woman who had romantic relationships with Caesar and Antony.

Chase-Riboud's third novel, *Echo of Lions* (1989), was inspired by the story of JOSEPH CINQUE, who in 1839 led a slave rebellion onboard the slave ship *Amistad* near the coast of Cuba. In 1994 she published *The President's Daughter*, a prequel to *Sally Hemings*. In 1996 the French government awarded her the Knighthood in Arts and Letters.

Riboud's published work also includes *Hottentot Venus: A Novel* (2003), which tells the tragic story of the South African heroine Sarah Baartman, who was taken to London at the age of twenty by an English surgeon. What follows is the tale of her racial and sexual exploitation at the hands of European imperialists. The Black Caucus of the American Library Association named the novel Best Fiction Book of 2004. Similarly, the fashioning of *Africa Rising* (1998), an eighteen-foot bronze memorial sculpture, was inspired by her desire to restore Baartman's human dignity. Chase-Riboud won the 1995 competition to create such a memorial for the colonial-era African burial ground discovered north of Wall Street in Manhattan in 1991.

Through her prolific artistic and literary career, Barbara Chase-Riboud has been able to offer international audiences an authentic African American literary voice and creative talent characterized by a sophistication that is her unforgettable trademark.

FURTHER READING
"Barbara (Dewayne Tosi) Chase-Riboud," in *Contemporary Authors (A Profile of the Author's Life and Works)* (2004).

Davis, Thadious M., and Trudier Harris, eds. *Afro-American Fiction Writers after 1955 (Dictionary of Literary Biography)*, vol. 33 (1984).

Farris, Phoebe, ed. *Women Artists of Color: A Bio-Critical Sourcebook to 20th Century Artists in the Americas* (1999).

Hine, Darlene Clark, Elsa Barkley Brown, and Rosalyn Terborg-Penn, eds. *Black Women in America: An Historical Encyclopedia* (1993).

McKee, Sarah. "Barbara Chase-Riboud," in *Contemporary African American Novelists: A Bio-Bibliographical Critical Sourcebook*, ed. Emmanuel S. Nelson (1999).

Selz, Peter Howard. *Barbara Chase-Riboud, Sculptor* (1999).

GINETTE CURRY

Chatmon, Sam (10 Jan. 1899–2 Feb. 1983), blues singer, guitarist, and arranger, was born in Bolton, Hinds County, Mississippi, on the John Gettis plantation near Jackson. Although some accounts identify 1897 or 1900 as his birth year, Chatmon's tombstone says 1899. He was one of eleven children—nine sons and two daughters—born to Henderson and Eliza Jackson Chatmon. Some accounts say there were thirteen children. Eliza Chatmon played the guitar. The grandson of a white planter and a black slave woman, Henderson Chatmon, a native of Terry, Mississippi, began to play the fiddle at square dances before he was freed from slavery. He lived to the age of 105. Rumors persist that Henderson Chatmon was the father of pioneering Delta bluesman CHARLEY PATTON, although he never acknowledged Patton as his son. Other rumors suggest that Patton was a cousin of the Chatmon children. At any rate, Patton was drawn to this immensely musical clan.

Sam Chatmon's upbringing was steeped in music. As a small boy, he would take a guitar, his mother's instrument, off the wall and play it while his family was working in the fields, then put it back before they returned. After his father deemed him old enough to play, "I go to playin' a piece, and I'd make a mistake. I was playin' a guitar. He said, 'Bring me a fiddle here, let me show you how that go.' And then me and him would sit down and play for maybe two hours" (Oakley, 52). The Chatmon family "played guitar, violin, tenor banjo, and mandolin, piano, saxophone, clarinet, just anything more or less borrowed, hired or picked up" (Oakley, 52). From a young age, Sam learned to play not only guitar, but banjo, mandolin, harmonica, and bass. He joined the family string band, which worked mostly for whites because area blacks generally could not afford to hire musicians. At some point during the 1920s, Sam Chatmon played with MA RAINEY and THOMAS A. DORSEY when they visited the area.

Around 1926, Sam Chatmon formed a guitar, fiddle, and vocals band with his brothers Lonnie and Armenter (known as Bo), and their friend Walter Vincson. They named the band the Mississippi Sheiks in honor of the wildly popular Rudolph Valentino movie *The Sheik* (1921). The Sheiks rapidly became famous throughout the Delta for their performances of blues, ragtime, and country songs. MUDDY WATERS reportedly once said, "I knowed the Mississippi Sheiks. Yessir. Walked ten miles to see them play. They was high-time ... makin' them good records, man" (Yazoo 2006, "Mississippi Sheiks," http://www.yazoorecords.com). Recording over seventy pieces on the Okeh, Paramount, and Bluebird labels, and sometimes touring beyond their home region, the Sheiks were able to reach a national audience. They did so especially with

"Sitting on Top of the World," their 1930 hit on Okeh that became a standard. It was eventually recorded by a wide variety of musical artists, including BIG BILL BROONZY, Bob Wills and His Texas Playboys, RAY CHARLES, Bob Dylan, Cream, and Willie Nelson. Another hit for the Sheiks was "Stop and Listen Blues." At the same time that he performed with the Sheiks, Bo Chatmon became well-known in his solo career as BO CARTER for his double-entrendre songs like "Banana in Your Fruit Basket" and "Please Warm My Weiner." Sam Chatmon, too, pursued a solo career, as a guitarist at Southern medicine shows.

The Mississippi Sheiks disbanded in 1935. However, in 1936, Bluebird recorded a set of duets between Lonnie and Sam Chatmon. Lonnie died during the late 1930s. From the 1940s onward, Sam and other family members moved to Hollandale, Washington County, Mississippi, to work on plantations. World War Two made it even more difficult than usual to make a living from music. An effort to launch a New Mississippi Sheiks was short-lived. Sam Chatmon married a woman named Elma Lue, who lived from 10 Apr. 1911 to 18 Mar. 1996. They had at least one child together, a son, Sam Jr., who became a bassist for ELMORE JAMES. After moving to Hollandale, Chatmon made his living as a sharecropper, carpenter, and laborer. However, starting in late 1950s, the folk and blues revival brought him out of his retirement from work as a professional musician. The "rediscovered" Chatmon signed on with the folk label Arhoolie in 1960. This was the first of several more folk labels he would work with, including Flying Fish. Outliving his former bandmates, including his brother Bo who died in 1964, Sam Chatmon became a well-known musical performer again, particularly under the rubric of folk blues.

Throughout the 1960s, '70s, and into the '80s, Sam Chatmon toured widely and continued to record. His guitar style evolved from an early twentieth-century sound to one affected by his long stays with fellow musicians on the West Coast and in Memphis, Tennessee. He played many well-known music festivals, including the Smithsonian Festival of American Folklife, Washington, D.C.; the Mariposa Fest, Toronto, Ontario, Canada; and the New Orleans Jazz and Heritage Festival. He toured with Jimmy Buffet and with the Blues Caravan. Many musicians were pleased to encounter Sam Chatmon, whose older work they already loved, or in some cases were hearing for the first time.

Sporting his signature cap and large white beard, Sam Chatmon continued to perform professionally until his death at age eighty-four in Hollandale. He was buried near his wife in Hollandale's Sanders Memorial Garden. His gravestone was paid for by acclaimed musician Bonnie Raitt through the Mount Zion Memorial Fund, a nonprofit that sought to honor acclaimed musicians lying in unmarked rural graves. The tombstone reads "SITTING ON TOP OF THE WORLD" and aptly identifies Chatmon as "one of the most important figures in American music," whose "contribution helped create the lyrical art form of the blues. A beloved friend and true gentleman" (Cheeseborough, 153). In 2008, the song "Sitting on Top of the World" was inducted into the Grammy Hall of Fame.

FURTHER READING

Materials on Sam Chatmon can be located in the collections of the Mississippi Department of Archives and History, available at http://mdah.state.ms.us/.

Beebie, Michael E. *Sam Chatmon: A Musical Biography* (1974).

Cheeseborough, Steve. *Blues Traveling: The Holy Sites of Delta Blues* (2004.)

Ford, Robert. *A Blues Bibliography* (2007).

Oakley, Giles. *The Devil's Music: A History of the Blues* (1997).

"Sam Chatmon." In *Mississippi Writers & Musicians*, available at http://www.mswritersandmusicians.com/.

DISCOGRAPHY

I Have to Paint My Face (Arhoolie, 1960).

Sam Chatmon: The Mississippi Sheik (Blue Goose, 1970).

Sam Chatmon's Advice (Rounder, 1979).

Sam Chatmon & His Bar-B-Q Boys (Flying Fish, 1980).

Sam Chatmon, 1970–1974 (Flyright, 1999).

MARY KRANE DERR

Chauvin, Louis (Feb. 1882?–26 Mar. 1908), ragtime pianist and composer, was born in St. Louis, Missouri, to Sylvester Chauvin, a musician who may have been born in Mexico, and Mary, an African American born in Missouri. Some sources give 13 March 1881 as Louis Chauvin's birth date. His death certificate merely states his age as "about 25." His first name was sometimes spelled "Lewis," and the family name was spelled variously as "Chovan," "Chouvan," "Chauvan," "Shovan" (as in the 1900 census), or "Showvan." Chauvin was about five feet five inches in height and light-skinned. The 1900 census listed him as black, but the 1880 census listed his parents as mulatto. Chauvin had no formal musical training and was musically illiterate. His brothers Sylvester, Abraham, and Peter, who

also became musicians, probably also lacked formal musical training.

Chauvin's musical activities were first reported in 1899, when he performed as a member of a singing and dancing group called the Mozart Quartette (*Indianapolis Freeman*, 27 May 1899). Also in the group was his boyhood friend Sam Patterson, later a close colleague of the ragtime composer SCOTT JOPLIN and a pianist in JAMES REESE EUROPE's Clef Club Orchestra. Chauvin and Patterson appeared on stage as a singing, dancing, and comic team for several years. In March and April 1903 they were featured in a musical play titled "Wait for the Dandy Coon," produced by the ragtime pioneer and saloon owner TOM TURPIN and directed by Joe Jordan, who was soon to become a major songwriter. Chauvin quickly gained recognition as a pianist of uncommon ability. He had superb technique and improvised using the most unusual harmonies. Patterson reported that Chauvin would routinely warm up with Sousa marches, covering the keyboard in octaves in contrary motion, playing in double-time. Patterson also said that Chauvin was always composing new music that was lost because, being musically illiterate, he could not write anything down. Patterson, as co-composer, however, did write down one of Chauvin's songs, "The Moon Is Shining in the Skies" (1903). Chauvin also had an acute musical memory and reportedly accompanied a show after a single hearing of the music. The ragtimer Charles Thompson recalled the admiration with which Chauvin and Scott Joplin were greeted in St. Louis: "Both Joplin and Chauvin had a string of followers as they strutted around the district" (Trebor Tichenor, "Chestnut Valley Days," *Rag Times* [Nov. 1971]: 3). Piano-playing contests were a major attraction in the ragtime world, and Chauvin usually won those he entered. He was billed as "The Black Paderewski," a reference to the acclaimed classical piano virtuoso Ignacy Paderewski.

In 1906, having moved to Chicago, Chauvin published another song, "Babe, It's Too Long Off," with lyrics by Elmer Bowman, a successful lyricist and stage performer partnered with the composer CHRIS SMITH. We do not know how Chauvin and Bowman became acquainted, but Bowman's renown must have been instrumental in obtaining the publication from M. Witmark, a major firm. Chauvin's two songs exhibit harmonic sophistications beyond what was typical for the time and style, but neither achieved any notice. Chauvin's fame today rests upon a single piano rag, "Heliotrope Bouquet, A Slow Drag Two Step," co-composed with Scott Joplin in Chicago and published in 1907 by Joplin's long-time publisher John Stark. Stark, in advertisements, described the work as "audible poetry of motion." Chauvin composed the first two sixteen-measure strains, and Joplin, who notated the entire piece, composed the last two. Chauvin's sections have a haunting quality making the rag unlike any other piece of the period. Joplin paid tribute to Chauvin by basing the first of his two strains on Chauvin's music. As fine as Joplin's strains are, they lack the exquisite beauty of Chauvin's. All told, Chauvin's contribution to this piece amounts to thirty-two measures, which, with the indicated repeats, amounts to less than three minutes of music. Yet those thirty-two measures constitute a minor masterpiece, attracting an inordinate amount of attention. The Pulitzer Prize–winning composer William Bolcom, for example, was so impressed with Chauvin that he wrote a rag in 1971 that he titled *Epitaph for Louis Chauvin*. As a recording pianist, Bolcom named his first ragtime LP album *Heliotrope Bouquet: Piano Rags 1900–1970* (1971). The highly regarded playwright Eric Overmyer, also fascinated by the music, wrote a play about Joplin and Chauvin, calling it *The Heliotrope Bouquet by Scott Joplin and Louis Chauvin* (1993). Music scholars have published analyses in an effort to understand and explain the magic of this piece, and the music remains a favorite among performers and audiences.

In early March of 1908 Chauvin was hospitalized in Chicago, fell into a coma, and died twenty-three days later. His dissolute lifestyle may have contributed to his early death; he reportedly drank alcohol excessively, took opium, and was an habitué of red-light districts during both his working hours as a musician and after-hours. His death certificate indicates that he died of multiple sclerosis, probably syphilitic, and inanition—that is, starvation—due to the coma. A modern medical diagnosis would probably not link multiple sclerosis to syphilis and would simply list the condition as a neurosyphilitic sclerosis. Regardless of the cause of death, the tiny sample we have of Chauvin's musical mind is sufficient for us to mourn his premature demise.

FURTHER READING

Berlin, Edward A. *King of Ragtime: Scott Joplin and His Era* (1994).

Blesh, Rudi, and Harriet Janis. *They All Played Ragtime* (1950).

Spencer, Frederick J. *Jazz and Death: Medical Profiles of Jazz Greats* (2002).

EDWARD A. BERLIN

Chavis, Benjamin Franklin, Jr. (22 Jan. 1948–), clergyman and civil rights activist, was born in Oxford, North Carolina, the son of Benjamin Chavis Sr., a lay minister at the local Episcopalian congregation, and Elisabath Ridley, a teacher at the black Central Orphanage School. Young Benjamin was descended from a prominent African American family that included JOHN CHAVIS, a wealthy landowner and the first black ordained preacher in the Presbyterian Church.

As a teenager Benjamin Chavis became actively involved with his parish, a role that led to his appointment as statewide youth coordinator for the Southern Christian Leadership Conference (SCLC), initiating his involvement in the civil rights movement and a lifelong commitment to African American youth. In the years following his education at St. Augustine's College in Raleigh he received a bachelor of arts degree in chemistry from the University of North Carolina at Charlotte, a master of divinity, magna cum laude, from Duke University, a doctor of ministry from Howard University, and completed course requirements for a doctor of philosophy from Union Theological Seminary. In 1969 he was appointed Southern regional program director of the United Church of Christ Commission for Racial Justice (UCC-CRJ). His first assignment was to Wilmington, North Carolina, where civil rights activists had gathered to defend black residents against violent Ku Klux Klan efforts to halt school desegregation. After a fire at a white-owned grocery store, several black activists, including Chavis, were arrested and charged with arson. During the ten-year legal battle that followed, Chavis and the "Wilmington Ten," as they came to be known, struggled to prove their innocence within a deeply prejudicial state court system.

In the first four months of 1972 Chavis was indicted or jailed and released more than fifteen times. By mid-1972 the Wilmington Ten were sentenced to a cumulative 282 years in prison. After four years of appeals Chavis and the ten entered prison in 1976. His dissertation, *Psalms from Prison* (1983), and his commentary on the judicial system, *An American Political Prisoner Appeals for Human Rights* (1978), were written or published during his incarceration. When three prosecution witnesses announced in 1979 that they had lied during the original trial, Chavis and his colleagues were at last released.

Upon leaving jail Chavis continued his work with the UCC-CRJ, seeking new methods through which to exorcise the racism he believed to be embedded within the American legal and economic systems. In

1985 he was named the executive director and CEO of the United Church of Christ Commission for Racial Justice. His success in that post led to his 1988 election to the vice presidency of the National Council of Churches of the USA. Throughout the 1980s Chavis developed an increasing concern for the environment and, in particular, the high frequency of hazardous waste sites being sited in low-income communities. After participating in a series of 1982 protests against the dumping of PCBs (polychlorinated biphenyls) in Warren County, North Carolina, Chavis commissioned a study under the auspices of the UCC to determine the precise relationship between existent toxic dumps and economically disadvantaged areas. With its shocking revelations about the prejudicial geography of industrial waste, that study, "Toxic Waste and Race in the United States of America" (1987), became one of the most significant events in the early history of the environmental justice movement. When he appeared before the House Subcommittee on Civil and Constitutional Rights of the Judiciary Committee in March 1993, Chavis's testimony included the first definition of "environmental racism."

Environmental racism is racial discrimination in environmental policy-making and enforcement of regulations and laws, the deliberate targeting of communities of color for toxic waste facilities, the official sanctioning of the presence of life threatening poisons and pollutants for communities of color, and the history of excluding people of color from leadership of the environmental movement (Chavis, xii).

Alongside his work with the UCC-CRJ, Chavis expanded his public profile through his nationally syndicated newspaper column and radio program, *Civil Rights Journal* from 1985 to 1993. Through this platform Chavis articulated his continuing frustration with the prevailing racism in American schools, prisons, courtrooms, and financial institutions. Although Chavis remained aligned with the UCC, his growing focus on the promotion of Afrocentric history and his repeated indictment of white power structures signaled his restlessness within mainline Protestantism. Nevertheless his aggressive pursuit of social justice for African Americans had impressed many of his peers, and in 1993 he was the youngest person ever appointed to be the executive director and CEO of the National Association for the Advancement of Colored People (NAACP).

During his sixteen months in that position Chavis focused on three areas of organizational development. First he emphasized the need for a viable economic infrastructure within the black community. After thousands of African Americans accused the Denny's restaurant chain of discriminatory service, Chavis invited that company to join forces with the NAACP, signing a multimillion-dollar economic covenant to initiate a series of corporate investments in African American businesses. The covenant improved Denny's public reputation and financed small business loans fostered by the NAACP. Second Chavis sought to address urban crime through a coalition between the NAACP and the nascent "Gang Truce" movement that had arisen following the 1992 Los Angeles riots. Third Chavis initiated a recruitment campaign among black youth, seeking to incorporate them into the institutional fight for social justice. Chavis's tenure with the NAACP saw a rapid growth in membership from about 475,000 to 650,000 members, with approximately 60 percent of those recruits under the age of thirty.

Although Chavis's youth and enthusiasm proved useful for the NAACP membership rolls, he had a fractious relationship with that organization's board of trustees. Disagreements about key issues, such as the North Atlantic Free Trade Agreement (NAFTA) and the environmental lobby, underlined for Chavis what he saw as the fundamental problems with institutional activism. His success defining and fighting environmental racism earned him his position as head of the largest civil rights organization in the United States; however, that organization could not reject the corporate and governmental sponsors that provided much of its financial and political support. Thus Chavis's rejection of NAFTA and his anxiety about corporate excess were outweighed by the exigencies of his new office. In addition Chavis's pursuit of young black America had led to a close relationship with LOUIS FARRAKHAN, the controversial leader of the Nation of Islam. The NAACP board discouraged public ties with Farrakhan owing to his anti-Semitism and exclusionary racial rhetoric. This growing discord between Chavis and the NAACP climaxed when it was discovered that he committed $332,000 in NAACP funds to settle a sexual harassment and discrimination claim against him. Married to Martha Rivera Chavis and the father of eight children, Chavis could not survive the political conflict alongside a personal embarrassment. The NAACP fired him in 1994.

Chavis did not take long to emerge from this defeat. In 1995 Farrakhan tapped him to be the national director for the Million Man March, which took place on 16 October 1995 in Washington, D.C. In response to the growing rate of black-on-black crime, Chavis organized this massive gathering of men to take a pledge of social and familial responsibility. Criticisms of the racially and gender-exclusive event were abundant, but for Chavis it initiated a new stage in his life. In that same year he became executive director and CEO of the National African American Leadership Summit (NAALS), an organization founded to create "operational unity" within the diffuse threads of the remaining civil rights movement.

Chavis's leadership of NAALS concluded in 1997 when he formally joined the Nation of Islam and changed his name to Benjamin Chavis-Muhammad. "During the last 40 years, God has called me into many different ministries, organizations, movements, struggles, trials, and tribulations, but through it all God has never left me alone," Chavis-Muhammad announced on 10 March 1997. "Today God is calling me again" (*Jet*, 6). Farrakhan quickly appointed Chavis-Muhammad East Coast regional minister of the Nation of Islam and minister of the historic Mosque Number Seven in Harlem, New York.

Chavis explained his conversion as a turn towards greater ritual discipline and racial solidarity, and did not interpret it as a rejection of any faith or creed: "The God of Judaism and the God of Christianity and the God of Islam is the same one God" (Muwakkil, 29). Nevertheless, many leaders in the African American Christian community were disappointed by the conversion, and perceived it as a betrayal of the ideals embodied within the mainstream civil rights movement. For his part Chavis-Muhammad used his affiliation with the Nation to connect with a new audience. In 2000 Chavis-Muhammad joined with the hip-hop music producer RUSSELL SIMMONS to found the Hip-Hop Summit Action Network (HSAN), a national coalition of hip-hop artists, recording industry executives, youth activists, and civil rights leaders focused on the education and political mobilization of young African Americans. Along with the HSAN board, which included Roc-a-Fella partners Jay-Z and Damon Dash, Bad Boy's SEAN "P. DIDDY" COMBS, and former presidential candidate the Reverend AL SHARPTON, Chavis Muhammad magnified HSAN's role as a leading African American lobbyist organization. During the 2004 national election cycle HSAN organized massive voter registration drives through concert events. In addition Chavis focused HSAN on the reformation of New York's Rockefeller drug laws, which impose lengthy sentences on first-time offenders.

FURTHER READING

Godwin, John L. *Black Wilmington and the North Carolina Way* (2000)

Mercadante, Linda A. "Questioning Chavis Muhammad," *Christian Century* (4–11 June 1997).

Muwakkil, Salim. "Answering the Call," *Black America* (31 Mar. 1997/13 Apr. 1997).

Myerson, Michael. *Nothing Could Be Finer* (1978)

Othow, Helen Chavis. *John Chavis: African American Patriot, Preacher, Teacher, and Mentor, 1763–1838* (2001).

Taylor, James Lance. "The Reverend Benjamin Chavis-Muhammad: From Wilmington to Washington, from Chavis to Muhammad," in *Religious Leaders and Faith Based Politics: Ten Profiles*, eds. Jo Renee Formicola and Hubert Morken (2001).

KATHRYN LOFTON

Chavis, John (1763–13 June 1838), Presbyterian minister and teacher, was born in Granville County, North Carolina; the names of his parents are unknown. He grew up as a free black near Mecklenberg, Virginia. By his own account, Chavis was born free and was a Revolutionary War army veteran. Details of his military service and the events of his life immediately following the war are not known, but he began his studies for the Presbyterian ministry in 1792 at the age of twenty-nine. According to an apocryphal account, one planter had a wager with another that it was impossible to educate a black man. In order to settle their dispute, they sent Chavis to the College of New Jersey (now Princeton University). More than likely, Chavis's religious fervor and potential for scholarship attracted the attention of Presbyterian leaders in Virginia, who believed a black clergyman might do a better job of evangelizing slaves and free blacks than white ministers.

During his three years at the College of New Jersey, Chavis studied under the private tutelage of the college president, John Witherspoon, who often instructed one or two black students and several Native Americans as well. Chavis's studies in New Jersey ended when Witherspoon died in 1794. The next year he resumed studies at Liberty Hall Academy (now Washington & Lee University) in Lexington, Virginia, also a Presbyterian school. Chavis completed his studies there in 1799, and when it licensed him to preach in early 1800, the Lexington Presbytery expressed hopes that he would serve the blacks of the community.

After leaving the Lexington Presbytery in 1801 Chavis served the Hanover, Virginia, Presbytery before going to work under the supervision of the Synod of Virginia in 1804. Ultimately, he also preached in Maryland and North Carolina. At the beginning of each new assignment, Presbyterian leaders admonished Chavis to focus his efforts on the evangelization of slaves and free blacks, but his preaching attracted large numbers of whites and hardly any blacks. In 1883 one white North Carolinian remembered Chavis as a "venerable old Negro preacher," who was "respected as a man ... familiar with the proprieties of social life, yet modest and unassuming, and sober in language and customs." Southern white admirers seemed to look beyond his race, while slaves and free blacks were unable to identify with one of their own who sounded and behaved like a white man.

By 1807 Chavis had opened a small school and devoted almost all of his attention to that endeavor. During the school's first year of operation he taught both white and black children together, but some white parents objected. The next year he advertised daytime classes for white students and evening classes for blacks. At different times, Chavis operated his school in Chatham, Wake, Orange, and Granville counties of North Carolina, and it attracted prominent white students, including the sons of the state's chief justice Leonard Henderson; James Horner, who later founded the Horner School in Oxford, North Carolina; Charles Manly, who later served as the state's governor; Willie P. Mangum, a prominent Whig senator; and Abram Rencher, who became governor of New Mexico.

Chavis charged low tuition rates, which kept his school full while providing ample money for his own support and that of his wife. By March 1828 he was able to boast that the enrollment had reached sixteen. The small, orderly school ran for about thirty years before political developments forced it to close. The 1831 insurrection of NAT TURNER created a climate of fear and distrust among white southerners that resulted in severe restrictions on the black population. The North Carolina legislature passed a law that prevented blacks from preaching or teaching, thus creating economic hardships for Chavis.

By 1832 the sixty-nine-year-old Chavis turned to the Orange, North Carolina, Presbytery for support. After careful study, the Presbytery resolved to take up a collection for his support. The sums forwarded to Chavis were never sufficient, and there is evidence that he found his situation extremely embarrassing. In 1833 he hoped to earn money for himself by publishing an essay entitled

"The Extent of the Atonement," but he needed the Presbytery to pay publication costs. Many other religious leaders had already written on the subject, and the Presbytery decided that such an essay would not be interesting enough to sell. Chavis continued to depend on them for charity throughout the remainder of his life. From October 1834 to April 1835 the Presbytery expended $81.95 for his support, but the sum was not always as generous. In the fall of 1835, when the Orange Presbytery divided, the new Roanoke Presbytery assumed Chavis's support. In 1837 it resolved to pay him fifty dollars annually.

John Chavis retained a close personal relationship with his former student, Senator Willie P. Mangum, and advised him to reject the demands of the abolitionists during the mid-1830s. His position on slavery was cautious because he feared for the plight of masses of black people who would face homelessness and uncertain futures. Chavis did not want them to be more miserable than they already were. His position seems startling, but no one was any more aware of the difficulties of living free than this impoverished man, who constantly depended on the charity of whites for support.

John Chavis died in North Carolina sometime between the April and October 1838 meetings of the Presbytery. At the October meeting, they resolved to continue support for his widow.

FURTHER READING

The Papers of Willie P. Mangum, in the Manuscript Collection of the University of North Carolina Library, contain letters that Chavis wrote to Mangum.
Berlin, Ira. *Slaves without Masters: The Free Negro in the Antebellum South* (1974).
Franklin, John Hope. *The Free Negro in North Carolina, 1790–1860* (1943).
Kaplan, Sidney, and Emma Nogrady Kaplan. *The Black Presence in the Era of Revolution*, rev. ed. (1989).
Shaw, G. C. *John Chavis, 1763–1838* (1931).
This entry is taken from the *American National Biography* and is published here with the permission of the American Council of Learned Societies.

THEODORE C. DELANEY

Chavis, Wilson Anthony "Boozoo" (23 Oct. 1930–5 May 2001), Zydeco musician and quarter-horse trainer, was born into a farming community in Dog Hill near Lake Charles, Louisiana, one of seven children, to Marceline Pete and Arthur Chavis, tenant farmers and entrepreneurs who managed a few well-known local horse circuits, or unregulated "bush" horse races. As a young boy he was given the inexplicable nickname Boozoo, which would remain his moniker throughout the entirety of his life. The first instrument Chavis learned to play was the harmonica, but he mastered the button accordion by watching his father, uncles, and Henry Martin, all well-known local musicians in southwest Louisiana. Although his parents separated when he was three years old, he remained in contact with his father and frequently attended the local house dances in Rayne and Dog Hill, where both his father and his great uncle Sidney Babineaux frequently played. At the age of twenty-one he married Leona Predium, a longtime friend from childhood, who would work alongside Boozoo breeding horses at their home in Dog Hill. The couple remained married for forty-nine years and had six children, three sons and three daughters. His three sons played in his band.

Chavis was best known for the single "Paper in My Shoe," which he recorded in 1954 with the local Goldband Records on its Folk Star label. The recording introduced to a national audience a unique regional musical genre known as Louisiana Zydeco. The song, which was about being too poor to buy a pair of socks, became popular after Imperial Records released it nationally. Although details about the recording of the hit single were the topic of controversy, it was believed that Goldband's owner Eddie Shuler sold over 100,000 copies of "Paper in My Shoe." Chavis, however, received almost no royalties from the song. Shuler, like many record producers of the era, did not hesitate to register his name along with Chavis's to receive credit for authoring the song. Shuler was listed on at least three other Chavis titles. Chavis neither forgot nor forgave his former producer's exploitation. In 1964, after recording a local hit, "Hamburger and Popcorn" (which Shuler again registered with BMI under his own name as the sole composer), Chavis ended his dealings with Goldband and walked away from the recording industry altogether. For twenty-five years Chavis remained a horse trainer and breeder and played at house dances and local clubs on the side.

In 1984 Chavis's wife, Leona, suggested that he return to recording. She had noticed that another musician was posing as Boozoo Chavis. Once, when driving to a horse race, Chavis and his wife heard a radio announcement promoting him as the musician scheduled to play at a local club. Leona suggested that if someone was to make money off of his name and fame that he should be the one to do it. Soon afterwards Chavis recorded a new single, "Dog Hill." He then signed a contract with Floyd Solae to record on the Ville Platte–based Maison de Soul label. Within three years, with the support of the label and his own unending energy, Chavis had jump-started his career and completed three albums. He recorded *Louisiana Zydeco Music* (1986), *Boozoo Zydeco* (1987), and *Zydeco Homebrew* (1988). The 1986 album included a new version of "Paper in My Shoe." In 1987 Chavis recorded an album with the more contemporary band Nathan and the Zydeco Cha-Cha's, which enabled him not only to share the top billing but also to meet the producers at Rounder Records of Cambridge, Massachusetts. By 1991 Chavis had recorded five albums with Rounder, Maison de Soul, and with the short-lived American Explorer series of Elektra Records. Chavis had finally garnered both a national and international audience. In 1994 he and relative newcomer Beau Jocque vied for the crown of King of Zydeco that became vacant with the deaths of Clifton Chenier and "Rockin" (Alton Rubin) Doopsie, the self-crowned Prince of Zydeco. The film *The Kingdom of Zydeco* by Robert Mugge (1994) and the subsequent book by Michael Tisserand, *The Kingdom of Zydeco* (1998), featured the rivalry between the Zydeco musicians.

Chavis remained dedicated to bringing authenticity to his music. He played full four- to six-hour sets during concerts even in his sixties. His dedication was so strong that even after losing two fingers from his left hand in a 1995 accident at his home at Dog Hill, Chavis still performed the following night in Washington, D.C. Known for his stamina and energetic performances, Chavis gave a music workshop in April 2001 at the Dewey Balfa Cajun and Creole Heritage Week at Lake Fausse Pointe State Park near St. Martinville, Louisiana, just two days prior to his experiencing a heart attack. While hospitalized in Austin, Texas, Chavis suffered a stroke and died. At the time he was completing what became his final album, *Down Home on Dog Hill* (2001).

Posthumously, Boozoo Chavis received the 2001 National Heritage Fellowship from the National Endowment for the Arts, considered the nation's highest honor in folk and traditional arts. In addition he was nominated by the Blues Foundation for the prestigious W.C. Handy Award in 2002 in the category of Best Blues Instrumentalist. Because of his commitment to the Creole house dance music style, many young musicians not only listen to his recordings and borrow his hard-playing accordion style but also honor him through their own versions of his music. Performers like JoJo Reed with his song "I Got It from Boo" ensured that Chavis's musical contributions will not be forgotten.

FURTHER READING

Ancelet, Barry Jean, and Elemore Morgan Jr. *Cajun and Creole Music Makers* (1999).

Bernard, Shane K. *Swamp Pop: Cajun and Creole Rhythm and Blues* (1996).

Coster, Rick. *Louisiana Music: A Journey from R&B to Zydeco, Jazz to Country, Blues to Gospel, Cajun Music to Swamp Pop to Carnival Music and Beyond* (2002).

Sandmel, Ben, and Rick Olivier. *Zydeco!* (1999).

Spitzer, Nicholas R. *Zydeco: Creole Music and Culture in Rural Louisiana*, film (1984).

Tisserand, Michael. *The Kingdom of Zydeco* (1998).

Obituary: *Baton Rouge Advocate*, 22 Aug. 2001.

DEMETRIA ROUGEAUX SHABAZZ

Cheatham, Doc (13 June 1905–2 June 1997), jazz musician, was born Aldophus Cheatham in Nashville, Tennessee, the son of Marshall Ney Cheatham, a barber, and Alice Anthony. The elder Cheatham was descended from Choctaw and Cherokee Indians who had settled in Cheatham County, Tennessee.

Cheatham began playing music with a youth band, the BFS Band (Bright Future Stars), at Philips Chapel in Nashville. Self-taught, he played several instruments, starting on drums before playing the cornet and later the soprano saxophone. Cheatham seems to have acquired the nickname "Doc" by performing at the local Meharry Medical College, where his mother worked as a lab assistant.

By the early 1920s, Cheatham was playing tenor saxophone in Nashville's Bijou Theater, a TOBA (Theater Owners Booking Association) outlet and the local venue for many of the classic blues singers of the time, including BESSIE SMITH, ETHEL WATERS, CLARA SMITH, and IDA COX. During a school vacation in 1924, Cheatham made his first trip out of Nashville to Atlantic City, New Jersey, and played a C melody saxophone with Charlie Johnson's orchestra at the Paradise Club. A later road excursion in 1925 with a small group landed Cheatham in Chicago, where the show disbanded and he was left to scramble for employment. It was in Chicago that Cheatham first became aware of New Orleans musicians and came under the influence of the cornetists FREDDIE KEPPARD, JOE OLIVER, and LOUIS ARMSTRONG; the discovery

caused him to concentrate on the cornet to the exclusion of all other instruments.

But Cheatham soon learned that his opportunities for employment in Chicago were limited; the city's entertainment during the 1920s was dominated by New Orleans–born musicians. This prompted him in 1927 to move to Philadelphia and then in 1928 to move to New York City, where he played briefly with CHICK WEBB's orchestra before accepting an offer from SAM WOODING, with whom Cheatham undertook his first tour of Europe (1929–1931). The Wooding tour established Cheatham as a lead trumpeter, a label that would identify and in some ways categorize him for the next thirty-five years. Lead trumpeters were the ex officio leaders of the band, but they often sacrificed greater recognition for anonymity since the star jazz soloists, the improvisers, usually claimed the public's attention.

Beginning in the 1930s Cheatham gradually solidified his reputation as a lead trumpet player with a number of big bands including McKinney's Cotton Pickers, led by DON REDMAN and later Benny Carter, as well as the orchestra of CAB CALLOWAY (with whom he spent eight years, 1931–1939). By the late 1930s, however, the traveling, the long nights, and an inadequate diet were beginning to take their toll on Cheatham's health. He was suffering from nervous exhaustion, and a routine physical examination toward the end of his stay with Calloway convinced him to take a hiatus from playing music. He returned to Nashville and began a convalescence that lasted eight months. Even though he was still not fully recovered, he made his way back to New York and eventually accepted work with TEDDY WILSON's band, although not in the lead trumpet position.

The public's diminishing interest in big bands and Cheatham's continuing problems with his own health led him to another break from performing during World War II. Between 1944 and 1946, in lieu of active military service he took a job in a U.S. post office on Long Island, handling GI wartime correspondence. During this time he played no music, but after leaving the post office job he gradually worked his way back, playing with the Eddie Heywood Sextet, a small combo that included MARY LOU WILLIAMS, VIC DICKENSON, John Simmons, Lem Davis, and BILLIE HOLIDAY on vocals.

It was during this period that Cheatham began to devote more of his time to teaching. By chance, one of his students, a Cuban trumpeter and bandleader, Marcellino Guerra, invited him to join his small Latin band. Latin music presented a new challenge for Cheatham and occupied much of his time for the next twenty years as he performed intermittently with orchestras led by Damaso Perez Prado, MACHITO, Ricardo Rey, and Bobbie Cruz. Cheatham also began a new chapter in his personal life. While touring Uruguay with Perez Prado in 1951, Cheatham met a young South American woman named Amanda (maiden name unknown), whom he married the following year on a return trip to Chile. Despite the great difference in their ages, the couple produced two children and remained married until the trumpeter's death. Cheatham's two earlier marriages, the first while he was still with Marion Hardy's group in Chicago in the late 1920s and the second to a Cotton Club chorine, were unsuccessful and childless. The names of his first two wives are unknown.

The 1950s were years of stylistic diversity, when Cheatham performed with groups led by WILBUR DE PARIS, Sammy Price, and Herbie Mann. In 1952 Cheatham began a long and productive association with George Wein, who at the time was operating jazz clubs in Boston. But the most rewarding chapter in Cheatham's long career began in the early 1960s when he continued a gradual transition from lead trumpeter and ensemble player to featured soloist, vocalist, and, eventually, leader. In 1966, at age sixty, he accepted an offer to join Benny Goodman and remained with the clarinetist into 1967. Goodman was suffering from back problems during this time, so the group did little touring, and Cheatham played only with the sextet, not with Goodman's big band.

The peripatetic Cheatham now seemed to be in demand everywhere that he performed, and he was especially revered during his frequent European tours of the 1970s and 1980s. As he became more confident in his gentle, melodic style of improvising, he gradually added distinctive vocal interpretations that provided some much needed rest from his trumpet playing. Now firmly established as a leader, he assumed the role of elder statesman of jazz and drew younger musicians and older admirers around him. His seventeen years at Sweet Basil's in New York (1980–1997) must be seen as one of the most enduring tenures of any jazz musician. By the early 1990s Cheatham had renewed his interest in New Orleans music—a direction that he first explored in the 1920s—and had formed a creative alliance with the young New Orleans trumpet star NICHOLAS PAYTON. The two had met by accident while performing with different bands on a cruise ship and developed an immediate rapport. Their celebrated 1997 recording, *Doc Cheatham & Nicholas Payton*, recorded two weeks before Cheatham's death, remains one of the most curious bigenerational collaborations in recent jazz history.

The story of Doc Cheatham parallels in many ways the diversity of jazz itself during its first century. His seventy-year career spans virtually every major development in the music, and his own development was a steady progression toward greater recognition as a jazz artist. Especially during the last two decades of his life he emerged as one of the most sought-after trumpeters and jazz personalities. As a slow starter and a truly humble individual (he waited until he was in his sixties before claiming to be a jazz musician), Cheatham was fortunate to have lived long enough to see his work recognized. The Cheatham/Payton appearances toward the end of his life introduced him to new and younger audiences, and he was clearly at a peak in his career when he died suddenly one night after completing a performance with Payton at Blues Alley in Washington, D.C.

FURTHER READING

Cheatham, Doc. *I Guess I'll Get the Papers and Go Home* (1995), ed. Alyn Shipton.

Schuller, Gunther. *Early Jazz: Its Roots and Musical Development* (1968)

Schuller, Gunther. *The Swing Era: The Development of Jazz, 1930–1945* (1989)

Shaw, Arnold. *52nd Street: The Street of Jazz* (1977)

Obituary: *New York Times*, 3 June 1997.

This entry is taken from the *American National Biography* and is published here with the permission of the American Council of Learned Societies.

CHARLES BLANCQ

Cheatham, Henry Plummer (27 Dec. 1857–29 Nov. 1935), congressman and public official, was born near Henderson, Granville (later Vance) County, North Carolina. All that is known of his parents is that one was a house slave. He attended local public schools and worked on farms during the 1860s and 1870s before graduating with honors from Shaw University in 1882. He became principal of the Plymouth Normal School for Negroes, a state-supported institution, and held this position from 1882 until 1884. He returned to Henderson and, after the retirement of the white Republican incumbent, won election as Vance County registrar of deeds, serving in this capacity from 1885 to 1888. During this time he also studied law, though he never established a practice.

Cheatham's career in national politics began in 1888. Unable to agree on a single candidate, delegates to the Republican convention for the Second Congressional District, the so-called Black Second, nominated both Cheatham and George A. Mebane, another African American. After Mebane's subsequent withdrawal, Cheatham had the edge over his Democratic opponent, Furnifold M. Simmons, because the district's African Americans and Republicans still voted in great numbers. Cheatham enjoyed a reputation as being responsible and courteous, but during the campaign he warned black constituents that local Democrats wanted to reestablish slavery. He narrowly won the election with 16,704 votes to Simmons's 16,051.

Cheatham took his seat in the Fifty-First Congress, which was controlled by Republicans. A member of the Education Committee, he introduced a bill for federal aid for education that received a favorable report but never reached the floor for debate. Supporting the interests of Carolina tobacco farmers, he endorsed the protectionist McKinley Tariff of 1890 and served on a House-Senate conference committee that considered the proposal. Cheatham also favored the Federal Elections Bill, introduced by Henry Cabot Lodge of Massachusetts, to safeguard the voting rights of African Americans, especially in southern states. Preferring personal contact in the committee room to delivering speeches, Cheatham did not speak on behalf of the measure on the floor but did address the House Republican caucus on the subject. The Lodge bill passed in the House but died in the Senate.

As a first-term congressman desiring reelection, Cheatham took special interest in federal patronage in his district, securing more than eighty appointments for his constituents. These were chiefly postal jobs, but he also helped to fill internal revenue, customs, and judicial positions in eastern North Carolina and secured the appointment of African Americans as census enumerators and clerks in Washington, D.C. Several of Cheatham's appointees performed poorly, however, and some were arrested for fraud and embezzlement. His parceling out of patronage alienated both whites, who complained of black domination, and certain African Americans, who did not believe that he had secured enough of the spoils for his own people.

By 1890 agricultural depression in the South had caused a decline in the proportion of black voters in Cheatham's district as the blacks sought opportunity elsewhere. The depression also increased demands from farmers for government aid. Accordingly Cheatham, addressing a primarily white audience in Wilson during the campaign, discussed neither the Federal Elections Bill nor the tariff but devoted himself mainly to depressed agricultural conditions. He also defended his patronage record in a manner calculated to avoid offending whites or exciting blacks, but at the same time he condemned the steel magnate Andrew Carnegie for importing laborers while neglecting to hire African Americans. Cheatham's successful appeal to white farmers helped to offset the black exodus from his district, allowing Cheatham, who had relocated to Littleton because of reapportionment, to defeat his last-minute Democratic challenger, James M. Mewborne, 16,943 votes to 15,713.

Cheatham's victory in 1890, the year of a Democratic landslide in House contests, earned him the distinction of being the only African American elected to the Fifty-second Congress. With Democrats in control, however, his influence diminished. Nevertheless Cheatham remained active. He persuaded a New Jersey Republican to propose an amendment to an appropriation bill to provide money for a black progress exhibit at the World's Columbian Exposition. Cheatham also introduced a bill, killed in committee, that proposed appropriating $100,000 "for the purpose of collecting, preparing, and publishing facts and statistics pertaining to the moral, industrial, and intellectual development and progress of the colored people of African descent residing in the United States." The fate of such endeavors led Cheatham to conclude that "whenever the colored people of this country ask for anything, something unfortunate intervenes to hinder their getting what they ask."

Cheatham won renomination by acclamation in 1892, and at that year's Republican National Convention he seconded President Benjamin Harrison's renomination in a brief speech. But the congressman's political base had been weakened by the general assembly's revisions of the state election law, which reduced the African American vote, and by the redrawing of political boundaries, which in effect destroyed the "Black Second," a citadel of Republican strength. As a result Cheatham lost the race to the Democrat Frederick A. Woodard, a Wilson lawyer and banker who drew the color line during the campaign and captured 13,925 votes to Cheatham's 11,812. Fraudulent election practices and the black discontent over patronage issues also hurt Cheatham, as did the presence of a Populist candidate who split the non-Democratic vote. The *Raleigh Signal*, a Republican newspaper, praised the defeated congressman as a "faithful public servant who has done all that he could for the whole state" and who "reflected great credit on his race, the Republican Party and himself."

Cheatham tried to mount a political comeback in 1894. After a prolonged and bitter battle for the Republican congressional nomination, he lost the hotly contested general election to Woodard by 9,413 to 14,721. As before, a Populist took a portion of the non-Democratic vote. Cheatham sought the congressional nomination again in 1896 but lost to his more militant brother-in-law, GEORGE H. WHITE, a lawyer and former state legislator, who defeated Woodard in the general election. Cheatham never again sought elected office but continued his political activity. President William McKinley in 1897 appointed him registrar of deeds for the District of Columbia, a position that Cheatham held until 1901, when he returned to Littleton. There he farmed and helped found a local hospital.

In 1907 Cheatham relocated to Oxford, North Carolina, and became superintendent of the North Carolina Orphanage for Negroes, which he had been instrumental in establishing in 1882. He held this post for the next twenty-eight years. Cheatham transformed the orphanage by means of both more effective administration and the construction of seven brick buildings with modern designs and facilities. He functioned as a benevolent father figure, disciplining the children and assigning each child tasks to perform in the cottages and on the farm operated by the orphanage. "No success without labor" was the creed by which Cheatham managed his orphanage and training school.

Cheatham was married twice: he had three children with Louise Cherry and three with Laura Joyner. He died in Oxford. Cheatham was one of North Carolina's most distinguished African American citizens. An educated, discreet, and diplomatic man, he impressed even the white Democrat Josephus Daniels, who remarked that he regarded Cheatham highly as a man who had gained the confidence of both races.

FURTHER READING

Anderson, Eric. *Race and Politics in North Carolina, 1872–1901: The Black Second* (1981).

Logan, Frenise A. *The Negro in North Carolina, 1876–1894* (1964).

Smith, Samuel D. *The Negro in Congress, 1870–1901* (1940).

Obituary: *Oxford (North Carolina) Public Ledger*, 3 Dec. 1935.

This entry is taken from the *American National Biography* and is published here with the permission of the American Council of Learned Societies.

LEONARD SCHLUP

Che-cho-ter (1811?–?), wife of the famous Seminole war leader Osceola, born in Alabama around 1802, was a Creek woman of Afro-Indian descent, also known as "Morning Dew." Che-cho-ter may have been the daughter of a former slave and a prominent Creek or Seminole man. She was one of two wives taken by Osceola during the turbulent years in which the United States first occupied the Florida Territory. During those years, the U.S. government was attempting to make the Florida Territory safe for the institution of slavery by evicting the Seminoles from their homeland.

Osceola was the son of an English trader, William Powell, and a Muscogee Indian woman of Creek heritage. The Seminoles, who first became prominent in European records during the late eighteenth century, were a nation of Florida Indians who had close ethnic and cultural ties to the Creeks of Georgia and Alabama. Historians believe that Osceola first saw and began pursuing Che-cho-ter late in 1826 in Florida when she was visiting a Seminole agency—a trading post set up by the U.S. government. She was probably about fifteen at the time, while Osceola was around twenty-two. By that age, Osceola had risen to the status of *tustenuggee* (subchief), an informal position in the Indian hierarchy characterized by having faithful followers—often young braves needing direction and wishing to learn how to make war or hunt.

The usual tradition would have consisted of having the bridegroom inform relatives of his choice to marry. Although Che-cho-ter was of Seminole-Creek ancestry, no record of her clan exists. Osceola's relatives would have then contacted Che-cho-ter's family, who would discuss the marriage with her. If she found the match acceptable, gifts would have been exchanged. On the night of the marriage, Osceola would have gone to Che-cho-ter's home to be received by his bride. Osceola and Che-cho-ter would then be considered husband and wife on the following day. After living with the wife's family for an undisclosed amount of time, the couple would then establish their own home. Historical records speculate that Osceola had a second wife, whose name is unknown. They also suggest that he may have fathered as many as four children, at least one of whom, a daughter, is believed to have been conceived by Che-cho-ter.

Congress began making appropriations in 1826 to aid the starving Seminoles relegated to reservation land, one of the many unfortunate side effects of the Treaty of Moultrie Creek. The document, signed in 1823 by thirty-two Seminoles (some signers were chiefs and some had no actual authority to sign), forced the Seminoles to relinquish all claims to Florida except for those pockets of acreage specifically designated for their use. In total, the Seminoles ceded 28,040,991 acres in exchange for what would amount to less than $120,000 over twenty years.

In his 1829 State of the Union message, President Andrew Jackson called for an Indian Removal Act to facilitate the relocation of Native American tribes living east of the Mississippi River to lands farther west. On 28 May 1830 this policy was eventually signed into law by Jackson as the Indian Removal Act of 1830. While the Indian Removal Act did not actually order the removal of any Native Americans, it did authorize the president to negotiate land-exchange treaties with tribes living within the boundaries of existing U.S. states. The United States had acquired a claim to a vast amount of land west of the Mississippi River in the Louisiana Purchase of 1803. Before the Indian Removal Act was passed, the U.S. government was already trying to remove all Indian tribes east of the Mississippi to this land, which was eventually known as the "Indian Territory" (present-day Oklahoma), in exchange for their historic eastern tribal lands. The Indian Removal Act greatly accelerated this land-exchange process.

By 1834 Osceola had witnessed the increasing antagonism between the Seminoles and whites and had begun to form his own strong views concerning the Indian Removal Act. While several incidents ignited Osceola's rage and helped precipitate violent actions leading up to the Second Seminole War, most notable and debatable is the supposed capture and kidnapping of Che-cho-ter in 1835. The abolitionist Joshua Giddings, who published *The Exiles of Florida* in 1858, repeated a story he had heard from M. M. Cohen in the *Quarterly Anti-Slavery Magazine*. In about 1824 Osceola took Che-cho-ter and their daughter to the Fort King trading post. While Osceola was busy trading, slave hunters seized Che-cho-ter and carried her off while the

daughter watched. This incident is the supposed basis for the argument between Osceola and General Wiley Thompson, the Indian agent in charge of the trading post. Sources claim that Osceola expressed outrage at Thompson's loose policy of allowing slave catchers to operate at the fort; it is also alleged that Osceola's angry outbursts against Thompson resulted in his arrest and placement into irons.

Historian Patricia R. Wickman suggests that while Osceola may have had a mixed-race wife, the chronology of the supposed events is unlikely, and the associations Osceola is supposed to have had with Thompson have been disproved, with many sources highly suspect. The sketchy details and unsubstantiated facts surrounding Che-cho-ter's ethnic heritage and subsequent kidnapping at Thompson's fort were initially suggested by historian Kenneth W. Porter in an article titled "The Episode of Osceola's Wife: Fact or Fiction?"

Little is known about Che-cho-ter and her family, although Osceola almost certainly lived with them during the early months of marriage. Critics believe that her family was of some importance and may have been affiliated with the Mikasuki family since there is additional evidence that Osceola was closely affiliated later in life with the Mikasukis. Although all Seminoles rallied around Osceola when he took the position of Seminole leader, his ties to the Mikasuki family were the strongest.

In late 1835 and throughout 1836 and 1837, the Second Seminole War progressed, resulting in Osceola's capture in 1837. Documentation related to Osceola's capture and subsequent death in 1838 suggests that he had two wives at his time of imprisonment. At the end of the Second Seminole War in 1842, many Indians were forced into the originally delegated "Indian Territory" in the West. Che-cho-ter's ultimate fate is unknown.

FURTHER READING

Covington, James W. *The Seminoles of Florida* (1993).
Hartley, William, and Ellen Hartley. *Osceola: The Unconquered Indian* (1973).
McNeer, May. *War Chief of the Seminoles* (1954).
Porter, Kenneth. "The Episode of Osceola's Wife: Fact or Fiction?," *Florida Historical Quarterly*, 26 (July 1947), 92–98.
Wickman, Patricia R. *Osceola's Legacy* (1991).

SYLVIA M. DESANTIS

Checker, Chubby (3 Oct. 1941–), singer and performer, was born Ernest Evans in Spring Gulley, Williamsburg County, South Carolina, one of three sons of a struggling tobacco farmer. The family moved to Philadelphia, Pennsylvania, when he was nine; there he attended Settlement Music School. He formed his first singing group at age eleven. Evans attended South Philadelphia High School, also the alma mater of teen pop idols Frankie Avalon and Fabian, and worked at a produce market where his boss gave him the nickname "Chubby." He also plucked chickens at Fresh Farm Poultry, and it was there that Kal Mann, a friend of the owner and cofounder of Cameo-Parkway Records, heard him sing and recommended him to Dick Clark, the host of the television show *American Bandstand*. Clark had asked Mann to write a novelty song for Christmas and find someone who sounded like FATS DOMINO to sing it. Mann wrote "Jingle Bells" and had Chubby Evans imitate Fats Domino. Dick Clark liked the song and sent it around as a Christmas greeting to all of his friends in the music business. Clark's wife came up with the second half of Chubby's stage name, "Checker," inspired by the parallel with Fats Domino: Fats-Chubby, Domino-Checker.

Chubby Checker performs in November 1961. His version of Hank Ballard's "The Twist" was a top hit that created a series of American dance fads. (AP Images.)

The song on which Chubby Checker built his career, "The Twist," was written in 1959 by Hank Ballard, a rock pioneer who merged gospel with rhythm and blues. Ballard recorded the song with his own band, the Midnighters, as the B side of a single, "Teardrops on Your Letter," which sold poorly. Dick Clark shopped the song around to another group who recorded a version he was not happy with and then offered it to seventeen-year-old Chubby Checker, who was still in high school at the time. Checker appeared on *American Bandstand*, dancing and miming "The Twist" to a prerecorded backing track, and the song was a huge hit in the summer of 1960. "The Twist" went to number one in the Billboard music charts, and when Chubby Checker rereleased the song over a year later, in the fall of 1961, it went to number one again. "The Twist" is the only song in rock music history to be a number one hit twice.

The success of "The Twist" was a product not only of the growing popularity of rock and roll music, but also the spread of television in general and *American Bandstand* in particular. Broadcast every Saturday at noon on WFIL-TV in Philadelphia, *American Bandstand* soon had an important impact on the record-buying habits of American teenagers. The format was simple: one hundred and fifty teenagers dancing to records, interrupted only by commercials and special appearances by popular singing stars. Philadelphia provided a convenient focal point for the burgeoning rock music industry, and the belief was that if a song were successful in "Philly," it would be popular nationwide. The conventional wisdom was self-fulfilling as *American Bandstand* served as a tastemaker with the capacity to promote music into households across the United States.

As important as *American Bandstand* was to popular music, it possibly had an even greater impact on dancing styles. Before, a dance style typically took around a year to move across the country, catching on in a new area as it became obsolete in others. Now, thanks to television, the impact was more immediate, and locally differentiated dancing styles became homogenized. This made Chubby Checker and the Twist into a cultural phenomenon. Numerous teen idols such as Bobby Rydell, Fabian, and Frankie Avalon also benefited from Dick Clark's *American Bandstand*, but Chubby Checker was one of very few who were black.

Not only Chubby Checker but also numerous other artists capitalized on the success of "The Twist." The Isley Brothers and Sam Cooke produced

Twist-related records, Atlantic Records released the album *Do the Twist with Ray Charles*, Joey Dee and the Starlighters recorded "Peppermint Twist," and Checker himself recorded "Let's Twist Again" for the summer of 1961. "The Twist" was also credited with taking rock and roll music across generational and social boundaries. The song was popular not only with teenagers, but also in adult discotheques in New York City such as the Stork Club, Barberry Room, and Peppermint Lounge, where rock music had not been played before. A *New York Times* article referred to the phenomenon as the first time "café society" had gone "slumming with such energy since its forays into Harlem in the Twenties," and it was on these terms the dance was analyzed. Psychiatrists were quoted describing the Twist as a "rite" that "approximated certain primitive ritual dances." The "wiping out of social distinctions" it enabled was said to have a "therapeutic effect," and even First Lady Jacqueline Kennedy was reported doing the Twist (*New York Times*, 19 Oct. 1961). But the Twist also had detractors. It was referred to as "synthetic sex turned into a spectator sport." Since what one twisted went unmentioned, it became a "hypocritical excuse for leers." The "pelvic movements" involved were associated with "African fertility dances" done "naked" (*New York Times*, 3 Dec. 1961).

Chubby Checker followed up "The Twist" with another number one gold record, "Pony Time" (1961), and then "Slow Twistin'" (1962) and "Twist It Up" (1963). He also appeared in several movies, including *Twist Around the Clock* (1961) and *Don't Knock the Twist* (1962), which were remakes of two of the first rock movies, *Rock Around the Clock* (1956) and *Don't Knock the Rock* (1956). Other films produced to cash in on the fad included *Doin' the Twist*, *Hey Let's Twist*, and *Viva La Twist!* In 1962 Chubby Checker received a Grammy for "Let's Twist Again," and according to one poll was even more popular than Elvis Presley (*The State*, 29 June 2003). That same year his future wife, Catherina Lodders of the Netherlands, won the Miss World contest. Chubby Checker and Catherina Lodders were married 12 April 1964 and raised three children.

Despite the fact that his career peaked with "The Twist," Chubby Checker remained a popular performer on the Oldies circuit—perhaps testimony to the song's impact. However, Chubby Checker was not inducted into the Rock and Roll Hall of Fame. Frustrated with being continually overlooked, in 2003 he began a personal campaign to be included.

However, critics insisted that credit for writing "The Twist" went to Hank Ballard, who was inducted in 1990, and without Dick Clark and *American Bandstand*, the song would never have been popular. Nevertheless, it is undoubtedly Chubby Checker with whom the song is most closely associated and without whose performance the song would not have had the same social and cultural impact.

FURTHER READING

Henke, James, Holly George-Warren, Anthony Decurtis, and Jim Miller, eds. *The Rolling Stone Illustrated History of Rock and Roll: The Definitive History of the Most Important Artists and Their Music* (1992).

Friedlander, Paul. *Rock and Roll: A Social History* (1996).

DISCOGRAPHY

Chubby Checker—Greatest Hits (Prime Cuts 2354).

WILLIAM DEJONG-LAMBERT

Chenault, Kenneth Irvine (2 June 1951–), lawyer and corporate leader, was born in Mineola, New York, to Hortenius Chenault, a dentist and a Morehouse and Howard University graduate, and Anne N. Quick, a dental hygienist and Howard alumna. The second of three brothers and one sister, Ken grew up in middle-class, mostly white Hempstead, Long Island, and attended the innovative, private Waldorf School in Garden City through twelfth grade. Although both his parents had graduated top in their classes, Kenneth was at first a middling student. He improved academically and became class president and captain of the track and basketball teams. He also avidly read biographies of famous people, including FREDERICK DOUGLASS, W. E. B. DUBOIS, and Winston Churchill.

Starting Springfield College on an athletic scholarship, he transferred under the mentorship of Waldorf's Peter Curran to Bowdoin College in Maine. There he joined two dozen black pioneers at the all-male (until 1972) and predominantly white elite college, graduating in 1973 with a B.A. in History, magna cum laude. He told a friend, "I've got to get into the system to help my people. If I get in, I can help somebody else" (*Ebony*, July 1997). Attending Harvard Law School, he became moot court champion and received a J.D. in 1976 (when he also got an American Express Gold card), joining the Massachusetts bar five years later. In 1977 Chenault married Kathryn Cassell, a Tufts University political science major and New York

University law student who became a United Negro College Fund lawyer. They lived in New York State with two sons, Kenneth Jr. and Kevin.

Chenault became an associate with the New York corporate law firm of Rogers & Wells from 1977 to 1979. Without an MBA, in 1979 he joined a Boston business consulting firm, Bain & Co., which familiarized him with large corporations, executives, and business strategies. Among his Bain mentors was a Harvard Law School classmate, the son of a former Michigan governor and a future Massachusetts governor, W. Mitt Romney, who takes credit for hiring Chenault, saying, "He was able to process a lot of conflict … cut through the confusion … arrive at very powerful … recommendations and then see them through to their implementation" (*Ebony*, July 1997).

In 1981 Chenault was hired as director of strategic planning for American Express Company in New York City, whose "membership has its privileges" branding of "charge" cards (payable monthly) versus credit cards (revolving payment) differentiated it from Visa and MasterCard. In 1983 he was promoted to vice president of Merchandise Services, a foundering division that he reorganized from a $150 million to a $500 million department. In 1984 he became general manager of Merchandise Service and senior vice president of AmEx Travel-Related Services (TRS), with green, gold, platinum, and travelers' cheques lines. In 1986 he became executive vice president and general manager of the platinum/gold card division. Under his leadership AmEx became the fifth leading direct marketer as he upscaled Merchandise Servicess to produce 20 percent yearly growth. But the old-line company, founded in 1850 and offering "charge cards" to compete with Diners Club since 1958, initially resisted his innovations.

In 1987 AmEx finally introduced for current members a credit card, Optima, to compete with Visa and MasterCard. While the company anticipated that existing AmEx members would be creditworthy, in fact, Optima defaults were twice as high as predicted, and company profits dropped. Although the Optima problems were not Chenault's responsibility, he recognized that AmEx was "arrogant and felt entitled" to customer patronage (*Current Biography*, 1998), and he instituted innovations such as linking cards to frequent flyer mileage. In 1988 Chenault became executive vice president of the Consumer Card and Financial Services Group, again producing record growth. *Black Enterprise* named him among the twenty-five "most powerful

black executives in corporate America." In 1990 his listing appeared in *Who's Who in America* and in 1992 *Who's Who among Black Americans*.

In 1990 Chenault became president of AmEx Consumer Card and Financial Services groups, and by 1991 he managed relations with all firms accepting AmEx cards. Then he faced the "Boston Fee Party," a revolt of one hundred restaurant owners unhappy with unresponsive AmEx treatment and steep transaction fees (3.5 percent vs. 2 percent for Visa and MasterCard). Chenault negotiated selective fee reductions for electronic transactions to keep the merchants as AmEx vendors and maintain the company's competitive position. He also began extending and downscaling the brand by reaching mass markets at Kmart, Sears, and Wal-Mart.

In 1993, when Harvey Golub became CEO, Chenault became president of American Express USA, and his attention to consumer trends and developments in computer technology improved AmEx's position. He increased company offerings to sixty co-branded cards. Merchants doubled to sixty thousand, with transaction fees of 2.7 percent. In 1994 the Optima True Grace card (later ended) was introduced, along with cards for groups like college students and seniors, though AmEx's share of card transactions fell from 22.9 percent in 1990 to 15.9 percent in 1996.

In 1995 Golub named Chenault vice chairman of AmEx. Early in his term Chenault had to "restructure" by laying off 15,800 jobs to cut $3 billion in costs, and he was recognized within the company as having handled the layoff professionally. Employment rose to 73,620 in 1997. In 1996 he became head of TRS International, and in 1997 AmEx market share rose for the first time in ten years. Even though AmEx faced falling share prices, card members grew to 54.3 million in 1998. In 1998 Visa still dominated the industry at 54 percent, with MasterCard at 28 percent, and AmEx at 13.7 percent, though antitrust efforts against Visa and MasterCard promised to reduce their market share.

In February 1997 Golub named Chenault president and chief operating officer, designated him heir apparent "as the primary internal candidate to succeed" as CEO when Golub retired in 2004, and placed Chenault on the company board. When it appeared that Chenault might become the first African American to run one of America's largest corporations, he remarked that it would be "naïve and untrue to say that race is not a factor in our society" but at AmEx, "I have been totally judged on my performance" (Smith, *Notable Black American*

Men, [1992], 192). In December 1998 *Business Week* ran a cover story on "The Rise of a Star."

In May 1999 Golub announced that Chenault would become CEO in 2001 when Golub stepped down three years early to enable his successor to increase his responsibilities within the company. In September 1999 Chenault became Black Enterprise Corporate Executive of the Year and appeared in *International Who's Who*. Although Franklin Delano Raines became the first black CEO of a Fortune 500 company in 1999, Chenault would become the first black CEO of a Dow Jones blue chip firm.

In January 2001 Chenault became AmEx CEO and, in April, chairman of the $22 billion enterprise. Early on he faced a financial crisis over write-offs of junk bonds. Soon after, he ably managed from afar the crisis at AmEx after the September 11 attack on the World Trade Center, evacuating the company headquarters in the nearby World Financial Center and helping 500,000 stranded cardholders by increasing credit limits. At an emotional meeting, he took command of comforting a shocked staff. "Ken epitomizes two attributes I think will be important here," said Golub. "One is courage and the other is composure" (*Business Week*, 29 Oct. 2001). Not long afterward, Chenault stood at George W. Bush's side at Ground Zero, stressing the need to improve security at airports and public sites, and he appeared with Mayor Rudolph Giuliani and Governor George Pataki on requests for federal funds to rebuild the city. In 2001 *Fortune* named him one of the fifty most powerful African American executives.

Chenault steered AmEx through the banking and credit crises of 2007 to 2010, when the company's stock price fell by one-third. Like other financial institutions, AmEx received significant government assistance, with $3.4 billion given in direct aid, as well as a government guarantee of $14 billion of AmEx's debt. The bailout enabled AmEx to rebound in quick order, becoming one of the first companies to pay back the federal government aid. By 2011 the company's stock price had risen to nearly $50, a little short of the $55 it had been when Chenault took over AmEx in 2001, in the final year of the Clinton economic boom. The BARACK OBAMA administration cultivated strong links with Chenault, and appointed him to the President's Council on Jobs and Competitiveness in 2011. The appointment raised some eyebrows among critics of the Wall Street bailout who noted that the previous year Chenault had presided over the restructuring of AmEx, shedding one percent of the workforce—550 employees—despite the company making $1.1 billion in the fourth quarter of 2010.

Following his philosophy that "part of being a leader is pulling people from disparate backgrounds together" and that minorities, "more than others, must give back to help our community and to ease the way of those who will follow" (Chenault, 11–12), Chenault is on the boards of Junior Achievement, the New York Medical Center, Bowdoin College, the NCAA, and the ARTHUR ASHE Institute for Urban Health. He was also named Corporate Arts Patron by the Harlem Studio Museum. Chenault belongs to the American Bar Association and the Council on Foreign Relations, and he has served on the boards of the Brooklyn Union Gas Company, IBM, and Quaker Oats. He received honorary degrees from Adelphi, Bowdoin, Howard, Morgan State, Notre Dame, and SUNY/Stony Brook. A team builder who shattered the glass ceiling, Chenault exemplifies his own dictum that "as barriers against us fall, we must not fail to move forward" (Chenault, 13).

FURTHER READING
Chenault, Kenneth. "Control What You Can: Your Own Integrity, Your Own Performance," in *Take a Lesson: Today's Black Achievers on How They Made It and What They Learned along the Way*, ed. Caroline Clarke (2001).
Byrne, John, and Heather Timmons. "Tough Times for a New CEO." *Business Week* (29 Oct. 2001).
Heberling, Michael E. *Modern Day CEOs: The Good, the Bad, and the Ugly* (2001).
Pierce, Ponchitta. "Kenneth Chenault, Blazing New Paths in Corporate America." *Ebony* (July 1997).

RICHARD SOBEL

Chenier, Clifton (25 June 1925–12 Dec. 1987), zydeco accordionist and singer, was born in Opelousas, Louisiana, the son of Joe Chenier, a sharecropper. His mother's name is not known. Clifton's father played the accordion in his free time. Maurice "Big" Chenier, Clifton's uncle, played guitar and fiddle and ran a popular small dance club in Louisiana. His neighbor Isaie Blasa gave Clifton an accordion in 1947, and his father gave him private lessons on the instrument. Clifton and his brother Cleveland began playing together in 1937, with Clifton on the accordion and Cleveland on a washboard-like instrument called a *frottoir*. The brothers were a popular dance hall act through the 1940s. Clifton continued to make music called la-la or house music but needed to work various other jobs to make a living, including working in the rice fields, cutting sugarcane, driving a refinery truck, and hauling refinery piping.

Chenier moved from Lake Charles, Louisiana, to New Iberia, Louisiana, in the mid-1940s and to Port Arthur, Texas, in 1947. His professional career received a significant boost with two local hit records titled "Clifton's Blues" and "Louisiana Stomp," which were recorded at a Lake Charles radio station and released on Elko Records in 1954. The next single, "Ay Tete Fille (Hey, Little Girl)," received national airplay. PROFESSOR LONGHAIR originally sang the song, and Specialty Records released Chenier's version in 1955. Chenier claimed his early influences were the accordion player Amede Ardoin, popular in the 1920s, the pop singer FATS DOMINO, Professor Longhair (Henry Roeland Byrd, aka Fess), and the blues artists MUDDY WATERS, LIGHTNIN' HOPKINS, and PEETIE WHEATSTRAW (William Bunch). The St. Louis blues guitarist Wheatstraw developed an elaborate folktale to explain his musical talents, a conceit that was later imitated by Chenier, who adopted the moniker "the King of Zydeco."

Chenier was able to work full time in music beginning in 1956. He played and toured with the Zydeco Ramblers and moved to record on the Chicago Chess record label. He was now touring full time, including a tour with ETTA JAMES. Chenier worked at every performance to create a visual spectacle and to encourage audience participation. He usually performed in a suit made of flamboyant fabric and wore a small cape, lined in red, over his shoulders, occasionally donning a red-lined gold crown to indicate his status as the Zydeco King. Some of his songs had physical actions in their titles, such as "Take off Your Dress," "Ride 'Em Cowboy," and "Louisiana Two-Step," and illustrated the importance of dance to the music. Foot stomping, two-stepping, and waltzing were encouraged at every performance. Clifton maintained that a show was not successful without a high level of audience participation. Chenier's son, Clayton Joseph, was born in 1957. His music was not received well throughout the country, and despite releasing singles throughout the late 1950s and early 1960s, none of the songs received the airplay of earlier hits. Chenier shifted record labels in the 1960s, when he recorded on the Arhoolie label.

Chenier's records for Arhoolie, beginning in the early 1960s, were a mix of traditional zydeco songs with songs that attempted to blend zydeco into a format for the mainstream rock and pop audience. *Louisiana Blues and Zydeco*, his first Arhoolie album released in January 1965, devoted one side to rhythm and blues recordings and the flip side to traditional Cajun French waltzes and two-step compositions.

Chenier's most popular songs include "Grand Texas (Jambalaya)," "Ay Tete Fille," and "I'm on My Way (Back Home to You)." Chenier organized a new group in 1976 called the Red Hot Louisiana Band that included the noted local musicians Paul Senegal and John Hart. The band's next album, *I'm Here*, won a Grammy Award in 1983. The award was special in many ways: it was the first award made to a Cajun and the first time zydeco music was recognized on national television on a popular awards program.

Chenier's influence was visible in the number of new zydeco music festivals that were created in the 1980s and 1990s across the country, from Suttle Lake, Oregon, to Escoheag, Rhode Island. Many music groups planned their stage show using Chenier's model. Zydeco artists in the United Kingdom, including the Zydeco Nubreedz member J. Paul Jr., cited Chenier's influence. Zydeco music was televised worldwide in the closing ceremonies of the 1996 Summer Olympics in Atlanta, Georgia. Chenier's rendition of the Cajun song "Grand Texas" was played as part of this performance, and this arrangement became a zydeco classic.

Chenier died of complications of diabetes in 1987. Despite the need for kidney dialysis twice a week, he continued to perform until a week before his death. After the King of Zydeco's death, Arhoolie released compilation compact discs of his early and later work as well as videos and DVDs of Clifton and the Red Hot Louisiana Band performing at various festivals across the United States. In the 2000s his son C. J. (Clayton Joseph) Chenier, who began performing with his father at age twenty-one, carried on Chenier's legacy, touring and playing his father's music with the backing of the original members of the Red Hot Louisiana Band.

FURTHER READING

Ancelet, Barry Jean, Elemore Morgan, and Ralph Rinzler. *Makers of Cajun Music/Musiciens Cadiens et Creoles* (1984).

Broven, John. *South to Louisiana: The Music of the Cajun Bayous* (1987).

Clifton Chenier: The King of Zydeco (1987).

Lichtenstein, Grace, and Laura Dankner. *Musical Gumbo: The Music of New Orleans* (1993).

Murphy, Michael, dir. *Dancing to New Orleans* (2003).

Savoy, Ann. *Cajun Music: Reflection of a People, Volume 1.* (1991).

Obituary: "Clifton Chenier Put Zydeco Music on the Map," *Lafayette (La.) Daily Advertiser*, 29 Dec. 1998.

DISCOGRAPHY

An Introduction to Clifton Chenier (Varese Sarabande/USA).

The Best of Clifton Chenier: The King of Zydeco and Louisiana Blues (Arhoolie) (CD/CASS 474).

Bogalusa Boogie (Arhoolie) (CD/CASS 347).

Bon Ton Roulet (Arhoolie) (CD/CASS 345).

Louisiana Blues and Zydeco (CD/9053) (with other artists).

Red Hot Louisiana Band (Arhoolie) (CASS 1078).

Zydeco Dynamite: The Clifton Chenier Anthology (Rhino/Wea Corporation).

PAMELA LEE GRAY

Cherokee Bill. *See* Goldsby, Crawford (Cherokee Bill).

Cherry, Don (18 Nov. 1936–19 Oct. 1995), jazz cornetist and composer, was born Donald Eugene Cherry in Oklahoma City. From an early age, music was a part of his life; when the family moved to Los Angeles in the mid-forties, his father worked as a bartender at the Plantation Club, the city's premier jazz club, and his mother played piano around the house.

When Cherry's family arrived in Los Angeles, the city was home to a vital modern jazz scene. Musicians like bassist CHARLES MINGUS, trumpeter HOWARD McGHEE, tenor saxophonists DEXTER GORDON and WARDELL GRAY, and pianist HAMPTON HAWES quickly absorbed the lessons of CHARLIE PARKER and DIZZY GILLESPIE, whose 1946 California jaunt fast became the stuff of bebop lore. A young Cherry gravitated toward jazz, eventually studying at Jefferson High School with Samuel Brown, who had taught Gray and Hawes, among others. Despite his father's protestations, by 1954 Cherry was working professionally, playing at the esteemed Lighthouse club and networking within the burgeoning community.

In 1956, Cherry made what would prove to be the most significant professional connection of his career, when he made the acquaintance of an eccentric Texan saxophonist named ORNETTE COLEMAN. A consummate original, the longhaired Coleman sported a trench coat in the Los Angeles heat, showing up at jam sessions with a white plastic saxophone and some remarkable ideas about melodic, harmonic, and rhythmic freedom in jazz.

In the Los Angeles scene, Coleman was an outcast, usually sticking around jam sessions just long enough to get thrown out. But Cherry, drummer BILLY HIGGINS, and tenor saxophonist James Clay found Coleman fascinating and began rehearsing with him in their spare time. In 1957 Cherry founded the Jazz Messiahs, a combo specializing in Coleman's compositions. Two years later Coleman and Cherry joined up with pianist Paul Bley and bassist Charlie Haden for a regular gig at the Hillcrest Club, which greatly heightened their public profile.

Over the next year Coleman's group went from local oddity to national lightning rod. Following two recordings for Lester Koenig's Contemporary label (*Something Else* and *Tomorrow is the Question!*), the Modern Jazz Quartet's JOHN LEWIS (1920–2001) took up their cause and secured the classic Coleman quartet (Coleman, Cherry, Higgins, and Haden) a deal with Atlantic Records. It was also around this time that Cherry began playing the pocket trumpet, which gave his already fragmentary brand of lyricism an added air of poignant mystery. Between a two-and-a-half-year stand at the Five Spot in New York that fast became the hottest ticket in jazz and the release of the portentously titled *The Shape of Jazz To Come*, the Coleman group found itself at the heart of a firestorm of controversy.

The charismatic Coleman may have been the figurehead of the new music, but it was arguably Cherry whose playing most aptly embodied its philosophy. Stringing together bits and pieces of ineluctable tunefulness with a seemingly capricious logic, Cherry's solos seemed to contain within them an entire musical language all their own. Coleman may have been responsible for the infectious themes and most incendiary blowing, but Cherry's playing was at once more radical and more palatable. He was often portrayed as the resourceful sidekick to Coleman's mad genius, but it might be more accurate to describe him as the muse of Ornette's ambitious enterprise.

Cherry continued to record with Coleman into the early sixties and was so much associated with Ornette that his record debut as a leader, the 1960s *The Avant Garde*, consisted primarily of Coleman tunes performed with the quartet's rhythm section. Significantly, though, the other horn on the date was JOHN COLTRANE, himself eagerly assimilating Coleman's innovations. This set the template for the next few years of Cherry's career, as he acted as a de facto ambassador for Coleman's music. As the revolution gained momentum, Cherry simultaneously spread the gospel and helped reinforce the music's original message, which he did also in the groups of SONNY ROLLINS, Steve Lacy, and ALBERT AYLER. During this same period, he also formed the New York Contemporary Five with ARCHIE SHEPP and John Tchicai, one of the most fully realized of all the era's cooperative ensembles.

In 1964 Cherry moved to Paris, where he began working with a host of European, South American, and African jazz musicians. He returned to New York to record 1965's *Complete Communion* for Blue Note and 1966's *Symphony for Improvisers*, a long-form, open-ended suite that many point to as the high watermark of his career as a leader. Yet at the same time, Cherry's concerns were becoming increasingly global in nature, as he traveled extensively, experimented with various world musics, and explored untrammeled music intimacy on *Mu, Parts One and Two* with drummer ED BLACKWELL, a fellow adherent to Coleman, who had replaced Higgins in the classic quartet and had appeared on Cherry's Blue Note triumphs.

The seventies saw Cherry continue in his chosen role of avant-garde jazz gypsy, splitting his time between teaching at Dartmouth College and travel abroad in Europe and the Middle East. During this time he established his identity apart from Coleman, with a series of international-minded projects that reflected his years overseas and voracious appetite for exotic musical traditions. *Codona*, his 1978 trio with multi-instrumentalist Collin Walcott and percussionist Nano Vascancelos, was one of his definitive statements and a prescient appreciation of the possibilities of a world music fusion.

In 1978 Cherry joined fellow Coleman alumni Dewey Redman (tenor sax), Charlie Haden, and Ed Blackwell to form Old and New Dreams, a group devoted to the musical legacy of the early Coleman groups. Far from being a cynical attempt to capitalize on their association with Coleman, this quartet served to clarify just how much of a role these musicians had played in formulating what had come to be seen as Ornette's signature sound. Playing a combination of fifties and sixties classics and originals by the group members, Old and New Dreams met with universal acclaim, whether for their festival appearances or their series of albums for ECM Records. Only after these former sidemen had proved their individuality apart from Ornette could their contributions to the Coleman sound be assessed objectively, and they be given their proper historical due.

Cherry continued to record with Old and New Dreams and as a leader throughout the eighties and nineties, including a brief stint on the major label A&M that found him reunited with James Clay for the straight-ahead *Art Deco* in 1988. That decade also found the trumpeter with rock artists ranging from Lou Reed to Bongwater, a testament to his curiosity.

Cherry also lived to see his daughter, Neneh, become a popular musician herself (as his son Eagle Eye would do some years after his death). He passed away from liver failure caused by hepatitis at Neneh's home in Malaga, Spain.

FURTHER READING

Davis, Francis. "Don Cherry Sees the World," in *In the Moment: Jazz in the 1980's* (1986).

Jost, Ekkehard. *Free Jazz* (1974)

Mandel, Howard. "Don Cherry: The World in His Pocket," *Downbeat*, 2 Jul. 1978.

Obituary: *New York Times*, 21 Oct. 1995.

NATHANIEL FRIEDMAN

Cherry, Frank S. (?–1965), pastor and religious leader, was born somewhere in the South; however, little is known about his early and adult life. He never went to school but managed to educate himself and learned both Hebrew and Yiddish. He also worked as a seaman, during which time he traveled all over the world. While overseas he claimed to have been appointed a prophet by God. He moved to Philadelphia, Pennsylvania, and founded the Church of God (Black Jews) in 1915. He probably married and fathered at least one child, Benjamin Cherry.

Cherry maintained that blacks, whom he also called Jews or Hebrews, descended from the Jews of the Bible, with Jacob as the father of all black people. Cherry was not the first African American to claim a Jewish ancestry for blacks. In 1896 William S. Crowdy had founded the Church of God and Saints of Christ, viewing its adherents as descendants of the twelve tribes of Israel. It must be noted that this "Black-Jewish" view emerged when American racism was at its peak and can be interpreted in part as a reaction against the perceived support of racial oppression by many white American Christians. Cherry accounted for the existence of the white race by claiming that Gehazi, a man who turned white when cursed by God, was the first white man (2 Kings 5:27). For him, God and the Jesus of the Bible were also black. Unlike other contemporary black leaders Cherry rejected any contact with whites and was especially radical in his racial position. Doctrinally the Church of God was a mixture of both Judaism and Christianity and considered the Hebrew Bible and the Talmud to be its sacred books. Thus, Cherry took most of his beliefs from the Old Testament and even taught Hebrew to his parishioners. Among the beliefs and practices the group appropriated from the Jewish tradition were the Jewish calendar, Passover, the (seventh-day) Sabbath, prohibition of divine and human images, and a taboo on the consumption of pork. Along with other Christians, Cherry affirmed Jesus as the savior of mankind, baptism, and the Second Coming of Christ. However he did not celebrate Christmas or Easter, and he replaced the Lord's Supper with Passover. Cherry adhered to many social and ecclesiastical tenets of the Protestant holiness churches. His members eschewed dancing, movies, divorce, and smoking. As a religious organization the Church of God appointed elders and male and female deacons. It also functioned somewhat as a sect and encouraged its parishioners to marry among themselves.

Cherry encouraged his black disciples to open their own businesses. In doing so he was following a common practice of contemporary black clergy and intellectuals who believed that blacks must reach economic self-reliance. Cherry demonstrated his concern for the material welfare of his members by helping to provide them with food, clothing, shelter, and medicine. His local congregation grew to four hundred members during his lifetime. When he died his son Benjamin replaced him as the head of the Church of God.

FURTHER READING

Fauset, Arthur Huff. *Black Gods of the Metropolis: Negro Religious Cults of the Urban North* (1971).
Gerber, Israel J. *The Heritage Seekers: American Blacks in Search of Jewish Identity* (1977).
Murphy, Larry, J. Gordon Melton, and Gary L. Ward, eds. *Encyclopedia of African American Religions* (1993).

DAVID MICHEL

Cherry, Gwen (27 Aug. 1923–7 Feb. 1979), the first African American woman elected to the Florida legislature, grew up (and was likely born) in Miami. Cherry earned her bachelor's degree from the predominantly black Florida AM University (FAMU) in 1946. She belonged to Sigma Gamma Rho, a black Greek-letter organization, and later served as legal counsel to the sorority from 1970 until 1970. Cherry obtained a master's degree from New York University in 1950. In the era of segregation, talented African Americans often left the South to obtain advanced degrees. Unlike many of them, Sawyer returned home to teach school, marry, and have children, before deciding to return to academic life. She earned a law degree cum laude in 1965 from FAMU, after serving as secretary of the Student Bar Association. She was the first black woman to practice law in Dade County, Florida.

A Democrat, Cherry was elected to the Florida House of Representatives in 1970 and won reelection four times. Known for her advocacy on behalf of women, the poor, and African Americans, Cherry became a widely popular figure in South Florida. In 1971, she helped to convene the Florida Women's Political Caucus to increase the participation and influence of women throughout the Sunshine State. Cherry explained that she wanted Florida to take the lead in demonstrating the political punch that women can pack in order to help society get its priorities in order. Typical of feminists of this era, Cherry expected that women would prioritize social concerns over economic and other matters. In 1972 her amendment adding discrimination based on sex to the existing prohibitions against discrimination because of race, color, religion, or national origin passed through the Florida House, 85–0. In that same year, she played a leading role in the Florida committee to elect African American Congresswoman SHIRLEY CHISHOLM to the U.S. presidency.

In 1973, when FAMU came under attack from the U.S. Health, Education, and Welfare Department for civil rights violations by not having enough whites on campus, Cherry defended her alma mater. She explained that African Americans needed an identity and that FAMU should be an institution that specializes in black accomplishments. She lamented that integration always seemed to mean that blacks lost their institutions and had to join white ones. The comment reflects the views of many black teachers who recognized that the Supreme Court's 1954 Brown decision, while laudable, meant in practice that black children too often lost their black role models and some sense of black identity as an unintended cost of integration.

Perhaps reflecting her urban origins, Cherry devoted much of her energy to fighting crime. She cofounded the Citizens' Crime Watch of Dade County, which served Miami. In 1973 Cherry joined her fellow state legislator Elaine Gordon and the activist Roxcy Bolton in pushing for the establishment of a rape crisis center, staffed by female lawyers and doctors, at Jackson Memorial Hospital in Miami. The women also wanted the public excluded from court sessions on rape cases, the right to study police officers' reports of rape investigations, and trained women to provide psychological support for victims. At the time, antirape activists were working to change the image of rape victims from "bad girls who asked for it" to victims of violent crime who deserved respectful treatment. Cherry's leadership put her on the cutting edge.

By the end of 1978, Cherry had set her sights on other political pursuits. She applied for a job on the Public Service Commission but failed to survive the nominating process. In February 1979, Cherry bled to death from a punctured aorta as the result of a car accident. Cherry, who rarely traveled alone and rarely traveled at night, attempted to cut across a grassy field at Florida State University (FSU) to get from a stadium parking lot to a road leading off campus. While moving at about 25–30 mph, she did not see a 15-foot-deep drainage ditch in the darkness and rolled her car into it. A FSU student found Cherry's body about midnight. The Florida Senate Democratic caucus paused in honor of Cherry and about eighty people gathered for a memorial service in the Florida House. Governor Bob Graham ordered flags lowered in the Capitol. A member of the Congregational denomination, Cherry had a private burial. She was survived by her husband, James, and children, Mary Elizabeth Barnett and William Sawyer Barnett. She was honored in 1985 by the National Bar Association Women Lawyers Division Dade County Chapter, which was renamed the Gwen S. Cherry Black Women Lawyers Association (GSCBWLA) in 1985 (http://www. gscbwla.org/). The Florida Women's Hall of Fame inducted Cherry in 1986.

FURTHER READING.

Gaskins, Rosa Mae. *A Bio-Bibliography of Gwendolyn Sawyer Cherry, 1923–1979* (1979).

Waters, Roderick Dion. *Sister Sawyer: The Life and Times of Gwendolyn Sawyer Cherry.* Ph.D. diss., Florida State University, 1994.

CARYN E. NEUMANN

Cherry, Henry C. (1836?–11 July 1885), carpenter, merchant, public official, and legislator, was born in Beaufort County, near Washington, North Carolina, of unnamed parents, probably free. Little is known of his early life or education, only that he was both free and literate when he moved to Tarboro, the Edgecombe County seat, in 1860, according to that year's federal census.

Within just a decade of his arrival in Tarboro, the mixed-race carpenter acquired significant social standing, a comfortable income, and political influence at both the local and state levels in the state's new Republican Party. Cherry's marriage in March 1861 to Mary Ann Jones (b. 1837) secured his place in the social ranks of the largely African American town. The daughter of a white Edgecombe planter and his free mistress, Miss Jones was the owner of her own house and a respected church leader. The rest of her husband's achievements came largely through his own extraordinary labors, both as a carpenter and the owner of a combination grocery and liquor establishment in Freedom Hill, an area on the outskirts of Tarboro first settled in 1865 by freed slaves, as well as an active and respected politician. In 1885, with Cherry's encouragement, the state's general assembly incorporated Freedom Hill as the Town of Princeville, making it the the state's first all African American municipality.

His wife had already borne two daughters through a liaison with a white planter, Henry G. Lloyd, whose will, probated in 1860, provided substantial legacies for all three. The Cherry family eventually included eight more children. At least three of the Cherrys' daughters graduated from college, including two who gained a measure of national fame as the wives of North Carolina congressmen and a third whose husband was a state legislator and nationally known physician. And if Cherry's own political ambitions were less far-reaching than those of his sons-in-law, he nonetheless gained statewide respect as an Edgecombe delegate to the 1868 convention that rewrote North Carolina's constitution and helped restore voting rights to the state's African American men.

In April 1868 Cherry was elected as a Republican member of the state's general assembly, the first of more than a dozen African Americans to represent Edgecombe County in the lower house, and among at least twenty African American legislators elected across the state that year. During two successive sessions of the general assembly, Cherry served with distinction on the House Committee on Penal Institutions, on that body's Claims Committee, and on the joint standing Finance Committee. He chose not to run again in the 1870 election, returning home instead to his family and business, and to pursue a new project, the establishment of the Tarboro Colored Institute.

Cherry and other local residents had recently appealed to the American Missionary Association

(AMA) to assign a schoolteacher to Tarboro for the education of the large population of African American children. Robert S. Taylor, a native of Jamaica, West Indies, was promptly certified by the AMA and began teaching in 1870 in the new Tarboro institute, constructed a year earlier by Cherry and his colleagues. Groomed by his new acquaintances, Taylor soon entered politics as well, serving two terms as state senator in the 1880s.

According to the 1870 federal census, Cherry, then thirty-four, owned real estate valued at $1,000 and another $200 in personal property. His family that year included five children at home, a figure which would grow to seven in 1880, the year after his wife's oldest daughter, Georgianna, a graduate of St. Augustine's College in Raleigh, married EUSTACE EDWARD GREEN, a Wilmington school principal soon to represent New Hanover County in the state house of representatives.

Henry Cherry's younger daughters, Louisa and Cora Lena, still in their teens, had attended Scotia Seminary and were both working as schoolteachers in 1880. In 1882 Louisa married the educator HENRY PLUMMER CHEATHAM of Henderson, soon to be elected to Congress from North Carolina's "Black Second" district in 1888. In 1887 Cora Lena married the former legislator GEORGE HENRY WHITE of New Bern, recently elected to his first term as solicitor (prosecutor) of North Carolina's Second Judicial District. In 1890 White was reelected solicitor, and in 1896 to the first of two terms in Congress, also from the Second District.

Cherry's family and his business interests were flourishing, and Cherry's own political career was not yet over. He was elected to several terms as a commissioner on the Tarboro Town Council, helping elect the city's first African American mayor, Franklin D. Dancy, in 1881. In addition to serving as town constable, Cherry was a member of the Fulton Fire Company, one of the state's earliest volunteer fire departments, formed in 1880.

In the spring of 1885 Henry Cherry contracted typhoid fever and struggled against its effects for two months. On 11 July 1885, at forty-eight years of age, he finally succumbed to the disease. Survivors included his wife, his three daughters, and five sons: Henry H., Charles C., William, Earnest A., and Clarence. The town's weekly newspaper described Cherry as "honest, straight forward, and lacking in the bitterness that marks the course of so many politicians" and as "command[ing] the confidence and respect of both races" (*Tarboro Southerner*, 16 July 1885).

FURTHER READING
Foner, Eric. *Freedom's Lawmakers: A Directory of Black Officeholders during Reconstruction* (1993).
Kenzer, Robert C. *Enterprising Southerners: Black Economic Success in North Carolina, 1865–1915* (1997).
Watson, Alan D. *Edgecombe County: A Brief History* (1979).
Obituary: *Tarboro Southerner*, 16 July 1885.

BENJAMIN R. JUSTESEN

Chesnutt, Charles Waddell (20 Jun. 1858–15 Nov. 1932), writer, was born in Cleveland, Ohio, the son of Andrew Jackson Chesnutt, a horse car driver, and Ann Maria Sampson. His parents were free African Americans who had left Fayetteville, North Carolina, in 1856 to escape the oppressiveness of life in a slave state and its sparse opportunity. They were married in Cleveland in 1857. During the Civil War, Chesnutt's father served four years as a teamster in the Union army, but the family returned to Fayetteville in 1866 because A. J. Chesnutt's father, Waddell Cade (a local white farm owner—the name Chesnutt came from A. J.'s mother, Ann), helped his son establish a grocery store there. Young Charles helped in the store and over the years heard many things there about southern life and folkways that he recorded or remembered and that later became part of or informed his writings. Charles attended the Howard School, which existed through the efforts of local black citizens and the Freedmen's Bureau, but after his father lost his store and moved to a nearby farm, Charles was forced at age fourteen to change his role in the school from that of eager pupil to pupil–teacher in order to help with family finances. He continued to read widely in various fields, especially in literature, thereby further educating himself.

Chesnutt began teaching in Charlotte, North Carolina, in 1872 and in the summers in other North and South Carolina communities. In the fall of 1877 he returned to Fayetteville to work in the new state normal school there. The following summer he married one of the school's teachers, Susan U. Perry, and the first of their four children was born the following spring. Though Chesnutt became principal of the normal school at age twenty-two and continued to study various subjects regularly, he felt restricted in opportunities and intellectually isolated in the post–Civil War South. In 1883 he used his self-taught ability to take shorthand at two hundred words per minute to escape, first to New York for a few months and then to Cleveland, where he was joined by his family in April 1884. He lived there the rest of his life.

The
Colonel's Dream

By
CHARLES W. CHESNUTT

New York
Doubleday, Page & Company
1905

The Colonel's Dream, written by Charles W. Chesnutt in 1905. (Courtesy of Documenting the American South, University of North Carolina at Chapel Hill Libraries.)

In Cleveland, Chesnutt worked as an office clerk and court reporter, passed the Ohio bar exam in 1887 (with the highest grade in his group), and established a prosperous legal stenography firm, eventually after several moves acquiring a fourteen-room home. More importantly, he worked at becoming a writer. He had been moving in that direction for some time, and in 1872 a local weekly Negro newspaper had published his condemnation of the reading of dime novels. The growth of his interest in literature and his ambition to become a writer are reflected in numerous entries in his journals during the 1870s and 1880s, especially as he became more and more aware of what had been written and was being written about the South and black people, subjects about which he felt confident of his own better knowledge and understanding. His journal entry for 29 May 1880 spoke of a purpose for his intended writing that would improve the South and all of its people. It included the declaration, "I think I must write a book." However, before he would accomplish that goal there were to be years of sketches, tales, and stories, beginning in 1885 published in various periodicals, including

eventually such widely known magazines as *Family Fiction, Puck, Overland Monthly, The Crisis, Southern Workman, Century, The Outlook, Youth's Companion*, and various newspapers in some of the nation's larger cities.

Chesnutt's most important breakthrough came with the publication of his tale "The Goophered Grapevine" in the *Atlantic Monthly* for August 1887. Although the editors did not then know the author's race, this was the first piece of short fiction published by an African American in a magazine with such prestige as to easily put the work before the majority of American readers. Chesnutt would publish short fiction and articles (both usually concerning racial matters) for much of the rest of his life, but very much tapering off after the early part of the twentieth century.

"The Goophered Grapevine" was the first of three of his stories in the *Atlantic Monthly* that focused on conjuring as an important aspect of black folklife. This is revealed in post–Civil War tales about earlier times in the Fayetteville area told by Uncle Julius, a shrewd and likable character who uses the stories to his own advantage and along the way also reveals much about what slavery meant in the daily concerns of its victims, of which he had been one. These three tales and four other Uncle Julius tales became Chesnutt's first book, *The Conjure Woman*, published by Houghton Mifflin (1899). In these stories Chesnutt broadened the range of racial realism in American literature, and all of his five volumes of fiction would deal with various facets of racial problems, with strong focusing on the experiences and points of view of his African American characters, though his concerns were always for both blacks and whites in American society and particularly in the South. The stories of his second book of fiction, *The Wife of His Youth and Other Stories of the Color Line*, also published by Houghton Mifflin (1899), are in most ways quite different from the conjure stories and illustrate the variety of Chesnutt's skill and art. They are more contemporary and less rural and folk oriented, with more focus (sometimes ironically) on middle-class African Americans, especially those with light skin color. About half of these stories are set in North Carolina, and about half in Ohio. As its title suggests, this book intended to demonstrate the complex difficulties and sensitivities of those who (like Chesnutt himself) were of obvious racially mixed blood in societies both north and south, in which they aspired to rise even in the face of uncertainties about how that would be viewed. Chesnutt had very light skin and few

Negroid features. He wrote about respect and injustice from personal concern and experience. These stories are sometimes tragic and sometimes comic, as he tried to write from a balanced and whole view of racial phenomena he had observed at close hand. Various reviews called attention to Chesnutt's presentation of African American characters in other than stereotypes and his making them of real interest and concern as individual human beings. Notable among such reviews was high praise from William Dean Howells in the *Atlantic Monthly* for May 1900, which took note of both of Chesnutt's volumes of fiction and of his biography of FREDERICK DOUGLASS (1899) in the Beacon Biographies Series. Howells also identified Chesnutt with various well-known contemporary writers of realistic fiction whom Howells championed.

On 30 September 1899 Chesnutt had closed his stenography business in order to pursue writing full time. In the autumn of 1900 Houghton Mifflin brought out *The House behind the Cedars*, the first of three novels Chesnutt would publish. It is a fuller and more straightforward exploration of some of the miscegenation themes that had been found in his second volume of stories. The primary setting of the novel is the Fayetteville area, and it focuses on the emotional and practical (and sometimes tragic) difficulties of relatively white African Americans who chose to pass as white in the post–Civil War South. Although Chesnutt himself chose not to pass even though he could have, he knew those who had done so and understood and sympathized with their motives. Another novel, *The Marrow of Tradition*, followed from Houghton Mifflin in October 1901. This work, with his largest cast and most complicated plot, also is set in North Carolina. It is based on the riot that occurred in Wilmington in 1898 when white supremacists took over the city government with accompanying violence against blacks. In addition to having concerns with racial justice, as had his first novel, this book also has some focus on the aspirations of African Americans who choose to participate in the more highly respected professions. However, this work is even more interracial, its principal characters are white, and there is more direct criticism of the white population. While Howells praised the straightforwardness of the novel's moral concerns, he was disturbed by its bitterness. It did not sell well enough for Chesnutt to continue his attempt to succeed as a full-time author, and he reopened his stenography business before the year was over.

While disappointment and the need to gain financial stability slowed Chesnutt's literary aspirations, he did publish one more novel. Another North Carolinian, Walter Hines Page, while an editor at Houghton Mifflin had praised Chesnutt's accuracy of local color and had assisted his progress. Now Page persuaded Chesnutt to leave Houghton Mifflin, even though his relations with that firm had been good, and in September 1905 (the year in which Thomas Dixon's racially negative novel *The Clansman* was a best-seller) Page's firm (Doubleday, Page & Company) brought out *The Colonel's Dream*. Its protagonist, a former Confederate officer, returns to his southeastern North Carolina hometown and proposes a plan to bring it out of the economic hardships caused by the Civil War and its aftermath. He is willing to invest his own resources, but the plan is rejected because of greed and racial prejudice in the community. Reflecting Chesnutt's continuing loving concern for the area where he had spent his formative years, this book is dedicated to "the great number of those who are seeking, in whatever manner or degree … to bring the forces of enlightenment to bear upon the vexed problems which harass the South."

However, the various-faceted message for the South (and the country as a whole) that pervades Chesnutt's fiction and nonfiction, particularly concerning economic and social justice in relation to race, was not being accepted by those for whom it was most intended. He now turned his efforts more to other aspects of his life, among them his family, his business, and his involvement in several cultural organizations in Cleveland. One of these was the prestigious bibliophilic Rowfant Club, which refused membership to this nationally respected author three times before finally admitting him in 1910. His satiric "Baxter's Procrustes" (*Atlantic Monthly*, June 1904) is based on that club, and many think it is his best-written story. His career as a writer resulted in his publishing between 1885 and 1931 sixty-one pieces of short fiction (including those in the two volumes); one biography; thirty-one speeches, articles, and essays; seven poems; and three novels. Also, he left unpublished a sizable correspondence, one play, six novels, fifty-three essays and speeches, eighteen short stories (most of which have now been published by Render), three journals, and one notebook.

Chesnutt's published fiction, particularly his five books, was his most important accomplishment both artistically and in his attempts to improve social (particularly racial) relations. However, in addition to his fiction, his early work as an educator, his stenographic work in Cleveland, and his other writings, he also was active in various other pursuits that gave him pleasure, visibility, influence, reputation, and opportunity. He put his concerns, his knowledge of the law, and his respected reputation and personality to good use in speaking out on political and legal matters locally and nationally, particularly when they concerned the rights of African Americans. Early in his career as a writer he had made the acquaintance of George Washington Cable and through this association had joined in the efforts of the Open-Letter Club, a project of several persons interested in and knowledgeable about the South to provide accurate information about that region and racial matters. Chesnutt was an active member of the National Association for the Advancement of Colored People (NAACP) in Cleveland and nationally, and there was mutual respect between him and both BOOKER T. WASHINGTON and W. E. B. DUBOIS. Though these two leaders took somewhat different approaches to the problems of African Americans and how best to solve them, Chesnutt saw merit in some aspects of the positions of both men and said so publicly, but also spoke up when he disagreed with them. He was a member of the General Committee of the NAACP and of Washington's Committee of Twelve for the Advancement of the Interests of the Negro Race. He addressed immediate socioeconomic problems and in various ways tried to promote awareness of and concern over the racial situation in America (particularly in the South—William Andrews has referred to his three novels as a New South trilogy). Chesnutt felt that the racial situation was undermining American democracy and that solutions to it would require sensitive understanding, ethical and moral conscience, and courage. In both his fiction and nonfiction his view of the proper future for African Americans was for gradual assimilation of them into the mainstream of American life through education and hard work. His three daughters and his one son all graduated from well-known colleges, and he lived to see them established in their chosen endeavors and moving into that mainstream, as he had in his way before them.

Though the major part of Chesnutt's literary career ended with the publication of *The Colonel's Dream* in 1905, respect for him as a pioneering writer continued. Among the recognition given him was an invitation to attend Mark Twain's seventieth birthday party at Delmonico's in New York in 1905 and membership in the National Arts Club in 1917. In 1913 Wilberforce University gave him an honorary degree, and in 1928 he was awarded the NAACP's prestigious Spingarn Medal for his "pioneer work as a literary artist depicting the life and struggle of Americans of Negro descent, and for his long and useful career as scholar, worker and freeman of one of America's greatest cities." That same year *The Conjure Woman* was republished by Houghton Mifflin in a special edition with a foreword by the literary critic and leader in racial concerns Joel Spingarn. In 1926 the committee to choose the first recipient of the newly established Harmon Foundation Award for the work of an African American writer during the preceding year recommended that the chronological stipulation be waived and the first award be given to Chesnutt to acknowledge his pioneering work and his continuing example to other African American writers. This was not allowed, and unfortunately Chesnutt never knew of this acknowledgment of high esteem from a distinguished panel of his literary peers both black and white.

Chesnutt was the first important African American writer whose primary genre was fiction and the first African American writer to be published primarily by major publishers and major periodicals. Writing and publishing during times that were not very socially, politically, or legally favorable to African Americans in general, Chesnutt wrote fiction to provide entertainment and to call attention to racism and social injustice, especially for middle-class light-skinned blacks and working-class blacks in small towns and the rural South. He believed that the sources of as well as the solutions to their problems were in the South, so he wrote about the South and in ways that he intended to be more accurate, realistic, and better than those of others using similar subject matter. He purposefully dealt with topics regarding racial problems, such as miscegenation, which he felt other southern writers were avoiding or mistreating. In doing this he used various literary devices, including accurate dialect and details of local color and black life, satire, humor, irony, pathos, and even first-person point of view for nonblack characters. However, while he wrote with unblinking truth and obvious strong social purpose, he also wrote without rancor and with attention to and faithful portrayal of both sides of problems, creating a variety of memorable characters. He especially hoped to counter the too often derogatory and stereotypical portrayal of black characters and to make readers more aware of the positive and often complex humanity and variety of African Americans, the mistreatment of minorities and their need for greater social justice, and the fallibility of human nature.

Sylvia Render has pointed out that Chesnutt promoted American ideals in popular American forms and in accord with accepted contemporary literary standards, and was published by very reputable firms. However, after his death his works were generally underread and undervalued until attention to them revived in the 1960s. In his Spingarn Medal acceptance Chesnutt said, "I didn't write my stories as Negro propaganda—propaganda is apt to be deadly to art—but I used the better types [of Negroes], confident that the truth would prove the most valuable propaganda." A few months later he wrote to JAMES WELDON JOHNSON, "I wrote the truth as I saw it, with no special catering to anybody's prejudices." He died in Cleveland.

FURTHER READING
The most important sources for unpublished Chesnutt writings and related materials are the Chesnutt collection of the Cravath Library at Fisk University and the Chesnutt papers at the Library of the Western Reserve Historical Society, Cleveland, Ohio.

Andrews, William L. *The Literary Career of Charles W. Chesnutt* (1980).

Chesnutt, Helen M. *Charles Waddell Chesnutt: Pioneer of the Color Line* (1952).

Ellison, Curtis W., and E. W. Metcalf Jr. *Charles W. Chesnutt: A Reference Guide* (1977).

Heermance, J. Noel. *Charles W. Chesnutt: America's First Great Black Novelist* (1974).

Keller, Frances Richardson. *An American Crusade: The Life of Charles Waddell Chesnutt* (1978).

Render, Sylvia Lyons. *Charles W. Chesnutt* (1980).

This entry is taken from the *American National Biography* and is published here with the permission of the American Council of Learned Societies.

JULIAN MASON

Chesnutt, Helen Maria (6 Dec. 1880–7 Aug. 1969), classicist and first African American to teach in the Cleveland, Ohio, secondary schools, was born in Fayetteville, North Carolina, the second daughter of CHARLES WADDELL CHESNUTT and Susan Chesnutt. Her parents had met while both were teaching at the Howard School in Fayetteville. Her father was a prominent African American novelist, short-story writer, lecturer, and lawyer. His fiction confronted prejudice, disfranchisement, segregation, and American stereotypes and racial mythologies. Her mother was a teacher who became a full-time homemaker after her children were born. Helen's paternal grandparents were free blacks who had emigrated from North Carolina to Cleveland, Ohio, in 1856 and were active in the Underground Railroad. Her paternal great-grandmothers were of mixed race, and probably her paternal great-grandfathers were white. Helen's father wrote about rejecting "passing" and the white hypocrisy toward miscegenation. She came from a long line of people who worked for integration, and in her lifetime she steadily continued their work. She grew up in a close-knit family with two sisters and a brother. Every evening, as the family sat around the sitting-room fireplace, her father read to the family books such as *Gulliver's Travels*, *Tom Brown's School Days*, *Little Women*, and *David Copperfield*. Because racial prejudice had made it difficult for him to receive a formal education, Charles Chesnutt was determined that his children would be well educated. By the time Helen was twelve, she could translate Virgil from Latin into English.

Chesnutt attended Cleveland public schools, which were integrated, and she graduated from Central High in 1897, when she was seventeen. It was at Central High that Chesnutt and her sister Ethel experienced the impact of the color line. A high school incident related in Chesnutt's biography of her father tells of the sisters realizing, "with shock and confusion that they were considered different from their classmates" (Chestnutt, 74). She reported that "One of their friends explained the situation 'after all, you are Negroes. We know that you are nice girls and everybody thinks the world of you; but Mother says that while it was all right for us to go together when we were younger now that we are growing up, we must consider Society, and we just can't go together any more'" (Chestnutt, 74–75). After this incident, the sisters' friend was no longer welcome at the Chesnutts' home.

Charles Chesnutt decided to send his daughters to college away from the prejudice of Cleveland, and since he considered New England the "cradle of democracy," he sent them to Smith College in Northampton, Massachusetts (Chesnutt, 76). No racial incidents involving the sisters were reported when they matriculated there. Often at white colleges and universities after the Civil War the question of where matriculating African American students would live and dine became an issue. As late as 1923, for example, some at Harvard University, where dormitories and dining rooms were integrated, took action to try to exclude African Americans. At Smith, the sisters apparently roomed together off-campus (as did some white students) at a "very pleasant student boarding-house highly recommended" by Smith president Laurenus Clark Seelye (Chesnutt, 80).

After graduating from Smith in 1902 with a major in Latin, Chesnutt returned to Cleveland to teach in the public schools. This is what her father wanted her to do, although she had applied to teach in Washington, D.C., and at Tuskegee University. Charles Chesnutt, concerned how his daughter would be received in the segregated South, prevailed upon her to return to Cleveland. Chesnutt explained to her father in a forthright letter that "I am not comfortable in Cleveland and never was, and I have always vowed that I would not settle down in that city … And now you ask me to return … I can't imagine anything more distasteful. I tell you all this because I want you to know exactly where I stand in this matter" (Chesnutt, 165). Despite her misgivings, ultimately her father's wishes prevailed and she reluctantly accepted his plan: "It seems to be up to me to do it. Well, I have stood a lot more than people give me credit for, and a few more blows won't materially affect my ultimate good" (Chesnutt, 165). Chesnutt returned to Cleveland and became the first African American to teach at a Cleveland secondary school. She secured a position teaching Latin at Central High and headed the school's foreign language department throughout her forty-one years of teaching. She was LANGSTON HUGHES's teacher, and he always remembered to send her a copy of each of his books.

Chesnutt did not marry and remained in her parents' home. In 1925, after studying summers in New York, she received a master's degree in the Classics from Columbia University. A classicist during a time when racist beliefs denied that there were African American classicists, she coauthored a Latin primer titled *The Road to Latin: A First Year Book* (1932). After her retirement from the Cleveland public school system, she wrote a biography of her father, *Charles Waddell Chesnutt, Pioneer of the Color Line* (1952).

In her retirement she continued to work for integration. She also served on the Cleveland Council on Human Relations, an organization that promoted understanding, "cooperation and mutual respect among all people and among the various religious, racial, social and cultural groups to which they belong" (*Plain Dealer*, 28 Jan. 1955). A quiet but determined trailblazer, she died at age eighty-nine in Cleveland Heights, Ohio.

FURTHER READING

Chesnutt, Helen M. *Charles Waddell Chesnutt, Pioneer of the Color Line* (1952).

Plain Dealer. "Retired Teacher to Write Story of Author-Father," 29 Aug. 1945.

Plain Dealer. "An Unusual Teacher," 30 Aug. 1945.

Obituary: *Plain Dealer*, 9 Apr. 1969.

LINDA SPENCER

Chester, Thomas Morris (11 May 1834–30 Sept. 1892), lawyer and Civil War correspondent, was born in Harrisburg, Pennsylvania, the son of George Chester and Jane Maria (maiden name unknown), restaurateurs. When, as a young man of eighteen, Chester decided to emigrate to Liberia, he wrote Martin H. Freeman, his former teacher at the Avery Institute in Pittsburgh, that his passion for liberty could no longer "submit to the insolent indignities and contemptuous conduct to which it has almost become natural for the colored people dishonorably to submit themselves." It was a bold assertion of independence for one who had come of age in a household long associated with the anticolonization sentiments of radical abolitionism. But the country's willingness to appease southern interests, symbolized by the passage of the Fugitive Slave Law in 1850, persuaded Chester, sometime before his 1853 graduation, to emigrate.

Anxious to recruit the son of such a prominent black family, leaders of the Pennsylvania Colonization Society led Chester to believe that he could complete his education in Monrovia. But the colony could not meet his needs, and within a year Chester was back in the United States where, with the support of the New York Colonization Society, he attended Thetford Academy in Vermont from 1854 to 1856. Following graduation Chester returned to Monrovia, where he became active in politics and published and edited the short-lived *Star of Liberia*, which appeared intermittently between 1859 and 1861. He also taught school at the new settlement of Robertsport and in Monrovia. During this period he made frequent trips back to the United States, under the auspices of the Colonization Society, to promote emigration to Liberia.

Continued troubles with political rivals in Monrovia persuaded Chester in 1861 to return to the United States where he continued to work for the cause of colonization. Abraham Lincoln's Emancipation Proclamation prompted him to delay his return to Liberia in early 1863. Chester headed the recruitment drive in central Pennsylvania for the two black Massachusetts regiments but ceased his activities when it became clear that blacks would not be appointed officers. Before resigning the civilian appointment, however, Chester became the first black to be given a captaincy in the Pennsylvania state militia when he raised a company to help defend the state capital against Confederate forces in the weeks before Gettysburg.

In 1864 Chester was employed by John Russell Young, editor of the *Philadelphia Press*, as a war correspondent attached to the Army of the James. He was the first and only African American to report on the war for a major daily newspaper. Chester's dispatches provide the most sustained accounts of black troop activity around Petersburg and Richmond in the last year of the war. He reported on the contributions of black troops to the war effort, sent moving accounts of the death and carnage of battle, and, with a rakish sense of humor, provided glimpses into camp life. Chester was one of the first reporters to enter Richmond, and with some bravado and a touch of irony he wrote his next dispatch seated in the chair of the Speaker of the Confederate House of Representatives. Chester remained in Richmond until June 1865, reporting on efforts to rebuild the city and on the activities of the African American community.

In 1866 Chester was commissioned by the Garnet League, the Harrisburg chapter of the Pennsylvania Equal Rights League, to undertake a fund-raising tour of Britain and the Continent. Even before his assignment with the *Press* Chester had been thinking of studying law in England and in 1863 had briefly visited London, where he made invaluable contacts in abolitionist circles. The tour was a rousing personal success although it is unclear exactly how much money he raised. During his visit to Russia, Chester was introduced to the royal court by Cassius M. Clay, U.S. minister to St. Petersburg. Chester was invited to join the annual review of the imperial guard and to dine with the royal family.

At the conclusion of his mission Chester applied and was admitted to Middle Temple, London, where he studied law from 1867 to 1870. In April 1870 he became the first African American to be called to the English bar. A few weeks later Chester argued his first case in the hallowed halls of the Old Bailey, defending a shoemaker charged with murder. Although all the evidence pointed to the defendant's guilt, Chester's skillful cross-examination saved his client from the gallows. The accused was sentenced instead to ten-year's penal servitude.

A few months after his return to the United States in mid-1870, Chester decided to settle in New Orleans, having been impressed with the level of black political power in the city. By the time of his arrival in 1871, the Republican Party was immobilized by factionalism and violence. On 1 January 1872, in the streets of New Orleans, Chester was shot (but not seriously wounded) by members of one of the political factions.

In 1873 Chester was admitted to the Louisiana bar, the first black man to be admitted according to contemporary news accounts, and he played a prominent role in many of the civil rights suits brought by blacks under the state's new antidiscrimination laws. In May 1873 he was commissioned a brigadier general in the Louisiana state militia by Governor William Kellogg. The militias had been formed by Republican administrations to fill the void left by departing federal troops. Two years later Kellogg appointed Chester superintendent of public education for the First Division, which included areas around New Orleans. The following year Chester was moved to head the Fifth Division with offices in Delta, Madison Parish. Chester retained both the rank of brigadier general and the position of superintendent until the return to power of the Democrats in 1876.

With the aid of powerful friends in Pennsylvania, particularly members of the Cameron family, Chester was appointed U.S. commissioner for New Orleans in 1878, a position he held for almost two years. In December 1882 he was sent, as an assistant to the U.S. attorney for the Eastern District of Texas, on a special mission to investigate political violence in the area. But disputes with Washington over payments for expenses led to the termination of his appointment before he had completed his investigation.

Chester married Florence Johnson, twenty-one years his junior, in 1879. Little else is known of his life except that in 1884 he was named president of the Wilmington, Wrightsville and Onslow Railroad, a company established by African Americans in North Carolina to build a rail system connecting the towns to important markets in Virginia. The plans never materialized, and Chester returned to his law practices in Louisiana and Pennsylvania. Chester died at his mother's home in Harrisburg of an apparent heart attack.

Chester was fiercely independent, driven by what he called "self respect and pride of race." As he told many audiences at home and abroad, he was descended from a long line of independent black men and women who had openly defied all forms of racial restrictions. In Liberia his work as editor and teacher contributed to the social and political life of Robertsport and Monrovia. In the United States he sought to push the country toward realizing the dream of full equality for all its people.

FURTHER READING

Letters from and about Chester are in the American Colonization Society papers at the Library of Congress; in the Simon Cameron papers, Historical Society of Dauphin County, Pennsylvania; in the Massachusetts Historical Society; in the archives of the Society of the Middle Temple, London; in Records of the General Agent (record group 60) at the National Archives; and in the Jacob C. White papers at the Moorland-Spingarn Library, Howard University.

Blackett, R. J. M. *Thomas Morris Chester: Black Civil War Correspondent* (1989).

This entry is taken from the *American National Biography* and is published here with the permission of the American Council of Learned Societies.

R. J. M. BLACKETT

Cheswell, Wentworth (11 Apr. 1746–8 Mar. 1817), teacher, coroner, scrivener, selectman, and justice of the peace, was born in New Market (now Newmarket), New Hampshire, the only child of Hopestill, a Portsmouth, New Hampshire, housewright, and Catherine Cheswell. The name is sometimes spelled "Cheswill." Wentworth's grandfather, Richard Cheswell, a black slave in Exeter, New Hampshire, purchased twenty acres of land from the Hilton Grant after he gained his freedom. The deed, dated 18 October 1716/17 (the discrepancy arises from the adoption of the Gregorian Calendar) is the earliest known deed in the state of New Hampshire showing land ownership by a black man. The land was located in what was to become the town of Newmarket. Richard's only child, Hopestill (1712–?), became a housewright and worked mostly in Portsmouth. He took part in building the John Paul Jones House as well as other important houses. Hopestill was active in local affairs, and he passed his love and knowledge of carpentry, agriculture, and community involvement to his son.

Wentworth Cheswell attended Dummer Academy in Byfield, Massachusetts, which was founded in 1763. It is likely, but not certain, that he was the first

African American to attend. He was educated by a Harvard graduate, William Moody, who taught Latin, Greek, swimming, horsemanship, and universal subjects. Cheswell's education was, in the terms of the day, "an unusual privilege for a country boy of that time" (Savage, 38–39). After completing his education Cheswell returned home to become a schoolmaster. In 1765 he purchased his first parcel of land from his father. By early 1767 he was an established landowner and the holder of a pew in the "New Alias Separate Meeting House," according to Rockingham County deed books.

Matrimony at age twenty-one was the next step. He married seventeen-year-old Mary Davis of Durham, New Hampshire, on 13 September 1767. Eleven months later Paul, the first of their thirteen children, was born. During the Revolutionary War the citizens of Newmarket, including Cheswell, were unequivocally for the patriotic cause. In April 1776, along with 162 other men, Cheswell signed the Association Test, which was a congressionally mandated assertion of willingness to oppose British acts of hostility—essentially, a loyalty oath. Signing was uncommon for a man of mixed descent, as the resolution specifically excluded "lunaticks, idiots, and negroes." Since the Association Test resolution preceded the formal Declaration of Independence by several months, the abundance of signatures submitted gave Congress assurance that their acts would be sanctioned and upheld by the country. Cheswell was also involved in building rafts to defend Portsmouth Harbor. He was elected town messenger for the Committee of Safety, which entrusted him to carry news to and from the Provincial Committee at Exeter. Paul Revere rode into Portsmouth to alert it of the impending arrival of the British frigate *Scarborough* and the sloop of war *Canseau*. Portsmouth sought help from neighboring communities, prompting Newmarket to hold a town meeting. There it was decided that thirty men should be sent to Portsmouth to help. Cheswell rode to Exeter to receive instructions from the committee on where the men were to be sent.

Cheswell enlisted on 29 September 1777. He served under Colonel John Langdon in a select company of "men of rank and position" called Langdon's Independent Company of Volunteers to bolster the Continental army at the Saratoga campaign. His only military service ended 31 October 1777. While his stint was brief when measured by later standards—he served one month and three days—it was not unusual at the time.

After his service in the war Cheswell returned to Newmarket and continued his work in local affairs. He also ran a store next to the old schoolhouse. Cheswell's career as a teacher was short-lived, but he remained concerned for the educational welfare of Newmarket's children. In 1776 the town chose five men to regulate the schools in town. Cheswell was one of them, becoming one of Newmarket's first school board members.

Cheswell was a man of many firsts. In 1801 Cheswell and several other men organized the first library in town, the Newmarket Social Library. Of the men who started this library, Cheswell had the most valuable estate, valued at more than thirteen thousand dollars at that time. In his will he states that "I also order and direct that my Library and collection of Manuscripts be kept safe and together.... if any should desire the use of any of the books and give caution to return the same again in reasonable time, they may be lent out to them, provided that only one book be out of said Library in the hands of any one at the same time" (Rockingham County Courthouse, Probate Office, Will #9508). He was a subscriber to Jeremy Belknap's three-volume *History of New Hampshire*. Belknap, who founded the Massachusetts Historical Society, quoted Cheswell more than once at great length, and they shared correspondence several times. And he may have been the first archaeologist in New Hampshire.

Cheswell's interest in his town and its history prompted him to copy all of the town records, including two congregational meetings that were held in Newmarket. He collected stories and took notes of town events as they occurred. This original work is still intact and is kept in the Milne Special Collections and Archives at the University of New Hampshire's Dimond Library. Cheswell's writing ability and legal knowledge were likely pivotal in his fellow townsmen's recommendation to appoint him justice of the peace for Rockingham County, and he served from 1805 until his death in 1817. He was responsible for executing deeds, wills, and legal documents and was a justice in the trial of causes.

In 1820 the New Hampshire senator David Lawrence Morril addressed Congress to oppose an item of legislation forbidding persons of mixed race to enter or become citizens of Missouri. In his speech Morril remarked that "In New Hampshire there was a yellow man by the name of Cheswell, who, with his family, were respectable in points of abilities, property and character. He held some of the first offices in the town in which he resided, was appointed Justice of the Peace for that county, and was perfectly competent to perform with ability all the duties of his various offices in the most prompt, accurate, and acceptable manner." Angrily Morril added, "But this family are forbidden to enter and live in Missouri" (Kaplan, 200).

In his will Cheswell requested that "the burying place in the orchard near my dwelling house be fenced with rocks, as I have laid out (if I should not live to finish it) and grave stones be provided for the graves therein." His daughter Martha, his last surviving heir, willed "the burying yard at my farm as now fenced in, for a burying place for all my connections and their descendants forever ... on the express condition that they and their heirs and assigns shall forever maintain and support the fence around said burying yard in as good condition as it now is." In accordance with their wishes, the gravestones have been restored or replicated over the last several years, as friends and family have recently discovered their heritage and connection to the Cheswells. On 8 March 1817 Wentworth Cheswell died from typhus fever. The Newmarket community mourned this vital, important, and influential man.

FURTHER READING

Getchell, Sylvia (Fitts). *The Tide Turns On the Lamprey: A History of Newmarket, New Hampshire* (1984).

Kaplan, Sidney, and Emma Nogrady Kaplan. *The Black Presence in the Era of the American Revolution* (1989).

Knoblock, Glenn A. *"Strong and Brave Fellows": New Hampshire's Black Soldiers and Sailors of the American Revolution, 1775–1784* (2003).

Sammons, Mark J., and Valerie Cunningham. *Black Portsmouth: Three Centuries of African-American Heritage* (2004).

Savage, John E. *The History of Newmarket* (1906).

Tuveson, Erik R. "'A People of Color': A Study of Race and Racial Identification in New Hampshire, 1750–1825," master's thesis, University of New Hampshire (1995).

RICHARD ALPERIN

Childers, Lulu Vere (28 Feb. 1870–6 Mar. 1946), singer and educator, was born in Dryridge, Kentucky, the daughter of Alexander Childers and Eliza Butler, former slaves. She studied voice at the Oberlin Conservatory of Music in Ohio and in 1896 was awarded a diploma that was replaced by a bachelor's degree in 1906, when the conservatory began granting degrees. The Oberlin Conservatory chapter of Pi Kappa Lambda, a national honor society, elected her a member in 1927. She studied voice further with Sydney Lloyd Wrightson at the Washington Conservatory of Music in Washington, D.C., with William Shakespeare, and with Oscar Devries at Chicago Musical College.

As a singer Childers enjoyed modest distinction. During her college years and shortly afterward, she performed in the Midwest with the Eckstein-Norton Music Company, a quartet of singers and their accompanist teamed with the concert pianist Harriet A. Gibbs. The group contributed their earnings to the development of a music conservatory at Eckstein-Norton University, an industrial school in Cane Springs, Kentucky. Childers rarely gave solo recitals, preferring solo parts in oratorios and other larger works. A review in the *Washington Bee* (2 June 1906) described her voice as "wonderfully sweet and sympathetic, a very pleasing contralto possessing a wide range, reaching the lower as well as the higher register with comparative ease."

Childers worked as a public schoolteacher in Ulrichsville, Ohio, from around 1896 to 1898, as the director of music at Wiley University in Marshall, Texas, from 1898 to 1900, and as the director of the music department and choral director at Knoxville College from 1900 to 1905. In 1905 Childers went to Howard University in Washington, D.C., as an instructor in methods and vocal music and the director of the choir. She faced a challenge at Howard, where it was unusual for a woman to be assigned the responsibility for heading a department and directing a choral organization. In a short time, however, she developed the university choir, which had been in existence since 1874, to a new level of competence and presented Mendelssohn's *Elijah*. With Childers as a soloist, along with HARRY T. BURLEIGH, Charlotte W. Murray, Sidney Woodward, and Pearl Barnes, the performance garnered positive reviews and drew favorable attention to the music program at Howard. Childers built Howard's music program to the point that the board of trustees, in the catalog of 1912, stated: "The work of the Music Department ... has grown in standard, excellence, and success, until the time has come when it should take some definite name under which it can realize many of the great possibilities which lie before it. It will, therefore, be designated, hereafter, ... as the Conservatory of Music of Howard University." Following a period of sustained growth, the conservatory became the School of Music in 1918. Childers also won community

support through her position as director of the choir at Plymouth Congregational Church.

Regular performances by the university choir of works such as Handel's *Messiah* (1912), Gabriel Pierne's *The Children's Crusade* (1915), and Samuel Coleridge-Taylor's *Hiawatha* (1919) were major events in the Washington community, as were the weekly vespers services offered to the public in Howard's Andrew Rankin Chapel. The Howard University orchestra, band, and women's and men's glee clubs flourished and made appearances in other cities. During Childers's tenure, the university presented William Gilbert and Arthur Sullivan's operetta *The Mikado* (1923), which Childers herself directed, and the operas *Il Trovatore* (1939), *Faust* (1940), and *I Pagliacci* (1942). Operatic productions were unusual for an undergraduate college, especially since, except for some soloists and members of the National Symphony Orchestra who joined the university symphony, the performers consisted entirely of faculty and students. Reviewing the production of *Faust*, Glenn D. Gunn, music critic of the *Times-Herald* (21 May 1939), wrote, "The choruses were brilliant, the ballet picturesque, the orchestra competent."

One additional activity that began under Childers and continued into later years was an annual recital series that brought outstanding musicians to the Washington community. The recitals drew large audiences and provided rare occasions in the rigidly segregated city of Washington, D.C., when black and white patrons sat together. One recital scheduled for the 1938–1939 concert series led to an event reported in newspapers worldwide. MARIAN ANDERSON, contralto, was contracted to appear in the series, and university officials, aware of Anderson's standing as an artist, sought a larger auditorium. After she was refused the use of facilities by the board of education and also by the Daughters of the American Revolution because of her race, she accepted the offer of Harold Ickes, secretary of the interior, to perform at the Lincoln Memorial, where she appeared on Easter Sunday 1939 before an audience of seventy-five thousand.

Childers's greatest contribution was the establishment of the Howard University School of Music. When she went to Howard, instruction in music was limited to precollege courses in piano and voice culture provided by one teacher. At her retirement Childers left in place the full-fledged School of Music, the largest and most comprehensive school of music in a historically black university and comparable in its offerings to many larger schools. In the process of transforming the music unit at Howard into a degree-granting program, she was a pioneer, for music had not yet achieved national status as a worthy member of the collegiate body. She trained many successful singers, one of whom, the soprano LILLIAN EVANTI, was the first African American to sing opera in Europe with an established company. Childers was described by her students and peers as "noble and regal in bearing," "meticulous to a fault," and "generous with her time and money."

Childers retired in 1940. She died at her home in Howell, Michigan. Howard University awarded her an honorary doctor of music degree in 1942 and named the classroom portion of the fine arts complex in her honor in 1956. LOIS MAILOU JONES, an artist and Howard University professor, painted a portrait of Childers, which was hung in the building in 1964.

FURTHER READING

Dyson, Walter. *Howard University: The Capstone of Negro Education, a History: 1867–1940* (1941).

Logan, Rayford W. *Howard University: The First Hundred Years, 1867–1967* (1969).

McGinty, Doris Evans. "Black Women in the Music of Washington, D.C., 1900–20," in *New Perspectives on Music: Essays in Honor of Eileen Southern*, ed. Josephine Wright with Samuel A. Floyd Jr. (1992).

This entry is taken from the *American National Biography* and is published here with the permission of the American Council of Learned Societies.

DORIS EVANS MCGINTY

Childress, Alice (12 Oct. 1916–14 Aug. 1994), playwright and actress, was born in Charleston, South Carolina, and brought up in Harlem, New York, by her grandmother Eliza Campbell White. Although Alice's grandmother had little or no formal education, she had a natural creative spirit, and fostered in her granddaughter a thirst for knowledge and an appreciation for the arts by exposing her to museums, galleries, libraries, theater, and concerts. She also encouraged Alice to role-play and create stories and skits, many of which grew out of Wednesday-night testimonials at Harlem's Salem Church. These testimonials, Alice later realized, allowed poor people in their community to relieve themselves of burdens linked to race, class, and gender biases.

Alice lived on 118th Street between Lenox and Fifth avenues and attended Public School 81 and the Julia Ward Howe Junior High School. She enrolled in Wadleigh High School, but dropped out after two years, forced to earn a living after the death of both her grandmother and mother in the early 1930s. Primarily self-taught, Alice worked as an assistant machinist, photo retoucher, domestic worker, salesperson, and insurance agent, jobs that tied her to working-class people who later found their way into her writing.

Unfulfilled by these odd jobs, Alice reinvented herself, gravitating toward theater because of her love of dialogue. In the 1930s she formed alliances with Harlem actors and won cameo roles in plays. During this time she met and married ALVIN CHILDRESS. Best known for his role as Amos Jones in the 1950s show *Amos 'n Andy*, Alvin Childress was one of the first African American actors to star on television. In 1935 a daughter, Jean, was born. The couple soon divorced but maintained a professional relationship throughout the 1940s, working side by side in the American Negro Theater (ANT), a training ground for black artists, including SIDNEY POITIER, OSSIE DAVIS, RUBY DEE, Frank Silvera, HILDA SIMMS, CANADA LEE, and Earle Hyman. Childress developed as an actress, director, and playwright at the ANT from 1941 to 1952. After work in several ANT productions, Childress starred on Broadway from 1944 to 1954 in *Anna Lucasta*, a play by Philip Yordan first staged at the ANT and costarring Alvin, Canada Lee, and FREDERICK O'NEAL. The play ran for 957 performances and earned Childress a Tony Award nomination.

While at the ANT, Childress responded to a call for more plays by, for, and about blacks. In 1949 she directed and starred in her first one-act play, *Florence*. One of Childress's major accomplishments during her tenure with the ANT was her role in the early 1950s in initiating guaranteed pay in advance for union off-Broadway contracts in New York. Childress's *Just a Little Simple* (based on the short story collection *Simple Speaks His Mind* by LANGSTON HUGHES) and *Gold through the Trees* (1952) were the first plays written by a black woman to be produced professionally and performed by unionized actors.

In 1955 Childress made theater history when she became the first African American woman to win an Obie Award, with *Trouble in Mind* (1955), which she directed off-Broadway at the Greenwich Mews Theater. In July 1957 she married the musician Nathan Woodard, with whom she collaborated on several creative projects. In 1966 Childress was awarded a two-year appointment to the Radcliffe Institute for Independent Study (now the Mary Ingraham Bunting Institute) at Harvard University, where she became friendly with the playwrights

Lillian Hellman and Tillie Olsen. While at Radcliffe she wrote *Wedding Band: A Love/Hate Story in Black and White*, a play about interracial love and the racism of laws barring marriage between blacks and whites.

In 1972 Childress and Joseph Papp codirected the *Wedding Band* for the New York Public Theater's Shakespeare Festival. Two years later she adapted *Wedding Band* for television. Childress's other plays include *String* (1969), *Wine in the Wilderness* (1969), *Mojo: A Black Love Story* (1970), *The World on a Hill* (1974), *When the Rattlesnake Sounds* (1975), *Let's Hear It for the Queen* (1976), a piece she wrote for her only grandchild, Marilyn Alice Lee, *A Portrait of Fannie Lou Hamer* (1978), *Sea Island Song*, renamed *Gullah* (1977 and 1981), and *Moms: A Praise Play for a Black Comedienne* (1986), based on the life of MOMS MABLEY. In an attempt to improve the quality of the lives of African Americans, Childress's plays underscore themes affecting the lives of American blacks: the need for self-determination and self-definition, the destructiveness of stereotypes, and the need for more creative, positive images.

Childress, who had spoken out against injustices in her column in *Freedom*, a newspaper edited by PAUL ROBESON, and in the *Baltimore Afro-American* (collected in *Like One of the Family: Conversations from a Domestic's Life* [1956]), became increasingly committed to the issue of poverty in America after her travels to Russia, China, and Ghana in the 1970s. She raised the social issues of poverty, addiction, child abuse, and racism in her fiction as well as in her dramatic works. Childress wrote a number of books, including three novels for young adults, *A Hero Ain't Nothin' but a Sandwich* (1973), which she later adapted as a screenplay; *Rainbow Jordan* (1981); and *Those Other People* (1989). Her novel for adults, *A Short Walk* (1979), traces black experiences in America from the MARCUS GARVEY movement through the 1940s. Like her plays, Childress's novels incorporate black history and emphasize the importance of relying upon ancestors for strength and guidance.

Childress garnered many honors, particularly for *Rainbow Jordan* and *A Hero Ain't Nothin' but a Sandwich*, which won a National Book Award nomination, the Lewis Carroll Shelf Award, and an American Library Association award for Best Young Adult Book. Childress was the recipient of the first Paul Robeson Award for Outstanding Contributions to the Performing Arts, a Radcliffe Alumnae Graduate Society Medal for Distinguished Achievement, a Lifetime Career Achievement Award from the Association for Theatre in Higher Education in 1993, and election to the Black Filmmakers Hall of Fame.

Childress's contributions to American life and letters are significant. Her novels created a much-needed space in American literature to view the dangers awaiting black adolescents in a hostile world. Her plays underscored her belief that black adults, too, were at great risk from the destructive forces in a racist society. She was an activist who saw a need for change and worked tirelessly both inside and outside of the theater to revolutionize American society. Childress, who died of cancer in 1994, wrote successfully for the American stage for over four decades and served as a major link in the development of African American theater.

FURTHER READING

Betsko, Kathleen, and Rachel Koenig, eds. *Interviews with Contemporary Women Playwrights* (1987).

Brown-Guillory, Elizabeth. "Interview with Alice Childress." *SAGE: A Scholarly Journal on Black Women* (1987).

Bryer, Jackson R., ed. *The Playwright's Art: Conversations with Contemporary American Dramatists* (1995).

Jennings, La Vinia Delois. *Alice Childress* (1995).

Jordan, Shirley M., ed. *Broken Silences: Interviews with Black and White Women Writers* (1993).

Obituary: *New York Times*, 19 Aug. 1994.

ELIZABETH BROWN-GUILLORY

Childress, Alvin (c. 1907–19 Apr. 1986), actor on stage, screen, television, and radio, was born in Meridian, Mississippi, where his father was a dentist and his mother a schoolteacher. Their names are not known. He attended Rust College in Holly Springs, Mississippi, where he received a B.A. in 1931. Though Childress had intended to become a doctor when he entered college, he moved to New York City only months after graduation to begin an acting career. He performed on Broadway in stylized, sometimes stereotypical, roles in such plays as *Savage Rhythm* (1932), *Brown Sugar* (1937), and *Two on an Island* (1940). He also appeared in a number of New York–produced all-black films, including *Dixie Love* (1933), *Hell's Alley* (1938), and *Keep Punching* (1939).

For a good deal of his career Childress was affiliated with Off-Broadway acting companies. He joined the Federal Theater Project, appearing in three of its 1937 New York productions at the Lafayette Theater: *Sweet Land*, *The Case of Philip*

Laurence, and *Haiti*. A long association with the American Negro Theater brought him featured stage roles, including that of Reverend Alfred Davidson in *Rain* (1941), Captain Tom in *Natural Man* (1941), and Noah in *Anna Lucasta* (1944). He also performed in many of the troupe's radio dramas, which were broadcast regionally on a New York radio station. He became a teacher of both stage and radio acting techniques for the company.

Childress is best remembered, however, for his role in the CBS television series *Amos 'n Andy*, which aired from 1951 to 1953. Adapted from the popular radio program, in which African American roles had been played by white performers affecting exaggerated accents, *Amos 'n Andy* came to television with an all-black cast. Childress, who had auditioned for all the male roles, was cast as Amos Jones, the soft-spoken, down-to-earth taxi driver who served as the show's narrator. Fearing that he was too light-skinned to be a credible black character, the producers insisted he play the role in blackface makeup. Amos was a pillar of the community, a dedicated family man, and a co-owner of a taxicab company in Harlem. However, he was the sole positive role model in a cast of characters who were otherwise portrayed as underhanded conmen, shiftless slackers, and shrewish women. Civil rights organizations, notably the National Association for the Advancement of Colored People (NAACP), waged a campaign against the presentation of these demeaning stereotypes. When Blatz Beer withdrew sponsorship at the end of 1952–1953 season, CBS dropped the series from its prime-time schedule.

Childress, however, defended *Amos 'n Andy*, telling an interviewer that he "didn't feel it harmed the Negro at all," pointing out that "the series had many episodes that showed the Negro with professions and businesses like attorneys, store owners, and so on, which they never had in TV or movies before." Along with other members of the cast, he predicted that canceling the show would have the overall negative effect of eliminating opportunities for black performers, ensuring that American television would develop as a "lily white" dramatic venue. This proved to be the case for almost two decades.

With *Amos 'n Andy* out of production, Childress moved to Los Angeles to attempt a film career but managed to appear in only two Hollywood features: the screen adaptation of *Anna Lucasta* (United Artists, 1959) and *The Man in the Net* (United Artists, 1959). His fortunes in decline, the veteran actor was forced to take a job as a parking lot attendant. Giving up on his hopes of remaining an actor, he took a civil-service examination and became a social worker for the county of Los Angeles.

In 1971 Childress was coaxed by producer Richard Alan Simmons into accepting a minor role in *Banyon*, a made-for-television movie. The 1970s saw a renaissance of situation comedy programs starring African American performers, many produced by Norman Lear's Tandem Productions. Lear helped revive Childress's show business career, offering him guest roles on three top-rated sitcoms: *Sanford and Son* (1972), *Good Times* (1974), and *The Jeffersons* (1976). These led to other television appearances as well as film opportunities. Childress performed character roles in such major studio releases as *The Day of the Locust* (1975), *The Bingo Long All-Stars and Motor Kings* (1976), and *The Main Event* (1979).

The actor developed a series of debilitating illnesses in the 1980s, including Parkinson's disease, diabetes, and pneumonia. He died in Inglewood, California.

FURTHER READING

Andrews, Bart, and Arghus Juilliard. *Holy Mackerel! The Story of Amos and Andy* (1986).
Ely, Melvin Patrick. *The Adventures of Amos 'n Andy: A Social History of an American Phenomenon* (1991).
Obituary: *Variety*, 30 Apr. 1986.
This entry is taken from the *American National Biography* and is published here with the permission of the American Council of Learned Societies.

DAVID MARC

Childs, Faith (8 Mar. 1951–), literary agent, was born Faith Hampton Childs in Washington, D.C., one of four children of Thomas Childs and Elizabeth Slade Childs, both public school English teachers who had attended Hampton University. Her father, a book collector, encouraged his daughter to learn about the world through reading, which Childs has credited for sparking her interest in literature. Following her graduation from high school, Childs studied history and political science at Clark University in Worcester, Massachusetts, graduating in 1973. Five years later she acquired a law degree at American University in Washington, D.C. Despite practicing law for several years in three different cities, Childs found herself, in her early thirties, in need of a drastic career change. The work, she has claimed, was simply not "intellectually challenging" (Sachs et al.), and she wished to "enter a life of the mind" (Baker,

p. 50) that her father had encouraged years earlier. A friend, the agent Jed Mattes, recommended literary representation to her, and referred her to his fellow agent Charlotte Sheedy. Childs apprenticed under Sheedy for four years and, despite an initially unsuccessful period in which she failed to sell a book for almost a year, she eventually left to start her own company, Faith Childs Literary Agency, Ltd. Her first major sale was PAULE MARSHALL's novel, *Daughters* (1991) to Atheneum Books.

At the time, the experiences of middle- and upper-class African Americans—in other words, people like Childs—were virtually nonexistent in literature, despite a relative increase in affluence among blacks. Understandably, most African American literature depicted struggle, violence, poverty, and oppression. "It's easy to sell a book like *Up from Slavery* because people are comfortable with that," Childs has said Baker, "but sophisticated, well-to-do black people" were deemed uninteresting by many publishers. For example, not long after founding her agency, Childs encountered difficulty trying to sell a memoir about a black man who had gone to Harvard. Perceptions within the publishing industry would change in the late 1980s and early '90s, however, with the success of commercial writers such as TERRY MCMILLAN (*Waiting to Exhale*, 1992) and E. Lynn Harris (*Invisible Life*, 1991), whose work appealed to the same underrepresented audience that Childs wanted to reach.

Besides addressing misconceptions about black readers, Childs has confronted stereotypes of black writers as well. Along with some of the more prominent African American agents (such as Marie Brown and Lawrence Jordan), she has worked to cultivate talented black writers and bring more attention to African American literature while, at the same time, discouraging the tendency to label the work (or her agency) as limited only to a black audience. To that end, Childs established an integrated list of authors. Over the years, her clients have included the Pulitzer Prize winner James Alan McPherson; the mystery writer Jill Churchill (author of *Anything Goes*, 1999); Valerie Wilson Wesley (author of *Ain't Nobody's Business If I Do* [1999] and the Tamara Hayle mystery series); Emily Bernard (author of *New York Times* Notable Book of the Year *Remember Me to Harlem: The Letters of Langston Hughes and Carl Van Vechten*, 2001); the novelist and essayist NATHAN MCCALL (*Them*, named by *Publishers Weekly* as one of the best novels of 2007); the novelist Benilde Little (*Acting Out*, 2003); the photo essayist Sylvia Plachy (who, along

with fellow client James Ridgway, authored *Red Light: Inside the Sex Industry* [1996], a provocative depiction of the pornography trade); the mythologist and biographer David Leeming (*Oxford Companion to World Mythology*, 2005); and the novelist David Haynes (*The Full Matilda*, 2004).

In addition, Childs has represented a number of books with an international focus (including Suketi Mehta's *Maximum City*, 2004), as well as those dealing with the multiracial backgrounds of African Americans (THULANI DAVIS's *My Confederate Kinfolk* [2006]; Emily Bernard's *Some of My Best Friends: Writing on Interracial Friendships* [2005]; and SHIRLEE TAYLOR HAIZLIP's *Finding Grace: Two Sisters and the Search for Meaning beyond the Color Line* [2004]). Because of her knowledge of the industry, Childs has been frequently interviewed in articles dealing with publishing events and trends that affect African American literature. For example, she weighed in on the controversy surrounding *The Help* (2009), a best-selling novel written by white author Kathryn Sockett that many (including Childs) felt presented a stereotypical depiction of African American servants.

While continuing to run her agency, Childs also helped to establish Women's Voices for Change, an advocacy group that seeks to redefine society's definitions and perceptions of menopausal women; she has been a frequent contributor to the organization's blog, often writing on literature and culture. She has also served as an advisor and board member for the nonprofit New Press, the PEN Open Book Committee, the Creative Writing Department of the New School, and the UpSouth Literary Book Festival in Harlem.

FURTHER READING
Arnold, Martin. "Literary Advocates for Black Voices." *New York Times*, 13 January 2000.
Baker, John F. "Faith Childs." In *Literary Agents: A Writer's Introduction* (1999), pp. 49–53.
Brown, Carolyn. "Writing a New Chapter in Book Publishing." *Black Enterprise*, Feb. 1995, pp. 108–118.
Covington, Heather. *Literary Divas: The Top 100+ African-American Women in Literature* (2006).
Foston, Nikitta A. "Black Male Authors: Smart, Sexy and Successful." *Ebony*, 1 Dec. 2002.
Rich, Mokoto. "A Southern Mirrored Window." *New York Times*, 2 Nov. 2009.
Sachs, Andrea, Barbara Dolan, and Nancy Williams. "Have Law Degree, Will Travel." *Time*, 11 Dec. 1989.
ROBERT REPINO

Childs, Francine C. (8 February 1940–), social activist and college professor, was born Francine Cheryl Childs to Margaret Frazier Thomas and Nathan Rogers in Wellington, Texas. Her grandparents John and Clara Frazier raised her. Childs attended the segregated Booker T. Washington School in Wellington. Although the school never had a gymnasium, Childs excelled as both a student and athlete. She was a star basketball player in high school and graduated valedictorian of her class in 1958.

After high school, Childs attended Paul Quinn College in Waco, Texas, where she earned a B.S. in Biology in 1962. Upon receiving her B.S. degree, Childs returned to teach at her alma mater, Booker T. Washington, for three years (1962–1965). Along with her teaching responsibilities, she also coached girl's basketball and track. Childs won a National Science Foundation Award at Prairie View A&M University during the summer of 1965. She later accepted a teaching position at Miel High School in Bastrop, Texas. In January 1967, she left Bastrop for McKinney, Texas, to serve as a residential director for Job Corps Center for Women. During her tenure, she pursued and earned an MEd in Sociology and Guidance Counseling at East Texas State University (now Texas A&M at Commerce). Childs then went on to Wiley College, where she served as the Dean of Women in 1970 and later as the Dean of Students in 1971. During this time, Childs pursued an Ed.D. from East Texas State University.

In 1974 Childs accepted a faculty position in the African American Studies department at Ohio University. She served as the chair of the department, started the first tutoring program for African American students, facilitated Sunday evening forums, advised the Black Student Union, and reinstituted the Black Faculty Caucus. Childs has published extensively in various peer review journals, books chapters, magazines, and newspapers. She has presented at academic conferences and has been a popular keynote and guest speaker for various school, church, and community events.

While at Ohio University, Dr. Childs became affectionately known as "Doc." She championed the cause of all students, fought for equity for faculty and staff, and engaged in extensive community outreach. In 1978 Childs went on a twenty-eight-day fast to protest multiple rapes and safety issues for women on campus. This individual act of bravery and sacrifice inspired hundreds of students, faculty, and staff at Ohio University to join her protest. Childs's activism was by no means limited to a hunger strike. She spent her entire career fighting for social, political, and economic justice. In 1978, hundreds gathered in front of Cutler Hall (which houses the offices of the president and top-level administrators at Ohio University) to participate in what was called "Community Pray-In." According to Alvin Hayes, a reporter from the student newspaper *The Post*, the speakers called on the university administrators to play a more prominent role in easing racial tensions in Athens. Childs was a prominent voice at this gathering. As a student of the work and lives of MARTIN LUTHER KING JR. and Mahatma Gandhi, Childs insisted that the gathering should take a nonviolent approach. Nevertheless, she was forceful in making her demands known to the administration. In fact, she passed out a list of concerns that she had previously presented to the administration that addressed the treatment of African American faculty and students by the university and the local community.

The church has played a pivotal role in Childs's life. Believing that equality is a hallmark of the black church, she has worked hard to live up to such values. She has clothed, fed, and provided financial, emotional, and spiritual support for students, not only at her own university, but all over the world. Countless students proclaimed that they would have not matriculated successfully through Ohio University without the aid of Childs. At the May 2010 Black Alumni Reunion, students from the 1980s and onward recounted the role that Childs played in their academic, social, and spiritual lives. Many indeed were moved to tears as Childs was honored at this event.

Childs officially retired from Ohio University in the fall of 2010.

FURTHER READING
Cochran, Shaylyn. "Professor Brings Rich Life Lessons to Students." *The Post*, 24 Feb. 2006.
Hayes, Alvin. "Problem of Racial Tension Raised at Pray-in." *Post*, 3 May 1978.
Rayford, Mary. "Celestial Singing at Athens' Mt. Zion Baptist Church." *Athens Magazine*, 1983.
Stettler, Lisa. "Childs: Understanding Need." *Athens News*, 29 Feb. 1985.

WINSOME CHUNNU-BRAYDA

Chiles, James Alexander (8 Jan. 1860–5 Apr. 1930), lawyer, was born in Richmond, Virginia, the son of slaves Richard C. and Martha A. Chiles. Immediately following the end of the Civil War a public school for blacks, known as the "Freedmen's

School," was opened in Ebenezer Baptist Church on Leigh Street in Richmond, and Chiles's family arranged for his admission to the school at the age of six. Chiles's father, Richard, had emerged by this time as a leader of the African American community in Richmond. During the Civil War Richard Chiles had worked in the War Department of the Confederate States of America (CSA), whose capital was at Richmond. On 2 April 1865, while CSA President Jefferson Davis was attending a worship service at St. Paul's Episcopal Church on Richmond's Capitol Square, Richard Chiles delivered to him a letter written by Confederate military commander General Robert E. Lee, who was then at Petersburg, Virginia. The letter notified President Davis that the capital at Richmond could no longer be defended by Confederate troops and urged that the city be evacuated immediately. Davis subsequently fled to Danville, Virginia, and then further south. After Lee's surrender at Appomattox, Virginia, Davis was arrested by Union troops in southern Georgia.

The Chiles family saw to young James's continuing education despite the deterioration of public schooling available to blacks in Richmond during the 1870s and 1880s. In the mid-1880s he entered Lincoln University in Pennsylvania, which had been founded in 1854 (as Ashmun Institute) to foster the higher education of African American males. In 1887 Chiles earned an AB degree from the college, which had been renamed in 1866 to honor President Abraham Lincoln. In the fall of 1887 Chiles moved to Ann Arbor, Michigan, and enrolled in the University of Michigan Law School. Chiles earned an LLB degree from the University of Michigan in 1889 and was also awarded an A.M. degree by Lincoln University in 1890.

After completing his education, Chiles initially returned to Richmond, Virginia. However, following his marriage in 1891 to Philadelphia schoolteacher Fannie J. Barnes, Chiles moved with his wife to Lexington, Kentucky. He quickly established a successful legal practice there and became a member of Lexington's Seventh Day Adventist Church.

James and Fannie Chiles had three children: M. L. ("Lilian") Gilpin of Richmond, Virginia; Richard Chiles of Washington, D.C.; and John R. Chiles of Richmond. While the children were growing up the family remained based in Lexington, but travel to Richmond was a regular event; the entire family maintained close ties to James Chiles's relatives there. Because of the Chiles's growing wealth and social ties to Richmond's elite black community, some of their visits to Richmond attracted the attention of that city's premier African American newspaper, *the Richmond Planet*. When Fannie and Lilian Chiles visited Richmond in the spring of 1906, for example, their arrival was prominently reported in *The Planet*; in July of that year, a photograph of young socialite Lilian Chiles was published on *The Planet's* front page.

In declining health in the late 1920s Chiles planned to relocate from Lexington to Richmond. In April 1930, while boarding a train to Richmond at the main rail station in Lexington, Chiles died suddenly. His body was taken by train to Richmond, where an elaborate funeral ceremony was held on 7 April 1930 at Ebenezer Baptist Church, where Chiles had attended school as a youngster. A cross-section of the city's African American social and professional leaders served as honorary pallbearers at the funeral.

FURTHER READING

Biographical information on James Alexander Chiles is available on a number of forms he completed, now at the University of Michigan's Bentley Historical Library in the University of Michigan Alumni Association's Necrology File. This information includes details on Chiles' Lincoln University degrees.

Johnson, W. D. *Biographical Sketches of Prominent Negro Men and Women of Kentucky* (1897).

Smith, J. Clay, Jr. *Emancipation: The Making of the Black Lawyer, 1944–1944* (1993).

LAURA M. CALKINS

Chinn, May Edward (15 Apr. 1896–1 Dec. 1980), physician and cancer researcher, was born in Great Barrington, Massachusetts, the daughter of William Lafayette Chinn, a former slave who had escaped to the North from a Virginia plantation, and Lulu Ann Evans, a domestic worker. William Chinn had unsteady employment because of racial discrimination, but occasionally worked at odd jobs and as a porter. Raised in New York City, May Chinn was educated in the city's public schools and at the Bordentown Manual Training and Industrial School (NJ), and she attended Morris High School in New York. A severe bout with osteomyelitis of the jaw plagued her as a child and required extensive medical treatment. Though her family's poverty forced her to drop out of high school in the eleventh grade for a factory job, she scored high enough on the entrance examination for Teachers' College at Columbia University a year later to be admitted to the class of 1921 without a high school diploma.

Chinn's early ambition was to be a musician. Despite the family's poor economic situation, her parents financed piano lessons that gave her some professional opportunity in music as a young adult. For several years in the early 1920s she was a piano-accompanist for the famed singer PAUL ROBESON, and she initially majored in music education at Columbia. She was the only African American and female in her music classes, and ridicule from one professor caused her to abandon music for study in the sciences. The switch to science, combined with her childhood experience of being treated for osteomyelitis, led to her decision to become a medical doctor. After graduating from Columbia with a B.S. degree in 1921, she was admitted to the Bellevue Hospital Medical College (now New York University Medical College) and in 1926 became its first African American woman graduate. In 1926 she was one of the first three African Americans to be accepted as interns at New York City's public Harlem Hospital. (The other two were men.)

Upon completion of her internship Chinn faced the color barrier confronted by all African American physicians; she could not gain admitting privileges for her patients at any hospital in New York City. She opened an office in a brownstone on Edgecombe Avenue in Harlem next to the Edgecombe Sanatorium, a private hospital owned and operated by a group of black physicians. In return for living and office space, she answered all-night emergency calls at the sanatorium. During the 1930s she studied dermatology and gynecology at the Post-Graduate Hospital Medical School in New York, and in 1933 she received an M.S. degree in Public Health from Columbia University. Chinn's interest in cancer research was elicited by the clinical experience of seeing so many patients in advanced stages of the disease, and this led to the development of a "fanatical preoccupation" in understanding and treating cancer. No hospital in New York City would allow her to do cancer work because of her race, but she was unofficially allowed to work with resident physicians at Memorial Hospital and was instructed in how to perform biopsies. Between 1928 and 1933 she studied cytological methods for the diagnosis of cancer under George Papanicolaou, developer of the Pap Smear test for cervical cancer. African American physicians in Harlem, having learned of her connection at Memorial and her training and clinical experience there, began to send her specimens for biopsies. In 1944 she was appointed to the staff of the Strang Clinic affiliated with Memorial and New York Infirmary Hospital. While working at the Strang Clinic over the next twenty-nine years, she helped to devise ways to detect cancer in asymptomatic patients. Her evaluation of patients' family histories to detect cancer in the early stages was recognized as a significant approach to cancer understanding and treatment at the time.

Over the course of her fifty-two-year career Chinn became a legend in Harlem. She was one of a handful of pioneering African American women in medicine in the mid-1920s through the 1930s and 1940s who overcame barriers of race and gender in medical school, in postgraduate training, and in gaining hospital appointments. In addition to her family medical practice and cancer work, she was a clinician and medical adviser in New York State Department of Health–supported day care centers in New York City (1960–1977) and a staff member of the New York Infirmary for Women and Children (1945–1956). As the physician assigned to escort fifty severely handicapped persons of the St. Jeanne Valois Guild of New York City to Paris, Lourdes, and Rome in 1961, she was granted a special audience with Pope John XXIII and in 1978 served as a medical consultant to 100 refugees from southern Africa who were attending colleges throughout the United States. After her retirement from private practice in 1977, Chinn continued to work in three Harlem day care centers sponsored by the state department of health.

Chinn's cancer research and clinical practice was recognized by her election as a member of the New York Academy of Sciences in 1954, and in 1957 she received a citation from the New York City Cancer Committee of the American Cancer Society. She was elected to the Society of Surgical Oncology in 1958, became a Fellow of the American Geriatrics Society in 1959, and was elected to medical membership of the American Society of Cytology in 1972 and as a Life Member of the American Academy of Family Physicians in 1977. In 1975 she was a founder of the SUSAN SMITH MCKINNEY STEWARD Medical Society, named for the first African American woman licensed to practice medicine in the state of New York. Chinn received a Teachers' College Distinguished Alumnus Award from Columbia University in May 1980 and an honorary doctor of science degree from New York University in June 1980. She died while attending a reception in Avery Hall at Columbia University.

FURTHER READING
Chinn's papers are housed in the Schomburg Center for Research in Black Culture of the New York Public Library.

Brozan, Nadine. "For a Doctor at 84, a Day to Remember." *New York Times*, 17 May 1980.

Davis, George. "A Healing Hand in Harlem." *New York Times Magazine*, 22 Apr. 1979.

Hill, Ruth Edmonds, ed. *The Black Women Oral History Project* (1991).

Obituary: *New York Times*, 3 Dec. 1980.

This entry is taken from the *American National Biography* and is published here with the permission of the American Council of Learned Societies.

ROBERT C. HAYDEN

Chisholm, Shirley (30 Nov. 1924–1 Jan. 2005), U.S. congresswoman, was born Shirley St. Hill in Brooklyn, New York, the eldest daughter of Charles St. Hill, a laborer born in British Guiana (now Guyana), and Ruby Seale, a seamstress born in Barbados. Shirley's first three years were spent in Brownsville, a predominantly Jewish area of Brooklyn. Finding the wages for unskilled factory work insufficient to care for three children properly, the St. Hills sent their three daughters to Barbados, where they lived with their maternal grandparents on the family farm. Shirley credits her grandmother Emily Seale with instilling in her a strong character and determination.

The girls returned to Brownsville in 1934, after their mother gave birth to another daughter. Despite the social and financial hardships of the Depression, Ruby encouraged her children to respect the values of civility, thrift, poise, humility, education, and spirituality, though the sisters endured a substantial amount of teasing in the neighborhood for upholding these values and the sense of decorum and respectability that their parents expected of them. Charles St. Hill's influence on Shirley's political development was also profound. His support for MARCUS GARVEY and his pride in his labor union were frequent dinner table discussion topics, and in her autobiography Chisholm recalls that she went to listen to many black nationalist orators with her father. In 1936 the family moved to the Bedford-Stuyvesant area of Brooklyn, where the Caribbean and southern black residents constituted about half of the population. Unaccustomed to the animosity blacks faced in that neighborhood, Shirley felt the sting of racial epithets for the first time. During this time she also became aware of racial discrimination, when her father's workdays in a burlap bag factory were inequitably reduced. As a result, Ruby was forced to find work as a domestic, leaving Shirley with the

In January 1972, Shirley Chisholm gained national recognition when she announced her intention to run for the presidency of the United States. (Library of Congress.)

responsibility of looking after the home and caring for her younger sisters. Shirley entered Girls High School in 1939 but was still guarded closely by her parents. Shy and self-conscious because of her West Indian accent, she became a voracious reader, maintained superior marks in school, and was elected vice president of a girl's honor society. Determined to pursue a career in teaching, one of the few career options available to black women at that time, Shirley entered Brooklyn College in September 1942. Motivated by her increasing awareness of the racism at the college, she shed her shyness, joined the debating society, and began to speak out on racial issues. She also became active in the Harriet Tubman Society for Negro History and formed Ipothia, a sorority for black women. Believing that "service is the rent we pay for the privilege of living on this earth" (a phrase also attributed to MARIAN WRIGHT EDELMAN), Shirley

St. Hill volunteered with the Urban League and the NAACP, in hospitals, and at a home for the aged. While still in college, she publicly challenged the mostly Irish American organization that ran Brooklyn's old Seventeenth Assembly District for ignoring issues of concern to African Americans, even though two-thirds of the district's constituents were black.

Despite graduating cum laude in 1946, Shirley had difficulty finding work, and she resented that whites with lesser qualifications appeared to have better job opportunities. Eventually hired as a classroom teacher at Mt. Calvary Child Care Center in Harlem, she later became the center's director. Concurrently she enrolled in the master's program in early childhood education at Columbia College, where she met fellow student and private investigator Conrad Chisholm, whom she married in 1949. Conrad Chisholm eventually became an investigator for the City of New York and was by her side through most of her political career until their divorce in 1977.

In 1953 she became director of the Friends in Need Nursery School in Brooklyn, but moved on after one year to become the director of the Hamilton-Madison Child Care Center on Manhattan's Lower East Side. By 1959 she had become a program consultant for the New York City Division of Day Care, but she continued her community work in Bedford-Stuyvesant, setting up youth programs for children, petitioning for better postal service and sanitation, and serving on the board of directors of the Albany Houses public housing project. Through these activities she became involved with New York's political clubs, which were organized by state assembly districts. In 1953 Chisholm joined with her political mentor Wesley McD. "Mac" Holder to help elect the first black judge in Brooklyn's history. Through that effort, the Bedford-Stuyvesant Political League (BSPL) was launched, and Chisholm remained active in this club as well as the regular Democratic organization. In 1958 Chisholm unsuccessfully challenged Mac Holder for the presidency of the BSPL, which caused a schism between them for ten years.

Chisholm was inactive on the political scene for two years following her loss to Mac Holder, but she soon returned to politics to help form the Unity Democratic Club. The primary goal of this club was to oust the white political machine of the Seventeenth Assembly District. Victorious in this mission, Unity became the official Democratic club for the district, and in 1964 Unity nominated Chisholm to fill a vacated seat in the New York State Assembly. She was elected to the assembly, but her victory was marred by her father's death during the campaign.

Chisholm soon earned a reputation in Albany as a maverick who voted her conscience and frequently went against the party line. During her tenure, she introduced more than fifty bills into the legislature, of which eight passed. The most notable of these was her creation of the SEEK (Search for Education, Elevation, and Knowledge) program, which enabled financially disadvantaged students to attend college. She also was a powerful advocate of extending unemployment insurance coverage to domestic employees and of providing state aid to day-care centers.

Determined to beat the political machine that had emerged in Brooklyn's newly created black-majority Twelfth District, Chisholm ran for Congress in 1968. Reuniting with Mac Holder, she campaigned with the slogan "Fighting Shirley Chisholm—Unbought and Unbossed." Emergency surgery for a stomach tumor caused Chisholm to lose some early ground to her opponent, the civil rights activist JAMES FARMER. Finding, however, that there were two and a half women for every man on the voter-registration rolls, Chisholm garnered the support of women's organizations. Her fluency in Spanish also attracted the Hispanic vote, thus providing an ultimately victorious block against her Republican opponent.

As a freshman representative to the Ninety-first Congress in 1969, Chisholm asked to be assigned to the House Education and Labor Committee. Instead, she was assigned to the Committee for Rural Development and Forestry, whose agenda was totally unrelated to the needs of her urban district. After failing in her attempts to enlist the support of more senior representatives, she defiantly approached the Speaker's dais to protest the assignment. Again, her diligence paid off, and she was reassigned to the Committee on Veterans Affairs. In 1971 she secured a seat on the powerful House Education and Labor Committee, which enabled her to focus on the economic and educational issues of greatest relevance to her constituents.

Chisholm became increasingly well known on Capitol Hill for her straightforward criticism of cozy bipartisan politics and the seniority system. In the late 1960s, the tap of Chisholm's trademark stiletto heels struck a dissonant chord in the boys club atmosphere of the U.S. Congress. Her unabashed and uncompromising liberalism also stood out, even in that relatively liberal era. She fought passionately for greater racial and gender equality, demanded a lowering of the voting age, spoke out against the Vietnam War, and supported the National Association for the Repeal of Abortion Laws. In 1970 Chisholm headed a coalition of women's groups to raise bail for a jailed Black Panther Party member.

Chisholm gained national recognition in January 1972, when she announced her intention to run for the presidency of the United States. Inspired by the young people with whom she maintained constant contact, she campaigned in six states while continuing to attend to her duties in Washington and Brooklyn. She did not receive the support of the Congressional Black Caucus, however, which severely dented her chance of winning the Democratic nomination. But her impressive showing of 151 votes to George McGovern's 1,415 constituted the largest number of convention votes cast for a female candidate in U.S. party political history.

Continuing to serve in the House of Representatives, Chisholm emerged as a powerful advocate for fair housing programs and the educational rights of the poor and racial minorities. Her most significant legislative achievement came in the mid 1970s, when she successfully led the opposition in Congress to President Ford's veto of federal support for state daycare services. By the time Chisholm retired from Congress in 1982, however, she had become less of a maverick, and, as a member of its Rules Committee, even something of a Capitol Hill insider.

She subsequently held faculty appointments at Mount Holyoke College, Massachusetts, where she taught politics and women's studies from 1983 to 1987, and at Spelman College in Atlanta, Georgia, where she was a visiting scholar in 1985. Chisholm authored two autobiographies, *Unbought and Unbossed* (1970) and *The Good Fight* (1973), and in 1984 she cofounded the National Political Congress of Black Women. In 1993 President Bill Clinton asked her to serve as U.S. Ambassador to Jamaica, but she declined the appointment for health reasons. Chisholm retired to Florida with her second husband, Arthur Hardwick, whom she married in 1977. Chisholm died on New Year's Day 2005.

Shirley Chisholm will be remembered as the woman warrior of American politics and as a champion for underrepresented Americans. CHARLES RANGEL and KWEISI MFUME, who followed her into Congress, attained greater political clout on Capitol Hill. JESSE JACKSON earned more votes and delegates in his 1984 and 1988 campaigns for the presidency. In each of these cases, however, their task was made easier by the precedents and the example set by Shirley Chisholm.

FURTHER READING
Chisholm, Shirley. *The Good Fight* (1973).
Chisholm, Shirley. *Unbought and Unbossed* (1970).
Gill, LaVerne McCain. *African American Women in Congress: Forming and Transforming History* (1997).
Hicks, Nancy. *The Honorable Shirley Chisholm, Congresswoman from Brooklyn* (1971).

PATRICIA E. CANSON

Christian, Barbara (12 Dec. 1943–25 June 2000), was born Barbara Theresa Christian in St. Thomas, Virgin Islands, one of six children of Alphonso Christian, a judge, and Ruth (maiden name unknown).

Christian was admitted to Marquette University in Wisconsin at the age of fifteen, graduating cum laude with a B.A. in 1963. She chose to continue studying literature at Columbia University in New York City, in part because of its proximity to Harlem and resonance with the legacy of the Harlem Renaissance writers, who were still largely foreign to the American literary canon during her term of study. Harlem was also a fertile center for political activism in the 1960s civil rights era and central to the creation of a new black intellectual elite whose activities centered around the bookstore run by LEWIS MICHEAUX, brother of black filmmaker OSCAR MICHEAUX. Christian was also said to have met LANGSTON HUGHES' personal secretary in Harlem, who first introduced her to ZORA NEALE HURSTON's masterpiece, *Her Eyes Were Watching God*.

Upon entering Columbia, Christian dedicated herself to the study of African American literatures, aware of the apparent absence of a black tradition. Her doctoral thesis, "Spirit Bloom in Harlem: The Search for a Black Aesthetic during the Harlem Renaissance: The Poetry of Claude McKay, Countee Cullen, and Jean Toomer," reflected her growing interest in defining the black literary tradition. During her graduate studies, Christian taught at the City College of the City University of New York (1965–1972), where she would become known as a pioneer of contemporary American literary feminism. At the City College, Christian was also an instructor in the SEEK program (Search for Education, Elevation, and Knowledge), which functioned to provide talented, underserved youth with access to higher education.

In 1970 she was awarded a Ph.D., with distinction, and a year later was appointed to the University of California (UC) at Berkeley as assistant professor.

She became the first African American woman to be granted tenure at UC–Berkeley in 1978. At Berkeley, Christian became central in establishing the African American Studies department, where she taught from 1972 until her death. She served as chairwoman of that department from 1978 until 1983 and went on to chair the campus's new ethnic studies doctoral program from 1986 to 1989.

Her awards include the American Women's Educators Association award (1982); the Louise Patterson African American Studies Award (1992, 1995); the Modern Language Association MELUS award for contribution to African American scholarship (1994); and the Gwendolyn Brooks Center award (1995).

Combining a rare love of literature with a dedication to political activism, she fought against U.S. intervention in Central America and the Caribbean and against U.S. support for apartheid in South Africa, and in 1993 she signed the call to Defend the Life of Abimael Guzman, imprisoned leader of the People's War in Peru and the Communist Party of Peru.

Professor Christian's groundbreaking first book, *Black Women Novelists: The Development of a Tradition*, was published in 1980. The text comprised the first comprehensive study of black women writers such as NELLA LARSEN, TONI MORRISON, and ALICE WALKER. In 1985 Christian published *Black Feminist Criticism: Perspectives on Black Women Writers*, another landmark study, featuring essays on the works of GWENDOLYN BROOKS, AUDRE LORDE, and GAYL JONES, among various others. In both works Christian argued against the trends in literary criticism to discount the contributions of black writers and argued for their inclusion in literary studies. To study black women writers is to probe the complex interrelationship of sexism and racism necessary in any study in literary criticism, Christian argued.

Professor Christian was known for her critical presence in the growing debates over the relationship between race and gender and insistence on the centrality and pivotal significance of black women not only within African American history, but also within social and political developments in America and American history at large. For Christian, the study of black literary traditions and movements was essential for all literary scholarly, so that the exclusivity of white authors in the literary canon could be effectively challenged and the canon effectively rewritten.

Throughout her career, Christian's focus contained a fine balance between literature and theory in a movement to ensure that African American literary traditions could bear continuity. In 1991 she was the first African American to win the university's Distinguished Teaching Award.

Professor Christian was married to poet David Henderson, author of *De Mayor of Harlem* and official biographer of JIMI HENDRIX. Christian died of lung cancer on 25 June 2000 at her home in Berkeley and is survived by her only daughter, Najuma.

Christian continued to receive professional accolades in the last year of her life, including Berkeley's highest honor, a citation for distinguished achievement and notable service to the university. The author of several books, she contributed dozens of articles and reviews to numerous scholarly journals and was asked to serve as editor of the contemporary section of the Norton Anthology of African American Literature, edited by HENRY LOUIS GATES JR. and NELLIE Y. MCKAY. In her *New York Times* obituary, Professor Gates, Jr. described her as "the senior figure among African-American feminists." In the same obituary the writer and critic ARNOLD RAMPERSAD praised her as a "major shaper and guide in the general area where the subjects of literature, race and feminism meet."

FURTHER READING
"Barbara T. Christian," Biography Resource Center, http://www.galenet.com/servlet/BioRC, 16 Feb. 2004.
"Barbara T. Christian," University of California, Berkeley: *What Good Teachers Say About Teaching*, http://teaching.berkeley.edu/goodteachers/christian.html, 16 Feb. 2004.
"Barbara Christian," 2001, University of California: *In Memoriam*, 19 Feb. 2004. Available at http://dynaweb.oac.cdlib.org:8088/dynaweb/uchist/public/inmemoriam/inmemoriam2001/%40Generic__BookTextView/484.
"Barbara Christian Bibliography," *Black Cultural Studies*, 17 Feb. 2004. Available at http://www.blackculturalstudies.org/christian/christian_biblio.html.
Kester-Shelton, Pamela. *Feminist Writers* (1996).
Obituary: *New York Times*, 9 July 2000.

ADEBE DERANGO-ADEM

Christian, Charlie (29 July 1916–2 Mar. 1942), musician, was born Charles Christian in Dallas, Texas, to parents whose names are unknown. His father was a blues guitarist and singer, and his mother was a pianist. The family moved to Oklahoma City when Christian was five, and he grew up there amid the diverse musical styles of the Southwest. Itinerant blues guitarists and singers played everywhere, and Christian also would have heard Texas blues bands, ethnic dance music, cowboy songs, rural banjo pickers, and white and black fiddle players, both in person and on radios and jukeboxes. Oklahoma City was home to WALTER PAGE's Blue Devils, and Christian heard LESTER "PREZ" YOUNG during Young's two tours with the group. Most of the mid- and southwestern jazz bands also played there. The early western swing bands often had electric guitarists who pioneered the improvised single-note lines that later typified Christian's jazz playing. Although he did not play in either his school's concert band or its symphony orchestra (they had no place for guitar), he did receive formal training in harmony. The writer RALPH ELLISON, a childhood neighbor and friend, remembered that the guitarist's group played light classics as well as the blues.

Christian played trumpet as a child, but he switched to guitar at age twelve and played in the family string band (his four brothers were musicians). He also occasionally played piano and bass during the early 1930s. He was familiar with the electric guitar by 1937 at the latest, probably introduced to it by EDDIE DURHAM, who was touring with the Count Basie band. Christian played professionally with a variety of territory bands, and by 1939 he enjoyed a growing reputation throughout the Southwest. The pianist MARY LOU WILLIAMS told the critic and record producer John Hammond about him, and Hammond arranged an audition with Benny Goodman, who was already considering adding an electric guitarist to his small group. Christian walked into the audition dressed in a purple shirt, bright green suit, and pointed yellow shoes—an affront to the bandleader's sartorial conservatism. But Hammond sneaked Christian onto the bandstand when Goodman was on a break, and Christian greatly impressed the leader with his playing. He joined Goodman in August 1939. Within two months Christian was featured on Goodman recordings like "Flying Home," "Rose Room," and "Seven Come Eleven," making an immediate impact on the jazz world.

Part of the appeal of course was the newness of the instrument and its sound. People were used to the sparer sound of an acoustic guitar, and Christian produced a beautiful bell-like tone with percussive qualities. With the electric guitar's amplification, other instruments could no longer drown out the instrument. From his first appearance on record, the genius of Christian's musical conception was clear. His solos consisted of long, uncluttered lines of eighth notes with a strong blues feeling. He played with a firm tone, flawless time, and a powerful sense of swing and drive. His playing always seemed logical and effortless, so "right" that it never failed to excite and interest. Like his contemporary Young, Christian was rooted in the blues tradition and sought to tell a story in his music. Like Young's, Christian's linear style also pointed toward later bebop innovations. Indeed bop players made some of Christian's favorite melodic figures their own.

Christian reached a temporary plateau in his development around 1940, but in 1941 he made a series of wonderfully relaxed and swinging chamber jazz recordings with the Edmond Hall Celeste Quartet, marked by unique double voicings and intricate rhythmic interplay with the young bassist Israel Crosby. Christian also spent much of the last year of his life playing regularly, often all night, at Minton's Playhouse on 118th Street in New York City with musical innovators like KENNY CLARKE and THELONIOUS MONK. His work during these sessions reveals that he was the most musically advanced and original of all these players, moving toward the language of bop as he stretched out his lines and intensified his already propulsive sense of swing.

By early 1942 Christian's was among the most important voices in all of jazz. But he collapsed with tuberculosis in mid-1941, and he spent the last months of his life in the Seaview Sanatorium on Staten Island, where he died.

Christian is a critical figure in the history of American music. His recordings are almost uniformly classic performances, and critics regard his solos as among the most creative in jazz for their eloquence and simplicity. His popularization of the electric guitar, finally, left a legacy that later spread to the blues, rhythm and blues, and rock and roll. Only twenty-five years old at his death, Christian changed the face of American popular music.

FURTHER READING

Collier, James Lincoln. *The Making of Jazz: A Comprehensive History* (1978).
Schuller, Gunther. *The Swing Era: The Development of Jazz, 1930–1945* (1989).
Tirro, Frank. *Jazz: A History*, 2d ed. (1993).
This entry is taken from the *American National Biography* and is published here with the permission of the American Council of Learned Societies.

RONALD P. DUFOUR

Christian, Marcus Bruce (8 Mar. 1900–21 Nov. 1976), poet, historian, civil rights activist, college instructor, and small businessman, was born in Houma (Mechanicsville), Louisiana, to Emanuel Banks Christian and Rebecca Harris. Christian was born into a family of teachers; both his father and grandfather had taught in rural Louisiana. The latter was a former slave who served as a director of the Lafourche Parish public school system during Reconstruction. Christian's mother died when he was three, and his father, who had tutored him, died ten years later. Little else is known of his early education. He moved with his siblings to New Orleans in 1919, where he worked as a chauffeur before opening his own dry cleaners business. During the 1920s he started writing and publishing poetry, and he studied in the evening division of the New Orleans public school system. The publication of more than a dozen of Christian's poems in *Opportunity* during the 1930s brought favorable remarks from W. E. B. DuBois, Langston Hughes, and other literary figures.

Marcus Christian is best remembered for his work as director of the Negro unit of the Federal Writer's Project (FWP) in Louisiana. Through the assistance of Lyle Saxon, a New Orleans author and head of the Louisiana FWP, Christian was appointed to the "Colored Project" of the program in 1936. Three years later Christian was named director, and the work he oversaw created a trove of folklore and history of African Americans in Louisiana. Christian's work informed much of the material about black Louisiana culture described in the *New Orleans City Guide* (1938), *Louisiana: A State Guide* (1941), and *Gumbo Ya-Ya* (1945). After his death, the Marcus Christian Collection at the University of New Orleans became best known among scholars for the voluminous, unpublished manuscript titled "The Negro in Louisiana" (later re-titled "A Black History of Louisiana"). Created as the culminating work of the "Negro unit," the 1128-page manuscript remains unpublished; however, the work and its accompanying research materials quickly made the Christian material one of the most consulted archival collections in New Orleans.

Christian sought employment with the Writer's Project by approaching Saxon directly. After reading some of his poetry, Saxon hired Christian and later introduced him to many famous African American authors. The "Negro unit" was housed at Dillard College (later Dillard University), and despite the difficulty of conducting research in libraries and archives during the Jim Crow era, the writers amassed a great amount of material. Much of the manuscript consisted of compilations and transcriptions of newspapers and other materials from the nineteenth century. The information about blacks that Saxon used in the state and city guides tended to offer rosier depictions of slavery and its aftermath. Since Christian's Negro unit enjoyed considerable autonomy, its interpretation of the effect of enslavement proved much more sophisticated and probing. World War II ended FWP financial support in 1943 but work remained to be completed on Christian's manuscript. The materials were kept at Dillard and Christian was awarded a Rosenwald fellowship (1943–1944) to complete the book. The work remained incomplete, however, and Christian worked as an assistant librarian at Dillard through the rest of the 1940s.

Christian married Ruth Morand in 1943, but the marriage ended three years later and produced no children.

With the death of Saxon in the mid-1940s, Christian lost a valuable patron. The 1950s found Christian struggling economically, and he delivered newspapers for many years. He balanced this menial labor by mining his research and publishing historical articles and poems in the *Louisiana Weekly*, the state's newspaper of record for the African American community. By the mid-1960s Christian had emerged as an elder among the leaders of Louisiana's modern civil rights movement, for whom Christian's research into the nineteenth-century Afro-Creole protest movement provided inspiration. Christian's greatest effect on the movement stemmed from his African American history articles published in the *Louisiana Weekly* as well as a few lectures broadcast via radio for black audiences. Christian connected the modern civil rights activists to Louisiana's nineteenth-century Afro-Creole protest tradition.

In the last several years of his life, during the 1970s, Christian entered the teaching profession and enthralled students in classrooms at the University of New Orleans as a special lecturer in English and history. History department members and others successfully advocated hiring Christian as an instructor even though he had never completed high school. Friends remembered these as his happiest years. Christian fell ill during one of his University of New Orleans class lectures and died in Charity Hospital.

Christian's legacy is perhaps best understood in relation to other writers. He was Louisiana's Zora Neale Hurston, researching and writing about the folkways and folk culture of Louisiana's African

Americans but above all he served as Louisiana's CARTER G. WOODSON. He labored for decades to amass the first substantial collection of African American historical materials for use by scholars, artists, and lay readers, restoring humanity, complexity, and agency to scholarly interpretations of Louisiana's African American history and culture.

FURTHER READING

A few vital finding aids and excerpts from Christian's work have been placed online. Christian scholar and advocate Rudolph Lewis developed the first online presence for Christian as part of *Chicken Bones: A Journal.* Available at http://www.nathanielturner.com/marcusbrucechristian.htm.

Marcus Christian Collection. Mss 11. Online Inventory. Special Collections, Earl K. Long Library, University of New Orleans. http://library.uno.edu/help/subguide/louis/inventories/011.htm.

Dent, Tom. "Marcus B. Christian: A Reminiscence and an Appreciation," *Black American Literature Forum*, 18:1 (1984).

Johnson, Jerah. "Marcus B. Christian and the WPA History of Black People in Louisiana," *Louisiana History* 20:2 (Spring 1979).

Redding, Joan. "The Dillard Project: The Black Unit of the Louisiana Writers' Project," *Louisiana History* 32:1 (Winter 1991).

Obituary: (New Orleans) *Times-Picayune*, 23 Nov. 1976.

MICHAEL MIZELL-NELSON

Christian-Christensen, Donna M. (19 Sept. 1945–), physician, politician, and delegate to the U.S. Congress, was born Donna Marie Christian in Teaneck, New Jersey, to Virginia Sterling Christian and retired Chief District Court Judge Almeric L. Christian, from St. Croix. Christian-Christensen's parents wanted their daughter to understand her cultural connections to the Virgin Islands, so she spent part of her adolescence in St. Croix. This time in St. Croix had a profound influence on Christian-Christensen's career and commitment to helping others.

Christian-Christensen returned to the United States to graduate from St. Mary's College in Notre Dame, Indiana, where she earned a B.S. degree in 1966. After reading a United Negro College Fund booklet about the lack of minorities in health care, she decided to enter the medical field. She attended George Washington University Medical School and earned an M.D. degree in 1970. From 1970 to 1971, Christian-Christensen worked an as intern at Pacific Medical Center in San Francisco, California, and saw a great need for women in adolescent

medicine. While thinking of the best way to help youths, she studied family medicine and finished her residency at Howard University Medical Center in 1974. In this same year, she married Carl Green and changed her name to Donna Christian-Green. They were married for six years and had two daughters, Rabiah Layla and Karida Yasmeen, before divorcing in 1980. Christian-Christensen remarried in 1988 to Chris Christensen and officially became Donna Christian-Christensen.

Even before she became a board certified physician in 1977, Christian-Christensen was eager to return to St. Croix and work in the health care system. She started as an emergency room physician in 1975 and then held various positions in the Virgin Islands Department of Health until 1980. From 1980 to 1985, she was the director of the Frederiksted Health Center in St. Croix. While she enjoyed this position, Christian-Christensen wanted her work to make more of a significant impact. Her desire for reform led to her entering the public service and serving as the vice chair of the U.S. Virgin Islands Democratic Territorial Committee in 1980. More political opportunities came her way, and she became a committeeperson to the Democratic Party in 1984, member of the U.S. Virgin Islands Board of Education from

Donna M. Christian-Christensen, delegate to the United States Congress, in an official photo.

1984 to 1986, and member of the U.S. Virgin Islands Status Commission from 1988 to 1992. Rallied by an outpouring of support, Christian-Christensen tried for a seat in Congress in 1992. Her bid was unsuccessful, but she ran again and won over incumbent Victor O. Frazer in 1996. As with the District of Columbia, the U.S. Virgin Islands' Member of Congress has only delegate status and cannot vote on issues presented before the full House. At the time of Christian-Christensen's election, the Republican majority in the House prevented delegates (all of whom were then Democrats) from even voting on Congressional Committees, but those rights were restored by the Democratic-led House in 2007. Devoting her full attention to politics, she retired from practicing medicine in January 1997.

Using her medical background as a legislator, Christian-Christensen has brought national attention to health care issues. In 2000 she participated in the first annual National Women's Health Week and promoted National HIV Testing Day. Two years later, she initiated the "State of Heart" campaign to educate African Americans on high blood pressure. Gathering additional political support, Christian-Christensen cosponsored a panel with Congresswoman SHEILA JACKSON LEE on African Americans and health care coverage in 2004 and held a press conference with the Reverend JESSE JACKSON, the Southern Christian Leadership Conference, the Association of Black Cardiologists, the NAACP, the Institute for the Advancement of Multicultural and Minority Medicine, and the National Pastors Network to address the numerous diseases affecting African Americans in 2007. One of these diseases, breast cancer, is a challenge that Christian-Christensen spoke about at the White House's Breast Cancer Awareness event in 2009. Her dedication to the passage of the Mammogram and MRI Availability Act, the Breast Cancer Patient Protection Act, the Breast Cancer Education and Awareness Act, and the Eliminating Disparities in Breast Cancer Treatment Act of 2009, ensure greater access to diagnosis and treatment.

Christian-Christensen has also been involved with several important economic and political achievements. She helped pass the New Markets Venture Capital Program Act of 2000, which helped people obtain employment, and has pushed for tax incentives for several years. As a member of the Congressional Black Caucus, she chairs the Health Braintrust and oversees the group's million dollar fund to stop the HIV/AIDS epidemic in African American communities.

As the first female physician in the U.S. Congress and first female delegate from the U.S. Virgin Islands, Christian-Christensen is a pioneering legislator. Her dedication to improving the conditions of various communities has garnered her success and many accolades, including being named by *Ebony* magazine as one of the "100 Most Influential Black Americans" in May 1997 and being the recipient of the National Innovator Award in 2002.

FURTHER READINGS

Christian-Christensen, Donna. "Donna Marie Christian-Christensen." *Notable Black American Women* (2002).

Corrigan, Janet M., Jill Eden, and Barbara M. Smith, eds. *Leadership by Example: Coordinating Government Roles in Improving Health Care Quality* (2002).

Ford, Lynne E., ed. *Encyclopedia of Women and American Politics* (2008).

DORSIA SMITH SILVA

Chuck D (Carlton Douglas Ridenhour) (1 Aug. 1960–), rapper, educator, and music entrepreneur, was born Carlton Douglas Ridenhour in Queens, New York, to Lorenzo and Judy Ridenhour, both political activists. Lorenzo worked as a warehouse manager before starting his own trucking company at age forty. Ridenhour's home was full of the sounds of jazz and R&B, and he grew up with an acute awareness of the political events of the 1960s as they unfolded: the murder of MEDGAR EVERS, the 1963 March on Washington, and the assassinations of the Kennedys, Black Panther leaders, MALCOLM X, and MARTIN LUTHER KING JR. The family, including his sister Lisa and brother Erik, moved from predominantly black Queensbridge to another largely black community in Roosevelt, Long Island, when Ridenhour was eleven. He spent the summers of 1970 and 1971 attending programs at Adelphi and Hofstra universities on the African American experience, further shaping his early sense of the importance of a unified black community. After graduating from Roosevelt Junior-Senior High School in 1979, Ridenhour enrolled at Adelphi to study graphic design. He designed posters for a variety of early hip-hop groups, and met Hank Shocklee while working as a DJ at the college radio station under the name Chuck D. With Shocklee and Bill Stephney he recorded several raps as the band Spectrum City. After recording the vocals for Shocklee's "Public Enemy No. 1," Chuck D attracted the attention of the producer Rick Rubin of Def Jam

Red black and green
Know what I mean
Don't believe the hype

An integral part of Chuck D's radicalism was his refusal to settle for existing media outlets and to encourage other artists to join in this resistance. He used his lyrics to address critics of his work, including black radio broadcasters, as in the single "Bring the Noise" from *It Takes a Nation*: "Radio stations I question their blackness / They call themselves black, but we'll see if they'll play this." In 1989 the motion picture director SPIKE LEE approached Chuck D to create a theme song for his film *Do the Right Thing*. The result, "Fight the Power," provided a haunting and ominous backdrop to Lee's story of racial tension in a Brooklyn neighborhood. Chuck D's radical lyrics challenged black youth to resist America's white power structure in positive ways and made waves around the world, along with Public Enemy's innovative use of strong beats over musical standards from a variety of genres. This created legal troubles for the group when Public Enemy's use of musical collage set the group squarely in the middle of music rights controversies that eventually resulted in less innovation in hip-hop scoring:

> Public Enemy's music was affected more than anybody's because we were taking thousands of sounds. If you separated the sounds, they wouldn't have been anything—they were unrecognizable. The sounds were all collaged together to make a sonic wall. Public Enemy was affected because it is too expensive to defend against a claim. So we had to change our whole style, the style of *It Takes a Nation* and *Fear of a Black Planet*, by 1991. (Chuck D, quoted in McLeod, 22)

In 1991, to protest the State of Arizona's refusal to observe King birthday, Public Enemy produced the video "By the Time I Get to Arizona," which culminated in images of politicians being gunned down in a manner similar to King's death. Chuck D stood by the video despite the controversy it incited, widening his role as spokesperson for the hip-hop movement. In 1996 he released a solo album, *Autobiography of Mista Chuck*, and the next year published his book *Fight the Power: Rap, Race and Reality*, cowritten with Yusef Jah. In 1999 Chuck D and Public Enemy broke from Def Jam and created their own label, Slam Jamz, in order to make use of the Internet as a mode of music distribution. Chuck D testified before the U.S. Congress

Chuck D, January 2005. The cofounder of the hip-hop group Public Enemy poses for photographers in Cannes, France. (AP Images.)

Records, at the time a fledgling hip-hop label. Chuck D initially resisted Rubin's aggressive efforts to sign him as lead vocalist, preferring to play a less prominent role in the group, but he eventually relented. With Terminator X, Flavor Flav, Professor Griff, and the Bomb Squad, Chuck D put out their first album under the name Public Enemy, *Yo! Bum Rush the Show* in 1987, followed by *It Takes a Nation of Millions to Hold Us Back* (1988) and *Fear of a Black Planet* (1990). *It Takes a Nation* catapulted Public Enemy to the forefront of hip-hop, gaining praise from media critics and African American listeners alike. The single "Don't Believe the Hype" from this album remains a seminal work of early hip-hop with its layered sound and critique of mainstream media. The final lyrics of the song express Chuck D's continual efforts to bypass corporate media to get his message out:

Rock the hard jams—treat it like a seminar
Teach the bourgeoisie, and rock the boulevard
Some say I'm negative
But they're not positive
But what I got to give …
The media says this

on 27 May 2000 and has appeared on several television news programs to discuss MP3 file sharing. After 2000 Chuck D made a habit of releasing his music via the Internet as well as on CD.

As a songwriter Chuck D never shied away from controversial topics. He cowrote several songs with the rappers Immortal Technique and DJ Green Lantern after the terrorist attacks of 11 September 2001, including "Bin Laden" (2005), which blamed the George W. Bush administration for 9/11. He also released several songs highly critical of President Bush just before the 2004 presidential elections, and his disgust seemed to reach a low point in "Hell No We Ain't Alright" from the album *New Whirl Odor* (2005), his response to the disorganized and slow-footed federal response to the devastation of New Orleans, Louisiana, and much of the Gulf Coast region by Hurricane Katrina in August 2005:

Son of a Bush, how you gonna trust that cat?
To fix the shit when help is stuck in Iraq?
Making war plans takin' more stands
In Afghanistan 2000 soldiers dyin' in the sand
But that's over there, right?
Now what's over here is a noise so loud
That some can't hear but on TV I can see
Bunches of people lookin' just like me.

Widely recognized as an iconic figure of hip-hop, Chuck D remained true to what he saw as the music's socially conscious roots and resisted the corporatization of rap music. He lectured regularly on "Rap, Race, Reality, and Technology" and downplayed his role as a grandfather of hip-hop. His democratic vision allowed for anyone to participate in musical creation, and his Web sites (rapstation.com and slamjamz.com) served to facilitate such involvement. He delighted in his own music being transformed by younger rappers in new mixes and continually urged young artists to be aware of their musical and historical roots. In his lectures he connected the contemporary hip-hop scene to the slavery and Jim Crow eras, when African Americans used music and rhythmic spoken word as code to communicate outside the white power structure. Chuck D appeared in many films and television programs, and lent his voice to the 2005 documentaries *Harlem Globetrotters: The Team That Changed the World* and *Bling: Consequences and Repercussions*, about the bloody African diamond trade.

In 2007 Public Enemy released their tenth album, *How You Sell Soul to a Soulless People Who Sold Their Soul?* They continued to tour throughout the globe in the years that followed, and in 2009

announced that they would release a new album, *Most of Our Heroes Don't Appear on a Stamp*, depending on support from their fans. While this unusual approach gave the group the freedom of not dealing with the record industry, the response from fans was tepid. By 2010 fans had contributed only $71,000 of the $250,000 Public Enemy had hoped to raise. In late 2011 Chuck D announced that the new album would finally be released in 2012. Through musical production, lectures, performances with Public Enemy, his Web sites, and his radio show on the left-leaning Air America network, *On the Real*, Chuck D remained a relevant and vital voice of hip-hop culture.

FURTHER READING

Chuck D, with Yusef Jah. *Fight the Power: Rap, Race and Reality* (1997).

McLeod, Kembrew. "How Copyright Law Changed Hip-Hop: An Interview with Public Enemy's Chuck D and Hank Shocklee," *Stay Free!* 20 (Fall 2002): 20–23.

ALICE KNOX EATON

Church, Robert Reed (18 June 1839–29 Aug. 1912), one of the first wealthy African Americans of the post-Emancipation era, was born in either Memphis, Tennessee, or Holly Springs, Mississippi, the son of a light-skinned house servant from Virginia, Emmeline, and her white Virginia-born master, Charles B. Church. Robert later said that his African heritage was slight. While giving testimony before a congressional committee holding hearings in response to the 1866 Memphis race riot, Church stated, "My father is a white man; my mother is as white as I am. Captain Church is my father; he used to have a packet line. My father owned my mother." Robert benefited from a paternity that went unacknowledged: "my father always gave me everything I wanted, although he does not openly recognize me." Captain Church owned steamships during the 1850s, making regular trips between Memphis and New Orleans, and he taught his son how to run the business. Beginning as a dishwasher, Robert progressed to cook and finally to steward, purchasing groceries wholesale, keeping accounts, and managing the provision of food, drink, and gambling on his father's boat.

The father instilled pride and a sense of honor in his son. "He taught me to defend myself," Robert recalled, "and urged me never to be a coward. 'If anybody strikes you, hit him back, and I'll stand by you.'" This advice was taken to heart by the violent-tempered Robert, who at various times as an adult pulled his pistol on a railroad conductor, a policeman, a sheriff, and a snowball-throwing crowd. Whenever Church felt threatened or discriminated against, he defended himself passionately. He was wounded at least three times, including once during the 1866 Memphis race riot when he was shot in the back of the head while defending his saloon from an Irish policeman who looted his whisky and $290 from his cash box.

When the Federal navy closed the Mississippi River to Confederate shipping in 1862, Church struck out on his own in Memphis. Having learned to manage liquor and gambling on the riverboats, he naturally turned to the saloon business and by the close of the Civil War had opened his own bar. In the years that followed, he traded up to a saloon and billiard hall. Church also continued a cordial relationship with his father, visiting him every Sunday.

An early slave marriage that took place in 1857 at the New Orleans end of the riverboat run, with Margaret Pico, had produced one child, a daughter, whose education Church financed; that marriage ended in separation. In Memphis, near the time of the Emancipation Proclamation of 1 January 1863, Church married a literate lady's maid, Louisa "Lou" Ayrers, whose master provided a trousseau purchased in New York and a wedding reception. Their first child, Mary, was born in September of that year. In later years she was educated at a preparatory school run by Antioch College in Ohio, earned degrees from Oberlin College, and became the social activist known as MARY CHURCH TERRELL, author of *A Colored Woman in a White World* (1940).

When Church and his second wife divorced, probably in 1870, Lou was given custody of Mary and her younger brother. After the divorce, Lou established a prosperous hairdressing shop for white ladies; she later moved the business to New York City, while Church stayed in Memphis. In 1885 Church married a college-educated school principal, Anna Wright, with whom he had two more children. One of them, ROBERT CHURCH JR., became a national black Republican patronage adviser to Republican presidents during the 1920s. The senior Robert Church gave little time to politics. He did let friends nominate him for city government in 1882 and 1886 but was soundly trounced by more popular black candidates and never engaged in politics again, except when he served as a delegate to the Republican Presidential Convention of 1900.

Church saw the yellow fever epidemics of 1878 and 1879 as opportunities for investment in city real estate. After first moving his family to northern safety, out of the plague-infested city, he returned to Memphis to purchase land and houses at distress sales, where panic-stricken Memphians sold property previously worth thousands of dollars for a few hundred. With his savings invested in bargain-priced real estate, Church emerged as a great landowner: he was said to have collected $6,000 a month from rents on property all across Memphis. His properties included undeveloped land, residential housing, and commercial buildings, some of them in the red-light district.

Myth and exaggeration invariably spring up in tales of high achievement. Many accounts say that Church bought the first $1,000 bond to restore the ruined credit of the defaulted 1885 city government, even though city records do not report his name among the first bond buyers. And virtually all popular accounts say that Church became the first black millionaire, although his real wealth seems not to have exceeded $700,000. The truth is that Church did invest in Memphis bonds, and he was certainly rich.

Church represented the black capitalism that BOOKER T. WASHINGTON advocated. Industry, thrift, and shrewd investment led to a family fortune that enriched the black community. At the end of the century, when African Americans were excluded from the segregated public parks in Memphis, Church built a park, playground, concert hall, and auditorium for blacks on Beale Street. Admission fees were generally charged, but free times opened the gates to all, and Thanksgiving dinners were served annually at Church Park for the poor. The wealth that Church made in real estate also helped to finance the first black-owned bank in Memphis. Solvent Savings Bank opened on Beale Street in 1906 with Church as president, sharing power with eighteen other black capitalists and community leaders. The bank remained sound at Church's death, but it eventually went bankrupt. Church died in Memphis.

Church never attended school, never wrote a letter, and never made a public speech, but he gained the respect and admiration of his community. "Church's life reads like a page torn from fiction," his obituary declared. And two of his five children became nationally prominent through their own efforts, which was no small accomplishment.

FURTHER READING

Hamilton, G. P. *The Bright Side of Memphis* (1908).
Church, Annette E., and Roberta Church. *The Robert R. Churches of Memphis* (1974).

Obituary: *Commercial Appeal*, 30 Aug. 1912.
This entry is taken from the *American National Biography* and is published here with the permission of the American Council of Learned Societies.

DAVID M. TUCKER

Church, Robert Reed, Jr. (26 Oct. 1885–17 Apr. 1952), politician and businessman, was born in Memphis, Tennessee, the son of ROBERT REED CHURCH, a banker and businessman, and Anna Sue Wright, a school principal. The wealth and prestige of his father afforded young Church opportunities not available to most African American children of his day. After attending a parochial school in Memphis and Oberlin Academy in Oberlin, Ohio, Church studied at Morgan Park Military Academy in Chicago, Illinois, and then enrolled in the Packard School of Business in New York City. He completed the business course and worked on Wall Street for several years before returning to Memphis in 1909 to help his father in the management of the Solvent Savings Bank and Trust Company and other family enterprises. In 1911 he married Sara Paroda Johnson, a schoolteacher; they had one child.

Church's rise to political power began in 1911, when, as a leader in the Colored Citizens Association of Memphis, he agreed to support Edward H. Crump, the successful Reform candidate for mayor, in exchange for pledges to build public parks and paved streets for blacks. The following year Church won a seat on the Tennessee delegation to the Republican National Convention and supported the renomination of President William Howard Taft. After the death of his father in 1912, Church and his sister, Annette Elaine Church, inherited rental property valued at more than a million dollars. Church was elected president of the bank in 1912 but resigned the following year to devote more time to politics and his real estate interests. Believing that members of his race could best achieve their goals through the ballot, he founded the Lincoln League in 1916 to encourage blacks to register to vote. He also used his personal funds to organize voting schools and to pay poll taxes. The league failed to elect its black candidate for Congress in 1916, but its ticket outpolled the regular Republican slate by a margin of 4 to 1.

In 1917 Church helped establish the Memphis branch of the National Association for the Advancement of Colored People (NAACP), the organization's first chapter in Tennessee. Elected to the national board of directors two years later, he represented branches of the NAACP in fourteen southern states. As racial antagonism intensified at the end of World War I, Church advised the mayor of Memphis that blacks would not instigate trouble in the city but would defend themselves if attacked. In 1920 white Republicans sought to curb Church's power by refusing him entry to the county convention in Memphis. Although Church and his supporters sent a delegation to the national convention and lost a seating contest before the Credentials Committee, he enhanced his standing with national Republican leaders by announcing that he would return to Tennessee and fight for recognition in the party. In the presidential election of 1920, Church's Black and Tan faction supplied the margin of votes that carried the Republican Party to victory in Memphis and in the state of Tennessee.

Church reached the height of his influence in the early 1920s. He maintained an office in Memphis on Beale Street, where the poor came for financial aid, politicians came for advice, and job seekers came for recommendations. Characterized as "a famed manipulator behind the scenes, a leading voice in the famed smoke-filled rooms in Republican high councils" (*Press-Scimitar*, 18 Apr. 1952), he influenced appointments of postmasters, judges, and other federal officials in Tennessee and neighboring southern states. Knowing that racial conditions in the South ruled out the acceptance of black appointees, he sought to recommend whites who would serve all citizens fairly and justly.

Although tendered two presidential appointments, Church declined them because he wanted to maintain his political independence. In local elections he generally supported the candidates of the Memphis political boss Crump, a white Democrat. Crump seldom engaged in race baiting or harassed blacks, and federal officials obligated to Church rarely interfered with Crump. In the 1920s and 1930s the city government of Memphis spent over $10 million on public improvements, school buildings, libraries, and health services for blacks. The federal government also completed two housing projects for blacks during the same period.

After winning a bitter seating contest at the Republican National Convention in 1928, Church later served on the committee to notify Herbert Hoover of his presidential nomination. Although never an admirer of Hoover, Church advised black voters to support the party ticket: "The Republican party offers us little. The Democratic party offers us nothing .... I choose the Republican party"

(*Chicago Defender*, 3 Nov. 1928). The following year he voiced displeasure with President Hoover's racial policies by refusing to serve on his national advisory committee. "Mr. President," he wrote to Hoover on 6 November 1929, "the Negro having stood the scorn of time can stand the indifference and neglect of even so good a man as you are."

With the election of a Democratic president in 1932, Church's influence rapidly declined. During the Depression the city government raised assessments on his property, and his rental income did not cover his tax bill. In 1938 he moved to Philadelphia to work in the political organization of the Pennsylvania Republican leader Joseph Pew. While maintaining his voting registration in Memphis, he later lived in Chicago and Washington, D.C. In 1941 the city of Memphis, which had claimed most of his property for nonpayment of taxes, sold his home at a tax sale. At the invitation of the black labor leader A. PHILIP RANDOLPH, Church accepted membership on a national board that lobbied for a permanent Fair Employment Practices Committee (FEPC). In 1944 Church organized and then chaired the Republican American Committee, a group of two hundred blacks who pressured Republicans in Congress to support the enactment of the FEPC and other civil rights legislation.

With the prospect of electing a Republican president and making a political comeback, Church returned to Memphis in the spring of 1952 to seek a seat on the Tennessee delegation to the Republican National Convention as a strong supporter of General Dwight D. Eisenhower for the presidential nomination. Church suffered a fatal heart attack in his Memphis hotel room during a telephone conversation with a friend about Republican politics.

At a time when lynch mobs posed a threat to blacks in the segregated South, Church boldly crusaded for civil rights and relied on the ballot box to secure public benefits for members of his race. "Born to wealth and acquiring more by astute management, Bob Church could have divorced himself from the problems of his people," the *Pittsburgh Courier* declared on 3 May 1952. "Instead, he unselfishly threw himself in the Negro's struggle and used his money, time and influence to further the interests of his people in their struggle for full citizenship in our Republic."

FURTHER READING

The Robert R. Church Family Papers are in the Mississippi Valley Collection at the University of Memphis Library, Memphis, Tennessee.

Church, Annette E., and Roberta Church. *The Robert R. Churches of Memphis* (1974).

Lee, George W. *Beale Street, Where the Blues Began* (1934).

McIlwaine, Shields. *Memphis down in Dixie* (1948).

Palmer, Pamela, ed. *The Robert R. Church Family of Memphis* (1979).

Obituaries: *Memphis Commercial Appeal* and *Memphis Press-Scimitar*, 18 Apr. 1952.

This entry is taken from the *American National Biography* and is published here with the permission of the American Council of Learned Societies.

THOMAS N. BOSCHERT

Cinqué (c. 1814–c. 1879), slave mutineer, was born Sengbe (also spelled Singbe and Sengbeh) Pieh in the village of Mani, in the Mende territory of Sierra Leone, Africa, the son of a rice farmer. His mother died when he was young, and at about the age of twenty-five he lived with his father, his wife, and his three children. One day while working alone in his rice field, he was seized by four members of the Vai tribe, often employed by Europeans to capture slaves for the market. He was taken to Lomboko, an island at the mouth of the Gallinas River on the coast of Sierra Leone, where he was purchased by Pedro Blanco, a Spanish slave trader, for sale in Cuba. He remained in Lomboko for three months in chains before Blanco filled the ship that was to transport him to Havana.

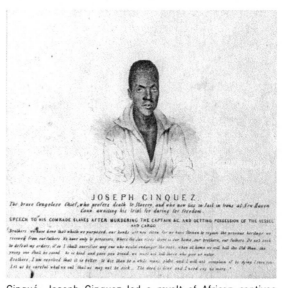

Cinqué. Joseph Cinquez led a revolt of African captives aboard the Spanish ship *Amistad* en route to Cuba in June 1839. (Library of Congress.)

Slavery was still legal in Cuba, but the trans-Atlantic trade in slaves had been abolished by international treaties in 1820. When Cinqué arrived he was thus technically contraband, but once landed he was legally a slave and was housed with many other recently transported Africans. Within ten days, he was purchased, along with forty-eight other able-bodied African men, by one of the leading Spanish dealers in Cuba, José Ruiz, who paid $450 each for them. Ruiz and a companion, Pedro Montes, who had made the more modest purchase of four children all under twelve years of age, loaded their fifty-three slaves on the schooner *Amistad* on 28 June 1839 and set sail for Puerto Príncipe, a short distance from Havana. Each slave had been provided with a false Spanish passport in case of search by English authorities while in transit. Alarmed by the cruel joke of the ship's cook, who communicated to the slaves that they were to be killed and eaten by the crew, Cinqué found a nail while exercising on deck and picked the lock on his iron collar. On the third night out, he freed his fellow slaves, all but three of whom were from Mende territory and spoke the same language. Arming themselves with machetes being shipped to the sugar plantations for cutting cane, the slaves quickly killed the cook and Ramón Ferrer, the captain. The two remaining crew members disappeared, presumably drowned trying to swim for shore. The mutineers, under Cinqué's command, then ordered their former owners Ruiz and Montes to steer the ship back to Africa. Montes, who had been a sea captain, was put at the helm and told to head into the rising sun, but the Spaniard reversed the course every night in hopes of being picked up and freed by Americans or Cubans. This zigzag route continued for sixty-three days, during which ten of the Africans died. At last on 26 August, the need for food and water forced Cinqué to order a landing at the next island they saw, which proved to be Long Island, New York.

The vessel was immediately seized by U.S. Navy officers, and on 29 August the mutineers were arrested for piracy and murder. Ruiz and Montes were set free; they demanded the return of the ship and its cargo, including the slaves, as their property. Because New York was a free state, Coast Guard Lt. Thomas Gedney, who had seized the schooner, had the *Amistad* towed to Connecticut, hoping to claim it and its forty-three surviving slaves as salvage. The Africans, including the four children, were jailed in New Haven while the courts undertook to clarify the local, national, and international issues involved. Lt. Gedney sued for possession of the boat

and all its cargo; Ruiz brought a separate suit for the return of his human property; and because Cuba was a possession of Spain, the Spanish government demanded that the slaves be returned to Havana to be tried for murder. President Martin Van Buren, seeking to maintain good diplomatic relations with Spain, supported the claim.

The trial of the Africans in the Circuit Court in Hartford on 17 September 1839 became a national sensation. The proslavery southern states opposed the freeing of the slaves, recognizing the threat to the institution on which their economy depended, and abolitionists in the North saw the case as an opportunity to promote their cause. The handsome, charismatic leader of the mutiny became a hero in the northern press, where his name took the form Cinqué (variously spelled Cinquè, Cinquez, or Cinquenzo, and sometimes embellished with the forename Joseph), and his status in Africa was elevated to royalty. William Cullen Bryant's poem "The African Chief," published in the *Emancipator* on 19 September 1839, said of him, "A prince among his tribe before, / *He could not be a slave*" (italics in the original). In the meantime, the Africans were kept in the New Haven jail, where they were given English lessons and instruction in Christianity. To help defray the costs of their incarceration, they were exhibited to the curious for twelve and a half cents a look. Both dignified and congenial, the Black Prince, as Cinqué was often called in the newspapers, cheerfully consented to perform native dances and turn somersaults on the lawn.

Lewis Tappan, a founder of the New York Anti-Slavery Society, organized an *Amistad* Committee to help free the prisoners and hired the prominent constitutional lawyer Roger Sherman Baldwin for their defense. Baldwin argued that they were not legally slaves but "kidnapped Africans" and that their mutiny was justified by "the inherent right of self defense." Cinqué delivered a speech so dramatically in his native Mende that it moved the audience even before it was translated for them. The Circuit Court found in favor of the Africans and ordered them freed. The Spanish government protested the decision and persuaded Secretary of State John Forsyth to direct the district attorney to appeal the case. President Van Buren issued an executive order to have the defendants transported to Cuba immediately if the appeal succeeded, thus preventing an appeal by the Africans. When the Federal District Court affirmed the Circuit Court's decision in January 1840, the government appealed again; in February of the next year the case was carried to the U.S. Supreme Court. The seventy-three-year-old former president John Quincy Adams, long an ardent supporter of abolition, was persuaded to join the defense, and his legendary eloquence carried the day. On 9 March, after trials that had dragged on for eighteen months, the Africans were once again declared free to return to Africa.

As the government refused to pay the costs of repatriation, several of the Africans went on a speaking tour, organized by the *Amistad* Committee, to raise money for their trip. Speaking in Mende, Cinqué was said to possess "a very graceful and animated manner" and became a popular spokesperson for the abolitionist cause. By November the mutineers, now reduced by death to thirty-five, had raised enough money for the long journey and embarked for Sierra Leone. They arrived in January 1842, accompanied by missionaries planning to establish a mission in Komende (spelled Kaw-Mendi in American sources), near Freetown. Cinqué continued inland to Mani in search of his family but, according to most reports, never saw them again. Little is known of his life after returning to Africa, but some accounts report that he made himself a powerful and prosperous chief among his people and even engaged in slave trading. Other versions have him returning to the mission to serve as an interpreter or returning there only in the last week of his life to die and be buried in the mission cemetery.

The leader of the only successful slave rebellion in American history, Cinqué set in motion a legal battle that was to provide an important precedent in American and international law. The *Amistad* case helped to establish the authority of the courts, and it constituted what the historian Howard Jones described as "an historic milestone in the long struggle against slavery and for the establishment of basic civil rights for everyone, regardless of color."

FURTHER READING

The principal collections of material related to Cinqué and the *Amistad* case are the Amistad Research Center in New Orleans, Louisiana; the Amistad collection of the New Haven Colony Historical Society Library in Connecticut; and the National Archives in Washington, D.C.

Baldwin, Simeon E. *The Captives of the Amistad* (1886).
Barber, John Warner. *A History of the Amistad Captives* (1840; repr. 2000).
Jones, Howard. *Mutiny on the Amistad: The Saga of a Slave Revolt and Its Impact on American Abolition, Law, and Diplomacy* (1987; repr. 1998).

This entry is taken from the *American National Biography* and is published here with the permission of the American Council of Learned Societies.

DENNIS WEPMAN

Clack, Doris Hargrett (24 Mar. 1928–22 Nov. 1995), educator, librarian, and activist, was born Doris Hargrett in Hyde Park, Florida, the daughter of Andrew Joshua Hargrett and Delia Leana Green, both educators. Clack was the eighth of nine children born into a nurturing family and in small, tightly knit African American village. The children were "fed a constant diet of positive life-sustaining sense of values," and she "learned many valuable lessons about community, trust, honesty, love of learning, faith in God" (Clack, 1995). Although her father died when Doris was three, his values of education, hard work, and a can-do attitude were instilled in her and her siblings by their mother. Experiencing economic hardship during the Great Depression, her mother was forced to send Doris to live with her older brother O. V. Hargrett for three years in Plant City, Florida. She rejoined the Hyde Park family at the age of nine.

Upon returning to Hyde Park, Doris was educated in the Wakulla County public schools, a system that was profoundly influenced by her father. Andrew Hargrett had projected "a charismatic personality to his children, and to others in the community, which encouraged them to pursue careers in education" (Hargrett, 17). Like her father, Doris believed she was called to teach. She graduated from Lincoln High School in Tallahassee and earned a bachelor's degree in English with a minor in Spanish and Social Studies from Florida A&M University in 1949.

In 1954 Clack married Harold Lee Clack; they had two sons. She considered Harold her "perfect soul-mate" (Clack, 1995), and he supported her educational pursuits. Clack earned a master's degree in Library Science from the University of Michigan in 1956 and then a Ph.D. in Library Science from the University of Pittsburgh in 1971 and 1973, respectively. She completed postgraduate and postdoctoral studies during the summer at Atlanta University in 1965, the University of Illinois in 1968, and the University of Toronto in 1979. Committed to a life of the mind, Clack felt it was important to never stop learning.

Pursuing her passion for teaching, Clack taught English, Spanish, and mathematics in Florida public high schools in Gadsden, Wakulla, and Leon coun-ties for seven years. Her library career began as a cataloger and then as head of technical services at Florida A&M University, where she was employed for fourteen years from 1955 to 1968. She was also employed as a senior cataloger at the Library of Congress in 1984. After completing her Ph.D. in Pittsburgh, she returned to Florida and taught cata-loging at Florida State University from 1973 to 1995. She held other teaching positions at the University of Pittsburgh and the University of Iowa, in 1978 and 1980, respectively; she also taught at the University of Missouri and the University of Maiduguri in Nigeria, West Africa, from 1987 to 1988.

Her students and colleagues acknowledged that Clack was an outstanding, enthusiastic educator who insisted on nothing but the best from her stu-dents. Bill Summers, dean of the School of Library and Information Studies at Florida State University from 1985 to 1994, "claimed that aspiring catalogers, when applying for positions, had only to say, 'I was taught by Doris Clack,' and no other credentials were needed. She insisted on quality performance, and didn't want to accept less than the best" (Wilkes, 118). Such high expectations thoroughly prepared her students for the workforce. Her insistence upon quality made a lasting impression on her colleagues as well. Stanton Biddle, a founding member with Clack of the African American Studies Librarians Section (AFAS) of the Association of College and Research Libraries, a division of the American Library Association, recalled that "Dr. Clack was an elegant, polished woman who believed in high standards and quality" (e-mail communication to author, 1 Feb. 2005).

Clack's scholarship made significant contri-butions to the profession. Her 1973 doctoral dis-sertation, "An Investigation into the Adequacy of the Library of Congress Subject Headings for Resources for Black Studies," transformed analysis of library resources concerning African Americans. She argued that the level of subject analysis of black-related materials was relatively low at the Library of Congress, and she strongly recommended that the library update its subject headings list to include rel-evant and current headings that adequately reflect the black experience. Doing so, she argued, would aid researchers in investigating African American topics. Clack published *Black Literature Resources: Analysis and Organization*, which was based on her dissertation, in 1975. As a result of Clack's research, the Library of Congress discontinued use of the term *Negro* and established *Afro-Americans* for people of African descent in the United States and *blacks* for those outside the United States. Clack continued to advocate improved access to black studies resources and to critique Library of Congress treatment of such materials throughout her professional career. Her other writings on the topic include "Collection Access through Subject Headings" (1989) in *Social Responsibility in Librarianship: Essays on Equality*, edited by Donnarae MacCann, and "Subject Access to African American Studies Resources in Online Catalogs: Issues and Answers" (1995) in the *Cataloging and Classification Quarterly*. In the early twenty-first century Clack's work continued in the African American Funnel Project, a collaborative effort of the Library of Congress and the AFAS. The Funnel Project was organized in 2000, and Clack's writings serve as a point of reference for its focus on improving subject access to black-related materials.

In the 1980s and 1990s Clack also advocated for improved access to periodical literature about the African American experience and expressed concern about the inadequacy of the various com-mercial indexing and abstracting services that were then indexing such literature. AFAS estab-lished an Indexing Project Committee to study the problem. However, the slow progress toward developing a research method was a concern to Clack. At a meeting of the AFAS in San Francisco in 1993 she encouraged members "to move the Indexing Project to an operational level beyond the organizational level" (Clack, American Library Association Archives, Record Series 22/25/5, Box 1). She further noted that the "project is crucial to the progress of access to African American resources and must be supported at all cost and be carried to completion." Again arguing the importance of the Indexing Project in "Where Are the African American Catalogers?" she warned, "Without dedi-cated visionaries with a perceived sense of urgency, information by and about African Americans could be lost to future generations" (*Proceedings of the Second National Conference of African American Librarians* [1995], 445). Although AFAS abandoned the Indexing Project two months after Clack's death, two librarians who had previously worked with her on the project became consultants for the produc-tion of the International Index to Black Periodicals, a full-text database with approximately 150 indexed periodicals. Clack had inspired them.

Believing that she had chosen a specialty in librarianship that was dynamic and forever changing, Clack had a strong sense of responsi-bility to impart knowledge beyond the classroom environment. She conducted workshops across the country to update professionals on changes in cataloging rules and practices. Six months prior to her death Clack accepted an invitation to conduct a cataloging workshop at Makerere University in Kampala, Uganda, in May 1995. She traveled to Uganda with her son Herek Clack at her own expense. The full-day workshop was outstanding, and those in attendance said they would never forget the applause, standing ovation, and smiles of approval. It was her delivery and enthusiasm for teaching that inspired others.

Clack was also recognized as an outstanding leader at Florida State University. The university president Dale W. Lick wrote to Clack: "During our recent Dr. Martin Luther King, Jr. Commemoration Convocation, I announced the establishment of the Commission on Pluralism at The Florida State University. I am asking you to serve on the commission as you will bring a varied perspective in helping to build a truly pluralistic university campus environment" (26 Jan. 1993).

Clack inspired many people who remember her elegance, her poise, her graciousness, her human spirit, and her insistence on high standards and quality. She died after an extended illness. The AFAS held a memorial tribute to her on 9 July 1996 at the Schomburg Center for Research in Black Culture in New York City during the Annual Conference of the American Library Association.

FURTHER READING

Andrew J. Hargrett II, Clack's brother, wrote the unpublished manuscript "A Brief History of the Andrew Hargrett Family." Clack's papers relating to AFAS activities are in the archives of the American Library Association in the University of Illinois Library. Clack's family has an unpublished manuscript obituary mostly written by Doris Clack.

"Doris Hargrett Clack: Not Subject to Classification," *American Libraries* 9 (Sept. 1978): 467.

Myall, Carolynne, and Ruth C. Carter, eds. *Portraits in Cataloging and Classification: Theorists, Educators, and Practitioners of the Late Twentieth Century* (1998).

Stone, Alva T. "Doris Hargrett Clack, 1928–1995: Educator, Gentle Activist, and Mentor," *Library Resources and Technical Services* (1996).

Wilkes, Angeline. "Doris Hargrett Clack, 1928–1995: Called to Teach," *Cataloging and Classification Quarterly* (1998).

Obituary: *Tallahassee Democrat*, 25 Nov. 1995.

DOROTHY A. WASHINGTON

Clamorgan, Cyprian (27 Apr. 1830–13 Nov. 1902), writer, adventurer, and perennial litigant, was born in St. Louis, Missouri, the grandson of Jacques Clamorgan, a French entrepreneur and land speculator. Jacques died in 1814, leaving as his heirs the four children he had fathered with his various slaves whom he then emancipated. One of those children, Apoline, was Cyprian Clamorgan's mother. Apoline never married. Instead, she lived with a series of white "protectors." A Catholic by upbringing in a deeply Catholic community, she presented each of her children for baptism at the Old Cathedral and revealed to the priest the name of the father so it could be entered in the baptismal register. However, she did not live long enough to have Cyprian baptized, and the identity of his father died with her.

Clamorgan and his siblings, Louis, Henry, and Louise, were left in the care of a white neighbor, Charles Collins. Henry had inherited land from an uncle, the others had shares of the real estate their mother had left them, and all had a right to the many land claims their grandfather had sought to have recognized. If the Board of Land Commissioners charged with sorting out Spanish and French land titles in the newly acquired Louisiana Territory had decided in Jacques Clamorgan's favor, his heirs would have been confirmed as the rightful owners of almost a million acres in Missouri and Arkansas.

Louise died young, but Collins did his best for Apoline's sons. Despite laws in Missouri severely restricting the access of African American children, free and enslaved, to education, Collins somehow arranged for their schooling. All three were literate, and Clamorgan became a voracious reader. Eventually Louis and Henry went into business as barbers. They married, bought homes, and became fixtures in St. Louis's growing free community of color. Clamorgan had no intention of staying close to home. He broke free of Collins's guardianship and traveled extensively. By 1849, though, he was back in St. Louis with his Irish-born wife, Joanna Stewart, and their infant son.

With a growing family to support, Clamorgan joined forces with his brothers. They pooled their money and opened what they advertised as St. Louis's most elegant and well-appointed "baths and barbering saloon." In a separate part of the establishment, presided over by the Clamorgan wives, customers could purchase everything from fine imported soaps and perfumes to costume jewelry and writing desks. The brothers prospered until disaster struck. In 1851 Louis succumbed to tuberculosis. He died intestate, and there was much bitter wrangling between Cyprian and Henry about the future of the business.

Clamorgan was soon off on his travels again, leaving his family to fend for itself. Given his complex racial ancestry, he had no difficulty reinventing himself as a white man. In Louisiana he embarked on a liaison with an English immigrant, Hebe White, which resulted in 1855 in the birth of a daughter, Mary Isabel. Although he sometimes referred to Hebe as his wife, Clamorgan still had a wife living in St. Louis. Hebe eventually married a Frenchman, Emile Soulier, who raised her child as his own, although Mary Isabel certainly knew the name of her biological father, even if she knew little else about him.

In 1858, back in St. Louis and reclaiming his identity as a man of color, Clamorgan published *The Colored Aristocracy of St. Louis*. On one level a penetrating analysis of the interplay of race and class in his native city, on another level it was a witty and irreverent look at the foibles of his friends and enemies. Cynical about the ability of organized abolition to effect far-reaching changes in American society, he placed his faith in the power of the almighty dollar, urging African Americans with money to use it to "buy" politicians and coerce white men who relied on their patronage to vote for candidates of their choosing. Money, Clamorgan insisted, spoke a universal language.

After the publication of his pamphlet—and perhaps because of it—Clamorgan soon left town again. He returned to Louisiana, and he was in New Orleans, living as a white man on the eve of the Civil War. After the war he continued roaming and was back in New Orleans in 1873. Two years later he moved to Illinois and in 1878 settled in St. Louis. Then he ventured down to Central America, perhaps to reconcile with his daughter, who had married and moved to Nicaragua. By 1881 he was in New York. A decade later he was in St. Louis again.

Over the decades Clamorgan kept himself afloat financially by pursuing his family's land claims. In addition to those he had inherited from his grandfather, there were others that had come his way from two of his uncles. His half brother, Louis, had begun suing back in the 1840s. After Louis's death, Clamorgan and Henry continued the battle. Initially they fought individuals who had appropriated various tracts of Clamorgan land. Unable to pay their legal fees, the brothers convinced various attorneys to act for them by promising them a share of anything they recovered. Inevitably some of those men sought to enrich themselves at the Clamorgans' expense, at which point the brothers

would initiate legal proceedings against them. They sued railroad companies that had laid track across their land. They even sued the U.S. government. Although they won the occasional victory, the sums they received were trifling compared to the millions that would have come their way if all their titles had been recognized.

Clamorgan spent his last years in St. Louis. His wife and their two sons predeceased him. His daughter had returned to the United States after the death of her husband, settled in Massachusetts, remarried, and passed into the white community. Henry died in 1883, but his widow and children lacked the means—and perhaps the inclination—to support Clamorgan. A lifelong Catholic, if not a particularly observant one, he turned to the church for help. In 1900 he was admitted to the Alexian Brothers' Hospital as a white man. Two years later he died in the poorhouse. He was listed in the death register as "colored," a designation he had embraced and rejected many times over the years. As for the "Clamorgan claims," the family was still fighting to have them recognized as late as 1910.

FURTHER READING
Winch, Julie, ed. *"The Colored Aristocracy of St. Louis" by Cyprian Clamorgan* (1999).

JULIE WINCH

Clark, Alexander G. (26 Feb. 1826–31 May 1891), businessman, Masonic leader, attorney, and diplomat, was born in Washington County, Pennsylvania, to John Clark, a freed slave, and Rebecca Darnes, who may have been born in Africa. He was educated in the Washington County public schools and in 1839 was sent to Cincinnati, Ohio, where he excelled in academic studies and learned barbering from his uncle, William Darnes. In October 1841 Clark headed south on the Ohio River aboard the steamer *George Washington*, where he worked as a barber. In May 1842 he settled in Muscatine (then called Bloomington), Iowa. In Muscatine, Clark began a profitable barbering business, supplied wood to Mississippi River steamboats, and invested in timberland and urban property. His real estate transactions made him wealthy, and his ethical practices won him a broad and positive reputation. On 8 October 1848 Clark married Catherine Griffin, a former slave, in Iowa City. The couple had five children who lived to adulthood and two others who died in infancy.

Meanwhile Clark's commitment to civil rights and social reform began to develop. While living in Muscatine in the 1840s, he became involved in a fugitive slave case. He sheltered a young black boy brought to Iowa from St. Louis who was threatened with capture and return to Missouri. Clark supported legal efforts that ultimately led to a state supreme court decision releasing the boy. Clark also devoted much of his life to the African Methodist Episcopal (AME) Church and PRINCE HALL Masonry. In 1849 he and three others founded the AME Church of Muscatine; he became its Sunday school superintendent in 1850. In 1851 he joined Prince Hall Lodge No. 1 in St. Louis. In 1853 he was elected a delegate from Iowa to the Rochester National Colored Convention, over which FREDERICK DOUGLASS presided.

Clark joined the Republican Party shortly after it was founded in 1854 and quickly gained a reputation as an eloquent orator on behalf of its principles. During the Civil War he traveled throughout the West, recruiting on behalf of the Union army. In the spring of 1863, Clark played a central role in organizing the First Iowa Colored Infantry, which later became the 60th USCT. When the unit returned to Muscatine in October 1865, Clark addressed the men and a mass of people who came to recognize the service of Iowa's black soldiers.

Clark emerged as a leader of the postwar civil rights movement when, in September 1867, his twelve-year-old daughter Susan was denied entrance to Public School No. 2 in Muscatine. Clark sued the school board, and in July 1868 the Iowa Supreme Court ruled that access to public schools could not be denied on the grounds of race, national origin, or religion.

Because of his shrewd business dealings, Clark was able to retire from barbering in 1868. Thereafter he lived comfortably and devoted his time to Prince Hall Masonry, civil rights, and the Republican Party. In February 1868 he chaired the first Convention of Colored Men meeting in Des Moines, Iowa, called to discuss proposed amendments eliminating the word "white" from five sections of the state constitution. In support of the amendments, Clark delivered a dramatic address invoking the memory of African American sacrifices in the Civil War. The convention in turn formally thanked Clark for his efforts, and on 8 December 1868 an amended constitution recognizing the equality that the convention and Clark had advocated went into effect. Also in 1868 Clark was elected deputy grand master of the Grand Lodge of Missouri and served as a vice president of the Iowa State Republican Party Convention. Upon the election of President Ulysses S. Grant, Clark was

a member of a committee that congratulated Grant on behalf of the African American people.

In 1869 Clark served as a delegate from Iowa to the Colored National Convention in Washington, D.C., where he was chair of the committee lobbying Congress for pension benefits for black veterans. He remained a stalwart of the Republican Party and continued as vice president of the Iowa State Republican Convention. When the Republican Party did not consume his attentions, he served the Masonic order. In 1869 Clark was elected grand master of the Missouri Lodge, and he later served as grand treasurer of the Missouri Grand Lodge.

When the Fifteenth Amendment to the federal Constitution—guaranteeing the right to vote regardless of race—was ratified in 1870, Clark delivered a celebrated speech hailing a new era of race relations. Two years later he served as a delegate-at-large from Iowa to the Republican National Convention in Philadelphia. Because of his loyal service to the party and his leadership in the African American community, President Grant nominated him in 1873 as consul to Aux Cayes, Haiti. Clark declined, citing the position's insufficient salary. That year he expanded his Masonic responsibilities, becoming chair of the committee on foreign correspondence. In 1874 he was again elected grand master.

In 1876 Clark was appointed by the Iowa State Convention of Colored Men as a delegate to the Philadelphia Centennial Exposition to gather information on the condition of African Americans. Clark also served as an alternate delegate from Iowa to the Republican National Convention. After the election, as the new Republican administration began to retreat from its commitment to racial equality, Clark publicly criticized President Rutherford B. Hayes's policies, marking the only time in Clark's career that he openly disagreed with his longtime party. Nevertheless, the next year he was back on the road, speaking throughout the Northwest and urging his kinsmen to remain loyal to the party of Abraham Lincoln. Meanwhile Clark pursued a crusade within Masonic ranks for equal recognition of African American Masons. At the National Masonic Convention in Chicago in September 1877, he won passage of a resolution on concurrent jurisdiction for African American Masonic lodges.

In August 1878 Clark's son Alex entered the University of Iowa Law School and the following year became its first black graduate. Clark's wife's death and his son's graduation in the same year (1879) set the senior Clark's life in new directions.

He began to take a more sober view of race relations in the United States, writing in the *Muscatine Evening Journal*, "This [Great] Exodus is forced upon our people as a last resort and the only one left" (21 January 1880). While some African American leaders (such as SOJOURNER TRUTH) welcomed the migrations as part of a movement toward full emancipation, others (such as Frederick Douglass) believed that migrations amounted to a retreat from the fight for equality. Clark reluctantly accepted the "exodus" as the only method remaining to achieve full freedom. After the election of James A. Garfield in November 1880, Clark approached the president-elect for a government position, but Garfield was assassinated before he made a decision.

Clark's international prominence within the AME Church grew. In September 1882 he served as a lay delegate from the United States at the first international Methodist Ecumenical Conference in London, England, which eventually led to the creation of the United Methodist Church. In December 1882 Clark became co-owner of the *Conservator*, the first black newspaper in Chicago and a periodical known for its nonsensationalist coverage of southern race relations. Under Clark, the paper became a radical voice of Republicanism. In 1883, when the Supreme Court struck down the 1875 Civil Rights Act banning discrimination in public accommodations, Clark, in the *Conservator*, denounced the decision. In 1884 Clark bought out his partners and over several years improved the paper's financial condition and increased its circulation and influence. He sold the paper on 15 March 1887 in the face of increasing competition. Nevertheless, Clark's editorial work earned him high esteem within the national African American community and newspaper publishing generally. In 1886 the National Press Association, a predominantly black organization which represented over 100 newspapers in the African American community, elected him treasurer and appointed him chair of the executive committee. The next year he prepared the program for the annual meeting of the association and was so successful that his colleagues insisted he remain in office.

At the same time Clark had begun yet another career. In 1883, at age fifty-seven, he entered the University of Iowa Law School "as an example to young men of my own race, that they, seeing what I have done, may take heart, and aim and strive for a higher and broader education in our best schools and become honored and useful members of our society" (Jackson, 49). He was popular with his classmates and was elected class treasurer, and his power as an orator spellbound his fellow students. He graduated in June 1884 and opened a law office in Chicago. Clark continued his intense involvement with the Masonic order. He organized the Hiram Grand Lodge of Iowa (1884), was elected to the Grand East Lodge (1884–1886), engineered the merger of his lodge with another African American lodge to form the United Grand Lodge of Iowa, and served as president of the United Grand Lodge. His Masonic activities earned him a reputation for clear thinking, thorough knowledge of Masonic history and law, effective oratory, and dedication to the welfare of his brethren.

On May Day 1886 some 340,000 workers struck nationwide. A labor protest in Chicago escalated into violence—the notorious Haymarket riots—awakening middle-class fears of class warfare. In an article for the July 1886 *A.M.E. Church Review*, Clark took his stand in the debate. Denouncing the recent "seditious and incendiary attacks upon law and order," Clark asserted that the "socialism" invoked during the Haymarket riots had little to do with the centuries-long tradition of social, political, and economic reform of which true socialism was a part. Recent violence and lawlessness, he said, was not "to be taken as a fair index of the spirit animating the knighthood of labor." Socialism, he said, "exists today only as driftwood, floating when the elaborately planned systems of Proudhon, Fourier, St. Simon, Owen, and Cabet went down…. The spirit of industrial capital is … auspiciously beginning to accord with the fraternal claims of labor." Finally, Clark argued, African Americans had nothing to gain by following socialism. "We want nothing of socialism or the Commune, the strike or the boycott, the mob or the riot. For us be it sufficient that we emulate the spirit and faith of Lincoln, Grant, Sumner, and their noble compeers" (Clark, 49–54).

On 8 August 1890 Clark began the last phase of a varied career when he was appointed U.S. minister and consul general to Liberia. His friends advised him against accepting the position. He was sixty-four years old, and Liberia had a reputation as an unhealthy posting. Clark understood the risks but viewed the post as his final contribution to his country and his people. He assumed his new position on 5 November 1890, and by March 1891 he was afflicted with fever. He suffered a number of bouts from then until 31 May 1891, when he died in Monrovia, the Liberian capital. Clark—known at the time as "the Toussaint L'Ouverture of the West"—was a man of wealth, boundless energy, and strong convictions who devoted much of his life to public service and used his powerful oratorical skills on behalf of social justice.

FURTHER READING

Briggs, John. "Iowa and the Diplomatic Service," *Iowa Journal of History and Politics* 19 (July 1921).

Clark, Alexander G. "Socialism," *A.M.E. Church Review* 3 (July 1886).

Iowa State Supreme Court Records (14 Apr. 1868) 24: 267–277.

Jackson, Marilyn. "Alexander Clark: A Rediscovered Black Leader," *Iowan* (Spring, 1975).

Laws, Joseph William. *Oration on the Life of Hon. Alexander Clark, Delivered by Rev. J. W. Laws of Keokuk, Iowa* (1891).

Simmons, William J. *Men of Mark: Eminent, Progressive, and Rising* (1968).

KENNETH J. BLUME

Clark, Charles Henry (15 Oct. 1855–?), pastor, educator, and entrepreneur, was born a slave in Christian Country, Kentucky. Clark never knew his biological father. While Clark was still a baby, his father escaped from slavery. His mother, Mary Clark, subsequently married Jerry Clark, who would join the Union army in 1860. Charles Henry Clark remained a slave for a total of nine years, and it was at the age of seven that the overseer's wife took him as her servant. She taught Clark to spell and initiated his path to literacy, but the outbreak of the Civil War would separate Clark from his teacher. During this period, Clark's mother moved from Kentucky to New Providence, Tennessee, to await her husband, Jerry Clark, who was returning from the army. Mary Clark had difficulty financially supporting her family, since her only income at this time came from her eldest son, George W. Clark. As a result, she and her eldest son hired themselves out to work on a farm owned by Jack Shelton in Trigg Country, Kentucky.

In 1864 Jerry Clark returned from the army and rejoined his family. He would lease a farm, move the family there, and hire a girl named Millie to help with the farm's demands. Millie knew how to read, and she taught both Clark and his brother, George, to read also. Several years later, Jerry Clark moved the family to Hopkinsville, Kentucky, where both Clark and his brother were hired out on the farm where they were born. Clark broke his leg there, and was forced to return home; he would never go back to that Hopkinsville farm. Meanwhile, poverty forced Jerry Clark to leave the city and reenter farm life for several years; Clark and his brother George would buy a house and enter school in Hopkinsville, which was approximately five miles from their home. George resolved that neither distance nor cost would prevent him and his brother from attaining an education, and he succeeded in paying both his and Clark's tuition. For three years, the brothers excelled in school and won numerous prizes. Charles Henry Clark managed to pass the county examination and was awarded a teacher's certificate. He taught at the Mount Zion Baptist Church near Hopkinsville for a number of years.

In 1876 Clark joined the Green Hill Baptist Church at Casky Station, Kentucky, which was pastored by Rev. C. G. Garrett. One week after his baptism, Clark was made church clerk, and a few months later he was elected to the office of deacon. He served in this capacity for five years. Once licensed to preach, Clark went from plantation to plantation preaching the scriptures and converting nonbelievers. He drew large crowds to his prayer meetings and was soon called by the church for examination in regard to his preaching and biblical knowledge. His trial sermon before the Green Hill Baptist Church was very well received and much talked about by older members and ministers of the church. By 1880 Clark had stopped teaching and devoted full attention to his ministry. It was also during 1880 that he married Maria Bridges from Canton, Trigg County, Kentucky. The two would have five children: Grant, Mattie, Mary, George, and Willie.

The Canton Baptist Church called Clark to ordination in September 1880. He served both the Rolling Mill Church and Center Furnace Baptist Church until 1884 when he was offered the pulpit at the Shepherd Street Baptist Church in Princeton, Kentucky. On 1 May 1886 he accepted the pastorate of the Fourth Street Baptist Church in Owensboro. He successfully preached there for seven years and nine months. In 1892 Clark was called to the pastorate of the Mount Olive Missionary Baptist Church in Nashville, Tennessee. Clark was there for seven-and-a-half years, and under his leadership the church flourished. Mount Olive boasted a membership of at least a thousand people, and the church managed to construct a $30,000 church building while incurring no debt. In 1920 Clark would be called to the pastorate of Ebenezer Missionary Baptist Church in Chicago, Illinois. Under his leadership, the church's mortgage was paid three years before its expired term. In August of 1929 Mrs. Clark died, and on 27 October 1930 Clark resigned from his duties as pastor at

Ebenezer Missionary Baptist Church. Little is known of Clark after this period.

Clark was one of the founding members of the National Baptist Publishing House; he was elected chairman by the board of managers and continually held that position. The publishing house was a success from its very conception. It held exclusive publishing rights to all church and Sunday-school literature for the National Baptist Convention; the house also owned property, machinery—including a Rotary Book Printing Press which cost $18,000—and stock estimated at $350,000. There were also about 150 clerks, stenographers, and skilled workmen employed at the publishing house.

Clark was also president of the Tennessee Baptist Convention and the National Baptist Sunday-School Congress, Moderator of the Cumberland River, South Kentucky, and Middle Tennessee District Association, and Commissioner of the Educational Convention of Negro Leaders (he was appointed by the governor of Tennessee). He was a director of the Penny Savings Bank of Nashville, treasurer of the Stone River Association, and an active member of the Board of Trustees of Roger Williams University and Howe Institute. He earned a Doctor of Divinity degree from Cadiz Normal and Theological College of Kentucky in 1890 and an honorary law degree from Roswell College, New Mexico.

FURTHER READING

Bacote, Samuel William, ed. "Charles Henry Clark," In *Who's Who among the Colored Baptists of the United States* (1980).

Ebenezer Missionary Baptist Church. *From a Rough Stone to a Polished Diamond* (1977).

Hurt, Reverend A. D., and Reverend T. J. Searcy. "Charles Henry Clark," In *The Beacon Lights of Tennessee Baptists* (1900).

ROCHELL ISAAC

Clark, Ed (6 May 1926–), pioneer of abstract painting, was born Edward Clark in the Storyville section of New Orleans, Louisiana. Little is known about his family, but they moved north during the Depression, and he was raised in Chicago.

Following service in the U.S. Air Force, Clark attended the School of the Art Institute of Chicago under the G.I. Bill from 1947 to 1951. At the Art Institute, he met abstract painter Joan Mitchell, with whom he developed a lifelong friendship, and the impressionist painter Louis Ritman, who was an encouraging instructor. During this period, Clark's work was traditional and figurative. But Clark's frustration with the Institute's academic restraints, such as the directive to avoid oils during this period, led him to create an experimental self-portrait that took two years to complete. The classic head-and-shoulders depiction was set against a Renaissance landscape consisting of subtle layers of stippled watercolors.

In 1952 Clark—like many other American artists—moved to Paris, where he continued his studies at L'Académie de la Grande Chaumière from 1952 to 1954. One of his teachers, Édouard Joseph Goerg, supported his experiments. Clark continued to produce traditional ink portraits and nudes but also began experimenting with abstract landscapes and oils, which led him to produce his first abstract paintings. In *The City* (1952), for example, Clark used curved and rectangular areas of muted color to convey the feel of urban dwellings.

Clark acknowledged that the work of Russian-born Nicolas de Staël, one of the most influential European artists of the post–World War II period, had a powerful impact on him. In particular, Clark was inspired by de Staël's *Parc des Princes (Les Grands Footballers)*, exhibited in 1952 at Salon d'Automne in Paris. He admired de Staël's movement away from the linear, geometric, quasi-cubist painting popular during the period and toward abstraction; he experimented with bold colors applied with a palette knife and layered on the canvas with great subtlety and sensitivity. Clark also cited the influence of Hans Hartung and Pierre Soulages's gestural abstractions; that is, abstractions that convey a sense of physical movement.

During his time in Paris, Clark was influenced not only by European painting but also by American jazz. As many in Paris did in the 1950s, Clark embraced the bebop of CHARLIE PARKER and DIZZY GILLESPIE, among others. Absorbing the spirit of jazz improvisation around him, Clark developed his own distinct style of large-scale paintings that combined energetic, passionate strokes with a cool sense of sophistication. He deemed jazz trumpeter MILES DAVIS as one of his inspirations as well.

After living in Paris for five years, Clark moved to New York City in 1956 and became a charter member of the Brata Gallery on East Tenth Street, joining such artists as Al Held, George Sugarman, and Helen Frankenthaler. Clark showed at the Brata Gallery until 1966, when he returned to France for three more years.

In 1956 Clark created his first extended "shaped" painting, an untitled oil on canvas work that exceeded the boundaries of its rectangular frame and continued onto overlapping and attached pieces of paper. He showed the work, which some considered the first of its kind, at the Brata Gallery's Christmas group show in 1957. Clark continued his *Untitled* series of oil on canvas paintings, some with paper collage on wood.

Clark continued to experiment with "shaped canvas," in which paintings were created on non-rectangular, irregular surfaces. Blurring the line between painting and sculpture, a shaped canvas called attention to the notion that a painting's surface always contains some degree of depth. The shaped canvas influenced contemporary art of the 1950s and 1960s and, as a result, gained the attention of art historians. Notable artists, including Frank Stella, Kenneth Noland, and Ellsworth Kelly, were among those exploring this radical interplay of imagery, construction, and composition. Although Clark was credited with the first shaped canvases, there was a precedent for such experiments: in the 1930s American artist Abraham Joel Tobias had created and exhibited abstract works—which he called "sculptural paintings"—integrating shaped canvases with inventive framing techniques. In the 1960s, Clark began painting abstract scenes using a technique that allowed him to move paint across the canvas quickly, creating broad, bold strokes of color. Clark's densely layered paint applications led him to use a method reminiscent of Jackson Pollock and Frankenthaler, artists who painted on large canvases placed on the floor. Clark applied the paint with his fists, with wide housepainter brushes, as well as with rags, rollers, and most often, various sizes of push brooms, which contributed to the sense of physicality in these works. These works often contained bands of color across the center portion of the canvas, engendering comparisons to landscape compositions. Speculating on the use in his art of the industrial push broom—perhaps a symbol of African American exploitation, in the opinion of one critic (Jacques, 35)—some critics have suggested that Clark may have been politically motivated in his choice of materials.

Beginning in the 1970s, Clark's travels to Nigeria, Crete, Brazil, New Mexico, Sicily, and Egypt, among other locales, inspired several series of paintings that captured elements of the distinctive atmosphere and sensibility of each place he visited. In the Sicilian series, produced in the 1970s, Clark rubbed pure, dry pigment into the canvas—similar to the techniques used by the Pueblo tribe of the American Southwest—with his hands, producing gentle, soft shapes and deep, cool tones that captured his impression of the island's spirit. By contrast, the Egyptian paintings, produced in the 1990s, possessed an earthier, more physical presence in both texture and sensibility. Clark employed thick layers of warm-toned acrylics and heavy strokes—applied with various-sized push brooms—to create curved and straight lines that moved across the canvas. He used a new language to describe an ancient landscape.

In a variation on the shaped canvas, Clark created his first oval painting while living in Vétheuil, France, in 1968. He went on to create elliptical, diamond-shaped, round, and square canvases that contained bold, broad strokes—sometimes in dark, ponderous colors; sometimes in light, ethereal tones. In a departure from the traditional stretched canvas hanging on a wall, his paintings sometimes were hung from the ceiling, as if floating in space.

Clark held teaching positions at a number of universities throughout his career. He was artist-in-residence and art instructor at the University of Delaware in 1969 and taught at the Art Institute of Chicago and the University of Oregon in 1973, the Skowhegan School of Painting and Sculpture in 1974, Ohio State University in 1976, Louisiana State University in 1978, and Syracuse University in 1980.

Clark's work was exhibited in many major U.S. cities and has been included in several collections around the world, including Boston's Museum of Fine Arts, Paris's Salon d'Automne, New York's Studio Museum in Harlem and the Whitney Museum, Washington, D.C.'s Hirshhorn Museum and Sculpture Garden and the Parish Gallery, and in galleries in Japan. In 2006, at the age of eighty, he exhibited in a show titled *Rebirth* at the G. R. N'Namdi Gallery in Chicago.

Clark received numerous honors and awards, including the Prix d'Othon Friesz from the Louvre in 1955, a National Endowment for the Arts grant in 1972, the Adolph and Esther Gottlieb Foundation Award in 1981, the Master Award from the National Endowment for the Arts in 1985, and the Art for Life honored artist award from the Rush Philanthropic Arts Foundation in 2000.

FURTHER READING

Jacques, Geoffrey, and David Hammons. *Quiet as It's Kept, Exhibition Catalog* (Vienna: Christine Konig Galerie, 2002).

Kinsella, Eileen. "The Rise of African American Art," *ARTnews* 102(8) (Sept. 2003).

Kinshasha, Holman Conwill. "African-American Artists in Paris," *American Art Review* 7(6) (Dec.–Jan. 1996).

Mercer, Valerie J. "The Studio Museum in Harlem: 25 Years of African-American Art," *American Art Review* (Feb.–Mar. 1995).

N'Namdi, George R., and Barbara Cavaliere, eds. *Edward Clark: For the Sake of the Search* (1997).

Tenabe, Gabriel. "Ed(ward) Clark," in Thomas Riggs, ed. *St. James Guide to Black Artists* (1997).

Wilson, Judith. "Edward Clark, Directions," *Art in America* 69(1) (1981).

GENEVIEVE SLOMSKI

Clark, Kenneth Bancroft (24 July 1914–1 May 2005), psychologist, was born in the Panama Canal Zone, the son of the Jamaican immigrants Miriam Hanson Clark and Arthur Bancroft Clark. In 1919, Miriam left her husband and brought Kenneth and his sister Beulah to New York City. He attended public schools in Harlem, which were fully integrated when he entered the first grade, but were almost wholly black by the time he finished sixth grade. Kenneth's mother, an active follower of MARCUS GARVEY, encouraged her son's interest in black history and his academic leanings, and confronted his guidance teacher for recommending that Kenneth attend a vocational high school. A determined woman, active in the garment workers' union, Miriam Clark persuaded the authorities to send Kenneth to George Washington High, a school with a reputation for academic excellence. In 1931

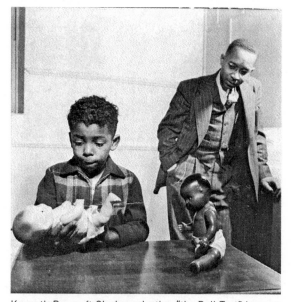

Kenneth Bancroft Clark conducting "the Doll Test" in 1947. Photograph by Gordon Parks. (AP Images.)

he won a scholarship to attend Howard University in Washington, D.C.

Clark attended Howard at time of great academic and ideological ferment on campus. The faculty, arguably the greatest "dream team" of black academics ever assembled, included the philosopher ALAIN LOCKE, the political scientist RALPH BUNCHE, and the sociologist E. FRANKLIN FRAZIER. CHARLES HAMILTON HOUSTON and WILLIAM HENRY HASTIE taught at Howard Law School in those years and numbered THURGOOD MARSHALL among their students. As editor of the *Hilltop*, the college newspaper, Clark immersed himself in the intellectual and political debates on campus and in 1935 was arrested for protesting segregation at the restaurant inside the U.S. Capitol building. Since Congress contributed to Howard's funding, several administrators proposed expelling the arrested students, but they were reprieved when Clark's mentor, Ralph Bunche, threatened to resign if such actions were taken. Clark graduated in 1931, remained at Howard to pursue a Master of Science degree, and taught in the Psychology Department at Howard for a year. He then moved to New York to pursue a PhD in Psychology at Columbia University, where his adviser discouraged him from choosing a "racial" topic for his dissertation for fear that it might harm his job chances. Clark's 1940 Ph.D., the first awarded to an African American at Columbia, was titled "Some Factors Influencing the Remembering of Prose Materials." He taught briefly at Hampton Institute, a black college in Virginia, and in 1942 became the first black instructor appointed to the faculty of the City College of New York. By then, Clark had begun collaborating on a study of racial self-identity in childhood with Mamie Katherine Phipps, a fellow Howard graduate whom he had married in 1938. They had eloped—Howard prohibited its undergraduates from marrying—and would later have two children, Kate Miriam Clark and Hilton Bancraft Clark. MAMIE PHIPPS CLARK had begun her study of children's perception of race in a class taught by her future husband at Howard and completed her dissertation on that topic at Columbia in 1943. Five years later, the Clarks established the Northside Center for Child Development. The Center provided a full range of psychological consulting and testing services for children, the first such agency in Harlem, and also carried out studies of racial self-identity in children.

One of these studies, now known simply as "the doll test," was to play a critical role in the NAACP's battle to end segregation. In the test, black children, aged between three and seven years old, were shown four identical dolls, two of them colored brown and two colored white, and asked to identify them as "Negro" or white. Three quarters of the children identified the dolls correctly. The psychologists then asked the children to give them the doll that they "liked best," or that looked "bad," or that is "a nice color," or that was most like themselves. Most of the black children studied expressed a preference for the white dolls, and rejected the black dolls; some did so in tears. The tests suggested to the Clarks that racial prejudice—and racial self-hatred—was fixed at an early age, and that only early intervention could prevent further psychic damage. In 1951, ROBERT L. CARTER of the NAACP's Legal Defense Fund (LDF) read of the Clarks' doll studies and urged Clark to serve as an expert scientific witness in their efforts to outlaw segregated schooling. Clark carried out the doll tests among black children in Clarendon County, South Carolina, one of the four cases later consolidated in *Brown v. Board of Education*. As in the previous tests, the majority of black children in the Clarendon study identified with the white dolls and rejected the black ones. Clark also served as the expert psychological witness in the South Carolina, Virginia, and Delaware cases that formed part of *Brown*. More importantly, he acted as a liaison between the LDF and academics who submitted to the Court a legal brief outlining the psychological and sociological evidence of segregation's harmful impact on children. In May 1954, Chief Justice Earl Warren wrote for a unanimous Court in *Brown* that segregation was inherently unequal. Footnote 11 of that opinion cites the work of Kenneth B. Clark as evidence that segregation "retarded the educational and mental development of Negro children." Warren added that such psychological knowledge had not been available to the Court in 1896 when it had rendered its "separate but equal" ruling in *Plessy v. Ferguson*. The Justices' acceptance of psychological and social scientific testimony was unprecedented, and provoked controversy, though mainly among those who already opposed integration.

After *Brown*, Clark attempted to bring the psychological arguments made famous in that decision to a broader audience. The results were mixed. His 1955 book, *Prejudice and Your Child*, sold poorly, but Clark was much more successful as a public intellectual. He appeared in *Commentary* and other liberal journals, and the national media anointed him *the* black academic, much as it had anointed his friend JAMES BALDWIN as *the* black writer,

and MARTIN LUTHER KING JR. as *the* civil rights leader. By 1963, when King, Baldwin, and thousands of lesser-known protestors had forced white Americans to look more deeply at the problems of racism, a second edition of *Prejudice and Your Child* found a larger audience. So, too, did Clark in a public television series, *The Negro and the Promise of American Life*, in which he interviewed the three most prominent African Americans of that era: Baldwin, King, and MALCOLM X. (Clark was a confidant of both King and Malcolm, and arranged the brief, but symbolic, meeting between the two leaders in 1964.) The interviews, published as *The Negro Protest* (1963), expressed Clark's belief that the United States had failed to live up to the promise of *Brown*. He envisioned only two ways in which America could avoid the racial explosions that would result from that unfulfilled promise: "One would be total oppression; the other total equality" (Keppel, *The Work of Democracy*, 138).

In the 1960s, Clark believed that latter goal was still possible. Harlem Youth Opportunities Unlimited (HARYOU), a grassroots antipoverty project which Clark founded, was influential in the growing intellectual and public policy debate about poverty. The project envisioned job training schemes, pre-school "academies," and a network of self-governing community councils dedicated to fighting poverty. Many of those programs were replicated in President Johnson's War on Poverty; HARYOU's pre-school academies, for example, served as the model for Head Start. Clark's experiences with HARYOU informed his most widely read book, *Dark Ghetto* (1965). He argued that America's inner cities were "colonies," exploited by the broader society's lack of interest in the educational, psychological, and economic well-being of African Americans. Until the nation responded to the institutionalized pathology of the ghetto with radical reforms, Clark concluded, America would "remain at the mercy of primitive, frightening, irrational attempts by prisoners in the ghetto to destroy their own prison" (Keppel, *Work of Democracy*, 159). Though some in the civil rights movement criticized the book's emphasis on black victimhood, others, notably black power advocates such as STOKELY CARMICHAEL, were influenced by *Dark Ghetto*'s discussion of African Americans' "colonial" status.

Clark did not advocate the separatist solutions offered by Carmichael, but America's retreat from the cause of racial justice in the 1970s and 1980s left him profoundly pessimistic about the future of civil rights. In 1990, he feared that the United States would never eradicate racism or achieve true integration. Looking back at the 1950s and 1960s, he shuddered at "how naïve we all were in our belief in the steady progress racial minorities would make through programs of litigation and education." Clark reflected that his life had been a "series of glorious defeats" (Clark, "Racial Progress and Retreat," 18).

Though it is true that the United States has far to go in achieving full integration, Dr. Clark's self-assessment seems unnecessarily negative. As the NAACP recognized in awarding him the Spingarn Medal in 1961, Clark's work as a psychologist was instrumental in the *Brown* decision, which set in motion an invigorated civil rights movement in the 1960s. It is also significant that in 1970–1971 Clark served as the first black president of the American Psychological Association and also received that organization's Gold Medal Award for "contributions by a psychologist in the public interest." Kenneth Clark served that public interest by arguing persistently, with dignity and passion, that only radical change could eradicate the deep-rooted scars of racism in American society. Clark died of cancer at his home in Hastings-on-Hudson, New York, on 1 May 2005.

FURTHER READING

Clark's papers are in the Library of Congress. Oral Histories of Kenneth and Mamie Phipps Clark are located in the Columbia University Oral History Program Collection in New York City.

American Psychologist Vol. 57, No. 1 (2002).

Clark, Kenneth B. "Racial Progress and Retreat," in *Race in America: The Struggle for Equality* Herbert Hill and James E. Jones Jr. (1993).

Keppel, Ben. *The Work of Democracy: Ralph Bunche, Kenneth B. Clark, Lorraine Hansberry, and the Cultural Politics of Race* (1995).

Kluger, Richard. *Simple Justice* (1977), chapter 14.

Markowitz, Gerald, and David Rosner. *Children, Race, and Power: Kenneth and Mamie Clark's Northside Center* (1996).

STEVEN J. NIVEN

Clark, Mamie Phipps (18 Oct. 1917–11 Aug. 1983), psychologist, activist, and children's advocate, was born in Hot Springs, Arkansas, the elder of two children born to Kate Florence Phipps and Dr. Harold Phipps. Dr. Phipps, who was a native of the West Indies, provided a privileged environment for his family in a time of entrenched racism. He owned his own medical practice and also managed a hotel and spa for elite black patrons in the resort town of Hot Springs.

Although Clark remembered a happy childhood, her father's status did not entirely shield her from the racist world around her. At the age of six, Clark experienced her first lynching. A black man was dragged through the streets of Hot Springs, taken out of town, and hanged. Clark did not witness the actual hanging, but the intense emotion of the experience remained with her for the rest of her life.

As a whole, however, Clark never felt she was harmed by the atmosphere in Hot Springs. The schools she attended were segregated, but she enjoyed them. After high school Clark enrolled in Howard University in Washington, D.C. Her trip to Washington was her first foray into the white world. She rode in a train compartment secured by her father, who instructed her never to leave it. Dr. Phipps arranged for the black porters to protect her, bring her food, and see that she arrived safely.

Clark was an excellent student in high school and especially proficient in math, her chosen field. At Howard, however, she realized just how much she had not been taught. Her classmates were from integrated schools in the West and in New England, and they had language skills and poise far beyond her own. Clark had to work hard to catch up. She took ten courses over two summers at Arkansas State to make up for her deficiencies. At the start of her junior year at Howard, Clark met her future husband, Dr. KENNETH BANCROFT CLARK, a master's student in psychology at Howard. Clark decided then to switch her major to psychology.

Mamie Phipps and Kenneth Clark were married on 14 April 1938. Clark graduated from Howard magna cum laude in 1938 and was awarded a graduate fellowship in psychology. While Mamie pursued her graduate studies, the Clarks had two children, Kate Miriam Clark and Hilton Bancroft Clark.

Clark centered her graduate work on the study of children and their development. At Howard, classes in child psychology were limited, so she took classes in nutrition and sociology and wrote her thesis on the "Development of Consciousness of Self in Negro Preschool Children." Her "lab" was the District of Columbia's segregated public schools, where she asked black children to draw themselves. When the children were instructed to color in their drawings, Clark discovered that they drew themselves as white. Even when offered crayons of several colors, the children did not draw themselves brown or black. Although the Clarks were unaware of it at the time, Mamie Clark's studies were laying the groundwork for the 1954 *Brown v. Board of Education* Supreme Court decision that reversed the "separate but equal" doctrine of *Plessy v. Ferguson* and ended segregation in America's public schools.

Between 1939 and 1940 the Clarks published three major articles on the subject of self-perception in black children. After completing her master's at Howard in 1940, Clark continued her studies at Columbia University in New York, where her husband was a professor. The two collaborated on further studies of black self-perception. In what became known as the "doll tests," Clark presented black children with two dolls—one black, one white—and asked the children which doll they preferred. More than half the children rejected the black doll. Clark's research led to the conclusion that segregation caused children to believe that being black was "bad," that black was not as "good" as white, and that they, as black children, could never be as "good" as white children. The results of Clark's tests were the genesis of the Clarks' belief that only desegregation could effect a positive change in the self-perception of black children.

In 1943 Clark was the first African American woman to be awarded a doctorate in Psychology from Columbia University and only the second African American in the university's history. Her husband was the first.

At the time the Clarks were pursuing their studies, federal and state assistance for blacks was nonexistent. Instead, private benevolent organizations assisted black students of promise. The Julius Rosenwald Foundation became the Clarks' benefactor. Rosenwald funds allowed them to focus their studies on the development of black consciousness at a time when few blacks could even attend an accredited college.

In 1943 Clark accepted a job at the American Public Health Association. She intended to continue her work on child development, but she soon found she was a phenomenon—and not one the professional world was ready to accept. She held a Ph.D. but she was still a black woman in a white world. She quickly left the Health Association and began working at the Riverdale Home for Children in New York, where she gave intelligence tests and achievement tests to abandoned children. Her work there led her to realize that the children were disturbed, but they were not unintelligent. In fact, many tested at very high intelligence levels. What they needed was emotional stability and

the opportunity to learn in a nurturing environment. In 1946, with a loan of $936 from her father, Clark established the Northside Center for Child Development in Harlem, New York. Clark's initial focus at Northside was to test children who had been placed in classes for the mentally retarded. As she suspected, the vast majority were bright enough to be in regular classes. Northside provided remedial classes and counseled both the children and their parents. Clark became an advocate for these children and demanded that they be placed back in their proper classes.

Meanwhile Dr. Kenneth Clark was becoming involved with the NAACP's attorneys, led by THURGOOD MARSHALL, in their fight to end segregation in public schools. The Clarks' published works were well regarded in the psychological community, and Mamie Clark was called on to present her results at one of the first desegregation trials in Virginia. In 1953, when the desegregation cases reached the Supreme Court, the now famous doll tests were a significant factor in the Court's decision to overturn *Plessy v. Ferguson*. Although some on the NAACP legal team felt doll tests and social science should play no role in a legal proceeding, the Clarks' testimony convinced Chief Justice Earl Warren that segregation generated feelings of inferiority in black children that might never be overcome. On 17 May 1954 the Court decided that the doctrine of "separate but equal" had no place in America's public schools.

After the conclusion of the *Brown v. Board of Education* trials, Mamie Clark devoted her time to the Northside Center. When the center was founded in 1946, the Clarks ran it with help from several volunteer psychologists and social workers. By 1976 the center had moved several times into larger and larger facilities to accommodate the demand for the center's services. The center served the entire Harlem community—black, white, and a substantial Hispanic population as well. Parents brought their children for psychiatric assessment, but the center was not limited to psychiatry. Clark's emphasis was always on remedial assistance for the whole family. If the child was hungry, the center provided food for the child and instructed the parents on how to access social services and food stamps. If the child was ill clothed, the center worked with welfare officials to provide proper clothing for the child. Once the reality of the family's social needs was acknowledged and improved, the children were equipped to move forward in their education. The center provided outreach as well by conducting teacher workshops on child development and sending staff into nursery schools to work with parents and teachers on everything from thinking skills to testing techniques to strategies on how to recognize and prevent child abuse.

Clark served on the board of many community organizations including Mount Sinai Medical Center, the New York Public Library, and the Museum of Modern Art. She retired from the Northside Center in 1979. Just three years after her retirement, Mamie Clark died of cancer at her home in New York at the age of sixty-five. Her many publications included *Changes in Primary Mental Abilities with Age*, published in 1944.

FURTHER READING:

Mamie Phipps Clark's papers, along with those of her husband, Kenneth Clark, are archived in the Library of Congress in Washington, D.C.

Clark, Kenneth. "The Effects of Segregation and the Consequences of Desegregation: A Social Science Statement," *Minnesota Law Review* 37 (1953).

Columbia University Libraries, Oral History Research Office. *Notable New Yorkers: Mamie Clark*, oral history interview with Mamie Clark (1976). Available online at http://www.columbia.edu/cu/lweb/digital/collections/.

Guthrie, Robert V. *Even the Rat Was White: A Historical View of Psychology* (1998).

Lyman, Darryl. *Great African-American Women* (1999).

Rangel, Charles. "In Honor of the Research and Contributions of the Late Dr. Kenneth B. Clark," *Congressional Record*, 5 May 2005.

Obituary: Smothers, Ronald. "Mamie Clark Dies; Psychologist Aided Blacks," *New York Times,* 12 Aug. 1983.

DONNA M. ABRUZZESE

Clark, Peter Humphries (1829–21 June 1925), educator, politician, and civil rights leader, was born in Cincinnati, Ohio, the son of Michael Clark, a barber, and his wife (name unknown). Clark was the product of a complex, mixed racial ancestry that formed the basis for a lifelong struggle to find a place for himself in both the white and African American worlds. The oral tradition of Peter Clark's family and of the Cincinnati African American community contends that Michael Clark was the son of the explorer William Clark, a Kentucky slaveowner who had children by his biracial slave Betty. Major Clark is said to have freed Betty and their children and settled them in Cincinnati. There she married and started another family with John Isom Gaines,

an affluent black man who owned a steamboat provisioning business. Though it was never authenticated, there is little doubt that Peter Clark himself believed the story of this genealogical connection was true. Quite light-complexioned and able to claim descent through a prominent white family, Peter Clark also had darker relatives to remind him of his African ancestry.

Clark's straddling of the color line was evident throughout his life. For example he belonged at the same time to local churches affiliated with the African Methodist Episcopal, white Unitarian, and Congregationalist denominations. That he felt completely comfortable in neither the white nor the black world contributed to the instability in his racial thought. At one time or another, and sometimes simultaneously, Clark advocated integrationist, separatist, and emigrationist strategies for African American advancement. Though perhaps less driven by complex personal backgrounds, other black leaders of the time also expressed contradictory responses to the problem they shared with Clark: finding an opening for blacks in a society at once democratic and thoroughly permeated by racism.

Clark had an extremely difficult time making a life for himself in antebellum Cincinnati's social climate of prejudice and discrimination. He had the best education available to an African American under the circumstances, graduating in 1846 from a segregated, private high school supported by white philanthropy. For years, however, he could not find dignified work consistent with his education and self-respect. He attempted an apprenticeship as a typemaker but quit because racial proscription blocked access to the status of craftsman. Then, though he felt cutting hair was undignified, he took over his father's barbershop, only to give that up when white customers demanded he not serve blacks. At this point, in 1848 or 1849, feeling that life in America offered no future for a black man, Clark began to consider emigration to West Africa. John McMiken, a wealthy white colonizationist from Cincinnati, arranged to send Clark and a party of one hundred blacks to a settlement on the Liberia–Sierra Leone border. Clark got no further than New Orleans. When he saw the filthy, unseaworthy schooner McMiken had commissioned for the journey, he returned to Cincinnati.

In 1852 Clark, who had been working without pay, seized the opportunity to become a salaried teacher in the segregated schools of Cincinnati. It was around this time that he finally gave up the idea of emigrating. In 1857 he rose from teacher to principal of a black elementary school, and in 1866 he became principal of the segregated high school. In addition to filling administrative and classroom duties, for many years he worked after school, without pay, training blacks for the teaching profession.

The movement for school desegregation among Ohio African Americans presented Clark with a formidable dilemma. In speeches and interviews in the black press, he acknowledged that desegregation would mean better schools for blacks. Yet he knew that black teachers would not be hired to teach white children, and this would mean a loss to the race of one of its few sources of dignified, intellectual, and well-paying employment. Furthermore, he did not believe that white teachers, even if unprejudiced, could be role models for black youth. For supporting the status quo in education when most blacks in Cincinnati strongly favored desegregation, Clark fell out of step with his own community. This, along with charges that he had bribed a witness in a political corruption case to save political allies from going to jail, led to his firing in 1886. He then worked briefly selling textbooks before becoming principal at the segregated State Normal and Industrial School at Huntsville, Alabama. He soon left there because, it was reported, he could not accept the harsh southern racial order. In 1888 he moved to somewhat more congenial St. Louis, where he taught in the black public schools until retiring in 1908.

Black education was Clark's most stable institutional base as a race leader; however, he was also deeply involved in politics as a campaign speaker, editor of ephemeral campaign newspapers, occasional candidate, and sometime recipient of patronage. He was a master of political oratory, known throughout the northern states for his emotional expositions of the evils of racism. Clark's political affiliations, however, shifted too often and unpredictably for him to emerge as a political boss. Clark quickly grew disillusioned when he found the Republicans unwilling to advance the political and legal promises of Reconstruction or reluctant to provide patronage jobs that would help free blacks from the constraints of a racist job market, both of which were evidence of prejudice within the party. In 1872 he began to search for alternatives. Clark became a Liberal Republican, then went back to being a Republican, then declared himself an independent, and then became affiliated with the Marxian socialist Workingmen's Party during the period of heightened class conflict in 1877–1878. He next returned to calling himself a Republican, only to announce in 1882 that he was a Democrat. In his political meandering, Clark found few reliable white allies. Furthermore he gained few significant personal rewards. He briefly served as a pensions agent under President Ulysses S. Grant and was appointed the first black trustee of Ohio State University by the Democratic governor George Hoadly in 1884.

It is not clear that Clark really wished to wield political power. Though he was ambitious for himself and his friends and frequently spoke of politics in practical terms as a struggle for jobs and money, there is little evidence that he wished to gain influence through personal control of such political assets as nominations and patronage. Whether he spoke of jobs or group empowerment in explaining his shifting political allegiances, Clark's goal in electoral politics was ultimately to achieve black inclusion in the American mainstream.

The last third of Clark's life was spent in an obscurity that is surprising considering the notoriety of his middle years. Having exhausted so many affiliations and strategies in the 1870s and 1880s, thereafter he seemed not to know where to turn for answers. After settling in St. Louis, Clark retreated from public life and rarely spoke out on racial issues. In the last decades of his life, he appears to have devoted himself entirely to teaching and to his family. Clark had married Frances Williams in 1854. They had three children: Herbert, who appears to have lived a precarious existence dependent on political jobs; Ernestine, the first black woman graduate of Cincinnati Normal School, who became a schoolteacher; and Consuelo, a graduate of Boston University Medical School, who was one of the first African American women doctors. Clark died in St. Louis.

Prominent in black public life from the 1850s through the 1880s, Clark is acclaimed for the dynamic but controversial leadership he brought both to the development of Cincinnati's segregated black public school system and to the creation of post-enfranchisement northern black political strategy. The legacy of his active, middle years, however, is uncertain. Clark helped widen the debate about black political strategy, and his ambivalence about desegregation prefigures some black nationalist ideologies of the twentieth century. Yet the instability of his views and affiliations undermined his influence, both in his own time and much later, when his life was briefly rediscovered during the black revolution of the mid-twentieth century. Clark's educational work made more durable, practical contributions: the teachers he trained worked in segregated school systems throughout the Ohio Valley until well into the twentieth century.

FURTHER READING

Clark, Dovie King. "Peter Humphries Clark," *Negro History Bulletin* 5 (1942): 176.

Gerber, David A. "Peter Humphries Clark: The Dialogue of Hope and Despair," in *Black Leaders of the Nineteenth Century*, ed. Leon Litwack and August Meier (1988).

Gutman, Herbert G. "Peter H. Clark: Pioneer Negro Socialist, 1877," *Journal of Negro Education* 34 (Fall 1965): 413–18.

Simmons, William J. *Men of Mark: Eminent, Progressive, and Rising* (1887).

Obituary: *St. Louis Argus*, 26 June 1925.

This entry is taken from the *American National Biography* and is published here with the permission of the American Council of Learned Societies.

DAVID A. GERBER

Clark, Robert (3 Oct. 1928–), educator and lawmaker, was born Robert George Clark in Ebenezer, Mississippi, the son of a schoolteacher. Little information about his parents or early life is known. He attended Jackson State College (later Jackson State University), which at that time was an unaccredited, publicly funded postsecondary school for blacks. After graduating from Jackson State College in 1953, Clark taught at Humphreys County Training School, Lexington Attendance Center, and other secondary schools in the Mississippi Delta. In addition to teaching he coached a number of boys' and girls' sports teams. Inspired by the *Brown v. Board of Education* decision, Clark decided to further his education. He enrolled in graduate school at Michigan State University, where in 1961 he earned his master's in administration and educational services. Because there were no available programs for black students in Mississippi's segregated public universities, a regional program, Southern Regional Education Board, paid his tuition out of state. For a time this allowed black students to attend graduate school while the state avoided lawsuits.

Upon his return to Mississippi, Clark became the athletic director at Saints Junior College. Later he served as director of Project Second Start, a federally funded poverty program. In 1966 he left his position at Lexington High School and began working full time at Second Start. When the poverty program received a grant of half a million dollars to create a job training program, he sought support from the public school system. The all-white school board refused to provide access to public facilities. Clark resigned from his job and decided to present himself as a candidate for county superintendent in 1966. To stymie him, J. P. Love, who represented Clark's home county in the Mississippi legislature, introduced legislation making the position of school superintendent appointive rather than elective.

Unable to run for school superintendent, Clark in 1967 sought to replace Love, a white planter who had served in the Mississippi legislature since 1956. Love's perpetual reelection, like that of many Mississippi legislators, rested upon the disenfranchisement of his black constituents. The state legislature had not had a black member since 1893. Love had first been elected to the legislature at a time when fewer than 1 percent of eligible black voters in Holmes County was registered to vote. Before the passage of the Voting Rights Act in 1965, only twenty of the nearly nine thousand potential black voters were registered in Holmes County. During that same period of black disenfranchisement, the number of white registered voters outnumbered the actual population of eligible white voters in the county.

The Mississippi Freedom Democratic Party was founded in 1964 to provide political education to black Mississippians and to challenge the legitimacy of the all-white Mississippi Democratic Party. When Clark ran for a seat in the state legislature in 1967, he did so as an Independent, utilizing the well-organized Holmes County Freedom Democratic Party. Unlike in other areas of Mississippi, where black workers primarily labored on white farms, there existed a large population of black landowners in Holmes County. In addition to the civil rights community of independent landowners, Clark sought support among black professionals who had been slow to join the grassroots organizing campaigns in the state.

Clark had not been active in the voting rights movement in Holmes County, but he descended from a long line of men who participated in the fullest level of political activity allowed their generation. His grandfather had chaired the Hinds County Republican Party during Reconstruction. A generation later Clark's father registered to vote, a step that a growing though still limited number of black Mississippians were willing to take in the postwar period. When the opportunity arose for Robert Clark to enter politics, he seized it. He had cast his first vote in the 1963 Freedom Vote, a parallel election sponsored by the Council of Federated Organizations, a coalition of the Congress of Racial Equality (CORE), the NAACP, the Southern Christian Leadership Conference (SCLC), and the Student Nonviolent Coordinating Committee (SNCC) in Mississippi. In 1966 he registered to vote. Clark cast his first official vote for himself in 1967.

A crossover candidate—because he drew support from black professionals like himself and the laborers and small farmers who had been most active in local organizing campaigns—Clark won election in 1967. He became the first black legislator in Mississippi since the demise of Reconstruction governments. Beginning in January 1968 Clark represented Attala, Holmes, and Yazoo counties, localities where the black population accounted for 65 percent of the entire voter population. As a result of legislative redistricting and the creation of multimember districts, another black representative did not win election and join Clark in the Mississippi statehouse until 1975. In 1971 he married Essie Austin; they had two children. Following her death, in 1997 Clark married Jo Ann Ross.

In 1982 Clark was instrumental in passing the Educational Reform Act, which established the first publicly funded kindergarten in Mississippi. That year Clark sought to represent the Second Congressional District in the U.S. Congress. Following the passage of the Voting Rights Act, the Mississippi legislature had redistricted the historic Second District, which had sent Mississippi's last black representative to Congress. Not until 1982 was the district returned to its original boundaries. Clark lost in his two attempts, 1981 and 1984, to represent the Second Congressional District, a seat later won by MIKE ESPY.

In 1992 Clark was selected speaker pro tempore of the Mississippi legislature. Eleven years later he retired from the Mississippi statehouse. Clark's son Bryant Clark succeeded his father. Robert Clark's election to the Mississippi statehouse in 1967 ended three-quarters of a century of all-white representation in the state legislature. In 2001 Mississippians elected 892 black government officials, the greatest number in the United States.

FURTHER READING

Campbell, Will D. *Robert G. Clark's Journey to the House: A Black Politician's Story* (2003).

Neilson, Melany. *Even Mississippi* (1989).

Parker, Frank R. *Black Votes Count: Political Empowerment in Mississippi after 1965* (1990).

Sewell, George A., and Margaret L. Dwight. *Mississippi Black History Makers* (1984).

RACHEL B. REINHARD

Clark, Septima P. (3 May 1898–15 Dec. 1987), educator, activist, and community leader, was born Septima Poinsette in Charleston, South Carolina, the second child of Peter Porcher Poinsette, a caterer, and Victoria Anderson, who took in laundry. Peter Poinsette emerged from slavery free of animosity or a spirit of rebellion but determined to serve others, to educate his children, and to follow Jesus Christ with a passion. Victoria Anderson Poinsette, who was born free and at one point lived in Haiti with relatives, boasted that she had never been a servant to any white family. Septima's parents met and married in Florida, later relocating to Charleston.

Septima graduated from Avery Institute in Charleston in 1916 and began teaching on Johns Island. She quickly learned that the educational season on the island was determined by the agricultural contracts between sharecroppers and landowners and that illiteracy and poverty contributed to a system akin to slavery. The children could only attend school in the brief period when they were not needed to plant or harvest. But the young people were aware of the world beyond Johns Island, and they wanted to learn to read and write in order to escape what they saw as a limited future. They came to her at night to learn to read and write, as did adults hoping to participate in church and fraternal functions. Poinsette came to see the clear discrepancy between the educational facilities for blacks and whites on the island; while she and another teacher looked after 130 students crammed into the crumbling Promiseland School, a nearby, neatly whitewashed school catered to only three white students. The white teacher at that school earned nearly three times Poinsette's salary.

In 1919 Poinsette returned to Charleston to teach at Avery Institute and became involved in a successful movement by the NAACP to secure black teachers for the public school system of the city of Charleston. While at Avery in 1920, she married Nerie Clark, a navy cook, with whom she had two children—Victoria, who lived for twenty-three months, and Nerie Clark Jr. Her in-laws became instrumental in the guardianship of Nerie Jr. after Nerie Sr. died in 1925, and Clark sought work in the public schools of Ohio, North Carolina, and South Carolina.

In 1929 Clark returned to Columbia, South Carolina, to work in the public schools. She also worked closely with the NAACP, which was pursuing a lawsuit to equalize the salaries of black and white public school teachers, and volunteered at a literacy program for black soldiers at nearby Camp Jackson. She joined with the Federated Women's Club and other civic groups in Columbia in developing a home for delinquent girls, creating an orphanage for black children, and assisting the elderly. Clark was accepted into Columbia's black society and also its social activities, and she earned her B.A. from Benedict College and her M.A. from the Hampton Institute. In 1947 she returned to Charleston to care for her elderly mother. Clark then resumed teaching in the greater Charleston area and became involved in the activities of the black branch of the YWCA. Her work with the YWCA raised the problem of the lack of recreational facilities and opportunities for the city's black girls and boys. It also brought her notoriety, since she befriended the ostracized Judge Waties Waring and Elizabeth Waring, prominent white Charlestonians who were shunned by most whites and some blacks because of their support of civil rights and social reform. Clark also resumed her work with the Charleston branch of the NAACP, and her refusal to deny her membership in that organization resulted in the Charleston school district firing her from her teaching job.

Clark learned of the Highlander Folk School in 1952 when a fellow YWCA worker encouraged her to attend the interracial institute in Monteagle, Tennessee. Clark attended Highlander during the summers of 1953 and 1954, excited to find a place in the South where progressive whites and blacks could meet and engage in dialogue about race. In 1954 and 1955 workshops on the *Brown* I and *Brown* II public school desegregation decisions brought civil rights leaders from across the South to Highlander to discuss how to work to implement the Supreme Court's rulings. By the summer of 1955 Clark began to focus on voting rights and brought activists from Charleston and the neighboring islands to Highlander with her. Among them was a former student, ESAU JENKINS, from Johns Island, who had attempted to register fellow islanders to vote and wanted assistance in mobilizing his community. After Highlander sponsored an adult literacy program under Clark's and Jenkins's direction on Johns Island, neighboring islands sought to establish their own citizenship schools to prepare black residents for registering and voting.

When Tennessee authorities forced Highlander to close in 1959, its citizenship school program and its foundation support was picked up by the Southern Christian Leadership Conference (SCLC). Under the direction of Clark, DOROTHY COTTON, and ANDREW YOUNG, the school was relocated to the McIntosh Center in southern Georgia. Along with Young and Cotton, Clark began a journey across the South informing black communities of the program and identifying candidates to attend a weeklong workshop in citizenship and public policy. These graduates then returned to their respective communities to establish citizenship schools, which helped African Americans pass the literacy tests required to vote in many southern states.

From 1960 to 1970 Clark worked with the SCLC in implementing citizenship programs that helped thousands of African Americans across the South. She also worked with other civil rights groups, like SNCC, in preparing citizens to register to vote. Following the passage of the Civil Rights Act in 1964 and especially after the 1965 Voting Rights Act, Clark personally witnessed the impact of the citizenship program on the political empowerment of black southerners. Many blacks who sought political offices following 1965 had been affiliated with some aspect of the citizenship program, as these schools enhanced the political and social progress of blacks in the deep South.

In 1970 Clark retired from the SCLC and conducted workshops for the American Friends Service Committee, organized day-care sites, raised funds for scholarships, and became a sought-after speaker on civil and women's rights. In her latter years she began to review her position as a woman in the movement and the contributions of women, realizing how seldom they were recognized or appreciated. Clark was elected to the same school board that had fired her years earlier, and she began receiving a plethora of national and regional awards, an honorary degree from the College of Charleston in 1978, and South Carolina's highest award, the Order of the Palmetto, in 1982.

On 15 December 1987 Clark, freedom fighter, educator, and community crusader, died in Charleston, South Carolina. By insisting an African Americans' citizenship rights, she helped pave the way for the 1965 Voting Rights Act and the subsequent upsurge in black political mobilization in the South.

FURTHER READING

The Septima P. Clark Papers are held in the Special Collections department of the Robert Scott Small

Library, College of Charleston, Charleston, South Carolina.

Clark, Septima P. *Echo in My Soul* (1962).

Brown, Cynthia S., ed. *Ready from Within: Septima Clark and the Civil Rights Movement* (1991).

McFadden, Grace J. "Septima P. Clark and the Struggle for Human Rights," in *Women in the Civil Rights Movement, Trailblazers and Torchbearers, 1941–1965*, ed. Vicki Crawford, Jacqueline A. Rouse, and Barbara A. Woods (1993).

Rouse, Jacqueline A. "'We Seek to Know … in Order to Speak the Truth': Nurturing Seeds of Discontent— Septima Clark and Participatory Leadership," in *Sisters in the Struggle, African American Women in the Civil Rights, Black Power Movement*, ed. Bettye Collier Thomas and V. P. Franklin (2001).

Obituary: *New York Times*, 17 Dec. 1987.

JACQUELINE A. ROUSE

Clark, Sonny (21 July 1931–13 Jan. 1963), jazz pianist, was born Conrad Yeatis (or Yetis) Clark in Herminie, Pennsylvania. His parents' names are unknown. Clark began to play the piano at age four. In 1943 his family moved to Pittsburgh, where, while continuing to study piano, he also played the vibraphone and bass in a high school band.

Following his mother's death, Clark traveled to Los Angeles in 1951 with his older brother, who was a professional pianist. Clark was briefly associated with most of the leading jazz musicians in the area, including the saxophonists WARDELL GRAY, Stan Getz, DEXTER GORDON, Art Pepper, and Zoot Sims; the trumpeter ART FARMER; the drummer Shelly Manne; the guitarist Barney Kessel; and the singer Anita O'Day. Early in 1953 he made his first recordings as a sideman with the vibraphonist Teddy Charles and then with Pepper. He joined the bassist OSCAR PETTIFORD's trio and traveled to San Francisco, where Clark also worked briefly with the tenor saxophonist Vido Musso and led his own trio at the Down Beat Club.

While in San Francisco, Clark met the clarinetist Buddy DeFranco. He recorded with an ad hoc big band accompanying DeFranco in Los Angeles in September, and around this time he replaced Kenny Drew in DeFranco's quartet. They toured Europe in January and February 1954 as part of the writer LEONARD FEATHER's "Jazz Club, USA" package. Clark made numerous recordings with the clarinetist, who said, "Sonny was a sweet little guy. He was just a nice, bright person. Great humor." By touring with DeFranco, Clark began to acquire a reputation beyond the Los Angeles area.

Early in 1956 Clark was once again based in the Los Angeles area, where he joined the bassist Howard Rumsey's Lighthouse All Stars, recorded the baritone saxophonist's Serge Chaloff's album *Blue Serge*, and participated in recordings by the alto saxophonist SONNY CRISS and the trombonist Frank Rosolino. In February 1957 he became a member of the singer DINAH WASHINGTON's accompanying trio, thereby gaining an opportunity to return to New York in April. At the club Birdland he led a trio with the bassist SAM JONES and the drummer ART TAYLOR. Later, around 1959, he performed at the Bohemia Club with the tenor saxophonist Johnny Griffin, the bassist WILBUR WARE, and the drummer PHILLY JOE JONES. Recordings from this period include his own albums *Dial "S" for Sonny*, *Sonny Clark Trio*, *Sonny's Crib* (all 1957), and *Cool Struttin'* (1958), as well as albums made with the tenor saxophonists SONNY ROLLINS (*The Sound of Sonny*), HANK MOBLEY (*Hank Mobley Sextet*), Johnny Griffin, and Clifford Jordan (all 1957).

Clark was largely inactive from 1959 into 1961, owing to a heroin addiction that had plagued him from a young age. His fellow jazz pianist and drug addict HAMPTON HAWES described this period: "Sonny and I earned ourselves a righteous moniker: the Gold Dust Twins…. We were strung as bad as you can get, way out on the edge and starting to burn people. The only reason we weren't in the park with the muggers was that we were musicians" (Hawes and Asher, 106). His occasional recordings during this period included the album *Sonny Clark Trio* (1960).

Clark was continually ill during the last two years of his life. Little is known of his nightclub work during this period apart from appearances in 1961 at the White Whale in Greenwich Village. Nonetheless, he made significant recordings, most notably *Leapin' and Lopin'* (1961), which is probably his finest album as a leader. He also served as a sideman for albums with the alto saxophonist JACKIE MCLEAN, the guitarist GRANT GREEN, and the tenor saxophonists IKE QUEBEC and DEXTER GORDON, including Gordon's *Go!* (1962). In late October 1962 Clark was hospitalized with a leg infection. He was released and performed at Junior's club on 11 and 12 January, but the following day, after a drug overdose, he suffered a fatal heart attack in New York City.

Although Clark composed a number of themes, few have entered the standard jazz repertoire. He is best remembered as a hard-bop pianist who amalgamated the principal styles of the pianists

BUD POWELL and HORACE SILVER, capturing the characteristic clarity and headlong rush of Powell's ever-changing single-note lines but also showing a strong affinity for Silver's willingness to repeat ideas and for his characteristically tuneful and relaxed use of swing riffs and piano blues formulas.

FURTHER READING

Hawes, Hampton, and Don Asher. *Raise Up Off Me: A Portrait of Hampton Hawes* (1974, 1979).

James, Michael. "Sonny Clark," *Jazz Monthly* 9 (May 1963).

Obituaries: *Jazz*, 2 February 1963; *Down Beat*, 28 February 1963; *Jazz Magazine*, no. 92, March 1963.

DISCOGRAPHY

Skovgaard, Ib, and Ebbe Traberg. *Some Clark Bars: Sonny Clark, a Discography* (1984).

This entry is taken from the *American National Biography* and is published here with the permission of the American Council of Learned Societies.

BARRY KERNFELD

Clarke, John Henrik (1 Jan. 1915–16 July 1998), scholar and activist, was born John Henry Clark in Union Springs, Alabama, the first of five children to John Clark and Willella (Willie) Mays, sharecroppers. Later Clarke changed the spelling of his name, dropping the "y" in Henry and replacing it with "ik" after the Norwegian playwright, Henrik Ibsen. He also added an "e" at the end of Clarke.

Clarke's great grandmother Mary, who lived to be 108, inspired him to study history. The young Clarke sat on her lap, listening to stories, and it was through her, he later said, that he first became aware of the word "Africa." Clarke grew up in the Baptist church and wanted to satisfy his intellectual curiosity regarding the Bible and its relationship to African people. Like a detective he searched the Bible looking for an image of God that looked like him. His dissatisfaction with what he found later helped him to produce one of his most famous short stories, "The Boy Who Painted Christ Black" (1940), which was translated into over a dozen languages.

Following the death of his mother in 1922 Clarke's family moved to Columbus, Georgia. Clarke did not attend school until the third grade because of his family's poverty, and since during the era of Jim Crow African Americans could not use public libraries across the South, Clarke had to develop creative ways to obtain information. He picked up used books and magazines from white

schools and took newspapers out of garbage cans. Occasionally, when employed by rich white families, Clarke borrowed books from them.

Like thousands of others Clarke grew tired of the bleakness and repression of the South and joined the Great Migration in search of a better future. Hopping a freight train Clarke and a friend, Roscoe Chester, hoboed to the North, first to Chicago and then in 1933 to New York City. Though the Depression still gripped the world Clarke found greater opportunities to grow in New York than were possible in Georgia. He and Chester lived on Manhattan's Lower Eastside, surviving on a diet of bread and sardines.

When he was eighteen Clarke was introduced to communist literature by a Russian, George Victor, and soon became active in the Young Communist League on the Lower Eastside. Clarke also joined the defense of the SCOTTSBORO BOYS and ANGELO HERNDON, organizing rallies and lectures throughout the city.

One of the most significant meetings that Clarke experienced during his early years in Harlem occurred at the New York Public Library. Before he left Georgia, Clarke had read and been greatly influenced by ARTHUR A. SCHOMBURG's essay "The Negro Digs Up His Past," which had appeared in *The New Negro*, an influential anthology edited by ALAIN LOCKE, a prominent figure in the Harlem Renaissance. This essay was Clarke's first exposure to the reality that African people had a history that was older than Europe, and it left him with many questions and a determination to meet its author. "I could not stomach the lies of world history, so I took some strategic steps in order to build a life of scholarship and activism in New York" (Clarke Papers, Funeral Program).

One afternoon Clarke decided to visit Schomburg, then curator of the "Division of Negro Literature" at the 135th Street Branch of the New York Public Library. Following their first meeting—Clarke interrupted Schomburg's lunch with a request to hear the story of African history—Schomburg took the young man under his wing, guiding him in his studies until his death in 1938. Despite the loss of his mentor Clarke found other black scholars to study under, most notably those at the Harlem History Club. Directed by Willis N. Huggins, the Harlem History Club (later the Edward Wilmont Blyden Society) served as Clarke's formal introduction to the study of history. Here he met other scholars like John G. Jackson, JOEL A. ROGERS, Charles Siefort, RICHARD B. MOORE, and

WILLIAM LEO HANSBERRY, among others, from all corners of the world. In addition to these studies Clarke also took writing classes sponsored by the Works Project Administration (WPA).

In 1941 Clarke was drafted into the U.S. Army Air Corps. At the end of World War II he received an honorable discharge and decided to continue his training as a scholar. His postwar years were productive. In 1948 he published his first volume of poetry, *Rebellion in Rhyme*. Around the same time, he enrolled at New York University on the G.I. Bill but was uninspired and withdrew. Clarke would not earn a degree until he was awarded a Ph.D. from Pacific Western University in 1995 for the completion of a competitive dissertation.

In 1958 he spent several months traveling across Ghana, Nigeria, and Togo. Clarke's African sojourn enabled him to understand the diversity and depth of African cultures, while allowing him to draw some parallels to his childhood in the South. It also provided him with the opportunity to see some of the new states that were emerging out of colonialism and the many challenges that they faced. In Ghana, Clarke freelanced for the *Ghana Evening News*, and it was his time in that country—with its rich land and ancient culture—that transformed his consciousness. Clarke saw both the triumph and the inevitable tragedy of Ghana. "I was frightened because I suspected that the colonial powers would not give up Africa very easily and that the first target of fragmentation would be Ghana. Unfortunately, history has proved me right"(Adams, 106).

On his way home from Africa, Clarke spent time in Britain, France, and Italy. He even attended the Second Congress of Black Writers and Artists in Paris in 1959, where he met African thinkers from around the world.

With the rise of black consciousness in the 1960s the demand for Clarke's expertise increased. For five years he directed the African Heritage program for HARYOU-ACT, the first antipoverty agency in Harlem, and served as a special consultant for the Columbia University–WCBS-TV series, "Black Heritage: The History of Afro-Americans." In 1969 Clarke joined Hunter College's faculty, where he established and chaired the department of black and Puerto Rican studies. There he built a comprehensive department, introducing new courses on African history, literature, and other previously neglected subjects.

He also had an instrumental role in shaping black studies departments around the country, most notably at Cornell University, where he served as distinguished visiting professor of African history. In 1983 Clarke was the recipient of the Thomas Hunter Professorship and in 1985 he retired from Hunter College as Professor Emeritus of African world history. In 1994 Clarke was awarded the Phelps-Stokes Fund's Aggrey Medal for his role "as a public philosopher and relentless critic of injustice and inequality."

Clarke published hundreds of articles and essays, authored approximately ten books, and edited over eighteen volumes. Some of his most popular works included *Notes for an African World Revolution* (1991), *Christopher Columbus and the African Holocaust* (1992), and *Who Betrayed the African Revolution?* (1991). Some of his edited works include *Harlem, A Community in Transition* (1964), *Malcolm X: The Man and His Times* (1969), *William Styron's Nat Turner: Ten Black Writers Respond* (1970), and *Marcus Garvey and the Vision of Africa* (1973). He also cofounded the Harlem Writers Guild—which nurtured such authors as JAMES BALDWIN, LORRAINE HANSBERRY, and MAYA ANGELOU—Freedomways, the African Heritage Studies Association, the National Council of Black Studies, the Association for the Study of Classical African Civilizations, the Black Academy of Arts and Letters, and the African American Scholar's Council.

Following his retirement from Hunter College, Clarke remained a sought-after lecturer. In 1997 the actor WESLEY SNIPES produced a documentary about Clarke's life, *A Great and Mighty Walk*, and professor Clinton Crawford of Brooklyn's Medgar Evers College offered a course, "The Life and Writings of John Henrik Clarke."

In 1993 Clarke donated approximately 10,000 volumes from his library to Clark Atlanta University and the university dedicated a wing of the Woodruff Library Center in his honor. Clarke's papers and other documents, however, were deposited at the Schomburg Center for Research in Black Culture. His heirs were his wife, Sybil Williams Clarke, whom he married on 21 September 1997, and his two children from a previous marriage (date and name of spouse unknown), Nzinga Marie Clarke and Sonni Kojo Clarke.

Clarke's profound grasp of history was impressive. He routinely delivered detailed lectures, replete with dates and numerous references, without notes. He received honorary degrees from the University of Denver, Colorado, the University of the District of Columbia, and, posthumously, from Medgar Evers College. Clarke maintained, without apology, that he was a black nationalist, a socialist, and a Pan-Africanist. He did not see any contradictions among these goals or ideals and often stated that the choice for African people throughout the world was simple: "Pan-Africanism or perish!"

FURTHER READING

The most extensive collection of primary material related to Clarke's life and work is to be found in the John Henrik Clarke collection at the Schomburg Center for Research in Black Culture of the New York Public Library.

Adams, Barbara Eleanor. *John Henrik Clarke: Master Teacher* (2000).

Harris, Robert L., Jr. *Journal of Negro History* 83 (Fall 1998).

Kelley, Robin D. G. *New York Times Magazine* (3 Jan. 1999).

Painter, Nell. *Crisis* (Sept.–Oct. 1998).

Obituaries: *New York Amsterdam News*, 23 July 1998; *New York Times*, 20 July 1998.

CHRISTOPHER WILLIAMS

Clarke, Kenny (9? Jan. 1914–26 Jan. 1985), jazz drummer and bandleader, was born Kenneth Clarke Spearman in Pittsburgh, Pennsylvania, the son of Charles Spearman and Martha Grace Scott. His birth date is almost always given as 9 January, but the writer Ursula Broschke Davis maintains that the actual date is 2 January. His mother played piano, and at a young age Kenny learned to play both this instrument and, in church, pump organ. Biographers concur that his boyhood was miserable, and he hid the experience behind rosy and contradictory memories. His father abandoned the family. When Kenny was around five years old, his mother died. Her companion, a Baptist preacher, placed him in the Coleman Industrial Home for Negro Boys in Pittsburgh, where he tried a few brass instruments before taking up drums. At about age eleven or twelve he resumed living with his stepfather. He attended several elementary schools and Herron Hill Junior High School before dropping out at age fifteen to become a professional musician. After an argument with his stepfather, he was placed in a foster home.

At sixteen years old, Kenny lived on his own, initially working day jobs while getting established in music. He was a local professional by age seventeen, drumming and occasionally playing piano. At one point he toured in a band that included the trumpeter ROY ELDRIDGE, and he briefly joined the Jeter-Pillars Orchestra in St. Louis before spending three years with Leroy Bradley's orchestra at the Cotton Club in Cincinnati.

Moving to New York City late in 1935, Clarke dropped his surname, thereafter working as Kenny Clarke. He doubled as a vibraphonist in a trio with his half-brother Frank Spearman, a bassist who also took Clarke as a surname to capitalize on his brother's newfound fame. Kenny Clarke played alongside the guitarist Freddie Greene in the tenor saxophonist Lonnie Simmons's band at the Black Cat in Greenwich Village. Still doubling on vibraphone, Clarke joined Edgar Hayes's band in April 1937, touring Europe from December 1937 to April 1938 and briefly working alongside the trumpeter DIZZY GILLESPIE. At some point Clarke joined the pianist CLAUDE HOPKINS's band; the chronology is uncertain.

Clarke became a member of Teddy Hill's big band, which included Gillespie. Hill puzzled over the drummer's abandonment of a steady four-beat rhythm on the bass drum in favor of irregular accents and reportedly asked, "What is this klook-mop stuff you're playing?" Hence his nickname, "Klook." Dissatisfied, Hill fired Clarke, who then performed with the reed player SIDNEY BECHET at the Long Cabin in Fonda, New York (c. Dec. 1939–Jan. 1940); they recorded together in February 1940. Later that year Clarke accompanied the singers Mildred Bailey and BILLIE HOLIDAY on record, joined Eldridge's band, and served as the house drummer at the Apollo Theater in Harlem.

Clarke spent the summer of 1941 in LOUIS ARMSTRONG's big band. He also toured with ELLA FITZGERALD, who was leading the memorial CHICK WEBB band, and recorded in a small band accompanying Fitzgerald in October 1941. That same year Hill, who had disbanded and taken a job managing Minton's Playhouse in Harlem, hired Clarke to lead the house band that included the trumpeter Joe Guy, the pianist THELONIOUS MONK, and the bassist Nick Fenton. Hill encouraged sitting in; the guitarist CHARLIE CHRISTIAN and Gillespie were regulars there, and many other renowned musicians appeared. In this setting Clarke collaborated with Monk in writing "Fly Right," which became a bebop standard under a new title, "Epistrophy." More generally the sessions became famous for demonstrations of virtuosity—unexpected harmonies, fast tempos, unusual keys—that discouraged those whose style did not fit in well. These experimental sounds were crucial to the development of bebop.

At Kelly's Stable in New York, Clarke led his own Kansas City Six, including Monk and the tenor saxophonist IKE QUEBEC, and then he played alongside Gillespie in the alto saxophonist Benny Carter's septet from 10 December 1941 to 4 February 1942. He joined RED ALLEN's band for performances in Chicago and Boston. In mid-1943 Clarke was drafted into the army. One year later, while stationed in Alabama, he married the singer CARMEN MCRAE. Absent without leave for 107 days, Clarke was captured and shipped overseas in September 1944. He played trombone and sang in Europe until his discharge in April 1946. Out of New York for three years, Clarke missed the full flowering of the bebop style, and MAX ROACH, not Clarke, became its foremost exponent on drums.

During his army service, Clarke was once again known as Spearman. Shortly after his discharge he became a Muslim and took the name Liaquat Ali Salaam. He replaced Roach in Gillespie's big band, and from May to September 1946 he made a series of classic bop recordings, including "Oop Bop Sh'Bam" and "One Bass Hit (Part 1)," with Gillespie's sextet. During this period Clarke also participated in a session with the saxophonist SONNY STITT; recorded "Epistrophy" and other titles with his own 52nd Street Boys, which included the trumpeter Fats Navarro and the pianist Bud Powell; and joined a recording session under Navarro's leadership.

After recording with Gillespie again in August 1947, Clarke joined Gillespie's big band in December, touring Europe from January to March 1948. Clarke considered this the finest musical experience of his life; unfortunately his drumming was not well captured on Gillespie's recordings. Clarke stayed in Paris, performing, teaching, recording, and helping Nicole Barclay organize the forthcoming Paris Jazz Festival. Returning to New York in August, Clarke joined TADD DAMERON's band at the Royal Roost and recorded with Dameron and numerous bebop all-stars between August 1948 and April 1949. Early in 1949 he played with the bassist OSCAR PETTIFORD's big band and trio, and he recorded the second of the trumpeter MILES DAVIS's *Birth of the Cool* sessions. Around this time or perhaps a bit later, Clarke became a heroin addict. He remained on narcotics at least into the 1960s, but unlike many of his colleagues, he was somehow a discreet user. Many people did not know that he was addicted, and he did not exhibit stereotypical characteristics, such as irresponsibility or exploitation of friendships.

Late in 1948 Clarke and McRae separated permanently. They had no children and divorced in 1956. He returned to Paris for the jazz festival in May 1949 as a member of another all-star bop ensemble, and in Zurich he gave a concert with the saxophonist CHARLIE PARKER and Davis. Again he stayed in Europe, touring Belgium with the pianist Bernard Peiffer and making Paris his home base. He worked there with the bassist Pierre Michelot and later toured to Tunis in a group that included the saxophonist JAMES MOODY and the singer Annie Ross. Clarke also toured Europe with Moody and Michelot under the saxophonist COLEMAN HAWKINS's leadership. Reunited with Bechet, he recorded "Klook's Blues" and "American Rhythm" in October 1949.

Clarke had a child from an affair with Ross. In 1951 they took their son to Pittsburgh to be raised by Clarke's brother Chuck Spearman. Clarke toured with the singer BILLY ECKSTINE and in August 1951 recorded with both Parker's quintet and the vibraphonist MILT JACKSON's quartet. With the pianist JOHN LEWIS replacing HORACE SILVER and the bassist PERCY HEATH replacing RAY BROWN, Jackson's quartet became the long-lived Modern Jazz Quartet. Clarke performed with this quartet at the first Newport Jazz Festival (with Silver in 1954) and recorded the albums *MJQ* (1952) and *Django* (1953–55), which exemplify his mastery of wire brushes on the drum set. But Clarke quarreled with Lewis over the quartet's artistic direction and leadership, and he quit the group around March 1955, saying, "I wouldn't be able to play the drums my way again after four or five years of playing eighteenth-century drawing-room jazz" (Hennessey, 100).

Clarke recorded prolifically during these years. In 1954 he contributed to numerous classic hard bop recordings under Davis's leadership, including "Solar," "Walkin'," "Airegin," "Oleo," and "Bags' Groove." He served as a talent scout and resident drummer for Savoy Records, to which he brought Silver, the saxophonists Pepper Adams and CANNONBALL ADDERLEY, and the trumpeter DONALD BYRD, among others. Clarke joined Pettiford's group at the Café Bohemia in mid-1955 and continued with Pettiford and the pianist PHINEAS NEWBORN at Basin Street West in March 1956.

At this point Clarke, exhausted from continuous studio and nightclub work, moved to Paris in search of a more relaxed life. Apart from a few brief periods, he spent the remainder of his life in Europe. He continued to record profusely. After working in Jacques Hélian's orchestra, he held long engagements in Paris at the Club St. Germain (1957–1958; 1963; early 1970s) and the Blue Note (1959–1962; 1964–1966), with regular breaks for concerts and tours throughout

Europe. Among his long-standing associates were the pianists Martial Solal, Bud Powell, René Urtreger, and Raymond Fol; the organists Lou Bennett and Eddy Louiss; the electric guitarists Jimmy Gourley and René Thomas; and the bassists Michelot, Michel Guadry, and Jimmy Woode. Organized variously into three- and four-piece rhythm sections, Clarke and these associates accompanied such soloists as the saxophonists LESTER YOUNG, STAN GETZ, DEXTER GORDON, Johnny Griffin, and Sonny Stitt; the trumpeter Gillespie; and the trombonist J. J. JOHNSON. The spirit of these years was later captured in the movie 'Round Midnight (1986). In 1962 Clarke settled east of Paris in Montreuil-sous-Bois and married Daisy Dina Wallbach; they had a son. Clarke was never able to take French citizenship. Instead, he renewed his residency status as an immigrant every three years.

With the arranger Francy Boland as co-leader, Clarke recorded The Golden Eight in 1961. This led to the formation of the Clarke-Boland Big Band. Widely recognized as Europe's finest jazz big band, the group began touring in 1966 and remained active to 1972. From 1967 to 1972 Clarke taught at the St. Germain–en–Laye Conservatoire, and from 1967 he also taught at the Kenny Clarke Drum School at the Selmer musical instrument company in Paris.

Clarke returned to the United States to receive a Duke Ellington Fellowship from Yale University (1972), to participate in a reunion of Gilliespie's band in Chicago (1976), to receive awards from the cities of Pittsburgh and New York, and to teach at the University of Pittsburgh (1979). He performed at jazz festivals throughout Europe until 1983. Having already suffered a heart attack in 1975, he died in Montreuil-sous-Bois.

Clarke is widely remembered as calm, kind, dignified, self-effacing, and quiet and as a complete professional. A generous teacher, he was infinitely patient, even with amateur musicians. He was only known to lose his composure when accompanying those few leading jazz musicians who could not keep a steady beat. His biographer Mike Hennessey, keen to establish the drummer's significance, uncritically accepts imprecise, exaggerated, and sometimes impossible claims. For example, he states that Clarke developed a new style of rhythm section playing with Simmons in 1936 after hearing the bassist JIMMY BLANTON's recordings with Duke Ellington, but these discs were made in 1940. It is impossible to know just what Clarke did because of undocumented events; the rapid interchange of ideas; the concurrent contributions of SID CATLETT, JO JONES, SHADOW WILSON, and other drummers; Clarke's own unsubstantiated claims; and Clarke's absence from the scene during army service while Roach made his mark in bebop. Nonetheless, no one questions his stature as one of the greatest and most innovative jazz drummers. The music educator Theodore Dennis Brown documents Clarke's achievements on the tracks with Bechet in 1940 and from amateur recordings made live at Minton's in 1941. In these recordings one can hear components of an overriding sense of musicality that distinguished Clarke's playing. He made such innovations as clicking the high hat cymbal closed on the backbeat (beats two and four of the measure); accenting in an improvisatory manner (and staying out of the bass player's way) by "dropping bombs" (irregular accents) on the bass drum rather than marking every beat with that drum; keeping a steady flowing sound on the ride cymbal; and articulating phrases in fragmented and asymmetrical ways in response to the improvising soloist.

FURTHER READING

A tape and transcript of Clarke's oral history, recorded by Helen Oakley Dance in 1977, are at the Institute of Jazz Studies, Newark, New Jersey.

Chilton, John. Sidney Bechet: The Wizard of Jazz (1987).

Haggerty, Michael, with Matthew Annenberg. A Flower for Kenny (1985).

Hennessey, Mike. Klook: The Story of Kenny Clarke (1990).

Obituary: New York Times, 27 Jan. 1985.

This entry is taken from the American National Biography and is published here with the permission of the American Council of Learned Societies.

BARRY KERNFELD

Clarke, Lewis G. (1815–1897), author and antislavery lecturer, was born into slavery on the plantation of his maternal grandfather, Samuel (some sources say William) Campbell, in Madison County, Kentucky. He was the son of Campbell's mixed-race slave daughter Letitia and her white Scottish-immigrant husband, Daniel Clarke, a soldier in the American Revolution. Lewis Clarke's middle name is variously recorded as either George or Garrand. Clarke's family history, which he traced back to the founding of the nation, inspired his quest for freedom and his subsequent dedication to the abolition cause in the North.

Clarke's first six years were spent with his parents and nine siblings and were the only family life and childhood he experienced. Betsey Campbell Banton, one of Campbell's white daughters and Clarke's maternal aunt, whom he likened to a "female Nero," claimed Clarke by right of dowry, taking him from his parents to her home in Lexington, Kentucky. Clarke saw his family only three times in the next ten years, a period that began what he called his "pilgrimage of suffering."

Subjected to beatings and mental cruelty and undernourished for nearly ten years, Clarke divided long days between serving the Banton family and spinning flax and hemp on a foot-wheel machine. From the age of ten, his chronic health problems were exacerbated by unremitting labor and Banton's policy of meting out food based on the measure of Clarke's production at the spinning wheel. Bouts of illness and exhaustion when he was unable to meet the imposed standard were occasioned by starvation and confinement in a drafty attic room. Sometime around 1831 the Bantons' years of bickering and violence ended in divorce. Their misfortune, however, was to Clarke's advantage. Banton "mortgaged" Clarke to Tom Kennedy to work in the tobacco fields, but as Clarke later recalled, even the brutality of an overseer, constant hunger, and heat exhaustion were preferable to servitude in the Banton home.

The death of Samuel Campbell in 1831 ruined any hope Clarke had of being reunited with his family. The patriarch's death precipitated a property struggle among Campbell's white descendants, leaving, against his promise of their freedom, his African American descendants to the vicissitudes of life in bondage. Clarke's family was dispersed at the auction block, each of his siblings and his mother sold to a different bidder. At Kennedy's death, Clarke, then about twenty, was transferred to Kennedy's son. Clarke then hired his time for twelve dollars a month, a system that permitted him to contract for his own labor and provide for his own keep, while remitting the net of his wages to Kennedy. Splitting rails, loading coal into furnaces, and peddling grass seed across the state line with a modicum of supervision provided Clarke with his first taste of freedom. Five years later, in 1840, the younger Kennedy died suddenly, and his executors auctioned off the estate. Because Clarke's "title" was entailed to multiple mortgages, it remained in probate for more than a year, permitting him to continue hiring his time.

Rumors soon mounted that Clarke was to be sent to Louisiana and sold into the lucrative slave market of the Deep South. To avoid this fate, Clarke and a companion attempted to escape bondage with Clarke disguised as a white master accompanied by a slave attendant. The ruse might have been successful, but they were forced to turn back, lacking confidence and confused by signposts they could not read.

Two weeks later, in August 1841, Clarke made his second bid for freedom. Under the guise of his independent employment, he traveled fifty miles to Lexington, where he made a clandestine visit to his youngest brother Cyrus. It was probably on this occasion that the seed was planted for Clarke's return for Cyrus the following year. From Lexington he headed due north toward the Ohio River; the next day he was in Aberdeen, across the Ohio River. Within a week he arrived in Cincinnati, where he found shelter among friends of the Underground Railroad. Not until November did he manage to locate his brother Milton (whose escape preceded Clarke's by a year), then living in Oberlin, Ohio. Greeted at his arrival in Oberlin by Milton and Ohio abolitionists, Clarke enjoyed a sense of family and community unknown to him since his earliest childhood. Engaged in the abolitionist cause, he became a speaker on a lecture circuit that took him throughout the North over the next twenty years.

Clarke risked capture by returning to Kentucky in July 1842 to rescue his brother Cyrus. Cyrus's unstable mental health, induced by terror and exacerbated by the increase in slave patrols and the fear of vigilante reprisal if caught, made the return journey particularly harrowing. Finally free, Cyrus comprised the third member of the celebrated fugitive slave brother trio, who turned their energies and talents toward aggressive campaigns both against slavery and for the elevation of their race.

Illiterate for the first few years after his escape from slavery, in 1845 Clarke dictated the account of his life in slavery to his white editor Joseph C. Lovejoy, himself one of a trio of abolitionist brothers. One year later Clarke's lightly amended narrative was republished together with the narrative of Milton Clarke, leaving to posterity the fundamental record of their family, *Narratives of the Sufferings of Lewis and Milton Clarke, Sons of a Soldier of the Revolution, during a Captivity of More Than Twenty Years among the Slaveholders of Kentucky, One of the So Called Christian States of North America. Dictated by Themselves.* The Clarkes's combined autobiographies immediately enjoyed critical praise and popular sales.

In the preface to Clarke's narrative, Lovejoy testified to his eloquence as a public speaker and his ability to move audiences with a "wave of deep feeling." No doubt this ability to tap into the current of nineteenth-century sentimentalism and to convey through the story of his life the atrocities of slavery brought Clarke to the attention of Harriet Beecher Stowe. Impressed by the narrative of Clarke's escape from Kentucky and the heroism exhibited in his return to the South for Cyrus, Stowe engaged Clarke for a series of interviews at her home. These meetings, she claimed several years later in *A Key to* Uncle Tom's Cabin (1853), not only provided her with factual material for her controversial novel but Clarke's personal, often Byronic, attributes, combined with those of FREDERICK DOUGLASS, also provided the character model upon which she based the courageous and defiant fugitive slave George Harris.

Around the time the Fugitive Slave Law of 1850 was passed, initiating the second and largest movement of blacks into Canada, Clarke left Ohio for Canada West (now Ontario), settling in Sandwich, where he invested in farmland and entered politics. Unlike the renowned fugitives WILLIAM WELLS BROWN or Douglass, who primarily confined their abolitionist activities to the United States, Clarke was more interested in promoting Canada West as the center for black settlement and antislavery resistance. His efforts to encourage black migration to Canada aimed at counteracting by force of representation what many perceived as the inevitable U.S. annexation of Canada. As an incentive to that end, he helped organize the Agricultural, Mechanical, and Educational Association of Canada West, a committee designed to educate and acculturate newly immigrant fugitives from slavery. Clarke became one of the association's trustees and a general traveling agent shortly after its charter on 1 March 1859.

Canadian census records show Clarke married and in residence in Windsor, Ontario, in 1861. He remained ambivalent about colonization for most of his life; his desire for a separate African American state in Canada, the Caribbean, South America, or Kansas was mitigated by his concern that emigration undermined black community and history, prolonging the dissipating effects of slavery. After the death of his wife, about whom little is known, Clarke sold his Canadian lands in 1874 and moved back to Oberlin, accompanied by his children. In the late 1870s or early 1880s he returned to Lexington, Kentucky, where he advocated agricultural labor and lived the remainder of his life. At Clarke's death the governor of

Kentucky ordered his body laid in state in the Civic Auditorium, where thousands paid tribute to his life and work, the first such honor accorded an African American in that state's history. His body was returned to Oberlin for burial, and his grave is marked by a headstone that memorializes him as "the original George Harris of Harriet Beecher Stowe's Book, *Uncle Tom's Cabin*."

FURTHER READING
Andrews, William L. *To Tell a Free Story: The First Century of Afro-American Autobiography, 1760–1865* (1988).
Vacheenas, Jean, and Betty Volk. "Born in Bondage: History of a Slave Family," *Negro History Bulletin* 36 (1973): 101–6.
This entry is taken from the *American National Biography* and is published here with the permission of the American Council of Learned Societies.

GREGORY S. JACKSON

Clarke, Milton (c. 1820–1901), antislavery memoirist and lecturer, Civil War veteran, and first black elected to the Common Council of Cambridge, Massachusetts, was one of ten children born into slavery in Madison County, Kentucky, on the plantation of his maternal grandfather Samuel Campbell. One of Milton's older brothers was the noted abolitionist LEWIS G. CLARKE. Also known as J. Milton Clark(e) and John M. Clark, Milton was the eighth child of Campbell's biracial daughter Letitia and her husband Daniel (or Donal), a Scotch-Irish widower who immigrated to America to fight the British for this country's freedom. The father's tales of battles at Bunker Hill and Valley Forge during the American Revolution were an inspiration for his sons' persistent struggle against slavery and for the education and uplift of their brethren. That struggle led them to escape slavery regardless of their sometimes privileged status and lighter skin, to join the Underground Railroad movement, to risk their lives to rescue others, and to speak out against slavery the rest of their free lives.

Coauthor with his brother of the *Narratives of the Sufferings of Lewis and Milton Clarke, Sons of a Soldier of the Revolution* (1846), Milton became a popular speaker partly as a result of the brisk sale of the book, which was circulated at abolitionist gatherings years before the Civil War. It is one of several books that historians credit with helping to solidify the abolitionist movement and win northern skeptics who suspected abolitionists of manufacturing stories for political purposes. The work is also considered among the first autobiographical accounts by former slaves, and FREDERICK DOUGLASS mentions it as a model for his own heralded memoir.

The narrative details the brothers' early years, which, for Milton, opens in the late 1820s when at age 6 he witnesses the auction off of the plantation and other property, including slaves, following the death of his grandfather Campbell. A few years earlier, Milton's older brother Lewis had been angrily taken away by one of Campbell's married daughters, who was jealous of another sister's dowry allotment. For Milton, the auction underscored the further dissolution of his family.

The Clarkes had experienced little mistreatment before Campbell's death. The wealthy planter had even promised his daughter and her children freedom in his will. After his death, however, his white heirs violated the will and it subsequently disappeared. Instead, the family auctioned off Milton's siblings despite protests from his father and Judith Campbell Logan, one of Campbell's daughters.

Fortunately, however, young Milton, with his mother, older sister Delia, infant brother Cyrus, and elderly and disabled father, relocated to Lexington to live with Judith, who had fought to prevent their sale. But a few years later Judith died, leaving the family in the hands of husband Joseph, a tanner, known for brutality. According to the narrative, Joseph's new wife Minerva, Judith's younger sister, joined her husband in arbitrarily whipping and beating slaves. After suffering several floggings in his attempts to save his older sister Delia from Logan's advances or to help his mother or to save himself from beatings, Milton survived to see Joseph Logan's property eventually sold to Logan's father, Deacon Logan. The deacon treated the boy well and appointed Milton, 13, his personal servant.

In 1833 Milton and his siblings were orphaned, following the death of his mother from cholera; her husband had died years earlier. Milton found solace teaching himself to play horns and the drums. Eventually Logan allowed Milton to hire himself out as a musician but demanded at least half his earnings. Still, the restricted travel and the chance to earn and save money exposed him to the possibility of freedom. He joined a band of musician slaves traveling by steamboat along the Ohio and Mississippi rivers, playing at balls and parties. The money came "easy" and "fast." Occasionally Milton came within earshot of public speakers reading aloud the "Declaration of Independence," and thoughts of his own freedom, an idea that

"might be just as good for me as others," were born. Though the deacon treated him relatively well, painful memories of early brutality and years of witnessing injustices heaped on others haunted him and he yearned for total freedom—as an ideal and a right.

Traveling as a musician aided other dreams. Longing to see his sister, who had been sold years before for resisting Logan's advances, Milton sought her whereabouts. He learned that she had been sold to a Frenchman in New Orleans whom she persuaded to marry her. After nearly eight years apart, Milton located his sister, now a wealthy widow. Delia asked Milton to accompany her to Kentucky to visit their remaining family. In the summer of 1839, she arrived in Lexington to discuss the purchase of Milton's and Cyrus's freedom. When Milton traveled to meet Delia for additional funds, he received a letter telling him she has died and left her property to him.

His attempt to claim the property was futile. The executor refused his claim because slaves were prohibited from inheriting property. Feeling desperate, in 1841, Milton headed north for Ohio and freedom in the company of his band of musicians. He reached Cincinnati, a hotbed of abolitionist activity and home to a prominent Congregationalist church and seminary. A year later his brother Lewis escaped and after many years apart the two were reunited in Oberlin.

Nicknamed "white slaves" because of their light-skinned appearance, Milton and Lewis became deeply involved with the antislavery movement, lecturing, plotting, and helping others, including their younger brother Cyrus, flee. Their involvement became so well known, and resented by slave catchers, that "Wanted!" posters were issued for their arrest. They spent the next years alluding capture and working with the Underground Railroad. It was also during this period that one of Milton's benefactors, despite the law, sent Milton to school, where he learned to read and write.

Eventually the brothers worked their way to the Boston area, where Milton spent a long and productive life. The two joined the Second Congregational Church, well known then for antislavery work. Through their acquaintance with the church's pastor, Reverend Joseph Lovejoy, also a publisher and brother-in-law of the famous Beecher family, Lewis's story was published in 1843; Milton's contribution was added in 1846. The book became popular enough for the brothers to earn a modest living. Novelist Harriet Beecher

Stowe learned of the family's experiences and drew from them and those of other fugitive slaves in her controversial book *Uncle Tom's Cabin*, which some say was partly responsible for sparking the Civil War.

Some years later, however, the brothers parted ways. Lewis returned to Ohio and then went north to Windsor, Ontario, Canada, after Congress enacted the Fugitive Slave Law of 1850. His brother Milton remained in Cambridge, Massachusetts, where, with the help of local merchant and abolitionist Aaron Safford, he flourished, finding stable work as a caterer and waiter. When the Civil War broke out, he enlisted in the 24th Massachusetts Regiment at age forty-three, returning to the Boston area after the war ended. In 1870, Aaron Safford, a member of the Cambridge Common Council who was preparing to end his term, appointed Milton to replace him. Clarke served out that term and was elected to a second in 1872, becoming the first black elected member of the council in the city's history. But soon after his election, he resigned to take a job as a bank messenger transporting money, which he held for nearly twenty years. Though risky, the job allowed him to support his wife and three sons, as well as his large extended family. He remained a popular speaker and continued to highlight the importance of racial uplift before state legislatures, conventions, and conferences, as well as at clubs and social gatherings.

After several years of declining health, Milton died at age eighty-two. Events of his life and accomplishments earned him a lengthy obituary in the *Cambridge Chronicle*. In addition, Milton Clarke's story, along with that of his brother Lewis, was retold along the Underground Railroad history trail in Cambridge.

FURTHER READING

Clarke, Lewis, and Milton Clarke. *Narrative of the Sufferings of Lewis and Milton Clarke, Sons of a Soldier of the Revolution, During a Captivity of More Than 20 Years Among the Slaveholders of Kentucky, One of the So-Called Christian States of North America. Dictated by Themselves* (1846). Available online at http://docsouth.unc.edu/neh/clarkes/clarkes.html.

"Death of A Noted Character: John Milton Clark Said to Have Been a White Slave—Served in the Civil War." *Cambridge Chronicle*, 2 March 1901.

Kennicott, Patrick C. "Black Persuaders in the Antislavery Movement." *Journal of Black Studies*, vol. 1, no. 1, Sept. 1970.

Vacheenas, Jean, and Betty Volk. "Born in Bondage: History of a Slave Family." *Negro History Bulletin*, vol. 36, no. 5, May 1973.

JANICE L. GREENE

Clarke, Yvette Diane (21 Nov. 1964–), member of the United States Congress, was born Yvette Diane Clarke in Brooklyn, New York, to the Jamaican immigrants Leslie Clarke, an engineer and architect, and Dr. Una S. T. Clarke, a daycare administrator and City Councilwoman. Born and raised in the Flatbush neighborhood of Brooklyn, Clarke graduated with honors from Edward R. Murrow High School in 1982 and earned a scholarship to Oberlin College in Ohio.

While in college, Clarke studied public policy and political science, and won an internship in 1983 with MAJOR R. OWENS, her local congressman. Moving back to New York in 1987, Clarke worked as a child-care specialist and as legislative aide to various elected city officials before becoming director of business development at the Bronx Overall Development Corporation.

By then the Clarke family had already made a foray into politics: Una Clarke became the first Caribbean-born woman to hold a public office in New York City when she became a City Council member in 1991, and ran unsuccessfully against Yvette's former employer, Major Owens, in the 2000 primary for his congressional seat. The following year, when her mother succumbed to term limits, Clarke ran for and won her Council seat, a heavily Caribbean district in Brooklyn. In 2004 she ran against Owens for the House of Representatives, but, like her mother, she lost.

When Owens retired in 2006, Clarke ran again for his seat in a hotly contested Democratic primary, which included a white city councilman and two other black candidates, including Owens's son. After winning the primary, Clarke easily defeated the Republican challenger in November 2006, securing the seat once held by SHIRLEY CHISHOLM, the first black woman elected to the U.S. Congress.

Clarke came under scrutiny during the 2006 election for falsely claiming that she graduated from Oberlin; though she attended the liberal arts college for four years, she fell short of a diploma, and finished her degree at Medgar Evers College in Brooklyn.

After taking a leave of absence for six weeks following uterine surgery in 2007, Clarke authored her first bill that October, one that sought to expedite background checks on legal immigrants seeking

American citizenship. During her first term, Clarke also cosponsored Representative CHARLIE RANGEL's largely symbolic bill that called for reinstatement of the draft. At the height of the unpopular Iraq war, Rangel and Clarke were seeking to show that the sacrifice of military service was disproportionately taken by working-class Americans in an all-volunteer army.

Following her reelection in 2008, Clarke was named the Congressional Black Caucus Whip. Befitting her platform interests in comprehensive immigration reform, affordable housing, and Caribbean concerns, Clarke kept a consistently liberal Democratic voting record and preserved close ties with labor unions. She was named to the Education and Labor, Small Business, and Homeland Security committees in her second term, and she was named chair of the Homeland Security Emerging Threats, Cybersecurity, Science and Technology subcommittee in 2009. Clarke maintained a vocal position in Homeland Security debates, often crossing the aisle to pass bills with Peter King, a Long Island Republican.

FURTHER READING

Hicks, Jonathan P. "Woman in the News: Yvette Diane Clarke; In Her Mother's Footsteps, and Now in Shirley Chisholm's, Too." *New York Times*, 14 Sept. 2006.

ADAM W. GREEN

Clash, Kevin (17 Sept. 1960–), puppeteer, children's entertainer, and voice of Elmo on public television's *Sesame Street*, was born in Baltimore, Maryland, the third of four children of George Clash, a flash welder operator, and Gladys Clash, a daycare provider. Clash grew up in Turner Station, Maryland, a mainly black, working-class, semirural community on Chesapeake Bay, ten miles from downtown Baltimore.

His interest in puppetry and in entertaining children began at an early age. He learned to understand children from living with his mother, who provided daycare in her own home. Clash observed children at close quarters and eventually learned how to entertain them. As a six-year-old, he became fascinated with children's puppet shows on television, sitting close to the screen trying to figure out how to make the puppets he saw on *Kukla, Fran & Ollie, Shari Lewis and Lamb Chop*, and, after 1970, *Sesame Street*. Both Gladys Clash, who taught her son to sew, and George Clash, a handyman and a keen artist, encouraged Kevin's interest

in using scraps of material to make puppets. They also shielded their son from criticism when his fascination with creating dolls and performing for children continued into his teenage years, a time when his male peers disdained such pursuits. An indifferent student, he nonetheless earned some local prominence in 1974, when he gave a presentation using puppets to explain developments in the Soviet Union to his junior high school class and, later, to the entire school. Local newspaper coverage resulted in Clash performing puppet shows on a regular basis at Baltimore's Inner Harbor. By 1977 he was performing regularly with *Caboose*, a children's television show hosted by Stu Kerr on Baltimore's CBS affiliate, a turn that led to guest spots on the nationally syndicated show *Captain Kangaroo*, with Bob Keehshan, an army buddy of Kerr's. Clash, who graduated from Dundalk High School in 1979, despite never attending college, appeared as "Kevin the College Student" on *Captain Kangaroo*. In 1979 Clash also began working with Kermit Love, a costume designer and creator of the *Sesame Street* characters Big Bird and Snuffleupagus. A visit to Love's workshop in New York City resulted in Clash appearing as Cookie Monster in the 1979 Macy's Thanksgiving Day Parade and then meeting with Jim Henson, creator of the Muppets. It did not initially, however, result in the full-time position on *Sesame Street* that Clash had hoped for. He moved to New York City that same year, working on *Captain Kangaroo*. After appearing as Goriddle Gorilla on the syndicated children's fantasy and variety show *The Great Space Coaster* in 1981, Clash began working as a puppeteer on *Sesame Street* in 1983. One day he was handed a rarely used red, furry hand puppet named Elmo, or "Baby Monster." By the time of the 1985–86 *Sesame Street* season, Clash had fashioned a major new character for the show. While one impetus for introducing Elmo was to have a regular red monster on the show in addition to the roster of yellow, blue, and green ones, *Sesame Street* was also seeking to appeal to its growing audience among preschoolers and toddlers. As a result, Elmo was cast with the personality of an enthusiastic and joyful three-and-a-half-year-old child, voiced by Clash in a falsetto. Despite efforts by television executives to tone down what they saw as the puppet's grating laugh, Clash persisted with Elmo's high-pitched chuckle, seeing it as part of the character's charm. Elmo's growing popularity with *Sesame Street* viewers, particularly the important under-four demographic,

Kevin Clash, the voice and movements behind *Sesame Street's* Elmo, poses for a picture with Elmo in New York City, August 2006. (AP Images.)

proved Clash right—as did his first Emmy Award for Outstanding Performer in a Children's Series in 1990. The award was largely for his work with Elmo, although Clash has provided the voice for other characters for *Sesame Street*, including Baby Natasha, Hoots the Owl, and Nobel Price.

Success with Elmo led to a large number of television credits for Clash, the most notable of which were the *Jim Henson Hour* (1989), *The Cosby Show* (1990), *The Torkelsons* (1991), and *Dinosaurs* (1991), as well as several animated movies in which he provided characters' voices, including *Teenage Mutant Ninja Turtles* (1990), *Teenage Mutant Ninja Turtles II: The Secret of the Ooze* (1991), and *Muppet Treasure Island* (1996). In 1993 Clash and his wife Genia had their only child: a daughter named Shannon. The couple would later divorce.

Elmo's massive popularity among young children became evident in 1996, when Tyco toys sold five million "Tickle Me Elmo" dolls in the run up to that year's holiday season. Shortages at some stores resulted in several well-publicized crushes as desperate shoppers fought each other for the plush red Elmo dolls, which vibrated and gave out Elmo's trademark high-pitched laugh when touched. The actress WHOOPI GOLDBERG later related to Clash, perhaps with tongue in cheek, that one shopper even pulled out some of Goldberg's dreadlocks in a mad rush to purchase one of the dolls. A TMX ("Tickle Me Elmo Extreme") doll released in 2006 sold well, but did not match the phenomenal success of its predecessor. The Tickle Me Elmo phenomenon led to the debut of "Elmo's World" in 1998, a self-contained fifteen-minute segment at the end of each *Sesame Street* episode targeted to two- to four-year-olds. Clash also serves as a coexecutive producer of the segment.

Clash has also provided the voice for Elmo and was coexecutive producer on an ABC television special celebrating thirty years of *Sesame Street*, *Elmopalooza* (1998), and a TV movie, *CinderElmo* (1998). The following year the full-length feature film *The Adventures of Elmo in Grouchland* (1999) was released in theaters. In 2001 Clash earned his second daytime Emmy Award for his work on *Sesame Street*, and won that award again in 2002, 2003, 2004, and 2005. In total, he won nine Emmy Awards between 1990 and 2006.

Clash's autobiography, *My Life as a Furry Red Monster: What Being Elmo Has Taught Me about Life, Love, and Laughing Out Loud*, appeared in 2006, enabling Clash to gain a little of the stardom of his more famous creation. The book also revealed to the broader public the little-known fact that Clash is a tall African American, whose natural voice is a rich baritone. From his earliest days in puppetry Clash had noticed that audiences, both black and white, express surprise when they discover he is black; and although none of the monsters on *Sesame Street* are of any particular ethnicity, he is amused when black people declare, "Elmo is a Brother!" (Lee, *New York Times*, Aug. 2006). Clash took a prominent role in launching *Takalani Sesame*, a South African version of *Sesame Street*, in 1999, which involved an eclectic array of characters that represented South Africa's ethnic diversity—for example, the voice of Elmo, renamed Neno, was done by a white Afrikaaner. Clash has also praised the show's inclusion of Kami, an HIV-positive character—a decision criticized by American conservatives opposed to the use of PBS funds in producing *Takalani Sesame*.

Like Elmo, Clash is an eternal optimist who sees the world as "a place of hope and possibility," a belief that encouraged him in November and December 2005 to bring Elmo and a host of other *Sesame Street* characters to New Orleans to entertain children affected by Hurricane Katrina (Clash, 194). In May 2007 Sesame Workshop promoted Clash to the position of senior creative adviser. In 2011 Clash was featured in a documentary film *Being Elmo: A Puppeteer's Journey*.

FURTHER READING

Clash, Kevin. *My Life as a Furry Red Monster: What Being Elmo Has Taught Me About Life, Love, and Laughing Out Loud* (2006).

Lee, Felicia. "Tickled Red to Be Elmo in a Rainbow World," *New York Times* (23 Aug. 2006).

"Sesame Street Principal Puppeteer Kevin Clash Makes Muppet Magic," *Jet* (March 1998).

KIRSTEN CONDRY AND
STEVEN J. NIVEN

Clay, Cassius Marcellus, Jr. *See* Ali, Muhammad.

Clay, William Lacy (Bill), Sr. (30 Apr. 1931–), politician, was born in St. Louis, Missouri, the fourth of seven children born to Irving Clay, a welder, and Luella (Hyatt) Clay, a homemaker. Growing up in a run-down tenement house with no indoor toilet, Clay would later note that a severe lack of basic facilities were afforded to the disenfranchised in the heavily black city, where thousands of residents lived in abject squalor, "just blocks from the downtown business district" (Clay, A Political Voice, p. 11).

While Clay attended St. Nicholas Catholic School, a black parochial school near his house, he worked as well, delivering newspapers at eight years old and selling scrap metal during World War II. By the time he was twelve, he was working at the Good Luck Store, a downtown retail men's clothing store, full-time during the summer and part-time during the school year.

Clay attributed his political awakening and activism to when, as an eighteen-year-old in 1949, he was falsely arrested on suspicion of abetting a double murder. The arresting officer took him into custody at his job, refused to enumerate the charges to either Clay or his employer, and physically abused him. His maternal aunt, who worked as a housecleaner and part-time nanny for one of the members of the board of police commissioners, called her employer, who sent two detectives to end the interrogation at the police house. Clay would later write that "the experience convinced me that survival and political influence are inseparable in American society" (Clay, *A Political Voice*, 14).

During his first year at St. Louis University, Clay was encouraged by his government professor to get involved in a local political campaign. Along with his then-girlfriend and future wife, Carol Ann Johnson, Clay began canvassing for two 18th Ward committee candidates. After graduating with a B.S. in History and Political Science, Clay was drafted into the army in 1953. While stationed at Fort McClellan in Alabama with the Army Chemical Corps, Clay organized a protest of the illegal discriminatory activities on the grounds, including a boycott of the barbershop and a forcible integration of the whites-only swimming pool.

Clay returned to St. Louis after his discharge in 1955, working for the federal government's mapping agency and selling insurance part-time. Continuing his newfound passion for activism, Clay received approval from the national NAACP office to organize a Youth Council chapter in St. Louis, and was elected president of the nascent group. Within the next year, the organization initiated a series of successful protests, forcing previously discriminatory restaurants to serve blacks, bread and dairy companies to hire black truck drivers, and chain supermarkets to employ black butchers.

Clay's first foray as a political candidate came when he ran for St. Louis's 26th Ward alderman, defeating the white incumbent, Bill Brady, in the March 1959 primary, and winning the seat a month later. Clay immediately set to work fighting the city's inherent discriminatory policies. He also continued his participation in equality demonstrations, most notably against the discriminatory hiring practices of Jefferson Bank. Along with members of the Congress of Racial Equality (CORE), Clay was arrested in October 1963 following a protest outside the bank, and served nearly four months in prison.

Through the 1960s, Clay balanced his position as an elected city official as well as a union business representative and educational director for a local steamfitter's union. Following congressional redistricting that resulted in a black-majority district of St. Louis, the longtime incumbent, Frank Karsten, chose to retire. Behind the endorsements of committeemen, wards, and black newspapers, Clay defeated a host of primary challengers for the 1968 Democratic nomination to the vacant seat. In the general election, he defeated Curtis Crawford, an African American Republican who had recently switched parties. As Clay described the race, while Crawford "advocated self-help projects for Negroes and a reduction in federal expenditures, closely following the Republican Party's national campaign platform, I continued to promote … racial equality and workers' rights" (*A Political Voice*, 166).

Clay easily won the election, becoming the first African American U.S. representative from Missouri. Along with seven other black representatives, including fellow freshmen SHIRLEY CHISHOLM and LOUIS STOKES, Clay helped found a congressional caucus in 1969 to "serve as a coordinating body on issues of special concern to the black community" (*Washington Afro-American*, 11 Nov. 1969); the caucus was officially named the Congressional Black Caucus by Representative CHARLES RANGEL in 1971.

Clay was reelected to his seat fifteen times until his retirement in 2001, when he was the third-most senior member of the House. Over that span, he kept labor issues at the forefront of his interests, serving on the Committee on Education and Labor for his entire career, and becoming the committee's ranking minority party member from 1995 through 2000. Clay also became the chair of the Post Office and Civil Service Committee from 1991 until 1995, when the new Republican majority cut it from the House.

Clay's legislative victories in Congress included his sponsorship of the Family and Medical Leave Act, one of the first major bills that Democratic President Bill Clinton signed into law in 1993; and an amendment to the 1939 Hatch Act, softening the stance on restrictions to the political activities of federal workers.

Clay suffered a handful of ethics controversies, including his involvement in the 1992 House banking scandal, in which he was one of 22 representatives reprimanded for receiving overdraft protection from the House bank. However, his popularity in Missouri's 1st congressional district remained untarnished, and he coasted to reelection that year.

His origins as a civil rights worker from the grass roots stood constant throughout his career. As if echoing his political awakening when he was eighteen years old, Clay outspokenly reaffirmed the need to speak for the disenfranchised in his 1982 congressional reelection bid, when the *New York Times* quoted him as saying, "I don't represent all people. I represent those who are in need of representation. I have no intention of representing those powerful interests who walk over the powerless people" (3 Aug. 1982). When Clay announced his intention to retire in 2000, his son, William Lacy Clay Jr., a Missouri state legislator for seventeen years, ran for his vacant seat and won. As well as his son, Clay had two daughters, Vicki and Michelle.

FURTHER READING

Clay, William L. *A Political Voice at the Grass Roots* (2004).

Clay, William L. *Just Permanent Interests: Black Americans in Congress, 1870–1991* (1992).

ADAM W. GREEN

Clayton, Buck (12 Nov. 1911–8 Dec. 1991), jazz trumpeter and arranger, was born Wilbur Dorsey Clayton in Parsons, Kansas, the son of Simeon Oliver Clayton, a musician, and Aritha Anne Dorsey, a schoolteacher, pianist, and singer. His father's church orchestra rehearsed at their home, and in his youth Clayton experimented with different instruments, learning their basic scales. He took piano lessons from ages six to eighteen. At about age sixteen he was deeply impressed by a trumpeter in GEORGE E. LEE's big band, and he decided to take up the instrument.

Before graduating from high school, Clayton hoboed by train to Los Angeles. Failing in his attempt to secure work as a musician, he returned home, resumed his schooling, and graduated, probably around 1932. On his second trip to Los Angeles, Clayton succeeded as a trumpeter, holding a long engagement in a dime-a-dance hall, the Red Mill, until it burned down. He then became a member of Charlie Echols's big band for over a year, during which time he began to learn to orchestrate for big bands. As work diminished for Echols, Clayton began performing on Hollywood movie soundtracks and at local clubs with Earl Dancer's band, until Dancer's habitual gambling problems forced the group to disband in 1934.

Clayton then secured a job as a bandleader in Shanghai, China. Just before departing, he and a dancer named Gladys Henderson (known as "Derb") obtained a marriage license, but they were unsure about marrying. DUKE ELLINGTON forced the issue by staging the marriage as a grand publicity event at Paramount Studios without Clayton's prior knowledge. Their marriage ended in divorce a few years later in New York City.

Clayton's band held residencies in Shanghai from 1934 into 1936. Returning once again to Los Angeles, he led bands but soon decided to seek the more challenging musical scene in New York City. En route in midsummer 1936, he stopped in Kansas City, Missouri, and met the pianist COUNT BASIE and his band. They had heard Clayton on radio broadcasts from California, and since the trumpeter HOT LIPS PAGE had recently left the group, Basie asked Clayton if he would join. Clayton went to Parsons to visit his family and then returned to Kansas City to join Basie at the Reno Club, thus becoming a featured soloist in what was about to become one of jazz's greatest ensembles.

A few months later Basie left on a tour designed to get the band in shape for New York. In Chicago the group had a disastrous experience trying to serve as the pit orchestra for a show at the Grand Terrace Ballroom, owing to the poor musical reading skills of some members of the ensemble, newly expanded to suit New York demands for a big band. Clayton, one of the best readers, wore his lip out trying to cover for others and hence was unable to appear on Basie's legendary small-group recording, made in Chicago in October 1936 under the name of Jones-Smith Inc., with the trumpeter Carl "Tatti" Smith taking Clayton's place.

On 24 December 1936 Basie made his debut in New York, where Clayton's wife, Derb, was then working. Soon afterward she left Clayton permanently. Over the next six years Clayton's career followed Basie's energetic routine of extensive national touring. During this time Clayton contributed memorable solos on "Swingin' at the Daisy Chain," "One O'Clock Jump," "Topsy" (all 1937), "Sent for You Yesterday," "Jumpin' at the Woodside" (both 1938), "Dickie's Dream" (1939), and "Goin' to Chicago Blues" (1941; arranged by Clayton). He appeared with the band in the film *Reveille with Beverly* (1943). Clayton occasionally recorded apart from Basie; the most notable of these sessions was as a sideman for singer BILLIE HOLIDAY in TEDDY WILSON's groups and in her own, including versions of "Why Was I Born?" "Getting Some Fun out of Life," "He's Funny That Way" (all 1937), "My First Impression of You," and "If Dreams Come True" (both 1938). Clayton became one of Holiday's closest friends; in her autobiography she called him "the prettiest man I'd ever seen."

Drafted into the army in November 1943, Clayton was stationed in New Jersey until the end of the war, playing in army bands. Early in 1946, soon after his discharge, he finally obtained his divorce from Derb and immediately married Patricia Roberta DeVigne; they had two children. In October 1946 he made the first of several tours with Jazz at the Philharmonic. The following year he established a sextet at Café Society in New York. From September 1949 to April 1950 Clayton toured Europe with his group.

After returning home, Clayton continued his work as a leader while also playing in the clarinetist Tony Parenti's Dixieland band and holding a residency at the Embers Club as a member of the pianist Joey Bushkin's quartet. In February 1953 he embarked on a lengthy European tour, working first with the clarinetist Mezz Mezzrow, continuing with the singer Frank Sinatra, and visiting Sweden with the singer BABS GONZALES.

Back in New York at year's end, Clayton was asked by the promoter John Hammond to head a series of long-playing jam sessions recorded for the Columbia label, including *The Huckle-Buck and Robbins' Nest* (1953). Extending to 1956, these sessions, together with contemporary ones recorded by fellow ex-Basie trombonist VIC DICKENSON for the Vanguard label, became the central documents of "mainstream jazz," amalgamating swing and Dixieland styles. During this period Clayton held further residencies in New York and made regional tours, including one with Bushkin. He appeared in the movie *The Benny Goodman Story* (1955) and toured with Benny Goodman to South America.

Clayton performed in April 1958 on the television series *The Subject Is Jazz*. Early in July he took part in the Newport Jazz Festival (preserved on the film *Jazz on a Summer's Day* [1958]), and made another television appearance on *Art Ford's Jazz Party* with Holiday's group. Late that same month he traveled with the promoter and pianist George Wein's band to the Brussels World's Fair, where they worked with the reed player SIDNEY BECHET. Clayton performed in London in September 1959. Later that year he joined the guitarist Eddie Condon's band in New York. He worked with the pianist Marian McPartland's trio, with Dickenson, and with the tenor saxophonist Bud Freeman. Sometimes he played in all-star swing and Dixieland bands at the Central Plaza and Stuyvesant Casino in New York.

During the first of his annual European tours during the 1960s, Clayton made the film *Buck Clayton and His All Stars* (1961) in Belgium. He toured with the singer JIMMY RUSHING in the summer of 1962. That November he went with Condon to Toronto, where he subsequently led his own band. Beginning in 1963 he often worked with the English trumpeter Humphrey Lyttelton during his European tours, moments of which were captured on the British television series *Jazz 625* (1965) and *Jazz Goes to College* (1966 and 1967). Clayton also toured Japan and Australia with Condon in 1964, and he participated in American jazz festivals.

Clayton suffered various illnesses from 1967 onward, including hernias, severe lip troubles, and later, a near-fatal ulcer. He virtually abandoned the trumpet and instead held day jobs of little interest to him. He managed to play trumpet for the film *L'Adventure* [*sic*] *du jazz* (1970), and he was interviewed for the film *Born to Swing* (1973). After undergoing major dental work in 1974, Clayton began to focus on writing arrangements. He resumed playing for a State Department–sponsored tour to Africa in 1977 but finally gave up playing after performing at the Grande Parade du Jazz in Nice in 1979.

From 1978 to 1982 Clayton taught at Hunter College, a campus of City University of New York. In 1983 he joined the Countsmen for a European tour, for which he served as leader, arranger, and conductor. After writing further arrangements for a small group, Clayton established his own big band in 1987. Writing many new scores for it, he remained active up to the weekend of his death in New York City.

Clayton was a controlled, tasteful, nearly perfect trumpeter who adopted moderated elements of LOUIS ARMSTRONG's style. He never achieved the mind-boggling originality and audacity of Armstrong in his melodies, but in his ever-present tunefulness he had the good taste to avoid Armstrong's propensity for gaudy technical displays.

Clayton complained that he came to hate the cup mute because Basie always wanted him to record with it (although Basie did not mind if Clayton played unmuted in public performance). Perhaps the truth is somewhat more complicated, since he used the device routinely in Basie's absence on the sessions with Holiday. The several aforementioned Holiday titles encapsulate his style, ranging from simple renderings of pop song melodies to tricky improvised lines, and from delicate muted embroideries barely heard beneath Holiday's voice to forceful, unmuted leadership of collectively improvised passages.

FURTHER READING

Clayton's oral history, taken by interviewer Stanley Dance (c. 1975), is at the Institute of Jazz Studies, Newark, New Jersey.

Clayton, Buck, with Nancy Miller Elliott. *Buck Clayton's Jazz World* (1986).

Chilton, John. *The Billie Holiday Story* (1975).

Dance, Stanley. *The World of Count Basie* (1980).

Hoefer, George. "A Brief Biography of Buck Clayton," *Down Beat*, 19 Jan. 1961: 16–17.

Weir, Bob. *Buck Clayton: A Discography* (1989).

Obituary: *New York Times*, 12 Dec. 1991.

This entry is taken from the *American National Biography* and is published here with the permission of the American Council of Learned Societies.

BARRY KERNFELD

Clayton, Eva McPherson (16 Sept. 1934–), first African American woman elected to the U.S. Congress from North Carolina, was born Eva McPherson in Chatham County, Georgia. The daughter of Thomas McPherson, an insurance agent, and Josephine Martin, a teacher, Eva attended Johnson C. Smith University in Charlotte, North Carolina, and earned her bachelor of science degree in Biology in 1955. In 1956 she married Theaoseus Clayton, also an alumnus of Johnson C. Smith. The Claytons had four children: Joanne, Theaoseus Jr., Martin, and Reuben.

Following their marriage both Eva Clayton and her husband pursued graduate degrees at North Carolina Central University in Durham. Theaoseus received his law degree in 1961, and Eva earned her master's of science in Biology and General Science in 1962. The young couple moved to Warrenton, North Carolina, where Theaoseus established himself as a lawyer and both became active in voter registration drives. Eva also pursued her law degree at the University of North Carolina, Chapel Hill School of Law and Government and became involved in the civil rights movement. She once picketed her husband's law office because the building he co-owned with his white partner had a segregated restaurant on the first floor. In 1968 Eva Clayton was encouraged by the civil rights activist VERNON JORDAN to run for the U.S. House of Representatives against the longtime white Democratic incumbent, L. H. Fountain of North Carolina's Second Congressional District. Clayton lost, receiving 30 percent of the vote, but her door-to-door campaign for black-voter registration increased voter registration in her district by 12 percent. After two years in law school Clayton became pregnant with her fourth child and decided to leave school. "I wasn't super enough to be a super mom," Clayton said in a 1993 interview, "My husband was supportive, but I felt enormously guilty. I think I would do it differently now. I think I would know how to demand more of my husband" (Gill, 209).

Following the birth of her fourth child Clayton decided not to return to school, but she became more active in a variety of community leadership positions in North Carolina. From 1968 to 1971 she worked to establish the Eastern North Carolina Development Corporation, through which she created some of the area's first day care facilities. In 1971 Clayton was appointed director of the newly established North Carolina Health Manpower Development Program at the University of North Carolina–Chapel Hill. The inter-institutional program was formed to address the shortage of health care professionals in North Carolina, especially among underrepresented minority populations.

From 1974 to 1976 Clayton served as executive director of the Soul City Foundation. The Soul City project was begun by the longtime civil rights activist and former Congress of Racial Equality (CORE) director FLOYD BIXLER MCKISSICK to develop a successful all-black town in Warren County, North Carolina. Although several Soul City programs were still in existence in the early twenty-first century, the project itself collapsed after federal funds were withdrawn in 1979.

In 1977 Governor Jim Hunt appointed Clayton the assistant secretary for natural resources for North Carolina, a position she held until 1981. Clayton then created a consulting company, Technical Resources International, Inc. (TRI), which she operated as president until 1992. Clayton did not forgo local politics for the business world, however. In 1982 she was elected chair of the Warren County Board of Commissioners, a position she held until 1990, when she was named Outstanding North Carolina County Commissioner.

Following the 1990 U.S. census, a number of states across the country redrew their voting districts to provide for better representation of growing minority populations. North Carolina gained two new majority-black congressional districts, immediately creating controversy but also positioning the state to have black representation for the first time since 1901. One of these districts, the First, included Clayton's Warren County, and she decided to once again run for U.S. Congress. In 1992 Clayton became one of seven candidates in the district's Democratic primary; she was one of five blacks and the only woman. Like many women running in 1992, described as the "Year of the Woman" in American politics, Clayton gained campaign funding and volunteer support from a number of national women's organizations and unions, such as the Teamsters Union. She was able to capitalize on her name recognition in the areas surrounding Warren County and advocated diversity in hiring practices, health care, and better employment across the new district. Clayton won in a runoff during the primaries and carried the general election with 61 percent of the vote.

In 1992 Clayton joined an unprecedented number of blacks and women in the 103rd Congress freshman class, to which she was also selected as president. She was the first woman and the first black to hold the position. Over the course of the next ten years in the House, Clayton developed a reputation for being a mature, assertive, friendly, and discerning leader within the Democratic Party. She was active on the Agriculture and Budget Committees, eventually becoming the ranking Democrat on the Department Operations, Oversight, Nutrition and Forestry Subcommittee. Clayton also served as chair of the House Rural Caucus. Known for her liberal positions Clayton supported social programs that provided crop subsidies, affordable housing, nutrition information, and food stamp assistance to the disadvantaged members of rural communities. When Hurricane Floyd battered North Carolina in 1999, Clayton was instrumental in securing federal relief for the area and provided support not just through legislation but also by dedicating her time and labor to assisting in the recovery efforts.

Clayton retired from the House in 2002 and was pleased to see her seat taken by her longtime friend and former campaign manager Frank W. Ballance, Jr. Ballance's election marked the first time in North Carolina history that a congressional seat passed from one African American to another. In 2003 Clayton was appointed special adviser to the director general of the Food and Agriculture Organization of the United Nations, addressing issues of world hunger. Following her three-year assignment in Rome, Italy, Clayton returned to North Carolina and began a "50 by 2015" campaign to reduce hunger in the state by 50 percent by the year 2015. Clayton worked with several organizations, including Second Harvest Food Banks and the Presbyterian Church (USA), to establish the North Carolina Hunger Forum, which began its statewide campaign in April 2007.

FURTHER READING

Betts, Jack. "Carrying on the Legacy—It's Been 100 Years since N.C. Sent a Black Person to Congress, Almost 50 Years for a Woman. Eva Clayton Is Hoping to Change All That," *Charlotte Observer*, 20 Sept. 1992.

Christensen, Rob. "Clayton to Retire in 2002," *Raleigh News and Observer*, 21 Nov. 2001.

Clayton, Dewy M., and Angela M. Stallings. "Black Women in Congress: Striking the Balance," *Journal of Black Studies*, vol. 30 (2000).

Gill, LaVerne McCain. *African American Women in Congress: Forming and Transforming History* (1997).

MONIKA R. ALSTON

Clayton, Mayme (4 Aug. 1923–13 Oct. 2006), librarian, bibliophile, and African Americana collector, was born Mayme Jewell Agnew at Van Buren, Arkansas, to Jerry and Mary Agnew. Jerry Agnew was a general store manager and the only African American merchant in town at the time. His wife Mary Knight Agnew was a homemaker. Upon graduation from high school, Mayme Agnew enrolled at Lincoln University in Missouri and later moved to New York. There, she met and married Andrew Lee Clayton in 1946. The couple had three sons. The Clayton family relocated to California, where Mayme Clayton graduated from the University of California, Berkeley, with a B.A. in History. She earned a master of library science degree through an external degree program run by Goddard College in Vermont in the 1970s and in 1983 was awarded a doctorate in Humanities from La Sierra University in Riverside, California.

Clayton's career led to several library positions, including work at the Doheny Library at the University of Southern California in 1952. Five years later she moved to the University of California, Los Angeles, to work as a law librarian for the next fifteen years. She served as consultant and founding member of the Afro-American Studies Center Library at UCLA, seeking to serve UCLA's African American student population during the Black Power era of the turbulent 1960s. Responsible for establishing and augmenting the collection, she sought to include out-of-print and rare books by those authors she deemed essential to support an African American studies program. The institution sought her expertise in establishing the Afro-American Studies Center Library, but at the time balked at funding these costly out-of-print resources. This intensified her desire to collect and preserve the African American primary sources that might otherwise have fallen into obscurity.

Clayton had been a private collector of African Americana for years and decided to expand this hobby into a more a formalized endeavor, known as the Western States Black Research and Educational Center. Since its inception in 1972, the collection has increased, offering content and scope that rival that of New York Public Library's prestigious Arthur A. Schomburg Center. Clayton amassed a collection said to be the largest of its kind on the West Coast. She single-handedly accumulated more than seventy-five thousand pieces of memorabilia and photographs, some dating back to the 1850s, more than ten thousand rare 33 rpm and 78 rpm phonograph record albums, and six hundred films dating back as early as 1916. Among those are films directed by OSCAR MICHEAUX, including the silent film *Body and Soul*, in which PAUL ROBESON made his acting debut. The vast collection also includes sheet music, movie posters, slave advertisements, newspaper clippings, family histories, and the flagship collection of more than thirty thousand books. Many of the books and other primary sources date back to the pre–Civil War era.

Clayton worked as a co-owner of Universal Bookstore at Hollywood in 1972. When the used bookstore eventually closed, its owners divided the remaining stock of books among themselves. Clayton claimed more than four thousand books on African American history and culture and was thus able to increase her private collection. Clayton was known by colleagues in the Antiquarian Society, as well as antique book dealers throughout the country, who alerted her to books and other materials of interest. A resourceful woman with acuity for finding for rare treasures, Clayton discovered a coveted first issue, dated November 1945, of *Ebony* magazine for just a dime at a garage sale. She scoured used bookstores throughout the United States, for many of her additions to the collection.

Mayme Clayton coedited and compiled the *Index to the Afro-American Rare Book Collection*, which serves as a selected list of the holdings in the Western States Black Research Center. The collection contains first editions, signed by such authors as ALEX HALEY, MARTIN LUTHER KING JR., ZORA NEALE HURSTON, PAUL LAURENCE DUNBAR, and BOOKER T. WASHINGTON. She also acquired handwritten correspondence by GEORGE WASHINGTON CARVER and a typewritten letter by JOSEPHINE BAKER. The library collection includes treasures such as a rare signed copy of PHILLIS WHEATLEY's 1773 *Poems on Various Subjects Religious and Moral*, which is considered the first book published by an American of African descent. Because a New York bookseller desperately needed the money, he sold the slim volume to Mayme Clayton for $600 in 1972. Although this was a steep price, Clayton managed to save the money to purchase this exceptionally rare find. Clayton used her own modest resources to purchase rare books, historical documents, papers, African American periodicals, and other ephemera from antique bookstores, secondhand stores, flea markets, and tag sales. For example, when she learned that an African American newspaper was going out of business, she purchased the collection of the newspaper's photographs. She rescued many other African American artifacts discarded from people's attics, basements, and even trash heaps. Clayton enthusiastically accumulated thousands of pieces of African American books and memorabilia during a time when her contemporaries had little interest in collecting materials from bygone eras because a portion of the artifacts and documents deal with the painful and unpleasant aspects in African American history and culture such as slavery and racism.

At her residence of more than sixty years, in the West Adams district of Los Angeles, California, Mayme Clayton stored her private collection, complemented by storage space in her two-car garage at the back of the house. Full to the rafters with stacks of books and extremely old documents, the old garage became vulnerable to insects, a leaky roof, mold, and theft. The collection since relocated to a more secure and spacious facility at the former Los Angeles Superior Court building at Culver City, California. In April 2004, Clayton's son Avery Clayton, an artist, retired teacher, and executive director of the Western States Black Research and Educational Center, began plans to develop a permanent, state-of-the-art research facility, library, and cultural center named for his mother.

Clayton received numerous awards, including the Paul Robeson Award and the Phoenix Award, and was one of the founders of the Black American Cinema Society. Mayme Clayton died of pancreatic cancer in 2006.

FURTHER READING

Clayton, Avery. "Mayme Clayton: Keeper of an American Legacy," *Western States Black Research and Educational Center (WSBREC) News* (1):9 (2003).

Western States Black Research and Educational Center, Mayme A. Clayton Library and Museum, http://www.wsbrec.org.

MELANIE THOMAS

Cleage, Albert Buford, Jr. *See* Agyeman, Jaramogi Abebe.

Cleage, Pearl (Michelle Cleage) (7 Dec. 1948–), writer, performance artist, and activist, was born in Springfield, Massachusetts, but grew up in Detroit, Michigan, as the younger of two daughters of ALBERT BUFORD CLEAGE JR., a minister, and Doris Graham Cleage, an elementary school teacher.

Pearl Cleage discusses her play *A Song for Coretta*, in Atlanta, 2007. (AP Images.)

Her father created his own religious denomination, the Black Nationalist Christian Church. His church, the Shrine of the Black Madonna, was most noted for its eighteen-foot pulpit portrait of a black Madonna painted by Glanton Dowdell. Cleage's parents bestowed upon her family an Afrocentric view of the world. She grew up surrounded by books and listening to political discussions about black liberation and empowerment. She and her sister Kristen were taught early on that growing up in a home of black middle-class privilege meant also having social and political responsibilities to contribute to the black community's liberation out of poverty, disenfranchisement, and racism.

A gifted student, Cleage attended Northwestern High School, where she excelled academically, graduating at the top of her class in 1966. Cleage enrolled in Howard University to study playwriting. Two of her early plays, *Hymn for the Rebels* (1968) and *Duet for Three Voices* (1969), were produced at the university. During the summer of 1969 Cleage attended a theater program at Yale University. At the end of the summer she decided not return to Howard University and relocated to Atlanta, Georgia. Her first job in Atlanta was working as a member of the field collections staff at the King Center, where she collected primary source data on the civil rights movement and transcribed MARTIN LUTHER KING JR.'s speeches as well as the speeches of other prominent civil rights leaders. After a brief courtship that year, she married Michael Lomax, a local politician who later became Fulton County Commission chairman. One daughter, Deignan Njeri, was born from this marriage. Cleage again took up her undergraduate studies, and in 1971 she graduated from Spelman College with a bachelor of arts in Drama. She continued her studies in Jamaica, where she took graduate courses at the University of the West Indies. The 1970s would see Cleage's entrance into radio and television media. From 1970 to 1971 she worked as a host and interviewer for *Black Viewpoints*, an educational television magazine show produced by Clark College for WETV Atlanta. In 1972 she worked as a writer and interviewer for *Ebony Beat Journal* for radio station WQXI Atlanta before becoming the program's head writer and associate producer. From 1972 to 1973 she worked for WXIA Atlanta as an executive producer. During this time Cleage published her first book, a collection of poetry titled *We Don't Need No Music* (1971), and a new dramatic work titled *The Sale* (1972) was performed at Spelman College. Growing up in a home of political activity (her

father ran for Michigan governor in 1962 on the Freedom Now ticket) was groundwork for her foray into Atlanta civic service and local politics. In 1974 she became the director of communications for the City of Atlanta, and later the press secretary and speechwriter for MAYNARD HOLBROOK JACKSON JR., the first black mayor of Atlanta. However, the stress and strain of trying to balance a life in political circles with domestic family circles as a political wife to Lomax and a mother took its toll on her marriage. In 1979 she and Lomax divorced.

In 1980 Cleage published her second collection of poetry, *Dear Dark Face: Portrait of a People*. The following year she joined Atlanta's Just Us Theatre Company as a playwright-in-residence, where she wrote several new works, including *Hospice* (1983), which was later produced in New York City by the New Federal Theatre. The production received five Audelco Awards, including a playwriting award for Cleage. In addition, her *puppetplay* (1983) opened the Negro Ensemble Company's theater season in New York City. Not only did Cleage's dramatic writings emerge on the national scene, but also her writing talents in other literary genres began to receive wider recognition. With the help of her friends, Cleage privately published an autobiographical short story titled "One for the Brothers" (1983). In 1986 she became the founding editor for *Catalyst* magazine, a literary publication, and two years later began writing a column in the *Atlanta Tribune*. Here she wrote commentaries about politics, racism, sexism, empowerment of women, and domestic violence. Numerous other essays about issues affecting the black community, but particularly those issues that affected black women, also appeared in national publications, such as *Essence* magazine and *Ms.* magazine. Cleage's *Atlanta Tribune* column garnered her a number of Outstanding Columnist awards from the Atlanta Association of Black Journalists, Atlanta Association of Media Women, and the Association of Southern Writers. She was also the recipient of numerous honors, grants, and awards, including a National Endowment of Arts Grant and a Georgia Council of the Arts Grant for her work as the artistic director of Just Us (1987–1994).

In 1989 Cleage published a collection of short stories for young adult readers, titled *The Brass Bed and Other Stories*. She wrote two of her most controversial works during the 1990s. The first, *Mad at Miles* (1990), was a collection of essays about domestic violence inspired by the jazz artist MILES DAVIS's confession that he had slapped his former wife, the actress CICELY TYSON. Three years later Cleage published another much discussed collection of essays, *Deals with the Devil and Other Reasons to Riot* (1993). Compiled from her *Atlanta Tribune* columns and other writings, it included her observations about the African American community, motherhood, sex, solitude, violence against women, and a host of newsmakers, including Anita Hill, EARVIN "MAGIC" JOHNSON JR., former president Bill Clinton, SPIKE LEE, the former Washington, D.C., mayor MARION SHEPILOV BARRY JR., and the U.S. Supreme Court justice CLARENCE THOMAS. She also wrote five new dramatic works. Two were one-act plays, *Chain* and *Late Bus to Mecca* (both 1992), which were produced in New York City by the Women's Project. *Chain* dramatized a family's desperate attempt to protect its daughter from urban violence by chaining her to a metal pipe. In *Late Bus to Mecca*, Cleage dramatized a chance encounter between a prostitute named Ava waiting for a friend and a woman who appeared to have been abused or is homeless. Appearing too emotionally shattered to speak, she listens while Ava, who speaks the only lines in the play, dispenses makeup tips and advice for living. Their encounter becomes a moment of sisterhood between two African American women. From 1994 until 1997, the Alliance Theatre in Atlanta produced three of her full-length plays—*Flyin' West* (1994), *Blues for Alabama Sky* (1995), and *Bourbon at the Border* (1997)—as part of an artistic collaboration between Cleage and the theater's artistic director Kenny Leon. *Flyin' West*, set in the historic midwestern all-black town of Nicodemus, Kansas, during the late nineteenth century, dramatized the lives of four women homesteaders. The play examined the issues of racial self-hatred, domestic violence, black nationalism, and the concept of what defines a family. From the 1990s through the early decades of the twenty-first century, the play was among the most produced African American plays in regional, college, and university theaters throughout the United States. *Blues for Alabama Sky* (1995) was set in the Harlem summer of 1930 and dramatized the lives of a gay costume designer, a nightclub singer, a social worker, a physician, and a laborer from Alabama. The play explored the issues of homosexuality in the black community, abortion, and the cultural schism between southern rural African Americans and northern urban blacks in the backdrop of the death of the Harlem Renaissance and the birth of the Great Depression. *Blues for Alabama Sky* was later produced by the Alliance Theatre as part of

the cultural activities of the 1996 Olympics held in Atlanta. *Bourbon at the Border* (1997) was set in the summer of 1995 in an apartment overlooking the Ambassador Bridge to Windsor, Ontario. The play portrayed the lives of a middle-aged couple, former civil rights workers, who have spent the years since the 1964 Mississippi Freedom Summer voter registration drive coping with survivor guilt, trying to heal the emotional scars of racism, and living with the continued disappointment of social injustice. During this time Cleage also participated in numerous playwright and scholar residencies at colleges and universities throughout the United States, including Spelman College, Smith College, Amherst College, Laney College, and Illinois State University.

Cleage and her longtime friend, the writer and performance artist Zaron Burnett Jr., cocreated a multimedia performance art piece called *Live at Club Zebra* (1991–1992). The piece, based on the 1920s speakeasies, was performed throughout Atlanta, including at the National Black Arts Festival, made appearances at the National Black Theatre Festival in Winston-Salem, North Carolina, and toured to New York City. In 1994 Cleage married Burnett in a small private ceremony. Three years later Cleage published her first novel, *What Looks Like Crazy on an Ordinary Day*. The book, which told the story of Ava Johnson (first seen in *Late Bus to Mecca*), an HIV-positive woman who returns home to Idlewood, Michigan, to be near her family, was chosen as a 1998 Oprah Book Club Selection.

Cleage's entrée into the world of fiction continued to flourish with the publication of four additional novels between 2001 and 2006. Her second novel, *I Wish I Had a Red Dress* (2001), continued the story of her Idlewood characters. For her remaining three novels she changed the locations to Atlanta, a city Cleage had called home for thirty-eight years. Her third novel, *Some Things I Never Thought I'd Do* (2003), introduced the urban warrior character Blue Hamilton, who was determined to create a safe urban Atlanta African American neighborhood. Next, *Babylon Sisters* (2005), also set in Atlanta, was about a mother-daughter relationship. Cleage's *Baby Brother Blues* (2006) featured the return of the fictional Blue Hamilton. In 2007, the book won an NAACP Image Award for Outstanding Literary Work in the area of fiction.

In 2006 OPRAH WINFREY commissioned Cleage to write a poem for Winfrey's three-day event celebrating African American sisterhood. *Celebration: We Speak Your Name* honored the contributions of twenty-four African American women. Begun by BILL COSBY and CAMILLE COSBY, the William and Camille Olivia Hanks Cosby Endowed Professorship in the women's studies department (2005–2007) at her alma mater Spelman College provided Cleage with a new venue for the development of experimental dramatic work. The play, *A Song for Coretta* (2007), was inspired by the sight of mourners standing in a line to pay their respects to the late CORETTA SCOTT KING.

When asked about her writing at a public lecture, Cleage said the following:

> The literary tradition that I embrace is one which endorses, even requires that the work have some relevance to the struggle of black people to be free. As a feminist, I also require that my work have something meaningful to say about gender issues (2002).

Whether she is writing poetry, drama, fiction, or nonfiction, Cleage has continued to write about racism and sexism, about powerful fictional women and principled fictional male urban heroes.

FURTHER READING

Giles, Freda Scott. *The Motion of Herstory: Three Plays by Pearl Cleage, African American Review,* vol. 31, no. 4, Contemporary Theatre Issue (Winter, 1997).

Perkins, Kathy, and Roberto, Uno, eds. *Contemporary Plays by Women of Color: An Anthology* (1996).

Roberts, Tara. "Pearls of Wisdom," *Essence,* vol. 28, no. 8 (Dec. 1997).

VANITA VACTOR

Cleaver, Eldridge (31 Aug. 1935–1 May 1998), Black Panther Party leader, was born Leroy Eldridge Cleaver in Wabbaseka, Arkansas, the third child of six born to Leroy Cleaver, a nightclub pianist and waiter, and Thelma (maiden name unknown), an elementary school teacher and janitor. After a brief stay in Phoenix, Arizona, the family moved in 1947 to East Los Angeles, where Leroy Cleaver, often abusive and violent toward Eldridge and his mother, eventually abandoned them. Soon afterward, Eldridge was arrested for the first time, for stealing a bicycle, and from 1949 until 1966 he spent most of his time in reform school and prison. At one reform school in 1950, he briefly converted to Roman Catholicism—less out of religious conviction, he later recalled, than because at that school most Catholics were black or Latino and most Protestants were white. In 1952 he was returned to reform school after being caught selling marijuana.

Eldridge Cleaver, Minister of Information for the Black Panther Party and presidential candidate for the Peace and Freedom Party speaking at the Woods-Brown Outdoor Theatre, American University, in Washington, D.C., October 1968,. (Library of Congress.)

In 1954, at age eighteen, Cleaver was convicted on a felony charge of selling marijuana and sent to prison. He would eventually spend time in Soledad, San Quentin, and Folsom prisons, and while he was incarcerated he began to take an interest in politics. The national controversy about *Brown v. Board of Education* (1954), the Supreme Court ruling outlawing school segregation, Cleaver recalled, "awakened me to my position in America and I began to form a concept of what it meant to be black in white America" (*Soul on Ice,* 3). When a white guard tore down a picture of a white woman Cleaver had pinned up in his cell and told him instead to post up a picture of a black woman, he became interested in how black men internalized racist standards of white beauty. The 1955 murder of EMMETT TILL, a young black boy from Chicago who was brutally killed in Mississippi for "wolf whistling" at a white woman, only increased Cleaver's obsession, especially when he found himself attracted to the woman in question after seeing her photograph. "Somehow," he writes in *Soul on Ice*, "I arrived at the conclusion that, as a matter of principle, it was of paramount importance for me to have an antagonistic, ruthless attitude towards white women" (13). At this time, Cleaver later recalled, he believed that rape, especially against white women, was a political act. Meanwhile, in 1958 Cleaver was arrested for the attempted rape of a nurse and again sent to prison. There he read voraciously, including works by Thomas Paine, Voltaire, Karl Marx, and RICHARD WRIGHT. He also joined the Nation of Islam, whose most prominent spokesman, MALCOLM X, had been, like Cleaver, a petty criminal who discovered radicalism and black nationalism in prison. When Malcolm split with the black Muslims, Cleaver supported him, and when Malcolm was killed in 1965—and supporters of the Nation of Islam were suspected—Cleaver began to write in order to "save myself" from the profound confusion caused by this traumatic event. His lawyer, Beverly Axelrod, took these essays, in which he most clearly articulated, and rejected, his earlier position on rape, to the editor of the liberal, Catholic *Ramparts* magazine, and they were later published in *Soul on Ice*.

In November 1966 Cleaver was paroled, in part because his writings had attracted the support of literary stars like Norman Mailer, and he became a writer and editor for *Ramparts*. At about the same time, Cleaver met HUEY NEWTON and BOBBY SEALE, who had founded the Black Panther Party in Oakland in 1966. Influenced by revolutionaries in China, Cuba, Algeria, and Vietnam, the Panthers blended black nationalism with socialism and propounded a militant struggle for black rights, an end to police brutality, and the right of armed self-defense. Cleaver joined the Panthers, becoming their minister of information (or propaganda chief), and under his direction, they developed a savvy propaganda image, notably in his now-famous slogan, "If you're not part of the solution, you're part of the problem." In May 1967 the police arrested Seale, Cleaver, and some thirty other Panthers in Sacramento for protesting a bill that would have outlawed carrying a loaded weapon. Five months later, after the police arrested Newton for killing an Oakland police officer, Cleaver helped organize the famous "Free Huey" campaign. This campaign, which convinced many that Newton was a political prisoner, dramatically increased awareness of the Panthers as it drew thousands of people to demonstrations. In December, Cleaver married his fellow Panther Kathleen Neal.

The year 1968 proved to be a fateful one for Cleaver. His prison essays were published as *Soul on Ice*, whose imagery and anger won him considerable literary fame. Maxwell Geismar writes in the introduction that Cleaver "rakes our favorite prejudices with the savage claws of his prose until our wounds are bare, our psyche is exposed, and we must either fight back or laugh with him for the service he has done for us" (xii). But both the local police and the national FBI continued their harassment of the Panthers. Seeking to destroy the militant organization, FBI director J. Edgar Hoover directed a campaign of infiltration, repression, and violence that eventually left most Panther leaders dead, in jail, or in exile. In April, Cleaver was involved in a Panther shoot-out in Oakland in which he and a police officer were wounded and Panther BOBBY HUTTON, aged seventeen, was killed. In response, the state revoked Cleaver's parole. In mid-June a California Superior Court justice released Cleaver from jail, calling him a "model parolee" victimized for his "undue eloquence in pursuing political goals." During this period Cleaver ran for U.S. president on the radical, California-based Peace and Freedom Party ticket. Shortly before he was due to return to jail in late November, he jumped his fifty-thousand-dollar bail, and on Christmas day, arrived in Cuba. For the next seven years Cleaver remained in exile in Cuba, North Korea, North Vietnam, China, Algeria, and, finally, France. In exile Eldridge and KATHLEEN CLEAVER had a son, Maceo, in 1969, and a daughter, Joju, in 1970.

In Algeria, Cleaver helped organize an international office for the Panthers, though his time in exile coincided with the organization's disintegration as a result of both massive government repression and internal dissension. On the West Coast, Seale and Newton, who had been released from prison in 1970, promoted community programs such as free breakfasts for children. Cleaver, more influential on the East Coast, emphasized the Panthers' militancy and the rhetoric of self-defense and revolution. In 1971 the Panthers expelled Cleaver, who, with Kathleen, then organized the short-lived Revolutionary People's Communication Network. The Algerian government, interested in closer ties to the United States, was growing uncomfortable with Cleaver's presence. Cleaver in turn became disillusioned with the Algerian government when it returned money donated to it by left-wing hijackers. In 1974, with the assistance of the French president,

Valery Giscard d'Estaing, Cleaver established legal residency in France. Soon thereafter he began to move to the right of the political and religious spectrum and reverted to Christianity after having a spiritual vision. In 1975, in a deal with the FBI, Cleaver returned to the United States to stand trial for the charges arising out of the 1968 shoot-out in Oakland. Eventually, the charges for attempted murder were dropped, though he was placed on probation for assault and sentenced to 1,200 hours of community service. By this time Cleaver had renounced his former radicalism and had become a born-again Christian, claiming that his travels in exile had made him appreciate American democracy and fear communism. In 1984 he declared that "I have taken an oath in my heart to oppose communism until the day I die."

In the late 1970s and early 1980s Cleaver seemed to flounder. As an attention-getting business venture, he developed the so-called Cleaver Sleeve— men's trousers with an exaggerated codpiece. For many, this symbolized the former Panther's decline. No longer an important African American spokesman, he had become a self-parody, trying to capitalize on his earlier fame and his emphasis (in his early prison writings) on his own sexuality as a political force. In 1985 his marriage ended in divorce. He was involved with various religious groups, including his own Eldridge Cleaver Crusades, a hybrid synthesis of Islam and Christianity he called "Christlam," the Reverend Sun Myung Moon's Unification Church, and the Mormons.

Cleaver attempted to explain his political metamorphosis in *Soul on Fire* (1978), and he ran unsuccessfully for public office several times. In 1984 he supported Ronald Reagan's bid for reelection and ran as an independent against the veteran African American Democratic congressman RON DELLUMS. Two years later Cleaver sought the Republican nomination for the U.S. senate seat in California, but again failed. His continued political marginalization was accompanied by a growing addiction to cocaine and in 1988 he was sentenced to probation after being convicted of cocaine possession and burglary. In 1992 he was again arrested for cocaine possession, although the charges were thrown out because the police had improperly arrested him. In 1994 he almost died from a severe blow on the head after an attack by another addict. Cleaver's response to this was to turn once again to evangelical Christianity.

In the late 1990s Cleaver's health declined, and he was diagnosed with both prostate cancer and diabetes. In May 1998 he died of a heart attack in suburban Los Angeles, where he had been working as a diversity consultant at a private college. For a moment in the mid-to late 1960s, Eldridge Cleaver's star burned more brightly than any of his contemporaries in the black nationalist movement. The sometimes bizarre political and personal meanderings of his later career cannot detract from the achievement of *Soul on Ice*, which conveyed on the written page the anger and resentment of young, urban blacks that exploded in the race rebellions of Watts, Detroit, and Newark.

FURTHER READING
Cleaver, Eldridge. *Soul on Fire* (1978).
Cleaver, Eldridge. *Soul on Ice* (1968).
Rout, Kathleen. *Eldridge Cleaver* (1991).
Obituaries: *New York Times* and *Washington Post*, 2 May 1998.

JACOB ZUMOFF

Cleaver, Emanuel (26 Oct. 1944–), mayor and U.S. Congressman, was born in tiny Waxahachie, Texas, into a family of preachers. He came of age in a public housing development near Wichita Falls, Texas, and attended the public schools there. For a time, he wished to pursue a life as a professional football player, but an injury prevented him from seeing that dream to fulfillment. Instead, he attended Texas A&M, from which he graduated in 1968. Falling back onto what was to some large degree the family business, Cleaver earned his Master of Divinity degree from St. Paul School of Theology in Kansas City, Missouri. There, at the behest of RALPH ABERNATHY, he established a chapter of the Southern Christian Leadership Conference. He was assigned to St. James Church, and under his guidance the tiny inner-city congregation (fewer than thirty regular attendees when Cleaver took over) soon blossomed into the one of the city's most thriving religious institutions.

Cleaver's political career began with a stint on the Kansas City Council. From there, he mounted a campaign in 1991 for mayor. He became the first African American in Kansas City to occupy that office, a feat made more remarkable by the majority white demographic of the city. He had reached out to whites, embarking on a campaign of home visits, and developed a broad coalition that cut across class and race boundaries. He served two terms, establishing a reputation as a conciliatory moderate. He also greatly improved the city's economic picture, attracting new businesses and growing the local economy. As money poured into Kansas City, Cleaver oversaw a massive city beautification project that made substantial enhancements to local attractions and essential infrastructure. He left office following his second term a successful and popular chief administrator and having served two terms as the president of the National Conference of Black Mayors. During his tenure with that organization, Cleaver engineered a partnership agreement with then-secretary of Housing and Urban Development under President Bill Clinton, Andrew Cuomo, to address the problem of declining urban centers. For its part, Kansas City named Emanuel Cleaver II Boulevard in his honor. In 2004 Cleaver sought the open seat in Missouri's Fifth Congressional District (mainly the Kansas City area). The race was a relatively close one in the Democratic stronghold, but Cleaver prevailed over his Republican opponent. In January 2005 Cleaver assumed his seat in the House of Representatives and began serving on a number of committees and subcommittees, including the Subcommittee on Housing and Community Opportunity and the Select Committee on Energy Independence and Global Warming, among numerous others.

Cleaver attracted some attention when he adamantly supported former first lady and New York senator Hillary Rodham Clinton over Illinois senator BARACK OBAMA in the hotly contested 2008 presidential election. Many of his colleagues in the Congressional Black Caucus also supported Senator Clinton in recognition of her and former President Bill Clinton's longtime support of civil rights. But Cleaver went so far as to suggest that so-called black superdelegates (that is, delegates whose votes were unattached to any specific primary contest) who supported Clinton had been exposed to abuse for their decision not to support the African American candidate.

As a representative, Cleaver had proven a reliable party vote, although not in the most liberal wing of the Democratic caucus. Notably, in 2009, he voted for a provision that would have allowed judges to modify mortgage principles in bankruptcy hearings (so-called cram-down legislation), an effort that was ultimately beaten back by the mortgage industry. He also voted yes on President Obama's administration's financial stimulus package and the bailout of the auto industry.

FURTHER READING

Freedman, Eric. *African Americans in Congress: A Documentary History* (2008).

Goldstein, David. "Cleaver: Black superdelegates backing Clinton are being 'threatened.'" *Kansas City Star*, 28 Feb. 2008.

JASON PHILIP MILLER

Cleaver, Kathleen (13 May 1945–), activist, educator, and lawyer, was born Kathleen Neal in Dallas, Texas, to Ernest Neal and Juette Johnson, educators. Activism and scholarship were staples of the Neal family home, as both of her parents held advanced degrees. Ernest and Juette met while attending the University of Michigan in the 1940s. Juette held a master's degree in mathematics, and Ernest earned a Ph.D. in Sociology. Ernest was working as a Wiley College sociology professor in Marshall, Texas, at the time of Kathleen's birth.

Shortly after Kathleen's birth, Ernest accepted a job at Tuskegee Institute, relocating the family to Alabama. In addition to Kathleen's early exposure to academia, her father's work in foreign aid promoted a family environment in which social progress was frequently discussed. At the age of nine Kathleen had already embarked upon a life of global travel and had an appreciation of diverse cultures. Her father's position with the foreign service led the family to locales such as India and the Philippines. The untimely death of her brother and her parents' eventual divorce led to Cleaver's return in 1958 to the United States, where she attended high school in the recently desegregated Baltimore public school system.

Living in countries such as India and the Philippines, places where people of color held

Kathleen Cleaver speaks at a news conference at New York City's Kennedy Airport in October 1971. (AP Images.)

leadership positions at all levels, shaped Kathleen's worldview and led to her interest in civil rights as a high school student. Drawn to the confrontation against racial injustice at sixteen years old, Kathleen longed to join the activist front lines. Her initiation into the movement in 1966 came at a time when methods of protest ran the gamut from nonviolent suit-and-tie sit-ins to bolder, overall-clad protesters with Afros advocating "black power" from behind dark sunglasses. Upon graduating from high school, Kathleen enrolled at Oberlin College and eventually transferred to Barnard College in New York City. In the summer of 1966 she joined the New York City chapter of the Student Nonviolent Coordinating Committee (SNCC) as a secretary. Ongoing riots in numerous urban cities and the passage of both the Civil Rights Act and the Voting Rights Act symbolized the tension between the hope found in the new laws and the ongoing frustration with the lack of social change resulting from new legal policies. During her time at SNCC, the office focused on community building, leadership development, and protesting the Vietnam War.

The following year Kathleen met her future husband, ELDRIDGE CLEAVER, while in Nashville on a conference at Fisk University aimed at uniting the various student groups with whom SNCC worked. Eldridge Cleaver was invited as a speaker. At the time of their introduction, the Black Panthers had yet to undergo their major chapter expansion across the country and were primarily based in California. Kathleen was familiar with some of the Panthers' protest actions, including the storming of the Sacramento statehouse and, more notably, the incident involving HUEY P. NEWTON and an Oakland police officer that resulted in the officer's death.

By November 1967 Kathleen relocated to California and joined the Black Panther Party for Self Defense, where she served as communications secretary. She married Eldridge Cleaver on 26 December 1967. Kathleen Cleaver became the first female member of the organization's Central Committee. She enjoyed the community-centered approach of the Panthers; however, her entry into that party came at a time of extreme duress. The group had been under constant surveillance and interrogation from local, state, and federal authorities. Only three months after their marriage, Eldridge Cleaver was involved in a shoot-out with local police and nearly killed. There were conflicts with police, Eldridge Cleaver's subsequent imprisonment, and the release of his autobiography, *Soul on Ice* (1968).

Cleaver left the country in 1969 to join Eldridge in Algeria, where he fled to avoid returning to prison. She was also pregnant with their first child, Maceo, at this time. The family remained in Algeria for four years, and during this time the Cleavers welcomed another child, Joju, to the family while on a visit to North Korea. During the couple's time abroad, the Federal Bureau of Investigation (FBI) used its Counterintelligence Program (COINTELPRO) to create rifts within radical political organizations such as the Black Panthers. The government's covert efforts destroyed the once-solid relationship between Newton and Eldridge Cleaver. Despite the rift in the organization, the Cleavers helped expand the Panthers by opening an international section in Algeria.

After almost a decade abroad, Cleaver returned to the United States in 1975 to assist Eldridge in resolving his legal issues. After reaching an agreement with authorities in 1980, Eldridge served an eight-month sentence and did community service. In the following few years Kathleen Cleaver decided to end her marriage to Eldridge and returned to school at Yale University in New Haven, Connecticut. She completed her B.A. in History in 1983 with summa cum laude and Phi Beta Kappa honors. She then went on to enroll in Yale's law school. Lawyers were an important staple in the life of the Panthers, and Cleaver had become intrigued by the profession and had developed an appreciation for the importance of legal expertise. She initially pursued a legal education in the hopes that she could help free wrongfully imprisoned political prisoners, many of them former Panthers. Upon completing the law degree in 1988, she joined the New York law firm Cravath, Swaine, and Moore, LLP, to learn more about litigation and trials. In 1991 she clerked in Philadelphia for the highly regarded African American judge A. LEON HIGGINBOTHAM, chief judge of the U.S. Court of Appeals for the Third Circuit.

Cleaver soon learned that her passion was for research and left the firm for a career in academia in 1993. She served as professor of public policy at Sarah Lawrence College and visiting professor at Benjamin N. Cardozo School of Law and was senior lecturer in law at Emory University and senior research associate at Yale University. Cleaver's courses built upon her abiding interest in the struggle of people of color across the African diaspora, including her class on citizenship, slavery, and the antislavery movement. Her writings appeared in publications such as the *Village Voice*, the *Boston Globe*, the *Critical Race Feminism Reader*, *Critical White Studies: Looking Behind the Mirror* (1997), and *The Promise of Multiculturalism: Education and Autonomy in the Twenty-first Century; A New Political Science Reader* (1998).

Cleaver realized her dream of helping to free wrongfully imprisoned political prisoners as a member of ELMER "GERONIMO" PRATT's legal team. Pratt was a former Panther comrade who had been wrongfully convicted of murder. Cleaver's aid to Pratt began with visits and letters during his incarceration and culminated in her position as a member of his legal team, which included Johnnie Cochran and Stuart Hanlon, that overturned the wrongful verdict in 1997. Playing a role in obtaining Pratt's freedom was a high point for Cleaver, who had long been known as one of the only Panthers to testify on Pratt's behalf at his trial in 1972. Cleaver was also a longtime supporter and outspoken advocate for the death row inmate MUMIA ABU-JAMAL, another former Panther member and political activist.

Cleaver also helped shape and preserve the legacy of Eldridge Cleaver, who died on 1 May 1998, as well as the Black Panther Party. She wrote the introduction to a book of photographs entitled *Black Panther 1968*, contributed a paper to *The Black Panther Party Reconsidered* (1997), edited *Liberation, Imagination, and the Black Panther Party* (2001) and created a film festival of the same name, and edited *Eldridge Cleaver in Target Zero: A Life in Writing* (2007). Her receipt of a number of prestigious fellowships, including the Bunting Institute of Radcliffe College, the W. E. B. DuBois Institute of Harvard University, the Center for Historical Analysis at Rutgers University, and the Schomburg Center for Research in Black Culture, helped her write perhaps her most important book, *Memories of Love and War*, the autobiography she began in 1974.

FURTHER READING

Cleaver, Kathleen Neal, and Susie Linfield. "The Education of Kathleen Neal Cleaver," *Transition* 77 (1998): 172–195.

Jones, Charles. *The Black Panther Party Reconsidered* (1997).

Rampell, Ed. "Third Degree: Kathleen Cleaver," *Los Angeles City Beat* (Feb. 2004).

JOCELYN L. WOMACK

Cleckley, Frank (1 Aug. 1940–), law professor and former West Virginia Supreme Court of Appeals Justice, was born Franklin Dorrah Cleckley in Newberry, South Carolina, the youngest of eleven children of Daniel Cleckley, a sawmill worker, and Ellen Dorrah Cleckley, a schoolteacher.

Justice Cleckley's family moved to Huntington, West Virginia, from South Carolina to join relatives seeking greater economic opportunities. Huntington was a railroad town with segregated neighborhoods, in a segregated State. After attending a segregated Catholic school and being taught by white nuns for a portion of grade school, he was educated in the public schools, and was a member of the first integrated class at Huntington High School.

A vivid memory of childhood, he later recalled, was when his father lost a portion of an arm working in a sawmill and received no compensation for his injury. The consequences of this devastating injury meant the obligation to earn a living now shifted largely to his mother, who supplemented her teaching salary cleaning homes and taking in laundry. The absence of a remedy for his father's injury also began the process of shaping the future lawyer's sense of fairness.

The decision to attend Anderson College (now Anderson University), Anderson, Indiana, was strongly influenced by his mother, an ordained minister in the Church of God (Anderson). Justice Cleckley served a summer internship with Congressman J. Edgar Rousch (D-Ind.) at the end of his degree program; Congressman Rousch encouraged his intern to consider attending law school in Indiana.

This recommendation, combined with a failure to receive any reply from the West Virginia University College of Law to his admission application, would help his efforts to emphasize the active recruitment of both minority and economically disadvantaged students when he became a West Virginia University (WVU) faculty member. With the option of attending law school in West Virginia closed, he attended law school at the University of Indiana, Bloomington, where he graduated with a J.D. in 1965.

Enlisting in the Navy, Justice Cleckley served in the Judge Advocate General Corps; here he specialized in the criminal defense of service members during the Vietnam War. This experience would provide a foundation for his expansive practice in criminal law; he also authored treatises on the law of evidence and the law of criminal procedure in West Virginia. For his final military assignment, he taught at the Navy Justice School, Newport, Rhode Island. During a posting in Long Beach, California, he met Cozette Scott, to whom he was married in 1967. The couple had two children, Shannon and Nichole; they were divorced in 1999.

After receiving an honorable discharge from the Navy, he was named a Martin Luther King Foundation Fellow by the Woodrow Wilson Fellowship Foundation for study in the United Kingdom at Exeter University, Exeter, England. Justice Cleckley's formal education was completed with the receipt of an LLM, or master's of law, from the Harvard Law School in 1969. During his LLM program he also worked as a Staff Attorney at the Community Legal Assistance Office in Cambridge, Massachusetts, which further sharpened his awareness of the impact of law on the lives of poor people and racial minorities, and the potential for effective representation having a progressive effect.

He joined the law faculty at WVU in 1969, as the first African American faculty member, and was appointed the Arthur B. Hodges Professor of Law in 1985. In addition to authoring multi-volume treatises on the law of evidence and criminal procedure, he maintained an extensive criminal and civil rights legal practice, frequently serving on a pro bono basis.

To further his earlier identified interest in advancing black involvement in higher education, and to further broad community understanding of issues of significance to African Americans among the WVU community, Justice Cleckley participated in the creation of a speaker series, coordinated through the WVU Center for Black Culture, and the Cleckley Foundation, which sponsored informal gatherings to facilitate applications to law school of racial minorities and economically disadvantaged persons. Justice Cleckley was encouraged in these efforts by his sister, Dr. Betty Cleckley, who served as a vice president at Marshall University, Huntington, West Virginia, for over thirty years, with an emphasis on multicultural affairs.

Significant for the development of the professional standing of the African American Bar in West Virginia, Justice Cleckley participated in the reestablishment of the Mountain State Bar to provide a professional legal organization for minorities who felt excluded from involvement in the mandatory West Virginia Bar Association. A central mission of the Mountain State Bar involved scholarship aid to disadvantaged students and to encourage outreach to poor West Virginia residents by lawyers who are members of the Association.

In 1987 Justice Cleckley was presented with the highest honor bestowed by the NAACP on a lawyer, the William Robert Ming Advocacy Award; the same year, the West Virginia State Conference of the NAACP awarded him the T.G. Nutter Award.

In 1994, he was appointed to an unexpired term on the West Virginia Supreme Court of Appeals; his appointment marked the first African American to serve on the only appellate court in West Virginia. The appointment, made by Governor Gaston Caperton, was to fill the remainder of the unexpired term of Justice Thomas Miller. Justice Miller, in turn, had served as a mentor to Justice Cleckley, engaging him in the drafting of procedural and evidentiary rules. At Justice Cleckley's swearing in ceremony, Governor Caperton characterized the appointment as the one of which he was the proudest.

During his term, from 1 September 1994 to 31 December 1996, Justice Cleckley authored over one hundred signed opinions. These are analyzed in "A Tribute to Franklin D. Cleckley: A Compendium of Essential Legal Principles from his Opinions as a Justice on the West Virginia Supreme Court of Appeals," which appeared in a special issue of the *West Virginia Law Review*, in 1998.

At the expiration of his Court appointment, Justice Cleckley returned to the faculty of West Virginia University where he continued his scholarship on evidence and criminal procedure, authoring new editions of his treatises which are the standard works of authority on these topics in West Virginia legal practice. He also coauthored a treatise on civil procedure. In 2003 Cleckley was one of the recipients of The American Inns of Court Professionalism Awards, an honor he shares with federal judge NATHANIEL R. JONES, among others, and which is awarded annually to a lawyer or judge "whose life and practice display sterling character and unquestioned integrity, coupled with ongoing dedication to the highest standards of the legal profession and the rule of law" (http://www.innsofcourt.org/Content/Default.aspx?Id=308). In addition he has been awarded the Civil Libertarian of the Year Award from the West Virginia Civil Liberties Union, the Thurgood Marshall Award from the West Virginia NAACP, and the West Virginia Human Rights Commission Civil Rights Award.

FURTHER READING

There are no public collections of Justice Cleckley's papers.

Davis, Robin Jean. "A Tribute to Franklin D. Cleckley: A Compendium of Essential Legal Principles from his Opinions as a Justice on the West Virginia Supreme Court of Appeals," *West Virginia Law Review* 100 (Special Issue) 1997–1998.

DALE P. OLSON

Clement, Rufus Early (26 June 1900–7 Nov. 1967), university president, was born in Salisbury, North Carolina, the son of George C. Clement, a bishop in the African Methodist Episcopal (AME) Zion church, and Emma Clarissa Williams, who in 1946 was the first black woman in the United States to be chosen as American Mother of the Year. A precocious youngster, Rufus attended public schools in Charlotte, North Carolina, and in Louisville, Kentucky, and graduated from Livingstone College in Salisbury with a B.A. at the age of nineteen. Three years later, in 1922, he received a B.D. from Garrett Biblical Institute in Evanston, Illinois. During that same year he received an M.A. from Northwestern University in Evanston and married Pearl Ann Johnson of Summer, Mississippi, with whom he had one child. In 1930 he also received a Ph.D. from Northwestern.

During Clement's years of graduate study he worked as an instructor, as a professor, and as a dean (in 1925) at Livingstone College, where he was instrumental in the college's obtaining accreditation. He also served as the pastor of an AME Zion church in Landis, North Carolina. Clement was a baseball coach at Livingstone and a football official of the Colored Intercollegiate Athletic Association. From 1931 to 1937, as dean of the Louisville Municipal College for Negroes, he helped the school obtain full accreditation. These accomplishments brought Clement to the attention of the board of trustees of Atlanta University, who selected him to be the university's sixth president. Clement held this position for the rest of his life—almost exactly thirty years. He eventually also became a trustee and forged a significant path for the university and for its surrounding community.

Having been recently restructured as a black graduate school close to several black undergraduate institutions (particularly Morehouse and Spelman) in Atlanta, the university joined the Georgia state university system in 1937 with the goal of enhancing the educational and cultural status of blacks. This allowed the university to serve as the hub of a complex of contiguous institutions that under Clement's administration became known officially as the Atlanta Center of Colleges (composed of Atlanta University, Morehouse College, Spelman College, Clark College, Morris Brown College,

and the Gammon Theological Seminary). Clement served as the chief administrator and leader of the initial nucleus and of the ultimate six-institution center that provided educational, cultural, and civic background for the historic national civil rights movement that was engendered and nurtured in Atlanta during the 1950s and 1960s. Furthermore, Clement's astute coordination and emphasis on cross-fertilization enabled the center to provide an extensive array of educational options, and it became known nationally for its autonomy and for the highly productive exchange of curricula and resources among its institutions.

During the 1940s the Clement administration expanded the accredited graduate schools and programs at Atlanta University to include library science, education, business administration, social work, and the People's College for adult education. One daunting task that Clement implemented in 1944 involved his forcibly retiring seventy-five-year-old W. E. B. DuBois, who had maintained an extremely impressive career at Atlanta University and had a strong national and local reputation as a brilliant scholar and an advocate for civil rights. In spite of strong opposition, Clement persisted in his contention that DuBois had reached retirement age and was not eligible for special considerations. This action further established Clement as a national role model leading a university guided by principles.

Throughout his career Clement held a belief that indirect action through professional and civic involvement could help ease racial tension. His life was a testament to that conviction, for he was active in numerous educational and professional associations. Principal among them are his memberships on the Council on Inter-Racial Cooperation, the Southern Regional Council—an advisory committee to the U.S. Office of Education—the Commission on Citizenship of the Association of American Colleges, the American Council on Education (second vice-president), the Commission on International Affairs, the World Confederation of the Teaching Profession (a National Education Association delegate), the Institute of International Education (trustee), the National Science Board, and the National Commission on Accrediting. In being elected to the school board for four consecutive terms, Clement became the first African American to be elected to public office in Atlanta since Reconstruction. He was also a charter member of the Georgia Science and Technology Commission, trustee of at least four colleges, trustee of the Phelps-

Stokes Fund, and president of the Conference of Presidents of Negro Land Grant Colleges.

An active writer and scholar, Clement served on the editorial board of *Phylon*. He was also a contributing editor of the *Journal of Negro Education* and was the author of articles on black education in a number of reference journals. Clement was involved extensively in civic affairs ranging from the Urban League, Planned Parenthood, and the National YMCA, to the U.S. Department of State's Advisory Council on African Affairs. His numerous awards included recognition from *Time* in 1966 as one of the fourteen most influential university presidents in America.

Clement's major contribution was his devotion to the role of higher education in enhancing the status of blacks and in the maintenance of democracy and world peace. He felt that educators and university administrators must fulfill the requirements of two roles simultaneously: one inside academia—guided by professional ethics and institutional policies—and the other outside—guided by humanitarian goals of service. Until his death in New York City, Clement showed that the two roles could be fulfilled effectively without contradiction.

FURTHER READING

Clement's papers are in the Robert R. Woodruff Library and in the Presidential Archives of Atlanta University. Clement's correspondence is in the General Education Board Papers, Rockefeller Archive Center, North Tarrytown, New York.

Bacote, Clarence A. *The Story of Atlanta University* (1969).

Obituaries: *New York Times* and *Atlanta Constitution*, 8 Nov. 1967; *Atlanta Daily World*, 8 and 12 Nov. 1967.

This entry is taken from the *American National Biography* and is published here with the permission of the American Council of Learned Societies.

CLYDE O. MCDANIEL

Clement, Samuel Spottford (13 Nov. 1861–?), politician and memoirist, was born a slave on a farm owned by James Adams in Pittsylvania County, Virginia. When Adams died shortly after Clement's birth, the boy, his mother, and two siblings were sold to a man named Tasswood Ward from nearby Campbell County. The family was treated harshly by the Wards, who beat them cruelly without warning for petty reasons.

On 8 April 1865 the workers in the field heard cannon fire and fighting from nearby Appomattox.

The next day the Confederate general Robert E. Lee surrendered to Ulysses S. Grant's Union forces to end the Civil War.

On Christmas morning of 1865 Clement and his family moved to a piece of land about fifteen miles from the Ward farm, where his father struck a deal under which he would clear the land and reap its harvest. The family continued to work on farms throughout Clement's youth, and though he was kept from work until he was fourteen, he also eventually took up farming. In the meantime his parents invested in his education, sending him to a school five miles away from his home. It was not long, however, before he was being harassed by white boys along the way, so he was taken out of school. Soon John McGoyett, a white Northerner, moved to town and taught the black children. The white planters in the area were not pleased with his presence, and after two years he was forced out of town. Clement was again left without a school to attend. Only after Virginia established a public school was Clement able to attend school for years without fear of its closing.

Clement went on to teach a night school for young people near the farm on which he worked during the day. He also delivered the mail for some time, but upon noticing that his friends who had moved to the North returned at Christmas with far more money than Clement could make in the South, he began to save and plan for his move to the North. However, for a time a combination of poor pay, illness, and bad spending habits kept him from carrying out his plan.

In 1883 Clement finally achieved his dream of moving north, when he found work in Steubenville, Ohio, where he lived off and on for most of his adult life. On 18 November 1890 Clement married Saphorna Braxton. On his way home to see his mother in the winter of 1891 Clement also made a sort of pilgrimage to see the site of Harper's Ferry and to pay his respects to the white abolitionist John Brown, whom he credited with freeing the slaves. Back in Steubenville, Clement worked as a coal miner, wagon driver, and church janitor, before he sought and won the position of town constable in 1895. He was the first black person to be elected to any political office in his county. According to his memoir Clement lost his second term because of his commitment to defending the law even when it offended powerful political foes. After his defeat he returned to working as a wagon driver.

The story of his life was written down by a young woman named Sarah Ovington and published in

Ohio in 1908 as the *Memoirs of Samuel Spottford Clement Relating Interesting Experiences in Days of Slavery and Freedom*. Beginning in the last days of slavery, Clement's life provides a perspective on the difficulties and possibilities black men encountered in the political life of the post–Civil War North.

FURTHER READING

Clement, Samuel Spottford. *Memoirs of Samuel Spottford Clement Relating Interesting Experiences in Days of Slavery and Freedom* (1908).

LAURA MURPHY

Clemente, Roberto (18 Aug. 1934–31 Dec. 1972), baseball player, was born Roberto Walker Clemente in Carolina, Puerto Rico, the son of Melchor Clemente, a sugar mill foreman, and Luisa Walker. Little is known of Roberto's early life. When he was fourteen, he played in exhibition games in Puerto Rico alongside Negro League and major league players. In 1952, during his first season with the Santurce Cangrejeros, Clemente impressed the Brooklyn Dodgers' scout Al Campanis. On his high school graduation in 1954 he signed with the Dodgers for $10,000 and was sent to their highest-level farm team, the Montreal Royals.

Roberto Clemente. Pittsburgh Pirates outfielder, poses for a portrait in 1957. (AP Images.)

The Dodgers took a risk by giving Clemente a year's seasoning at Montreal because of baseball's rules at the time, which stated that players receiving bonuses above $4,000 had to be kept on a team's major league roster during their initial summers or else become eligible for selection by other teams in the minor league draft at season's end. In eighty-seven games for the Royals, Clemente batted .257 with two home runs and twelve runs batted in, statistics that seemed hardly good enough to attract outside attention. Nevertheless the Dodgers' gamble backfired. The former Dodgers' president Branch Rickey, then general manager of the Pittsburgh Pirates and a shrewd finder of talented young players, chose Clemente as the draft's first selection. Before joining the Pirates in 1955, Clemente played another winter season for Pedrin Zorilla's Santurce team. In the outfield with the future Hall of Famer WILLIE MAYS and the former Homestead Grays slugger Bob Thurman, Clemente continued to develop his knowledge and skills. These former Negro Leaguers, along with James "Buster" Clarkson, made the young Puerto Rican their special project. After helping his team win the Caribbean championships in Venezuela, Clemente joined the Pirates in Florida for spring training.

Forced into segregated sleeping quarters and denied the opportunity to travel and eat with his teammates, Clemente encountered more virulent prejudice than he had experienced before. His refusal to submit meekly to such arrangements probably led to his reputation as a hothead.

Clemente's 1955 rookie season was unremarkable, but in his second year the graceful five foot eleven inch, 185-pound outfielder realized some of the potential that the Dodgers, Rickey, and others had predicted for him by batting .311 while driving in 60 runs. Marked by injuries, his next three years with Pittsburgh saw him tail off from his sophomore season. Although Clemente's batting average improved each of these three years, it remained under .300; as a right fielder, however, he displayed confidence, daring, a thorough knowledge of National League ballparks, and a virtually matchless throwing arm.

In 1960 he had his best year yet in the major leagues. He played superlatively in the field, batted .314 (with 179 hits and sixteen home runs), scored 89 runs, drove in ninety-four runs, and was named to his first National League all-star team. Sportswriters began comparing Clemente with Mays, whom many considered the best National League player of the time. But Clemente finished eighth in the voting for the most valuable player award that autumn. According to his teammate Bill Mazeroski, the snub left him bitter and hurt.

In 1961 Clemente improved again, coming into his own as a hitter. That season he led the league in batting at .351, had more than 200 hits for the first time, scored 100 runs (batting in 89), and posted an outstanding .559 slugging average. Still, much of his bitterness remained.

"Latin American Negro ballplayers," he said, "are treated today much like all Negroes were treated in baseball in the early days of the broken color barrier. They are subjected to prejudices and stamped with generalizations. Because they speak Spanish among themselves, they are set off as a minority within a minority. And they bear the brunt of the sport's remaining racial prejudices."

Voicing a sentiment widely held by African American and Hispanic athletes of his day, Clemente argued that "the Latin player doesn't get the recognition he deserves. Neither does the Negro unless he does something really spectacular." Clemente fought that stereotyping the rest of his life, both on and off the field.

An intense, driven man, Clemente channeled much of his passion into his playing. His body paid for his reckless style. He suffered from a curved spine, hematomas, a paratyphoid infection, bone chips, and tension headaches, as well as everyday bruises, strains, and injuries. The contrast between his grace on the field and his frequent inability to play stirred a frequently heard complaint that Latinos, and especially Clemente, "couldn't take it."

Gradually Clemente overcame these racial and cultural obstacles. Already a sports hero in Puerto Rico and the Caribbean basin where he starred in winter ball, he won the respect and admiration of Pittsburgh fans and others wherever he competed. Throughout the 1960s, along with Mays and HENRY AARON, Clemente became the standard of excellence for National League outfielders. He led the league in batting three times, recording averages of .339 in 1964, .329 in 1965, and .357 in 1967. He twice topped the league in hits, with 211 in 1964 and 209 in 1967. He became a standout clutch hitter, a legitimate extra-base slugger, and a skilled batter at getting on base. In 1966 and 1967 he both scored and batted in more than 100 runs. And in every season but one during the 1960s he was named to the league's all-star team.

In 1964 Clemente married Vera Cristina Zabala, and they had three children. Finally in 1971 Clemente achieved the greater recognition that he felt he deserved, after leading the Pirates to a World Series championship. He collected twelve hits and a .414 batting average, with two home runs, two doubles, and a triple over seven games. Voted the series's most valuable player, he made several exceptional fielding plays. Moreover, with the Pirates trailing the Baltimore Orioles two games to none, his hustle on a routine groundball caused the Orioles pitcher Mike Cuellar to throw wildly to first base and allow the Pirates to break the third game open, reversing the series's momentum. Afterward Clemente told the press that at first sportswriters "thought Latins were inferior to the American people. Now they know they can't be sarcastic about Latins, which is something I have fought for all my life." In two World Series, Clemente hit safely in all the games in which he played, ending with a .362 average.

On 30 September 1972 Clemente hit a double off the New York Mets pitcher Jon Matlack for his 3,000th hit in regular season play, making him only the eleventh major league player to reach that plateau at the time. The hit marked his last regular season at bat.

During his eighteen seasons with Pittsburgh, Clemente was one of baseball's premier hitters, with four batting titles, 240 home runs, 1,305 runs batted in, 1,416 runs scored, and a career .317 average. A fixture in the National League's all-star lineup and the league's 1966 most valuable player, Clemente also won twelve Gold Gloves for his fielding. Among all outfielders in modern baseball, his throwing arm is known as one of the best.

Clemente was a U.S. citizen, but his sense of himself as Puerto Rican was paramount. Like other ballplayers from the islands, he felt an obligation, despite his many injuries, to play winter ball for his countrymen. After playing during fifteen winters, he sat out in 1972–1973 to manage Puerto Rico's team in the Mundiales, the world amateur baseball championships. He spent November and December with the team in Nicaragua. "When we went to Nicaragua that November," Vera Clemente recalled in an unpublished interview, "Roberto saw himself in the boys in the streets—without shoes, living in a one-room house with ten people—much like it had been when his father worked for the sugar mill in Carolina."

After the Clementes returned to Puerto Rico, an earthquake rocked Managua. He and his wife spearheaded relief efforts organized on the island. When reports surfaced of the Nicaraguan National Guard pilfering aid shipments, Clemente decided to fly there himself to be sure that the relief reached those in need. But his plane, which took off on New Year's Eve 1972, plunged into the waters off San Juan. Clemente's body was never recovered.

As early as 1964 Clemente had conceived of building a sports city for the children of Puerto Rico. His death was the catalyst for the creation of Ciudad Deportiva, a sporting complex financed by government donations of land and corporate and private financial contributions.

In 1971 the Baseball Writers Association of America waived its five-year waiting period and overwhelmingly elected Clemente to the National Baseball Hall of Fame. Lou Gehrig was the only other player for whom the waiting period had been dismissed. Clemente was the first Latin ballplayer enshrined in Cooperstown. As time passed, Clemente became a legendary figure wherever baseball is played throughout the Caribbean basin and in Hispanic communities in the United States. If Babe Ruth is the classic hero for baseball's pre-integration era, and JACKIE ROBINSON the modern game's pioneer, Clemente was the paladin for Latin Americans in the "American" pastime.

FURTHER READING

Christine, Bill. *Roberto* (1973).

Musick, Phil. *Who Was Roberto? A Biography of Roberto Clemente* (1974).

Wagenheim, Kal. *Clemente!* (1973).

Obituary: *New York Times*, 2 Jan. 1973.

This entry is taken from the *American National Biography* and is published here with the permission of the American Council of Learned Societies.

ROB RUCK

Clemons, Michael "Pinball" (15 Jan. 1965–), Canadian Football League player, coach, sports executive, and philanthropist, was born Michael Lutrell Clemons in Dunedin, Florida, to Anna O'Neal and Willy James Clemons. The diminutive Clemons earned his nickname in the CFL because, according to Bill O'Billovich, the Toronto Argonauts' head coach, he resembled a pinball when bouncing off of would-be tacklers. His parents never married; Anna raised Michael, while Willy stayed largely at the periphery of his son's life. Later, Anna married and gave birth to Kelli, while her new husband added two children of his own to the family.

Clemons grew up in the projects of a predominantly black, working-class community. His family and neighbors struggled economically; at one point, Clemons—an excellent student and math whiz—even helped his mother's boyfriend run a numbers racket. Still, Clemons and his mother were devout attendees of the local Baptist church, and Clemons became a professed Christian at the age of eight. Around the same time, he became a star running back for the Dunedin Golden Eagles, a football team sponsored by the Police Athletic League. When he left the team at age eleven, the Eagles retired his number. Clemons also excelled at soccer and baseball, but favored the more "methodical and intense" (Clemons, 1999, 14) nature of football. His success continued at Dunedin High, where he split time at running back with larger players but still gained 1,000 yards rushing in his junior year. Few colleges expressed interest because Clemons was barely five feet six inches, almost half a foot shorter than the average running back. Thanks to his grades, Columbia and Harvard were among the suitors, but the College of William and Mary in Williamsburg, Virginia, was the first to offer a full scholarship after Dunedin's coach George Hemond convinced the school's recruiter to watch a video of Clemons.

While Clemons struggled with the adjustment, his first season with The Tribe earned him Freshman of the Year honors for 1983. After the school year ended, he returned home to work a seasonal job with the aerospace division of Honeywell, a career he expected to keep permanently upon graduating from college. That summer, he began dating Diane Lee, whom he would eventually marry in 1991. The couple had three daughters, Rachel, Raven, and Rylie. While his sophomore year was lost to injury, Clemons blossomed the following year under his running-back coach and mentor Derwyn Cox, only the second black coach in William and Mary's history. Clemons broke school records in receiving and became a co-captain, while the team improved for the third straight year. In his final season, the team went 9–2, while Clemons amassed more than 2,000 all-purpose yards. For his entire college career, he gained 4,778 yards and was named a Division 1-AA All American. Despite the success, Clemons did not impress many teams at the NFL Scouting Combine in Indianapolis the following spring. Not only did his size remain a concern, but nagging injuries prevented him from performing well.

While preparing to be a working professional with Honeywell, Clemons acquired an agent in the event that he was selected in the NFL draft. The Kansas City Chiefs selected him as the 218th player, but Clemons saw limited action with the team due to injuries and a players strike in 1987. He finished the year with only 19 punt returns for 162 yards. In 1988 Clemons was cut by both the Chiefs and the Tampa Bay Buccaneers within a span of about two weeks.

After continuing to work on his degree and then returning to his life in Florida, Clemons was beginning to accept that his chance to play professional football had passed. But in 1989 the Argonauts reached out to his agent and invited him to play. Over the following decade Clemons would emerge as one of the most prolific offensive weapons in the history of the Canadian game. In the CFL, Clemons's size would not be as much of a factor. With its wider field, deeper end zones, and greater emphasis on passing (thanks to there being only three downs instead of four), the game was well-suited to quick, agile players who had been deemed too small for the NFL, such as Doug Flutie and Henry "Gizmo" Williams. Moreover, there would be more opportunities for a return specialist such as Clemons; in the CFL, missed field goals can be returned in what is considered by many fans to be the game's most exciting play. (In contrast, returned field goals have taken place only a handful of times in the history of the NFL.)

In his first game with the Argonauts, Clemons had an amazing return of about forty yards, only to fumble the ball after taking a hit. But from there, his career took off. After an occasionally brilliant rookie season, Clemons went on to win Most Outstanding Player honors in 1990 thanks to a record-setting 3,300 all-purpose yards. In 1991, Clemons teamed up with Raghib "The Rocket" Ismail to lead the Argos to a victory in the Grey Cup. Over the next few years, Clemons became the face of the franchise, although the team itself, thanks to league-wide financial woes and mismanagement, constantly changed ownership, coaches, and personnel. Clemons also reached out to the community, participating in charity organizations aimed at improving the lives of disadvantaged youths, including Athletes in Action, Youth for Christ, and Horizons for Youth. His activities earned him the Tom Pate Memorial Award twice (1993 and 1996), honoring his sportsmanship and philanthropy.

It was not until the Argonauts signed quarterback Doug Flutie in 1996 that they returned to the Grey Cup. Flutie and Clemons became an effective duo, leading the team to two consecutive championships. In the 1997 playoffs, they combined for what Clemons refers to as the signature play of his career, a catch-and-run that resulted in a winning touchdown against Montreal. That same year, he

managed to break his own record with over 3,800 total yards. Once Flutie left for the NFL, however, the team began a steady decline into mediocrity.

Clemons vowed that 2000 would be his final year. That season, under a new owner, Sherwood Schwarz, and new coach, John Huard, the team got off to one of its worst starts ever, prompting Huard to quit halfway through the season. What followed was one of the most unusual personnel moves in the history of professional sports. Schwarz, desperate to spark new life in the team, asked Clemons to retire early so that he could become the new coach. Clemons reluctantly agreed. At the time of his retirement, he had amassed 25,396 all-purpose yards, a pro football record. He had accumulated 5,000+ yards in rushing, receiving, kickoff, and punt returns, something no other athlete has done. Thanks to these accomplishments, the respect that Clemons had earned made up for his lack of experience, and the team went 5–2 under his leadership to just barely miss the playoffs.

Clemons coached again in 2001, but the team failed to make the postseason, and Clemons decided to take the position of team president. This made room for CFL legend Sam "The Rifle" Etcheverry to take over as coach. However, in a situation similar to what happened in 2000, Clemons was once again asked to replace the coach following a slow start to the season. He led the team to an uneven record throughout 2002 and 2003, prompting criticism that he was more of a motivator and a figurehead than a legitimate coach, and that the team ownership had mismanaged the entire situation. Making things more difficult, the Argos entered the 2004 season with newly acquired Damon Allen, a forty year old quarterback recovering from an injury. Clemons managed to steer the team through a difficult season and into the playoffs, where Toronto began a run that culminated in a 27–19 victory over the British Columbia Lions in the Grey Cup. Three years before TONY DUNGY would accomplish the feat in the NFL, Clemons had become the first black coach to win a professional football championship in the era of integrated sports. He led the team through 2007, compiling fifty-seven wins before becoming the Argonauts chief executive. In 2008, he became vice chair, handling community relations.

Clemons's popularity in the Toronto area following his football career was sustained by his philanthropic work, a commitment that took up so much of his time during his playing days that his coach advised him to scale back his efforts. Among his organizations are the Argos Foundation: Stop the Violence (founded 2005); Christian Blind Mission International (for which he is a spokesman); and Free the Children. In February 2006, Clemons became Chair of the Youth Challenge Fund, which raises money for select neighborhoods in Toronto. In 2007 he started the Michael "Pinball" Clemons Foundation, another organization dedicated to providing educational and economic opportunities for disadvantaged youths. In 2010 the Michael Clemons Foundation partnered with Free the Children to begin building 131 schools in Africa. He also has participated in outreach programs through the Argonauts; one initiative, for example, recruits professional football players to mentor prison inmates. He has also worked as a motivational speaker and is a partner with Simply Kids, a business specializing in baby food, diapers, and related accessories for infants.

FURTHER READING

Clemons, Michael "Pinball." *All Heart: My Story* (1999).

Ito, Gail. "Clemons, Michael 'Pinball' (1965-)." The Black Past: Remembered and Reclaimed. http://www.blackpast.org/.

Lefko, Perry. *Pinball: The Making of a Canadian Hero* (2006).

Roberts, Rob. "The Torontonians: Pinball Clemons, Do-Gooder." *National Post*, 18 Dec. 2009.

ROBERT REPINO

Cleveland, James Edward (5 Dec. 1932–9 Feb. 1991), gospel singer, arranger, and minister, was born in Chicago, Illinois, to Benjamin Cleveland, an employee of the federal Works Progress Administration, and Rosie (Lee) Cleveland. Cleveland's father and grandmother, Annie Hicks, raised him. Hicks was a devout member of the Pilgrim Baptist Church and choir, where pianist and composer THOMAS A. DORSEY served as choir director. During the Depression, James delivered newspapers to neighbors such as the gospel legend MAHALIA JACKSON. By the age of five he had a desire to play the piano like his childhood idol ROBERTA MARTIN of the Roberta Martin Singers. Since his family was too poor to afford a piano, he used his windowsill as an imaginary keyboard on which to master scales and chords. The church organist, Lucy Smith, provided Cleveland with formal instruction, and Roberta Martin took an early interest in his career. At the age of eight, Cleveland was granted his first piano solo by director Dorsey, the father of modern gospel.

As a young singer, James was a soprano with a sweet, stirring voice. As his voice began to deepen during puberty, he may have damaged his larynx in a futile effort to reach notes that were out of his range. The resulting raspy vocal quality became a hallmark of his sound as distinctive as the gravelly yet appealing voice of LOUIS ARMSTRONG. In 1948 Cleveland's skill as a composer of gospel lyrics gained recognition after Martin performed his song "Grace Is Sufficient" at the Baptist convention. Following this success, Martin agreed to pay Cleveland forty dollars for his compositions. The following year, Cleveland joined the Gospelaires, a group started by Bessie Folk and Norsalus McKissack, both former members of the Roberta Martin Singers. With the Gospelaires Cleveland made his first recording, "Oh, What a Time," on the Apollo label in 1950.

Cleveland brought his talents as a pianist, singer, or composer to various venues during the 1950s—including a tour with Mahalia Jackson. In 1953 he became pianist for the Caravans, a group formed by ALBERTINA WALKER, and he scored another hit, "The Solid Rock." In 1960, after starting his own group, the Gospel Chimes, Cleveland accepted an offer from the Reverend C. L. FRANKLIN to direct Franklin's choir at the New Bethel Baptist Church in Detroit. At that time, Franklin reigned as one of the most popular black preachers in the United States; the choir served largely as an opening act for his dynamic sermons. Cleveland also gave voice lessons to Franklin's nine-year-old daughter, ARETHA FRANKLIN, who later collaborated with Cleveland on the Grammy Award-winning album *Amazing Grace* before establishing herself as "Queen of Soul." During this time, Cleveland recorded his first major album, *Love of God*, with Detroit's Voices of Tabernacle Choir. Herman Lubinsky, owner of the independent Savoy Records, recognized Cleveland's unique talent and signed the gospel singer; their relationship proved to be a fruitful one that spanned almost three decades.

By the late 1950s the groups that had popularized gospel during the World War II era—mostly male-dominated quartets such as the Dixie Hummingbirds, the Soul Stirrers, and the Five Blind Boys—were in decline. By the 1960s many young gospel artists such as SAM COOKE, LOU RAWLS, and WILSON PICKETT were forsaking gospel choirs for rhythm and blues groups. The crossover promised a larger audience and greater financial rewards. During this period of secularization, Cleveland not only remained true to his gospel roots but also returned to using large choirs (which would not fit in older recording studios) and to interspersing sermonettes into many of his songs in order to recreate the church atmosphere on his recordings. And at a time when many middle-class black churches were shunning the ecstatic worship services and exuberant singing of an earlier time in favor of more sedate and "dignified" modes of expression, Cleveland moved closer to the religious abandon found in sanctified denominations. Though formally a member of the Baptist Church, he became a licensed minister with the Church of God in Christ and began using the title Reverend.

In 1963 Cleveland released his third album, *Peace Be Still*, which he recorded with the 300-voice Angelic Choir of Nutley, New Jersey. The size of the choir was unprecedented in the annals of gospel recording. Cleveland transformed the title song, a sixteenth-century madrigal, into a soulful supplication in which his words—partly spoken and partly sung—offered a prayer and the choir's refrain carried it to heaven. The song remained on the charts for fifteen years and sold over 750,000 copies during an era when selling 5,000 records represented a hit for a gospel song. Cleveland, now the "Crown Prince of Gospel," moved to Los Angeles to become the pastor of the Greater Harvest Baptist Church. Although both he and the acclaimed SHIRLEY CAESAR were lifting gospel music to new heights during this period, Cleveland wanted to create an innovative forum where gospel artists could better learn and practice their craft. Thus, in 1968 he launched the Gospel Music Workshop of America (GMWA). Eventually the GMWA expanded to 150 chapters with nearly 30,000 members, including the young gospel superstar Kirk Franklin.

Cleveland formed a new choir called the James Cleveland Singers, and ultimately founded a new congregation in 1970 called the Cornerstone Institutional Baptist Church, but he continued to record with great choirs around the country. In 1974 he won the first of three Grammy Awards for his album *In the Ghetto*. He followed with *Live at the Carnegie Hall* (1977) and *Lord, Let Me Be an Instrument* (1980). With these achievements, major record companies again approached him and nightclubs in Las Vegas and other large venues offered him lucrative sums for engagements. He rejected them all, arguing that his reasons were both religious and racially motivated. As for his recordings, he refused to allow his work to be used for white corporate profit. Regarding nightclubs, he did not believe that the spirituality of his performances should be mixed with the secular vices of drinking and gambling inherent in the casino experience.

However, Cleveland participated in a number of projects that were not strictly related to gospel. He worked with QUINCY JONES on the soundtrack to *Roots*, and assisted on the soundtracks for *The Idolmaker*, the comedy *The Blues Brothers*, and the opera *Porgy and Bess* with RAY CHARLES and Cleo Laine. He raised money for civil rights organizations such as JESSE JACKSON's Operation PUSH, and accepted awards from the NAACP. His aversion to secular songs did not abate his appetite for an extravagant home in Beverly Hills, nor his love of expensive clothes and luxury cars. Nevertheless, gospel was his life. His marriage (about which almost nothing is known) produced one child, Lashone, who lived with her mother after the couple divorced. He made over one hundred records, six of them gold, wrote more than 400 gospel songs, many of them standards, and became the first gospel singer to receive a star on the Walk of Fame in Hollywood. After he died of heart failure at the age of fifty-nine, there were struggles within his church to determine the disposition of its property. Several lawsuits were filed against his estate. Cleveland's legacy, however, transcended such secular and mundane issues. His death and life contributed to the ongoing debates concerning the "true" nature of gospel music. And to this his work speaks most eloquently—not through rhetoric of any kind, but through hundreds of excellent examples of gospel at its best.

FURTHER READING
The papers of James Cleveland are not yet publicly available.

Broughton, Viv. *Black Gospel* (1985).

Heilbut, Anthony. *The Gospel Sound: Good News and Bad Times* (1971).

Obituaries: *New York Times* 11 Feb. 1991; *Independent (London)* 11 Feb. 1991; *Washington Post*, 13 Feb. 1991; *Billboard*, 23 Feb. 1991.

SHOLOMO B. LEVY

Clifford, Carrie Williams (1862–11 Nov. 1934), poet, clubwoman, and political activist, was born in Chillicothe, Ohio, the daughter of Mary Evans and Joshua T. Williams, whose occupation is now unknown. In 1870 the family moved to Columbus, Ohio, where Mary Evans opened a successful wigmaking business that operated for over twenty years. Carrie Williams attended the first integrated school in Columbus. Whether she pursued higher education is unknown; however it is known that during the 1880s she taught in Parkersburg, West Virginia.

In 1886, at the age of twenty-four, she married William H. Clifford, a two-term Republican state representative from Cleveland. They would have two sons. As part of the black middle class in Cleveland, Clifford and her husband socialized with other important black figures such as CHARLES W. CHESNUTT and George A. Meyers. BOOKER T. WASHINGTON and W. E. B. DuBois made frequent appearances in Cleveland, joining the Cliffords for dinner and entertainment. While living in Cleveland, Clifford joined the Friday Night Study Club and helped found the Minerva Reading Club, which met twice a month. The club members eventually applied for membership to the National Association of Colored Women's (NACW) Clubs. Clifford attended the National Convention at Chicago in August 1899, where she was elected the third recording secretary of the NACW.

After meeting with Mrs. Jerome Jeffries, the National Organizer from the NACW in July of 1901, Clifford founded the Ohio State Federation of Colored Women's Clubs. The first state convention was held in December of that year. The women met at Mt. Zion Congregational Church in Cleveland with two representatives from outside the local area. Clifford was elected as the first president of the state organization. The organization grew quickly, adding eight cities to its list of represented clubs by its second convention in 1902. The following year Clifford, used her personal finances to start the organization's publication, *The Queen's Garden*. At the state convention that year in Xenia, the Ohio State Federation voted to continue the publication of the newsletter and allocated funds for it. Clifford edited a collection of women's essays titled *Sowing for Others to Reap: A Collection of Papers of Vital Importance to the Race*.

Clifford remained president of the Ohio State Federation until 1905. During this time she also held a position as the editor-in-chief of the Women's Department in the black-owned and -operated newspaper, the *Cleveland Journal*. In 1905 Carrie convinced the *Cleveland Journal*, typically only a four- to six-page paper, to print a twelve-page issue focused entirely on women's issues. MARGARET MURRAY WASHINGTON, the wife of Booker T. Washington, MARY CHURCH TERRELL, and many others had by-lines in the "Woman's Edition" of the *Journal*. Additionally Clifford regularly contributed

to larger national publications, such as the *Colored American Magazine* and *Alexander's Magazine*. One article, published in the *Colored American* in 1905, documented her mother's successful business career, and because of it Clifford was invited to deliver a speech at the National Negro Business League's Convention in New York City, drawing the attention of the *New York Times*.

As an advocate of women's suffrage Clifford was involved in the larger political events of her time. By 1906 both she and her husband had become members of the Niagara Movement. At the second convention held at Harpers Ferry, West Virginia, however, the women were excluded from the regular meetings. In response Clifford organized nightly meetings, which included WILLIAM MONROE TROTTER and JESSE MAX BARBER. Clifford was specifically asked to help recruit women for the Niagara Movement. By the third annual meeting in 1907, over half of the 800 delegates present were women. Clifford also proposed that the Niagara Movement merge with the Afro-American Council in order to strengthen its position. Clifford's dedication to the movement did not waver, even after the movement had been blacklisted by Booker T. Washington.

In 1908 Clifford moved with her two sons to Washington, D.C., to be with her husband, who had taken a position as an auditor in the War Department. In 1910 Clifford was invited to join the Committee of One Hundred of the NAACP. In addition to working at the national level, Clifford also worked to create the local chapter. In 1911 Clifford and Mary Church Terrell met with President William Howard Taft to present anti-lynching resolutions. Eventually Clifford was elected to an administrative post in the local chapter of the NAACP. She later became head of the NAACP's Juvenile Department and created a card game to teach children about important black figures.

In 1911, at the age of fifty, Clifford privately published her first volume of poetry, *Race Rhymes*. In addition to this volume of poetry, Clifford had several poems published in the *Crisis* and *Opportunity*. She also participated in several literary contests, at first as a contestant and later as a judge. Beginning in 1920 Clifford began to actively work toward the publication of her second volume of poetry, *The Widening Light*, which was published in 1922 and focused on issues of race and protest. Clifford continued her work within the NAACP until her husband's death in 1929; she died five years later.

FURTHER READING

Carrie Williams Clifford's papers are in the private family collection in the care of Rosemary Clifford McDaniel.

Carter, Linda M. "Carrie Williams Clifford," *Notable Black American Women, Book II* (1996).

Meyer, Jimmy E. W. "Carrie Williams Clifford," *African-American Women: A Biographical Dictionary* (1993).

Mohr, Diane L. "Carrie Williams Clifford," *The Black Renaissance in Washington D.C. 1920–1930's.* Available from http://www.dclibrary.org/blkren/bios/cliffordcw.html.

Smith, J. Clay, Jr. *Emancipation: The Making of the Black Lawyer, 1844–1944* (1999).

KIMBERLY A. SISSON

Clifford, John Robert (12 Sept. 1848–6 Oct. 1933), newspaper editor and civil rights lawyer, was born in Williamsport, Virginia (later West Virginia), the youngest of three sons born to Isaac Clifford, a farmer, and Mary Satilpa Kent, free blacks living in Hardy County. John Robert joined the Union army on 3 March 1865, rising to the rank of corporal in the 13th U.S. Heavy Artillery. After serving in Kentucky, Tennessee, and eastern Virginia under General Ulysses S. Grant, Clifford volunteered for service at Chicago, Illinois.

After the Civil War, Clifford remained in Chicago, staying from 1865 to 1868 with the Honorable John J. Healy, an acquaintance of his father, and graduating from Chicago High School. Clifford worked as a barber before going to live with an uncle in Zeno, Muskingum County, Ohio, where he attended a school taught by Miss Effie McKnight and received a diploma from a writing school conducted by a Professor D. A. White. Between 1870 and 1871 Clifford conducted a writing school for nearly one hundred students in Wheeling, West Virginia, and later in Martin's Ferry, Ohio. Clifford returned to West Virginia and entered Storer College at Harper's Ferry in 1873. At the age of twenty-five, in August of 1874, the young college student witnessed an event that would have a profound effect on his life: the lynching of a young black man named John Tallifero in nearby Martinsburg. Tallifero's murder sparked a chain of events that placed Clifford in direct conflict with local Republican leaders and led to a lifelong commitment to fighting for equal rights.

After graduating from Storer College in 1876 Clifford began teaching at the Sumner School in Martinsburg. In December 1876 he married a fellow Storer graduate, Mary Franklin of Harpers Ferry, West Virginia, in a ceremony performed by Nathan Brackett, the president of Storer College. The Cliffords had eleven children, several of whom died before reaching adulthood.

In the early 1880s Clifford became a member of the Knights of Wise Men, an African American fraternal organization whose national membership included JOHN ROY LYNCH, JOHN WESLEY CROMWELL, and HENRY MCNEAL TURNER. Clifford gave the address at the 1882 meeting held in Atlanta, Georgia. The organization afforded him the opportunity to discuss with prominent African Americans throughout the country the inequity that blacks faced in America. In that same year Clifford became the proprietor and editor of the first African American newspaper in West Virginia, the *Pioneer Press*. Publicized as a "Republican" newspaper, the *Press* was used as an organ through which to inform and educate blacks, as well as to criticize the changes taking place in the Republican Party after Reconstruction.

Animosity between Clifford and local Republican Party leaders increased when George F. Evans, who had been involved in the Tallifero lynching, was appointed postmaster of Martinsburg in 1874. Clifford expressed his opposition openly in the *Press*, encouraging 132 black voters to petition the Committee on Post-Offices and Post Roads of the U.S. Senate in protest of Evans's confirmation. He also threw his support behind the Democratic candidate, J. Nelson Wisner. In response, party leaders attempted to have Clifford fired from his position as teacher and principal at the Sumner School and began a campaign to shut down his paper. When delegates at the state Republican convention, held at Martinsburg in May, elected Clifford as a delegate-at-large to the national convention at Chicago, local leaders went from delegation to delegation, changing the votes and eliminating him. From 1884 on Clifford advocated "independent" voting, a political stance that angered many black West Virginians as well as local party leaders.

Clifford's opposition to local Republican leaders, his vocal demands for political, economic, and social equality for blacks, and his refusal to "accommodate" white politicians resulted not only in his exclusion from public office but also in attempts by his enemies to imprison and physically harm him. In addition class differences, political ideology, and Clifford's outspoken criticisms of the black community, notably what he felt was a lack of education and morality among local black preachers, served to separate him from many local blacks.

Tension increased in 1887 after Clifford passed the bar exam (having studied with J. Nelson Wisner) and became the first practicing African American lawyer in the state. In 1993 Clifford argued two cases before the courts challenging West Virginia's "separate but equal" school system. In *Martin v. Morgan County Board of Education*, Clifford asked the circuit court for an order compelling the board of education to admit black students to white schools in circumstances where no black schools existed. In the second case, *Williams v. Tucker County Board of Education*, after the board set the length of the school term for white schools at eight months and for the black school at five months, Clifford advised a black teacher in Coketon, West Virginia, Carrie Williams, to teach the entire eight months and then sue the board for her wages. In court Clifford argued that state law required school terms for black and white students to be equal and so the board owed Williams three months' salary. Both cases went before the West Virginia Supreme Court. In 1896 the court ruled against Clifford in the Martin case, stating that the West Virginia Constitution required separate schools. The Williams case, however, proved a victory. In one of the few, if not the first, cases in the South to state that discrimination on the basis of color was illegal, in 1898 the West Virginia Supreme Court ruled in favor of Carrie Williams. The decision upheld the law requiring equal terms in the state and established equal pay for teachers regardless of their color, attracting highly educated black teachers to the state and challenging nearby states to provide equal pay as well.

Between those two rulings Clifford led another battle against segregation in West Virginia. Although an 1879 U.S. Supreme Court decision in *Strauder v. West Virginia* gave blacks the right to serve on juries, the courts routinely failed to empanel African Americans. When Clifford attempted to empanel blacks in Martinsburg, the Berkeley County prosecutor, U. S. G. Pitzer, struck him three times with the "weights of justice" often found in courtrooms, knocking Clifford down each time and forcing blood to run into his shoes. No action was taken against Pitzer for this assault. Blacks did indeed sit on the jury, but Clifford lost the case. However when Pitzer ran for the state legislature in 1898 Clifford stood in the town square with the shirt he'd worn in court the day of Pitzer's attack, quite literally "waving the bloody shirt" and helping to send Pitzer down to defeat in the election.

Clifford was a grand master of the West Virginia Masons, and served as a lecturer for the state of West Virginia, teaching summer institutes for African American teachers in the state. He served as the state commissioner of the colored department of the New Orleans Exposition, and was the only black member of the West Virginia State Editorial Association. He played an active role in both the American Negro Academy and the Niagara Movement, making the arrangements for the historic Harper's Ferry meeting in 1906. In 1908 he joined ALEXANDER WALTERS, WILLIAM MONROE TROTTER, and Reverend J. Milton Waldron to form the National Negro-American Political League (later the National Independent Political League) and served as its president from 1911 to 1913. Clifford helped to form the West Virginia Civic League in 1915, the forerunner to the NAACP in West Virginia.

Hailed as the "dean of black editors," Clifford published the *Pioneer Press* for thirty-five years. When it closed in 1917 it was the longest-running black newspaper in the United States. Clifford died from injuries he sustained after falling down the stairs in his home at the age of eighty-five. Originally buried in Mount Hope Cemetery in Martinsburg, Clifford was re-interred in Arlington National Cemetery in 1954.

FURTHER READING

Evans, Willis. *History of Berkeley County, West Virginia* (1928)

Langhenry, Randy. "The Life and Times of John R. Clifford: A Pioneer Black Journalist," in *Honoring Our Past: Proceedings of the First Two Conferences of West Virginia's Black History*, ed. Joe William Trotter Jr. and Ancella Bickley (1993).

Moss, Alfred. *The American Negro Academy: Voice of the Talented Tenth* (1981).

Simmons, William J. *Men of Mark: Eminent, Progressive and Rising* (1887).

Smith, J. Clay, Jr. *Emancipation: The Making of the Black Lawyer, 1844–1944* (1993).

Obituary: *Martinsburg Journal*, 6 Oct. 1933.

CONNIE PARK RICE

Clifton, Lucille (27 June 1936–13 Feb. 2010), poet, author of children's literature, and memoirist, was born in Depew, New York, to Samuel L. Sayles, a steel mill worker, and Thelma Moore Sayles, a homemaker, laundry worker, and amateur poet. Born Thelma Lucille Sayles, she was named for one of her father's ancestors, the daughter of a woman

Lucille Clifton was a 2000 National Book Awards finalist for her poetry collection *Blessing the Boats: New and Selected Poems 1988–2000.* (AP Images.)

kidnapped from Dahomey (later Benin), West Africa, in 1822 and enslaved in Virginia. This early Lucille had been executed for killing the white man who had fathered her son.

In 1953 Clifton became the first member of her family to graduate from high school. She attended Howard University on scholarship as a drama major for two years, from 1953 to 1955, meeting writers such as AMIRI BARAKA (then LeRoi Jones), STERLING ALLEN BROWN, and TONI MORRISON (then Chloe Wofford). Clifton chose to leave Howard, telling her family that she wanted to write poetry. She then attended Fredonia State Teachers College (later the State University of New York) graduating from there in 1955. It was also where she met her future husband, Fred James Clifton. They were married in 1958 and had six children together.

From 1958 to 1960 Clifton worked as a claims clerk for the state of New York's Employment Division in Buffalo, and then from 1960 to 1971 in the Office of Education in Washington, D.C.

Meanwhile Clifton was crafting her poetic style, one marked by the use of the vernacular, concrete images, strongly drawn images, and a lack of standardized punctuation and capitalization. Clifton's poetry draws heavily upon African American oral traditions as well as her family's personal history. Most often written in free verse, her poetry is stark and emotional. In a writers' group she shared her work with the author ISHMAEL REED, who then passed it on to the poet ROBERT EARL HAYDEN, who became the first editor to publish her poetry.

In 1969 Hayden nominated Clifton for the Young Women's–Young Men's Hebrew Association Poetry Center Discovery Award, which she won. The award led to the publication of her first book of poetry, *Good Times*, in 1969, which was nominated by the *New York Times* as one of the ten best books of the year. She published two books of children's literature in 1970 that were picture books of verse: *The Black ABC's* and *Some of the Days of Everett Anderson*; the character of Everett Anderson would appear in seven more books. These were the first of more than twenty children's books that Clifton would write. These early publications all contributed to her growing reputation as a writer, a reputation enhanced when Clifton received creative writing fellowships from the National Endowment for the Arts, first in 1970 and again in 1973. The two next collections of poetry were *Good News about the Earth* in 1972 and *An Ordinary Woman* in 1974. The themes found in the latter book relate to the extraordinary lives led by the "ordinary" women of history. This continues one of Clifton's themes, exploring women's history, including HARRIET TUBMAN and SOJOURNER TRUTH. Following the success of *Good Times*, Clifton became writer-in-residence at Coppin State College in Baltimore, Maryland, a post she held until 1974.

In 1976 Clifton published *Generations: A Memoir*, in which she traced her family's line back to West Africa and told the stories of her ancestors in first-person narratives. Clifton was named Maryland's poet laureate in 1979 and served in that post until 1985. Early in her tenure as poet laureate she published her next collection of poetry, *Two-Headed Woman*, in 1980, which won the University of Massachusetts Press Juniper Prize. She was named visiting writer at the Columbia University School of the Arts in 1982 and at George Washington University in 1983. Later she taught at the University of California–Santa Cruz (1985–1989) and then at St. Mary's College of Maryland (1989–1991), where she served as distinguished professor of humanities.

Clifton gathered her first four volumes of poetry and the memoir *Generations* in a 1987 collected works anthology titled *Good Woman: Poems and a Memoir*. That same year she also published *Next: New Poems*, a collection which contained many poems mourning the loss of some of the people closest to her, including her mother, who had died twenty-eight years earlier on 13 February 1959, and her husband, who had died at age forty-nine on 10 November 1984. Both *Good Woman* and *Next* received Pulitzer Prize nominations, making Clifton the only author to have had two books of poetry nominated for the Pulitzer Prize in the same year.

Clifton's output over the last two decades of the twentieth century was prolific: she published *Quilting: Poems, 1987–1990* in 1991; *The Book of Light* in 1993; *The Terrible Stories* (which was nominated for the National Book Award) in 1996; and *Blessing the Boats: New and Selected Poems, 1988–2000* in 2000, which won the award. She was also appointed a chancellor of the Academy of American Poets in 1999. Her poems have been reprinted in more than a hundred anthologies, and she appeared on numerous television shows, including Bill Moyers's series *The Power of the Word*, which originally aired during the fall of 1989.

Clifton's poetry has been widely read and celebrated, earning her many prestigious awards. She won the American Poetry Society's Shelley Memorial Prize in 1991–1992, the Charity Randall Prize from the International Poetry Forum in 1991, and the Jerome J. Shestack Poetry Prize from the *American Poetry Review* in 1988. She was elected a chancellor of the Academy of American Poets in 1999. A prolific and celebrated writer, Clifton published another collection of poems titled *Mercy* in 2004. Clifton wrote often about the strength and dignity found in African American families, in the roots of those families themselves, and the strength that individuals can find within themselves, giving voice to what many experience. She retired from St. Mary's College in 2005 and was given the title professor emeritus. Clifton died in Baltimore at the age of seventy-three.

FURTHER READING

Lucille Clifton's papers are housed in the Special Collections Department, Raymond Danowski Poetry Library, Emory University, in Atlanta, Georgia.

Holliday, Hilary. *Wild Blessings: The Poetry of Lucille Clifton* (2004).

Hull, Akasha. "In Her Own Images: Lucille Clifton and the Bible," in *Dwelling in Possibility: Women Poets and Critics on Poetry*, ed. Yopie Prins and Maeera Shreiber (1997).

Lupton, Mary Jane. *Lucille Clifton: Her Life and Letters* (2006).

Madhubuti, Haki. "Lucille Clifton: Warm Water, Greased Legs, and Dangerous Poetry," in *Black Women Writers (1950–1980): A Critical Evaluation*, ed. Mari Evans (1984).

AMY SPARKS KOLKER

Clinton, George (22 July 1940–), singer, songwriter, producer, and leader of Parliament-Funkadelic, was born in Kannapolis, North Carolina, the eldest of Julia Keaton's nine children. His father's name is unknown, but Clinton had moved to Plainfield, New Jersey, by the time he was a teenager. While straightening hair at a local barbershop, Clinton began singing doo-wop in the back room with a group called the Parliaments. Formed in 1955, they modeled themselves after the hit makers FRANKIE

George Clinton performs during the Jerry Lewis Labor Day Telethon in Beverly Hills, California, in September 2005. (AP Images.)

LYMON and the Teenagers, and they spent the next decade on the competitive R&B circuit. Although they recorded sparingly during this period, the group's repeated trips to Detroit helped Clinton establish himself as a producer and songwriter with the Motown Records subsidiary Jobete. In 1964 the Parliaments themselves signed with Motown, but it was for Revilot Records that the group scored an R&B hit in 1967 with the gospel-drenched "(I Wanna) Testify," sung by Clinton. In the late 1960s, prompted not only by disagreements with their record company but also by Clinton's interest in the rock movements emerging from Detroit, San Francisco, and elsewhere, the group changed its artistic direction and called itself Funkadelic. Building on the psychedelic iconography and improvised music favored by rockers like Frank Zappa and JIMI HENDRIX, Clinton transformed his former group into a loud, freaky ensemble that played extended, mind-tripping material that blended rock, soul, and jazz. The new band grew to include virtuoso players like Eddie Hazel, Bernie Worrell, and Bootsy Collins, and coalesced around Clinton's eccentric vision. Funkadelic's early albums, recorded for Westbound Records, reflected both a desire to push the boundaries of black musical expression and a deep engagement (both intellectual and emotional) with political issues as broad as black political equality and as pointed as the Vietnam War. Albums like *Maggot Brain* (1971), *America Eats Its Young* (1972), and *Cosmic Slop* (1973) mixed love ballads with war protests, burning funk jams with philosophical journeys of the mind and spirit, all in search of Clinton's envisioned "one nation under a groove." Although Funkadelic achieved limited commercial success during this period, its impact on the music world (particularly within the context of Black Power) was substantial.

Clinton found greater success with Parliament, a dance-oriented group that ran simultaneously to Funkadelic and featured most of the same membership. With Parliament, the overt commentaries that were so prominent in Funkadelic's work were made more subtle, and the albums were constructed around a series of alternate-reality visions of time, space, and identity that owed a debt to the conception of a "collective unconscious" articulated by Clinton's intellectual hero, Carl Jung. Faced with the difficult moment after the civil rights and Black Power movements, when internal fractures and external repression left both goals and spirits diminished, Clinton and Parliament offered inventive jazz-inflected visions of black freedom that included the lost continent of Atlantis, or an alien "Mothership" swinging down (like the "sweet chariot" of slave days) to take its children home. Their musical and lyrical futurism, combined with a firm grounding in African American traditions, created a potent mixture. The group created an ongoing series of characters (such as the rhythmless, cocaine-fueled Sir Nose D'Voidoffunk or his nemesis, and bearer of the "uncut funk," Star Child), whose stories crisscrossed around the deep grooves of Parliament's music. Clinton himself found a fitting alter ego in the mad scientist Dr. Funkenstein. Indeed, though the philosophical underpinnings of Parliament's work were heavy, even dense, the intoxicating rhythms and compelling melodies made the group far more commercially accessible than Funkadelic. Far from being in conflict, the band actively juxtaposed the complex polyrhythm and memorable melodic structures in creative tandem: as their song "Aqua Boogie (A Psychoalphadiscobetabioaquadoloop)" suggested, "with the rhythm it takes to dance to what we have to live through, you can dance underwater and not get wet."

Clinton's ambitious scope was not only reflected on his albums. Apart from Parliament and Funkadelic, at least three other successful groups were part of the "P-Funk" universe, including Bootsy's Rubber Band and the Brides of Funkenstein. In addition, P-Funk shows were legendary spectacles with stage props (including, for a time, a descending, glowing Mothership), outlandish costumes, and as many as thirty musicians on stage at one time. These shows, which often lasted more than four hours, were full-blast expressions of Clinton's experimental, communal concept, and were also among the reasons why, by the late 1970s, the band was no longer economically viable. This excess, its accompanying drug use, and personnel departures meant that even after Parliament hits such as "Flash Light" and "Give Up the Funk (Tear the Roof off the Sucker)," and a resurgence of Funkadelic with disco-era hits such as "Knee Deep," the Mothership was grounded by the early 1980s. Although Clinton scored a surprise monster hit in 1983 with "Atomic Dog," and later recorded for PRINCE's Paisley Park label, his musical presence during the decade was primarily as an important influence on the funk, R&B, and hip-hop artists of the day.

It was through hip-hop that Clinton made his resurgence. In the early 1990s the Los Angeles–based "G-Funk" movement, which took both its name and much of its musical foundation from Parliament-Funkadelic, helped return Clinton to national prominence. DR. DRE, perhaps the genre's most popular producer, used Clinton samples as the foundation of much of his smash 1993 album *The Chronic*, and many other popular West Coast rappers such as ICE CUBE, SNOOP DOGGY DOGG, and Coolio utilized the rolling beats and party atmosphere of Clinton's recorded work. Alternative rockers the Red Hot Chili Peppers also championed Clinton, hiring him to produce one of their albums. This fame helped Clinton relaunch his own career; one album, a 1994 compilation called *Greatest Funkin' Hits*, contained versions of P-Funk classics remixed by some of Clinton's gangsta-rap fans.

In 1997 Parliament-Funkadelic was inducted by Prince into the Rock and Roll Hall of Fame. The award was a testament to the group's widespread influence, as its deeply funky music and sophisticated themes have resonated across many genres and eras. Clinton continued to record and tour into the 2000s and has remained one of the most respected living figures in American music. His genius marked him as one of the culture's most truly inventive musical figures.

FURTHER READING

Bush, John. "George Clinton," "Funkadelic," and "Parliament," in *All Music Guide to R&B and Soul*, ed. Vladimir Bogdanov (2003).

Mills, David, et al., eds. *George Clinton and P-Funk: An Oral History* (1998).

Vincent, Rickey (foreword by George Clinton). *Funk: The Music, the People and the Power of the One* (1996).

Werner, Craig. *A Change Is Gonna Come: Music, Race and the Soul of America* (1999)

CHARLES L. HUGHES

Clyburn, James Enos (21 July 1940–), Congressman from South Carolina's Sixth District, was born in Sumter County, South Carolina, the son of Enos Lloyd Clyburn and Almeta (Dizzley) Clyburn. Clyburn's parents met while his mother was attending Mather Academy, a private secondary school for African Americans in Camden, South Carolina. Clyburn's father was a minister in the Church of God, and, after marrying James's mother Almeta, he accepted the pastorate of a church in Sumter, South Carolina, which would allow both him and his wife to attend Morris College in Sumter. Clyburn would later describe both his parents as having a "tremendous thirst for education," and he would credit their commitment to learning and their struggles to obtain college degrees as the inspiration behind his lifelong dedication to seeking equal opportunities for South Carolinians and Americans in general (interview with James Clyburn, 20 Nov. 2006).

Clyburn's mother finished Morris College in three years, but chose to operate a beauty shop and raise children in lieu of pursuing a career in teaching. Despite a distinguished academic record, Clyburn's father was not allowed to earn a degree from Morris College because it was discovered that he had never finished high school. In fact, African Americans of his generation in Kershaw County, South Carolina (the elder Clyburn's home), were only allowed to attend school through the seventh grade. Clyburn's father would not tell his son that he had not completed his college degree until a few months before his death in 1978, because he did not want James to assume it was acceptable not to finish college. Clyburn's father was posthumously awarded a degree by Morris College a decade after his son entered Congress.

Growing up as the son of a minister in the segregated South Carolina of the 1940s and 1950s, Clyburn was on the front line of the civil rights movement. He was personally acquainted with the plaintiffs from neighboring Clarendon County in the case of *Briggs v. Elliot*, which was later consolidated with subsequent civil rights cases in the U.S. Supreme Court as *Brown v. Board of Education*. Clyburn's father was active, though not outspoken, in the civil rights movement; nevertheless, the family lived in fear of reprisals from segregationists. At age twelve, Clyburn told a family friend and customer in his mother's beauty shop that he wanted to be in politics and government when he grew up. She responded, "Son, don't you ever let anybody else hear you say that again," because such aspirations were bound to be disappointed and would trigger hostility from whites (interview, 20 Nov. 2006). Clyburn's mother told him to ignore this admonition, and Clyburn would tell this story in his speech accepting election as the majority whip in the U.S. House of Representatives in 2006.

Clyburn graduated from Mather Academy in 1957 and went on to South Carolina State University in Orangeburg, South Carolina. While at South Carolina State, Clyburn was active in student politics, and he participated in the lunch-counter sit-ins in Orangeburg in the spring of 1960. Clyburn was jailed for participating in the sit-ins, and while in jail he met his future wife, fellow sit-in participant

Emily England. They were married on 24 June 1961, and eventually had three daughters.

Clyburn received a B.S. from South Carolina State in 1962, and went on to work as a teacher, employment counselor, and executive director of the South Carolina State Commission for Farm Workers. Clyburn ran unsuccessfully for the South Carolina legislature from Charleston County in 1970, the only Democrat in an eleven-candidate countywide slate to lose. Clyburn would reportedly later confess that he was considered too young and too brash to be elected in South Carolina at that time.

In 1971 newly elected South Carolina Governor John C. West asked Clyburn to serve as one of his advisers. Clyburn at first demurred, believing he was not a "good fit" with the popular white governor. Clyburn changed his mind when West told him, "If I were black, and had as much on the ball as you have, I'd be much more militant than you are" (interview, 20 Nov. 2006). In accepting the position, Clyburn became the first African American adviser to a South Carolina governor since Reconstruction.

Clyburn served as assistant to the governor for human resources from 1971 to 1974, helping organize the South Carolina Human Affairs Commission in 1972. In 1974 Clyburn was named the second commissioner of the South Carolina Human Affairs Commission. He remained at the head of the Human Affairs Commission for eighteen years, expanding the commission's investigatory and enforcement authority with respect to employment and housing discrimination in South Carolina. Clyburn ran unsuccessfully for South Carolina secretary of state in 1978 and 1986.

Prior to the 1992 election, South Carolina's Sixth Congressional District was redrawn to become a majority African American district. Clyburn secured the Democratic nomination for the seat, and defeated prominent Republican attorney John R. Chase in the general election, becoming the first African American to be elected to Congress from South Carolina since the nineteenth century.

Clyburn quickly rose through the ranks in the U.S. House of Representatives in the 1990s, and he was elected co-president of the freshman class in 1993, chair of the Congressional Black Caucus in 1998, vice chair of the House Democratic Caucus in 2002, and Democratic Caucus chair in 2005. After the Democrats took control of the House in November 2006, Clyburn was elected majority whip, the third most powerful position in the House. Clyburn was the second African American to serve as majority whip, which is the highest Congressional office ever held by an African American.

Known for his considerable negotiating skills and a willingness to seek compromise on major issues, Clyburn's tenure as chair of the Congressional Black Caucus was hailed as the beginning of a new era of pragmatism for African Americans in Congress. A staunch advocate of constituent interest and what some termed "pork barrel" projects, Clyburn promoted education, healthcare, and rural economic development in eastern South Carolina, one of the poorest areas in the state. Because of his prominence among South Carolina Democrats, Clyburn earned the sobriquet "Carolina Kingmaker" in the 2000 and 2004 presidential elections.

FURTHER READING

James Clyburn's papers are housed in the Miller F. Whittaker Library at South Carolina State University in Orangeburg, South Carolina.

Interview with James Clyburn, 20 November 2006 (audiotape), collection of the E. N. Zeigler South Carolina History Room, Florence County Library, Florence, South Carolina.

Derfner, Jeremy. "The New Black Caucus," *American Prospect*, 27 March 2000.

BENJAMIN T. ZEIGLER

Coachman, Alice (9 Nov. 1923–), track-and-field athlete, was the fifth of ten children born to Fred "Doc" and Evelyn Coachman in Albany, Georgia. She was primarily raised by her great-grandmother and maternal grandmother and endured the difficulties of impoverishment. As a child, she participated in music and dance and was active in sports. Like many other African American women, she competed in basketball and track in junior high, where she came to the attention of Coach Henry E. Lash at Madison High School.

It was at this point that Coachman made a leap and became part of what was fast becoming a track-and-field dynasty when she transferred to the Tuskegee Institute in Tuskegee, Alabama, where she was trained by the renowned coach CLEVELAND ABBOTT. Founded by BOOKER T. WASHINGTON in 1881 as a teacher's college, Tuskegee was one of the first black institutions to embrace women's athletics, and Abbott's team dominated the national track scene for decades, winning fourteen national outdoor titles, nine consecutively. When Coachman graduated from high school, she stayed at the Tuskegee Institute and obtained a certificate in tailoring in 1946. In 1947 she transferred to Albany State College, having earned

Alice Coachman cleared the bar at five feet to win the running high jump at the Women's National Track Meet in Grand Rapids, Iowa, in July 1948. (AP Images.)

the nickname the "Tuskegee Flash." From 1939 to 1948 she competed in the high jump, 50-meter dash, 100-meter dash, and many relay teams. At Tuskegee she won ten consecutive national outdoor high-jump titles. In 1946 she was the first African American selected for the All-American team.

Coachman joined the 1948 U.S. Olympic team along with eight other black women—nine of twelve women on the Olympic track-and-field team were African American that year. This stood in marked contrast to the 1932 and 1936 Games, when the black sprinters LOUISE STOKES and TIDYE PICKETT were included in the team, but not selected to run. At the 1948 London games, Coachman competed in the high jump with severe back pains caused by a twisted ovary, but nevertheless she won the gold medal on her first jump. Coachman jumped 5 feet 6¼ inches, a feat that was both an Olympic and an American record. She was the first African American woman to win a gold medal. Audrey Patterson of Tennessee State, another black college with a standout women's track-and-field program, won a second Olympic medal when she got a bronze in the 200 meters.

Coachman and Patterson were the only American track-and-field women to earn medals.

When Coachman returned home, she was honored with a parade, recognition dinners, and a meeting with President Harry S. Truman. Still, given America's deep segregation and racism, Coachman was not allowed to speak at the ceremony in her honor at the segregated Albany Municipal Auditorium in Georgia. Coachman felt the weight of her responsibility to excel, later saying that "if I had gone to the Games and failed, there wouldn't have been anyone to follow in my footsteps" (McElroy, 14). Her gold medal performance, along with Patterson's bronze medal, served to legitimate the start-up track programs at black schools. Her achievement was a great source of pride to black America, struggling under segregation and moving toward civil rights.

Although Coachman turned in a superlative performance at the 1948 Olympics and received a lot of attention in the years immediately following her win, her name quickly faded from public conversations. Track, like basketball, which had held great public interest in the 1920s and early 1930s, was by mid-century considered a "masculine" sport unsuited to properly feminine athletes. Stereotypes of race and gender intersected in devastating ways at this time and no doubt had an effect on Coachman's life. Women who competed in track were ridiculed as "muscle molls" or amazons, and it was a common view that women who succeeded in this sport were not "normal" women.

African American women, including Coachman, withstood this kind of ridicule and prevailed to occupy a central place in track and field. They stepped up to the challenge when middle-class white women had largely backed down, and they began a long tradition of national and international excellence. Track participation was a double-edged sword for African American women. On one hand, performances like Coachman's or those of Mae Faggs and WILMA RUDOLPH a little later demonstrated that African American women could excel at an endeavor valued by American culture: winning medals in an increasingly nationalistic Olympic games. On the other hand, because these achievements were in a "masculine" sport, it reinforced racist and sexist stereotypes of black women as less "feminine" than middle-class white women.

Because of her age and perhaps because of a growing ambivalence in American culture toward women's participation in track and field, Coachman retired from competition in 1948 and focused on her education. She received a degree in Home Economics and Science from Albany State College in 1949. She became the first black female athletic champion to sign a product endorsement for a multinational corporation, Coca-Cola, in 1952. For many years Coachman taught physical education and trained other women athletes, first at a high school in Albany, Georgia. She also taught at Southern Carolina State College, Albany State College, and Tuskegee High School. After her retirement she lived with her second husband, Frank Davis, in Alabama. Coachman established the Alice Coachman Track and Field Foundation in 1994, a nonprofit organization for young athletes and retired Olympians. Despite the stigmatization of women's participation in track and field in mid-century, Coachman's legacy has opened the way for beloved American track stars, such as Evelyn Ashford, FLORENCE GRIFFITH-JOYNER, Gwen Torrance, Gayle Devers, JACKIE JOYNER-KERSEE, and MARION JONES. Coachman has been honored with memberships in eight halls of fame, including the National Track and Field Hall of Fame, the Georgia Sports Hall of Fame, and the Albany Sports Hall of Fame.

FURTHER READING
Cahn, Susan K. *Coming on Strong: Gender and Sexuality in Twentieth-Century Women's Sport* (1994).
Emerson, A. D. *Olympians against the Wind: The Black American Female Difference* (1999).
McElroy, Kathleen. "Somewhere to Run," in *Nike Is a Goddess: The History of Women in Sports* (1998).
Rhoden, William C. "Good Things Happening for One Who Decided to Wait," *New York Times*, April 27, 1995.
Vertinsky, Patricia, and Gwendolyn Captain. "More Myth Than History: American Culture and Representations of the Black Female's Athletic Ability." *Journal of Sport History* 25, no. 3 (1998): 532–561.

LESLIE HEYWOOD

Cobb, Charles E., Jr. (23 June 1943–), poet, journalist, and activist, was born in Washington, D.C., the oldest of four children of Charles E. Cobb Sr., a Methodist minister, and Martha Kendrick Cobb. His father's ministry kept the family on the move, and they lived in Kentucky, North Carolina, Massachusetts, and other states. Cobb attended Howard University in 1961 and 1962, leaving after his freshman year for Mississippi to organize and register black voters as a member of the Student Nonviolent Coordinating Committee (SNCC). Five years in southern cities with SNCC provided Cobb with a sense of purpose, of "determining and doing a work that is mine … living a life that is mine" ("Whose Society Is This?," quoted in Williams). In his first volume of poetry, *In the Furrows of the World* (1967), Cobb chronicles the often violent struggles of the civil rights movement with poems and photos of protests, lynchings, field work, and militant opposition to white supremacy. Like many of his contemporaries in the Black Arts Movement, such as AMIRI BARAKA and NIKKI GIOVANNI, Cobb experimented with minimal punctuation, capitalization, and deliberate misspellings as a way of upending the established social and political order. He notes the irony of the war in Vietnam and the war at home:

where
LITTLE CHILDREN
COME DOWN
BLOWN APART
IN PIECES
cause they're the Enemy too (*Furrows*, 47)

From his 1967 trip to Hanoi came the poem "To Vietnam," in which Cobb reflects that in the United States, "wind has never sung song / of nation in my black face" (*Furrows*, 51). In "L.A.— The Order of Things," he confronts police brutality in the Watts riots in Los Angeles: "The Best Ghetto In the Country/where/they/should understand/ lawful expression" (*Furrows*, 13–14) and ends his volume with a call for unity in the black community, to "dig ourselves in the mirror" (*Furrows*, 54) and "destroy white oppression" (*Furrows*, 53). In 1968 Cobb returned to Washington, D.C., where he worked with the Drum and Spear Press, a black publisher. His work with Drum and Spear took him to Tanzania, where he developed a broader vision of African American identity as it relates to Africa. As he wrote in *African Notebook: Views on Returning "Home"* (1971), African Americans "have no really fixed collective relationship to Africa except in the vague, highly romanticized sense of being 'lost brothers'" (quoted in Williams). *African Notebook* marks Cobb's shift in focus from poetry to journalism, though he published one more book of poetry, *Everywhere Is Yours*, also in 1971. In "Nation No. 3" from this volume, Cobb explores the yearning African American relationship to the African continent:

In searching, stumble to you Africa,
as a child torn from the womb,
slung to die, as without milk.
Minds eye wanders to where I have never been in looking
for where we can be (quoted in Williams).

Cobb's work in Africa led him to work on the U.S. House of Representatives Subcommittee on Africa in the mid-seventies. Cobb studied journalism at the University without Walls at Howard University from 1973 until 1976. From 1974 to 1976 he worked as a Capitol Hill reporter for WHUR radio, then reported on foreign affairs for National Public Radio until 1979. From that time on he worked as a freelance reporter for various news outlets, including *Black Enterprise* magazine, PBS's *Frontline*, and the Africa News Service.

Beginning in 1985 Cobb wrote regularly for *National Geographic* magazine on a wide array of subjects related to black culture, including Bahia, "the most African of Brazilian states," blues culture from Mississippi to Chicago, and conflicting responses to tourism and development in Harlem. In "Traveling the Blues Highway" (1999), Cobb drew on his family history to illuminate the dying art of blues music, starting with his great-grandfather Samuel Reuben Kendrick, who founded a farming community called New Africa in Mississippi in 1888. He also told the story of his great-aunt Hattie Kendrick, who hired THURGOOD MARSHALL in her successful suit against the Cairo, Illinois, school board regarding unequal salaries for black teachers. Cobb's work with *National Geographic* also included reporting on environmental issues.

Cobb reunited with his old friend ROBERT P. MOSES, from their days as SNCC voting rights activists to publish *Radical Equations: Civil Rights from Mississippi to the Algebra Project* (2001). Widely praised as a call to action through math education in poor communities, the book deftly wove the political activism of the 1960s with Moses's work on the Algebra Project, a growing nationwide movement of educational empowerment. Though the book was written in the first person from Moses's point of view, Cobb was nevertheless listed as coauthor, and in the acknowledgments Moses stated that "This story has been unfolding for the past forty years, but it took Charlie to get it told" (222).

Cobb continued his work in international journalism as senior writer and diplomatic correspondent for allAfrica.com. He wrote about the Montgomery bus boycott for the Smithsonian Institution Traveling Exhibition Service (2005) and served as speaker on the topic of journalism in the African diaspora at the African Diaspora Heritage Trail Conference in 2006. With his wife, Ann L. Chinn, Cobb had one daughter, Zora Nomnikelo, born in 1993, and a stepson, Kenn Blagurn. Cobb's enduring interests in African cultures around the world continued to inform his work, and he provided a vibrant voice for black empowerment.

FURTHER READING

Cobb, Charles E., Jr., with Robert P. Moses. *Radical Equations: Civil Rights from Mississippi to the Algebra Project* (2001).

Cobb, Charles E. "Whose Society Is This?," in *Thoughts of Young Radicals* (1966).

Cobb, Charlie. *In the Furrows of the World* (1967).

Williams, Clara R. *Dictionary of Literary Biography, Volume 41: Afro-American Poets Since 1955*, ed. Trudier Harris (1985).

ALICE KNOX EATON

Cobb, James Adlai (1876–14 Oct. 1958), lawyer, judge, professor of law, and civil rights activist, was born on a plantation near Shreveport, Louisiana. Nothing is known about Cobb's parents, except that his mother was white and his father black. Orphaned at an early age, Cobb worked various jobs and was eventually able to save enough money to attend private schools. Cobb studied at Straight University (later Dillard University) in New Orleans and Fisk University in Nashville, Tennessee. After relocating to Washington, D.C., Cobb continued his education and graduated from Howard University with a bachelor of law degree in 1899. In 1900 Cobb was awarded a J.D. from Howard University School of Law.

Cobb was admitted to the Washington, D.C., bar in 1901 and began practicing law. His practice primarily involved handling racial discrimination cases on behalf of black Americans. In 1907 Cobb was appointed special assistant in the U.S. Department of Justice, and later made his way to the office of U.S. Attorney. As the first African American to be appointed as an assistant U.S. attorney in the legal department of the Department of Justice, between 1907 and 1915, Cobb handled several cases that were prosecuted under the 1906 Food and Drug Act. He was known for his zealous prosecution style and affiliation with the Republican Party.

In 1915, after resigning from his post at the Department of Justice, Cobb continued his affiliation with the Republican Party and attended the Republican National Convention as a delegate in 1920 and 1924. He also returned to private law practice and later established the law firm of Cobb, Howard, and Hayes. As one of the most influential law firms in the county, Cobb, Howard, and Hayes hired and trained black lawyers in the D.C. area who had experienced difficulty obtaining jobs with other Washington-area law firms. The clientele of the firm constituted a diverse population.

In 1915 the Supreme Court began to strike down Jim Crow laws. The landmark decisions in several cases encouraged black plaintiffs to file lawsuits challenging racial discrimination. In 1916 Cobb joined the faculty of Howard University's School of Law, where he taught courses in constitutional law. His expertise in the area of constitutional law led Cobb to represent plaintiffs in cases that involved racial discrimination. *Buchanan v. Warley* (1917) was Cobb's first case involving housing discrimination. The lawsuit was brought by an African American who alleged that a Louisville, Kentucky, housing ordinance fostered housing segregation. Cobb, along with the lawyers T. Gillis Nutter and W. Ashbie Hawkins, argued that the ordinance

requiring blacks and whites to live in separate areas violated the Fourteenth Amendment of the Constitution. On 5 November 1917 the U.S. Supreme Court ruled in favor of Cobb's clients and struck down the Louisville ordinance.

In 1923 Cobb was appointed as vice dean of the Howard University School of Law. He served in this capacity until 1929, when he was removed from the position due to personal conflict with the university's president Mordecai W. Johnson. Cobb remained actively involved with Howard until 1938.

Cobb's participation and political affiliation with the Republican Party paved the way for President Calvin Coolidge to appoint him to a judgeship in the District of Columbia's Municipal Court in 1926. Cobb succeeded the first African American appointed to a full federal judgeship, Robert H. Terrell. Cobb was re-appointed to a second term by President Herbert Hoover; however, he was not reappointed by Democratic President Franklin Delano Roosevelt when Cobb's term ended in 1934.

In 1931, during a speaking engagement at the National Bar Association Convention in Cleveland, Ohio, Cobb called for Congress to pass the pending Anti-Lynching Bill. In his speech Cobb argued

Lynching is murder plus something else, namely anarchy, if the State dealt with the situation there could be no lynching, or if so, a trial of those committing lynching acts would be had. If the nation has constitutional powers to call its citizens to arms to fight its battle, then it has power to go into any part of its territory to protect the lives and property of those citizens ("Anti-Lynching Bills Constitutional Says Judge Cobb at Cleveland Bar Association Convention," *Washington World*, 14 Aug. 1931).

In 1935 Cobb returned to full-time practice in his law firm. He served as counsel on significant cases involving constitutional issues, including *Nixon v. Herndon* (1927), which involved a Texas statute that barred blacks from voting in Democratic primary elections. The U.S. Supreme Court ruled in favor of Cobb's client and held the statute an unconstitutional violation of the Fourteenth Amendment.

Because of his outstanding work as an educator, judge, lawyer, and community activist, the Washington Bar Association honored Cobb with a tribute in January 1940. In 1955 he received the Howard University Achievement Award for Distinguished Post-Graduate Service in the Field of Law. He served as a board member of the NAACP, the Urban League, and the local Selective Service

Board, and as a trustee of the Washington Public Library. In his last will and testament Cobb established a charitable trust in the amount of $300,000 at Howard University and its Law School as a scholarship fund for students.

FURTHER READING

Significant documents related to Cobb's career are located in the Moorland Springarn Research Center at Howard University, Washington, D.C.

DONNAMARIA CULBRETH

Cobb, Jewell Plummer (27 Jan. 1924–), research biologist, educator, and college administrator, was born in Chicago. Her mother, Carriebel Cole, was a physical education teacher who taught interpretive dance in the public schools. Her father, Frank Victor Plummer, a physician, graduated from Cornell University in 1908 and subsequently from Rush Medical School in Chicago. He was an early member of Alpha Phi Alpha, the first national Greek letter fraternity for black men.

The Plummer family strongly emphasized education. Cobb's parents' circle of friends included black writers, historians, and artists. As a member of the upper middle class, she enjoyed many more educational, cultural, and social advantages than did most African American children of that era. She had access to a library in her home that included scientific texts belonging to her father. Not surprisingly, Cobb developed an early interest in science. Her interest in biology developed when she was a high school sophomore studying cells under a microscope. In high school she succeeded academically and was a member of her school's honor society.

Following her graduation in 1941, Cobb attended the University of Michigan at Ann Arbor. Black students at the University of Michigan at that time were not allowed to live in dormitories with white students and were denied certain courses of study. After three semesters at the predominately white school she transferred to Talledega College, a historically black college in Talledega, Alabama. She had to restart her college education because Talledega did not accept her credits from the University of Michigan. Nevertheless, she fulfilled requirements for graduation in three and a half years and emerged in 1944 with a bachelor of arts degree in biology.

Cobb's path to graduate school was not smooth. The graduate school at New York University accepted Cobb during her final year at Talledega but at first denied her application for financial aid. When she demonstrated her credentials and her determination during a face-to-face interview, the fellowship committee relented and awarded her a five-year fellowship for graduate study. She earned a master's degree in Cell Physiology in 1947, followed by a Ph.D. in Cell Biology three years later. Cobb spent the next two years at the National Cancer Institute in Bethesda, Maryland, on a postdoctoral fellowship.

Cobb's research interests centered on the behavior of living cells in tissue culture. She was particularly interested in melanocytes, the skin cells that carry melanin, the pigment that gives skin its color. One of her research projects examined the protection that melanin affords from the harmful effects of the sun. She also studied the effects of chemicals on cancerous cells, searching for chemical agents that would inhibit the growth of cells. Such agents have the potential to become drugs for cancer chemotherapy in humans.

For two years following her postdoctoral fellowship, Cobb was an instructor of anatomy and director of the Tissue Culture Laboratory at the University of Illinois. She returned to New York University in 1954 to continue her basic research in cancer chemotherapy. That year she married Roy Raul Cobb, an insurance salesman, whom she divorced in 1967. The couple had one child.

From 1955 until 1960 Cobb was instructor and later assistant professor of research surgery at New York University. During this period she also taught at Hunter College in New York City. From 1960 to 1969 Cobb was professor of biology at Sarah Lawrence College in Bronxville, New York. She taught biology and continued her research agenda. In 1969 she moved to Connecticut College in New London, Connecticut, to become dean and professor of zoology. At Connecticut College, Cobb established a program to assist minority students pursuing careers in medicine and dentistry. This program, designed to increase the number of black physicians and black dentists in New England, became a model for similar programs at other colleges.

In 1976 Cobb left Connecticut College to accept a position as dean and professor of biological sciences at Douglass College of Rutgers University. In 1979 she was nominated for the position of president of Hunter College in New York City. A group of prominent female scientists supported her candidacy, calling Cobb "an outstanding model for minority students and women" (*New York Times*, 16 Sept. 1979). Despite widespread support, her candidacy failed to garner the nine votes of the board of trustees needed to win the appointment. In 1981, two years after her unsuccessful candidacy for president of Hunter, Cobb was appointed president of California

State University at Fullerton. She was the third president of the sixth largest campus in the California State University system, and she served from 1981 until 1990. After retiring from the presidency, Cobb was appointed trustee professor at California State University in Los Angeles, a position that enabled her to continue her lifelong efforts to motivate minorities to study science and engineering.

Among Cobb's numerous awards and honors were more than a score of honorary degrees from prestigious educational institutions. Two buildings, one at Douglass College and another at California State University at Fullerton, bear her name. In 1993 the National Academy of Sciences awarded Cobb its Lifetime Achievement Award for Contributions to the Advancement of Women and Underrepresented Minorities.

FURTHER READING

Brown, Mitchell C. *The Faces of Science: African Americans in the Sciences* (2005). Also available at http://www. princeton.edu/~mcbrown/display/cobb/html.

"Jewell Plummer Cobb, 1924–, American Cell Biologist," in *Notable Twentieth Century Scientists* vol. 1, ed. Emily J. McMurray (1995): 369–370.

Smith, Jessie Carney. *Black Firsts: 4,000 Ground-Breaking and Pioneering Historical Events*, 2nd ed. (2003).

BENJAMIN A. JACKSON

Cobb, Ned. *See* Shaw, Nate (Ned Cobb).

Cobb, William Montague (12 Oct. 1904–20 Nov. 1990), physical anthropologist and anatomist, was born in Washington, D.C., the son of William Elmer Cobb, a printer, and Alexzine Montague. Experiencing racial segregation in education, he graduated in 1921 from Dunbar High School, an elite college-preparatory school for African Americans. Cobb attended Amherst College, where he pursued a classical education in arts and sciences, graduating in 1925. After graduation he received a Blodgett Scholarship to study biology at Woods Hole Marine Biology Laboratory in Massachusetts. There he met the Howard University biologist ERNEST EVERETT JUST and decided to attend Howard University's College of Medicine. At the time, Howard was undergoing a transformation as-its first African American president, MORDECAI JOHNSON, attempted to place the university under greater African American control. Showing great academic promise, Cobb was groomed to become

William Montague Cobb, a physical anthropologist and anatomist, published many articles and also edited the *Journal of the National Medical Association* for twenty-eight years. (Courtesy of University of Massachusetts, Amherst.)

a new member of the faculty. After receiving his medical degree in 1929, he was sent to Cleveland for postgraduate study at Western Reserve University.

Even before he could read, Cobb had been intrigued by pictures of human biological variation, or "race." At Western Reserve he pursued this interest by studying anatomy and the emerging discipline of physical anthropology under T. Wingate Todd, who amassed one of the two most extensive research collections of human skeletons in the United States, the Hamman-Todd Collection. Cobb spent two years at Western Reserve, earning a doctoral degree in 1932 on the basis of a thesis that inventoried skeletal material available for anthropological study in the United States. He was the first and, until the early 1950s, the only African American to earn a Ph.D. in Physical Anthropology.

In 1932 Cobb returned to Howard University as professor of anatomy, intent on establishing a skeletal collection for the use of African American scientists. He prepared more than seven hundred skeletons from cadavers and compiled documentation on three hundred more. Through his efforts, the Cobb Collection at Howard grew to become comparable to the Hamman-Todd Collection and the Terry Collection at the Smithsonian Institution—an irreplaceable resource for studying the remains of Washington's poor from the Great Depression. Such skulls were particularly valuable because they provided a unique record of past states of sickness and health.

During his early years on the Howard faculty, Cobb continued to work on skeletal collections. His work resulted in important publications on the cranio-facial union, showing how the cranial portion of the skull grows relatively fast and remains stable after birth, while the facial portion grows relatively slowly and can be modified by the environment. He also undertook a massive study of cranial suture closure, showing that it is an unreliable estimator of skeletal age. In the 1930s many Americans believed that the emerging preeminence of African American sprinters and broad-jumpers in Olympic competition was due to racial anatomy. Cobb refuted this view by carefully measuring African American Olympic athletes and comparing their measurements to European American and African American skeletal averages. JESSE OWENS's measurements, for example, turned out to be more "typical" of European Americans than of African Americans, showing that racial biology and behavior are not fixed. This important finding had broad application outside athletics.

Cobb believed that African Americans represented a population whose physical and intellectual vigor had been enhanced by the evolutionary bottleneck of slavery. Slave-traders had selected superior physical specimens to transport to the Americas, and of these, only the strongest had survived the new diseases and brutal labor they encountered there. Considering the social barriers, their achievements were extraordinary. Furthermore, he believed that African Americans were highly adaptable and would become more genetically varied as social barriers to racial mixing crumbled. These views were intended to counteract prevailing views that African Americans were inferior because they had been insufficiently exposed to European American culture.

Cobb also undertook to show how racism and segregation were exacting a biological toll on African Americans and, through the added cost of separate and unequal health care, a financial toll on all Americans. He worked diligently for the racial integration of American hospitals and medical schools. To this end, he created the Imhotep National Conference on Hospital Integration, which met annually from 1957 through 1963, ending with the passage of the 1964 Civil Rights Act. Cobb was invited to attend the formal signing of the 1965 Medicare Bill, which the conference had promoted. On the subject of race, he published many articles in both popular and scientific journals, especially the *Journal of the National Medical Association*, which he edited for twenty-eight years. Among his associates in the integration effort were RALPH BUNCHE and W. E. B. DuBois. He was among the first physical anthropologists to direct the resources of that discipline toward social problems.

Cobb graduated from Howard in the same year that the American Association of Physical Anthropologists was founded; he contributed actively to the association in its formative years and was its president (1957–1959). As Cobb matured professionally, he rose to prominence in other anthropological and medical organizations, serving as president of the National Medical Association (1964–1965) and the National Association for the Advancement of Colored People (1976–1982). He chaired the department of anatomy at Howard University College of Medicine from 1949 until 1969, when he became distinguished professor, then distinguished professor emeritus in 1973.

Cobb was accomplished in the arts as well as science, playing violin and reciting literature and poetry, often in class. He was remembered by associates as a well-rounded Renaissance man. Later in life, his humanistic side flourished as he philosophized about the duality of human nature. Cobb presented his last professional paper in 1987. In his lifetime he received more than one hundred awards, published more than one thousand articles, and taught several thousand students. He died in Washington, D.C.

FURTHER READING

Documents relating to Cobb, including transcripts of interviews, are in the Moorland-Spingarn Research Center at Howard University.

Rankin-Hill, Lesley M., and Michael L. Blakey. "W. Montague Cobb (1904–1990): Physical Anthropologist, Anatomist and Activist." *American Anthropologist* 96, no. 1 (1996): 74–96.

Obituary: *American Journal of Physical Anthropology* 92 (1993): 545–548.

This entry is taken from the *American National Biography* and is published here with the permission of the American Council of Learned Societies.

PAUL A. ERICKSON

Coburn, John P. (1811–21 Jan. 1873), abolitionist and businessman, was born in Boston, Massachusetts, to John and Mary Coburn. Nothing is known about his upbringing and little about his parents and family. During the 1820s Coburn labored as a housewright and by 1830 had established a clothing business, probably with his white father, on Brattle Street. He married Emeline Gray, a New Hampshire native, and joined with his brother-in-law Ira S. Gray, a well-known light-skinned gambler, to establish a successful gaming parlor. Coburn remained in the clothing business into the mid 1860s, when he changed the name of his company to W.T. Coburn Clothing Store, after his adopted son, Wendell T. By the early 1850s he had acquired substantial real estate holdings in the city—with one house worth $4,000 and another valued at $3,000—and possessed one thousand dollars of personal property.

As one of the most successful African Americans on the north side of Beacon Hill, where most of the city's black population resided, Coburn quickly emerged as a community leader. His various properties on or near Beacon Hill, especially at Coburn Court, also provided residences for many relatives, business associates, and black abolitionists who, because of rampant discrimination, could not live elsewhere in the city. Even Boston's most successful black barber, John J. Smith—who had moved to Boston from Virginia in 1840—for a time lived with the Coburns at their Southac Street residence. The 1840 city tax records also reveal that other black abolitionists, such as Joshua B. Smith (who would become Boston's most successful caterer), Frederick G. Barbadoes, and J. Milton Clarke (a former slave who escaped from Kentucky in 1842), lived at one of the Coburn homes.

In 1838 Coburn joined with PRIMUS HALL and twenty-eight others to petition the city council for funds to expand the Abiel Smith School, the only Boston school open to African American children. Coburn and his colleagues clearly opposed segregation but bowed to white opinion, believing that it represented the best practical way to increase "facilities for the instruction of our youth" (Hall, et al., Petition). He helped organize "August First" celebrations—to commemorate the end of British slavery—and in 1845 became treasurer of the New England Freedom Association, a group founded in 1842 or 1843 to assist fugitive slaves. Joshua B. Smith served as vice president of the organization, which also counted WILLIAM C. NELL, the city's leading black abolitionist, as a member.

While Coburn's membership in the famed "Boston Vigilance Committee" is uncertain, he and other city blacks took the lead in assisting fugitive slaves long before adoption of the hated 1850 Fugitive Slave Law. When marshals seized SHADRACK MINKINS (also known as Frederick Wilkins or Jenkins) on 15 February 1851, Coburn and his allies swung into action. Minkins, who had fled enslavement in Norfolk, Virginia, worked in Boston for about four months before his capture, and his rescue became one of the earliest tests of the new federal Fugitive Slave Law and the 1850 Compromise, a package of congressional legislation that sought to prevent a rupture of the Union over the issue of slavery. Within three hours of Minkins's seizure, Coburn and other black abolitionists rushed the courthouse, freed him, and eventually spirited the former Virginia slave away to freedom in Canada. Federal and state officials, incensed at the well-orchestrated defiance, pledged to convict all those involved in the rescue. Coburn and two other merchants posted a three-thousand-dollar bond for one of the first men arrested in the case, and about two weeks later marshals arrested Coburn—along with the black lawyer Robert Morris—for their roles in the incident. In all, ten men had been charged for participating in the rescue, but prosecutors failed to convict any of them.

The next year ROBERT MORRIS and CHARLES L. REMOND, a black abolitionist from Salem, Massachusetts, unsuccessfully petitioned the state legislature to charter a militia company. Their effort, one of many that blacks made during the 1850s, not only represented an expression of racial pride but also reflected growing anticipation of increased conflict over fugitive slaves, if not a more general war over slavery. In February 1853 Morris led renewed efforts by Coburn and other local blacks to obtain official authorization for their unit. Morris, who had been the lead attorney in the famed *Roberts v. City of Boston* school desegregation case, appeared before a committee of the state constitutional convention then in session to justify the request for an official charter for the proposed militia company. He pointed to a colonial law that compelled blacks to serve in the militia, but the convention remained unmoved and rebuffed the petition.

In June 1853 sixty-five black Bostonians petitioned the convention to amend the constitution "to remove the disabilities of colored citizens from holding military commissions and serving in the militia" (Nell, 103). The convention rejected the new request "on the ground that it could not be granted without bringing Massachusetts into conflict with the United States Constitution and the laws of the land." The Commonwealth's attorney general Rufus Choate ruled that because the federal government barred blacks from serving in the militia, the state could not enroll them, "*the color cleaves to them*" (Nell, 108). Coburn and twenty-two other blacks rejected the Commonwealth's refusal to recognize their militia unit as a violation of the state constitution, "which knows nothing of the complexion of the people." Additionally, they asserted that the federal Constitution did not discriminate based on color and "not a sentence or a syllable" could be found "recognizing any distinctions among the citizens of the States, collectively or individually, but they are all placed on the same equality" (Nell, 108–109). The convention and the legislature remained defiant, rejected the new petition, and refused to even record its presentation. Nevertheless, Boston blacks formed the unit, christened it the Massasoit Guards, and in 1855 elected Coburn as its captain.

After the Republican Party nominated Abraham Lincoln for president in 1860, Coburn joined with LEWIS HAYDEN (a close associate of Governor John A. Andrew), Mark R. De Mortié (a black businessman who later became sutler for the 54th Massachusetts Regiment), and other politically active blacks to form the "West Boston Colored Wide Awakes" and promote Lincoln and Republicans. One hundred forty-four men, fully uniformed and equipped, joined the organization and chose Coburn as their commander. Coburn and his family remained in Boston after the Civil War, where he continued his successful business ventures, joined the East Cambridge Land Company (incorporated in 1861), and according to an obituary notice in the *Boston Evening Transcript* (22 Jan. 1873), died, leaving behind an "ample fortune."

FURTHER READING

Collison, Gary. *Shadrack Minkins: From Fugitive Slave to Citizen* (1997)

Ferris, William Henry. *The African Abroad: Or, His Evolution in Western Civilization* (1913).

Grover, Kathryn, and Janine V. da Silva. *Historic Resource Study* (2002).

Hall, Primus, et al. "Petition of 6 Aug. 1838." City of Boston Archives, City Council Series 1.4.

Horton, James O., and Lois E. Horton. *Black Bostonians* (1999).

Nell, William Cooper. *Colored Patriots of the American Revolution* (1855).

Ripley, C. Peter, et al., eds. *The Black Abolitionist Papers* (1985–1992).

DONALD YACOVONE

Cochran, Johnnie (2 Oct. 1937–29 Mar. 2005), attorney, was born Johnnie L. Cochran Jr. in Shreveport, Louisiana, the son of Johnnie L. Cochran Sr. and Harriet Bass. In the fall of 1943 Johnnie Cochran Sr. moved his family from Louisiana to the Bay Area of California, seeking to escape the racial segregation of the Deep South and in search of greater opportunities. World War II had created thousands of new jobs, and Cochran Sr. found employment in a shipyard. An excellent salesman, he also became an agent for Golden State Mutual, California's leading black-owned insurance company.

After the war Cochran Sr. went to work full time for Golden State in Los Angeles, where the company had its headquarters. Johnnie Cochran Jr. attended the academically challenging Los Angeles High School before entering the University of California at Los Angeles in 1955. As a business administration major he again found himself enmeshed in a highly competitive academic environment. As an undergraduate he worked part-time selling insurance and in the post office. Upon his graduation in 1959 he married Barbara Jean Berry, with whom he had two daughters. Cochran sought admission to Loyola University School of Law because it offered excellent training and because its schedule was hospitable to students who needed to work. In his last year of law school Cochran obtained a position as a law clerk in the office of the Los Angeles city attorney. Late in 1962 he learned that he had passed the bar, and on 10 January 1963 he was sworn in as a member of the California bar.

The newly minted lawyer went to work full time as a deputy city attorney with the Criminal Division of the Los Angeles City Attorney's office. He had a flair for trial work, and during his early years in that office he argued a large number of cases involving a variety of offenses. But as he gained experience Cochran came increasingly to be called upon to argue so-called 148 cases, cases in which a defendant, often a battered and bruised African American or Latino, would be brought into the courtroom to face charges that included "resisting arrest" or "interfering with an officer in the performance of his duties." The police usually suggested that the defendant's injuries were the result of the application of reasonable force necessary to subdue him and effect his arrest.

Cochran found it increasingly difficult in his role as city attorney to bolster police testimony that he believed to be bogus and to discredit the accounts of events offered by the defendants, many of whom were black men. In the end he resolved the dilemma by leaving the city attorney's office in 1965.

Five years of successful practice followed; then in 1970 he took a case that brought him widespread notice. Barbara Deadwyler was eight months pregnant. Believing that she was going into labor, she asked her husband, Leonard, to rush her to the hospital. Leonard tied a white cloth to the antenna of their car, a signal to the police in their native Georgia that a driver needed assistance. As he sped to the hospital, a police car fell in behind him and signaled for him to pull over. A policeman approached with gun drawn; only then, according to Barbara Deadwyler, did she and her husband realize they were being pursued, not assisted. The officer leaned into the car. Deadwyler asked him to escort them to the hospital. The gun discharged. Deadwyler's dying words were, "But she's having a baby." Cochran took the case, pressing a charge of negligence, but a coroner's inquest accepted the police explanation that the car had lurched, causing the officer to fire his weapon. Despite losing the case Cochran drew favorable attention from black Angelenos by speaking powerfully against police practices that treated blacks as "the other," an alien and dangerous horde not to be accorded the assumption of decent motives or innocent needs.

In 1972 Cochran took on the case of GERONIMO PRATT, which would occupy him for the next twenty-seven years. Upon his return from the Vietnam War to a racially divided United States, Pratt had joined the Black Panthers and risen to a position of leadership only to find himself charged with murder, robbery, and aggravated assault. Evidence produced years later that led to Pratt's release established that the Panthers had been heavily infiltrated by police informants and that the testimony offered against Pratt at trial had been fabricated. Pratt was convicted, but Cochran continued to be involved for decades in the struggle to secure his freedom. Following a successful appeal of his conviction, Pratt was released from prison in 1997.

Cochran and his wife Barbara were divorced in 1977, and in 1985 he married Sylvia Dale. After a brief return to government as assistant district attorney for Los Angeles County from 1978 to 1980 Cochran returned to private practice. One year later he took on the case of Ron Settles, a star black football player at the University of Southern California who had been jailed after a minor traffic stop and was later found dead in his cell, allegedly a suicide by hanging. Cochran, representing the young man's parents in a wrongful death suit, had the body exhumed and was able to establish that Settles had died as the result of a police choke hold. The family received a settlement of $780,000.

By the early 1990s Cochran was a successful attorney with thirty years' experience and was contemplating retirement when he was approached about working a murder case that was rapidly gripping the nation's attention. On 12 June 1994 Nicole Brown Simpson, the ex-wife of the retired professional football player O. J. SIMPSON, and Ron Goldman were murdered. Shortly thereafter Simpson was arrested and charged with the double homicide. When Simpson asked Cochran to take the lead in his defense, a team of some of the best lawyers in the country was assembled, including the DNA experts Barry Scheck and Peter Nuefeld, and the noted defense attorney F. Lee Bailey. Cochran built the defense around the theme that had driven his career: official negligence and malfeasance. Although Simpson was the defendant, Cochran put the Los Angeles Police Department on trial. He and his team suggested that incompetence tainted the prosecution's evidence and that malice had driven the police to the hasty identification of Simpson as the chief and only suspect. Building on an opening provided by F. Lee Bailey's cross-examination of Mark Fuhrman, one of the investigating officers, Cochran was able to establish that Fuhrman had lied under oath and that he had a history of racial animus. In his summation Cochran implored the largely minority jury to look at the case in light of their history with and personal experience of the Los Angeles Police Department's abuse of the black community. In the end the jury rendered a quick and highly controversial verdict, finding Simpson not guilty.

The trial made Cochran a national celebrity. He hosted a television show and appeared frequently as a legal commentator in various forums. The most important consequence of the trial was that he expanded his practice, with its theme of social justice, to a national stage. In the years after the trial the Cochran firm grew to 120 lawyers in eight states. More than $4 million was won in a Nashville police abuse case; almost $1 million was secured on behalf of women and minority firefighters in Battle Creek, Michigan; and New York paid a major settlement in the 1997 Abner Louima case, involving a Haitian immigrant sodomized in a police station bathroom by a police officer wielding a plunger.

In 1977 the Los Angeles Criminal Courts Bar Association named Cochran Criminal Trial Lawyer of the year. He was inducted into the Inner Circle of Advocates, an organization composed of one hundred of the nation's elite plaintiff lawyers. His autobiography, *Journey to Justice* (1996), became a national best-seller. After a brief battle with brain cancer Cochran died at his Los Angeles home.

FURTHER READING

Cochran, Johnnie, with Tim Rutten. *Journey to Justice* (1996).

Cochran, Johnnie, with David Fisher. *A Lawyer's Life* (2002).

Fleming, Robert. "Johnnie Cochran—Interview," *Black Issues Book Review* (Nov.–Dec. 2002).

JOHN R. HOWARD

Cockrel, Kenneth V. (5 Nov. 1938–25 April 1989), activist, attorney, community organizer, police reformer, and Detroit City Councilman, was born Kenneth Vern Cockrel in predominantly black Royal Oak Township, Michigan, to Sye Cockrel, an automobile assembly worker, and Cynthia, (maiden name unknown). Sye Cockrel left school after the sixth grade, while his wife was the first African American female to graduate from Lincoln High School, in the suburban Detroit community of Ferndale, Michigan.

Kenneth was the second eldest of five siblings (along with Sye, Jesse, Novella, and Shirley) and after the children lost both of their parents in late 1950—within one month of each other—his siblings were then separated as a family unit and each sent to live with different relatives. Ken was sent off to live with his uncle and aunt, Golden and Beatrice Kennedy in Detroit's Jefferies Housing Projects; his early teenage years displayed a lively and diligent work ethic signified by the accomplishment of his highly successful newspaper delivery route. His stylish personality assisted in convincing the affluent route customers to mail their weekly charges to his home instead of him going door to door collecting.

In his junior year, Ken dropped out of high school to join the U.S. Air Force. He received an honorable discharge in 1959 and returned to school at Wayne State University in Detroit, which at that time had a recruitment program for adult students who lacked a formal high school diploma.

In order to earn his way through college, Cockrel worked as a Detroit *News* circulation department "jumper," a truck driver's assistant delivering the newspapers to distribution points and newsstands, with his friend, activist Mike Hamlin. In the classroom, he developed a deep passion for Marxist-Leninist thought, and his personal style reflected his radical ideological contempt for the capitalist system; he sported a large Afro hairstyle, blue jeans, army boots, an army style knapsack and stylish hat or black beret. In 1963, as a Wayne State University undergraduate student, Cockrel once got into a heated, extemporaneous debate with MALCOLM X, who nonetheless complimented Ken's aggressive and articulate rapid-fire speaking style.

Upon matriculation with a Bachelor of Arts degree in 1964, Cockrel entered the Wayne State University Law School and earned his J.D. in 1967. Cockrel also married his first wife, Carol W. White, a teacher in the Detroit Public Schools. The couple had a son, Kenneth V. Cockrel Jr., born in 1966, who in 2005 was elected president of the Detroit City Council. Cockrel and his wife divorced in 1973.

As a young attorney, Cockrel's personal adopted mission was to draw attention to the social and legal inequality faced by many of Detroit's black and urban residents and was appointed the position of research director for the North Woodward Interfaith Organization, a community organization serving for the betterment of Detroit. In June, 1969, Cockrel was one of the eight founders of the legally incorporated workers activist organization, The League of Revolutionary Black Workers (LRBW). This organization was formed after a series of wildcat worker strikes in retaliation for ill treatment of black workers by abusive factory floor supervisors, of which ninety-five percent were white. The LRBW promoted political education and strategies which sought to change the social inequities on the shop floor and in the neighborhoods where workers lived.

In 1969, Cockrel was selected to be the co-attorney with good friend Justin Ravitz in the legal defense of a well publicized, politically, and racially charged criminal case, in which members of the Republic of New Africa, a controversial black separatist group, were accused of assault with the intent to kill in the March 29th incident in which two Detroit Police Officers were shot, one fatally, the other critically. On the night of the police shooting, 147 RNA members were exiting a meeting at the New Bethel Baptist Church and when the police were fired upon by an unknown assailant, police returned gunfire and wounded five RNA members; the other members were detained and held without being formally charged until a black Detroit Recorders Court Judge, George Crockett, came to the police station, and ordered the processing of the prisoners and then released 142 of the arrested held on writs of habeas corpus, a deed that infuriated the Detroit Police Officers Association union. Prosecutors charged four defendants and decided on having two separate trials for each pair of defendants: New Bethel One and New Bethel Two. Cockrel was appointed co-attorney along with his very good friend Justin Ravitz; the two were popularly known as Butch and Sundance in reference to characters in a popular Hollywood movie. Cockrel and Ravitz successfully represented defendant Alfred Hibbet in the New Bethel One trial and he was acquitted, but not before Cockrel was held in contempt for calling the white judge a number of derogatory, racially charged names at the bail hearing because he felt the judge was setting an unreasonable bail amount of fifty thousand dollars for Mr. Hibbet. The contempt charges were dropped immediately after the trial.

The following year, Cockrel was appointed to defend a black hourly autoworker, James Johnson Jr., who was accused of shooting his white Chrysler Corporation supervisor and two others on the shop floor. Cockrel argued that his client was driven to a state of insanity because of the racial discrimination and accompanying stress he experienced in his job. The defendant was acquitted, but was ordered to a state mental facility for five years.

Cockrel also worked with diligence to correct the problem of jury malpractice within the Wayne County, Michigan Jury Commission, in which the protocol was to assemble juries that were white, male, and middle class. Cockrel also worked diligently to correct the injustice problem of prisoner overcrowding at the Wayne County jail.

In 1973, Cockrel gained significant recognition for securing the acquittal of a black teenager, Hayward Brown, who was accused of two separate shootings involving Detroit Police officers, which resulted in the death of one officer and the wounding of five others. Cockrel argued successfully that the young black defendant acted in self-defense, against an often hostile undercover unit of the Detroit Police Department. This decoy unit, known by its acronym STRESS (Stop the Robberies and Enjoy Safe Streets) was deeply distrusted and scorned by inner city blacks in Detroit. Over the

course of two years, a total of seventeen victims, mostly black, were fatally shot by STRESS officers. Soon after Brown's acquittal, the notorious Detroit Police STRESS unit was dismantled. Cockrel was the driving force behind the elimination of the brutally dangerous police decoy unit.

In 1977, Cockrel ran for public office and was elected to the Detroit City Council, where he served one term. Unwilling to wait for change, he became disillusioned with committee style city governance. Cockrel didn't seek a second term in office and later publicly admitted that he felt he was politically neutralized by the machine style politics of Detroit Mayor COLEMAN A. YOUNG.

Cockrel married his second wife Shelia Murphy in 1978. She was also a community organizer and social reformer who was later elected to Detroit's City Council. The couple had one daughter, Katherine, born in 1985.

After his tenure in city government, Cockrel continued working as a trial lawyer and in 1988 joined the prestigious Detroit law firm, Sommers, Schwartz, Silver, Schwartz. Cockrel died suddenly of a heart attack, at only age fifty, in 1989. His passing came as a shock to the entire Detroit community, and was much discussed in the Detroit media. Well known Detroit News columnist Pete Waldmeir wrote that "Ken was one of the chosen ones; a lean mean child of the city, who burst on Detroit in the '60s like a bargeful of Fourth of July fireworks; not one fist, but both fists clenched in defiance of racial and human injustice in any shape or form."

Twelve hundred people from all walks of life came to his memorial service. Eulogies were offered by many, including the Mayor of Detroit, Coleman Young, Michigan Governor James Blanchard, and Michigan Supreme Court Justice DENNIS ARCHER. His bereaved wife Sheila eulogized her late husband in a note read by a family friend Gregory Hicks at the memorial service, "Ken's legacy to his family, his community and his city is encompassed in his shining integrity, his fierce passion for justice and his unwavering opposition to racism and economic inequality" (Detroit News). The memorial service was covered extensively by print, broadcast, and radio media.

Other commentators remembered Cockrel as an articulate, rapid fire speaker, and community activist who rose from the streets of Detroit's inner city to become one of the city's most respected attorneys. Cockrel also received several awards in recognition of his achievements as a civil rights lawyer and his refusal to compromise his ideals.

Among these were the Distinguished Achievement Medal of the Detroit branch of the NAACP in 1973 and the Frank D. Reeves Award from the National Conference of Black Lawyers in 1976.

FURTHER READING

Kenneth Cockrel's papers are housed in the Kenneth V. and Sheila M. Cockrel Collection, part of the Damon J. Keith Collection of African American Legal History, at the Walter P. Reuther Library at Wayne State University in Detroit.

Georgakas, Dan, and Surkin Marvin. *Detroit, I Do Mind Dying: A Study in Urban Revolution* (1998).

Geschwender, James A. Class, *Race and Worker Insurgency: The League of Revolutionary Black Workers* (1977).

Jefferies, Judson, ed. *Black Power: Beauty in the Belly of the Beast* (2006).

Thompson, Heather Ann. *Whose Detroit?: Politics, Labor, and Race in a Modern American City* (2001).

Obituary: *Detroit News,* 26 April 1989.

KENNETH J. HREHA

Coffee (fl. 1712), or Cuffee, slave insurrectionist, was the reported leader of the first major slave rebellion in the American colonies. His name means "son born on a Friday" in the Akan language of Gold Coast Africans. The Akan, known in the era of the slave trade as Coromantees, were reputed to resist enslavement with great bravery and ferocity. In the early eighteenth century, slavery had become an integral part of the economy of New York City, with an active slave market and a regular influx of slave labor from Africa. As the slave population grew, treatment of slaves became increasingly brutal, as British colonists attempted to make slave labor as productive in the North as it was in the South. Unlike slaves on southern plantations, however, slaves in New York City lived in densely populated areas and had many more opportunities to meet with one another and plan organized resistance. On the night of 6 April 1712, Coffee led more than twenty African and two Native American slaves in organized violent resistance against their masters in lower Manhattan. They began by setting fire to a shed belonging to Coffee's master, Peter Vandilbourgh, then attacked the white men who came out to stop the fire. The slaves killed at least nine men, using knives, hatchets, and guns, and they wounded six others before fleeing into the woods. It took two days for the colonial militias of lower Manhattan and Westchester to capture the slaves. According to Governor Robert Hunter's report, six of the slaves committed suicide before being apprehended; twenty-one more were publicly executed by "the most exemplary punishment ... that could be possibly thought of" including being burned alive, hanging, and being "broke on the wheel" (Singer).

Curiously, Coffee apparently escaped punishment along with one other slave through "services provided to the British Crown" (Rucker, 88), possibly as a translator. Walter Rucker discusses the involvement of Peter the Doctor, a "conjurer" in the New York rebellion, attributing the audacity of the slaves' resistance to a shared belief in the power of a powder that the conjurer rubbed on the slaves' clothing before they took action. Coffee's Rebellion, as the 1712 revolt became known, prompted Governor Hunter and other lawmakers to enact tougher laws restricting slaves' nighttime activities and their possession of firearms. There were also harsher penalties for escape attempts, as well as a law requiring slave owners who wished to free their slaves to pay a fee of two hundred pounds. Despite this crackdown, Coffee and his fellow rebels were not forgotten. Their example may have inspired another violent slave rebellion in Manhattan in 1741. Historians differ in their interpretation of the events of 1741, when more than thirty slaves were hanged or burned to death and more than seventy deported after a series of fires were set and rumors of a conspiracy rocked the city. Many whites were also implicated in the supposed conspiracy and put to death; whether white New Yorkers were responding to an actual insurrection or to their own fears of a repeat of Coffee's Rebellion remains a mystery.

FURTHER READING

Africans in America, available online at http://www. pbs. org/wgbh/aia (1998).

Bolden, Tonya. *Strong Men Keep Coming: The Book of African American Men* (1999).

Rucker, Walter. "Conjure, Magic, and Power: The Influence of Afro-Atlantic Religious Practices on Slave Resistance and Rebellion," *Journal of Black Studies* (2001).

Singer, Alan, ed. *New York and Slavery: Complicity and Resistance.* "1712–1719. The New York Slave Revolt," New York State Council for the Social Studies, (2005). Available online at http://www.nyscss.org.

ALICE KNOX EATON

Coffey, Cornelius Robinson (6 Sept. 1903–2 Mar. 1994), aviator, was born in Newport, Arkansas, a farming community on the banks of the White River. Although the names of his parents are now unknown, Coffey recalled in 1993 that "my daddy was a railroad man in the days when an Afro-American could hook a train together and drive a locomotive from the roundhouse to the station, but he could never become a full-fledged engineer" (*Chicago Tribune*, 25 July 1993). Cornelius Coffey, however, would spend a large portion of his life suspended in the air operating the controls of an airplane. This was a time when even to dream of being a pilot was considered preposterous for a black youth growing up in segregated Arkansas. In order to escape such limitations imposed on blacks in the Jim Crow South, the family sought new opportunities first in Nebraska, and then ultimately in Chicago in 1923.

Shortly after arriving in Chicago, Coffey studied automotive technology at the city's Lincoln Automotive Institute. After completing his training in 1926, he soon landed a job as a mechanic. He not only understood the relative similarity of internal combustion engines in automobiles and aircraft but also saw that the burgeoning aircraft industry would need experienced mechanics; however, he needed flight school certification. After being enthralled by Charles Lindbergh's solo flight to Paris in 1927, Coffey made his first unlicensed solo flight in a Waco 9, a state-of-the-art biplane, at Akers Airfield in the northwest suburbs of Chicago in 1928. He enrolled in the Curtis Wright Flying Service Aeronautics Training School; but upon arrival for class, he and his friend JOHN C. ROBINSON were both refused admission because of their skin color.

Both men, employees of Elmwood Park Chevrolet (owned by Emil Mack, who was a white businessman), advised the school that it would be vulnerable to litigation if they did not admit the two mechanics. The school relented, and Coffey and Robinson would go on to finish at the top of their class. Coffey completed a master mechanic course for Airframe and Engine (A&E) and in 1931 became the first African American to achieve the A&E certification from the Civil Aviation Authority (CAA). Six years later, in 1937, he established the Coffey School of Aviation on the far southwest side of Chicago. That year Robinson and Coffey flew from Chicago to Washington, D.C., to meet Senator Harry S. Truman and Congressman Everett Dirksen to ensure that the Coffey School would play a role in the U.S. government's preparations for war. The pilots also sought the support of First Lady Eleanor Roosevelt. As a result of these lobbying efforts and petitions sent to the U.S. Civil Aeronautics Administration, President Franklin Roosevelt approved the Coffey School to train African American civilian pilots. Ultimately the Coffey School would train more than 1,000 African American pilots. Coffey's personal instruction and leadership would provide preliminary preparation for the military aviation training program at the Tuskegee Institute in Tuskegee, Alabama.

With the invasion of Ethiopia by Mussolini's fascist army in 1935, plans had been negotiated by Coffey and Robinson with his highness Haille Selassie's threatened government that would have had John Robinson serving as the personal pilot for the Emperor and Coffey operating the school to train Ethiopian pilots. These plans, however, were ultimately dashed.

In 1939 Coffey, with the encouraging assistance of a recent student-wife of two years (Willa Beatrice Brown), founded the National Negro Airmen Association of America (NNAAA). After military service units were integrated they dropped the word Negro from this association's appellation. Coffey and the NNAAA also initiated the first National Negro Air Show in Chicago. Once the United States entered World War II, Coffey was commissioned an officer. Then he assisted in training cadets in the military training program that ultimately produced the pilots better known as the "Tuskegee Airmen."

After the war, Coffey began a career as an instructor at the Lewis School of Aeronautics in Lockport, Illinois. He was then hired as an instructor in the Dunbar Vocational High School program, where he would train many young men who would go on to become the first black commercial aviation mechanics.

Coffey's achievements were many. He was the first black person to hold CAA/FAA (Civil Aviation Authority/Federal Aviation Authority) certification both as a pilot and as a mechanic. He was a recipient of the Charles Taylor Master Mechanic Award from the FAA and was the first African American to have an aerial navigation intersection named after him by the FAA (the "Coffey fix," a way point located on the Victor 7 airway over Lake Calumet, which provides electronic course guidance to Chicago Midway Airport runway thirty-one). He also designed a carburetor heater that prevented icing and allowed planes to fly in inclement weather. This practical remedy is still in use on aircraft today. He was the first black person to establish and operate an aeronautical school, the only noncollegiate-affiliated aviation school to become a part of the Civilian Pilot Training Program. His pioneering endeavors led to the integration of black pilots into the commercial aviation industry. In his later years Cornelius continued to have an active presence in aviation. As a designated mechanic examiner he retained his certification to administer tests to civilian and military personnel seeking to be certified as licensed civilian mechanics. He continued this FAA-sanctioned responsibility until into his nineties.

FURTHER READING

Gubert, Betty Kaplan, Miriam Sawyer, and Caroline M. Fannin. *Distinguished African Americans in Aviation and Space Science* (2002).

Hardesty, Von, and Dominick Pisano. *Black Wings: The American Black in Aviation* (1984).

Jakeman, Robert J. *The Divided Skies: Establishing Segregated Flight Training at Tuskegee, Alabama, 1934–42* (1992).

Peters, Raymond Eugene, and Clinton M. Arnold. *Blacks in Aviation* (1975).

Smith, Jessie Carney. *Black Firsts: 4,000 Groundbreaking and Pioneering Historical Events* (2003).

Obituaries: *Chicago Tribune*, 4 Mar. 1994; *Jet*, 21 Mar. 1994.

JIM GARRETT

Coggs, Pauline Redmond (1 Feb. 1912–17 July 2005), social worker, educator, and civil rights activist, was born Josephine Pauline Redmond in Paris, Kentucky, the daughter of Josephine B. Scott, an educator, and John B. Redmond, a prominent Methodist minister and educator, both formerly from Mississippi. The third of four children, Redmond relocated to several Midwestern cities with her family as a youngster before eventually settling in Chicago, Illinois, after her father gained a pastoral assignment to St. Mark's Methodist Church. John Redmond's deep involvement in community affairs and Josephine's unwavering commitment to self-improvement made a lasting impression on the young Pauline. As she recalled years later, "my father was the kind of minister deeply concerned about everything that happened to his congregation, and he would get up in the middle of the night and go out into those harsh Chicago winters and see someone who had died because one of his parishioners asked him to

come. My mother had very definite beliefs about the education of young people and never strayed from them" (Coggs, interview by author, 12 Feb. 2000). The Redmonds also instilled in their children a fierce sense of self-definition and social responsibility; all four children later became active in the civil rights struggle and the social, political, and economic issues that affected their communities.

After graduating from high school in 1930 Redmond attended the University of Chicago, earning a dual bachelor's degree in Sociology and Psychology before going on to win a fellowship to attend the master's degree program in Social Work at the University of Pittsburgh. It was while taking courses at the University of Pittsburgh that she began to take a keen interest in the issues shaping the lives of urban youth. After graduating in 1936 she returned home to Chicago, where she landed employment at the local Urban League chapter as the director of youth activities. Not long afterward she plunged herself into a variety of activities, creating job training programs and statewide conferences for struggling young black people.

Meanwhile her work as a caseworker consultant for the Urban League introduced her to the issues of vital concern to black youth at the time, and as her concerns over the plight of young people grew, so too did her interests in progressive politics deepen. By 1938 Redmond had created the National Conference of Negro Youth and attended the Second World Youth Congress gathering in Poughkeepsie, New York, as a delegate for the Chicago Urban League. While attending the seven-day sessions covering a variety of issues ranging from the collective prevention of war to the economic and social status of youth, she found a community of social reformers in the fields of civil rights and social welfare, including DOROTHY HEIGHT, TED STRONG, ANGELO HERNDON, and Virginia Anderson. All of these individuals possessed extensive ties to their respective communities, embraced progressive politics, and were deeply engaged in grassroots organizing of youth activities to challenge racism, unemployment, and poverty during the period. However, her involvement in the radical youth movement also exposed her to decades of domestic surveillance and harassment from the Federal Bureau of Investigation.

In 1940 Redmond's organizing of activities in Chicago attracted the attention of the National Council of Negro Women founder MARY MCLEOD BETHUNE, who offered her a position with the national advisory committee of the National Youth

Administration in Washington, D.C. About a year after gaining this appointment she moved to the Office of Civilian Defense, where she worked as a race relations adviser before being named to the top leadership position at the Washington Urban League in 1943. Her appointment was significant because she was the first African American woman to head an Urban League branch. As executive director she quickly gained a national reputation as an adept social reformer, developing revolutionary programs to address the housing and employment woes facing the urban, poor populations living in the nation's capital. While serving in such capacities, she met First Lady Eleanor Roosevelt and the human rights activist PAULI MURRAY, establishing friendships that lasted well into the twentieth century.

In 1942 her life entered a new phase when she married Theodore Washington Coggs, a graduate of Howard University. After her husband returned home from serving in the U.S. Army during World War II, Pauline Coggs relocated to Madison, Wisconsin, where she taught in the department of sociology at the state university while Theodore attended law school. Upon her husband's graduation from the law school in the late 1940s, the pair moved to Milwaukee, where Pauline Coggs received an appointment as a social worker for the Milwaukee public school system while attaining tenure as a professor with the University of Wisconsin–Extension School of Social Welfare. She also continued to address the plight of young African Americans in Wisconsin, serving on the city's welfare council and the governor's commission on human rights during the period. In 1959 Coggs was selected along with thirteen other residents by the Milwaukee mayor to study bouts of discrimination encountered by black city dwellers after a shootout between a young black man and law enforcement officials heightened racial tensions in the town.

Coggs remained active in the public sphere after her husband's death in 1968, working to revive the Milwaukee branch of the National Association for the Advancement of Colored People and serving as the midwest regional coordinator for the National Association of Social Workers. At the same time she became the charter member and first president of the Epsilon Kappa Omega chapter of Alpha Kappa Alpha Sorority. In 2001 Coggs suffered a series of strokes and died four years later, leaving behind her son Gregory and his wife, one grandson, and three great-grandchildren.

Her reputation as a trailblazer for racial advancement and social reform garnered the respect of her friends and foes throughout her lifetime. Of Coggs's lifelong efforts to get individuals and organizations to work toward realizing social change, one contemporary noted, "she had a unique skill at facilitating dialogue between various age groups and made everyone feel good, even the people who needed to change their behavior" (*Milwaukee Journal Sentinel*, 28 July 2005).

FURTHER READING

Crawford, Vicki L., Jacqueline Anne Rouse, and Barbara Woods, eds. *Women in the Civil Rights Movement: Trailblazers and Torchbearers, 1941–1965* (1990).

Fleming, G. James, and Christian E. Burckel, eds. *Who's Who in Colored America: An Illustrated Biographical Directory of Notable Living Persons of African Descent in the United States* (1950).

Murray, Pauli. *Song in a Weary Throat: An American Pilgrimage* (1987).

Shaw, Stephanie J. *What a Woman Ought to Be and to Do: Black Professional Women Workers during the Jim Crow Era* (1996).

White, Deborah Gray. *Too Heavy a Load: Black Women in Defense of Themselves, 1894–1994* (1999).

Obituary: *Milwaukee Journal Sentinel*, 28 July 2005.

ROBERT F. JEFFERSON

Cohen, Walter L. (22 Jan. 1860–29 Dec. 1930), businessman and politician, was born a free person of color in New Orleans, Louisiana, the son of Bernard Cohen and Amelia Bingaman, a free woman of color. Although Cohen's father was Jewish, he was raised as and remained throughout his life a Roman Catholic. His parents died when he was in the fourth grade, whereupon he had to quit school, though he later attended Straight University in New Orleans for several years. As a boy Cohen became a cigar maker and later worked in a saloon. His entrée into the world of politics came during the period of Reconstruction, when he worked as a page in the state legislature, then meeting in New Orleans. There, Cohen became acquainted with several influential black Republicans, among them OSCAR J. DUNN, C. C. ANTOINE, and P. B. S. PINCHBACK. Pinchback, founder of and dominant figure in the city's Fourth Ward Republican organization, in particular helped steer Cohen into the patronage system that has always been the bread and butter of Louisiana politics.

Cohen joined Pinchback's organization and around 1885 received his first political appointment as a night inspector on the riverfront. Although the end of Reconstruction forced many older black Republicans into retirement, Cohen's star continued to rise. Appointed as secretary of the Republican State Central Committee, he became its most powerful member before President Herbert Hoover removed him in the late 1920s. Cohen was made a U.S. inspector in New Orleans in 1889 and later was promoted to lieutenant of inspectors, serving until 1893. His most important federal position came in 1898, when he was named register of the United States Land Office in New Orleans. In 1904, however, when the time came for Cohen to be reappointed, he was opposed by F. B. Williams, the Republican State Central Committee chairman and leader of the "lily white" faction. Cohen, who was head of the state's "black and tan" Republicans (Cohen himself was very light skinned), asked his friend and mentor, BOOKER T. WASHINGTON, then the most influential spokesman for black Americans, to intercede on his behalf. Washington appealed directly to President Theodore Roosevelt and, with additional pressure from Pinchback, secured Cohen's reappointment to the post, which President William Howard Taft later abolished in 1910.

Finding himself without a political position but not without influence, in 1910 Cohen, along with a few partners, organized the People's Benevolent Life Insurance Company and became president of the firm, a position he held until his death. The company remained profitable for decades. By 1942, when it had become People's Industrial Life Insurance, the firm had more than $300,000 in assets and total insurance in force of about $6 million.

Cohen had other business ventures as well. In 1914 he established the People's Drug Store on South Rampart Street, an area where many black residents lived. Putting his political networking skills to good business use, Cohen contacted local benevolent and fraternal organizations and asked them to include his store on their lists of druggists. He also installed a soda fountain and an ice cream parlor—both popular with his customers—and he hired a physician to be present from 9 A.M. until 7 P.M. in case someone in the store needed medical attention. Cohen's efforts to make People's Drug Store the best drugstore for blacks in the city were so successful that eventually he expanded into a second location. In addition, from 1910 to 1912

Cohen was a partner in a roof garden business at the Pythian Temple, ultimately leaving because of differences with one of his partners. In many of these endeavors Cohen secured the endorsement of Washington, who engaged Cohen as his primary contact and representative in Louisiana, particularly in relation to the activities of Washington's National Negro Business League.

In 1920 Cohen's first wife, the former Wilhelmina Selden, whom he had married in 1882 and with whom he had had at least two children, died. Soon thereafter he married Antonia Manade from nearby Lutcher, Louisiana. Then, in 1924, he received his final political appointment—but not without a struggle. President Warren G. Harding's choice of Cohen for the post of controller of the Port of New Orleans was vehemently opposed by white southerners, and the U.S. Senate rejected Cohen three times before Harding's successor, Calvin Coolidge, finally pushed the appointment through. Political opposition to Cohen came in other forms as well. His opponents—primarily white southerners who simply could not abide the inclusion of blacks in the social and political realm—often accused Cohen of wrongdoing, but it is impossible to determine, given the bias of his detractors, if any of the various charges was warranted. In 1925, in the midst of Prohibition, Cohen and fifty-two white officials were indicted for accepting bribes to allow liquor to be smuggled through the Port of New Orleans. At his trial, Cohen was found not guilty.

An active party member throughout his life and a confidant of many top party leaders, Cohen attended every Republican National Convention from 1896 through 1928. He was a member (and for many years president) of the Iroquois Literary and Social Club, an elite Republican organization founded in 1899, and from the late 1890s on he served as president of the prestigious Société d'Economique, arguably the most exclusive black organization in the United States at that time. Cohen was also a member of the National Association for the Advancement of Colored People, the Knights of Pythias, Odd Fellows, and Elks. He died in New Orleans.

Cohen's political and business careers bridged the years from Reconstruction to the Great Depression, a period that witnessed a stunning rise followed by a precipitous fall in political power for African Americans. His life is representative also of the emergence of independent businesses and organizations as championed by Booker T.

Washington. Cohen was indeed, as his obituary in the *Louisiana Weekly* described him, the last of the city's "Old Guard."

FURTHER READING

Cohen's private papers are not available to the public, but correspondence with Booker T. Washington and Emmett J. Scott can be found in the Washington papers at the Library of Congress and at Tuskegee University.

Ingham, John N., and Lynne B. Feldman. *African-American Business Leaders* (1994).

Rousseve, Charles B. *The Negro in Louisiana: Aspects of His History and His Literature* (1937).

Obituaries: *New Orleans Times-Picayune*, 30 Dec. 1930; *Louisiana Weekly*, 3 Jan. 1931.

This entry is taken from the *American National Biography* and is published here with the permission of the American Council of Learned Societies.

JOHN N. INGHAM

Coincoin, Marie-Thérèse (Marie-Thérèse dit Coincoin, Marie-Thérèse Coin Coin, Marie-Thérèse Metoyer) (1742?–c. 1820), slave, agriculturalist, and head of a dynasty, was probably born in Natchitoches, Louisiana, near what was then the border between Spanish Texas and French Louisiana, although it is possible that she was born in Africa and came to Louisiana as a young child. Her name definitely originated in Africa, but no convincing argument has been made that traces it to one particular location. She was baptized in 1742 as the slave of Louis Juchereau de St. Denis, the founder of Natchitoches which was the first permanent settlement in Louisiana. In 1756 she was inherited by the widow of St. Denis, and then became the property of the widow's son, Pierre Antoine de St. Denis Jr., in 1758, ending up the slave of the de Soto family. Between 1761 and 1766 she had three black children—Marie Thérèze Don Manuel, Françoise, and Jean Joseph. In 1767 a white French merchant, Claude Thomas Pierre Metoyer, known as Pierre, arrived in Natchitoches and Coincoin was loaned to him by her owner. They quickly entered into a relationship. Between 1768 and 1784 they had ten children including AUGUSTIN METOYER and LOUIS METOYER.

Relationships between black women and white men were semiauthorized, given a customary rather than legal status, through the Louisianan system of *placage*, in which white men provided for free women of color in return for sexual favors. A white man living openly with a black slave as a common-law wife in a shared household was more unusual, and aroused the disapproval of the Catholic Church. In 1777 Father Luis de Quintanilla, the local priest, complained to local authorities about their relationship. While this caused a scandal at the time, the intervention of Madame de Soto, and then Pierre's purchase and manumission of Coincoin in 1778, eased the situation. The children that Coincoin bore Pierre when enslaved remained the property of her owner, and between 1776 and 1780 Pierre set about buying his enslaved children from the de Soto family.

Coincoin, Pierre, and their children lived together for the next decade. This was a period of financial and familial stability, although Coincoin's three oldest children remained enslaved. As well as occupying herself with her children, Coincoin was probably in charge of running the plantation household, and given that Pierre was one of the wealthiest men in Natchitoches Parish, she probably had enslaved servants to undertake the heavier housework, and had very little or no contact with agricultural work.

However, this phase of Coincoin's life was soon to end. In 1786 Pierre succumbed to pressure to marry a suitable white French woman, and his relationship with Coincoin ended. It was apparently an amicable split, as upon her departure from their household, he gave her a plot of land close to his plantation on the Cane River, south of Natchitoches, and an annuity of 120 piastres. Here, Coincoin, now at least forty years old and the mother of thirteen children, finally became completely independent. She built a house, and earned a living through agriculture. In 1793 Coincoin petitioned for and was granted more land by the Spanish government. It seems likely that she undertook the cultivation of tobacco and indigo on these plots, both requiring intense production and skilled processing, although her later purchase in 1807 of three sheep suggests she was also raising animals. Those amongst her children who were born after her liberation and were therefore free accompanied her, and she welcomed other family members into her home. Tradition has it that Coincoin was knowledgeable about native medicinal plants, and she may also have been involved in bear trapping for skins and grease. Archaeological excavations at the location of her home reveal a quantity of pots made locally by Native Americans, which were associated with the bear oil trade.

Initially, Coincoin must have undertaken most of the work at the plantation herself, as she is not recorded in the 1787 Slave Census as owning any slaves, and at the time the free children who accompanied her were just ten, four, and two years of age. Her other children with Pierre were still owned by him (although he eventually liberated them all), but her oldest children, born before her relationship with Pierre, were still enslaved, as were the other close members of her family. In 1790 Coincoin began the process of remedying this situation through loaning her daughter Thereze and Thereze's son Joseph from their (and her former) owner. She bought them in 1797, by which time she had bought and freed Catiche, the illegitimate daughter of her son Louis Metoyer in 1794, who was already living in her household. In 1795, she bought, and presumably freed, her own sister Marie Louise.

As well as buying family members to liberate them, Coincoin also bought slaves to work the land she owned. In the 1795 Slave Census she is recorded as owning five slaves and, by 1816 when she divided her property among her children, she had twelve slaves, six women and six men. These slaves—Jean Baptiste, Harry, Marguerite, Marie Jeanne, Constance, Louis, Froisine, Marianne, Marcellino, Jean Noel, Marie Louise, and Hilaire—appear in earlier records, so we can trace some family ties between them. Oral tradition in the Cane River Creole community has it that Coincoin was a good owner who never hit her slaves, and although we cannot be certain of this, the presence of family groups and equal numbers of men and women suggests that the slave community at her plantation was settled and stable.

As well as dividing her slaves amongst her children in 1816, Coincoin also sold her main plot of land on the Cane River to a white neighbor. Her decision may have been influenced by her closest neighbor, another free black called NICHOLAS DOCLAS, who sold his plantation and died that year. Coincoin and Doclas were at one time two of only a handful of free people of African descent in Natchitoches Parish, and lived next to each other for fourteen years. Traditional accounts report that she moved to live with her son Louis at his nearby plantation, but it is probable that she moved to another community of free blacks, as she appears in the 1820 census living with another free woman of color aged over forty-five, and a free man of color aged over forty-five. She may of course have moved in with Louis at his large plantation home at a later date, when she must have been extremely old. There is no record of the date or location of her death, though it is presumed that it must have been fairly soon after 1820.

Coincoin was an independent black woman in a world dominated by white men. She adapted successfully to all the situations that life presented to her; from being the concubine and housekeeper of a rich white man, she became a profitable agriculturalist and businesswoman in her own right. She retained her African identity in her name, and used her earnings to liberate many members of her family and provide for their future. She raised her children to become some of the wealthiest and most respected people along the Cane River, and amongst the richest free people of color in the United States at the beginning of the nineteenth century. Many of Coincoin's descendents remained in Natchitoches Parish where they retained a distinct identity. At the beginning of the twenty-first century they were known as the Cane River Creoles. They played a key role in preserving the story of Coincoin, as have several historical novels, including *Isle of Canes* by Elizabeth Shown Mills (2004). Coincoin's exceptional life survives in local archives and Louisiana oral traditions, embodying the hard work, versatility, and family values shared by many black women of the colonial era.

FURTHER READING

Surviving records of Coincoin's life are in the Natchitoches Parish Courthouse, Natchitoches, Louisiana, and at the Cammie G. Henry Research Center, Northwestern State University, Natchitoches.

Kein, Sybil, ed. *Creole: The History and Legacy of Louisiana's Free People of Color* (2000).

MacDonald, K. C., D. W. Morgan, F. Handley, A. L. Lee, and E. Morley. "The Archaeology of Local Myths and Heritage Tourism: The Case of Cane River's Melrose Plantation." In S. Shennan, R. Layton, and P. Stone, eds., *The Future of the Past: Papers in Honour of Peter Ucko*, 127–142 (2006).

Mills, Gary B. *The Forgotten People: Cane River's Creoles of Color* (1977).

Morgan, David, Kevin MacDonald, and Fiona Handley. "Economics and Authenticity: A Collision of Interpretations in Cane River National Heritage Area, Louisiana." In *The George Wright Forum*, 44–61 (2006).

FIONA J. L. HANDLEY

Coker, Daniel (1780?–1835?), a founder of the African Methodist Episcopal church, author, and educator, was born a slave in Frederick County, Maryland, the son of Susan Coker, a white indentured servant, and Edward Wright, a black slave belonging to the same plantation owner, whose name is unknown. Daniel Coker was educated with his master's son, who refused to go to school without his slave. When Coker was in his early teens he escaped to New York City where he joined the Methodist Church and was ordained as a lay minister.

Empowered by his education and ordination, Coker returned to Maryland in 1801 to become the first African American teacher at the African Academy, a school founded by the Baltimore Abolition Society for the education of free blacks. He was the first black licensed minister in Baltimore, and the spiritual leader of an independent prayer meeting formed by black Methodists dissatisfied with their position within the white Methodist church. But because the twenty-one-year-old Coker was still legally a slave, he was forced to remain in hiding until a Quaker abolitionist purchased and freed him. In 1806 Coker founded the Daniel Coker School, which by 1810 had an enrollment of one hundred fifty African American students.

In 1810 Coker wrote *A Dialogue between a Virginian and an African Minister*, generally considered the first published antislavery tract written by an African American. In this pamphlet, Coker exposed the failure of white Methodists to address the evils of slavery and refuted the notion that the Bible defended the institution. "But the question," Coker argued, "is concerning the liberty of a man. The man himself claims it as his own property. He pleads (and I think in truth) that it was originally his own; and he has never forfeited, nor alienated it; and therefore, by the common laws of justice and humanity, it is still his own." In 1814, responding to the continued failure of Baltimore's white Methodists to grant ministries or autonomy to African American Methodists, Coker led the trustees of the black Methodist congregation in withdrawing entirely from the white Methodist Church and in buying their own church.

During this time, Coker frequently communicated with the Reverend RICHARD ALLEN, another African American Methodist minister, whose struggles to form a separate black church in Philadelphia paralleled Coker's efforts in Baltimore. Coker's "Sermon Delivered Extempore in the African Bethel Church in the City of Baltimore," delivered on 21 January 1816, was a response to Allen's labors on behalf of black Methodism in Philadelphia.

Rev. Daniel Coker.

Daniel Coker in a portrait included in James A. Handy's *Scraps of African Methodist Episcopal History*, 1902. (Courtesy of Documenting the American South, The University of North Carolina at Chapel Hill Libraries.)

In 1816 Baltimore's black Methodists met with their brethren from Pennsylvania, New Jersey, and Delaware and combined their separate churches into a single denomination, the African Methodist Episcopal Church. Richard Allen was elected chairman of the convention with Coker as vice chairman. Because Coker was one of the few participants who could read and write, the task of drafting the convention's resolutions fell to him.

After Coker and Allen were both elected bishops, Allen insisted the new denomination needed only one and, according to many accounts, offered to resign. In a second election on 11 April 1816, Allen was chosen sole bishop. Coker was made pastor of Bethel, Baltimore's AME church, but for unknown reasons he was expelled from the AME within two years and reduced to a life of itinerant preaching.

Inspired by an earlier meeting with PAUL CUFFE SR., a pathbreaking black businessman and ship builder who had come to Baltimore in 1812 seeking support for his plan to transport free blacks to Sierra

Leone, Coker allied himself with the American Colonization Society. In 1820 Coker set out for Sierra Leone in the company of Samuel Bacon and John P. Bankson representing the federal government and Samuel Crozer, an agent for the colonization society and eighty-three black emigrés. Envisioning himself as a Christian pilgrim, Coker kept a detailed record of the voyage, later published in Baltimore as the *Journal of Daniel Coker, A Descendant of Africa, from the Time of Leaving New York in the Ship Elizabeth, Capt. Sebor, On a Voyage for Sherbro, in Africa, in Company with Three Agents and about Ninety Persons of Colour* (1820). In the new settlement's early days, Coker served as a justice of the peace, held church services, and acted as a mediator between the white agents and black emigrants. The initial optimism of the voyagers was soon eroded by torrential rains, malaria, and polluted water. Within months, the U.S. government and ACS agents had died, leaving Coker in charge of the struggling settlement. But Coker's close ties with the white agents before their deaths undermined his authority with the surviving black settlers, and when they moved to their permanent settlement in Liberia in 1821 they left him behind. In 1821 Coker's wife, Maria (d. 1824), and his three sons sailed from Baltimore and joined him in Sierra Leone.

In 1822 the governor of Sierra Leone made Coker the superintendent of Hastings, a village that functioned as a repatriation center for West Africans retrieved from coastal slave traders after the abolition of the slave trade. In Hastings, Coker continued to preach, eventually seceding from the AME Church and founding the West African Methodist denomination. He died in Sierra Leone.

The trajectory of Coker's life is salient, in part, because it intersected with a number of important institutions—slavery, the AME, and the American Colonization Society. But it is the power of his voice as one of a small number of literate African Americans in the early national period that remains his most potent legacy. "May the time speedily come," Coker wrote in his Baltimore sermon, arguing for the formation of a separate black church, "when we shall see our brethren come flocking to us like doves to their windows. And we as a band of brethren, shall sit down under our own vine to worship, and none to make us afraid."

FURTHER READING

Because there is no biography of Daniel Coker, his own writings remain the richest source of information about his life and thought. The *Journal of Daniel Coker* is available on microfilm at the New York Public Library. Coker's second *Journal* written in Africa and covering the period from April 1821 to September 1821 is in the Library of Congress, Manuscripts Division.

Aptheker, Herbert. *A Documentary History of the Negro People in the United States*, vol. 1 (1973).

Coan, Josephus R. "Daniel Coker: Nineteenth-Century Black Church Organizer, Educator, and Missionary." *Journal of the Interdenominational Theological Seminary* 1 (1975): 17–31.

This entry is taken from the *American National Biography* and is published here with the permission of the American Council of Learned Societies.

MARY F. COREY

Coker, Marie Jones Austin Dickerson (20 Apr. 1906–19 Jan. 1993), aviator, dancer, and musician, was born in Muskogee, Oklahoma, the fifth of seven children to Sarah Ragsdale and a father surnamed Jones. Official records such as census records from 1930 and the Social Security Death Index list her birth year as 1906, but family records, photographs, and anecdotal evidence indicate her birth year as between 1900 and 1903. After she was widowed Marie's mother left Muskogee for Los Angeles, California, along with Marie and some of her siblings, where they settled in a vibrant, multiracial neighborhood in East Los Angeles. When Marie's mother married David Austin, a former guitarist for the singer SISSIERETTA JONES (Black Patti) in 1910, Marie took her stepfather's surname, Austin.

Coker attended and graduated from Central High School in Los Angeles and was the first in her immediate family to attain a high school diploma. She was a precocious child, particularly in music. She first began taking music lessons at the age of thirteen, and by age fifteen she gave piano performances and offered piano lessons throughout the East Los Angeles neighborhood in which she lived.

In the early 1920s, Coker married a man named Dickerson. It was a short-lived marriage, as Marie married not for love but rather to gain greater independence from her protective parents. She began singing in local nightclubs shortly after her marriage. She was also a talented dancer, and appeared at a number of nightclubs in and around Los Angeles, especially those along the famed Central Avenue strip, and for a period of time appeared at the famous Cotton Club in Harlem.

In 1929, after her performance at a Los Angeles–area club, a group of black aviators attending the show talked with Coker. After a lengthy conversation during which they became impressed with Coker's intelligence and her interest in flying, they invited her to take flying lessons at the recently formed BESSIE COLEMAN Aero Club, an organization created by the pilot William Powell to promote flying among blacks and named in honor of the first black person and first black woman to fly in the United States. After Coleman's untimely death in a plane crash in 1926, Powell and other black pilots wanted to ensure that blacks, and especially black women, continued in her footsteps. Coker took lessons with JAMES HERMAN BANNING, a pioneering aviator who, along with THOMAS COX ALLEN, was the first black man to make the transcontinental flight across the United States in 1934, flying from Los Angeles to New York in forty-two days. Coker was among the first students to take lessons at the Bessie Coleman Aero Club, learning to fly on a World War I vintage Curtiss OX5 water-cooled plane. The zenith of Coker's flying career was her membership in the "Five Blackbirds," a group led by the aviator William Powell and which included the aviator HUBERT F. JULIAN. The Blackbirds' best-known performances were in September 1931 and in December 1931 in Los Angeles. During the 1931 performance, they flew before a crowd of 15,000 people.

Coker gave up flying in the 1930s and again focused on her first love, her career in music and dance. She performed with actors such as Alec Lovejoy and Idah Brown and with the singer Teddy Peters in a series of all black musical revues, performing with an ensemble cast of fifty dancers and singers under the direction of Blossom Wilson and Harry Heber. Coker was often cited as the greatest black "shake" or "shimmy" dancer on the American stage in the 1930s. She later performed in USO shows during World War II in Hawaii, and immediately after the war toured with an all-woman band in which she played bass and piano, and sang and danced. It was during this period that she met and married Henry Coker, a renowned jazz trombonist who played with, among others, Benny Carter, the Count Basie Orchestra and RAY CHARLES. Marie's marriage to Henry Coker ended in divorce in the 1960s.

Coker retired from performing in the late 1950s. She thereafter spent several years as a successful realtor, and in 1967 she moved to Mexico City, Mexico, where she lived among a thriving expatriate community until returning to the United States in the late 1970s. She died of complications of emphysema in Los Angeles.

Coker made her a mark as an aviator in the early days of flight. She was a multitalented woman who also excelled as a dancer, musician, and businesswoman. She moved between her diverse careers with an ease and grace that is not frequently seen.

FURTHER READING

Much of the information in this article was gathered through a number of interviews with members of Coker's family.

Bryant, Clora, et al., eds. *Central Avenue Sounds: Jazz in Los Angeles* (1999).

Hardesty, Von, and Dominic Pisano. *Black Wings: The American Black in Aviation Washington* (1983).

Hart, Phillip S. *Flying Free: America's First Black Aviators* (1996).

Powell, William. *Black Aviator: The Story of William J. Powell* (1994).

LOLITA K. BUCKNER INNISS

Colbert, J. B. (28 June 1861–14 Dec. 1936), a minister who helped consolidate the African Methodist Episcopal Zion (AMEZ) Church in the postbellum South, was born Jesse B. Colbert in Cedar Creek township, Lancaster County, South Carolina, the son of farm laborers Tillman Colbert and Mariah House Colbert. Neither of his parents could read, but they made sure their children attended school (1870 and 1880 Census, Kentucky Death Certificate). Colbert attended county schools until the age of eighteen and then entered Lancaster High School, originally called the Pettey High School after its founder and principal, Rev. (later Bishop) Charles Calvin Pettey, pastor of the Lancaster Courthouse AMEZ church.

After teaching school himself in South Carolina, Colbert entered Livingstone College in Salisbury, North Carolina, in January 1883, shortly after it was established by DR. JOSEPH CHARLES PRICE, who served as president from 1882 to 1888. Bishop JAMES WALKER HOOD recorded that Colbert was converted the third day after beginning studies there, a decision and experience critical to full church membership during that period.

Colbert was first licensed as a local preacher in Concord, North Carolina, in 1884 and the following year took up assignment as an itinerant preacher for the Indian Hill Circuit of the church's South Carolina conference. In 1886 Colbert was ordained a deacon by Bishop S. T. Jones, and in 1888 he was ordained as an elder, stationed at Rock Hill, South Carolina. The same year on 3 July he married Margaret A. Davis, in Rowan County, North Carolina (NC Marriage Index, cf. 1910 Census). He then spent a few months assigned to the Fort Lawn circuit, before being transferred by Bishop Jones to the New England Conference, where Bishop Hood, presiding over the North-East Episcopal District, appointed him to the church at Derby, Connecticut.

Hood observed with approval that during his work in the Carolinas, Colbert in one year at Rock Hill raised more general funds than were ever raised by any of his predecessors and built a splendid frame church, while in his short time on the Fort Lawn circuit, he accomplished "a glorious revival," with many souls added to the church, and the parsonage was "handsomely repaired" (Hood, 256–257). During the half century following the Civil War, stabilizing each local church's finances and establishing permanent buildings that secured respect from the surrounding community while instilling confidence in the membership were important goals for every African American denomination active in the southern states.

Continuing to meet Bishop Hood's high expectations, Colbert liquidated a long-standing debt during the first of his two years in Derby. The second year he pursued a course of theology at Yale Divinity School. Hood transferred Colbert to First Church, Providence, Rhode Island, a difficult assignment, suited to his demonstrated abilities. The church had been forced three years earlier to sell its building to make way for railroad improvements. The church was located in a hall, and older members passed away while younger members lost interest. Those who remained doubted they would ever rebuild. Colbert began with a church lot, for which his predecessor had paid $4,500, and $3,000 in the bank. Eighteen months later a vestry was completed (dedicated by Bishop Hood, 26 November 1893), at a cost of over $12,000, of which $5,300 remained to be paid off in February 1894.

In 1892, while still in Providence, Colbert first served as a ministerial delegate to the church's quadrennial general conference. He was minister at Galbraith AMEZ Church in Washington, DC, when the 1896 general conference called upon him to organize the Varick Christian Endeavor Society, which he served as president. This effort was part of a larger interdenominational movement, begun by Rev. Francis E. Clark, at Williston Congregational Church in Portland, Maine, 2

February 1881. By 1927 some form of Christian Endeavor was adopted by eighty-nine evangelical religious denominations "to promote an earnest Christian life among its members, to increase their mutual acquaintance, and to make them more useful in the service to God." In four years Colbert oversaw the creation of six hundred local societies within the AMEZ Church, ha ving a membership of thirty thousand. During this time, Colbert moved to St. Louis, Missouri.

Because of the efforts of Colbert, his contemporaries, and the generation that taught them, the church had grown from about 5,000 to 528,461 members, plus another 125,000 adherents who had not made a profession of faith or experienced conversion, sustaining 4,841 church buildings and 2,902 ordained ministers. From its pre-war concentration in New York, New England, and the Midwest, the church was by the year 1900 represented in twenty-eight states, with the largest membership in North Carolina (111,949), Alabama (79,231), South Carolina (45,880), and Florida (14,791). Colbert was among the incorporators of AMEZ Publication House in 1899.

In September 1901 Colbert served as one of fourteen delegates representing the AMEZ church at the Third Ecumenical Methodist Conference at City Road Chapel, London, a gathering of most Methodist denominations throughout the world. Subsequently, he served as pastor of Walters AMEZ Church, Chicago, where he and his wife were living in 1910. Colbert moved to Louisville, Kentucky, in 1911, where he remained for the last twenty-five years of his life, residing at 2330 East Walnut Street. Initially, he served as presiding elder of the Louisville district of the church in Kentucky.

Colbert was signatory to a statement by "eighteen bishops and fifty-seven ministers of the gospel" along with a number of leading educators and "leaders of the colored race" who met in Washington, D.C., 12 March 1912, to bitterly denounce President William Howard Taft's re-election bid and endorse the nomination of Theodore Roosevelt as the best hope to restore the Republican Party (*The Washington Bee*, 16 March 1912, 1).

He was active in promoting the new "colored branches" of the Louisville public library, ten years old in 1915, and in 1916 hosted the church's twenty-fifth quadrennial general conference in Louisville. Considered a candidate for bishop in 1912, when no bishops were elected—after a stand-off between conservatives and progressives within the church—Colbert was not among those elected in 1916. His colleague, Rev. George Clement, was elected bishop that year, making his home in Louisville.

By 1918 Colbert was listed as an attorney, in addition to his AMEZ responsibilities, but by 1930 he considered the practice of law to be his primary profession. By 1925 he was also manager of the National Employment Bureau, and in 1928 he sought qualified teachers for assignment through the National Colored Teachers Agency, advertised in the Proceedings of the Kentucky Negro Education Association that same year. When he died in 1936 the flags in Louisville were flown at half staff, but existing scholarship on community life of the segregated black population in Louisville sheds little light on the content of his law practice or personal associations and accomplishments.

FURTHER READING

DuBois, W. E. B. *The Negro Church* (1903).

Hood, James Walker. *One Hundred Years of the African Methodist Episcopal Zion Church; or, The Centennial of African Methodism* (1895).

Martin, Sandy Dwayne. *For God and Race: The Religious and Political Leadership of AMEZ Bishop James Walker Hood* (1999).

Smith, J. Clay, Jr. *Emancipation. The Making of the Black Lawyer, 1844–1944* (1999).

CHARLES ROSENBERG

Cole, Allen Eugene (1 Sept. 1883–6 Feb. 1970), photographer and fraternal leader, was born in Kearneysville, West Virginia, the eleventh of thirteen children of Allen Cole, a wagon maker, blacksmith, and carpenter, and Sarah Jenkins Cole. The Cole family numbered among the 4,045 African Americans in Jefferson County, West Virginia's most populous county in 1880. Although he came from a humble background, the elder Cole was able to send some of his children to Storer College in Harpers Ferry, eight miles east of Kearneysville. Allen "Allie" Cole was enrolled at Storer in October 1900, following his older brother Hughes and older sister Lucy, both of whom attended in the early 1890s. The first school of higher education for African Americans in West Virginia, Storer College was founded in Harpers Ferry in 1867 under the condition that it did not discriminate by race, gender, or color. At Storer, Cole completed courses in industrial arts, mathematics, pedagogy, and West Virginia and American history and literature, which was then a typical education at many black colleges and universities. Cole excelled at Storer, receiving a scholarship in 1904 and participating in the oratorical contest during the June 1904 commencement ceremonies.

After graduating from Storer in 1905, Cole moved to Cincinnati, Ohio, and worked as a laborer, houseman, bellman, and porter. He eventually worked with the attorney Justis Carter in real estate. After trying to gain admission to law school, he eventually settled for a correspondence course in business law. He joined one of the many fraternal organizations in Cincinnati, the Royal Arch Masonry, and became a loyal member of the Prince White Lodge No. 1, serving on its publicity committee. The Masons helped to formalize his organizational skills and provided a network for Cole and other members for social, political, and economic mobility. Cole married Frances Tillie Lightfoot in Cincinnati on 1 June 1909. They had no children. The Coles settled into the West End section of the city's downtown, occasionally moving from one apartment house to another. By 1912 Cole and his wife had moved to the Walnut Hills section of the city, an area of middle-class blacks.

The real estate ventures of Cole and the attorney Carter included investments in property in Washington, D.C., Chicago, and New York City as well as in Cincinnati. However, their ventures proved to be unsuccessful. After an injury prevented him from regaining a job as a railroad porter, Cole set out for Cleveland, Ohio. In 1917 he moved into a boardinghouse in the Cedar-Central community on the East Side owned by his wife's cousin, Emma Findley. His wife, Frances, did not immediately join him in Cleveland. In 1917 Cole began working as a waiter at the Cleveland Athletic Club. He first became secretary to the headwaiter and then was promoted to headwaiter himself, a position in which he remained for ten years. While working at the club Cole met Joseph Opet, manager of the Frank Moore Photographic Studio. Cole worked as a custodian at the studio in exchange for lessons in photography. He effectively apprenticed under Opet for six years until the studio came under new management and moved to another location.

Cole established himself as a professional photographer in 1919, ordering his own equipment and opening a residential studio in his home at East 103rd Street. In 1922 he moved to 9904 Cedar Avenue and opened a larger studio in his home there. Shortly thereafter Cole decided that he could earn more per hour as a studio photographer than working tables at the Cleveland Athletic Club for an entire day. The African American community on the east side of Cleveland, the Cedar Avenue community in particular, needed a residential photographer. Although Cole was not the first African American photographer in the city, he was a formidable presence among a new generation of cameramen that focused their lenses on the East Side's emerging middle class.

Cole's predecessors were the Chesnutt brothers, E. Nelson Ellis, and Robert Smith. As the African American population increased, so did the number of photographers. Cole partnered with the lithographer Chester Horton, doing portraits and commercial jobs, and used his fraternal contacts to persuade organizations, churches, and businesses that their meetings and conferences should be photographed. Cole photographed the twentieth national convention of the NAACP when that historic meeting was held in Cleveland in 1929. He also capitalized on the holiday season by advertising photographs as Christmas gifts. In his studio Cole made portraits of migrants newly arrived to the East Side. He was invited into homes to photograph children's birthday parties, New Year's celebrations, family gatherings, and intimate portraits, and was hired by insurance companies, attorneys, and families to photograph the deceased at funeral homes and even in the city morgue.

By the late 1920s Cole's photographic business was well under way. He had already turned his attention to other activities. Cole was familiar with all branches of Masonry and continued in Cleveland the fraternal activities that he had started while living in Cincinnati. In 1925 he was elected Exalted Ruler of the Improved Benevolent and Protective Order of Elks of the World, King Tut Lodge. The King Tut Lodge was established in 1923 and was the second Elks Lodge in Cleveland. Cole was also a member of the Excelsior Lodge No. 11 PRINCE HALL Masons, serving as past master.

In 1939 Allen Cole and other businessmen in the East Side formed the Progressive Business Alliance. Its predecessors were the Cleveland Association of Colored Men, formed in 1908, and the Cleveland Businessmen's Association, formed in 1925. The Progressive Business Alliance held trade shows and hosted a weekly radio program, the *Negro Business Hour*. In 1954 Cole was honored by the organization with its annual award for outstanding contributions to the Alliance. However, Cole's contributions to business went further than the Alliance. In the early 1930s he did photographic work pro bono for the new weekly *Call and Post* newspaper. Throughout the 1930s, a time of economic hardship for African Americans, Cole bartered for his services and even allowed people to pay whenever they could, thereby endearing him to many in the community.

In the 1930s Cole was a member of the Future Outlook League (FOL), an organization that boycotted those white-owned businesses and companies that were patronized by African Americans but refused to hire them as employees. The FOL's motto was "Don't Buy Where You Can't Work." Founded in 1935 and headed by John O. Holly, the FOL was so successful with its campaigns aimed at neighborhood stores, utility companies, and statewide corporations that its strategies were adopted by African Americans throughout Ohio and western Pennsylvania.

It was during the 1930s that Cole adopted the slogan, "Somebody, Somewhere, Wants Your Photograph." He posted this slogan on a huge billboard in the yard of his Cedar Avenue studio and attached portraits of his clients. Cole continued his studio and freelance work into the early 1960s. Although ill health slowed his activities, he nevertheless remained a popular photographer and was influential among a post–World War II class of African American photographers.

Well into his eighties Cole continued to work in his studio so that he could provide for his wife, Frances, in case of his death. Constant companions for sixty years, the Coles navigated their photography studio through the migration of the 1920s, the Depression of the 1930s, World War II, and the modern civil rights era. After months of illnesses that kept him bedridden, Allen Cole died in Cleveland in 1970 leaving thousands of photographs, negatives, films, and paintings covering more than forty years of significant cultural production and history. It was nearly a decade before the breadth of his photographic influence and documentation of African American life in Cleveland was widely known and appreciated.

FURTHER READING

Allen E. Cole's papers and photograph collection are housed at the Western Reserve Historical Society in Cleveland, Ohio.

Black, Samuel W. *African American Photographers of Cleveland, 1930–1965* (1996).

Davis, Russell H. *Black Americans in Cleveland: From George Peake to Carl B. Stokes, 1796–1969* (1972).

Martin, Olivia, ed. *"Somebody, Somewhere, Wants Your Photograph": A Selection from the Work of Allen E. Cole (1883–1970), Photographer of Cleveland's Black Community* (1980).

SAMUEL W. BLACK

Cole, Bob (1 July 1868–2 Aug. 1911), actor, director, and composer, was born Robert Allen Cole Jr. in Athens, Georgia, the son of Robert Allen Cole Sr., a successful carpenter and political activist. Nothing is known about Cole's mother. Cole received musical training in Athens and finished elementary school after his family moved to Atlanta. He made his first stage appearance in Chicago, performing in Sam T. Jack's *The Creole Show* in 1891; later he became the show's stage manager. Around 1893 Cole and his stage partner, Stella Wiley, moved to New York, where they performed in vaudeville. Cole and Wiley may have married, but there is no evidence, and in any event by the end of the 1890s they had parted company. Returning to Jack's *Creole Show*, Cole soon emerged as the headliner, developing his popular stage character, the tramp Willy Wayside. During the mid-1890s he formed the first school for black performers in New York City, the All-Star Stock Company. This group, working out of Worth's Museum, became the center for many future productions.

Cole joined BLACK PATTI's Troubadours as a performer and songwriter in 1895. His music gained rapid popularity and he soon found himself writing songs for groups such as the Georgia Jubilee Singers (c. 1895), the show *Black America* (c. 1896), and the popular singer May Irwin. By 1896 his music and performance in Black Patti's Troubadours' production of *At Jolly Cooney-Island* had become popular, prompting him to ask the producers for a raise. Denied the increase, Cole bolted from the show, taking with him a number of talented artists. He then created *A Trip to Coontown* (1897–1901) with BILL JOHNSON.

A Trip to Coontown proved to be significant for two reasons: it was the first show on Broadway to be written, produced, and managed by African Americans, and it was the first black-produced show to break with the minstrel tradition. Although he was "labeled a disturber and was blackballed" by white producers (Riis, *Just before Jazz*, 28), Cole enjoyed a successful tour of *A Trip to Coontown* throughout the United States. In establishing the production company, Cole enunciated his goals: "We are going to have our own shows. We are going to write them ourselves, we are going to have our own stage managers, our own orchestra leader and our own manager out front to count up. No divided houses—our race must be seated from the boxes back" (Foster, 48).

Around 1902 Cole dissolved his relationship with Billy Johnson and began working with J. ROSAMOND JOHNSON, the brother of the writer and poet JAMES WELDON JOHNSON. For the next decade Cole abandoned the tramp figure Willy Wayside in his vaudeville shows, opting instead for performances in black tie and coattails. Cole and Johnson were credited with initiating a few trends in music, such as the use of eye, moon, and tree images in songs. They emerged as one of the most popular black musical comedy duos, appearing in New York and London, from around 1903 to 1905. Their act, wrote James Weldon Johnson, "started a vogue of acts consisting of two men in dress suits and a piano" (*Along This Way*, 188).

Cole was one of the most versatile performers in early black theater. A good singer and an excellent dancer, he was, according to James Weldon Johnson, "able to play several musical instruments" (*Black Manhattan*, 98). He wrote more than 150 songs for over a dozen shows. While many of these might be regarded as "coon songs," others were romantic ballads devoid of references to race. He authored such popular hits as "Under the Bamboo Tree," "Congo-Love Song," "The Conjure Man," "Gimme de Leavin's," and "The Maid with the Dreamy Eyes."

Cole also wrote songs for his own shows: *The Shoo Fly Regiment* (1905–1907) and *The Red Moon* (1908–1909). *The Shoo Fly Regiment* depicted African American university students and teachers who enlisted in the military during the Spanish-American War. Cole portrayed the janitor, Hunter Wilson, providing comic relief. *The Red Moon*, which costarred ABBIE MITCHELL and later AIDA OVERTON WALKER, dealt with a scheme to recover a kidnapped African Indian princess. Cole also wrote an unpublished libretto, *The Czar of Czam*.

In 1911 Cole collapsed from what was probably syphilis, although the disease would not be the cause of his death. While recuperating near Catskill, New York, he drowned in an apparent suicide.

FURTHER READING

Foster, Will. "Pioneers of the Stage: Memoirs of William Foster," in *1928 Edition of the Official World of Colored Artists*, ed. Theophilus Lewis (1928).

Riis, Thomas L. "'Bob' Cole: His Life and His Legacy to Black Musical Theatre," *Black Perspective in Music* 13 (Fall 1985).

Riis, Thomas L. *Just before Jazz: Black Musical Theatre in New York, 1890 to 1915* (1989).

Riis, Thomas L. *More than Just Minstrel Shows: The Rise of Black Musical Theatre at the Turn of the Century* (1992).

Obituaries: *Chicago Defender* and *Indianapolis Freeman*, 12 Aug. 1911.
This entry is taken from the *American National Biography* and is published here with the permission of the American Council of Learned Societies.

DAVID KRASNER

Cole, Cozy (17 Oct. 1909–29 Jan. 1981), jazz percussionist, was born William Randolph Cole in East Orange, New Jersey. He was led into a musical career by his three brothers, all of whom were jazz musicians. Cole took up the drums when he was a young boy, and he continued to study the instrument in high school. He began playing professionally as a teenager before attending Wilberforce College in Ohio for two years.

In 1926 Cole moved to New York City, where he continued his study of jazz percussion with Billy Gladstone and Charlie Brooks, two noted drummers in the New York jazz scene of the 1920s. In 1928 he was hired by the clarinetist and bandleader Wilbur Sweatman and then led his own group before joining several prominent jazz bands in the 1930s. During that decade Cole performed and recorded with bands led by JELLY ROLL MORTON, BLANCHE CALLOWAY, Benny Carter, Willie Bryant, Jonah Jones, and STUFF SMITH. Cole made his first records at age twenty with Jelly Roll Morton's Red Hot Peppers.

In 1939 Cole gained national recognition as a performer with CAB CALLOWAY's famed band. Cole stayed with Calloway for four years and was featured on many of Calloway's recordings, including "Crescendo in Drums," "Paradiddle," and "Ratamacue." In 1943 Cole joined the CBS Orchestra, becoming one of the first African Americans on a radio network musical staff. In the same year, Cole was featured in the Broadway musical *Carmen Jones*, an adaptation of Bizet's *Carmen*. His volcanic drum solo in "Beat Out Dat Rhythm on a Drum" in the show brought him recognition in the theater world. "I think I'm the only drummer to have been featured in a big Broadway show with his name on the program," he later said (*New York Times*, 31 Jan. 1981).

Although it was an unusual step for a professional musician, in 1943 Cole entered the Juilliard School of Music, where he studied musical theory, harmony, piano, timpani, and drums. In 1944 he appeared with Benny Goodman's band in the stage production of *Seven Lively Arts* and recorded "Thru for the Night" and "Concerto for Cozy" as a leader, and "St. Louis Blues" with Roy Eldridge.

In 1945 Cole left both Juilliard and the CBS Orchestra and began a four-year period of freelancing with various bands in New York City. In 1949 he joined EARL HINES, Jack Teagarden, and BARNEY BIGARD in LOUIS ARMSTRONG's All Stars and toured with the group for more than four years. During that period he was featured in *The Glenn Miller Story* (1954) and other films with Armstrong; he toured with the All Stars in Europe in 1949 and 1952.

In 1953, following his tenure with the Armstrong band, Cole opened a drum school in New York City with Gene Krupa and recorded several pieces as a leader, including "Drum Fantasy" in 1954. From 1955 to 1958 he appeared regularly at the Metropole, a New York City nightclub, and on Arthur Godfrey's radio show. During that period Cole also toured Europe with an all-star band led by Jack Teagarden and Earl Hines. In 1958 Cole made a solo record, "Topsy," that became an unexpected hit and gave his name considerable commercial value. More than 1 million copies of the record were sold, enabling him to tour with his own group in the late 1950s and early 1960s. In 1962 he was sent by the State Department on a tour of Africa. Through the 1960s Cole's band was one of the most popular regular performers in New York City's nightclubs.

In 1969 Cole rejoined the trumpeter Jonah Jones in a quintet with which he played through the end of his career. He retired from performing in 1976, when he became an artist in residence and student lecturer at Capital University in Columbus, Ohio. At Capital, Cole continued his lifelong study of music, expanding his knowledge to include arranging, piano, and harmony. He died in Columbus.

Cole was one of the most versatile drummers in jazz history. He mastered virtually every style in jazz, including swing, bebop, and the popular form featured in Broadway musicals and on radio. Cole was also known for his deep knowledge of music and percussion and for his ability to deliver precise yet explosive drum solos.

FURTHER READING
Dance, Stanley. *The World of Swing* (1974).
Obituary: *New York Times*, 31 Jan. 1981.
This entry is taken from the *American National Biography* and is published here with the permission of the American Council of Learned Societies.

THADDEUS RUSSELL

Cole, Johnnetta (19 Oct. 1936–), anthropologist, educator, and college president, was born Johnnetta Betsch in Jacksonville, Florida, the second of three children to Mary Frances Lewis, an English teacher, and John Thomas Betsch Sr., an insurance executive. Johnnetta grew up in one of Florida's most prominent African American families; her great-grandfather, Abraham Lincoln Lewis, co-founded the Afro-American Life Insurance Company, Florida's first insurance company. An ambitious and civic-minded businessman, Lewis established several black institutions, including the colored branch of the public library, the Lincoln Golf and Country Club, and the seaside resort known as American Beach, the only beach allowing blacks in north Florida. Johnnetta's childhood was shaped by competing influences: her supportive family and community, and the racist attitudes and institutions of the Jim Crow South. Educated in segregated public and private schools, Johnnetta credits the influence of her teachers and her family friend MARY MCLEOD BETHUNE with encouraging her educational and moral development. Her family's active participation in civic works was fostered by

strong ties to the church and a fundamental belief in community service, an attitude voiced by A.-L. Lewis, and often repeated by Johnnetta as "Doing for others is just the rent you gotta pay for living on this earth."

Johnnetta excelled academically and entered Fisk University at the age of fifteen. A year later she joined her older sister Marvyne at Oberlin College in Ohio, where she switched her concentration from medicine to the social sciences. After receiving a B.A. in Sociology in 1957, she began graduate work at Northwestern University in Chicago, Illinois. Under the tutelage of the anthropologist Melville Herskovits, who had taught KATHERINE DUNHAM two decades earlier, Johnnetta earned an M.A. (1959) and a Ph.D. (1967) in Anthropology. In a 1993 *Chicago Tribune* interview, she attributed her academic success in part to her family and friends back home: "It was wonderful to listen to old black folk who had not been educated themselves, say: 'Look at sister. Just look at sister. She is getting all that education.'" While at Northwestern, she met Robert Cole, a white graduate student in economics from Iowa. Over the objections of both their

Johnetta Cole, president of Bennett College in Greensboro, North Carolina, second from right, applauds during a news conference in October 2003. (AP Images.)

families, the couple married in 1960 and had three sons, David, Aaron, and Ethan Che. They divorced in 1982. In 1970, after several years teaching anthropology and directing the black studies program at Washington State University, Cole was offered a tenured position at the University of Massachusetts, Amherst. She remained at UMass for the next thirteen years, during which time she taught anthropology and played a key role in establishing a black studies program. She served for a time as associate provost and was asked to head a panel that proposed university-wide curricula reform. In 1983 she took a teaching position at Hunter College in New York City, where she also directed the Latin American and Caribbean studies program.

Cole became one of the most influential figures in higher education when, in 1987, she became the first African American female president of Spelman College, a women's liberal arts school in Atlanta and one of the most prestigious of the nation's historically black colleges and universities. Founded in 1881 by two white Christian missionary women from New England, Spelman has graduated several generations of black women, including ALICE WALKER and MARIAN WRIGHT EDELMAN. Cole's appointment, already a noteworthy affair, proved a sensation when, on the weekend of her inauguration, CAMILLE and BILL COSBY donated $20 million to Spelman, setting the tone—and expectations—for her administration. Cole met the challenge, dramatically raising both the college's financial holdings and its public profile. Cole later estimated that she spent half of her time at Spelman raising money. The return on her investment was unmistakable. During her presidency, the college's endowment increased from $41 million to $143 million. Cosby's gift, the largest ever personal donation to a black college or university, and Cole's leadership encouraged a $1 million donation from OPRAH WINFREY, followed in 1992 by a $37 million gift from the DeWitt Wallace Fund, the largest donation ever made to a black college. The college's visibility received an additional boost when Cosby modeled Hillman College, the fictional setting for his *Cosby Show* spin-off, *A Different World*, after Spelman. The television show, which ran from 1987 to 1993, filmed its exterior shots on campus, introducing Spelman to millions of Americans each week. In 1992, *U.S. News and World Report* ranked Spelman the top liberal arts college in the South.

With the money she raised, Cole built up Spelman's physical plant, endowed scholarships and professorships, and established a mentoring program matching students with executives at local companies. She opened the Office of Community Service, making service central to Spelman's mission. Cole, who managed to teach an anthropology class each year, was known for her accessibility and visibility on campus, and when she nicknamed herself "Sister President," the students immediately embraced the title, and their president. Her success at Spelman was due in part to her interdisciplinary approach to scholarship and governance and to her experience articulating the practical and theoretical needs of emerging programs in black studies and women's studies. She introduced a clear set of priorities: building job networks for black women, introducing community service into leadership training, and expanding the notion of diversity to include differences *within* African American and women's communities. Cole embodied each of these efforts, fashioning a public identity that combined elements and attitudes from different worlds. Moving easily between the southern black vernacular of her childhood and a formal academic speaking style, Cole is equally comfortable in the classroom and the boardroom. Even her fashion choices challenge the prevailing image of the woman in the gray-flannel suit: "Johnnetta includes at least one detail that defies conformity—a carved ivory Janus-faced pendant, made as the emblem of a Liberian secret society; a cowrie-studded belt; or fabric hand-woven by a friend" (Bateson, 25–26).

Shortly after arriving at Spelman in 1987, Cole married the public health administrator Arthur J. Robinson Jr. and became stepmother to his two sons. Johnnetta and Art had been childhood playmates who, after forty years, were reunited when news of Cole's appointment prompted Art to look up his old friend. In 1992 she was honored with an appointment to President-Elect Bill Clinton's transition team. As cluster coordinator for education, labor, and the arts and humanities, she was responsible for the review of the Department of Education budget, personnel, and programs. Soon after her appointment, however, she was subjected to attacks that her supporters likened to McCarthyism. Allegations that she was a pro-Communist, pro-Cuban, pro-Palestinian radical effectively bumped her from the list of candidates under consideration for education secretary.

In 1997, after serving for ten years, Cole resigned as president of Spelman. When asked about Cole's decision, Bill Cosby, perhaps overdramatically, told the *Atlanta Journal-Constitution*, "I'm not happy. To me it's as if DIZZY GILLESPIE, MILES

DAVIS, SARAH VAUGHAN, CARMEN MCRAE, and ELLA FITZGERALD had all died on the same day." In 1998 she returned to teaching, taking a position at Emory University, and in 2002 put off retirement plans in order to accept the presidency of the financially beleaguered Bennett College in Greensboro, North Carolina, the only remaining black women's college in the nation other than Spelman.

Cole's scholarly work, which includes fieldwork studies in Cuba, Haiti, Grenada, Liberia, and the United States, has contributed rigorous analyses of race, gender, and labor to the field of cultural anthropology. Through her teaching and publishing, she has bridged disciplines, bringing together scholars from anthropology, African American studies, women's studies, African studies, and Latin American studies. She has written and edited numerous books, beginning with *Anthropology for the Eighties: Introductory Readings* (1982). Her many trips to Cuba resulted in *Race Towards Equality* (1986), and she broke new ground in women's studies with *All American Women: Lines That Divide, Ties That Bind* (1986). Another anthology, *Anthropology for the Nineties: Introductory Readings* (1988), continues to be used in the classroom and beyond. During her reign at Spelman, Cole produced *Conversations: Straight Talk with America's Sister President* (1993) and *Dream the Boldest Dreams: And Other Lessons of Life* (1997), two folksy books directed at a general audience. In 2003 she returned to scholarly publication with *Gender Talk: Sexism, Power, and Politics in the African American Community*, cowritten with BEVERLY GUY-SHEFTALL.

Cole's charisma and innovative approaches to problem solving have made her a popular choice for appointments to both corporate and nonprofit boards. She has sat on the boards of directors of Merck and Company, Home Depot, and Coca-Cola, where she was the first female board member in the company's history. She has served as a trustee of several colleges and universities and in leadership positions at the Rockefeller Foundation, the Martin Luther King Center for Nonviolent Social Change, the Points of Light Foundation, the Feminist Press, the United Negro College Fund, and the American Council on Education. She has been awarded more than forty honorary degrees and has received dozens of honors from a wide range of organizations.

When *Essence* magazine asked Cole in 1997 to describe her goals, she replied, "I dream I come onto campus and on top of Rockefeller Hall ... every inch of space is covered with young women flapping their arms, convinced they can fly. We must make these young African American women believe they indeed can fly, can do the impossible."

Cole stepped down as head of Bennett College in 2007 to serve as chair of Bennett's Johnnetta B. Cole Global Diversity and Inclusion Institute. In February 2009, the Smithsonian Institution appointed Cole as the new director of the National Museum of African Art.

FURTHER READING

Cole, Johnnetta. *Conversations: Straight Talk with America's Sister President* (1993).
Bateson, Mary Catherine. *Composing a Life* (1989).

LISA E. RIVO

Cole, Maria Hawkins (1 Aug. 1922–10 July 2012), singer, writer, and socialite, was born Maria Hawkins in the Roxbury section of Boston, Massachusetts. Her father, Mingo Hawkins, was a mail carrier with the U.S. Postal Service, which at the time was considered a prestigious position for an African American; her mother, Carol Saunders, was from Bermuda. Maria was born the second of three daughters, and when she was only two years old her mother died while giving birth to her youngest sister, Carol. Immediately all three girls were sent to live with their father's sister, Dr. CHARLOTTE HAWKINS BROWN, who was the founder and president of the Palmer Memorial Institute, the nation's most distinguished finishing school for blacks. There Cole was exposed to the likes of Dr. W. E. B. DuBOIS, MARY McCLEOD BETHUNE, and even Eleanor Roosevelt, among other noteworthy guests.

As a student at the Palmer Memorial Institute, Cole was trained in piano and music, and graduated as the salutatorian in 1938, at which time she was allowed by her aunt to attend the school of her choice, as long as that choice did not take her back to Boston and her father. Cole, however, had made up her mind that music and the entertainment industry was what most interested her. She wanted to become a jazz singer and chose to attended Boston Clerical College, where she performed with a local orchestra. She was later offered a chance to sing for two months in New York. Against her family's wishes she accepted a job singing with Benny Carter's band, which she did under the stage name Marie Winter. Her aunt Charlotte had other plans for her, however, and arranged a secretarial job for her with Dr. MORDECAI JOHNSON, a family friend and distinguished leader of Howard University in Washington, D.C. She worked there briefly but later returned to New York to resume her singing career.

In 1943 Cole married First Lieutenant Spurgeon Neal Ellington, a Tuskegee Airman of the famed 332nd Fighter Group who served during World War II; he died two years later during a routine training mission. The climax of Cole's short performing career came when she was offered a job with the DUKE ELLINGTON orchestra. Prior to joining Ellington she worked briefly with COUNT BASIE and FLETCHER HENDERSON.

In 1948 she married the singer and entertainer NAT KING COLE, who was regarded as one of the greatest entertainers of the twentieth century. It was the second marriage for both of them. Although he was still married when they met he was enthralled by her beauty after seeing her perform in 1946. Nat Cole eventually divorced his wife and became engaged to Maria Ellington. Their wedding took place in New York's famed Abyssinian Baptist Church and was officiated by the pastor Reverend Doctor ADAM CLAYTON POWELL JR. More than three thousand people crowded into the sanctuary and an even larger crowd spilled into the streets. The marriage ceremony received wide acclaim and numerous celebrities were in attendance, including BILL ROBINSON, HAZEL SCOTT, SARAH VAUGHAN, and MAXINE SULLIVAN.

Dr. Charlotte Hawkins Brown did not attend the wedding because of her objection to her niece marrying an entertainer. Despite the snub Maria Cole later gave a benefit concert to raise funds for the school. In 1948 the Coles purchased a twenty-room Tudor mansion valued at $85,000 in the exclusive Hancock Park area of Los Angeles, where they had to face the anger of several white residents who at first feared the presence of a black family in their neighborhood. The Coles later adopted Maria's youngest sister's daughter, Carol "Cookie," when her parents died. In 1950 Cole gave birth to another daughter, NATALIE COLE, who would go on to become a renowned singer in her own right.

Despite their fame and success, by 1951 the Coles were in debt to the Internal Revenue Service and were bailed out by her aunt Dr. Brown and by Capitol Records. Meanwhile, Maria Cole played an important role in her husband's career, from selecting his wardrobe to setting the salaries of his performers. She also traveled with him all over the world, leaving her older sister Charlotte to care for all of her children. In 1959 the couple adopted a son, Nat Kelly, and in 1961 became the proud parents to twin daughters, Timolin and Casey.

Upon her husband's death in 1965 Cole established the Nat "King" Cole Cancer Fund in memory of her husband with the intended purpose of furthering medical research into the causes of and possible cures for cancer. She served as a trustee of the fund. She also produced a version of JAMES BALDWIN's play *Amen Corner* with coproducer Frank Silvera on Broadway in 1965, and coauthored a book about her husband in 1971, *Nat King Cole: An Intimate Biography*.

Cole eventually remarried, in 1969, to Gary DeVore and moved back to Massachusetts. The marriage ended in divorce and she continued to live either in her home in the Berkshires of Massachusetts or in Boston's Back Bay area. She was involved in various philanthropic endeavors, such as the Boston Symphony Orchestra board of overseers, board of visitors of the Medical School at Boston University, board of directors of the American Cancer Society–Massachusetts Division, and the board of trustees at the Northfield Mount Hermon School, after which Dr. Brown had patterned Palmer Memorial Institute.

Cole was largely responsible for helping to enlarge the Nat King Cole legacy and remained financially involved in the scope and direction of his music. She eventually relocated to Florida, where she lived close to her twin daughters and grandchildren. She continued to enjoy traveling and kept busy with various charitable endeavors.

Cole died of cancer in Boca Raton, Florida, in 2012. She was 89.

FURTHER READING

Brookes, Ian. "Nat King Cole," in *African American Lives* (2004).

Cole, Maria, with Louis Robinson. *Nat King Cole: An Intimate Biography* (1971).

Cole, Natalie. *Angel on My Shoulder* (2000).

Epstein, Daniel Mark. *Nat King Cole* (1999).

Smith, Jessie Carney. "Maria Cole," in *Notable Black American Women, Book II* (1996).

Wadelington, Charles W., and Richard F. Knapp. *Charlotte Hawkins Brown—What One Young African American Woman Could Do and Palmer Memorial Institute* (1999).

Young, A. S., ed. *The Incomparable Nat King Cole—His Career, His Life, His Legacy* (1965).

ANDRE D. VANN

Cole, Nat King (17 Mar. 1917?–15 Feb. 1965), pianist and singer, was born Nathaniel Adams Coles in Montgomery, Alabama, the son of the Reverend

Edward James Coles Sr., a Baptist minister, and Perlina Adams Coles, choir leader and organist at her husband's church. The family, which included Nat's brother, Edward Jr. ("Eddie"), and sisters Eddie Mae and Evelyn, moved to Chicago when Nat was about four years old, where his brothers Isaac ("Ike") and Lionel ("Freddie") were born. All the Coles children demonstrated musical talent, each playing piano and organ at their father's services and singing in the church choir. Nat was especially precocious, capable at the age of four of a two-handed rendition of "Yes, We Have No Bananas" on the family piano. From the age of twelve he received formal piano training.

Nat grew up on Chicago's South Side, the heartland of Prohibition jazz culture, and attended Wendell Phillips High School. Grounded in gospel at home, he was enthralled by Chicago's jazz milieu, which influenced his organ playing in church; his father often admonished him to "tone it down." During this formative period of his musical development, he was listening avidly to jazz emanating from nightclubs, often from the alleys outside. Both EARL "FATHA" HINES, then playing a residency at Chicago's Grand Terrace ballroom, and TEDDY WILSON were significant influences. In about 1935 Nat abandoned school to concentrate on his musical career. While still a teenager, he organized two jazz groups: a big band, the Rogues of Rhythm, and a quintet, Nat Coles and His Royal Dukes. Drawing on Hines's band style, these groups played at school dances and other local venues. (Some speculated that Nat had illicitly acquired arrangements from the Hines book, the catalog of band arrangements that constituted its unique repertoire.) Nat Coles's big band later challenged Hines's band to a "cutting contest" at the Savoy Ballroom (a competition between bands vying to outperform each other with the result determined by the audience), and, remarkably, Coles's band won. In 1936 Nat's brother Eddie assembled the Solid Swingers with musicians from the old big band and Nat as pianist. The new band obtained a six-month residency at Chicago's Club Panama and recorded, with little recognition, four sides for Decca's "race records" Sepia Series (a category of recordings marketed specifically to a black audience). In the same year Nat and Eddie toured with the revue *Shuffle Along*. On tour Nat met Nadine Robinson, a dancer in the show, and they were married in Ypsilanti, Michigan, in 1937. When the show eventually folded, in Long Beach, California, Nat and Nadine remained there.

The employment prospects for black musicians in Los Angeles were bleaker than in Chicago, and

Nat King Cole, pianist and singer, in New York City, c. June 1947. (© William P. Gottlieb; www.jazzphotos.com.)

Nat later described the impecunious circumstances in which he "played every beer joint from San Diego to Bakersfield." He took such work as he could find, usually as a soloist, playing, as one biographer put it, "in joints with out-of-tune pianos, keys that didn't work, and audiences that didn't listen" (Gourse, 25). At other times he would "sit in" with jazz musicians with whom he was beginning to establish a significant local reputation. It was at this time that he wrote what would become one of his trademark songs, "Straighten Up and Fly Right," with a lyric derived from one of his father's sermons.

In 1937 Nat formed a trio with the guitarist Oscar Moore and the double bassist Wesley Prince (later Jimmy Miller), called King Cole and His Swingsters and, subsequently, the King Cole Trio, marking his name change from "Coles" to "Cole." Such a combo was quite unusual at a time when the big bands of the Swing Era held sway, especially since the band excluded drums and featured electric guitar. The trio secured a residency at the Swannee Inn in Los Angeles, and it was there that Cole began to sing, apparently in response to audience requests. He made several significant recordings in the early 1940s, including a trio session in 1942 with LESTER YOUNG (tenor saxophone) and Red Callender (bass). From 1943 he recorded for the fledgling Capitol label. What made these recordings so distinctive was the trio's intensely responsive interplay, especially between Cole and Moore, and the tightly driven sense of swing behind Cole's elegantly felicitous piano. In addition to the trio's instrumental performances, Cole's role as a vocalist became increasingly prominent on recordings such as "Straighten Up and Fly Right" (1943), "(Get Your Kicks on) Route 66" (1944), "Sweet Lorraine" (1944), and "It's Only a Paper Moon" (1944). With the postwar rise of the starring vocalist, Cole switched emphasis from jazz pianist to "stand-up" singer. Cole, the "accidental" vocalist, possessed a warm baritone with a dark-grained timbre, an immaculate enunciation, and a seemingly effortless naturalism conveying intimacy and charm.

With "The Christmas Song" (1946), what was by then virtually an obligatory vocal was accompanied by a lavish orchestral arrangement that typically characterized the trio's subsequent sound, exemplified on such recordings as "I Love You (for Sentimental Reasons)" (1946), "Nature Boy" (1948), and "Mona Lisa" (1950). These records, all number-one hits, signaled a shift away from Cole's trio jazz toward luscious orchestral ballads. Cole's record sales for Capitol were so great that the company's new tower building was known as "the house that Nat built." More hits in a similar vein followed, including "Unforgettable" (1951), "When I Fall in Love" (1957), and "Let There Be Love" (1962), and much of Cole's work during this period was produced with arrangements by Billy May, Nelson Riddle, and Gordon Jenkins. The trio consequently became sidelined and eventually disbanded in 1955. Cole intermittently returned to a trio format, notably for the album *After Midnight* (1957), with John Collins (guitar), Charlie Harris (bass), and Lee Young (drums).

Cole divorced Nadine in 1948, having met Maria (Marie) Hawkins Ellington, a singer. Nat and Maria were married by the Reverend Doctor Adam Clayton Powell Jr. at Harlem's Abyssinian Baptist church that same year. They had a daughter, Natalie Maria Cole ("Sweetie"), in 1950 and later adopted another, Carol ("Cookie"). In 1959 they adopted a son, Nat Kelly, and in 1961 they had twin daughters, Timolin and Casey. Maria was often credited, or criticized, for her influential role in the subsequent direction of her husband's career.

Cole also appeared in several films in the 1950s, notably as himself in the biographical short *The Nat King Cole Story* (1955) and as the composer W. C. Handy in *St. Louis Blues* (1958). In 1956 Cole became one of the first black performers to star in his own television series, *The Nat King Cole Show*, but despite favorable ratings, sponsors were reluctant to back a black performer, and, consequently, the show soon failed. He had already met racial prejudice in his career. In 1949 he bought a house in the exclusively white Hancock Park district of Los Angeles, where residents attempted to oust him, and in 1956 racist agitators assaulted him onstage at a concert in Birmingham, Alabama. Nevertheless, Cole could appear aloof from or at odds with civil rights activism, and he was criticized for complacency, especially as a highly successful crossover star reluctant to have his career tainted by any association with racial politics. For some, however, he had merely adopted a different strategy to militancy though his demonstrable commitment to racial equality went largely unpublicized. A heavy smoker throughout his life, Cole died of lung cancer at St. John's Hospital in Santa Monica, California.

Cole's standing remains anomalous and comprises two conflicting reputations. He was an extraordinarily innovative jazz pianist whose influential trio work played a vanguard role in validating small-group jazz, often denigrated as "cocktail lounge" music. With the trio's demise, however, this reputation became largely eclipsed by his spectacular popularity in the commercial mainstream. To his detractors, Cole had reneged on jazz and betrayed his talent as an instrumentalist for facile success as a pop singer. Certainly, Cole is now better known for his voice than his piano playing, and his recordings are more frequently categorized as "easy listening" than as jazz, a view that, unfortunately, traduces some of Cole's most distinctive popular recordings. Nevertheless, many would agree with Oscar Moore's "jazz epitaph" for Cole, reported in *Down Beat*: "I never thought Nat would become really important as a *singer*. To me, the cat was always a crazy piano player" (25 Mar. 1965).

FURTHER READING

Cole, Maria, with Louie Robinson. *Nat King Cole: An Intimate Biography* (1971).

Epstein, Daniel Mark. *Nat King Cole* (1999).

Gourse, Leslie. *Unforgettable: The Life and Mystique of Nat King Cole* (1991).

Haskins, James, with Kathleen Benson. *Nat King Cole: The Man and His Music* (1986).

"Nat 'King' Cole, 1917–1965." *Down Beat* 32, no. 7 (25 Mar. 1965): 14.

Obituary: *New York Times*, 16 Feb. 1965.

DISCOGRAPHY

Teubig, Klaus. *Straighten Up and Fly Right: A Chronology and Discography of Nat "King" Cole* (1994).

IAN BROOKES

Cole, Natalie (6 Feb. 1950–), entertainer, singer, and author, was born Stephanie Maria Cole to the singers NAT KING COLE and MARIA HAWKINS COLE; her name was later changed to Natalie, but her father called her "Sweetie." She was one of five children raised in the Cole household in Los Angeles. Her parents had already adopted Carol "Cookie" Cole, Maria's niece, before Natalie was born, and in 1959 they adopted a son, Nat Kelly. In 1961 the number of Natalie's siblings grew to four when her mother had twin girls, Casey and Timolin. The family lived in a Tudor-style mansion in fashionable Hancock Park. Although they were initially greeted harshly by their all-white neighbors, eventually they were accepted.

Natalie grew up accustomed to meeting creative artists such as SARAH VAUGHAN, ARETHA FRANKLIN, ELLA FITZGERALD, DUKE ELLINGTON, Nancy Wilson, and many other musicians, songwriters, and music professionals. At the age of six she sang on a Christmas album, and a year later sang with Cookie and her father on "*Ain't She Sweet.*" Her musical tastes extended from BILLIE HOLIDAY to the Beatles. Her father encouraged her talent and musical ambitions, and even wrote a part for her in a nightclub act. She attended the best private schools and graduated in 1968 from the Northfield Mount Hermon School in Massachusetts.

In 1965 Cole's father died of lung cancer and her world changed. First she aspired to become a doctor, but while studying child psychology at the University of Massachusetts at Amherst she continued to sing and perform in a local band. After earning a B.A. in 1972 she decided to follow in her parents' footsteps and become an entertainer. Despite her legendary father's name and reputation she was determined to create her own singing style, one based on gospel and rhythm and blues, rather than the love songs that made her father famous. She debuted as a solo artist in 1973, and in 1975 she received a recording contract from Capitol Records, her father's label. Her first album, *Inseparable*, was released in 1975 and earned her two Grammy Awards and a gold record. In 1974 she met Marvin Yancey, a producer and songwriter; they married in 1976 and had a son. Yancey was also a minister in Chicago at the Fountain of Life Baptist Church. Although she had been raised a staunch Episcopalian Cole left that denomination in order to be baptized at the Third Baptist Church in Chicago. The strain of work, marriage, and a longing to return to California proved too strong, and in 1978 she and her husband separated and were later divorced.

Natalie Cole performs in New York City in August 2001. (AP Images.)

During the 1980s Cole experienced many highs and lows in both her personal and professional life. As early as 1983 she made several failed attempts to overcome drug addiction. Her mother began to care for her son and later was appointed by the courts to supervise her estate. She was admitted into the Hazelden drug treatment center and remained there for six months. She emerged resolved and determined to never again allow substance abuse to hinder her career. In 1987 she signed a recording contract with Elektra and produced such greats as "Everlasting," "I Live for Your Love," "Pink Cadillac," and in 1989 "Good To Be Back." In that same year she married Andre Fischer, became a stepmother to his three children, and hosted a talent show before their marriage ended in divorce.

By the 1990s her career was soaring with the release of an album, *Unforgettable with Love* (1992), a salute to her father's music that eventually went platinum and earned her seven Grammy Awards. In 1994 she made her movie debut in *Lily in Winter* on the USA Cable Network. She also maintained an active tour schedule throughout much of the late 1990s.

Natalie Cole was the recipient of numerous awards, including some ten Grammy Awards and numerous nominations; the Soul Train Best Single (Female) Award, 1987; three NAACP Image Awards, 1992; two American Music Awards, 1992; and an honorary degree from the Berklee College of Music, 1995. She spent much of her professional career involved in public service and various charities that included the Children's Diabetes Foundation, the Rainforests Foundation, the American Red Cross, and the Minority AIDS Project. She was a member of the Delta Sigma Theta Sorority, Inc. In 2000 she wrote her autobiography titled *Angel on My Shoulder* and also released her *Greatest Hits, Volume I* album.

FURTHER READING

Cole, Natalie M. *Angel on My Shoulder* (2000).
Nicholson, Dolores. "Natalie Maria Cole," in *Notable Black American Women, Book II* (1996).
Press, Skip. *Natalie and Nat King Cole* (1995).

ANDRE D. VANN

Cole, Rebecca (16 Mar. 1846–14 Aug. 1922), physician, organization founder, and social reformer, was born in Philadelphia, Pennsylvania, the second of five children all listed as "mulatto" in the 1880 U.S. census. Her parents' names are not known. In 1863 Rebecca completed a rigorous curriculum that included Latin, Greek, and mathematics at the Institute for Colored Youth, an all-black high school.

In 1867 Cole became the first black graduate of the Women's Medical College of Pennsylvania and the second formally trained African American woman physician in the United States. Dr. Ann Preston, the first woman dean of a medical school, served as Cole's preceptor, overseeing her thesis essay, "The Eye and Its Appendages." The Women's Medical College, founded by Quaker abolitionists and temperance reformers in 1850 as the Female Medical College of Pennsylvania, was the world's first medical school for women. By 1900 at least ten African American women had received their medical degrees from the school.

After completion of her M.D., Cole was appointed resident physician at the New York Infirmary for Indigent Women and Children, a New York City hospital founded in 1857 by America's first woman physician, Elizabeth Blackwell, her sister, the surgeon Emily Blackwell, and Marie Zakrzewska, a German- and American-trained doctor. Cole worked as a "sanitary visitor," making house calls to families in slum neighborhoods and giving practical advice about prenatal and infant care and basic hygiene.

In the early 1870s Cole practiced medicine for a short time in Columbia, South Carolina, before taking a position as superintendent of the Government House for Children and Old Women in Washington, D.C. She then returned to Philadelphia, serving as superintendent of a shelter for the homeless until 1873, when she co-founded the Women's Directory Center. The center offered free medical and legal services to poor women, and according to its charter, programs aiding in "the prevention of feticide and infanticide and the evils connected with baby farming by rendering assistance to women in cases of approaching maternity and of desertion or abandonment of mothers and by aiding magistrates and others entrusted with police powers in preventing or punishing [such] crimes" (quoted in Hine, 113).

A sought-after lecturer on public health, Cole boldly countered W. E. B. DuBois's claim that high mortality rates for blacks were due to an ignorance of hygiene. In an article published shortly before the turn of the century in *The Woman's Eye*, a clubwoman's journal, Cole argued that the spread of disease within the African American community was due to the unwillingness of white doctors to take proper medical histories of black patients.

Until the mid-nineteenth century, American medicine had been essentially unregulated. Doctors underwent less training than ministers and did not need a license to practice. Women benefited from the ease with which proprietary medical schools were given charters; between 1860 and 1900, nineteen medical schools for women were founded. During this same period, the number of women physicians rose from fewer than 200 to more than 7,000, or around 5 percent of American doctors (a percentage not surpassed until the 1970s). American women, of course, had long been practicing healing, as had African Americans of both genders. The earliest known African American physician was JAMES DURHAM, a slave born in 1762. The first African American to receive a formal medical degree, JAMES MCCUNE SMITH, did so in Scotland in 1837. Ten years later, DAVID J. PECK became the first black to get an M.D. from an American medical school.

In 1890, 909 African American physicians were in practice; of these 115 were women, including Rebecca Cole. Beginning with REBECCA CRUMPLER, America's first black woman doctor, these pioneers composed one of the earliest groups of African American professional women. Despite the dual barriers of race and gender, many of these women worked outside their private practices in helping underserved populations of women and children and blacks barred from segregated facilities. Often denied privileges at existing institutions, these trailblazers established an array of health care institutions. In 1881 SUSAN SMITH MCKINNEY STEWARD cofounded a black hospital, the Brooklyn Women's Homeopathic Hospital and Dispensary. Eight years later, CAROLINE STILL WILEY ANDERSON, the daughter of abolitionist WILLIAM STILL, cofounded the Berean Manual Training and Industrial School in Philadelphia. After years of treating patients at her home, MATILDA ARABELLA EVANS established the first African American hospital in Columbia, South Carolina. LUCY HUGHES BROWN and SARAH GARLAND JONES founded black hospitals and training schools in, respectively, Charleston, South Carolina, and Richmond, Virginia. The first woman to practice medicine in Alabama, HALLE TANNER DILLON JOHNSON, daughter of BENJAMIN TUCKER TANNER and sister of HENRY OSSAWA TANNER, established a dispensary and nurses' training school while serving as resident physician at Tuskegee Institute.

By the last decades of Cole's career, however, the number of African American women physicians declined dramatically. The 1920 U.S. census lists only sixty-five African American women physicians. The professionalization and standardization of medicine further marginalized blacks and women, who were generally excluded from key organizations. Coeducation, which resulted in the closure of scores of women's schools and training facilities, further curbed the number of women physicians and dismantled much of the institutional and intellectual infrastructure that had supported late-nineteenth-century women doctors. Male African American doctors weathered these changes fairly well, as they now had access to a number of black medical schools and hospitals; in 1920 black male doctors numbered 3,885.

In 1922, Rebecca Cole died after fifty years of practicing medicine. Her career and the contributions of the first wave of black women physicians illustrate that had opportunities been available, black women might have further invigorated the practice of medicine with their collaborative and community-based approach to health care.

FURTHER READING
Hine, Darlene Clark. "Co-Laborers in the Work of the Lord" in *"Send Us a Lady Physician": Women Doctors in America*, ed. Ruth Abrams (1985).

Wells, Susan. *Out of the Dead House: Nineteenth-Century Women Physicians and the Writing of Medicine* (2001).

LISA E. RIVO

Cole, Robert A. (8 Oct. 1882–26 July 1956), insurance entrepreneur, was born Robert Alexander Cole in the small Tennessee town of Mount Carmel to former slaves Robert and Narcissa Cole. Cole grew up in a community of poor cotton sharecroppers, but his childhood was a happy one. Cole worked on the farm with his seven brothers and sisters. He was only able to complete four years of formal education. Around 1899 Cole moved to Kentucky and quickly advanced as a foreman in a machine shop. However, he chafed under southern racial proscriptions and migrated to Chicago in 1905. He eventually secured employment with the Pullman Company as a sleeping car porter. In his twenty years as a porter Cole listened closely to traveling businessmen and often asked questions. He also formed valuable professional and social relationships with prominent blacks, such as the successful undertaker and policy king Daniel McKee Jackson. He gained an invaluable business education to match his ambition and used his social connections to cement his success.

In the mid-1920s Jackson and black Chicago entrepreneur Otto Stevenson formed a burial insurance association, which they called the Metropolitan Funeral System Association (MFSA). Although the MFSA became popular with poor and working-class Chicagoans, it suffered from many of the problems that plagued early black insurance concerns, particularly the inability to obtain capital or credit from white banks. It did not base its premium on age or inquire about previous health conditions, and it ran into serious financial problems less than a year after it began. Stevenson bowed out of the association, and Jackson approached Cole with a business proposition. Jackson had come to trust and admire Cole's business sense; Cole, who enjoyed a reputation as a skilled gambler, had successfully managed one of Jackson's largest gambling houses since 1925.

In 1927 Cole took the largest gamble of his life and bought the MFSA from Jackson for $500. Immediately Cole set about reforming and modernizing the MFSA's business practices. He instituted an age-based premium and required a detailed application that asked health questions. He placed skilled, educated, and ambitious blacks who had suffered continued discrimination in their efforts to secure jobs in the professional fields in key positions in the MFSA. He also started the Metropolitan Funeral Parlors next door to the MFSA, and it grew to become one of the largest black-owned funeral businesses in Illinois under the skillful management of his wife, Mary, a licensed mortician.

The Great Depression represented a daunting challenge for every business owner. However, Cole kept the MFSA afloat by using gambling winnings for working capital, and black Chicagoans who got by on New Deal federal assistance and jobs were able to keep up with their small premium payments. While most businesses failed during the Depression, the MFSA actually surpassed its previous growth. Its net premium income increased from $394,000 to $567,000 between 1935 and 1939. Cole, affectionately known as "King Cole," also invested in and contributed to community and social institutions, such as the radio show "All Negro Radio Hour," *Bronzeman* magazine, and a Negro League baseball team, the Chicago American Giants, which was once owned by RUBE FOSTER.

In 1949 he built the upscale Parkway Ballroom and Parkway Dining Room near the MFSA offices. His community spirit extended beyond the black community, and the MFSA purchased over $1 million worth of war bonds during World War II. In 1946 the MFSA changed its name to the Metropolitan Mutual Assurance Company of Chicago. In 1952 the company changed its name again to Chicago Metropolitan Assurance Company (CMAC) and Cole expanded its operations to southern Illinois and nearby states such as Indiana and Missouri.

Although Cole went to great lengths to cultivate a positive public persona, personal problems with his wife, Mary, became public in early December 1955. Police arrested Mary and charged her with extortion after she and two men allegedly held two MFSA executive officers at gunpoint and demanded $20,000. She was eventually acquitted of all charges although it was widely believed that she had stolen the $20,000 and had also extorted money from Cole and his businesses. The charges against Mary did not affect CMAC's profitability or expansion, but the scandal deeply embarrassed the normally unflappable Cole. He went into seclusion, his health faltered, and he died less than a year later.

At the time of Cole's death CMAC had grown from a nearly bankrupt $500 company to one worth over $10 million. Cole and his company illustrated the ingenuity of black entrepreneurs who were forced to provide services to a neglected market and create innovative ways to capitalize and market

their businesses in a racist business environment that limited blacks' access to business capital, education, and experience. Though he had little formal education, Cole's ingenuity, business acumen, and dedication to the black community made him a successful entrepreneur.

FURTHER READING
Weems, Robert E., Jr. "Robert A. Cole and the Metropolitan Funeral System Association: A Profile of a Civic Minded African-American Businessman," *Journal of Negro History* 78.1 (Winter 1993).

SHENNETTE GARRETT

Cole-Talbert, Florence O. (17 June 1890–3 Apr. 1961), operatic soprano and music educator, was born in Detroit, Michigan, into a musically prominent family. Her father, Thomas A. Cole, was a talented bass who was also known as a fine dramatic reader. Sadie (Chandler) Cole, her mother, was a mezzo-soprano who had studied at Fisk University in Nashville, Tennessee, and had toured with the famous Fisk Jubilee Singers. Cole's maternal grandmother, Mrs. Hatfield-Chandler, was a patron of the arts who sang soprano in Cincinnati's first African American choir. With such a rich musical heritage, it was predictable that Cole would begin piano lessons at a very early age. Her family relocated to Los Angeles in 1898. At age twelve Cole was accomplished enough to accompany her mother in recitals and in public concerts and to teach younger children piano basics.

While a student at Los Angeles High School, where she studied ancient and modern languages and music theory, Cole joined the Glee Club and became its first African American soloist. Cole's considerable talents in piano performance were apparent when, at age sixteen, she was chosen to accompany Madame E. AZALIA HACKLEY, the famous African American classical soprano. Hackley and Cole's high school teachers encouraged her to concentrate on voice. This encouragement, along with experiencing a production of *Aida* at age fifteen, caused Cole to set a personal goal of becoming an opera singer and performing the title role of *Aida*. The only African American in her high school graduating class of more than two hundred, Cole was selected as the soloist for the 1910 commencement exercises.

After graduation from high school Cole enrolled at the University of Southern California (USC) College of Music, where she majored in music and studied oratorio. Cole completed the music course at USC and became affiliated with the Midland Lyceum Bureau, touring nationally with Hahn's Jubilee Singers. While on tour she met Wendell P. Talbert, a talented pianist and composer who had studied at Oberlin College and graduated from Wilberforce University. They subsequently married and performed together for a time, but the marriage was short-lived. By 1916 the couple had separated. Cole-Talbert's career turned from the classics to a more modern repertoire, and she moved to Chicago. She continued her vocal training at the Chicago Musical College and completed her voice studies in one year rather than the usual four years.

Cole-Talbert received numerous honors, including the school's prestigious Diamond Medal for outstanding achievement in vocal studies and for the highest grade point average in her class. She was the first African American to be selected as graduation soloist, and her performance of "Caro Nome" from *Rigoletto* was accompanied by the Chicago Symphony Orchestra. From 1916 through the early 1920s Cole-Talbert performed a varied repertory that included arias, spirituals, and contemporary songs throughout the United States. On 18 April 1918 Cole-Talbert made her New York debut at Aeolian Hall to rave reviews. A cover story about Cole-Talbert was featured in the first issue of *Half-Century Magazine* in 1919, and she was the subject of a special issue of *Music Master Magazine* published in March 1919.

It was during this period that she also recorded. In 1919 she recorded Eva Dell'Acqua's "Villanelle" for Broome, the first black-owned label. In 1922–1923 she released on the Black Swan label "Bell Song" from *Lakmé* (by Leo Delibes), "Il Bacio" (by Luigi Arditi), and "The Last Rose of Summer" from *Martha* (by Friedrich von Flotow). All of these recordings were later reissued by Paramount.

In 1925 Cole-Talbert went to Europe for further study. During the two years she was in Europe, most of her studies and recitals were in Italy and France. She accomplished one of her early personal goals when she debuted in the title role of *Aida* at the Communale Theatre in Cozenza, Italy. Upon her return to the United States in 1927, Cole-Talbert resumed her career as a recitalist and concert artist and began teaching voice to students. In spite of her enormous success and critical acclaim in European operatic circles, her indisputable talent, and the barriers she broke in the music field, Cole-Talbert was never able to break free from the restrictions imposed by race in mainstream professional opera in America.

The year 1930 brought many changes to Cole-Talbert's life. She became a college professor at Bishop College in Marshall, Texas, where she was the first African American director of music. She was the head of the voice department at Fisk University in Nashville, Tennessee. Later she chaired the voice department of Tuskegee Institute during WILLIAM L. DAWSON's tenure, a time of expansion of the Tuskegee music program.

On 27 August 1930, she was married a second time, to Dr. Benjamin F. McCleave, a prominent Memphis physician and dentist who had four children. In assuming this new maternal role, Cole-Talbert cut back on her touring schedule and became more active in her Memphis studio teaching voice. Among her students was the mezzo-soprano Vera Little.

During both her performing and teaching careers, Cole-Talbert was active in professional music associations, and she was also a civic leader. She became a charter member of the National Association of Negro Musicians (NANM) in 1919, and she chaired and served on various NANM committees, such as the Conference of Artists and the Voice Conference. In Memphis, she cofounded the Memphis Music Association with Mrs. T. H. Watkins. Through this association she brought singers such as MARIAN ANDERSON and ROLAND HAYES to Memphis.

Cole-Talbert collaborated with ALICE DUNBAR-NELSON, her sorority sister, in composing the national hymn for the Delta Sigma Theta Sorority in 1924. She was a founder of the Christian Science Society Church of Memphis. She also held memberships in the Elite Club and the Women's Medical Auxiliary of the National Medical Association.

In 1953 the National Negro Opera Guild, and its founder Mary Cardwell Dawson, bestowed the title "The First Lady in Grand Opera" upon Cole-Talbert. She was presented this honor because of her contributions as an opera singer, mentor to younger artists like Marian Anderson, arranger of spirituals, music educator, vocal coach, and community leader. Cole-Talbert died in 1961 in Memphis, Tennessee.

FURTHER READING

Cole-Talbert's scrapbook and other materials are held by her stepdaughter Gladys McCleave Johnson in Compton, California. Florence Cole Berg, her niece, has other photographs and clippings.

Smith, Jessie Carney, ed. *Notable Black American Women, Book II* (1996).

Turner, Patricia. "In Retrospect: Florence Cole Talbert, Our Divine Florence," *Black Perspective in Music* (Spring 1984).

Obituary: *Los Angeles Sentinel,* 17 Apr. 1961.

PAULETTE COLEMAN

Coleman, Anita Scott (1890–1960), writer and poet, was born in Guaymas, Sonora, Mexico, one of two children to Mary Ann and William Henry Scott. Scott was a buffalo soldier stationed at Fort Elliott, located in the eastern Texas panhandle. According to some sources, Coleman's mother was a slave whom her father had purchased and emancipated. She worked as an on-base laundress and later took work in private life as a domestic. When William Henry left service, the family relocated briefly to Mexico, but Mary's poor health (she apparently suffered from a weak heart) convinced them to return to the States to homestead in New Mexico. The family was politically engaged, if not actively involved in politics, and Scott was a member of some of the local fraternal societies and much interested in the "race question" of the day.

Coleman attended local schools in Silver City, including Silver City High School, and eventually settled on a career in education. She attended the Normal School in Silver City and graduated in 1909, thus embarking on a teaching career that lasted until around 1916. In that year, she met and married James Harold Coleman, a photographer and printmaker, and retired from teaching work. Sometime in 1926 the couple moved to Los Angeles, California. Together, they had four children.

In Los Angeles, Coleman took on various jobs to make ends meet, principle among them was running a boarding house for wayward youths. She also undertook a career as a writer of poetry, essays, and short fiction. Her first forays into creative writing took place sometime before 1920. Among her early work, "The Little Grey House" was perhaps most important. A story about the struggle of African Americans in the western United States to become homeowners, "House" is typical of much of Coleman's work and artistic concerns.

Coleman wrote about the meaning of race and the ways in which it intersected and clashed with the dominant white culture of the time. Her stories concern lynching, African American art and music (jazz especially), discrimination, and gender inequality. Her stories and poems found an audience, and she published her work in such journals as *Half-Century Magazine* (1919, 1920, 1922), *Crisis* (1926, 1927, 1933), *The Messenger* (1928), and *Opportunity* (1930, 1931), to name but a few. Her stories and poems were awarded a number of journal prizes. Though she never lived in New York, she came to be considered a significant voice in the Harlem Renaissance.

In 1937 she published a volume of poetry, *Small Wisdom*. In 1940 her poem "Baptism" won the Robert Browning Award sponsored by the University of Redlands and subsequently saw publication in JOHN H. SENGSTACKE's *Chicago Defender*. A second poetry volume, *Reason for Singing*, appeared in 1948. Besides questions of race, her poetry often treated subjects having to do with military life and the sacrifices of soldiers, especially black soldiers in a time when those sacrifices were either ignored or considered offensive. A children's book, *The Singing Bells*, was published after her death in 1961.

Aside from these publication dates and the names of journals that her work appeared in, very little is known of Coleman's life. When she died sometime in 1960 she had been nearly completely forgotten as a literary figure. A renewal of critical and biographical interest in the early 1990s, however, has stoked interest in this important figure in the history of African American literature in the American West.

FURTHER READING

Champion, Laurie. *American Women Writers, 1900–1945: A Bio-Bibliographical Critical Sourcebook* (2000).

Mitchell, Verner. "A Family Answers the Call: Anita Scott Coleman, Literature, and War." *International Journal of the Humanities* (2008).

JASON PHILIP MILLER

Coleman, Bessie (26 Jan. 1892–30 Apr. 1926), aviator, was born Elizabeth Coleman in Atlanta, Texas, the daughter of George Coleman, a day laborer of predominantly Indian descent, and Susan (maiden name unknown), an African American domestic and farmworker. While Bessie was still very young, the family moved to Waxahachie, Texas, where they built a three-room house on a quarter-acre of land. She was seven when her father left his family to return to the Indian Territory (Oklahoma). The Coleman household was Baptist, and Bessie was an avid reader who became particularly interested in BOOKER T. WASHINGTON, HARRIET TUBMAN, and PAUL LAURENCE DUNBAR. After finishing high school, she studied for one semester at Langston Industrial College, in Langston, Oklahoma.

Between 1912 and 1917 Coleman joined her two brothers in Chicago, where she studied manicuring at Burnham's School of Beauty Culture and worked at the White Sox Barber Shop. She supplemented her income by running a chili parlor on the corner of Twenty-fifth and Indiana avenues. In 1917 she married Claude Glenn. It was during this time that her brother Johnny related World War I stories to her about women flying planes in France. She decided that this would be her ambition. Coleman was rejected by a number of American aviation schools because of her race and sex. ROBERT ABBOTT, the founder of the *Chicago Defender*, a newspaper dedicated to black interests, suggested that she study aviation in France; she left the United States in November 1920. With Abbott and the banker JESSE BINGA's financial assistance, she studied at the School of Aviation run by the Caudron Aircraft Manufacturing Company in Le Crotoy. She later trained in Paris under a French pilot who reportedly shot down thirty-one German planes in World War I. Coleman's plane of choice was the 130-horsepower Nieuport de Chasse.

On 15 June 1921 Coleman received her pilot's license, number 18310, the first awarded to an American woman by the French Federation Aeronautique Internationale, and she became the only licensed African American woman pilot in the world. She returned to the United States in September 1921 but went back to Europe to study in Germany, where she received the first flying license granted to an American woman. She returned to the United States in August 1922.

With her goal of obtaining a pilot's license fulfilled, Coleman then sought to become an accomplished stunt and exhibition pilot. Barnstorming was the aviation fashion of the day, and Coleman decided to become part of these aerial acrobatics. United States air shows were attended by thousands of people. Sponsored by Abbott and Binga, Coleman made her first air show appearance at Curtiss Field in Garden City, Long Island, New York, during Labor Day weekend 1922 flying a Curtiss aeroplane. She then appeared at an air show at Checkerboard Airdrome in Chicago on 15 October. By this time Coleman had purchased three army surplus Curtiss biplanes.

Coleman's third exhibition was held in Gary, Indiana, where she met David Behncke, the founder and president of the International Airline

Bessie Coleman, seen here in the early 1920s, was the first African American woman to fly an airplane. After no American school would admit her, she learned to speak French so that she could train at a flight school in Paris. (Google Images.)

Pilots Association, who became her manager. The Gary exhibition was supervised by Reynolds McKenzie, an African American real estate dealer. There Coleman made a parachute jump after a white woman changed her mind.

On 4 February 1923, while Coleman was flying from municipal flying field in Santa Monica, California, to Los Angeles on her first exhibition flight on the Pacific Coast, her Curtiss JN-4 "Jenny" biplane engine failed, and she plunged 300 feet to the ground. The airplane was completely demolished, and Coleman had to be cut from the wreckage. During her recuperation she went on the lecture circuit and resumed flying as soon as she was able. Newspapers reported that she planned to establish a commercial passenger flight service.

Using Houston as her base, Coleman performed at air shows in Columbus, Ohio; Waxahachie and Austin, Texas; Memphis, Tennessee; and Wharton and Cambridge, Massachusetts. She thrilled crowds and became widely known for her flying outfit, which consisted of a pilot's cap, helmet, and goggles, a Sam Browne belt, long jacket and pants, white shirt and tie, and high boots. In 1924 Coast Firestone Rubber Company of California hired Coleman to do aerial advertising.

While recuperating from another airplane accident, which occurred during a race from San Diego to Long Beach, Coleman reflected on her third goal, opening the field to African Americans by establishing an aviation school in Los Angeles. She lectured to church and school groups and attended private dinners, speaking on the opportunities for blacks in aviation. She appeared in a number of documentary news films, and Coleman reportedly was scheduled to appear in *The Flying Ace*, billed as the "greatest airplane mystery thriller ever made"; it was produced in 1926 and featured an all-black cast.

In late April 1926 Coleman was in Florida at the invitation of the Negro Welfare League of Jacksonville to perform in an air show in Orlando for the annual First of May celebration. When the Orlando Chamber of Commerce informed her that African Americans would not be allowed to view her performance, she refused to participate in the show until "the Jim Crow order had been revoked and aviators had been sent up to drop placards letting the members of our race know they could come into the field" (Marjorie Kritz, "Bessie Coleman, Aviator Pioneer," undated leaflet, U.S. Department of Transportation). William D. Wills, Coleman's publicity agent and mechanic, flew her Jenny plane from Texas because local agencies would not rent a plane to a black person. Mechanical problems had occurred during the flight from Texas, and on the morning of Friday, 30 April, at Paxon Field, during a practice run, after the plane had been in the air only twelve minutes and had reached 3,000 feet, Wills, who was at the instruments, attempted to complete a nosedive, but the plane did not right itself. Though safety conscious, Coleman apparently had failed to secure her seat belt or wear a parachute. "Brave Bessie" was catapulted out of the plane and fell to her death. The plane continued in a downward spiral and crashed; Wills was also killed. Members of the Eighth Regiment of the Illinois National Guard served as pallbearers at Coleman's funeral in Chicago.

Coleman's place in aviation history is secure. In 1929 William J. Powell, author of *Black Wings* (1934), organized the Bessie Coleman School in Los Angeles. Bessie Coleman Aero Clubs, which promoted interest in aviation within the African American community, soon sprang up all across the United States, and the *Bessie Coleman Aero News*, a monthly periodical edited by Powell, first appeared in May 1930. On Labor Day 1931 the Bessie Coleman Aero Club sponsored the first all-black air show in the United States. Every Memorial Day African American aviators fly over her gravesite at Lincoln Cemetery in Chicago in single-file nose low to allow women passengers to drop flowers on her grave. The Chicago mayor HAROLD WASHINGTON proclaimed 26 April 1986 Bessie Coleman Day. Also in 1986 the Federal Aviation Administration created the Bessie Intersection, located forty miles west of Chicago's O'Hare Airport, in her honor. She is included in a monument to African American aviators, *Black Americans in Flight*, at Lambert-St. Louis International Airport. On 27 April 1994 a U.S. Postal Service Bessie Coleman commemorative stamp was issued. She continues to be an inspiration to young African American women.

FURTHER READING

Freydberg, Elizabeth. *Bessie Coleman: The Brownskin Lady Bird* (1994).

Patterson, Elois. *Memoirs of the Late Bessie Coleman, Aviatrix: Pioneer of the Negro People in Aviation* (1969).

Rich, Doris L. *Queen Bess: Daredevil Aviator* (1993).

Obituary: *Chicago Defender*, 8 May 1926.

This entry is taken from the *American National Biography* and is published here with the permission of the American Council of Learned Societies.

CONSTANCE PORTER UZELAC

Coleman, Bill (4 Aug. 1904–24 Aug. 1981), jazz musician, was born William Johnson Coleman in Centerville, Kentucky, the son of Robert Henry Coleman, a cook, and Roberta Johnson, a seamstress. Coleman's parents had separated by the time he was five, and he grew up with his mother and aunt in Crawfordsville, Indiana. When he was seven, he moved with his mother to Cincinnati, a popular stop on the Theater Owners' Booking Association circuit and a city that hosted traveling circuses, riverboats, jug bands, and medicine shows. He saw the blues singers MAMIE SMITH, MA RAINEY, and BESSIE SMITH at local vaudeville houses. When he was fourteen, he joined a band organized to teach young boys music, and he began playing alto saxophone. At seventeen he took piano lessons and did some singing. A year later, he bought a cornet he saw in a pawnshop window. While earning money in a variety of odd jobs, he taught himself the instrument and began to perform at social gatherings. He also started to play with the trombonist J. C. HIGGINBOTHAM, the pianist Edgar Hayes, and others at area roadhouses. He led his own group (as Professor Johnson Coleman and His Band) for an engagement in Richmond, Indiana, and he played weekends at a vacation camp in Kalamazoo, Michigan.

In 1923 Coleman joined the Clarence Paige orchestra and traveled more widely. He heard players such as LOUIS ARMSTRONG with FLETCHER HENDERSON on a 1925 recording of "Money Blues," and REX STEWART with the Henderson band in 1926. By this time, Coleman had married his first wife, Madelyn Grant, in 1925. In early 1927 he joined the Lloyd Scott orchestra for six months, first on tour and then playing at New York's Savoy Ballroom. In New York he heard the DUKE ELLINGTON band and Armstrong play in person for the first time. The Scott group toured extensively. Coleman struggled to earn a living over the next five years, playing for theater shows, at black dances in places like the Renaissance Ballroom, and occasionally as an accompanist at dancing schools. But he also played in groups led by Cecil Scott (1929–1930), HORACE HENDERSON (1930), Charlie Johnson (1930), and LUIS RUSSELL (1929, 1931–1932). In 1933 he went overseas for the first time with LUCKY MILLINDER's group. When he returned, he joined Benny Carter's orchestra and played at the Apollo, the Harlem Club, and the Empire Ballroom. He joined the Teddy Hill group in January 1934, and he recorded with Hill and with FATS WALLER.

In September 1935 Coleman became one of the first American jazz musicians to seek escape from American racism by moving to Paris, where he found "a mellow, cultural city where you were accepted for what you were!" (Carr et al., 99). He worked with the dancer and bandleader Freddy Taylor in 1935 and 1936, and he recorded with Willie Lewis's band in 1936. In January 1936 he made his first recordings under his own name. He traveled to India with Leon Abbey's band (1936–1937), returning to Paris to record in July 1937 with the guitarist Django Reinhardt and the trombonist DICKY WELLS and in November 1937 with the violinist Stéphane Grappelli. He traveled to Egypt with the Harlem Rhythm Makers (1938–1940); in March 1939 he played at the wedding of Muhammed Reza Pahlevi, the future shah of Iran, in Cairo. On jazz standards like "I Got Rhythm," recorded with Reinhardt, Coleman played with "light phrasing and almost translucent tone" (Liam Keating, liner notes to Charly Records' 1993 CD issue of Wells and Coleman, *Swingin' in Paris*); he also exhibited an "irrepressible vivacity" and the elegant sensitivity that made him increasingly popular throughout Europe.

Coleman returned to New York City in March 1940. He continued to tour widely and record often, playing with Carter and Fats Waller (1940), TEDDY WILSON (1940–1941), ANDY KIRK (1941–1942), Ellis Larkins (1943), MARY LOU WILLIAMS (trio and orchestra, 1944), JOHN KIRBY (1945), SY OLIVER (1946–1947), and Billy Kyle (1947–1948). He made recordings with most of these groups, highlighted by a series of excellent solos with Carter's group on "Embraceable You," "But Not for Me," and "Lady Be Good," among others. He also recorded with LESTER YOUNG for Commodore Records in 1942 and 1944. In March 1945 he recorded in Los Angeles with the Capitol International Jazzmen, a group that included Carter, COLEMAN HAWKINS, NAT "KING" COLE, and the drummer MAX ROACH. He also continued to perform abroad, touring the Philippines and Japan with a USO group during 1945.

Invited to play at the opening of a new club in Paris, Coleman returned to Europe in December 1948. He remained in France for the rest of his life. His lyrical playing, lively singing, and open personality made him enormously popular throughout France and Europe. He played often in Belgium, Germany, and especially Switzerland at festivals, in concerts, and on television programs, and he recorded extensively with both European and American jazz artists. By now he had divorced his first wife, and in Paris in October 1953 he married his second wife, Lily Renee Yersin, who took over the managem ent of his career. He had no children from either marriage. He returned for brief visits to the United States in 1954 and 1958, only to be reminded in several ugly incidents of the pervasive racial prejudice that had driven him away.

Despite mounting health problems, Coleman toured and recorded in the 1960s and 1970s, playing in England in 1966 and 1967 and recording with the tenor saxophonist BEN WEBSTER. In 1968 he was elected to the French Academy of Jazz; in 1969 he realized a lifelong ambition by playing in the band accompanying Duke Ellington during Ellington's appearance on French television. In 1971 the U.S. Cultural Center's African programming office engaged him to go to West Africa to familiarize the National Orchestra of the Ivory Coast with jazz. In 1972 the French celebrated his jubilee (fifty years of playing the trumpet) with articles in jazz magazines, appearances on TV, and recognition throughout the country, and in 1974 the government made him a knight of the Order of Merit, the second-highest official distinction in France. He lived his last few years in the village of Cadeillan and died in Toulouse.

Like all trumpet players of his generation, Coleman was greatly influenced by Armstrong. But he gradually developed his own style and voice and became noted for his elegant, fluid phrasing, lovely melodic ideas, ease in the upper register, and relaxed approach. Essentially a swing player, he remained musically adventurous, even adopting some bop ideas during the 1940s and 1950s. Perhaps his greatest contribution to jazz, though, lies in his work as "a modern-time troubadour," an ambassador of jazz to the rest of the world.

FURTHER READING

Coleman, Bill. *Trumpet Story* (1981).
Carr, Ian, et al. *Jazz: The Essential Companion* (1987).
Harrison, Max, et al. *The Essential Jazz Recordings*, vol. 1, *Ragtime to Swing* (1984).
Obituary: *Jazz Journal International*, Nov. 1981.

DISCOGRAPHY

The Complete Commodore Jazz Recordings, vol. 2 (1988).

This entry is taken from the *American National Biography* and is published here with the permission of the American Council of Learned Societies.

RONALD P. DUFOUR

Coleman, Gary (8 Feb. 1968–28 May 2010), actor and performer, was born in Zion, Illinois, and adopted by W. G. Coleman, a laborer, and Edmonia Sue, a nurse. Coleman suffered a kidney disorder that required numerous surgeries (he had two by the time he was five years old) and daily dialysis. The disorder, a form of nephritis called glomerulonephritis, inhibited his physical growth, and he never grew above four feet eight inches. Coleman attended local schools, but even as a child he had begun acting in local commercials, one for a bank's toy drive.

This work, along with Coleman's cherubic appearance and the fact that he could "play young," brought him to the attention of casting directors. In 1978 he was spotted by the Normal Lear production company and asked to audition for an updated version of the *Little Rascals* series. The show fell through after the pilot was filmed, but Lear felt strongly enough about Coleman to ask him to appear in some of his other successful series, including *The Jeffersons* and *Good Times*. Reaction to Coleman was so positive that network executives felt they could build a show around him, the result of which was *Different Strokes*. The show premiered on the National Broadcasting Company (NBC) network in 1978, and Coleman quickly became a star and nationally known figure.

Different Strokes was very much a creature of its time, and would no doubt raise the eyebrows of at least some of today's television audiences. In it, Coleman played Arnold Jackson, one of two young boys adopted by their mother's former employer, a millionaire named Philip Drummond. Early episodes of the program were built around the white liberal Drummond proving himself as a capable father figure to his young African American wards while also showcasing a palatable form of white patrician wisdom and guidance. Arnold's older brother, Willis (played by Todd Bridges), was often portrayed as sulky and mistrusting, while Arnold played for laughs and affection as a kind of fish-out-of-water microhustler. Some critics accused the show of perpetuating stereotypes of African Americans as in need of rescue by well-meaning (and father-like) whites while portraying blacks as either clowns, teddy bears, or schemers. *Different Strokes* also became known for a number of episodes that dealt with serious social topics like drug abuse and, in one notorious instance, child molestation. The show was an enormous hit for the network, running until 1985 on NBC and from 1985 to 1986 on the American Broadcasting Company (ABC) network where it migrated after cancelation. At the height of the show's popularity, Coleman was earning a remarkable $100,000 per episode, much of which he gave over to his parents.

Such was Coleman's celebrity that he became a familiar figure on television and in the movies. In 1979 he starred in *The Kid from Left Field* on NBC and the feature film *The Fish That Saved Pittsburgh*, appearing with JULIUS ERVING, FLIP WILSON, and DEBBIE ALLEN, among many others. In 1982 he played *The Kid with the Broken Halo*, another television movie that became the basis for a short-lived Saturday morning cartoon (also in 1982), in which Coleman portrayed an angel-in-training not much different from the character he played on *Different Strokes*. He also made a number of guest appearances as himself, for example on a 1984 Dean Martin Celebrity Roast and the 1987 fortieth anniversary broadcast of the *It's Howdy Doody Time* show.

After 1986, and a change in networks, *Different Strokes* came to an end, and with it an end to Coleman's good fortunes. A limited performer, Coleman had difficulty finding new parts. More, a change in audience taste led many to associate him (perhaps unfairly) with the sentimental and moralizing tone of much of prime-time television of the day. In just a few years, he was broke. He sued his parents in 1989 for misuse of his fortune and was awarded $1.3 million. Along with the fates of his fellow cast members Todd Bridges (who became addicted to drugs and was later arrested and tried for attempted murder) and Dana Plato (who also suffered drug addiction and committed suicide by overdose in 1999), Coleman's name became something of a watchword about the dangers of child celebrity.

Meanwhile, Coleman's health worsened. He was forced to undergo dialysis more and more often (at one point, four times a day). The expense of his surgeries was exorbitant, and he took work wherever and however he could to make ends meet. He fell into a depression and later admitted to attempting suicide on more than one occasion. In 1998 he was working as a security guard at a movie studio. An off-lot incident with an aggressive fan led to an assault charge when Coleman punched the fan in the nose. In 1999 he filed for bankruptcy and in 2005 removed to a small town near Salt Lake City, Utah. But more troubles and strife followed. Coleman wanted to sue the producers of the popular Broadway show *Avenue Q* for basing a character around him, but apparently never found a lawyer willing to take the case. He was cited in 2007 on a disorderly charge stemming from an argument with his fiancé, Shannon Price, an actress. A year later, the couple was married, but the union (at least in the legal sense) didn't last. They appeared on an episode of the syndicated *Divorce Court* program in 2008 and divorced later that same year but then continued to live together. A year later, 2009, both he and Price were cited for disorderly conduct following another domestic incident. In 2010 Coleman was booked on a charge of domestic assault but was soon released. Meantime, he was cited numerous times for reckless driving, a few of the incidents stemming from arguments with over-eager fans.

On 26 May 2010 Coleman was admitted to Utah Valley Regional Medical Center in Provo, Utah, after a fall inside his residence left him with a traumatic brain injury. His condition quickly grew worse, and on 28 May, Price ordered his life support switched off. Even his final arrangements, though, were haunted by dispute and grievance. Though some media sources speculated that Price had played a role in Coleman's accident and death, a medical examination later held that no foul play could be determined. His funeral services were canceled following a dispute between his family and Price. A judge finally released his remains for cremation, but the disposition of his ashes was, as of February 2011, still a matter before the courts.

FURTHER READING

Bogle, Donald. *Primetime Blues: African Americans on Network Television* (2001).
Obituary: *People*, 28 May 2010.

JASON PHILIP MILLER

Coleman, L. Zenobia (21 Jan. 1898–3 May 1999), librarian, library director, and educator, was born Louie Zenobia Coleman to Joseph and Alice Hunter Coleman at Childersburg, Alabama. Joseph was a farm laborer, and Alice was a homemaker and helped on the family farm. Zenobia Coleman earned a B.A. degree in Education at Talladega College in 1921 and continued her studies in education at the University of Chicago during the mid-to late 1920s. Coleman's first professional position was at Bricks Junior College in Brick, North Carolina (later the Franklinton Center), where she worked as a teacher and librarian from 1924 to 1932. In 1936 she graduated from Columbia University Library School, earning the bachelor of science degree in Library Science. She received a fellowship for advanced study through the General Education Board Fellowship, an academic award program funded by the Rockefeller agency. The scholarship fund provided financial aid to African American and white students from rural, southern communities during the early first half of the twentieth century. The General Education Board's objective was to enroll such students into graduate programs at northern academic institutions, provide financial support for travel, tuition, and living expenses, and to prepare them for careers as teachers, administrators, health care providers, librarians, and other professional vocations where there was a shortage of qualified and trained personnel. L. Zenobia Coleman earned the M.A. in Library Science in 1943 at Columbia University, completing a thesis titled "Changes Needed in the Library of a Small Liberal Arts College to Meet the Needs of the New Curriculum."

Her distinguished thirty-six-year tenure began at Tougaloo College in 1933, where she served as director of Eva Hills Eastman Library. Founded on a former cotton plantation in 1869 by the American Missionary Association, Tougaloo College is one of Mississippi's oldest private colleges, and its aim was to serve the higher education needs of Mississippi's African American students right after the Civil War. In the early 1930s Tougaloo's library collections had about 9,000 volumes, thanks to donations from individual benefactors and foundations. By the time Coleman retired, the library's collections had grown to 55,000 volumes, including the Emory Ross Collection of Africana, a 3,000-volume special collection of materials by and about African Americans. She retired from Tougaloo College in 1969, but as librarian emerita she supervised the planning and construction of the college's new library facility, which opened in 1972. The library was officially named for Coleman in May 1974, and during the following year she and other supporters at Tougaloo established the L. Zenobia Coleman Endowed Scholarship Fund to help raise money in support of general scholarships.

Earnestly concerned about librarianship and participation in its professional activities, Coleman supported the value of reading and helped to establish libraries in many African American high schools in Mississippi. She was appointed to the advisory board to establish the George Washington Carver Branch Public Library at Jackson, Mississippi, in 1949, and the following year the library opened in a duplex at 144 Davis Street. Carver Library was Jackson's first public library for African Americans.

Coleman cofounded the graduate chapter of the African American sorority Alpha Kappa Alpha at Tougaloo College. She was a member of the Mississippi Association of Teachers of Colored Schools, National Educational Association, American Association of University Professors, Mississippi Association of Teachers in Negro Schools, the Women's Fellowship Club, the Association of College Libraries, and was honored with lifetime membership in the American Library Association in 1973. She was listed in *Who's Who among Colleges and Universities*, *Who's Who in American Education*, and *Who's Who in Colored Americans*. Coleman also authored several journal articles in education and library science publications.

Coleman was a pioneer in establishing libraries and facilitating access to books in rural Mississippi African American high schools during the 1920s and 1930s and faithfully advocated for black representation in local and national professional library associations. Coleman gained the respect of her peers by demanding professional recognition in the face of racism and discrimination. Her selflessness, courageousness, and pride in the library profession helped to establish the path of opportunity for African American professionals in the field of library science. By displaying her commitment to excellence and scholarship, Coleman served as a role model and mentor to educators and librarians in Mississippi and beyond. She died at her residence at Childersburg, Alabama, at the age of 101.

FURTHER READING

L. Zenobia Coleman's papers are housed at the Tougaloo College Archives in the L. Zenobia Coleman Library (Mississippi).

Beilke, Jayne. *"Deserving to Go Further": Philanthropic Fellowships, African American Women, and the Development of Higher Educational Leadership in the South, 1930–1954* (1999).

"Coleman, L. Zenobia," in *Notable Black American Women, Book II* (1995).

Mississippi Library Association, Historical Committee. *A History, 1909–1968* (1968).

Peebles, Margarete, and J. B. Howell. *A History of Mississippi Libraries* (1975).

Rhodes, Lelia Gaston. *See How They Ran: A Bibliographic Profile of Some Mississippi Librarians, 1930's–1970's* (1977).

MELANIE R. THOMAS

Coleman, Lucretia Newman (18? ?–?), writer and educator, was born in Dresden, Ontario, Canada, the fourth child of William and Nancy Newman. Little is known of her family, and the exact dates of her birth and death are unknown, but she was most likely born sometime in the mid-nineteenth century. As a young woman, she accompanied her father to the West Indies for missionary work, then returned to the United States when he became pastor of a church in Cincinnati, Ohio. Following her father's death, she moved to Appleton, Wisconsin, where she looked after her invalid mother for thirteen months. Upon her mother's death, Lucretia Newman became the head of the household for her siblings. After her early education she completed a course of scientific study at Lawrence University in Appleton before finding work as a high school music teacher and as a clerk in a dry goods store.

In 1883 Coleman was named assistant secretary and bookkeeper for the African Methodist Episcopal (AME) Church. That year she also published her first literary offering, a poem, "Lucille of Montana," which appeared in several issues of the journal *Our Women and Children*. Her works were recognized by such journals as *The American Baptist* and were praised as scholarly and eloquent. She also produced articles for the *A.M.E. Review*, which furthered her reputation as a gifted scientific and philosophical writer.

Coleman's association with the AME Church proved advantageous when she published a book-length work around 1890 through the Sunday School Union. A biography, *Poor Ben: A Story of Real Life* (1890), it detailed the life and noble Christianity of BENJAMIN WILLIAM ARNETT JR., the seventeenth bishop of the AME Church. She wrote of a man who became the first African American to serve as foreman of an otherwise all-white jury. A forceful and compelling speaker, Arnett, as portrayed by Coleman, labored vigorously to improve the spiritual and political landscape of Ohio. She dedicated the volume to the "colored young men and women in America," hoping that Arnett's story would inspire them.

Although Coleman herself remains an obscure figure in history, her literary efforts, lauded by publishers across the country, helped to motivate and elevate the standards for the turn-of-the-century African American press.

FURTHER READING

Coleman, Lucretia Newman. *Poor Ben: A Story of Real Life* (1890).

Dann, Martin E. *The Black Press, 1927–1890* (1977).

Dunnigan, Alice E. "Early History of Negro Journalism," *Negro History Bulletin* 28 (Summer 1965).

Majors, Monroe A. *Noted Negro Women* (1893).

Mossell, Mrs. N. F. *The Work of the Afro-American Woman* (1894).

Penn, Irvine Garland. *The Afro-American Press and Its Editors* (1891).

Scruggs, Lawson A. *Women of Distinction* (1893).

ROXANNE Y. SCHWAB

Coleman, Maude B. (1879–25 Feb. 1953), politician, clubwoman, and welfare worker, was born in the Piedmont region of Virginia to Frances Dearing in approximately 1879. During her youth, the Dearing family moved to Harrisburg, where Maud was educated in the Harrisburg school system. Later in life she attended the University of Pennsylvania. On 5 September 1897 Maude B. Dearing married John W. Coleman in Harrisburg, Pennsylvania. They had one child, Priscilla Coleman, who died in infancy.

Throughout her adult life, Coleman was a driving force in Harrisburg's African American community. During World War I she worked tirelessly in support of African American troops and received a commendation from General Cornelius Vanderbilt for her service. This success in community organizing encouraged Coleman to become a founding member of the Phyllis Wheatley Colored Harrisburg Branch of the Young Women's Christian Association in 1920. Coleman participated in and led a variety of social reform organizations, including the Dauphin County Tuberculosis Society, the Rebecca Aldridge Civic Club of Harrisburg, and the Pennsylvania State Organization of Social Workers.

Maude Coleman's influence spread beyond Harrisburg during the 1920s due to her outspoken political activism and leadership of the Pennsylvania State Federation of Colored Women's Clubs. In 1922 Coleman vigorously campaigned throughout the state in an effort to gain passage of the Dyer Anti-Lynching Bill in the United States Congress. She skillfully utilized her position as state organizer for the Federation of Colored Women's Club to build a strong political following. Coleman was later elected district vice president and president of the organization. Coleman also played an active role in local and state politics. She was a charter member of the Pennsylvania State Council of Republican Women and the Dauphin County Council of Republican Women.

Coleman's prominence in the African American community and loyalty to the Republican Party was rewarded by the Republican governor Gifford Pinchot in 1925 with her appointment as an

Interracial Consultant in the Bureau of Social Work. As one of the first African Americans appointed to a state patronage position, Coleman worked to secure jobs for African Americans in the state Department of Welfare and served as a consultant in all areas of interracial concern. During a 1937 fight to integrate steel mills in western Pennsylvania, Coleman was brought in to negotiate with executives and successfully secured jobs for African American workers. Though difficult to quantify, the impact of her appointment cannot be discounted. In her autobiography, DOROTHY HEIGHT, the president of the National Council of Negro Women (NCNW), remembered the thrill of hearing Coleman speak to a meeting of the State Federation and her pride in seeing an African American woman as a member of the state government. Though Height did not remember Coleman's position, she recalled that her speech "kept me awake most of the night. The words haunted me." Coleman retained her patronage job until her death, serving for over thirty-five years and under eight different governors.

By the 1930s Maude Coleman was a well-known figure throughout the eastern United States. Still active in local issues, during 1936 she led a group of African American leaders in forming a disaster committee when Harrisburg was inundated by heavy flooding, and was president of the auxiliary to the Harrisburg branch of the NAACP. On the national stage she was named the director of the Colored Women's Eastern Division of the Republican Party. During the campaign she traveled throughout the eastern seaboard as part of a "flying squadron" of speakers who spoke in support of the Alf Landon/Frank Knox ticket. As a lifelong Republican, Coleman consistently pressured the party to be more inclusive and actively campaigned for increased representation for African Americans in party leadership.

From the 1940s Coleman remained a prominent voice in statewide and national social reform and civil rights activities. During World War II, Coleman renewed her efforts on behalf of the armed services by participating in protests against the segregation of the National Guard and worked to improve African American access to defense jobs. In an effort to build on the gains made by African Americans during the war, she authored a book, *The History of the Negro in Pennsylvania*, published by the Department of Welfare in 1947, and became an outspoken advocate of desegregation. In an impassioned appeal to the readers of the *Philadelphia Tribune*, Coleman invoked the participation of African American soldiers and reminded

readers that segregation voided democratic principles. Though Coleman had contemplated retirement in the early 1950s, she remained employed as Interracial Consultant to the Department of Welfare until her death on 25 February 1953.

FURTHER READING

Coleman, Maude B. "Integrated Housing Is True Democracy," *Philadelphia Tribune*, 30 May 1950.

Height, Dorothy. *Open Wide the Freedom Gates: A Memoir* (2005).

Obituary: *Philadelphia Tribune*, 28 Feb. 1953.

JENNIFER REED FRY

Coleman, Ornette (19 Mar. 1930–), jazz innovator, saxophonist, composer, and trumpeter, was born Randolph Denard Ornette Coleman, in Fort Worth, Texas, the youngest of four children of Randolph Coleman, a cook, mechanic, and baseball player, and Rosa (maiden name unknown), a clerk and seamstress. Ornette's early life was marked by family tragedy: his oldest brother, Allen, died in the 1940s; his oldest sister, Vera, died as an adolescent; and his father died when Ornette was only seven. His surviving sister, Truvenza Coleman Leach, was a trombonist and vocalist who performed under the name Trudy Coleman.

Ornette Coleman, October 1960. (Library of Congress.)

Ornette began playing the alto saxophone in 1944 after his mother purchased an instrument with the agreement that he would get a job. A year later, at age fifteen, he began to play professionally. The saxophonists Dewey Redman and Prince Lashay and the drummer Charles Moffett were among the first musicians with whom Coleman played, and they remained close collaborators throughout his career. Coleman, who was primarily self-taught, developed an unorthodox approach to music that marked his entire progress as an improviser and composer. He took an extraordinarily fluid approach to tonality, which he incorporated into his enigmatic "harmolodic" theory of music. Coleman's idiosyncratic sense of intonation dates from his earliest studies of the saxophone, when he "realized that you could play sharp or flat in tune" (Litweiler, 25).

Most of Coleman's early employment was in gutbucket honky-tonks, which were often fronts for gambling houses where violence was frequent. These gigs were lucrative, and Coleman, who made as much as one hundred dollars a week, became his family's primary wage earner. He also added to his technical knowledge of music while at I. M. Terrell High School (where the saxophonists KING CURTIS and Sonny Simmons were classmates) and with instruction from his cousin, James Jordan, and a local tenor sax hero, Red Connors (who, according to Coleman, once bested LESTER YOUNG in a jam session). Under Connors's tutelage, Coleman learned bebop compositions and switched to tenor sax. As an RB saxophonist, Coleman was a honker in the style of BIG JAY McNEELY, delighting audiences with his squealing and screaming saxophone and gyrating body. The ecstatic blues voice Coleman developed in these early performances remained an important part of his artistry. Coleman grew dissatisfied with the limitations of Fort Worth. His discomfort was not just in music; his overall aesthetic sensibility was out of step with his environs. One night, while playing alto in Red Connors's band at a gig in a white establishment, Coleman strayed from the melody of "Stardust" and was shouted down by a patron. Coleman later recalled another hostile encounter in Forth Worth: "I had a beard and my hair was thicker than it is now [it was also straightened and long] and this fellow came up to me and said, 'Say, boy, you can really play saxophone. I imagine where you come from they call you mister, don't they? ... It's an honor to shake your hand because you're really a saxophone player—but you're still a nigger to me'" (Spellman, 93–94).

In 1949 Coleman left Fort Worth to tour with a minstrel band led by "Silas Green from New Orleans." The tour was a disaster. Coleman found the show's uninspired repertoire full of "white Dixieland tunes," the comedians "like Uncle Tom minstrels," (Spellman, 99–100) and the venues even more violent than those in Fort Worth. Worse, the band hated the way he played. After sharing his musical ideas with the other saxophonist, Coleman was fired, accused of trying to make the other horn player into a bebop musician. Stranded in Natchez, Mississippi, by happenstance, Coleman made his first recordings (now lost) in 1949 of rhythm and blues. He then joined the R & B singer Clarence Samuel's band. While in this band, Ornette was led outside by a young woman, ostensibly to meet some admirers, only to be beaten and kicked by several huge men who also smashed his horn, apparently because his playing offended them. But Coleman's playing attracted staunch admirers from among New Orleans's elite musicians, including Ellis Marsalis (father of WYNTON MARSALIS), Alvin Batiste, and EDWARD BLACKWELL. Coleman next joined Pee Wee Crayton and landed in Los Angeles in 1950, where he stayed until 1959.

In Los Angeles, Coleman developed a group sound with a group of musicians that included Blackwell, DON CHERRY, and BILLY HIGGINS, all of whom later accompanied him to national attention. He supported himself with odd jobs and care packages from his mother while studying music theory and rehearsing his compositions with sympathetic musicians. In 1954 he married the poet JAYNE CORTEZ, and two years later their son, Ornette Denardo, was born. The marriage ended in divorce in 1964, though they had separated six years earlier. (Denardo, who began recording and performing with his father when he was only ten years old, took over management of his father's business, Harmolodic Inc., in 1983.) Coleman's music was highly controversial, and he found few opportunities for performance, but with the help of the bassist Red Mitchell, Coleman made his first recordings as a bandleader in 1958 for Contemporary Records.

JOHN LEWIS, leader of the Modern Jazz Quartet, became an ardent supporter of Coleman's music and used his influence to have Coleman and his protégé, Don Cherry, participate in the Lenox School of Jazz during the summer of 1959, where he gained other enthusiastic and influential supporters, including the composer Gunther Schuller and the jazz critic Martin Williams, who saw to it that Coleman's group was booked at the important Five Spot Café in New York City. The two-week engagement at the Five Spot was extended to two months. Coleman's performances quickly became the stuff of legend, attracting many important musicians, artists, and critics, some of whom proclaimed Coleman a genius and the most original saxophonist since CHARLIE PARKER; others thought that he was a charlatan.

Coleman was suddenly in demand for performances and recordings. His position as one of the handful of bona fide jazz innovators was solidified by 1961 after the release of several recordings with his quartet. He reached a new height of notoriety and controversy with a groundbreaking recording, *Free Jazz*, featuring two quartets playing simultaneously. This recording gave its name to the Free Jazz movement, which includes Coleman, JOHN COLTRANE, CECIL TAYLOR, and ALBERT AYLER among its preeminent exponents.

When Coleman realized that he was earning less money than white artists who drew smaller audiences, he tripled his fees, effectively pricing himself out of work. In 1962, at the height of his popularity, Coleman withdrew from the professional music scene, although he occasionally sat in with musicians whom he admired, including John Coltrane, who paid Coleman for lessons in his harmolodic theory. Coleman also taught himself to play the violin and the trumpet, which he showcased upon his return to performing and recording in 1965. Coleman's increased virtuosity on the alto saxophone and the fact that he learned to play the trumpet and violin almost completely without recourse to conventional techniques led many erstwhile detractors to recognize his unusual creativity.

In the 1970s and 1980s Coleman's scope as a composer and bandleader widened. In an attempt to gain work permits in England as a concert musician rather than as a jazz musician, Coleman began writing music for chamber groups and eventually for symphony orchestras. His most important symphonic work is *Skies of America* (1972); his most celebrated chamber piece, "The Country That Gave the Freedom Symbol to America," premiered at the *Festival d'Automne* in Paris in 1989. In 1972 Coleman visited Nigeria, and the following year he recorded with the Master Musicians of Joujouka in the Moroccan Rif Mountains. This music avoids clichés, crosses musical and cultural boundaries, and demonstrates Coleman's ideal of subsuming the soloist in the ensemble performance. Based upon this experience, he formed a new band, Prime Time, that featured the guitarist James "Blood" Ulmer, and the bassist Jamaladeen Tacuma. Prime Time included a doubled rhythm section (bass, drums, guitar, and keyboards) and used rock textures, country-and-western rhythms, funk grooves, and anything else Coleman found useful. In many ways this electric, eclectic band covered some of the same ground as MILES DAVIS did with his various fusion bands.

Coleman has continued to perform with musicians from different nations and traditions and to incorporate dancers, rappers, video artists, contortionists, and even body piercing into his shows. He was voted Artist of the Year in *Down Beat*'s 1998 International Critics Poll and has received numerous honors, including induction into the *Down Beat* Jazz Hall of Fame (1969) and the French Order of Arts and Letters (1998), two fellowships from the Guggenheim Memorial Foundation (1967, 1972), and one from the MacArthur Foundation (1994). Ten years after his last album, Coleman released *Sound Grammar* in 2006 to widespread acclaim. Recorded live in Germany in 2005 with his son Denardo on percussion, it won the Pulitzer Prize for music in 2007. In the same year, Coleman won a Lifetime Achievement Grammy Award.

FURTHER READING

Litweiler, John. *Ornette Coleman: A Harmolodic Life* (1992).

MacRae, Barry. *Ornette Coleman* (1988).

Spellman, A. B. *Black Music, Four Lives* (1973).

Wilson, Peter Niklas. *Ornette Coleman: His Life and Music* (1999).

DISCOGRAPHY

Cuscuna, Michael, and David Wild. *Ornette Coleman 1958–1979: A Discography* (1980).

SALIM WASHINGTON

Coleman, Steve (20 Sept. 1956–), alto saxophonist, band leader, and educator, was born on Chicago's South Side. While Coleman has chosen not to reveal many details about his childhood, he has underscored his father's love of jazz and his encouragement of his son's violin study in elementary school. At fourteen Coleman switched to the alto saxophone, but rejected his father's advice to explore CHARLIE PARKER. Instead, Coleman adopted Maceo Parker, a saxophonist in JAMES BROWN's band, as his idol. He then organized a group of schoolmates in a funk band that emulated the Brown sound.

During his freshman year at Illinois Wesleyan University, Coleman experienced a watershed moment. The school's jazz band rejected his candidacy, citing his lack of proficiency in improvisation. This rejection moved Coleman to study Charlie Parker's recordings in the hopes of acquiring Parker's seemingly intuitive ability for spontaneous innovation. He combined an immersion in Parker's music with formal instruction from the saxophonists Bunky Green and VON FREEMAN. Lessons with Von Freeman provided Coleman with a mentor who had performed with SUN RA, an avant-garde keyboardist and composer. Sun Ra was a pioneer in the sense that he founded and led big bands with a large degree of freewheeling improvisatory freedom—a freedom shaped by Sun Ra's conviction that jazz ought to be music deeply reflective of the spiritual values of ancient Egypt. Much of Coleman's post-1990 big band music could be described in identical terms.

Coleman moved from Chicago to New York in 1978. He performed regularly in the THAD JONES–Mel Lewis big band and worked in many of the most innovative jazz big bands of the early 1980s, including those led by SAM RIVERS, CECIL PERCIVAL TAYLOR, and David Murray. His playing attracted international attention when he shifted from big band contexts to performing and recording as the sole saxophonist in various small groups led by the English bassist Dave Holland. A highly acclaimed series of five albums by the Holland ensembles on the prestigious ECM record label brought Coleman widespread recognition.

During the 1980s, Coleman also formed both his own group and a musical collective. His band, Five Elements, began in 1981 as an experiment in combining funk with elements of bop and free jazz. Inspired by the earlier African American, avantgarde jazz collectives AACM in Chicago and BAG in St. Louis, in 1985 Coleman founded the musical collective M-Base ("micro-basic array of structured extemporization") as an informal jazz academy and music publishing vehicle. It appealed to musicians who wanted to maintain the spirit of radical musical experimentation during a decade marked by widespread musical and political conservatism. Among M-Base's shifting members were the vocalist Cassandra Wilson and the saxophonist Greg Osby. Both Five Elements and M-Base continued their activities into the twenty-first century.

Coleman led a variety of his own bands in addition to Five Elements, including the Metrics, a group synthesizing the sounds of jazz instrumentalists with hip-hop rappers. He also worked with the Mystic Rhythm Society, an ensemble emphasizing Caribbean, African, and Southern Indian instrumentation and musical concepts, and Council of Balance, a thirty-piece big band. All of these units were well documented on various albums released under the RCA label. Jazz critics and fans alike loved the recordings, but RCA seemed unclear as to how to market them effectively. The label dropped Coleman in the 1990s. His subsequent recordings have been on the French label Label Bleu. Among his earlier major recordings on RCA still sometimes available internationally are *The Sonic Language of Myth: Believing, Learning, Knowing* and *Genesis and Opening of the Way*.

The Sign and the Seal, a collaboration of Coleman's Mystic Rhythm Society with the Cuban folkloric group AfroCuba de Matanzas, released in 1996, reflected a new direction in his music: the album was an intense exploration of the musical meeting ground of his jazz with Afro-Caribbean, West African, Egyptian, and Indian sacred traditional musical forms. Through extensive travel and performance in those areas with his band, Coleman learned to infuse his jazz compositions with tonal colors and rhythms found in various sacred musical traditions. He engaged in a rich cross-cultural exchange of musical ideas that had blossomed in jazz since the 1960s. By seeking compositional procedures, musical methodologies grounded in the sacred cosmologies, and numerologies active in those traditional musical cultures, Coleman also added a new dimension to the sixties' spirit of crosscultural jazz experimentation. His interest in Egyptian numerology led to his creating computer software programs based on symbolic numerical ratios of note values that challenged his band.

Coleman reinvented jazz in the 1990s as no one had ever done before: as a form of musical research and expression that centrally transmitted the metaphysics of cultures beyond America. This was jazz as ritualistic spiritual transmission as well as improvised musical entertainment, an idea alien to most modern jazz fans. In addition to instrumentalists, his bands in the 1990s frequently included dancers and rappers. This approach presented concert audiences with a multidimensional aesthetic and spiritual experience that Coleman saw as akin to Cuban and West African religious rituals.

After a brief stint teaching music at the University of California, Berkeley, the twenty-first century found Coleman touring internationally in support of an ambitious big band album, *Lucidarium*. The Canadian filmmaker Eve-Marie Breglia produced a documentary DVD, *Elements of One*, a film of Coleman's band touring around the world. Coleman's place among the major innovators in jazz history seemed assured, as his experimentation with forging cross-cultural meeting grounds found a parallel in the larger arena of nonmusical affairs where globalization and cultural hybridization were ongoing issues. He also made a mark in jazz history through his imaginative merger of the looping structures of funk and rap music with improvised jazz.

FURTHER READING

Fischlin, Daniel. *The Other Side of Nowhere: Jazz, Improvisation, and Communities in Dialogue* (2004).

Ratliff, Ben. "A Jazz Guerrilla Blows Back In, Spreading Ideas," *New York Times* (18 Aug. 2002).

NORMAN WEINSTEIN

Coleman, Warren Clay (25 Mar. 1849–31 Mar. 1904), businessman, was born a slave in Cabarrus County, North Carolina, the son of Rufus C. Barringer, a white lawyer and politician, and Roxanna Coleman. Little is known about his parents, but as a youngster he learned the shoemaker's trade and also barbering. After the Civil War he briefly attended Howard University in Washington, D.C., hawking jewelry

Warren Clay Coleman, c. 1899. (Library of Congress.)

to pay for his board and room. He also worked as an itinerant salesman in North Carolina. Coleman saved his earnings and in 1869 he purchased a 130-acre farm in Cabarrus County, paying $600 for the well-timbered land. In 1870 he was listed in the census as the proprietor of a small grocery store in the town of Concord, North Carolina, with a total estate of $800 in real and personal property. During the same period he also began purchasing low-priced rental houses in and around Concord, paying between $125 and $300, and renting them for between $.50 and $1.25 per week. He continued this real estate activity for many years, and according to one estimate he eventually owned nearly one hundred rental houses. In 1873 he married Jane E. Jones, a native of Alabama, in a church wedding. He later became a trustee of the African Methodist Episcopal Zion Church.

During the late 1870s and early 1880s Coleman engaged in a variety of business enterprises, including a barbershop, a bakery, and a grocery store. He advertised in the *Concord Times* in 1880 that he specialized in selling teas, coffee, sugar, syrups, home and imported molasses, cakes, and candies. In 1881 he purchased a lot on Main Street in Concord and later opened a mercantile store, but only four years later he was temporarily put out of business by a disastrous fire. He rebuilt, and in 1890 the business was worth $5,000, a large enterprise when compared to other black-owned businesses of the time. Coleman had become one of the most prosperous African Americans in North Carolina. In 1896, near the end of a depression, Coleman decided to construct a cotton mill in Concord, to be operated by blacks. Toward that end he wrote BOOKER T. WASHINGTON to solicit funds. "The books have been open for subscriptions only a very short time," he wrote, "and shows upwards of the amount of $10,000, already subscribed, with a steady increase and a bright future" (Harlan, vol. 4, 117). In 1898 Coleman opened the Coleman Manufacturing Company, beginning not only with subscriptions from blacks but also with a loan in 1899 from the wealthy white tobacco magnate Benjamin Duke for the purchase of new machinery. The company manufactured cotton goods and yarn. In 1900, according to a report issued by the National Negro Business League, Coleman employed 230 black workers, possessed a 270-horsepower Corliss engine and a three-story brick building, and boasted assets worth $100,000. "Our business grows more and more," he said in 1902, and the next year he was employing about 350 black workers. Coleman billed his company as a cooperative venture, one that would help the race. In the entire South in this period there were only a small number of black manufacturers (including the brick maker Richard Fitzgerald of Durham and the doll maker RICHARD HENRY BOYD of Nashville). Black textile companies were especially rare and typically short-lived.

Coleman's enterprise began to experience difficulties even as it reached its zenith. Inefficient machinery, insufficient materials, inexperienced management, and untrained workers, compounded by marketing problems and the belief in the southern Piedmont that cotton mill management and labor should be controlled by whites, caused the company to become unstable. Coleman's untimely death in Concord brought the experiment to an end, and the Coleman Manufacturing Company was sold to whites, who subsequently employed white operatives.

While establishing an all-black enterprise, Coleman had sought the support of whites, especially Washington Duke, who purchased stock in the company. He believed, as did his acquaintance Washington, that a successful business enterprise would reveal to those of the "white race who are our friends" that blacks were on the rise. "Coleman was a colored man of great energy and great force of character," the *Concord Times* said the day after his death. "He was always respectful to white people and maintained pleasant relations with the white population generally."

FURTHER READING

Harlan, Louis, ed. *Booker T. Washington Papers*, 14 vols. (1972–1989).

Rouse, J. E. *The Noble Experiment of Warren C. Coleman* (1972).

Thompson, Holland. *From the Cotton Field to the Cotton Mill* (1906).

Obituary: *Concord Times*, 1 Apr. 1904.

This entry is taken from the *American National Biography* and is published here with the permission of the American Council of Learned Societies.

LOREN SCHWENINGER

Coleman, William T., Jr. (7 July 1920–), lawyer and public official, was born William Thaddeus Coleman Jr. in the Germantown district of Philadelphia, Pennsylvania, the son of William Thaddeus Coleman, a social worker, and Laura Beatrice Mason. His was a middle-class family with many of its members engaged in teaching, social work, and the church. Coleman attended an all-black elementary school in Germantown and a predominantly white high school, in which he was one of seven African American students.

Having harbored an ambition since childhood to be a lawyer, Coleman entered Harvard Law School in 1941 after graduating with a B.A. degree summa cum laude from the University of Pennsylvania. Wartime service in the U.S. Army Air Corps interrupted his legal studies, which he completed in 1946 by gaining his LLB degree magna cum laude, first in his class. He married Lovida Hardin in 1945; they would have three children. On leaving Harvard after an additional year of study, Coleman discovered that Philadelphia law firms refused to employ an African American, regardless of his qualifications, and he secured employment instead as law secretary to a judge on the Court of Appeals for the Third Circuit.

In 1948 Coleman became a Supreme Court clerk to Justice Felix Frankfurter. He was the first African American to hold such a position. At the end of his clerkship, Frankfurter wrote Coleman, "What I can say of you with great confidence is what was Justice Holmes's ultimate praise of a man: 'I bet on him'" (Kluger, 293). With employment in Philadelphia law firms still closed to him, Coleman then moved to New York City and joined Paul, Weiss, the only multiracial practice on Wall Street. In 1950 he began a long association with the NAACP Legal Defense and Educational Fund (LDF) when THURGOOD MARSHALL recruited him as a member of the team working on the school desegregation cases. Coleman's knowledge of Frankfurter was invaluable, but so was more generally the "cold-eyed counsel" (Kluger, 292) that he offered Marshall as a close adviser. He was, for example, skeptical of the LDF's reliance on the use of the social-science findings of KENNETH B. CLARK and others to prove the harm of segregation. In 1955 he also advocated, though with some reluctance, that the LDF support the argument in favor of a gradual implementation of the Supreme Court's school desegregation decision the previous year in *Brown* v. *Board of Education*.

In 1952 Coleman joined what would later become Dilworth, Paxson, Kalish, Levy & Coleman as the first African American member of a white law firm in Philadelphia; he became a partner in 1966. His expertise involved corporate law and antitrust litigation, particularly in connection with transportation. The success he enjoyed in law brought invitations to join the board of mass-transit operations, airline corporations, and other major concerns.

Continuing his work for the LDF, Coleman defended civil rights activists at the height of the freedom struggle, including sit-in protesters and freedom riders. He acted as cocounsel on *McLaughlin v. Florida* (1964), in which he successfully argued that state laws against interracial cohabitation were unconstitutional. Outside his LDF work, and following his involvement in earlier efforts that had ended in failure, in 1965 Coleman represented the Commonwealth of Pennsylvania in a lawsuit against Girard College in Philadelphia, which practiced segregationist policies; the suit was fully and successfully concluded in 1968. Less successful was the outcome of an LDF case concerning the need for interdistrict desegregation plans to tackle racial disparities in schools. The 4–4 vote of the Supreme Court in the case *Richmond School Board v. Virginia Board of Education* (1973) left standing the decision of the lower court against interdistrict plans. Coleman became LDF president in 1971.

Coleman was a Republican with a probusiness philosophy, a position unusual within the LDF. He began his career as a public official in 1959 when President Dwight Eisenhower named him to the President's Commission on Employment Policy, designed to increase minority representation in the civil service. In 1964 he was appointed senior consultant and assistant counsel to the Warren Commission, which investigated the assassination of President John F. Kennedy. Coleman accepted other public appointments, including membership of the National Commission on Productivity and the Phase II Price Commission during the Nixon administration. In 1973, however, he declined an invitation from Attorney General Elliott Richardson, with whom he had worked when both were Frankfurter's clerks, to become Watergate special prosecutor.

In March 1975 Coleman became the second African American to be appointed a member of a presidential cabinet, when Gerald Ford named him as secretary of transportation. At the Department of Transportation he was a pioneer in seeking to create an integrated national policy, releasing in 1977 what the *Washington Post* described as "a remarkable study on trends and choices in transportation" (23 Jan. 1977). His successor, Brock Adams, decided not to follow the course suggested by this report, however. Many other initiatives by Coleman faced difficulties because of the conflict between Congress and the White House that characterized the Ford administration as a whole.

Coleman advocated the development of user fees to reduce the sector's reliance on government subsidy, but Congress declined to cut transportation appropriations, as much as doubling the levels of expenditure recommended by the administration. An example of this conflict involved the railroad industry, with Congress maintaining subsidies to an extent considered unwise by Coleman. Other key decisions taken by Coleman at Transportation included his determination that automobile manufacturers should not be required to install air bags, fearing consumer opposition to government interference; his approval of landings by supersonic airplanes at U.S. airports; and his support for the construction of two deep-water ports in the Gulf of Mexico to facilitate oil imports by supertanker.

Following Ford's defeat by Jimmy Carter, Coleman returned to private practice with the firm O'Melveny & Myers, while continuing his work on civil rights cases, acting as LDF chair from 1977 to 1997. His most high-profile case was not directly on behalf of the LDF, however. In *Bob Jones University v. United States* (1983), Chief Justice Warren Burger invited him to speak for the defendant when the Reagan-era Department of Justice decided to support the plaintiff. Coleman successfully argued before the Supreme Court that it was permissible for the Internal Revenue Service to withhold tax exemptions from private educational institutions, like Bob Jones University, that practiced racially discriminatory policies. Coleman's opposition to the Reagan administration in the case underscored his increasingly critical view of the Republican Party's approach to race.

One of the most influential lawyers in the nation who over many years made significant contributions to the protection of civil rights, as well as to public life more generally, Coleman received the Presidential Medal of Freedom in 1995.

FURTHER READING
Greenberg, Jack. *Crusaders in the Courts: How a Dedicated Band of Lawyers Fought for the Civil Rights Revolution* (1994).
Kluger, Richard. *Simple Justice: The History of "Brown v. Board of Education" and Black America's Struggle for Justice* (1975).

ROBERT MASON

Coles, Honi (2 Apr. 1911–12 Nov. 1992), tap dancer, raconteur, and stage, vaudeville, and television performer, was born Charles Coles in Philadelphia, Pennsylvania, the son of George Coles and Isabel (maiden name unknown). He learned to tap-dance on the streets of Philadelphia, where dancers challenged each other in time-step "cutting" contests, and he made his New York debut at the Lafayette Theater in 1931 as one of the Three Millers, a group that performed over-the-tops, barrel turns, and wings on six-foot-high pedestals. After discovering that his partners had hired another dancer to replace him, Coles retreated to Philadelphia, determined to perfect his technique. He returned to New York City in 1934, confident and skilled in his ability to cram several steps into a bar of music. Performing at the Harlem Opera House and at the Apollo Theater, Coles was reputed to have the fastest feet in show business. And at the Hoofer's Club, where only the most serious tap dancers gathered to compete, he was hailed as one of the most graceful dancers ever seen.

From 1936 to 1939 Coles performed with the Lucky Seven Trio, who tapped on large cubes that looked like dice. The group went through ten costume changes in the course of their act. Touring with the big swing bands of COUNT BASIE and DUKE ELLINGTON, the six foot two inch Coles polished his style, melding high-speed tapping with an elegant yet close-to-the-floor style where the legs and feet did the work. In 1940 as a soloist with CAB CALLOWAY's orchestra, Coles met Cholly Atkins, a jazz tap dancer who later choreographed for the best rhythm and blues singing groups of the 1960s. Atkins was an expert wing dancer, while Coles's specialty was precision. They combined their talents after the war by forming the class act of Coles & Atkins. Wearing handsomely tailored suits, the duo opened with a fast-paced song-and-tap number, then moved into a precision swing dance and soft-shoe, finishing with a tap challenge in which each showcased his specialty. Their classic soft-shoe, danced to "Taking a Chance on Love" played at an extremely slow tempo, was a nonchalant tossing off of smooth slides and gliding turns in crystal-cut precision. Coles performed speedy, swinging, and rhythmically complex combinations in his solos, which anticipated the prolonged cadences of bebop that extended the duration of steps past the usual eight-bar phrase. In 1944 Coles married Marion Evelyn Edwards, a dancer in the Number One chorus at the Apollo Theater; they had two children.

Through the 1940s Coles and Atkins appeared with the big bands of Calloway, LOUIS ARMSTRONG, LIONEL HAMPTON, Charlie Barnet, BILLY ECKSTINE, and Count Basie. In 1949 at the Ziegfeld Theater in the Broadway musical *Gentlemen Prefer Blondes*, Coles and Atkins stopped the show with the Jule Styne number "Mamie Is Mimi," to which choreographer Agnes de Mille had added a ballet dancer. By the time the show closed in 1952 the big-band era was drawing to a close and a new style of balletic Broadway dance that integrated choreography into the musical plot became the popular form over tap dance. Though Coles opened the Dancecraft studio on Fifty-second Street in New York City in 1954 or 1955 with the tap dancer Pete Nugent, there was a steady decrease of interest in tap dancing in the 1950s. "No work, no money. Tap had dropped dead," Coles remembered of that decade.

Coles and Atkins broke up in 1960. For the next sixteen years Coles worked as production stage manager for the Apollo Theater, with duties that included introducing other acts. He served as president of the Negro Actors Guild and continued his association with the Copasetics, a tapping fraternity named in honor of BILL ROBINSON, which he had helped to found in 1949. At the Newport Jazz Festival in 1962 Coles was in the forefront of the tap revival that brought veteran members of the Copasetics back to the stage. He joined the touring company of *Bubblin' Brown Sugar* in 1976 and regained his stride as a soloist, performing at Carnegie Hall and Town Hall. After receiving a standing ovation for his performance in the Joffrey Ballet production of Agnes de Mille's "Conversations on the Dance" in 1978, Coles firmly placed tap dance in the world of concert dance. In 1983 at age seventy-two he received both the Tony and Drama Desk awards for best featured actor and dancer in a musical for the Broadway hit *My One and Only*. Jack Kroll in *Newsweek* called Coles "Brilliant!" in that musical, adding that his feet had "the delicacy and power of a master pianist's hands."

Coles was a tap dancer of extraordinary elegance whose personal style and technical precision epitomized the class-act dancer. "Honi makes butterflies look clumsy. He was my Fred Astaire," the singer LENA HORNE said of Coles. The historian Sally Sommer wrote that Coles was "a supreme illusionist … he appeared to float and do nothing at all while his feet chattered complex rhythms below." He was also a master teacher who preached, "If you can walk, you can tap." As an untiring advocate of tap dancing, Coles often claimed that tap dancing was the only dance art form that America could claim as its own. He was awarded the *Dance* magazine award in 1985, the Capezio Award for lifetime achievement in dance in 1988, and the National Medal of the Arts in 1991. Coles last appeared as master of ceremonies at the Colorado Tap Festival with his former partner Atkins, performing up to the end of a long and rhythmically brilliant career. He died in New York City.

Coles appeared in the films *The Cotton Club* (1984) and *Dirty Dancing* (1987) and in the documentaries *Great Feats of Feet*, *Charles Honi Coles: The Class Act of Tap*, and *Milt and Honi*. His television appearances included "The Tap Dance Kid," "Mr. Griffin and Me," "Conversations in Dance," "Charleston," "Archives of a Master," and Dance in America's "Tap Dance in America" for PBS. Coles & Atkins's classic soft-shoe can be seen in the 1963 *Camera Three* television program "Over the Top with Bebop," narrated by the jazz historian Marshall Stearns.

FURTHER READING

Malone, Jaqui. *Steppin' on the Blues* (1996).

Sommer, Sally. "Smooth and Mellow," *International Tap Association Journal* (Spring 1990).

Stearns, Marshall, and Jean Stearns. *Jazz Dance: The Story of American Vernacular Dance* (1968).

Obituary: *New York Times*, 13 Nov. 1992.

This entry is taken from the *American National Biography* and is published here with the permission of the American Council of Learned Societies.

CONSTANCE VALIS HILL

Coles, Solomon Melvin (21 Feb. 1844–18 Feb. 1924), minister and educator, was born a slave in Petersburg, Virginia, to Charles and Nancy Coles, both of whom worked on the Pryor family farm in Dinwiddie County. Even though antebellum southern states excluded slaves from education, Coles learned the basics of reading and writing from the sympathetic sheriff of Dinwiddie County, H. J. Heartwell. After the Civil War, Coles moved to Connecticut and enrolled in the Guilford Institute. After graduating in 1869 Coles sought to continue his education by attending Pennsylvania's Lincoln University, from which he took a bachelor of arts in 1872 and a master of arts in 1874. A year later he earned his bachelor of divinity from Yale University.

Coles recognized what a rare thing it was for an African American to obtain a formal education in a time when access to universities and higher degrees for blacks remained limited. Like many of his contemporaries, Coles considered education to be the most important method for rising out of economic poverty and combating racial prejudices in a country that sought to keep African Americans in an inferior social status. Coles claimed that even

after the Civil War and the abolition of slavery, "ignorance" was "the instrument" that "the masters at the South" used to "hold his slaves today" (Jordan, 7). By entering the ministry Coles hoped to reach his people and help those less fortunate in the South to receive an education. He became the first African American to graduate from the Yale seminary school, in 1875.

Coles began his ministry by working for the American Missionary Association of the Congregationalist Churches. He found that poverty and lack of education were the major problems that plagued his people, and he refused to accept missionary assignments in Liberia, Africa, specifying instead to the Association that he wanted missionary assignments in either the South or West, where the poverty rate tended to be high and access to education especially limited. In 1877 Coles was ordained as a minister in Goliad, Texas, and he went on to accept an assignment in Corpus Christi, after members of the Congregational church there requested a minister and teacher for the local black population.

When Coles arrived, however, he found that the public school for African Americans did not have a teacher and remained closed. Therefore Coles established a private school, at the beginning taking on fifty students, in which he also served as teacher. He continued to work as a minister, but Coles had made a conscious decision to devote his work to teaching. In 1878 he became both a teacher and a principal for the Free Public School, Colored, because he was the only person to apply for the position. By 1880 Coles was working full-time in public education. His private school closed, and another minister replaced him in the Congregational church.

As a full-time teacher and principal Coles lobbied for equal educational opportunities and facilities for black schools and equal salary for black teachers and administrators. Between the years 1883 and 1887 Coles participated in state conventions—later known as the Teachers State Association of Texas—that demanded equal funding for black public schools, and he witnessed the growth of student attendance in Corpus Christi. Coles had postponed marriage in his earlier years due to financial reasons, but in 1887 he married M. Cornelia Lewis. The couple had two daughters, Iphigenia and Emma May. Emma May, an infant, died in 1891, as did her mother, Cornelia. Coles continued to dedicate his life to education. In his final years he moved to Oberlin, Ohio. In 1925, a year after his death, the Free Public School was renamed Solomon M. Coles in honor of his fifteen years of serving the educational needs of the black community in Corpus Christi, Texas.

Before the civil rights movement took effect in Corpus Christi and the rest of the country, Coles sought equal education rights for the African American community in the city. He demanded equal facilities and equal funding for black children and equal wages for black educators in Texas. His legacy sheds light on the early civil rights activists and black educators whose history is often clouded by those of the twentieth century. Solomon M. Coles remains an important part of Corpus Christi's past, a reminder of the fight undertaken by one African American community in order to receive an equal education.

FURTHER READING

Jordan, Edna. *Black Tracks to Texas: Solomon Melvin Coles—From Slave to Educator* (1977).

MADALYN ARD

Colescott, Robert (26 Aug. 1925–), painter, was born Robert Hutton Colescott in Oakland, California, to parents whose names are not now known but who were both trained musicians, one as a pianist, and the other, as a classically trained violist and sometime band mate of LOUIS ARMSTRONG. His parents had moved from New Orleans to Oakland in 1919. As a child Robert was initially drawn to music, playing the drums and performing in local bands, but quite quickly he realized that his real gift was for drawing and painting.

Before receiving his formal education Colescott met the sculptor SARGENT CLAUDE JOHNSON through his father who, in order to supplement his income as a musician, worked as a porter on the Southern Pacific railroad, where Johnson was one of his co-workers. The sculptor became a family friend and a role model for Robert. After serving for nearly four years in the army in France during World War II, Colescott studied at the University of California, Berkeley, where he received a B.A. in Art in 1949, and a MFA in 1951. In 1949 Colescott traveled to Paris, where he studied with Fernand Léger, an artist whose commitment to figurative art had a tremendous influence on the young artist. Léger's work, which combined the styles of cubism and futurism but emphasized the human figure, inspired Colescott to develop a style that integrated expressive gestures and figurative drawing.

After completing his master's degree Colescott moved to the Pacific Northwest, settling first in Seattle, where he taught art in public schools from 1953 to 1957. He then moved to Portland, Oregon, to take a post as associate professor of art at the state university. It was in Portland that Colescott's career was first firmly established. In 1961 he was part of the inaugural group exhibition at the Fountain Gallery where, in 1963, he had his first solo show. In paintings of this period Colescott focused mainly on the relationship between figures, landscapes, and still lifes while incorporating aspects of pop art and minimalism. In the following years however, Colescott's painting was revolutionized by his travels to Egypt. Between 1964 and 1966 he lived in Cairo, first as an artist-in-residence at the American Research Center and then as a professor at the American University. Colescott's was energized by Egypt's ancient art, specifically by its strong narrative tradition, by its vivid color and sense of pattern, and by its monumentality.

Colescott moved to Paris in 1967, the year he introduced satire and irony into his work as a way to critique American culture from an African American perspective. In 1970 he moved back to the San Francisco Bay Area, where he developed his characteristic style. Working in a figurative-narrative form Colescott began to appropriate images from the history of art and popular culture in order to present satirical interpretations of contemporary society. For example, in *George Washington Carver Crossing the Delaware: Page from an American History Textbook* (1975), he quoted Emanuel Leutze's famous patriotic painting but substituted GEORGE WASHINGTON CARVER for George Washington and included a host of stereotypes derived from antebellum culture along with contemporary images to suggest the persistence of those older stereotypes. By inserting African Americans into canonical paintings, including works by Manet, Picasso, de Kooning, and other avant-garde European painters, Colescott critiqued the history of race relations in the United States and the exclusivity of the Western art tradition. Colescott's work treated racial and sexual stereotypes candidly and, while some had difficulty accepting his frankness, others praised his "skillful combination of humor and seriousness as opening new approaches to issues of race, gender, and power" (Roberts, 18).

During the 1970s Colescott taught at various art programs in California. In the early 1980s he moved to the Southwest to take a post at the University of Arizona, Tucson. He continued to paint in a figurative-narrative style and to employ satire to address issues of race and history but he began to move away from the use of canonical works and to examine questions of beauty and power as they related to gender. He received three National Endowment for the Arts grants, in 1976, 1980, and 1983.

Colescott's work received more audience recognition in the late 1980s as developments in the art world began to highlight his pioneering early work. In 1987 he spent a year at the Roswell Foundation Artist's Residency program in New Mexico, where his work prospered. His palette grew richer, his compositions bolder, and his commitment to exploring the interrelationship between the history of art and the inequities in contemporary society became more refined.

In 1985 he received a Guggenheim Foundation grant. Four years later the city of Houston declared 8 December Robert Colescott Day. In 1990 he was appointed by the regents of the University of Arizona to the Endowed Regents' Professorship in Fine Arts. In 1993 the National Council for the Arts named him Artist/Teacher of the Year. Colescott received two honorary doctorates in fine art, one from the San Francisco Art Institute in 1994 and another from the College of Art at the Maryland Institute in 1997. Also in 1997 he was selected to represent the United States at the forty-seventh Biennale in Venice, Italy, making him the first African American artist to have a solo exhibition at that show. The exhibition, *Robert Colescott: Recent Paintings, 1987–1997*, traveled for two years after its debut in Venice. Colescott received over eighty solo exhibitions, including a touring retrospective, *Robert Colescott: A Retrospective, 1975–1986*, which traveled the United States from 1987 to 1989. He participated in more than 160 group exhibitions, and his work could be found in the collection of over forty major American museums.

FURTHER READING

Bloemink, Barbara J., and Lisa Gail Collins. *Re/righting History: Counternarratives by Contemporary African-American Artists* (1999).

Karlstrom, Paul. "Interview with Robert Colescott, 14 April 1999," Smithsonian Archives of AmericanArt (1999). Accessible online at http://www.aaa.si.edu/collections/oralhistories/transcripts/colesc99.htm.

Roberts, Miriam. *Robert Colescott: Recent Paintings* (1997).

Sims, Lowery S. *Robert Colescott: A Retrospective 1975–1986* (1987).

GLENDA CARPIO

Collette, Buddy (6 Aug. 1921–19 Sep. 2010), alto and tenor saxophonist, clarinetist, flutist, bandleader, arranger, composer, music teacher, and one of the leading jazz musicians in Los Angeles since the early 1940s, was born William Marcell Collette in Los Angeles, California. He was the son of Willie Hugh Collette, who came from Knoxville, Tennessee, and drove a garbage truck. Both he and a brother dabbled in music. Collette's mother, Goldie Marie Dorris, came from Kansas City and sang in church. She had a degree in cosmetology but was primarily a homemaker. Collette had an older sister, Doris, and a younger brother, Patrick. As a child he took piano lessons, but rebelled against further lessons on the instrument after coming under the sway of big band recordings, which inspired him to take up the saxophone. Collette bought his first horn at the age of eleven, using money he made shining shoes. At twelve, he was leading a band of fellow Watts youngsters, using a library of cast-off arrangements he had purchased.

Collette's early influences included the Woodman brothers, who were musically precocious and had a teenage band slightly older than Collette's. One of the brothers, Britt Woodman, would become a renowned trombonist, best known as a member of the DUKE ELLINGTON Orchestra. In his teens Collette sought out ever more demanding teachers, and he soon became influential as a link between his mentors and other young musicians in Los Angeles, branching out into black neighborhoods beyond Watts. He met CHARLES MINGUS, a contemporary who was studying cello, when both were around twelve years old. Collette urged Mingus to switch to double bass so he could play jazz, which he did immediately, kicking off one of the greatest careers in jazz history. Collette was soon mastering the clarinet and different sizes of saxophones and playing with increasingly professional bands. By age eighteen he was a seasoned performer, working with other future stars including Mingus, the drummer Chico Hamilton, and the bass and tuba player Red Callender.

At nineteen Collette got his first regular job, with a "novelty band" led by "Cee Pee" Johnson. This band was popular in Los Angeles, and was hired for several big-budget Hollywood films. Among these were the Ginger Rogers vehicles *Kitty Foyle* (1940), and *Tom, Dick, and Harry* (1941). In the Fred Astaire–Rita Hayworth picture *You'll Never Get Rich* (1941), a lyrical off-screen clarinet introduces a moody nocturnal scene that evolves into an upbeat specialty number with the young Collette

Buddy Collette, right, and Dr. Richard Birkemeier, Associate Dean of the College of the Arts at Cal State Long Beach, share a laugh on campus on 25 September 1996. (AP Images.)

playing the instrument while prone on a cot. He was also heard in the classic *Citizen Kane* (1941), in which director Orson Welles took the unheard of step of filming the band "live" (albeit briefly) in a party scene. Collette thus became one of the few major jazz musicians to get high-profile exposure in films first and records only after.

During World War II Collette served on a naval base near San Francisco. Unwilling to play the unwieldy baritone saxophone in the marching band, he was relegated to the base's number two band, which played the less desirable functions and also did latrine duty. However, Collette, though only twenty at the time, drilled his inferior musicians until he had a crack ensemble that was soon asked to play for dances and other prime assignments, to the consternation of the more favored band on base, which was led by Marshall Royal and featured several future jazz stars.

After the war Collette became a central figure in a burgeoning jazz scene on Central Avenue in Los Angeles, which gradually became the closest thing New York had to serious competition as a jazz scene. He recorded during this period under

the leadership of BENNY CARTER, LOUIS JORDAN, Charles Mingus, GERALD WILSON, and others. Collette had begun teaching music in early adolescence, and in the 1950s he became a leading jazz pedagogue. He was crucial to the musical development of several younger jazz giants, particularly wind players. Among them were ERIC DOLPHY, SONNY CRISS, and Charles Lloyd.

Collette became a racial pioneer in the early1950s, when he was hired for the house band of the television show *You Bet Your Life*, starring Groucho Marx. The first African American to break into this medium, he was nicknamed "the JACKIE ROBINSON of the Networks." Marx featured Collette heavily on his show, boasting on air about having a prominent jazz musician in the band.

In the 1950s Collette was very active in the advancement of African Americans in Los Angeles, working for the amalgamation of the white and black musicians unions there. He was also a committed social progressive, unafraid to stick by unpopular causes and people. A friend and admirer of PAUL ROBESON's, he continued to perform and socialize with him after the singer fell afoul of the U.S. government. Collette also aided the American Civil Liberties Union in Los Angeles, playing at their functions with pickup groups he organized.

The 1950s and early 1960s were the prime of Buddy Collette's long career. He made his first recordings as a leader in 1956 (*Man of Many Parts*), following this up the following year with *Nice Day with Buddy Collette* and several other recordings. On his own sessions he often played flute, clarinet, and both alto and tenor saxophones. He was also adept on several instruments he did not play in public, including baritone saxophone and bass clarinet. His sessions as a leader frequently featured his own expert arrangements, and on these Collette often utilized innovative instrumental combinations. On *The Swinging Shepherds* (1959) he and three other flutists played alto and bass flutes as well as the standard "C" flute, trading solos and playing four-part ensembles over a rhythm section. Here, as on all his recordings as a leader, Collette was notably generous with his hired colleagues in soloing opportunities.

Collette's profile as a jazz star grew when he became the first woodwind player in an influential quintet led by his old friend, the drummer Chico Hamilton. This groundbreaking ensemble, formed in 1955, included the cello, not a standard jazz instrument, and no piano or brass. Collette often played flute with this band, which became renowned for its light, sophisticated sound. Their unique musical sound became quite popular. For a time, the flute virtually dominated Collette's career. In addition to *The Swinging Shepherds* he appeared on a 1957 album called *Flute Fraternity*, on which he and Herbie Mann traded solos on flute, clarinet, and saxophones.

Between his work with Hamilton and his projects as a leader Collette became very prominent in the Hollywood scene, and this led to an ever-widening range of opportunities. He became a preferred player in bands led by Nelson Riddle and Billy May, leading arrangers and conductors of the period. He was often a soloist in bands backing Frank Sinatra, who collected Collette's recordings and brought him to the inauguration of President John F. Kennedy in 1961. Later that year he traveled to Italy, where he was featured heavily at the San Remo Festival and appeared extensively on television. Collette instantaneously became a musical celebrity in Italy, and he stayed on to do a great deal more performing. In 1963 Collette was asked to go to New York to work with ELLA FITZGERALD

as the conductor on some recordings. He was quite successful there, and considered relocating to New York, but returned home to care for his family.

In the 1960s and 1970s, as musical tastes changed, many jazz musicians fell on hard times, but Collette, having become so well established as a studio musician, continued to work steadily. In 1967 Collette reentered the television studios, where he was a regular on *The Danny Kaye Show*, *The Carol Burnett Show*, *Trapper John, M.D.*, and others into the 1970s. After many years of giving private lessons to younger musicians such as the flutist James Newton, in 1972 Collette began a four-year stint at California State University at Los Angeles; he also taught at other institutions of higher learning, including Loyola Marymount University.

The 1980s and 1990s found Collette continuing to play, compose, arrange, conduct, and teach with vigor. He returned to Italy in 1988, and while there recorded the album *Flute Talk* with his former student James Newton. Collette's performances during this second sojourn in Italy led to demands for further appearances there and elsewhere in Europe. He suggested to Chico Hamilton that they re-form their original 1956 quintet; this band was greeted with great acclaim in Italy, and recorded *Reunion* in Milan in 1989. Collette was treated like visiting royalty and making a great deal of money during this second stay in Europe. He stayed on, working in Holland with a mixed band of Dutch and American musicians. However, as always, he gravitated home to Los Angeles.

In 1990 Collette organized a big band and brought it to El Camino College in Torrance, California. His flute solo on his original "Blues in Torrance," from the recording made "live" on this occasion, shows him in exceptional form in his late sixties. Two further live recordings were made under his leadership in 1996; another big band date, in Washington, D.C., and *Jazz for Thousand Oaks*, with an octet. Collette's composing also deepened during this late phase of his career, with such excellent compositions as "Magali," which was quickly adopted by the trumpeter CLARK TERRY and other peers.

Collette's playing remained vital and versatile through most of the 1990s. A 1998 stroke left Collette physically impaired on his left side and ended his performing, possibly permanently. However, he retained his powers of speech and continued to teach and appear on panel discussions. He regained the use of his left arm with the aid of constraint induced movement therapy, a testament to his extraordinary resilience, will power, and optimism.

Although Collette was always highly disciplined and clean-living, his life was tinged with sadness as many of his friends, colleagues, and students succumbed to drug addiction and other depredations. Collette's family life also suffered, as his wife, Lou, a former chorus dancer, succumbed to alcoholism in the 1950s. The two separated and ultimately divorced, by which time Collette had been raising a son and two daughters as a single parent for several years. He also has numerous grandchildren and great-grandchildren.

As both bandleader and composer, Collette did notable work in swing, bebop, commercial, and post-bop genres and settings. He was an innovator, but a subtle innovator, and never self-aggrandizing. In duets and ensembles, he was peerless. For example, on the song "Speak Low" on his longtime friend Red Callender's album *Red Callender Speaks Low*, the interplay between the leader's tuba and Collette's flute is outstanding. Numerous similar examples can be heard on his other recordings. If not among the greatest composers in jazz, he is certainly in the first rank of arrangers for jazz bands.

Collette's sound on his instruments was always highly varied, reflecting his masterful technique and constant study. On flute, he employed a wide vibrato on ballads, a "straighter" sound elsewhere. His clarinet work was often limpid and crystalline, though he could switch to a rough, gutty sound at will. His saxophone sound displayed a similar range, and he also could suddenly switch to a veiled, almost smoky timbre on his flute and reed instruments. Unlike some wind players, whose characteristic timbres were connected with particular ranges on the instruments (perhaps betraying some technical limitation) Collette could employ a complete gamut of sounds across all registers, using variety on his horns purely for aesthetic effect, never as a novelty.

Gentlemanly, urbane, and immensely disciplined, Buddy Collette never pushed himself to the forefront as a soloist or front man, and his renown was never as great as his talents merited. He was always something of a man behind the scenes, focused more on excellence than on stardom. However, jazz cognoscenti and the many musicians influenced by him can attest to his stature as one of the greatest figures to come to prominence in jazz during the 1950s. Collette died in Los Angeles on 19 September 2010, at the age of eighty-nine.

FURTHER READING

Buddy Collette's life and career are well documented, thanks to his coauthorship of a personally revealing and musically detailed memoir, and his participation in other oral history projects. He also figures in the life stories of a wide and distinguished array of other musicians, particularly those from, or active in, Los Angeles.

Collette, Buddy, with Steven Isoardi. *Jazz Generations: A Life in American Music and Society* (2000).

Bryant, Clora, Buddy Collette, et al., eds., *Central Avenue Sounds: Jazz in Los Angeles* (1998).

Mingus, Charles. *Beneath the Underdog* (1971).

ELLIOTT S. HURWITT

Collier, Holt (1846–1 Aug. 1936), slave, soldier, hunter, guide, and pioneer, was born on Home Hill plantation, Jefferson County, Mississippi, the son of slaves Harrison and Daphne Collier. Little is known of Daphne Collier, although it is believed that she had some Native American ancestry. In 1815 Harrison Collier accompanied the famed General Thomas Hinds when he fought alongside General Andrew Jackson during the War of 1812 at the Battle of New Orleans. As house servants the Colliers maintained a higher status on the plantation, and from all indications young Holt was a favorite of the Hinds family. At age ten he was taken into the upriver wilderness to serve as a juvenile valet and hostler on Plum Ridge plantation in what would later become known as Washington County in the Mississippi Delta.

At Plum Ridge plantation Holt was trained to hunt and kill anything that could be used as food for the growing slave population. He became so proficient with both the long gun and the pistol that he could shoot equally well from his left or right shoulder. He is credited with killing his first bear at the age of ten. Holt mastered the geography of the delta swamps during the next four years.

As a young boy Holt heard stories of his father's service with General Hinds. When the Civil War erupted in 1861 the general's son and grandson, Howell Hinds and Thomas Hinds, joined the Confederacy. The fourteen-year-old Holt—in the spirit of adventure—ran away to join the two men. In time he became an unofficial soldier in the Confederate army, serving as a cavalryman and scout for Perry Evans's Texas Rangers in the very hunting grounds he had learned as a boy. He served with far more distinction than did either of the men he sought to serve. Collier remains the only soldier of African descent to be officially recognized by any of the Confederate states as a combat veteran.

After the war Collier returned to an impoverished Plum Ridge plantation a free man. He rejoined the Hinds family in an effort to survive the effects of the conflict. The years following the war were difficult and poverty knew no racial barriers. The region was occupied by federal forces and the Freedman's Bureau took charge of the workforce. The officer in charge of the bureau in 1866 was Captain James A. King, an abolitionist from Newton, Iowa. Soon after being involved in an altercation with the elderly and crippled Howell Hinds, Captain King's lifeless body was found submerged in the swampy canebrakes—disposed of in the manner used by the Texas Rangers. Collier was arrested and charged with King's murder but was acquitted by a military court-martial in Vicksburg. Not able to return to Washington County for fear of retribution from the occupying forces, Collier joined his former comrades and traveled to Texas, where he became a cowboy for the next two years.

In 1868 Collier was told of the murder of Howell Hinds on the streets of Greenville. Seeking vengeance Collier returned to Mississippi but was met and detained several times by authorities eager to coerce a confession for the unresolved murder of James A. King. To avoid further prosecution Collier moved into the swamps and sought to earn a living by providing meat to the growing workforce of the new timber, railroad, and levy building industries. In this endeavor he earned large sums of money and became a highly respected citizen of the Mississippi Delta community.

Collier hunted the wilderness area of the lower Mississippi Valley for more than thirty years, blazing trails through uncharted and unexplored territory. He is credited with killing more than 3,000 bears during his lifetime.

During non-hunting seasons Collier served as a lawman and was involved in several gunfights. But for the death of King and the resulting prosecution, he was never punished. One particularly notable incident was the gunfight at Washburn's Ferry, during which Collier outdrew the notorious Louisiana double murderer deputy-turned-outlaw Travis Elmore Sage.

By the turn of the century the black bear population had been reduced significantly due to hunting and a reduction of its habitat. Collier's services as a professional guide were in demand by wealthy men who sought to participate in the excitement of a bear hunt before the bear population became totally denuded. One of those men was President Theodore Roosevelt. Collier was chosen to guide Roosevelt on a bear hunt in the lower Mississippi Delta along the banks of the Little Sunflower River. On 14 November 1902, following a grueling chase and difficult fight, Collier single-handedly captured a large adult black bear and tied it to a tree for Roosevelt to kill. Roosevelt refused to kill the tethered animal.

Cartoonists and reporters had a field day with the story, which was published for several days in major newspapers throughout the country. Although the press lampooned Roosevelt, it was highly complimentary of Collier and spoke of him in almost heroic terms for the superhuman effort of capturing the bear. Within days the cartoonist Clifford Berryman of the *Washington Post* had published several cartoons depicting the tethered bear as a small, delightful creature. Brooklyn store owner Morris Michtom was inspired by the image and designed a toy bear he called "Teddy's bear." The resulting phenomenon of the famous and ever-popular Teddy Bear continues around the world even today.

Roosevelt was so impressed with Collier that he called him the best guide and hunter he had ever seen. He pledged to return for another hunt with Collier, and did so in 1907 in Louisiana. The hosts of the 1907 hunt put the famous hunter Ben Lilly in charge and relegated Collier to serve as his second, presumably because Lilly was white. However, after twelve unsuccessful days, Roosevelt put Collier in charge and the next morning, Roosevelt succeeded in killing a trophy black bear that had eluded him so long. In appreciation of the success of the hunt, Roosevelt had a special Winchester rifle sent to Collier, and though Collier never learned to read or write or sign his own name, it is known that they corresponded several times.

The 1902 Mississippi hunt is unquestionably the most famous hunt ever to occur on American soil. In time Collier would be the subject of six national publications. The news coverage he received in 1902 and the national magazine publications issued soon thereafter made Collier the first nationally known sportsman of African descent. Though Collier's relationship with Roosevelt insures his lasting fame, being the one person most responsible for the event that spawned the Teddy Bear places his legacy alongside pioneers and hunters of national and world renown.

FURTHER READING

Buchanan, Minor Ferris. *Holt Collier: His Life, His Roosevelt Hunts, and the Origin of the Teddy Bear* (2002).

                    MINOR FERRIS BUCHANAN

Collier, Nathan White (14 May 1871–20 Feb. 1941), college president and educator, was born in Augusta, Georgia, to Madison Jordan Collier and Frances (Tyler) Collier. He attended Georgia public schools and worked with his father as a brick mason. Graduating from Ware High School in 1887, he first found work as an apprentice at the Georgia Baptist Printing Office. In 1890 Collier enrolled at Atlanta University, where he met his lifelong friend and college roommate, JAMES WELDON JOHNSON. Upon graduating from Atlanta University with honors in 1894, Collier was offered a summer teaching position at the Georgia State Industrial College. Instead, he accepted a position as principal and chair of ancient languages at Florida Baptist Academy. Rooted in the Baptist tradition, Florida Baptist was founded in 1892 by the Reverend Matthew Gilbert, the Reverend J. T. Brown, and SARAH BLOCKER in Jacksonville, Florida. By 1896 the academy's financial and administrative woes culminated in a crisis as the founders Gilbert and Brown resigned. Collier and Sarah Ann Blocker, however, were determined to persevere and save the school from closing. Collier became the institution's president, serving from 1896 to 1941, and Blocker became vice president, principal of the normal department, registrar, and dean of women, serving from 1892 to 1943.

In 1898 Collier recruited several notable faculty to Florida Baptist Academy, including the educator Mary White Blocker and the musician and composer JOHN ROSAMOND JOHNSON, who composed the music to the black national anthem, "Lift Every Voice and Sing," written by his brother James Weldon Johnson. Collier increased student enrollment and changed the name of the institution to Florida Baptist College. Support from Jacksonville's African American community facilitated relocation of the institution from the basement of Bethel Baptist Institutional church to East Jacksonville, where the school purchased a three-story building. There Collier and Blocker attempted to replicate the educational aims and programs of the Tuskegee Institute founder BOOKER T. WASHINGTON. They reclaimed the original name of the institution (Florida Baptist Academy) and adopted the motto "Knowledge in the mind, divine love in the heart and skill in the hand," which encompassed Washington's ideals for industrial education.

The Jacksonville fire of 1901 devastated the city and severely hampered Collier's fund-raising efforts. He did, however, secure funds by 1910 from the General Education Board established by John D. Rockefeller and the Slater Education Fund. He received additional financial support from the Women's American Baptist Home Mission Society, the Florida Baptist Convention, the local Jacksonville community, and friends such as the millionaire realtor Carl G. Fisher.

Despite the efforts of Collier and Blocker, in its early years Florida Baptist Academy was constantly plagued with overcrowded facilities, a shortage of housing, and insufficient resources to accommodate long student waiting lists. To rectify this situation, Collier led a very successful fund-raising drive that eradicated all outstanding institutional debts and increased the visibility of the campus across the nation. For example, in 1901 President Theodore Roosevelt selected Florida Baptist Academy as the premier site of African American higher learning in the state of Florida. Roosevelt made a presidential speech from this campus in 1905. In 1917 Collier purchased a former plantation home in St. Augustine, Florida, as the new site for Florida Baptist Academy. The relocation occurred primarily because of a request from the St. Augustine Chamber of Commerce, which offered land and financial considerations. In 1918 Collier successfully led efforts to amend the institution's charter to reflect full college status and instituted another name change from Florida Baptist Academy to Florida Normal and Industrial Institute (FNII). By 1921 the institution owned more than four acres of land and consisted of one main building and three smaller buildings.

While working to establish FNII, Collier also continued his own education, earning a doctorate in Literature from Alabama's Selma University in May of 1918. Collier and Blocker also participated in numerous national and local educational events. Although wartime exigencies during the First World War created financial difficulties and decreased student enrollment, Collier led a major fund-raising campaign to increase FNII's institutional buildings and facilities. He transformed FNII with the construction of a new library, new gymnasium, laundry facilities, boys' and girls' dormitories, updated farm equipment, trades buildings, an improved water-sewer system, and drainage and millinery equipment. Collier was also active in community efforts during the war, and on 5 June 1918 he formally accepted a victory flag from the U.S. government on behalf of the city of Jacksonville. He received this flag for his leadership role in assisting to raise $298,000 in the nation's Third Liberty Loan Campaign. Collier also made significant alterations to the FNII curriculum to include industrial, liberal arts, and science courses. His greatest contribution was to the education and training of African American teachers throughout the state of Florida during the 1920s and 1930s. By 1935 FNII was renowned for training African American teachers who taught at various institutions throughout the nation.

Dedicated to the survival of the college, during the 1930s Collier cashed in his life insurance policy to supplement the institution's budget shortfalls as financial support dwindled. Collier and his vice president Sarah Ann Blocker also voluntarily suspended their annual teaching incomes. Both lived on the institution's campus and used their salaries to pay teachers and to sustain the institution.

Collier and Blocker's students included several prominent African Americans, including the playwright and novelist ZORA NEALE HURSTON (who attended the college in 1901, although she did not graduate), the social worker EARTHA MARY MAGDALENE WHITE, the businessmen Charles Anderson and Moses Samuel Adams, and the attorney Pope D. Billups. Highly respected by his peers and by the General Education Board, Collier was offered presidential positions at several other African American institutions, including Florida Agricultural and Mechanical University (FAMU), but he remained dedicated to FNII. Collier's efforts adversely affected his health and caused him to be bedridden in 1940. He returned to Augusta, Georgia, later in 1940 but continued ministering to the demands of the institution until his death in February 1941. He never married.

The Florida legislature issued a declaration of regret upon his passing and formally recognized him as one of the nation's premier African American educators. Politicians and local and national newspapers formally issued statements of regret upon Collier's passing. His funeral was held in St. Augustine, Florida, and he was buried on the campus of FNII. Sarah Ann Blocker was later buried next to him in 1943. In 1941, FNII merged with Florida Memorial College, formerly known as Florida Baptist Institute, established in Live Oak in 1879. The institution became known as Florida Normal and Industrial Memorial Institute in 1941. Following several name changes, in 1968 the institution was renamed Florida Memorial College and moved to Miami. In 2004, the institution became known as Florida Memorial University. Florida Memorial University named the Nathan White Collier Library in honor of Dr. Nathan White Collier and issues the Nathan White Collier Award for outstanding community service. Florida Memorial University is accredited by the Commisson on Colleges of the Southern Association of Colleges and Schools.

FURTHER READING

McKinney, George P. *History of the Black Baptists in Florida, 1850–1985* (1987).

Neyland, Leedell W., and Gilbert Porter Neyland. *History of the Florida Teachers Association* (1977).

ROSE C. THEVENIN

Collins, Addie Mae (18 Apr. 1949–15 Sep. 1963), schoolgirl and terrorist bombing victim, was born in Birmingham, Alabama, the seventh of eight surviving children of Oscar Collins, a busboy in a Chinese restaurant, and Aline Collins, a domestic. Addie Mae grew up in a small four-room house on a dirt road in Sixth Court West, one of Birmingham's poorest neighborhoods. When her parents separated, making an already difficult home life even harder, Addie Mae and her sisters Janie and Sarah helped the family finances by going door to door after school, selling cotton aprons and potholders that their mother made. Interviewed by the *Birmingham News* in April 2001, her sisters recalled that Addie Mae was a quiet—but by no means shy or timid—child who emerged as the peacemaker whenever quarrels broke out in the family. "She just always wanted us to love one another and treat each other right," her younger sister Sarah remembered.

In 1955 Addie Mae entered Brunetta C. Hill Elementary School in downtown Birmingham. Like all schools in Alabama, Hill Elementary remained segregated despite the U.S. Supreme Court's *Brown v. Board of Education* school desegregation ruling the previous year. She enjoyed drawing, reading, and math; played Simon Says, softball, and hopscotch with her friends; and was a member of the school band. On Sundays she regularly attended services and sang in the youth choir at Birmingham's Sixteenth Street Baptist, the chosen church of the city's growing black middle-class that also included working-class congregants like the Collinses. Sarah Collins later told the *New York Times* that because of their poverty, her family was looked down upon by many of the wealthier children at Birmingham's most elite black church.

On Sunday, 15 September 1963, as on most Sundays, Addie Mae Collins readied herself for Sunday school and church, and with four of her siblings she walked the sixteen blocks to Sixteenth Street. Because they were late for Sunday school, Addie Mae and Sarah waited in the basement ladies' lounge for the main eleven o'clock church service to begin. Around ten o'clock the sisters were joined by DENISE MCNAIR, eleven, and CAROLE ROBERTSON and CYNTHIA WESLEY, both fourteen, who had just left their Sunday school service, where the lesson had been "The Love That Forgives." Along with Addie Mae, the three girls were supposed to act as ushers and sing in the youth choir that day for a special Youth Day service instituted by Sixteenth Street's young minister, the Reverend John Cross. Around 10:22 A.M., Sarah Collins later recalled, Addie Mae was standing with her friends looking out of the restroom window to Sixteenth Street below. The girls were tending each other's hair and clothing; Addie was helping to tie the sash on Denise McNair's dress.

At that moment a massive explosion ripped through the church. The blast was powerful enough to eject a driver from his car outside the church and to blow the door off the shop of a nearby dry cleaner. Dynamite placed by white supremacists earlier that morning had exploded, demolishing a stone foundation wall that was thirty inches thick. The east and west walls of Sixteenth Street Baptist collapsed against each other. Inside the church Sarah Collins, badly burned and blinded by flying glass, called out for her sister Addie but never received a reply. Addie Mae Collins, Cynthia Wesley, Carole Robertson, and Denise McNair had all perished in the blast; their bodies had been broken by falling concrete slabs and were charred beyond recognition. Remarkably, no one else died, although several children and adults were badly burned and injured. Soon, the shell-shocked congregants were joined by family members who had either heard or heard about the explosion and rushed to Sixteenth Street to find their loved ones in the rubble.

Outside the church and throughout Birmingham, predominantly African American crowds gathered to vent their anger at the senseless killings. Few of the protesters were inclined at that moment to heed the admonitions of the Reverend Cross, who asked them to disperse, go home, and pray for those who had planted the dynamite. Birmingham's overwhelmingly white police force had used excessive force in subduing teenage civil rights protesters earlier that summer. And for more than a decade the police had done nothing to halt or solve nearly fifty dynamite attacks on black homes. One patrolman had shot Johnny Robinson, a sixteen-year-old African American protester, in the back, killing him instantly. Later that day in northwest Birmingham, two white teenagers on a motorbike fired at two black schoolboys, James Ware, sixteen, and his thirteen-year-old brother, Virgil, who were cycling home on their bicycles. Shot in the chest and jaw, Virgil died instantly; his murderers were later sentenced to seven months in the county jail but were released on probation.

In Sixth Court West, the Collins family struggled to come to terms with the loss of Addie Mae, and they also feared for Sarah, who had lost her right eye, was badly scarred, and remained in the hospital. Too numb to feel any hatred towards her children's attackers, Aline Collins stoically told the press of her relief that only one of her five children who had been at the church that morning had died. Civil rights leader MARTIN LUTHER KING JR. condemned the atrocity in a telegram to President John F. Kennedy, demanding that the federal government take immediate steps to prevent "the worst racial holocaust this nation has ever seen" (cited in McWhorter, 530). King's telegram to George Wallace, Alabama's defiantly segregationist and racist governor, directly blamed him for the murders. "The blood of our little children is on your hands," he told Wallace (cited in McWhorter, 530). King's deputy, RALPH ABERNATHY, recognized, however, that responsibility lay not only in Tuscaloosa, where Wallace had encouraged militant white supremacists and condemned the peaceful civil rights demonstrations, but also in Washington, D.C., where a timid Kennedy administration had failed to enforce the Constitution for fear of losing Southern white support.

Global outrage at the murder of four innocent girls did, in fact, spur the White House to action in a way that the assassination four months earlier of MEDGAR EVERS, or the 1955 lynching of fourteen-year-old EMMETT TILL, had not. Along with the King-led March on Washington in August 1963, the bombing made passage of the long-awaited civil rights bill much more likely. However, more murders—especially the assassination of President Kennedy and the 1964 slaying of civil rights workers JAMES CHANEY, Andrew Goodman, and Michael Schwerner—would take place before the bill's final passage. The federal government, and in particular the FBI, were certainly culpable for the failure to prosecute the perpetrators of any of those murders until 1977. That year Robert "Dynamite Bob" Chambliss, long suspected of involvement in several bombings and of being the ringleader of the Sixteenth Street bombers, was found guilty of murder in a state trial. Chambliss, who died in jail in 1985, was one of four Ku Klux Klansmen named by the FBI in their initial investigation of the case; another, Herman Cash, died in 1994 before he could be put on trial. Even though the FBI had, since 1964, possessed incriminating audiotapes of the two other men, Thomas Blanton and Bobby Frank Cherry, they chose not to share them with the Alabama prosecutor. Blanton was later found guilty in an April 2001 trial, having enjoyed thirty-eight years of freedom because the FBI withheld evidence. Cherry, who most likely planted the bomb, was indicted with Blanton; but on the basis of mental incompetence, he did not stand trial.

While some in Birmingham believed the Blanton trial would provide closure, Sarah Collins Rudolph, Addie Mae Collins's younger sister, who testified at the trial, did not find much solace. Indeed, the tragedy of her sister's senseless murder was compounded three years before Blanton's trial. The cemetery in which Addie Mae was buried was not well kept, and in January 1998, wishing to transfer her remains to another site, the Collins family discovered that their daughter was not in her assigned grave. In the late 1990s, Addie Mae Collins's niece founded a youth center in Birmingham and named it after her aunt, not only as a memorial but also to highlight the center's goals of building positive attitudes, developing talents, and helping children in crisis to learn to deal with adversity.

FURTHER READING

McWhorter, Diane. *Carry Me Home: Birmingham, Alabama: The Climactic Battle of the Civil Rights Revolution* (2001).

Mendelsohn, Jack. *The Martyrs: Sixteen Who Gave Their Lives for Racial Justice* (1966).

Sikora, Frank. *Until Justice Rolls Down: The Birmingham Church Bombing Case* (1991).

STEVEN J. NIVEN

Collins, Albert (3 Oct. 1932–24 Nov. 1993), guitarist and singer, was born in Leona, Texas, a very small town about thirteen miles from Normangee. Little

is known about his family, but they had apparently moved to Houston by the time Albert was nine years old. His first exposure to guitar was through his uncle, Campbell Collins, who was a minister. Albert was initially drawn to the sounds of piano and organ and had some instruction in each of those instruments. As a teenager his instrument was stolen, and he reverted to guitar. An older cousin named Willow Young played lap-style guitar with a knife and introduced Collins to the open-tuning technique (which involves tuning a guitar to an actual chord) that he would use throughout his career. This particular minor-chord tuning would heavily influence his unique phrasing. Another relative on his mother's side was LIGHTNIN' HOPKINS, a very popular bluesman in Texas who went on to international fame. Hopkins would perform at family gatherings or "associations," as they were called at the time. Collins absorbed much of Hopkins's music as well as the music of JOHN LEE HOOKER, whose "Boogie Chillen" was the first song he learned to play on guitar.

It was the big band sound that really grabbed Collins's attention, however. He was attracted to the sounds of horns and listened to the Dorsey Brothers' and JIMMIE LUNCEFORD's big bands on the radio. Texas guitarists such as T-BONE WALKER, Clarence "Gatemouth" Brown, and LOWELL FULSON recorded and traveled with large bands, and Collins was able to see them perform live after hearing them on the radio. Collins formed his own band called the Rhythm Rockers in 1950 and played around Houston. The band member and alto saxophonist Henry Hayes tutored Collins in the rudiments of jazz, which would later help him with his trademark horn arrangements. Gatemouth Brown was a particular influence, and he encouraged Collins to play a Fender electric solid-body guitar, which was relatively new at the time. A solid-body guitar could be played through an amplifier at louder volumes without the unwanted squeal and feedback common to hollow-bodied instruments. After seeing Brown play, Collins also began using a capo, a clamping device that allows the guitarist to play in an open position anywhere on the neck and can be moved to different frets to change keys. Like Brown, he fretted primarily with the second and third fingers of his left hand and picked the strings with the bare fingers of his right. This approach gave him the percussive attack and the snap so identifiable in his style.

Collins regarded the acquisition of his Fender Esquire guitar in 1952 as the moment he became a professional musician. He had been playing weekends as a teenager, but it wasn't until he traveled through the South backing singer Piney Brown that he began forging his signature sound. A meeting with the already successful B.B. KING cemented Collins's quest to develop his own sound; King told him that finding his own identity would serve him well.

Collins eventually returned to Houston and worked a series of day jobs while playing at night. He recorded his first single, "The Freeze," in 1958 on the small Kangaroo label ("Collins Shuffle" was the B-side.). The single was successful locally, and Collins began sharing bills with Gatemouth Brown, T-Bone Walker, and Guitar Slim (EDDIE JONES). Guitar Slim was known as a showman and would walk into the crowd with a long cord on his electric guitar. Collins later claimed he had already employed this technique after seeing the jazz saxophonist CECIL JAMES "BIG JAY" McNEELY stroll through the audience. Using a one-hundred-foot-long cord was another trademark Collins utilized throughout his career. Two years later, he recorded the single "Defrost," with "Albert's Alley" on the B-side, for Hall Records. In 1962 Collins recorded "Frosty," which became a million-selling single. Besides his fellow Texan FREDDIE KING, no other blues guitarist enjoyed such success with instrumental hit records. The use of chilly titles such as "Don't Lose Your Cool," "Ice Pickin'," and "Cold Snap" were became a Collins signature.

In 1966 Collins moved to Kansas City, which was a jazz stronghold. There he met guitarists WES MONTGOMERY, GRANT GREEN, and George Benson. However, it was jazz organists such as Jimmy Smith, Brother Jack McDuff, and especially Jimmy McGriff who most excited and inspired him. McGriff would later contribute to some of Collins's recordings.

By now, Collins's uniquely conversational style—the sort of musical phrasing that is cadenced like speaking—was strongly in place, and his success was spilling beyond the Houston region. His approach to lead and rhythm guitar was informed as much by jazz organists and horn players as by other blues guitarists such as Albert King. Collins was of the next generation of electric blues guitarists after T-Bone Walker, Gatemouth Brown, and B. B. King. His cool, modern approach added funk and jazz to the blues, and this was not lost on many up-and-coming guitarists who coveted his records and style. One such guitarist was JIMI HENDRIX, who met Collins when Hendrix was around seventeen

and was traveling the Chitlin Circuit, backing acts such as the Isley Brothers, LITTLE RICHARD, and IKE TURNER and TINA TURNER. Collins actually replaced Hendrix in Little Richard's band for a short time. Collins was a link between the first electric bluesmen and the psychedelic blues of Hendrix. Hendrix had studied Collins's records, and during his career he would perform and record an homage to Collins called "Drivin' South." It started as a funky blues jam and often culminated in fuzztone-laden, free-form psychedelia.

Collins moved back to Houston in 1968 to focus on his blues music. Shortly thereafter, Bob Hite, an avid record collector and lead singer for the blues-rock group Canned Heat, sought Collins out when his band was in the area. Hite got Collins a deal with Imperial Records, and Collins recorded three albums for the label and relocated to Los Angeles. The records were moderately successful, and Collins developed his vocal skills and his abilities to mimic many sounds with his guitar. In addition to his conversational phrasing, Collins could make his guitar sound out actual words by the notes he played. He established himself on the concert hall circuit and played venues like the legendary Fillmore Auditorium, sharing billings with hugely popular rock acts such as Hendrix, the Allman Brothers Band, and Grand Funk Railroad.

After leaving Imperial, Collins briefly recorded for the Tumbleweed label run by producer Bill Symczyk. Discouraged and tired, he left music for a year to be a construction worker and truck driver. His wife, Gwendolyn, whom he'd met in Kansas City (although the date of their marriage is not known), recognized that music was his true calling and urged him to go back to playing full-time. After a successful tour in Scandinavia, he was signed to Alligator Records and finally realized his fullest potential. Playing and singing a mixture of blues and funk, Collins's forceful playing and wry vocals catapulted him to the top of the blues heap. Songs such as "Conversation with Collins" and "Master Charge" were cowritten with his wife.

In 1985 Collins performed at Live Aid with George Thorogood and the Destroyers and was seen on television worldwide by millions. He also recorded the Grammy-winning "Showdown" with the singer-guitarists Robert Cray and Johnny Copeland. In 1986 he appeared in television commercials with the actor Bruce Willis, and in 1987 Collins made a cameo appearance in the film *Adventures in Babysitting*. Around this time, Collins relocated to Las Vegas.

After recording seven albums, Albert left Alligator in 1989 to record for Pointblank, a subsidiary of Virgin Records. He continued to tour the world playing festivals, concerts, and clubs. The Fender company honored him with his own signature model Telecaster guitar. In the late 1980s and early 1990s he recorded with such artists as B. B. King, David Bowie, Gary Moore, and Jack Bruce, among others. In 1993 he was diagnosed with lung cancer and died less than six months later. He was known variously as "The Master of the Telecaster," "The Ice Man," and "The Houston Twister." Of the legions of blues guitarists, no one has forged a more chilling, powerful, and individual sound than Albert Collins.

FURTHER READING

Forte, Dan. "Blues Meltdown: The Power of Albert Collins," *Guitar Player Magazine* (1988).

Harris, Sheldon. *Blues Who's Who* (1979, 1993).

Milkowski, Bill. "Mr. Freeze," *Guitar World Magazine* (1990).

Obrecht, Jas. "Albert Collins, the Iceman Speaketh," *Guitar Player Magazine* (1993).

Welding, Pete. Liner notes from the LP *Truckin' with Albert Collins* (1970).

DISCOGRAPHY

Truckin' with Albert Collins (Blue Thumb, 1970).

Ice Pickin' (Alligator, 1978).

Cold Snap (Alligator, 1986).

The Complete Imperial Recordings (1991).

MARK S. MAULUCCI

Collins, Cardiss Robertson (24 Sept. 1931–), U.S. Congresswoman, was born Cardiss Hortense Robertson in Saint Louis, Missouri. She was the only child of Rosie and Finley Robertson, a domestic worker and a manual laborer, respectively. Cardiss's parents came from two different families with the same surname of Robertson. Rosie Robertson grew up on the Whiteville, Tennessee, farm of her great-grandfather, an ex-slave named Erastus White. Cardiss's parents separated during her infancy. Cardiss and her mother were so poor that their two-room apartment lacked a gas stove and refrigerator. They moved to Detroit when Cardiss was ten.

After graduating from the Detroit High School of Commerce, Cardiss moved to her maternal grandmother's home in Chicago. Initially a mattress factory seamstress, she eventually worked as stenographer for a carnival equipment business and then the Illinois Department of Labor. Attending night school courses at Northwestern University for twelve years, she achieved a business certificate in 1966 and a professional accounting diploma in 1967. She was employed as a secretary, accountant, and finally revenue auditor in the Illinois Department of Revenue. She belonged to Friendship Baptist Church.

On 5 August 1958, Cardiss Robertson wed George Washington Collins. A World War Two veteran and a prison guard, he was a rising star in Democratic politics on Chicago's majority-black West Side. The couple's only child, Kevin, was born in 1959. While her mother took care of Kevin, Cardiss Collins continued to work outside the home, as the family needed her income. She served as committeewoman of the 24th Ward Regular Democratic Organization and assisted with her husband's successful campaigns for committeeman, alderman, and then, in 1970, U.S. Representative to the 7th District of Illinois. In Congress, he was known for his reserve and his advocacy for black military personnel.

On 8 December 1972, George Collins died with forty-four others in the crash of a United Airlines flight from Washington, D.C., as it approached Chicago's Midway Airport. Also killed were CBS-TV's Michelle Clark, one of the first African American women network correspondents, and Dorothy Hunt, wife of Watergate conspirator E. Howard Hunt. The crash was later determined to be from crew error and mechanical failure. Cardiss Collins, suddenly a widow and single parent, was overwhelmed with shock and grief.

Although she was reluctant at first, Chicago Mayor Richard J. Daley and others asked her to run for her husband's seat. With 92 percent of the vote, Cardiss Collins became the first African American woman to represent Illinois and indeed any state in the Midwest, and became only the fourth black woman to enter the U.S. House of Representatives, following SHIRLEY CHISHOLM (D-NY), BARBARA JORDAN (D-TX), and YVONNE BURKE (D-CA). Asian Pacific American Patsy Mink (D-HI) was the first woman of color elected to Congress. Collins's son, then in his early teens, hesitated to move away from his familiar surroundings. They agreed that he would stay in Chicago with his grandmother.

Between 5 June 1973 and 3 January 1997, starting with the 93rd Congress and continuing to the 104th, Cardiss Collins was readily elected a total of twelve times to represent the 7th District of Illinois. At first reserved and uncertain of Congressional procedures, she grew to be a more assertive leader and one who served her constituents' interests with increasing independence from the Chicago Democratic machine.

In her first term, Cardiss Collins was appointed to the Committee on Government Operations (later renamed Government Reform and Oversight). Serving on this committee throughout her time in office, Collins eventually chaired its Manpower and Housing as well as Government Activities and Transportation (GAT) subcommittees. While leading GAT, Collins advocated for better regulation of toxic material transport and air safety. Indictments followed her 1987 investigation of charges that Eastern Airlines willfully neglected plane safety equipment. She brought about higher participation of women- and minority-owned businesses in airport concessions as well as improvements in the national aviation security system.

Collins had stints on the International Relations (later Foreign Affairs) Committee (1975–1980) and the District of Columbia Committee (1977–1979). She was the second woman to chair the Congressional Black Caucus (1979–1981) and at one point was secretary of the Congressional Caucus on Women's Issues. She joined the Energy and Commerce (later Commerce) Committee (1981–1997) and became the first woman and first African American to chair its Commerce, Consumer Protection, and Competitiveness Subcommittee (1991–1995). By the 104th Congress (1995–1997), she was Ranking Democrat on the full committee, as well as the first woman and first African American to become a Democratic Whip-at-Large.

Cardiss Collins achieved numerous other milestones during her twenty-four years as a U.S. Representative. She called for funding cuts to federal agencies that did not comply with federal civil rights provisions (1985) and introduced the Non-Discrimination Act (1986) to boost minority opportunities in the advertising industry. During the 1990s, she authored a law that made screening mammography available to more women on Medicare and sponsored the Medicaid Infant Mortality Act. She helped to expand Medicaid coverage for PAP smears and infant mortality reduction and Medicare coverage for screening mammograms; tripled the number of child care centers for federal workers; started the Office of Minority Health in the National Institutes of Health; designated October as National Breast Cancer Awareness Month; and brought about the Family and Medical Leave and Child Safety Protection Acts. She was inducted into the Women's Sports Hall of Fame in 1994 for her promotion of women's college athletics.

Cardiss Collins retired from Congress in 1996 at age sixty-five, at first returning to Chicago, then moving back to Alexandria, Virginia. While enjoying more time with her son and granddaughter, Candice, she stayed in public service. She continued her memberships in Alexandria's Alfred Street Baptist Church, the NAACP, the Chicago Urban League, the National Council of Negro Women, the Black Women's Agenda, the Coalition of 100 Black Women, Alpha Kappa Alpha, and Alpha Gamma Phi. In 2004, Nielsen Media Research appointed Collins chair of a task force to ensure that people of color were fairly represented in the compilation of television ratings. As Rep. Marcy Kaptur (D-OH), noted, Cardiss Collins was remarkable among national politicians for her "lower working class origins" and her unshowy but diligent and productive commitment to underrepresented Americans (Kaptur, 183–193).

FURTHER READING

"Cardiss Collins," and "George Washington Collins." *Black Americans in Congress.* Available at http://baic.house.gov/.

"Cardiss Collins" and "George Washington Collins." *Biographical Directory of the United States Congress, 1774–Present.* Available at http://bioguide.congress.gov.

"Cardiss Collins." National Visionary Leadership Project. Available at http://www.visionaryproject.org/collinscardiss/.

Kaptur, Marcy. *Women in Congress: A Twentieth Century Odyssey.* Congressional Quarterly, 1996.

MARY KRANE DERR

Collins, George Washington (5 Mar. 1925–8 Dec. 1972), United States congressman, was born in the poor North Side Chicago neighborhood of what would later be known as Cabrini-Green to Washington and Leanna Collins. Collins graduated from Waller High School in 1943, and immediately entered the armed forces as a private. He served for three years in the army, stationed with the Engineer Corps in the South Pacific until he was discharged as a sergeant in 1946. Upon returning to the states, Collins entered Central Y.M.C.A. College in Chicago, and graduated in 1954, going on to receive his business law degree from Northwestern University three years later.

Collins began his career in civil service and involvement in the Chicago Democratic Party machine in the 1950s while still in graduate school. He was appointed precinct captain in 1954 for Chicago's 24th Ward on the West Side, and later served as deputy sheriff of Cook County from 1958 to 1961. In August 1958, his first year in the Sheriff Department, he married Cardiss Robertson, with whom he had a son, Kevin, the following year.

Along with being an administrative assistant at the Chicago Board of Health, Collins also became secretary to Alderman Benjamin Lewis of the 24th Ward, a district that had moved from Jewish to heavily black over the preceding years. When Lewis was mysteriously—and gruesomely—killed in his office, midterm in 1963, Collins succeeded him and remained alderman through the decade.

Another untimely death in office preceded Collins's next step in public service, when U.S. Congressman Daniel J. Ronan passed away during his third term in August 1969. Collins ran for the vacant seat, which comprised the largely African American West Side and two working-class white suburbs. With the influential power of the party machine and Mayor Richard J. Daley behind him, Collins won the runoff for the unexpired term. The following year, in the race for the full term, Collins easily defeated his primary opponent, Brenetta Howell, a social worker and community activist, and his Republican counterpart, a white engineer and steel executive, in the general election.

Though Collins's stay in Congress was short, he was an immediate advocate for legislation that would benefit poor urban residents, a sizable portion of his constituents. He stumped for a federal highway bill that would fund mass transit and aid the city's disenfranchised affected by road construction; introduced a bill requiring the Treasury Department to provide free tax preparation for low-income residents; and sought to reform the Federal Housing Administration after a panel on his Government Operations committee found that low-income homeowners had been defrauded by speculators and brokers.

Collins was one of nine Congressional Black Caucus members who toured military bases in the early 1970s to investigate allegations of racial discrimination.

When the findings of the 1970 census led to a court-ordered redistricting in Illinois, Collins's congressional seat was folded into another. His reelection in 1972 was doubtful; the popular former representative Frank Annunzio had entered the primary race against Collins for the seat in Chicago's new 7th district. Seeking to ease racial tension between the mayor's office and the African American leadership of the city, Daley threw his support behind Collins, and pressured Annunzio to run for a different seat, in the largely Polish American 11th district.

On 8 December 1972, just a month after his reelection victory, Collins was flying home from Washington, DC, to Chicago to oversee the purchasing of toys for thousands of children expected at his district's official Christmas party; just before Midway Airport, the plane crashed into four homes in the North Side, killing most of the people on board, including Collins.

A week later, his funeral at Greater Galilee Baptist Church gathered some of the rising black members of Congress and other political dignitaries, including JESSE JACKSON, CHARLES RANGEL, SHIRLEY CHISHOLM, Adlai Stevenson, and the future House Speaker Tip O'Neill. Daley, CBC chairman LOUIS STOKES, and RONALD DELLUMS were among the eulogizers.

His widow, CARDISS COLLINS, who had worked for twenty-four years as an auditor in the Illinois Revenue Department, received the backing of the 24th Ward, and entered and won the special election to fill her late husband's seat; she served in Congress until 1996. Chicago named a high school after Collins posthumously.

FURTHER READING
Hunt, Ridgley. "Blacks Bid Collins Emotional Farewell," Chicago Tribune, 15 Dec. 1972.

ADAM W. GREEN

Collins, Hannibal (c. 1800–?), a sailor during the War of 1812, fought in the Battle of Lake Erie with Commodore Oliver Hazard Perry. Little is known about Collins's personal life although it is possible he was born into slavery in Newport, Rhode Island, or the surrounding area. As of the 1790 Census there were still over nine hundred slaves in the state, which pursued a policy of gradual emancipation after 1784. Hannibal may have been a slave for less than a decade of his life, although this is not certain. The 1810 Federal Census does detail two white Collins families in Newport that either owned slaves or had black persons residing in their household; the entry for John Collins details just one person of color in his household, whereas that of Job Collins details seven. Although not specifically identified as such, these individuals may have been slaves. However, the same census details three free black families by the name of Collins that also resided in Newport, those of Vital and Dyer Collins, each with one additional member in their household, and, a more likely possibility, that of Selina Collins and the six other members of his (or her, as the gender of Selina is undetermined) household. The assertion by a Perry family historian that Hannibal Collins was freed from slavery prior to his service in the War of 1812 makes it all the more likely that he was a member of the Selina Collins household in 1810.

Like most of the details of his life, the military service of Hannibal Collins also lacks documentation and is based largely on oral history. Collins is alleged to have served under Commodore Perry on Lake Erie, making it likely that he was one of 150 men serving at Newport, Rhode Island, including African Americans such as NEWPORT HAZARD, who volunteered to accompany Perry when he was transferred to Erie, Pennsylvania, in March 1813 to take command of the newly formed Lake Erie squadron of vessels. Given his youth, Collins likely served as a ship's boy and may have even waited on Perry himself. The role of ship's boy in the sailing navy was well established, being filled by youths, both white and black, under the age of eighteen; it was their task to wait on a ship's officers in a servant capacity and act as messengers in noncombat situations, and, during times of action, to perform the dangerous task of a "powder monkey," carrying gunpowder from the ship's magazine to the various gun stations on a ship when they needed replenishment in the heat of battle. No matter what his position may have been, the service of Hannibal Collins is indicative of the overall role played by blacks in manning naval vessels during the war, comprising anywhere from 10 to 20 percent of a ship's complement. Because crew records for the War of 1812 are often missing or incomplete, the black contribution to the war effort has been seldom studied and has been largely forgotten.

Upon his arrival to the Great Lakes, Hannibal Collins was assigned to the twenty-gun brig *Lawrence*, the flagship of Perry's fleet, and it was on this ship that he took part in the decisive Battle of Lake Erie on 10 September 1813. Although Perry's fleet easily outgunned his British adversaries, the failure of the captain of his other twenty-gun brig, the *Niagara*, to join the battle left him and the men of the *Lawrence* to battle the enemy fleet with little support for the course of two hours. At a critical point in the battle, with many killed and wounded aboard his heavily damaged flagship, Perry decided to transfer his command to the *Niagara*, which lagged far behind and was yet to join in the fight. To do so, four of the men from the *Lawrence*, Newport natives William Taylor, the ship's sailing master, and Hannibal Collins among them, joined Perry in the ship's cutter and rowed him to the *Niagara*. This was a bold move and the cutter took heavy British fire, but Perry and his small crew managed to make it to the *Niagara* unscathed. With a new ship and a fresh crew, Commodore Perry sailed to join the battle once again and soon turned the tide toward victory. When the fighting was over at the end of the day, the enemy fleet had been captured and the British were thereby swept from control of Lake Erie and the vital surrounding territory; it was one of the most celebrated American victories of the War of 1812.

At an unknown time following the Battle of Lake Erie, Hannibal Collins returned to Newport and here he likely resided for the rest of his life. It may be that Collins earned a living after the war as a sailor or in a related maritime trade, and one can easily imagine the exciting stories he related of his service under Perry to the many sailors and stevedores employed on the docks of the city's bustling waterfront. However, after 1840 the records regarding Collins are silent and he disappears from history.

FURTHER READING

Altoff, Gerard T. *Amongst My Best Men: African-Americans and the War of 1812* (1996).

Copes, Jan M. "The Perry Family: A Newport Naval Dynasty of the Early Republic," *Newport History*, Vol. 66, Part Two, Fall 1994, No. 227.

GLENN ALLEN KNOBLOCK

Collins, Janet (2 Mar. 1917–28 May 2003), prima ballerina, modern dancer, choreographer, teacher, and painter, was born Janet Fay Collins in New Orleans, the daughter of Ernest Lee Collins, a tailor, and Alma de Lavallade (the noted dancer CARMEN DE LAVALLADE was a first cousin on this side of the family), a seamstress. At the age of four Collins moved to Los Angeles with her family, which included three sisters and one brother. In Los Angeles, Collins had trouble being accepted into "whites-only" dance studios, so she worked with private tutors. Her first formal ballet lessons were at a Catholic community center at the age of ten.

When she was fifteen Collins auditioned for the prestigious Ballet Russe de Monte Carlo led by the legendary Leonide Massine. Collins was accepted, but only on the condition that she stay in the corps

Janet Collins in 1951. (Library of Congress.)

de ballet and that she paint her face white to blend in with the other dancers. Heartbroken, Collins refused.

While still in high school Collins performed in vaudeville as an adagio dancer, a ballerina who usually dances with a male partner and focuses on balance and perfection of form. Then as now the field of dance was competitive, so she majored in art at Los Angeles City College, then transferred to the Los Angeles Art Center School on a scholarship. She continued to study ballet with Mia Slavenska, Adolph Bolm (who had once partnered Anna Pavlova), Carlotta Tamon, and Dorothy Lyndall. She studied Spanish dance with Carmelita Maracci and modern dance with Lester Horton. In 1940 Collins was principal dancer in the musicals *Run Little Chillun* and *The Mikado in Swing*, performed in Los Angeles. In the early 1940s she performed with the companies of KATHERINE DUNHAM and Horton. Her partner was Talley Beatty, with whom she toured in a nightclub act, *Rea and Rico Deguera*. They had to rehearse in dance studios early in the mornings because blacks were not allowed in during regular hours. In 1943 Collins performed with Dunham's dance company in the all-black film musical *Stormy Weather*. In 1945 Collins won a Julius Rosenwald Fellowship for $1,800, which made it possible for her to attend the San

Francisco School of Ballet. She also worked on her own choreography and in 1947 completed *Spirituals*, her most famous work. Collins was featured dancer in "Rendezvous in Rio," choreographed by Jack Cole, in the film *The Thrill of Brazil* (1946), but she continued to choreograph several dances on liturgical themes, honoring both her African American and French ancestries. She loved the music of Mozart and Bach. In 1947 she choreographed *Blackamoor, Eine Kleine Nachtmusik, Protest, Apres le Mardi Gras,* and *Spirituals*. On 3 November 1948 Collins gave a concert at the Las Palmas Theater in Los Angeles. Critics praised not only her "rare talent ... of reaching out to her audiences and making them share emotions that her characters are portraying" but also the costumes that she had designed herself (*Los Angeles Daily News*, 1948).

With hopes of greater financial success—she had been living on proceeds from her paintings—Collins arrived in New York City in 1949 with only two hundred dollars. Almost immediately she auditioned for a showcase of young dance artists at the YM-YWHA on Ninety-Second Street. Her dance, to a Mozart rondo, drew spontaneous enthusiastic applause. In May 1949 *Dance* magazine named her the "Most Outstanding Debutante of the Season." The dance critic John Martin of the *New York Times* described Collins's style as sharp and precise, establishing communicative contact with the audience with a "wonderful sense of aliveness ... the most exciting young dancer who has flashed across the current scene in a long time" (27 Feb. 1949). That same year she choreographed *Juba* and *Three Psalms*.

The choreographer Hanya Holm cast Collins in Cole Porter's musical *Out of This World*, which opened on Broadway on 2 December 1950. Collins's relatively small role of "Night" drew rave reviews from critics, who said that in the entire show she was the only one who was truly "out of this world" (*Saturday Evening Press*). Collins studied modern dance with Holm and ballet with Anthony Tudor and Margaret Craske. She received a merit award and was named "Young Woman of the Year" by *Mademoiselle* magazine in 1950. The following year she won the Donaldson Award for the best dancer on Broadway in the 1950–1951 season. She also choreographed *Moi J'Aime Toi, Chere*.

Collins's Broadway performances drew the attention of the ballet master of the Metropolitan Opera, Zachary Solov, who was choreographing a new production of Verdi's *Aida*. Her body "just speaks," he said and persuaded the Met management to hire her (Lewin, 69). With this position,

Collins made history as the Metropolitan Opera's first full-time African American prima ballerina with a regular contract as a member of the company. She electrified audiences as the Ethiopian slave in the dances during the Triumphal Scene in the second act of *Aida*, which premiered on 13 November 1951. Her success led to roles as a gypsy dancer in *Carmen*, as the Queen of the Night, on pointe, in "The Dance of the Hours" in *La Gioconda*, both in 1952, and as lead dancer in the bacchanal in *Samson et Dalila* in 1953.

Collins later recalled that she was treated well at the Met, was recognized for her talent, and had a dressing room on the first floor, where the other stars had theirs. She toured with the Met across the United States and in Canada but was not allowed to appear in the South on the same stage as white dancers. Even in Canada, Collins was refused entrance into a restaurant. When the Met was closed for vacation, Collins toured the country performing her own choreography under contract with Columbia Artists Management. To rest from all the touring and to find greater fulfillment, Collins resigned from the Met in 1954.

By 1957 Collins was teaching dance as rehabilitation for students at St. Joseph's School for the Deaf in the Bronx. Her innovative teaching methods derived from her belief in deaf children's innate gifts for pantomime; as dance was a "mute and living art form," it could be better adapted to the children's needs, rather than the other way around (Lewin, 70). In 1958 Collins joined the faculty of Marymount Manhattan College and the following year also joined the faculty of Manhattanville College of the Sacred Heart in Purchase, New York, both Roman Catholic institutions. A devout Catholic, Collins choreographed liturgical dances for her students. *Genesis*, for which Collins had commissioned music by Heitor Villa-Lobos, premiered at Marymount Manhattan College in 1965.

By 1970 Collins was living in California and teaching at Scripps College and the Mafundi Institute. She choreographed the dances in Verdi's *Nabucco* for the San Francisco Opera. In 1973 she choreographed *Song, Fire Weaver, Sunday and Sister James*, and *Birds of Peace and Pride*. Her *Canticle of the Elements* premiered in New York in 1974, performed by the Alvin Ailey Dance Company. That year Collins moved to Seattle to be near her sisters and to concentrate on painting pictures of religious subjects from the New Testament.

Periods of ill health in the late 1990s prompted Collins to move to Arlington, Texas, to be near her brother and sister-in-law in Fort Worth. She continued to paint and read the Bible and served on the board of Ballet Arlington. It is likely that she never married (though some sources state she was once briefly married), and she had no children. She died in Fort Worth at the age of eighty-six.

Collins left a rich legacy of inspiration for African Americans in the rarefied worlds of ballet and modern dance. The dancer and painter Geoffrey Holder said, "She gave everybody hope" (*New York Times*, 31 May 2003). Arthur Mitchell, founder of the Dance Theater of Harlem, was inspired by Collins's example and became premier danseur with the New York City Ballet. Collins's cousin Carmen de Lavallade was awed by Collins and inherited her dancing role in *Aida*. By believing that "dancing is not about self, but about seeking and communicating fundamental truths," Collins succeeded in overcoming racial barriers to bring the beauty and joy of dance to all (*Fort Worth Star-Telegram*, 9 Oct. 2000).

FURTHER READING

Janet Collins's archives are in the New York Public Library Dance Collection in the Performing Arts Library at Lincoln Center.

Lewin, Yael. "Janet Collins: A Spirit That Knows No Bounds," *Dance* (Feb. 1997).

Milligan, Jessie. "Led by Artistic Passion, Janet Collins Broke the Color Barrier in Dance," *Fort Worth Star-Telegram* (9 Oct. 2000).

Obituary: *New York Times*, 31 May 2003.

THERESE DUZINKIEWICZ BAKER

Collins, Julia C. (?–25 Nov. 1865), novelist, essayist, and teacher, was the married name of an African American woman whose maiden name and place and date of birth are unknown. Collins is best known for her novel *The Curse of Caste; or the Slave Bride*, which was originally serialized in the *Christian Recorder*, the weekly newspaper of the African Methodist Episcopal (AME) Church, between February and September 1865. Some scholars regard *The Curse of Caste* as the first non-autobiographical novel written by an African American woman to appear in print.

Nothing is known of Collins's life before April 1864, when a letter to the *Christian Recorder* mentioned that she was to serve as schoolteacher for the African American children in the small north-central Pennsylvania city of Williamsport. The same issue of the newspaper also printed

Collins's first known published work, a nonfiction essay titled "Mental Improvement." By January 1865 she had published five additional essays in the newspaper: "School Teaching," "Intelligent Women," "Originality of Ideas," "Life Is Earnest," and "Memory and Imagination." All of the essays are rather didactic and deal to some degree with self-improvement. While most of the essays' recommendations might apply to either black or white audiences, some of Collins's language, as well as the venue in which she chose to publish, clearly indicate her commitment to reaching members of her own community with a message of racial uplift and empowerment. The AME Church was at the time the largest and most influential black organization in the United States, and the *Christian Recorder* was one of only a few black newspapers with a wide national distribution, so Collins must have realized that she would reach large numbers of black readers.

Collins's personal life remains shrouded in mystery. Although she published in an AME newspaper Collins only became a church member on her deathbed. It is not known whether she had previously affiliated with another denomination. Her husband, variously identified as Stephen C. Collins or Simon C. Collins, was an African American barber who served in the Sixth Infantry Regiment of the United States Colored Troops during the Civil War. Barbering and schoolteaching were among the higher-status occupations available to African Americans in the nineteenth century, suggesting that the Collinses were well connected and well respected within Williamsport's small African American community. Julia's writing and Stephen/Simon's later involvement with local and regional black civic organizations lend credence to that conclusion. They appear to have had at least one child together, Emma or Annie Collins, who was born around 1862 and was buried in Williamsport after her death in 1889. Since Stephen/Simon had been married previously, it remains unclear whether another daughter, Sadie Collins, born around 1858, was Julia's or not. While Stephen/Simon seems to have lived in Williamsport as early as 1850 and remained in the area into the 1880s, no records indicate how long Julia may have lived there before April 1864 or where else she may have resided. For some time between June 1864 and January 1865 Julia may have been a resident of Oswego or Owego, New York, but she returned to Williamsport by February 1865 and appears to have remained there until her death.

The first chapter of her pioneering novel, *The Curse of Caste*, appeared on 25 February 1865, about one month after the publication of her final nonfiction essay. The novel is a melodramatic work set in the mid-nineteenth-century United States. Through the lives and experiences of a very light-skinned, mixed-race mother and daughter, *The Curse of Caste* addresses themes of hidden African ancestry, interracial romance and marriage, and the injustices of American slavery and racism. The thirty-first and final published chapter clearly was leading readers toward the climax and resolution of the plot, but readers were denied the conclusion of the novel by Collins's death from tuberculosis.

FURTHER READING

Collins, Julia C. *The Curse of Caste; or the Slave Bride: A Rediscovered African American Novel*, ed. William L. Andrews and Mitch Kachun (2006).

MITCH KACHUN

Collins, Kathleen (18 Mar. 1942–18 Sept. 1988), playwright, screenwriter, novelist, filmmaker, educator, was born Kathleen Conwell in Jersey City, New Jersey, daughter of Frank and Loretta Conwell. Her father was employed as a mortician prior to being appointed as the principal of a New Jersey school. Conwell attended Skidmore College in Sarasota Springs, New York, where in 1963 she earned a Bachelor of Arts degree in Philosophy and Religion. Upon graduating from college she became active with the Student Nonviolent Coordinating Committee's (SNCC) initiative to advance voter registration in the South, where African Americans had been historically discouraged from voting. Conwell attended graduate school in Paris, France, where in 1966 she earned an M.A. in French Literature and Cinema through the Middlebury College program at the Sorbonne.

Upon completing her graduate studies in Paris, Conwell returned to New York, where she had attended college and promptly began working as a member of the editorial and production staff at WNET Radio, a public broadcasting service station. Recounting her tenure in France, life as a young wife, and her experiences with SNCC, Conwell began to compose stories and scripts. In 1974, her marriage to Douglas Collins ended in divorce, yet it marked the beginning of another stage in her life and career. The newly divorced Collins became a professor of film history and screenwriting at the City University of New York and, prompted by student, resumed work on a script adapted from the fiction of the Jewish writer Henry H. Roth. In 1980, her completed film adaptation was entitled *The Cruz Brothers and Mrs. Malloy*, which won first prize in the Sinking Creek Independent Film Festival (now known as the Nashville Film Festival). This project established Collins as the first African American woman to write, direct, and produce a full-length feature film. Later, Collins won first prize at the 1982 Figueira da Foz International Film Festival in Portugal for *Losing Ground*, a comedy about the marital challenges experienced by a young African American couple; the script is included in *Screenplays of the African American Experience* (2008), edited by Phyllis Rauch Klotman. In addition to the acclaim she received at film festivals around the world, Collins's films have also appeared on The Learning Channel and the Public Broadcasting Station.

Meanwhile, Collins was also busy producing plays. She cited LORRAINE HANSBERRY as an inspiration for her work. In 1981, she produced *In the Midnight Hour*, about an African American middle-class family at the onset of the civil rights movement. *The Brothers* (1982), garnered national and international attention for Collins; it was selected as one of the twelve outstanding plays of the season by the Theater Communications Group, one of the best plays of the year by the AUDELCO Awards Committee, as a finalist for the Susan Blackburn International Prize in Playwriting, and was published in Margaret B. Wilkerson's *Nine Plays by Black Women* in 1986. In 1984, The American Place Theater commissioned *The Reading*, a one-act play in which Collins explores the conflicts between African American and white women. The following year she composed *Begin the Beguine*, a collection of one-act plays, at the Richard Allen Center for Culture and the Arts in New York. Also in 1985, Collins penned a play about Bessie Coleman, the first African American female aviator, entitled *Only the Sky Is Free*, and in 1986 she wrote *While Older Men Speak*. Collins presented a black female perspective on issues of family and adversity; furthermore, her work sought to examine and expose the humanity in each character.

Collins was married in 1987 to Alfred E. Prettyman, whom she had originally met in 1983. The couple had been wedded only one week when Collins learned she had cancer. On Sunday, 18 September 1988, at the age of forty-six, Collins died at Memorial Hospital in New York. Her memorial service was held at the internationally renowned Riverside Church, where Dr. MARTIN LUTHER KING JR., Nelson Mandela, and Fidel Castro have been guest speakers. Collins had one daughter, Nina; two sons, Asa Hale and Emilio; one stepdaughter, Meryl Prettyman; and one stepson, Evan Prettyman. In 1988 Collins completed the final draft of her first novel entitled *Lollie: A Suburban Tale*, her sixth stage play, *Waiting for Jane*, and by the summer she had completed a new screenplay, *Conversations with Julie*, which explores the topic of a mother and daughter coming to terms with separation.

FURTHER READING

Klotman, Phyllis. *Screenplays of African American Experience* (2008).

Mountain, Chandra Tyler. "Kathleen Conwell Collins," in Yolanda Williams Page, ed., *Encyclopedia of African American Women Writers* (2007).

Obituary: *New York Times*, 24 Sept. 1988.

SAFIYA DALILAH HOSKINS

Collins, Marva Delores (31 Aug. 1936–), teacher, educator, and entrepreneur, was born Marva Delores Nettles in Monroeville, Alabama, the daughter of Henry Knight Jr., an entrepreneur, and Bessie Maye Knight Nettles, a housewife. A child of the Depression and segregated schools, Collins recalls the talk of grown-ups about "how times were hard and there was no money" (Collins and Tamarkin, 32), but she remembered that the Depression had little impact on her childhood.

Her father was one of the "richest black men in Monroeville" (Collins and Tamarkin, 32). Their house was one of the "finest" in the black section of Monroeville with "polished wood floors" and "store-bought furniture." Her mother dressed her "like a doll in ruffled, ribboned dresses and crisply pleated store-bought school dresses tied in back with an ironed sash." Her classmates for the most part wore homemade clothes from empty twenty-five pound flour sacks that came from her father's grocery store (Collins and Tamarkin, 32).

Her father was the strongest influence in her life until her parents separated when Collins was twelve. At that time he remained in Monroeville while Collins and her mother moved to Atmore, Alabama, where her mother remarried and had another daughter, Cynthia (Collins and Tamarkin, 38).

Her paternal grandparents remained an essential part of her life. It was her Grandma Knight who quoted proverbs to her as a child, the same proverbs she used with students she taught. Her mother's sister introduced Collins to Shakespeare's

Macbeth, a work Collins taught to elementary-age students at her school. Two teachers at her elementary school influenced the way she related to her students. Her first grade teacher rapped her fingers with a ruler when she made a mistake. Her fourth grade teacher, whom Collins described as "a patient, good teacher" (Collins and Tamarkin, 45), had students work at the blackboard so mistakes could be corrected immediately. The "rapper" convinced Collins to praise her students' efforts rather than punish their mistakes, and the other convinced Collins that students needed immediate feedback for their schoolwork. These became part of Collins's methodology for teaching.

Her tenth grade teacher influenced her respect and demand for proper speech, pronunciation, and grammar, which also became a mainstay of Collins's methodology. Collins graduated first from Escambia County Training School and then in 1957 from Clark College (now Clark Atlanta University) in Atlanta, where she majored in secretarial sciences.

"If you went to college in Alabama, you were a celebrity. The minister had you stand in church and all the people would give you a quarter or fifty cents, what they could. You didn't get into trouble because in your mind's eye you could see all those people caring about you, depending on you" (Lankin, 75).

She taught typing, shorthand, bookkeeping, and business law for two years at the Monroe County Training School in Monroeville, Alabama. In 1959 she moved to Chicago and got a job as a medical secretary at Mt. Sinai Hospital. She met Clarence Collins, a draftsman, and they married on 4 September 1960. The couple had three children, Eric (1962), Patrick (1965), and Cynthia Beth (1968).

From 1960 to 1975 Collins served as an elementary school teacher starting as a substitute, but spending most of her years at Delano Elementary School in Chicago's West Side Garfield Park area, teaching students who had been labeled as having learning disabilities or behavioral problems.

Through the years, Collins found herself becoming frustrated with the system, its curriculum, and her teaching colleagues. She mixed classical and progressive methodologies, teaching phonics and using classics such as *Aesop's Fables*, *Grimm's Fairy Tales*, and Shakespeare's *Macbeth* rather than the prescribed sight-readers.

Such obstinacy did not gain Collins any friends with her teaching colleagues, and by the beginning of the 1974 school year Collins had decided to focus solely on her students and teaching her way. By the end of the year, Collins had decided she could no longer work in public education. That summer a group of women interested in establishing a private elementary school in the Garfield Park area approached Collins about being its director. The president of a community college on the West Side agreed to let them use a basement classroom, rent free, and provided typewriters and mimeograph machines. Further assistance from the Alternative Schools Network allowed the Daniel Hale Williams Westside Preparatory School to open on 8 September 1975 with four students, including Collins's daughter Cynthia, and a monthly tuition of $60 (Collins and Tamarkin, 80).

By January the student enrollment had tripled, and Collins found herself teaching in a one-room schoolhouse. By the end of the school year, Collins had decided to move the school out of the community college and become truly independent. Her supportive husband remodeled the upstairs apartment in their two-flat home using the $5,000 she had taken from her pension fund. Desks and materials came from loans and donations. In September 1976 Westside Preparatory opened in Collins' home with eighteen students (Collins and Tamarkin, 130).

As Collins began receiving publicity from local media outlets such as *The Chicago Sun Times*, *The Chicago Defender*, and local television programs the school gained more attention and requests from additional students, but was at capacity at the Collins home. In 1979, *60 Minutes* did a segment on the school, which resulted in a financial bonanza. More than $50,000 came in from donations, and a movie production company paid $75,000 for the rights to her story. The money allowed Collins to move Westside Prep to the second floor of an essentially vacant old bank building. In September 1980 the school opened with two hundred students and a waiting list of more than five hundred. By this time Collins was also securing funds through speaking engagements and seminars, but tuition remained the most reliable source of income for the school. Parents formed an association to deal with fundraising and delinquent tuition.

Collins had also hired and trained three additional teachers. The 1980–1981 year proved to be a transition for Collins. A student body of two hundred meant complexity, which meant Collins had to accept administrative duties she didn't want.

She saw herself as a teacher, not as a principal, but administrative decisions needed to be made, and Collins was the only one who could make them. Many of her decisions were not popular. Teachers who refused to follow her methodology were fired. Parents who could but wouldn't pay their children's tuition found their children dismissed from the school.

In September 1981 Westside Preparatory School moved into its own permanent facilities, two adjoining buildings on the outskirts of Garfield Park. The television movie *The Marva Collins Story* starring CICELY TYSON and MORGAN FREEMAN debuted. By 1990 Collins had worked with a parent group in Cincinnati, Ohio, and a Marva Collins Prep school had opened. In 1991 the Sate of Oklahoma hired Collins to design a teacher-training program. Collins eventually named her daughter headmistress of Westside Prep as she became more involved in training and seminar activities.

In 2004 Collins was awarded the National Humanities Award by President George W. Bush. In June 2008 Cynthia Collins announced that Westside Preparatory would be closing due to the economic downturn. Tuition was $550 a month and enrollment was down to twenty-eight students. It was planned for the school to reopen at a later date and to continue offering online material for home-schooling; however, Cynthia Collins died shortly after the school closed.

FURTHER READING

Collins, Marva, and Ciia Tamarkin. *Marva Collins' Way* (1990).

Hine, Darlene Clark, ed. *Black Women in American: An Historic Encyclopedia Vol. 1* (1993).

Lankin, Brian. *I Dream a World* (1989).

Mallegg, Kristin B., ed. *Who's Who among African Americans* (2010).

Paarham, Marti. "Marva Collins School to Close." *Jet*, June 2008.

Kinnon, Jay Bennett. "Marva Collins: The Collins Creed." *Ebony*, December 1996.

CLARANNE PERKINS

Collins, Newton Isaac, Sr. (1826–1907), former slave and landowner in central Texas at a time when few southern blacks owned land, was born a slave in Birmingham, Alabama, in 1826. The literate son of a slave mother and an Irish slaveholder father, Collins was freed in Alabama and traveled to Manor, Texas, in the mid-1800s as a skilled carpenter.

At the time he left Alabama, Collins was likely one of an estimated 500,000 free blacks in the United States in the decade before the Civil War. Free blacks were never a large population in Texas; in the 1860 census they numbered fewer than 400 but may have been twice that many. Free blacks, nevertheless, made a significant contribution to the early history of Texas. When Collins arrived in Manor, Texas, in 1863, however, he was reenslaved.

He may have married his wife, Sarah Elizabeth Harrington, at a Methodist church in the Austin area before he was emancipated again after the Civil War.

Collins became one of the 25 percent of African Americans in Texas who owned land in the postwar period. "Literacy rose dramatically through the late nineteenth century" in Texas, "notably in cities and towns, where black schools, though segregated, helped provide African Americans with the skills they needed. … However, most African Americans in Texas remained in rural areas as sharecroppers or tenant farmers, mired in poverty and peonage. Impoverished, lacking access to decent schools, and facing a deteriorating racial situation, their daily lives hardly seemed to improve with the end of slavery" (Wintz, 2006). Determined not to be swept up in the strife that affected other African American Texans, in 1872 Collins purchased a homesteaded tract of 92.5 acres of land situated in Austin's Mueller Development from an heir of Henry Warnell, a survivor of the Battle of the Alamo.

It's unclear how he held on to the $1,800 in gold coins that he'd brought with him to Texas or if it was the same money that he'd saved and arrived with in 1863. But that amount of money bought the land. He later flourished as a construction business owner, and he traded in some of that property in 1891 to buy 506 acres of farmland in Pilot Knob, near what is now McKinney Falls State Park in Travis County. That land sits near the intersection of U.S. Highway 183 and Farm Road 812, eight miles southeast of Austin in southern Travis County. Pilot Knob was named for the remains of a volcano and was settled by families like Collins's, who moved to Texas after the Civil War. In 1907, the Pilot Knob school had two teachers and ninety-nine students. In the 1940s, one church and a few houses marked the community.

A road where the community once sat is currently named for Dee Gabriel Collins, the youngest of the seven children born to Newton Collins and his wife. Collins deeded about seventy-two acres to each of his children and helped each one of them build a home. He sent for his sister and her sons in Alabama. But within a year or two, his sister died, and he raised his two nephews along with his own children.

At a time when black teachers were not hired with state funds, Collins built a school and a church for blacks and hired a teacher and a preacher. His legacy of perseverance and self-determination trickled down to his progeny. Dee Gabriel Collins was the grandfather of ADA C. ANDERSON, the grand dame of Austin's African American community and a local cultural arts doyenne. Anderson founded an educational program in the arts and helped to integrate the city's recreational facilities in the 1960s.

In 2009 Anderson discovered maps that showed Collins's ownership of land that she grew up playing on as a child. Part of that land now houses the Austin Children's Shelter, and in February 2010 a stretch of greenbelt was dedicated to Collins in honor of his contribution to Austin's local education and religious community.

FURTHER READING

Barnes, L. Diane. "Free African Americans before the Civil War (South)." In *Encyclopedia of African American History, 1619–1895: From the Colonial Period to the Age of Frederick Douglass*, ed. Paul Finkelman (2006).

Wintz, Cary D. "Texas." *Encyclopedia of African American History, 1619–1895: From the Colonial Period to the Age of Frederick Douglass*, ed. Paul Finkelman (2006).

JOSHUNDA SANDERS

Collins, Sam "Crying" (11 Aug. 1887–20 Oct. 1949), blues musician, was born in Louisiana, and raised in McComb, Mississippi, fifteen miles north of the Louisiana border. While familial and personal details of Collins's life remain sparse, he has achieved an affirmed place in the cannon of American blues singers.

Collins's hometown lies beyond the Mississippi Delta, the region famed for giving rise to legendary blues artists such as ROBERT JOHNSON. Yet the notion that the Delta was the only area rich in blues talent is a mythological one. In reality, much of Mississippi proved fertile ground for gifted blues performers.

Collins is best known for his unique vocalization, characterized by a rich, emotive, somewhat feminine timbre, often described as "falsetto." In songs like the mournful "Jailhouse Blues," he calls

to mind female singers of the era such as BESSIE SMITH. Clearly, Collins's keening, plaintive style is attributable to the appellation "Crying Sam."

Compositional innovation was not the hallmark of Collins's career. His repertoire consisted of standard blues songs such as "Hesitation Blues," as well as other commonly known gospel, folk, pop, and hokum numbers. On renditions like "It Won't Be Long," Collins did little to alter his rhythmic delivery from that of the gospel song book in which the song first appeared.

Collins recorded a version of the prison folk song "Midnight Special," releasing "The Midnight Special Blues" in 1929, five years prior to Lead Belly's immortalized recording. Again, Collins maintains a traditional treatment of the song, similar to one recorded by country artist Dave "Pistol Pete" Cutrell in 1926. However, Collins's version does contain one notable detail: his is the first to name the woman in the narrative "Little Nora."

Collins's guitar technique was generally simplistic, sometimes consisting of a single string method. At other times he used a bottleneck or knife, conjuring a discordant, untuned effect. Yet, it is likely that the lack of tuning was a deliberate, stylistic gesture. Although Collins was not a blues innovator comparable to Charley Patton, his rare, "haunting" lyricism and impassioned, though ingenuous, unison accompaniment on guitar, defines his signature style.

In the long decades between Reconstruction and Civil Rights, Mississippi was steeped in an exacting system of social and economic apartheid, by which the white minority (within the state) dominated. Employment options for black men generally consisted of hard manual labor, or the certain financial quagmire of sharecropping. Thus, a migratory pattern emerged, with many black men adopting a transitory lifestyle in order to search for better opportunities. Musicians of the day were not inured to these realities. Thus, the romanticized figure of the wandering or "rambling" blues man emerged, and by 1924 Collins was among those who traveled the region, performing in juke joints and barrelhouses. What, if any, other occupation he may have undertaken to supplement this activity is unclear.

Collins made his first recording of the song "Jail house Blues" in 1927. Varying sources list his initial label as Gennett, others as Black Patti. Black Patti contracted their discs through Gennett, as the company had no recording facilities of its own; thus, it is likely that both labels released copies of

"Jail House Blues" that year. A July 2, 1927 Black Patti ad for the record in the Chicago Defender announces: "Here he is, Crying Sam Collins and his Git-Fiddle … Sam cries and weeps out loud, does he make his old Git-Fiddle weep and moan 'And how!'" Collins made additional recordings for ARC in 1931.

Despite putting fifty titles on wax during a period of more than four years, only nineteen of Collins's songs were actually released. Many of the same songs were issued simultaneously by various labels, forcing Collins to adopt numerous pseudonyms to give the appearance of being a different performer for each one. His most commonly known alias was "Jim Foster," the name he recorded under for Champion and Silvertone. For Banner, Oriole, Perfect, and Romeo records he became "Salty Dog Sam," for the Bell label he was "Big Boy Woods," and for Conqueror music he recorded as "Bunny Carter."

King Solomon Hill (Joe Holmes) also hailed from McComb. He and Collins often performed together, and they, along with a third musician, Willard Thomas, were mutually influential of one another's styles. Both Collins and Hill sang in an upper register and played bottleneck (slide) guitar. In fact, the two men sounded so similar on certain recordings, that it was rumored that "King Solomon Hill" was simply another of Collins's pseudonyms. However, close examination of their guitar playing shows significant technical differences, and this along with differing dates and locations of death, suffice to disprove the myth.

Toward the end of the 1920s the once furious sale of race records met a sharp decline. Sam Collins migrated to Chicago in the late 1930s, died there of heart disease, and was buried in Worth, Illinois. Though Collins has not gained a gilded place in blues history, his extensive recordings remain important. Given the fact that so "little is known about his life," (Charters, 122) these recordings help solidify Collins's legacy, as all traces of his existence might have been lost without them.

FURTHER READING

Charters, Samuel B. *The Blues Makers* (1977).
Komara, Edward M. *Encyclopedia of the Blues* (2006).
Leonard, Hal (Jim O'Neal). *All Music Guide to the Blues: The Definitive Guide to the Blues*, Book Beat, Edition 3 (2003).
Oakley, Giles. *The Devil's Music: A History of the Blues* (1976).
Oliver, Paul. *The Story of the Blues* (1998).

DISCOGRAPHY

Crying Sam Collins and His Git-Fiddle: Jailhouse Blues (Yazoo records #1079).
Wirz, Stefan. *Sam Collins Discography*. Available at http://wirz.de/music/collifrm.htm.

CAMILLE A. COLLINS

Coltrane, Alice McLeod (27 Aug. 1937–12 Jan. 2007), keyboardist, harpist, and composer, was born Alice McLeod in Detroit, Michigan, the daughter of Solon and Anne McLeod, and grew up in a musically oriented family. Her brother, Ernie Farrow, played bass in the jazz groups of Terry Gibbs, Stan Getz, and YUSEF LATEEF. Beginning piano at the age of seven and studying classical music, Alice later attended Cass Technical High School in Detroit and played piano in church. Her achievements led to a scholarship to the Detroit Institute of Technology. Her most important influences in classical music during this time were the works of Beethoven, Rachmaninoff, Stravinsky, and Tchaikovsky. Eventually Alice followed her brother into jazz and became a bebop pianist for musicians such as KENNY BURRELL and Lateef, eventually traveling to Europe to study with BUD POWELL in 1959. She moved to New York in the early 1960s. During a stint as a sideperson for Gibbs in 1962–1963, she met JOHN COLTRANE. She and Coltrane married in 1965, and they had three sons. Alice also had a daughter from a previous relationship.

In 1966 Alice Coltrane replaced McCOY TYNER in John Coltrane's band, bringing her characteristic "rhythmically ambiguous arpeggios and … pulsing thickness of texture" to the group (Chris Kelsey, Scott Yanow, and Thom Jurek, online *All Music Guide*). Influenced by her predecessor's modal piano style, Alice also followed the advice of her husband, who encouraged her to unlock her playing potential: "Branch out, open up, play your instrument. You have a whole left register—use it. You have an upper register—use it. Play your instrument entirely" (Rivelli, 123). After John's death in 1967, Alice added the harp and the Wurlitzer organ to her repertoire, forming her own group and leading recording sessions. From this foundation Alice Coltrane created a distinctive and immediately recognizable sound throughout the next thirty years that transcended both jazz and her earlier training in classical music while incorporating her childhood African American gospel background and her later Eastern mysticism.

Using members from her husband's group—including PHAROAH SANDERS (reeds), Jimmy

Garrison (bass), RASHIED ALI (drums), and Ben Riley (drums)—Alice recorded *A Monastic Trio* for Impulse! Records in 1968. A year later she released *Huntington Ashram Monastery* (also on Impulse!) with the bassist Ron Carter and the drummer Ali. With her two 1970 albums *Ptah, the El Daoud* and *Journey in Satchidananda*, Coltrane came to be regarded as a strong performer and composer well outside her husband's shadow. These albums also saw an increased shift toward Eastern influences, especially with the album and song titles as well as the use of the tamboura and oud, common Middle Eastern instruments. Both records peaked at number thirteen on the Billboard Jazz Album charts in 1971, anticipating her classic album *Universal Consciousness*.

Recorded in the spring of 1971, *Universal Consciousness* blended Coltrane's interest in spirituality with improvised and composed soundscapes that fused her early classical training—notably Stravinsky—with her jazz background, producing a work of art with the deeply functional purpose stated in its title. Written by Coltrane, the liner notes explain how in her journey to the East she had completed her "Sadhana" (spiritual struggle) and explored cities and temples in India and Ceylon. Thus the album becomes a window into the spiritual envelopment that she underwent in her travels to Asia. In what the critic Thom Jurek labeled as "breathtaking," the opening title track sets Coltrane's harp and organ playing against a backdrop of Jack DeJohnette's drumming, Garrison's bass, and the work of the violinists John Blair, Leroy Jenkins, Julius Brand, and Joan Kalisch. The string players were chosen because of their association with jazz and were characterized by Coltrane as sounding like "a symphony of celestial strings" (Coltrane, *Universal Consciousness* liner notes). String arrangement-transcriptions were done by the composer/saxophonist ORNETTE COLEMAN. The opening track presents the beginning of the journey, a cleansing where the "soul must pass before it finally reaches that exalted state of Absolute Consciousness" (Coltrane, *Universal Consciousness* liner notes). The second and sixth tracks are Coltrane and Ali duets. Finally, on "Sita Ram," Coltrane employs Clifford Jarvis on drums and uses Tulsi on tamboura. The popular reach of this album is illustrated with its peak position of nine on Billboard's Jazz Albums charts and 190 on the Pop Albums charts.

Recorded later that year, *World Galaxy* continued in the direction set forth by *Universal Consciousness*, what Jurek labeled "spiritual jazz" (online *All Music Guide*). Coltrane chose the bassist Reggie Workman, the violinist Jenkins, the timpanist Elayne Jones, the saxophonist Frank Lowe, and the drummer Riley as well as a string orchestra. She recorded John Coltrane standards for the opening and closing tracks, "My Favorite Things" (Oscar Hammerstein and Richard Rodgers) and his classic "A Love Supreme." The latter track continued in the spiritual direction of its author John Coltrane with a spoken word poem by Alice Coltrane's guru Satchidananda.

After 1973's *Lord of Lords*, which reached number nine on the Billboard Jazz Albums charts, Coltrane recorded a jazz-fusion record with the rock guitarist Carlos Santana. *Illuminations* appeared at number thirty-three on Billboard's Black Albums charts, fifteen on Jazz Albums, and seventy-nine on Pop Albums. She finished the 1970s with *Eternity* (1975), the spiritually charged *Radha-Krisna Nama Sankirtana* (1976), and the live recording *Transfiguration* (1978). After a few sporadic performances in the 1980s, Coltrane began performing again in the late 1990s and released the critically acclaimed *Translinear Light* in 2004 on Impulse!. That album reached number ten on Top Jazz Albums in *Billboard*. Produced by her son Ravi, the record included past collaborators such as DeJohnette and Charlie Haden and featured Coltrane on piano, organ, and synthesizer. Set upon releasing *Sacred Language of Ascension* in 2007, Coltrane unfortunately passed away on 12 January 2007, leaving a rich musical legacy.

FURTHER READING

Coltrane, Alice. *Universal Consciousness*; liner notes (1971).

Dahl, Linda. *Stormy Weather: The Music and Lives of a Century of Jazzwomen* (1984).

Kahn, Ashley. *The House That Trane Built: The Story of Impulse Records* (2006).

Kelsey, Chris, Scott Yanow, and Thom Jurek. Available *All Music Guide*, http://www.allmusicguide.com/cg/amg.dll?p=amg&sql=11:avfwxqr5ldse~T1.

Rivelli, Pauline. "Alice Coltrane—Interview by Pauline Rivelli," in *Giants of Black Music*, ed. Pauline Rivelli and Robert Levin (1980).

Wilmer, Valerie. *As Serious as Your Life: John Coltrane and Beyond* (1977).

DANIEL ROBERT MCCLURE

Coltrane, John William (23 Sept. 1926–17 July 1967), musician, composer, and bandleader, was born in Hamlet, North Carolina, the son of John Robert Coltrane, a tailor and amateur musician, and Alice

John William Coltrane in 1964. (AP Images.)

Gertrude Blair. A few months after John's birth, the Coltranes moved to nearby High Point to live with his maternal grandfather, the Reverend William Blair. Alice, who had studied music at Livingstone College, accompanied her father's choir on piano. The young Coltrane grew up in a secure middle-class environment in which both religion and music were highly valued. At age twelve he began studying alto horn, then the clarinet, and joined the High Point Community Band. From the outset, Coltrane practiced constantly, a pattern that he sustained throughout his life. By 1942 he was playing clarinet and alto saxophone in his high school band.

After graduating from high school in 1943, Coltrane moved to Philadelphia, Pennsylvania, where he worked as a laborer in a sugar-refining factory and studied saxophone at the Ornstein School of Music. He made his professional debut in 1945, and in August of that year was drafted into the U.S. Navy. He was posted to Hawaii, where he played clarinet in naval marching and dance bands. Discharged in 1946, Coltrane returned to Philadelphia, resumed his studies at the Ornstein School, and made a living playing saxophone in rhythm-and-blues bands. This was the beginning of a long and thorough musical apprenticeship.

Coltrane developed his distinctive style in a variety of musical contexts. In 1947 and 1948 he toured with the jazz-influenced rhythm and blues group of Eddie "Cleanhead" Vinson, playing tenor saxophone for the first time. In 1949 he joined the influential DIZZY GILLESPIE Big Band and stayed with Gillespie when the band was reduced to a sextet. Coltrane made his recording debut with Gillespie in 1950. In 1952 and 1953 Coltrane was back on the rhythm and blues circuit with EARL BOSTIC, and in 1953 he joined the JOHNNY HODGES band. By 1955 Coltrane had developed an identifiable style that combined technical virtuosity with a unique tone. His potential was recognized by the trumpeter MILES DAVIS, who invited the saxophonist to join his quintet in 1955. This band was one of the key jazz groups of the mid 1950s and joining it transformed Coltrane's career. The quintet toured widely and recorded frequently, and the consequent exposure enhanced his reputation. Within a week of joining Davis in the autumn of 1955, Coltrane married Naima Austin, becoming stepfather to her daughter, Syeeda. By March 1957, Coltrane's alcohol abuse and heroin addiction had so affected his reliability that Davis dismissed him as a permanent member of the group, but Coltrane continued playing intermittently with Davis until 1960. In the ensuing nine months Coltrane rid himself of his addictions and completed his musical apprenticeship with a lengthy residency at the Five Spot Café in New York as part of the THELONIOUS MONK Quartet. Monk pushed Coltrane to the limit of his creativity. His lengthy solos were characterized by a persistent, relentless, rapid-fire outpouring of notes, to which the description "sheets of sound" would subsequently be applied. Coltrane's music was evolving rapidly. At the end of his gig with Monk, he rejoined Miles Davis as part of a sextet that included CANNONBALL ADDERLEY. This group recorded two seminal albums, *Milestones* (1958) and, with Bill Evans in the band, the more subtle and atmospheric *Kind of Blue* (1959).

By early 1960 it was clearly time for Coltrane to leave Davis and form his own band. Coltrane had been recording prolifically under his own name since the mid-1950s, initially for Prestige and then for the much more influential Atlantic label. Important albums like *Giant Steps*, recorded in 1959 and consisting entirely of Coltrane compositions, and *Coltrane Jazz*, recorded later that same year, further enhanced his reputation, raised his profile, and prepared the way for the launch of his solo career. The John Coltrane Quartet was formed as a permanent unit in April 1960.

The personnel of the band fluctuated during 1960, but when the pianist McCoy Tyner and the drummer Elvin Jones joined the group, Coltrane had the nucleus of the classic quartet that would be at the heart of his musical existence for the next five years. The bassist Jimmy Garrison joined in 1961, the same year in which Coltrane signed a lucrative contract with Impulse Records. The Impulse years produced a rich and diverse musical legacy including an album of ballads, sessions with Duke Ellington and with the singer Johnny Hartman, as well as the larger ensemble used on *Africa/Brass*, which reflected the influence of African rhythms and Indian concepts of improvisation.

However, the music with which Coltrane and the quartet were more usually associated was exemplified by the sessions recorded live at the Village Vanguard in New York in November 1961. On *Chasin' the Trane*, Coltrane, spurred on by the ferocious, fragmented, polyrhythmic drumming of Elvin Jones, unleashed an impassioned fifteen-minute solo full of honks, screams, and tonal distortions. This aspect of Coltrane's music met with a mixed reception among both audiences and critics. Some hailed him as an innovator, every bit as important as Louis Armstrong in the 1920s or Charlie Parker in the 1940s. Others, expecting nothing more demanding than renditions of Coltrane's commercially successful and relatively accessible 1960 recording of *My Favorite Things*, were appalled by what they heard and dismissed it as "anti-jazz" and "musical nonsense."

There was also disagreement concerning the extramusical significance of Coltrane's music. Some critics sought to link him with those younger African American musicians who, influenced by the ideas of the 1960s Black Power movement, identified their art as a revolutionary black music through which they could express their pain, their anger, and their condemnation of American society. Coltrane's position on issues of this kind was ambivalent. Arguably, if his music had any extramusical content, it lay in its visionary, spiritual quality rather than in any sociopolitical sensibility. It was no coincidence that, by the mid-1960s, Coltrane was releasing albums with titles like *Meditations*, *Ascension*, and *A Love Supreme*. Elvin Jones confirms that Coltrane's music "wasn't any protest against anything. John was all love. Everything that he did was out of his love for music, and his love for people" (*Jazz Journal* 28. 4 [1975], 4–5). This same love led Coltrane to record his composition *Alabama* following the death of four young African American girls in a 1963 bombing incident in a Birmingham, Alabama, church. The piece is a lament for the children, and its mood of sadness and desolation constitutes an eloquent response to their death.

In December 1964 the quartet recorded the four-part suite *A Love Supreme*. The suite, a testament to the continuing richness of their musical creativity and empathy and an expression of Coltrane's religious beliefs, received almost unanimous critical praise and rapidly became Coltrane's most celebrated album. In 1965 *Down Beat* magazine named *A Love Supreme* Record of the Year in both its Readers' poll and its International Critics' poll. Coltrane also won awards in the Tenor and Soprano Saxophone categories, was elected to the magazine's Hall of Fame, and named as Jazzman of the Year. Rather than rest on his laurels and exploit his fame, Coltrane moved the creative goalposts. In June 1965 he recorded *Ascension*, on which the quartet was augmented by such leading avant-garde players as Archie Shepp and Pharoah Sanders. The eleven-strong ensemble played a forty-minute piece in which uncompromising solos alternated with overpowering group improvisation, without much in the way of rhythm, melody, or harmony to anchor it.

Coltrane continued to explore the outer limits of improvised music. This musical policy, and a decision to expand the quartet, was not to the liking of all the original group members. McCoy Tyner left the band in December 1965, followed by Elvin Jones in March 1966. For the next year Coltrane recorded and toured with a group in which Jimmy Garrison remained on bass, with Pharoah Sanders on saxophone and Rashied Ali on drums. The piano chair was taken by Coltrane's partner, Alice McLeod Coltrane, who became his second wife in August 1966, following his divorce from Naima. Between 1964 and 1967 the couple had three sons.

At the age of forty, Coltrane had found happiness in his personal life and was still at the height of his creative powers. He had completed a remarkable musical journey, from rhythm and blues via bebop to the cutting edge of the contemporary avant-garde movement. A series of duets he recorded with Rashied Ali in February 1967, subsequently issued as *Interstellar Space*, show his tenor playing to be as fierce and uncompromising as ever, but there is also a serenity and lyricism to the music. Whether this was a pointer to the future, or simply another episode in the juxtaposition of anguish and tranquillity evident in so much of Coltrane's music, remains uncertain. John Coltrane died of liver cancer in the Huntington Hospital in Huntington, Long Island.

Since his death, no single figure has dominated the jazz scene the way Coltrane did in the 1960s. He remains one of a select group of jazz musicians who evolved artistically throughout their careers and whose personal growth and development moved the music forward in significant ways. Into the twenty-first century Coltrane's influence remains profound. Long before the term "world music" came into vogue, Coltrane had shown the way by absorbing elements of Indian and African music. His move away from a chordal to a scalar approach helped change the face of jazz improvisation. His unsurpassed instrumental technique and his remarkable ability as an improviser have inspired generations of jazz musicians. Coltrane is dead, but he lives on in his remarkable legacy of recorded work and in his continuing influence on the contemporary jazz scene.

FURTHER READING

Porter, Lewis. *John Coltrane: His Life and Music* (1998).
Priestley, Brian. *John Coltrane* (1987).
Thomas, J. C. *Chasin' the Trane: The Music and Mystique of John Coltrane* (1975).
Obituary: *New York Times*, 18 July 1967.

DISCOGRAPHY

Fujioka, Yasuhiro. *John Coltrane: A Discography and Musical Biography* (1995)

JOHN RUNCIE

Colvin, Claudette (5 Sept. 1939–), civil rights activist and nurse's aide, was born Claudette Austin in Birmingham, Alabama. The daughter of Mary Jane Gadson and C. P. Austin, she was raised by her great-aunt and great-uncle, Mary Ann Colvin and Q. P. Colvin, the former a maid and the latter a "yard boy," or outdoor domestic.

When Colvin was eight, she and her guardians moved to Montgomery, Alabama, where she attended Booker T. Washington High School. In February 1955 her classes were devoted to "Negro History month," with a focus on current racial injustice in Montgomery. On her way home from school on 2 March 1955, she sat in the rear of the bus, far behind the ten seats that were automatically reserved for whites. A 1900 Montgomery city ordinance stipulated that conductors were given the power to assign seats in order to ensure racial segregation, but that no passengers would be required to give up their seat to stand if the bus was crowded. In accordance with long-standing custom, however, when the bus became full of commuters the driver demanded that Colvin move to accommodate a white person, despite there being no spare seats. Her adamant refusal led to her being arrested and taken to the adult city jail.

On 18 March 1955, represented by the African American lawyer Fred Gray in Montgomery County juvenile court, she pleaded not guilty to breaking the segregation ordinance, disturbing the peace and assaulting the arresting policemen. Colvin was found guilty of all charges, declared a ward of the state, and sentenced to indefinite probation. The outcome of the trial prompted a minority of the community to independently boycott the city buses. During the early 1950s, a local civic organization the Women's Political Council (WPC), led by Jo Ann Robinson, protested frequently to the three Montgomery City commissioners about mistreatment of black customers by the Montgomery

Claudette Colvin is seen at age 15 in this undated file photo taken around the year 1953. (AP Images.)

City Lines bus company. The group's search for a case to initiate a mass boycott led the WPC to investigate Claudette's background and temperament. The Montgomery chapter National Association for the Advancement of Colored People leader, E[dgar] D[aniel] Nixon, also reviewed her case, while his group raised money to appeal her conviction.

On 6 May 1955, Colvin's case went to Montgomery Circuit Court, and two of the three charges against Claudette were dropped. The remaining conviction for "assaulting" the two officers gave her a criminal record. Colvin believed that she was rejected by Montgomery Civil Rights movement leaders as a test case due to her youth, dark skin tone, and the fact that she became pregnant by a married man. She was expelled from school due to her pregnancy, giving birth to son Raymond on 29 March 1956. Colvin did, however, take part in the Montgomery bus boycott of 1 December 1955 to 20 December 1956. On 11 May 1956, Colvin testified in the federal lawsuit *Browder v. Gayle*. The three-judge panel in the landmark case concluded that the Montgomery segregation codes denied and deprived plaintiffs and African American citizens of the equal protection of the laws and due process of law secured by the Fourteenth amendment.

Colvin held a series of short-term jobs in restaurants, but was fired from a series of positions due to her white employers' learning about her "criminal" activities. In 1957 Colvin passed her General Education Diploma, a high school equivalency test, and enrolled at Alabama State College. She dropped out after one year due to dissatisfaction with the courses offered. She lived alternately between New York City and Montgomery, working as a live-in domestic in the North and a maid in the South. Her second son, Randy, was born in 1960, after which she refused to take part in civil rights activities, due in part to caution over being persecuted or losing employment. She moved to New York permanently in 1968.

Colvin retired to the Bronx in 2004, after thirty-five years of working as a nurse's aide in a Manhattan nursing home. She agreed to publicize her civil rights activities only after retirement. Colvin's arrest was one of many test cases considered by the NAACP of those who opposed racial segregation on the bus system. Her action predated the Rosa Parks case, which was widely publicized and led to her being considered the "mother" of the civil rights movement. Colvin's struggle graphically illustrates both the contribution of the young and women, and the problems of racism and class-based conflict in the nascent civil rights movement.

FURTHER READING

Branch, Taylor. *Parting the Waters: America in the King Years, 1954–1963* (1988).

Garrow, David J., and Jo Ann Gibson Robinson. *Montgomery Bus Boycott: Women Who Started It* (1987).

Gray, Fred D. *Bus Ride to Justice* (1994).

Hoose, Philip M. *Claudette Colvin: Twice toward Justice* (2009).

Wright, Roberta Hughes. *The Birth of the Montgomery Bus Boycott* (1991).

RUTH E. MARTIN

Combs, Osie V., Jr. (1949–), U.S. naval officer and naval engineer, was born in Texas. Nothing is known of his parents, nor even his specific place and date of birth. He graduated from Texas City High School in 1967, then attended Prairie View A&M University from 1967 to 1971, graduating with a B.A. in Electrical Engineering. One of his school's most distinguished graduates, Combs was named Outstanding Student Engineer of the Year by the Texas Society of Professional Engineers and Outstanding Senior Engineer while at Prairie View.

Combs also joined the Naval Reserve Officers Training Corps (NROTC), serving with the future navy vice admiral David Brewer while at Prairie View. Upon completing his undergraduate degree, Combs served for four years in the navy, joining the crew of the aircraft carrier *Coral Sea* as assistant boilers officer prior to its deployment to Vietnam in November 1971. Two weeks after returning to Texas from his first overseas tour of duty, on 30 July 1972, Combs married Iris Parks in Matagorda County, Texas. They had two children. Combs served a second Vietnam deployment aboard the aircraft carrier from March to November 1973. Upon returning stateside, he enrolled at the Massachusetts Institute of Technology (MIT) in 1974, earning a combined master's degree in Mechanical Engineering and a naval engineer's degree in Naval Architecture in 1977.

Following his graduation from MIT, Combs continued in his naval career at the Norfolk Naval Shipyard in Virginia as surface and submarine ship superintendent and deck officer as well as backup docking officer from 1977 to 1981. Because the base at Norfolk was the navy's main home port on the Atlantic coast, Combs gained valuable maintenance and construction experience there. He also became interested in the Submarine Force and the intricate machinery employed aboard the boats. He earned his Gold Dolphins—insignia awarded to officers who have learned the complete submarine systems and are officially qualified as "submariners"—and served as engineering duty officer aboard the missile boat *Woodrow Wilson* in 1980, the beginning of a long and far-reaching association with the underwater navy. After completing the Program Managers Course at Defense Systems Management College, Combs was assigned in 1981 as assistant project officer for the *Los Angeles* class attack submarine (the 688 class) building program at the Newport News Shipbuilding Yard in Virginia in the office of the supervisor of shipbuilding, conversion, and repair. In helping to oversee this program, first begun in 1976, Combs contributed to the building of the navy's most numerous and, at the time, technologically advanced fast-attack submarines, which became the mainstay of the Submarine Force. The history of the 688 class of submarines also proved important to the navy's continued efforts to improve racial diversity at all levels. Not only was Combs involved in their building as a black engineer, but C. A. TZOMES became the first black submarine commander when he was named skipper of the 688-class *Houston* in 1983.

His time at Newport News completed, Combs served his last tour of sea duty aboard the submarine tender *Proteus* from 1983 to 1985 as repair officer. While stationed at Guam and on extended deployments to Subic Bay, the Indian Ocean, Singapore, and Australia, Combs gained valuable field experience working with both missile and fast-attack submarines in the Pacific Fleet. In close contact with submarine commanders and engineering officers, he gained an understanding of the unique operational requirements of a submarine on deployment as well as of the technological improvements that might be needed in the future to ensure successful mission outcomes.

Once back in the United States, Combs returned to duty in naval development and construction, serving as program manager for the large-scale vehicle (LSV) autonomous submarine program. Working on this new craft, a quarter-scale model for research and development of the future *Seawolf* class submarine, from 1985 to 1988 proved vital in Combs's future duties and provided a platform for future submarine research and development that evolved into the world's largest unmanned submarine in the early twenty-first century. Combs's succeeding duty was both prominent and challenging. In 1988 he was named assistant program manager for design and construction of the Submarine Force's newest boat, the *Seawolf* class of submarines. This program produced the first submarine

designed and built from top to bottom since the early 1960s. Planning commenced in 1982, and the first keel was laid in 1989 under Combs's watch. Built of an advanced type of steel, capable of reaching a depth of two thousand feet, and heavily armed with a combination of fifty torpedoes or missiles, the *Seawolf* was renowned for its stealth. Indeed it was said to be quieter at its tactical speed of twenty-five knots than a *Los Angeles* class boat at its moorings. Combs served as assistant program manager until 1990, as project officer for construction from 1990 to 1992 while work was progressing on the first boat in the class, and as overall program manager from 1992 to 1995.

However, the *Seawolf* program came under fire soon after Combs's arrival for reasons beyond his control. With the fall of the Berlin Wall in 1989, followed by the collapse of the Soviet Union and the official end of the cold war in late 1991, the navy's latest submarine was viewed as suddenly outdated, designed for a threat that was now overstated, and perhaps most important, too costly. After much debate both in Congress and in the press, the original twenty-nine submarines in the program were reduced to twelve and subsequently to just three in 1993. These ships, the *Seawolf*, the *Connecticut*, and the *Jimmy Carter*, were subsequently commissioned from 1997 to 2006. Though the *Seawolf* program was severely curtailed, some of its elements later were incorporated into its less costly replacement, the *Virginia* class attack boats. Combs's management of the *Seawolf* program was highly respected in navy circles, and his work there and directing the 688-class construction and LSV programs are indicators of the quiet impact he had in building and developing some of the most prominent defense weapons.

Combs's subsequent service, though out of the public spotlight, was equally distinguished. Elevated to flag rank in 1995, Rear Admiral Combs served from 1995 to 1996 first as chief engineer and then as program director, C4ISR (command, control, communications, computers, and intelligence and information technology for the twenty-first century), at Space and Naval Warfare Systems Command (SPAWARSYSCOM) in San Diego. From 1997 to 1998 he was vice commander at SPAWARSYSCOM, and from 1998 to 2004 he served as deputy commander for submarines at Naval Sea Systems Command in Washington, D.C. A recipient of the Legion of Merit, the Meritorious Service Medal with Gold Star, the Navy Commendation Medal, and other navy unit and private sector awards, Combs retired from the navy in 2005 and settled in Virginia.

FURTHER READING

Massachusetts Institute of Technology. Osie Combs, NavEng 1977. http://oe.mit.edu/content/view/28/67/.

Real African American Heroes. Rear Admiral Osie V. Combs. http://www.raahistory.com/military/navy/combs.htm (2005).

GLENN ALLEN KNOBLOCK

Combs, Sean (4 Nov. 1969–), hip-hop producer and businessman, was born Sean John Combs in Harlem in New York City to Melvin and Janice Combs. Combs's childhood years were spent in Harlem, where his father worked for the Board of Education and as a cab driver. His mother was a model. Eager to provide for his family, Melvin Combs succumbed to the lure of criminal activity, which ultimately led to his murder in 1973. In 1982 Janice moved her family to suburban Mount Vernon, New York, in an effort to escape the growing violence and unemployment in Harlem.

Following her husband's death, Janice worked as a teacher's assistant, bus driver, and night attendant for children with cerebral palsy. His mother's determination to provide for her family influenced Combs to work after school beginning at age twelve. Too young to formally apply for his own paper route, Combs convinced an older friend to take on a second route, which Combs would complete. In return Combs gave his friend a percentage of his earnings.

In 1987 Combs graduated from Mount St. Michael High School in the Bronx and entered Howard University in Washington, D.C., as a business administration major. During his time at Howard, Combs seized the opportunity to indulge in his entrepreneurial inclinations. He organized and hosted weekend dance parties and established a shuttle service for students between the airport and campus.

In 1989 Combs met Andre Harwell, president of Uptown Records. Impressed with Combs's work ethic and ability to interpret the music and cultural interests of urban youth, Harwell offered Combs an internship. Determined to make an impression, Combs hired young adults to flood New York City with promotional materials for artists like Jodeci and Mary J. Blige. The success of this inventive advertising campaign earned him a promotion to director of Artist & Repertoire at the age of

nineteen, making him one of the youngest record executives in the history of the music industry. This position allowed Combs to continue to build successful careers for artists such as Father MC, Mary J. Blige, and Jodeci. When he was dismissed from Uptown, Combs capitalized on his relationships and creativity to found Bad Boy Records in 1993.

Initially based out of Combs's home, Bad Boy eventually turned into a multibillion-dollar, multifaceted organization. The genesis of Bad Boy allowed Combs to reinvent himself. With the new label came a new title: "Puffy" (or "Puff Daddy"). His quick temper and his desire to portray a tough image on the football field led to the coinage of the nickname, which described Combs' tendency to react strongly when something did not go his way.

After encountering some difficulty in signing potentially high-profile artists to the Bad Boy label, as well as witnessing the growing popularity of West Coast rap, Combs signed a former member of the rap group EPMD, Craig Mack, to the Bad Boy label. In 1994 Mack's single "Flava in Ya Ear" reached *Billboard*'s top-ten singles chart. In the same year, "Ready to Die" by NOTORIOUS BIG. went double platinum and helped reinvigorate the reputation of East Coast hip-hop culture.

In 1997, at the height of Bad Boy's success, Combs suffered the loss of friend and artist Notorious B.I.G., whose murder was shrouded in mystery. Later in the same year, Combs released his first solo album, *No Way Out*, which featured the single "I'll Be Missing You," a tribute to the fallen rapper. The record marked Combs's debut as a successful solo hip-hop artist and influenced the sound of popular music by combining R&B sounds with rhythmic and cultural components of hip-hop. Combs helped create a more mainstream and arguably more commercial form of rap. Reviews of his debut criticized Combs for watering down and overcommercializing rap by sampling and capitalizing on past hit songs such as the Police's "Every Breath You Take" in "I'll be Missing You." However, the records produced by Bad Boy promoted hip-hop to a wide audience and helped that burgeoning musical form gain mass appeal in previously unexplored markets.

Combs used his talents as an entertainer and entrepreneur to pursue ventures in the restaurant business, fashion, film, and television production. In 1997 Combs opened a Caribbean-Soul restaurant chain in Manhattan and Atlanta named after his eldest son, Justin, and launched the clothing line "Sean John," which won him the 2000 Council of Fashion Designers of America's award for Menswear Designer of the Year.

From 1999 to 2001, however, legal difficulties overshadowed Combs's flourishing career. He was acquitted of gun possession and bribery charges in 1999 for a shooting in a Manhattan nightclub. In 2001 Combs appeared in the movies *Monster's Ball* and *Made*. A year later he produced MTV's *Making the Band* reality television series. In 2004 he starred as Walter Lee Young in a Broadway revival of LORRAINE HANSBERRY's *A Raisin in the Sun*.

Combs's success in the music industry brought him fame and fortune. As early as 1995 he received numerous awards recognizing both his musical and entrepreneurial accomplishments, including the ASCAP Songwriter of the Year. "I'll Be Missing You" won the Grammy Award for Best Rap Performance by a Duo or Group. In 1998 *No Way Out* won the Grammy for Album of the Year. In 2002 Combs was named one of the forty wealthiest people under age forty by *Forbes* magazine. Combs's entrepreneurship extended into social service and civic participation. He founded Daddy's House in 1995 to offer tutoring and life-skills training to Harlem youth, and in 2000 he raised more than $2 million for charity when he ran in the New York City Marathon. He was also engaged in politics. During the 2004 presidential election, Combs and other celebrities developed the "Vote or Die" campaign to encourage young people to vote.

Combs's understanding of American urban culture allowed him to become one of the most successful entrepreneurs in U.S. history. His success in the music industry led to other business ventures based on his personal interests, developing a visual image to complement the Bad Boy sound. In June 2007 Combs received the Fragrance Foundation Recognition Award for his fragrance for males *Unforgivable*. He was only the second African American, after MICHAEL JORDAN, to be so honored. Meanwhile, Combs and Bad Boy World Entertainment had success in the television market. Home Box Office's *The Bad Boys of Comedy* and MTV's *Diddy TV* were two television series created by Combs in 2006 and 2007, respectively. Each show displayed another side of the hip-hop mogul, solidifying his influence and contribution to American popular culture. Diddy's prodigious output continued unabated into the second decade of the 21st century. He launched his own reality TV series, *I Want to Work for Diddy*, on VH-1 in 2008 and 2009; received accolades for his role as Walter Lee Younger in a television adaptaion of LORRAINE HANSBERRY's

A Raisin in the Sun (2009), and in 2010 he released his fifth album, *Last Train to Paris*, on Bad Boy Records. Diddy's business interests continued to diversify, and he added a lucrative deal with Ciroc Vodka and the beverage giant Diageo. In 2011 *Forbes* magazine listed Diddy as the nation's wealthiest hip-hop artist, and predicted that either he or rival JAY-Z would likely become hip-hop's first billionaire.

FURTHER READING

Ro, Ronin. *Bad Boy: The Influence of Sean "Puffy" Combs on the Music Industry* (2001).
Shapiro, Peter. *The Rough Guide to Hip-Hop: The Definitive Guide to Hip-Hop from Grand Master Flash to Outkast and Beyond* (2005).

VONZELE DAVID REED

Commodore, Chester, Sr. (22 Aug. 1914–10 Apr. 2004), political and editorial cartoonist, was born Chesterfield Commodore in Racine, Wisconsin, the fourth of five children of Elizabeth "Bessie" Fite and Pascal "Pat" Commodore, a Creole laborer and model maker from Louisiana. One Commodore ancestor, Peter D. Thomas of Racine, a former slave, was the first elected black official in Wisconsin.

The family resided with Bessie Commodore's mother, Della, in her Racine boarding house until 1923 when the three girls and their parents moved to Chicago where Pat could pursue better employment opportunities. Chester, as he was known, remained with his grandmother and his older brother until 1927 when he joined his parents.

Commodore grew up in a culturally stimulating environment. Because of its convenient proximity to Chicago and Milwaukee and because black entertainers, in preintegration years, were not allowed above the first floor of the Chicago and Milwaukee hotels where they appeared, Della Fite's house provided temporary respite for many entertainers such as the Will Mastin Trio with SAMMY DAVIS JR., ETHEL WATERS, and BILL "BOJANGLES" ROBINSON (Bojangles taught Chester and his siblings some dance steps.)

John Prophet, called Uncle John, a nontransient resident of Della's boarding house, was an artist who first saw Commodore's primal talent. Drawing his first cartoon at age five, Commodore spent hours with Prophet at his grandmother's dining room table, learning techniques that matured into his immense talent.

Observing performers through his ingenuous although perspicacious eyes, Commodore developed an ability to isolate distinguishing features.

With the help of his mentor, he honed his exceptional abilities. In 1927 in Chicago, Commodore enrolled in Tilden Technical High School, holding no doubt that he would pursue an artistic career. Much to his chagrin, however, he discovered that black students were only given domestic and manual training to prepare for the only employment areas opened to them. Although Commodore was denied access to art classes during his high school years, he turned each class into an art course, drawing rather than doing class-related assignments.

Growing up, Commodore viewed black cartoonists such as expatriate OLIVER HARRINGTON and Jay Jackson as his inspirations. Part of the artist's young life was spent in Minneapolis, where he formed a friendship with photographer GORDON PARKS SR.

By fifteen years old, frustrated by limited opportunities, Commodore made a prophetic decision. He gathered his drawings into an improvised portfolio and took the first step on his eventual career path. Without an appointment, Commodore crossed the Chicago Defender threshold to naively request an audience with publisher ROBERT S. ABBOTT. Mr. Abbott's secretary, whether through empathy for the scrawny teen or out of amusement, convinced Mr. Abbott to see him.

Inside the office, Commodore steeled himself to meet the imposing figure. Taking a seat, he advised the publisher of his desire to draw for the *Defender*. Respecting the fortitude of the youth, Mr. Abbott perused the novice's makeshift portfolio. Once finished, Mr. Abbott, after a protracted gaze into the young, imploring eyes, asked whether Commodore had completed high school. In response to the student's "no," the publisher instructed him to go back, finish, and then come to see him. Unfortunately, Abbott died in 1945, three years before Commodore began his half-century at the *Defender*, becoming the most recognized African American political cartoonist of the time. (Before he was hired at the *Defender* during a printers' strike, Commodore held a number of menial jobs, culminating at the Pullman Company.) During his years at the *Defender* (1948–2004 with a break in the 1960s), Commodore drew up to seven strips per day, including the Ravings of Prof. Doodle, So What!, the Sparks, and Bungleton Green, the oldest black strip in the country. Commodore's works were published in several other newspapers.

In the 1930s while pursuing work as a cartoonist, Commodore was summoned to the Minneapolis Sun's publisher's office where he had been hired, over the telephone, as an illustrator. When he arrived, however, after examining the color of Commodore's skin, the publisher told him there was no job.

With his pen, Commodore became a crusader for civil rights, decrying ethnic, racial, and economic prejudices. (His hammer/anvil cartoon of the Supreme Court's 1954 *Brown* decision against school segregation became an iconic representation for integration.) Commodore described himself as a "champion of the little guy," drawing attention to injustices against all ethnic groups and the disenfranchised, both at home and abroad. His work garnered many awards, including the National Conference of Christians and Jews' National Media Medallion, and seven Best Cartoon awards from the National Newspaper Publishers Association. Nominated twelve times for the Pulitzer Prize that eluded his grasp (although he received twelve honorable mentions), Commodore and his white peers, including Dick Locher, Herblock, John Feschetti, and Bill Mauldin, were baffled and angered by this blatant slight.

Commodore's cartoons were often predictors rather than testimonial as he often had visions or premonitions, dictating his days' illustration. The cartoon subject would amazingly become a news item within a day or two.

A talented railroad model maker, Commodore created train engines, cars, and diorama from discarded items: beer and coffee cans and shirt cardboards. His exceptionally accurate models (in tandem with his cartoons) were displayed at the Chicago Museum of Science and Industry, the Library of Congress, and other repositories.

Married three times, Commodore had two sons, Chester Jr. and Phillip, with his first wife, Marie Bazel (1937?). Little is known of his second, short-lived marriage. His third wife, Marcia Buchanan (1955), came into his life with two children, William B. Hutchins and Lorin Nails-Smooté, both of whom he helped raise. He was a dedicated grandfather to their seven offspring. (Marcia's sister was DR. GLORIA B. EVANS.)

Marcia became Commodore's muse. In each of his cartoons, beginning about 1968, he drew a stylized "M," honoring their union. Although Marcia died fourteen years before Commodore, he never developed another relationship, beginning each day in communion with her spirit.

A very compassionate man, Commodore had few enemies, but he did antagonize Chicago's Sheriff Joe Woods. The artist drew Woods in Klan clothing, with "Woods' Vigilantes," suggesting law enforcement contributed to Chicago's 1960s unrest. Woods accused Commodore of yellow journalism.

President Nixon and J. Edgar Hoover were among many who requested his cartoons for their archives. A number of younger cartoonists credit Commodore as having drawn them to the art form.

Commodore semiretired and he and Marcia moved to Colorado in 1981. However, he continued to submit cartoons to the *Defender* and other papers until four days before his death in Colorado Springs.

Noting that through the mid-twentieth century the white press drew black faces as solid black cue balls with big white lips, big noses, and circular eyes, Commodore strove, successfully, to change that image. Civil rights activist JULIAN BOND credited Commodore as one of the "pioneers in reversing this trend" of negatively stereotyping blacks in the press (Julian Bond, narrator, *Pleading Our Own Cause: The Black Press in America*).

FURTHER READING

Chester Commodore's Papers are held in the Vivian G. Harsh Research Collection of Afro-American History and Literature, Chicago Public Library, Chicago, Illinois.

Brooks, Charles. *The Best Editorial Cartoons of the Year* (1974–75, 1995–98, 1999–2001, 2003).

Burns, Ben. *Nitty Gritty: A White Editor in Black Journalism* (1996).

Goldstein, Nancy. *Jackie Ormes: The First African American Woman Cartoonist* (2008).

Nelson, Stanley. *The Black Press: Soldiers without Swords* (1998).

Waters, Enoch P. *American Diary* (1987).

Obituary: *Chicago Tribune*, 14 April 2004.

LORIN NAILS-SMOOTE

Cone, James Hal (5 Aug. 1938–), theologian, was born in Fordyce, Arkansas, the son of Charles "Charlie" Madison Cone, a woodcutter, and Lucy Cone. Cone was the youngest of three children. When Cone was just a year old his family moved to Beardon, Arkansas, a rural town of roughly 800 whites and 400 blacks. He only achieved a sixth-grade education, but his natural intelligence and courage led him to later challenge racial segregation, a lifetime commitment to racial justice that included his participation in a school desegregation case and his opposition to racial coercion in the Jim Crow South.

Cone's early education took place in segregated schools that often employed teachers without college degrees. What they lacked in formal training, however, Cone's teachers made up for in life-affirming qualities. He recalls that his first-grade teacher often hugged him, making him "feel loved." Cone did not know what it meant to be hated in a classroom until college, when he attended integrated schools in the North where his professors made it a habit to question the intellectual and moral capacities of African Americans. However, his attendance at Macedonia African Methodist Episcopal (AME) Church during his youth embedded a biblical stamp on Cone's self-worth. The small congregation allowed Cone to serve as its pastor when he was only sixteen, and the young Cone came to believe that he was part of a larger spiritual story—just as Isaiah and Amos had a purpose, so did he and other black folks as they struggled for dignity and equality. The combination of Cone's home, school, and church upbringing awakened his burgeoning intellectual courage and scholarly commitments.

In 1954 Cone graduated from high school and attended Shorter Junior College, a small two-year college of the African Methodist Episcopal Church. He soon transferred to Philander Smith, another Methodist college in Little Rock, Arkansas. There Cone encountered Plato, Socrates, Luther, Kant, and Hegel for the first time, all the while remaining interested in "Negro history." He also wrestled with the writings of W. E. B. DuBois, BOOKER T. WASHINGTON, and FREDERICK DOUGLASS. In 1958 Cone married Rose Hampton and traveled to Illinois to attend Garrett Biblical Seminary. Cone's expectations that northern whites would welcome him were quickly dispelled when he was refused service at a barber shop because he was black. Cone struggled through his first semester, working hard to obtain Cs in an openly hostile climate. Though frequently humiliated by his professors' racial taunts, Cone struggled on and by his senior year had become a straight-A student and was awarded a bachelor of divinity degree. Cone went on to become Garrett's first black Ph.D. candidate, earning his master's and doctoral degrees from Garrett–Northwestern.

From 1964 to 1966 Cone taught theology at Philander Smith in Arkansas, but found it somewhat stifling. Just as his father resented white segregationists who controlled the lumber business, Cone began to resent the limitations imposed by the white-controlled Methodist college. In 1966 he left Philander for a position at Adrian College in

Illinois. It was during this time that Cone found his theological voice; that is, he located Christ in black people's struggle for justice. Living in a town with only fifty or so black residents, Cone drafted his pivotal essay, "Christianity and Black Power." Cone brought the essay to the Black Methodists for Church Renewal Conference in Cincinnati in 1968. While there he met STOKELY CARMICHAEL and the influential black scholar C. ERIC LINCOLN, who agreed to read Cone's work. Lincoln was impressed with Cone's arresting article, and the two discussed it late into the next morning.

Two months later, on 4 April 1968, MARTIN LUTHER KING JR. was assassinated. In the wake of the murder of this greatest American advocate of nonviolent activism, many blacks began to gravitate to the Black Power movement. Cone was no exception, and he continued his theological quest to reconcile Black Power with the Christian gospel. The fruit of this labor was the seminal work, *Black Theology and Black Power* (1969). Cone wrote the book in one month during the summer of 1968 in the basement of his brother's church. Inspired and indignant, Cone's writing of *Black Theology and Black Power* constituted a "conversion experience" for its author, who saw in it a final separation from white theology and his rebirth in black theology. Cone's text was part of a broader movement throughout the Americas in which theologians argued that God is active in history and favors the oppressed in their struggle for liberation. The Peruvian theologian Gustavo Gutierrez formalized the field of liberation theology in Latin America, arguing that God sided with the oppressed against economic domination. Cone's book was the first published work systematically to articulate a theology of liberation in its insistence that God identified with African Americans' struggle for freedom and equality. The book received instant critical attention, and Cone followed up with his second work *A Black Theology of Liberation* (1971). Although these works were well received among black religious scholars, many felt that Cone relied too heavily on European frameworks and white theologians. Cone responded with *The Spirituals and the Blues* (1972), which related the history of the black freedom struggles to the biblical quest for salvation.

Roughly around the time that *Black Theology and Black Power* was published, in January 1969, Cone joined the faculty at New York's Union Theological Seminary. At Union, Cone taught alongside influential scholars such as JAMES MELVIN WASHINGTON, CORNEL WEST, and James Forbes. It was the young West who convinced Cone to use Marxist theory as a tool in his broader theological analysis. During the spring of 1976, Gutierrez was a visiting professor at Union and further expanded Cone's theological connection with Third World struggles. Cone's theological perspective enlarged as he established links between Third World struggles, women's equality, and black theology.

In 1977, while he was a teacher at Union, Cone's marriage to Rose Carmichael ended in divorce. He and Rose had two sons, Michael and Charles. Cone married Sondra Gibson in 1979, but she died of cancer in 1983. Throughout these years Cone remained at Union, where he held the position of Charles A. Briggs Distinguished Professor of Systematic Theology and influenced a "second" generation of black theologians, such as his former student Dwight Hopkins, who was the author of several works on black theology. In 1998 the University of Chicago held a national conference on the thirtieth anniversary of Cone's *Black Theology and Black Power*. Leading scholars argued that Cone's work redefined the field of theology insofar as he challenged both the black church and theologians to place the black quest for equality at the center of their work. Cone published numerous other works, including *Martin & Malcolm & America: A Dream or a Nightmare* (1991) and *The Risks of Faith: The Emergence of a Black Theology of Liberation* (1999).

FURTHER READING
Cone, James. *My Soul Looks Back* (1986).
Hopkins, Dwight, ed. *Black Faith and Public Talk: Critical Essays on James H. Cone's Black Theology and Black Power* (1999).

CARL MIRRA

Conner, Jeffie Obrea Allen (17 Aug. 1895–10 June 1972), teacher, home economist, administrator, and civil rights activist, was born in Harrison, Texas, to Jeff D. and Meddie Lillian Estelle Allen. She was the oldest of their three children. Jeffie's father was an early graduate of Prairie View State Normal and Industrial College, established in 1876, and both her mother and maternal grandmother were teachers. When Jeffie was eleven years old her parents sent her to Mary Allen Seminary in Crocket, Texas, a school founded by Presbyterians in 1886 for the education of black girls. Her mother, an alumna of the school, considered it superior to the segregated public schools of the time. After two years at the seminary Jeffie scored exceedingly high marks on her entrance exams for Prairie View and began college as a thirteen-year-old sophomore in 1912. In 1914, at the age of fifteen, she graduated with a teaching certificate.

Conner began her teaching career in Clifton, Texas, but possessed with drive and ambition, she found employment as a home demonstration agent for the U.S. Department of Agriculture in 1918 and remained with the agency for the next seventeen years. Home demonstration agents were part of the agricultural extension service established by Congress in the 1914 Smith-Lever Act and the 1917 Smith-Hughes Act. As an agent, she assisted "in diffusing … useful and practical information on subjects relating to … home economics" (Wallace, 197). Specifically she provided poor women with training in home management, gardening, and sanitation. The agency was segregated so Conner's clients were rural black farmwomen who hauled water from the source to their homes, did their laundry by hand, and lived without electricity and other amenities. Conner's detailed field notes commented on cotton harvests, land acquisition by some of her client families, and the advent of indoor plumbing in rural farm homes. In 1924 she instituted a significant health advance in McLennan County known as the sanitary drinking cup project, in which she coordinated the making of 1700 individual tin cups by county schoolchildren. The project served to decrease the incidence of communicable diseases in the rural county population by replacing a shared water dipper with individual cups and by having children carry home to their families a message regarding the importance of sanitation and the curtailment of disease.

At age twenty-eight Jeffie Allen wed Dr. George Sherman Conner, a fifty-nine year-old widower and a well-established physician in Waco, Texas. The two met after Jeffie began attending New Hope Baptist Church with her sister and brother-in-law. Financially secure, Dr. Conner asked his wife to quit her job as an extension agent and become a full-time homemaker. She refused and continued her career, and in 1930 after seven years of marriage, she surprised her husband by telling him she was going to get a bachelor's degree in home economics. This decision required her to return to Prairie View for the next three years. Dr. Conner supported his wife's professional success and desire to upgrade her academic credentials and in 1933 she received a bachelor of science degree and returned to work full-time as a county agent. In 1935 Connor became district supervisor to both black and white county agents, making her one of the highest-ranking black female workers in the state of Texas. Her promotion also resulted in a larger area of travel, one that occasionally required her to stay overnight away from home. Hotels, however, did not accommodate black clientele, but Conner was not a person to be discouraged and she appointed female hosts from each county under her supervision so that in the event of an overnight stay she had pre-arranged accommodations. Even though her work became even more demanding, Conner managed to return home to her husband every weekend. In 1939, after sixteen years of marriage, her husband died on Valentine's Day and she never remarried.

A year after her husband's death Conner enrolled in Prairie View to complete her master's degree in home economics. Upon her graduation in 1944 she returned to work as a home demonstration agent. In 1948 she changed careers and took a job as supervisor of McLennan County's thirty-five "colored" schools. Conner quickly realized that the facilities she supervised were significantly deficient in terms of teacher's salaries, quality of textbooks, and physical plant. After assessing the situation she determined that consolidation of the thirty-five schools into fourteen larger ones would increase both the available funds and efficiency, thus benefiting the student population. Her reform efforts were successful, and she retired in 1957 at the age of sixty-two.

In a speech to the Texas Federation of Colored Women's Clubs, Conner summed up her philosophy in the following words: "It is my belief that we (club women) would do well to identify ourselves with organized efforts of agencies to solve the social, health, and community problems of mankind." In her later years she worked tirelessly for public school integration, and in 1967 Governor John Connally appointed her to the Committee on Public School Education. She was also active in the civil rights movement and endorsed the NAACP, participating in demonstrations, controversial meetings, and public speaking. Among her many honors was a citation for outstanding service from Prairie View A&M College, Zeta Beta Phi Woman of the Year, and an honorary doctor of humanities degree from Paul Quinn College. Jeffie Obrea Allen Conner died at the age of seventy-seven.

FURTHER READING

George S. and Jeffie O. A. Conner's papers are held in the Texas Collection, Baylor University, Waco, Texas, and in the Women's Collection, Texas Woman's University, Denton, Texas.

Wallace, Patricia Ward. *A Spirit So Rare: A History of the Women of Waco* (1984).

Winegarten, Ruth. *Black Texas Women* (1996).

Obituary: *Waco Tribune*, 10 June 1972.

DIANNE DENTICE

Connerly, Ward (15 June 1939–), Republican political activist and businessman, was born Wardell Anthony Connerly in Leesville, Louisiana, the son of Roy Connerly and Grace Soniea. Roy Connerly left the family when Ward was two years old, and Ward's mother died when he was four. After the death of his mother, Connerly was sent to live with Bertha Soniea, his maternal aunt and her husband James Louis in Sacramento, California. Later, at the age of twelve, his grandmother, Mary Soniea relocated to Sacramento and gained custody of Ward.

After graduating from Grant Union High School in 1957, Ward Connerly entered American River Junior College that same year. He transferred to Sacramento State College in 1959, one of fifty blacks out of a total of two thousand students. In 1962 he earned a B.A. degree with honors in Political Science. At Sacramento State, Connerly became the first black student to pledge to the all-white Delta Phi Omega fraternity, and later he became an honorary member of Sigma Phi Epsilon fraternity. He also served as student body president. While participating in campus causes, Connerly expanded his activism to the larger Sacramento community through campaigning against housing discrimination, which resulted in a bill to ban the practice in the state.

He married Ilene Crews in 1963, and they had two children and two grandchildren.

Connerly's college experiences prepared him for future political activism. He studied the 1964 Republican National Convention in which Barry Goldwater won the presidential nomination. He related to some of Goldwater's positions on issues. For example, Ward agreed with the Republican philosophy about the benefits of free enterprise to earn financial freedom. In 1968 Connerly began his association with California State Senator Pete Wilson, the future governor of California. At the time, Wilson was the chairman of the Assembly Committee on Urban Affairs and Housing. Wilson asked Connerly to serve as Wilson's chief consultant. In that role, Connerly and Wilson devised a plan to give low-income housing residents ownership of their housing developments. By 1973, with the encouragement of Wilson (and

in partnership with his wife) Connerly had left government and founded the firm of Connerly & Associates, a consulting and land-use planning company. During the next twenty years, the company flourished and Connerly became a successful businessman, gaining membership in the Rotary Club of Sacramento and becoming a lifetime member of the California Building Industry Hall of Fame.

In 1993 Connerly was appointed to the California Board of Regents where he asserted his opposition to affirmative action. The policy of attempting to redress discrimination in hiring, government contracting, and school admissions was first suggested by President John F. Kennedy in 1961. In 1965 President Lyndon Johnson made it federal law when he issued Executive Order 11246, which prohibited federal contractors and federally assisted construction contractors and subcontractors—those who generated over $10,000 per year in government business—from discriminatory employment decisions based on race, color, religion, and sex. The policy was later amended to take steps to address educational disparities among minority students.

Connerly became more interested in the issue of affirmative action in 1994 after Jerry and Ellen Cook contacted him. Jerry Cook, a statistician, presented Connerly with data showing that whites and Asians were being systematically denied admission despite having better grades and test scores than many of those admitted. The medical school at the University of California—San Diego had rejected their son. After listening to their story and doing further research, Connerly became convinced that affirmative action as practiced in the University of California system amounted to reverse discrimination.

Connerly became a major advocate of a state initiative, Proposition 209, which proposed abolishing racial preferences in hiring and contracting by January 1996 and to end racial preferences in college admissions by January 1997. The measure also banned the use of preferential treatment based on sex, color, ethnicity, or national origin in local or state governments, public universities, colleges, or other instruments of government. Connerly's proposition to end racial preferences in college admissions also included a recommendation to increase outreach efforts to attract low-income students.

The movement for the amendment to the state constitution was initiated by a group of academics who solicited Connerly's involvement and were intent on putting a measure on the ballot banning preferential treatment in admissions and hiring by any state public employer, school, or contractor. Reluctant at first, Connerly joined the movement in 1995 and became the chairman of the California Civil Rights Initiative Campaign. Proposition 209 was supported by California voters by more than a 50 percent majority; it overturned affirmative action policies in state government. Once the California initiative was in place, Connerly took his movement to end affirmative action to the national level. In 1997 he formed the American Civil Rights Institute (ACRI), and in conjunction with this Institute, Connerly also formed the American Civil Rights Coalition as the nonprofit lobbying and initiative-introducing arm of ACRI.

Between 1997 and 1999 Connerly spearheaded moves to pass similar affirmative-action bans in Houston, Texas, and Florida. His efforts failed in Texas, but Florida Governor Jeb Bush issued executive orders banning many affirmative action programs. Through a program called One Florida, key portions of Connerly's proposal were implemented. Also, in July of 1997 Connerly's ACRI began to agitate for the addition of a multiracial category on the federal census and other government forms that collect racial data. He aligned himself with the multiracial movement, which culminated in the Racial Privacy Initiative. As Proposition 54, it was introduced to California voters in 2003. This initiative sought to prohibit the state government from using race, ethnicity, color, or national origin to classify students, employees, or public contractors. It did not prohibit classification by sex. Critics felt that the measure would make it difficult to track housing discrimination, racial profiling activities, and racial data for determining health treatment. The measure gained only 36 percent of the vote when placed before California voters in October 2003.

Not to be deterred by the measure's failure, Connerly continued to actively campaign to abolish affirmative action. Following the 2003 Supreme Court rulings in *Gratz v. Bollinger* and *Grutter v. Bollinger*, (a case in which the U.S. Supreme Court upheld the affirmative action admissions policy of the University of Michigan), Jennifer Gratz invited Connerly to Michigan to support a measure similar to the 1996 California amendment to ban affirmative action. Joining forces with the two plaintiffs in the case, Gratz and Barbara Grutter, Connerly led the campaign to effectively end all affirmative-action related programs in the state. The Michigan Civil Rights Initiative appeared on the November 2006 Michigan ballot and passed with 58 percent of the vote.

Connerly could best be described as Republican with a libertarian bent, with a multiracial ancestry (black, Irish, French, and Choctaw). His libertarian philosophy led him to support domestic partner benefits for gay and lesbian couples in all state universities to avoid discrimination against anyone. Connerly was an influential and controversial figure in America. He illustrated that blacks are not monolithic in their political views; rather, they often had diverse social, economic, and political viewpoints.

FURTHER READING

Bearack, Barry. "Questions of Race Run Deep for Foe of Preferences," *New York Times*, 27 July 1997.

Black Enterprise (Nov. 1995).

Christian Science Monitor, 16 Nov. 1999.

Chronicle of Higher Education, 28 July 1995.

Connerly, Ward. *Creating Equal: My Fight Against Race Preferences* (2002).

Gale Research. *Contemporary Black Biography*, volume 14 (1997).

JULUETTE BARTLETT PACK

Conyers, John F., Jr. (16 May 1929–), U.S. congressman, was born in Detroit, Michigan, the first of five children of John Conyers Sr., a factory auto painter who became an international representative for the United Automobile Workers, and Lucille Simpson. John Conyers Sr.'s progressive politics proved a major influence on his son's life and career. Conyers grew up in a predominantly Italian American neighborhood in East Detroit and graduated from the city's Samson Elementary School in 1943, the year of a major race riot in the city. The riot and his father's political activism shaped Conyers's political consciousness, but his primary interest as a teenager was jazz. An accomplished trumpet player, he included among his friends in high school SONNY STITT, MILT JACKSON, and BETTY CARTER, who all pursued careers in music. Unchallenged by his school work, Conyers spent much of his time in pool halls when not playing music. He nonetheless graduated in 1947 from Detroit's Northwestern High School.

Unable to afford college for his son, John Conyers Sr. secured for him a job as a welder at Lincoln Motor Company. The younger Conyers also began studying at night at Wayne State University. He served in the Army National Guard from 1948 to 1950, the U.S. Army from 1950 to 1954, including service in Korea in 1951, and the U.S. Army Reserves from 1954 to 1957 as an officer in the U.S. Army Corps of Engineers. He earned several combat and merit citations. Although he had set out to be an engineer, by the time he graduated with a B.A. from Wayne State in 1957, Conyers had decided on a career in law. He earned a J.D. degree in 1958, also from Wayne State University. Conyers began his political career as an undergraduate at Wayne State, where he was active in Detroit's Young Democrats Club. From December 1958 to May 1961 he served as a legislative assistant to Michigan representative John D. Dingell, during which time he was also a senior partner in the law firm of Conyers, Bell, and Townsend. In October 1961 Michigan governor John B. Swainson appointed Conyers a referee for the state's Workman's Compensation Department. When redistricting created a second black majority congressional district in Detroit in 1964, Conyers entered the race. Campaigning on a platform of

"equality, jobs, and peace," he won his first election to the U.S. Congress by a slight margin and became the second black man to serve as congressman from Michigan, following the Democrat from the Thirteenth District, Charles C. Diggs Jr., who was elected ten years earlier. In subsequent years Conyers won reelection by increasing margins. By 2007 he had served in Congress for forty-three years, longer than any other African American. In June 1990 Conyers married Monica Esters. They had two sons.

Conyers began his congressional career in support of the antipoverty and civil rights reforms proposed by President Lyndon Baines Johnson. In 1965 Conyers became the first African American member of the House Judiciary Committee, and he used that platform during the 1960s to support federal protection of civil rights workers and full implementation of the 1965 Voting Rights Act. He was also one of the earliest critics of the Vietnam War. In

John Conyers Jr. The ranking Democrat on the House Judiciary Committee, Conyers meets with reporters in October 1988. (AP Images.)

May 1965 he was one of only seven congressmen and three senators who opposed Johnson's escalation of American military involvement in Indochina. In the decades that followed Conyers emerged as one of the most outspoken critics of American military adventurism not only in Southeast Asia but also in the Caribbean and Central and South America. As critical of President Richard Nixon's foreign policies as he was of Johnson's, Conyers appeared as number thirteen on Nixon's notorious 1973 "enemies list," which included his fellow congressman RONALD DELLUMS, the actor Paul Newman, and the journalists Daniel Schorr and Mary McGrory. Conyers's role as one of the leaders of the Congressional Black Caucus, which he helped found in 1969, and his criticisms of Nixon's "benign neglect" of civil rights were also factors in Nixon's hostility toward him. In 1974 Conyers was a member of the House Judiciary Committee that recommended impeachment of the president following the Watergate scandal.

Conyers, who had supported the liberal congressman Morris Udall for the Democratic presidential nomination in 1976, was critical of President Jimmy Carter's domestic policies, particularly his unwillingness to support greater economic assistance to urban centers like Detroit, which suffered greatly from high unemployment in the 1970s and 1980s. A leading advocate of increases in the minimum wage and the 1978 Humphrey-Hawkins Act, which committed the nation to a policy of full employment, Conyers in 1979 introduced a house bill that would have lowered the normal work week to thirty-five hours and would have required employers to pay double for overtime. The bill did not become law, but it indicated that Conyers was one of the few members of Congress—Dellums was another—whose politics might reasonably be described as socialist.

In spite of Republican success in recapturing both the presidency, under Ronald Reagan, and the Senate in 1980, the House remained under Democratic control until 1994, leaving Conyers as one of the most powerful figures in Congress, notably on the Judiciary Committee. During his time in the majority on that committee, Conyers initiated a national study on police brutality, helped introduce the Alcohol Warning Label Act of 1988 and the Violence against Women Act of 1994, and conducted hearings in several cities on police violence, racially motivated violence, and racial profiling. An advocate of prison reform, he held a series of public meetings to hear testimony by both former inmates

and staff regarding the sexual misconduct of male guards in Michigan prisons. As a result Michigan prisons began to restrict male correctional officers from guarding women in private quarters. Conyers also created a job fair for ex-offenders in conjunction with the City of Detroit Employment Connection. This innovative partnership was established to reduce the recidivism rate among ex-offenders and to ensure their access to adequate employment once released from prison. Conyers was a persistent opponent of the death penalty.

Conyers opposed much of the foreign policy of the Reagan and George H. W. Bush administrations, notably the attempt to build a "Star Wars" antiballistic missile defense shield, the 1983 invasion of Grenada (for which he called for Reagan's impeachment), and the illegal funding of the right-wing Contras in Nicaragua. Long a supporter of the African National Congress, he chided the Reagan and Bush administrations' complicity with South Africa's apartheid regime. President Reagan did, however, sign into law in 1983 the MARTIN LUTHER KING JR. Holiday Act, a bill Conyers had first introduced in Congress in 1968, shortly after King's assassination. A jazz aficionado, Conyers was instrumental in the passage of the Jazz Preservation Act of 1987, which denotes jazz's classification as a national American treasure. Social justice issues and economic opportunity remained the focal points of Conyers's platform. The civil rights advocate and activist ROSA PARKS worked in several of his political campaigns and was employed for more than two decades in his Detroit office. In 1988 the House of Representatives appointed Conyers one of the managers to conduct the impeachment proceedings against Alcee Lamar Hastings, judge of the U.S. District Court for the Southern District of Florida. In January 1989 Conyers introduced H.R. Bill 40, which led to the creation of the Commission to Study Reparation Proposals for the African American Act. This bill was intended to prompt the federal government to undertake an official study of the impact of slavery on the nation as a whole, African Americans in particular. Although the bill made limited progress, Conyers introduced it in every legislative session. He was also the most prominent lawmaker who lobbied to free MUMIA ABU-JAMAL, the convicted murderer of a Philadelphia police officer.

When the Democratic Party lost control of the House in 1995, Conyers remained in Congress (he failed in two attempts to become mayor of Detroit). Conyers, who had supported the former California governor Jerry Brown against Bill Clinton in the 1992 Democratic primaries, nonetheless became one of President Clinton's strongest allies during efforts by the Republican majority to impeach the president following revelations that he had lied about an affair with an intern.

In response to problems experienced by voters during the 2000 presidential election, Conyers cowrote the comprehensive election reform legislation to end discriminatory election practices that was enacted in October 2002. This bill advanced civil rights and protected voting rights, among other provisions, by establishing federal voting rights standards for election machines and requiring that voting sites be made accessible to those with disabilities. For more than three decades Conyers led efforts in Congress to reform the health care system. He was founder and chairman of the Congressional Universal Health Care Task Force, a forty-five-member caucus whose mission was to secure universal health care legislation. Following the terrorist attacks in New York City and Washington, D.C., on 11 September 2001, Conyers supported some of the George W. Bush administration's efforts to prevent terrorism but expressed concern that elements of the administration's Homeland Security Act infringed on the civil liberties and civil rights of American citizens and residents. He also campaigned in the early 2000s to publicize the growing humanitarian crisis in Sudan and supported debt relief for Mozambique and other African countries. Committed to reestablishing democracy in Haiti, he criticized President George W. Bush's efforts to keep Haitian refugees from entering the United States. In the 108th Congress he cosponsored the Haitian Economic Recovering Act (the Hero Act), whose goal was to grant duty-free status to Haitian products. Believing that there were no weapons of mass destruction in Iraq, Conyers opposed the 2003 invasion of that country (Conyers had also opposed the 1991 Gulf War). Additionally he spoke at several antiwar demonstrations, both in the lead up to the war, when his opposition was a minority view in the nation, and afterward, when the failure to find weapons of mass destruction and the descent of Iraq into civil war had moved a majority of Americans toward Conyers's position.

In 2006, when Democrats won control of the House of Representatives for the first time in twelve years, Conyers became chair of the House Judiciary Committee. A few weeks before taking up the committee gavel in January 2007, however, he was accused of violating House ethics rules by asking his staff to work on his political campaigns and to babysit and chauffeur his children. Conyers admitted to a lack of clarity in his communications with staff members regarding their responsibilities, and no formal charges were brought.

Conyers, who was awarded the NAACP's Spingarn medal in 2007, again chaired the House Judiciary Committee from January 2007 until the Democratic Party's loss of Congress to the Republicans in 2010. A consistent liberal voice against the Bush administration's domestic and foreign policies in its final two years, Conyers promoted the idea of a "Truth and Reconciliation Committee" to investigate free speech and human rights abuses by the Bush administration. At the beginning of the 111th Congress in January 2009, Conyers introduced six major bills, including a proposal to establish a National Commission on Presidential War Powers and Civil Liberties; amendments to the Bankruptcy Code to make it easier to modify the terms of a home mortgage in foreclosure; measures to protect and expand voting rights, including the establishment of an Election Day federal holiday; and the establishment of a commission to study the institution of slavery, its continued effects on modern day society, and the issue of reparations.

While many members of the Congressional Black Caucus gravitated towards Senator Hillary Clinton (D-NY) in the 2008 Democratic Primaries, Conyers was the first member of the CBC to endorse Senator BARACK OBAMA (D-IL). This has not, however, prevented Conyers from criticizing the President for his failure to close Guantanamo Detention Center; for failing to bring American soldiers home from Afghanistan; and for attempting to seek common ground with Republicans in Congress to the detriment of Democratic priorities. His anger at Obama was particularly pointed on health care, due to the President's abandonment of the single payer option, Obama's support for which had been a major factor in Conyers' initial endorsement of him. Conyers also criticized the President's readiness to cut entitlement programs during the 2011 budget and debt ceiling crisis. In November 2012 Conyers was elected to his 24th term in Congress, winning 83 percent of the vote in his district.

FURTHER READING

Ehrenhalt, Alan, ed. *Politics in America: Members of Congress in Washington and at Home* (1983).
Salser, Mark R. *Black Americans in Congress* (1991).

Tate, Katherine. *Black Faces in the Mirror: African Americans and Their Representatives in the U.S. Congress* (2003).

FRED LINDSEY

Cook, Coralie Franklin (1861–25 Aug. 1942), educator and club woman, was born Coralie Franklin in Lexington, Virginia, a daughter of Albert Franklin and Mary E. (maiden name unknown). During or immediately after the Civil War the family moved to Harper's Ferry, West Virginia, where Coralie attended the Normal Department at Storer College, graduating in 1872. She continued her education at Storer and graduated from the Academic Department in 1880. A gifted elocutionist she was described by JOHN WESLEY CROMWELL, on a visit to Harper's Ferry in 1877, as "an elocutionist of grace, skill and power" (*Journal of Negro History*, July 1923). Franklin went on to attend Emerson College in Boston, the Shoemaker School of Oratory in Philadelphia, and the Martha's Vineyard Summer Institute of Oratory in Massachusetts. Franklin then returned to West Virginia and her alma mater, where she taught elocution at Storer College from 1882 to 1893, becoming one of the school's first black teachers.

While teaching at Storer, in January 1887, she began writing the Women's Column for the Martinsburg *Pioneer Press*, a paper owned and edited by her sister Mary's husband, JOHN R. CLIFFORD. The column contained articles on women's issues from other newspapers as well as original writings by Cook and other women throughout the state. In July of that same year Cook became one of the founders and president of Mount Hope Woman's Christian Temperance Union at Harper's Ferry, the only known African American branch of the organization in West Virginia. Reports on the organization also appeared in the *Press*.

From 1891 to 1900 Franklin taught English and elocution at Howard University in Washington, D.C., later becoming chair of oratory and founder of the School of Expression, a forerunner to the Washington Conservatory of Music and School of Expression founded by HARRIET GIBBS MARSHALL in 1903. In 1893 she became superintendent of the Washington, D.C., Home for Destitute Colored Women and Children, leading her to resign her position at Storer College and relocate to the District of Columbia. Although eager to move on, Harper's Ferry and Storer College remained in her heart. In letters to the *Storer Record*, the college newspaper, Franklin wrote, "I am busy and happy in my new field of labor. In spirit I mingle with teachers and pupils of you each day. Whatever of discouragement or distress may come to you, I share with you and whatever of success or encouragement is yours is mine also" (Feb. 1894). Her devotion to Storer led to her appointment as a trustee in 1894; she was one of the first women to hold that position.

In Washington, Franklin became involved in the women's club movement, joining the D.C. branch of the National League of Colored Women. When she presented a paper for the League at the Women's Congress of the Atlanta Exposition held in Atlanta in 1895, leading periodicals of the time claimed that "no finer paper was presented during the entire Congress" (*Harper's Bazaar*, 2 Nov. 1895) and that "the beautifully composed address was perfectly delivered and was remarkable for its rhetorical finish" (*Atlanta Constitution*, 10 Oct. 1895). In 1896 Franklin led the D.C. Colored Women's League on a pilgrimage to John Brown's Fort at Harper's Ferry. That same year she was part of a joint committee of fourteen women who met to consider a plan for a merger between the National League of Colored Women and the National Federation of African American women and played a vital role in the new organization, the National Association of Colored Women (NACW).

In August 1899 Franklin married GEORGE WILLIAM COOK, an educator, secretary-treasurer, and member of the board of trustees at Howard University. The couple had one son, George Will Jr. After her marriage Coralie Franklin Cook worked to improve education and achieve social justice through women and civil rights, community, and educational organizations. She was a delegate to the Susan B. Anthony Eightieth Anniversary Mass Meeting held in Washington, D.C., in 1900. In 1904, at a meeting of the NACW in St. Louis, Missouri, members selected Cook, MARY CHURCH TERRELL, JOSEPHINE B. BRUCE, and MARGARET MURRAY WASHINGTON to attend the International Congress of Women held in Berlin, Germany. In 1915 Cook addressed the Panama Pacific Exhibition held in San Francisco.

Around 1913 George and Coralie Franklin Cook became members of the Baha'i Faith. They were attracted to the Baha'i principles of the unity of mankind in peace without animosity or prejudice and equality between men and women. In 1914 she wrote, "Weary and heart sore, discouraged with the Churches that close their doors to them, the silent pulpits that should thunder forth in trumpet tones against the iniquities in the pews, it were strange indeed if the Baha'i teachings wakened no response of great hope in the hearts of colored people" (quoted in Darlene Clark Hine, et al., *Black Women in America*, 1993, 63).

Unlike many black women in the early years of the suffrage movement, Cook encouraged interracial cooperation. She remained a suffragist but her views on interracial cooperation changed when black women faced discrimination from the National Women's Suffrage Association. In August 1915 Cook wrote an essay for the *Crisis* titled "Votes for Mothers" in which she wrote, "Disfranchisement because of sex is curiously like disfranchisement because of color. It cripples the individual, it handicaps progress, it sets limitations upon mental and spiritual development." Other publications include "A Slave for Life" in the June 1929 issue of *Opportunity*.

Cook served on the District of Columbia board of education from 1914 to 1926, a time of increasing racial tension in the city. Cook continued to use her oratory skills, addressing the Fourth Pan-African Conference in New York City in 1927. She also belonged to the Delta Sigma Theta Sorority, the Free Baptist Women's Missionary Society, the Book Lovers Club, the Board of Public Welfare, the National District Social Hygiene Association, the Juvenile Protection Association, and the Red Cross.

Throughout her life, Coralie Franklin Cook envisioned a better world, with opportunities for all. Upon her death, in a last remembrance to her alma mater, she established a scholarship at Storer College.

FURTHER READING

Cash, Floris Barnett. *African American Women and Social Action: Clubwomen and Volunteerism from Jim Crow to the New Deal, 1896–1936* (2001).

Moore, Jacqueline M. *Leading the Race: The Transformation of the Black Elite in the Nation's Capital, 1880–1920* (1999).

Salem, Dorothy C. *To Better Our World: Black Women in Organized Reform, 1890–1920* (1990).

CONNIE PARK RICE

Cook, Fields (1814–?), slave narrative author, minister, and politician, was born in rural tidewater Virginia. All that is known about Cook's early life appears in an unpublished, handwritten, thirty-two-page autobiographical narrative, which is the only surviving memoir written by a slave while still in the South. Unlike nearly all of the autobiographical memoirs written by nineteenth-century African American slaves, Cook's narrative is not addressed to a Northern abolitionist audience, but rather was written solely for the author's "own benefit in future years." Cook may also have had a larger audience in mind, since he promises at one point "to be candid before an enli[ghtened] community," though it is possible that he intended his children and grandchildren to read it. The narrative also makes clear Cook's extensive knowledge of the Scriptures, and it may have served as a guide for his later work as a minister.

Episodic, occasionally rambling, and often vague in its details, Cook's memoir is nonetheless revealing of the inner life and experiences of a thirty-three-year-old black Virginian, who never directly acknowledges whether he is free or a slave. (Census materials indicate that he was a slave.) Although he does not provide the name of his parents or siblings, Cook recalls that his mother "had brought us up to stand greatly in fear of her." He also discusses two events from childhood that made a profound impression on him. In the first, as a young child he was badly scalded by an overturned coffeepot. The second was the ending of a close childhood friendship with a white boy, perhaps the son of his master, whom he had thought of as a brother. Constant companions until Fields was sent out to work and his friend was sent to school, the two boys remained close. The white boy taught him to read and write, but one day, Cook recalled, his friend "began to feel some what a man and like the peafowl in a [brood] of chickens he began to raise his feathers and boast of the superiority which he had over me." Later in life Cook forgave his friend, who had become a Christian.

The rest of Cook's narrative deals mainly with the various trials in his life that resulted in his salvation as a Christian and in his removal to Richmond. He notes several near-death experiences: he was chased and bitten by wild dogs, was thrown from a horse at speed, and was badly injured unloading pine rails, an accident that confined him to bed for six weeks. Cook's survival of these incidents further persuaded him that a benevolent God had spared him. He also describes the sins and folly of his youth, including his love of dancing and his obsession with women, although at first an intense shyness prevented him from acting upon his desires. Engaged to a local woman in the early 1830s, Cook successfully petitioned his master to leave for Richmond when the relationship ended in 1834. There on Christmas Day 1835 Cook met Mary, the woman he later married, though not until after she had been baptized in the First Baptist Church of Richmond and he had promised her that he also would become a Christian. It is unknown whether the couple had children.

At the time that he completed his memoir in February 1847 Cook believed that God had called him to the ministry. He was unable to preach the gospel, however, because of the laws prohibiting blacks from preaching that had been enacted by the Virginia legislature in the wake of the NAT TURNER rebellion in 1831. Cook greatly resented Turner, "who had better never been born," and blamed him for the wave of terror and violent white reprisals against African Americans that swept the Virginia countryside after the rebellion. In 1853 Cook's owner manumitted him and allowed him to remain in Richmond, where he worked as a barber and medical doctor. A property owner even before he gained his freedom, Cook owned personal property worth $2,400 on the eve of the Civil War and was well known and respected by leaders of both races in Richmond and its environs. By then he had also realized his dream of becoming a lay preacher and was active in Richmond's First African Baptist Church.

Cook was prominent in black political circles in Richmond at the end of the Civil War. In early June 1865 he helped organize a meeting at the First African Baptist Church to protest the ill-treatment of black soldiers in the Union army, and he chaired a meeting about that issue with President Andrew Johnson and O. O. Howard, commissioner of the Freedman's Bureau. As a result of this meeting the army eased curfew restrictions on black soldiers and set up military tribunals that allowed African Americans to testify.

Around this time Cook began working as a cashier in the Freedman's Savings Bank and was a prime mover in several mass meetings of black freemen in 1865, notably at Richmond in June and at Alexandria in August. Although Cook has generally been portrayed as one of the more conservative black leaders of Virginia's Reconstruction, he was sufficiently outspoken on the rights of freemen to receive on the final day of the Alexandria meeting an anonymous letter containing a death threat. Upon receiving it Cook addressed his fellow delegates, telling them to ignore the letter and that he would gladly give up his life for the freemen's cause. In May 1867 Judge John C. Underwood appointed Cook and five other black men to serve on the federal grand jury that indicted Jefferson Davis, former president of the Confederacy, for treason.

Cook was also prominent in the efforts to establish a biracial Republican Party in Virginia in the late 1860s, and he generally adopted a conservative position on all matters, except for the right of black males to vote. He was, however, opposed to women's suffrage, and at one party meeting he protested the seating of a female observer. He strongly opposed the confiscation of Confederate property, chastised rural black Republicans for their radicalism, and was an ally of John Minor Botts, a former Whig congressman who led the conservative faction of the Virginia Republican Party. Cook's endorsement of cooperation with white Virginian conservatives was not shared by most black Republicans in the state, who generally followed the more radical approach of the Norfolk Republican THOMAS BAYNE. Out of step with the prevailing radical mood among black Republicans, Cook ran for the U.S. Congress in 1869 as an independent. In spite of significant backing from prominent white conservatives, he lost and never again sought political office.

It is unknown when Fields Cook died, though it may have been around 1902, when the Library of Congress acquired the only existing copy of his narrative from an unknown donor. Though it does not compare in style and sophistication to those of FREDERICK DOUGLASS or HARRIET JACOBS, Cook's autobiography provides a rare glimpse into the life of a black, conservative, evangelical man in the antebellum South.

FURTHER READING
The manuscript of Fields Cook's narrative can be found in the Library of Congress, Washington, D.C.; the text is available online at http://docsouth.unc.edu/neh/fields/fields.html.

Bratton, Mary Jo Jackson. "Fields' Observations: The Slave Narrative of a Nineteenth Century Virginian," *Virginia Magazine of History and Biography* 88 (1980).

Calhoon, Robert M. *Evangelicals and Conservatives in the Early South, 1740–1861* (1988).

STEVEN J. NIVEN

Cook, George F. T. (18 June 1835–7 Aug. 1912), educator, was born free in Washington, D.C., to the Reverend JOHN FRANCIS COOK, who ran a free school for African Americans in that city. The name of George's mother is not recorded, but his elder brother, JOHN FRANCIS COOK JR., also was active in education and political circles in Washington after the Civil War. Born into slavery the Reverend

Cook had gained his freedom by the time his sons were born. As pastor of the city's Fifteenth Street Presbyterian Church and a founding member of the Grand United Order of Odd Fellows he was also prominent in Washington's black religious and fraternal organizations.

In September 1835, when George was only three months old, Reverend Cook was forced to close his school and flee Washington with his family when he learned that a white mob was planning to attack him. The "Snow Riot," as it came to be known, caused the temporary closing of all black schools in the city, and was part of the widespread white backlash against black education that followed the rebellion led by NAT TURNER, a literate slave, in nearby Virginia in 1831. When Reverend Cook returned with his family to Washington in 1836 he reopened his school as Union Seminary and played a key role in restoring black education in the nation's capital, despite the opposition of the city's white churches. George and his elder brother were among his first pupils at Union Seminary and as teenagers became their father's assistants. When Reverend Cook died in 1855 his sons returned to Washington from their studies at Oberlin College in Ohio to take over the running of the school, although John left in 1857 to teach for three years in New Orleans.

Washington's African American population exploded between 1860 and 1865 as thousands of runaway slaves, contrabands of war, and ambitious Northern blacks fled to the city in search of work. Since privately funded schools like George Cook's were unable to cope with this influx, and since the various missionary societies had just begun their work to educate the freedmen, in 1862 Congress moved to enact a law establishing the District's first "colored" public school system. The system was to be funded by 10 percent of the taxes levied on Washington's black property holders, but because this raised only eight hundred dollars over two years, the city's first public school did not open until 1864. The following year the Negro Board of Trustees of the District Schools appointed its first superintendent, A. E. Newton, who served until 1868, at which time Cook, who at the time was working as a Republican Party organizer in the South, was appointed to the post.

From the beginning of his tenure Cook was forced to navigate the complexities of the District's governance and the partisan politics of Reconstruction. In 1869 the Republicans in Congress passed a law that would have abolished the separate public school systems in the District and replaced them with a unitary system without regard to race. Blacks in Washington strongly opposed the measure, which would almost certainly have cost Cook his job, and, because the city at that time had a white majority, would have resulted in an all-white school board. Under pressure from many black citizens of the District, President Andrew Johnson refused to sign the bill into law. Cook also survived several reorganizations of the District's government. In 1873, when control of the schools was transferred from the Department of the Interior to an autonomous District of Columbia government, Cook maintained his position as Superintendent of Negro Schools. He also survived a further reorganization of the District the following year, when the city's administration was placed in the hands of three commissioners appointed by Congress.

Despite these early administrative challenges Cook enjoyed a high degree of autonomy in his thirty-two years as superintendent of the District's black schools. At first, when the public school population was little more than 2,500, he appointed many of his former pupils to teach in the normal and graded school, but as the system expanded he began to attract many of the most talented black educators in the nation. Among those he appointed to positions in the District's schools were FRANCIS L. CARDOZO, a graduate of Glasgow University who served as secretary of state of South Carolina during Reconstruction; MARY JANE PATTERSON, the first black woman to graduate in classics from Oberlin; Richard T. Greener, Harvard's first black graduate; ROBERT H. TERRELL, also a Harvard graduate, who later became the first African American appointed as a municipal court judge; and the writer ANNA JULIA COOPER, also an Oberlin graduate, who received her doctorate from the Sorbonne. The exceptionally talented staff that Cook assembled to teach in the District's schools undoubtedly testifies to his skills as an administrator, though it also tends to indicate the lack of alternative professional opportunities for academically gifted African Americans in the late nineteenth century.

In July 1900 Cook resigned when a single white superintendent was appointed to lead the District's black and white school systems. Although there would continue to be a black assistant superintendent with responsibility for the city's black schools, Cook refused to accept such an obvious demotion. His lengthy tenure as Washington's foremost black educator helped make that city's black public school system the best in the nation; it also placed George Cook firmly among the city's black elite. An 1895 survey estimated his personal worth at fifty thousand dollars, though that figure was only one-fourth as much as the worth of his brother John, the city's wealthiest black resident at that time. George F. T. Cook's legacy to an entire generation of black Washingtonians, however, was priceless. He died, aged seventy-seven, after a brief illness.

FURTHER READING

Gatewood, Willard B. *Aristocrats of Color: The Black Elite, 1880–1920* (1990).

Wormley, G. Smith. "Educators of the First Half Century of Public Schools in the District of Columbia," *Journal of Negro History* 17 (Apr. 1932).

Obituary: *Crisis*, Jan. 1913.

STEVEN J. NIVEN

Cook, George William (7 Jan. 1855–20 Aug. 1931), educator and civil rights leader, was born a slave in Winchester, Virginia. The names of his parents are unknown. In May 1862 the Cook family, which included seven children, became war refugees after the Union capture of Winchester. The family eventually settled in Harrisburg, Pennsylvania, where young Cook's most important early experience as a free person was working as a servant for David D. Mumma, a Pennsylvania state legislator. Permitted to use the Mumma family library, Cook developed the ambition to seek higher education, which would have remained beyond his grasp except for several fortunate events.

After he moved to New York in 1871, Cook learned about Howard University from the Reverend HENRY HIGHLAND GARNET, a black abolitionist and Howard trustee. Then, in the course of working for a physician, Cook met the reformer George B. Cheever, a classmate of Henry Wadsworth Longfellow and Oliver Wendell Holmes. Cheever was so impressed by Cook's eagerness for higher education that he paid Cook's tuition to Howard for one year. Cook entered the Preparatory Department (the university's high school) in 1874, graduated three years later, and entered Howard's College Department. Graduating as valedictorian in 1881, he went on to earn an M.A. from Howard in 1886, an LLB in 1898, and an LLM in 1899.

Widely regarded as "one of the pillars of Howard University," Cook began his career as a tutor of mathematics and as assistant principal of the Normal Department in 1881. Eight years later he became the principal of the Normal Department, a large but diverse unit of the university. The department reflected the educational improvisation necessary to meet the extraordinary needs of the recently emancipated slaves who attended the institution in its early years, including elementary, secondary, and some college-level instruction, as well as courses in music, industrial arts, bookkeeping, and typing. In 1899 the university decided to deemphasize precollegiate work and reorganized the Normal Department into a professional teachers college like the one founded at Columbia University in 1892. Lewis Baxter Moore was appointed dean of the new Teachers College, and Cook, whose major interest was in business education, served from 1899 to 1905 as the dean of the department responsible for commercial subjects.

As a professor of civics and commercial law from 1902 to 1928, Cook wanted to develop a stable business college at Howard; such a college was not realized in his lifetime. The Commercial College was limited to offering secondary-level subjects (1905–1919), and when these courses were terminated in 1919, Cook succeeded in having commercial subjects included in the new Junior College. When the Junior College was abolished in 1925, Cook was appointed professor of commercial law and international law (which he had taught in the Commercial College since its establishment) in the College of Liberal Arts.

Although Cook's ambitions for business education at Howard were thwarted, he nevertheless became a successful administrator of the university. He was appointed business manager in 1908 and, a year later, secretary of the university and of its board of trustees. For a decade he was the highest-ranking black official at Howard. Respected for his business and administrative ability, Cook was also a civic leader. President Theodore Roosevelt appointed Cook a member of the District of Columbia Board of Charities in 1904, and the District of Columbia Commissioners in 1907 appointed Cook the first superintendent of Washington's school for delinquent black children at Blue Plains, D.C. Cook's wife, Coralie Franklin (CORALIE COOK), whom he had married in 1899, was a member of the District of Columbia Board of Education.

Cook became a national figure through his work with the NAACP. From 1912 to 1931 he was treasurer of the nation's largest and most active NAACP branch, in Washington, D.C. He was elected to the NAACP's national board of directors in 1914 and served until his death. Cook was at the center of the controversy during World War I to establish a camp for black officers. The War

Department had made provisions to train white officers but maintained that no facilities were available for training black officers. Working closely with Joel Spingarn, the white president of the NAACP, with Dean WILLIAM PICKENS of Morgan College (now Morgan State University), and with George W. Cabaniss of Washington, Cook was the crucial link among the NAACP, the university, and the black civic leadership of Washington. Acting on his own, Cook offered the campus of Howard University as a training camp. After Cook and others organized the Central Committee of Negro College Men, which recruited qualified candidates for the proposed camp, the War Department finally agreed to establish the Colored Officers Training Camp at Fort Des Moines and a Student Army Training Camp at Howard, which trained 1,786 men. Although the army maintained its policy of racial segregation, the NAACP won one of its early public policy victories in the fight for black officers.

Associated with Howard University for fifty-eight years, Cook served under ten presidents and was an important part of the institution's emergence from a Freedmen's Bureau experiment to a respected university. He retired in 1928, was elected secretary of the General Alumni Association, and continued to live on the campus until his death. Cook died in Philadelphia, Pennsylvania, after a short illness at his summer home in Asbury Park, New Jersey. Funeral services were held in Andrew Rankin Memorial Chapel at Howard on 24 August 1931. He was buried in Lincoln Cemetery, Washington, D.C., and was survived by his wife and a son. Howard named a men's dormitory in Cook's honor in 1940.

FURTHER READING

Cook's papers are in the Manuscript Division of the Moorland-Spingarn Research Center, Howard University, Washington, D.C.

Dyson, Walter. *Howard University: The Capstone of Negro Education* (1941).

Logan, Rayford W. *Howard University: The First Hundred Years, 1867–1967* (1969).

This entry is taken from the *American National Biography* and is published here with the permission of the American Council of Learned Societies.

MICHAEL R. WINSTON

Cook, John Francis (1810?–21 Mar. 1855), educator and clergyman, was born a slave in the District of Columbia. His mother was Laurena Browning Cook, but his father's identity is unknown. His mother's sister, ALETHIA BROWNING TANNER, was clearly a dominant influence in his early life. Although she was a slave, her owner allowed her to hire out her own time, and by operating a profitable vegetable market in Washington, D.C., she acquired the money to purchase her own freedom as well as that of her sister and about twenty-one other relatives and acquaintances, including her nephew. Freed at the age of sixteen, Cook apprenticed himself to a shoemaker in order to earn the money to repay his aunt.

He completed his apprenticeship in 1831 but abandoned shoemaking because of an injured shoulder. He secured a job as a messenger in the office of the United States Land Commissioner where a white employee, John Wilson, recognized his ability and encouraged him to acquire an education. In his spare time Cook learned to read and write. He attended a school for blacks known as Smothers School but was largely self-educated. In 1834 he assumed charge of the Smothers School and changed its name to Union Seminary.

Cook headed the seminary for the next two decades, except for the year 1835 when an outbreak of antiblack violence in Washington, D.C., known as the Snow riot, resulted in extensive damage to the school and prompted him and other free blacks to flee the city. For a year he lived near Philadelphia, Pennsylvania, with a friend, the businessman and moral reformer WILLIAM WHIPPER, whom he had met at various conventions of free blacks who gathered periodically to address the problems of both slaves and freed persons. Cook had made his first appearance as a delegate to such a convention in New York City in 1834. The following year he served as secretary of a similar gathering in Philadelphia, during which delegates petitioned the federal government to extend full rights to free blacks and to grant immediate emancipation to all slaves. The Philadelphia convention also launched the American Moral Reform Society, created to address "education, temperance, economy and universal liberty," an enterprise enthusiastically supported by Cook. Through his participation in the convention movement, Cook became acquainted with prominent free blacks throughout the United States.

After returning to Washington, D.C., in 1836 Cook resumed direction of Union Seminary. The building underwent extensive renovations to repair damage resulting from the Snow riot; once these were complete, the school's reputation, as well as Cook's, began to grow. During some years there were more than 100 students in attendance. Among them were the two mixed-race daughters of Vice President Richard M. Johnson.

A deeply religious individual, Cook increasingly manifested interest in church affairs after his return to Washington. Associated initially with the African Methodist Episcopal (AME) Church, he occasionally filled the pulpit of Israel AME Church and was a founder and trustee of Union Bethel AME Church. In 1840, however, Cook withdrew his membership from Union Bethel and became affiliated with the Presbyterian Church. The reasons for his transfer of denominational allegiance are unclear, but it appears that the influence of a white friend, John C. Smith, minister of the Fourth Presbyterian Church of Washington, figured in Cook's decision. When racial tensions in the wake of the Snow riot made it impossible for Fourth Presbyterian to hold a Sabbath school for black children, Smith pressed for the establishment of an all-black Presbyterian congregation in the city and promoted Cook as the one to head it. At Smith's urging, the District of Columbia Presbytery approved the organization of a "colored Presbyterian church," and a group of free blacks meeting at Union Seminary late in 1841 chose Cook as pastor. For the next eighteen months he prepared for the rigorous examinations that he had to pass in order to be ordained. In 1843, less than two decades after receiving his freedom, Cook became the first black person in the District of Columbia to be officially ordained as a minister in the Presbyterian Church. His congregation was known as the First Colored Presbyterian Church of Washington.

For the rest of his life Cook devoted his abundant energies to his church and school. In addition to his teaching duties, he presided over his fledgling congregation, preached, held prayer meetings, organized a Sunday school library and abstinence society, assisted in the formation of the first black ministerial association in the District, and engaged in a variety of fund-raising activities. The latter enabled the congregation to construct a sizable church on Fifteenth Street in 1852, and the name was changed to the Fifteenth Street Presbyterian Church. By the time of his death in Washington, D.C., the church had 120 members, including many of the capital city's most prominent people of color.

Despite the demands of running the church and school, Cook was involved in a wide variety of civic and social uplift activities among blacks.

A charter member of the local lodge of the Grand United Order of Odd Fellows, he was a prominent figure in the temperance movement and a founder of Harmony Cemetery for blacks in Washington. Widely respected by both blacks and whites, he possessed a reputation for unimpeachable integrity and public spiritedness.

Cook was married twice. With his first wife, Jane Mann, a woman of African Indian ancestry, he had six children. Upon her death he married Jane Le Count of Philadelphia; they had one child. The children who lived to adulthood became leaders in their own communities. Among them, JOHN F. COOK JR. was a public official and reputedly the wealthiest African American in the District of Columbia at that time; GEORGE F. T. COOK headed for many years D.C.'s separate colored school system; and Samuel Le Count Cook graduated from the University of Michigan Medical School and was a physician in the District.

FURTHER READING

The Cook Family Papers are in the Moorland-Spingarn Research Center, Howard University, Washington, D.C.

Gatewood, Willard B. "John Francis Cook: Antebellum Black Presbyterian," *American Presbyterians: Journal of Presbyterian History* 67 (Fall 1989): 221–30.

Green, Constance M. *The Secret City: A History of Race Relations in the Nation's Capital* (1967).

This entry is taken from the *American National Biography* and is published here with the permission of the American Council of Learned Societies.

WILLARD B. GATEWOOD

Cook, John Francis, Jr. (21 Sept. 1833–20 Jan. 1910), public official and businessman, was born in Washington, D.C., the son of the prominent African American clergyman and educator JOHN FRANCIS COOK (1810?–1855) and Jane Mann. Educated first at his father's school, Union Seminary, he later attended Oberlin College in Ohio from 1853 to 1855. Upon the death of their father, he and his brother GEORGE F. T. COOK, also a student at Oberlin, returned to Washington to assume direction of Union Seminary. Except for a brief tenure in New Orleans as a schoolteacher, John Cook was connected with the seminary until it ceased operation in 1867 after the District of Columbia opened public schools for blacks. While his brother remained in the education field and was for many years superintendent of the "separate colored school system" in the District of Columbia,

John Cook embarked upon a career in government service, Republican politics, and business.

In 1867 Cook secured a clerkship in the office of the District tax collector. A staunch advocate of universal male suffrage, he was elected the following year to the Washington board of aldermen in the first election in which blacks were allowed to vote. From 1869 to 1876 he also served as a justice of the peace. After 1868 until his death, he wielded considerable influence in local Republican politics and served as a delegate to the party's national conventions in 1872 and 1880. Careful to cultivate influential friends in Congress and the White House, Cook was appointed District tax collector by President Ulysses S. Grant in 1874 and retained the office for the next decade. Although he later served as jury commissioner in 1889 and was a member of the Board of Children's Guardians for almost two decades beginning in 1892, his tenure as a prominent District official ended when he left the tax collector's office.

During his years as a city official Cook began to accumulate what ultimately became a sizable fortune. By the turn of the century he was reputed to be one of the wealthiest black men in the United States. One knowledgeable observer estimated that his net worth in 1895 was in excess of $200,000. Four years later Cook built a large brick and stone home on Sixteenth Street, described as the most commodious house in Washington owned by an African American. Much of his wealth was derived from wise investments in real estate, including some located in the heart of the city's business district. Known as leaders of Washington's "black 400," Cook and his wife continued to be included in the *Elite List*, a forerunner of the *Social Register*, long after other upper-class blacks had been dropped.

Despite occasional criticism of his family's alleged penchant for social exclusiveness, Cook remained solidly identified with the black community and with various efforts to promote its welfare. For many years he was a trustee of the Home for Destitute Colored Women and Children in Washington. Throughout his career Cook was an effective advocate of civil rights and vigorously opposed Jim Crow practices in the District. Although he had abandoned education as a career, he remained deeply interested in educational matters. He used his influence to win greater public support for black schools, especially after his appointment to the District board of education upon its reorganization in 1906, a position he retained until a few months before his death. No

educational institution attracted more of his support than Howard University. A member of the university's board of trustees for thirty-five years (1875–1910), Cook served on its executive committee and on several occasions as its chairman.

Cook was associated with various social and cultural organizations in the District. A conspicuous figure in fraternal circles, he was for a dozen years grand master of the Eureka Lodge, the oldest and most prestigious chapter of Prince Hall Freemasonry in the Washington area. Also, like his father, Cook took an active interest in the Harmony Cemetery Association. A man of "refined" musical taste, he served as president of the Coleridge-Taylor Choral Society, an organization chartered in 1903 "to diffuse among the masses a higher musical culture and appreciation for the works that tend to refine and cultivate." The society sponsored American tours in 1904 and 1906 by the black British composer, Samuel Coleridge-Taylor, for whom it was named. Cook took an interest in the preservation of African American history. As a trustee of the FREDERICK DOUGLASS Memorial and Historical Association, he labored to preserve the home of Frederick Douglass, Cedar Hill, as a historic monument. He and his family were staunch members of the church founded by his father, Fifteenth Street Presbyterian.

Cook was married to Helen Elizabeth Appo of an old and well-known Philadelphia, Pennsylvania, family; they had five children. Prominent in the formation of the National Association of Colored Women, Helen Cook was described by FANNIE BARRIER WILLIAMS as "a noted example and inspiration to women of her own social standing in the serious work of social reform." John Cook died in Washington, D.C. Like his father, he was for half a century one of the most influential members of the large and expanding African American community in the nation's capital.

FURTHER READING

The Cook Family Papers are in the Moorland-Spingarn Research Center, Howard University.

Gatewood, Willard B. *Aristocrats of Color: The Black Elite, 1880–1920* (1990).

Green, Constance M. *The Secret City: A History of Race Relations in the Nation's Capital* (1967).

Obituary: *Washington Bee,* 29 Jan. 1910.

This entry is taken from the *American National Biography* and is published here with the permission of the American Council of Learned Societies.

WILLARD B. GATEWOOD

Cook, Joyce Mitchell (28 Oct. 1933–), philosopher and educator, was born in Sharon, Pennsylvania, the ninth of twelve children of the Reverend Isaac William Mitchell Sr., a minister of the Church of God (headquartered in Anderson, Indiana), and Mary Belle Christman Mitchell, a homemaker. Cook was briefly married to J. Lawrence Cook, M.D. Cook holds the distinction of being the first African American woman to receive a Ph.D. in Philosophy in the United States. She was also the first woman appointed to teach in the department of philosophy at Yale College (September 1959 to June 1961) and the first African American woman to teach philosophy at Howard University (September 1966 to June 1968 and September 1970 to June 1976).

Cook's early education took place in the Sharon public school system. After reading a biography of Madame Curie, Cook decided to study chemistry, but as an undergraduate at Bryn Mawr College she became interested in philosophy. Cook graduated from that institution—where she was one of only two black students—in 1955 with an AB in Philosophy with honors. Her first philosophy class was taught by Isabelle Stearns, the only woman philosopher at Bryn Mawr College at the time and later the director of Cook's honors thesis on Benedictus de Spinoza, whom she studied because of her interest in his geometrical method. Cook also studied under Geddes MacGregor, a Scotsman who taught her medieval philosophy. Cook was passionate not only about philosophy but had a deep and abiding love of classical music, and was particularly fond of the works of the Polish piano composer and pianist Frederic Chopin.

Cook wrote to Harvard University, indicating her interest in pursuing graduate studies, but was advised to try Radcliffe College. Instead of contacting Radcliffe, Cook applied to Yale University and was accepted the same year that she graduated from Bryn Mawr (1955). Meanwhile Cook also applied to Oxford University, which she attended between 1955 and 1957, writing a letter to Yale requesting that it hold her dossier until she reapplied. She went to Oxford because she admired the English language and English literature. When she reapplied to Yale she was accepted. She received her B.A. in 1957 from Oxford with high honors in a double major, Philosophy and Psychology. She was awarded an M.A. from Oxford in 1961. While at Oxford, Cook studied with the leading analytic philosopher Peter Strawson. She was also introduced to the ethics side of the analytical school of philosophy while attending informal lectures given by John Austin, a prominent British linguistic philosopher. Cook's tutors were Mary Warnock, who sent Cook to Strawson, which was an indication of Warnock's confidence in Cook's philosophical acumen, and B.A. Farrell, who taught philosophy of mind.

After graduating from Oxford, Cook entered Yale in 1957, where she was one of a handful of women students in the graduate school to study philosophy. Cook stayed at Yale for four years, and during the last two (1959–1961) she served as a teaching assistant in philosophy. This marked the first time that a woman was appointed to teach in Yale College in a field other than foreign languages. During those same two years she worked as the managing editor of the prestigious philosophy journal *Review of Metaphysics*, edited by the eminent American philosopher Paul Weiss, who showed a great deal of confidence in Cook's editorial abilities. She also worked at Yale University Press. Cook studied with such well-known philosophers as Wilfrid Sellars, F. S. C. Northrop, Rulon Wells, and John Smith. Although she was not a convert to Weiss's brand of metaphysical speculation, partly due to the influence of Oxford's view of philosophy, Cook learned from Weiss his dedication to philosophy, his care for his children, and his extraordinary industry. Weiss also hired Cook during her first year at Yale to be a reader for his undergraduate philosophy of art class.

Cook described herself as "always primarily interested in ethics" (Yancy, 271). Specializing in value theory, which Cook says includes branches of logic "insofar as logic is interested in what constitutes a good argument" (Yancy, 272), Cook wrote a dissertation titled "A Critical Examination of Stephen C. Pepper's Theory of Value." Pepper was a well-known American philosopher who wrote on ethics and aesthetics, among other philosophical topics. Cook graduated from Yale with her Ph.D. in 1965.

In addition to the teaching experiences noted above, Cook also taught for two years at Connecticut College (1968–1970) and one year at Wellesley College (1961–1962). For about a year and a half Cook also worked for the State Department, where she served as an analyst covering the affairs of various African countries. After leaving the State Department, she worked for the now defunct Office of Economic Opportunity. Though she left governmental work in 1966 she returned to it when she worked at the White House under President Jimmy Carter for four years (1977–1981), where she served as an editor/writer, writing special correspondence for the president and supervising a staff of twelve writers. In 2004 Cook was the recipient of an ALAIN LOCKE Excellence Award in African Philosophy, presented at Howard University. The award was given in part for Cook's early attempts to articulate, philosophically, the meaning of black philosophy. In the early 1970s, during the formative historical period when only a small number of black philosophers were working toward defining the discursive field of black philosophy, Cook was actively involved in a number of significant panel and conference discussions on the conceptual parameters of black philosophy. During that period she also served for two years on the Program Committee of the American Philosophical Association, Eastern Division, as well as on its Committee on Blacks in Philosophy

Given the paucity of African American women in the field of philosophy, the low percentage of African Americans in the field of philosophy more generally, and the paucity of women studying philosophy in the United States in the 1950s, Joyce Mitchell Cook is a significant pioneer in the field of American philosophy.

FURTHER READING

Cook, Joyce Mitchell. "A Critical Examination of Stephen C. Pepper's Theory of Value," Ph.D. diss., Yale University (1965).

Cook, Joyce Mitchell. "The Examined Life," *Bryn Mawr College Alumnae Bulletin* (Oct. 1973).

Cook, Joyce Mitchell. "The Nature and Nurture of Intelligence," *Philosophical Forum*, vol. 9, nos. 2–3 (Winter–Spring, 1977–1978).

Yancy, George. *African-American Philosophers: 17 Conversations* (1998).

GEORGE YANCY

Cook, Vivian E. J. (6 Oct. 1889–28 July 1977), educator, was born Vivian Elma Johnson in Colliersville, Tennessee, the daughter of Spencer Johnson, a farmer, and Caroline Alley, a teacher. One of eight children, Vivian grew up under the enterprising spirit of her parents, both of whom were born in slavery. That her mother was the first black schoolteacher in Fayette County, Tennessee, set a special standard of achievement for Vivian and her seven siblings. The family moved to Memphis when she was very young, and the decision was made to favor the girls with a higher education. All four were to graduate from college, but Vivian, thanks to the financial assistance of a brother, the inventor and railway postal clerk Thomas W. Johnson, was able to attend Howard University and later earn a master's degree in English from Columbia University.

In 1912, the year of her graduation from Howard, Vivian accepted a post at Tuskegee Institute under BOOKER T. WASHINGTON, which was the beginning of her teaching career. Over one summer session at Tuskegee she directed the Children's House, a demonstration school where visiting black educators could observe teaching methods. Though extended an invitation from Washington to return to Tuskegee for a second year, she chose instead to take a post in 1913 in Cincinnati under the principalship of an educator who had observed her at the Children's House. Vivian's year in Cincinnati was followed by several years as an English teacher at Sumner High in St. Louis, then one of the leading black high schools in the nation. In 1918 she married Ralph Victor Cook, a graduate in engineering from Cornell and a member of the prominent Cook family of Washington, D.C., whom she had met in graduate school at Columbia in 1917, the summer in which she received her master's degree. The couple had one son, who died in infancy.

Teaching science and English, Cook joined her husband, who headed mechanical drawing, at Baltimore's Colored High School, which was later named Frederick Douglass High School. While teaching in Baltimore in 1921, she called a meeting of African American women to found the Epsilon Omega Chapter, Alpha Kappa Alpha Sorority, the first chapter of this sorority on the East Coast, which she headed for two years. Three years later Cook organized the Baltimore branch of the National Association of College Women and later served as its president for two terms, from 1933 to 1937. Meanwhile she found time to do additional graduate work at the University of Chicago.

With relatively deep roots in Baltimore by the 1930s, she cofounded in 1933 the Philomathian Club, which was established to honor outstanding women of color. By then in her early forties, Cook was emerging as a figure of national reputation in black America, exchanging correspondence with MARY McLEOD BETHUNE, perhaps the most distinguished black female educator of the period, and with MORDECAI JOHNSON, the president of Howard University.

With Ralph Cook a member of the Boule, a social club of black men that boasted the memberships of the civil rights pioneer W. E. B. DuBOIS and the chemist PERCY JULIAN, and with Vivian Cook a power in a number of women's organizations, the couple's social network was among the most influential in black America. But both were mainly committed to the uplift of their people. As such, they were members of what DuBois called "the talented tenth," that minority of gifted blacks who would use their considerable talent to help raise their people as a whole, which was what Cook had in mind when she used the word "service."

Cook promoted African American history and culture before it was fashionable to do so, annually helping to sponsor programs for that purpose. Together with other educators in the Baltimore community, Cook brought distinguished students of the arts, such as ALAIN LOCKE, the first black Rhodes scholar and a leading theorist of black culture, to Baltimore to lecture. In addition, as chair of the Art Committee of the Cooperative Women's Civic League, Cook led initiatives for the work of black artists to be exhibited at the Baltimore Museum of Art. Infrequently she saw, but frequently she corresponded with, the great storyteller and folklorist WILLIAM JOHN FAULKNER, who was married to a relative of Cook's husband.

Despite the barriers of race in the segregated environment in which she worked, Cook commanded attention and respect from white people. In fact she was the first woman of any race to serve as counselor in the Baltimore school system, and she went on to become the first black woman to hold an administrative post in a secondary school. In addition, after serving as vice principal and principal of Baltimore schools, she became principal of Dunbar High School, the largest school in the state with its 3,800 students. In her first year as principal of Dunbar, Cook was given the Future Teachers of America Award of Merit. In 1949 she received the Howard University Alumni Medal for Achievement in Education. During the years of her distinguished principalship at Dunbar from 1951 to 1956, she was also a member of the National Executive Board of the Association for the Study of Negro Life and History. There could be no better illustration of Cook's stature in those years than when future Supreme Court justice THURGOOD MARSHALL, with already more than twenty victories before the Supreme Court, paid tribute to Cook at Grace Memorial Church in Baltimore on 20 January 1952.

After her retirement from Dunbar in 1956, Cook became assistant director of practice teaching in the Teacher-Education Department of Morgan State College in Baltimore. By then she was a widely recognized pioneer in education and in forwarding black history, civil rights, civic affairs, and women's rights. Cook stands as one of the foremost champions of women's rights not so much by preachment as by having demonstrated that women, despite racial and other barriers imposed on them, can perform with brilliance. More than that, she is distinguished for having founded important institutions that have endured after her death in Baltimore.

FURTHER READING
Cook's papers are housed at the Moorland-Spingarn Collection at Howard University.
"Vivian E. J. Cook: Pioneer Educator—Civic and Social Leader," *Baltimore Afro-American*, 27–31 Jan. and 3–7 Feb. 1976.
Obituary: *Baltimore Sun*, 1 Aug. 1977.
This entry is taken from the *American National Biography* and is published here with the permission of the American Council of Learned Societies.

STERLING STUCKEY

Cook, Will Marion (27 Jan. 1869–20 July 1944), composer and librettist, was born in Washington, D.C., the son of John Hartwell Cook, a professor of law at Howard University, and Marion Isabel Lewis, a sewing instructor. He received classical violin training at the Oberlin Conservatory of Music (1884–1887). For approximately the next decade he presumably studied violin and composition with the German violinist Joseph Joachim at the Hochschule für Musik in Berlin (1888–1889?), and he continued harmony and counterpoint training under Antonín Dvořák and John White at the National Conservatory of Music in New York City (1893–1895?).

Cook was a prolific composer whose instrumentals and songs were closely related to the craze for cakewalking and two-stepping. His first musical success began with the show *Clorindy, the Origin of the Cakewalk* (1898), which he originally wrote for the vaudevillian comedians BERT WILLIAMS and GEORGE WILLIAM WALKER, although it was first performed with ERNEST HOGAN in the lead. This landmark production departed from the minstrel tradition in two ways: first, by employing syncopated ragtime music; and second, by introducing the cakewalk to Broadway audiences. The show, which opened at the Casino Roof Garden Theatre in New York, emerged along with BOB COLE's *A Trip to Coontown* as one of the first all-black shows to play in a major Broadway theater, and Cook became the first black conductor of a white theater orchestra. The author JAMES WELDON

JOHNSON noted that Cook "was the first competent composer to take what was then known as rag-time and work it out in a musicianly way" (Johnson, 103). The show's star, ABBIE MITCHELL, became Cook's wife in 1899. They were divorced in 1906, but continued to work together in show business; they had two children. *Clorindy* presented songs that countered minstrel stereotypes. Whereas many of the tunes, notably "Hottes' Coon in Dixie" and "Who Dat Say Chicken in Dis Crowd?," continued in the minstrel tradition, others, such as the choral "On Emancipation Day" and the hauntingly lyrical "Ghost Ship" (unpublished), were stirring tunes that reflected black pride and the pain of the Middle Passage. The production played throughout the summer of 1898 at the Casino in New York. After a brief but successful tour the show was incorporated into the Williams and Walker Company as part of their vaudeville routine.

In the first decade of the twentieth century Cook emerged as an original, if sometimes erratic, genius of musical comedy. He teamed with PAUL LAURENCE DUNBAR, Alex Rogers, Joe Jordan, Williams and Walker, Jesse Shipp, CECIL MACK, James Rosamond Johnson, and James Weldon Johnson to produce some of the most popular musical shows, vaudeville, and hit tunes. Cook's next three productions, *The Casino Girl* (1900), *The Policy Players* (1900), and *Jes Lak White Fo'ks* (1900), failed to duplicate his *Clorindy* success, but his fortunes turned upward when he created the music for Williams and Walker's *In Dahomey* (1902–1905), *Abyssinia* (1906–1907), and *Bandana Land* (1907–1909). *In Dahomey* opened successfully in New York, establishing the Williams and Walker Company as the premier black musical comedy troupe for the remainder of the decade. In addition, the show toured throughout Great Britain during the 1903–1904 season.

In 1910 Cook formed the New York Syncopated Orchestra, which toured the United States that same year. He also formed the orchestra known as the Clef Club in 1912, a group of black musicians and entertainers. Both the Syncopated Orchestra and the Clef Club performed a mixture of Cook's music, as well as popular and classical music. His most popular songs, along with those from *Clorindy*, were "Swing Along," a satiric choral piece on relations between blacks and whites, "Mandy Lou," "Red, Red Rose," "Exhortation: A Negro Sermon," "Brown Skin Baby Mine," "Darktown Is Out Tonight," "Nobody Knows the Trouble I

See," and "The Rain Song." In 1918 Cook moved his Syncopated Orchestra to Europe, and he was largely instrumental in creating the vogue for black musicians there and in England.

Cook's classical musical education proved a mixed blessing. Endowed with tremendous talent, his refusal to tolerate racism in the white world and show business egos in his own circles alienated him from many friends and colleagues. During the last two decades of his life Cook's productivity declined, but he did compose *In Darkydom* (1914) and fragments of a Negro folk opera called *St. Louis Woman* (1929). He also wrote spirituals, such as "Troubled in Mind" (1929), and during World War II he and his son Will Mercer Cook composed patriotic songs.

Abbie Mitchell referred to him as "a giant in experience, a sincere student of music in spite of all statements to the contrary, notwithstanding his eccentricities, his erratic temperament, which in later years caused him many disappointments, much poverty, loss of influence, contacts and friends and a deep sorrow" (Mercer Cook Papers). He died in New York City's Harlem Hospital.

FURTHER READING

Valuable sources of information on Cook include the Mercer Cook Papers, Moorland-Spingarn Research Center, Howard University; the Theatre Museum, London; the Music Division, Library of Congress; and the Billy Rose Theatre Collection at the New York Public Library for the Performing Arts, Lincoln Center.

Johnson, James Weldon. *Black Manhattan* (1930).

Peterson, Bernard L. *A Century of Musicals in Black and White* (1993).

Riis, Thomas L. *Just before Jazz* (1989).

Riis, Thomas L. *More than Just Minstrel Shows* (1992).

Sampson, Henry T. *Blacks in Blackface* (1980).

Obituary: *New York Times*, 21 July 1944.

This entry is taken from the *American National Biography* and is published here with the permission of the American Council of Learned Societies.

DAVID KRASNER

Cooke, Charles "Doc" (3 Sept. 1891–25 Dec. 1958), arranger, composer, and bandleader, was born Charles Leonidas Cooke in Louisville, Kentucky. Little is known of Cooke's early years. He attended Louisville and Detroit public schools and was active as a composer and arranger in Detroit before 1910. Cooke scored an early hit in 1918, when his song "I've Got the Blue Ridge Blues" (words by Charles Mason; cocomposed by Richard Mason) was included in *Sinbad*, a successful show featuring a young Al Jolson.

By 1920 Cooke was based in Chicago, where he quickly became a leading theatrical and cabaret bandleader and worked as musical director at Riverside Park. He was in residence at Paddy Harmon's Dreamland Ballroom from 1922 to 1927 before moving to Chicago's Municipal Pier in the summers and the Casino at White City during the colder months. His orchestra was broadcasting live from White City over station WBCN by May 1927. Cooke continued his education during these years and earned a doctor of musical arts degree from the Chicago Musical College in 1926.

Like many of the most highly regarded bandleaders of the era, Cooke was recruited to make jazz recordings in the 1920s. His twenty-one released sides were recorded for three leading labels and under four different ensemble names. First came six sides for the Gennett Company of Richmond, Indiana, recorded in January 1924 by Cook's Dreamland Orchestra, a twelve-piece ensemble. Cookie's Gingersnaps, a smaller version of the same band, made another four sides in June 1926 for Okeh. Cook and his Dreamland Orchestra (named for the popular ballroom), now back to full strength, recorded five sides for Columbia in July and December 1926. A final six pieces were recorded for Columbia in June 1927 and March 1928 as "Doc" Cook and his fourteen Doctors of Syncopation. Why his last name was given in truncated form is not known; it may have originated as an error and become too troublesome to correct.

Most of the material Cooke's bands covered on their recordings was somewhat undistinguished novelty and other pop material of the period that nonetheless left room for "hot" solo breaks by the better jazz soloists in the band. A few of the pieces were by some of the best songwriters of the era, such as JELLY ROLL MORTON and FATS WALLER, but were generally not their choicest material. Among the popular successes for the band was "Here Comes the Hot Tamale Man," which they recorded in both vocal and instrumental versions. Their best jazz record was "Willie the Weeper," which is sometimes included in anthologies of jazz records from its era. The song has an infectious Latin beat, a memorable tuba line, and a wailing clarinet line by Jimmie Noone.

Cooke's ensembles were renowned for their technical expertise, and the section players were required to be fully trained reading musicians. Cooke may have compromised slightly in the interest of featuring hot soloists, although the two most famous of these, the clarinetist Noone and the cornetist FREDDIE KEPPARD, both from New Orleans, probably would not have been hired if they could play only by ear.

Cooke moved to New York in 1930 and was soon among the busiest music arrangers in the city. At first he was involved primarily in theatrical music, initially in African American shows such as *Brown Buddies* (1930) and *Yeah Man* (May 1932). His orchestral work *Sketches of the Deep South* was performed at an American Society of Composers, Authors, and Publishers (ASCAP) Silver Jubilee concert in 1939. He became perhaps the most sought-after arranger for shows with African American themes and stars, including *The Hot Mikado* (1939) and *Cabin in the Sky* (1942). He found success in the white show world as well, writing arrangements for the comedy team Olsen and Johnson in their *Sons o' Fun* (1941), for Eddie Cantor's *Banjo Eyes* (1941), and for younger performers, such as Jackie Gleason in his *Follow the Girls* (1944). He was a staff arranger for a number of years for both the RKO theater chain and for New York's Radio City Music Hall. Cooke also did a great deal of work for the impresario Billy Rose between about 1930 and 1950. Some of his arrangements for Rose survived in the Performing Arts Library at Lincoln Center (in the New York Public Library). They showed him to have been an assured, sophisticated craftsman. During the 1940s Cooke became less active and moved to New Jersey for a prolonged semiretirement.

Cooke's relationship with the songwriter and publisher W. C. HANDY was particularly close and lasted for decades. The two made their last recordings together for the Audio Archives label in 1952, which included Handy's daughter, the singer Katherine Handy Lewis, and a small choir. Handy played cornet and sang on these sessions and also recounted anecdotes from his long life. Cooke acted as pianist for the sessions and may have done some arranging work as well. By this time Handy had been completely blind for a number of years, so his ability to continue such work was understandably limited to dictating or playing ideas. Cooke and Handy also co-composed some of their last songs together, including "Big Stick Blues March" in 1951 and "Newspaperman's Blues" in 1954. When the latter was published, Handy predicted that it would be his company's biggest hit; but this was standard show business puffery. Upon his death Cooke left a wife, a sister, and other relations, none of whom were named in his obituaries.

As a composer, Cooke was versatile if not notably inspired. Few of his songs were hits, although "Blame It on the Blues," "Messin' Around," and "Lovin' You the Way I Do" all enjoyed some measure of success. Unfortunately, he seems not to have found much opportunity to work in the larger compositional forms or to take full advantage of his classical training. Although Cooke was never the subject of a recorded anthology in modern times, his recordings could be heard on the French-produced compact disc *Jimmie Noone, 1923–1928* (Classics CD, 1991).

FURTHER READING

Chilton, John. *Who's Who of Jazz: Storyville to Swing Street* (1972).

Southern, Eileen. *Biographical Dictionary of Afro-American and African Musicians* (1982).

ELLIOTT HURWITT

Cooke, Marvel Jackson (4 Apr. 1903–29 Nov. 2000), was born in Mankato, Minnesota. Although her father, Madison Jackson, was an attorney—the first black member of the South Dakota bar—he could not build a practice in the overwhelmingly white community in which they lived, so he instead became a Pullman porter. Her mother, Amy Wood, was a former cook and teacher. Her father was a socialist, and her mother was a close friend of W. E. B. DuBois, circumstances that helped Cooke acquire an early commitment to political activism. Her political consciousness was also raised by personal experiences of overt racism. When the family moved into an all-white neighborhood, their new neighbors demonstrated outside the house. As a student Cooke qualified for a War Department job as a translator but was demoted to file clerk when her race was discovered; she wrote to her state senator, however, and was reassigned to her original position.

At the University of Minnesota, Cooke helped found a chapter of Alpha Kappa Alpha, studied literature, wrote poetry, and committed herself to writing and civil rights activism. After her graduation in 1925, she moved to Harlem and began working as an editorial assistant for the *Crisis*. She rented an apartment at Harlem's most prestigious address, 409 Edgecombe Avenue, and soon became part of the intellectual and cultural ferment of the Harlem Renaissance. Her friends included the poet LANGSTON HUGHES, the novelist and *Crisis*

literary editor JESSIE REDMON FAUSET, the actor PAUL ROBESON, the future executive director of the NAACP ROY WILKINS (to whom she was briefly engaged), and the star athlete Cecil Cooke, whom she married in 1929.

A year before her marriage, Cooke took a job with New York's leading black newspaper, the *Amsterdam News*, as secretary to the women's editor. After their marriage, however, the Cookes moved to Greensboro, North Carolina, where Marvel Cooke taught history, English, and Latin at North Carolina Agricultural and Technical College. The couple had no children. Two years later they moved back to New York, and Cooke returned to the *Amsterdam News*, first as editor of a short-lived feature, then as the paper's first female news reporter. At the *News*, Cooke countered the paper's tendency to print sensational stories by conducting serious investigations of poor working conditions, euthanasia, and crime. She helped organize a writer's group to encourage literary creation and a local branch of the American Newspaper Guild. When the paper's owner challenged this action, the guild members picketed, the first black workers in the United States to picket a black-owned business. In 1936 Cooke joined the Communist Party. In 1939 she covered MARIAN ANDERSON's historic concert at the Lincoln Memorial and the opening of *Gone with the Wind*, which she criticized for its portrayal of black characters.

In 1940 Cooke left the *Amsterdam News*, and in 1942 she became assistant managing editor of the *People's Voice*, a militant new paper created by ADAM CLAYTON POWELL JR. The *Voice's* editorial policy treated race relations "within the larger context of a [class-and-ideology-based] people's movement composed of labor and the political left, both white and Negro" (Robbins, 132). When the managing editor resigned, Cooke assumed his responsibilities without any increase in pay or official recognition of her new function. She also worked closely with the paper's theatrical editor, FREDI WASHINGTON, whose regular columns included some of the era's most penetrating critiques of theatrical representations of race. According to Cooke, she recruited Washington into the Communist Party, and they were both fired in 1947, shortly before the paper folded, for political as well as economic reasons.

In 1950 Cooke became a reporter for the *Daily Compass*, a leftist paper based in New York, making history by becoming the first African American woman to join the staff of a white newspaper. Here Cooke wrote her famous series of stories on the "Bronx Slave Market," which investigated working conditions for black women who stood on street corners in the Bronx waiting to be hired by "local housewives looking for bargains in human labor" (quoted in Shapiro, 245). Cooke next published reports on prostitution and teenage drug use. Her investigations of labor exploitation and drug addiction prompted reform initiatives by the Domestic Workers Union and the city of New York. In 1952 the *Daily Compass* folded, and Cooke's career as a journalist came to an end.

A year later Cooke was called to testify before the Permanent Subcommittee on Investigations. The subcommittee was interested in information regarding one of Cooke's *People's Voice* colleagues, but Cooke refused to cooperate, pleading the Fifth Amendment. Also that year Cooke became New York director of the Council of Arts, Sciences, and Professions. Presumably blacklisted, Cooke was unemployed from 1955 until 1960, at which time she was hired by the New York surgeon Samuel Rosen to work in his office. Cooke left this position in 1968, becoming, as she later reported, "a nice little housewife" (Currie interview). Cooke entered public life, however, in 1969, as national legal defense secretary for the ANGELA DAVIS Defense Committee. In 1971 Cooke became associated with the National Council for American-Soviet Friendship, serving as national vice chair in the 1980s. Cecil Cooke died in 1978, and Marvel Cooke lived alone in their Harlem apartment until her own death from leukemia. Ten years before her death, however, the journalist Kathleen Currie conducted seven in-depth interviews with Cooke concerning her life and career, available on the Washington Press Club Foundation Web site.

FURTHER READING

The *People's Voice* 1942–1948 is available on microfilm at the Schomburg Center for Research in Black Culture, New York Public Library.

Mills, Kay. *A Place in the News: From the Women's Pages to the Front Page* (1988).

Robbins, Richard. "Counter-Assertion in the New York Negro Press," *Phylon* 10.2 (1949): 126–136.

Shapiro, Bruce, ed. *Shaking the Foundations: 200 Years of Investigative Journalism in America* (2003).

Streitmatter, Rodger. *Raising Her Voice: African-American Women Journalists Who Changed History* (1994).

Obituary: *New York Times*, 10 Dec. 2000.

CHERYL BLACK

Cooke, Sam (22 Jan. 1931–11 Dec. 1964), singer-songwriter, was born Samuel Cook in Clarksdale, Mississippi, the son of Charles Cook, a minister in the Church of Christ (Holiness), and Annie May Carl. After Sam's father lost his position as houseboy for a wealthy cotton farmer as a result of the Great Depression, the family migrated to Chicago, where Reverend Cook became assistant pastor of Christ Temple (Holiness) and a laborer in the stockyards. The family lived in Bronzeville, Chicago's severely overcrowded and impoverished black section. Young Sam was educated at nearby schools and gained musical experience by sneaking into taverns to hear pop tunes but mostly by hearing and singing gospel music at church. There he started a gospel group, the Singing Children; later he joined the Teenage Highway QC's and became more widely known throughout the nation. He graduated from Wendell Phillips High School in 1948. About that time he spent ninety days in jail on a morals charge that stemmed from a paternity suit.

Cooke's first major break came when R. H. Harris, lead singer of the famous Soul Stirrers, retired and Cooke replaced him, thus embarking on the possibility of becoming a major gospel star, dressing in elaborate suits and performing as a singing minister to a growing flock of gospel adherents. First there were hurdles to overcome. Cooke's introduction

Sam Cooke performs at the Copacabana nightclub in New York City. (AP Images.)

to the Soul Stirrers was a trial-by-fire, as competing groups and highly critical audiences and record promoters were skeptical of his skills. After Cooke became a Soul Stirrer, the group, on Cooke's recommendation, began to aim performances at "Sister Flute," the archetypal black female churchgoer who, once aroused by gospel singing, would ignite the congregation into sacred ecstasy. Cooke's formal, conversational style of singing and his handsome looks initially failed to move older parishioners, but he greatly excited teenage girls, normally an indifferent audience to gospel appeals.

Cooke also had to win over the group's record promoter, Art Rupe of Specialty Records in Los Angeles. Upset that the Soul Stirrers had lost their star, Rupe demanded near perfection during Cooke's first marathon recording session in 1951. The resulting album included Cooke's first hit with the group, "Jesus Gave Me Water," and one of his own songs, "Until Jesus Calls Me Home." Enthusiasm and overwhelming sales brought the group back into the studio a second time in 1952. During this session Cook introduced his trademark "yodel" effect, which would help establish his career. Another first was the birth of a child to his longtime sweetheart, Barbara Campbell, in 1953. Although Cooke acknowledged paternity and paid child support, he did not marry Campbell. Over the next few years Cooke toured constantly with the Soul Stirrers, singing at churches, stadiums, and religious conventions before pushing on to the next engagement the following day. Cooke's distinctive yodeling of lyrics helped to elevate the group's popularity as never before. At an engagement in Fresno, California, Cooke met Dolorous Mohawk and after a whirlwind romance married her in 1953. Mohawk had a young child from a previous marriage. After they married she moved to Chicago to wait for Cooke while he traveled with the group.

Specialty Records had a very successful line of popular music featuring such innovative stars as Lloyd Price, PERCY MAYFIELD, and, later, Larry Williams and Jesse Belvin. In 1955 Rupe hired Robert "Bumps" Blackwell to sign and arrange new talent, including the immortal LITTLE RICHARD. The Soul Stirrers continued to sell records in the middle 1950s and celebrated their twenty-fifth anniversary in 1955. Cooke was becoming restless, however, and more keenly interested in making money. In June 1956 he agreed to make some "cross over" pop records for Rupe. During several undistinguished forays into popular music, a personal crisis ensued. His wife, distraught with loneliness, attempted suicide. Cooke went to her side but was soon back on the road. It was also around this time that he added an "e" to his name.

In 1957, after a dispute with Rupe, Cooke and Blackwell, now his manager, took masters of a song called "You Send Me" to a new label, Keen Records. Despite a cover version by white artist Teresa Brewer, Cooke's version sold a reported 1.7 million copies, ascended to the top of the charts, and stayed in the mix for more than six months. Ed Sullivan invited Cooke to appear on his Sunday night show, squeezed him in for only a few seconds before the credits, then received outraged letters from thousands of black Americans. Impressed as well as contrite, Sullivan reinvited Cook for a full performance. Over the next two years Cooke scored with such hits as "I Love You for Sentimental Reasons," "Only Sixteen," "Win Your Love for Me," and even the improbable "Everybody Loves to Cha-Cha-Cha."

Despite his success, Cooke was beset by problems. He divorced his wife, who was later killed in a car accident, and then had a child with another woman. Rupe hit him with numerous lawsuits. A heralded appearance at New York's Copacabana club was a fiasco. At a restaurant on the New Jersey turnpike waitresses refused to serve him, even as his songs were playing on the jukebox. One positive event was a reconciliation with Barbara Campbell, and the two were married.

In 1960, Cooke, by now a major star, signed a lucrative contract with RCA. Able to arrange and produce his own songs, Cooke created such pop masterpieces as "Wonderful World," "Chain Gang," "Sad Mood," "Having a Party," "Bring It on Home to Me," "Another Saturday Night," and "Twisting the Night Away." He also produced records for his own label, Sar Records, and ran KAGs Music, a publishing company.

Cooke's second marriage gradually drifted into one of convenience, and while his popularity remained high, his personal life declined. On 11 December 1964 he was shot to death in Hollywood, California, by Bertha Franklin, a motel keeper, under very mysterious circumstances. Although police classified the shooting as self-defense, many black Americans regarded their determination with suspicion. Daniel Wolff, Cooke's biographer, has pointed to a number of discrepancies in the official story and posited alternative explanations.

Cooke's funeral in Chicago was attended by more than 200,000 fans of both gospel and pop. Shortly after his death a new song, "A Change Is

Gonna Come," became a big hit and pointed to a fusion of gospel music and social awareness. This style was later successfully broached by such disciples as MARVIN GAYE, OTIS REDDING, and CURTIS MAYFIELD.

FURTHER READING

Boyer, Edward J. "The Soulful Legacy of Sam Cooke," *Los Angeles Times*, 23 Dec. 1994.

Guralnick, Peter. *Dream Boogie: The Triumph of Sam Cooke* (2005).

McEwen, Joe. *Sam Cooke: A Biography in Words and Pictures* (1977).

Santoro, Gene. "Sam Cooke," *Nation*, 13 Mar. 1995.

Wolff, Daniel. *You Send Me: The Life and Times of Sam Cooke* (1995).

Obituaries: *New York Times* and *Los Angeles Times*, 12 Dec. 1964.

This entry is taken from the *American National Biography* and is published here with the permission of the American Council of Learned Societies.

GRAHAM RUSSELL HODGES

Cooke, William E. "Washboard Bill" (4 July 1905–27 Apr. 2003), washboard musician, raconteur, and hobo, was born William Edgar Givens in the sawmill town of Dupont, Florida. His mother ran a "juke joint," a tavern where the music and the liquor flowed. Little other information about his parents is available. As a boy, Givens would watch the dancing and listen to the music through a hole in the wall of his sleeping room. It was in this manner that he discovered rhythm. He practiced on buckets and pots around the house and gave little shows for his siblings and the neighborhood children.

At a young age, he was adopted by his preacher grandfather, who changed the boy's name to William Edward Cooke. He left his grandfather's home in 1917 and made his way to south Florida, working odd jobs, including clearing land for roads, among these the great Dixie Highway, U.S. 1. In 1931 he took to the rails, hoboing throughout the South and Midwest. He felt that God had called him to be a hobo, and this is what he told his mother, who by then was a preacher. Not liking the idea of her son becoming a hobo, she disinherited him. She would have preferred that he settle down and marry the piano player in her church.

The rails were a lonely life, where the blues were felt, where one would wake up hungry and go to bed hungry. Yet Cooke made his way, working for families along the countryside in exchange for food and a place to sleep. He traveled until about 1940, when he landed in New York City.

While working in a restaurant in the city, Cooke met Jiving Washboard Jimmy, a musician whose rhythm section included a washboard, cymbals, and cowbells. Cooke's love of rhythm was reignited, and he was inspired to make his own washboard instrument, something different. He improved upon Washboard Jimmy's design, creating a rhythm device out of two washboards, three cymbals, a ship's bell, and a cowbell. Calling himself "Washboard," Cooke became a musician.

The musician's union would not accept him because the washboard was not considered a musical instrument. Convinced that it was indeed an instrument that could accompany almost anything, Cooke found himself accompanying some of the greats of the blues and jazz scene in New York, including the guitarist BROWNIE MCGHEE and the harmonica player SONNY TERRY. So popular was the washboard that Pete Seeger arranged in 1956 to have Cooke record with McGhee and Terry for the *Washboard Band—Country Dance Music* album on the Folkways label. The album sold lightly, but the washboard was now considered a blues and folk instrument. Between 1946 and the late 1960s Cooke stayed in New York, playing his washboard device in jazz, blues, folk, and bluegrass bands. He wintered in Palm Beach, Florida, at times playing at the train station, at other times playing for parties in the homes of the wealthy.

Cooke suffered a heart attack in 1964 that put him on welfare, and he did jail time in 1967 for shooting his abusive son-in-law. In December 1972, for health reasons, he made West Palm Beach his home. There he continued to play washboard and ukulele at the train station and at a corner on Clematis Street. He entertained visitors with his stories about hoboing and playing music, and would sing jazz standards, peppered with vaudeville, blues, and novelty tunes. He even wrote some of his own songs, such as "Everybody Talks about Sunshine Florida, but West Palm Beach's the Place for Me." He spiced up his conversation with similes such as "I'm as happy as a mosquito in a nudist colony."

One of Cooke's striking features was his style of dressing in a suit with a brightly colored tie, a handkerchief in his pocket, and frequently a derby hat topping off the ensemble. He wanted to look sharp, hoping to attract attention visually as well as aurally.

It was important to Cooke to tell his story, especially about his experiences as "Hobo Bill." Hoping his stories could be made into a movie, he wrote some of them down and recorded others, which were then transcribed, forming a book-length manuscript that remains unpublished. Transcripts of interviews, photographs, and sound recordings are housed in the Florida Folklife Collection of the Florida State Archive in Tallahassee.

Cooke's declining health and welfare became a cause for concern in the West Palm Beach community. In 1988 he became a citywide celebrity, playing at the annual Fourth of July celebration and being honored with a birthday cake and a limousine ride to the festival. He became a city treasure and was esteemed by doctors and lawyers, who provided services to Cooke free of charge. In 1992 he received a Florida Heritage Award for preserving the art of washboard playing and storytelling.

Cooke played his favorite street corner until a day in 2002 when he collapsed. He had a pacemaker installed, but it was discovered he had inoperable colon cancer. He was transferred to a nursing home, where he died.

William E. ("Washboard Bill") Cooke was a "historical touchstone" in a region of Florida that had a particularly transient population. His legendary music making contributed to the rich history of African American folk and popular music.

FURTHER READING

Information about Cooke may be found in Jan
  Rosenberg's field notes, "Washboard Bill Cooke,"
  dated August 1987–May 1988. Part of the Florida
  Folklife Program, the notes are located in the
  Florida State Archives, Tallahassee.
Minor, Emily J. "Someone's Missing on Clematis
  Sidewalk," *Palm Beach Post*, 30 Jan. 2003.
Obituary: *Palm Beach Post*, 30 Apr. 2003.

JAN ROSENBERG

Coons, Orlando (1 Nov. 1915–7 Sept. 1998), gymnast and coach, was born in south central Ohio and raised in Summithill, the son of Blaine Coons, a farmer, and Grace (maiden name unknown), a barber. When Orlando was seven years old his grandfather sold the family farm and he and his mother moved from Summithill to Los Angeles, California. At age fourteen he first saw a champion gymnast perform when he used a complimentary pass to the Los Angeles Athletic Club. Although the sport aroused his interest, he lacked the means to train for it. Orlando graduated from Jefferson High School.

Coons went on to find work in the Civilian Conservation Corps, a job that landed him in San Diego in 1935. In 1938 he enrolled at San Diego State College, majoring in engineering. He worked odd jobs to support himself, among them pouring cement for sidewalks and providing room service at the U.S. Grant Hotel. As a member of the freshman track and field team his specialties were the hurdles and pole vault. However when the coach, Charles E. Peterson, saw him working out on the high bar, he decided that Coons's athletic skills were better utilized on the fledgling gymnastics team. Without prior notification Peterson made arrangements to enter Coons in a gymnastic meet near Los Angeles. Though Coons's first competition was personally disappointing he felt motivated to commit himself more seriously to the sport.

Concentrating on the rings and high bar Coons won consecutive all-around gymnastic competitions at the California College Athletic Association (CCAA) Championships in 1939 and 1940. At the 1945 Amateur Athletic Union (AAU) Southern Pacific section competition in Los Angeles he again took the all-around crown.

In 1940 Coons married Nellie Marguerite Cheaves. A deformed big toe, the result of a childhood injury, prevented Coons from serving in World War II. During the war years Coons found full-time employment as an aircraft and engine mechanic at the federal government's North Island Naval Air Station in San Diego, a place where he had previously worked as a janitor. Meanwhile he attended classes part-time at San Diego State College and served as the student gymnastics coach, the first African American to hold a teaching position at the college. In 1948, his last year as a college coach, he lead his gymnasts to the CCAA team championship.

In 1950 Coons completed his undergraduate degree at the University of California at Berkeley, earning a B.S. in Engineering, after which he returned to San Diego. Nicknamed the "Old Man of the Mesa," though he was only thirty-one, Coons placed first at four meets in 1948 and was ranked thirteenth by the AAU. His sixth-place ranking in 1950 earned him a berth on the U.S. national team, although he did not compete in the 1951 Pan American Games because he felt he could not afford the seven hundred dollars to travel to Buenos Aires, Argentina. He did, however, compete in other venues with foreign athletes and was named as an alternate on the 1952 U.S. Olympic Team.

For two decades the largely self-taught Coons was probably the best gymnast on the West Coast. He did not cease competing until 1960. That year, at age forty-five, he was once again ranked thirteen by the AAU. Coons never received due recognition from sports writers or the black press, an omission that seems especially grievous since he was probably the first black gymnast to compete successfully on the national level and the first black gymnastics coach at a predominantly white college or university. Another reason Coons's role as a pioneering black gymnast may have been temporarily overlooked was because he was fair skinned and was often mistaken for white or Latino.

Coons worked for thirty-seven years as an aeronautical aerospace engineer at the navy's North Island Naval Air Station. His work there—first as an engineer investigating airplane crashes and later as a supervisor of aircraft engineers—made him a standout among African American engineers of his era. Ironically it was Coons's work as a helicopter weapons engineer, rather than as a gymnast, that occasioned coverage in *Ebony* magazine's July 1968 issue. Coons's engineering job gave him the stability necessary to extend his athletic career as well as support his wife, Nellie Coons, and their four children, all of whom grew to share their father's love of sports and community service.

Coons played an active role in San Diego's inner-city communities. Nearly every week for some fifty years he taught gymnastics and tumbling to thousands of budding athletes at San Diego–area YMCAs. He also volunteered as a gymnastics coach for the city's Park and Recreation Department, at public elementary and high schools, and at the Girls Club of San Diego located in the city's predominantly black and Hispanic Logan Heights community. Coons's coaching philosophy held that sports training developed character and leadership skills. "They learn to discipline themselves," he told the *San Diego Union*, "and then doing that they can lead others" (Sutter, D-2).

Coons died at the age of eighty-two of cancer at his home in the Valencia Park section of San Diego. Following his death a tribute to him was read by Congressman Bob Filner on the floor of the U.S. House of Representatives.

FURTHER READING

Anders, Rea. "History of the Black Male Gymnast in Collegiate Gymnastics," *International Gymnast* (Mar. 1978).

Sutter, Janet. "Learning about Life's Twists, Turns," *San Diego Union*, 17 July 1988.

Obituaries: *La Prensa San Diego*, 11 Sept. 1998; *San Diego Union-Tribune*, 12 Sept. 1998.

ROBERT FIKES JR.

Cooper, Ada Augusta Newton (4 Feb. 1860–18 Sept. 1899), writer, temperance advocate, and educator, was born Ada Augusta Newton in Brooklyn, New York, the eldest of the three children of Alexander Herritage Newton, a trained mason, and Olivia Augusta (Hamilton) Newton, who was the eldest daughter of ROBERT HAMILTON, the radical abolitionist and owner and editor of the *Weekly Anglo-African* newspaper. When Ada was eight years old her mother died and shortly thereafter her father, a recently licensed preacher of the African Methodist Episcopal (AME) denomination, was directed by the AME leadership to manage the church at Pennington, New Jersey. This was the first of dozens of appointments for Newton, and Ada's early years were characterized by constant travel from city to city as her father's ministry took him to all regions of the country. Despite the incessant moving, Ada received a good elementary education.

Ada worked closely with her father on church matters. Indeed she enjoyed his full confidence on personal family matters as well. After consultation with Ada and receipt of her approval, Newton made the decision to marry Lula L. Campbell in Arkansas in 1876.

Cooper continued to assist her father in his work as an itinerant AME preacher and made her home with him and his new family. By the time she was seventeen she had already begun to submit articles to the *Christian Recorder*, the official newspaper of the AME Church. A young correspondent, she nonetheless gave a full report to the *Christian Recorder* on the progress of her father's efforts to strengthen African American Methodism in Algiers, Louisiana, where the family was living in 1877. Cooper noted the significant rise in church membership and proudly boasted that the Sabbath school had become "the finest … in the State of Louisiana" (*Christian Recorder*, 10 May 1877). In praising the work of bolstering circulation of the paper accomplished by her stepmother, who was the Algiers agent for the *Christian Recorder*, Cooper reported that "she sells as many papers as are sent her, and could sell as many more if she but had them …. The people take quite an interest in the paper simply because it is edited and published by their own color" (*Christian Recorder*, 10 May 1877).

The U.S. census of 1880 records the Newton family residing in North Carolina. During this period Cooper was a student at Shaw University in Raleigh, a Baptist institution founded in 1865 and the first historically black college in the South. It is unclear exactly when Cooper became a student at Shaw, but her name appears in the university academic catalog as early as 1875 as a student in the Classical Department. She is still listed as a student in the Classical Department during the school terms of 1877 through 1879, and in the school term for 1880–1881 she is listed among the female students in the Scientific Department. In addition to completing the necessary course work for her studies in these areas, Cooper also served as one of several assistant teachers, a special honor reserved for only a few "appointed by the Faculty from among the Pupils" (Shaw University Archives, University Academic Catalogs, 1875–1882). Cooper was clearly an inspired student and gifted young teacher, and she seems to have fulfilled the promise of excellence that her father anticipated in her from an early age.

While Cooper was completing her education at Shaw, her father established a permanent family home in Camden, New Jersey, despite his responsibilities for the management of churches in Morristown, Madison, and other New Jersey towns. It was therefore with great happiness that sometime during the late 1880s he welcomed Ada to New Jersey with her husband, the Reverend Albert A. B. Cooper (the exact date of their marriage is unknown), who had just been appointed to the AME Bethel Church in South Camden.

In addition to her many church activities, Cooper was passionately devoted to temperance work. The temperance movement gained much support in the northern black community during the post-Reconstruction years. Within southern black communities, however, temperance advocacy was a more complex issue. Among Freedmen's Bureau agents working in the South it was commonly known that freed people generally did not drink spirits, but were opposed to a movement that sought to restrict individual freedom of choice in the matter. The movement nevertheless had strong support in some quarters. The school terms for 1892–1894 at Shaw University included a Missionary Training School with a faculty member dedicated to instruction in "Temperance and Social Purity." In an article titled "Intemperance," Cooper warned her readers against the "fatal evil" that she perceived in the drinking of alcohol. She imbued her writing with an emotional,

biblical force characteristic of the time: "the cup that has the glow of a ruby 'biteth like a serpent and stingeth like an adder'" (*Christian Recorder*, 25 Oct 1877).

Little is known of the later years of Cooper's life. She was eulogized by her bereaved father in his 1910 autobiography. Extolling her virtues as a loving, dutiful daughter and teacher and his tireless helper in the many obligations he fulfilled on behalf of his AME ministry, Newton recorded the passing of his beloved daughter in 1899 in Orange, New Jersey.

FURTHER READING
Information on Cooper is in the Shaw University Archives, available at www.shawuniversity.edu/Archives/DigitalArchives.htm.
Newton, Alexander Herritage. *Out of the Briars: An Autobiography and Sketch of the Twenty-ninth Regiment Connecticut Volunteers, by A. H. Newton* (1910, repr. 1969).
Williams, Gilbert Anthony. *The Christian Recorder, Newspaper of the African Methodist Episcopal Church: History of a Forum for Ideas, 1854–1902* (1996).

DEBRA JACKSON

Cooper, Andy "Lefty" (24 Apr. 1896–3 June 1941), baseball player, was born Andrew Lewis Cooper in Waco, Texas. Almost nothing is known about Cooper's parents or childhood. In fact, beyond his baseball career, Cooper is something of an anonymous figure, and the general dearth of reliable records makes it difficult to paint a clear picture of the man. Given such relative obscurity, his 2006 election to the Baseball Hall of Fame along with sixteen other black baseball players and executives surprised some experts. So unheralded was Cooper that, even though he was deemed worthy of induction into the Hall of Fame, his name is hardly mentioned in *Shades of Glory* (2006), Lawrence D. Hogan's retrospective of the Negro Leagues, published by the Hall of Fame in conjunction with *National Geographic*. While Cooper's selection elicited some controversy, there is no denying that he fashioned an exceptionally successful playing career that placed him among the top ten in most Negro Leagues statistical pitching categories.

Despite his impressive statistical achievements, Cooper might have been lost to the dustbin of history but for the efforts of Dick Clark, a baseball enthusiast from Ypsilanti, Michigan. A member of the Society of American Baseball Research (SABR),

Clark was asked to help compile baseball box scores from Detroit papers of the early 1920s. As Clark worked, Cooper's numbers began to stand out. Eager to learn more and certain that others would be interested as well, Clark began to search for as much information as he could find while compiling his statistical database. The career he helped uncover was impressive even if some of the details were missing.

Cooper was described as a big, left-handed pitcher, standing 6'2" and weighing around 220 pounds. Throughout his career the southpaw proved remarkably durable. In the typical five-game series played by Negro League teams, Cooper often started two of the games and relieved in one or two others. He won ten or more games seven times in his career, the equivalent of winning twenty games in the modern Major Leagues. Utilizing a broad array of pitches that included a curveball, a screwball, and a slider, Cooper was recognized as a master at changing speeds to keep opposing hitters off balance.

Cooper excelled for the Detroit Stars from 1920 to 1927. In 1923 the crafty left-hander emerged as the dominant ace of the Detroit staff, winning fifteen games and saving six more. Four brilliant seasons followed, including a thirteen-win campaign in 1926. His combination of pitching skill and durability earned him a place at the top of every one of Detroit's career statistical pitching categories. Such dazzling success was no small feat for a Detroit pitcher. Cooper thrived despite playing home games at Mack Park, an east side Detroit field that was regarded as especially friendly to hitters.

Cooper was so highly valued that the Kansas City Monarchs sent five players to Detroit to acquire him for the 1928 season. Cooper notched eleven wins for the Monarchs that year. In 1929 he won thirteen games, helping the Monarchs clinch the Negro National League pennant. He enjoyed one more successful season in Detroit before returning to Kansas City for the 1931 season.

On the downside of his career thereafter, Cooper could still outwit opposing batters when given the chance. During a 1931 barnstorming tour, the future Major League pitcher Elden Auker played against the Monarchs. After facing both Cooper and the pitcher SATCHEL PAIGE, Auker estimated that Cooper was at least as good as if not better than Paige. If nothing else, Auker was certain that Cooper threw a superior curveball and would have been a big winner in the Major Leagues.

Although his pitching appearances were infrequent, Cooper was still a valuable asset for the Monarchs and was named the team's manager in 1937. Presiding over a talented team that featured Paige, the hitter BUCK O'NEIL, and the pitcher HILTON SMITH, Cooper led the Monarchs to three pennants between 1937 and 1940. Smith, inducted into the Hall of Fame in 2001, recalled that Cooper was one of the greatest influences on his career. O'Neil remembered Cooper as a sort of father figure, a man who seemed to understand every nuance of the game of baseball and who took the young hitter out to dinner to help him break down pitchers. Having left the mound for good in 1939, Cooper seemed poised for an equally successful managerial career. It was not to be.

In 1940 Cooper unexpectedly became ill and returned to Waco to stay with his mother. He left behind an eleven-year-old son, Andy Cooper Jr., whose mother had died while he was a baby. The younger Cooper, who moved in with relatives, was swimming at a local YMCA when he was informed that his father had died of heart failure. Interviewed prior to ceremonies at Cooperstown, Andy Cooper Jr. recalled little of his late father as a baseball player, though he had spent two seasons traveling with him as a batboy for the Monarchs. Instead, he remembered a jovial man with a happy-go-lucky attitude who was always willing to give some time to his son.

Ultimately, however, baseball is the only arena in which Cooper's legacy can honestly be judged. His career mark of 116 wins and 57 losses was one of the finest in Negro League history. He is the leagues' all-time leader in saves, with twenty-nine. Though Negro Leagues statistical records are always somewhat questionable, his numbers compare favorably to the best of his peers. While he never enjoyed the fame of Paige, Cooper has increasingly been recognized as one of the best left-handed pitchers in the history of the Negro Leagues. Clark labeled him the best black pitcher ever to play in Detroit for the Stars or the Tigers.

FURTHER READING

Bruce, Janet. *The Kansas City Monarchs: Champions of Black Baseball* (1985).

Lester, Larry, Sammy Miller, and Dick Clark. *Black Baseball in Detroit* (2000).

O'Neil, Buck, with Steve Wulf, and David Conrads. *I Was Right on Time* (1996).

Riley, James A. *The Biographical Encyclopedia of the Negro Baseball Leagues* (2002).

NATHAN M. CORZINE

Cooper, Anna Julia Haywood (10 Aug. 1858?–27 Feb. 1964), educator, writer, and activist, was born Anna Julia Haywood in Raleigh, North Carolina, to Hannah Stanley, the slave of George Washington Haywood, who was probably Anna's father. Anna exhibited a love of books and a gift for learning early in her childhood. Hannah was hired out as a nursemaid to a successful local lawyer, whose family most likely assisted her daughter in learning to read and write. Most important, however, was Anna's mother herself, who although illiterate, encouraged her daughter's education.

In 1867 Anna was one of the first students admitted to St. Augustine's Normal School and Collegiate Institute, a recently founded Episcopal school for newly freed slaves. At age nine she found herself tutoring students older than herself and decided to earn her teaching credentials. At St. Augustine's Anna first confronted the gender imbalance in education, challenging the exclusion of women from

Anna Julia Haywood Cooper, principal of the renowned M Street High School in Washington, D.C. (Courtesy of Documenting the American South, University of North Carolina at Chapel Hill Libraries.)

courses in theology and classics. In 1877, at the age of nineteen, Anna married George A. G. Cooper, a theology student and teacher at St. Augustine's who was fourteen years her senior. Social mores of the time barred married women from teaching, so Cooper gave up her budding teaching career. When George died two years later, however, Anna felt free to continue her teaching career. Proficient in classics and mathematics, she enrolled in Oberlin College in Ohio in 1881 and was awarded a tuition scholarship. Cooper took on the mantle of "race woman," defending and advocating for blacks, and demanded the inclusion of women in the "gentlemen's course." Cooper earned a B.A. from Oberlin in 1884, placing her, along with MARY CHURCH TERRELL, among the first four African American women to earn a bachelor's degree. She followed this with an M.S. in Mathematics in 1887.

After a brief teaching stint at Wilberforce University in Ohio and a year teaching at her alma mater, St. Augustine, Cooper was invited in 1887 by the superintendent of Colored Schools in Washington, D.C., to join the faculty at Washington Colored High School (soon after renamed the M Street Colored H.S. and, in 1916, Paul Laurence Dunbar H.S.). In Washington, Cooper and Mary Church (Terrell), who also took a teaching position at the school, boarded in the home of, and were influenced by, the Pan-Africanist clergyman ALEXANDER CRUMMELL.

In 1892 Cooper published *A Voice from the South by a Black Woman of the South*, a collection of essays widely acknowledged as the first black feminist treatise. Cooper held the view that black women were especially suited for raising the status of the black community, more so than black men. Cooper's perspective was unique in the vehemence of her assertion that "only the BLACK WOMAN can say 'when and where I enter ... the whole *Negro race enters with me*'" (Cooper, 31). She became widely known on the lecture circuit, espousing many of the themes of the black club women's movement, such as education and culture as beacons on the path to black self-improvement. Cooper also helped edit *The Southland*, a magazine founded in 1890 by JOSEPH C. PRICE.

In 1892 Cooper cofounded the Colored Women's League to encourage black women's collective approach to the race's problems. As the Colored Women's League corresponding secretary, she addressed the World's Congress of Representative Women in Chicago in 1893. Her comments during a special session titled "The Intellectual Progress of Colored Women of the United States Since Emancipation" addressed the need for inclusiveness in tending to the needs of a broad range of women.

In 1900 Cooper served on the executive committee of the first Pan-African Conference in London, and she was one of two women invited to address the conference. She was certainly understating her role when she described herself simply as a globetrotter. She was the first and only woman elected to the American Negro Academy, an organization of artists and scholars dedicated to the publication of works in defense of the race, and whose members included PAUL LAURENCE DUNBAR, KELLY MILLER, ALAIN LOCKE, ARTHUR SCHOMBURG, WILLIAM PICKENS, W. E. B. DuBOIS, FRANCIS J. GRIMKÉ, Alexander Crummell, and CARTER G. WOODSON. In 1902 Cooper became principal of M Street High School. This position was not without its challenges from the elites of Washington, D.C. Cooper transformed the school into one of the best for black students. Contrary to BOOKER T. WASHINGTON's educational philosophy of vocational and industrial training, Cooper insisted on a college preparatory curriculum for her students. Her insistence on this curriculum was met with resistance, and her leadership of M Street was challenged by disagreement over the appropriate educational course for black students. In 1902–1903 DuBois delivered a speech at the M Street School critical of the school's timidity toward expansive curricula. In response, advocates of the Washingtonian perspective spurred what became known as "the M Street High School Controversy." The school board levied an array of charges against Cooper in order to discredit her.

As Annette Eaton, a former M Street student explained, Cooper's tenure as principal fell victim to race and gender politics in Washington, D.C. Eaton noted the obstacles Cooper faced, pointing out that the white power structure clearly took issue with Cooper's audacity in preparing black students for college and believing that black students could easily match white students' achievement. Eaton also observed that the sexism Cooper encountered stemmed from three main causes: her ambition to succeed beyond the role of principal, her status as a married (though widowed) woman in a profession, and gossip regarding Cooper's rumored relationship with a male boarder, John Love, in her home.

Cooper had taken in John Love and his sister as foster children after they were orphaned. Both Love and his sister continued to board with Cooper as adults, along with four other female teachers. Although theirs was a close relationship, scholars speculate that Cooper declined Love's later marriage proposal, perhaps owing to the age difference or to the impropriety of marriage after being Love's guardian. The confluence of the school board's racism and the community's sexist views of her personal life—two forms of discrimination about which Cooper was quite vocal—forced her resignation as principal of M Street in 1906, after a year of disparaging testimony. Though hounded out of the position of principal, Cooper returned to the school to teach Latin four years later.

Cooper's industriousness in Washington, D.C., was not limited to her role as principal. Impervious to segregationist policies, Cooper helped found, in 1905, the Colored Women's YWCA and, in 1912, the Colored YMCA. Black women's clubs were instrumental in establishing YWCA branches in areas where there were no support services for black women moving from rural, southern communities to the North. Upon the death of her half-brother in 1915, Cooper adopted his five grandchildren, interrupting the doctoral studies at Columbia University that she had begun in 1911. After enrolling the children in boarding school in 1924, Cooper left for Paris to complete her degree at the University of Paris. She finished her dissertation, "The Attitude of France toward Slavery in the Revolution," in 1925 and, at age sixty-seven, became the fourth African American woman to receive a Ph.D.

After retiring from teaching at Paul Laurence Dunbar in 1930, Cooper became the second president of Frelinghuysen University, an educational institution for black adults founded in 1917. Cooper paid tribute to the role her mother played in her educational achievement by creating the Hannah Stanley Opportunity School, annexed to Frelinghuysen, despite Cooper's many efforts to keep it open. Frelinghuysen, with economic problems and loss of accreditation, became the Frelinghuysen Group of Schools for Colored Working People, with Cooper as registrar, until it closed in the 1950s. Cooper maintained a scholarly writing life until her death at the age of 105 in Washington, D.C. A consummate race woman, Cooper serves as an examplar "of what one black women can do if given access to the halls of academe" (HENRY LOUIS GATES JR., Norton Anthology of African American Literature, 554).

FURTHER READING
Cooper's papers are housed in the Moorland-
    Spingarn Research Center, Howard University,
    Washington, D.C.

Cooper, Anna Julia. *A Voice from the South: By a Black Woman of the South*, with an introduction by Mary Helen Washington (1988).

Cooper, Anna Julia, Charles Lemert, and Esme Bhan, eds. *The Voice of Anna Julia Cooper: Including a Voice from the South and Other Important Essays, Papers, and Letters* (1998).

Hutchinson, Louise Daniel, and Anacostia Neighborhood Museum. *Anna Julia Cooper: A Voice from the South* (1982).

Johnson, Karen Ann. *Uplifting the Women and the Race: The Lives, Educational Philosophies, and Social Activism of Anna Julia Cooper and Nannie Helen Burroughs* (2000).

White, Deborah Gray. *Too Heavy a Load: Black Women in Defense of Themselves, 1884–1994* (1999).

KIMBERLY SPRINGER

Cooper, Arthur (1789–20 Mar. 1853), African Methodist Episcopal (AME) elder and leader in the African American community on Nantucket, was born on the plantation of David Ricketts on the outskirts of Alexandria, Virginia, where he was called George. The names of his parents are unknown.

There are conflicting accounts as to when Cooper fled Virginia. It is also unclear whether he fled with his wife, or whether he married a free woman in New Bedford, Massachusetts. (Little is known about his wife, Mary, other than her birth year of 1785.) All accounts do agree that he fled from Virginia with other fugitives on the packet ship *Regulator*, which hailed from New Bedford. Shortly after his arrival in New Bedford, George assumed the name Arthur Cooper and the following year, the Coopers' first child, Eliza Ann, was born. Sons Cyrus and Randolph were born in 1812 and 1814, respectively. Randolph was probably named for fellow fugitive William Mason, who changed his name to John Randolph. It is not known how Cooper made his living in New Bedford or if it was during this time that he learned to read and write. A third son, Robert, was born in 1818.

The family moved to Nantucket around 1820 when Arthur Cooper was in his early thirties. They rented a house on Angola Street in an African American community on the outskirts of town called New Guinea. Cooper was most likely a laborer, but in what industry is unknown. He may well have worked on the docks of both New Bedford and Nantucket.

In October 1822 bounty hunters came to Nantucket to capture Arthur and Mary Cooper. According to the census of 1820, Cooper's owner,

David Ricketts, had eight slaves, so the loss of Cooper and possibly Mary, too, was significant enough for him to hire Camillus Griffiths, a bounty hunter, to track them down. Griffiths tried, but for some reason failed, to get a warrant from Judge Davis in Boston to apprehend Mary and Arthur Cooper. However, a federal marshal, Colonel Harris, sent a deputy named Bass to accompany the hunters to Nantucket.

Word spread quickly across the small island that a band of bounty hunters had arrived for the Coopers, and so when the slave-catchers showed up at the Cooper house before sunrise the next day, they found a crowd of their black neighbors had already gathered there to protect the family of six. George Washington, a cow herder, ran to fetch several prominent white men, among them the Quakers William Mitchell, Thomas and Sylvanus Macy, and Oliver C. Gardner, neighbors on nearby Vestal Street. These men hurried to the scene to prevent the violence that would occur if the strangers attempted to break into the Cooper house and take the family into custody.

The white Nantucketers attempted to defuse the situation by engaging the bounty hunters in conversation about the legality of their undertaking and by demanding to see legal documents, which they then questioned the authenticity of. Next to arrive at the scene was Nantucket magistrate Alfred Folger, who continued to delay the proceedings. He threatened to arrest the slave-catchers. They, in turn, insisted that Folger order the crowd to disperse and uphold federal law pertaining to the return of fugitive slaves.

The delaying tactics in front of the house gave the Coopers time to escape out the back of the house, disguised in Quaker garb provided by Thomas M. Macy and his brother-in-law, Oliver Gardner. The Coopers made their way in the half-light to Gardner's house on Vestal Street, where they remained in hiding for five or six weeks. Only five days after the harrowing escape and while still in hiding, Mary gave birth to their fourth son, Arthur Jr. After the danger had passed, the Coopers returned to their house on Angola Street, never again to be harassed by slave-catchers.

One more child, Harriet, was born to Arthur and Mary in 1824. Mary died two years later in 1826. One year later Arthur married Lucinda Gordon, who had been captured in Africa at the age of eighteen. She was taken to South Carolina and later sold to a man in Newport, Rhode Island. It is not known when she became free or when and under what circumstances she came to Nantucket. Lucinda wore the mark of slavery in the shape of a brand on her forehead.

During this time Cooper supplemented his income by acting as a labor scout for the whale ships of George and Joseph Starbuck. By 1833 he had saved enough money to buy the house on Angola Street, where he had been living.

Cooper was a respected man in the Nantucket community. In 1832 he became one of the three founders of the African Methodist Episcopal Church on West York Street, known locally as the Zion Church. He remained a church elder for many years and residents recalled seeing him walking around Nantucket dressed in Quaker garb.

Cooper was politically active in temperance, abolition, and anti-colonization movements. The Zion Church was a site of temperance meetings for the New Guinea community. Cooper believed that the schemes to send blacks back to Africa were unfair and unjust. In August 1831 he was chosen to chair a meeting to register opposition to the American Colonization Society. He sent a report of the meeting to be published in the *Liberator*, the abolitionist newspaper founded by William Lloyd Garrison, then in its first year. In 1840 when Eunice Ross applied to attend Nantucket High School but was denied owing to her color, Cooper was active in the protest. In 1842 he was among ten black citizens who ran unsuccessfully for the school committee. He also signed a petition presented to the state legislature in 1845 asking for equal access to public education. The activism of the Nantucket black community led to the first state law in the nation to guarantee equal education to all, passed in March 1845.

Arthur Cooper died at the age of sixty-four. His wife, Lucy, who had survived the Middle Passage, lived past the age of 100.

FURTHER READING

Grover, Kathryn. *The Fugitives Gibraltar: Escaping Slaves and Abolitionism in New Bedford, Massachusetts* (2001).

Karttunen, Francis. *The Other Islanders: People Who Pulled Nantucket's Oars* (2005).

White, Barbara. *The African School: The African School and the Integration of Nantucket Public Schools, 1825–1847* (1978).

BARBARA A. WHITE

Cooper, Chuck (29 Sept. 1926–5 Feb. 1984), basketball player, was born Charles Henry Cooper in Pittsburgh, Pennsylvania, the youngest of five children of Daniel Webster Cooper, a mailman, and Emma Caroline Brown, a schoolteacher.

Cooper played basketball at Westinghouse High School in segregated East Pittsburgh. After graduating in February 1944, Cooper attended West Virginia State College, a historically black institution. He played basketball from 1944 to 1945, until he was drafted into the U.S. Navy. He served from July 1945 to October 1946.

Upon leaving the Navy, Cooper attended Duquesne University in Pittsburgh on the GI Bill and graduated in 1950 with a B.S. in Education. Although Duquesne was a predominantly white university, it was an early leader in the recruitment of black athletes. Cooper made the basketball team, The Dukes, when only a freshman. He was their first black starter and an All-American. As captain in 1949–1950, he led the team to twenty-three wins and six losses. The overall record of seventy-eight wins and nineteen losses over the four years he played included two prestigious National Invitational Tournament (NIT) appearances. Cooper's number 15 is one of only five retired numbers in Duquesne basketball history, and in 1964 he was selected for the Duquesne All-Time team. Cooper experienced racism as a player for Duquesne. In December 1946 the University of Tennessee team walked off the court when Chuck Davies, the Duquesne coach, refused to promise not to play Cooper. Every game played in the South set a precedent for mixed-race events, and the Deep South was off-limits.

Cooper was the first African American to be drafted into the National Basketball Association (NBA) by Walter Brown, owner of the Boston Celtics, on 25 April 1950, after a three-week stint with the Harlem Globetrotters. Brown famously said, "I don't give a damn if he's striped or plaid or polka-dot," and signed Cooper for $7500. EARL FRANCIS LLOYD, selected by the Washington Capitols a few rounds after Cooper in the 1950 NBA draft, would, however, be the first African American to play in the league. The six-foot-five Cooper played forward for the Celtics from 1 November 1950 to 1954. If Cooper was refused service in a restaurant, his Celtics teammates refused to eat there as well. He married Patsy Jane Ware, a nurse, on 18 August 1951.

In 1954 Cooper was traded to the Milwaukee Hawks, where he played for one year. He divorced at that time, and there were no children from the marriage. The Hawks moved to St. Louis for the 1954–55 season. Cooper was released and signed with the Fort Wayne Indiana Pistons for his final NBA season (1956). His career average was 6.7 points per game. In 1956 and 1957 he played for the Harlem Magicians, an offshoot of the Globetrotters.

Cooper married Irva Lee on 28 March 1957, and they had four children. They moved to Minnesota in 1959, and in 1961 he earned an M.S. in Social Work from the University of Minnesota. Returning to Pittsburgh, he held several positions as a social worker between 1966 and 1971, including acting executive director of Community Action of Pittsburgh (CAP), coordinator for Pittsburgh Community Action, and planning director of the Health and Welfare Association for Allegheny County. In 1970, Pittsburgh's mayor, Pete Flaherty, appointed Cooper the first black director of the Department of City Parks and Recreation. Cooper then became the urban affairs officer for the Community Affairs Department at the Pittsburgh National Bank (1971–1984), where he was responsible for overseeing the bank's compliance with the Community Reinvestment Act.

After retiring from basketball, Cooper felt that racism was a reason he was not offered a coaching position. He downplayed his role as a pioneer, deferring to JACKIE ROBINSON (who broke baseball's color line in 1947) as the groundbreaker for black professional athletes. Cooper was inducted into the Duquesne Hall of Fame in 1970, and was chosen as one of the 100 Most Distinguished Living Alumni in 1978. In 1974 he was inducted into the Pennsylvania Sports Hall of Fame. In 1983 Duquesne established a Chuck Cooper Award for basketball underclassmen. Copper's legacy as a community leader was highlighted on 26 February 1991 when the Pittsburgh City Council declared Chuck Cooper Day, honoring him for his devotion to recreation for young people. In 2000, the Boston Celtics raised a special banner with Cooper's number 11, on the 50th anniversary of his selection in the 1950 draft.

Cooper was a pioneer as a member of the Boston Celtics, but his dedication to ending racial discrimination and improving life in the black community was his true legacy. He served on the boards of trustees for the Citizen's Advisory Committee on Desegregation, the Urban League, the Hospital Council of Western Pennsylvania, and the Boy Scouts. As the first, and at the time the only, black professional at the Pittsburgh National Bank, Cooper was committed to meeting the bank's affirmative action goals and developing minority connections. Cooper was described by teammates and coworkers as a kind and gentlemanly person. He died of liver cancer.

FURTHER READING

Rust, Art, and Edna Rust. *Art Rust's Illustrated History of the Black Athlete* (1985).

Thomas, Ron. *They Cleared the Lane: The NBA's Black Pioneers* (2002).

Sachare, Alex, ed. *The Official NBA Basketball Encyclopedia*, 2d ed. (1989).

Obituaries: *Boston Globe*, 7 Feb. 1984; *New York Times*, 7 Feb. 1984.

JANE BRODSKY FITZPATRICK

Cooper, Clarence, Jr. (1934–1978), newspaper editor for the *Chicago Messenger* in the mid-1950s, novelist, and a key figure of the black crime fiction movement of the 1960s, was born in Detroit, Michigan. Little is known about Cooper's early life—neither his actual date of birth nor his parents' names and occupations. Even his education is unknown. All that is known is that he was a boyhood friend of MALCOLM X, became an editor and writer for the *Chicago Messenger*, got married, developed a heroin addiction, and served two years in Iona Penitentiary all before the age of twenty-seven.

In 1960 Cooper published his first novel, *The Scene*, to almost universal critical praise. Set in a nameless ghetto populated by junkies, prostitutes, detectives, dealers, and pimps, *The Scene* was a powerful portrait of the heroin drug trade and black urban life in the postwar period. As the reviewer from the *New York Herald Tribune* stated: "Not even Nelson Algren's *The Man with the Golden Arm* burns with the ferocious intensity you'll find here. [Cooper] writes with a personal authority that can only be called shattering and the searing exactness of one who has lived through the horror" (Bullock, 13). As Cooper would himself admit, this novel offered him an opportunity to work through in fiction the psychological dynamics of heroin addiction. "I didn't know why I had been a user. I found the reason in the hearts and souls of the people I had created in *The Scene*" (Bullock, 13).

In 1960 Cooper also published *The Syndicate* under the pseudonym of Robert Chestnut. The story of a hit man who finds himself caught in the middle of a hunt for a missing half-million dollars, *The Syndicate* is a hard-boiled novel in the tradition of Dashiell Hammett's first novel, *Red Harvest*. Featuring a wise-cracking gun-for-hire ensnared in a web of social forces, variously represented by mob bosses, crooked cops, femme fatales, and sexually deviant nightclub owners, *The Syndicate* illustrates Cooper's flair for reworking the American noir tradition.

But by the time these two novels were published, Cooper was serving another prison sentence. Unable to find a reputable publisher for his work, Cooper wrote a series of novels for Chicago-based publisher Regency Books, helmed by science fiction writer Harlan Ellison. A pulp press which had published the likes of Jim Thompson, Robert Bloch, and Philip José Farmer, Regency published Cooper's third novel, *Weed*, in 1961. Consisting of the interlocking stories of a Korean War veteran, an aging detective, and the prostitute they both love, and infused with rhythms and sounds of bebop jazz, *Weed* lyrically portrays working-class people struggling to find meaning in their everyday lives. A year after releasing *Weed*, Cooper published *The Dark Messenger*, a semi-autobiographical novel about his experiences as a writer and editor for the *Chicago Messenger*. Containing extended debates about the complex relationship between black middle-class social climbers and the working-class masses they ostensibly represent, *The Dark Messenger* is the story of a young reporter named Lee Merriweather who must come to terms with the corruption and sensationalism of the black press. A scathing denunciation of what Cooper perceived as the opportunistic nature of black publishing, the novel offers a chilling vision of how some African American newspapers exploit stories of black-on-black violence to hock their literary goods. Cooper followed this novel with *Black!: Two Short Novels* in 1963, composed of the novellas *Yet Princes Follow* and *Not We Many*. With its cast of archetypal street characters, including a corrupt preacher, a pimp trickster, a goldbricking con artist, and a Greek chorus of hipsters, *Yet Princes Follow* was Cooper's most straightforward satire of ghetto street life and the swindler opportunists that populate it. In direct contrast to this work was *Not We Many*, the story of a mulatto man from Harlem on a search to find meaning in the doctrines of the Nation of Islam. Cooper's most didactic piece of fiction, *Not We Many* was deeply critical of the racial and sexual chauvinism of the Islam practiced in inner-city neighborhoods. Since *Weed*, *The Dark Messenger*, and *Black!* were published as paperback originals, they received little critical attention. In the introduction to *Black!*, Harlan Ellison wrote: "Clarence Cooper Jr. is black, and cannot get along with the world. No special star shone at his birth to tell anyone either that another dark face or a special talent had come to stare at us and wonder what place it could find for itself. He had to find his own voice for his own message, and that message is here, in these two stories" (*Black!*, 1).

Released from prison in the early 1960s and disillusioned by the lack of reception to his work, Cooper spent much of his time in lower Manhattan, falling into a world of drug addiction and petty theft. But in 1967 Cooper published his final and finest book, *The Farm*. A first-person narrative about an addict named John who is serving out his sentence in a federal rehabilitation center, *The Farm* was Cooper's most ambitious and experimental novel. *The Farm* received mostly negative reviews, as its readers were dissatisfied with Cooper's occasional tendency toward overwriting and strained metaphors. A book which traces John's increasing sexual obsession with a fellow female prisoner named Joyce, *The Farm* fully developed a theme which had been implicit in all of Cooper's work, the dialectic between trauma and memory. Like TONI MORRISON's *Beloved* or William Faulkner's *The Sound and the Fury*, Cooper's *The Farm* revealed that the past is never really past, and that the specters that haunt are every bit as real in the present.

During his life Cooper was not considered an important figure in the canon of black literature. After *The Farm* failed to recapture the positive attention that *The Scene* had enjoyed, Cooper fell into obscurity, dying poor at the Twenty-third Street YMCA in New York City. Although he never attracted the following that fellow black crime writers ROBERT BECK (Iceberg Slim) or DONALD GOINES achieved, Cooper has nevertheless developed a lasting underground following. In a 1968 review of *The Farm* in *Negro Digest*, William Barrow wrote: "There is a small coterie of readers who swear by Clarence Cooper Jr. He is, they maintain, one of the most underrated writers in America, a RICHARD WRIGHT of the revolutionary era" (Barrow, 94). Cooper's works were republished in the 1990s as part of the Old School Books series as well as by the British-based Payback Press.

FURTHER READING

Cooper, Clarence. *Black!: Two Short Novels* (1963).
Cooper, Clarence. *The Scene* (1960, 1996).
Barrow, William. *Negro Digest* 17 (May 1968).
Bullock, Florence Haxton. *New York Herald Tribune Book Review*, 28 Feb. 1960.

JUSTIN DAVID GIFFORD

Cooper, Edward Elder (June 1859–9 July 1908), journalist, businessman, and civil rights organization leader, was born into slavery, probably near Smyrna, Tennessee, to unnamed parents, and apparently orphaned soon afterward. Little is known of his childhood, except that Cooper moved at an early age to Nashville, where he was educated at the old barracks school for African American children on Knowles Street, later the nucleus of Fisk University.

Cooper later recalled working on a farm for two years before he began selling newspapers on passenger trains. He also worked briefly as a hotel waiter in Philadelphia, Pennsylvania, during the Centennial Exposition there in 1876. About 1877 Cooper migrated to Indianapolis, Indiana, where he worked as a book-seller and became one of the first African Americans to graduate from the city's Shortridge High School in 1882. He began working for the Railway Mail Service, and soon rose to chief clerk on the Louisville-to-Indianapolis route, but left in 1886 amid allegations of mail tampering.

The business of journalism was his preferred profession, and one at which he showed considerable talent. Cooper helped create three of the nation's better-known African American weekly newspapers of the nineteenth century: the Indianapolis *Colored World*, co-founded with Edwin F. Horn in 1882; the Indianapolis *Freeman*, launched in 1888; and the Washington, D.C., *Colored American*, founded in 1893. Though a perfectly adequate writer in his own right, Cooper preferred to hire other writers, including such gifted female writers as Lucy Wilmot Smith and Lillian Thomas Fox, and to concentrate instead on handling front office affairs.

His first experiment, the *Colored World*, was not a financial success, and Cooper soon turned over its operation to the schoolteacher Levi E. Christy in 1885. He then worked briefly as manager of the *Baptist Watch-Tower*, published in Evansville, Indiana. His next attempt, the *Freeman*, emerged as a daring, eight-page illustrated newspaper, using correspondents from around the nation and winning rave reviews from observers. In 1891, the editor and author I. Garland Penn called the *Freeman* "tho in its infancy … the leading paper of the race," and it was compared favorably to *Harper's Weekly* for the quality of its cartoons and writing and its focus on regional and national news (Penn, 336).

Financial problems finally forced Cooper to sell the newspaper in 1892 to one of his creditors, a prosperous local barber named GEORGE L. KNOX, for whom he continued to work. Under Knox's ownership, the *Freeman* remained stable and a fixture

of Indianapolis journalism well into the 1920s, and he painted a friendly if ambiguous portrait of Cooper in his memoirs, published in 1979. Others in Indianapolis were less kind than Knox. The *World*, for instance, in 1891 decried Cooper's business methods and called him "a positive detriment to the race" (*Indianapolis World*, 26 Dec. 1891).

In 1893 Cooper left journalism to work in the Indiana legislature, before moving to Washington, D.C., with his bride, the former Tenie Porter of Kentucky, whom he had wed by 1893. It is not known if they had children. In August of that same year, Cooper's single most enduring venture appeared in the nation's capital, a distinctive new weekly billing itself optimistically as "A National Negro Newspaper." Cooper listed himself as president and general manager. His Indiana colleague, Richard W. Thompson, once the managing editor of the *World*, was the most notable of a series of editors at the *Colored American*, succeeding Thomas J. Calloway and Jesse Lawson in that capacity. The *Colored American*, well-illustrated and well-written, succeeded beyond all expectations, reportedly achieving a paid circulation of twelve thousand by 1901. It became a determined editorial supporter of the accommodationist policies of BOOKER T. WASHINGTON and an enthusiastic booster of many African American politicians, including the nation's only African American congressman at the time, the North Carolina Republican GEORGE HENRY WHITE; U.S. Treasury Register Judson W. Lyons; and former congressman HENRY PLUMMER CHEATHAM, then recorder of deeds for the District of Columbia.

Cooper was initially active in the new National Afro-American Council, a precursor of the NAACP founded in 1898, presiding over the local council, attending its annual national meetings, and serving until 1901 on the national executive committee of the early civil rights organization. He was also active in the National Afro-American Press Association, and championed both organizations in his newspaper, which appears to have been subsidized quietly by Booker T. Washington. In 1902 Cooper contributed a rare article, on the assassination of President McKinley, to an anthology of works on social and political issues. But success as a publisher did not teach Cooper to live within his means, and by late 1904, the *Colored American* was out of business, despite Cooper's pleas to Washington and others to rescue the flagging operation. Cooper blamed cash flow problems on delinquent advertisers and subscribers; others blamed his extravagance. His

1905 attempt to merge the paper into the *Colored Catholic Herald* lasted only one issue. Desperate, Cooper was forced to seek employment as a clerk with the District of Columbia Commission, as was noted by his rival, W. Calvin Chase, editor of Washington's *Bee*. In 1907 Cooper became a special agent of the U. S. Census Bureau and briefly toured the South to collect religious statistics among poor African Americans there.

By 1908 Cooper's short-lived Colored American Novelty Company, which he had founded around 1905, had failed; his last position was performing unspecified duties for a Washington, D.C., steamboat company. A minor stroke in the spring of 1908 left him weakened, although he worked almost until the day of his death in July. Survivors included his wife and an unnamed sister and brother. Cooper was forty-nine and penniless, the victim of overextended dreams and bad luck.

His modest home funeral was paid for by his friends, but drew a distinguished crowd to pay tribute, including pallbearers JOHN C. DANCY, Judson W. Lyons, Judge Robert H. Terrell, and RALPH WALDO TYLER. His obituary in Knox's *Freeman* called Cooper "greatly loved by all who ever worked for him … for none were so genial, of such rare good nature, of supreme wit and tact in troublesome times." Cooper's mission in life, the newspaper continued, "was to spread printer's ink over men—to make 'big Negroes' greater, mediocre Negroes of some consequence, and little Negroes worth noticing—by a liberal use of printer's ink" (*Indianapolis Freeman*, 18 July 1908).

FURTHER READING

No collection exists of Edward Elder Cooper's papers, although more than fifty of his letters (1889–1907) can be found in the Booker T. Washington Papers, Library of Congress, along with a number of letters to the Ohio political leader George A. Myers (Myers Papers, Ohio Historical Society). Cooper's only signed article appeared in *Twentieth Century Negro Literature, or a Cyclopedia of Vital Topics Relating to the American Negro*, ed. Daniel W. Culp (1902).

Knox, George L. *Slave and Freeman, The Autobiography of George L. Knox* (1979).

Suggs, Henry F., ed. *The Black Press in the Middle West* (1996).

Thornbrough, Emma Lou. *The Negro in Indiana before 1900: A Study of a Minority* (1982).

Penn, I. Garland. *The Afro-American Press and Its Editors* (1891).

Obituary: *Indianapolis Freeman*, 18 July 1908.

BENJAMIN R. JUSTESEN

Cooper, George Clinton (7 Sep. 1916–20 May 2002), pioneer black naval officer, was born in Washington, North Carolina, the eighth of eleven children of Edward L. Cooper, a sheet metal worker, and Laura J. Cooper, a homemaker. One of the eleven siblings died in infancy; the remaining ten became college graduates. During his upbringing in North Carolina, Cooper often faced the tribulations of southern racism. He went to segregated schools and learned from his parents that he had to go out of his way to avoid conflict with whites. Once, when Cooper was eight or nine years old, he got into a fight with a white boy. As he put it, "It was the wrong day for him to call me a 'nigger,' and we had it out" (Stillwell, 76). Cooper's father had to smooth things over with the boy's father to avoid the incident's escalation. When he worked as a bellhop in a local hotel, Cooper often endured unpleasant comments from hotel guests and reluctantly swallowed his pride. As his mother told him, "Son, it ain't no sin being colored, but it's darned inconvenient" (Stillwell, 86).

From his father Cooper learned a work ethic and from his mother a sense of compassion and humanity. The senior Cooper, who ran a sheet metal shop in Washington, passed on to his son the idea that an individual has to produce things that customers are willing to buy. Cooper enrolled in 1934 in Hampton Institute, Hampton, Virginia, to study metalwork. The school, now Hampton University, was founded after the Civil War for the education and training of black students. While he was pursuing his degree, Cooper worked as a waiter on campus and was also part of the various singing groups that presented black spirituals to outside groups on behalf of the school. During his time as an undergraduate, Cooper met Margarett Gillespie, a student in Hampton's library science program. They were married in December 1939 and subsequently had one child. Their daughter, Peggy Cooper Davis, became a judge and law school professor.

After the Coopers' marriage, the couple moved to North Carolina, where George briefly did sheet metal work. However, as the United States geared up for World War II, metal for civilian use became scarce, so Cooper turned to government work. In 1941 he started as an instructor in sheet metal work at the War Production and Training Center in Wilberforce, Ohio, and in 1942 became a civilian instructor at the Naval Training School established on the campus of his alma mater. During the course of his time at Hampton, Cooper enlisted in the navy as a chief petty officer and continued to instruct navy enlisted personnel.

The commanding officer of the school, Commander E. Hall Downes, was so impressed by Cooper's ability that he recommended him for the navy's first training course for African American officers. The class convened at Great Lakes, Illinois, in January 1944. Of the sixteen officer candidates enrolled in the course, Cooper was one of twelve commissioned as ensigns; a thirteenth became a warrant officer. At the time the navy had more than 100,000 black enlisted personnel. The men who became the pioneer officers in March 1944 were the forerunners of thousands of black naval officers commissioned in the many years since then. In the 1970s the first officers retroactively achieved a group identity when they were dubbed the Golden Thirteen. In one of his first days in uniform as an officer, Cooper walked through the railroad station in Chicago and observed that people came to a quiet stop wherever he was: they had never before seen a black naval officer.

After being commissioned, Cooper reported back to Hampton, where Downes installed him as the personnel officer and supervisor of training. Once, while Cooper was away from the school, a white sailor directed a derogatory remark at him. Cooper was ready to respond physically, but his wife, Peg, grabbed his arm and said, "George, it's not worth it" (Stillwell, 89). It was the only time he lost his cool in such a situation. However, he often reached out to white enlisted personnel, calling them into his office when they had deaths or illnesses in their families. As Cooper remembered, "You start empathizing with this guy, and he begins to see you as a human being and not as a black son of a bitch with a shingle on his shoulder" (Stillwell, 89).

With the end of World War II, Cooper left the service but remained at Hampton Institute as a member of the civilian faculty. In that position he coordinated the activities of thirty-seven instructors who were teaching trade school students. He remained at the school until 1952 when he moved to Dayton, Ohio, where he and a partner, Cal Crawford, established Finer Services, Inc., a company that engaged in interior cleaning and decorating. In the mid-1950s he transferred to the city government of Dayton to become a housing inspector, applying the knowledge he had acquired in a number of trades involved in construction. As

with his experience reaching out to white sailors during his navy time, Cooper sought to change the attitudes of prejudiced coworkers by both offering friendship and demonstrating competence. Cooper moved up the ladder in the Dayton city government before returning to the field of education in 1964. He joined the staff of Antioch College in Yellow Springs, Ohio, where he was involved in the school's extramural department and later as director of the international work-study program, which involved a worldwide program of study and work for foreign professionals. In 1970 he returned to government work as the first black department head in the city of Dayton. He was director of the Department of Human Resources, which encompassed parks and recreation, human rehabilitation, social services, and consumer services.

Following his retirement from city government in 1981, Cooper devoted himself to a variety of civic enterprises in the Dayton area, including the Community Action Agency, which fostered training and job opportunities for youths, and the establishment of a local diversity council. For many years he and fellow members of the Golden Thirteen attended annual meetings of the National Naval Officers Association, a group of black professionals of the navy, marine corps, and coast guard. The pioneers were invariably saluted for serving as role models for all those who followed. Cooper died in Centerville, Ohio.

FURTHER READING

Cooper, George C. *Reminiscences of George C. Cooper, Member of the Golden Thirteen* (1989).

Stillwell, Paul, ed. *The Golden Thirteen: Recollections of the First Black Naval Officers* (1993).

Obituary: *Los Angeles Times,* 28 May 2002.

PAUL STILLWELL

Cooper, J. California (c.1945–), playwright, short fiction writer, and novelist, was born Joan Cooper in Berkeley, California, the daughter of Joseph and Maxine Rosemary Cooper. Unapologetically protective of her private life, little is known about Cooper's personal information, including her birth date. At least two explanations have surfaced in separate interviews regarding her use of "California" as part of her professional name. One is that its incorporation is the result of an observation made earlier in her career that her works resembled those of Tennessee Williams, a twentieth-century

American writer who appropriated the name of his father's home state as his own. Another explanation is that because Cooper has kept her personal life so closely guarded, she felt the need to give the public something of herself; thus, she gave them California. In addition to Northern California, Cooper has resided in various areas of the United States, including Texas, Alaska, and Oregon. She is the mother of Paris A. Williams.

Cooper's writing career began in early childhood. Like many little girls, Cooper played with paper dolls as a child. However, her fascination with them lasted into late adolescence, so her mother took them away when she became eighteen years old. In an attempt to satisfy the needs of her vivid imagination, she began to write down the stories she could have lost with the loss of her dolls. It is not surprising then that her professional debut as a writer would manifest in the form of plays. Although she doubted the quality of her own early work, Cooper continued to write stories. Eventually she gained enough confidence to present her plays to the Black Repertory Theater in Berkeley, California. After the first production, a play entitled *How Now?*, Cooper discovered that her work was appealing to others and she continued to allow her plays to be staged in other venues, including college campuses and public television and radio stations. In the mid-1970s Cooper's play, *Strangers*, was staged at the San Francisco Theater of Fine Arts. This event became the turning point in Cooper's career. In addition to earning the distinction of Black Playwright of the Year in 1978, Cooper also caught the attention of the acclaimed Pulitzer Prize winning novelist, ALICE WALKER, who encouraged her to consider rewriting her plays as short stories. Walker was so impressed with her work that she offered Cooper the opportunity to publish at Wild Trees Press, Walker's new publishing company that was dedicated to the cause of promoting writing that foregrounded a feminist perspective. The result was the publication of *A Piece of Mine* (1984), Cooper's first published book and Wild Trees Press's most successful endeavor.

Most of Cooper's work can be distinguished by her conspicuous employment of oral expression. Her narrators speak directly to the reader, rendering folksy, parable-like stories that are meant to both entertain and instruct. Although she has often been criticized for saturating her works with preachy and overmoralizing narration, Cooper's fiction has developed a significant following. Her stories are, as novelist TERRY McMILLAN observes

in the *New York Times Book Review* (8 November 1987), "in their own gossipy, circuitous, roundabout way, the stories [that] enchant you because they are not stories; they are the truth reconstructed." In *A Piece of Mine*, for example, several stories focus on African American women who, while futilely seeking true intimacy with emotionally unavailable men, stumble upon self-love, often realizing for the first time an authentic inner strength. Although *A Piece of Mine* remains as one of Cooper's most popular works, it is her second short story collection, *Homemade Love* (1986), that earned Cooper the American Book Award in 1989. A decade later, "Funny Valentines," a story from this collection, became the basis for a made for cable television movie entitled *Funny Valentines* (1999), a film directed by celebrated African American woman filmmaker Julie Dash. In 1987, Cooper moved to Marshall, Texas, where she completed her third collection of short stories, *Some Soul to Keep* (1987). Over the next twenty years, Cooper produced four more short story collections: *The Matter Is Life* (1991), *Some Love, Some Pain, Sometime* (1995), *The Future Has a Past* (2001), and *Wild Stars Seeking Midnight Suns* (2006).

Following the success of her earlier short story collections, Cooper decided to extend her professional repertoire to include novel writing. In 1991 her first novel, *Family*, achieved notable success among a diverse reading audience. The novel's setting and thematic focus placed her fiction in the company of other African American women writers of late twentieth century such as TONI MORRISON, author of *Beloved* (1987), and Sherley Anne Williams, author of *Dessa Rose* (1986), whose works contributed to a popular new genre of African American literature dubbed the neo-slave narrative. True to the elements of this contemporary literary style, Cooper's *Family* reimagines the American slave's existence, often infusing the characters with sufficient enough personal agency to rebel against oppression. In *In Search of Satisfaction* (1994) and *The Wake of the Wind* (1998), Cooper chronicles the experiences of African American women and their families during the years following the Civil War. In her fourth and fifth novels, *Some People, Some Other Place* (2006) and *Life Is Short, but Wide* (2009), the settings shift from the rural post-Civil War southern states of her earlier novels to the twentieth century Midwest. Similar to her earlier fiction, these latter two novels explore the themes of love, morality, and desire among multiple generations of African American women.

A master storyteller, Cooper's short stories and novels reveal her commitment to extending words of wisdom, comfort, and renewal to her readers. Through her employment of call and response patterns and black verbal artistry, her works can be viewed as a celebration of the African American oral tradition that is reminiscent of the fiction of Harlem Renaissance authors ZORA NEALE HURSTON and LANGSTON HUGHES.

FURTHER READING

Carroll, Denolyn. "Sometimes I Cry, Sometimes I Laugh: J. California Coopers Spins Tales of Common Folk Who Insist on Being Heard." *Black Issues Book Review*, 2004.

Carroll, Rebecca. *I Know What the Red Clay Looks Like: The Voice and Vision of Black American Women Writers* (1994).

McMillan, Terry. "Life Goes On and Don't You Forget It," *New York Times*, 8 November 1987.

CYNTHIA DOWNING BRYANT

Cooper, Jack Leroy (18 Sept. 1888–12 Jan. 1970), radio personality and advertising executive, was most likely the first black announcer in the history of broadcasting, on the air as early as 1924. His successful radio career would span four decades and make him a wealthy man. Cooper did not come from an entertainment background. Born in Memphis, Tennessee, he was one of ten children of William and Lavina Cooper. Jack Cooper quit school after the fifth grade to help support his impoverished family. He held a number of low-paying jobs and for a time got interested in boxing, winning more than a hundred bouts as a welterweight fighter. But he found his calling on the vaudeville stage, where he became a singer and dancer, beginning in 1905 and continuing well into the 1920s. He was more than just a performer, writing and producing skits and entire shows, often in collaboration with his first wife Estelle (sometimes called Estella), who was also a performer. He parlayed that talent into a job as a columnist and theater critic for the *Chicago Defender* newspaper, but his heart was in performing, and he hoped to find a job in the new medium of radio. In the days before audiotape was in use, radio stations eagerly sought live talent. Although there were a handful of black performers in early radio, the vast majority were white, as were all the announcers. Cooper was determined to change that. He persuaded station WCAP (later known as WRC) in Washington, D.C., to hire him as an entertainer, doing the comedy skits, dialects, and impersonations that had made him popular in vaudeville. The station did not pay him much, and he quickly grew tired of being a comedian, but he realized that radio was what he wanted to do with his life. When he returned to Chicago, he decided to plan for a career in broadcasting.

That plan came to fruition on 3 November 1929 when Jack Cooper debuted with his own show, *The All Negro Hour*, on station WSBC (World Storage Battery Company), having convinced the station's owner Joseph Silverstein that there was a large black audience in Chicago not being served by any of the other stations. Silverstein leased time to people who wanted to do a radio show, and Cooper made use of that arrangement. *The All Negro Hour* was a one-hour variety show, and this time Cooper was not restricted to performing comedy sketches. He booked his own guests, wrote much of the material, directed the skits, and above all, he did the announcing. Later his show would include some of the first newscasts aimed at black listeners, using content from the *Chicago Defender*. What was unique about Cooper's new show was the respect it showed for black performers and listeners. At a time when the radio programs that featured blacks tended to place them in stereotyped roles, Cooper refused to perform any skits that demeaned people of color (Newman, 55). He also tried to combat the myth that white listeners would have no interest in a show with an all-black cast. While black listeners were his primary target audience, he made his show appealing to the white audience, too.

By this time Cooper was divorced from Estelle, and had married Billie, who worked with him at WSBC. Nothing else is known of his second wife, and the marriage did not last long, as he married Gertrude (Roberts), also a performer, in 1938.

By the mid-1930s Cooper had gone from doing only one hour a week to being on WSBC three days a week. By 1937 he was on the air Monday through Friday. In addition to doing his variety show with its comedy routines, he became known for his disc jockey show. Having an announcer playing phonograph records was still a relatively new concept; most stations still relied on orchestras and live vocalists. Stations solely devoted to black audiences would not go on the air until 1948, but Cooper was ahead of his time, and his listeners loved the music he played, an eclectic blend of music by black performers—blues, dance music, even some gospel. When he was not on the air, he wrote and produced commercials for his sponsors, and his work was so much in demand that he was able to open his own production company and advertising agency.

Jack Cooper was a role model for many young African Americans who wanted to go into broadcasting, and he mentored a number of them over the years. By the late 1940s he had become so popular as a broadcaster that the media reported that his annual salary was $185,000 (Newman, 56). Cooper prided himself on speaking in a style that reflected an educated person, but he did so with such warmth that he was known as "the voice with the smile" (Jackson, 11).

While he made a lot of money in broadcasting, he always had time for community service; he raised money for black charities and volunteered his time on various committees that were involved with interracial understanding, earning awards for doing so. Starting in 1938 he began broadcasting a program called *Search for Missing Persons*, which helped to reunite listeners with those people they had lost touch with over the years. In the late 1940s Cooper began producing an educational program called *Listen Chicago*, a current events forum for the black audience, featuring the day's top news makers. At a time when there still were no entirely black-owned and-staffed radio stations, he was able to employ a number of local black performers to appear on his shows. One of his favorite performers was his third wife, Gertrude (Trudy), who was a talented musician in her own right. She also helped him to run his advertising agency.

By the 1950s his health began to decline, and he developed vision problems that led to blindness. He retired from radio in 1959 and died from a heart condition in January of 1970 at the age of 81. In the twenty-first century, when all-black radio stations are common and black music is loved by both white and black audiences, few people remember Cooper. Yet it was largely as a result of his success in Chicago that stations in other cities began to offer programming with more appeal to blacks. Jack L. Cooper was a pioneering voice for African Americans, a respected businessman, entertainer, and disc jockey who paved the way for acceptance of blacks in broadcasting.

FURTHER READING

Jackson, Jay. "The Voice with a Smile," *Negro Digest* (Feb. 1945).

Newman, Mark. *Entrepreneurs of Profit and Pride— From Black Appeal Radio to Radio Soul* (1988).

Ottley, Roi. "From Poverty to 90 Suits—Saga of a Negro in Radio," *Chicago Tribune*, 10 Jan. 1954.

Williams, Gilbert A. *Legendary Pioneers of Black Radio* (1998).

Obituary: "Last Rites Held for City's First Black DJ," *South Side (IL) Bulletin*, 21 Jan. 1970.

DONNA L. HALPER

Cooper, John Walcott (18 Jan. 1871–17 Apr. 1966), ventriloquist, was born in Brooklyn, New York, to John W. Cooper Sr. and Annie Morris. Cooper's parents died when he was still a child, and at the age of thirteen he began to care for himself by working as an exercise boy at the stables of the Sheepshead Bay Race Track in New York City. At the age of fifteen Cooper began singing tenor with a troupe called the Southern Jubilee Singers. After seeing performances by two white vaudeville ventriloquists, Harry Bryant and Al O. Duncan, Cooper became interested in the art of ventriloquism. While continuing to perform with the Southern Jubilee Singers, he began to focus his attention on becoming a professional ventriloquist. His first documented ventriloquist performance was with the Southern Jubilee Singers in Hamilton, Ontario, in 1894. He was twenty-three years old. As he toured with the singers, his ventriloquist act was incorporated into their performances, and he was soon credited during performances as a "ventriloquist and mimicist."

Cooper finally got his big break in May 1901, when he joined the Rusco and Holland Big Minstrel Festival and performed for forty-five weeks as a "special feature." In 1902, after a successful tour, W. A. Rusco signed Cooper as a principal feature with Richards and Pringle's Famous Georgia Minstrels. Cooper performed his ventriloquist act in the second part. One of few actors who used special scenery that he designed and built himself, Cooper appeared on stage as a barber and called his act "Fun in a Barbershop." In his original barbershop skit Cooper employed five characters and a parrot on a perch. He was the only ventriloquist performing the barbershop skit, and his barbershop for white folks became the talk of the vaudeville stage.

Cooper continued to perform through the early 1900s on the vaudeville circuit, billed as the Black Napoleon of Ventriloquism, the Great Cooper, the Only Colored Ventriloquist in the World, America's Representative Colored Ventriloquist, and Cooper the Great Ventriloquist. With his success two more African American ventriloquists made the move to mainstream vaudeville, Frank Rogers, who worked with two dummies, one black and one white; and Johnny Woods, who worked with his dummy Little Henry. Cooper retired his barbershop act and began to perform with one ventriloquist dummy named Sam. The idea of performing with one dummy came to Cooper when he witnessed a performance by Arthur Prince in 1919.

After this change Cooper continued to perform on the vaudeville circuit and in lodge halls, private clubs, and churches. In 1924 he performed with the Summer Chautauqua, a performing arts festival, at the Abyssinian Baptist Church, where ADAM CLAYTON POWELL was pastor. In 1928 Cooper and his second wife, Juliana St. Bernard, had their only child, Joan Cooper.

With the decline of the vaudeville circuit in the 1930s, Cooper toured with the Major Bowes Second Anniversary Revue, performing under the name Hezekiah Jones in the vaudeville houses that remained. He was not the star of the show and therefore was permitted to change identities. Cooper wanted to get out of the limelight, and changing his name was a way to relax. He also employed a different Sam than he had previously used. The new dummy was billed as the Colored Charlie McCarthy because of its resemblance to Edgar Bergen's dummy. (And indeed they were built by the same artist.)

In the 1940s Cooper toured the United States as part of the United Service Organizations (USO) Camp Shows. At the end of 1949 he was still involved with a hospital unit for the USO, and he continued to perform throughout the next decade. In 1953, at the age of eighty-two, he headlined a show for the Old Folks Home of the Colored Actors Guild and also performed at Hubert's Museum in New York City. In 1960 Cooper's wife, Juliana, died, and he retired from show business at the age of eighty-nine.

FURTHER READING

Burns, Stanley. *Other Voices: Ventriloquism from B.C. to T.V.* (2000)

Fax, Elton C. "John Walcott Cooper," in *Africana: The Encyclopedia of the African and African American Experience*, 2nd ed., ed. Kwame Anthony Apiah and Henry Louis Gates Jr. (2003).

CHARLIE T. TOMLINSON

Cooper, Tarzan (30 Aug. 1907–19 Dec. 1980), professional basketball player, was born Charles Theodore Cooper in Newark, Delaware, the son of Theodore Cooper and Evelyn (whose maiden name is unknown). He was a standout for the Central High School basketball team in Philadelphia, Pennsylvania, where he graduated in 1925. Cooper immediately began a twenty-year career in professional basketball,

playing initially with the Philadelphia Panther Pros in 1925, then going on to star for the all-black Philadelphia Giants from 1926 to 1929. ROBERT DOUGLAS, owner of the famed all-black professional team the New York Renaissance, spotted Cooper in a game at Philadelphia and signed him the next day to play for his team. Cooper then began an eleven-year stint with the Rens, named for their home court, the Renaissance Ballroom in Harlem. Over these eleven years the Rens earned a record of 1,303 wins and 203 losses.

At six feet, four inches, Cooper was considered a giant for his era. Howie Evans, sports editor of the *New York Amsterdam News*, noted in 1977 that "his hands were like giant shovels, and held more than their share of his 215 pounds." Cooper's large size earned him the nickname "Tarzan." He played center and was often considered the Rens's most valuable player. Joe Lapchick, center of the Original Celtics of New York City, considered Cooper both the best center in professional basketball and the best center he had ever played against.

In the 1932–1933 season, the Renaissance team earned a record of 127–7, including a winning streak of 88 consecutive games. From 1932 to 1936 just seven players constituted the Renaissance team: Cooper, Eyre "Bruiser" Saitch, James "Pappy" Ricks, William "Wee Willie" Smith, John "Casey" Holt, Bill Yancey, and CLARENCE "FATS" JENKINS. The "Magnificent Seven," as the Rens were called, consistently defeated the Original Celtics, the top white team of the day. For example, in 1933 the Rens topped the Original Celtics in seven out of eight meetings.

The teamwork and style of play exhibited by the Rens became their trademark. Known for their passing ability, the Rens rarely dribbled the ball down the court. Instead, their fast breaks consisted of quick passes from player to player, resulting in a scored basket. The Rens were also known for their endurance on the court, rarely calling a time-out in a game. This forced the opposing team to play to exhaustion and use up their own time-outs. The Rens's playing ability attracted crowds of up to fifteen thousand, both black and white. Nonetheless, they faced many forms of prejudice and discrimination while on the road.

During the Great Depression the Rens became a barnstorming team, traveling to the Midwest and the South to play amateur and professional teams, both black and white. Douglas purchased a custom-made bus for his players to travel in. The bus often served as a restaurant and a hotel for the team, as discrimination prevented the players from being served or housed in many places. In addition the team would set up headquarters in a large city such as Indianapolis, travel up to two hundred miles to a game, and then return to the city afterward. The Rens regularly played and defeated white teams that belonged to the National Basketball League (NBL), such as Oshkosh, Sheboygan, and Fort Wayne. During Cooper's era professional basketball remained segregated by team, although black and white teams played each other.

Cooper served as the leader of the Rens squad that won the World Professional Championship in 1939. In the 1938–1939 season the Rens had accumulated 112 wins and only 7 losses. Having defeated both the New York Yankees basketball team and the Harlem Globetrotters in preliminary games, the Rens became the first World Professional titleholders by defeating the Oshkosh All-Stars, the 1939 NBL Champions, by a score of 34–25.

Gas rationing and travel restrictions during World War II forced Douglas to cut back on the number of away games. Many of the Rens traveled the relatively short distance from New York City to Washington, D.C., on the weekends to play as Washington Bears during the war. In 1943, with Cooper serving as player-coach, the Bears went 66–0 and entered the World Professional Championship in Chicago. With a 38–30 win over the Dayton Bombers behind them, they defeated the Oshkosh All-Stars 43–31 to win the 1943 title.

In 1963 the famed 1932–1933 Renaissance team, of which Cooper was a member, was inducted into the Naismith Memorial Basketball Hall of Fame in Springfield, Massachusetts. Through the efforts of Eddie Younger, a former Ren, Cooper was the first Renaissance player to be inducted into the Hall of Fame in May 1977. Cooper was nearly seventy years old at his induction ceremony. As witness to his popularity and playing ability forty years earlier, hundreds of supporters traveled to Springfield to witness his induction, including the former Rens owner and coach Douglas.

As Evans stated in the *New York Amsterdam News* in May 1977, "It is because of Tarz, there was a Baylor, a Wilt, a Doctor J, and all the others still to come." Following his professional basketball career, Cooper worked in the Philadelphia Navy Yard. He also volunteered his time as a basketball instructor at the Philadelphia YMCA. Cooper died at home in Philadelphia. He was divorced and had no children, and the name of his wife and the dates of their marriage and divorce are unknown.

FURTHER READING
Cooper's file is at the Naismith Memorial Basketball Hall of Fame, Springfield, Massachusetts. Important primary sources on Cooper and the Renaissance team include hundreds of articles in the *New York Amsterdam News*, the *Pittsburgh Courier*, the *Chicago Defender*, and other black newspapers.
Ashe, Arthur R., Jr., with Kip Branch, Ocania Chalk, and Francis Harris. *A Hard Road to Glory: A History of the African-American Athlete*, vol. 2, 1919–1945 (1988).
Dickey, Glenn. *The History of Professional Basketball since 1896* (1982).
Peterson, Robert W. *Cages to Jump Shots: Pro Basketball's Early Years* (1990).
This entry is taken from the *American National Biography* and is published here with the permission of the American Council of Learned Societies.

SUSAN J. RAYL

Cooper, Thomas (1771–1832), slave and minister, was born in Maryland. The names of his parents are unknown. For the first twenty-five years of his life Cooper was known as "Notly." He escaped to Philadelphia, Pennsylvania, around 1800 and took the name John Smith. Employed at a lumberyard, he married a free black woman and had four children. Around this time Cooper's identity was betrayed by a friend. He was separated from his family and sent to Washington, D.C., to be sold at auction. He managed to escape and, with the help of a friend, return to Philadelphia, where he was reunited with his family. Still in danger of recapture, Cooper concealed himself at the home of a Quaker, where he stayed for a week while his master attempted to locate him.

Cooper fled to New Jersey, where he was hired by a farmer. His whereabouts were again discovered, and Cooper escaped by ship to Boston, eventually sending for his family. Around this time he changed his name from John Smith to Thomas Cooper.

Cooper became a Methodist preacher and visited the West Indies and Nova Scotia. In 1817 he moved with his family to London, where he met with philanthropists in the hopes of eventually pursuing his missionary work in Africa. During his year and a half in London, Cooper published *The African Pilgrim Hymns*, a selection of hymns in a duodecimo volume. He also became a popular preacher. On 3 November 1818, just before his departure for Africa, Cooper gave a farewell sermon. His speech was advertised on handbills and was reportedly attended by several thousand people.

Cooper and his family arrived in Sierra Leone, where he immediately threw himself into his ministerial work. After two or three years he became ill with fever and died, leaving his family penniless and stranded. Cooper's wife and children eventually made their way back to London and then to Philadelphia.

Isaac T. Hopper, a friend of Cooper's from Philadelphia, published the *Narrative of the Life of Thomas Cooper* in New York in 1832. In his preface Hopper testifies to Cooper's "sobriety and general good character." The *Narrative* went through at least four editions. The *Narrative of the Life of Thomas Cooper* is characteristic of early slave narratives in its emphasis on adventure and religion rather than on racial identity and abolition. Hopper, in describing Cooper's life, dwells less on the physical miseries of slavery than on Cooper's near escapes and his missionary work.

FURTHER READING

Hopper, Isaac T. *Narrative of the Life of Thomas Cooper* (1832).

Starling, Marion Wilson. *The Slave Narrative: Its Place in American History* (1946, 1981).

JULIA LEE

John Anthony Copeland Jr., a contemporary of John Brown. (Library of Congress.)

Copeland, John Anthony, Jr. (15 Aug. 1834–16 Dec. 1859), abolitionist, was born free in Raleigh, North Carolina, the son of John Anthony Copeland, a carpenter and joiner emancipated in childhood upon the death of his white owner-father, and a freeborn biracial woman, Delilah Evans, a domestic worker. In 1843, impelled by the increasing proscription of free blacks in North Carolina, the Copelands moved to the heavily abolitionist Oberlin, a key station on the Underground Railroad, in northern Ohio. Taking advantage of the exceptional egalitarianism, his parents acquired their own home and reared eight children. Copeland, who was the eldest child, attended the preparatory department of Oberlin College in 1854–1855 and pursued his father's trades. A newspaper editor in a neighboring town wrote that young Copeland was regarded as an "orderly and well-disposed citizen."

According to the 1894 autobiography of John Mercer Langston, a leading black townsman, Copeland regularly attended meetings of blacks in Oberlin to hear fugitive slaves narrate their histories and he expressed "by the deep scowl of his countenance, the moist condition of his eyes and the quivering of his lips, how deeply he was moved." In September 1858 news that slave catchers had seized John Price, a Kentucky fugitive, galvanized the community. With rifle in hand, Copeland joined the throng of students and townspeople who surged into a hotel in nearby Wellington, where Price's captors had taken him to await the southbound train. At length, as an angry crowd of some five hundred demanded the fugitive's release, Copeland helped push through armed guards into the hotel where a small company of men wrested Price from the slave catchers. Later, Copeland reportedly escorted Price to Canada. Copeland was among the thirty-seven men indicted (two of whom, CHARLES H. LANGSTON and Simeon Bushnell, were convicted) for violating the Fugitive Slave Law in what became known as the Oberlin-Wellington Rescue Case. Perhaps because of his militancy in the rescue and the treatment he could expect because of his race, Copeland refused to surrender. The rescue intensified black militancy and Copeland joined the Oberlin Anti-Slavery Society, part of a new statewide black organization. His fellow society member and kinsman by marriage, Lewis Sheridan Leary, a twenty-four-year-old harnessmaker and an unindicted rescuer himself, exhorted: "Men must suffer for a good cause." In the autumn of 1859 when John Brown signaled his allies of his readiness to launch a direct assault on slavery, Leary, who had met Brown months before in Cleveland, persuaded Copeland to co-enlist. Copeland vowed "to assist in giving that freedom to at least a few of my poor and enslaved brethren who have been most foully and unjustly deprived of their liberty."

Copeland and Leary had barely reached Brown's hideout when Brown set his plan in motion. On the night of 16 October 1859, Brown led eighteen volunteers, the five black recruits among them, in an attack on the federal arsenal at Harpers Ferry, Virginia. Before midnight, Brown seized the rifle works, a major target, and left his white lieutenant John Henry Kagi and Copeland, later reinforced by Leary, to garrison it. The following afternoon, surrounded and under fierce attack by an overwhelming armed force, the three made a desperate effort to escape across the rapids of the Shenandoah River. Both Kagi and Leary were shot and mortally wounded. Discovered hiding behind jutting rocks in mid-river, Copeland surrendered and was taken into custody, narrowly escaping lynching through the intervention of a local physician.

White northern opinion of the raid was initially divided between Republicans who largely disavowed it and Democrats who pronounced it an abolitionist-Republican conspiracy. Federal marshal Matthew Johnson of Cleveland visited Copeland in jail and emerged with a purported "confession"—actually fabricated from letters found in Brown's hideout—that implicated in Brown's plot prominent figures connected with the Oberlin-Wellington case.

Copeland was convicted of murder and of inciting slaves to rebellion and, like the other captured raiders, was sentenced to death. But just as the imprisoned Brown's eloquence and stoicism helped to transform his own image from madman to Christian martyr, Copeland's conduct challenged racist assumptions of black inferiority. Even the presiding judge and the special prosecutor at his trial, both white Virginians, later would vouch for Copeland's courage and poise, with the latter adding intelligence as well. "There was a dignity to him that I could not help liking," the judge would confess. "He was always manly." The eulogy at a funeral service for Copeland in Oberlin on Christmas Day praised the Supreme Being for granting African Americans a "not less firm, heroic and Christlike champion" at Harpers Ferry than whites had in "the immortal John Brown." African Americans throughout the North applauded, in the words of the Ohio State Anti-Slavery Society, "the noble and Christ-like John Brown and his compatriots."

In poignant letters from prison Copeland urged family and friends to remember that his death was in a holy cause, asserting that he blamed no one for his fate and expressing confidence that history would vindicate his actions. Even though the raid had not succeeded in freeing the slaves, Copeland told his best friend, Elias Green, that it was "the prelude to that great event." Copeland died on the scaffold in Charlestown, Virginia. He never married and had no children.

FURTHER READING

Several of Copeland's letters are in the executive papers on the Brown raid in the Virginia State Library and in the Oswald Garrison Villard Collection in the Columbia University Library.

Cheek, William, and Aimee Lee Cheek. *John Mercer Langston and the Fight for Black Freedom* (1989).

Oates, Stephen B. *To Purge This Land with Blood: A Biography of John Brown* (1970; 2nd ed., 1984).

Quarles, Benjamin. *Allies for Freedom: Blacks and John Brown* (1974).

This entry is taken from the *American National Biography* and is published here with the permission of the American Council of Learned Societies.

WILLIAM CHEEK AND
AIMEE LEE CHEEK

Coppin, Fanny Jackson (1837–21 Jan. 1913), educator, civic and religious leader, and feminist, was born a slave in Washington, D.C., the daughter of Lucy Jackson. Her father's name and the details of her early childhood are unknown. However, by the time she was age ten, her aunt Sarah Orr Clark had purchased her freedom, and Jackson went to live with relatives in New Bedford, Massachusetts. By 1851 she and her relatives had moved to Newport, Rhode Island, where Jackson was employed as a domestic by George Henry Calvert, a descendant of Lord Baltimore, the settler of Maryland. Jackson's salary enabled her to afford one hour of private tutoring three times a week. Near the end of her six-year stay with the Calverts, she briefly attended the segregated public schools of Newport. In 1859 Jackson enrolled at the Rhode Island State Normal School

Fanny Jackson Coppin, the first female principal of the prestigious Institute for Colored Youth in Philadelphia. (Library of Congress.)

in Bristol. In addition to the normal course, she also studied French privately. Funded by her aunt Sarah and scholarships from Bishop DANIEL ALEXANDER PAYNE of the African Methodist Episcopal (AME) Church and Oberlin College, Jackson was able to enroll in the ladies department of Oberlin in 1860. She also helped to pay for her education by working during her years at Oberlin. By 1861 Jackson transferred into the collegiate department at Oberlin, where she distinguished herself and actively participated in student life. Her outstanding academic achievements resulted in her being chosen as the first African American student teacher of Oberlin's preparatory department. In addition, Jackson was chosen as class poet and graduated in 1865 with an AB degree, becoming the second African American woman in the nation to receive such a degree. After graduating from Oberlin, Jackson accepted the position of principal of the female department of the prestigious Institute for Colored Youth (ICY) in Philadelphia. Founded by the Society of Friends in 1837 as a high school for African Americans, the ICY offered a preparatory department,

separate secondary-school departments for males and females, and a teacher training course. Jackson's ability as a teacher and as a principal was immediately recognized by the Quaker managers as well as the African American community. Her skills in public speaking and elocution were reflected in the improved speaking of the female students. By the end of her first year, the enrollment of the girls' secondary school nearly doubled from forty-two to eighty, and the school reported fewer dropouts. By 1869, when Ebenezer Bassett, the principal for the entire school, was appointed the U.S. minister to Haiti by President Ulysses S. Grant, Jackson was promoted to head the entire school. This promotion was extremely significant because no woman at this time headed a coeducational institution that had both male and female faculty.

Immediately after Jackson became principal of the ICY, many changes that reflected her educational and personal philosophies began to appear at the school. She believed that if respect were given to students it would be returned by the students to the teachers. Thus, she abolished corporal punishment at the school. Academic performance at the school was so high that the institution averaged thirty visitors a week in 1869. Jackson also believed in fostering close relationships between the faculty, students, managers, and parents. She began sending monthly conduct papers to parents to inform them of their children's character, attendance, and recitations. Monthly meetings were also held with parents of ICY students. Managers began sponsoring teas for the school's upper-level students and teachers to stimulate conversation and fellowship. Her devotion to the ICY was so great that she remained as principal for the next twenty-one years.

In 1878 Jackson began a regular column titled "Women's Department" in the *Christian Recorder*, the newspaper of the AME Church. Through her column she was able to reach African American women of all income levels. She reported the achievements of women in education, employment, and other areas and also discussed cases of discrimination against black women. Jackson was always concerned about gender discrimination as well as racial discrimination and stressed to her female readers that they should pursue the same professions and occupations as men and not simply enter traditional female-dominated fields. In 1881 Jackson married LEVI JENKINS COPPIN, an AME minister at least fifteen years her junior.

Coppin's greatest contribution to the ICY was the establishment of an industrial department.

She was stimulated to take action after visiting the Centennial Exposition in Philadelphia (1876), which emphasized education and national progress; she was particularly impressed by the exhibition of the Moscow Imperial Technical School's Victor Della Vos, who demonstrated his newly developed approaches to the teaching of the mechanical arts. She became acutely aware of the need to prepare African American youth for an increasingly industrial nation, and so she began to campaign for a department of industrial arts at the ICY. Her idea, though, was a hard sell. The Quaker managers did not want to incur additional expenses for expansion of the institution, and African Americans were apprehensive about what was being proposed by Coppin. Many of the leading families in Philadelphia who sent their children to the ICY had a tradition of classical education and affiliations with prestigious literary societies, and they were reluctant to embrace a form of education that appeared more practical in nature. Nevertheless, the industrial department finally opened in 1889, although it failed to offer the advanced classes that Coppin had proposed, such as mechanical drawing and engineering. Instead, the department offered only carpentry, bricklaying, shoemaking, printing, and plastering for men, and millinery, dressmaking, and cooking for women. By 1892 typing and stenography were added to the curriculum. The industrial department was a great success. As the only institution in Philadelphia to offer industrial training for African Americans, the ICY had 87 students enrolled in the new department and 325 on a waiting list just two months after the department opened.

During Coppin's tenure as principal of the ICY, her normal students were so sought after that most were able to pass teacher examinations and secure employment successfully after only two years in secondary school. By 1890 three-fourths of the African American teachers in Philadelphia and Camden, New Jersey, were ICY graduates. Many of the institute's students also pursued the professions.

In addition to her school work, Coppin was extremely active in the African Methodist Episcopal Church. She was elected president of the local Women's Mite Missionary Society and later became national president of the Women's Home and Foreign Missionary Society. In addition, she was on the board of managers of the Home for the Aged and Infirm Colored People in Philadelphia for over thirty years (1881–1913), and she was elected vice president of the National Association of Colored Women in 1897.

In 1902 Coppin retired from the institute and accompanied her husband, who had been elected bishop of the Fourteenth Episcopal District of South Africa in 1900, to Capetown. They returned to Philadelphia in the spring of 1904. Bishop Coppin was then appointed to the Seventh Episcopal District, which encompassed South Carolina and Alabama. Coppin, who had frequently traveled with her husband, made the trip to South Carolina; however, the South African trip had severely affected her health, and by 1905 her health had deteriorated to such an extent that she was primarily confined to her Philadelphia home for the remaining years of her life. She died in Philadelphia.

FURTHER READING

Primary documents concerning Coppin's Oberlin years are available in the Oberlin College Archives. Documents from her years as principal at the ICY are available at the Friend's Historical Library, Swarthmore College.

Coppin, Fanny Jackson. *Reminiscences of School Life, and Hints on Teaching* (1913; repr. 1987, 1995).

Perkins, Linda M. *Fanny Jackson Coppin and the Institute for Colored Youth, 1865–1902* (1987).

Obituary: *Philadelphia Tribune*, 1 Feb. 1913.

This entry is taken from the *American National Biography* and is published here with the permission of the American Council of Learned Societies.

LINDA M. PERKINS

Coppin, Levi Jenkins (24 Dec. 1848–25 June 1924), clergyman, educator, and author, was born in Fredericktown, Maryland, or as he put it in his autobiography, "Frederick Town." He was born on the eastern shore of Maryland, the birthplace of Frederick Douglass, but was freeborn, one of eight children of John Coppin, probably a farmer, and Jane Lilly, a homemaker. His father was a member of the African Methodist Episcopal (AME) Church. There were no schools where he could get an advanced education, so he was homeschooled by his mother, and tutored privately by Quakers in Wilmington, Delaware, who prepared him for a career in teaching. He then began teaching in Smyrna, Delaware, and occasionally served as a preacher. A personal tragedy, however, pushed him toward the ministry. In September 1875 he married Martha Grinnage, a young schoolteacher from Wilmington, Delaware, and they soon had a son. But the baby was only nine months old when he suddenly died, followed eighteen days later by Coppin's wife. Overwhelmed with grief, Coppin wanted to leave Wilmington as soon as possible and gave up teaching to accept the call to ministry.

In late 1876 (some sources say early 1877) Coppin was licensed to preach by the Rev. John F. Thomas, the pastor of Bethel Church in Wilmington. Coppin was sent to Philadelphia, and his first job was at the City Mission, a group of three small churches, which comprised a "circuit." In addition to his pastorial work, Coppin also taught Sunday School and worked toward increasing the membership until the Mission became a self-supporting "Station." After becoming a deacon in 1879, he was transferred to the mother church, Bethel Church or "Big Bethel," in Baltimore, where the pastor, the Rev. George C. Whitfield was dying. Coppin served as an assistant until Whitfield's death, at which point he became acting pastor. According to the *Christian Recorder* (23 Oct. 1884), Coppin did a heroic job taking over from Whitfield and at the next pulpit he filled: "Levi J. Coppin, a young man, took his place, and afterwards was sent to the next largest and oldest station, Bethel Church, Baltimore. Did he not do a grand work, holding that church by his power as a preacher and administrator of law equal to his older and experienced predecessor?"

Always an avid student, Coppin continued his education, studying theology at the Protestant Episcopal Divinity School in Philadelphia, from which he graduated with distinction in 1887. In 1889 he received a Doctorate of Divinity from Wilberforce University in Ohio. His personal life had also improved by this time. He met Fanny Jackson, the first African American woman who in 1869 became the principal of the Institute for Colored Youth in Philadelphia. They married in December 1887. FANNY COPPIN was a tireless advocate for black education, and kept her job even after her marriage to Coppin. She continued to be actively involved with education, leaving the profession only when she accompanied her husband on missionary work in South Africa.

In May 1888 Coppin became the second editor of the prestigious *AME Church Review*, founded in 1884, which was described as a "literary journal, devoted to religious, moral, scientific, and social questions.... [It] has a circulation of three thousand, and it goes to all parts of the United States, to Africa, Europe, Canada ... British Guiana, Hayti, and Santo Domingo" (Morris, 315). Serving until May 1896, his editing work earned him considerable praise. In a retrospective on the *Review*'s first

quarter century, J. Albert Johnson paid special tribute to Coppin, commending his editorial and managerial skills, his dedication to increasing the circulation of the *Review*, his ability to get excellent writers, and insistence on accuracy. Johnson had watched Coppin's preaching evolve over the years. His riveting sermons were both thought-provoking and memorable. And as for his personal traits, Johnson noted that Coppin impressed nearly everyone who met him as a truly Christian man. He was "a man of strong convictions ... [with] the courage necessary to express them in language understandable of the people" (Johnson, 388–89).

By 1900 Coppin had been named a bishop, the thirtieth in the church's history. That year he and his wife left for South Africa, where he became the first resident AME bishop. His South African assignment proved difficult, coming in the midst of the Boer War. Because it was a British colony, Coppin raised the jealousy and suspicions of the white Anglican pastors. The bishop's efforts to ordain black ministers and build churches and schools threatened the white elites. Because the Coppins sought more educational opportunities for blacks, the British rulers saw their work as dangerous and feared that these black missionaries from America would empower the natives to such a degree that they would rebel against white rule. Despite the obstacles, Coppin and his wife successfully completed their South African work. By 1902 they had established about forty churches, and opened Bethel Institute, a new school in Cape Town that could offer college preparatory courses.

The Coppins returned from South Africa in 1904, partly because of Fanny Coppin's declining health. Levi Coppin continued to preach. His publications included *The Relation of Baptized Children to the Church* (1890), *Key to Scriptural Interpretation* (1895), *Observations of Persons and Things in South Africa 1900–1904* (n.d.), and *Fifty-Two Suggestive Sermon Syllabi* (1910). His autobiography, *Unwritten History*, was published in 1919. He also wrote a number of hymns and gospel songs for the church.

Fanny Coppin passed away on 21 January 1913. On 1 August 1914 Levi Coppin married Melissa E. Thompson (some sources say Evelyn Melissa Thompson), a doctor. At the time he wrote his autobiography, Coppin and his wife had a daughter three and a half years old. Coppin died in Philadelphia on 25 June 1924. He had spoken out against slavery, defended the intelligence and ability of African Americans, advocated for better schools, and devoted his life to helping the AME

Church become a major force in the black community throughout the United States and around the world.

FURTHER READING
Coppin, Levi Jenkins. *Unwritten History* (1919).
"Exterminating the Boers: Bishop Coppin of South Africa Says They Are Being Wiped off the Face of the Earth," *New York Times*, 27 Jan. 1902.
"History of the *AME Review*," *AME Church Review* 25 (Apr. 1909).
Johnson, J. Albert. "An Estimate of Dr. Coppin as Editor," *AME Church Review* 25 (Apr. 1909).
"Levi Jenkins Coppin: Editor of Our Leading Magazine the *Review*," *Cleveland Gazette*, 12 Jan. 1889.
Morris, John T. "History and Development of Negro Journalism," *AME Church Review* 6 (Jan. 1890).
Obituary: *Chicago Defender*, 5 July 1924.

DONNA HALPER

Corbin, Joseph Carter (26 Mar. 1833–9 Jan. 1911), educator and journalist, was born in Chillicothe, Ohio, the son of William Corbin and Susan, both Virginia-born former slaves. Corbin's parents eventually settled in Cincinnati to raise their family of twelve children. Corbin attended school sporadically because of economic circumstances (one of his classmates was JOHN MERCER LANGSTON), though his family emphasized education. In the late 1840s Corbin and his older sister Elizabeth moved to Louisville, Kentucky, where their father had family. Both lived with the Reverend Henry Adams, the pastor of the black First Baptist Church. Though the 1850 census takers listed him as a cook, Corbin taught at least some of the time in a school supported by Adams.

Thirsty for further education, Corbin traveled north to Ohio University, where he earned a B.A. in 1853 and an M.A. in 1856. He settled in Cincinnati, worked as a bank messenger and steward, gained prominence as a mason, and became active in the education and uplift efforts of the lively black community. Along with JOHN PATTERSON SAMPSON, Charles W. Ball, H. P. Leonard, and the Reverend GEORGE WASHINGTON WILLIAMS, Corbin founded the weekly *Colored Citizen*, a regional newspaper in operation between 1863 and 1869. Referred to in the *Christian Recorder* (24 Sept. 1864) as "Cincinnati's most accomplished musician," Corbin directed the choir at the dedication of Union Baptist Church.

Corbin married Mary Jane Ward, a Kentucky-born dressmaker, on 11 September 1866. They had three children. The couple lived in Cincinnati with Ward's widowed sister Eliza Gaines. Corbin was promoted from messenger to clerk, but hoping the West would offer more opportunities, the family moved to Little Rock, Arkansas, around 1870. Corbin worked for the *Arkansas Republican*, a party paper centered on Reconstruction, and parlayed his journalistic support into an appointment with the Little Rock post office.

In 1873 Corbin was appointed Arkansas's superintendent of public instruction. This position, which also called for him to lead the University of Arkansas Board of Trustees, was tumultuous from the beginning, as Reconstruction in Arkansas was quickly crumbling. Still, he set up an exploratory committee to found a black college in the Arkansas system, Branch Normal College (now the University of Arkansas at Pine Bluff). By 1875 Corbin had left Arkansas to teach and help administer the young Lincoln Institute in neighboring Missouri. Nonetheless, when the Arkansas governor Augustus Garland offered an appointment at the newly created Branch Normal, Corbin took the job and in August 1875 moved his family to Pine Bluff.

Though Branch Normal, which was affiliated with the normal school department of Arkansas Industrial University, was housed for close to a decade in a single rented building and began with only seven students, it gave Corbin a chance to build an institution from scratch. As principal, sole teacher, and custodian between 1875 and 1882, he oversaw all aspects of the school and taught Greek and Latin (he was multilingual) as well as his old passion, music, and a newer passion, mathematics. For several decades his short pieces on math appeared in periodicals ranging from *Barnes' Educational School Visitors* to the *Mathematical Gazette*.

Branch Normal initially focused on training black teachers for black schools in part because, in the language of a circular Corbin sent to the *Recorder*, "one of the great needs of the colored population in Arkansas is a supply of well qualified teachers for the county schools" (*Christian Recorder*). In addition to developing degree programs, Corbin in the early 1880s spearheaded the creation of short-term institutes, an innovation praised in the national black press. He campaigned actively and eventually secured funding for the college's first permanent building, which opened in 1882, and a women's dormitory, which opened in 1887. His focus on teacher training also led him in 1898 to help found the Teachers of Negro Youth, which evolved into the Arkansas Teachers Association and eventually merged with the Arkansas Education Association in 1969.

Corbin oversaw the construction of the first college buildings, as well as the addition of trade school programs (some of which were taught by his daughter Louisa Corbin, who also served as the matron of the first women's dormitory). Although Branch Normal granted a handful of bachelor's degrees prior to 1885, it remained essentially a junior college and teacher licensing facility until 1930. However, tensions between Corbin and the board of trustees grew throughout the 1890s. Corbin had long taken a liberal view of the state's policy toward "normal beneficiaries" to waive tuition at normal schools for a certain number of poor students who would go on to teach. Some blacks were suspicious of the matriculation fees Branch Normal charged (as did all other state schools) even when tuition was waived, and some whites raised questions about whether Corbin's application of the normal beneficiary policy was appropriate.

Corbin also offended the local Democratic politician Clifton R. Breckinridge by supporting his Republican challenger John M. Clayton. Historian Thomas Rothrock made a convincing case that Breckinridge harassed Corbin and gradually took over control of the college's governing board. In 1893, after narrowly deciding to allow Corbin to continue as principal, the board brought in a white teacher to superintend the school's industrial curriculum and handle all funds. Corbin was eventually ousted in 1902, though he stayed in Pine Bluff with his sister-in-law and daughter. Perhaps because of the increasing tension at Branch Normal, Corbin's wife and two sons settled in Chicago.

Corbin remained active in education. He was president of the Colored Teachers of Negro Youth in 1902 and 1903. One source also notes that he worked with Ouachita Baptist College for a time, but by 1905 he had accepted an invitation to return to Pine Bluff as the principal of Merrill High School. Now widowed, he lived with his son William. He left Merrill in 1910 to begin a private correspondence school. He died in Pine Bluff. An important early journalist and educator, Corbin made significant and lasting contributions to public education in Arkansas.

FURTHER READING

Some of Corbin's papers regarding Branch Normal are in the University of Arkansas Special Collections.

Preston, Izola. "Joseph Carter Corbin," in *Arkansas Biography: A Collection of Notable Lives*, ed. Nancy A. Williams (2000).

Rothrock, Thomas. "Joseph Carter Corbin and Negro Education in the University of Arkansas," *Arkansas Historical Quarterly* (Winter 1971).

Obituary: *American Mathematical Monthly*, Feb. 1911.

                                    ERIC GARDNER

Corbitt, Ted (31 Jan. 1919–12 Dec. 2007), long-distance runner and physical therapist, was born Theodore Corbitt near Dunbarton, South Carolina, to John Henry Corbitt, a farmer and railroad worker, and Alma Bing Corbitt, a seamstress and union official. Though small in stature, the young Corbitt helped on the family farm, plowing and picking crops, forging a work ethic that would become the trademark of his athletic career. While white children rode the bus, Corbitt walked the dusty roads back and forth to school. At age nine his family moved to Cincinnati, Ohio, where he won his first races in school competitions. He graduated from Cincinnati's Woodward High School in 1938 and enrolled in University of Cincinnati that fall. There he joined the track and cross-country teams, trying every running event from 100 yards to two miles. He graduated in 1942 with a degree in Education. Corbitt was drafted into the U.S. Army and sent to the Pacific in August 1945, but World War II ended before he saw combat.

Returning to the United States in 1946, he moved to New York City, where he married Ruth Butler, the sister of a Cincinnati friend. They remained married until her death in 1989. They had one son, Gary, born in 1950. In 1949 Corbitt was hired as a physical therapist at the Institute for the Crippled and Disabled (later the International Center for the Disabled), where he worked until his retirement in 1993. He earned a master's degree from New York University in 1950 in Physical Therapy. In addition he taught courses in physical therapy at Columbia University, New York University, and other colleges.

As a high school student Corbitt had read a newspaper article about Ellison "Tarzan" Brown, the Narragansett Indian who won the Boston Marathon in 1936. Corbitt said, "The idea of running such a long distance intrigued me," vowing, "One day I'll run the Boston Marathon just to see if I can" (Lewis). His opportunity didn't come until 1951, when he made his marathon debut in Boston at age thirty-two. He finished in fifteenth place with a respectable time of 2:48:42. From then on he was hooked on distance running. Corbitt ran two more marathons in the following months. In 1952 he was the third American finisher (sixth overall) at Boston and won a spot on the U.S. Olympic team. In Helsinki on 27 July 1952 he became the first African American to compete in the Olympic marathon, finishing forty-fourth with a time of 2:51:09. He participated in the Olympic marathon trials twice more, missing a spot on his second U.S. team by one place in 1956.

When Corbitt began his marathon career, little was known about scientific training methods, so he developed his own approach that emphasized overdistance runs. Preparing for a marathon, he typically completed at least one thirty-mile run. Corbitt soon became known for his prodigious training feats such as circling Manhattan—twice. His weekly mileage often totaled more than 200 miles. To fit his running with his full-time job he ran twelve miles to work in the morning and then back home in the evening.

The remarkable endurance built up on his long training runs produced impressive results. He set American records for 25, 40, and 50 miles (in 1966), and 100 miles (in 1969), and 24 hours on the track (in 1973). He won the American and Canadian marathon championships in 1954 and 1955, respectively. He also won U.S. titles at 30 kilometers in 1956 and 1957, and at 50 miles in 1968. Corbitt finished an incredible 199 races at the marathon distance or beyond, winning thirty-three times.

In the sport of distance running, an "ultramarathon" is any race longer than 26.2 miles. Because he was the first American to do well in international ultradistance races such as the London to Brighton race in England and encouraged Americans to organize races beyond the 26.2-mile marathon distance, some have called him the "father of American ultramarathoning." He won his first ultra race in 1959—a thirty-mile run he organized for the New York Road Runners Club. In 1962 he traveled to England to take part in the 52.5-mile London to Brighton race, the premier ultradistance event of the time. He finished fourth that year and returned four more times, placing second three times.

At an age when most men had retired from athletic competition, Corbitt continued to set new marks. He won the U.S. 50-mile national championship in 5:39:43 at the age of forty-nine. At fifty he covered 100 miles in the American record time

of 13:33:06. He ran 134.7 miles in a 24-hour race at age fifty-four. Although asthma forced him to stop competitive running in 1974 he continued to participate in distance events by walking. At age eighty-two he logged 303 miles in a six-day race.

Corbitt's greatest contributions to the sport of distance running were behind the scenes. As the first president of the New York Road Runners Club in 1958, Corbitt's prestige lent credibility to the organization that later would sponsor the New York City Marathon and hundreds of other races. In 1960 he was elected the third president of the Road Runners Club of America (of which the New York club, NYRRC, is a regional affiliate). In this capacity he developed meticulous standards for measuring race courses more accurately. As the "running boom" took off during the 1970s Corbitt oversaw certification of hundreds of distance race courses. His 1964 booklet, "Measuring Road Running Courses," was considered the "bible" for race directors. Corbitt also lobbied for creation of a "masters" division for runners older than forty.

Corbitt's many contributions to American distance running were recognized in 1998 when he was among the initial five runners inducted into the National Distance Running Hall of Fame. He was the first man selected for the Ultrarunning Hall of Fame in 2004. The hall was created by the American Ultrarunning Association in 2004; Corbitt and Sandra Kiddy were the first athletes to be inducted. A New York City twenty-four hour race was named in his honor. Corbitt died in 2007, leaving an indelible mark as father of American running.

FURTHER READING

Corbitt, Ted. "A Willingness to Suffer," in *First Marathons*, ed. Gail Kislevitz (1998).

Chodes, John. *Corbitt: The Story of Ted Corbitt, Long Distance Runner* (1974).

Lewis, Barry. "On Any Given Sunday," *Running Times* (July–Aug. 2002).

Obituary: *New York Times*, 13 Sept. 2007.

PAUL T. MURRAY

Cornely, Paul Bertau (9 Mar. 1906–9 Feb. 2002), physician and public health activist, was born in Point-á-Pitre, Guadeloupe, French West Indies, the son of Eleodore Cornely and Adrienne Mellon. When he was three years old, his family moved to Santurce, Puerto Rico. In 1920 the family relocated to Harlem for one year and then moved to Detroit, where his father found work in an auto plant.

After attending Detroit City College, Cornely transferred to the University of Michigan. He earned his AB in 1928 and his M.D. in 1932, both from the University of Michigan, where he was one of 4 blacks in a medical school class of 250 students. Unable to get an internship in the North, he spent a year at the segregated Lincoln Hospital in Durham, North Carolina. He intended to continue with specialty training in surgery, but effectively barred from a residency, he returned to the University of Michigan to study public health. In 1934 he completed his doctoral work, became a naturalized American citizen, and married Mae Juanita Stewart. The couple had one son.

Hired as an assistant professor at the Howard University College of Medicine in 1934, Cornely was promoted to associate professor after one year. In 1943 he became chair of bacteriology, preventive medicine, and public health. He was promoted to full professor in 1947 and went on to become chair of community health practice in 1950.

During World War II he worked with the American Social Hygiene Association on the problem of venereal disease in the black population. After the war, as a consultant to the National Urban League, he found proportionately fewer hospital beds available to blacks, in the North as well as in the South. He served as the director of Freedman's Hospital (now Howard University Hospital) in Washington, D.C., from 1947 to 1958.

Cornely's work on health economics in the 1940s and 1950s demonstrated that African American physicians worked harder and for lower compensation than their white counterparts, and his findings on relative health indicators and access to medical care provided important ammunition to the civil rights movement in its struggle against discrimination in health care. He helped lead the effort to desegregate General Hospital in Washington, D.C., and he collaborated with the national leadership of the NAACP to organize the Imhotep Conferences (named after the Egyptian god of medicine), which between 1956 and 1963 were dedicated to promoting expanding opportunities for blacks in the medical profession. During the same period Cornely helped the newly independent African nations of Sierra Leone and Ghana establish health professional schools.

In 1961 Cornely was elected president of the Physicians Forum, a New York–based organization that had been demonized by the American Medical Association and some conservative politicians because its membership included communists and it advocated a national health plan. Although his political views differed in many ways, Cornely was willing to affiliate with this group because it vocally opposed racial discrimination and supported universal access to medical care.

With other progressive doctors, Cornely picketed the 1963 convention of the American Medical Association (AMA). This public protest by physicians brought increased attention to the AMA's policy of recognizing southern state medical societies that excluded blacks, a policy the organization changed soon afterwards. Cornely also served as Washington coordinator for the medical contingent of the 1963 civil rights March on Washington.

He helped found the Medical Committee for Human Rights (MCHR), whose initial purpose was to provide medical care to civil rights activists in the South during the "Freedom Summer" of 1964. The MCHR later developed a broader range of interests, including the rights of psychiatric patients and the health needs of incarcerated people. The ultimate measure of Cornely's importance in public health was his 1969 election as president of the American Public Health Association (APHA). The first African American to occupy this position, he served from 1970 to 1972. As APHA president-elect he continued to challenge the AMA's commitment to public health, and he hailed the largely black National Medical Association for its successes in improving the circumstances of African American physicians. After touring California's Central Valley in June 1969, Cornely and other APHA leaders reported that the health needs of agricultural workers—mainly Hispanic and white—were as urgent as those of the urban poor.

Cornely's 1970 APHA presidential address demonstrated the complexity of this man and the passion of his beliefs. He spoke strongly in favor of national health insurance and against discrimination in health care. Similarly he expressed opposition to the war in Vietnam and support for domestic programs intended to fight poverty. At the same time, though, he called for a more spiritual approach to the public sphere. He decried consumerism and crass materialism in American culture and spoke with abhorrence of growing sexual permissiveness and tolerance of obscene expression.

As APHA president, Cornely urged President Richard Nixon to sign federal legislation that would expand access to childhood vaccinations. In 1971 Cornely was appointed to a panel of congressional consultants on the National Cancer Act, the initiative associated with Nixon that came to be known as the "War on Cancer." A member of the

Presidential Commission on Population Growth and the American Future (known as the Rockefeller Commission for its chair, John D. Rockefeller III), Cornely dissented from several of its conclusions. He opposed easing information on contraceptives to minors and liberalizing abortion laws. In keeping with these views, Cornely denied that overpopulation was a problem and instead called for wiser stewardship of the earth's resources. In his 1972 speech accepting the APHA's highest honor, the Sedgwick Medal, he reiterated the themes of his presidential address. When Secretary of Health, Education, and Welfare Caspar Weinberger spoke at the 1973 APHA convention, Cornely led a vocal protest against the Nixon administration's announced cutbacks in child health funding and impoundment of federal funds allocated by Congress for federal health programs.

Cornely regarded his views on abortion and teenage sex as consistent with his concerns for the environment and for access to health care, all derived from his commitment to the Catholic Church. He was a leading lay member of the Washington archdiocese and of Opus Dei, the society known for its devotion to the pope and its commitment to conservative causes.

In the mid-1970s Cornely resigned from his longtime position at Howard to become assistant to the director of the United Mine Workers Welfare and Retirement Fund. Several officers of the fund had been indicted on corruption charges, and Cornely was called in to help restore its integrity.

Cornely received honorary degrees from the University of Michigan in 1968 and Howard University in 1992. During his retirement Cornely, who lived with his wife in the Maryland suburbs of Washington, D.C., remained a vocal spokesman for the causes he had always espoused.

FURTHER READING

Cornely's papers are at the National Library of Medicine, in the Howard University Archives, and in the possession of family members.

Brickman, Jane Pacht. "'Medical McCarthyism': The Physicians Forum and the Cold War," *Journal of the History of Medicine and Allied Sciences* (1994).

Morais, Herbert M. *The History of the Afro-American in Medicine* (1978).

Reynolds, P. Preston. "Hospitals and Civil Rights, 1945–1963: The Case of *Simkins v. Moses H. Cone Memorial Hospital*," *Annals of Internal Medicine* (1997).

EDWARD T. MORMAN

Cornish, Samuel Eli (c. 1795–6 Nov. 1858), clergyman and newspaper editor, was born in Sussex County, Delaware, the son of free black parents. Cornish was educated after 1815 in Philadelphia, where he studied for the ministry with John Gloucester, pastor of the First African Presbyterian Church. During Gloucester's illness, Cornish served as minister to the church for a year. In this brief tenure Cornish learned much about the tenuous finances of black churches, knowledge that would serve him later. Cornish gained a probationary license to preach from the Presbyterian synod in 1819. He then spent six months as missionary to slaves on Maryland's Eastern Shore, where his license gave him greater credibility than most black preachers enjoyed. In 1821 he moved to New York City, where he worked in the blighted Lower East Side ghetto around Bancker Street and organized the first black Presbyterian congregation in New York, the New Demeter Street Presbyterian Church. Ordained in 1822, Cornish preached at New Demeter until 1828, while itinerating among blacks in New York and New Jersey. In 1824 he married Jane Livingston; they had four children.

In 1827 Cornish and JOHN BROWN RUSSWURM established *Freedom's Journal*, the first black newspaper in the United States. The editors combined local news and black history with condemnations of slavery and colonization. After several months, Cornish resigned to devote more time to his ministry. Russwurm operated the newspaper until he left abruptly for Africa in 1829. The same year, Cornish initiated *Rights of All*, which lasted less than a year. Eight years later, Cornish became editor of the *Colored American*, remaining in that post until 1839.

In his newspaper editorials, ministry, and personal life, Cornish emphasized the importance of education, hard work, thrift, and agricultural labor for the progress of African Americans. He first advocated agriculture for black uplift in 1837 in the *Colored American*. He offered to distribute two-thousand acres of land on the banks of the Delaware River in New Jersey to blacks willing to leave the city to become independent farmers. Vehemently opposed to colonization, in 1840 he coauthored with THEODORE S. WRIGHT a lengthy diatribe against the American Colonization Society entitled *The Colonization Scheme Considered, in Its Rejection by the Coloured People—in Its Tendency to Uphold Caste—in Its Unfitness for Christianizing and Civilizing the Aborigines of Africa and for Putting a Stop to the African Slave Trade.*

Cornish was a key participant in many of the reform movements of the antebellum period, serving as agent for the New York African Free Schools (1827–1829), member of the executive committees of the American Anti-Slavery Society and the New York State Vigilance Committee, manager of the American Bible Society (1835) and Union Missionary Society (1842), and a founder, executive committee member, and vice president of the American Missionary Association (1848–1858). A founder of the New York City Phoenix Society for mutual aid and education of urban blacks, Cornish had an active role in the early black national convention movement.

Cornish often disagreed with his colleagues. Although an organizer of the American Moral Reform Society, he left it because he felt it acted too slowly on racial issues. While active in the New York City Vigilance Committee, he opposed the controversial methods of one of its leaders, DAVID RUGGLES. In 1838 Ruggles used the pages of the *Colored American* without Cornish's permission to accuse a black New York City landlord of slave trading. A resulting lawsuit for libel threatened the financial viability of the newspaper. Cornish blamed Ruggles for the incident, which badly divided the local antislavery community. In 1840 he forced Ruggles to resign as head of the New York State Vigilance Committee.

In the late 1830s and 1840s Cornish took a number of controversial positions. He objected to William Lloyd Garrison's anticlerical tone and left the American Anti-Slavery Society for the American and Foreign Anti-Slavery Society. Later he left the AFASS over its support of the Liberty Party because it would not back black political candidates. In 1839 he opposed the formation of an antislavery political party. In the late 1840s he disagreed strongly with the development of exclusively black conventions and political activity because he did not believe in racially separate movements. He disdained the Pan-African movement of the 1850s because of its support of colonization.

Cornish's Presbyterian affiliation caused problems for him. As the denomination grew more conservative and identified with colonization projects, Cornish sought refuge as an activist minister. In addition to his tenure at New Demeter, Cornish was pastor of Gloucester's Philadelphia church from 1831 to 1832 and in 1843 ministered to the activist Negro Presbyterian Church in Newark. In 1845 he organized and pastored the Emmanuel Church in New York City, where he remained until 1847.

In his personal life, Cornish suffered discrimination and tragedy. Although he regarded New York City as his home, racial discrimination against his children forced his departure in 1838 for Belleville, New Jersey, and then in 1840 for Newark. Cornish outlived his wife and three of his children. In 1855 he moved to Brooklyn, where he died. Despite his individualized politics and membership in a conservative denomination, Cornish sustained black abolitionist institutions while pioneering black journalism.

FURTHER READING

Cornish's papers can be found in C. Peter Ripley et al., eds., *The Black Abolitionist Papers*, microfilm ed. (1981–1983).

Pease, Jane H., and William H. Pease. *Bound with Them in Chains: A Biographical History of the Antislavery Movement* (1972).

Swift, David Everett. *Black Prophets of Justice: Activist Clergy before the Civil War* (1989).

This entry is taken from the *American National Biography* and is published here with the permission of the American Council of Learned Societies.

GRAHAM RUSSELL HODGES

Corrothers, James David (2 July 1869–12 Feb. 1917), journalist, poet, and clergyman, was born in Chain Lake Settlement, Cass County, Michigan, a colony first settled by fugitive slaves in the 1840s. His parents were James Richard Carruthers (the spelling was later changed by Corrothers), a black soldier in the Union army, and Maggie Churchman, of French and Madagascan descent, who died when Corrothers was born. Corrothers was legally adopted by his paternal grandfather, a pious and respected man of Cherokee and Scotch-Irish origins, who raised young Corrothers in relative poverty. They lived in several roughneck towns along the eastern shore of Lake Michigan, where Corrothers attended school and became aware of racial hostility. When he was just a boy family members introduced him to a rich vein of African American folk tales that he would later draw upon for a number of his dialect sketches.

Working in his teens variously as a sawmill hand, hotel menial, coachman, pantryman on a lake steamer, and bootblack in Chicago, Corrothers also worked hard to teach himself to read and write. Settling in Chicago in the early 1890s, he was first befriended by the crusading journalist Henry D. Lloyd and then by the temperance reformer Frances E. Willard. Sponsored by Willard, he sporadically attended a preparatory school at Northwestern University for two years and then spent a year at Bennett College in Greensboro, North Carolina. By this time he was beginning his own first tentative efforts as a poet.

Returning to Chicago, Corrothers married Fannie Clemens in 1894; they had two children. In a profession where opportunities to write for the black press were scant and white editors were distinctly inhospitable to an aspiring black journalist, Corrothers struggled to establish his career as a freelance writer for various Chicago newspapers. Overcoming his initial distaste for dialect speech and spurred by the example of his friend PAUL LAURENCE DUNBAR, he took advantage of an offer in 1896 to write a series of prose sketches and poems in black dialect for the *Chicago Evening Journal*.

Unable to find sufficient newspaper employment because of his color, Corrothers accepted a call to enter the ministry in the African Methodist Episcopal (AME) church in 1898. In the same year, as he embarked on his first pastorate in Bath, New York, he lost his wife and youngest son to consumption. At this time he also undertook his literary career in earnest, placing a dialect poem in *The Century*. With the interest and support of the editor Richard Watson Gilder, he received modest recognition by publishing his poetry with some regularity in that magazine. Over a period of several years at the turn of the century, his poems also appeared in the *Colored American*, the *Criterion*, the *Southern Workman*, the *New York Sunday Herald*, and the *Philadelphia Inquirer*. This achievement culminated in 1902 with the publication by Funk and Wagnalls of *The Black Cat Club*, his best known work.

At the same time Corrothers continued his career in the ministry. Following several pastoral appointments in New Jersey, he was accused of an inappropriate relationship with a young woman in the congregation and of plotting, as he put it, "to ruin my bishop's good name." This incident led to his expulsion from the church in 1902, followed by an interval of extreme despair and irregular employment in the New York City area. Subsequently he became a Baptist, and in the period from 1904 to about 1914 he pursued an active ministry in that faith with a series of pastorates in Virginia, Michigan, Washington, D.C., and Massachusetts. In 1906 he married Rosina B. Harvey; they had one son.

Along with his clerical responsibilities, Corrothers sustained a busy literary life as a poet. Although his reputation has been overshadowed by the prominence of contemporaries like CHARLES CHESNUTT, W. E. B. DuBois, JAMES WELDON JOHNSON, and Dunbar, in his time he earned more than modest celebrity for his dialect poetry. Converting to the Presbyterian faith, he was appointed in 1915 to a parish in West Chester, Pennsylvania, where he finally found a degree of calm and stability. In 1916 he published his autobiography, *In Spite of the Handicap*. A year later he died of a stroke in West Chester at the age of forty-seven.

Although best known as a dialect poet and often excelling in that form, Corrothers was never entirely comfortable in the role. Educated mainly among white children, he observed that before his introduction to black life in Chicago he was "not used to colored people" and "never talked Negro dialect." He was particularly sensitive at the beginning of his literary career to the invidious distinction between what he referred to as the "dis" and "dat" of black vernacular speech and his own strong preference for refined standard English. Needing income, however, Corrothers sought to take advantage of the popularity of the fashion of dialect writing. To accomplish this, he was obliged to learn literary dialect when he began publishing the prose sketches and verse that were collected in *The Black Cat Club*. Although he later expressed his regret for having produced that material, he developed an uncanny range within the dialect, from the shallow doggerel of pieces like "De Cahvin'" (the bloody carvings of a razor fight) to the moving lyrical appeal of poems like "Way in de Woods and Nobody Dah" to social resistance pieces like "An Indignation Dinner." He continued to publish dialect poems even when he came under the influence of Algernon Charles Swinburne and focused the latter part of his career on what he termed "a higher class of work" in "literary English." The non-dialectal works that he wrote later in his career, including two volumes of poems he is alleged to have written but that have not been recovered, were little noticed. More recently, his autobiography has been criticized for its tendency to harshly characterize other African Americans, while his dialect poetry, despite the cultural and social limits that the genre poses from a contemporary perspective, is thought to rank among the best of its kind.

Writing at the turn of the century in an era of extreme racial prejudice and discrimination, Corrothers was pessimistic about his chances for success. His own turn to a sustaining religious faith was repeatedly tested by racial hostility and by what he increasingly came to believe was spiteful behavior among his own people, especially in his painful experiences with the church. His autobiography clearly reveals the underlying tensions between expressions of sentimental feeling on the one hand and a strong commitment to the values of respectful behavior and intellectual accomplishment on the other.

FURTHER READING

Corrothers, James David. *In Spite of the Handicap* (1916).

Bruce, Dickson D. *Black American Writing from the Nadir* (1989).

Redmond, Eugene B. *Drumvoices: The Mission of Afro-American Poetry, a Critical History* (1983).

This entry is taken from the *American National Biography* and is published here with the permission of the American Council of Learned Societies.

WILLIAM C. FISCHER

Cortez, Jayne (10 May 1936–), poet and performance artist, was born, one of three children, in Fort Huachuca, Arizona, an army base where her father was stationed. Her maternal grandfather served in the U.S. military in the Philippines, where he met and married Julia Cortez, for whom the poet was named.

At Fort Huachuca, Cortez attended a segregated one-room school with African American and Native American children. When Cortez was seven, her family moved to San Diego, where they lived for a year with her maternal grandfather, and then to West Los Angeles, where she attended school with African American and Japanese American children returning from internment camps. Cortez spent most of her teenage years in Watts, attending a primarily white junior high school just outside the neighborhood. She graduated from Manual Arts High School, where she studied drawing, painting, design, piano, bass, cello, and music theory. She briefly attended Compton Junior College and studied drama at Ebony Showcase in Los Angeles.

In addition to her formal education, Cortez was informally educated in African American music and oral traditions, and these forms strongly shape her poetry. Her parents owned many jazz records, and she grew up listening to ELLA FITZGERALD, BILLIE HOLIDAY, LENA HORNE, DUKE ELLINGTON, COUNT BASIE, JIMMY LUNCEFORD, CHARLIE PARKER, and THELONIUS MONK. She also remembers: "We played the Dozens, signified, told jokes, and performed for each other …. We did it constantly.

It was an everyday ritual. Oral poetry in an oral atmosphere" (Melhem, *Heroism*, 200).

In 1954, at the age of eighteen, Cortez married the jazz musician ORNETTE COLEMAN. In 1956 they had a son, Denardo, who began playing the drums at age six and made his recording debut with his father at age ten. Denardo was a long-standing member of the Firespitters, Cortez's jazz band. The ten years between Cortez's marriage to Ornette Coleman and their divorce in 1964 have not been clearly documented, with the exception of Denardo's birth and Cortez's work on Mississippi voter registration in 1963 and 1964. During this time Cortez would have been caring for her young son, but there is evidence that she was also working. She told D. H. Melhem that her empathy for working-class and women's struggles worldwide was connected to her own experiences as a factory worker:

I worked in a shirt factory; then I worked in a belt factory; and I worked in other factories. I also worked as a waitress, a telephone operator, and an office worker, typing and operating business machines. I learned a lot from women in the factories. We talked about many, many things. I got advice and tips on how to confront reality. How to be an independent woman. How to get your heels clicking when you're being abused. How to cook. What to do about health problems. It was a real sisterhood. (Heroism, 201)

It seems most likely that Cortez would have been doing this work as a young wife and mother who had not yet developed her own career as an artist.

In 1964 Cortez cofounded the Watts Repertory Theater Company, an offshoot of the community-based arts organization Studio Watts Workshop, and although she moved to New York City in 1967, she served as artistic director of the company until 1970. She published her first poetry collection, *Pissstained Stairs and the Monkey Man's Wares*, in 1969, dedicating it to the company. Cortez composed these poems for performance, and in them she employs African American speech patterns to play the music and lives of BESSIE SMITH, LEADBELLY, Charlie Parker, Ornette Coleman, CLIFFORD BROWN, SUN RA, BILLIE HOLIDAY, JOHN COLTRANE, and FATS NAVARRO. The literary critic T. J. Anderson observed that "Cortez's references to African American musicians are a means of acknowledging the critical role African American music has played in the spiritual and historical development of the black community" (124).

Cortez founded Bola Press to control the creation and dissemination of her own work, and she published *Festivals and Funerals* (1971), *Scarifications* (1973), *Mouth on Paper* (1977), *Firespitter* (1982), and *Poetic Magnetic* (1991), most of which include drawings by the sculptor and printmaker MEL EDWARDS, whom she married in 1975. Other books include *Coagulations: New and Selected Poems* (1984), *Somewhere in Advance of Nowhere* (1997), and *A Jazz Fan Looks Back* (2002). In 1975 Strata East Records released Cortez's first recording, *Celebrations and Solitudes: The Poetry of Jane Cortez*. Bola Press released the recordings *Unsubmissive Blues* (1980), *There It Is* (1982), *Maintain Control* (1986), *Everywhere Drums* (1991), *Cheerful and Optimistic* (1994), and *Borders of Disorderly Time* (2003), while Harmolodic-Verve released *Taking the Blues Back Home* in 1997. Many of these recordings feature the Firespitters jazz band.

Cortez's poems remained committed to music, especially jazz. Her work was also affiliated with surrealism as a ritualistic means of disrupting complacent perception to access the real. She said: "I use dreams, the subconscious, and real objects, and I open up the body and use organs, and I sink them into words, and I ritualize them and fuse them into events. I guess the poetry is like a festival. Everything can be transformed" (Melhem, "A *MELUS* Profile," 75). She chanted, invoked, and improvised in surprising ways. Her themes varied: she wrote praise poems in the African tradition; she wrote about oppression and revolution, love, and sexuality; and she engaged African global cultures and world politics.

Cortez's poetic innovations were recognized with numerous grants and awards, including an American Book Award in 1980. She gave performances and lectures all over the world, including at the Museum of Modern Art, the Berlin Jazz Festival, and the Fourth World Congress on Women. She was also committed to international cultural work. In 1991 she founded the Organization of Women Writers of Africa with the Ghanian writer Ama Ata Aidoo, and she coordinated major events, such as the annual Yari Yari International Conference of Women Writers of African Descent.

In a prescient review of Cortez's first collection, NIKKI GIOVANNI characterized the importance of Cortez's poems: "We haven't had many jazz poets who got inside the music and the people who created it. We poet about them, but not of them. And this is Cortez's strength. She can wail from Theodore Navarro to Leadbelly to Ornette and

never lose a beat and never make a mistake. She's a genius" (97). Cortez's voice was a jazz instrument, innovative and accessible, individual and communal. She played her instrument to preach to us and to reach us.

FURTHER READING

Anderson, T. J., III. *Notes to Make the Sound Come Right: Four Innovators of Jazz Poetry* (2004).

Giovanni, Nikki. "Review of *Pissstained Stairs and the Monkey Man's Wares* by Jayne Cortez." *Negro Digest* (Dec. 1969).

Melhem, D. H. *Heroism in the New Black Poetry: Introductions and Interviews* (1990).

Melhem, D. H. "A *MELUS* Profile and Interview: Jayne Cortez." *MELUS* (Spring 1996).

Pettis, Joyce. "Jayne Cortez (1936–)," in *African American Poets: Lives, Works, and Sources* (2002).

Woodson, Jon. "Jayne Cortez," in *Dictionary of Literary Biography*, vol. 41, *Afro-American Poets since 1955*, ed. Trudier Harris and Thadious M. Davis (1985).

JENNIFER DRAKE

Cortor, Eldzier (10 Jan. 1916–), artist, was born in Richmond, Virginia, to John and Ophelia Cortor. The following year the Cortors moved to Chicago, Illinois, as part of the Great Migration. In 1910 fewer than 50,000 blacks lived in Chicago; by 1920 the number had tripled. In search of a better education and environment for their son, the Cortors first moved to the South Side, home to a thriving African American community. John Cortor operated a modest business installing electricity into homes and repairing small electrical appliances; he eventually saved enough to open a grocery store and earned the luxury of indulging in his favorite pastimes. A motorcycle enthusiast and a sportsman, he also learned to pilot a small airplane. He belonged to a group of pioneering African American pilots and prided himself on the fruits of his practical brand of hard work, ingenuity, and self-determination. Though John Cortor was not in favor of Eldzier's becoming an artist, he provided the blueprint. Eldzier Cortor had many mentors outside of his home, but surely his first model was the father who determined his own future through the attainment of goals that he had set for himself.

Cortor enjoyed Leslie Rogers's comic strip *Bungleton Green*, which appeared weekly in the *Chicago Defender*. He would copy the strip and dream of one day making his own. Catherine Irving, the editor of the *Chicago Bee*, was a neighbor and friend, and she gave Cortor his first watercolor set, which he kept until he began to study at the School of the Art Institute of Chicago.

With John Cortor's continuing prosperity the family moved to the West Side, and Eldzier attended Medill Junior High School. Miss Wilson, his art teacher, had been a student with Elmer Simms Campbell, a cartoonist with fans throughout black America. Unlike the burlesque images drawn by whites, Campbell depicted likable African Americans. Miss Wilson introduced Cortor to Simms, and subsequently they began a correspondence.

In the Depression black Chicagoans were well represented among the jobless and homeless, and the city's largest black bank closed its doors. John Cortor's businesses suffered, and he was forced to return his family to the predominantly black South Side. Eldzier entered Englewood High School along with fellow students Charles White and Charles Sebree, who also became artists. Ultimately Cortor left high school to work in his father's electrical business, continuing to study at night. When he finished high school he started evening classes at the School of the Art Institute. He still planned to be a cartoonist because he believed that painting should be "left to the Gods." By 1935 he had saved enough money to begin day classes, and he enrolled as a full-time student. His most influential teacher was Kathleen Blackshear, a white Texan with a love of African art.

Kathleen Blackshear secured a scholarship on Cortor's behalf and even purchased his equipment. She demanded much from her students: she insisted that they closely examine the Old Masters such as Rembrandt, Frans Hals, and El Greco to learn composition. She dissected these works, illuminating their details and requiring her students to reconstruct paintings as if they were the painters. For similar reasons Blackshear also had her students sketch African sculpture: she wanted them to understand its powerful aesthetic. Cortor could see that a man was in the details, having left his mortal fingerprints and ungodly ragmarks. Furthermore, in African art Cortor recognized a beauty that he could claim as heritage. The influence of African art is ever present in his work.

By the time he was twenty-two Cortor was that very rare thing—a working artist. He was an easel painter for the Works Project Administration. In 1938 he was painting the life of Chicagoans in the slums where they lived, and his work was placed in area public schools. During his tenure at the WPA, Cortor also met George Neal, who was the spiritual advisor of a group of young painters. Neal encouraged young artists to record their life and neighborhoods in an exacting way, to document figuratively rather than abstractly. Cortor was profoundly affected and agreed that an abstract style would not serve him quite as well.

In December 1940 the South Side Community Art Center opened in Chicago. The center was dedicated in a nationally broadcast ceremony attended by the first lady, Eleanor Roosevelt. Cortor taught at the center, which attracted black artists in the fields of theater, dance, literature, painting, and sculpture; it is still in existence today. Henry Avery, MARGARET G. BURROUGHS, CHARLES SEBREE, HUGHIE LEE-SMITH, ARCHIBALD MOTLEY JR., and CHARLES WHITE were among the artists who frequented the South Side Community Center. Another member of the vibrant Chicago scene was HORACE CAYTON, a historian and coauthor of *Black Metropolis* (1945) who also wrote extensively on African retentions in the speech of the Sea Islands' Gullah people and their grave-decorating customs. Cayton's scholarship piqued Cortor's interest in African American history and in particular in African survivals across the diaspora.

In 1944 Cortor received a Julius Rosenwald Fellowship enabling him to live and work on the Sea Islands to learn and record Gullah customs in his art. Cortor's Sea Islands work was purchased by Howard University. When Cortor returned to Chicago he saw a major exhibition of classical French painting that helped cement his own goals: he would achieve something epic and unique in the representation of black Americans. His desire to perfect his technique, to work through problems in paint chemistry, took him to New York, where he studied at Columbia University (with a concentration in lithography) and at the Pratt Graphic Art Center. He created striking studies of tall nude black women, celebrating the particular beauty of African American women. His women were long, lyrical, sculptural, and pensive and were situated in simple interiors surrounded by the paraphernalia of their lives.

Cortor's painting of women earned him popular attention and artistic acclaim. *Southern Gate*, a 1942 oil on canvas (one of his best-known paintings) was placed in the Smithsonian Museum of American Art in Washington, D.C. In 1945 *The Bathers* won the annual prize at the Art Institute of Chicago. In 1946 *Life* magazine published one of his nude studies. In 1947 *Americana* received honorable mention, and Cortor was awarded the Purchase Prize at the

Carnegie Institute Annual Show. In the same year the artist's work was mentioned in Sinclair Lewis's novel *Kingsblood Royal*, in which a character says that if he were a "colored man" he would certainly have a "'Cortor' on his wall." In 1949 Cortor was awarded a Guggenheim Fellowship and traveled to Cuba, Jamaica, and Haiti. He remained in Haiti for two years and taught drawing at the Centre d'Art in Port-au-Prince. He admired Haitian art with its proprietary blend of Western culture, Catholicism, and the Afro-Haitian religion of Vodun.

Cortor created series of paintings and prints organized around artistic, symbolic, and metaphoric themes; among them are *The Jewels*, *The Rooms*, *Classical Studies*, and *Souvenirs*. In *Cuban Souvenir*, an oil on canvas, a woman sits in the corner of a room; through the open window behind her we see a small crescent moon that shines its light on the sea. She silently holds a pretty flowered fan, and its pink colors rhyme with the rose in her hair and the faint shade of pink dabbed across her bottom lip. These colors highlight her beautiful, dark brown skin, which is luminescent in the room's darkness. In *Remembrances*, a 1939 tempera on a gessoed surface, the female figure wears a dainty cross around her neck and a simply buttoned dress. She leans against a brick wall that overlooks a small valley of rooftops. Her elbow intrudes into her basket, which is overfull with a framed photograph and a few bottles. The painting is romantic and mysterious and suggests, in title and image, nostalgia for a time past.

Cortor's skills were widely esteemed. Described by Cedric Dover in the 1960 survey text *American Negro Art* as a "poet of poignancy," Cortor painted in lavish, thick strokes that created bas-relief depth on his works' surfaces. Yet Cortor declared the paintbrush insensitive and has always returned to the pen and pencil to create graphic art. When Willard Motley was asked about Cortor, he said that whether it's a lithograph, palette knife portrait, painting done with a paint tube technique, murals worked out on a small scale, or sketches in simple lines and living moods, Cortor's work is unmistakable.

FURTHER READING

Bearden, Romare, and Harry Henderson. *A History of African American Artists from 1792 to the Present* (1992).

Dover, Cedric. *American Negro Art* (1960).

Driskell, David. *Narratives of African American Art and Identity* (1998).

Fax, Elton C. *Seventeen Black Artists* (1971).

Fine, Elsa Honig. *The Afro-American Artist: A Search for Identity* (1982).

Lewis, Samella. *African American Art and Artists* (1994).

Locke, Alain. *The Negro in Art: Pictorial Record of the Negro Artist and of the Negro Theme in Art* (1940).

Patton, Sharon F., ed. *Three Masters: Eldzier Cortor, Hughie Lee-Smith, Archibald John Motley, Jr.* (1988).

JOYE VAILES SHEPPERD

Cosby, Bill (12 July 1937–), actor and comedian, was born William Henry Cosby Jr. in Germantown, Philadelphia, the son of William Henry Cosby Sr., a U.S. Navy mess steward, and Anna Pearl Cosby. Many of the vicissitudes of Cosby's childhood in the poverty-stricken Richard Allen housing projects would be transformed later into fodder for his hilarious comedy routines and television shows. As a youngster, Cosby worked many hours shining shoes and performing menial tasks at a local grocery. He attended the Germantown High School for Gifted Students, where he was elected captain of the track and football teams.

At age nineteen, Cosby dropped out of school and enlisted in the U.S. Navy, in which he served for four years (1956–1960). During his stint in the

Bill Cosby in August 1972, starring in *The New Bill Cosby Show*. (AP Images.)

navy, he managed to earn his high school equivalency diploma through correspondence and studied physical therapy. In 1960, with four years of military service under his belt, Cosby received a scholarship to the College of Education at Temple University in Philadelphia, where he majored in physical education. At Temple, Cosby earned a living as a bartender at local nightclubs. Inspired by comedy pioneers like Mel Brooks and Carl Reiner—and having always casually told jokes to friends and teammates—Cosby decided to try his hand as a comedian. In 1962, after he had appeared at various coffeehouses in Philadelphia, the Gaslight Café in New York's Greenwich Village booked Cosby for an engagement. He received a glowing review in the *New York Times*. Encouraged, Cosby began polishing and honing his act with the help of his friend Roy Silver, who would eventually become his manager. In 1962 Cosby dropped out of school to focus more intensely on the comedy circuit. On 25 January 1964 he married CAMILLE HANKS [COSBY], and the couple had five children: Erika, Erinn, Ennis, Ensa, and Evin. Cosby made his television debut in 1965 on the *Tonight Show* with Johnny Carson. The appearance brought him headlining engagements at popular nightclubs nationwide, including the hungry i in San Francisco, Mr. Kelly's in Chicago, the Flamingo in Las Vegas, and Harrah's at Lake Tahoe.

In sharp contrast to the explicit, anti-authoritarian routines of such contemporaries as George Carlin and RICHARD PRYOR, Cosby's comedic style avoided cursing. He gained a reputation for his congenial anecdotes about everyday foibles and family issues. A master storyteller with a strong gift for physical comedy and exaggerated impersonations, Cosby became known as "the Negro comedian who doesn't use racial material" (Cohen, 64). He would record eighteen comedy records over the course of his career, including *Bill Cosby Is a Very Funny Fellow* (1963), *To Russell, My Brother Whom I Slept With* (1968), and *My Father Confused Me, What Should I Do?* (1977). These records captured the spirit of his live comedy routines, selling 12 million copies and, over time, earning him eight Grammy awards.

Cosby's flair for comedy brought him to the attention of the television producer Sheldon Leonard, who cast him, as Alexander Scott, opposite the white actor Robert Culp in the NBC adventure-comedy series *I Spy* (1965). Playing a Temple University graduate and a Rhodes Scholar able to speak seven languages, Cosby became the first black actor to land a continuing role in a network series. He won three Emmy awards during the show's immensely popular three-year run. His national visibility garnered him a weeklong stand-up engagement at the Apollo Theater in Harlem, and in 1969 he took home his fourth Emmy for *The Bill Cosby Special*. A lifelong aficionado of black music and himself a jazz musician, Cosby became the president of the Rhythm and Blues Hall of Fame in 1968.

In the following years Cosby struggled to maintain a hit on network television. He starred as a physical education teacher Chet Kincaid on *The Bill Cosby Show* (1968), which ran to lukewarm reviews for three years. In 1972 Cosby launched a comedy-variety show called *The New Bill Cosby Show*, which lasted only a year, until May 1973. A short-lived sitcom, *Cos* (1976), was excoriated by critics. In 1973 he fared substantially better by creating and providing voice-overs for a cartoon series, *Fat Albert and the Cosby Kids*. Set in an inner city junkyard, the humorous show aimed to teach children creative solutions for everyday problems and ran for nearly eleven years.

In the 1970s Cosby cultivated his interests in education and child psychology to earn his bachelor's degree in Sociology from Temple University and a master's and doctorate in Education from the University of Massachusetts. He made guest appearances on children's television shows, such as *The Electric Company, Captain Kangaroo*, and *Pinwheel*. He launched a film career, starring in movies like *Hickey and Boggs* (1972), *Mother Jugs and Speed* (1976), *California Suite* (1978), and *The Devil and Max Devlin* (1981). Alongside his friend SIDNEY POITIER, Cosby starred in several successful crime-caper films: *Uptown Saturday Night* (1974), *Let's Do It Again* (1975), and *A Piece of the Action* (1977). In 1982 he starred in a feature film version of his comedy act, *Bill Cosby: Himself*.

In 1984 Cosby created the comedy series *The Cosby Show* for NBC. The show followed the life and times of the obstetrician Heathcliff "Cliff" Huxtable; his wife, Claire, a lawyer; and their five children. Buoyed by sharp writing and universal story lines, the show broke all Nielsen records to emerge as the top-rated family show for most of its eight-year run. Winning numerous Emmy awards and NAACP Image awards, *The Cosby Show* helped revitalize the stagnant sitcom genre in the early 1980s.

The success of *The Cosby Show* also triggered long-standing debates about the direction of black representation in the media. Many critics felt that the show's vision of black upward mobility was little more than a fairy tale that misdirected popular attention away from the increasing socioeconomic and political decline of African Americans in the Reagan era. Cosby's stated goal in representing upwardly mobile African Americans was to show that "we have the same kinds of wants and needs as other American families" (Smith, 165).

The Cosby Show received a massive syndication deal in 1988 and was seen regularly on television. In 1988 Cosby also produced a television spin-off about life in an all-black college, called A Different World. Although his feature films during this period, such as Leonard Part VI (1988), Ghost Dad (1990), and Meteor Man (1993), were critically lambasted, Cosby would emerge as a literary powerhouse with successful books on family, aging, and relationships, such as Fatherhood, Time Flies, and Love and Marriage.

Cosby was recruited in the 1980s as a product spokesman for several major companies, including General Foods and Kodak. Along with his wife, the comedian also emerged as a humanitarian when he donated $20 million to Spelman College—the largest personal contribution ever given to a black college or university. Among his other charitable contributions were $1.3 million to be divided among Fisk University in Nashville, Tennessee, Florida A&M, Howard University in Washington, D.C., and Shaw University in Raleigh, North Carolina, as well as $325,000 to Central State University in Wilberforce, Ohio. In the 1990s he became part owner of the New Jersey Nets basketball team. Cosby was drawn into the deal by the team's sponsorship of a trust fund benefiting inner-city youth. One of the highest paid African American performers, Cosby also announced his intention to buy NBC in the 1990s, which did not come to fruition.

Cosby's television ventures in the 1990s pale in comparison to the success of The Cosby Show. A remake of the Groucho Marx game show You Bet Your Life was a flop in 1992. The Cosby Mysteries, patterned after Angela Lansbury's Murder She Wrote, received a lukewarm response in 1994. In that same year Cosby appeared in the television movie I Spy Returns. Somewhat more successful was Cosby in 1996, a sitcom that placed the comedy legend in more familiar environs. Playing a retiree living in Queens, he was reunited with Phylicia Rashad, the actress who had played his wife on The Cosby Show. In 1996 Cosby appeared with Robin Williams in the film Jack, and in 2000 he produced Men of Honor, a movie starring Cuba Gooding Jr. as CARL BRASHEAR, the first African American

U.S. Navy diver. Cosby's easy rapport with children came to the fore in two television shows, Kids Say the Darnedest Things, which he hosted in 1998, and Little Bill (1999), for which he was executive producer.

Cosby's popular image was dented somewhat in the late 1990s, when a woman named Autumn Jackson claimed to be his illegitimate daughter and demanded money from him. Cosby admitted publicly that he had an affair in 1974 with Jackson's mother, Shawn Thompson Upshaw, and that he had been paying her money to remain quiet about the relationship. Nonetheless, the comedian denied paternity—even agreeing during the trial to take a paternity test. Jackson refused. She was later convicted of extortion. Then, in 1997, Cosby's twenty-seven-year-old son, Ennis, part of the inspiration for the character Theo in The Cosby Show, was murdered in Los Angeles by a man attempting to rob him. The man was later arrested and convicted.

In 2002 NBC ran a reunion special of The Cosby Show that brought the cast together in celebration of the longevity and good humor of a comedy legend. Beyond his well-documented—and much-needed—ability to make people laugh, however, Bill Cosby's greatest legacy may well be in his charitable contributions. In addition to providing several historically black colleges with much needed funds, Cosby and his wife, Camille, have established one of the world's greatest private collections of African American art. The Cosbys' collection is intended to end the neglect of black artists, including JACOB LAWRENCE, HENRY OSSAWA TANNER, ELIZABETH CATLETT, and AUGUSTA SAVAGE, who were ignored or marginalized in their own time. In 2001 DAVID DRISKELL, curator of the collection, published The Other Side of Color: African American Art in the Collection of Camille O. and William H. Cosby, Jr. (2001). In recognition of his lifetime achievements, Cosby was awarded the nation's highest civilian honor, the Presidential Medal of Freedom, in 2002.

On May 17, 2004, Cosby gave a speech to the NAACP on the fiftieth anniversary of the historic Brown vs. Board of Education decision. He argued, with flourishes of comic brio, that there was a widespread failure in parenting, accountability, and leadership in segments of the black community.

In the aftermath of Cosby's speech, support and opprobrium were heard in almost equal measure. On one hand, he was congratulated on his courageousness, while on the other, criticized for failing to take into account social and economic deprivation. Yet this was no departure from the norm for

Cosby. It merely marked a new stage in his mission to educate (while entertaining) about the need for discipline and strong parenting.

FURTHER READING

Adler, Bill. *The Cosby Wit: His Life and Humor* (1986).
Cohen, Joel H. *Cool Cos: The Story of Bill Cosby* (1969).
Latham, Caroline. *Bill Cosby for Real* (1985).
Rosenberg, Robert. *Bill Cosby: The Changing Black Image* (1991).
Smith, Ronald L. *Cosby: The Life of a Comedy Legend* (1997).

DISCOGRAPHY

The Best of Bill Cosby (Warner Bros. 1798).
More of the Best of Bill Cosby (Warner Bros. 1836).
20th Century Masters: The Millennium Collection: The Best of Bill Cosby (MCA 112610).

JASON KING

Cosby, Camille (20 Mar. 1944–), educator, author, and philanthropist, was born Camille Olivia Hanks in Washington, D.C., to Guy Hanks, a chemist who earned an M.A. from Fisk University, and Catherine Hanks, a nursery school owner and Howard University graduate. Camille, the eldest of four siblings, attended a series of parochial schools, starting with St. Cyprian's Elementary School in Washington, D.C. She then attended St. Cecilia Academy, also in Washington, and completed her secondary education at Ursuline Academy in Bethesda, Maryland.

Although Camille Hanks had displayed an earlier interest in biology, Latin, and algebra, when she entered the University of Maryland at the age of eighteen she decided to major in psychology. During her sophomore year she was introduced to a twenty-six year old up-and-coming comedian named BILL COSBY. On their second date the young comedian proposed, and the couple was married ten months later, on 25 January 1964. About this same time Bill Cosby landed the lead role as Alexander Scott on the television series *I Spy*. Camille Cosby left school, and the couple moved to Los Angeles. As her husband's career took off she became his trusted and able business partner, managing a growing enterprise that eventually included two television series—*The Cosby Show* (aired 1984–1992) and *A Different World* (aired 1987–1993)several movies, regular comedy shows, recordings, commercials, book ventures, and a growing number of philanthropic activities. During this time the Cosbys also started their family. The couple had four daughters, Erika, Erinn, Evin, and Ensa, and one son, Ennis.

After six years in Los Angeles the Cosbys moved to Amherst, Massachusetts. It was while living in this college town and overseeing her children's education that Cosby decided to continue her own education as well.

Cosby enrolled at the University of Massachusetts and in 1980 earned an M.A. in Education. While conducting her thesis research on historically black colleges and universities (HBCUs), Cosby concluded that each of the eight institutions she visited was suffering from declining enrollment and lack of financial support. In response the Cosbys initiated the largest philanthropic movement in the history of HBCUs. In 1988 they gave the largest-ever personal gift to a black institution, donating twenty million dollars to Spelman College, then under the leadership of JOHNNETTA COLE. By 1994 it was estimated that the Cosbys had donated over seventy million dollars to various predominantly black colleges and universities. In turn these institutions recognized the Cosbys' commitment to supporting educational opportunities for African Americans. In January of 1996 Spelman College opened the Camille Olivia Hanks Cosby Academic Center. Both Spelman and Howard University awarded Cosby honorary doctorates.

In 1992 Cosby earned a Ph.D. in Education from the University of Massachusetts, and two years later she published *Television's Imageable Influences: The Self-Perception of Young African Americans*, based on her doctoral studies. In this book Cosby investigated the effect of television's negative images of blacks on the self-perception of young African Americans. "What I found out," Cosby explained, "is that these negative imageries are affecting our young people, and they are affecting them negatively" (Johnson, 13).

After completing her doctoral work, providing more diverse images of African American life and culture to counter the negative images perpetuated in the media became one of Cosby's most passionate missions. As art collectors, Cosby and her husband have amassed over 300 pieces of art from the African diaspora that document the African and African American influence on American culture. Pieces from the Cosbys' extensive art collection were showcased in the 2001 book, *The Other Side of Color: African American Art in the Collection of Camille O. and William H. Cosby, Jr.*, written by the longtime family friend and curator of the Cosby art collection, the artist and scholar DAVID DRISKELL. As part of Camille Cosby's ongoing commitment to present more complex images of

African Americans, in 1994 she became an executive producer for the documentary *No Dream Deferred*, which chronicled the experiences of Thelma and Wesley Williams, entrepreneurs who used their catering business as an opportunity to mentor young people. Cosby realized that the Williamses provided positive images for young African Americans and showed how young people could excel if given a constructive, affirming, and disciplined environment.

In 1995 Cosby coproduced, with Judith Rutherford James, the play *Having Our Say*, a dramatization of the best selling autobiography of BESSIE DELANY AND SADIE DELANY, two North Carolina sisters. "They really articulate the history of America," Cosby explained, "They lived through the establishment of Jim Crow laws and [HOMER ADOLPH] Plessy v. Ferguson. They knew people like Dr. ANNA JULIA COOPER and W. E. B. DUBOIS and BOOKER T. WASHINGTON. ... These events are their life experiences" (Fitzgerald, 24). The two-person play starring Mary Alice and Gloria Foster received three Tony nominations after it moved to Broadway, and it was made into a 1999 television film starring DIAHANN CARROLL and RUBY DEE, which earned the prestigious Peabody Award.

Tragically, in January 1997 the Cosbys' son, Ennis, was shot and killed while changing a tire on a Los Angeles freeway. Although diagnosed with dyslexia, Ennis was pursuing a Ph.D. in Special Education at Columbia University and planned to open a school for children with learning disabilities. Ennis's perseverance and altruism were memorialized in the 2000 documentary *Ennis's Gift*, for which Camille Cosby served as the executive producer. The film revealed how Ennis came to understand that he had dyslexia but could still succeed in school. The documentary introduced dozens of people, including actors, scientists, and business leaders, who were diagnosed with learning differences, but who refused to be limited by those differences.

Cosby also cofounded, with the television journalist RENEE FRANCINE POUSSAINT, the National Visionary Leadership Project, a Washington, D.C.-based, intergenerational program devoted to collecting, preserving, and disseminating the stories of African American elders. The project resulted in the publication of *A Wealth of Wisdom* (2004), a collection of stories documenting the experiences of more than fifty prominent African Americans. In 2004 Cosby served as a co-executive producer for the film *Fat Albert*.

Cosby's commitment to education as well as to celebrating African American history and ensuring its future embodied the adage that with great gifts come great responsibilities. Cosby insisted, however, that she was not a leader, but rather a vehicle for social change, "I want to do my part in helping people to change their negative attitudes about us as a people, and hopefully, if we have any negative attitudes about ourselves, I want to help change those, too" (Fitzgerald, 25).

FURTHER READING

Fitzgerald, Sharon. "Catalyst Camille," *American Visions* (Dec. 1994).

Johnson, Robert E. "Millionairess Camille Cosby Says She Had to Earn Ph.D. Degree Because 'You Have to Do What You Urge Others to Do,'" *Jet* (15 June 1992).

Oliver, Stephanie. "Camille Cosby: An Intimate Portrait," *Essence* (1 Dec. 1989).

Williams, Lena. "At Home with Camille Cosby," *New York Times*, 15 Dec. 1994.

SHIRLEY C. MOODY

Cose, Ellis Jonathan (20 Feb. 1952–), journalist, editor, and novelist, was born in Chicago, the son of Raney Cose, a poorly educated employee of a laundry service, and Jetta Cameron. He spent his youth in the Henry Horner Homes high-rise housing project on Chicago's West Side, but as an adolescent he was inspired by the civil rights movement of the 1960s and strongly sensed he had something to contribute to the betterment of society. As a senior at Lane Technical High School, Cose was challenged by an English teacher whose class he was failing, and he responded by composing a two-hundred-page collection of essays on racial and social issues. This collection so impressed the teacher that she referred him to Illinois' poet laureate at the time, GWENDOLYN BROOKS, who asked Cose to join her writing group.

In 1968, with the aid of a scholarship, Cose enrolled at the University of Illinois at Chicago (UIC), where he wrote commentaries in the student newspaper. He gathered some of these commentaries and forwarded them to Ralph Otwell, managing editor of the *Chicago Sun-Times*. On the strength of what he and the editor Jim Hoge read, Otwell hired Cose in 1970 to write a column in its school edition and later in its regular edition, making Cose at age nineteen the youngest columnist in the newspaper's history.

Cose honed his skills as a columnist, national correspondent, and editor at the *Chicago Sun-Times*, where he became the resident voice of the city's African American community. He completed his undergraduate degree in psychology at UIC in 1972. He left the newspaper in 1977 and pursued graduate study at George Washington University, where he earned a master's degree in science technology and public policy in 1978. While in the Washington, D.C., area, he was director of energy policy studies for the Joint Center for Political Studies, a black think tank, from 1977 to 1979, and he produced two monographs for the center: *Energy and the Urban Crisis* (1978) and *Energy and Equity: Some Social Concerns* (1979).

Cose returned to journalism full time when he became an editorial writer and columnist for the *Detroit Free Press* in 1979. His two-year stint there ended when he was named a resident fellow at the National Academy of Sciences and the National Research Council in 1981. Also during the late 1970s and the early 1980s he occasionally published articles on race, urban problems, and labor-management issues in *Time* magazine and *USA Today*.

In 1983 Cose published his first commercial trade book, *Decentralizing Energy Decisions: The Rebirth of Community Power*, which concerned the nation's struggle with the new realities of the energy crisis. That same year Cose became president of the Institute for Journalism Education at the University of California at Berkeley, a post he held until 1986. The institute published his coauthored twenty-two-page monograph *Minorities Research: Minority Journalists and Newsroom Opportunity* (1987), which examined the scarcity of racial minorities in American newsrooms. In 1987 he moved on to a similar position as president of the Gannett Center for Media Studies at Columbia University. His experience and expertise on the culture of American journalism was evident in his next book, *The Press* (1989), which was largely based on interviews with corporate leaders of the print journalism industry. The book was generally favored by reviewers, including Ron Rosenbaum of the *New York Times*, who pointed out that its stories recounting strained relations between black reporters and their white editors broke fresh ground.

Cose returned to the private sector from 1991 to 1993 as chair of the editorial board of the *New York Daily News*. Beginning in the early 1990s he contributed articles, and reviews, mainly dealing with issues of race and society, to *Time* magazine, *Newsday*, *USA Today*, *Media Studies Journal*, *Business and Society Review*, *Civil Rights Journal*, *Black Enterprise*, *Essence* magazine, the *Boston Globe*, and the *New York Times*. The majority of his published articles appeared in the pages of *Newsweek* magazine, where he became a contributing editor in 1993. In 1992 he married Lee Llambelis; they had one daughter.

Cose spent more than two years researching and writing his next book, a well-received history of the nation's immigration policy titled *A Nation of Strangers: Prejudice, Politics, and the Populating of America* (1992). The following year he published the best-seller *The Rage of a Privileged Class* (1993), which was featured in a *Newsweek* magazine cover story that focused on the predicament of the black middle class striving for success but hampered and tormented by persistent racism. Moving from racism, Cose next tackled the perplexing issue of gender discrimination and gender relations in *A Man's World: How Real Is Male Privilege—and How High Is Its Price?* (1995). The book was translated for publication in Japan and Korea. He returned to the problem of racism in American society with *Color-Blind: Seeing beyond Race in a Race-Obsessed World* (1997), which benefited from interviews, contrasting experiences of Americans and foreigners, and his own proposals for fostering a "race-neutral" situation in the United States. For *The Darden Dilemma: 12 Black Writers on Justice, Race, and Conflicting Loyalties* (1997), Cose compiled a collection of essays by black journalists and legal experts—among them CLARENCE PAGE, ROGER WILKINS, Anita Hill, and Wade Henderson—to address issues relating to African Americans and the criminal justice system.

In 1998 Cose published a courtroom novel, *The Best Defense*, which highlighted the racial angles of a case in which an unemployed white man, an alleged victim of workplace affirmative action, kills his Hispanic replacement and is defended by a black female attorney, the main character. In yet another switch, Cose returned to harsh reality with another best-selling, critically acclaimed work of nonfiction, *The Envy of the World: On Being a Black Man in America* (2002), which formed the basis of a special segment on National Public Radio. In his next book, *A Bone to Pick: Of Forgiveness, Reconciliation, Reparation, and Revenge* (2004), Cose examined how societies and individuals around the world responded to violence, human rights abuses, and personal traumas, and he concluded that recognition and exposure of such tragic events is a necessary prerequisite to healing and the redress of social wrongs. Cose was the recipient of awards from the Illinois UPI, the Association of

Black Journalists, and the Gustavus Myers Center for the Study of Bigotry and Human Rights.

FURTHER READING

Mari, Christopher. "Cose, Ellis," in *World Authors, 1990–1995* (1999).

Martin, Jonathan. "Ellis Cose," in *Contemporary Black Biography*, vol. 5 (1994).

Nix, Will. "Ellis Cose," *Publishers Weekly* (23 Mar. 1992).

ROBERT FIKES JR.

Costen, James Hutten (5 Oct. 1931–11 Apr. 2003), Presbyterian pastor and educator, was born in Omaha, Nebraska, one of three children born to Baptist parents Mary Lou Brookings Costen, a homemaker, and William Theodore Costen, a railroad worker. At the encouragement of his dying father, who was impressed with the personal discipline instilled by Costen's Catholic school education, Costen was baptized into the Roman Catholic Church at the age of seven. Costen attended Catholic elementary and junior high schools, and he considered the priesthood. When Costen was sixteen, however, a Presbyterian congregation moved to temporary quarters across the street from the Costen house, and its pastor, the Reverend Charles Tyler, began to exert a strong influence on him. Costen joined the Presbyterian Church and began to think about a calling as a Presbyterian pastor.

When Costen graduated from Omaha's Central High School in 1949, a high school counselor suggested that he apply for a job in a local meat packing plant. The Reverend Charles Tyler, however, advised Costen to attend college, and Tyler arranged for the Omaha Presbytery to help fund his education. Costen then enrolled in Johnson C. Smith University in Charlotte, North Carolina, where he briefly played football and where he earned the nickname "Omaha" for his hometown. He met MELVA WILSON during his sophomore year, and they married the day before Costen graduated in 1953. They eventually had two sons and one daughter, James Jr., Craig, and Cheryl.

Costen stayed on after college to earn his divinity degree from the Johnson C. Smith Theological Seminary. In 1955 Costen was ordained as a minister of the United Presbyterian Church, USA, and installed as pastor of Mount Pisgah Church in Rocky Mount, North Carolina, where he continued his education and became involved in local politics. Costen became the first African American to enroll in Southeastern Baptist Theological Seminary in nearby Wake Forest, North Carolina, where he graduated in 1963 with a master's of theology (ThM) in religious education with a thesis entitled "The Stewardship of Possessions in Pauline Thought." Costen narrowly lost an election for mayor of Rocky Mount, but his political involvement put him in touch with the Reverend MARTIN LUTHER KING JR., and in 1965 the Costen family moved to Atlanta, Georgia, where Costen began to recruit members for an interracial new church development in an area that had been experiencing "white flight." Three months later Costen was installed as the organizing pastor of the Church of the Master.

In 1968 the United Presbyterian Church General Assembly voted to close Costen's alma mater, the Johnson C. Smith Theological Seminary, owing to financial difficulties and a declining enrollment, and Costen led a grassroots fight to keep the seminary open. Through his efforts, the seminary stayed open and moved to the Atlanta campus of the Interdenominational Theological Center (ITC), an ecumenical consortium of five seminaries. In 1969 Johnson C. Smith University awarded Costen an honorary doctor of divinity degree, the first of thirteen honorary degrees he would receive. Later that year, the newly relocated seminary asked Costen to serve as dean.

A 1974 visit to Kenya prompted Costen to begin to help Kenyan Presbyterians study at Johnson C. Smith Theological Seminary, and his efforts eventually helped educate more than forty ministers of the Presbyterian Church of East Africa (PCEA).

Throughout his career, Costen had been active in the "northern" United Presbyterian Church, which had been separated from its southern counterpart, the Presbyterian Church (U.S.), since the Civil War. He served on numerous national committees, including the General Assembly Nominating Committee, the Task Force on Reunion, and the board of directors for the Presbyterian Foundation. In 1982 Costen was elected as Moderator of the General Assembly of the United Presbyterian Church (U.S.A.), and a year later he helped lead the two churches into their 1983 reunion to become the Presbyterian Church (USA). In 1983 Costen become the fifth president of the ITC, a post he held until his retirement in 1997. In 1994 ITC completed and dedicated its new $3 million administrative and classroom building as the James H. Costen Lifelong Education Center.

When Costen retired from the Interdenominational Theological Center in 1997, the ITC had become the largest predominantly black seminary in the world, as its enrollment burgeoned from 175 to 400 students and its annual budget swelled from $1.7 million to $6 million. That year the ITC established an endowment fund to honor Costen, and it published *The Costen Legacy*, a retrospective of his twenty-eight years of service to the institution.

Costen continued his work for social justice. In 1998 he helped draft an open letter from prominent African American Presbyterians to the Presbyterian Church (USA), likening its poor treatment of sexual minorities, including gays and lesbians, to its earlier racial discrimination against African Americans. In 1999 Johnson C. Smith University honored Costen as a Distinguished Alumnus, and the General Assembly of the Presbyterian Church (USA) gave Costen its Award for Excellence in Theological Education. In addition to his remarkable service to the Presbyterian Church, to his schools, and to his communities, Costen chaired several boards of trustees, the Boggs Academy of Keysville Georgia, the Harbison Development Corporation, the Association of Theological Schools in North America (its first African American president), and the Fund for Theological Education (for fifteen years).

During Costen's retirement, he volunteered as a development officer for Kenya's Presbyterian University and its Pastoral Institute, run by the Presbyterian Church of East Africa and located in Kikuyu, Kenya, outside Nairobi. He raised more than $2 million for a school library and for a faculty-staff housing facility that was dedicated in honor of Costen and his wife just a month before his death. Costen's poor health kept him from attending the dedication, but his wife, Melva, and son James Jr. attended in his place. Soon afterwards, Costen died from renal and heart failure. Costen's friend and colleague Oscar McCloud preached at his funeral, held 22 April 2003, at the Martin Luther King Jr. International Chapel at Morehouse College in Atlanta.

FURTHER READING

The Presbyterian Historical Society in Philadelphia and the Woodruff Library at the Interdenominational Theological Center in Atlanta contain important archival material related to Costen and his work.

Anonymous. "James H. Costen—Pastor/ Administrator," in *Black Presbyterians in Ministry*, ed. Frank T. Wilson Sr. (1979).

Costen, Melva Wilson. "Dedication" in *In Spirit and in Truth: The Music of African American Worship* (2004).

Troutman, Joseph E., and John C. Diamond, eds. *The Costen Legacy* (1997).

Wilson, Agnes T. "Four Black Moderators," in *Periscopes 2: Black Presbyterians—Yesterday, Today, and Tomorrow: 175 Years of Ministry, 1807–1982* (1982).

Obituaries: *Presbyterian Outlook*, 5–12 May 2003; *Christian Century*, 3 May 2003.

DAVID B. MCCARTHY

Costen, Melva Wilson (29 May 1933–), musician, educator, and prominent Presbyterian, was born Melva Ruby Wilson in Due West, South Carolina, one of five children of Azzie Lee Ellis Wilson and John Theodore Wilson Sr., both of whom were college graduates and teachers. Because the local black public schools were unaccredited, her parents sent her to a black boarding school, Harbison Junior College in Irmo, South Carolina, at the age of fourteen. Two years later, at the age of sixteen, she entered Johnson C. Smith University in Charlotte, North Carolina. There she met fellow student JAMES HUTTEN COSTEN. She graduated with a B.A. in Education in 1952 and married Jim Costen the day before he graduated in 1953. They eventually had two sons and one daughter, James Jr., Craig, and Cheryl.

Costen taught elementary school in the Mecklenburg County school system from 1952 to 1955, the year her husband's job took them to Rocky Mount, North Carolina. From 1955 to 1956 she taught elementary school in nearby Edgecombe County, and from 1959 to 1965 she worked as an elementary and music teacher in Nashville, North Carolina. In 1961 she enrolled in the University of North Carolina at Chapel Hill, where she received her MAT in Music Education in 1964. From 1965 to 1973 Costen served as an itinerant music teacher for the Atlanta public school system. In 1973 Atlanta's Slater School named her Teacher of the Year.

In 1973 the president of the Interdenominational Theological Center (ITC), Oswald P. Bronson Sr., attended a worship service where Costen gave a dramatic presentation that included a liturgical dance. After the service Bronson offered Costen a position as assistant professor at ITC, which she soon accepted. Also in 1973 she was ordained as an elder at the Presbyterian Church of the Master. That same year Costen enrolled at Georgia State University, where she received her Ph.D. in Curriculum and Instruction in 1978 for her dissertation "A

Comparative Description of Curricular Offerings in Church Music Degree Programs at Accredited Protestant Theological Seminaries in the United States."

Costen soon became known for her curricular revisions at ITC, where she was named Teacher of the Year in 1975 and Helmar Emil Nielsen Professor of Worship and Music in 1988. During her thirty-two years at ITC, she established a master of arts in church music degree program and led the Research Project on African American Christian Worship Traditions.

Costen sought to fill a void in the scholarship about African American church music. In 1992 she co-edited *The Black Christian Worship Experience*, and a year later Abingdon Press published her pioneering *African American Christian Worship*. In 1999 she served as consulting editor for *African American Worship: Faith Looking Forward*. Her 2004 book, *In Spirit and in Truth: The Music of African American Worship*, recapitulated a lifetime of scholarship. Her books were widely adopted as textbooks in theological seminaries.

Costen was active in numerous committees of the Presbyterian Church. In 1977 she was elected to the Board of the Joint Office of Worship, a cooperative effort of the "northern" United Presbyterian Church (U.S.A.) and the "southern" Presbyterian Church (U.S.). When those two denominations reunited in 1983, after a rift that dated back to the Civil War, Costen served on the committee to plan the worship for the new denomination's inaugural General Assembly in Atlanta, and she led the eight-hundred-voice choir at its opening worship celebration. From 1984 to 1990 Costen chaired the committee to publish a new hymnal for the reunited Presbyterian Church (USA), and the resultant *Presbyterian Hymnal: Hymns, Psalms, and Spiritual Songs* (1990) included several of her musical arrangements of African American spirituals. In her work on several national committees for the Presbyterian Church (USA), she helped develop a new Directory for Worship as part of the denomination's constitution, the *Book of Order*. She also served on the national committees that published the Presbyterian *Book of Common Worship* (1993), *The African American Heritage Hymnal* (2001), and *Holy Is the Lord: Music for the Lord's Day* (2002). In 2000 she was elected to the Presbyterian Church General Assembly Nominating Committee, and in 2002 she was appointed to the Presbyterian Church (USA) Mission Initiative Steering Committee. In 2004 she was named to the Atlanta Ecumenical Planning Committee for the meeting of the U.S. Conference for the World Council of Churches.

In addition to her work for the Presbyterian Church (USA), Costen served in several other regional and national leadership positions. She served as regional director of the National Association of Negro Musicians from 1973 to 1975, as cochair of the choral division of the District V Georgia Music Educators Association from 1981 to 1982, as a board member of the Presbyterian Association of Musicians (PAM) from 1982 to 1986, and as a board member of the Liturgical Conference from 1985 to 1991 and again from 1999 to 2003. From 1996 to 1999 she served as artistic director for the Atlanta Olympics. She was also active in the Hymn Society in the United States and Canada, was elected to membership in the North American Academy of Liturgy in 2001, and maintained membership in the College Music Society.

In 1974 Costen made the first of several trips to Kenya with her husband, and she shared in his philanthropic work with the Presbyterian Church of East Africa and its Presbyterian University and Pastoral Institute of Kenya, located in Kikuyu, Kenya, outside Nairobi. In March 2003 she and her son James Jr. traveled to Kenya with a delegation of fifteen people for the dedication of a faculty-staff housing complex that was dedicated in honor of James H. and Melva W. Costen. Her husband had been scheduled to lead the delegation, but emergency hospitalization prevented his attendance. He died in an Atlanta hospital on 11 April 2003 from renal and heart failure.

Costen's many honors included two honorary doctor of human letters degrees, one from Wilson College in Chambersburg, Pennsylvania, and one from Erskine College in her native city, Due West, South Carolina. On 7 May 2005 Costen retired after thirty-two years of "shaping and guiding the theological education of hundreds of students—emphasizing the integral relationship between music and worship in the church, particularly in the black church experience; underscoring the importance of inclusive liturgical language, and expanding the definition of worship" (Sanders, 2005). Through her teaching, her writing, and her hymnals, Costen established a legacy of a deepened awareness of the rich diversity and global scope of Christianity's musical heritage.

FURTHER READING

The Presbyterian Historical Society in Philadelphia and the Atlanta University Center (home to the Interdenominational Theological Center) contain important archival material related to Costen and her work.

Sanders, Alvelyn J. "Legacy in Song: Professor's Reach Extends Far beyond the Halls of ITC," *Atlanta Journal-Constitution*, 7 May 2005.

DAVID B. MCCARTHY

Coston, Julia Ringwood (late nineteenth century–early twentieth century?), journalist and publisher, was born in an unknown year in the latter half of the nineteenth century in Warrenton, Virginia. Little is known about her early childhood, except that the Ringwood family moved to Washington, D.C., when she was still an infant and that she attended school there. However, in her final year of studies, Julia's mother fell ill and so the young woman was obliged to look for work to help the family make ends meet. Taking a position as governess in the home of a military general, Julia was exposed to the lifestyles of a wealthy family for perhaps the first time, and she was most likely able to continue her studies.

While working as a governess Julia met William Hilary Coston, who was raised in Rhode Island and Connecticut. At sixteen Coston had obtained a privileged position of "janitorship" at Hopkins Grammar School, Yale Preparatory, which he attended for several years, later attending Wilberforce University

Julia Ringwood Coston began publishing *Ringwood's Afro-American Journal of Fashion* in 1891. (Schomburg Center for Research in Black Culture, New York Public Library.)

and Yale Divinity School. The couple married in the spring of 1886, while Coston was still a graduate student at Yale, and then moved to Cleveland, Ohio, where William served as a minister at St. Andrew's Episcopal Church. Julia gave birth to two children, Julia in 1888, and William Hilary Jr. in 1890. The couple enjoyed a happy marriage, "mutually and justly proud of each other." In the opinion of her early biographer, Coston represented "that pearl of pearl, a good woman, whose price is far above rubies … a faithful, affectionate, earnest, Christian wife, who fills her position in his household and congregation with the dignity and grace which appertain thereto."

In 1891 Coston launched *Ringwood's Afro-American Journal of Fashion*, a twelve-page journal for "refined ladies" and the country's first magazine published exclusively for black women. The magazine offered illustrations of modern fashions including "the latest Parisian ladies gowns." In addition, it usually included a romance story and advice on household and lifestyle matters. Features also included, according to one reader, "biographical sketches of prominent ladies of the race and promising young misses, edited by the Mrs. M. C. Church Terrel of Washington, DC." (This is most likely a reference to MARY CHURCH TERRELL, the prominent civil rights and women's activist.) Other sections of the magazine included "Plain Talk to Our Girls," "Mother's Corner," "Literary Department," and "Home Department," all described as being "well-edited by educated colored women," according to the *Philadelphia Recorder*.

In 1893 Coston, who was said to have "an intense desire" to see colored faces in the pages of women's magazines since the time she was a young girl, also launched *Ringwood's Home Magazine*, which was in print until at least 1895. Interestingly, the historian Lawson Scruggs gave Coston's husband much of the credit for the success of both publications, writing, "Mrs. Coston has received much sympathy, encouragement and help from her husband, whose practical experience has enabled him to suggest plans and methods for the realization of that cherished desire of her heart which will forever distinguish her among Afro-American women." Julia shared with her husband a dedication to the Christian uplift of the race. Lawson Scruggs described her (quoting from the words of one of Julia's friends) as "a loveable woman whose actuating desire is to serve the highest interests of the women of today, that their lives may be made more helpful by giving them modest publicity, and thus present them as worthy models for the emulation of our growing womanhood." As one reader wrote in praise of *Ringwood's Afro-American Journal of Fashion*, it was "pure, yet simple, characterizing the sublime force of education, of woman's prosperity." Indeed, Julia Coston was interested in upholding what she called a "true womanhood" of sanctity and purity, and she directed scathing criticism toward women writers of her day, novelists in particular, who had lost touch with what she viewed as woman's "essential femininity."

As others had done long before the Civil War Coston defended the character of African American women by advancing orthodox views of womanhood:

Recently, there has appeared in the world of letters a certain class of women writers who have thrown off the veil of modesty, and who, in the name of reform, pose as martyrs, sacrificing themselves to a great work. To all such would-be missionaries it may be admissible to hint that the loss of one chaste womanly woman does more harm than any number of novels can ever do good. … Only an utter lack of femininity could make it possible for a woman to stand before the world and proclaim its vice. The women who are truly loved, know naught of woman's rights and universal suffrage. … They are not troubled with the affairs of State, nor are they agents of reform. They are women, adorable women, into whose minds has crept no vicious longing for publicity, no hunger to usurp the sphere of men.

On issues of great importance to many white female reformers of the late nineteenth century, Coston espoused ultra-orthodox positions. "Women have so many rights that are truly theirs, so many opportunities for influence upon the great world, that they may stop and consider, not how to obtain more, but how to make the best use of what already is theirs. … Politicians, lawyers and financiers can all be recruited from the ranks of men, but where are we to find the softening, refining influences of life if our women cease to be such?"

Coston's life and the fate of her magazines after 1895 are a mystery. Despite her publications' widespread notoriety and apparent popularity, no copies of either are known to survive. As for Coston herself: "She may not have a monument of bronze or marble erected to perpetuate a grateful memory," wrote her first biographer, accurately foreseeing Coston's future historical neglect, "but she will live … in the pure and exalted lives of the grand women of the dawning future."

FURTHER READING

Bolden, Tonya. *The Book of African-American Women: 150 Crusaders, Creators, and Uplifters* (1996).

Majors, Monroe A. *Noted Negro Women: Their Triumphs and Activities* (c. 1893).

Scruggs, Lawson Andrew. *Women of Distinction: Remarkable in Works and Invincible in Character* (1893).

KRISTAL BRENT ZOOK

Cotter, Joseph Seamon, Sr. (2 Feb. 1861–14 Mar. 1949), author, teacher, and civic leader, was born in Bardstown, Kentucky, the son of Michael (also spelled Micheil) Cotter, a boardinghouse owner who was known as an avid reader, and Martha Vaughn. Cotter was raised largely by his mother, a freeborn woman of mixed English, Cherokee, and African heritage. It was from her naturally dramatic manner—she orally composed poems and plays as she worked at chores—that he acquired his love of language and stories. Having taught herself, she also taught her son to read and enrolled him in school. When he was eight, however, economic necessity forced him to drop out of school to begin work at various jobs, first in a brickyard, then in a distillery, and finally as a ragpicker and a teamster. Until age twenty-two, manual labor consumed much of Cotter's life.

The friendship of the prominent black Louisville educator William T. Peyton, who sensed Cotter's natural intelligence, inspired Cotter's enrollment in night school in 1883. His talent and discipline are indicated by the fact that after less than a year of studies he was teaching. He began his career as an educator in Cloverport, Kentucky, staying there until 1887. He then conducted a private school for two years. After teaching at the Western Colored School in Louisville, Kentucky, from 1889 to 1893, Cotter founded and served as principal of the Paul Laurence Dunbar School in Louisville. He remained there until 1911—during his most fruitful years as a poet—and then became principal of the Samuel Coleridge-Taylor School, where he remained until his retirement in 1942.

Cotter would be remembered in Louisville primarily as an educator, but his life held much more, both privately and professionally. In 1891 he married Maria Cox of Louisville. Despite the demands of his teaching and administrative duties, he began to work more diligently at the poetry that would be the source of his national reputation. His first published work, *A Rhyming* (1895), showed the strong influence of early English lyrics, including the ballad and the sonnet, but by the time this volume saw print, Cotter was moving in a different direction. On Thanksgiving Day 1894, having already acquired a burgeoning reputation as a local poet, Cotter hosted his fellow poet PAUL LAURENCE DUNBAR on his first visit to the South and discovered not only an enduring friendship but also a new style that would both distinguish him individually and link him to a larger tradition. Excited by Dunbar's incorporation of African American dialect into poetry, Cotter, sensing the appropriateness of this language to the oral storytelling tradition into which he had been born, often followed the same practice in his own career, beginning with his second collection, *Links of Friendship* (1898). He also adopted Dunbar's practice of writing poems in praise of African American leaders, as in "Frederick Douglass," "Dr. Booker T. Washington to the National Negro Business League," and "The Race Welcomes Dr. W. E. B. DuBois as Its Leader." Cotter never entirely gave up experimenting with more established English forms and language, however. If in his era African American poetry fell into three schools—the dialect poetry of Dunbar, the protest tradition of DuBois, and "literary" work that was couched in European forms and expressed noble sentiments—Cotter ultimately participated in all three.

Cotter experimented with other genres as well. *Caleb, the Degenerate* (1903), his only play, was written in blank verse and was practically unperformable. It attempted to express dramatically many of the views endorsed by Washington in his conservative 1895 Atlanta Exposition speech, which encouraged African Americans to be content with their current lot as laborers and to concentrate on vocational education. Cotter's *Negro Tales* (1912), a mixture of prose genres that constituted his only fiction outside of newspapers, came immediately after his prolific period at the Dunbar School. It was one of only four collections of fiction by African American writers to appear nationally between 1906 and 1922. Then, while moving in new political directions in the second half of his life, Cotter embraced DuBois's call for African American intellectual achievement. Cotter published his *Collected Poems* (1938) and *Sequel to "The Pied Piper of Hamelin," and Other Poems* (1939)—on the whole, his best work—near the end of his teaching career.

Cotter was without family in his last years. His firstborn son, who bore his name, had been a promising poet before his death from tuberculosis at age twenty-three. Cotter's other two children also predeceased him, as did his wife. But he lost himself in his community. Aside from his teaching and writing, he was also active in the NAACP, the Kentucky Negro Educational Association, the Story-Tellers League, and the Authors League of America, and he served as director of the Louisville Colored Orphans Home Society. He helped organize African American neighborhoods in Louisville, and his initiation of storytelling contests for local children grew into a national movement and earned him a place in *Who's Who in America* in 1919, during an era when African Americans were rare in those ranks. The teacher-poet was remembered in Louisville as a humanitarian who devoted himself to the younger generation, as when in writing a community creed he advised his fellow citizens: "Let us lose ourselves in the welfare of our children." Even more characteristically, in "The Negro Child and the Story Book" (*Collected Poems*) he praised the power of the imagination in the lives of the young.

Cotter died at his home in Louisville, a pillar of his community and a minor but essential figure in his field. Although the aesthetic quality of his work is inconsistent, he combined wide-ranging formal and stylistic approaches with a thematic concern for both the universal human condition and the particular needs of his race. During the seemingly fallow period between the turn-of-the-century eclipse of figures such as Dunbar and CHARLES CHESNUTT and the beginnings of the Harlem Renaissance, he held the small but already significant ground that had been gained in the field of African American letters.

FURTHER READING
Cotter's papers are in the Western Branch of the Louisville Free Public Library.
Cotter, Joseph S. *Negroes and Others at Work and Play* (1947).
Cotter, Joseph S. *A White Song and a Black One* (1909).
Shockley, Ann Allen. "Joseph S. Cotter, Sr.: Biographical Sketch of a Black Louisville Bard," *College Language Association Journal* 18 (Mar. 1975).
This entry is taken from the *American National Biography* and is published here with the permission of the American Council of Learned Societies.

W. FARRELL O'GORMAN

Cotten, Elizabeth (c. 5 Jan. 1893–29 June 1987), folksinger, was born near Chapel Hill, North Carolina, the daughter of George Nevills, a day laborer and part-time farmer, and Louise (maiden name unknown), a domestic worker. Her parents' blue-collar jobs were tied to the largely agrarian economy that supported the black community in Orange County. One of five children, "Libba" Cotten's formal education did not extend beyond elementary school. She was attracted to music as a child, and began to play her older brother Claude's banjo and guitar shortly after the turn of the century, teaching herself to tune and play both instruments left-handed (upside down). She was exposed to a wide variety of music during a fruitful and creative period for southern music. Blues was just beginning to emerge, and the ballads that developed in the United States, country dance tunes, minstrel show songs, and sacred songs were all commonly heard. Around this time Cotten wrote two songs—"Freight Train" and "I'm Going Away"—for which she later became famous.

She remained involved with music making for her family and neighbors until 1906, when she joined the Baptist church. A year later she married a local man, Frank Cotten; they had one child. Just shy of her fifteenth birthday Elizabeth Cotten put down her instruments and settled into a conventional domestic life of housework and child rearing.

Cotten and her family made Chapel Hill their home until 1940, when they journeyed northward, settling in Washington, D.C., the mecca for so many black Americans from central North Carolina. After working in a series of short-term domestic jobs Cotten providentially met Ruth Crawford Seeger, who invited her to become her family's housekeeper. Seeger's family included her husband, the famed music ethnologist Charles Seeger, and their children, Peter, Mike, and Peggy. For over forty years Cotten had not played music at all, but in the company of the Seeger family her talents were eventually uncovered.

For many years Cotten occasionally played a guitar around the Seeger household, usually for her own amusement but sometimes for visitors. Two of the children, Peggy and Mike, became involved with learning and playing different styles of folk music. By the mid-1950s, at the dawn of the "folk revival," they began to build professional music careers and sometimes included songs—most notably "Freight Train"—as part of their repertoire. During a 1957 tour of England, Peggy regularly played "Freight Train," and the song quickly circulated among local singers. Startled to hear her music performed outside her immediate circle of friends and encouraged by the burgeoning market for folk musicians, Cotten launched her own professional music career when she was in her mid-sixties. In 1958 Mike Seeger recorded her on an album called *Folksongs and Instrumentals with Guitar* for Folkways Records.

By 1960 Cotten had established herself as a regular performer at folk festivals throughout the United States and Canada and was identified with "Freight Train." During this period Cotten recorded *Negro Folk Songs and Tunes* for Folkways and *Freight Train and Other North Carolina Folk Songs and Tunes* for Smithsonian/Folkways. She often appeared at the early folk festivals at UCLA and the University of Chicago and at clubs such as the Gas Light Coffee House and Gerdes Folk City in New York City.

Cotten continued performing into the early 1980s as one of the few black women on the folk music circuit. She received a Heritage Fellowship from the National Endowment for the Arts in 1984. In 1985 she recorded *Elizabeth Cotten Alive* (Arhoolie), which won a Grammy Award for best traditional folk album. Washington, D.C., remained her home until she moved to Syracuse, New York, in the early 1980s to be closer to relatives. Cotten remained in upstate New York until her death in Syracuse.

FURTHER READING

Coy, Carol. "Elizabeth Cotten," *Folk Scene*, Apr. 1974: 14–17.

Harrison, Sheldon. *Blues Who's Who* (1979).

This entry is taken from the *American National Biography* and is published here with the permission of the American Council of Learned Societies.

KIP LORNELL

Cotton, Dorothy Foreman (9 June 1930–), civil rights activist, educator, and motivational speaker, was born Dorothy Lee Foreman, one of four girls of Maggie Pelham and Claude Foreman, a laborer, in Goldsboro, North Carolina. After graduating from Dillard High School in Goldsboro, she was encouraged by one of her high school English teachers to enroll at Shaw University in Raleigh, North Carolina, where she began her undergraduate education. Along with several other jobs she took to enable her education at Shaw, Dorothy worked as the housekeeper for the president of the institution, Robert Prentiss Daniel, and his wife, Blanche Daniel. Because the couple had no children and because of Cotton's efficiency as a worker, in 1950 when Robert Daniel became president of

Virginia State College in Petersburg, Cotton, who had become part housekeeper and part daughter, accompanied the couple and completed her education at Virginia State.

Cotton earned an AB degree in 1954 from Virginia State with a major in English and a minor in Library Science. In 1955 she married George Junius Cotton, a native of Petersburg, and soon thereafter she began graduate work at Boston University. She chose Boston as the location for study in part because of her childhood fascination with a radio soap opera that featured Boston's Beacon Hill. Working during the summer months, Cotton earned a master's degree in Special Education in August 1960. That same month she left Petersburg for Atlanta, Georgia, to work with MARTIN LUTHER KING JR. and the Southern Christian Leadership Conference (SCLC) as director of education. Although the move to Atlanta was intended to be temporary, Cotton became committed to the civil rights movement and did not return to Petersburg. As a consequence her marriage to George Cotton dissolved. There were no children, and the couple divorced in 1978.

Cotton's work in Petersburg at Gillfield Baptist Church, pastored then by WYATT TEE WALKER, had prepared her for the position at SCLC. An active member of the Gillfield congregation, Cotton was also secretary of the local chapter of the National Association for the Advancement of Colored People, of which Walker was president. She also participated in the Petersburg movement, formed to desegregate the local library that expanded to desegregate other public accommodations. In late 1959 King spoke in Petersburg and subsequently invited Walker to come to Atlanta to help with the organization of SCLC. On the condition that two of his colleagues in the local movement, Jim Woods and Cotton, accompany him, Walker accepted King's offer and moved to Atlanta. It was at this point that Cotton's full involvement in the civil rights struggle began.

Cotton's job as director of education included organizing and conducting workshops in nonviolence and directing the Citizenship Education Program (CEP). The training in nonviolence was in its earliest stages, however, and was primarily focused on preparing demonstrators to withstand verbal and physical abuse during marches and sit-ins without retaliating. Supported by a grant from the United Church of Christ, the CEP included training for voter education, literacy, and voter registration but with the overarching goal of developing local leadership and promoting social change through nonviolence and self-empowerment. With Cotton as director and ANDREW JACKSON YOUNG JR. as administrator, the CEP set up citizenship schools in eleven southern states. Through the hard work of workshop participants like FANNIE LOU HAMER and staff members like SEPTIMA P. CLARK, citizenship schools enabled the registration of hundreds of thousands of voters who ushered in the New South.

Following her work with SCLC, Cotton in the 1970s served as vice president for field operations for the Martin Luther King Jr. Center for Nonviolent Social Change. From 1978 to 1981 she was southeastern regional director for ACTION, which administers volunteer programs for the U.S. government, and from 1982 to 1991 she was director of student activities at Cornell University. She then became a motivational speaker and trainer, conducting workshops on a number of issues, including nonviolence, multiculturalism, diversity, and personal and spiritual growth, and writing a book describing the CEP. She received honorary doctorates from the University of New Rochelle, Spelman College in Atlanta, and the University of New England.

FURTHER READING

Branch, Taylor. At Canaan's Edge: America in the King Years, 1965–1968 (2006).

Garrow, David J. Bearing the Cross: Martin Luther King, Jr., and the Southern Christian Leadership Conference (1986).

Ling, Peter J. "Gender and Generation: Manhood at the Southern Christian Leadership Conference," Gender and the Civil Rights Movement, ed. Peter J. Ling and Sharon Montieth (2004).

Young, Andrew. An Easy Burden: The Civil Rights Movement and the Transformation of America (1996).

ALMA JEAN BILLINGSLEA BROWN

Council, Mildred "Mama Dip" (10 April 1929–), businesswoman, chef, restaurateur, and community activist, was born Mildred Edna Cotten in Baldwin Township, Chatham County, North Carolina. The youngest daughter in a family of seven children, she was raised by her father Ed Cotten, a farmer and voice teacher. Council's mother Effie Edwards Cotten, a teacher trained at Bennett College in Greensboro, North Carolina, died at age thirty-four when her daughter was twenty-three months old. Mildred Council was nicknamed "Dip" by her brothers and sisters because her long arms allowed her to reach deep into the rain barrel and retrieve a dipper full of water, even when the barrel was low.

Council recalled as a significant moment the day in 1938 when her father asked her to stay home and "fix a little something to eat" while the rest of the family worked in the fields (*Mama Dip's Kitchen*, 2).

From a young age Council loved to cook, which she learned by watching Roland Norwood, a family friend, and her older sisters who were adept at "dump cooking," a method requiring neither recipes nor measurements. Instructions were passed orally, from cook to cook, just as other American folk traditions were transmitted from generation to generation. Dump cooking used local ingredients—either farm or homegrown—that were well seasoned, simply prepared, and eaten fresh. The cook improvised with available ingredients, rather than following a recipe. This culinary improvisation was similar to the creative impulse in African American quilts and musical forms such as jazz and the blues.

Mildred Council's childhood in the 1930s and 1940s was grounded in Chatham County and its world of close family ties, church, school, and farm chores. Council's vivid memories of these worlds are captured in the introductions of her two publications, *Mama Dip's Kitchen* (1999) and *Mama Dip's Family Cookbook* (2005). Council lived in a self-sufficient African American community, where family and neighbors planted gardens and fields, made hominy and molasses, and built their own furniture, homes, and outbuildings. Between their many chores, the Cotten children invented their own games and entertainment as they explored the nearby woods, meadows, and fishing holes.

Despite the challenges of life in the Depression-era Jim Crow South, Ed Cotten protected his family from poverty and the sting of racial prejudice. Not comfortable accepting charity or exposing his children to ridicule, he accepted government-issued canned meat and yellow corn meal only once. After all, the Cottens knew they could make do with tastier homegrown meat and cornmeal, even in the toughest of times. Cotten instilled strong values in his children, beginning each day with a prayer to express thanks for their blessings. Mildred Council fondly remembered homecoming feasts at the Hamlet Chapel Methodist Episcopal Christian Church, where "dinner on the ground" was served on outdoor tables covered with fried chicken, vegetables, and pies and cakes as far as the eye could see.

The Cotten children began their education in the one-room Baldwin School, where a single teacher taught all grades. Later they attended high school in Pittsboro, and in 1945 the family moved to Chapel Hill when Ed Cotten purchased a home there. Mildred Council reluctantly attended beauty school, one of the few employment opportunities other than domestic work for young black women. Although she worked briefly in the business, Council's true passion lay in cooking.

In 1945 Mildred met Joe Council, who had recently been released from the army. The couple married in 1947, and they had eight children between 1949 and 1957. Mildred Council's professional life as a cook and businesswoman began soon after marriage. She worked in the University of North Carolina dining hall, at the Carolina Coffee Shop, as a cook in fraternity houses and private homes, and in her in-laws' restaurant in Chapel Hill. These jobs provided valuable experience for Council's later ventures. Like many working black women, Mildred Council was the main breadwinner for her family. She worked a double-day as she cooked, cleaned, ironed, and washed clothes for students, "did hair" for neighbors, and cared for her own family in the evening. Joe Council worked part-time in his parents' restaurant, Bill's Bar-B-Q, and was also employed at a local lumber mill. Their marriage ended in divorce in the mid-1970s.

In 1976 George Tate, the first black realtor in Chapel Hill, encouraged Mildred Council to take over a failing restaurant on Rosemary Street. Council agreed, and with only $64 in hand, she purchased groceries to prepare breakfast for opening day. Her customers ate everything, and with the money from that first successful meal, Council returned to the grocery to buy supplies for lunch, and after lunch once more to buy supplies for dinner. With her first day's profit of $135, Dip's Country Kitchen was launched. Over the years Mildred Council expanded her business through catering and specialty food production. In 1998 Council purchased land to build her own restaurant, "Mama Dip's Kitchen," which opened in 1999. Her children, grandchildren, and great-grandchildren all worked in the restaurant.

Mildred Council's discovery by media and culinary writers began with an enthusiastic review of her restaurant in 1985 by Craig Claiborne in the *New York Times*. Council went on to frequent appearances on the Food Network, a cable television division dedicated to food programming, and was also a popular guest on the home-shopping television network, QVC. When Mildred Council appeared on QVC in the 1990s, *Mama Dip's Kitchen*, her first cookbook, sold out after only minutes on the air. In 2000 North Carolina governor Jim Hunt presented Council with the Order of the Longleaf Pine, the highest honor given to citizens of the state. In 2002 Council won the North Carolina Small Business Award, followed by Chapel Hill's naming 16 May "Mama Dip Cotten Council Day."

Mama Dip's remained a culinary landmark in Chapel Hill. Both locals and visitors enjoyed fried chicken, catfish, "chitlins," eastern North Carolina–style barbecue, beef stew, gumbo, and pork chops. Vegetables of all kinds were served plate-style and in casseroles, along with hot biscuits, yeast rolls, cornbread, and a wide selection of cakes, cobblers, puddings, and pies. Council's food bridged differences of race, class, and ethnicity among her customers. Her restaurant attracted an eclectic mix of customers that included university students, sports coaches, professors, businessmen and women, and laborers. Mildred Council's goal was to "Put a Taste of the South in Your Mouth," a slogan she used for over three decades. She was also known for her long record of volunteer work and community service. Reared in a loving family during difficult times in the South, Mildred Council's life as an exemplary mother, wife, philanthropist, entrepreneur, and symbol of Southern and African American foodways was without parallel.

FURTHER READING

Mildred Council's papers and an oral history interview conducted by UNC's Southern Oral History Program are housed in the Southern Historical Collection, Wilson Library, University of North Carolina at Chapel Hill.

Council, Mildred. *Mama Dip's Kitchen* (1999).

Council, Mildred. *Mama Dip's Family Cookbook* (2005).

Council, Annette M. *The Recipe: Have a Seat at Our Table* (2006).

Harris, Jessica. *The Welcome Table: African-American Heritage Cooking* (1995).

MARCIE COHEN FERRIS

Councill, William Hooper (12 July 1848–17 Apr. 1909), educator, was born in Fayetteville, North Carolina, the son of William Councill and Mary Jane (maiden name unknown), slaves. In 1854 Councill's father escaped to freedom in Canada, leaving his wife and children to be dispersed in the South by slave traders. In 1863 young William, his mother, and his youngest brother escaped from a plantation in northern Alabama to a U.S. Army camp in Chattanooga, Tennessee. Councill attended a freedmen's school in Stevenson, Alabama, from 1865 to 1867 and later was tutored at night in Latin, physics, chemistry, and mathematics. In 1867 he established a school for freedmen in Jackson County and in 1869 began another in Madison County, laboring under the constant threat of Ku Klux Klan violence.

As a young man, Councill made contacts and received appointments that established him as an emerging black Republican leader in Alabama. He was active in the state's African Methodist Episcopal Church, the Prince Hall Masons, and the Independent Order of Immaculates and the Pallbearers. Councill also organized branches of the National Labor Union, served as secretary of the 1873 National Equal Rights convention, and attended the 1874 Chattanooga Convention of Republicans. Ambitious for political office, he served as chief enrolling clerk of the Alabama legislature from 1872 to 1874 and narrowly lost his bid for a seat in the legislature in 1874. That same year Councill abandoned the Republican Party, an action that alienated him from most Alabama blacks and even provoked death threats. Councill nevertheless believed that blacks should work with Democrats rather than simply distrusting them. "The republican party will grow tired of you," he warned, "and like the bat who was disowned by the beasts and not recognized by the birds, you will find favor with neither democrats or republicans" (Sherer, 34). To woo him back into the Republican ranks, President Ulysses S. Grant appointed Councill receiver general of the Land Office of the Northern District of Alabama in 1875. Councill refused the post.

Councill's star ascended as a Democrat. In 1875 he became the first principal of the State Normal and Industrial School in Huntsville, Alabama, a school that preceded and rivaled BOOKER T. WASHINGTON's Tuskegee Institute, which was founded six years later. From 1877 to 1884 Councill also published the *Huntsville Herald* in an effort to espouse his political opinions. In 1879 he attended the National Conference of Colored Men in Nashville. During these years he read law, and he was admitted to the Alabama bar in 1883, although he never actually practiced. More accommodating to whites than Washington, Councill thrived until April 1885, when he was accused of raping a twelve-year-old student and then assaulting her uncle. Although he was later acquitted, Huntsville blacks, already dissatisfied with Councill's accommodationism, called for his expulsion. He retained his position, but as a result of the controversy, northern philanthropists shifted their support from Huntsville to Tuskegee.

In 1887 Councill became involved in two other crises that ultimately forced him to resign. In the first he filed a suit before the Interstate Commerce Commission (ICC) against the Atlantic Railroad Company for excluding him from a first-class coach on a trip between Tennessee and Georgia. While the ICC sided with Councill, ordering separate if equal treatment on railroads, this ruling went unenforced. The second case resulted when several of Councill's students attempted to sit in the first-class coach on a trip between Huntsville and Decatur. Whites accused Councill "of forcing social equality," and he resigned under pressure from Huntsville Normal, only to be reappointed principal in 1888.

These incidents convinced Councill of the importance of placating whites. Afterward he espoused accommodationist views openly, without Washington's long-term political agendas. Whereas Washington looked to northern philanthropists for support, Councill sought the largesse of white southerners. He believed that once blacks "proved" themselves, whites would treat them fairly. "Councill's error," according to the historian Robert G. Sherer, "was betting on the wrong horse, not gambling" (41). Still, for a time Councill's strategy worked.

Huntsville Normal, not Tuskegee, first received funds from the 1890 Morrill Act, and in 1891 the school relocated to Normal, north of Huntsville, and was renamed Alabama State Agricultural and Mechanical College for Negroes. (In 1948 it became Alabama Agricultural and Mechanical College.) Gradually after 1895, however, Washington outmaneuvered Councill for state funds, and in 1896 Tuskegee acquired Alabama's state agricultural experiment station for blacks. By 1900 Washington, who reaped large donations for Tuskegee from northerners, distanced himself from Councill because of his "reputation of simply toadying to the Southern white people" (Meier, 110).

White supremacists, however, applauded Councill as a "good" Negro. In 1900 John Temple Graves described him as "the wisest, the most thoughtful and the most eloquent Negro of his time—as discreet as [Booker T.] Washington, a deeper thinker and a much more eloquent man. But for one hour of the Atlanta Exposition, Councill would stand to-day where Washington stands—as the recognized leader of his race" (Southern Society, 50). In 1905 William Benjamin Smith likewise praised Councill as "that most able and eloquent Negroid," one who admitted that whites never would grant blacks equal economic, political, social, and civil rights (xiii).

Vacillating between the promotion of industrial training and literary education as well as between accommodationism and militancy, Councill never became a race leader of Washington's stature. Nevertheless, he published *The Negro Laborer: A Word to Him* (1887), *Lamp of Wisdom; or, Race History Illuminated* (1898), *Negro Development in the South* (1901), *Bright Side of the Southern Question* (1903), and *The Young Negro of 1864; the Young Negro of 1904: The Problem Then; the Problem Now* (1904) as well as many articles concerning questions of race.

Councill's accommodationism and "unctuous sycophancy" (Meier, 77) toward whites concealed his anger at the circumscribed world of late nineteenth-century blacks. As early as 1893 he expressed bitterness at the limited avenues for racial progress, encouraging blacks to emigrate to Africa. Four years later he attacked lynching and longed for the return of racial harmony that allegedly existed under slavery. In 1899 Councill blamed the new generation of whites for inhibiting black progress. Evaluating Councill out of context, historians have often overvalued his opportunism and undervalued both his realism and his ideological and financial commitment to his school and blacks in general. In 1901, for example, Councill explained "that the salvation of the negro in this country depends upon drawing the social lines tighter, ... North and South. The moment they become slack the white man becomes brutal—the negro goes down forever" (Hackney, 185). Nonetheless, Councill, who died in Normal, is remembered for his pragmatic accommodationism, one that encouraged blacks to trust and cooperate with whites, a strategy that ultimately guaranteed their second-class citizenship.

FURTHER READING

Some of Councill's letters are in the Governor's Office Records at the Alabama Department of Archives and History and in the Booker T. Washington Papers at the Library of Congress.

Bond, Horace Mann. *Negro Education in Alabama: A Study in Cotton and Steel* (1939).

Hackney, Sheldon. *Populism to Progressivism in Alabama* (1969).

Meier, August. *Negro Thought in America, 1880–1915: Racial Ideologies in the Age of Booker T. Washington* (1963).

Sherer, Robert G. *Subordination or Liberation? The Development and Conflicting Theories of Black Education in Nineteenth Century Alabama* (1977).

Smith, William Benjamin. *The Color Line* (1905).

Southern Society for the Promotion of the Study of Race Conditions and Problems in the South. *Race Problems of the South* (1900).

Thorpe, Earl Endris. "William Hooper Councill," *Negro History Bulletin* 19 (1956): 85–86, 89.

This entry is taken from the *American National Biography* and is published here with the permission of the American Council of Learned Societies.

JOHN DAVID SMITH

Cousins, Laura Cheatham (14 June 1927–), mathematician, computer programmer, and consultant, was born Laura Cheatham on the west side of Philadelphia, Pennsylvania, the youngest of three daughters of Gertrude Richey and James Hammond Cheatham. Gertrude was born in Williamston, South Carolina, in 1888 to Mary Roberts and Mak Richey, who sent her to the Atlanta Baptist Female Seminary (now Spelman College) in Atlanta, Georgia, from grade school through normal school. After receiving her teaching certificate, Gertrude took a job in Anderson, South Carolina, where she married James Hammond Cheatham, son of a wealthy white plantation owner, James Hammond Freeman, and a Cherokee woman named Emma Lenier. Previously married to a man of mixed race named Cheatham, Lenier had a long-established liaison with James Hammond Freeman, with whom she had five children. James Hammond Cheatham, unable to take his biological father's name because of concubinage laws, was apparently taught to read and write by his father and also owned property apparently given to him by his father. Shortly after marrying, the Cheathams moved to Philadelphia in about 1920 to educate their children, settling in the prosperous black community in West Philadelphia.

Laura, who was born in a nearby Women's Hospital, described her black neighbors as upwardly mobile, even during the Depression. There was a physician and a dentist, both with practices in their homes, and two pharmacists with their own stores. Although her neighborhood was primarily African American, the first school she attended, Baris Elementary School, had a student body that was evenly divided between whites and blacks. Laura recalled that all the schools were probably racially integrated, but the teachers were almost all white, with the exception of those in North Philadelphia, the only location where a black teacher could be hired. A curious and persistent child, Laura could read and had her own library card at age four. She learned to play piano as a young girl but soon switched to double bass because she wanted to join the All-Philadelphia Youth Orchestra, where she ended up playing throughout her junior high and high school years. In 1944 she graduated from Overbrook High School, third in a class of three hundred, and received a full academic scholarship to Temple University, where she would major in math and minor in physics.

Her father died in 1947 at the end of her junior year at Temple, and she subsequently withdrew from school. She went to New York, where she worked for a while and then married William (Bill) Cousins, a fellow Philadelphian and former Tuskegee Airman. Cousins and her husband moved back to Philadelphia, where she enrolled in night school at Temple to complete her B.S. in Mathematics. By 1951 the couple had produced two children, Philip and Leslie Cousins. Intent on a scientific career, Cousins began applying for positions with computer companies. In 1955 her first interview with IBM went well until she revealed she was married; she was told that the company did not hire married women. Another interview, with UNIVAC, proved successful, and she worked under the direction of Grace Murray Hopper. She joined a group of programmers, mostly mathematicians, who developed a computer program that could translate a whole set of programmer's instructions into binary language. Cousins worked on the FLOW-MATIC B-0, an important compiler and predecessor of COBOL (Common Business Oriented Language).

In addition, she and other manufacturers and users served on the American Standards Committee of the international Codasyl Committee to assure that COBOL would be a universal computer language. Cousins was one of a few African Americans—and possibly the only African American woman—to work on the UNIVAC 1 (specifically the UNIVAC Serial #3), the first general-purpose electronic stored-program computer built in the United States. Roughly five to seven years into her job with the team, Hopper unexpectedly announced that it was time to hire a "Negro," to which Laura ultimately replied, "You already have one in me." Her colleagues had assumed she was white. Although Cousins had no intention of "passing for white," she also did not announce her racial identity, especially in light of being turned down by IBM because she was married. Cousins left UNIVAC after ten years. She taught COBOL for many years, built specified software, and worked as a consultant to the U.S. Navy Department, Unisys, Sigma, many cities and principalities, and as a private consultant to smaller companies.

CAMILLE HAZEUR

Couvent, Marie Bernard (c. 1757–29 June 1837), philanthropist and founding benefactor of the oldest continuously operating black Catholic school in the United States, was born Justine Fervin in Guinea, West Africa. In early childhood she was brought to San Domingue and enslaved. Little is known about her youth or at what stage in her life she began calling herself Marie. What is known is that she received no formal education and was brought to New Orleans as a slave before securing her freedom. By the 1820s she was living as a free woman in the Faubourg Marigny district of the city, the wife of a carpenter, a free black man named Gabriel Bernard Couvent.

A devout Catholic, Couvent and her husband regularly attended Mass at St. Louis Cathedral. There she established a relationship with Constantine Manehault, a priest who was to become her lifelong friend and religious director.

With no children to support, the Couvents lived comfortably and amassed substantial savings. They owned several properties around the city as well as a small number of slaves. Yet despite their prosperity—and though protected by Louisiana's comparatively progressive legal and economic codes—they could not overcome their social status as free people of color, which in the eyes of many of their white neighbors rendered them little better than slaves.

When Gabriel died on 22 May 1829 at the age of seventy-one, Marie seized the opportunity to use his wealth to improve the situation of free blacks in Louisiana. Gabriel had left the entirety of his considerable estate to Marie who, on the advice of Father Manehault, began to entertain thoughts of establishing a Catholic school for poor free-born orphans of color. In 1832 she dictated her will to reflect this ambition, leaving the majority of her real estate holdings to serve as school buildings: "I bequeath and order that my land at the corner of Grand Hommes (Dauphine) and Union (Touro) Streets be dedicated and used in perpetuity for the establishment of a free school for orphans of color of the Faubourg Marigny. This said school is to be operated under the direction of Reverend Father

Manehault … or under the supervision of his successors in office" (Hine, 288).

Establishing a school for indigent people of color was a pioneering feat in antebellum Louisiana. The state's public schools did not admit black students, and before Reconstruction only a handful were educated in private schools or by private tutors. Even the wealthiest black families had to send their children to New England or Europe in search of a formal education.

What little is known of her intentions suggests that Couvent saw the school as a tool to uplift people of color. Certainly her own lack of formal education—she remained illiterate throughout her life—marks a powerful contrast to the skills and knowledge her school was founded to impart.

Couvent died in New Orleans at the age of eighty. Henry Fletcher, a free man of color, was named executor of her will. However, over the next few years he appeared uninterested in fulfilling those duties. Nothing was done to further Couvent's wish to establish the school. After more than a decade of delays Father Manehault decided the project could wait no longer and finally solicited the help of François Lacroix, a prominent citizen of New Orleans, to put pressure on Fletcher and restore momentum to plans for the school. Lacroix assembled notable free men of color such as Emilien Brule, Adolphe Duhart, Nelson Fouche, and Barthelemy Rey, who in 1848 formed a lobbying group known as the Society for the Instruction of Indigent Orphans. The Society soon succeeded in bringing Fletcher to court to explain the delays. Manehault, Lacroix, and the members of the Society insisted that Fletcher account for the several small houses Couvent had specified in her will as the site for the school and eventually succeeded in forcing the executor to turn over these properties to them. With these buildings finally in their possession, things finally began to move quickly. Within months, the École des Orphelins de Couleur was opened at the corner of Union and Grand Hommes streets, in New Orleans's Third District.

While most accounts blame Fletcher for the prolonged stagnation of Couvent's plan, others have noted the prejudice of the city administration, a prejudice Fletcher may have been intimidated by. Even the oversight of Father Manehault, a respected leader in the Catholic church, was not enough to overcome local officials' reservations about establishing a school for free people of color within the city's limits. Indeed, in the eleven years between

Couvent's death and the opening of her school in 1848, the city had continued to restrict access to education for people of color even as it expanded educational opportunities for its white residents. In 1841 New Orleans had established its free public school system, yet systematically excluded people of color from it.

The Couvent School's opening, then, marked the end of a long period of conflict and opposition and the school's first governors had to fight hard to maintain it in its first years. As Couvent's will had dictated, the orphanage was placed under the supervision of Father Manehault, who quickly set about soliciting bequests to enlarge the original financial endowment. Uniquely, its initial endowment grew largely from the donation of free black benefactors such as Arisitide Mary who left five thousand dollars to the school in his will. It was only as its reputation grew that the school began to receive grudging financial support from the city and state, including an 1854 state appropriation of two thousand dollars.

In step with the school's growing financial security the number of students attending Couvent grew steadily throughout the antebellum period. It expanded its student population, accepting orphans and non-orphans alike and extended its catchment area beyond the Third District. While wealthier families were encouraged to make a donation, the school was free of charge for most of its students. Yet despite rarely charging tuition, the school quickly gained a reputation for the quality of its instruction. Classes were taught in both French and English, and additional courses were offered in Spanish language and literature. Its first teacher was Félicie Cailloux, who was soon joined by four or five other full-time instructors, all persons of color drawn from prominent families. In 1852 ARMAND LANUSSE, the first African American to compile an anthology of poetry, became its principal. In time its alumni could boast a number of distinguished civic leaders such as ERNEST N. MORIAL, the first African American mayor of New Orleans.

The outcome of the Civil War eroded some of the school's purpose. During Reconstruction the New Orleans school system began to accept black students and so attendance at the Couvent School began to decline and then dwindle. By 1884 things had fallen so far that the school was in serious danger of closing, only saved from ruin through the efforts of a group of civic leaders who stabilized its finances and helped it to adapt to the new postwar realities.

The Couvent School operated as the Holy Redeemer School and was the oldest continuing black Catholic school in the country until it at last closed in 1994. Its founder, Marie Bernard Couvent, lies buried in the nearby St. Louis Cemetery.

FURTHER READING

Desdunes, Rodolphe Lucien. *Our People and Our History: Fifty Creole Portraits* (2001).

Hine, Darlene Clark, ed. *Black Women in America: An Historical Encyclopedia* (1993).

Logan, Rayford W., and Michael R. Winston, eds. *Dictionary of American Negro Biography* (1982).

RICHARD J. BELL

Cowans, Adger W. (19 Sept. 1936–), photographer, was born in Columbus, Ohio. Details about Cowans's upbringing and early education are difficult to come by. He attended local schools and around 1954 matriculated to Ohio University, where he undertook a study of photography. There he fell under the influence and tutelage of the great Clarence White Jr., one of the founders (along with Alfred Stieglitz and others) of the Photo-Secession movement, which helped to solidify photography as a legitimate art form. He earned a bachelor of fine arts degree in Photography in 1958 and subsequently enlisted in the U.S. Navy, which he served as a photographer until his discharge in 1960.

Upon leaving military service, Cowans removed to New York, intent on pursuing a career in photography. There he landed a job at *Life* magazine, at the time perhaps the most famous and widely distributed photo magazine in the United States. With *Life*, Cowans served as assistant to GORDON PARKS SR., whose twenty-year tenure with the magazine made him one of the legends of American photography. Cowans also met and worked with Henry Clarke, whose fashion photography with *Vogue* Cowan both admired and was influenced by. Cowan continued to learn his craft. During the early sixties, he trained his lens on the doings of the burgeoning civil rights movement. His reputation grew, and increasingly he came to attention of prize committees and critics alike. In 1962 he won a grant from the John Hay Whitney Foundation, which sought to support artists and creators from culturally and ethnically diverse backgrounds who might not otherwise be able to pursue their work. The grant—and the growing attention to his photographs—allowed Cowans to do just that. By 1963 he was able to quit magazine work and go freelance.

The year 1965 saw Cowans's first solo exhibit. For some time he had been part of a Boston-based photography collective called the Heliographers, and it was through them that he mounted his first show in New York. It was the first of many such exhibits, both in New York and elsewhere in the United States and abroad. A year later his photographs appeared in Dakar, Senegal, at the First World Festival of Negro Arts, where he was one of only sixteen African Americans represented. In 1968 he was part of a group show at the New York Met.

Some of Cowans's most popular and widely viewed photographs, however, came from his work in the motion picture and film industry. Around 1965 Cowan began to work as a still photographer on the set of feature films. Those stills were subsequently used either in publicity for the film or appeared alongside reviews or feature stories in newspapers and magazines. Cowans's extensive work in the field is too lengthy to do justice to here, but among the films that he has shot are *Panic in Needle Park* (1971), *Eyes of Laura Mars* (1978), *On Golden Pond* (1981), *The Cotton Club* (1984), *Dirty Dancing* (1987), *The Ice Storm* (1997), and many, many others. Though they may not realize it, anyone who has looked at the "Movies" section of the *New York Times* or other similar magazine or newspaper film section has almost certainly seen some of Cowans's work. His photographs have likewise appeared in numerous journals and magazines, including *Time*, *Look*, *Essence*, and *Harper's*, to name but a few. Cowans also occasionally did turns as a guest lecturer at various colleges and universities, among them the University of Michigan and the Université des Antilles et de la Guyane. His photos reside in the collections of the NAACP, Schomburg Center, and Howard University, again among many, many others. In the twenty-first century Cowans continued to work in film and as a freelance artist, living in New York City.

FURTHER READING

Deborah, Willis. *Reflections in Black: A History of Black Photographers 1840 to the Present* (2000).

Krantz, Les, ed. *American Photographers* (1989).

JASON PHILIP MILLER

Cox, Elbert Frank (5 Dec. 1895–28 Nov. 1969), mathematician, was born in Evansville, Indiana, the son of Johnson D. Cox, a high school principal, and Eugenia D. Talbot. From an early age Elbert demonstrated tremendous talent as a violinist and was offered a scholarship to study in Europe at the Prague Conservatory of Music. Instead he opted for a career in mathematics, and he received an AB from Indiana University in 1917. Cox became assistant principal and mathematics teacher at Alves Street School in Henderson, Kentucky, but resigned the next year to enlist in the U.S. Army. He spent the last six months of World War I in France as a clerk and was discharged in 1919 with the rank of sergeant.

That same year, Cox was appointed chairman of the department of natural sciences at Shaw University in Raleigh, North Carolina. He left Shaw to enroll at Cornell University, where he was awarded a graduate scholarship in mathematics in 1922 and an Erastus Brooks Fellowship two years later. Cox spent the fall semester of 1924 as a traveling fellow at Canada's McGill University in order to work with William Lloyd Garrison Williams, a former Cornell professor who was Cox's dissertation committee chairman. Cox's doctoral work focused on the polynomial solutions of the difference equation $af(x+1)+bf(x)=F(x)$, where "$F(x)$" represents the Euler function, the number of integers that are not greater than x and that share no common factor with x other than 1. To this end he adopted the symbolic methods of the Danish mathematician Niels Erik Nörlund and of the French mathematician Edouard Lucas concerning Bernoulli numbers, which take the form $B_0+B_1x/1!+B_2x^2/2!+ \ldots$ and are used as coefficients in power series of the form $a_0+a_1x+a_2x^2+ \ldots +a_nx^n+ \ldots$, where a represents a Bernoulli number.

In 1925 Cox's dissertation was accepted by Cornell. As a result of Williams's efforts, it was also accepted by the Imperial University in Sendai, Japan, thus making Cox the first person of African descent in the world to receive a Ph.D. in pure mathematics. This achievement is all the more impressive when one considers that by 1925 fewer than fifty African Americans had received doctorates of any kind. Moreover, prevailing racial attitudes in the United States had forced many of them to go abroad to undertake their graduate studies. Cox's accomplishment helped make it possible for other black mathematicians, such as Dudley Welcon Woodard, William Waldron Shiefflin Claytor, MARJORIE LEE BROWN, EVELYN BOYD GRANVILLE, and DAVID BLACKWELL, to receive their doctorates from American universities. By becoming the second black to receive a doctorate from Cornell (THOMAS WYATT TURNER, who received his Ph.D. in biology in 1921, was the first), Cox also helped to open the door a little wider for black doctoral candidates at that school. By 1943 an additional twenty-three blacks had received doctorates from Cornell, including seven who received their degrees in either mathematics or physics.

In 1925 Cox accepted a position as a professor of physics at West Virginia State College, at the time a poorly funded segregated institution without a science library. In 1928, the year after he married Beulah P. Kaufman, with whom he had three children, Cox taught both physics and mathematics, but he left the next year to become an associate professor of mathematics at Howard University. During World War II he contributed to the American war effort by teaching engineering science and war management at Howard from 1942 to 1944 and by serving as head of a specialized training program for the army from 1943 to 1945. In 1947, the same year that he was promoted to full professor, he assisted in overhauling Howard's grading system. In 1949 he served briefly as chair of the mathematics department, and in 1956 he assumed the chairmanship again. In 1957 the departments of mathematics and physics were merged, and Cox chaired the combined department until 1961. He retired in 1966 with the reputation of having supervised more master's theses than any other member of Howard's faculty.

Throughout his academic career Cox carried a heavy teaching load as well as substantial administrative and advising duties. These factors effectively prevented him from publishing anything more than "The Polynomial Solution of the Difference Equation $af(x+1)+bf(x)=F(x)$" (*Tohoku Mathematical Journal* 39 [1934]: 327–348), a revised version of his dissertation that offered a better understanding of generalized Euler polynomials of both higher and lower order. Cox planned to spend his retirement writing about mathematics, but his health prevented him from doing so. He died in Washington, D.C.

Cox was a member of the American Mathematical Society, the American Physical Society, the American Physics Institute, and Beta Kappa Chi, Pi Mu Epsilon, and Sigma Pi Sigma education fraternities. Though a private person, he possessed an excellent speaking voice and often served as an after-dinner speaker. By becoming the first African American to earn a doctorate in pure mathematics, Cox helped many other black scholars make a career in that discipline. As a teacher and thesis adviser he inspired and helped dozens of promising young black mathematicians achieve success in their chosen field.

FURTHER READING
Bruno, Leonard C. "Elbert Frank Cox," in *Notable Twentieth Century Scientists*, ed. Emily J. McMurray (1995).
Giles-Giron, Jacqueline. "Black Pioneers in Mathematics: Brown, Granville, Cox, Claytor, and Blackwell," *MAA Focus* (Jan.–Feb. 1991): 18 and 21.
Greene, Harry W. *Holders of Doctorates among American Negroes: An Educational and Social Study of Negroes Who Have Earned Doctoral Degrees in Course, 1876–1943* (1947).
Newell, Virginia K., et al., eds. *Black Mathematicians and Their Works* (1980).
Obituary: *Washington Post*, 2 Dec. 1969.
This entry is taken from the *American National Biography* and is published here with the permission of the American Council of Learned Societies.

CHARLES W. CAREY JR.

Cox, Ida (25 Feb. 1896–10 Nov. 1967), blues singer, was born Ida Prather in Toccoa, Stephens County, Georgia, of parents whose names have not been recorded. In Cedartown, Georgia, where she spent her childhood, Prather sang in the African Methodist church choir. At age fourteen she left home to tour with the White and Clark Black & Tan Minstrels, playing "Topsy" roles. She subsequently joined other companies, including the Rabbit Foot Minstrels and Pete Werley's Florida Cotton Blossom Minstrels. She married three times. Her first husband, Adler Cox, whom she married about 1916, was a trumpeter with the Florida Blossoms Minstrel Show; he died in World War I. The date of her second marriage, to Eugene Williams, is unknown; the couple had a daughter. Her third husband was Texan Jesse "Tiny" Crump, a pianist and organist who may be heard performing on some of her recordings and who also shared management responsibilities with her.

By 1922 Cox was solidly established as a star performer. With Crump, she led her own touring tent show throughout the South from 1929 into the 1930s. That revue, *Raisin' Cain*, was chosen to be the first show from the Theatre Owners' Booking Circuit to open at New York's Apollo Theater. Difficult times after the stock market crash forced Cox and Crump to reorganize and seek bookings as far away as the West Coast before bringing the show, under the title *Darktown Scandals*, to the Midwest. Still, Cox never ceased barnstorming through the South in the late 1930s and into the 1940s.

Her performances maintained a high-class tone. They were constructed on a simple formula: three letters in each name (i.e., Cox, Ida), three jokes between songs, and three songs. With regal bearing, dignity, and a beauty that combined glamour and sophistication, she came across as a blues queen in every way. Audiences saw her as "always a lady," even though her often salty lyrics were laced with sexual allusions and sly humor directed at men. The most distinctive aspect of her work was the frequent use of macabre formulas; her work has been characterized as death-focused blues. Though she could be imperious and demanding, she was known as a fair employer and a good manager.

Working the clubs and theaters over the course of a quarter century, mostly in the Southeast, she performed with headliners such as JELLY ROLL MORTON, in Atlanta around 1920; KING OLIVER, in Chicago; and BESSIE SMITH, in the 1934 revue *Fan Waves*. At the invitation of John Hammond, she took part in the 1939 Carnegie Hall concert *From Spirituals to Swing*.

From 1923 to 1929 she recorded extensively for Paramount with the pianist LOVIE AUSTIN ("Any Woman's Blues") but not exclusively, as the company claimed. Under an assortment of aliases—Julia/Julius Powers, Jane Smith, Velma Bradley, Kate Lewis—she also cut sides for Harmograph and Silvertone. Her output included more than seventy titles. These early recordings suffer from inferior sound, but backed up by Austin and her Blues Serenaders, as well as other outstanding musicians such as Tommy Ladnier and Jim Bryant—and later COLEMAN HAWKINS and FLETCHER HENDERSON—they reveal a high level of artistry.

In her phrasing she had an expressive habit of displacing the normal word stress in a way that intensified the rhythmic pulse and held the listener's attention. Outstanding titles from the 1923 and 1924 sessions include "Death Letter Blues," "Chicago Monkey Man Blues," "Wild Women Don't Have the Blues," and "Kentucky Man Blues." By 1925 and 1926, at her artistic peak, she recorded "Mississippi River Blues," "Coffin Blues," and "Rambling Blues." Following a ten-year hiatus, she recorded for Vocalion-Okeh with LIONEL HAMPTON, HOT LIPS PAGE, J. C. HIGGINBOTHAM, JAMES P. JOHNSON, and CHARLIE CHRISTIAN ("Four Day Creep").

Following a stroke in 1945 she retired in 1949 to Knoxville, Tennessee, where she lived with her daughter until her death. Between 1940 and 1960 Cox performed only intermittently and reluctantly, as she became increasingly active in church work. After a hiatus of more than twenty years, she returned to the recording studio in 1961 for a final album, *Blues for Rampart Street*, with an all-star band including Coleman Hawkins and ROY ELDRIDGE. The album featured a persuasive new version of "Death Letter Blues." Even though her voice had faded, the *New York Times* reviewer John Wilson praised the greater "artfulness of her phrasing" (10 Sept. 1961). Sammy Price, the blues pianist who took the place of Crump on that final recording, commented on her "flowing blues sound," the "good melodic lines, words that make sense, decent diction" (Harrison, 238). The brief revival of her career ended when she suffered another stroke in 1965 in Knoxville.

A classic blues singer known in the 1920s and 1930s for the ability to communicate feeling and bring out her own personality in performance, Cox was sometimes billed as the Uncrowned Queen of the Blues and the Sepia Mae West. Possessed of a regal stage presence and a strong, resonant voice with a touch of nasal quality, coupled with a "salty cynicism all her own," she was most effective in traditional-form blues songs, notably her own blues compositions and those of Austin, with whom she regularly performed and recorded in the early 1920s.

FURTHER READING
Carr, Ian, et al. *Jazz, the Essential Companion* (1987).
Harrison, Daphne D. *Black Pearls: Blues Queens of the 1920s* (1988).
Oliver, Paul. *Conversation with the Blues* (1965).
Stewart-Baxter, Derrick. *Ma Rainey and the Classic Blues Singers* (1970).
Obituary: *New York Times*, 12 Nov. 1967.
This entry is taken from the *American National Biography* and is published here with the permission of the American Council of Learned Societies.

LOUIS E. AULD

Cox, Minnie (5 Feb. 1869–1933), postmaster and businesswoman, was born Minnie M. Geddings in Lexington, Mississippi, one of two daughters of William Geddings and his wife Mary (maiden name unknown). Her parents' occupations have not been recorded, and little is known about Minnie's early life in Holmes County on the eastern edge of the Mississippi Delta. In the mid-1880s she left Lexington for Nashville, Tennessee, where she enrolled at Fisk University.

MRS. MINNIE M. COX.
THE EFFICIENT INDIANOLA, MISSISSIPPI, POSTMISTRESS.

Minnie Cox, first African American female postmaster. (Library of Congress.)

Upon graduating—probably around 1888—with a teacher's certificate Geddings returned to Lexington to teach in the town's public schools. On 31 October 1889 she married WAYNE WELLINGTON COX, the principal of the Indianola public schools in nearby Sunflower County. The Coxes had one daughter, Ethel.

In 1891 Republican president Benjamin Harrison appointed Minnie Cox as the nation's first African American female postmaster. In a state where the Democratic Party controlled virtually all local political patronage and at a time when the reach of the federal government into everyday life was minimal, postmasterships were among the only significant federal positions available to Mississippi Republicans. Although Harrison's defeat by the Democrat Grover Cleveland in the 1892 presidential election resulted in Cox's replacement by a white Democrat in 1893, the Republican William McKinley reappointed her as Indianola's postmaster in May 1897.

Three years later McKinley promoted Cox from a fourth-class appointment to a third-class appointment and increased her annual salary to $1,100. While that figure was close to the national average it was more than twice the average salary for Southerners (both black and white) and at least ten times the annual income of her African American customers. Any notion that her appointment represented an advance for "black power" should be seen in perspective, however. Cox was one of only five black third-class postmasters in the entire state of Mississippi, whose population in 1900 was 60 percent black. Indianola, like much of the Delta, was more than 80 percent African American.

There was a general consensus among the three thousand citizens of Sunflower County who used her post office that Cox performed her duties with due diligence. She worked a seven-day week, and even the white postal inspector for the county—a die-hard Democrat—declared Cox's office "a model of efficiency, tidiness, and good service" (Gatewood, 49). Cox was mindful to avoid potential conflicts with her white customers, installed a telephone at her own expense, and used her own money to help out customers of both races who fell behind in their payments of box rents. In 1902, however, a national depression—which hit the Delta particularly hard—and political tensions brought Cox to national prominence. In 1900 three-quarters of Southern blacks were either sharecroppers or tenants on white-owned land; in the Delta, the Coxes were among only a handful of African Americans who owned more than a few acres of the rich cotton-growing lands that dominated Mississippi's economy. The worldwide economic depression of the 1890s, however, precipitated a decline in the demand for and price of cotton, forcing a growing number of Mississippi's white landowners into sharecropping, farm tenancy, and debt peonage, just like their black neighbors. Wealth and landownership was increasingly in the hands of a tiny number of Delta planters. In response, James K. Vardaman, a blunt-speaking newspaperman, launched a bid for the governorship of Mississippi in 1902 on a platform of taxing the planters who lorded it over the common whites, but also of ensuring that the historical economic and social distance between blacks and whites was restored. He promised to do so by ending all state-supported education for blacks, repealing the Fourteenth and Fifteenth Amendments, and by ending the "menace to white civilization" posed in Sunflower County by the postmastership of Minnie M. Cox (Gatewood, 53). In the fall of 1902 Vardaman made several campaign stops in Indianola, where he rebuked the town's white citizens for "tolerating a Negro wench as postmaster," and for "receiving mail at the hands of a coon" (Gatewood, 55, 58). Vardaman warned that any degree of political power encouraged blacks to see themselves as the social equals of whites. By a bizarre and perverse—but for white voters stunningly effective—twist of logic, Vardaman concluded that such social equality encouraged black men to rape white women and girls.

The Coxes' relative wealth and power at a time of declining white economic fortune appears to have unhinged Indianola whites who had previously indicated no overt hostility towards them. Shortly after one of Vardaman's incendiary speeches, a group of angry Indianola whites condemned Cox for allowing "crap-shooting darkies" in the lobby of her post office where white women and children gathered, viewing the situation as an incitement of black men to rape. A petition demanding that Cox be removed from office, forcibly if necessary, gained many signatures. Tensions between the races had visibly worsened by November 1902, but Wayne Cox, who had considerable experience in dealing with local white leaders, attempted to secure a compromise that would allow his wife to remain in office until 1904, to be replaced then by a white Democrat. Cox insisted, however, that his wife's replacement could not be one of those who were actively seeking her removal. Indianola whites appeared in no mood to compromise; both the mayor and the sheriff refused to offer Cox their protection. Fearing violence and the closing of the post office, and because she felt a "deep interest in the town and its people," Cox offered her resignation to the postmaster general in Washington in December 1902 (Gatewood, 58).

Cox's resignation did not resolve matters, in part because Vardaman continued to stoke racial tensions in his gubernatorial bid, but also because President Theodore Roosevelt made a stand in defense of federal authority and civil rights against mob rule. He refused to accept Cox's resignation, instead ordering the Indianola Post Office to be closed on 1 January 1903. Cox would continue to draw her salary. Mississippi whites were outraged. The mood in Indianola had turned so ugly that Cox was forced to leave the town for Birmingham, Alabama, on 5 January 1903, under threat of violence. One group of whites threatened to break her neck if she attempted to return. For several months Vardaman, the Southern white press, and Southern Democratic leaders in Congress lambasted Roosevelt for his actions, viewing the Cox affair as a cynical attempt by the president to curry favor with black voters in the North and to defeat the growing "lily-white" tendency among Southern Republicans. Roosevelt continued to insist,

however, that the Indianola Post Office remain closed. In the fall of 1903 Vardaman was elected governor of Mississippi, primarily because of his avowedly "anti-Minnie Cox platform" (Gatewood, 66). In January 1904, when Cox made it clear to the president that she would not be a candidate for reappointment as postmaster, Roosevelt duly reopened the Indianola Post Office with a new postmaster, William B. Martin, a white Democrat. This was somewhat less of a victory for the Vardaman forces than it first appeared, however, since Roosevelt insisted on Wayne Cox's recommendation that the new postmaster could not be someone who had agitated to remove Minnie Cox. Martin had been a friend and staunch defender of the Coxes throughout their ordeal, which ended in February 1904, when Minnie Cox returned to Indianola from exile in Birmingham.

Vardaman's election victory exhibited the determination of Mississippi Democrats to uphold white supremacy at all costs, but Minnie Cox was one of the few African Americans who successfully challenged the Vardaman insistence that whites should master blacks. True to the ideals of her friend BOOKER T. WASHINGTON, she abandoned overt political activism for business opportunity. A few months after her return to Indianola she helped her husband to found the Delta Penny Savings Bank, which rapidly became the largest black financial institution in Mississippi and was for a time recognized as the second largest black-owned bank in the world. Although the wealth that the couple amassed came largely from the deposits and hard labors of many thousands of African Americans in the Delta, many of the same Sunflower County whites who had violently opposed her as postmaster deposited their money in the Coxes' bank. In 1910 the couple founded the Mississippi Beneficial Insurance Company, popularly known as Mississippi Life, which, like C. C. SPAULDING's North Carolina Mutual Insurance Company, provided health and retirement policies to African Americans, because white companies like Prudential refused to accept the "risk" of black policy holders.

Upon her husband's death in 1916 Cox assumed the position of secretary-treasurer of Mississippi Life, and she helped the company to its peak of four hundred employees and an annual income of half a million dollars three years later. In the 1920s she sold her controlling interest in the company to the Standard Life Company of Atlanta and moved to Memphis, Tennessee, where in 1925 she married George Hamilton of Rockford, Illinois. At the time of her death in 1933 she was one of the wealthiest black women in America, though the investors and former post office customers in Indianola did not fare so well. The Delta Penny Savings Bank was forced to close in 1928, a victim of the stock market crash and the great Mississippi floods of 1927.

The attempt to remove Cox from the postmastership of Indianola in 1902 signaled the determination of Mississippians like James K. Vardaman that they were "not going to let niggers hold office" (Gatewood, 58). Regrettably, it would take Congress another six decades to pay heed to the testimony of another Sunflower County native, FANNIE LOU HAMER, and pass the Civil Rights Act of 1964 and the Voting Rights Act of 1965, ensuring all Americans the full and equal rights of citizenship denied to Minnie Cox.

FURTHER READING

Gatewood, Willard B. "Theodore Roosevelt and the Indianola Affair," *Journal of Negro History* 53.1 (Jan. 1968).

Hemphill, Marie. *Fevers, Floods and Faith: A History of Sunflower County, Mississippi, 1844–1976* (1980).

STEVEN J. NIVEN

Cox, Oliver Cromwell (24 Aug. 1901–4 Sept. 1974), sociologist, was born in Port of Spain, Trinidad, in what was then the British West Indies. His father, William Raphael Cox, was the captain and customs officer of a revenue schooner, a position that secured a modicum of social and financial security for his wife, Virginia Blake, and their five children. William Cox had five additional children with Oliver's stepmother, Louisa. Oliver's uncle, Reginald W. Vidale, the headmaster of St. Thomas Boys' School in Port of Spain who later became a councilman and alderman, took primary charge of Oliver's early education and rearing.

He was a bright student, but he did not win one of St. Thomas's coveted scholarships to study in England. Because his father would only finance the education of his eldest son, Cox briefly attended a local agricultural college before securing a position as a clerk in a department store. In 1919, to further his education, he took the initiative of emigrating to the United States, where he lived with his brother Ethelbert in Chicago. Since diplomas from West Indian institutions were not routinely recognized by American colleges, Cox was forced to complete a course of study at the Central YMCA High School in Chicago. After graduating in 1924 he entered Crane Junior College and earned an

associate's degree two years later. During this period he worked part time at La Salle and Steven's Hotel and as an "assistant engineer," a common euphemism that could include any manner of janitorial or mechanical work.

In 1925 Cox became a licensed stenographer, perhaps after studying at the Lewis Institute. He is also believed to have taken courses at the Chicago Art Institute. By 1927, when he entered Northwestern University, it is clear that he had settled on a legal career. In 1929 he graduated with a bachelor of science in law degree. However, shortly after receiving his degree he was stricken with polio, which left him paralyzed in both legs for the rest of his life. Though he achieved a level of mobility and independence with the aid of crutches, his aspirations to become a lawyer were dashed, and he set his sights on a somewhat less physically active career in academia.

Just as the effects of the Depression were beginning to be felt, Cox entered the University of Chicago as a graduate student in economics. He studied under Frank Hyneman Knight, one of the founders of the "Chicago School" of economics and the translator of Max Weber's *General Economic History*. In his studies Cox gained an appreciation for Weber's comparative and historical approach, which came to underlie much of his own later work. In those days the writings of Karl Marx and Friedrich Engels were included on a long list of required reading for all students at the University of Chicago. Though Cox insisted that he was not a Marxist, he was a socialist, and his thinking on the question of race rests on the premise of a Marxian dialectical materialism in which political and social change is driven by the economic forces of class struggle.

After receiving an M.A. in economics in the spring of 1932, Cox abruptly shifted to the study of sociology. "I felt that if economics did not explain what I wanted to know," he wrote, "if economics did not explain the coming of the depression; if economics did not help me to understand that great [economic change], then I felt that I did not need it. Thus, I changed over to sociology" (Hunter, "Biographical Sketch," 251). Cox's M.A. thesis had dealt with workingmen's compensation in the United States, suggesting a sensitivity for those injured on the job, but apparently Cox was more interested in understanding the larger societal forces that crippled the lives of people of color. His primary influences in the sociology department were Ellsworth Faris, whose views about the differences between Jews and Negroes figure prominently in Cox's work, and William F. Ogburn, who, as Cox's adviser, is most likely responsible for the statistical methodology Cox used in his dissertation, "Factors Affecting the Marital Status of Negroes in the United States."

Cox received his Ph.D. in Sociology in 1938. Two other black social scientists produced by the University of Chicago during those years were E. FRANKLIN FRAZIER, author of *The Negro Family in the United States* (1939), and ST. CLAIR DRAKE, who wrote *Black Metropolis* (1945) with HORACE CAYTON JR. In contrast to Frazier, who worked more comfortably within the analytical parameters exemplified by the University of Chicago, Cox felt intellectually inhibited in what he described as an academic environment with many kind liberals who were nonetheless "sternly opposed to Negroes taking such initiative as would move them along faster than a proper pace; and they would rather turn conservative than tolerate independent thinking or acting Negroes" (McAuley, 39).

Despite his credentials in economics and sociology, Cox could not find a permanent teaching position at any of the white research colleges or universities. He had worked briefly as a senior statistician for the Chicago Park District and held a short teaching assignment at Louisville Municipal College, and in 1938 he accepted a position at Wiley College, a small black Baptist school in Marshall, Texas. There he taught economics and directed the school's poorly funded Bureau of Social Research. In 1944 he took a position at Tuskegee Institute in Alabama, one of the flagships of the black college system. But the focus at Tuskegee was on industrial and vocational education, and few students were interested in the graduate-level sociology courses that Cox offered as a laboratory for his ideas. Nevertheless, Cox remained active in a variety of professional societies and managed to publish frequently.

In 1948 Cox completed his magnum opus, *Caste, Class, and Race*. The first third of the book is a refutation of the notion that the racial category in America is similar to the caste system in India, an idea that was in great ascendancy. He argues that "race prejudice is not an individual idiosyncrasy; it is a social attribute" (xxxi), one that is inextricably linked to class and created as a capitalist justification for economic exploitation. This challenged the prevailing view put forth by the Swedish economist and sociologist Gunnar Myrdal in *An American Dilemma: The Negro Problem and Modern Democracy* (1944), which evaded class by attributing racism to problems in the "American Creed." Cox won the George Washington Carver award from black social scientists for *Caste, Class, and Race*, and his ideas resonated with radical intellectuals for generations, but the book never received wide recognition and went out of print soon after it appeared.

In 1949 Cox left Tuskegee to teach at Lincoln University in Missouri. Shortly after arriving there he published "The Leadership of Booker T. Washington," a searing appraisal of Tuskegee's founder, whom he referred to as a "collaborator" who "never fully lost the attitude of the favorite slave," and who did not really lead black people as much as he diverted them. While at Lincoln, Cox wrote *The Foundations of Capitalism* (1959), *Capitalism and American Leadership* (1962), and *Capitalism as a System* (1964). In this trilogy on communism he meticulously traces the development of capitalism from ancient Venice to modern multinational corporations; he fully develops the nexus between capitalism and racism; and he explores the political and sociological implications of capitalism on theories of cultural assimilation, intolerance, and racial prejudice.

Although Cox was never politically active, as a theorist he critiqued events of the civil rights movement from the 1950s through the early 1970s. He articulated the belief that the goals of this movement were intellectually shallow and therefore insufficient because they only demanded rights within the existing capitalist framework. "Protest ideology never brings the social system itself into question. It envisages only an indiscriminate inclusion of Negroes in the general society as it is" (Cox, "The Programs of Negro Civil Rights Organizations," *Journal of Negro Education* [Summer 1951], 360).

Cox's most controversial and misunderstood ideas pertain to the distinction he drew between anti-Semitism and racism. Cox argued that anti-Semitism is a form of social intolerance in which society refuses to accept Jews unless they completely assimilate, that is, unless they cease to be Jews. On the other hand he believed racial prejudice has an opposite intent: to prevent the assimilation or integration of black people. As Cox expresses it, "The dominant group or ruling class does not like the Jew at all, but it likes the Negro in his place" (*Caste, Class, and Race*, 401). Cox expands on this idea in his essay "Race Prejudice and Intolerance—A Distinction" (*Social Forces*, Dec. 1945). In his last article, published shortly before his death in 1974, Cox carries this position further to argue that black people should reject black nationalist movements and campaigns for cultural pluralism or diversity because "Negroes do not have a culture in the same sense that Jews have one" ("Jewish Self-Interest in 'Black Pluralism,'" *Sociological Quarterly* [Spring 1974], 189). Cox favored assimilation as an intermediary step toward some form of color-blind socialism. In his view, pursuing separatism or promoting cultural pluralism obfuscates the interests of the proletariat. Cox's opinions evoked both sharp criticism from such African American intellectuals as HAROLD CRUSE and charges of anti-Semitism by Jewish leaders.

Cox published more than forty articles and four seminal books over his thirty-five-year career. Like his Trinidadian compatriots Henry Sylvester Williams, C. L. R. JAMES, GEORGE PADMORE, and Eric Williams, Cox saw racism as an ideological problem that he fought with the strength of his intellect. With the notable exception of W. E. B. DuBOIS, few African American sociologists have been more influential.

FURTHER READING

Blackwell, James, and Morris Janowitz, eds. *Black Sociologists: Historical and Contemporary Perspectives* (1974).

Hunter, Herbert M. "Oliver C. Cox: A Biographical Sketch of His Life and Work," *Phylon* 44, no. 4 (1960).

Hunter, Herbert M., ed. *The Sociology of Oliver C. Cox* (2000).

Hunter, Herbert M., and Sameer Y. Abraham, eds. *Race, Class, and the World System: The Sociology of Oliver C. Cox* (1987).

Hier, Sean P. "The Forgotten Architect: Cox, Wallerstein and World-System Theory," *Race and Class* 42, no. 3 (2001).

McAuley, Christopher A. *The Mind of Oliver C. Cox* (2004)

Reed, Adolph, Jr. "Race and Class in the Work of Oliver Cromwell Cox," *Monthly Review* 52, no. 9 (2001).

SHOLOMO B. LEVY

Cox, Wayne Wellington (8 Aug. 1864–Apr. 1916), teacher, landowner, and businessman, was born to Caroline Cox (sometimes recorded as Caroline Griffin) on the Griffin plantation near Ebenezer, in Holmes County, Mississippi, on the eastern edge of the Yazoo-Mississippi Delta. The name of Wayne's father is unknown, but several accounts suggest that his mother was widowed either shortly before or shortly after her son was born.

From an early age, perhaps as early as three or four, Cox worked in the cotton fields of the Griffith plantation alongside his mother. During the years of Reconstruction he benefited from the establishment of the first state-supported public schools for African American children in Mississippi. Though the school year was only a few weeks long, Cox displayed a precocious talent at the Holmes County School, and by age eleven he had completed all of the courses on offer in the school's rudimentary curriculum. In 1875 he won a scholarship to study at Alcorn Agricultural and Mechanical College, the recently opened state university for blacks in Port Gibson, Mississippi, and he supported himself for three years by working on the college farm. He returned to Holmes County in 1877, however, a year shy of graduation, to help support his mother, who was ill. Though only thirteen Cox had already taken on the responsibilities of manhood. Perhaps emboldened by his early experience of self-sufficiency, he clashed with a prominent white man in Ebenezer. Though the confrontation was a relatively minor one, such seemingly innocuous incidents could have devastating repercussions for self-confident young black men in the Delta in the late 1870s, as EMMETT TILL would discover more than seventy years later. Cox wisely left Ebenezer and found work nearby as a mail clerk in the Lexington post office. In 1878 he began teaching in the Holmes County public schools, where, at the age of only sixteen, he became principal in 1880. Having saved enough money Cox returned to Alcorn A&M in 1881 with the intention of completing his studies. By late 1883, however, a lack of funds again forced Cox to quit Alcorn, never to return as a student.

Having walked more than 120 miles of rough road from Port Gibson, Cox arrived in Indianola, Sunflower County, on 1 January 1884, with only seventy-five cents to his name. Teaching, this time in the Indianola public schools, again provided Cox with enough to live on, and he began to save money from his salary to invest in land. Not yet twenty, but ambitious and optimistic, Cox resolved to carve out a new life for himself in the still undeveloped lands in the Delta counties west of Holmes County. In this he shared the dream of a large number of former slaves, like ISAIAH T. MONTGOMERY, who in the 1870s and 1880s saw opportunities in the swampy, heavily wooded Delta counties of Sunflower, Bolivar, and Coahoma. The name "Coahoma" was taken from the Choctaw word for "red panther," because red panthers, along with timber wolves, bears, snakes, and alligators, awaited those black pioneers seeking to clear their property of dense woods and forbidding cane brakes that reached nearly twenty feet high.

Once the land was secured and cleared, usually by the labor of entire black families, the landowners could finally hope to farm the Delta's rich, dark, alluvial soil, which was ideal for cotton production. By 1887 Cox had saved five hundred dollars, and he invested it in land in Sunflower County, purchasing 160 acres—which was, though Cox probably did not know it, the average acreage of black-owned farms in the Delta. The average white-owned farm was nearly five times larger. By the early 1900s, however, Cox had greatly expanded his landholdings to several thousand acres, frequently buying and selling properties on his way to becoming one of the largest black landowners in the state.

Cox's fortunes as a landowner stood in sharp contrast to those of most blacks in the Delta at the turn of the twentieth century. A sharp decline in cotton prices in the late 1880s was part of a general agricultural depression that struck particularly hard in the American South and West. Black landowners—as well as many whites—found themselves increasingly indebted to landlords and local furnishing merchants. Sharecropping or renting became increasingly prevalent for both races. Many black landowners were forced to sell their land to timber companies or to the Louisville, New Orleans, and Texas Railroad, which had become a powerful force in the Delta. Thus, even though two-thirds of all landowners in the Delta in 1900 were black, black farmers owned only around 10 percent of the region's rich cotton-growing land. Their farms were as a rule not only much smaller than the large plantations owned by whites but also much less fertile and productive.

There are several reasons why Cox prospered while most other black farmers failed. As a teacher and after 1890 as a postal clerk for the Railway Mail Service, Cox could depend on a relatively steady income to tide him over when the price of cotton was unfavorable. Moreover, his extensive education favored him in his negotiations with white lawyers, landowners, and merchants. By contrast, more than a third of black Delta landowners at this time were illiterate, a great disadvantage in a highly litigious, contract-based society. Finally, at a time when Mississippi whites were steadily eroding the political rights of the state's black majority, Cox was a prominent black Republican who served as Indianola's sole African American alderman in the 1890s and early 1900s, a post that helped forge business contacts and relationships with the most powerful of Sunflower County whites, many of whom were his neighbors in Indianola's wealthiest neighborhood.

Several biographies note the important role of Cox's wife, MINNIE COX, formerly Minnie M. Geddings, in furthering his business career. The Coxes, who married in 1889, had one daughter, Ethel Grant Cox. The political campaign that forced Minnie Cox from her position as Indianola's postmaster in 1903 signaled the increasing determination of Mississippi Democrats to remove African Americans from public life, but it did not deter Wayne Cox from continuing his business activities. After his wife returned from exile in 1904, she helped Cox to establish the Delta Penny Savings Bank of Indianola, which rapidly became the largest black-owned bank in the state. Cox served as the bank's chief cashier, and within several years he had made it the second largest black-owned bank in the nation. The bank provided a refuge for African American landowners, renters, and sharecroppers in a relatively hostile economic world. Another Cox business venture, the Mississippi Loan, Improvement, and Industrial Company of Indianola, offered small business loans to budding black entrepreneurs in the Delta. Cox also served as secretary-treasurer of the Woodmen of Union, a Mississippi-based fraternal organization that boasted seven thousand members.

In 1909 Cox and his wife founded the Mississippi Beneficial Insurance Company, with Wayne Cox as secretary and treasurer. "Mississippi Life," as it was commonly known, struggled in its early years. Insuring the lives of the Delta's black inhabitants was, because of their poverty and economic insecurity, a quite risky business, but by 1915 Cox had helped place Mississippi Life on a secure footing. That year Cox also fought off efforts by state banking regulators to close the Delta Penny Savings Bank and five other black-owned banks. Cox ultimately persuaded two white banks in Indianola to endorse his efforts at Delta Penny, which remained open when all the other black-owned banks in the state were closed by the regulators. The exertion of keeping his two businesses afloat took its physical toll on Cox, however. In early winter 1916 Cox spent a couple of weeks at the exclusive sanatorium in Stafford Springs, Mississippi—in a cottage separate from the white patients—but later moved to Tuskegee Hospital in Alabama, where he died, at the age of only fifty-five, in April 1916.

In the view of many of his contemporaries, both black and white, Wayne Wellington Cox was the "best business man in the State of the Mississippi" (G. P. Hamilton, *Beacon Lights of the Race* [1911], 219). He was known for his fierce work ethic, which he shared with thousands of black men and women in the Delta. That Cox succeeded at a time when most of his contemporaries were forced into sharecropping or debt peonage was not simply a matter of luck, however. His extensive education and his leadership role in Republican politics proved invaluable in his negotiations with the handful of wealthy white planters and merchants who came to dominate the Delta by the end of the nineteenth century. Yet the same power structure that tolerated—and even encouraged—black entrepreneurs like Wayne Cox and Isaiah T. Montgomery ensured that these men were the exception to the rule. A decade after Cox's death, three-quarters of the Delta's population was black but only 2 percent of the cultivated land in the Delta was owned by black farmers.

FURTHER READING

Cobb, James C. *The Most Southern Place on Earth: The Mississippi Delta and the Roots of Regional Identity* (1992).

Hemphill, Marie. *Fevers, Floods, and Faith: A History of Sunflower County, Mississippi, 1844–1976* (1980).

Willis, John C. *Forgotten Time: The Yazoo-Mississippi Delta after the Civil War* (2000).

STEVEN J. NIVEN

Craft, Juanita Jewel Shanks (9 Feb. 1902–6 Aug. 1985), civil rights activist, was born Juanita Jewel Shanks in Round Rock, Texas, the daughter of David Shanks, a school principal, and Eliza Balfour, a teacher and seamstress. Juanita was the granddaughter of slaves. Her early childhood education began with an introduction to the primary school curriculum by her father. She graduated from Anderson High School in Austin, Texas, in 1919. Although Craft's family home in Austin was merely blocks away from the campus of the University of Texas at Austin, she could not attend that university because she was African American. Craft enrolled in her father's alma mater, Prairie View State Normal and Industrial College (now Prairie View A&M University). She resented being forced to attend the school that had been designated by the Texas State Education Board as a university for African Americans because it was segregated and she knew she would receive an inferior education.

Craft attended Prairie View for approximately two years, graduating in May 1921 with a certificate in dressmaking and millinery. She later transferred to the all-black, coeducational Samuel Houston College in Austin, where she attended "summer normals," a teacher training program, in 1921, and earned a teaching certificate in that same year to teach elementary education.

Craft's career in education was short-lived because of her intense dissatisfaction with the salary of $55 per month that she received as a second grade teacher. She shifted to the textile industry and pursued a career as a dressmaker and milliner, but was sidetracked by an early marriage to her childhood sweetheart, Charles Floyd Langham, from 1922 to 1925. The marriage to Charles was troubled; Juanita was reared to be independent and industrious and Charles found that problematic and often refused to give Juanita money for sewing items. To avoid arguing with her husband, Juanita secured employment as a drugstore clerk in Galveston, Texas, where they lived. Juanita divorced Charles in 1925 after he became angry about her purchasing a coat.

In 1925 Craft relocated to Dallas, where she secured employment as a bell maid at the city's famed Adolphus Hotel. Her father severely criticized her for accepting what he saw as a demeaning position in a place that he believed promoted promiscuity and drinking. Craft stated in an interview with Chandler Vaughn in 1981 that she never belittled herself in her position as a bell maid even though African Americans could not even enter through the front door of the hotel. The experiences at the hotel enlightened Craft. She met several prominent African Americans and whites who visited the hotel, including Eleanor Roosevelt, Charles Lindbergh, DUKE ELLINGTON, and LOUIS ARMSTRONG. During her nine years at the hotel, Craft earned a respectable salary that was subsidized by tips and an informal introduction to culture, politics, and entertainment.

Craft learned early in life that it was her duty to challenge segregation and to seek an egalitarian way of life as outlined by the Constitution. However, her active role in fighting discrimination was spurred by a personal tragedy. In late 1918 her mother contracted tuberculosis and required immediate medical attention. Craft, then sixteen years old, traveled with her mother to the Tubercular State Hospital in San Angelo, Texas, but Eliza Shanks was denied treatment because of her race. Shortly afterward Shanks died of tuberculosis-related complications.

Her mother's death and the early instruction by her parents to refuse second-class citizenship because of her race led Craft to campaign against racism and discrimination.

Craft's civil rights activism began formally in 1935, when she joined the Dallas branch of the National Association for the Advancement of Colored People (NAACP). Her early involvement centered on fieldwork; she was responsible for increasing the membership rolls of the local chapter in Dallas that had declined significantly during the 1920s and 1930s. NAACP membership in Texas waned after World War I because of the red scare and the revival of the Ku Klux Klan. Many African Americans in Dallas feared the conservative political oligarchy that controlled the city and gave approval to the robed militants. On 2 October 1937 Juanita married Johnnie Edward Craft, a salesman, a marriage that was to last until Johnnie's death in 1950; they had no children.

The political activism of the New Deal years and the upsurge of African American political activity during World War II enabled Juanita Craft to revitalize failing NAACP branches and chapters, while the increased prosperity of the war years enabled more members to pay their dues. By 1946 the Dallas branch was credited with more than seven thousand paid memberships, up from twelve hundred in 1942. A local activist in Dallas, Donald Jones, recalled that the membership campaigns were "like a blood transfusion" awakening people to "The Fight Is On!" a slogan that Craft charismatically chanted at rallies in Dallas and throughout Texas (Gillette, 29; Winegarten, 244–245).

Craft was quite effective as a grassroots fieldworker, but when she coupled her dynamic oratorical abilities with the administrative talents of the Houston fieldworker LULU WHITE, the results were even more effective and dramatic. White was executive secretary of the Houston branch of the NAACP and a key member in the statewide organization. The pair traveled from city to city, often going to small rural towns, where they would call meetings and organize branches. They traveled in White's car with a small caliber handgun for protection because they never knew when they would be accused of stirring up race problems and might encounter a violent aggressor. The two women utilized different strategies to gain recruits. White had worked with the NAACP for a longer time, so her mode of operation often entailed establishing the branch, then drawing on the resources of the national organization and enlisting help from other state and local offices. Craft's more direct approach centered on writing individuals who were interested in establishing a local chapter and instructing them on how to organize. She explained that after the core group obtained fifty members, it could apply for a charter and be nationally recognized.

Craft was also an electoral pioneer. Two years after the U.S. Supreme Court's 1944 ruling in *Smith v. Allwright* that Texas's all-white Democratic Party primary was unconstitutional, Craft became the first African American woman to vote in a Democratic Party election in Dallas County.

Craft's early career as a successful fieldworker elevated her in 1946 to the position of youth council adviser of the Dallas NAACP. She cherished this role because she believed that the fight for an egalitarian society lay in the hands of younger African Americans. Craft organized the Dallas Youth Council into an active branch of dues-paying youth and college-aged campaigners for justice. In one of its first actions, the student-based arm of the NAACP challenged segregation at the University of Texas. HEMAN M. SWEATT, a Houston letter carrier, applied to the University of Texas Law School and was denied admission because he was an African American. Craft quickly organized Youth Council members, who raised money and protested in support of Sweatt. In part because of the students' efforts, the Supreme Court ruled in favor of Sweatt in the landmark case *Sweatt v. Painter* (1950), paving the way for future desegregation cases leading up to *Brown v. Board of Education of Topeka* in 1954.

In the 1950s Craft also led a cadre of young activists in protest against the Texas State Fair, one of the nation's largest, which restricted admission of African Americans to only one day. The second Monday in October was designated Negro Achievement Day, the day African Americans could enjoy the fair. Over the course of five days when the fair opened in 1955, African American Youth Council members attempted to patronize the fair, but they were resisted by white fair workers, who told them to come back on their day. The Youth Council, under the direction of Craft, printed protest signs that read "This Is Negro Aggrievement Day—Keep Out" and "Don't Sell Your Pride for a Segregated Ride—Keep Out" and boycotted the state fair on 17 October 1955. The youths circulated handbills to patrons who were not aware of the boycott, informing them that patronizing the fair would bring disgrace and humiliation to African American patrons.

Although the protest did not force the state fair organizers to immediately desegregate, the financial losses caused by Craft's boycott along with the broader changes brought on by the civil rights movement, notably the 1964 Civil Rights Act, ultimately forced it to integrate all facilities and attractions in the mid-1960s.

Juanita Craft remained dedicated to combating discrimination, educating young people, and achieving the egalitarian promise of the Constitution during her tenure as a Dallas City Council member from 1970 to 1979. She received several awards from the NAACP and in 1984 the Eleanor Roosevelt Humanitarian Award. Her commitment to civic duty was also recognized by Presidents Kennedy, Johnson, and Carter, who each invited her to the White House in recognition to her service to civil and political activism.

Juanita Craft died 6 August 1985, and was buried next to her father in Evergreen Memorial Cemetery in Austin, Texas.

FURTHER READING

Information on Craft is in the Juanita Craft Collection, Center for American History, University of Texas at Austin, and the Juanita Craft Collection, Texas/Dallas History Archives Collection, Dallas Public Library, Dallas.

Craft, Juanita Jewel. "Interview with Juanita Jewel Craft," by Dorothy R. Robinson (20 January 1977), in *The Black Women History Project* (1991).

Gillette, Michael L. "The NAACP in Texas, 1937–1957." Ph.D. diss., University of Texas at Austin (1984).

Winegarten, Ruthe. *Black Texas Women: 150 Years of Trial and Triumph* (1995).

Vaughan, Chandler, ed. *A Child, the Earth, and a Tree of Many Seasons: The Voice of Juanita Craft* (1982).

YVONNE DAVIS FREAR

Craft, William and Ellen Craft (1824–28 Jan. 1900) and (1826–1891), escaped slaves, abolitionists, teachers, entrepreneurs, and autobiographers, were born into slavery in antebellum central Georgia. William recalled little of his father and mother, who, along with a brother and a sister, were sold away "at separate times, to different persons" by his first master, a merchant named Craft (Craft, 8). Ellen was the daughter of Maria, a mixed-race slave, and James Smith, a white planter from Clinton, Georgia. Like her mother, Ellen was raised as a house servant until she was given, at age eleven, as a wedding present to her white half-sister Eliza, the wife of Robert Collins, a wealthy businessman and railroad builder in Macon, Georgia. While Ellen was serving as a lady's maid and seamstress in the Collins mansion, William was brought to Macon by a bank officer named Ira Taylor.

William was much in demand for his carpentry skills, as his first master had apprenticed him to learn this trade. Like other male slaves in urban areas who possessed specialized knowledge, he was "hired out," in this case to work for a white carpenter in town. He waited tables to earn his board and handed over a monthly percentage of his pay to Taylor while pocketing the rest. An accomplished seamstress, Ellen may have saved money from handiwork produced at night after her required duties were done. By the late 1840s both had attained physical mobility, economic self-sufficiency—and for William, a rudimentary reading ability—assets that proved crucial to their success in their escape from slavery.

William and Ellen met around 1846 and quickly fell in love. They agonized, however, over their inability to live together and to procure a Christian marriage. They were equally troubled by the dismal prospects for any children they might have. So long as Ellen remained enslaved, the Crafts' children would suffer the brutalities of slavery—unrelenting and unrequited toil, crowded and unsanitary living conditions, whippings, perhaps rape by the master, and the auction block. By 1848 the couple had decided to escape to the North.

They strategically planned to make their escape during the Christmas holidays, when it was customary for slaveholders to relax surveillance of their "property," releasing their slaves from work for several days. The vigilance of the "paterollers"—who patrolled the countryside and monitored the activities of bound and free blacks traveling between plantations—also eased during the holidays. Fear of recapture, separation, punishment, and sale, however, must have weighed heavily on the couple, who were well aware of whites' anxieties about unchaperoned blacks. The Crafts' justifiable fears would have been heightened by the tense atmosphere of suspicion that resulted from such slave uprisings as those led by NAT TURNER in Virginia in 1831 and by DENMARK VESEY in Charleston, South Carolina, in 1822. The Crafts thus decided to increase their prospects for success by using camouflage, a timeworn yet often effective diversion for runaways. Ellen took advantage of her light-skinned complexion by posing as a chronically ill, albeit prosperous, southern gentleman named William Johnson. She cut her hair, put on a suit and spectacles, layered bandages around her face to conceal her beardless chin, hung her arm lifelessly in a sling to avoid having to write, and topped the whole costume with an elegant, status-announcing beaver hat. William was darker in skin color and facial features, so they devised for him to accompany his "master" as a slave valet. Under the ruse of seeking treatment for "Johnson's" various ailments, the couple conspired to travel to Philadelphia, where slavery was outlawed. After William obtained a pass from his master on the pretext of accompanying Ellen to visit her dying mother, they were ready.

On 20 December 1848, as southern protocol demanded, they boarded separate compartments on the same Macon-to-Savannah railroad that Ellen's current owner had built. On Christmas Day, after a few near exposures and close calls, they arrived in Philadelphia. The Crafts arrived in Boston several weeks later, in January 1849. Unlike other escaped slaves who fled at night following the North Star, lived off berries, and held close to riverbeds and ditches, William and Ellen Craft had traveled openly up the eastern seaboard, tempting fate with overnight stays at hotels swarming with southern planters.

For two years the Crafts were the darlings of northern abolitionists. They settled in Boston, the center of the American antislavery movement, where they lived in the dynamic African American enclave on Beacon Hill. The Crafts became sought-after participants at abolition meetings throughout New England, although in keeping with social convention, Ellen rarely spoke. They were familiar figures at the African Meeting House at Eight Smith Court (known around Boston as "the Black Faneuil Hall"), and at the integrated Charles Street AME Church. William was elected vice president of the League of Freedom, a group organized to protect fugitive slaves. In their private life, the Crafts established a model Victorian household. Possessed of an endearing shyness and delicacy, Ellen remained home but also earned a little "by the needle." White union members blocked William from plying his carpentry trade, but he sustained a modest used furniture business. This must have further romanticized him to Boston abolitionists, who well remembered the black abolitionist DAVID WALKER's used clothing business located decades earlier on Brattle Street in Cambridge.

The Crafts were surrounded by a pantheon of notables, including Lewis Hayden, the businessman, former slave, and Underground Railroad conductor who temporarily boarded the couple in his home; WILLIAM WELLS BROWN, the fugitive slave and novelist, who coached the pair for public appearances; the historian WILLIAM COOPER NELL; the lawyer and integration and antislavery activist ROBERT MORRIS; and the influential white reformers William Lloyd Garrison and Lydia Maria Child, who covered the couple extensively in their widely circulating newspapers the *Liberator* and the *National Anti-Slavery Standard*. At the peak of the Crafts' celebrity, Robert Hayden opened his home to celebrate at last the couple's Christian marriage.

Passage of the Fugitive Slave Law by Congress in September 1850 revealed the illusory quality of the Crafts' peaceful lives. In the North, fugitive and free blacks alike had always been imperiled by bounty hunters who abducted them back to the prison-house of slavery with impunity. With the Fugitive Slave Law, however, the federal government itself mandated extradition of escaped slaves to their owners, and punished those who harbored runaways with imprisonment and stiff fines. The biracial Vigilance Committee posted handbills on 24 April 1851 warning Boston's black citizens to "Keep a Sharp Look Out" for human "HOUNDS" engaged in "KIDNAPPING, CATCHING AND KEEPING SLAVES." The Crafts' owners issued a warrant for their arrest and sent two men, John Hughes and Willis Knight, to confiscate the now-famous couple. Thus began a cat-and-mouse chase during which William and Ellen lived separately and were moved frequently from one safe house to another. Bostonians largely resisted Hughes and Knight, hurling trash and epithets, and even jailing them, and Hughes and Knight eventually quit in fear and exasperation and returned to Georgia. The damage to the Crafts' sense of security was irreparable, however, and in November 1851 they sailed to Liverpool, England, by way of a packet from Halifax, Nova Scotia.

The couple bought a home in 1857 on Cambridge Road in Hammersmith, a suburb west of London, and traveled throughout England and Scotland, lecturing against slavery. The Crafts were active in benevolent groups such as the London Emancipation Society and the British and Foreign Freedman's Aid Society, and they hobnobbed with transatlantic reformers such as Harriet Martineau and Sarah Parker Remond. British abolitionists raised money to enroll them in the experimental Ockham School, which combined manual training with a liberal arts education. At the London World's Fair in 1851, the Crafts staged a silent antislavery protest in the American exhibit and scandalized their former countrymen by walking arm-in-arm with white abolitionists. When a rumor began circulating that Ellen wanted to return to the South, she responded with an open letter in the antislavery press, asserting, "I had much rather starve in England, a free woman, than be a slave for the best man that ever breathed upon the American continent" (*Anti-Slavery Advocate* [Dec. 1852], 22). The culmination of the Crafts' overseas fame was the publication in 1860 of *Running 1,000 Miles for Freedom*, their recollection of bondage, escape, and pursuit by slave catchers in the North. In 1865 some of the proceeds from the book financed bringing Ellen's mother from post–Civil War Georgia to England.

While the Crafts were thankful to their "antislavery friends" for spiriting them to safety in England and for supporting them while they found their bearings, they were determined to be self-reliant. William tried several business schemes and twice sailed to Benin for prolonged visits in unsuccessful moves to end slavery there, to open an African mission school, and to establish trade links with Britain. After the Civil War ended, homesickness and their concern for the newly freed slaves inspired another move. The Crafts returned to the United States with their two youngest children, Ellen and Alfred, and their oldest son, Charles, then a teenager. Their two middle children, William Jr. and Brougham, briefly remained in England for their educations.

After a triumphant reunion with Boston friends in 1869, the Crafts returned to Georgia after nineteen years in exile. After a school they had opened in South Carolina was burned down by the Ku Klux Klan, William, in 1871, began raising money from Bostonians for the Woodville Cooperative Farm School, an Ockham-style school and plantation in Ways Station, Georgia, outside Savannah. Five years later after the Crafts were accused by white neighbors of misspending funds and keeping sloppy records, they lost contributors. William sued for libel in Boston, but lost the case. The school closed in 1878. Ellen, who spent her last years with her daughter in Charleston, South Carolina, died in 1891. She was buried on the grounds of the Woodville Cooperative Farm School. After his wife's death, William struggled to make his mortgage payments amid lowering crop prices and escalating Jim Crow policies. In 1899 the banks repossessed his land and he died a year later in Charleston.

The Crafts' story has been imaginatively used by a number of authors, including their contemporaries William Wells Brown (in *Clotel*, 1853) and Lydia Maria Child (in *The Freedman's Book*, 1865),

and Harriet Beecher Stowe, borrowed heavily from the Crafts' saga for plot and characterization in *Uncle Tom's Cabin* (1852). During the Harlem Renaissance, the poet and playwright GEORGIA DOUGLAS JOHNSON revisited the Crafts' story in her work. The Crafts' descendants, continuing the couple's commitment to racial advancement, became influential leaders and professionals. Many of the Boston places frequented by the Crafts have been designated national historic sites on the African American Heritage Trail. In London a plaque commemorates the site where these tireless "campaigners against slavery" once lived, on a street now called "Craft Court."

FURTHER READING

Letters from William and Ellen Craft are housed in the National Archives in Washington, D.C., and in the Boston Public Library's Anti-Slavery Manuscripts Collection.

Craft, William, and Ellen Craft. *Running 1,000 Miles for Freedom: The Narrative of William and Ellen Craft* (1860).

Blackett, R. J. M. *Beating against the Barriers: The Lives of Six Nineteenth-Century Afro-Americans* (1986).

Blackett, R. J. M. *Building an Antislavery Wall: Black Americans in the Atlantic Abolitionist Movement, 1830–1860* (1983).

McCaskill, Barbara. "'Yours Very Truly': Ellen Craft—The Fugitive as Text and Artifact," *African American Review*, Winter 1994.

Sterling, Dorothy. *Black Foremothers: Three Lives* (1988)

Still, William. *The Underground Rail Road* (1872).

BARBARA MCCASKILL

Crafts, Hannah (?–?) is pseudonym of an unidentified writer about whom no biographical information is known. The author of the novel *The Bondwoman's Narrative* (c. 1853–1861), she may have chosen the pseudonym Hannah Crafts as a tribute to ELLEN CRAFT, who escaped from slavery in 1848 disguised as a white male. There is no evidence that Crafts tried to publish *The Bondwoman's Narrative* and though it reached the *New York Times* best-seller list in 2002, she remains an invisible woman. The heroine of the novel calls herself a "repository of secrets" (11), privy to the sins and stories of her masters and mistresses, and the novel has yet to yield its greatest secret: the author's historical identity.

Circumstantial and textual evidence strongly suggest that the author was a woman, a slave of a North Carolinian named John Hill Wheeler, of mixed race, and familiar with the works of FREDERICK DOUGLASS, Harriet Beecher Stowe, Charles Dickens, Sir Walter Scott, and Charlotte Brontë. The intimate relationship between mistress and slave explored in the novel suggests the author's experience of slavery is first-hand, and her tendency to introduce characters as people first, and blacks second, indicates that she was African American. If the slave narrator's voice is then authentic, *The Bondwoman's Narrative* would be the first novel written by a female fugitive slave and would be, most likely, the first novel written by an African American woman. In addition it is our first "unedited, unaffected, unglossed, unaided" glimpse into the mind of a fugitive slave, as HENRY LOUIS GATES JR. explains in his introduction to the 2002 edition of the novel (xxxiii). Perhaps because the text was not filtered through an abolitionist editor, *The Bondwoman's Narrative* complicates traditional abolitionist-approved narratives that tend to present a unified slave community; in the novel slave-characters make class distinctions amongst themselves, and an internal slave hierarchy emerges.

The novel's subtitle identifies Crafts as "a Fugitive Slave, Recently Escaped from North Carolina," and the description of the novel manuscript in a 2001 auction catalog calls the author "a mulatto, born in Virginia" (Crafts, xi). Of course we also have the self-description of the narrator: "I am neither clever, nor learned, nor talented. When a child they used to scold and find fault with me because they said I was dull and stupid. ... I had none of that quickness and animation which are so much admired in children, but rather a silent unobtrusive way of observing things and events" (5). We might seek Crafts's biography in the details of the fictionalized autobiography: the author certainly claims in the preface that she has simply "relat[ed] events as they occurred" (3). But this claim is just token and formulaic: *The Bondwoman's Narrative* is a novel in the first person, albeit one likely drawing on the author's life experience.

In florid Victorian style Crafts tells the story of Hannah, a light-skinned house-slave whose new mistress is passing for white. Together they flee the blackmail of a villainous lawyer, Mr. Trappe, and after the melodramatic death of her mistress Hannah works as a maid to the unpleasant Mrs. Wheeler. She escapes when threatened with a forced marriage to a field slave and eventually reaches safety in the North, where she marries a New Jersey minister and begins work as a schoolteacher in a free

black community. Crafts borrows from Dickens's *Bleak House*, scatters biblical and classical allusions throughout, and uses the religious, gothic, and sentimental conventions of nineteenth-century fiction, combining portents, old portraits, and cursed trees with coincidences, heroines, and villains. While the blending of fact and fiction has made the historical trail even harder for scholars to trace, we see that Crafts's fictionalizing was also a challenge to the expectations of her own time: "Veracity was everything in an ex-slave's tale, essential both to its critical and commercial success and to its political efficacy within the movement," Gates reminds us in his introduction to the novel (lxiv).

The modern-day verification of a slave narrative, and the search for "Hannah Crafts," began in 2001, when Gates noticed a listing for an unpublished manuscript in an auction catalog. Apparently dating from the 1850s, the clothbound manuscript had sat for more than fifty years in the collection of the late DOROTHY PORTER WESLEY, a Howard University librarian. She had bought the manuscript from Emily Driscoll in 1948 for eighty-five dollars, and their exchange of letters about the item acknowledges its first-hand knowledge of plantation life in Virginia, and the "substratum of fact" upon which the fictionalized biography rests (Crafts, xx). Driscoll herself had bought the book from a trader, who had picked it up in New Jersey—the state in which the heroine of the novel ends her journey. Before completing this manuscript's long passage from antebellum production to 2002 publication, Gates bought it at auction and began a process of detective work, seeking to authenticate the holograph and determine the identity of its author. Experts examined ink, paper, punctuation, and handwriting, and dated the book between 1853 and 1861.

One specialist concluded that the author was a "relatively young, African-American woman who was deeply religious and had obvious literacy skills, although eccentric punctuation and occasional misspellings suggest someone who struggled to become educated" (Crafts, xxxi). Sifting through the evidence Gates and his fellow scholars also speculated that Crafts may have passed for white after achieving freedom, or may have married one Thomas Vincent and taught Sunday school in New Jersey at a black Methodist church. But biographical details remain elusive. Indeed the narrator herself acknowledges that her "descent could not be readily traced" (6). As was the case with many slaves the problem of identity may have been a reality for Crafts herself, whose heroine remarks in the first chapter of *The Bondwoman's Narrative*: "Of my relatives I knew nothing. No one ever spoke of my father or mother" (5). We find in the elusive "Hannah Crafts" what her heroine observes in Mrs. De Vincent—"a mystery, something indefinable about her" (27).

FURTHER READING

Crafts, Hannah. *The Bondwoman's Narrative*, with introduction by Henry Louis Gates Jr. (2002).

Gates, Henry Louis, Jr., and Hollis Robbins, eds. *In Search of Hannah Crafts: Critical Essays on The Bondwoman's Narrative* (2004).

Townshend, Dale. "Speaking of Darkness: Gothic and the History of the African American Slave-Woman in Hannah Crafts' *The Bondwoman's Narrative*," in *Victorian Gothic*, ed. Karen Sayer and Rosemary Mitchell (2003).

Williams, Adebayo. "Of Human Bondage and Literary Triumphs: Hannah Crafts and the Morphology of the Slave Narrative," *Research in African Literatures* 34.1 (2003).

ZOE TRODD

Crafus, Richard (1779–7 Feb. 1831), sailor and prisoner of war leader, was born in Salem, Massachusetts, or vicinity and was also known as Richard Seavers. His status as a free man or slave prior to his seafaring service is unknown. In 1814 Crafus, aged twenty-three, was a sailor on the Baltimore privateer schooner *Requin* when she was captured by British warships off Bordeaux, France, on 6 March 1814. According to one obituary, however, Crafus had joined the British Navy at about age sixteen. When or how he returned to the United States is uncertain. While little is known about Crafus before his capture, he was likely an accomplished sailor and, at six feet three inches or six feet five inches in height, surely a dominant figure among the *Requin's* crew. His size and forceful personality would be traits that brought Crafus to prominence during his time as a prisoner of war.

The service of black men such as Crafus, JOHN DAVIS, JOHN JOHNSON, and others as sailors in the U.S. Navy and privateering vessels during the War of 1812, though significant, has largely been forgotten. The contributions of black sailors have been lost amidst the epic retelling of the naval battles that defined the war in which they themselves were participants, such as the victory of the USS *Constitution* over the British frigate *HMS Guerriere* and the victory of the privateer *Prince de Neuchatel*

over *HMS Endymion*. Black seamen were by this time such a part of the fabric of America's maritime culture and industry that their contributions in manning U.S. vessels was not considered unusual. They served in any variety of shipboard positions, from lowly cabin boy, to ordinary and able-bodied seaman, and even to higher positions below the level of captain, such as first, second, or third mate. While black sailors seldom obtained command positions because of their race on ships owned by outside interests, blacks that served as captains of their own vessels, especially in the South, were not unheard of. Indeed, many white ship captains of this period, though prejudiced to some degree, were likely more than happy to overlook a prospective crewman's race if he were able to haul a line, furl the sails, or could capably man the helm. It was these qualities that many captains wanted, color or nationality aside. If, as the historian Christopher George suggests, Richard Crafus may have been a runaway slave, it is likely that the commander of the privateer *Requin* cared little and was probably satisfied to have such a man as part of his crew.

Upon his capture, Crafus was sent to imprisonment in Britain on one of the prison hulks at Chatham. Six months later, in October 1814, he was transferred to the most notorious prisoner of war camp of them all, Dartmoor Prison. Located on an isolated and windswept moor in Princetown, County of Devon, the prison would eventually house some 6,000 American prisoners, of which about a sixth were African Americans. From the start Crafus quickly gained the sobriquet "King Dick" for the manner in which he carried his authority. Dartmoor Prison consisted of seven different prison blocks, each with doors leading from one block to the next. From afar, the notorious prison, formed by three large concentric walls, bore the appearance of a maze from which there was no escape.

Indeed, escape attempts there were seldom successful. At first, blacks and whites were imprisoned together and freely mingled throughout the prison with no reported problems. However, as was the case with American soldiers and sailors imprisoned by the British during the Revolution, the men organized themselves by rank within their prison society and blacks soon found out, likely to no surprise, that they were on the lowest rung of the social ladder.

At first the number of African Americans imprisoned at Dartmoor was small, but the situation changed as the war continued and Britain captured increasing numbers of American privateers. With more and more blacks arriving each day, white resentment grew and whatever interracial comradeship that may have existed fell by the wayside.

As in any prison society, gaining sufficient food, clothing, and other wares became a primary way of survival, but with the influx of so many blacks, white American prisoners resorted to old habits and stereotypes and soon accused the black prisoners of thievery. Some white prisoners demanded that British prison officials segregate the black prisoners, which the British did, assigning the black sailors to the upper level of Number Four block. There "King Dick" held sway, making daily rounds among about 450 black sailors to see that they were properly disciplined, and settling disputes between them as needed, as well as taking the lead in both entertainment and mercantile operations.

According to an American surgeon who witnessed Crafus's rule: "This black Hercules commands respect, and his subjects tremble in his presence. … When he goes the rounds, he puts on a large bearskin cap, and carries in his hand a huge club. If any of his men are dirty, drunken, or grossly negligent, he threatens them with a beating, and if they are saucy, they are sure to receive one" (*Liberator*, 26 Feb. 1831).

In the course of these later events "King Dick" taught boxing skills to his men, as well as overseeing the operations of gambling tables and black participation in the prisoners' food market. He ruled fairly to all, blacks and whites, and was remembered as "a man of good standing" who exercised "it to a good purpose" (*Liberator*, 26 Feb. 1831).

Because the doors between prison blocks were kept open and men freely passed from one block to another, more than one opportunity presented itself for assassination. Occasional attempts to dethrone him were handily put down. In one case, when attacked by several black prisoners, Crafus picked up the smallest by the feet and thumped the others with him. With his towering size, made all the more formidable by his signature bearskin grenadier's cap and club, "King Dick" easily survived his 249 days of imprisonment at Dartmoor Prison and deserves recognition for both his successful leadership of imprisoned black sailors and for helping many of them to survive the ordeal.

Following the war and his return to America, Crafus settled in Boston sometime around 1826 and was prominent in that city's black society. Though the full details of the rest of his life, as well as his death, are uncertain, Richard Crafus, aka Richard Seavers, formerly "King Dick" and "Big Dick," lived in the Botolph Street area and died at age fifty-two, likely from pneumonia, as a result of exposure.

FURTHER READING
Bolster, W. Jeffrey. *Black Jacks—African American Seamen in the Age of Sail* (1997).
Doyle, Robert C. *Making Experience Count: American POW Narratives from the Colonial Wars to Vietnam* (2000). Available at http://usafa.af.mil/df/dfh/docs/Harmon43.doc.
Fabels, Robin. "Self Help in Dartmoor: Black and White Prisoners in the War of 1812," *Journal of the Early Republic* 9.2 (Summer 1989): 165–190.
George, Christopher T. *African-American Sailors Served-in Our Nation's "Private Navy."* Available at-http://www.baltimoremd.com/monuments/blacksatsea.html.

GLENN ALLEN KNOBLOCK

Craig, Douglas (1860?–11 Feb. 1936), Gallaudet University handyman, was born to parents about whom nothing is known, perhaps in the vicinity of Washington, D.C. In 1870, when he was about nine years old, he wandered from the National Association for the Relief of Destitute Colored Women and Children in Washington and was found on a cold winter night on the streets by Senator Aaron Cragin of New Hampshire. Cragin soon realized that the boy was deaf and took him to Columbia Institution for the Instruction of the Deaf and Dumb (later Gallaudet University). Compassion for blacks was not new for Senator Cragin; fifteen years earlier, in a 4 August 1856 speech, he argued passionately in support of Charles Sumner of Massachusetts, the Senate's leading opponent of slavery who had been beaten almost to death with a cane by Congressman Preston Brooks of South Carolina. Cragin also knew that there was only one place in Washington, D.C., where Douglas could be properly educated: the Kendall School. It is likely that Cragin knew Amos Kendall, the former postmaster general for Presidents Andrew Jackson and Martin Van Buren, who founded the school in 1857 with a mission to provide education for deaf students. The first superintendent was Dr. Edward Miner Gallaudet, the son of Thomas H. Gallaudet, the nation's leading exponent of aid to the deaf.

Soon the young child had been named Douglas Craig, likely after Cragin and FREDERICK DOUGLASS, who at the time owned and edited the *New National Era*, a weekly newspaper in

Washington, D.C. Douglass was also a benefactor of the facility that Craig had fled. He lived over the Kendall School's stable and attended classes, but it is not clear at what grade levels. Craig remained there for eight years and apparently remained on the school's honor roll. Despite his performance, the school's business manager decided that he had grown too large to share classes with younger students and should not remain enrolled. It is not clear how many other black children were at the school at the time, or if race rather then size or age was the real issue behind Craig's removal. He could have been sent to the Knapp School in Baltimore, which admitted black deaf students in an integrated setting, but no one chose that option for Craig. Rather than turn out this strong and healthy young man, the school instead officially hired him as a yardman. He soon became a "community icon" at Gallaudet, as the school had been renamed. Some at the school referred to him as a "Topsy" because he often "growled," others called him Douglas Craig, "M.M.," which had two meanings. The first referred to "Master of Mail" because he frequently rode his bicycle, nicknamed the Fast Flying Virginian (F.F.V.), to Union Train Station to pick up the campus mail. The appellation also meant "Master of Mechanics," referring to Craig's reputation as a "jack of all trades." Craig fixed virtually everything on campus, including the school tower clock.

There are many stories about Douglas's interaction with staff, faculty, and students but none more memorable than his collecting one dollar from students as they arrived on campus with their heavy trunks. Douglas would lift the trunks, haul them to the students' rooms, and then ask the student for one dollar. Most students agreed to pay this price and Douglas had his own special way of marking each one so that he could give the same dollar back to the student when he or she left campus. When plays were held in the auditorium Douglas was called upon to hoist and lower the heavy drop curtain on the stage; but he also had his own stage where in the early evenings he often joined students in the reading room. He was fluent in American Sign Language, but did not read lips well. Students in the reading room always met him with laughter because of his quiet humor, pronounced smell of cologne, and his announcing that he was off to see his girlfriend in Baltimore. A trusted soul on the campus, he also served as the campus Cupid, delivering love notes for students. Campus legend maintained that

he proposed to every black cook in the school's kitchen and did indeed often visit a female friend in Baltimore. Late in life, on 21 April 1920, Craig married a deaf black woman named Katie Jones of Washington, D.C. The wedding was quite a celebration, attended by many faculty and students at the Calvary Episcopal Church in Washington, D.C. Douglas wore a suit and white gloves and received more attention than the bride. After the wedding Craig moved off campus with his wife, but only a stone's throw away, and he could see the campus from his Camp Meade Cottage housing unit. By 1928, however, his wife had fallen ill and died. After her burial Douglas bought a burial lot next to her at the Harmony Cemetery and moved back to the only home he knew on the Gallaudet campus.

For sixty-five years Douglas was very much a part of the university. On 11 February 1936 a Western Union telegram was sent to Catherine Gallaudet, informing her that Craig had died at the Freedman "Colored" Hospital in Washington, D.C. (later Howard University Hospital). The president of the university, Percival Hall, wrote a detailed letter to Katherine Gallaudet (daughter of E. M. Gallaudet, one of the cofounders of Kendall Green) noting that a "proper and impressive funeral was held for Douglas in the College Chapel and many students, faculty and friends attended" (Gallaudet, "Letter from President Hall regarding the Death of Douglas Craig," 20 Feb. 1936). He was buried in the Harmony Cemetery next to his wife. In 1960 the interments were moved to Hyattsville, Maryland, as part of a relocation of the entire cemetery.

In 1978 a street on the campus was named in his honor and as of 2004, a photo of him hangs in the lobby of the Kendall School, the K–12 division of Gallaudet University.

FURTHER READING

Gallaudet Archives, Gallaudet University, Washington, D.C.

Gannon, Jack R. *Deaf Heritage: A Narrative History of Deaf America* (1981).

Stewart, Roy J. "Douglas Craig, M. M.," Recollection in *Buff and Blue*.

Obituary: *Buff and Blue*, 27 Feb. 1936.

MARIETA JOYNER

Craig, Lulu Mae Sadler (12 Aug. 1868–25 Sept. 1972), educator, writer, and community leader, was born Lulu Mae Sadler, in Platte County, Missouri, the daughter of Harriet Ellen Samuels, a homemaker, and Meride George Sadler, a farmer and laborer. Both were former slaves. As a young man, Lulu's father ran away from the Foley plantation and his slave owner to join the military and fought for his freedom with the Second Kansas Colored Infantry, Volunteers for the Union in the Civil War. Meride registered in the military under his slave name Foley and reclaimed his father's name of Sadler after the war.

When Sadler was a little boy his mother, whose name was China, was tied to a tree to be whipped by her angry slave owner. Lulu's grandfather, Meride Sr., ran to China's rescue and threw an axe that landed close to the slave master Foley's head. To punish him, Foley sold him down river and Lulu's grandfather was never heard from again.

When Craig was four, the family moved to Kansas and in 1878 settled in Nicodemus. Nicodemus was an all-black colony in northwestern Kansas founded in 1877 by a group of "Exodusters," former slaves who left the South and migrated west in pursuit of a better life. The Sadler family was among the early settlers lured to the Kansas plains by promises of free land and freedom from the racism that continued to prevail during the Reconstruction period.

Sadler and her family survived under tough conditions. They had no plows, so they used their hands for planting. Food was scarce. The Sadlers and other residents who had horses and wagons traveled long distances to other towns to ask for donations of food and supplies for their community. By 1880 the Sadlers were among the more than four hundred people who called Nicodemus home.

At fifteen years old, Craig attended one of Kansas's first colleges and befriended a classmate, GEORGE WASHINGTON CARVER, the famous African American scientist. Craig graduated from State Teachers College in Emporia, Kansas, with a teacher's certificate and taught grades one through eight in Nicodemus. With no formal teaching program guidelines and few teaching supplies, such as books, blackboards, and slates, Craig worked hard at educating her students under primitive conditions.

In 1886 Lulu married Sanford Craig, a carpenter; they had eight children. They remained in Nicodemus for approximately twenty-eight more years. Rare for a woman during this period, Lulu Craig served on the Nicodemus election board beginning on 12 November 1914.

In April 1915 Craig and her extended family, including her parents and her brother, left Nicodemus. They stepped out on faith and were among the first hundred African Americans who shaped a homestead out of the hostile prairie land known as "the dry," approximately eleven miles south of Manzanola, Colorado. Upon their arrival, lumber to build a shelter was scarce, so instead they dug into the prairie. The families knew that dugouts would hold their homestead title. Craig's first Colorado home was a hole six feet deep. It kept them cool in the summer and warm in the winter. The prairie winds were strong, but no wind could penetrate it.

The lack of irrigation made farming a challenge. The Craigs and the Sadlers managed to produce crops of vegetables with the help of a white neighbor who let them use his well. Craig stayed in touch with her friend Carver, and he explained carefully to her which weeds were good for food. Eventually the dugouts were replaced with more permanent structures. The settlers built a schoolhouse, which gave them a community meeting place for church, school, and other activities. Craig organized a Sunday school and a literary society. She was proud of the fact that many of her former students advanced to local high schools nearby. The family's economic security was ensured when official title for her land was issued to her name on 3 January 1922. Unfortunately, the community dwindled in the 1930s during the Great Depression, when many of the young men moved away to find work. The school closed in 1932, effectively ending her teaching career when the Manzanola school district rejected her application based on race.

A member of the Colorado's Writer's Club and known to be a prolific writer, Craig continued to write stories and poetry. Craig wrote about Nicodemus and Colorado. One of her manuscripts, "A History of Nicodemus: Graham County, Kansas" is preserved at the Kenneth Spencer Research Library at the University of Kansas. Barbara Brenner and Don Bolognese's *Wagon Wheels*, a work of historical fiction for the elementary school readers, is based on a story documented in Mrs. Craig's Nicodemus memoirs.

On 12 August 1970 five generations of the Craig family and numerous friends traveled from all over the United States to the farm home south of Manzanola to honor Craig on her 102nd birthday. As she intently and graciously greeted her guests, the celebration was filmed by Harry Belafonte Enterprises, produced and directed by the Academy Award winner Richard Kaplan. Kaplan used the story to develop a living history of the American West and demonstrate how many black families emerged from slavery, settled in the West, and contributed to its development. The documentary *Happy Birthday Mrs. Craig* (1970) features interviews with Craig and numerous family members. Their candid stories provide important historical insight. The film is a standard resource in many women's studies and African American studies programs. It is an impressive story of an American family and its determination to survive with dignity.

Craig was the matriarch of her close-knit family for thirty-one years after her husband died in 1941. She modeled the family mantra, "We are one." No matter how distant geographically, they all remained a family. Craig was 104 years old at the time of her death; in addition to her eight children, she had thirteen grandchildren, twenty-five great grandchildren, and six great-great grandchildren. Intelligent, communicative, and a real pioneer through rugged times, she made her transition from this world with positive memories of the past and hopes for her family's and humankind's future. Craig was a successful educator in Kansas and Colorado for fifty-five years and a respected community pillar, and her positive attitude explains her success in her interactions with people. She was intuitively guided by her Christian faith and practiced the biblical rule: "do unto others as you would have them do unto you." Craig was a grand lady with a nurturing spirit who left a legacy of hard work, endurance, and a desire of peace for humankind.

FURTHER READING

Craig's manuscript "A History of Nicodemus: Graham County, Kansas" is in the Kenneth Spencer Research Library at the University of Kansas.

Brenner, Barbara, and Don Bolognese. *Wagon Wheels* (1993).

Kaplan, Richard. *Happy Birthday Mrs. Craig*, Filmmakers Library. Available at http://www.filmakers.com/indivs/HappyBirthdayCraig.htm (1970).

Katz, William Loren. *Black Women of the Old West* (1995).

Obituary: *Rocky Ford Colorado Daily Gazette*, 26 Sept. 1972.

ANTOINETTE BROUSSARD FARMER

Craigen, Joseph A. (2 Apr. 1896–21 June 1962), attorney and cofounder of the Michigan Federated Democratic Club (MFDC), was born in British Guiana (Guyana), South America. Little is known about his life prior to his emigration from the colony. Because Craigen grew up near Spanish-speaking countries such as Venezuela, he became bilingual at an early age. During World War I he served in the United States Navy as a Spanish interpreter stationed in Muscle Shoals, Alabama. At the end of the war he migrated to Detroit where he worked in the automobile industry and became active in MARCUS GARVEY's Universal Negro Improvement Association (UNIA).

The Detroit UNIA had more than 4,000 members in the 1920s, making it one of the largest divisions of the organization. As was true for other northern cities where the UNIA had a considerable presence, African American migrants from the South comprised much of the rank and file of the organization, while its leaders, like Craigen, came largely from the Caribbean. In 1923 Craigen served as president of a Detroit division of the UNIA and later as executive secretary, acting in some official capacity for the organization over a seven-year period. He and leaders of other major divisions held the International Convention of the Negro Peoples of the World in Detroit to express the stability of the organization in the wake of Garvey's 1925 conviction for mail fraud. The United States government deported Garvey back to Jamaica in 1927, and Craigen was among those who met with him aboard ship immediately prior to his departure. Craigen attended the UNIA convention in Kingston in 1929. He professed the continued support of the Detroit division and his conviction in Africa's redemption with Garvey as the redeemer. The two would later have disagreements, which led to Craigen's unsuccessful attempt to found a splinter organization.

With the decline of Garveyism, Craigen turned to partisan politics and with Harold Bledsoe and Charles Diggs Sr. founded the Michigan Federated Democratic Club (MFDC) in 1930, one of the first black Democratic political organizations in the nation. Craigen acted as the first general secretary. The organization's support of Democratic candidates conflicted with the political aims of Detroit's old guard black leadership, which stood solidly in the Republican camp, as did most African American voters. The employment of many black men in the auto industry by Republican Henry Ford, who expected his workers to vote according to his wishes, increased the opposition to the MFDC. Craigen supported labor unions, which were backed by the Democratic Party. Also politicians such as Frank Murphy, who presided as judge over the trial of OSSIAN SWEET encouraged Craigen to work for the party.

When candidates backed by the MFDC won elections and responded by rewarding blacks with patronage positions, the organization gained members in earnest, mostly those who previously had not voted or were dissatisfied Republicans. The Depression severely affected Detroit's black community, and in 1933 Craigen led the MFDC in protest of discrimination against the application of the National Recovery Act (NRA). He organized black voters in Detroit's mayoralty race and helped obtain patronage positions in the county government.

Craigen became the first black constable of Detroit's Seventh Ward and in 1934 was elected secretary of the First Congressional district. Michigan governor Frank Murphy appointed Craigen deputy labor commissioner after he obtained a law degree in 1937. Although he had the highest civil service examination scores when reviewed by the state, when Murphy lost his gubernatorial bid for reelection in 1939, Craigen lost his position. The black community loudly protested his firing to the new governor, but a court injunction and an appeal of the Labor Commission's decision both proved unsuccessful. Craigen also failed in his 1938 bid to obtain a U.S. congressional seat as a delegate from the Thirteenth District, which contained the heavily African American First and Third Wards of Detroit.

In 1938 Craigen led the committee that sponsored a voter registration drive consisting of mass meetings and direct-mail campaigns that increased black voters in Detroit. His party loyalty was rewarded when a local probate court judge appointed him probate registrar at an annual salary of four thousand dollars, an astronomical amount for most black men in the city. In 1940 he campaigned throughout the state for Franklin Roosevelt and Michigan gubernatorial candidate Democrat Murray VanWagoner. In 1941 the latter reappointed Craigen as deputy labor commissioner, the position he kept for the remainder of his life.

Craigen suffered setbacks during his long career as a civil servant and a politician. Hindered by the fierce competition for the few patronage positions available to blacks, he had to contend with the erratic nature of partisan state politics and dissension in the ranks of the Democratic Party as well. Political infighting kept him from obtaining the federal appointment that he and others expected him to receive because of his loyalty to the party.

While African Americans affiliation with the Democratic Party remained insignificant prior to the 1936 presidential elections, Craigen had little trouble virtually dominating the course of Democratic politics in Detroit's black community. Factions would emerge within the MFDC, often forcing Craigen to the courts to maintain control of the organization he had played a central role in founding. His command of the MFDC grew increasingly difficult as blacks swelled the ranks of the Democratic Party and established rival organizations and Craigen encountered personal rivals of his own.

Craigen played an active role in the nation's second oldest African American fraternity, Kappa Alpha Psi, and under his direction the Detroit branch of the organization became a political as well as a social club. He used the fraternity as a vehicle to mentor young black men, advocate human rights, and to end discrimination in education and housing. Craigen's ubiquitous role would earn him the sobriquet "Mr. Kappa."

Craigen died in 1962, just as his native country was first experiencing self-rule. Although a naturalized citizen, Craigen retained an allegiance to his homeland. He visited Guyana after World War II and was a member of one of Detroit's pioneer associations of West Indian immigrants. When a political feud with Charles Diggs Sr. led Diggs to attack Craigen's loyalty to America, Craigen refused to renounce his West Indian roots. Diggs resented Craigen's control of the MFDC and his ability to obtain patronage positions from white political leaders in the Democratic Party. But he also expressed his steadfast belief in the ideals of American citizenship and continued his efforts to ensure that African Americans attained their full rights as citizens.

FURTHER READING

The records and papers of Joseph Craigen are not publicly available. The most scholarly study of his leadership of Detroit's black Democrats is an unpublished paper by the author, "'I Have Made Good As a Stranger in Your Lands': Joseph A. Craigen and African America Politics in Detroit" (2004).

Levine, David Allan. *Internal Combustion: The Races in Detroit, 1915–1926* (1976).

Stein, Judith. *The World of Marcus Garvey: Race and Class in Modern Society* (1986).

Thomas, Richard W. *Life for Us Is What We Make It: Building Black Community in Detroit, 1915–1945* (1992).

KATHRYN L. BEARD

Crawford, Anthony P. (Jan. 1860–21 Oct. 1916), businessman, landowner, farmer, and lynching victim, was born into slavery in Abbeville, South Carolina, the youngest son of Thomas and Louisa, slaves on the plantation of Ben Crawford in Abbeville, South Carolina. After Emancipation and Ben Crawford's death, his widow Rebecca may have bequeathed land to her former slave, Thomas, Anthony's father. Thomas continued to acquire land, and in 1873 he purchased 181 acres of fertile land from Samuel McGowan, a former Confederate general and South Carolina Supreme Court Justice. Thomas Crawford's "homeplace" was located in an alluvial valley, approximately seven miles west of the town of Abbeville. The rich land was flanked on the east by Little River and on the west by Penny Creek.

While Crawford's brothers worked the family farm, Anthony was sent to school, walking seven miles to and from school each day. Seventeen-year-old Anthony was the only one able to sign his name; his brothers could only scratch out Xs. As he grew older he built a thriving farming enterprise. Aided at first by a gift of land from his father, his farming business eventually made him the wealthiest African American in Abbeville County. He shrewdly financed

Anthony P. Crawford, c. 1910. (Library of Congress.)

his business by taking out mortgages on his equipment and supplies and repaid every loan on schedule. On 15 December 1904 the *Abbeville Medium* wrote that Crawford's "homeplace" included 427 acres of "the prettiest cotton land" in Abbeville County. It comfortably accommodated homes for his nine married children, and included "six horses, 12 heads of cattle, 18 hogs, two good wagons, a McCormick rake and a new top buggy."

Resourceful in business and farming, Crawford proved equally inventive when it came to his family's education. While the date of his marriage to his wife Phoebe is not known, records reveal that they had thirteen children. Because state law barred black children from state supported schools, Crawford built one, the Abbeville School, for his own children and for others in the community on his own property. Crawford was also the chief financial supporter and secretary of Cypress Chapel African Methodist Episcopal (AME) church. He once sat on a federal jury and, on 4 October 1894, was an assistant marshal of a parade through the center of Abbeville, composed of hundreds of black members of the Industrial Union of Abbeville County, which he had cofounded. The Industrial Union was formed "to promote the material, moral and intellectual advancement of the colored people." Although cotton still reigned as the region's staple crop, Crawford had diversified his crops well before 1900. In addition to cotton, he grew melons and corn, produced syrup, and raised mules. But various economic crises—and the boll weevil—threatened the area's economic stability. In 1911 the United States enacted the Cotton Reduction Act to control the amount of cotton produced and to stabilize prices. Coupled with the economically crippling effects of World War I, during which many of the ports through which Southern farmers exported cotton to Europe were closed off, the price of cotton began to plummet and tensions steadily rose. In Abbeville, as elsewhere in the South, the threat of violence against blacks grew as a number of factors converged to tear at the socioeconomic fabric of the town. Crawford's comfortable life became increasingly irritating to his white neighbors. Although he was wealthy Anthony Crawford was expected to adhere to the racist codes that governed black life during and following Reconstruction. Blacks were to know their place and always be deferential and obsequious around whites. Crawford did not accept this idea of submissive inferiority, and a comment he made to a friend one day summed up his defiant attitude: "The day a white man hits me is the day I die." Demonstrating his literacy and wealth, much to the chagrin of his white neighbors, Crawford purchased an ad in the *Abbeville Press & Banner* in 1908. In it he thanked the whites who had offered support after his sons had an altercation with white neighbors: "To those who opposed and differed with us I have nothing but a friendly feeling. For individuals as well as nations sometimes differ," he wrote in his "card of thanks."

On the morning of Saturday, 21 October 1916 Crawford brought two wagonloads of cotton and a wagonload of seed into the Abbeville town square to sell. He left his place in line at the cotton gin and took a load of seed over to W. D. Barksdale's general store. Barksdale offered Crawford eighty-five cents per bushel, and Crawford responded that he had been offered more for his load elsewhere. Barksdale called Crawford a liar, and Crawford reportedly called Barksdale a cheat. Crawford backed out of the store. A store clerk flew out of Barksdale's with an axe handle, and Crawford started to make his way back to the cotton gin where he had left his loads. Police Chief Johnson arrested Crawford and put him in the municipal jail. By this time a crowd was gathering. White people streamed out of every store and across the square to give Crawford a whipping. However, Police Chief Johnson collected fifteen dollars bail from Crawford and let him out a side door. While Crawford was arranging his bail, Barksdale was enlisting the help of McKinney Cann, a notorious strong-arm in the town, to give Crawford a beating for daring to challenge a white man. As Crawford made his way back to the gin to recover his loads, a mob had again formed and was headed toward him. Crawford ran into the boiler room of the gin to hide. He found a four-pound hammer to defend himself. As Cann entered the boiler room with the mob behind him, Crawford smashed the white thug's skull with the hammer. Crawford was then hit on the head with a rock.

The mob, which included three of Cann's brothers, pushed Crawford outside to the street. Backing up, trying to defend himself over a stretch of fifty feet, Crawford took on six members of the mob, beating them rather badly before being stabbed in the back. The gin superintendent and two furniture dealers tried to prevent the beating, but as Crawford lay in the street, two hundred men kicked and beat him unconscious. For forty-five minutes Sheriff R. M. Burts implored his constituents not to "tarnish his reputation and violate his oath of office" by lynching Crawford. Finally after promising Lester and Jack Cann that Crawford would not be moved until their brother's condition had stabilized, Burts was allowed to remove the bloodied Crawford to the county jail.

At the jail Mayor Gamble, who was also a doctor, was summoned to treat Crawford. Sheriff Burts urged Crawford to leave town, but Crawford refused. While Crawford lay dying in the jail cell, Abbeville whites again assembled, fearing Sheriff Burts was going to whisk Crawford away on the 4 o'clock train. Crawford managed to hand his bank book to a relative and said "I thought I was a good citizen." The crowd stormed the jail, took the sheriff's keys and dragged the beaten Crawford back out into the street. The cheering mob then thrashed and pummeled Crawford. They dragged his body through the black section of town as a warning to his brethren. Although Crawford was dead long before the rioters arrived at the fairgrounds on the edge of Abbeville, the mob hanged him from a towering southern pine and riddled his swaying body with several hundred bullets. At the time of his death, Anthony Crawford's estate was worth over twenty-five thousand dollars.

In the aftermath of the lynching some enraged whites threatened to expel all blacks from the town and closed all black businesses except one, which was spared with the help of a prominent white citizen. Alfred Ellison, a prominent African American citizen in Abbeville (and grandfather of the author RALPH ELLISON) appealed to white town leaders to stop the violence. Progressive Republican governor Richard Manning conducted a thorough investigation of the lynching and despite identifying the main perpetrators of the violence, a grand jury decided that no one would be tried for the murder. News of the lynching spread across the country and was covered by the *Defender* in Chicago and the *New York Evening Post*. The New York *Independent* dispatched NAACP secretary Roy Nash, who conducted a four-month investigation.

Many of Crawford's children stayed in Abbeville, but others fled the South, as did many other Southern blacks, horrified by Crawford's lynching. In March 1923, as economic conditions in the town continued to deteriorate, six of Crawford's children took out a mortgage for $2,305 from the People's Savings Bank in Abbeville. The entire 427 acres of property was put up as security for the loan. In 1929, when the mortgage was not paid off, the bank filed for a foreclosure. The property was put under W. M. Barnwell and L. C. Haskell as receivers, who auctioned it off in March 1929—Crawford's 427 acres brought $504.

On 13 June 2005 U.S. senators Mary Landrieu and George Allen sponsored and the Senate adopted Resolution 39, which acknowledged that "at least 4,742 people, predominantly African-Americans, were reportedly lynched in the United States between 1882 and 1968." Over one hundred members of the Crawford family attended the proceedings and received a formal apology from the U.S. Senate for failing to enact antilynching legislation.

FURTHER READING

Finnegan, Terence. *The Equal of Some White Men and the Superior of Others: Masculinity and the 1916 Lynching of Anthony Crawford in Abbeville, South Carolina.*

Governor Richard I. Manning. Manning Papers, 1915–1919, South Carolina Department of Archives and History.

Johnson, Doria Dee. *The Lynching of Anthony Crawford* (1998).

Nash, Roy. "The Lynching of Anthony Crawford: South Carolina Declares an End to Mob Rule," New York *Independent*, 11 Dec. 1916.

Schweninger, Loren. *Black Property Owners in the South 1790–1915* (1997).

Spierenburg, Peter, ed. *Modern Europe and America* (1998).

Spierenburg, Peter, ed. *Men and Violence: Gender, Honor and Rituals in Modern Europe and America* (1998).

Ware, Lowry. *Old Abbeville: Scenes of the Past of a Town Where Old Time Things are Not Forgotten* (1992).

CAROLINE DEVOE

Crawford, James (1810 or 1811–20 Oct. 1888), fugitive slave, Baptist minister, and abolitionist leader on Nantucket Island, Massachusetts, was born the son of his wealthy white owner and Mary, one of his father's slaves on a plantation in Virginia. No account has been found yet which reveals his father's name or how James Crawford himself was named. Though stories about how and when he escaped slavery are in conflict, all of them agree that his white half brother broke his promise to their dying father to free Crawford. Instead, Crawford was sent into the fields to work. His obituary in the Nantucket *Inquirer and Mirror* claimed that he escaped the first time by running to Florida to live among the Seminole Indians for two years as a preacher. The same account claimed that his half brother, then the master of the plantation,

"spent a fortune" to recapture him and then "strung him up by the thumbs" as a punishment. Another account asserted that when he was sixteen years old he escaped by sea to Canada. Whatever the specific details, all the accounts agree that he did eventually escape by sea to the North and ended up in Canada, where he decided to pass for white. He was described as having the "merriest blue eyes and dimples." Crawford worked for several years as a cook on board ships. In a letter to the local Nantucket newspaper in 1937, Arthur C. Brock asserted that Crawford had worked as a cook for his grandfather, Captain Peter Coffin Brock.

Crawford converted to Christianity when he heard Edward Taylor preach at the Seamen's Bethel in Boston. Crawford later said that Taylor's preaching also convinced him that he should abandon his seafaring life. He settled in Providence, Rhode Island, where he worked as a jeweler. While in Providence—the exact date is unknown—he married his first wife, Ann Williams, a fugitive slave from South Carolina. Their only child, Juliana, was born there. Sometime while living in Providence, Crawford became gravely ill and decided to devote the rest of his life to God's service. There are conflicting accounts about when he learned to read. One account claimed that his white father had taught him in secret. According to another, he learned to read in Providence while studying for the ministry. He became a minister, first as a Methodist and then as a Baptist. His obituary claimed that he became an ardent abolitionist while living in Providence and rendered "valuable assistance to many a fugitive slave."

His ministerial duties took him to Nantucket in 1848 at a time when the African Baptist Church there had ceased to exist because of dwindling membership. He became the minister of a reorganized Baptist congregation, which occupied the African Meeting House. Crawford moved his family—which by then included his seventy-year-old mother, Mary, who had evidently been released from slavery, perhaps because of her advanced age and dementia—to the island. Since the church could not afford to pay him a salary, Crawford supported himself as a barber with a shop on the south side of Main Street. His customers were both black and white.

Julia Ward Williams, one of Ann Crawford's three sisters, had also escaped slavery and married the famous black abolitionist HENRY HIGHLAND GARNET. The third sister, Dianna Read, however, remained a slave, as did her daughter, Cornelia.

Word came to Nantucket in 1857 or 1858, via Henry Highland Garnet, that Dianna and Cornelia were to be put up for sale by John N. Maffit of Wilmington, North Carolina. Crawford began negotiations with Maffit for their purchase—$1,900 for both women. But before negotiations had been finalized, a second letter arrived from Garnet, then in Jamaica, informing the Crawfords that young Cornelia had already been sold and that Dianna's sale was also imminent. Northern Quakers, undoubtedly informed of the situation by Nantucket's Quaker community, circulated calls for donations to enable the purchase of Cornelia and Dianna. Crawford even gave up his ministerial duties in order to devote all his time to fund-raising, which took him on speaking tours as far away as Canada. Sufficient money was raised to purchase Dianna, and unknown channels brought her north. It took longer to raise $1,000 to purchase Cornelia. Nearly half the amount was raised in England by the efforts of the Richardson family of Newcastle and by a Miss Hilditch of Shrewsbury. The prominent New York abolitionist Lewis Tappan also donated almost $500. With the necessary funds in hand, Crawford himself journeyed south in February 1858, once again passing as a white man. The journey was fraught with danger as he was a fugitive and risked being reenslaved if he were caught. According to his own account, he "trembled for his safety" throughout the journey. He never explained how he succeeded in obtaining Cornelia, but related that on his return, still passing for white, he traveled in first class while Cornelia traveled in the baggage car.

The two considered themselves to be fugitives, even though Crawford apparently purchased his niece legally. Perhaps he feared that since he was himself a fugitive from slavery, authorities would not honor the sale if his true status were uncovered. Stopping in New Bedford, Massachusetts, a haven for runaway slaves, they were greeted warmly, according to the New Bedford *Mercury*, despite the fact that Cornelia had been purchased "for so much gold." They then proceeded to Nantucket, where Cornelia was reunited with her mother and her aunt. Unfortunately, Crawford's wife Ann died that year at the age of fifty-four. He then married Ann's sister, Dianna Read, newly freed from slavery as a result of his fund-raising efforts. Dianna lived only two more years, dying in 1860 at the age of forty-six; Crawford's mother, Mary, died that same year, age eighty-three.

Cornelia Williams Read continued to live on the island with Crawford, who was her rescuer, uncle, and now her stepfather. She married WILLIAM GOULD on 22 November 1865, with Crawford officiating. Gould was a runaway slave who was taken as contraband in 1862 off the coast of Wilmington, North Carolina, and served in the Union navy. The two had known each other in childhood, probably in Wilmington, and left the island for Dedham, Massachusetts, where they raised eight children. They named one son Frederick Crawford Gould, in honor of Crawford, and another Herbert Richardson Gould, in honor of the English couple who had donated to Cornelia's escape.

In 1868 Juliana, Crawford's only child, died at age twenty-nine; she had married Edward J. Godfrey on Nantucket. The same year Crawford married again, this time to a widow living on the island, Rebecca Elaw Pierce. She was the daughter of the Methodist preacher ZILPHA ELAW. Crawford died twenty years later at the age of seventy-seven. His obituary reported that he had served as a pastor on Nantucket longer than any other, and to date his record of forty-one years of service is unbroken. The local paper described him as "one of our best known and highly respected citizens."

FURTHER READING

Gould, William B., IV. *Diary of a Contraband: The Civil War Passage of a Black Sailor* (2002).

Karttunen, Francis. *The Other Islanders: People Who Pulled Nantucket's Oars* (2005).

Nantucket Historical Association Archives. Available online at http://www.nha.org.

Obituary: Nantucket *Inquirer and Mirror* (25 Oct. 1888).

BARBARA A. WHITE

Creed, Cortlandt Van Rensselaer

Creed, Cortlandt Van Rensselaer (Jan. 1833– 9 Aug. 1900), physician and the first African American graduate of Yale, was born in New Haven, Connecticut, to West Indian native John William Creed (a custodian and caterer at Yale College) and Vashti Duplex Creed (the daughter of the Revolutionary War hero Prince Duplex, who had been born a slave). John and Vashti Creed's wedding had been officiated by Reverend Leonard Bacon, a professor of theology at Yale and an abolitionist. Cortlandt Creed was named after the Yale alumnus Cortlandt Van Rensselaer, scion of an old New York Dutch family who was a Presbyterian minister among freed and enslaved African Americans in Virginia and a member of the American Colonization Society, whom it is likely that John Creed knew as a student. Cortlandt Van Rensselaer Creed was the first African American to take a degree from Yale, earning the M.D. in 1857. He served as a military surgeon during the Civil War, established medical practices in Brooklyn, New York, and New Haven, and was consulted as a medical expert after the shooting of President Garfield.

Cortlandt Creed was the beneficiary of aspirational parents. A native of Connecticut, his mother's father, PRINCE DUPLEX, in addition to serving in the War of Independence, for which he earned manumission and a federal pension, later moved some of his family to western New York state in order to establish a homestead farm. His mother was the first African American teacher at the Temple Street School in New Haven. His maternal uncle, Prince Duplex Jr., was one of the founders of the African United Ecclesiastical Society, which led to the creation of Temple Street Church. His son, EDWARD P. DUPLEX, moved to California, becoming a successful businessman and the first African American elected to office west of the Mississippi River. Cortlandt Creed's father, born in the West Indies, sought admission to Yale College but was refused. Nonetheless, the father established himself as a successful New Haven businessman and property owner.

Cortlandt Creed was educated at the New Haven Lancasterian School (where he was probably one of a very few African American students) before apprenticing to the New Haven physician Dr. George Buddington. (At this period in the training of physicians, a baccalaureate degree was not required for admission to medical school.) In 1854 Creed was accepted into Yale Medical School, even though Yale College still refused to admit black students. His admission may have been enabled by a changing political climate in Connecticut, with moderate abolitionists controlling the state's general assembly and Yale's president Theodore Dwight Woolsey supportive of African American citizens. In contrast to the contested admission of MARTIN R. DELANY and two other African Americans to Harvard Medical School in 1850, Creed's admission to Yale apparently evoked no public dissent. In January of 1857, Creed took his oral exams having completed a written thesis on blood, earning his M.D. During his studies at Yale, Creed wrote to FREDERICK DOUGLASS expressing his interest in practicing medicine in Jamaica or Liberia, plans that did not come to pass. Nonetheless, his medical career exhibited an ethos of professional service and humanitarianism.

In the years that followed, Creed established successful mixed-race medical practices in New Haven and briefly in Brooklyn. With the beginning of the Civil War in 1861, Creed volunteered for military service in the Connecticut Volunteers but was turned down because of his race. However, by 1863 President Lincoln authorized the recruitment of black soldiers, and Creed served as a field surgeon in the 30th Connecticut Volunteer Infantry Regiment (a company of African Americans) until the war's end. In 1879 Creed was commissioned as a first lieutenant and assistant surgeon in the Fifth Battalion of the Connecticut Guard. He was admitted to the Connecticut Medical Society in 1885. In 1881 when U.S. President James Garfield was shot, Creed was consulted by federal authorities seeking advice on how to find the bullet before conducting surgery, a specialized expertise that he likely acquired as a military surgeon.

Creed married his first wife, Drucilla Wright (1836?–1864) in 1854, with whom he had four sons; after her death, he married Mary A. Paul (1839–1908) in 1865, who gave birth to four daughters and two sons. Creed died of Bright's disease in New Haven in August 1900. Many of Creed's descendents still live in New Haven and have distinguished themselves professionally, a further testimony to their ancestors' enduring aspirations and emphasis on education.

FURTHER READING

"Descendents of Prince Duplex." *Tompkins County NYGenWeb* (2010). http://nytompki.org/Genie/duplex/duplex_register/d3.htm#i3.

Patton, Curtis L. "Early African American Presence in New Haven and Yale University." In *Edward Bouchet: The First African-American Doctorate*, ed. Ronald E. Mickens, 1–18. (2002).

THOMAS LAWRENCE LONG

Crews, William Henry (11 Oct. 1843 or 1845?–1912?), teacher, farmer, public official, and three-term state legislator, was born a slave in Granville County, North Carolina, near the county seat of Oxford, to unnamed unknown parents. Little is known of his childhood, except that he received a limited education before the Civil War, probably because of his preferred status as the property, and possibly the son, of a prosperous white planter named Benjamin Crews. One account of Crews's early life says he was taken from his slave mother "at the age of two years and reared by a white family whose name he bore" (Edmonds, 102). He is also said to have attended both private and public schools in Oxford, where he grew up.

By 1870 Crews's education had enabled him to begin work as a schoolteacher in Oxford, even as he also ran his own farm and worked as a carpenter. Beginning in 1874 Crews embarked on a career of public service that lasted for the next quarter of a century, becoming one of ten African Americans elected to the North Carolina general assembly from predominantly black Granville County between 1868 and 1898. In 1874 Crews and his colleague Hanson Truman Hughes were elected to the North Carolina House of Representatives by Granville voters, where Crews served until the 1874–1875 general assembly. In 1876 Crews was reelected to the chamber, this time with his colleague Henry Clay Rogers, and served until the 1876–1877 general assembly, with Hughes representing the Twenty-First District (Granville) in the state Senate.

More than a decade later, in 1892, Crews was once again selected as the Republican house nominee for Granville, narrowly defeating both a white Democrat and a white Populist candidate in a three-way race. While in the general assembly, he served on the House Education Committee and the Committee on Insane Asylums. Yet it was his Crews's record of public service at the local level, much of it accomplished after the formal end of Reconstruction and before the so-called "fusion" era of the 1890s, when Populists and Republicans united to defeat the state's Democrats, that was little short of astonishing. Crews reportedly ran for office in Granville County for twenty-three years without suffering a single defeat. Elected a county justice of the peace in 1878, he held that post for three years, and he served for fourteen years as a town constable in Oxford and as a deputy sheriff in Granville County. He also served as both a street commissioner in Oxford and a member of the local school committee. Active in his the local Missionary Baptist Church, he served as church treasurer for sixteen years and auditor of the denomination's Shiloh Association. He also was chairman of the Granville County Republican executive committee in the 1870s.

On 10 March 1870 Crews married Sarah E. Taylor, a schoolteacher. The couple had at least nine children: seven daughters, Bessie, Georgia, Lily, Martha, Minnie, Sarah, and Willie; and two sons, Vernen and Hiram. Crews had at least one other son, William H. Crews Jr., who followed his father into statewide politics. In 1894 the younger Crews

won his father's Granville County seat in the legislature by a narrow majority of eleven votes, and then served in two successive general assemblies before leaving office. During the 1895 session, he gained a measure of statewide notoriety for proposing, successfully, that the general assembly adjourn early on Friday, 21 February, out of respect for the death of the abolitionist FREDERICK DOUGLASS. Angry Democrats labeled this adjournment an insult to George Washington, whose birthday on 22 February fell that year on Saturday, a half-day of work. In 1896 the younger Crews served as an alternate delegate from the Fifth Congressional District to the Republican National Convention in Saint Louis, in 1896, at which William McKinley was nominated for president, and he won reelection to a second legislative term that fall, serving his final term in the 1897 general assembly.

Neither Crews legislator sought re-election in 1898, the year in which a Democratic landslide fueled by antiblack sentiment swept most Republicans and Populists out of office in Granville and across the state. Dismayed by the advent of white supremacist politics in North Carolina and the imminent disfranchisement of most black voters there, the elder Crews soon moved to Washington, D.C., to accept a minor federal appointment in the McKinley administration.

In 1899 the elder Crews was listed in the Washington city directory as a clerk at the Bureau of Pensions, a position he held until about 1910. His family remained in Oxford until after 1900, at which time they joined him in the nation's capital, according to the 1910 census. Crews appears to have died in Washington sometime after 1912, the last year he was listed in the directory; his daughter Minnie, studying to become a pharmacist, lived with him. The 1920 census lists his wife as a widow, living with a married daughter.

FURTHER READING

Edmonds, Helen G. *The Negro and Fusion Politics in North Carolina, 1894–1901* (1951).

Foner, Eric. *Freedom's Lawmakers: A Directory of Black Officeholders during Reconstruction* (1993).

Kenzer, Robert C. *Enterprising Southerners: Black Economic Success in North Carolina, 1865–1915* (1997).

BENJAMIN R. JUSTESEN

Crichlow, Ernest T. (19 June 1914–10 Nov. 2005), painter, illustrator, and graphic artist, was born in Brooklyn, New York, the second oldest of nine children of Herbert and Irene Crichlow, immigrants from Barbados. Using his bricklaying and plastering skills, Crichlow's father made beautiful, patterned ceiling decorations that Ernest recalled as his earliest artistic inspiration. In the 1920s Crichlow won his first artistic commission: a neighborhood preacher paid him and a close friend to paint a black Jesus on a window shade. Not only did this assignment encourage Crichlow to pursue a career in art, it also marked the beginning of his work with black subjects.

Realizing Crichlow's artistic potential, his art teachers at Haaren High School in Brooklyn raised money for a scholarship for him to attend the School of Commercial Illustrating and Advertising Art in Manhattan. In a 1968 interview, Crichlow recalled that he left school during "the height of the Depression," but whether this was after attending the art school in Manhattan or whether it was even before completing high school is not known. Apparently unable to find work after leaving school, Crichlow attended free night classes at the Art Students League, where he interacted with both black and white artists and further developed his artistic skills.

At the Art Students League, Crichlow studied European modernism and began experimenting with abstraction. Although his mature work maintains a sophisticated engagement with cubist spatial and figurative distortion, he quickly realized that pure abstraction did not suit him. This realization came after observing his parents' reaction to his work. Although they took pride in their son's talents, Crichlow felt that his abstract work did not really communicate with them. At that point he decided to develop figural compositions that would interest and inspire his family and community.

Aware of the burgeoning Harlem artistic community of the mid-1930s, Crichlow met the sculptor AUGUSTA SAVAGE, who had studied in Paris for several years. As an assistant supervisor for the Works Progress Administration's Federal Art Project (FAP) and later director of the Harlem Community Art Center, Savage dedicated her career to encouraging and teaching young black artists. Crichlow enrolled in Savage's art classes, which included JACOB ARMSTEAD LAWRENCE, GWENDOLYN KNIGHT, and Norman Lewis. He learned lithography, etching, and casein and egg tempera, and soon joined the FAP, where he excelled as a teacher, muralist, and printmaker. The FAP was a national program and assigned Crichlow to its North Carolina Art Project in Greensboro.

While working for the FAP, Crichlow made what would become his most famous work of art—a lithograph titled Lovers (1938). The ironically titled print depicted a tightly enclosed space containing a hooded Ku Klux Klansman clutching a black woman around the waist and lifting her skirt. Crichlow was particularly interested in black women as symbols of strength and courage; in the print, with a controlled expression and deft arms, the woman attempted to unmask her perpetrator with one hand and grab onto a chair leg or stick with the other, poised to strike back. Crichlow implicated the professional classes in this form of racial violence by exposing the Klansman's pinstriped suit under his robe. While the Klan sought to legitimize its criminal assaults on blacks by professing to protect white women from what they deemed the brutal and lascivious black man, Crichlow reversed the scenario to represent the historical reality of the vulnerability of black women at the hands of socially and economically empowered white men. As was noted in his 2005 Washington Post obituary, Crichlow was unwilling to present African Americans as victims; instead, his courageous woman embodied black resistance to white brutality.

Crichlow displayed this work and others at exhibitions held at the Harlem Community Center (1938), the New York World's Fair (1939), the Augusta Savage Studios (1939), and the American Negro Exposition in Chicago (1940). In December 1941 Crichlow was included in an important show of African American art at the Downtown Gallery in Manhattan. His Lovers hung beside works by time-honored masters such as HENRY OSSAWA TANNER and important contemporaries including ELDZIER CORTOR, ELLIS WILSON, and CHARLES HENRY ALSTON. The ACA gallery in New York held Crichlow's first one-person exhibition in 1960.

Crichlow married Dorothy Kley in 1952, and they had a son, Anthony. Dorothy Crichlow's work as a microbiologist provided a stable income for the family while Crichlow took sporadic jobs as an illustrator and educator. In the mid-1940s he had begun illustrating children's literature: Lorraine and Jerrold Beam's Two Is a Team (1945) promoted racial tolerance; Dorothy Sterling's Freedom Train: The Story of Harriet Tubman (1954) focused on the Underground Railroad's famous conductor; and Judith Griffin's The Magic Mirrors (1971) was a fable about an African princess. Crichlow transformed the image of the black child in children's literature from "little black Sambos" to sensitively rendered and individualized boys and girls.

In 1958, with artists Jacob Lawrence, Tom Feelings, and Vivian Keys, Crichlow founded the Fulton Art Fair in the Bedford-Stuyvesant area of Brooklyn. The fair showcased local artists and provided an important meeting and exhibition space for black artists. To create further opportunities for African American artists, Crichlow, ROMARE BEARDEN, and Norman Lewis opened the Cinque Gallery in downtown Manhattan in 1969. They exhibited the work of ethnic minority groups under the age of thirty. As gallery and museum institutions generally excluded the work of minority artists, the Cinque Gallery became a vital asset for them.

Crichlow returned to teaching in 1979, when he joined the faculty at the Art Students League, retiring in 1994. In 1980 he received national recognition for his long and honorable career when President Jimmy Carter held a reception at the White House for the National Conference of Artists, an organization founded in 1959 to promote black art and culture. Carter honored ten individuals including Crichlow, Lawrence, LOIS MAILOU JONES, and ARCHIBALD JOHN MOTLEY JR., as the most important African American visual artists of the twentieth century. Crichlow died in Fort Greene, Brooklyn, at the age of ninety-one.

FURTHER READING
Ernest Crichlow's papers are housed in the Archives of American Art, Smithsonian Institution, Washington, D.C.
Doherty, M. Stephen, et al. *Alone in a Crowd: Prints of the 1930s–40s by African-American Artists* (1992).
Messinger, Lisa Mintz, Lisa Gail Collins, and Rachel Mustalish. *African-American Artists, 1929–1945: Prints, Drawings, and Paintings in the Metropolitan Museum of Art* (2003).
Obituary: *Washington Post*, 14 Nov. 2005.

PHOEBE WOLFSKILL

Criss, Sonny (23 Oct. 1927–19 Nov. 1977), jazz alto saxophonist, was born William Criss in Memphis, Tennessee, the son of Lucy B.; her maiden name and her husband's name are unknown. Criss began playing saxophone at age eleven. In 1942 his family moved to Los Angeles, where he attended Jefferson High School and performed with his fellow students HAMPTON HAWES, a pianist, and CECIL (later known as "Big Jay") MCNEELY, a tenor saxophonist. Criss studied music with Samuel Browne, who also taught the trumpeter Art Farmer and the tenor

saxophonist DEXTER GORDON. He transferred to the Polytechnic High School, again with Hawes, and while in school worked with the pianist in a quartet at the Last Word, a nightclub. Criss may have married in the mid-1940s. Details are unknown, apart from his mention of a son who returned from service in Vietnam around 1966.

Criss first toured around 1945, going to Chicago to play with the rhythm and blues drummer Johnny Otis's band. From February to March 1946 Criss sat in with the alto saxophonist CHARLIE PARKER's quintet, which included MILES DAVIS, at Club Finale. He was also a member, along with Parker and the tenor saxophonist Teddy Edwards, of the trumpeter HOWARD MCGHEE's band at the same club from March through May 1946, at Billy Berg's Swing Club early in July, and then at the Hi-De-Ho Club.

Criss joined the trumpeter Al Killian's band at Billy Berg's in April 1947. His early recordings include solos on "Groovin' High" and "Hot House" as a member of McGhee's All Stars at Gene Norman's Just Jazz concert in Pasadena on 29 April 1947 and on "The Hunt," "Bopera," "Jeronimo," and "Bop after Hours" as a member of the Bopland Boys, a nine-piece group including the tenor saxophonist WARDELL GRAY, McGhee, Gordon, and Hawes, performing at a Hollywood Jazz Concert on 6 July 1947. During this period Criss toured with Killian to Portland, Oregon, Seattle, and San Francisco before returning to Los Angeles, where the group recorded with the singer BILLY ECKSTINE.

Criss left Killian's band early in 1948. He began rehearsing with the trumpeter GERALD WILSON's orchestra in autumn 1948 but soon left when the opportunity arose to tour nationally with Jazz at the Philharmonic from November 1948 through June 1949. During breaks from this affiliation, Criss concurrently toured the East Coast from New York to Miami Beach in a small group with the tenor saxophonist Flip Phillips, a long-term member of Jazz at the Philharmonic. In mid-June 1949 Criss worked with Phillips in Chicago.

Returning to the West Coast, Criss recorded in Los Angeles as the leader of a quartet including Hawes in September 1949. In the fall he joined Edwards, Gordon, and Hawes as a member of the house band at Bop City in San Francisco, and through the latter part of 1949 he performed at the Lighthouse in Hermosa Beach, California, in a quintet with Edwards, Hawes, the bassist Howard Rumsey, and the drummer Larry Bunker. He was one of Gray's Los Angeles All Stars at the Hula-Hut Club in August 1950.

In association with Jazz at the Philharmonic, Criss toured nationally from 1950 to 1951 in a distinguished septet comprising the trumpeter Joe Newman, the trombonist Benny Green, the saxophonists Criss and EDDIE "LOCKJAW" DAVIS, the pianist Bobby Tucker, the bassist Tommy Potter, and the drummer KENNY CLARKE. The septet accompanied Eckstine but also performed on its own, and one such performance was recorded in concert on 12 October 1951. An almost maniacally inspired Criss dominates this session, released posthumously as *Intermission Riff* under his own name on the strength of his playing.

Early in 1952 Criss was among a rotating pool of musicians who played with the baritone saxophonist Gerry Mulligan on Monday nights at the Haig club on Wilshire Boulevard. That summer he was heard at the Trade Wind Club in Inglewood, California; the surviving recordings also include Parker, the trumpeter Chet Baker, and the pianist Al Haig. Severely impaired by alcoholism, Criss struggled for work over the next few years, at times performing in striptease houses. After joining Stan Kenton's Jazz Showcase package tour in 1955 (not as a member of Kenton's band), Criss toured with the drummer Buddy Rich on and off for five years. Rich's quintet, which at times included the pianists WYNTON KELLY or Kenny Drew, often worked in resort areas, including Miami Beach.

Late in 1959 or early the next year, Criss returned to Los Angeles. He made a guest appearance with Hawes's trio on an episode of the *Jazz on Stage* television series in about 1960. In 1961 he failed to find any work, and the following year he traveled to Europe. As a fresh face on the European jazz scene, Criss performed with Clarke in the film *Le glaive et la balance* (1962) and with the pianist Henri Renaud at the Trois Mailletz nightclub in Paris (1963), but by 1964 he was again struggling for work. These problems continued in early 1965 with his return to Los Angeles, where his scant earnings came from occasional performances at Shelly's Manne-Hole and REDD FOXX's club and, in early 1966, at Marty's nightclub.

Criss's career moved forward in 1966, when he signed a contract with Prestige Records. His first album, *This Is Criss!* was recorded in October 1966 and helped him secure engagements in New York at the Village Vanguard and the Museum of Modern Art. Further albums included *Up, Up, and Away*

in 1967 and *Sonny's Dream (New Birth of the Cool)* in 1968, and in the latter year he performed at the Newport Jazz Festival. His contract with Prestige was abruptly canceled when he showed up drunk for his eighth session in 1969.

From 1970 through 1974 Criss was devoted to community service, giving concerts for schoolchildren at the Hollywood Bowl and working as an alcohol rehabilitation counselor. He also toured Europe in 1973 and 1974, and he began to make further recordings, including the albums *Crisscraft*, *Saturday Morning*, and *Out of Nowhere*, all in 1975. Shortly before a scheduled performance in Tokyo, he committed suicide with a gun at his home in Los Angeles. Given his recent success, after a career impeded by alcohol and other personal problems and after decades of struggling for opportunities to perform, this action seemed inexplicable. Eleven years later Criss's mother revealed that he had been suffering from stomach cancer but told no one and kept playing until finally he could no longer face the pain.

The writer Thomas Owens called Criss "another of Parker's disciples," noting that the saxophonist borrowed certain melodic phrases from Parker but had a sweeter tone and a "fast and automatically applied vibrato [that] was more typical of swing than of bebop .... The chief source of tension in his playing was his disconcerting unconcern for, or perhaps inability to keep track of, the meter .... Eventually, however, he solved his rhythmic and harmonic problems and developed into an excellent soloist" (48–50). Unlike many who received Parker's technically minded musical message, Criss also shared Parker's deep feeling for blues phrases, which he inserted into any manner of tune. The ballad "Sweet Lorraine" on his album *At the Crossroads* (1959) provides a particularly striking example. Within the erudite context of the bop tradition, he delivered these blues formulas in a somewhat rawer form than did Parker himself. On mature recordings from the mid-1960s and mid-1970s, Criss was most creative when improvising at a leisurely pace, as, for example, in his renditions of "Black Coffee" on *This Is Criss!*, "Willow Weep for Me" on *Up, Up, and Away*, and "Blues in My Heart" on *Crisscraft*.

FURTHER READING

Gordon, Robert. *Jazz West Coast: The Los Angeles Jazz Scene of the 1950s* (1986).

Owens, Thomas. *Bebop: The Music and Its Players* (1995).

Salemann, Dieter, et al. *Sonny Criss: Solography, Discographical Informations, Band Routes, Engagements in Chronological Order* (1987).

Obituaries: *Los Angeles Times*, 20 Nov. 1977; *New York Times*, 21 Nov. 1977; *Down Beat*, 26 Jan. 1978.

This entry is taken from the *American National Biography* and is published here with the permission of the American Council of Learned Societies.

BARRY KERNFELD

Crite, Allan Rohan (20 Mar. 1910–6 Sept. 2007), a painter of African, Native American, and European ancestry who recorded the people, architecture, and daily life of African Americans in Boston's Roxbury and South End districts, was born in 1910 in North Plainfield, New Jersey, to Oscar William Crite and Annamae Palmer Crite. He was the only one of four children to survive infancy. While he was still a baby, his family moved to Boston so that his father could pursue a degree in engineering. Crite graduated from Boston Latin High School in 1920. Although offered a scholarship by the Yale University School of Art, Crite elected to remain in Boston to help his mother attend to his father, who had suffered a stroke. He attended the Boston School of the Museum of Fine Arts on scholarship, studying industrial design as well as drawing and painting before graduating in 1936. The school encouraged precision, a quality that can be seen in Crite's art. For the next few decades, Crite supplemented his formal education by visiting the libraries, galleries, and museums of Boston. In 1968 he earned a B.A. from the Harvard University Extension School. Suffolk University awarded him an honorary doctorate in 1979.

Crite became one of the few African Americans to get hired as an artist by the Roosevelt Administration's New Deal during the Great Depression. He enjoyed a brief tenure in 1934 on the Public Works of Art Project (PWAP), the first federal art program, and participated in the Works Progress Administration (WPA) Federal Art Project in 1936. The two experiences provided him with financial support and a number of important exhibition opportunities. He exhibited as part of PWAP at the Corcoran Gallery of Art in Washington, D.C., and as part of the WPA at the Museum of Modern Art in New York City in 1936. In the late 1930s, Crite began giving lectures on the liturgical arts and worked for fourteen months in New York City for the Rambusch Decorating Company. He designed a large mural for St. Augustine's Church in Brooklyn. Crite then accepted a job as an engineering draftsman with the Boston Naval Shipyard in 1940 and remained in this position for the next thirty years.

The roughly two dozen works that Crite produced for the government art projects were an extension of a series of images of African American urban life in Boston that the artist began around 1930 and completed in the 1940s. These are Crite's most acclaimed works. Collectively known as the "Neighborhood Series," these documentary-style pictures feature street scenes, portraits of the artist's friends and family, and images of local church life. The content of his works is conveyed through Crite's attention to configurations on the surface, the details of the brick, the color of the wood, and the texture of the hair. His paintings and drawings are a repository of faithfully taken notes of everyday activities or seemingly insignificant moments. For example, *Last Game at Dusk* (1939) shows children playing near a stoop before being called home for dinner. Crite's goal in producing these pictures was to provide a visual alternative to the dominant images of African Americans as jazz players, gamblers, or backwoods Southerners. Crite's idealized impressions of African Americans may relate to the Boston School artists' shared philosophy that spiritual or moral beauty is best conveyed through aestheticized depictions. His desire to present uplifting images of African Americans' urban life also relates closely with the goals of the Harlem Renaissance. Although Crite did not participate in the Harlem Renaissance directly, his works share the desire felt by many black artists to convey the humanity of black people to white America.

After completing the Neighborhood Series, Crite produced a book of Christian images in 1944 that reflected his devout Episcopalian religious faith. The pictures do not visually elaborate a text but rather serve as a medium of expression, from musical rhythm into visual rhythm. In subsequent years, he produced a range of oil paintings, watercolors, drawings, and prints that captured the parades, games, conversations, and work with expressive lines and vivid colors. He continued to produce religious works and also served as a mentor to young artists. Crite spent his life in Boston, primarily in the South End on Columbus Avenue, before succumbing to natural causes at the age of ninety-seven.

FURTHER READING

Crite, Allan Rohan. *Were You There When They Crucified My Lord: A Negro Spiritual in Illustrations* (1944).

Caro, Julie Levin. *Allan Rohan Crite: Artist-Reporter of the African American Community* (2001).

CARYN E. NEUMANN

Crocker, Frankie (18 Dec. 1937–21 Oct. 2000), DJ and broadcasting executive, was born Frank Michael Crocker in Buffalo, New York, the only child of Mrs. Frances Crocker. There is some disagreement about his date of birth, which some sources have reported as 1940. Little is known about his early life; only that he began his career as a DJ while still a prelaw student at the University of Buffalo and also attended the University of Southern California. In the early 1960s Crocker was hired by WUFO, a local daytime AM station that served Buffalo's black community. During this time he developed his rich vocal delivery and created the smooth, confident persona that would attract listeners and give him the platform to ascend to larger markets such as New York City, where he established himself in the early 1960s at R&B station WWRL. In 1969 he became the first black DJ at all-white AM powerhouse WMCA.

As a DJ, Crocker gained notoriety for his rhyming monologue, which he would recite over a slow blues riff. He asked his listeners to get "more dip in your hip, more glide in your stride" (http://www.powerhouseradio.com/frankiecrocker.html). He unapologetically introduced himself as the "Eighth Wonder of the World," and "tall, tan and fly," and teased his female listeners with the line, "If I'm all you've got, I'm all you need" (http://www.powerhouseradio.com/frankiecrocker.html). His provocative, sensual radio act sometimes ended with an invitation for the ladies in the audience to take a bath with him. He would use running water sound effects, and even light a candle in his studio to set the mood. His mellifluous voice permeated the New York airwaves with his famous tagline, "And remember: Whenever Frankie Crocker isn't on your radio, your radio really isn't on" (*Jet*, 6 Nov. 2000, 98). He was also strongly identified by his sign-off music, "Moody's Mood for Love." He acquired many nicknames at different points in his career, including "Chief Rocker," "Hollywood," and "Love Man." And although his playfully sexual verbal repertoire made him the top DJ in New York, his lasting influence was not as an on-air personality but as a program director.

Crocker made history in 1972 after arriving at Harlem radio station WBLS. Within a few years of becoming its program director, he had positioned WBLS as the number one–rated radio station and himself as the number-one disc jockey in New York. In the most significant market in the country, he had supplanted historically powerful top-forty station WABC. He mixed Latin, pop, R&B, and even rock music styles to create an innovative new radio format, which he called "urban contemporary." He presciently understood the need for radio to reach across musical platforms to appeal to all cultural, racial, and economic segments of society in the era immediately after the civil rights movement, Vietnam, and the Black Arts Movement. His willingness to play extended tracks made him a key figure in promoting early disco. Soon, top-forty radio stations in both large and small markets around the country followed suit and emulated the format, which would later evolve into CHR (Contemporary Hit Radio) and then "Churban"— soon to become the most dominant format in all radio broadcasting.

Because of the celebrity status he had attained, he got the opportunity to try his hand at acting, appearing in five films, including *Cleopatra Jones* (1973), *Five on the Black Hand Side* (1973), and *Darktown Strutters* (1975). He also made recordings with the Heart and Soul Orchestra for Neil Bogart's groundbreaking Casablanca label, whose star artist was dance diva Donna Summer. In 1976 Crocker left WBLS under a dark cloud of scandal when he was indicted and convicted in Newark, New Jersey, of lying to a federal grand jury during the payola investigations of that decade, which centered on bribes of drugs and money given to radio DJs and executives by record companies in order to obtain airplay for their artists. The conviction was later overturned.

Then in 1979, at the height of the decadent disco era, he made a flamboyant return to WBLS riding a white horse onto the dance floor of New York's infamous Studio 54. His eclectic blend of music programming in the late 1970s and early 1980s included white rock bands such as Devo and Blondie, the sophisticated ballads of LUTHER VANDROSS, and Argentinean rhythms of saxophonist Gato Barbieri. He even interviewed Australian Olivia Newton-John and promoted her 1981 dance hit "Physical."

During the 1980s Crocker hosted the television programs *Friday Night Videos* and *Solid Gold* and appeared in the film *Breakin' 2: Electric Boogaloo*

(1984). He was also among the first video jockeys (or VJs), hired by cable television's VH1 channel in 1985.

After working in Chicago and St. Louis, he was brought back to WBLS as program director again in 1994. The station had experienced a precipitous fall in the ratings and Crocker redirected the format away from the eighteen- to thirty-four-year-old demographic toward a larger adult audience. Always the innovator, in 1997 Crocker started frankiecrocker.com, an early Internet-based radio Web site that provided a diverse blend of music, artist interviews, and personal information.

In the late 1990s he became a born-again Christian and in 1998 promoted a national day of prayer to reject the excesses he saw in contemporary society, which he believed were manifested by the popularity of shock-value programs hosted by such broadcasters as Jerry Springer and Howard Stern as well as by the sex scandal involving President Bill Clinton and Monica Lewinsky.

Before his October 2000 death in Miami from pancreatic cancer, Crocker worked in California in gospel radio and as a syndicated weekend countdown host for "Classic Soul Countdown." His enormous influence on broadcasting was acknowledged at the 19 March 2001 Rock and Roll Hall of Fame induction ceremony at New York's Waldorf Astoria Hotel and in 2002 at the Buffalo Broadcast Pioneers Hall of Fame.

FURTHER READING

Barlow, William. *Voice Over: The Making of Black Radio* (1999).

Fong-Torres, Ben. *The Hits Just Keep On Coming: The History of Top 40 Radio* (1998).

Obituaries: *New York Times*, 24 Oct. 2000; *Jet*, 6 Nov. 2000; *Village Voice*, 7 Nov. 2000; *New York Beacon*, 6 Dec. 2000.

SAM LORBER

Crockett, George William, Jr. (10 Aug. 1909–7 Sept. 1997), activist, attorney, judge, and United States congressman, was born in Jacksonville, Duval County, Florida, the son of Minnie Amelia Jenkins and George William Crockett Sr. The former was a licensed public school teacher, and the latter a railroad carpenter for the Atlantic Coast Line Railroad and Baptist church pastor.

George Crockett Jr. graduated from Morehouse College in 1931, and the University of Michigan Law School in 1934, before returning to Jacksonville. He was one of a small number of practicing African American attorneys in Florida at this time. In 1934 he married Ethelene Crockett, with whom he would have three children, Elizabeth Crockett Hicks, George W. Crockett III, and Ethelene Crockett Jones.

Initiating a lifetime at the forefront of the civil rights legal struggle, Crockett was the first African American lawyer employed by the U.S. Department of Labor, from 1939 to 1943. He also participated in the 1937 founding of the country's first racially integrated bar association, the National Lawyers Guild (NLG), and twelve years later helped found the first integrated bar firm, Goodman, Crockett, Eden, and Robb.

In 1949, Crockett defended eleven Communist Party leaders accused of violating the Smith Act, namely advocating the overthrow of the federal government. At the end of the trial, Judge Harold Medina sentenced Crockett to jail for alleged contempt of court. He narrowly avoided being disbarred and ultimately served a four-month sentence in Ashland, Kentucky, prison in 1952.

Crockett's principled representation of politically controversial defendants sparked his commitment to provide leadership for the NLG, which had been designated a possible "Communist-Front" by the Federal Government. He developed the Guild Committee to Assist Southern Lawyers (CASL) in 1962. CASL organized southern projects for northern lawyers who wanted to support racial integration and voting rights cases. He was also part of the Mississippi project, a coalition developed by leading civil rights organizations during the Freedom Summer of 1964.

From his 1966 election as a judge on Detroit's criminal court, Crockett became an outspoken advocate of equal justice in a system that failed to accord key due process rights to poor black defendants. His most notable case came in 1969, when he was woken before dawn by news that a sniper firing from a church had killed a Detroit policeman and that the police had arrested over 140 people in the church. Terming it a "collective punishment" mass arrest, Judge Crockett released over one hundred supposed black separatists for lack of probable cause, a case representative of a judicial career that drew praise from the local black community and opprobrium from the white press. In 1974 he was elected Chief Justice of the Detroit Recorder's Court, until his retirement in 1978.

After his wife's death in 1978, he married Harriet Clark Harris in 1980. In the same year he ran for public office in Michigan's 13th Congressional District, a staunchly Democratic area within the city limits of Detroit. He received 92 percent of the vote in the 1980 special election, winning by the same margin in the general election for the 97th Congress a year later.

As a member of the Africa subcommittee in Foreign Affairs, Crockett became an outspoken opponent of South Africa's racist apartheid regime. He called for economic sanctions against the country, and authored the [Nelson] Mandela Freedom resolution that was passed by both Houses in 1984. Crockett also demonstrated against apartheid outside the South African embassy in Washington, D.C., for which he spent a night in jail alongside Detroit MAYOR COLEMAN A. YOUNG.

Between 1987 and 1991, Crockett chaired the Foreign Affairs Subcommittee on Western Hemisphere Affairs, which oversaw policy in the Caribbean and Latin America. Through this role he denounced the Republican Ronald Reagan administration's policy of public support and covert military and financial assistance to the Nicaraguan Contras. The Contras had been implicated in serious human rights violations during their attempts to overthrow the socialist Sandinista National Liberation Front government. Crockett retired from the House of Representatives at the end of his fifth term in January 1991.

George Crockett's eventful life encompassed being jailed in federal prison and working within Congress to enact reform of U.S. prisons and the justice system as a whole. In his roles as attorney, judge, and congressman, he maintained a deep commitment to defending constitutional liberties. His defense of the neglected and unpopular within society focused on combating racial inequalities and political persecution, expanding in later years to incorporate international human rights issues. He died in Washington, D.C.

FURTHER READING

George Crockett's legislative papers are housed in the Moorland-Springarn Research Center, Howard University, in Washington, D.C. His court papers are held at the Walter P. Reuther Library Archives of Labor and Urban Affairs in Detroit, Michigan.

Georgakas, Dan, and Marvin Surkin. *Detroit: I Do Mind Dying: A Study in Urban Revolution* (1999).

Moon, Elaine. *Untold Tales, Unsung Heroes: Oral History of Detroit's African-American Community, 1918–67* (1993).

Obituary: Thomas, Robert M. "George W. Crockett Dies at 88; Was a Civil Rights Crusader," *New York Times*, 15 Sept. 1997.

RUTH E. MARTIN

Crogman, William Henry (5 May 1841–16 Oct. 1931), sailor and classics professor, political activist and first black president of Atlanta's Clark University, was born on St. Martin's in the Caribbean, the son of William Crogman, Sr. and Charlotte Chippendale. A small tropical island in the West Indies' northern Leewards, St. Martin's was occupied jointly by two colonial powers in William Crogman's childhood days, and its sugar plantations had kept slave labor alive. While the French in the North abolished the "peculiar institution" in 1848, the Dutch in the South followed suit only in 1863. Observing slavery intact may have alerted young Crogman to the necessity of serving his race while the reality of at least a partial abolition increased his confidence that even the most adverse circumstances could be overcome. However, before an ambitious intellectual career catapulted Crogman to the top of the African American "Talented Tenth," he would roam the world's oceans for more than a decade.

An orphan at age twelve, William Crogman took to the sea when he turned fourteen. B. L. Boomer, mate under the first captain to hire Crogman, became friends with the boy and introduced him to his family in Massachusetts. Two of the Boomer brothers commanded their own vessels, and in their service Crogman's itinerary reached from the United States to South America and from the ports of Europe to those of Bombay and Calcutta. In 1866, somewhere on the high seas of the Indian Ocean, Crogman gave in to B. L. Boomer's admonitions and determined to get an education. Moving to the United States with his friend, the thrifty seaman spent the next two years saving up his hard-earned wages until he could afford to enroll at Pierce Academy in Middleborough, Massachusetts, in 1868.

Although the landlords of this New England town refused him lodging, their racism could not impede the twenty-seven-year-old's stellar achievements in the classroom. Crogman attracted the personal attention of the school's principal and surpassed his fellow students in English, French, and bookkeeping classes. After his graduation in 1870 Crogman's desire to uplift the freedmen of the post-Civil War South brought him to Orangeburg, South Carolina, where he secured a position as English instructor at Claflin University. A devout member of the Methodist Episcopal Church, Crogman thus became the first black professor in any school sponsored by this denomination. Over the course of the next three years, Crogman's academic pursuits sparked an active interest in the classical languages. When his persistent self study of Latin eventually proved unsatisfying, he matriculated at Atlanta University. In 1876, he completed the four-year course in Greek and Latin a full twelve months ahead of schedule. Yet Crogman gained more from these early years in Georgia than a fluency in these ancient languages, as he also met and married his fellow Atlanta graduate Lavinia C. Mott. The couple would raise three daughters and five sons and their marriage would last for more than half a century.

Atlanta remained the focus of William Crogman's life for the next forty-five years. Clark University hired him on the spot and in 1880 Crogman became Professor of Classical Languages, a position he would hold until his retirement. In these years, hundreds of his Greek and Latin students fanned out across the South to help in the elevation of their race as teachers and priests. Among the honors bestowed upon the mild and diligent instructor were two honorary doctoral degrees, and he was chosen to represent his race in the 1895 Cotton States Exhibition.

While Crogman's life as teacher and family man was grounded in Georgia's capital, his budding career as a public orator took him across the South and on to the Midwest and East of the United States between 1883 and 1896. Most notably, he was invited in 1883 to deliver two addresses at Plymouth Church in Brooklyn, New York, which was then headed by the famous clergyman and reformer Henry Ward Beecher. In photographs of the time, the slender-framed William Crogman is always elegantly clad, his receding hairline and graying mustache framing a boyish face behind wire-rimmed glasses. On his journeys across the segregating nation, even this gentle "aristocrat of color" encountered racism at the hands of restaurant owners, who refused to let him dine with white colleagues, or train conductors, who would force African Americans to overpay and yield better seats to white passengers. Yet there are few mentions of segregation and lynchings in his *Talks for the Times* (1896), a collection of his orations, and *Progress of a Race; or the Remarkable Advancement of the American Negro*, a history book he coauthored in 1897 (reissued 1902). Rather than list the obstacles blacks still had to overcome, Crogman asserted their "manhood" in the face of such attacks. Hoping to crush demeaning preconceptions of "the Negro," he would list African Americans' astounding achievements in spite of de jure and de facto racial discrimination. To illustrate his points, he mined the rich quarry of classical and biblical heritage for metaphors. Indicating the scope of their accomplishments, he would liken FREDERICK DOUGLASS to a Spartan warrior and the toils of former slaves to those of Jesus Christ. Additional imagery from Shakespeare and the romantic poets betrays the profound learning of a man admired by his colleagues for his voluminous library.

Crogman, however, did protest the Jim Crow system in private. As the twentieth century approached, the aging classics professor refused to ride on segregated trains and elevators, preferring even to climb countless flights of stairs to the top of ten-story buildings in downtown Atlanta.

In the contemporary debate surrounding the value of intellectual versus manual training for African Americans, William Crogman upheld a Christian education as the highest ideal attainable. To Crogman, this entailed maintaining sturdy morals coupled with compassion and forgiveness, providing an optimistic black elite with a classical education, and enabling the general population through industrial education. Later, he came to promote a broader education for the black masses. In support of this new goal, he and his former Atlanta classmate, RICHARD R. WRIGHT, advocated the establishment of the American Negro Academy (ANA) in the 1890s. Crogman was the first to approach the future ANA figure head, ALEXANDER CRUMMELL, about this project. When Crogman became Clark University's first black president in 1903 and stayed in office until 1910, his administration consequently removed industrial training from the curriculum.

In 1921, an eighty-year-old William H. Crogman resigned from his professorship at Clark University. The Crogmans now went to live with their daughters, spending time in turn in Philadelphia, Atlanta, and finally Kansas City. When William Crogman died there at age ninety, he had lost his eyesight to a lifetime of reading. After mere days, Lavinia Crogman followed her husband, who had not only spent years battling the popular misconception of blacks' intellectual inferiority by mastering Greek and Latin—at the time, the gauge of humanity—but also employed his classical education toward the advancement of his race. The Crogmans are buried in Atlanta, Georgia.

FURTHER READING

Crogman, W. H. *Talks for the Times* (1896).

Crogman, William H., and J. W. Gibson. *Progress of a Race; or the Remarkable Advancement of the American Negro: From the Bondage of Slavery, Ignorance and Poverty to the Freedom of Citizenship, Intelligence, Affluence, Honor and Trust.* Revised and enlarged (1902).

Ronnick, Michele Valerie. "William Henry Crogman (1841–1931)," *Classical Outlook* 77 pp. 67–68 (2000).

Obituary: Hershaw, L. M., et al. "Notes," *Journal of Negro History* 19.2: 211–224 (1934).

MATHIAS HANSES

Cromwell, Adelaide M. (27 Nov. 1919–), educator and sociologist, was born in Washington, D.C., on Thanksgiving Day, the only child of Yetta Elizabeth Mavritte and JOHN W. CROMWELL JR. Her father, a Phi Beta Kappa graduate of Dartmouth College in 1906, was the first black to become a practicing certified public accountant.

Adelaide McGuinn Cromwell grew up in a prominent family of educators in Washington, D.C. An only child, she grew up in a large townhouse on Thirteenth Street in the northwest portion of Washington, where she lived with her parents and her father's three sisters, two of whom were schoolteachers. Although she was surrounded by adults, it was her aunt OTELIA CROMWELL, the eldest of her father's siblings, who became an enduringly influential figure.

Named after her maternal grandmother, Adelaide (Addy) Mavritte, Adelaide Cromwell and her mother often spent weekends with her maternal grandparents who lived in Burrville, in the then rural northeast area of Washington, D.C. Her grandfather, William Mavritte, was a Baptist minister and a bricklayer by trade. In addition to her grandparents, her mother's close-knit family consisted of numerous great-aunts, aunts and uncles, and first and second cousins, including Senator EDWARD BROOKE of Massachusetts. Cromwell's paternal grandfather, JOHN WESLEY CROMWELL, a civil servant, educator, historian, lawyer, and editor and owner of the *People's Advocate*, was an influential figure among Washington's intellectual elite. Born into slavery in Virginia, his family settled in Philadelphia, Pennsylvania, in 1851, where he graduated from the Institute for Colored Youth. Cromwell's book *Unveiled Voices, Unvarnished Memories: The Cromwell Family in Slavery and Segregation, 1692–1972* (2007), explored the life of her grandfather, John Wesley Cromwell Sr., and her family history as told through the letters, journals, and other documents that her grandfather had kept throughout his life.

Cromwell first entered school as a second-grader at the Lucretia Mott Elementary school and eventually attended Garrison Elementary. Then she attended Garnet-Patterson Junior High School and Dunbar High School, graduating from Dunbar in 1936. In the fall of 1936, at the age of sixteen, Cromwell entered Smith College, where her aunt, Otelia Cromwell, had been the first African American graduate in 1900.

While an undergraduate at Smith, she discovered her various aptitudes and interests, including zoology. Her abiding interest in sociology was especially influenced by her relationships with Professor Frank H. Hankins and Professor Gladys Bryson. When she was a junior at Smith, she was interviewed for Dr. E. FRANKLIN FRAZIER's *Negro Youth at the Crossways: Their Personality Development in the Middle States* (1940). Later, as president of the Sociology Club, she invited Dr. Frazier to speak at Smith. In her senior year she wrote a prizewinning honors thesis titled, "Class Stratification in Negro Society as Portrayed through a Study of Negro Adolescent Girls in Washington, D.C."

Cromwell graduated cum laude from Smith College in 1940 with an AB in Sociology. Later, she was elected into the Smith College chapter of Phi Beta Kappa. After graduation, Cromwell moved to Philadelphia and entered the graduate program in sociology at the University of Pennsylvania. It was here that she pursued her study of Africa; one of her classmates was Kwame Nkrumah, the first president of Ghana.

In 1941, after earning an M.A. in Sociology from the University of Pennsylvania, Cromwell entered the graduate program in social work at Bryn Mawr. She spent the next two years in the classroom and in the field, where her placements included the public welfare department, the Sleighton Farms School for Girls, and the Red Cross. After receiving a Certificate in social case work from Bryn Mawr, Cromwell was invited to serve as the executive director of the Urban League of Englewood, New Jersey.

While at the Urban League, Dr. Frazier Cromwell to teach a course in African American history at Hunter College. Dr. Frazier had originally been asked to teach this course in response to requests by the college's black students for a black professor. As an adjunct member of the faculty, Cromwell became the first African American professor at Hunter College.

It was also during this period that Cromwell met and married HENRY AARON HILL, a chemist with a Ph.D. in Organic Chemistry from the Massachusetts Institute of Technology (MIT). They had one son, Anthony Cromwell Hill, who would eventually graduate from Harvard and become a journalist and filmmaker in Boston.

After her marriage in 1943, Cromwell relocated to Boston and entered the doctoral program in sociology at Harvard. While pursuing her studies at Harvard she was also an instructor for two years at her alma mater, Smith College. The teaching position at Smith was followed by her appointment as a teaching fellow for two eminent Harvard professors, the historian Oscar Handlin and the sociologist Talcott Parsons. With Professor Talcott Parsons as her dissertation adviser, Cromwell wrote her dissertation, "The Negro Upper Class in Boston—its Development and Present Social Structure" (1952). In 1994 an updated and revised version of this work was published by the University of Arkansas Press as *The Other Brahmins: Boston's Black Upper Class, 1750–1950*.

In 1951 Cromwell began her long affiliation with Boston University (BU) when she joined the sociology department. Cromwell's interest in Africa led to her joining a select group of colleagues who created the African studies program at Boston University in 1953. BU's African studies program was one of only a handful of graduate programs solely devoted to Africa at that time. BU's program was unique in that it focused on contemporary Africa and the complex issues facing the countries in an increasingly modern and postcolonial Africa. Cromwell left teaching soon after the program was established to take on the pivotal role of administrative director of BU's African studies program, now known as the African Studies Center of Boston University.

As the African studies program became firmly established, Cromwell returned to her teaching and research in BU's sociology department. Responding to a student's comment about the racist treatment of material in various courses, she created the graduate program in African American studies, modeling it after the successful African studies program she was so instrumental in developing in the 1950s. In 1969 Cromwell was appointed director of the African American

studies program at BU, the oldest such graduate-level program in the nation.

During the course of her career, Cromwell traveled to Africa on several occasions. In 1959 she was recruited by the anthropologist ST. CLAIR DRAKE JR. as a visiting lecturer in the department of sociology at the University of Legon in Ghana. While on a visit to Sierra Leone during this time, she met the educator and writer Adelaide Smith Casely Hayford, who became the subject of Cromwell's own favorite publication, *An African Victorian Feminist: The Life and Times of Adelaide Smith Casely Hayford, 1868–1960* (1986).

In 1962 Cromwell was the organizer and one of four U.S. delegates to the Seminar on Social Work in West Africa, held in Legon, Ghana. This seminar addressed social welfare activities and social problems in West Africa and was sponsored by the Department of Social Welfare and Community Development of the Republic of Ghana, and the Department of Sociology of the University of Ghana. Cromwell discussed the role of social workers in newly independent West African countries in her paper, "The Administrative Structure for Social Welfare in West Africa," presented to more than fifty delegates from Ghana, Guinea, Ivory Coast, Nigeria, Sierra Leone, Togo, the United Kingdom, and the United States. In 1964 Cromwell was appointed to a five-member committee commissioned by the Methodist Church in America to assess the state of higher education in what was then the Belgian Congo.

In 1983 Cromwell was instrumental in organizing the seminar "Dynamics of the African/Afro-American Connection: From Dependency to Self-Reliance" with colleagues from the University of Sierra Leone and the University of Liberia. The seminar included many distinguished African scholars of that time, and the delegates who participated were from Ghana, the Ivory Coast, Liberia, Nigeria, Senegal, and Sierra Leone. Held at the University of Liberia, the seminar was designed to assess and develop means to improve communication between Africans and African Americans. In addition to the paper she contributed to the seminar, "Continuing Mechanisms for Discourse," she also edited *Dynamics of the African/Afro-American Connection: From Dependency to Self-Reliance* (1987), the collection of papers presented at the seminar.

Throughout her career, Cromwell received several presidential appointments, honorary degrees, and awards. She was appointed by President John F. Kennedy as a delegate to the Dahomey Independence Celebration. President Lyndon B.

Johnson appointed her to the National Endowment for the Humanities, and she was appointed to the Board of Foreign Scholarships by President Jimmy Carter. Governor Christian Herter appointed Cromwell to the Massachusetts Advisory Committee on Correction, where she served from 1955 through 1968. Among her awards are honorary degrees from the University of Southeastern Massachusetts (1971), George Washington University (1989), and Boston University (1995). In 1971 she received the Smith College Medal, "awarded annually to alumnae who, in the judgment of the trustees, exemplify the true purpose of a liberal arts education through both their work and their lives." Additional awards include a Citation from the National Order of Cote d'Ivoire, the TransAfrica African Freedom Award (1983), the Carter G. Woodson Scholars Medallion from the Association for the Study of African American Life and History, and the Smithsonian National Museum of American History Life Achievement Award (1999).

Cromwell has been a singular force throughout her distinguished career as an educator, sociologist, social worker, author, and mentor. As a tireless pioneer in the fields of African and African American studies, she has sought to strengthen collaborations with African colleagues, especially as they relate to issues of social welfare. The African American studies program she created at Boston University has served as an important foundation for many students who now have prominent careers in academics, business, the judiciary, law, medicine, and social work. In acknowledgment of her many contributions to the school, Boston University awarded her an honorary degree in 1995, and established the Adelaide Cromwell Suite, seminar rooms in its African studies building.

FURTHER READING

Cromwell, Adelaide M. *An African Victorian Feminist: The Life and Times of Adelaide Smith Casely Hayford, 1868–1960* (1986).

Cromwell, Adelaide M. *The Other Brahmins: Boston's Black Upper Class, 1750–1950* (1994).

Cromwell, Adelaide M. *Unveiled Voices, Unvarnished Memories: The Cromwell Family in Slavery and Segregation, 1692–1972* (2007).

BARBARA A. BURG

Cromwell, John W., Jr. (2 Sept. 1883–16 Dec. 1971), educator and the first African American Certified Public Accountant (CPA), was born in the District of Columbia to JOHN WESLEY CROMWELL SR.

and Lucy A. McGuinn. His grandfather, Willis H. Cromwell, had purchased his family's freedom from slavery and moved from Virginia to Philadelphia, Pennsylvania, in 1851. Cromwell's father was a leader in the African American community, an 1874 graduate of Howard University School of Law, the publisher of the *People's Advocate* newspaper, one of the first two African American clerks in the federal government, a prolific writer, and a public school teacher and principal in Washington, D.C.

John Jr. absorbed his family's values of education, achievement, and responsibility to the black community. He attended the preparatory high school at Howard University and entered Dartmouth College in 1902 at a time when fewer than a dozen African Americans had graduated from that latter institution. In 1900 his sister, Otelia, had become the first black graduate of Smith College. At Dartmouth he studied Latin, German, and the sciences, was elected to Phi Beta Kappa, and was the top science graduate in the class of 1906. He completed a master's degree at Dartmouth in 1907 and took a one-year position reserved for Dartmouth's top science student at General Electric in Lynn, Massachusetts. He then returned to the District of Columbia to teach mathematics, German, and Latin at Dunbar High School.

In 1918 Cromwell married Yetta Mavritte, a cousin of EDWARD W. BROOKE, the Republican senator from Massachusetts from 1968 to 1980. The marriage ended in divorce in the early 1940s. His only child, a daughter, ADELAIDE McGUINN CROMWELL, was born on 27 November 1919. Cromwell considered pursuing a Ph.D. at the University of Chicago, where he had spent the summer of 1916 as a graduate student, but decided that it would entail too much time far away from his family. Instead he decided to pursue the CPA credential, possibly having developed an interest in business during his stint at General Electric.

In 1921 it was no easy task for an African American to become a CPA. Though the professional requirements varied by state, most states set educational prerequisites and all of them mandated passage of the uniform CPA examination. Because training in business, especially accounting, was scarce at black colleges, it was difficult to meet the education requirement. Although at the time Howard University had a better-developed accounting curriculum than did any other black college, it employed only one accounting professor. Passing the examination was also notoriously difficult and required perseverance and significant independent study. Without a doubt, however, the most daunting challenge was meeting the experience requirement. With the exception of one or two Jewish-owned firms in New York City, in the 1920s no white-owned firms would hire African Americans.

Cromwell overcame this barrier by taking the CPA examination in New Hampshire, which did not initially require experience working for a CPA. Later he returned to Washington, but upon finding that there were too few African American–owned businesses to allow a black CPA to sustain a living, he returned to teaching at Dunbar. There his students included a number of young people who would go on to noteworthy careers, among them ROBERT WEAVER, the first Secretary of Housing and Urban Development; STERLING BROWN, writer and professor at Howard University; and Mercer Cooke, who became the United States ambassador to Nigeria and Senegal.

In 1930 Cromwell became the controller, or chief accountant, at Howard University, where he remained until 1932, at which time he returned to teaching and to his private accounting practice. His client list was limited by the small size of the African American business community, but as the only African American CPA in the District, he helped many black-owned businesses thrive by providing them with financial advice in a time when few African Americans had business training. He became the accountant for several of the largest black-owned businesses in town, including the *Afro-American Newspaper*, the Industrial Bank, McGuire's Funeral Home, the African Methodist Episcopal (AME) Church, and Harrison's Restaurant, a popular gathering spot for Howard University faculty.

Rapidly changing tax laws in the 1930s and 1940s, along with skyrocketing tax rates for the wealthy, expanded Cromwell's practice to include tax services for individuals. African American doctors, lawyers, and schoolteachers converged on the Cromwell household during tax season as he prepared tax returns for the black middle class.

Cromwell rarely discussed racial prejudice, but his daughter reported that he did resent it when potential clients preferred to have a low-level white clerk provide them with financial services rather than hiring Cromwell, a certified public accountant. Although the African Methodist Episcopal Church hired him to do its accounting, St. Luke's Episcopalian Church, to which the family belonged, would not.

In the decades when white-owned CPA firms would not hire African Americans and offer them the necessary experience to earn their CPA licenses, John W. Cromwell trained some other pioneering African American CPAs, including Bert W. Smith Jr., who went on to form what became one of the largest black-owned CPA firms in the District. Nonetheless nearly forty years passed between the time John Cromwell became a CPA in New Hampshire and when the first CPA license was granted by the District of Columbia to an African American.

An avid bridge player, a game that he learned at Dartmouth, in 1932 Cromwell helped found the American Bridge Association. He was also a member of the national Capital Lodge of the Elks and Omega Psi Phi fraternity.

Cromwell died of a heart attack at the age of eighty-eight.

FURTHER READING

Hammond, Theresa A. *A White-Collar Profession: African American Certified Public Accountants since 1921* (2002).

Obituaries: *Washington Post*, 22 Dec. 1971; *Jet*, 6 Jan. 1972.

THERESA A. HAMMOND

Cromwell, John Wesley (5 Sept. 1846–14 Apr. 1927), lawyer and historian, was born a slave in Portsmouth, Virginia, the son of Willis Hodges Cromwell, a ferry operator, and Elizabeth Carney. In 1851 Cromwell's father purchased the family's freedom and moved to West Philadelphia, Pennsylvania, where Cromwell attended public school. In 1856 he was admitted to the Preparatory Department of the Institute of Colored Youth. Graduating in 1864, he embarked on a teaching career. He taught in Columbia, Pennsylvania, and in 1865 opened a private school in Portsmouth, Virginia. Cromwell left teaching temporarily after an assault in which he was shot at and his school burned down. He returned to Philadelphia, Pennsylvania, and was employed by the Baltimore Association for the Moral and Intellectual Improvement of Colored People. Then he served as an agent for the American Missionary Association and went back to Virginia. In 1867 he became active in local politics, serving as a delegate to the first Republican convention in Richmond.

After his short political career, Cromwell returned to teaching. He taught in Withersville, Richmond, Southhampton, and Columbia, Virginia. In 1871 he moved to Washington, D.C., and enrolled in Howard University's law school. While at Howard, he passed the civil service examination for the Treasury Department. In 1873 Cromwell married Lucy A. McGuinn of Richmond; they had seven children. In 1874 he graduated and was admitted to the bar. He also accepted a position as chief examiner of the money order department and later become the registrar of money order accounts, a position he held until 1885. Cromwell practiced law from his admission to the bar until 1892, and he earned the distinction of being the first African American to argue a case before the Interstate Commerce Commission. In 1895 he was appointed by BLANCHE K. BRUCE, an African American from Mississippi who served in the U.S. Senate during Reconstruction, as honorary commissioner of the Department of Colored Exhibits in the Cotton Centennial Exhibition at New Orleans. Despite his governmental duties, Cromwell actively engaged in social and educational causes. In 1875 he founded the Virginia Educational Organization, consisting of black teachers throughout the state, to whom he delivered "An Address on the Difficulties of the Colored Youth in Obtaining an Education in the Virginias" in Richmond; he served as president of this organization for eight years. In 1876 he founded *People's Advocate*, a weekly newspaper in Alexandria. The paper moved to Washington, D.C., in 1877, and Cromwell ran the paper until 1884. During these years he argued that African Americans should patronize black tradespeople exclusively, that black students and teachers would perform best in all-black schools, and that industrial education should be fostered.

In the 1880s Cromwell became involved in the nascent Black History movement. In 1881 he joined DANIEL ALEXANDER PAYNE, a bishop in the African Methodist Episcopal Church, in founding the Bethel Literary and Historical Association. A forum in which black intellectuals discussed issues of black advancement, the Bethel Literary and Historical Association's membership included many of the District of Columbia's most prominent black citizens. Cromwell later wrote the organization's history, *History of the Bethel Literary and Historical Association* (1896).

In 1897 Cromwell played a prominent role in establishing the American Negro Academy (ANA). Founded by ALEXANDER CRUMMELL, a classical scholar and minister educated at Cambridge University, the ANA sought to promote scholarship, educate youth, establish an archive to document the work of black authors, and publish an annual anthology to foster increased intellectual production by black scholars. Present at the founding meeting of the organization on 5 March 1897, Cromwell served as the organization's corresponding secretary from 1897 to 1919. In this capacity he handled all materials printed and distributed by the organization and used his position to promote the publication of the annual. From 1901 to 1909, despite teaching and serving as principal of several District of Columbia schools, including Briggs, Garnet, Banneker, and Crummell, Cromwell also found time to edit the *Washington Record*, a weekly newspaper. In 1910 he and James Robert Lincoln Diggs, a Baltimore businessman, established the American Negro Monograph Company. Although this publishing concern lasted only eleven months, it managed to publish four papers, two of which were written by members of the ANA. In 1919 Cromwell became president of the ANA, but his advanced age and the members' waning interest in the organization's goals forced him to resign by 1920.

Cromwell's reputation as a writer and amateur historian blossomed during the first two decades of the twentieth century. He occasionally published papers for the ANA, for example, "The Early Negro Convention Movement" (1904), an overview of the convention movement among African Americans from 1817 to the 1860s, and "The Challenge of the Disfranchised: A Plea for the Enforcement of the Fifteenth Amendment" (1924), an analysis of African American disfranchisement from the end of Reconstruction through the early 1920s. In 1914 he published his first full-length monograph, *The Negro in American History*. It covered the history of African Americans from the slave trade through Reconstruction and its aftermath. The second portion of the text featured biographical sketches of notable African Americans, such as PHILLIS WHEATLEY, BENJAMIN BANNEKER, SOJOURNER TRUTH, and FREDERICK DOUGLASS.

CARTER G. WOODSON founded the Association for the Study of Negro Life and History in 1915 and its organ, the *Journal of Negro History* (*JNH*), in 1916. Cromwell published two articles in the *JNH*, "The Aftermath of NAT TURNER's Insurrection" (1920), an assessment of the effect Turner's 1831 slave rebellion in Southampton, Virginia, had on the social, political, and economic control of slaves in the South; and "First Negro Churches in the District of Columbia" (1922), a survey of the development of black churches in the District of Columbia from colonial times until the 1920s. Cromwell died at his home in Washington, D.C. He was survived by his second wife, Annie E.

Cromwell, whom he had married in 1892, and his seven children.

Cromwell thrived as both a self-made man and a race man, combining advocacy for the collective uplift of African Americans with a belief in educational advancement and intellectual achievement. His historical work placed him at the nexus of the preprofessional and professional milieus in African American scholarship.

FURTHER READING

The main corpus of Cromwell's papers is in the possession of Adelaide Cromwell, director of the Afro-American Studies Center, Boston University. Another smaller collection is housed at the Moorland Spingarn Research Center, Howard University, Washington, D.C.

Meier, August. *Negro Thought in America, 1880–1915* (1988).

Moss, Alfred A., Jr. *The American Negro Academy: Voice of the Talented Tenth* (1981).

Simmons, William J. *Men of Mark: Eminent, Progressive, and Rising* (1887).

Obituaries: "Notes," *Journal of Negro History* 12 (July 1927): 563–566; and *Washington Evening Star*, 15 Apr. 1927.

This entry is taken from the *American National Biography* and is published here with the permission of the American Council of Learned Societies.

STEPHEN GILROY HALL

Cromwell, Oliver (24 May 1753–1853), Revolutionary War soldier, was born in Black Horse (now Columbus) in Burlington County, New Jersey. Nothing is known of his family except that, of light complexion and likely of mixed descent, Cromwell was never a slave. He was reared by John Hutchins, a farmer. Cromwell himself worked the land until he joined the Continental army in late 1776 at the age of twenty-three, serving in the Second New Jersey Regiment, under the command of Colonel Israel Shreve.

The service of Oliver Cromwell in the American Revolution as a free black from New Jersey is well worth noting. Although black men, both free and slave, such as PRINCE WHIPPLE and LONDON DAILEY, served in relatively high numbers in New England regiments, such was not the case for regiments raised in the middle and southern colonies. In New Jersey blacks were generally forbidden to serve, and in one location, Shrewsbury, all blacks were required to turn in any weapons they owned "until the present troubles are settled" (Quarles, 17).

Even at the height of the war in 1779, New Jersey passed a law restricting service in state militia regiments to whites only.

Cromwell was probably allowed to serve in the army because of two factors: the light complexion of his skin and his residence in Burlington County. Located in the Delaware Valley area, this county had the largest black population in all of New Jersey's five counties and has been called the "Cradle of Emancipation" because of its close connection with the Quakers in nearby Pennsylvania. Even though New Jersey often restricted the service of blacks in the military, it was not wholly indifferent to the plight of its slave population; in 1778 Governor William Livingston asked the state assembly to pass a manumission law, believing the institution of slavery to be wholly inconsistent with the ideals of liberty and freedom.

The specifics of Oliver Cromwell's activities during the war are unknown. There is nothing to indicate that he did not serve on an even basis with his white fellow soldiers in the Second New Jersey Regiment. Surely he shared the long and exhaustive marches in all types of weather, both devastating cold and extreme heat; a threadbare and tattered uniform and worn-out shoes resulting from his hard service, and a frequent lack of available replacement clothing; and a diet that oftentimes was lacking in both quality and quantity. This was the life of a typical Revolutionary War soldier.

Then, of course, there were the battles that Oliver Cromwell experienced. By the time Cromwell joined his regiment it had already seen its share of heavy fighting in the Canadian campaign and subsequent retreat. He saw his first battle action in October 1776 when his regiment and others of Washington's main army were being hotly pursued by the British in a race across New Jersey. It may even be that a desperate call to arms all across the state to fight the invaders was what inspired Cromwell to join the army. He saw more action on 25–26 December 1776 when he participated in Washington's historic crossing of the Delaware River and the subsequent smashing victory over the Hessians at the Battle of Trenton. Cromwell went on to serve for six years during the war, taking part in the battles at Princeton—where he humorously stated that the Americans "knocked the British about lively" (Kaplan and Kaplan, 54)—Brandywine, Monmouth, and Yorktown. About the last of these battles, where the British general Cornwallis surrendered, Cromwell claimed to have witnessed the last man killed.

Though Cromwell and the Second New Jersey Regiment were now done fighting, their part in the drama of the Revolution was not yet over. On 1 January 1781 Pennsylvania troops mutinied over shortages in food, pay, and clothing and successfully negotiated with state and congressional officials to gain concessions. Perhaps emboldened by their success, New Jersey's troops did the same thing, staging a mutiny on 20 January. However, the New Jersey troops achieved nothing. General Washington, determined to quell future mutinies, dealt harshly with the mutineers, arresting the ringleaders and executing two of them for treason.

On 5 June 1783 Private Oliver Cromwell's service in the Second New Jersey Regiment came to an end when he was discharged with the Badge of Merit, a certificate signed by George Washington himself, attesting to Cromwell's faithful years of service. Although Cromwell's regiment took part in a mutiny, the reputation of most of its soldiers remained untarnished in the eyes of Washington. In stark contrast to this was Washington's low regard for the colonel of the Second New Jersey, Israel Shreve, who was viewed by the general as a poor leader of men and one who did little to deal with his mutinous troops. Because of this, Washington refused to promote Shreve to higher rank.

His war service ended, Cromwell owned and operated a hundred-acre farm outside Burlington, New Jersey. In his old age he moved to Burlington proper, establishing a residence at 114 East Union Street. Though he could not read or write, Cromwell was a well-known and respected resident in town, and he was greatly helped by his fellow citizens when he applied for a pension on the basis of his military service. He died in 1853 at the age of one hundred and is buried in the Broad Street Methodist Cemetery.

FURTHER READING

Kaplan, Sidney, and Emma Nogrady Kaplan. *The Black Presence in the Era of the American Revolution*, rev. ed. (1989).

Quarles, Benjamin. *The Negro in the American Revolution* (1961).

GLENN ALLEN KNOBLOCK

Cromwell, Oliver (fl. 1875–1889), paramilitary leader and agrarian activist, was born of unknown parentage, perhaps in Mississippi. He appears in the historical record on two occasions. The first was in the bloody political conflict known as the "campaign of 1875," when white Democrats used tactics ranging from fraud to intimidation to violence and assassinations to wrest control of state government from the Republican Party.

In early September 1875, Cromwell traveled to the town of Clinton in Hinds County, Mississippi, to address a gathering of at least six hundred black men—some sources claim there were more than a thousand—who had organized into armed, paramilitary political clubs to defend their families, the black community, and the few remaining white Republicans against violent intimidation by white Democrats and their allies. Like other communities in the central part of the Magnolia State, a slight majority of citizens in Clinton were African American. Black Clintonians, notably CHARLES CALDWELL, had served in the state constitutional convention of 1869, and other blacks held office at state and county level. The presence of federal troops and the support of Mississippi's radical Republican Governor Adelbert Ames had helped secure the voting rights of African Americans and the election of BLANCHE KELSO BRUCE to the U.S. Senate in 1874. White Democrats had made clear, however, that they intended to win the 1875 state and local elections "at all hazards" (Hahn, 299). One Democratic Party official summarized his party's campaign as follows:

1. Organize a solidly Democrat front.
2. Intimidate Negroes if persuasion fails.
3. Stuff the ballot box with Democrat tickets.
4. Destroy Republican tickets.
5. Substitute Democratic for Republican tickets for illiterate Negroes.
6. If these plans do not work, then count out the Republicans and count the Democrats in (Ferguson).

Cromwell was determined to resist such naked intimidation. He may have adopted the name of England's onetime military ruler—or, though less likely, he may have been inspired by an African American Revolutionary War soldier also named OLIVER CROMWELL. Either way, the Cromwell who appeared in Clinton on 4 September 1875 had an imposing military bearing, and may, like many Reconstruction-era activists, have fought as a Union soldier in the Civil War. Cromwell addressed the assembled black Republicans while mounted on a horse, wearing a plumed hat and carrying a cavalry saber. Cromwell's saber rattling and the show of force by Hinds County's black Republicans were immediately challenged by an armed force of one hundred white Democrats who confronted them. A shot was fired, resulting in a confusing melee, in which several blacks and a few whites were killed. Outnumbered, the white Democrats escaped, but swiftly formed heavily armed squads that, over the following weeks, traveled throughout the county, killing as many as fifty African Americans and forcing others to flee the county.

Cromwell remained, however, and was active in the armed militia movement sponsored by Governor Ames following the "Clinton Riot," as Democrats called it. In late September 1875, the Republican-dominated legislature passed the "Gatling Gun bill," to provide arms to the citizens of Hinds County and other Mississippi communities who were being terrorized by paramilitary "white line" groups, such as the Ku Klux Klan. Cromwell received a supply of sixty breech-loading muskets in October 1875, as did other black leaders. Despite the best efforts of Governor Ames and militia leaders like Cromwell to defend black communities in the weeks leading up to the election, white Democrats ultimately won by pursuing a program of electoral "fraud, intimidation, and violence," that were, in the view of one observer, "without a parallel in the annals of history" (Hahn, 302). On Election Day 1875, thousands of blacks who had voted in earlier elections remained at home for fear of being attacked, or cast their ballots for Democrats for the same reason. In Hinds County and elsewhere in Mississippi, black Republicans were driven from office. Like other radical black activists who survived the violent purges of the self-styled white "redeemers" in 1875 and 1876, Oliver Cromwell appears to have gone underground.

Cromwell next appears in the historical record as an organizer for the Colored Farmers' Alliance in Leflore County in the Mississippi Delta in the summer of 1889. The economy and politics of Leflore County was shaped by its demography: eighty-five percent of its population was black. Thousands of African Americans had come to the county in the late 1870s and 1880s, hoping to carve out for themselves some of the richest cotton-growing land in the nation. Desiring social stability and in need of black labor to clear swamps and forests and to pick cotton, white planters in Leflore and other Delta counties reached a political compromise with the black majority in the decade after 1875. African Americans could continue to vote and to hold minor political office, while white Democrats were guaranteed majorities in all local offices and controlled the most important financial, legal, and police posts. The falling price of cotton, a succession of floods and droughts, and the general agricultural depression that began in the late 1880s would break this fragile political consensus in the Delta. Fearing the loss of their land and of being forced by indebtedness into renting or sharecropping, black and white farmers joined racially separate organizations—the Colored Farmers' Alliance (CFA) and the Southern Farmers' Alliance to fight for economic survival.

As a CFA agent, Cromwell visited the most remote parts of Leflore County, urging black farmers to join Colored Farmers' Alliance and to stop trading with local white merchants whose high prices, rent, and credit charges made it impossible for them to get out of debt. Cromwell persuaded many black farmers to instead buy farm supplies and other goods from the Durant Cooperative Store, owned by the Southern Farmers' Alliance in Holmes County, thirty miles away, southeast of the Delta. Cromwell's actions concerned white merchants in Leflore County who feared that they would lose a vital means of controlling black labor. Even more disturbing to the Delta elite was what they considered rabble-rousing political speeches that Cromwell made in his efforts to gain adherents to the CFA cause.

In August 1889, white planters began circulating rumors that Cromwell was an untrustworthy former convict—which was quite possibly true given his earlier militancy during Reconstruction. They also stated that Cromwell was more concerned in furthering the interests of the Durant Cooperative Store and in lining his own pockets with membership dues than with helping the economically threatened black farmers. Whether that was true or not, some black farmers believed it. A large number of African Americans in Leflore County, however, placed greater faith in Cromwell and the CFA than in their paternalistic landlords. In early September 1889, Colored Alliancemen from throughout the county met at the hamlet of Shell Mound in Leflore County to elect Cromwell their leader and to proclaim in a manifesto signed by "Three Thousand Armed Men" that they would defend Cromwell should whites attempt to kill or capture him as they had earlier threatened.

After seventy-five armed Alliancemen delivered their manifesto, white leaders in Leflore sent their women and children out of the county, gathered huge stockpiles of weapons, and recruited supporters from neighboring counties. Both the planters and the Colored Alliancemen appealed to Governor Robert Lowry to prevent a race war, but it soon became apparent that the governor was no honest broker. Lowry ordered the Mississippi National Guard into the camp near the Tallahatchie River where the Alliancemen were gathered early on 1 September 1889. The guardsmen arrested forty CFA members and handed them over to the white posse. Reports vary on how many Alliance members and their families were killed by the white posse. The most conservative estimate claims that at least six African Americans were killed; other observers claim that as many as one hundred blacks perished. Most likely, the number was around twenty-five to thirty, including several prominent leaders of the Colored Farmers' Alliance, but women and children were also shot at point-blank range when the posse broke into several black homes. It is worth noting that no whites are reported to have been shot during the Leflore County massacre and that many of the blacks arrested and killed were unarmed. Cromwell and his allies had exaggerated their firepower, and Delta whites had all too readily believed that such weapons of mass destruction existed.

Yet again Oliver Cromwell escaped capture, fleeing south even before the National Guard units had arrived from the North. He was spotted in Jackson, Mississippi, on 1 September, but he was never heard of again. Following Cromwell's departure and the Leflore County massacre, the Colored Farmers' Alliance crumbled in the Delta, though it would continue to grow in other parts of the South. White planters in the Leflore County forced the Durant Cooperative Store to stop selling goods or lending money to Colored Farmers' Alliance members and threatened the lives of the few remaining CFA activists. The brief compromise of political fusion gave way in 1890 to a more rigid color line in Mississippi's new state constitution, which disfranchised all but a tiny percentage of black voters. This new constitution proved to be the most tragic legacy of Oliver Cromwell's defiance. In 1892, only twenty-eight black men in Leflore County were allowed to register to vote. Widespread disfranchisement would remain in force until the 1960s, when a new generation of activists like AARON E. HENRY and FANNIE LOU HAMER completed the work that Oliver Cromwell and others had begun nine decades earlier.

FURTHER READING

For information on the Clinton riot, see U.S. Congress, *Report of the Select Committee to Inquire into the Mississippi Election of 1875* (1875).

Ferguson, Beth. *Raymond: A History, 1821–1876* (1976).

Hahn, Steven. *A Nation under Our Feet: Black Political Struggles in the Rural South from Slavery to the Great Migration* (2003).

Willis, John C. *Forgotten Time: The Yazoo–Mississippi Delta after the Civil War* (2000).

STEVEN J. NIVEN

Cromwell, Otelia (8 Apr. 1874–25 Apr. 1972), educator and scholar, was born in Washington, D.C., the first child of JOHN WESLEY CROMWELL and Lucy McGuinn Cromwell. Her father was a lawyer, editor of the *People's Advocate*, and for most of his life a teacher and principal in the district public schools. Her mother died when she was twelve, leaving this eldest of six children with a responsibility for their welfare that she would exercise for the rest of her life. Cromwell received her education in the public schools of Washington, D.C., including the M Street High School, predecessor of the well-known Dunbar High School. After graduating from the Miner Normal School in Washington, she taught for six years in the public schools before entering Smith College in Northampton, Massachusetts. When she completed her degree in 1900 she became the college's first African American graduate.

Upon returning to the district, Cromwell once again taught in the public schools—briefly at the elementary level, later at the high school level at M Street and then at Armstrong High School until 1922. Meanwhile she pursued graduate study, receiving an M.A. in English from Columbia University in 1910 and a Ph.D. in English from Yale University in 1926. Her dissertation, *Thomas Heywood, Dramatist: A Study in Elizabethan Drama of Everyday Life*, was published by the Yale University Press in 1928. In 1923 she was promoted from teacher of English to the head of the department of English and history in the senior and junior high schools. In 1929 she was initiated into Phi Beta Kappa at Smith College, which did not have a chapter when she was a student. In 1930, after the Miner Normal School had been upgraded to a four-year college, Cromwell was appointed professor of the division of English language and literature, where she remained until her retirement in 1944. She then began what would become her major scholarly work, a biography of the Quaker abolitionist and women's rights advocate Lucretia Mott. Her other publications included *Readings from Negro Authors for Schools and Colleges*, published in 1931, which she edited with EVA BEATRICE DYKES and LORENZO DOW TURNER. Together they were at the time the only three African Americans with doctorates in English, and their work was one of the first collections of its kind published in the United States. Cromwell also published essays and book reviews in numerous professional journals.

In 1923 Cromwell was invited to be a member of the board of directors of the *Encyclopedia of the Negro* under the chairmanship of Anson Phelps Stokes. In addition to W. E. B. DuBois, the board included among its nineteen members only one other woman, Florence Read, the president of Spelman College. Cromwell was a consummate scholar as well as an extraordinary teacher. For her time she was well traveled, having spent a summer studying at the Wahrendorf Tochterschule in Rostock, Germany, and later made two additional trips to Europe and England. In 1950, at the seventy-fifth anniversary of the founding of Smith College, she was one of the ten recipients of an honorary degree, and since 1989 Smith College has celebrated Otelia Cromwell Day to increase awareness of the diversity that exists within that community.

The following statement appeared in the minutes of the Board of Education of the District of Columbia on 16 February 1944:

> The excellence of Professor Cromwell's training was reflected in her teaching. She developed among her students a keen appreciation of beauty and truth. ... She daily emphasized the value of thoroughness and open-mindedness in her own classroom preparation. ... The influence she exerted in her position cannot be easily estimated. Encouraging students to pursue graduate work in leading universities, stimulating them to write. She was never too busy to listen to their problems.

Cromwell was a most distinguished personage—tall and gray-haired most of her adult life, as well as soft-spoken—and she abided by a strict code of ethics and principles. While others were more vocal in their reactions against the discriminatory practices of the day, Cromwell responded by refusing to patronize the stores in Washington because of their treatment of black customers and by not riding on the public transportation—she walked or took taxis because no blacks were employed as conductors and motormen. She was a life member of the NAACP and a member of the Smith College Alumnae Association, the Association of University Women, the Writers Club, Modern Language Association, and St. Luke's Episcopal Church in Washington, D.C. Cromwell never married and lived all her life in the family home. Her personal philosophy could be summed up in this quote to her father: "Ambition for place or fame is not my besetting folly." She died at her home in Washington, D.C.

FURTHER READING
Obituary: *Washington Post*, 28 Apr. 1972.

ADELAIDE M. CROMWELL

Cromwell, Robert I. (1830–1880), physician, editor, abolitionist, activist, and Reconstruction politician, was a native of Virginia who migrated to New Orleans, determined to fight the disenfranchisement of blacks. Nothing is known of Cromwell's upbringing and childhood except that he was born free. Educated in Wisconsin, Cromwell also spent time in the West Indies before settling in New Orleans in 1864. Cromwell was an outspoken proponent of black rights, known for employing controversial rhetoric, and was not averse to the idea of a race war between blacks and whites during Reconstruction.

In 1863, the militant Cromwell wrote to Secretary of War Edwin M. Stanton, seeking to raise black troops in the North. Cromwell moved to New Orleans in January of 1864 and quickly entered the political circles of Louisiana, participating in a number of pivotal events that helped shape the politics and civil rights of Reconstruction Louisiana. Although never serving in the Louisiana state Senate or House of Representatives, Cromwell was active in the political circles of Louisiana. Cromwell served on numerous committees and boards and was actively engaged with notable black politicians such as P. B. S. PINCHBACK, OSCAR JAMES DUNN, and CAESAR CARPENTIER ANTOINE. Most notably, Cromwell represented the Second District of New Orleans during the 1865 Republican Convention in New Orleans, which marked the official beginning of the Republican Party in Louisiana. As one of the delegates from New Orleans, Cromwell helped develop the Republican Party's platform in Louisiana. Cromwell was also present at the 1865 convention that sought black suffrage. In a heated exchange during the constitutional convention of 1868 with Pinchback, a black politician and fellow delegate, Cromwell exclaimed that blacks "will rule until the last one of us goes down forever" (Tunnell, 145). Always controversial, Cromwell openly spoke of his dislike of mixed-race individuals, deeming those of mixed ancestry not worthy of working with or for. Furthermore, Cromwell once noted that whites who disapproved of the Louisiana Bill of Rights, which he helped to shape, "could leave the country and go to Venezuela or elsewhere" (Tunnell, 119).

In July 1866, during the New Orleans Riot, Cromwell was arrested, assaulted, and robbed by the New Orleans police after being forced to leap out of a window by a mob of former Confederates, Democrats, and policemen. According to W. E. B. DuBois in *Black Reconstruction in America, 1860–1880*, forty-eight people were killed by the angry mob. After the incident, he searched out the policeman who instigated the event and worked to bring the issue before the courts. While working to gather information concerning his own assault, Cromwell was once again arrested. After being released, Cromwell presented the issue to the U.S. commissioner R. H. Shannon. Subsequently charges were brought against the member of the police force, who, as a result of Cromwell's charges, was jailed.

In 1867, Cromwell composed and published a letter in the *New Orleans Tribune* on 14 April 1865, titled "The Colored People of Louisiana and the Ten Rebel States." The aim of the letter was "to instruct, interest, and enlighten freedmen and new voters" (Lewis, 194). In 1868, as a member of the Constitutional Convention, Cromwell was an architect in developing the Louisiana State Constitution. Specifically, he helped shape bills regarding land ownership and marriage. In developing a provision regarding the purchasing of land and acreage, Cromwell sought to protect the newly freed black population by working to limit the amount of acreage an individual could buy. This in turn protected the poor black population from the influence of wealthy landowners. Specifically, the measure stated an individual could only purchase between five and one hundred acres.

Most notably, though, Cromwell was one of four delegates to propose the Louisiana Bill of Rights that granted blacks the same rights as whites in Louisiana. The bill was debated and passed on 2–3 January 1868. The constitutional convention adjourned on 9 March 1868. The census of 1870 shows Cromwell owned eight hundred dollars' worth of real estate. He also operated a boarding-house in New Orleans in 1871 and in 1880. Cromwell furthered his influence by establishing the newspaper the *Negro Gazette*. In 1880 Cromwell was "reported to have been hung" in Texas.

FURTHER READING

Foner, Eric. *Freedom's Lawmakers: A Directory of Black Officeholders during Reconstruction* (1996).

Vincent, Charles. *Black Legislators in Louisiana during Reconstruction* (1976).

MICHAEL RISTICH

Crosse, Rupert (29 Nov. 1928–5 Mar. 1973), actor, was born in New York City, though some biographies give his place of birth as the Caribbean island of Nevis. Little is known of Crosse's parents or siblings, but when Crosse was seven years old, his father, a schoolteacher, died, and he was sent to Nevis to be raised by his grandparents. He came from a family of teachers and preachers who could trace their ancestry on the island back 200 years. His grandfather, also a schoolmaster, strongly influenced Crosse, making sure that he received a solid education.

After several years Crosse returned to New York City, where he attended Benjamin Franklin High School. During his high school years, he had a variety of odd jobs, including loading boxcars for a railroad. Eventually he left school to work as a packer in New York's garment district until he was drafted. He served with the U.S. infantry in Germany and Japan for two years.

Upon leaving the service and completing his high school education, Crosse entered Bloomfield College and Seminary in New Jersey intending to become a minister. Then he transferred to Brooklyn College, part of the City University of New York. He still had not finally settled on a career at this point, as evidenced by the variety of jobs he held, including machinist, construction worker, and recreation counselor.

Crosse had his first sustained education in theater when he enrolled at the Tamara Daykarhanova School for the Stage, where he studied acting. His first professional appearance was in the Equity Library Theatre 1952 production of Moss Hart's *Climate of Eden*, an adaptation of a novel written by the Guyanese writer Edgar Mittelholzer.

Crosse then joined John Cassavetes' acting workshop, where in 1959 he helped to create and appeared in Cassavetes' *Shadows*, an experiment in improvisational acting and directing in film (though the film appeared improvised; it was actually scripted). Financed by Cassavetes and made in New York City, outside the Hollywood studio system, *Shadows* was a low-budget production, shot in black-and-white, with a jazz soundtrack by CHARLES MINGUS. Featuring the actors from Cassavetes' workshop, the story, set in Manhattan, was about a biracial romance between the light-skinned Lelia Goldoni, who falls in love with a white man, Anthony Ray. However, when he learns that she is African American, he rejects her. Winner of five awards including the Critics Award at the Cannes Film Festival in 1960, *Shadows* is considered by film scholars and critics to be one of the most influential movies of American independent cinema of the time.

In 1959 Crosse left New York and moved to Hollywood to guest on *Johnny Staccato*, a crime drama television series starring Cassavetes. He also made another television appearance that same year in *Have Gun Will Travel*. His first major motion picture appearance was also with Cassavetes in *Too Late Blues* in 1961. The film, Cassavetes's major studio directorial debut, was a low-key drama about a jazz musician and starred Bobby Darin, Stella Stevens, and Seymour Cassel. Crosse played Baby Jackson, a minor character.

Crosse's ability to speak French and to assume Spanish as well as various African and Jamaican accents increased the variety of his roles. Over the next few years, the 6'4", ruggedly handsome actor worked steadily in television, film, and stage productions. In 1963 he appeared in *The Alfred Hitchcock Hour* in a pilot episode for a series called "Diagnosis: Danger." The episode starred Michael Parks as Daniel Dana and Crosse as Dr. Paul Mackey. Directed by Sydney Pollack, produced and written by Roland Kibbee, the series was panned and dropped. Parks and Crosse worked together again in 1965 in *The Wild Seed*, directed by Brian G. Hutton. In 1966 Crosse appeared as Nobuk in *To Trap a Spy*, a film which was expanded from the original pilot for the television series, *The Man From U.N.C.L.E.* In 1967 he appeared in the comedy/Western *Waterhole #3* and another Western, *Ride in the Whirlwind*, directed by Monte Hellman and written by Jack Nicholson. Nicholson also starred in the production. During these years Crosse guest-starred in several popular television series, including *Ben Casey*, *I Spy*, *Bonanza*, *Felony Squad*, *Dr. Kildare*, and *That Girl*.

In 1968 Crosse appeared in an Actors Studio-West production of *Echoes* at UCLA, where his performance was hailed as "superb"(*Los Angeles Times*, 6 Feb. 1968). In the audience was the director Mark Rydell. Months later Rydell cast him in *The Reivers*, signing him for the role of Ned McCaslin. His other stage credits from this time include *Blood Knot*, by Athol Fugard in 1964, *Sweet Bird of Youth*, *Hatful of Rain*, and *In White America*. It was, however, *The Reivers* that would bring Crosse his greatest acclaim.

The Reivers, adapted from William Faulkner's final novel, was a coming-of-age story about eleven-year-old Lucius McCaslin (Mitch Vogel) who goes on a journey with the hired hand Boon Hogganbeck (Steve McQueen) and Ned McCaslin (Crosse), Lucius's distant cousin. Boon "borrows" Lucius's grandfather's automobile, and the three travel from Mississippi to Memphis, visit a brothel, and trade the car in for a racehorse. In an interview with Crosse in 1971, the critic Cecil Smith described his performance as a "superb realization of a free spirited black man at the turn of the century" (*Los Angeles Times*, 10 Oct. 1971). For his performance Crosse became the first African American performer to be nominated for an Academy Award for Best Supporting Actor.

In 1972 Crosse married Christopher Lynn Calloway, the daughter of CAB CALLOWAY, at the home of Elois Davis. Not having been to Nevis since childhood, he returned there with his bride for a brief holiday. They had a son, Rupert Crosse Jr.

In 1973 Crosse was cast as Mulhall in *The Last Detail*, which starred his friend Jack Nicholson; however, he became terminally ill with cancer and died before shooting began, at the age of forty-five, at his sister's home in Nevis, West Indies.

FURTHER READING

Bogle, Dick. *Blacks in American Films and Television: An Encyclopedia* (1988).

Lehman, Jeffrey, ed. *The African American Almanac* (2003).

Obituary: *Jet*, 29 Mar. 1973.

ANNA CHRISTIAN

Crossland, John R. A. (24 Apr. 1864–12 Sept. 1950), physician and diplomat, was born near Bennettsville, South Carolina, to parents whose names are not recorded, and who may have been slaves or freed slaves. At an early age, he moved with his parents to St. Joseph, Missouri, where he was educated in that city's public schools.

A gifted student, Crossland later graduated from Shaw University in Raleigh, North Carolina, before completing his medical studies at Meharry Medical College in Nashville, Tennessee. He practiced medicine and surgery for twelve years in both Missouri and Kingstree, South Carolina, where he also served for a brief period as assistant postmaster. He also served as city physician for several years in St. Joseph.

Crossland also became active in Republican Party politics in Missouri, and by 1901, had become a member-at-large of that state's Republican central committee. He was also elected president of the Negro Republican State League. As a member of the national executive committee of the nonpartisan National Afro-American Council, a newly formed national civil rights organization, Crossland was chosen as a member of an official delegation to visit President William McKinley after his second inauguration in March 1901. Although still largely unknown outside Missouri, Dr. Crossland then actively began to seek appointment to a federal office, after obtaining recommendations from Booker T. Washington and others, and even seeking assistance from the new U.S. vice president, Theodore Roosevelt.

After Roosevelt became president in September 1901, he reportedly considered Crossland for the post of recorder of deeds for the District of Columbia, before naming him in January 1902 as the new U.S. minister and consul general to Liberia, succeeding OWEN L. W. SMITH of North Carolina. After his confirmation by the U.S. Senate, Crossland arrived in Monrovia in May 1902 and presented his credentials to the Liberian government. He quickly became embroiled, however, in an embarrassing scandal, reported by the *Atlanta Constitution* (26 Dec. 1902) as involving allegations of theft, housebreaking, and wife-stealing, and apparently involving another member of the U.S. legation in Monrovia. Unconfirmed reports also circulated that Crossland kept a loaded pistol in his desk drawer at the U.S. embassy, and that on one occasion, he had fired a pistol at an attacker armed with a razor.

In December 1902, the government of Liberia demanded that the State Department recall Crossland; after being given leave of absence to return home, he left Monrovia in disgrace in January 1903. After his subsequent resignation, Crossland was succeeded as U.S. minister to Liberia by Reverend Ernest Lyon of Maryland. Rumors of the scandal prompted a rare written apology from BOOKER T. WASHINGTON to President Theodore Roosevelt for having earlier recommended Crossland, "the only one I have recommended about whose character I was not sure" (letter dated 1 December 1902).

Upon returning to Missouri, Crossland was involved in another violent incident in September 1904, in which he was reportedly shot and seriously wounded, according to local newspaper reports. He did, however, remain active in Republican politics for many years, and served as an alternate delegate-at-large to the Republican national conventions of 1908 and 1916.

In September 1921, Crossland was appointed as a special expert by the U.S. Veterans Bureau's Negro Training Section, to look after the interests of African American soldiers and sailors entitled to benefits under relief laws for their wartime service. In this capacity he often visited Tuskegee, Alabama, where he helped establish the nation's first black hospital for veterans at the Tuskegee Institute.

Crossland was married four times. He wed his first wife, Ada, a native of Kentucky, in 1891; they had one son, John R. A. Crossland Jr., born in Missouri in 1892. After Ada's death, Crossland married Laura F. Pearson of St. Joseph in December 1914. By 1920, Crossland was married to his third wife, Myrtle, a Missouri native. He married his fourth wife, Hattie, a native of South Carolina, in 1927.

Crossland died at age eighty-five of pneumonia and complications of other diseases, in the State Hospital at St. Joseph, Missouri.

FURTHER READING
"Crossland, J. R. A." in *The National Cyclopedia of American Biography*, Volume 14 (1910).

BENJAMIN R. JUSTESEN

Crosswaith, Frank Rudolph (16 July 1892–17 June 1965), labor leader, was born in Frederiksted, Saint Croix, Virgin Islands, the son of William Ignatius Crosswaith, a painter, and Anne Eliza (maiden name unknown). He left school at thirteen and immigrated in 1910 to the United States, where he joined the U.S. Navy as a mess boy. In 1915 he married Alma E. Besard; they had four children. Settling in New York City, Crosswaith worked as an elevator operator during the day and at night attended the Rand School of Social Science, a socialist educational center.

While at the Rand School, Crosswaith encountered two influences that changed his life: the teachings of the socialist leader Eugene V. Debs and the radical politics of the New Negroes, a group of young African Americans in Harlem who had begun speaking out against the accommodating policies of their elders. Upon his graduation in 1918, Crosswaith began a long career of socialist political activity and part-time teaching at the Rand School.

Crosswaith was convinced that if black workers could win acceptance in labor unions, job competition among the races would end and all workers could unite against their common enemies. In pursuit of this goal, he devoted much of his career to a succession of organizations, many short-lived and underfunded, designed to introduce black workers to the labor movement and persuade white unions to accept them. The first such effort was the Friends of Negro Freedom (FNF), which Crosswaith joined in 1920. The FNF provided a useful discussion forum for Crosswaith and other black activists, but it had little effect. After campaigning against the black nationalist MARCUS GARVEY in 1922, it disbanded.

Next came the Trade Union Committee for Organizing Negro Workers (TUC), set up in 1925 with the backing of the New York Urban League, the Garland Fund, the National Association for the Advancement of Colored People, and several socialist unions. Crosswaith became executive secretary; one historian calls him "the real sparkplug" of the organization. The TUC managed to persuade a few unions to accept a handful of black members, and it started to organize the city's thirty thousand laundry workers, two-thirds of whom were black women. It also stirred Harlem with a campaign for housing reform, but with insufficient funding and minimal support from mainstream labor leaders, the TUC dissolved in 1926.

By then Crosswaith had become involved in a new undertaking, the Brotherhood of Sleeping Car Porters (BSCP). A. PHILIP RANDOLPH, the founder, hired Crosswaith part time as his special assistant in 1925. A year later, when the TUC closed down, Crosswaith began to work for the BSCP full time as its first professional organizer. His association with the union ended in October 1928, when he and another employee accused the secretary-treasurer of taking BSCP funds and implied that Randolph had known about the wrongdoing. An investigation cleared the official, and both Crosswaith and his ally were forced to resign. Crosswaith then became an organizer for the International Ladies' Garment Workers' Union (ILGWU), a position he held for the rest of his career.

Crosswaith polled few votes in his repeated campaigns on the Socialist Party ticket for Harlem's congressional seat and various state offices; furthermore the United Colored Socialists of America that he established in 1928 soon dissolved. Nevertheless, Crosswaith won recognition within the party, earning the title "the Negro Debs." His impassioned oratory made him, according to one of his contemporaries, "one of the most effective Socialist speakers in the party," and he made many national lecture tours. He also wrote a column in the *Chicago Defender*, contributed articles and reviews to the *Messenger*, and in 1931 published a pamphlet, *The Negro and Socialism*, which was one of the few party publications aimed specifically at blacks.

Crosswaith continued to battle union discrimination, urging not only membership for blacks but equal treatment once they were admitted. He edited the Negro Labor News Service from 1932 to 1934 and in 1935 was chosen to head the Negro Labor Committee (NLC), created by the ILGWU to open American Federation of Labor (AFL) unions to black workers. Crosswaith made progress in several trades, including meat cutters, painters, and cafeteria employees. He also played a major role in the Socialist Party's National Negro Work Committee (NNWC) and ran the NNWC's Harlem Labor Center, established in 1937 to educate black workers about unionism. Nevertheless, even in the more open atmosphere created by the National Labor Relations Act, most unions remained racially exclusive.

In 1941 Crosswaith joined Randolph in planning a march on Washington to protest discrimination in defense work; he was among those who met with President Franklin D. Roosevelt and were told that their plan was a "bad and unintelligent" idea. However, the group held its ground, calling the march off only after Roosevelt issued an executive order prohibiting discrimination in defense industries. In 1942, when Randolph was unable to accept Mayor Fiorello La Guardia's offer of a position on the New York City Housing Authority, Crosswaith was chosen to serve instead.

During these years Crosswaith became increasingly concerned about communist influence in the labor movement. He opposed the Congress of Industrial Organizations (CIO) and the National Negro Congress because of their left-wing connections. Having joined the American Labor Party (ALP) in 1936, he resigned from the Socialist Party in 1941 and helped found the anticommunist Union for Democratic Action. Then, along with other anticommunists, he left the ALP in 1944 for the new Liberal Party. In 1952 he chaired a new national Negro Labor Committee, USA, organized by seventy-five unions both to promote black unionism and to counter communist agitation among blacks. He died in New York City.

Crosswaith spent most of his life trying to bring black workers into the American labor movement. He faced formidable obstacles in the resistance of most unions to integration and in the Socialist Party's reluctance to highlight the unique problems of black workers. His anti-communism in later life cut him off from some potential allies, but for more than three decades he enriched American dialogue by testifying in word and deed to the fundamental connection of two compelling goals: working-class solidarity and racial justice.

FURTHER READING

Information about Crosswaith's career is in the papers of the Negro Labor Committee at the Schomburg Branch of the New York Public Library and of the Socialist Party of America at Duke University, Durham, North Carolina.

Anderson, Jervis A. *Philip Randolph: A Biographical Portrait* (1973)

Foner, Philip S. *Organized Labor and the Black Worker, 1619–1973* (1974).

Kornweibel, Theodore, Jr. *No Crystal Stair: Black Life and the "Messenger," 1917–1928* (1975).

Marcus, Irwin M. "Frank Crosswaith: Black Socialist, Labor Leader, and Reformer," *Negro History Bulletin* 37 (Aug.–Sept. 1974): 287–88.

Obituary: *New York Times*, 18 June 1965.

This entry is taken from the *American National Biography* and is published here with the permission of the American Council of Learned Societies.

SANDRA OPDYCKE

Crosthwait, David Nelson, Jr. (27 May 1898–25 Feb. 1976), mechanical engineer and inventor, was born in Nashville, Tennessee, the son of Dr. David Nelson Crosthwait and Minnie Harris. He attended elementary school and graduated from high school in Kansas City, Missouri.

Crosthwait received a B.S. in Mechanical Engineering from Purdue University in 1913. That same year he began lifelong employment with the C.A. Dunham Company (later Dunham-Bush) in Chicago, where he distinguished himself nationally in the field of heating, ventilation, and air-conditioning (HVAC) technology. By 1915 he had been appointed to the position of engineering supervisor, and by 1919 he had risen to the position of research engineer. In 1920 Crosthwait received an M.S. in Engineering from Purdue.

In 1925 Crosthwait became director of research at Dunham, overseeing heat-transfer research, steam-transport research, and temperature-control systems. In 1930 he was designated a senior technical consultant and adviser at Dunham-Bush. Crosthwait married E. Madolyn Towels in 1930;

they had one son, who died at age six. After the death of his wife, Crosthwait married Blanche Ford in 1941.

Between 1930 and 1969, when he retired, Crosthwait conducted research on heating systems. He developed techniques to reduce noise caused by steam and noncondensable gases in heating systems. A signal achievement was his design of the heating system for the seventy-story main building of Rockefeller Center in New York City.

Crosthwait received thirty-four U.S. patents and eighty foreign patents relating to the design, installation, and testing of heating, ventilation, and air-conditioning systems for large buildings. His U.S. patents included an apparatus for returning water to boiling (1920), a method and apparatus for setting thermostats (1928), a differential vacuum pump (1930), a freezing temperature indicator (1932), a method of steam heating from a central station (1934), a vacuum heating system (1935), a one-pipe heating system (1937), heat balances (1940), a unit heater and air conditioner (1941), a window thermostat (1944), and a balance-resistance-type temperature control (1947).

Crosthwait's achievements and contributions to the HVAC field were recognized with the award of a medal by the National Technical Association in 1936. In 1971 he became the first African American to be elected a fellow of the American Society of Heating, Refrigerating, and Air-Conditioning Engineers.

As a recognized specialist in his field, Crosthwait contributed to the HVAC literature. His first article, "Heating System Vacuum," was published in *Power* in 1919. He was a contributor to chapters in the 1939, 1959, and 1967 editions of the *American Society of Heating and Ventilation Engineers Guide*. His technical writings also appeared in the *Heating and Ventilation* magazine and in other industrial engineering publications.

Crosthwait was active in the National Society of Professional Engineers and in the American Association for the Advancement of Science. In community and civic affairs he served on the executive committee of the North West Comprehensive Health Planning Commission in Michigan City, Indiana, and as president of the Michigan City Redevelopment Commission. On his retirement from Dunham-Bush in 1969, Crosthwait became an instructor at Purdue University, where he taught a course on steam heat theory and applications. He died, after a brief hospital stay, in Michigan City, Indiana.

FURTHER READING
American Men and Women of Science, 12th ed. (1971).
Ploski, Harry A., and James Williams. *The Negro Almanac: A Reference Work on the Afro American* (1976).
Obituary: *Michigan City (Indiana) News Dispatch*, 25 Feb. 1976.

This entry is taken from the *American National Biography* and is published here with the permission of the American Council of Learned Societies.

ROBERT C. HAYDEN

Crothers, Scatman (23 May 1910–23 Nov. 1986), actor, singer, musician, and composer, was born Benjamin Sherman Crothers in Terre Haute, Indiana, the youngest of five children of Benjamin Crothers, a clothing store owner and odd jobber from Jonesboro, Arkansas, and Fredonia Lewis Crothers. Crothers's mother bought him his first drum, which, along with the guitar, he taught himself to play. Although unable to read music, he began street performing for small change at age seven. Crothers encountered discrimination in largely segregated Terre Haute when black players were barred from the high school football team. Responding with what would soon become his characteristic blend of superficial accommodation and subversive disregard of racist standards, he tolerated such discrimination as a temporary situation and became the "yell leader" for school pep rallies. At the same time, he flouted segregation by using his winning personality to frequent "whites only" restaurants. As he later recalled, "I did a lot of things that blacks didn't do in my hometown" (Haskins, 31–32).

Influenced by vaudeville shows, Crothers became an entertainer at a local roadhouse, dropped out of high school in the tenth grade, and continued to transgress racial barriers through interracial dating. He soon became the band director of Montague's Kentucky Serenaders, a traveling band, worked with blues musician T-BONE WALKER, and met LOUIS ARMSTRONG, who impressed Crothers with his powerful voice and vocal "scat" style. Already scatting, Crothers developed his style further and left the band in 1931. He soon became a fixture on Dayton, Ohio's WFMK radio station, where he was first called "Scat Man" after the program director asked him to provide a snappier name than Sherman, as he was then known. "Call me 'Scat Man,' because I do quite a bit of scattin'," Crothers reportedly responded, and the name stuck.

For the next several years Crothers played with different bands throughout the Midwest, including JIMMIE LUNCEFORD's group. In between gigs he worked in hotels to support himself. At this time Crothers became the first black performer to appear at the Moonlight Gardens club in Springfield, Ohio, and the first black guest to stay at the Jefferson Hotel in Peoria, Illinois. Drawing on his own experience and abilities, Crothers formed his own group, Scat Man and His Band, in 1936, which played mostly for white audiences but also frequented black-and-tan clubs for mixed clienteles. In April 1936 he met Helen Sullivan, a white waitress at one of the clubs, and on 15 July 1937 they were married in Cleveland, Ohio, after being rebuffed by a judge in Canton, Ohio. The interracial marriage created controversy within their families. Although Crothers's parents died without meeting Helen, the couple established a lifelong commitment.

Now billed as "The Original Scat Man and His Band," Crothers and his musicians traveled together throughout the Midwest and East for the next few years, while Helen stayed at home rather than fuel racial tension by traveling with the band. Audiences soon became familiar with Crothers's theme song, "I Am the Scat Man," penned by Sulky Davis, and his incorporation of bebop into the band's largely swing repertoire. He frequently played the Chicago Loop along with jazz luminaries like DIZZY GILLESPIE. Upon a suggestion from his manager Bert Gervis, Crothers reformed his band into a trio and headed for Hollywood in 1944. He played at Hollywood clubs and performed in his first play, *Insults of 1944*, at the Playtime Theater in Los Angeles. He also performed for soldiers at the Hollywood Canteen in 1944 before once again expanding his band and resuming a national tour. This time Helen accompanied him despite the discrimination the interracial couple encountered on a regular basis. At this time Crothers began to write his own songs. His first, titled "Truly I Do," was completed in 1945 and reflected his love for Helen. In 1948 he recorded his first single, Phil Harris's "Chattanooga Shoe Shine Boy," for RCA-Victor. The recording brought him increased attention, and he followed it with Riff Charles's "Dead Man's Blues" for Capitol Records, which offered him a contract in 1948.

Returning to Los Angeles, Crothers and his wife had a daughter, Donna, in 1949. Crothers worked as a traveling musician while Helen and Donna settled in a small house in a black Los Angeles neighborhood. In 1949 Crothers took a stand against segregation in Las Vegas when he refused to enter a club through the kitchen. He broke another racial barrier that year when he became the first black man to secure a regular spot on a Los Angeles television show, Paramount's *Dixie Showboat*. This led to more television, particularly *The Colgate Comedy Hour*, and to radio work, where his distinctive voice was soon in demand. His first significant film appearance was in *Meet Me at the Fair* (1952) with Dan Dailey. The role of Enoch was remarkable in its substance at a time when most roles for blacks in Hollywood were limited and often demeaning. The movie also included some of Crothers's original songs. He then composed for and performed songs in *The Return of Gilbert and Sullivan* (1950) and *East of Sumatra* (1953).

Crothers's work ethic was relentless, and he continued to travel and perform, including appearances in the Los Angeles Valley area, Las Vegas, and at Harlem's famous Apollo Theater. He also recorded several singles for Capitol Records during this period, including "On the Sunny Side of the Street," his own compositions "Blue Eyed Sally" and "I'd Rather Be a Hummingbird," and the timely tunes "Television Blues" and "The Atom Bomb Blues." However, Crothers finally refused to play Las Vegas after again encountering segregation there in the early 1950s. In the late 1950s, he continued to make several television appearances and released an album titled *Rock and Roll with Scatman* for High Fidelity Records. In 1957 he began traveling overseas with the USO, where he met Bob Hope and developed a strong interest in golf.

Throughout the 1960s, Crothers traveled and performed in television and film. Though he did not participate directly in the civil rights movement, he continued to break down barriers, and in 1967 he was the first black entertainer to appear at the Forge in Glendale, California. He appeared in the films *Hello Dolly!* (1969) and *The Great White Hope* (1970), and in 1970 he was featured as the swinging Scat Cat in Walt Disney's *The Aristocats*. This role led to more vocal work, including the voice of MEADOWLARK LEMON in various children's television movies featuring the animated Harlem Globetrotters (1970–1972) and the title character of *Hong Kong Phooey* (1974–1976).

In the 1970s, when black actors began to gain more opportunities, he appeared as Big Ben in *Lady Sings the Blues* (1972), the gangster Lewis in *The King of Marvin Gardens* (1972), and Turkle in *One Flew Over the Cuckoo's Nest* (1975). He finally achieved fame in his role as Louie on NBC's television series *Chico and the Man* (1974–1977), which showcased his optimism and genial humor. His participation in the controversial animated feature *Coonskin* (1975) and his turn as a Pullman porter in *Silver Streak* (1976) raised accusations of "Uncle Tomism" during a time of elevated racial consciousness, but his lifelong refusal to bow to racism and his role as Mingo in the miniseries *Roots* (1976) belied this.

Crothers's appearances in increasingly complex roles suggested that he was becoming as skilled an actor as he was a musician, and he welcomed parts of many different kinds. He merged his talents in 1978 in his touring revue, *The Scatman Crothers Show*, and continued to appear on television variety shows and in celebrity golf tournaments. His reputation as a strong character actor with a charismatic screen presence was established further in 1980 in his role in Stanley Kubrick's *The Shining* (1980), for which he won Best Supporting Actor from the Academy of Science Fiction, Fantasy and Horror Films and an NAACP Image Award, and as the MC Doc Lynch in Clint Eastwood's *Bronco Billy* (1980). In 1981 he was honored with a star on the Hollywood Walk of Fame, and he continued to perform on television and in film for the next few years, most notably in Steven Spielberg's segment in *Twilight Zone: The Movie* (1983). Scatman Crothers died of cancer in Van Nuys, California, after a lifetime of musical performances, appearances in forty-six films and more than eighty-four television programs, and as the voice of many popular cartoon characters. For many, his life exemplified faith, optimism, and the courage to ignore or overcome racial barriers. He was posthumously inducted into the Black Filmmakers Hall of Fame in 1987.

FURTHER READING

Haskins, Jim. *Scatman: An Authorized Biography of Scatman Crothers* (1991).
"Scatman Crothers: After 50 Years in Show Biz, an 'Overnight' Success," *Ebony* (July 1978).
Obituary: *New York Times*, 23 Nov. 1986.

JILL SILOS

Crouch, Andrae (1 July 1942–), gospel singer, composer, and pastor, was born Andrae Edward Crouch in Los Angeles, California. As a child, his musical talents were cultivated under the church ministry of his parents, Benjamin and Catherine Crouch.

He also benefited from attending Pentecostal services at the Emmanuel Church of God in Christ, where his great-uncle, Bishop Samuel M. Crouch, was the pastor. Crouch's upbringing was enhanced not only by his experiences singing and playing in church but also through his exposure to an array of musical styles such as jazz, blues, rock and roll, and European classical music. At the age of fourteen, he drew from these multiple influences to pen his first composition, "The Blood Will Never Lose Its Power," which would become a classic gospel piece (Darden, 276–278).

During his teenage years, he formed vocal ensembles with several of his siblings, most notably his twin sister, Sandra. He labeled one of these groups the COGICS, an acronymic tribute to the Church of God in Christ. This predominantly African American Pentecostal organization had provided him with early support and would serve as a spiritual and musical training ground for gospel luminaries such as Walter and EDWIN HAWKINS, the Clark Sisters, and Vanessa Bell Armstrong (Boyer, 24). By 1965 the COGICS had disbanded, and Crouch put together a male vocal group to perform his compositions. Crouch began a steady rise to prominence in the mid-1960s. His new group, Andrae Crouch and the Disciples, garnered critical acclaim along the West Coast and soon signed a record deal with Light Records, an upstart gospel music label (Darden, 278).

A pivotal figure in the history of gospel music, Crouch quickly established himself as a prolific songwriter and a highly influential performer. As his career began to blossom, he found himself remarkably well positioned to capitalize on the folk music movements of the 1960s, which brought a renewed quest for the values of peace, freedom, and social justice (Cusic, 126–127). This era also saw an increase in youth involvement in Christianity through the charismatic revival, which supported livelier, more participatory forms of religious worship, and the Jesus movement, in which churchgoers craved more accessible varieties of Christian music (Darden, 278). With their infusions of rock and pop elements, Crouch's gospel compositions effectively resonated with the ethos of their time and place. His early successes included the release of his first album, *Take the Message Everywhere* (1968), produced by Ralph Carmichael for Light Records (Darden, 278).

Andrae Crouch is best known for his numerous recordings and compositions in the 1970s. With the Disciples, he achieved unprecedented acclaim for a gospel artist, recording best-selling albums such as *Take Me Back, This Is Another Day, Soulfully, Keep On Singing*, and *Live in London* for the contemporary Christian market. Many of his compositions from this period became gospel standards that were sung in black and white churches across the United States. Songs such as "My Tribute" and "Bless His Holy Name" exemplify the Crouch-inspired trend characterized by an emphasis on "praise and worship" music during church services and revivals. Thus, Crouch was at the forefront of a movement focused more on the musical exaltation of Jesus Christ than on the recounting of human struggles (Darden, 280).

Crouch became a source of controversy to gospel music devotees who felt his songs relied too heavily on secular musical influences. Crouch also weathered tough critiques from conservative listeners who felt his music diluted the sound of traditional black gospel music. However, the harsh words of Crouch's critics were generally outnumbered by positive reviews from his fans and peers in the contemporary Christian music industry. Indeed, many Christian musical artists rode the coattails of Crouch's prosperity. For example, gospel singer Danniebell Hall enjoyed a successful solo career after first gaining popularity as a member of Crouch's Disciples (Darden, 278).

As early as 1970 Crouch was composing and performing gospel music full-time. Early in that decade, his group was among the first of its kind to appear on *The Tonight Show with Johnny Carson* (Cusic, 128). Crouch enjoyed tremendous popularity through songs such as "Through It All" and "I Don't Know Why Jesus Loved Me," which seemed to strike a perfect balance between old and new gospel music sounds. These contemporary gospel pieces succeeded in retaining the time-honored, Jesus-centered message of the Bible while delivering it by way of a popular musical style that appealed to audiences across generational and racial divides (Heilbut, 247).

In 1981 Crouch dissolved the Disciples to concentrate on other endeavors, including an ambitious solo career that yielded albums such as *Don't Give Up* and *No Time to Lose*, which were released in the first half of the decade. At this stage in his professional life, he also supplemented his gospel projects with collaborative endeavors involving a number of renowned secular artists such as Madonna, STEVIE WONDER, and MICHAEL JACKSON. Among his multiple accolades, Crouch received an Academy Award for his work with QUINCY JONES on the movie soundtrack for *The Color Purple*. Ten years after the release of *No Time to Lose*, Crouch won two Grammy awards for his 1994 solo album *Mercy*. Several gospel artists who experienced success in the 1990s, including Yolanda Adams, Vickie Winans, and Donnie McClurkin, acknowledged an enormous debt to Crouch for his musical innovations (Heilbut, 281).

The mid-1990s marked a watershed in Crouch's life. Following in the footsteps of his father, who passed away in 1992, Crouch became the new pastor of Christ Memorial Church of God in Christ in Pacoima, California. Overseeing hundreds of congregants, Crouch began devoting much of his time to pastoral duties and to outreach programs serving disadvantaged members of his community. Having launched his own record company, Slave Records, Crouch remained a highly respected elder in Christian music arenas. In 1997 he found time to release *Pray*, an album that was widely praised among gospel music enthusiasts. That same year, he received an honorary doctorate from Berklee College of Music. In June 2004 Crouch succeeded MAHALIA JACKSON and JAMES EDWARD CLEVELAND by becoming only the third gospel artist to be given a star on the Hollywood Walk of Fame.

FURTHER READING

Crouch, Andrae, with Nina Ball. *Through It All* (1974).

Boyer, Horace Clarence. "A Comparative Analysis of Traditional and Contemporary Gospel Music," in *More Than Dancing*, ed. Irene V. Jackson (1985).

Boyer, Horace Clarence. *How Sweet the Sound: The Golden Age of Gospel* (1995).

Cusic, Don. *The Sound of Light: A History of Gospel Music* (1990).

Darden, Robert. *People Get Ready!: A New History of Black Gospel Music* (2004).

Heilbut, Anthony. *The Gospel Sound: Good News and Bad Times* (1971).

DISCOGRAPHY

Andrae Crouch and the Disciples Keep On Singin' (Lexicon Music, 1971).

The Andrae Crouch Songbook: 40 Favorite Andrae Crouch Songs (Lexicon Music, 1976).

The Best of Andrae: Andrae Crouch and the Disciples (Lexicon Music, 1975).

Mercy (Qwest, 1994).

No Time to Lose (Lexicon Music, 1984).

Pray (Qwest, 1997).

Soulfully (Lexicon Music, 1972).

Take Me Back (Lexicon Music, 1975).

MELVIN L. BUTLER

Crouch, Hubert Branch, Sr. (7 Dec. 1906–17 Oct. 1980), educator, was born in Jacksonville, Texas, the fifth of seven children of George W. Crouch, a Methodist minister, and Mary Ragsdale Crouch. Known by the nickname "Red," Crouch graduated from Frederick Douglass High School in Jacksonville in 1923, but his family would relocate twenty-six miles to the north in Tyler, Texas, which he considered his hometown.

In Tyler, the Crouches lived in a home with a view of Texas College, a historically black school run by the Colored Methodist Episcopal Church (later known as the Christian Methodist Episcopal Church). In 1927 Crouch earned a B.A. in Biology from Texas College. His father, an elder in the church, wanted him to teach at the school after graduation. Instead, Crouch left for Dallas for a brief but lucrative stint selling insurance. Crouch would later forgo insurance sales for a future in science and education, applying to graduate school at Iowa State College, now Iowa State University (ISU) in Ames, Iowa, an overwhelmingly rural college town. In December 1930 ISU awarded him a Master of Science in Protozoology.

In 1930, while still a student at ISU, Crouch married Mildred Shipp, with whom he would later have two children. Shipp was the granddaughter of Archie and Nancy Martin, former slaves, housing advocates, and influential members of Ames's small black community. The Martins worked on behalf of black students to convince the college's administration to change its racially discriminatory housing practices, and their efforts eventually led to greater housing opportunities for African Americans. Moreover, for three decades, the Martins housed, mentored, and befriended many of ISU's black students and affiliates, including Crouch, the botanist George Washington Carver, the scientist and U.S. Naval Academy professor SAMUEL PROCTOR MASSIE JR., and former Tuskegee Institute professor FREDERICK DOUGLASS PATTERSON. In 2004, ISU named a new dormitory after the Martins.

Although Crouch had studied agriculture during the early 1930s, and was on leave of absence from West Virginia State College in Institute, West Virginia, he began his academic career at Kentucky State College in Frankfort in 1930 when he was appointed assistant professor of biology and, in 1932, acting head of the Natural Sciences and Mathematics Department. At the time, the college's new administration was implementing major changes in the department including upgrades of the undergraduate program with new equipment, integrated courses, additional student extracurricular activities, and plans to require higher faculty qualifications.

Accordingly, Crouch returned to Iowa State College to pursue a doctorate beginning in 1934. In 1935, he was awarded a General Education Board Fellowship of $110 per month to complete his education, and in March 1936, an additional $90 per month to cover expenses stemming from the birth of his second child, and the illness of his wife. He received his Ph.D. in Parasitology on 15 June 1936. He returned to Kentucky State College in the fall of 1936. While there, Crouch established the Council of Science Teachers within the Kentucky Negro Education Association and in 1938 made history as the first black to present a paper to the Kentucky Academy of Sciences. His paper was entitled "The Fauna of Fermentation Residents from Distilleries." In 1938, Crouch held the position of chairman of the Division of Arts and Sciences.

Early in his career, Crouch headed the Kentucky Syphilis Service (1939–1943) and during part of the summer of 1939, he collaborated briefly on venereal disease research with distinguished researcher William A. Hinton, Harvard Medical School's first black professor and the developer of the Hinton test for syphilis. In 1939, Crouch also investigated venereal diseases at the U.S. Marine Hospital on Staten Island.

In 1944 Crouch was appointed professor and head of the Biology Department, and director of the Science Division at Tennessee State University. In 1951 he became the first full dean of its graduate school. During nearly three decades at Tennessee State, Crouch initiated the first graduate program in the sciences, developed a high-quality undergraduate program, and was recognized for his contributions as an administrator, teacher, and scholar with research published in scientific journals.

Crouch's most enduring and far-reaching achievement was cofounding the National Institute of Science (NIS) with Dr. Thomas W. Turner, then a professor and head of the Biology Department at Hampton Institute. In 1931, while attending the National Association for Research in Science Teaching Conference held in New York, Crouch conceived the idea to form an organization of black scientists and educators after noticing that he, his wife, Mildred, and perhaps one other person were the only African Americans in attendance.

For the next several years, Crouch traveled up and down the East Coast and throughout the South strategizing with fellow educators and scientists, and attending meetings and conferences in his quest to bring the national organization into being. In 1943, after innumerable conversations, letters, and hours of planning and coordination, their work culminated in the formal establishment of the NIS by vote of ten scientists representing eight historically black colleges. Crouch's drive and inspiration had been central to the development and success of the nascent association. He infused it with innovative ideas including establishing a scientific supply house as an enterprise of a black college; creating a marine vacation laboratory for biology teachers; developing professional exchange programs; conducting surveys of private industries to determine their willingness and reactions to hiring African American scientists; forging closer relations between industry and black colleges; greater use of grants; and creating a more equitable distribution of funds provided by the federal government under the Hatch-Adams Acts of 1887 and 1906, and under the Purnell Act of 1925.

African American scientists were already actively engaged in major governmental research efforts, including the Manhattan Project, Synthetic Rubber Program, Radar/Microwave Program, and the American Red Cross Blood Donor Project. Nonetheless, membership in the wider scientific community and most national and professional organizations was withheld or restricted because of racial discrimination. Crouch helped establish the NIS to fill the void created by the white institutions, and in so doing provided a forum for blacks and other scientists to share and discuss their achievements, research, and academic interests. Formerly called the National Association of Science Teachers in Negro Colleges (NASTINC), the NIS upgraded science education and research at historically black institutions and enhanced professional development and opportunities for black scientists.

While dedicated to his students, academia, and research, Crouch devoted his intellect and passion to civic endeavors as well. For nine years, he served as chairman and vice chairman of Nashville's Metro Development and Housing Agency. He was a member of the Metro Action and Metro Planning Commissions, the Nashville Area Chamber of Commerce, and the Salvation Army advisory board. He was also Nashville chapter president of Frontiers International, a nonprofit, community service organization, and executive secretary of the American Men of Science (1943–1948). He was a member of Sigma Zi, a national science organization; the Nashville Urban League Board, which he helped bring to Middle Tennessee; and Chi Boule, an exclusive fraternity of prominent African American men. Crouch held life memberships in the NAACP and Kappa Alpha Psi fraternity.

In 1972, with his health failing, Crouch retired from Tennessee State University after 28 years of service and from chairing the Metropolitan Development and Housing Board. He died eight years later, two months before his seventy-fourth birthday, and is buried in Nashville's Greenwood Cemetery. In 1980 TSU renamed the graduate school building Hubert B. Crouch Hall to recognize his outstanding work on behalf of students and the school. The Davidson County, Tennessee, seat of the Nashville–Davidson County Metropolitan Government named Crouch Drive in his honor, and Shipp Drive was named for his wife, Mildred, who was an educator, community volunteer, and the first female and first African American appointee to the Nashville Civil Service Commission.

FURTHER READING

King, William M. "Hubert Branch Crouch and the Origins of the National Institute of Science," *Journal of Negro History,* vol. 79, issue 1 (1994).

Obituaries: *Tennessean,* 19 October 1980, 1 April 2007.

DEBRA A. VARNADO

Crouch, Stanley (14 Dec. 1945–), journalist, music critic, and novelist, was born in Los Angeles to James Crouch, an absentee father, and Emma Bea Crouch, a domestic worker. Crouch's early education was in the Los Angeles public schools, where he was a highly successful student. Crouch began writing stories at the age of eight, read widely in the classics from his early years in secondary school, and was active in the civil rights movement in junior high school.

After graduation from high school Crouch attended several California junior colleges. At East Los Angeles Junior College he became involved in a poverty program in which he taught a literacy class. Witnessing the Watts riots in 1965 made Crouch even more of an activist, and he became a Black Nationalist—although he would in short time come to oppose the movement. From 1965 to 1967 Crouch was an actor and playwright at Studio Watts and the Watts Repertory Theatre Company. During this time he was greatly influenced by the writings of the novelist RALPH ELLISON and ALBERT MURRAY, a contrarian critic and public intellectual. It was mainly because of Murray's influence that Crouch turned from the Black Nationalist movement, which he found too radical in the face of his new, more conservative leanings.

From his mother Crouch had learned to value personal aspiration and the importance of not being imprisoned by class. No doubt those values, his own audacious spirit, and the temper of the times played a large role in his achievements as a young man. Despite his lack of a college degree, Crouch obtained a teaching position at the prestigious Claremont colleges. While teaching English at Claremont's Pomona College and black studies at Pitzer College from 1968 to 1975, Crouch wrote poetry and played the drums. His artistic interests and particularly his passion for music were a driving force. Seeking a broader cultural perspective he left California and moved in 1975 to New York City, where he wrote, performed as a drummer, and promoted jazz performances. In 1979 Crouch became the jazz critic for the *Village Voice*, a position he held until 1988. He also wrote for *Esquire*, the *New York Daily News*, the *New Republic*, and the *New Yorker*. In 1995 Crouch married the sculptor Gloria Nixon.

Stanley Crouch's public life and expressions became increasingly colorful and controversial in the late 1980s and 1990s. As a musician and music critic, Crouch was initially a fan of progressive jazz, but just as his earlier radical political views grew increasingly conservative, so too did his views on music. An early supporter, promoter, and mentor of the jazz trumpeter WYNTON MARSALIS in the late seventies and early eighties, Crouch maintained his supportive role of the highly talented and traditional Marsalis. Crouch turned, however, from many of his other early enthusiasms, particularly his interest in avant-garde jazz. In 1987 Crouch became a music consultant at Lincoln Center.

Given Crouch's view that African Americans should avoid activity in which they promote self-segregation, it is hardly surprising that in the 1990s Crouch began to attack rap and hip-hop music. Critical of what he saw as the music's lack of artistic value, its negative portrayal of women, and its celebration of a criminal lifestyle, Crouch found many supporters for his perspective that young people have enough problems without being encouraged to be violent, irresponsible, and contemptuous of women.

In 1990 Oxford University Press published a collection of Crouch's essays, *Notes of a Hanging Judge: Essays and Reviews, 1979–1989,* in which Crouch attacked highly popular, even iconic, figures in the public and literary worlds, such as TONI MORRISON and SPIKE LEE. In Crouch's view these writers and artists were undermining the African American community through what he perceived as their unwillingness to see black Americans as anything other than victims. In the same vein, he decried their portrayal of black society as falsely homogeneous and thus lacking in authenticity. On several occasions, Crouch's literary feuds became physical as well as verbal: he punched the jazz critic Howard Mandel after an argument at the First Annual Jazz Award and slapped the literary critic Dale Peck in a Greenwich Village restaurant after Peck wrote an unfavorable review of Crouch's first novel *Don't the Moon Look Lonesome.*

In addition to his columns in the *New York Daily News* and articles in various magazines, Crouch's nonfiction publications include *The All-American Skin Game, or, The Decoy of Race: The Long and the Short of It, 1990–1994* (1995); *Always in Pursuit: Fresh American Perspectives, 1995–1997* (1998); *One Shot Harris: The Photographs of Charles "Teenie" Harris* (2002); and *The Artificial White Man: Essays on Authenticity* (2004). These writings reveal an iconoclastic side, in which Crouch further confirmed his ability to confuse and confound with attacks on varied targets including ALEX HALEY, Phillip Roth, MALCOLM X, LOUIS FARRAKHAN, and the theory of Afrocentrism, that is balanced by an ability to offer praise as well as dissent. In addition to his ongoing support of Wynton Marsalis, Crouch wrote tributes to many artists, including Ralph Ellison, CHARLIE PARKER, and DUKE ELLINGTON. Of particular note is the piece on Ellington that appeared in a 1996 special edition of the *New Yorker*, "Black in America." Additionally, *One Shot Harris* presents a hardly positive but nevertheless convincing view of the influence of popular culture on modern society.

In 2000 Crouch published his first novel, *Don't the Moon Look Lonesome: A Novel in Blues and Swing.* The novel is set in New York City and features Carla, a blonde blues singer, and her boyfriend Maxwell, a black saxophone player. The novel, like Crouch's life, was the subject of controversy, not so much for its themes of interracial romance and the significance of art in the modern world as for its style. As the subtitle suggests the novel is almost a montage of song, dialogue, polemic, commentary, and rhyme. Sometimes *Don't the Moon Look Lonesome* soars; sometimes it does not. Thus the novel becomes a metaphor for Stanley Crouch's

role in public life—to demand attention, sometimes effectively, sometimes not—and for American life in the twenty-first century.

FURTHER READING

Beck, Stefan. "Authenticity Blues," *The New Criterion* (2004).

ALICE DRUM

Crowders, Reuben. *See* Hogan, Ernest.

Crowdy, William Saunders (1847–1908), founder of the Church of God and Saints of Christ (CGSC), was born on a slave plantation in Maryland. Crowdy escaped in 1863 and joined the Union army, in which he was assigned to the Quartermaster Corps as a cook for the officers. After the war he purchased a small farm in Guthrie, Oklahoma. Crowdy put his skills as a cook to use with the Santa Fe railroad, which frequently took him to Kansas City, Missouri. There he met a young widow, Lovey Yates Higgins, at a church fair and married her around 1880. At some point in the mid-to-late 1880s, the couple moved to a farm in Oklahoma with their three children, Mattie Leah (who died soon afterwards), Isaac, and August. Crowdy served as a deacon in the Baptist church but does not seem to have been regarded as unusually pious or knowledgeable on religious matters. His biographer and granddaughter, Beersheba Crowdy Walker, tells us that he had been an "ardent Mason" (Walker, 2–4).

Crowdy experienced the vision that defined his calling in 1893. He saw tables descending from the ceiling of a large room, each bearing the name of a denomination—Methodist, Baptist, and so forth. Each table was soiled with vomit, the Baptist table having the most sickening filth of all. Then he saw a little table, clean and white, coming down, with the name "Church of God and Saints of Christ" on it. After reaching the floor, this little table grew larger until it filled the whole room, crowding out the filthy tables. Seven keys, each with a distinctive point of doctrine or practice inscribed on it with corresponding scripture references, lay on the clean table. Then he was shown a Bible and was instructed to eat it. Through this experience, the entire Bible "from Genesis to Revelations was indelibly written in him, chapter and verse, line by line" (Walker, 6–8).

Crowdy began preaching on the street in Guthrie, surprising himself with his ability to quote chapter and verse from the Bible. He took up itinerant preaching full-time in 1896, attracting a sizable following in several towns throughout Oklahoma, Kansas, and Texas. Though he preached that "Christ was black," many of his early converts in these western towns were white people. According to a newspaper account in 1898, the CGSC was a racial "conglomeration such as probably was never before amalgamated in any one religious body," and Crowdy's followers claimed "that they are doing more than any other force being brought to bear in eradication of the color line" (Salt Lake City *Broad-Ax*, 6 Aug. 1898). Not surprisingly, though, his message also attracted heated, sometimes violent, opposition. He was arrested twenty-two times.

His calling to be "The World's Evangelist" then took him to Chicago, where he preached on State Street and was arrested repeatedly. In part to legitimize his public status as a preacher and avoid the frequent arrests, Crowdy began establishing a more formal organizational structure for his movement. He appointed a Presbytery Board and introduced a ceremony for his ordination and anointing as bishop and executive head of the organization. A constitution was adopted in 1898 at the CGSC first General Annual Assembly held in Emporia, Kansas.

As would MARCUS GARVEY soon thereafter, Crowdy proved masterful at using an array of offices, titles, auxiliary organizations, uniforms, ceremonies, parades, and grand assemblies to build his followers' sense of dignity, purpose, and identity as a distinct people of singular significance. The Daughters of Jerusalem and Sisters of Mercy, one of the church's most important auxiliaries, and the first to be assigned a uniform, was organized at the 1898 assembly. They undertook charitable work and visited the sick, "leaving them with money and clothes according to the spirit of Jesus' sayings" (Walker, 16). Additional departments would include the Sabbath School, the choir, the Sons of Abraham men's group, and the YPIL youth group, and participation in them became one of the eleven basic commitments required of CGSC members.

Crowdy's organizational thoroughness and attention to detail in following biblical practices was part of a restorationist view of history. The prophet was regarded as the "Elijah" promised in Malachi 4:5 to appear before the "great and dreadful day of the Lord" to prepare the way for the liberation of his people. The CGSC, as the "clean table" that would eventually displace the "filthy tables" and go on to fill the whole room, was thus a latter-day restoration of the true church that would lead to the apocalyptic coming of the kingdom of God. This re-embodiment of the biblical people of God who "keep the commandments of God and the faith of Jesus" required recovery of neglected worship practices drawn from both Old and New Testaments. Of the seven keys revealed in Crowdy's vision of 1893, four have to do with church rites, such as the use of unleavened bread and water (not wine) for Christ's body and blood, foot washing, and the "Holy Kiss." Crowdy taught that fidelity to the Ten Commandments required observance of the Sabbath on the seventh day of the week (which he considered to be Saturday). This practice, along with annual observance of the "High Days" of the Hebrew scripture, such as Passover and Yom Kippur, became a major point distinguishing the CGSC from the dominant Protestant denominations.

In 1899 Prophet Crowdy turned his attention to the eastern cities, where the CGSC took on a fuller and more definite profile as a holistic program for African American development in the face of tightening oppression. In Philadelphia, Pennsylvania, Crowdy riled opposition from the city's ministers by preaching the sinfulness of keeping Sunday rather than God's seventh day Sabbath, Saturday, and of using wine for communion, which he said made people "drunkards." Some of the "most influential ministers" in the city circulated a petition to have the prophet run out of town and presented it to Mayor Samuel Howell Ashbridge. The mayor responded that the city could use "more Crowdys," in fact if he had "ten more like him" he would "soon be able to clean up the city" (Walker, 29).

Crowdy made Philadelphia his headquarters, saying that the Lord's instruction for him here was to "dig down deep and drive stakes." Long estranged from his first wife, Crowdy united here with Hallie Booker, with whom he had two children, William and Isabella (Walker, 26, 39, 55). During his three years in Philadelphia he began publishing the *Weekly Prophet*. He also acquired forty acres in Belleville, Virginia, on which the church set up an industrial school and a cooperative farm where widows and orphans could live and work. Crowdy also launched several cooperative stores in Philadelphia, beginning with the Noah's Ark Store, which stocked dry goods. He then expanded his enterprises to include several types of stores, including grocery, wood and coal, and photography, as well as a restaurant, a barber shop, and a printing shop. By 1903 membership in the Philadelphia church had surpassed two thousand (Walker, 39–40, 44).

The Prophet envisioned the CGSC spreading among people of African descent throughout the world. In 1903 he ordained a Xhosa sailor, Albert Christian, as a bishop and commissioned him to preach the CGSC message in his homeland of South Africa. Several tabernacles were established there under Christian's leadership, and subsequently the CGSC also planted a smaller presence in Jamaica (Bradford, 173–174).

After the outbreak of a smallpox epidemic in Philadelphia in 1903, Crowdy moved his home base to Washington, D.C., where the church began businesses parallel to those in Philadelphia. Thus, in the two cities with the largest concentrations of African American population at that time, as well as in rural Virginia, Crowdy and the CGSC had created a broad range of cooperative enterprises, thereby structuring economic opportunity and self-determination for a proscribed people.

Crowdy drew extensively on the Hebrew scriptures as well as the New Testament to forge an alternative program for social and economic empowerment as well as religious renewal during the nadir of race relations in America. By the time of his death in 1908, CGSC adherents numbered in the tens of thousands, with communities in southern Africa and the West Indies as well as the United States. In 1904 Crowdy suffered the first of a series of strokes. Nevertheless he continued to travel, appear at public gatherings, and exert authority until his death. In contrast to some other charismatic leaders, Crowdy left behind a movement with staying power. The heirs of Crowdy have diverged, however, with some tabernacles more explicitly Christian in manner and emphasis, and others highlighting Jewish characteristics.

FURTHER READING

The Kansas State Historical Society in Topeka, Kansas, holds a collection of primary documents relating to Crowdy and the CGSC.

Bradford, Charles E. *Sabbath Roots: The African Connection* (1999).

Walker, Beersheba Crowdy. *Life and Works of William Saunders Crowdy* (1955).

Wynia, Elly M. *The Church of God and Saints of Christ: The Rise of the Black Jews* (1994).

DOUGLAS MORGAN

Crudup, Arthur (24 Aug. 1905–28 Mar. 1974), blues singer and songwriter, was born in Forest, Mississippi, between Jackson and Meridian, the son of Minnie Louise Crudup, an unmarried domestic worker. His father was reputed to be a musician, but Crudup recalled seeing him only twice. Raised by his mother in poverty, Crudup began singing both blues and religious music around age ten. In 1916 he and his mother moved to Indianapolis. After she became ill, Crudup dropped out of school and took a job in a foundry at age thirteen.

According to his own account Crudup did not start playing guitar until around 1937, by which time he had returned to the South, married and divorced his first wife, Annie Bell Reed, and taken work as a farmhand. Supposedly he found a guitar with only two strings and one by one added the other four while picking up rudimentary chords from a local musician known as "Papa Harvey." Despite his limited skills on guitar, Crudup found musical employment, supplementing his weekday job by playing at weekend dances.

In 1939 or 1940 Crudup went to Chicago, possibly on tour with a gospel group. Unable to find a steady job, he took to music in desperation, playing the streets for handouts. In 1941, as Crudup was trying to make enough money to return south, the recording artist Peter "Doctor" Clayton heard him playing on the street and summoned the veteran race-record producer Lester Melrose to hear him. Melrose offered Crudup $10 to play a "house party" that evening. The house party, actually an audition, included TAMPA RED, BIG BILL BROONZY, Lil Green, LONNIE JOHNSON, MEMPHIS MINNIE, WASHBOARD SAM, and others—the cream of Chicago blues talent at that time. After the audition, Melrose signed Crudup to two contracts: one as recording artist, the other as songwriter. On 11 September 1941 Crudup cut his first four sides for RCA Victor's Bluebird subsidiary. He played an acoustic guitar and was accompanied by Joe McCoy, who did a vocal imitation of a bass. Three of the sides, "Death Valley Blues," "If I Get Lucky," and "Black Pony Blues," are now considered classic examples of down-home blues.

The records sold well, and on 15 April 1942 Crudup was called back for a second Bluebird session, this time playing an electric guitar and accompanied by the noted session bassist Ransom Knowling. The session yielded six issued sides, including one of the greatest of all train blues, "Mean Old 'Frisco Blues." A 15 December 1944 Chicago session with the drummer Melvin Draper produced another blues that would become traditional, "Rock Me Mama." During World War II, Crudup was one of the only blues artists included in the U.S. Armed Forces Radio Services transcription series, although his songs were wrongly credited to "Art Crudux."

A postwar session in February 1946 with the drummer Armand "Jump" Jackson yielded "So Glad You're Mine" and "Ethel Mae," also considered classics, released on RCA Victor. A September 1946 session, teaming Crudup with Knowling and the drummer Judge Riley, produced Crudup's best-known song, "That's All Right [Mama]," a candidate, according to some critics, for the first rock and roll recording. The successful trio stayed together through 1952, putting out notable hits, "Train Fare Blues," "Hand Me Down My Walking Cane" (also known as "Look on Yonder Wall"), "Shout, Sister, Shout," and "My Baby Left Me."

Crudup received payments for each session, but the money from record sales went to Melrose and RCA, so from 1941 to 1945 Crudup alternated between menial day jobs in Chicago and farmwork in Mississippi.

While in Chicago, Crudup married again, but little is known about his second wife. Crudup told family members years later that she had been murdered. On one of his trips back to Forest, Mississippi, after the death of his second wife, Crudup bumped into Annie Bell, his first wife, whose second husband had also died under violent circumstances. A year later, probably around 1945, Crudup moved back to Mississippi, remarried Annie Bell, and resumed full-time farming. With seven children from Annie Bell's second marriage, the Crudups went on to have five children of their own (one of whom died in infancy) and remained together until Annie Bell died in 1963. Crudup remained a part-time musician, performing on *King Biscuit Time*, a popular midday show on KFFA Radio in Helena, Arkansas, in the mid-1940s. He struck up an informal musical collaboration with the *King Biscuit* star SONNY BOY WILLIAMSON No. 2 and in 1948 met the slide guitarist ELMORE JAMES, who was living in Belzoni, Mississippi. Crudup, Williamson, and James began playing together informally in what must have been one of the most formidable blues trios ever assembled.

Crudup did further recording in the South in 1952, 1953, and 1954, but his style was dated, and the records met with minimal success. Discouraged, he withdrew from recording, ironically, at the same time Elvis Presley remade "That's All Right Mama," helping to touch off the rock and roll revolution that Crudup is thought by some to have fathered.

Around 1954 Crudup left Mississippi and began contracting and transporting migrant labor for seasonal farmwork near Orlando, Florida, and Franktown, Virginia, where he eventually settled. In 1959 he recorded an album, *Mean Ol' Frisco*, released on the Fire label, but it did little for Crudup, and Fire went bankrupt soon after. As the 1960s began, he continued to live in Franktown on Virginia's Delmarva Peninsula, performing every so often in his own small dance hall, built next to his house, or sitting in with his sons' band, the Malibus.

As the nationwide blues revival gathered steam in the 1960s, Robert Koester, who had been recording rediscovered blues artists, wrote Crudup to propose a session in Chicago. Crudup accepted and went to Chicago in 1967 to appear at the University of Chicago's Rhythm and Blues Festival and record for Koester's Delmark label. Signing with Dick Waterman's booking agency, Crudup successfully made the transition to the blues-revival festival circuit, playing major U.S. festivals and touring Europe and Australia to much acclaim.

Meanwhile Waterman, the American Guild of Artists and Composers, and other concerned parties sought to help Crudup collect royalties he was long due. Although no final settlement was ever reached, Broadcast Music Incorporated (BMI) did make a substantial payment to Crudup. Ironically, the end of his poverty coincided with the end of his life. Diagnosed with insulin-dependent diabetes in 1972, he suffered a series of small heart attacks starting about that same time. He was being treated for heart trouble at a hospital in Nassawadox, Virginia, when he suffered a fatal heart attack. He was buried in Franktown.

Best known in rock history as Presley's idol, Arthur "Big Boy" Crudup was a transitional artist whose recordings bridged the era of down-home Delta blues and the dawn of electric blues. If he had a larger role in the beginnings of rock, it was in bringing electric guitar blues to the forefront as a marketable sound for the recording industry. In his heyday Crudup recorded more than eighty sides, which sold primarily to the African American blues and rhythm and blues markets. A limited guitarist who favored the key of E, he tended to rework the same instrumental figures time and again, which for better or for worse made his music consistent and predictable.

Despite his hulking size, Crudup had a keen, high-pitched voice that retained traces of the field holler. With early help from Tampa Red, Crudup found that he had a remarkable talent for blues composition. Although Crudup himself became a symbol of economic exploitation and racial injustice, his songs became staples for blues, rock, and even country artists, including Presley, Creedence Clearwater Revival, and B. B. KING.

FURTHER READING
Leadbitter, Mike. "Big Boy Crudup," *Blues Unlimited* 75 (Sept. 1970): 16–18.
McKee, Margaret, and Fred Chisenhall. *Beale Black and Blue: Life and Music on Black America's Main Street* (1981).
Obituary: *Living Blues* 16 (Spring 1974): 5.

This entry is taken from the *American National Biography* and is published here with the permission of the American Council of Learned Societies.

BILL MCCULLOCH AND
BARRY LEE PEARSON

Crum, George (July 1828–22 July 1914), best known as the reputed inventor of the potato chip, who established his own restaurant in the resort community of Saratoga Springs, New York. His ancestry and ethnicity are a matter of speculation; he may have been best described in *Saratoga Springs, New York: A Brief History* as "of thoroughly mixed American blood." He is generally reported in census data from 1850 to 1880 as mulatto and in later censuses as black. It is commonly said that his mother was of Native American descent and that he "looked Indian."

Crum was born in Malta, New York, to Abraham (or Abram) Speck and his wife Catherine. Although oral accounts suggest Speck was from Kentucky and possibly had been enslaved there, the 1820 Federal Census shows a "Free Colored Person" male, age twenty-six to forty-five, of that name, living in New York, and the 1840 Census shows a free colored person of the same name heading a household of nine. The 1800 census records "Abraham Speck, a Free Negro" living in Watervliet in Albany County, head of a family of four—quite possibly George Crum's paternal grandfather and probably the Abraham Speck who served in the Albany County Militia during the Revolutionary War. Catherine Speck is variously described as a Stockbridge Indian, a Huron, or from "the St. Regis tribe." Oral traditions recall Abraham Speck as mulatto or Native American and as a jockey, who may have used the name Crum professionally.

George Crum is reputed to have said he chose his surname because a crumb is bigger than a speck. He alternated both surnames in succeeding

censuses and consistently reported that both his parents were born in New York. He sometimes referred to himself as having Spanish and German blood. There are no significant records of his childhood. Although it has been published that he "knew ridicule as a child" on account of his mixed ancestry, this is pure speculation based on other lives and common stereotypes.

As a young man, Crum worked in the Adirondack Mountains as a guide, known as an excellent hunter and fisherman. Throughout his life, these occupations and that of farmer were reported to the federal census as his occupation. He apparently did not consider chef to be his primary calling. He did learn to cook from a Frenchman, a frequent companion in the woods. In 1850 George Speck was a blacksmith in Minden, New York, living with his younger sister Catherine (1850 Census). George Crum and his sister, Catherine Wicks (or Weeks), known as "Aunt Katie," were in charge of the kitchen at Moon's Lake House when it was opened in 1853 by Cary Moon, on Saratoga Lake. The city catered to summer visitors, including future and former presidents, governors, members of congress, and a variety of wealthy bankers, industrialists, and professionals, with a series of luxury establishments along the lakefront.

There are many stories of how the potato chip was invented. A standard legend is that in the summer of 1853 a dissatisfied customer, perhaps Cornelius Vanderbilt (a regular at Moon's), sent some fried potatoes back to the kitchen, complaining that they were not sufficiently crunchy, or perhaps not salty enough, or too thick. Crum sliced some potatoes very thin, deep-fried them, added copious salt, and returned them to Vanderbilt (or whoever it was), who was delighted and asked for more.

Other accounts suggest Katie Wicks may have been the inventor. She took credit for it in an 1899 interview and is further credited in her 1917 obituary. Her brother, still living in 1899, did not dispute it, nor is he known to have taken credit for the potato chip; David Mitchell, director of the Brookside Museum in Saratoga County, observed that Crum was "not a humble man." Accounts that George Crum personally invented the potato chip first appeared in the 1930s and in late twentieth century publicity of the late-blooming snack food industry.

Katie Wicks is said to have invented the chip while slicing potatoes and frying crullers, when a potato slice fell into the hot oil. Crum, according to this story, tasted the chip, asking, "That's good, how did you make it?" Hearing her account of the accident, Crum replied, "That's a good accident. We'll have plenty of these." It is also possible that she obtained the recipe from a French chef at the nearby San Souci. Neither Crum nor anyone else became the proprietor of a major potato chip manufacturer or applied for a patent. Chips were made in small local establishments at least until 1895, and nationally distributed brands did not appear until the 1930s and later. They appeared on the menu at the Lake House as "Saratoga Chips."

Crum opened his own restaurant, Crum's House, in 1860, at the south end of the lake. He owned his own home on a nearby hill, with a small porch overlooking the water, and raised as much of the food served as possible on his own farm. By some accounts he had five wives, who with others of his extended family were the primary employees of his establishment. However, every census from 1860 to 1900 shows him living with the same wife, whose name was recorded as Hester or Esther. Local accounts are that she was from an Indian reservation in Wisconsin. His clients included financier Jay Gould, lawyer and hotel operator Henry Hilton, and William H. Vanderbilt, son of the railroad magnate, but he ran his business on a first-come, first-served basis.

A reminiscence published in 1928 observed that being an Indian, Crum never departed from the rules of his establishment; "guests were obliged to wait their turn, the millionaire as well as the wage earner" ("Reminiscences of Saratoga," compiled by Cornelius E. Durkee, *The Saratogian*, 1927–1928). Gould was once kept waiting more than an hour when the restaurant was crowded. Hilton insisted he would wait in the front yard for two hours to be served at Crum's House. Vanderbilt is reputed to have admired Crum because he was able to cook canvass back ducks in exactly the manner the wealthy guest desired. Presidents Chester Arthur and Grover Cleveland were among his guests, as were many governors. Crum served what he called "potato crunches" in baskets on each table and sold take-out under the name "Saratoga Chips."

A woman named Nancy Hegamore, commonly known as Nance, born in New York of mixed German and Indian ancestry, but listed in the census as black, or mulatto, or whatever Crum was listed as each time, was Crum's business manager, cashier, bartender, and headwaiter. In later years, he came to lean on her ability to superintend the business, and she was still part of his

household in 1910. He closed the restaurant after thirty years and lived another twenty-four years, dying at the age of eighty-six in 1914. Invention is seldom the product of one person having a unique idea: George Crum's real and mythical role in the invention of the potato chip shows how a man and a woman, both skilled chefs, probably a mix of African, European, and Native American ancestry, interacting with tourists, tycoons, entrepreneurs, and woodsmen, gave rise to a new snack food that rose to real prominence in American life almost a century later.

FURTHER READING

Bradley, Hugh. *Such Was Saratoga* (1975).

Burhans, Dirk E. *Crunch! A History of the Great American Potato Chip* (2008).

D'Imperio, Chuck. *Great Graves of Upstate New York* (2007).

Lamont, William J., Jr. "Potato Chips Are Big Business." *Spudlines*, March 2006, Vol. 44, No. 1.

CHARLES ROSENBERG

Crum, William Demos (1859–c. Nov. 1912), physician and politician, was born near Orangeburg, South Carolina. Born free and the youngest of seven children in a family with German African ancestry, he matured on an Orangeburg plantation, which his father, Darius, had inherited from his German father, who had settled in South Carolina in the early nineteenth century. The Crums owned and used forty-three slaves to farm their plantation, yet the close of the Civil War marked the death of Darius and their fortune.

The dissolution of the family fortune drove Crum's older brothers north in search of employment, but they helped him get an education. He graduated in 1875 from Avery Normal Institute in Charleston, South Carolina, and briefly attended the University of South Carolina shortly thereafter. In 1881 he obtained an M.D. degree from Howard University, establishing a medical practice in Charleston two years later. After setting up his medical practice Crum married Ellen Craft who, like him, was free born and formally educated.

By 1900 Crum had joined the black elite community in Charleston, including sundry charities, the African Methodist Episcopal Zion (AMEZ) Church, the local hospital for blacks (which he led), the Avery Normal Institute Board of Trustees, various business ventures, and the Republican Party. One business venture—director of the black Department of the Charleston and West Indian

Exposition in 1901—garnered him the opportunity to cement his relationship with BOOKER T. WASHINGTON, Crum's friend and political mentor. Washington employed his extraordinary influence with President Theodore Roosevelt to elevate Crum's name to the federal level and in the Republican Party.

Like Booker T. Washington, Crum exhorted social responsibility over equality. Thus his rise to power was not without resistance from both blacks and whites. Preaching the politics of acquiescence and compromise, he served as chairman of the Republican Party for more than twenty years and as a delegate to every Republican National Convention from 1884 until 1904.

Moreover President Benjamin Harrison appointed Crum postmaster of Charleston in 1892, but the opposition of white Charlestonians forced Harrison to rescind the appointment. Two years later Crum was selected as the Republican candidate for U.S. Senator, but lost by a wide margin to Benjamin Tillman, the guru of South Carolina's Democratic Party. When the position of Collector of Internal Revenue was left vacant by the death of Eugene Alonzo Webster, generally acknowledged as Republican Party boss, on 17 September 1901 Washington implored Roosevelt to grant the position to Crum. However, Washington's pleas fell upon deaf ears and Roosevelt gave the position to Loomis Blalock, a white manufacturer, though he did assure Washington that he would grant Crum some other available position.

Meanwhile, black Republicans in South Carolina vocalized increasing disillusionment over Roosevelt's distribution of federal positions. When R. M. Wallace's death in September 1902 left the collector to the port of Charleston position vacant, Washington advised Roosevelt to appoint Crum, and this time Roosevelt agreed. In November 1902 Crum replaced Wallace. While this announcement engendered collegiality among many Republicans, it also marked the beginning of a protracted and invidious battle by Southern white Democrats to defeat Crum's confirmation.

When Crum's appointment finally reached the Senate, a delegation from Charleston argued that he was woefully incompetent: He was "colored," did not represent the citizens of Charleston or the state, and was a vapid opportunist. Roosevelt requested that Washington investigate Crum's fitness to serve in public office and, not surprisingly, he found that Crum's color constituted the primary objection of the opposition. Consequently, Roosevelt gave the collectorship to Crum in March 1903 and used several interim appointments to keep him in the position until Senate confirmation in 1905. Crum performed his duties with efficiency and racial conciliation; he used a white deputy director to serve whites who refused to work for him and gave jobs to the less recalcitrant whites to pacify them.

Although Crum continued to draw criticism, he worked inconspicuously but effectively the next four years after confirmation. He doubled annual receipts while maintaining his medical practice and large business ventures. In 1908 Roosevelt reappointed Crum to another term, but the political vitriol from the South prevented him from completing it. William Howard Taft's election in 1908 signaled the end of White House support for Crum. He had become the symbol of the "Negro Question," which Roosevelt and Taft had desperately sought to defuse. Once again, they turned to Washington for advice and he, once again, delivered. He persuaded Crum to vacate the collectorship in March 1909 at the end of his term.

With aplomb and grace, the unflappable Crum retired with "Roosevelt, his 'chief and friend'" to his medical practice and private life. Under pressure from Washington not to forget Crum's forced resignation, Taft named Crum minister to Liberia in May 1910. He worked diligently to attenuate Liberia's debts and resolve boundary disputes. He encouraged trade with the United States as the main vehicle to ameliorate the country's social and economic plights.

Unfortunately Crum's stay in Liberia proved fleeting; he contracted an African fever and sailed with his wife to Charleston in September 1912. He died fewer than three months later. His life and death reenacted a central paradox and tragedy in African American life. He relied upon conciliation and appeasement to navigate nineteenth- and early-twentieth-century America, stoically repressing his hurt and the pains of his people.

FURTHER READING
Gatewood, Willard B. "William D. Crum: A Negro in Politics," *Journal of Negro History* 53 (1968).
Logan, Rayford W., and Michael R. Winston, eds. *Dictionary of American Negro Biography* (1982).
FLOYD OGBURN JR.

Crummell, Alexander (3 Mar. 1819–10 Sept. 1898), clergyman, activist, and Pan-Africanist, was born in New York City, the son of Charity Hicks, a freeborn woman of Long Island, New York, and Boston

Crummell, an African of the Temne people, probably from the region that is now Sierra Leone. Boston Crummell had been captured and brought to the United States as a youth. The circumstances of his emancipation are not clear, but it is said that he simply refused to serve his New York owners any longer after reaching adulthood. Boston Crummell established a small oyster house in the African Quarter of New York. Alexander Crummell received his basic education at the African Free School in Manhattan. In 1835 he traveled to Canaan, New Hampshire, along with his friends Thomas Sidney and HENRY HIGHLAND GARNET, to attend the newly established Noyes Academy, but shortly after their arrival the school was destroyed by local residents angered by its policy of integration. He resumed his education at the Oneida Institute, in upstate New York. Later, rejected by the General Theological Seminary of the Protestant Episcopal Church in New York City for purely racial reasons, Crummell sought out private instruction from sympathetic clergymen in Providence and Boston, attended lectures unofficially at Yale University, and was elevated to the status of deacon in 1842.

Crummell was ordained a priest in 1844, but there were few among the Episcopal clergy who accorded him the respect due his office. As a young pastor in Providence, Rhode Island, during 1841 and 1842, he began to show the stubbornness, pride, and intellectual toughness that were his prime temperamental traits. Sometime in 1841 he married Sarah Mabitt Elston. Their first child was born and died during the scant year the Crummells spent in attempting to develop a congregation in Philadelphia in 1844. They later had at least five children. The young couple moved to New York in 1845 but was continually dogged by poverty, hunger, and racial discrimination.

Crummell had participated in the antislavery movement from the time he was a boy, when he worked in the New York offices of the American Anti-Slavery Society. He was the New England correspondent for the *Colored American* in the early 1840s and participated in the convention movement among black Americans. Crummell belonged to that faction of black activists who identified themselves as "race men," working through separate organizations for the specific interests of people of African descent.

After a fire in 1847 Crummell went to England to raise funds for a new church by lecturing on the antislavery circuit. With the support of distinguished British philanthropists, he established a fund for the church, but he also set up a separate fund to support his apparently long-standing ambition to study at Oxford or Cambridge. Crummell's experiences in England were comparatively pleasant despite poverty, illness, and the minor humiliations and thoughtless condescensions he and his family occasionally experienced. He was admitted to Queens' College, Cambridge, though his studies were disrupted by ill health, the difficult pregnancies of his wife, and the death of one of his children. He was further distracted by his travels on the antislavery circuit, which extended far from Cambridge. While uncompromisingly militant in his opposition to slavery, he did not present himself as an authority on the conditions of the slaves, often preferring to focus his lectures on the problem of "caste" encountered by the free black community.

Crummell was awarded the bachelor's degree by special examination in the spring of 1853. Early that summer, he surprised many of his supporters when he left for Liberia, West Africa, as a missionary under the financial sponsorship of the Protestant Episcopal Church. Crummell's opposition to colonization was well known, but he explained that he wished to bring up his children within the political institutions of black men.

Crummell's prickly disposition and contentious temperament were not improved by the rigors of frontier life. He suffered from heart ailments, fevers, varicose veins, and "liver complaint." Nonetheless he demonstrated tremendous energy, often embarking on long treks into the bush, working variously as a farmer, preacher, schoolmaster, politician, and small businessman, and toiling over vitriolic lucubrations regarding his enemies. He quarreled constantly and bitterly with his bishop, John Payne, a white man from Virginia, accusing him of color prejudice and condescension. Payne accused Crummell of conspiring to usurp his authority and of refusing to work with the native population. It is said, however, that Crummell was an effective preacher before native audiences and that, as administrator of the agricultural school at Cape Palmas, he met with remarkable success.

Although Crummell claimed he had no political ambitions, it is clear he hoped to have an influence on the political philosophy and intellectual life of the society. He envisioned a career as a scholar statesman and pinned his hopes on the new college that was to be erected in Monrovia. His cultural ideals and political ideology were revealed in speeches delivered in Liberia over the next decade. "The Relations and Duty of Free Colored

Men in America to Africa" (1860) is an excellent illustration of his Christian black nationalist sentiments. Another essay, "The Responsibility of the First Fathers of a Country for Its Future Life and Destiny" (1863), reveals Crummell's vision of himself as a founding father of the republic. Crummell's uplift ideology was consistent with ideas expressed in the Constitution of the African Civilization Society drafted by American black nationalists in 1861 and anticipated the aims of MARCUS GARVEY's Universal Negro Improvement movement of the 1920s.

Crummell's marriage was never a happy one, and he was frequently alienated from his wife and children. At the time of her death in 1878, Sarah was living separately from him in New York. Crummell's dealings with associates, both clerical and lay, went no better than his domestic affairs during these years. He nonetheless continued to produce letters, sermons, and public addresses in a style both graceful and strong, which are among the most polished examples of African American literature in the nineteenth century.

In 1861 and 1862 Crummell toured and lectured widely in the United States on behalf of the American Colonization Society and in support of the nascent Liberia College. Upon his return to Liberia he was appointed to the professorship of English and moral philosophy at Liberia College. Crummell was not happy with the supervisory requirements of a professor's life, and he had differences with the college president, JOSEPH JENKINS ROBERTS. He left the college for several months in 1865, claiming the need to look after the fortunes of his daughters, who were studying at Oberlin College in Ohio, but he also used the occasion to embark on another speaking tour in the United States, and on his return, he was relieved of his professorial duties.

Frustrated in his ambitions, Crummell submitted to the discipline of the church hierarchy and turned his attention to missionary work outside Monrovia. He published occasional letters in the Episcopal journal, *Spirit of Missions*, describing his preaching and travels in the backcountry. Crummell was committed to a policy of educating and intermarrying with the native population. He supported the assimilationist policies of President EDWARD JAMES ROYE, opposing Roberts and the Republican Party, whom he denounced as a "venal mulatto elite" dedicated to keeping the natives in a permanently inferior status. In 1871, when Liberia experienced its first coup, led by the Roberts faction, Roye was assassinated, and Crummell fled the country.

In 1872 Crummell became rector of St. Mary's Church in Washington, D.C. Seven years later he established the congregation of St. Luke's, which he served until his retirement in 1894. During this time, he was often embroiled in ecclesiastical controversies but continued to write on a variety of social and religious issues. His essay, "The Black Woman of the South: Her Neglects and Her Needs" (1883), outlines a program of moral and industrial education for the masses of poor black women to compensate for the ravages of slavery, anticipating the issues addressed by MARY CHURCH TERRELL, president of the National Association of Colored Women. Always an advocate of strong central government in the tradition of Alexander Hamilton and John Jay, he was critical of the democratic principles of Thomas Jefferson. In an undated sermon written in the 1880s, he expressed the opinion that "the nation's existence is endangered by insane political excitements." He believed it was the destiny of African Americans to offer a conservative balance to the radical tendencies of certain European immigrant groups.

Crummell was married in 1880 to Jennie Simpson, who played an active role in his church and social life. After his retirement from St. Luke's, Crummell was granted a lectureship at Howard University. He served as president of the Colored Minister's Union of Washington, D.C., worked actively in the Episcopal Church on behalf of its African American membership, and traveled and lectured widely. His address "The Solution of Problems, the Duty and Destiny of Man" at Wilberforce University in 1895 was a call for ceaseless intellectual struggle. In *The Souls of Black Folk* (1903), W. E. B. DuBois recalled the impression Crummell made at Wilberforce: "Instinctively I bowed before this man, as one bows before the prophets of the world. Some seer he seemed, that came not from the crimson Past or the gray To-come, but from the pulsing Now" (216).

In 1897 Crummell founded the American Negro Academy, an institution opposed to the educational policies of BOOKER T. WASHINGTON and committed to the vindication of the African race through scholarly publication. Although Crummell was an advocate of industrial education, he was just as strong a proponent of classical studies, the social sciences, and the liberal arts. The American Negro Academy program reflected

Crummell's dedication to the development of independent black institutions, the promotion of stable nuclear families, and the development of individual character.

Crummell remained intellectually active until his death at Red Bank, New Jersey. His essays and addresses provide a unique if somewhat sardonic perspective on nineteenth-century intellectual life. Crummell published three books during his lifetime: *The Future of Africa* (1862), *The Greatness of Christ and Other Sermons* (1882), and *Africa and America* (1891). The best summation of his racial chauvinism is his sermon on "The Destined Superiority of the Negro" (1877). While Crummell contributed substantially to the African American protest tradition, it would diminish the importance of his legacy to view him primarily as a racial protest writer. His writings, for the most part addressed to black audiences, are most often concerned with the relationship of human nature to the concept of authority, the importance of traditions and institutions to human existence, and the defense of literary culture.

FURTHER READING

Crummell's sermons have been preserved in the collections of the Schomburg Center for Research in Black Culture of the New York Public Library. Collections of his letters are held in the Archives of the Episcopal Church in Austin, Texas, Cuttington University College in Liberia, the Library of Congress, and the Jay Family Papers at Columbia University.

Moses, Wilson J. *Alexander Crummell: A Study of Civilization and Discontent* (1989).

Oldfield, John. *Alexander Crummell and the Creation of an African American Church in Liberia* (1990).

Rigsby, Gregory. *Alexander Crummell: Pioneer in Nineteenth-Century Pan-African Thought* (1987).

Obituary: *Colored American*, 24 Sept. 1898.

This entry is taken from the *American National Biography* and is published here with the permission of the American Council of Learned Societies.

WILSON J. MOSES

Crumpler, Rebecca Davis Lee (8 Feb. 1831–9 Mar. 1895), physician, was born Rebecca Davis in Delaware, the daughter of Absolum Davis and Matilda Webber. Little is known of her early life, except that she was raised in Pennsylvania by an aunt who was often sought out by sick neighbors and whose kind attention to the sufferings of others had a great impact on her appreciative and impressionable niece. By 1852 Crumpler had moved to Charlestown, Massachusetts (near Cambridge), and for the next eight years worked as a nurse for various doctors there. Her lack of formal training did not distinguish her from other nurses at the time, as the first U.S. school for nurses did not open until 1873. In 1860, bearing letters of recommendation from her physician-employers, Crumpler sought admittance to the M.D. program at New England Female Medical College (NEFMC). The first black medical school in the United States would not open until 1868, and in antebellum America medical school administrators routinely denied entrance to blacks, both male and female. Yet the trustees of New England Female Medical College admitted Crumpler to their four-year medical curriculum in 1860.

In 1860 only about 300 of the 54,543 physicians in the United States were women with medical degrees. None were black women. American physicians were only gradually finding medical degrees necessary to their work; many still trained in apprenticeships, and most states had no licensing requirements. No records remain of Crumpler's first three years at NEFMC or of the struggles she may have endured to gain admittance or to remain enrolled. Her later writings give no indication that she was aware of her status as the first black woman M.D. in the United States; indeed, until the late twentieth century, scholars had assigned that distinction to REBECCA COLE, who received her degree from the Woman's Medical College of Pennsylvania in 1867, three years behind Crumpler. It seems likely that Crumpler attended medical school less to enable her to practice as a physician than to improve her nursing skills. She would later argue, for example, that "woman should study the mechanism of the human structure ... before assuming the office of nurse" (Crumpler, 3).

On 24 February 1864 Crumpler and her two white classmates, Mary Lockwood Allen and Elizabeth Kimball, came before the four faculty members to undergo their final, oral examinations. Each candidate had had at least three years of preparatory coursework, written a thesis, and paid her graduation fees, all standard for the time. At the conclusion of the exam, the faculty voted to recommend Crumpler and her two classmates to the board of trustees, but they recorded some hesitation with regard to Crumpler's recommendation. "Deficiencies" in Crumpler's education and what the faculty regarded as her "slow progress" in medical school led the faculty to note that "*some of us have hesitated very seriously in recommending her.*" In spite of their reservations, the faculty deferred to "the wishes of the Trustees & the present state of public feeling," suggesting that the faculty had felt pressured to pass Crumpler. The minutes of that meeting offer no further explanation. It is possible that the doctors for whom Crumpler had worked before entering medical school had put pressure on the faculty. Nevertheless, on 1 March the trustees conferred the "Doctress of Medicine" degree upon Crumpler, whom the trustees identified as "Mrs. Rebecca Lee, negress." According to NEFMC statistics, in this period only about 35 percent of all women who attended the college completed the degree program. With Crumpler's graduation, the number of NEFMC graduates totaled forty-eight women. The college would close in 1873 without graduating another black woman. At around the time of her graduation she married Arthur Crumpler, but further details about him or their marriage are unknown except that Arthur outlived Rebecca.

Crumpler remained in Boston after graduation to practice and for a time sought additional training at an unspecified location in the "British Dominion." She specialized in caring for women and children, particularly poor ones. At the end of the Civil War she moved to Richmond, Virginia, to do what she considered "real missionary work," treating black patients through an arrangement with the Freedmen's Bureau (Crumpler, 3). Many southern blacks, particularly former slaves, found themselves without medical care after leaving the plantation. The resulting need led Crumpler and other black physicians to offer such care; it also encouraged many more blacks to seek formal medical training. White missionary groups as well as black community groups were instrumental in founding, in the late nineteenth century, the first black medical schools in the United States. Yet despite the need for them, black practitioners were not usually welcome in the postwar south. There is some indication that Crumpler herself was not well received in Richmond. One source suggests that "men doctors snubbed her, druggists balked at filling her prescriptions, and some people wisecracked that the M.D. behind her name stood for nothing more than 'Mule Driver'" ("Outstanding Women Doctors," *Ebony* [May 1964], 68).

By 1869 Crumpler had returned to Boston, where she practiced with "renewed vigor," perhaps because she felt more at home in the community where she had been trained. She lived, for a time at least, at 67 Joy Street on Beacon Hill, then a predominantly black neighborhood. By 1880 she and her husband had moved to Hyde Park, Massachusetts, where the residents apparently were less in need of her services. She appears not to have been in active practice in 1883, the year she published *A Book of Medical Discourses* to advise women on medical care for themselves and their children. That she dedicated the volume to mothers and nurses seems a further indication that she viewed her medical training primarily as preparation for her nursing work. According to her death certificate, she died in Fairview, Massachusetts, still a resident of Hyde Park. Although much of Rebecca Lee Crumpler's life remains hidden, and in spite of her exclusion from most histories of American medicine, many have drawn inspiration from her achievements, as evidenced by the name of one of the first medical societies for black women: the Rebecca Lee Society.

FURTHER READING

Records of Crumpler's education at NEFMC are held at the Boston University Archives. A meager bit of information on her is available at the Archives and Special Collections on Women in Medicine at the Medical College of Pennsylvania, gathered as part of the Black Women Physicians Project.

Crumpler, Rebecca. *A Book of Medical Discourses in Two Parts* (1883).

Wells, Susan. *Out of the Dead House: Nineteenth-Century Women Physicians and the Writing of Medicine* (2001).

This entry is taken from the *American National Biography* and is published here with the permission of the American Council of Learned Societies.

SARAH K. A. PFATTEICHER

Cruse, Harold W. (8 Mar. 1916–25 Mar. 2005), writer and educator, was born in Petersburg, Virginia, to parents about whom little is known but who were only briefly married before Harold's father took his young son to New York City during the black migration to the North. The elder Cruse found work as a custodian with the Long Island Railroad; however, he soon realized the he could not care for a small child alone and placed Harold with a foster family in Queens. During the Harlem Renaissance of the 1920s his foster mother, Aunt Henrietta, instilled a love for the black theater in the young Harold, frequently taking him to performances. With the coming of the Depression the family lost their home and was forced to move into an apartment in Harlem, where Cruse became more deeply immersed in black culture. There he would witness performances by DUKE ELLINGTON, CAB CALLOWAY, BILL ROBINSON, and FLORENCE MILLS, which left him with "the indelible impression that black theatrical art was not only unique but inimitable" (Cruse, *Rebellion or Revolution?*, 11).

Cruse attended P.S. 139, FREDERICK DOUGLASS Junior High School, where COUNTÉE CULLEN taught English. JAMES BALDWIN, Cruse's much more popular rival, was only a few grades behind. With the coming of World War II, Cruse served as a quartermaster in an all-black army unit stationed in various parts of Europe and North Africa. During his tour of duty he saw performances by JOSEPHINE BAKER. In Italy Cruse received his first exposure to communist philosophy from soldiers debating the virtues and detriments of various political systems. Cruse was persuaded by the blistering critique of capitalism presented by Marxist intellectuals, whose ideas would have a profound influence on the trajectory of his political development.

Upon returning to the United States, Cruse completed his formal education in New York at the Washington Carver School on 125th Street, run by the African American poet GWENDOLYN BENNETT, who was married to one of Harlem's leading black communists, OTTO HUISWOOD. It was at the school that Cruse first heard African American thinkers such as W. E. B. DUBOIS expound on racial and economic issues. He briefly attended the City College of New York on the G. I. Bill but left within his first year of study. In 1946 Cruse joined the Communist Party and also the Lincoln-Douglas Club. He became a cultural critic for the *Daily Worker* and the *New York Labor Press*. Cruse perceived that the party leadership appreciated the way he expounded on the racist and imperialist implications of such vehicles as the film *King Solomon's Mines* (1950) and a Broadway revival of *Green Pastures* (1951). However, he felt pressure to sublimate any race consciousness or black cultural pride in order to promote the party's belief in a common class struggle. This refusal to tote the official party line on race, he believed, led to his marginalization.

Many African American creative artists passed through the Communist Party during the postwar years, including RICHARD WRIGHT, PAUL ROBESON, CHESTER HIMES, and CLAUDE MCKAY. Yet Cruse was perhaps the most probing in his criticisms of the party and controversial in his conclusions—particularly as they related to the role of Jews and the character of West Indian militancy. He wrote, "Jews were also able to play a three-way game inside the Communist leftwing: as 'Americanized' Jews, á la [Michael] Gold; as Jewish Jews; and as pro-Zionist, nationalistic Jews. Left-wing Jews were able to drop their Jewishness and pick it up whenever it suited them" (*Crisis*, 57). Blacks, Cruse argued, were expected to be good color-blind comrades. Cruse characterized West Indian activists as Anglophiles who were conservative at home and radical abroad and who were not in racial solidarity with African Americans. They "preferred to be revolutionary Marxist first, a West Indian second, and a Negro last" (*Crisis*, 130).

Critics including Ernest Kaiser, archivist at the New York Public Library's Schomburg Center, and the historian Winston James took Cruse to task for his many factual errors, analytical mistakes, and for his apparent prejudices, but all acknowledged that there were tensions and a troubling dynamic pervading the interethnic and intraracial relationships in the Communist Party, and they all recognize the profound debt owed to Cruse for raising such important questions. Cruse conceded that there were "many flaws" in *The Crisis of the Negro Intellectual* (1967), but he explained that "the real intent of this book was to inject into the civil rights movement by polemical force a new level of criticism at any cost" (James, 264). After Cruse left the party in 1953 he struggled to find a forum for his ideas until 1957, when *Précence Africaine*, a journal of the Society of African Culture located in Paris, agreed to publish "An Afro-American's Cultural Views." In this article Cruse stakes out an ideological position which asserts that the dilemma African Americans face is "fundamentally a cultural one," rather than political or economic—though all three forces are, in his view, inextricably related. However, he argues that because blacks suffer from what he terms an "imitation complex" driven by a desire for social integration rather than for true equality, they have not sufficiently developed or supported their own cultural institutions. This lack of cultural aspiration, in turn, has a deleterious effect on many other aspects of life.

In 1960 Cruse was a member of a delegation to Cuba that included the historian JOHN HENRICK CLARKE and fellow writer Leroi Jones (AMIRI BARAKA). Both Cruse and Baraka thought that they saw in Castro's experiment a paradigm for the black struggle in America, though only Baraka was successful in publishing his memoir of the trip, "Cubra

Libre." Back in the United States, Cruse worked for *Freedomways*, a quarterly edited by SHIRLEY GRAHAM DUBOIS and JOHN HENRIK CLARKE, and he published several insightful essays, including "Marxism and the Negro" and "The Economics of Black Nationalism" in the *Liberator*. In 1964 Cruse severed his ties with the *Liberator* while he was in the hospital following an ulcer attack. He cited a conflict in "editorial policy" as the reason for his departure, but he later elaborated that these journals did not possess ideological clarity or political independence and were controlled by old guard liberals.

Ironically, in 1965 Cruse found himself playing a supporting role to Baraka in the creation of the Black Arts Repertory Theatre and School (BARTS) in Harlem, where Cruse was increasingly seen as the old guard to a new generation of black radicals. The emergence of the Black Arts Movement might have satisfied Cruse's cultural imperative, but being led by Baraka, whom Cruse saw as a brash upstart, the movement did not have the theoretical depth that Cruse would have preferred. Yet, Baraka's poetry and plays, and his book *Blues People* (1963), earned him accolades and grant funding that Cruse could only yearn for. During the 1960s Cruse wrote two plays and a musical; like many of his essays and reviews, they were rejected by publishers. Thus, as the Afrocentrists Baraka and MAULANA KARENGA emerged as leading voices of the Black Arts Movement, Cruse was forced to settle for being an occasional writer, director, and stage manager at BARTS.

Cruse's place in the pantheon of African American intellectuals of the twentieth century was secured in 1967 with the publication of *The Crisis of the Negro Intellectual*. For all of its problems it was the most searing, exhaustive, and thought-provoking treatise of its kind, and it became an instant classic. Suddenly Cruse had the visibility and academic credibility that had eluded him for two decades. In 1968 the University of Michigan in Ann Arbor appointed him a visiting professor. He became a leading force in the creation of the university's Center for Afro-American and African Studies; he lectured widely; and his essays began to appear in various anthologies of black thought. Upon his 1977 promotion to the rank of full professor, he became the first African American in the nation to attain that status at an American university without the benefit of a college degree.

Rebellion or Revolution? (1968) was published on the heels of his newly found fame and was largely a montage of his earlier work. The most perceptive essays, from which the title derives, analyze the race riots that engulfed many black communities during the 1960s. Cruse laments that the riots were little more than misdirected, self-destructive outbursts. He argues that despite some of the inflammatory rhetoric, these unorganized rebellions were in fact a pathetic plea for integration into the capitalist system, rather than a revolutionary movement to abolish capitalism. The onus for this sad state of affairs was once again placed at the feet of black leaders who failed to develop and apply a set of truly revolutionary ideas. Almost twenty years later Cruse published *Plural but Equal: A Critical Study of Black and Minorities and America's Plural Society* (1987). The arc of his analysis had not changed, but its scope had broadened to cover events of the 1970s and 1980s and fix them within his existing theoretical framework. The central tenet of this text harkens back to his earliest writings and signals to the future the message that social integration and cultural assimilation are pipe dreams that divert African Americans from devising culturally based strategies for equality. The same year that this book appeared Cruse became professor emeritus at the University of Michigan and entered a low-profile retirement.

Cruse's legacy is perhaps best seen in the generation of African American thinkers who are still grappling with the monumental questions he raised and who must inevitably respond to the ideas set forth in his work. Among more recent African American intellectuals, for example, CORNEL WEST pays homage to Cruse in his most quoted and reprinted essay "The Dilemma of the Black Intellectual." Although West and others reach different conclusions, they still struggle with the problem that Cruse best articulated.

FURTHER READING

The Harold Cruse Papers are housed at the Tamiment Library of New York University. Additional primary material on some of the organizations that Cruse was affiliated with can be found at the Schomburg Center for Research in Black Cultures of the New York Public Library.

Cruse, Harold. *The Crisis of the Negro Intellectual* (1967).

Cruse, Harold. *Rebellion or Revolution?* (1968).

Cruse, Harold. *Plural but Equal* (1987).

Cobb, William Jelani, ed. *The Essential Harold Cruse: A Reader* (2002).

James, Winston. *Holding Aloft the Banner of Ethiopia: Caribbean Radicalism in America* (1998).

Kelley, Robin D. G. *Freedom Dreams: The Black Radical Imagination* (2002).

Watts, Jerry Garfio. *Heroism and the Black Intellectual* (1994).

Obituary: *Washington Post,* 29 Mar. 2005.

SHOLOMO B. LEVY

Crutchfield, John William (25 Mar. 1910–31 May 1993), baseball player, was the second child born to John Henry Crutchfield, a coalminer, and Carrie Kirby, a housewife, in Ardmore, Missouri. After spending his formative years and briefly going to college in his hometown of Moberly, Missouri, Crutchfield began a fifteen-year career in the Negro Leagues, beginning with the Birmingham Black Barons in 1930. In his first league game, the diminutive 5'7", 155-pound outfielder homered, giving pitcher SATCHEL PAIGE the win and earning himself a spot in the daily lineup.

After briefly playing with the Indianapolis ABCs for the 1931 season, Crutchfield jumped to the Pittsburgh Crawfords for the 1932 campaign, earning $150.00 a month and playing alongside the finest Negro League outfielders of the day, including COOL PAPA BELL and TED STRONG. To supplement his baseball salary, Crutchfield also worked as a hotel bellhop and shined shoes.

Overshadowed by a powerhouse lineup that included Hall of Famers Bell, JOSH GIBSON, Satchel Paige, JUDY JOHNSON, and OSCAR CHARLESTON, Crutchfield shined with superb defensive skills and his infectious and lovable personality.

Although never a "league-leading" caliber player in any single category, Crutchfield demonstrated better-than-average skills in almost every aspect of play. What he lacked offensively, he made up for defensively. He became, in essence, the epitome of the well-rounded ballplayer—a solid everyday performer.

Crutchfield earned three East–West All Star game appearances while with the Crawfords. Even though he was 0 for 3 in the 1934 classic, it was his ninth-inning perfect throw home on a Red Parnell pop fly that led to the tagging of Mule Suttles at home plate that gave the East and Satchel Paige the 1–0 win.

To this day some baseball historians consider Crutchfield's catch in the eighth inning of the 1935 East–West game "the greatest catch ever." Slugger BIZ MACKEY ripped a towering drive into the right-centerfield gap. With Crutchfield and centerfielder Bell giving chase, Crutchfield leaped in the air and caught the ball at the last instant with his bare hand!

In 1936, Crutchfield hit .265 and was 5 for 17 in an exhibition series against major leaguers that included pitcher Bob Feller. The number three vote-getter among outfielders for the 1936 East–West Game, Crutchfield was 0 for 2 in another lackluster offensive showing.

During the decline of the Pittsburgh Crawfords' reign after the 1936 season, Crutchfield journeyed through the Negro Leagues with several other teams.

In 1937, with the Newark Eagles, he hit a career best of .313. The following season his average dipped to .270, but he is credited for his continued great defensive play. The winter of 1938–1939 found Crutchfield playing in the inaugural season of the Puerto Rican League. In 1939, with the Toledo Crawfords, his average dipped to a meager .105.

At the start of the 1940 season with the Indianapolis Crawfords, Crutchfield retired, citing personal reasons. He returned to the Chicago American Giants in 1941 and averaged .297. Fifth among outfielders in All-Star game voting, Crutchfield went 1 for 3 as the backup left-fielder for the West, his only hit in ten All-Star game plate appearances. The thirty-two-year-old veteran averaged .242 in 1942.

Crutchfield served thirteen months in the Army beginning in 1943. Back to baseball in 1944, he played briefly with the Cleveland Buckeyes, but returned to Chicago for the bulk of the season, batting .254. He hit .300 the next season in his final year of play.

After retiring from baseball, Crutchfield married his wife Julia in 1947 and worked for the U.S Postal Service for twenty-six years. He died in Chicago in 1993 at the age of eighty-three.

FURTHER READING

Lester, Larry. *Black Baseball's National Showcase* (2001).

Loverro, Thom. *The Encyclopedia of Negro League Baseball* (2003).

Riley, James A. *The Biographical Encyclopedia of the Negro Baseball Leagues* (1994).

BYRON MOTLEY

Cruz, Celia (21 Oct. 1925–16 July 2003), singer, popularly known as the Queen of Salsa, was born Ursula Hilaria Celia Caridad Cruz Alfonso in the Santo Suárez neighborhood of Havana, Cuba, the second daughter of Catalina "Ollita" Alfonso, a housewife, and Simón Cruz, a railroad stoker.

From an early age, Cruz was drawn to music. She was born into an era in Cuba where musical styles such as *guaguanco* and *guaracha* carried West African rhythms into the streets. One of the first styles she was drawn to was Cuban *sons*, languid tropical ballads sung by popular radio singers, and she was particularly influenced by Paulina Alvarez. Argentine tangos by Carlos Gardel were also among her favorites. Despite her father's disapproval, Cruz's mother and her aunt Ana, two major figures in her life, encouraged her to sing.

More profoundly, however, Cruz came to learn about her own African roots when she stole away with a young cousin to Havana's pre-Lenten carnivals in the 1930s. There, she heard Bembé, folkloric Cuban music infused with Yoruban rhythms and sung in Lucumi, a traditional African language. "Later I would realize that the music during those ceremonies would forever give me inspiration" (Cruz, 2). She described the Bembé music as "a beautiful way of expressing my African roots" (26).

Cruz's first public appearance was in 1947, when her cousin entered her in a singing competition on a local radio show called *La Hora de Té* ("Tea Time"). Cruz donned her favorite dress and white patent leather shoes, and then she rode the bus to the radio station. She sang a tango called "Nostalgia" and won first prize—a fancy cake baked by one of Havana's finest bakeries. This sweet reward was just the beginning of many radio show successes and a long list of accolades that would mark her career.

In the early 1940s Cruz became known at all the major radio stations in Havana, and she helped her family pay bills by singing promotional spots for very little money. If she was overworked, she didn't mind; she loved to perform whenever she could. As a teenager Cruz performed with bands in Havana's burgeoning music scene. Cruz's first dream, encouraged by her father, was to be a teacher. But after her initial success and popularity, her most beloved teacher encouraged the young Cruz to pursue singing professionally. In 1951 Cruz became known to a wider audience when she was cast in *Sun Sun Ba Baé*, a musical extravaganza at Havana's Sans Souci nightclub. The show drew heavily from Cuba's African tradition. As lead singer, Cruz won raves singing in Lucumi. The overwhelmingly successful show soon moved to the famed Tropicana nightclub.

Greater acclaim would come in 1950 when she began performing with Cuba's most popular band, the Sonora Matancera. Her success led to several tours throughout Latin America with famous artists such as JOSEPHINE BAKER. The band was largely responsible for popularizing Cuban music around the world, and Cruz became known for her first signature song, "Burundanga." In 1957 Cruz traveled to New York City for the first time to receive her first gold record for "Burundanga." While there, she was scheduled to perform at the St. Nicholas Arena with the Cuban bandleader MACHITO and his orchestra, but the concert was shut down when the crowd grew too big for the venue and a melee ensued. Her fans began calling her *La Guarachera de Cuba*, the *guaracha* woman of Cuba, which was the accolade she held closest to her heart.

Just as Cruz was achieving fame with the Sonora Matancera, Cuba was thrust into a revolutionary war. Cruz returned after a lengthy international tour in 1959 to a much-changed Cuba. Fidel Castro had gained control of the island nation, and soon Havana's vibrant music scene was overwrought with government controls. Cruz was asked to perform at a state-sponsored concert at the Tropicana that year. Although she performed, she refused to meet Castro or be paid. "[Castro's] presence revolted me … I refused to become another act in his circus" (82). Conflicted with a deep love for her country and her family, on 14 July 1960 Cruz left Cuba to perform in Mexico. She never returned to Cuba.

After a year in Mexico, Cruz moved to Los Angeles to perform at the Palladium without the Sonora Matancera. In early 1962 she reunited with the band in New York City. In April of that year she married the Sonora's trumpeter, Pedro Knight, with whom she shared the rest of her life. The couple had no children.

Cruz continued to perform and record in New York City. On 18 June 1962 she became the first Latin-born woman to perform at Carnegie Hall, and in 1964 she debuted at Harlem's Apollo Theater. In 1965 she left the Sonora Matancera and began to work with other Latin American musicians such as Tito Puente. However, the popularity of Cuban music entered a period of decline, and Cruz's record sales began to slump. It was not until the early 1970s that Cruz's next significant contribution began to take shape. Together with the flutist Johnny Pacheco and the Fania All-Stars, Cruz revived popular Latin American music with a fast-paced hybrid form that became known as salsa.

The new group performed in Zaire during the celebrations for the MUHAMMAD ALI and JOE FRAZIER heavyweight boxing championship. Cruz and the All-Stars captivated the African audience alongside legendary African American performers JAMES BROWN, B. B. KING, and the Pointer Sisters. Cruz sang her signature hit "Quimbara" and the seminal Cuban song "Guantanamera," and she was overwhelmed when the audience sang along with her. "I was amazed that my version of the Cuban classic made it all the way into the heart of Africa" (141).

Known for her energetic performance style, eccentric outfits, and tireless work ethic, Cruz propelled herself into the hearts of Latin American audiences with her signature exclamation, "*Azucar!*" ("Sugar!"), which she used to punctuate her songs. She achieved legendary status around the world as the Queen of Salsa, but to Cuban exiles she symbolized the Cuban culture that was lost to the revolution.

Cruz continued to record major hits and appear in television and film through 2002. Along with two Grammy and four Latin Grammy awards, Cruz's many honors included a Smithsonian Institution Lifetime Achievement Award, a Congressional Gold Medal, and the President's Award for the National Endowment of the Arts.

She died of cancer in 2003. Hundreds of thousands of her fans flocked to three public viewings of her body in New York City and Miami.

FURTHER READING

Cruz, Celia, and Ana Cristina Reymundo. *Celia: My Life* (2004).

Hamill, Pete. "Celia Nunca Regreso (Celia Never Returned)," *Letras Libres* (31 July 2005).

Marceles, Eduardo. *Azucar: The Celia Cruz Biography* (2004).

Moscatel, Susana. "*La Politica Invade el Entretenimiento* (Politics Invade Entertainment)," *Siempre* (28 July 2005).

JUAN CARLOS RODRIGUEZ

Cuffe, Paul (17 Jan. 1759–7 Sept. 1817), Atlantic trader and early African colonizationist, was born on Cuttyhunk Island off southern Massachusetts, one of ten children of Kofi (later Cuffe) Slocum, a freed slave originally from West Africa's Gold Coast, and Ruth Moses Slocum, a Wampanoag Native American, both farmers. Kofi Slocum's Quaker master freed him in the mid-1740s and, although he was excluded by race from membership in the Society of Friends, Kofi and Ruth Slocum lived by Quaker principles—hard work, frugality, and honesty. This diligence paid off in the 1766 purchase of a 116-acre farm in Dartmouth, Massachusetts, on Buzzard's Bay. At his death in 1772 Kofi bequeathed the farm to his sons Paul and John. Taking his father's African name, Cuffe, and respecting his dual (Native American and African American) identity, the self-educated Cuffe sought his fortune at sea. Whaling was open to men of any race, so Paul worked on Atlantic whalers during his adolescent years. From this, he turned to maritime trading and, during the American Revolution, he was briefly jailed for running the British blockade of the colonies. When Massachusetts passed new tax levies in 1780, Cuffe joined his brother and five other Dartmouth free blacks in a petition protesting their "having No vote or Influence in the Election with those that tax us" because of being "Chiefly of the African Extraction" (Thomas, 9–10). He was jailed again, but his persistence brought reduction of the Cuffe brothers' tax debt in 1781. Two years later Cuffe married Alice Pequit, a Pequot Indian from Martha's Vineyard; by the end of the century the couple had seven children. He built a school to ensure that racial discrimination would not deny his children and others a

From a Drawing by JOHN POLE, M. D. of Bristol, Eng.

Paul Cuffe in an engraving from a drawing by John Pole of Bristol, England. Cuffe was one of the richest African Americans of his day, owned a large farm, and built ships large enough to conduct international trade. (© New Bedford Whaling Museum.)

formal education. Through the 1790s and into the 1800s Cuffe invested in a gristmill and store but he amassed his considerable wealth through maritime ventures. He worked closely with the Rotch family of New Bedford, Massachusetts, owners of a bank and financiers of whaling operations; he bought and built ships, developing his own maritime enterprise that involved trading the length of the U.S. Atlantic coast, with trips to the Caribbean and Europe; and he developed contacts around the Atlantic rim. For business partners as well as crew, he preferred his extended family of blacks and Native Americans.

Cuffe became aware of African colonization through the intellectual circles he encountered during his travels along the Atlantic coast. Since 1787 British philanthropists had been working to build a settlement of former slaves in Sierra Leone, on Africa's west coast, and British and American acts to end Atlantic slave trading in 1808 focused greater attention on the effort. Cuffe grew to share a belief with philanthropists on both sides of the Atlantic that slave trading had damaged Africa's moral foundation, but that African American colonists could bring Christianity to "uplift" African populations and in time replace the trade in humans with a commerce lucrative to the colonists and their supporters in the United States and Great Britain. He thus developed a plan to transport moral, religious, and industrious blacks across the Atlantic to begin the process of development while he worked to persuade people in the United States to support the effort.

To test the feasibility of such an effort, early in 1811 Cuffe loaded his brig, *Traveller*, with merchandise from Philadelphia and sailed to Freetown, Sierra Leone, his first voyage to Africa. Although English merchants profiting from the trade with Sierra Leone disapproved of Cuffe's intervention and worked against his designs, he ended his visit confident that African Americans could establish a prosperous colony in Africa. After venturing to Liverpool to gain British support for his "civilizing mission," Cuffe returned to Freetown. Late in 1811 he founded the Friendly Society of Sierra Leone, a cooperative black organization intended to encourage "the Black Settlers of Sierra Leone, and the Natives of Africa generally, in the Cultivation of their Soil, by the Sale of their Produce" (Harris, 55). Black colonists, English philanthropists, and the British government voiced approval.

Cuffe hoped to send at least one vessel each year to Sierra Leone, transporting African American settlers and goods to the colony and returning with marketable African products. As he talked about the venture in the United States, he stimulated black feelings of Pan-Africanism and brought new energy to African American thinking on emigration. The timing was not good, however. Because war with Great Britain was imminent, the U.S. House of Representatives refused Cuffe permission to trade with the British colony. He was forced to wait out the War of 1812, tending to family, business, and religious matters while urging the government to end the war and open trade. Once the war ended, Cuffe put his plans into action. On 10 December 1815 he sailed for Africa's west coast on the *Traveller* with a commercial cargo and thirty-eight African Americans, twenty of them children, intent on making a new life in Sierra Leone. This constituted the first, black-initiated "back to Africa" effort in U.S. history.

Cuffe failed to profit from the venture, but he obtained land for the settlers, and his enthusiasm for colonization grew. With racial tensions rising in the United States, as poor whites reacted to competition from growing numbers of free blacks, Cuffe believed still more strongly that only in Africa, away from white animosity, could African Americans "rise to be a people" (Thomas, 119). He soon was pressing for the United States to free its slaves and then colonize them on land they could own in Africa. It was an expensive proposition that, in the end, neither free blacks nor Cuffe and his supporters could finance. Ironically, as Cuffe's enthusiasm for colonization was growing, so was that of some white Americans, many with less philanthropic motives. Their new American Colonization Society, with government backing, would establish in 1821 the West African settlement for American free blacks that eventually would become the nation of Liberia. Cuffe did not live to witness that effort. In 1817, after a period of deteriorating health, he died at his Massachusetts farm.

W. E. B. DuBois and Marcus Garvey are considered among the major advocates of Pan-Africanist thinking in the United States for their early-twentieth-century recognition of the transatlantic plight of persons of African descent. A full century earlier, Paul Cuffe had courageously advocated this position and had taken the first concrete steps toward its realization. For this reason, Cuffe should be recognized as one of the fathers of American Pan-Africanism and one of the most successful black entrepreneurs of his generation.

FURTHER READING

Most of Paul Cuffe's letters and logs are housed in the New Bedford, Massachusetts, Free Public Library and the Old Darmouth (Massachusetts) Historical Society.

Harris, Sheldon H. *Paul Cuffe: Black America and the African Return* (1972).

Thomas, Lamont D. *Rise to Be a People: A Biography of Paul Cuffe* (1986).

Wiggins, Rosalind Cobb, ed. *Captain Paul Cuffe's Logs and Letters, 1808–1817: A Black Quaker's "Voice from Within the Veil"* (1996).

DONALD R. WRIGHT

Cullen, Countée (30 May 1903?–9 Jan. 1946), poet and playwright, was the son of Elizabeth Thomas Lucas. The name of his father is not known. The place of his birth has been variously cited as Louisville, Kentucky, New York City, and Baltimore,

Countée Cullen in Central Park, 1941. (Library of Congress.)

Maryland. Although in later years Cullen claimed to have been born in New York City, it probably was Louisville, which he consistently named as his birthplace in his youth and which he wrote on his registration form for New York University. His mother died in Louisville in 1940.

In 1916 Cullen was enrolled in Public School Number 27 in the Bronx, New York, under the name of Countee L. Porter, with no accent on the first "e." At that time he was living with Amanda Porter, who generally is assumed to have been his grandmother. Shortly after she died in October 1917, Countee went to live with the Reverend FREDERICK ASHBURY CULLEN, pastor of Salem Methodist Episcopal Church in Harlem, and his wife, the former Carolyn Belle Mitchell. Countee was never formally adopted by the Cullens, but he later claimed them as his natural parents and in 1918 assumed the name Countée P. (Porter) Cullen. In 1925 he dropped the middle initial.

Cullen was an outstanding student in every school he attended. He entered the respected, almost exclusively white, Dewitt Clinton High School for boys in Manhattan in 1918. He became a member of the Arista honor society, and in his senior year he received the Magpie Cup in recognition of his achievements. He served as vice president of the senior class and was associate editor of the 1921 *Magpie*, the school's literary magazine, and editor of the *Clinton News*. He won an oratorical contest sponsored by the film actor Douglas Fairbanks and served as treasurer of the Inter-High School Poetry Society and as chairperson of the Senior Publications Committee. His poetry appeared regularly in school publications and he received wider public recognition in 1921 when his poem, "I Have a Rendezvous with Life," won first prize in a citywide contest sponsored by the Empire Federation of Women's Clubs. At New York University, which Cullen attended on a New York State Regents scholarship, he was elected to Phi Beta Kappa in his junior year and received a bachelor's degree in 1925. His poems were published frequently in the school magazine, *The Arch*, of which he eventually became poetry editor. In 1926 he received a master's degree from Harvard University and won the *Crisis* magazine award in poetry.

When Cullen's first collection of poetry, *Color*, was published in 1925 during his senior year at New York University, he had already achieved national fame. His poems had been published in *Bookman*, *American Mercury*, *Harper's*, *Century*, the *Nation*, *Poetry*, the *Crisis*, the *Messenger*, *Palms*, and *Opportunity*. He had won second prize in 1923 in the Witter Bynner Undergraduate Poetry Contest sponsored by the Poetry Society of America. He placed second in that contest again in 1924 but won first prize in 1925, when he also won the John Reed Memorial Prize awarded by *Poetry* magazine.

Color received universal critical acclaim. ALAIN LOCKE wrote in *Opportunity*: "Ladies and Gentlemen! A genius! Posterity will laugh at us if we do not proclaim him now. COLOR transcends all of the limiting qualifications that might be brought forward if it were merely a work of talent" (Jan. 1926). The volume contains epitaphs, only two of which could be considered racial; love poems; and poems on other traditional subjects. But the significant theme—as the title implies—was race, and it was the poems dealing with racial subjects that captured the attention of the critics. Cullen was praised for portraying the experience of African Americans in the vocabulary and poetic forms of the classical tradition but with a personal intimacy. His second volume of poetry, *Copper Sun*, published in 1927 also by Harper and Brothers (the publisher of all his books), won first prize in literature from the Harmon Foundation. There are fewer racial poems in this collection than in *Color*; however, they express an anger that was not so pronounced in the earlier volume. The majority of the poems in *Copper Sun* deal with life and love and other traditional themes of nineteenth-century poetry.

Cullen edited the October 1926 special issue of *Palms* devoted to African American poets, and he collected and edited *Caroling Dusk* in 1927, an anthology of poetry by African Americans. Cullen was by this time generally recognized by critics and the public as the leading literary figure of the Harlem Renaissance. GERALD EARLY in *My Soul's High Song* (1991) said, "He was, indeed, a boy wonder, a young handsome black Ariel ascending, a boyish, brown-skinned titan who, in the early and mid-twenties, embodied many of the hopes, aspirations, and maturing expressive possibilities of his people."

Cullen said that he wanted to be known as a poet, not a "Negro poet." This did not affect his popularity, although some Harlem Renaissance writers, including LANGSTON HUGHES, interpreted this to mean that he wanted to deny his race, an interpretation endorsed by some later scholars. A reading of his poetry reveals this view to be unfounded. In fact his major poems, and most of those still being printed in anthologies, have racial themes. Cullen expounded his view in the *Brooklyn Eagle* (10 Feb. 1924):

If I am going to be a poet at all, I am going to be POET and not NEGRO POET. This is what has hindered the development of artists among us. Their one note has been the concern with their race. That is all very well, none of us can get away from it. I cannot at times. You will see it in my verse. The consciousness of this is too poignant at times. I cannot escape it. But what I mean is this: I shall not write of negro subjects for the purpose of propaganda. That is not what a poet is concerned with. Of course, when the emotion rising out of the fact that I am a negro is strong, I express it. But that is another matter.

From 1926 to 1928 Cullen was assistant editor to CHARLES S. JOHNSON of *Opportunity* (subtitled "A Journal of Negro Life"), for which he also wrote a feature column, "The Dark Tower." In his reviews and commentaries, on one hand he called upon African American writers to create a representative and respectable race literature, and on the other hand he insisted that the African American artist should not be bound by race or restricted to racial themes.

The year 1928 was a watershed for Cullen. He received a Guggenheim Fellowship to study in Paris, the third volume of his poetry, *The Ballad of a Brown Girl*, was published, and, after a long courtship, he married Nina Yolande DuBois. Her father, W. E. B. DuBois, the exponent of the "Talented Tenth" concept, rejoiced at bringing the young genius into his family. The wedding, performed by Cullen's foster father, was the social event of the decade in Harlem. After a brief honeymoon in Philadelphia, Cullen left for Paris and was soon joined by his bride. The couple experienced difficulties from the beginning. Finally, after informing her father that Cullen had confessed that he was sexually attracted to men, Nina Yolande sued for divorce, which was obtained in Paris in 1930.

Cullen continued to write and publish after 1928, but his works were no longer universally acclaimed. *The Black Christ and Other Poems*, completed under the Guggenheim Fellowship, was published in 1929 while he was abroad. His only novel, *One Way to Heaven*, was published in 1932, and *The Medea and Some Poems* in 1935. He wrote two books for juveniles, *The Lost Zoo* (1940) and *My Lives and How I Lost Them* (1942). His stage adaptation of *One Way to Heaven* was produced by several amateur and professional theater groups but remained one of his several unpublished plays. Critics gave these works mixed reviews at best.

Cullen's reputation as a writer rests on his poetry. His novel is not an important work, and it received little attention from the critics. He rejected so-called jazz and free-style as inappropriate forms of poetic expression. He was a romantic lyric poet and a great admirer of John Keats and Edna St. Vincent Millay. While his arch traditionalism and lack of originality in style had been seen in *Color* as minor flaws, they came to be viewed as major deficiencies in his later works.

Cullen's fall from grace with the critics had little effect on his popularity. He remained much in demand for lectures and readings by both white and black groups. In 1931 alone he read his poetry and lectured in various institutions in seventeen states and Canada. Some of his poems were set to music by Charles Marsh, Virgil Thomson, William Schuman, William Lawrence, MARGARET BONDS, and others. However, even though he continued to live with his foster father, royalties and lecture fees were insufficient income for subsistence. He searched for academic positions and was offered professorships at Sam Huston College (named for an Iowa farmer, not the Texas senator), Dillard University, Fisk University, Tougaloo College, and West Virginia State College. There is no clear explanation of why he did not accept any of the positions. In 1932 he became a substitute teacher in New York public schools and became a full-time teacher of English and French at Frederick Douglass Junior High School in 1934, a position he held until his death (caused by complications of high blood pressure) in New York City, and where he taught and inspired the future novelist and essayist JAMES BALDWIN.

Cullen married Ida Mae Roberson in 1940, and they apparently enjoyed a happy married life. Cullen's chief creative interest during the last year of his life was in writing the script for *St. Louis Woman*, a musical based on ARNA BONTEMPS's novel *God Sends Sunday*. With music by Harold Arlen and lyrics by Johnny Mercer, *St. Louis Woman* opened on Broadway on 30 March 1946. Although the production was opposed by WALTER WHITE of the National Association for the Advancement of Colored People and some other civil rights activists as an unfavorable representation of African Americans, it ran for four months and was revived several times by amateurs and one professional group between 1959 and 1980. *On These I Stand*, a collection of poems that Cullen had selected as his best, was published posthumously in 1947. The 135th Street Branch of the New York Public Library was named for Cullen in 1951, and a public school in New York City and one in Chicago also bear his name. For a few brief years Cullen was the most celebrated African American writer in the nation and by many accounts is considered one of the major voices of the Harlem Renaissance.

FURTHER READING

Countée Cullen's personal papers are in the Amistad Research Center at Tulane University and the James Weldon Johnson Collection in Beinecke Library at Yale University.

Early, Gerald, ed. *My Soul's High Song: The Collected Writings of Countee Cullen, Voice of the Harlem Renaissance* (1991).

Ferguson, Blanche E. *Countee Cullen and the Negro Renaissance* (1966).

Perry, Margaret. *A Bio-Bibliography of Countée P. Cullen, 1903–1946* (1971).

Shucard, Alan R. *Countee Cullen* (1984).

Obituaries: *New York Herald Tribune*, 10 Jan. 1946; *New York Times*, 10 and 12 Jan. 1946; *Negro History Bulletin* 14 (Feb. 1946): 98.

This entry is taken from the *American National Biography* and is published here with the permission of the American Council of Learned Societies.

CLIFTON H. JOHNSON

Cullen, Frederick Ashbury (1868–25 May 1946), minister and Harlem civil rights leader, was born in Fairmount (Somerset County), Maryland, the son of Isaac and Emmeline Williams Cullen, who had been slaves. The youngest of eleven children, Cullen grew up in poverty, his father having passed away two months after his birth. He moved to Baltimore with his mother at age twelve and worked for a physician while attending Maryland State Normal School (later Towson University). He then taught public school in Fairmount for two years before entering Morgan College (later Morgan State University), an Episcopalian seminary in Baltimore; between his first and second year of studies, he also worked as a waiter in Atlantic City, New Jersey. He had received a preacher's license while in Fairmount and was ordained in 1900.

Cullen's religious awakening had taken place in September 1894, at Sharp Street Methodist Episcopal Church in Baltimore, and he had preached his first sermon at Fairmount Centennial Methodist Church. His first assignment consisted of a two-church circuit, Boyer's Chapel and Willis's Chapel, in Catlin, Maryland. Although the Catlin church board initially objected to his appointment, deeming him too young for the job, he ultimately earned its approval, successfully leading the parish from 1900 to 1902. His achievements included improving the parish finances, initiating a music program, and effecting a degree of reconciliation between his two congregations (the two chapels represented factions that had formed during a trustees' dispute prior to Cullen's hiring). The superintendent of his district then intended to transfer him to a church in Pennsylvania, but the bishop reassigned him to St. Mark's Church, a predominantly black congregation in New York City. The last-minute reassignment brought Cullen to the city where he would work and reside for the rest of his life.

As an assistant to senior pastor William H. Brooks, Cullen was asked to tend to "Salem Chapel," St. Mark's storefront mission in Harlem, New York. On his first day as its pastor, 20 April 1902, he preached to an audience of three women, and the collection netted a total of nineteen cents. Aided by the New York City Church Extension and Missionary Society, Cullen expanded his congregation by focusing on Sunday-school recruitment, befriending local children by participating in their games and favoring them with sweets. As the children became involved with his church, so, too, did their parents.

In August 1902 the mission moved to a house on 124th Street. Despite hostile neighbors and a February 1904 fire, the Salem church flourished, and it was promoted to independent status in 1908. The congregation then relocated to a property at Lenox Avenue and 133d Street, where it resided until 1924. Later Salem took possession of a West Harlem edifice formerly occupied by predominantly white Calvary Methodist Episcopal Church. During the early 1920s Salem Methodist Episcopal Church counted over twenty-five hundred names on its rolls (with a youth group of over two hundred members) and was solidly established as one of Harlem's largest and most influential institutions.

During a vacation in 1906 or 1907, Cullen was introduced to Carolyn Belle Mitchell, a soprano and pianist based in Baltimore. After a short engagement they were married at Salem, and she assisted him with his duties there until her death in 1932. The Cullens were childless until they unofficially adopted a teenager named Countée Porter sometime prior to 1919. As COUNTÉE CULLEN, the boy became a prominent lyric poet and a star of the Harlem Renaissance.

Frederick Cullen enjoyed a close relationship with his son, who composed at least two poems in his honor ("Fruit of the Flower" and "Lines for My Father, Dad"); an enthusiastic traveler, the elder Cullen relished their annual joint visits to Europe and the Middle East between 1926 and 1939. Their family became ranked among Harlem's cultural elite, and Countée Cullen's 1928 wedding (to Yolande DuBois, daughter of W. E. B. DuBois) was a social extravaganza with a guest list of twelve hundred.

At the height of his career, Frederick Cullen was regarded as a major force in the black community. His ministries paired evangelistic fervor with initiatives for social justice and extracurricular programs for Harlem children. By the time of Cullen's retirement, the church offered more than three dozen activities and clubs for young people; the most prominent of these was the Salem Crescent Athletic Club, whose alumni included champion boxer SUGAR RAY ROBINSON. The church also raised tuition funds for a number of its youths, sending them to schools such as Atlanta's Gammon Theological Seminary, which awarded Cullen an honorary doctorate. In addition, Cullen battled crime through strategies such as visiting brothels incognito, subsequently badgering their proprietors with the observations he had collected in order to pressure them toward more seemly business practices. Cullen also supported the development of the National Urban League, a merger of three smaller social service agencies into a single, substantially more effective organization.

Cullen also provided counsel to the founders of churches such as Epworth Methodist Episcopal, and his church hosted the "World Gospel Feast" parties led by the charismatic and controversial George W. Becton. A fierce believer in interdenominational cooperation, Cullen worked closely with other powerful religious leaders such as ADAM CLAYTON POWELL SR. (head of Abyssinian Baptist) and Hutchens C. Bishop (rector of St. Philip's Protestant Episcopal) during his tenure as president of the Harlem branch of the NAACP, this branch having been established in 1910. Under his watch, the chapter grew to more than one thousand members; its accomplishments included successfully petitioning the New York City government to appoint its first African American policeman, Samuel J. Battle (later New York's first African American sergeant, lieutenant, and parole commissioner) in 1911. With other NAACP leaders, he organized protest demonstrations and raised legal aid funds for cases such as that of the SCOTTSBORO BOYS.

Cullen led his church for four decades, until ill health forced him to step down. According to his autobiography, he retired on 14 April 1942, but other records cite 1943 or 1944 as the year in question. Cullen outlived both his wife and son, dying at home in New York City at the age of seventy-eight.

FURTHER READING

Cullen, Frederick Ashbury. *From Barefoot Town to Jerusalem* (n.d.).

Early, Gerald. Introduction to *My Soul's High Song: The Collected Writings of Countée Cullen, Voice of the Harlem Renaissance* (1991).

Faturoti, Ambrose Olumuyiwa. "Church Leadership in Harlem: Responsibility and Discernment," in *Renaissance Collage* (2004), available online at http://xroads.virginia.edu/~MA03/faturoti/harlem/.

Powers, Peter. "'The Singing Man Who Must Be Reckoned With': Private Desire and Public Responsibility in the Poetry of Countée Cullen," *African American Review* 34.4 (Winter, 2000).

Obituary: *New York Times*, 27 May 1946.

PEG DUTHIE

Cumbo, Marion (1 Mar. 1899–17 Sept. 1990), cellist, was born in New York City. Cumbo was inspired to pursue music by the careers of the great cellist Pablo Casals and the violinist and black musical comedy composer WILL MARION COOK. He was educated in the city's public schools as well as at the Martin-Smith School of Music, where he became a protégé of Minnie Brown, and at the Institute of Musical Art (later the Juilliard School of Music), where he studied with Willem Willeke. He also studied with Leonard Jeter and Bruno Steindl in Chicago, Illinois. In 1920 Cumbo received special recognition as a featured soloist at the annual convention of the National Association of Negro Musicians in New York.

During the 1920s Cumbo became a part of the Negro String Quartet, with Felix Weir as first violinist, Arthur Boyd as second violinist, HALL JOHNSON as violist, and Cumbo as cellist. They originally played informally in homes two or three times a week, rehearsing Mozart, Haydn, and Beethoven quartets. Later they performed concerts in New York, Washington, D.C., and Philadelphia, where they appeared with singer MARIAN ANDERSON. The quartet also accompanied singer ROLAND HAYES in a Carnegie Hall recital rendering of Negro spirituals arranged by Johnson. Cumbo expressed the desire to show that blacks could be identified with high art instead of high crime as usually portrayed in the media.

Cumbo worked in both concert and theatrical venues. He was a soloist with the Philadelphia Concert Orchestra, a black symphonic group founded in 1905 with Gilbert Anderson as its conductor. In the late 1940s he performed with the African American musical director EVERETT ASTOR LEE's Cosmopolitan Little Symphony, and in the 1970s he played with the Senior Musicians' Orchestra of AFM Local 802. During the interims he performed in the pit orchestras for the Midnight Frolics revue at the Amsterdam Theatre (1919) and in the 1922–1924 touring company of NOBLE SISSLE and EUBIE BLAKE's Broadway musical *Shuffle Along*.

Other Broadway productions in which he performed were the *Chocolate Dandies* of 1924, *Brown Buddies* of 1930, *Blackbirds* of 1938, and *Hot Mikado* of 1939. He also played in various vaudeville shows and appeared with both the Johnson and the EVA ALBERTA JESSYE choral ensembles.

Cumbo came of age as a "New Negro" striving for equal access to the symphonic stage. To address this dilemma he became a part of a racially inclusive ensemble known as the Symphony of the New World (1964–1978). Lee led his nearly half-black orchestra into performances of the European works of Brahms, Mendelssohn, and Saint-Saëns, as well as the African American works of WILLIAM GRANT STILL, Howard Swanson, and ULYSSES SIMPSON KAY. To provide more performing opportunities for black symphonic players, Cumbo and his impresario wife, Clarissa Burton Cumbo, established Triad Presentations in 1970, which presented annual concerts at Alice Tully Hall. Cumbo represented a pioneering artist who bridged the concert and theatrical worlds while enhancing the performing status and opportunities for blacks in America.

MARVA GRIFFIN CARTER

Cummings, Blondell (22 Oct. 1949–), dancer, choreographer, artistic director, educator, and activist, was born in Effingham, South Carolina, the eldest of three daughters of Jack Cummings and Carrie Cummings, sharecroppers who grew tobacco and cotton. When Blondell was a year old, the Cummingses, like many African American families of the mid-twentieth century, migrated to the North. While both her parents had relatives who previously moved to New York, it was Jack who followed two of his four church-singing brothers to the city to pursue careers in the commercial music industry. Upon the family's arrival in Harlem, Jack found work as a taxi driver, and Carrie earned a living as a domestic and later completed school to become a health-care professional. Cummings described her upbringing as very strict and typical of most black families. Her mother was the disciplinarian, and while her father was not an authoritarian, together they ran a stable household with the support of family and friends who lived in the neighborhood. She had plenty of cousins and extended family from South Carolina who lived in Harlem and were there to reinforce her strong connection to the black community.

It was during her childhood that Cummings developed an appreciation for music and dance. Coming from a family of aunts, uncles, and cousins who were singers, and being a part of a junior high school choir and orchestra, she was connected to music from an early age. Dance was an integral aspect of her upbringing as well. During a time when jazz, the Lindy hop and jitterbug, and the Savoy and Renaissance ballrooms were popular, dance was everywhere in Harlem. Cummings's parents and neighbors danced socially, and she participated in African dance classes at the local community center. Programs offered by the Police Athletic League introduced her to modern dance and further cultivated her interest in the art.

Cummings's father wanted her to become a lawyer, and her mother saw a future for her in teaching, but Cummings was convinced that a career in the arts, particularly dance, was her calling. Nevertheless, she felt a responsibility to pursue higher education. She attended New York University's School of Education and later matriculated at Lehman College for graduate work, where she studied film and photography. While pursuing her studies, Cummings found ways to integrate art with academics. She studied dance at the Martha Graham, José Limón, and Alvin Ailey schools. Her training was eclectic. Among the African American dance legends she studied with were Walter Knicks of the KATHERINE DUNHAM Dance Company, PEARL PRIMUS, Mary Hinkson, ALVIN AILEY, Rod Rodgers, TALLEY BEATTY, and Eleo Pomare. Her extensive training in modern dance was developed through her education directly with Martha Graham, Alwin Nikolais in the Martha Graham technique, Merce Cunningham, Erick Hawkins, and the Lester Horton technique.

Beginning in the 1970s Cummings redefined modern dance by placing her identity and cultural experiences at the center of what would be considered a European American modern dance style. She became a renegade, going against the restraints of both traditional African American and European American concert dance. Her choreography was categorized variously as modern dance, experimental dance, and performance art. She was known for blending dance, theater, dialogue, storytelling, "freeze-frame" gesture, mime, photography, video, and personal reflections to create unique performance pieces that fall into the genre of postmodern dance. Influenced by the music of Philip Glass and Steve Wright, Cummings was drawn to the postmodern aesthetic because of its combination of both traditional and nontraditional approaches to art.

The universal dynamics of relationships, emotions, community, and family influenced her work, and she approached choreography from a personal, social, political, historical, and anthropological perspective. She was noted for her strong characterization and acting ability and was most recognized for her solo performances; however, out of the more than fifty dances she created, many were group works.

Cummings's career, going back to the 1960s, crossed over broad terrain in the arts world, as performer, administrator, producer, videographer, choreographer, educator, and activist. In the late 1960s she co-founded the Video Exchange with friend David Schiller to document dance works. It was also with Schiller that she started a theater company and produced dance and poetry performances around New York City. Most notably, she started the dance performance series at the Merce Cunningham Dance Studio. During this period she also danced with Richard Bull, Kai Takei, the New York Chamber Dance Company, the New Jersey Repertory Company, and Rod Rodgers's dance companies. In 1969 she joined the Meredith Monk/The House dance company and performed in *Juice* (1969), *Needle Brain Lloyd and the System's Kid* (1970), *Vessel* (1971), *Education of the Girlchild* (1973), *Chacon* (1974), *Venice/Milan* (1976), and *Quarry* (1976). She performed with Nimbus Dance Theatre Company and Bill T. Jones's Everybodyworks as well.

Cummings toured throughout the United States, Europe, Asia, and Africa. Some of her most recognized dances included *Point of Reference* (1971), *The Ladies and Me* (1979), *A Friend* (1980), *A Friend II* (1980), *Chicken Soup* (1981), *Food For Thought* (1983), *The Art of War/Nine Situations* (1984), *A Nun Story* (1986), *To Colette, Too* (1987), *For J.B.* (1990), *Omadele and Giuseppe* (1991), *Women in the Dunes* (1995), and *100% Cotton/Natural Fiber* (1998). Other works include *The Relationship Series, Basic*

Strategies I through V, Cycle, He Searched from Wall to Wall, Passing Images, and *3B49.*

Cummings was the founder of several long-term projects inspired by discussion groups and workshops. Among them are the Cycle Arts Foundation (1978), inspired by a dance work about the menstrual cycle, menopause, bonding and sharing rituals, and art-making; the Menopause Project (1993); and the Boomer Project (2002).

Cummings never married and had no children. She received numerous honors and awards throughout her career, and was recognized by the National Endowment for the Arts, the Asian Cultural Council, the U.S.-Japan Friendship Commission, the Harkness Center for the Arts, the New York Foundation for the Arts, and the Jerome Foundation. She was also the recipient of Guggenheim and Robert Rauschenberg fellowships.

FURTHER READING

Dixon, Brenda. "Blondell Cummings: The Ladies and Me," *Drama Review* 24.4 (December 1980).

Goler, Veta. "Living with the Doors Open: An Interview with Blondell Cummings," *High Performance* 69–70 (Spring–Summer 1995).

PRINCESS MHOON COOPER

Cummings, Elijah E. (18 Jan. 1951–), congressman, was born Elijah Eugene Cummings in Baltimore, Maryland, the son of Robert Cummings, a chemical plant worker, and Ruth Cummings, a homemaker. A product of a working-class family in West Baltimore, Cummings did well in high school, serving in student government as president of his senior class. He graduated from Baltimore City College High School in 1969. After high school Cummings was accepted into Howard University in Washington, D.C. There, Cummings developed an interest in politics and law and continued his participation in student government as sophomore class president, treasurer, and president. In fact, Cummings did so well academically that he was a recipient of the prestigious Phi Beta Kappa key. After graduating in 1973 with a B.A. in Political Science, Cummings returned to Maryland, where he enrolled in law school at the University of Maryland. In 1976, Cummings received his J.D. and entered private practice. He was married twice, first to Joyce Cummings, with whom he had two daughters. In 2008 he married Dr. Maya Rockeymoore, a public policy analyst.

Cummings embarked on a successful legal career in 1976 following his law school graduation.

He became chief judge of the Maryland Moot Court Board; however, the lure of politics beckoned. In 1982 Cummings was elected to the 39th district in the Maryland House of Delegates. He served his West Baltimore district in the House from 1983 until 1996. His career in the Maryland House of Delegates included becoming the first African American Speaker Pro Tem in Maryland's history. Representing an urban district, Cummings focused on the needs of African Americans and the poor. His priority interests were education, crime, police misuses of power, empowerment, and HIV-AIDS prevention. Priding himself on professionalism and congeniality, Cummings made his name as an likable, effective, and dedicated legislator on both sides of the aisle. An unexpected political development, however, provided Cummings with a golden opportunity to take his talents to a higher plane.

When the prominent congressman and head of the Congressional Black Caucus, Kweisi Mfume, announced his retirement from the U.S. House in February 1996 to lead the NAACP, Cummings quickly jumped into the race to succeed him. In a crowded field of more than two dozen challengers in the Democratic primary, Cummings bested the field with nearly 40 percent of the vote. In the special election to represent the 7th Congressional District, Cummings easily beat his Republican rival, Kenneth Konder, with 81 percent of the vote. He assumed office on 16 April 1996 to complete the remainder of Mfume's unexpired term.

Once in Congress, Cummings continued his agenda of promoting the interests of African Americans, poor people, and urban-dwellers. Cummings has served on several committees in Congress, including Transportation and Infrastructure; Railroads, Pipelines, and Hazardous Materials; and Aviation. He also has served as chair of the subcommittee on the Coast Guard and Maritime Transportation. Beyond his responsibilities in those areas, Cummings has taken a leading role on the House Committee on Oversight and Government Reform, where he has moved to remove waste, fraud, and abuse from the federal government. Cummings has also taken leadership roles with the Congressional Black Caucus and the Joint Economic Committee and the House Task Force on Health Care Reform. Cummings has not faced strong electoral opposition and has won every reelection campaign easily. Generally considered a liberal politician, Cummings has taken strong stands against American drug policy, the war in Iraq, and American port security. Further,

Cummings has used his stature, both in Baltimore and Washington, to participate in various organizations and institutions, such as Morgan State University Board of Regents, the Maryland Zoo Board of Trustees, and the Baltimore Area Council of the Boy Scouts of America Board of Directors, among others. He is active in church related activities and maritime education efforts.

Unlike many of the more established black members of the House, Cummings was an early supporter of BARACK OBAMA's presidential bid in 2007 and vigorously worked to help the then-U.S. senator win the 2008 Democratic nomination and defeat the Republican John McCain in the general election. Once discussed as a prospect for the U.S. Senate in 2006, to replace Senator Paul Sarbanes, Cummings decided to stay in the House, where he has enjoyed increasing respect and responsibility. He has been a leader on reforming the financial industry and was a strong ally of President Obama in passing the historic health care reform act of 2010.

FURTHER READING

Editorial, "Elijah L. Cummings: A Fine Representative, a Strong Role Model," *Baltimore Sun*, 31 Oct. 1999.

U.S. Congress, House, Committee on House Administration of the U.S. House of Representatives. *Black Americans in Congress, 1870–2007* (2008).

DARYL A. CARTER

Cummings, Ida Rebecca (17 Mar. 1867–8 Nov. 1958), educator, fraternal leader, and clubwoman, was born in Baltimore, Maryland. Her mother, Eliza Davage Cummings, of the second generation of her family to enjoy freedom from slavery, operated a boarding house at the family residence. Her father, Henry Cummings, also born free, was a hotel chef and owner of a catering business. Cummings received her early education from the Oblate Sisters of Providence, the nation's first order of black nuns. Subsequently she attended Baltimore's public school for black children and Hampton Institute. She earned a B.A. from Morgan State College in Baltimore and later studied at Bennett College in Greensboro, North Carolina, and at Columbia University.

Like many in the small postbellum black middle class, the Cummings family felt a responsibility to improve the lot of less fortunate members of their race. This expectation was reinforced by the family church, Metropolitan Methodist, which had played a role in the Underground Railroad and operated a school for blacks prior to the Civil War.

Obtaining an education and breaking new ground in service to the community was part of the fabric of the Cummings family life. Cummings's grandmother, Sidney Hall Davage, was influential in the development of the Centenary Biblical Institute, from which Morgan State College evolved. In 1889 Ida Cummings's brother, Harry, an alumnus of Lincoln University, was one of the first two blacks to graduate from the University of Maryland School of Law. A year later he became the first black elected to the Baltimore City Council. Another brother, Aaron, was the first black supervisor in Baltimore's postal service. Cummings's mother and aunt worked for community uplift through their church and the racially segregated branch of the YWCA. As a young child Cummings accompanied her mother throughout the city soliciting funds for Morgan State College. In recognition of her success, a dormitory at the school is named in honor of Mrs. Cummings. In an era when the majority of African Americans were minimally educated and employed as laborers, Cummings family members were business people, clergymen, civil servants, and educators.

Cummings followed the family tradition. By 1900 she was teaching in a Baltimore primary school. After a year she moved to Chicago to study at the Chicago Kindergarten College, an institution that pioneered the concept of pre-primary education. Returning to Baltimore she enrolled at the Baltimore Kindergarten College, after which she became Baltimore's first certified kindergarten teacher. Before the establishment of kindergartens in Baltimore, countless children too young to attend primary school were left at home unattended. By the 1920 school year seventy-four children were enrolled in "Miss Ida's" kindergarten. With the help of two assistants Cummings taught an average of fifty-four students each day. For thirty-seven years Cummings provided supervised child care and a foundation for and appreciation of learning to Baltimore youth. These were her goals in the classroom and in the larger community.

Throughout her lifetime Cummings affiliated with organizations whose purpose was to improve education, health care, housing, and social activities for the children of the poor. One such organization was the Frances E. W. Harper Temple of Elks, of which she was the founder and Daughter Ruler for twenty-nine years. Cummings also served as the Elks' state director of the Department of Education and the national chairperson of the Child Welfare Department. In recognition of her work on behalf of children, she was appointed to the board of directors of Cheltenham School, Maryland's residential facility for black juvenile delinquents.

Long active with the YWCA in Baltimore, Cummings, along with her mother and aunt, organized members of that group and formed the Colored Empty Stocking and Fresh Air Circle. One of its purposes was to provide Christmas gifts for needy children. The group also raised funds and paid rural families, at $1.50 weekly per child, to board city children in their homes for the summer months. In this manner, poor children living in substandard city housing gained exposure to a healthier environment for a few months of the year. During the forty years of the group's existence, Cummings served as president. A major accomplishment of her administration was the purchase of a farm. With the assistance of volunteers, a summer camp was built and staffed. From 1904 to 1907 more than five thousand children were served by the Fresh Air Circle.

An active member of the National Association of Colored Women (NACW), Cummings was corresponding secretary from 1912 to 1914 and chaired the planning committee for the tenth annual convention, which Baltimore hosted in 1916, when MARGARET MURRAY WASHINGTON, the widow of BOOKER T. WASHINGTON, was president of the NACW. During this convention, at which Cummings was elected vice president, symposia on lynching and women's suffrage were presented. Featured speakers included MADAME C. J. WALKER, who gave an address on business activities for black women, FANNIE JACKSON COPPIN, who spoke on women as educators, and Cummings, who addressed "What the Kindergarten Does for the Child."

Although officially retired in 1937, Cummings remained active in the field of education, teaching Sunday school and serving as a trustee of Bennett College and as the first female among the twenty-four-member board of trustees of Morgan State College. She maintained an interest in politics and was president of the Republican Women's League. Cummings, who was unmarried and childless, died in Baltimore at the age of ninety-one. Never wealthy, she made small bequests to the schools and organizations she had supported throughout her lifetime. More than four hundred civic, religious, fraternal, and educational leaders participated in her funeral service, a tribute to her positive influence on countless Baltimoreans.

FURTHER READING

Many of the primary sources on which this entry is based remain in the possession of Cummings family members. The original manumission record for Sidney Hall Davage and the original *Report of the Colored Empty Stocking and Fresh Air Circle, 1904–1907* are deposited in the Beulah Davis Room, Soper Library, Morgan State University.

Greene, Suzanne Ellery. "Black Republicans on the Baltimore City Council, 1890–1931," *Maryland Historical Magazine* 74 (Sept. 1979).

Neverdon-Morton, Cynthia. *Afro-American Women of the South and the Advancement of the Race, 1895–1925* (1989).

Wesley, Charles Harris. *The History of the National Association of Colored Women's Club* (1984).

Wilson, Edward N. *The History of Morgan State College: A Century of Purpose in Action 1867–1967* (1975).

Obituary: *Baltimore Evening Sun* and *Baltimore Afro-American*, 10 Nov. 1958.

DONNA TYLER HOLLIE

Cummings, Michael (28 Nov. 1945–), quilter and textile artist, was born Michael Arthur Cummings in Los Angeles, California, to Arthur Cummings, who worked for the U.S. Postal Service, and Dorothy Dent Cummings Goodson. He was the oldest of three children, including sisters Phyllis and Monica. Cummings attended Fremont High School and Los Angeles City College.

In 1970 Cummings moved to New York, where he attended the Art Students League and later earned a BA in American Art History at Empire College of the State University of New York. His early art mediums were painting, shadow boxes, and collage. The collage and mixed media work of ROMARE BEARDEN and appliquéd banners, such as those created by the Fon of the Republic of Benin, were early artistic influences on Cummings, who once made a fabric banner. He saw the potential to explore art through fabric and quilts, also appreciating that fabrics could be folded, shipped, and stored more easily than framed artwork.

Cummings began quilting in 1973 when he was twenty-eight. Searching the family tree, he found no grandmother, aunt, or other relative who quilted. He taught himself by viewing the techniques of other quilters on display in local exhibits and by reading how-to books and quilt magazines. Vivian Ayers-Allen, the Pulitzer Prize–nominated poet and mother of the entertainers DEBBIE ALLEN and Phylicia Ayers-Allen Rashad, was the first gallery owner to display Cummings's quilts, in her Texas gallery.

In 1986 Cummings answered a classified ad that CAROLYN MAZLOOMI placed in a national quilting magazine seeking to correspond with other African American quilters. Cummings and others who responded later became founding members of the Women of Color Quilters Network (WOCQN), the first national African American quilting organization. WOCQN's objectives included fostering and preserving quilt making among African Americans, encouraging research into African American quilt history, and offering authentic African American quilts to museums and galleries for exhibition. WOCQN membership grew to more than twelve hundred.

From the early 1980s through the 2000s, Cummings lived and quilted in an 1886 three-story house in Harlem. Before retiring, Cummings was employed by the New York State Council on the Arts, and he worked on quilts during carefully planned personal hours.

Known for his extraordinarily large quilts, some as tall as ten feet, Cummings used cottons, silks, African prints, dyed fabrics, found objects, sequins, beads, and buttons, among other materials. Of his quilt making, he says in the catalog *Spirits of the Cloth* (1998) that he is "concerned as much with art as with craft. The narrative themes in my quilts are constructed sometimes with dense designs, making statements that can be humorous or somber. The juxtaposition of contrasting colors dominates my creative thought process, both in technique and in design development."

Cummings also earned critical acclaim for his quilt series, in which he explores the same idea many times in a narrative sequence or in a variety of creative executions. For instance, the three-piece *Haitian Boat People* (1987) was inspired by news reports of hundreds of desperate Haitians who undertook perilous sea voyages to gain unauthorized entry into the United States. The three machine-appliquéd quilts in this work were made of cotton and synthetic fabrics and beads. Yemoja, a sea goddess in the Yoruba (Nigeria) religion and the religions practiced across the African diaspora, appears in each quilt. In the first quilt she pushes the Haitians' raft out to sea. In the second quilt she guides their journey to the United States. In the last,

haunting quilt, she is horrified that she cannot save the drowning Haitians whose raft has capsized.

Another work, the *African Jazz Series* (1990), is a twelve-piece collection that illustrates a musical trio featuring a shade-wearing piano player, a saxophonist, and a bass player. Each quilt varies in size, some measuring six feet by eight feet and others six feet by nine feet, proportions that accommodate Cummings's representation of the tall bass violin. This quilt also inspired a 1997 quilt created for the House of Seagram's Absolut Vodka advertising series in which a bottle of the popular alcohol substitutes for the bass violin.

Cummings also created a mini-quilt series, *The Children of Egungun* (1992). The Yoruba people honor and celebrate the *egungun*, masked ancestral spirits that return to earth to protect and guide family members. Each of Cummings's quilts, which are 2.5 feet by 3.3 feet, illustrates a masked *egungun* child in multifabric strip dress and represents spirits, such as the queen, the king, the trickster, and wisdom. Other Cummings quilt series include *Egyptian Mythology* (1980s), *Sioux Indian Tribes* (1992), *Navajo Women* (1992), *Take My Brother Home* (1993), the four-piece *Haitian Mermaid* series (1996), the *Butterflies* series (2000), and the *Josephine Baker* series (2000).

Important single quilts by Cummings include *Grandma's Porch* (1986), a ten-foot quilt depicting his grandmother standing on her front porch in one of her actual housecoats. *I'll Fly Away* (1992) is a quilt featuring HARRIET TUBMAN; *Clara's Garden* (1994) is a seven-foot quilt of a loving churchwoman in her best Sunday dress and lace hat; *Christ Bearing the Cross* (2003) features an African Christ; and *Satin Doll* (2005), his first quilt with text, honors jazz singers.

Over the years Cummings built an impressive exhibition record, participating in more than fifteen solo and sixty group exhibitions of quilts, traditional arts, and contemporary design. Cummings's works are in the permanent collections of the Museum of Arts and Designs in New York, the California Afro-American Museum in Los Angeles, the Getty Center for Education in the Arts in Los Angeles, the National Underground Railroad Freedom Center, the Schomberg Center for Research in Black Culture, the Smithsonian Institution Renwick Gallery, and the Studio Museum in Harlem. Cummings also explored ways to expose his quilts to newer audiences. In 1987 his quilts appeared in a series of Eastman Kodak film advertisements. In 1995 Hallmark Cards licensed two of Cummings's quilts for its African American greeting card line called Mahogany. In 2000 he illustrated the children's book *In the Hollow of Your Hand: Slave Lullabies*, by Alice McGill.

Cummings commented in 2000 that being a male quilter placed him in a "unique position." He said that his quilting "forces people to reassess what they think men can and cannot do. And if you dig a little deeper, you'll learn that in Africa and other non-Western places, men have been the ones who created and worked with fabric—for centuries" (www. michaelcummings.com/biography.html).

FURTHER READING

Benberry, Cuesta. *Always There: The African American Presence in American Quilts* (1992).

Brathwaite, Kwame. "Masters of the Quilt Opens in Harlem," *New York Beacon*, 19 Apr. 2000.

Freeman, Roland. *A Communion of the Spirits: African American Quilters, Preservers, and Their Stories* (1997)

Grudin, Eva Ungar. *Stitching Memories: African-American Story Quilts* (1990).

National Afro-American Museum and Cultural Center. *Uncommon Beauty in Common Objects: The Legacy of African American Craft Art* (1993).

Raynor, Vivien. "A Quilter's Hand with Dazzling Images," *New York Times*, 23 Aug. 1992.

KYRA E. HICKS

Cundieff, Rusty (13 Dec. 1960–), filmmaker and screenwriter, was born George Arthur Cundieff in Pittsburgh, Pennsylvania. He was one of two children born to John and Christina, who would later appear in one of their son's most well known films. He attended local schools and matriculated at Loyola University in New Orleans, where he studied journalism, but soon changed course and enrolled at the University of Southern California, where he was a member of Alpha Phi Alpha, the traditionally black college fraternity, and from which he graduated in 1982 with a bachelor's degree in Religious Studies.

Somewhere along the line Cundieff was bitten by the performance bug. Upon graduating from USC, he began doing stand-up comedy around Los Angeles, where he met and rubbed elbows with some of the young black comics who themselves were soon starring in feature films and television series, particularly the WAYANS brothers. He also began picking up small parts on television, notably an appearance on *Benson*. He also appeared in episodes of *What's Happening Now?* and *MacGruder*

and Loud (both 1985). That same year he joined the daytime soap opera *Days of Our Lives* and played the role of Theo Carver for a year before leaving the program. Around this time, Cundieff met and married Trina Davis. The couple went on to have two children.

Meanwhile, Cundieff continued work in film and television. He continued to act, though usually in small parts, appearing on the popular series *Thirtysomething* (1990) and the SPIKE LEE movie *School Daze* (1988). He also tried his hand at screenwriting, cowriting the sequel to the smash hip-hop comedy *House Party* (1990) and its sequel, *House Party II* (1991). He directed a number of music videos, as well, including some for Neil Young. Cundieff made his directorial debut in 1994 with the "mockumentary" *Fear of a Black Hat*. The film purports to follow the rise and fall and rise of a hardcore rap group called *Niggaz with Hats* (one of whom, Ice Cold, is played by Cundieff himself). The movie performed well on the festival circuit—including at the Sundance Film Festival—and fared well among critics, but it was given only limited release by its studio and never made back even its million-dollar budget. Still, Cundieff was establishing himself as a young, resourceful director to watch.

His next feature, *Tales from the Hood*, was an African American–oriented spoof of horror anthology films produced by Spike Lee. The movie features a trio of drug dealers lured to a funeral home for a drug pick-up by the mysterious and sinister mortician Mr. Simms, who proceeds to regale them with terrifying tales with ironic and darkly comic twists. Among the film's sequences are "Boys Do Get Bruised" and "KKK Comeuppance." Cundieff found small roles for his mother and father in the movie. *Tales from the Hood* went on to become a modest hit, earning nearly $12 million on a $6 million budget.

In 1997, Cundieff directed *Sprung*, a low-budget romantic comedy that again proved a modest moneymaker. Since that time, he has continued to write and direct for both film and television. He worked with the filmmaker and liberal provocateur Michael Moore for his short-lived but critically acclaimed program *TV Nation* (1994–1997). He directed numerous episodes of the hit *Chappelle's Show* (2003–2006) and *The Wanda Sykes Show* (2009–2010). In 2009 he wrote an episode of *CSI: NY*, one in the family of long-running TV police procedurals. Another motion picture effort, *Movie 43*, was slated for a 2010 release but was delayed.

FURTHER READING

Alexander, George. *Why We Make Movies: Black Filmmakers Talk about the Magic of Cinema* (2003).

Donalson, Melvin. *Black Directors in Hollywood* (2003).

JASON PHILIP MILLER

Cuney, Norris Wright (12 May 1846–3 Mar. 1897), politician, labor leader, and community leader, was born one of eight slave children in Austin County, Texas, to a prominent white planter and politician, Philip Minor Cuney, and Adeline Stuart, a slave of mixed race birth. In the decade prior to the Civil War Cuney's father began manumitting his slave children, sending Norris Wright and his two brothers to the black abolitionist GEORGE B. VASHON's Wylie Street School for Colored Youth in Pittsburgh, Pennsylvania. During the Civil War Cuney left school to work on riverboats on the Mississippi River. Following the war he joined members of his extended family in Galveston, Texas, where he entered politics. One brother, Joseph, also earned an enviable reputation in Galveston. On 5 July 1871 Cuney married Adeline Dowdy, who was the progeny of a white planter and slave mother. They had two children, Maud (who attended the New England Conservatory of Music) and Lloyd Garrison. Cuney's accomplishments were many and varied, including serving as collector of customs for Galveston, chairman of the Texas Republican Party, city alderman, water commissioner, union leader, grand master of the Prince Hall Freemasonry, and active member of the AME Church.

Cuney became the political protégé of George T. Ruby, a northern-born free black man, who after the Civil War came to Texas as part of the Freeman's Bureau. During Reconstruction Ruby became president of the Union League, a predominantly black organization that aided newly freed slaves in becoming citizens and protecting their rights. From his position of de facto leadership of black Texans, Ruby rose to a position of power and influence within the fledging Republican Party, becoming an important ally of Radical Republican Governor Edmund J. Davis, and one of only two African Americans elected to the state senate during Reconstruction. Cuney aided Ruby in that effort and served as president of the Galveston Union League. Ruby arranged for his appointment as the first black Sergeant of Arms of the Texas Legislature. As Reconstruction began to unravel, Ruby left Texas to pursue a journalism career in New Orleans and Cuney began to fill the void. Upon the death of former governor Davis, Cuney assumed party leadership, becoming National Committeeman in 1884.

As Cuney took over party leadership, black Republican options in Texas and all across the South were diminishing every day. He was determined to maintain the party's viability and that of the African American voter and won the respect of colleagues across the state and nation. One anonymous AME Church visitor to Galveston offered high praise for Cuney's abilities and leadership:

> Fortunately, we have a man for leader worthy of the confidence imposed in him; I allude to Mr. N. W. Cuney, who is no stranger to the political world. He it was who so gallantly and skillfully led the Blaine wing of the Texas delegation in opposition to General Mallay; an enthusiastic Arthur man and Collector of this Port. Mr. Cuney is respected and esteemed by the better class of both races. Two years ago he and Mr. W. H. Washington were elected members of the City Council. Both are candidates for re-election, and, it is hoped, will be elected. Mr. Cuney is recognized by all to be of the leaders of that body, and it would be a public loss if he were defeated. (*Christian Recorder*, 19 Mar. 1885).

Although he was a Republican, Cuney pursued "fusion" with third parties and dissident breakaway Democratic groups, influence over national policies regarding Texas, and through patronage. In 1892, for example, Cuney's Republican Party fused with dissident Democrats led by George Clark against incumbent governor Jim Hogg. And although Republicans would not gain high state office during the late nineteenth century, they remained active until their virtual disfranchisement with the establishment of the all-white primary and passage of the poll tax in 1905.

Republican candidates may not have won state office in Texas or other Southern states, but they won the presidency in five out of seven elections following the Civil War. Cuney made sure that Texas Republicans, who were overwhelmingly African American, played an important role at national conventions. Presidential candidates sought Cuney's support, he served on important national committees, and developed friendships and alliances with many within party leadership. In 1884 Cuney was one of a small group of delegates chosen to notify James G. Blaine that he had won the Republican nomination. In 1888 he led the Texas delegation to the national convention to support Benjamin Harrison for president. Harrison won the election and rewarded

Cuney with the appointment as collector of customs for the port of Galveston, arguably the most important appointment any African American received following the Civil War. As leader of the party Cuney controlled political patronage and appointed some whites but mostly blacks to important positions.

Cuney became active in Galveston city politics, gaining election as alderman in 1883 and 1885. He developed a close friendship and alliance with Robert Fulton, Galveston's mayor. Alderman Cuney effectively led a campaign to root out corruption in city contracts and fought to improve education for black youth. The area of education brought Cuney more criticism from whites than almost any other issue in his career. In 1883 a wealthy businessperson named George Ball bequeathed $50,000 to Galveston for the creation of the city's first high school. Cuney convinced the council to integrate the school. The reaction of whites in Galveston was immediate and angry: Ball's heirs threatened to withdraw the money and the council reversed its earlier decision. Although defeated in that effort Cuney was able to convince the council to build an equivalent high school (Central High) for blacks, the first such school in Texas.

In the late nineteenth century the port of Galveston rivaled New Orleans in cotton shipments. There were two unskilled Longshoreman's Unions, one white and one black, and one skilled union, the Screwmen Benevolent Association, which allowed only white membership. Screwmen, led by a contracting stevedore, operated complicated devices that packed cotton into the hulls of ships, and the more skilled the Screwmen the more money the shipper made. Their skill gave the union the ability to gain high wages and shorter work hours for its membership, but in doing so created ill feeling on the part of shippers and the Galveston Cotton Exchange that comprised many of the city's leading businesspeople. In 1882 tensions between the union and the shippers increased dramatically after the union led a "work holiday" in support of a shorter workday and reduced load. Cuney saw an opportunity for black dockworkers, spent $2,500 of his own money to buy the equipment, and created the rival black Screwmen Union (SBA #2). He successfully approached the Cotton Exchange for permission to contract with shippers and received guarantees that his men have an equal opportunity on Galveston's docks. The appearance of black skilled workers on the docks, with police protection led the white union to call a strike, which continued for over four months before the membership voted to return to

work. Cuney had successfully filled the vacuum left by striking white workers, the union received high praise from shippers, and it established a permanent presence on Galveston's docks.

Cuney's amazing political career ended in 1896 when whites within the Texas Republican Party gained enough strength to oust him from leadership. He died early the following year after a long illness.

FURTHER READING

Barr, Alwyn. *Black Texans: A History of African Americans in Texas, 1528–1995* (1998).

Cuney-Hare, Maud. *Norris Wright Cuney: A Tribune of the Black People* (1936, repr. 1995).

Hales, Douglas. *A Southern Family in White and Black: The Cuneys of Texas* (2003).

DOUGLAS HALES

Cuney-Hare, Maud (16 Feb. 1874–14 Feb. 1936), musician, author, and educator, was born Maud Cuney in Galveston, Texas, to NORRIS WRIGHT CUNEY, a prominent Republican politician and entrepreneur, and Adelina Dowdie Cuney, a public school teacher, soprano vocalist, and community activist. Both of Cuney's parents were born slaves of mixed racial parentage, and both gained freedom, education, social clout, and considerable financial advantage as the acknowledged offspring of their fathers. This, in addition to Norris Wright Cuney's political success with the Texas Republican Party, situated the Cuney family solidly among the Texan black elite. Cuney describes her early home life as one that was comfortable and markedly pleasant, and she praises both of her parents for instilling in her and in her younger brother, Lloyd Garrison Cuney, the values of education, racial pride, and social obligation.

Following her graduation from Central High School in 1890, Cuney moved to Boston, Massachusetts, where she enrolled in the New England Conservatory of Music. Her major was the pianoforte, though she was an eclectic musician whose talents included voice and violin. At the conservatory, Cuney studied under such renowned instructors as Edwin Klahre, Martin Roeder, and Edwin Ludwig. In addition to music, Cuney showed great promise and interest in the literary and dramatic arts. After completing her musical studies at the conservatory, Cuney enrolled at the Lowell Institute of Harvard University, where she studied English literature.

In Boston, Cuney met the city's intellectual and social black elite. She was a regular member of a prestigious social group known as the Charles Street Circle (or the West End Set), whose members included JOSEPHINE ST. PIERRE RUFFIN and W. E. B. DUBOIS. For a brief time, Cuney and DuBois were engaged to be married. Although the engagement dissolved, the two remained lifelong friends and collaborators in intellectual, artistic, and activist pursuits.

In 1898 Cuney married J. Frank McKinley, a physician more than twenty years her senior. The two relocated to Chicago, where McKinley, who was biracial, hoped for them to "pass" as a Spanish American couple. In 1900 Cuney gave birth to a daughter, Vera, who indeed was identified as a Spanish American on her birth certificate. Disputes over the ethics of passing caused strife in the McKinley marriage. Despite her temporary compliance, Cuney was staunchly opposed to passing. In 1902, McKinley filed for divorce and won custody of Vera.

After the divorce, Cuney returned to Boston, where in 1904 she married William Parker Hare, a descendant of a moneyed family of Boston's black elite. At this point, she changed her surname to Cuney-Hare, and it was under this name that the majority of her professional work would be acknowledged.

In Boston, Cuney-Hare resumed her musical career, performing publicly as a pianist and delivering lectures on literature and music of the African diaspora. Cuney-Hare regularly collaborated with William Howard Richardson, a Canadian-born baritone vocalist who shared her interest in the origins and trajectories of the music of the African diaspora. They performed together for more than twenty years, touring domestically and abroad.

Cuney-Hare's flourishing musical career did not coincide with an abatement of her social or political initiatives. In 1907 she was among the first women to join the antisegregationist Niagara Movement, the forerunner to the National Association for the Advancement of Colored People (NAACP). In 1910, when DuBois launched the NAACP's charter publication, the Crisis: A Record of the Darker Races, Cuney-Hare became its musical editor. In later years, when her eclectic career and exhausting performance schedule prevented her from continuing in this full-time position, Cuney-Hare contributed to the publication by submitting articles and reviews.

In 1913, the Crisis Publishing Company published Cuney-Hare's first full-length text, a biography of her father called Norris Wright Cuney: A Tribune of the Black People. Though sentimental, Cuney-Hare's work was thoroughly researched and provided both personal insight to and a documented account of an important if often overlooked historical figure. In 1918, Cuney-Hare edited an anthology of poems titled The Message of the Trees: An Anthology of Leaves and Branches. The compilation celebrated the place of nature and beauty in the human world. It included a broad range of poets, both men and women, canonical and obscure, and of both British and American nationality. Uncharacteristically for Cuney-Hare, only one black poet's work (PAUL LAURENCE DUNBAR's "The Haunted Oak") was included in the extensive survey. She dedicated the book to her daughter, Vera, who had died after a long illness in 1908.

Cuney-Hare saw the arts as integral to the project of racial uplift, and in 1926 she used private funds to found the Allied Arts Centre, a nonprofit, community-based organization in Boston. The center facilitated a number of art, music, and drama groups and housed a small theater (aptly named the Little Theatre) as well. While predominantly African American in its constituency, the Allied Arts Centre was explicitly an inclusive interracial organization, founded on the principle of combating racial prejudice through conscientious artistic work. Cuney-Hare's contributions to the center were practical as well as financial and conceptual. She served as managing director of the center, in addition to which she lectured, gave recitals, and produced plays.

With the Little Theatre of the Allied Arts Centre in mind, Cuney-Hare wrote the script for her play, Antar of Araby, in 1929. The play told a romantic tale of the historical Arab/Abyssinian slave poet Antar, whose valor outshines and disproves presuppositions ascribed to his color. According to Cuney-Hare's stage directions, Antar "must be of dark complexion, but [give] an impression of wealth and magnificence" (34). In 1930, a year after its publication and first performance, Antar was anthologized in WILLIS RICHARDSON's Plays and Pageants from the Life of the Negro.

Cuney-Hare's lifetime of scholarly and artistic work culminated in 1936 with her final publication, a comprehensive musical anthropology called Negro Musicians and Their Music. Identifying such elements as ritual, dance, mysticism, and entertainment as valid and integral components of musical production, Cuney-Hare validated Afrocentric trends and influences in the musical arts and reclaimed a legitimate space for people of African descent within discourses of "high art." The book drew upon Cuney-Hare's extensive primary research from a number of countries and territories, including Mexico, the Virgin Islands, Puerto Rico, and Cuba. Musical scores, photographs, and artistic reproductions were included at length alongside her narrative analyses. Unfortunately, Cuney-Hare died on 14 February 1936, of a cancerous tumor, just before the final proofs for *Negro Musicians* were sent to the publisher. Despite the general approval and critical acclaim given *Negro Musicians*, sales were low, and the book soon became obscure. Later critics attributed this failure to a number of causes, including posthumous publication and the continuing economic effects of the Depression (Hales, 137).

Though most remembered as a musician, Cuney-Hare excelled in a number of careers and was an influential and visionary figure in African American history. Various themes from Cuney-Hare's life and writing—from the idea of diasporic continuity (as in *Negro Musicians*) to the celebration of the black body as beautiful (as in *Antar*) to the empowering potential of a community art forum—foreshadowed social, academic, and artistic movements that would more fully flourish in the latter half of the twentieth century. In the late 1990s, both *Norris Wright Cuney* and *Negro Musicians* were "rediscovered" and republished as part of HENRY LOUIS GATES JR.'s series devoted to African American women writers from 1910 to 1940.

FURTHER READING

A noteworthy collection of Maud Cuney-Hare's original sheet music is available at Clark Atlanta University Special Collections, and a series of her "Music and Art" columns appear in the *Crisis: A Record of the Darker Races*, in issues dating between 1910 and 1935.

DuBois, W. E. B. *The Autobiography of W. E. B. DuBois: A Soliloquy on Viewing My Life from the Last Decade of Its First Century* (1968).

Gatewood, Willard B. *Aristocrats of Color: The Black Elite, 1880–1920* (1993).

Hales, Douglas. *A Southern Family in White and Black: The Cuneys of Texas* (2003).

Hunter, Tera W. "Introduction," in *Norris Wright Cuney: A Tribune of the Black People*, by Maud Cuney-Hare, 2d ed. (1995).

Love, Josephine Harreld. "Introduction," in *Negro Musicians and Their Music*, by Maud Cuney-Hare, 2d ed. (1996).

Woodson, Carter G. "The Cuney Family," in *Negro History Bulletin* 11, no. 6 (Mar. 1948).

AIDA AHMED HUSSEN

Cunningham, Edgar V., Sr. (11 Dec. 1910–27 Feb. 1980), possibly the first African American Eagle Scout, was born in New Orleans, Louisiana. Shortly after his birth he moved with his family to Waterloo, Iowa. Waterloo was home to African Americans who, around the World War I era, fled the Jim Crow laws and limited economic opportunities of the Deep South to work in railroad, meatpacking, and manufacturing industries in Iowa, which was also the location of an early branch of the National Association for the Advancement of Colored People (NAACP), established in 1921. Cunningham later married Susie Ann Rockett on 14 September 1931, and together they had five children.

Cunningham was quite possibly the first African American to achieve the rank of Eagle Scout, the highest and most prestigious rank awarded by the Boys Scouts of America. The Boy Scouts of America was established in 1910 as an organization to help young men develop their citizenship, discipline, and character through service and physical activity, and there were increasing levels or ranks that could be achieved as the scouts studied, matured, and demonstrated their knowledge and proficiency. The rank of Eagle Scout began being awarded in 1912.

Cunningham's accomplishment broke a significant barrier. Though the Boy Scouts did not keep specific records about ethnicity, in the early years of boy scouting, the presence of African American scouts was controversial, and a substantial number of Boy Scout troops across the country were segregated. It was often up to local council approval to permit African American scout troops, which gave southern whites on the local councils leverage to reject potential African American scouts. Some southern whites feared that white scouts would not want to voluntarily participate alongside African American scouts. A specific concern involved African American scouts wearing the same Boy Scout uniforms as white scouts. Because of these impediments, before 1926, there were few African American scouts in the South in particular. However, in 1926, the Boy Scouts of America collaborated with the Laura Spelman Rockefeller Foundation to sponsor a campaign to recruit more African American boys.

Cunningham achieved the rank of Eagle Scout on 8 June 1926, as a member of Troop 12, guided by his scoutmaster, James Lincoln Page. Page was a World War I veteran who rose to the rank of sergeant. He led two Boy Scout troops composed entirely of African Americans, Troops 9 and 12, based in Waterloo. There is a possibility, since the Boy Scouts of America did not keep records on the race of its members, that Cunningham may not have been the first black Eagle Scout, although he was, at least, certainly among one of the earliest African Americans to reach that rank. Lending greater credence to his claim of being first, Cunningham also received a handwritten letter from President Calvin Coolidge, a Boy Scout supporter whose sons were also boy scouts, congratulating Cunningham on his achievement.

Cunningham later worked at the John Deere and Chamberlain Manufacturing Corporation. In 1976, his son, Walter Cunningham, a prominent educator, was selected as the first African American high school principal in Iowa. Edgar Cunningham's former Boy Scout troop reunited in 1978, a reunion also attended by his former scoutmaster, James Lincoln Page. At that reunion, Cunningham paid tribute to Page for his support and encouragement. Cunningham died in February 1980 at the age of sixty-nine. Two months later, the Winnebago Council of Boy Scouts in Iowa formally acknowledged Cunningham's achievement. Cunningham's family had also been working to gain greater official recognition for Cunningham. Cunningham soon posthumously received recognition for his achievements from the governor of Iowa, Tom Vilsack, as well as the city of Waterloo. Despite its belated recognition of racial minorities within its ranks, the Boy Scouts came under fire in the 1990s, after banning homosexuals, agnostics, and atheists from becoming scouts or scout leaders, in effect reopening the debate over equal access in the Boy Scouts of America.

FURTHER READING

Macleod, David I. *Building Character in the American Boy: The Boy Scouts, YMCA, and Their Forerunners, 1870–1920* (1983).

Silag, Bill, ed. *Outside in: African-American History in Iowa, 1938–2000* (2001).

KRISTAL L. ENTER

Current, Gloster B. (26 Apr. 1913–3 July 1997), civil rights advocate, musician, and minister, was one of six children born to Earsey Bryant Current and John T. Current, a bank employee, in Indianapolis, Indiana. He grew up in Chicago and Detroit and credited the "outspokenness" of his parents and his grandfather the Reverend Gloster Bryant for his long career in the struggle for black rights (*New York Times*, 9 July 1997). Current's mother was an

officer in the Women's Society of Christian Service, a black women's Methodist organization, and both parents played active roles in their local church. Gloster attended the Detroit Institute of Musical Art and in 1941 received an AB degree from West Virginia State College, near Charleston. In 1951, he earned a master's degree in Public Administration from Wayne State College in Detroit.

On 6 September 1941, he married Leontine "Teenie" Turpeau of Cincinnati, whom Current had met at West Virginia State, and the couple moved to Detroit where they had three children before divorcing in 1955. The next year, Current's former wife married James Kelly, a Methodist minister, and eventually rose to become the first black woman ordained a bishop in the United Methodist Church. In 1957, Current married Rebecca Busch of New York, but had no further children.

As a very young man, Current began building a career as a musician, a talent he probably acquired from his mother who played the piano. By 1932, he had gained attention for his performances at Detroit's YMCA musicale and songfest group. By 1936 "Gloster Current and his Nightingales" began performing in Detroit and Chicago, gaining many fans. Based in Detroit's Paradise Valley community, the Nightingales began playing throughout Michigan, Ohio, and the Midwest, rivaling WILLIAM "BILL" McKINNEY's Cotton Pickers—also based in Detroit—in popularity. Photographs of Current, who played the xylophone, and his band, appeared in the *Chicago Defender*, which referred to Gloster as the "young maestro of swing" (*Chicago Defender*, 5 Aug. 1939). The Nightingales produced a smooth and "scintillating" sound that by 1938 earned the band praise as "internationally famous" (*Chicago Defender*, 1 Oct. 1938). The Nightingales also broke ground in 1936 by being one of the few black traveling bands that included a female member. They first featured Ellariz Thompson, a saxophonist and singer, and in 1939 hired top vocalist "Jerry" Mitchell. Later, when Current attended college, he headed the Gloster Current West Virginia State Collegians where he played saxophone and the xylophone.

After college, however, a performer's career lost its appeal for Current. In part, he probably had come to disdain the road life of a musician, especially with a new bride and a family on the way. The "one-night stands, bad food, insulting treatment," and Jim Crow practices that made finding even a bad hotel nearly impossible for black musicians, likely drove him away from a career in music

(Current, "Duke Ellington," 175). Beginning in 1936, Current already had developed other interests. He had been campaign manager for C. Le Bron Simmons, a lawyer and Wayne County candidate for the Michigan state senate on the Farmer-Labor ticket and, inspired by a speech delivered in Detroit by Juanita Jackson Mitchell, joined and then became president of the Detroit NAACP Youth Council, beginning an association with the civil rights organization that would continue for nearly fifty years. For a time, he combined his two great passions by having his band play at NAACP Youth Council events. But by 1939, his future was being shaped by the racism that infected Detroit. As NAACP Youth Council head, Current and several friends swore out a warrant for the arrest of a local restaurateur who had refused to serve them because of their race, claiming that the practice violated a state anti-discrimination law.

In 1941, Current became executive secretary of the NAACP's Detroit branch, serving there until 1946, during one of the greatest crisis periods in the city's history. The war industry brought a huge southern African American and white population to Detroit. Efforts to alleviate terribly overcrowded conditions among African Americans brought out the resentment of local and migrant whites. In February 1942, when the city and federal government was about to open the SOJOURNER TRUTH Defense Homes housing project for black residents, white Detroiters rebelled. An alliance of local Polish residents, former white southerners, and "fascist-minded white citizens" (*Chicago Defender*, 7 Mar. 1942) blocked all attempts by blacks to move into the housing project. Klansmen burned a cross on the project's grounds and thugs armed with clubs patrolled the streets to insure that no black would move into the facility. Led by Congressman Rudolph Tenerowicz, Joseph Buffa—a realtor—and Father Constantine Dziuk, a Polish priest, and backed by the city's police who refused to protect black residents, white resistance stymied Mayor Edward J. Jeffries's efforts to settle the conflict. Unable or unwilling to resolve the crisis, Jeffries turned the entire matter over to the federal government to defend a project built with federal dollars to house defense plant workers. Current, who tried to bring calm by urging blacks not to resort to violence, helped organize the Sojourner Truth Citizen's Committee to defend black interests and also worked to get bail reduced or charges dismissed for blacks arrested during the riots, especially for those arrested while trying to defend themselves. Current's NAACP branch office

also collected funds for those injured by whites and for the legal defense of the accused. One man who appeared before a judge to answer charges of disorderly conduct said: "I have two boys in the U.S. Army fighting for these people (the whites) and you can sentence me to any years you want, but when I get out I am going to start fighting again just where I left off" (*Chicago Defender*, 14 Mar. 1942). With federal support and Current's leadership, blacks finally began moving into the facility in April.

Racial tensions in Detroit simmered over the next year and exploded in June 1943. Early in the month, 25,000 white Detroit defense plan workers staged a wildcat strike over the promotion of three black employees. "I'd rather see Hitler and Hirohito win the war than work beside a nigger on the assembly line," one agitator screamed at fellow strikers (White, 225). Opposition to integrated housing, fear of miscegenation, scarce resources, and unshakable belief in the racial inferiority of blacks erupted into near warlike conditions on 21 June when rumors spread through the city that a black man had raped a white woman. Whites destroyed black-owned vehicles and businesses, and beat any African American who had the misfortune to be caught out on the street. After word that a patrolman had been shot and wounded by a black shooter, the police organized an assault on the Vernor Apartments—occupied by African Americans—with machine guns and tear gas, terrorizing innocent residents and pillaging the residences, taking whatever property that suited them. The devastation, according to THURGOOD MARSHALL, "resembles a battlefield" (White, 229). By the close of the riots, thirty-four people had been killed. Twenty-five of the dead were black and of those, seventeen had been killed by the police. Six hundred people were injured, and over one million dollars' worth of damage (an enormous sum in 1943) had taken place. Eighty-five percent of all those arrested during the riots were black. Only the arrival of army units restored an uneasy calm to the city. With much justification, the NAACP placed blame for the riots and the devastation squarely on the police, which it described as a "fifth column," alluding to their alleged disloyalty to basic American values in wartime. Current's NAACP office collected evidence that some police even held blacks so that white rioters could beat them.

In response to the riots, a committee formed, which included Current's former ally C. Le Bron Simmons, to offer legal assistance to those victimized by the riots. Additionally, Current, heads of other city civil rights organizations, and WALTER FRANCIS WHITE—NAACP national executive secretary—met with Michigan governor Harry S. Kelly and other officials to investigate the causes of the riots and to reform the police. Current took advantage of the anger over the insurrection by whites to increase membership and contributions to the Detroit branch of the NAACP. By the close of 1943, Current had signed up over 20,000 NAACP members and gathered over $13,000 in contributions. Additionally, the dynamic Current forged strong bonds with black trade union leaders, played a leading role in Detroit's Citizens Committee for Jobs in War Industry, and helped build a strong relationship between the NAACP and the United Auto Workers union. His work on behalf of black labor and his handling of the NAACP branch during the riots and his work with Walter Francis White and Thurgood Marshall brought him to the attention of the national office in New York and in 1946 he was made director of branches, a position he filled with energy and enthusiasm until 1977.

In his new position, Current traveled throughout the country, visiting NAACP branch offices and assessing their programs and efficiency. In 1948, he met with Thurgood Marshall in Indianapolis to discuss the possibility of challenging the state's segregated public school system. But under the directorships of White and ROY WILKINS, Current headed the NAACP's effort to purge the association of American Communist party influence. The Party made African Americans a special target of their appeals and Current worked especially hard to prevent Communists from gaining adherents among NAACP youth and college chapters. The NAACP believed that association with Communists, or even radical critics like former NAACP founder W. E. B. DuBois would severely damage the organization's effectiveness and invite recriminations by Congress or the FBI. Even PAUL ROBESON's 1946 "American Crusade" for a federal anti-lynching law failed to gain NAACP support. Current accused Robeson and his supporters of using "the Negro issue as an opportunity to foist their opinions on other matters on the unsuspecting public" (Duberman, 307).

Current remained a central figure in the NAACP's New York office and served as Roy Wilkins's "talent scout," responsible for finding prospective NAACP board members who reflected Wilkins's interests and goals (Jonas, 145). He worked to build the membership, establish new association branches in areas outside of the South, where the NAACP remained strongest, and headed association fund raising drives. He also worked with branch offices in major cities to pressure retailers like Sears & Roebuck or Montgomery Ward to hire African Americans, even setting up picket lines if necessary. Often, when newspaper reporters needed an official NAACP reaction to a lynching or other racist outrage, they turned to Current. He worked closely with MEDGAR EVERS and was the last person to speak with him before Evers's assassination. In 1963, Current joined with comedian-activist DICK GREGORY to head a march of ten thousand in Gary, Indiana, to protest housing segregation. Current addressed the crowd exclaiming that "the black man wants only that to which he is entitled. … he wants only to be free" (*Chicago Defender*, 16 Sept. 1963).

During the Nixon presidency, he spoke out against the administration's attempts to pack the Supreme Court with weak and racially prejudiced nominees. NAACP official and chronicler Gilbert Jonas considered Current to be one of the association's most talented and respected leaders, but often found him demanding and overbearing. According to Jonas, who headed the association's development program, Current "riddled" him "with criticism for more than a decade until he was convinced that my work was worthwhile" (Jonas, 465).

Current became director of branches and administrator in 1976 and 1977, and then deputy to the executive director in 1977 as the NAACP's board fought to force executive director Roy Wilkins into retirement. Current himself retired in 1978, but the new executive director BENJAMIN LAWSON HOOKS asked him to serve on the association's board until 1983. Current, however, who had been an assistant pastor at St. Paul's United Methodist Church since 1953, spent most of his time as the full-time minister of the Westchester Community Church in the Bronx, remaining there until 1983. From 1985 to 1995, he was the organist of St. Paul's United Methodist Church in Jamaica, Queens. He also had been appointed to the New York State Minority Committee on Aging and served on the board of the National Caucus and Committee on Black Aged. He was a board member, then vice president and president, of the United Methodist City Society and a member of the General Board of Discipleship of the United Methodist Church. He received an alumni award from West Virginia State College, and honorary degrees from historically black Rust College in Holly Springs, Mississippi, and Bethune Cookman College in Dayton Beach, Florida. He received a "living legacy" award from the National

Caucus on Black Aged and recognition from the National Association of Negro Musicians. He spent his final years in Hollis, New York, and died of leukemia and pneumonia at the North Shore University Hospital at Cornell University.

FURTHER READING

Current, Angella. *Breaking Barriers: An African American Family and the Methodist Story* (2001).

Current, Gloster B. "Duke Ellington," *Black Perspective in Music* 2:2 (Autumn 1974).

Current, Gloster B. "Paul Robeson," *Black Perspective in Music* 4:3 (Autumn 1976).

Duberman, Martin B. *Paul Robeson* (1988).

Gilbert, Jonas. *Freedom's Sword: The NAACP and the Struggle against Racism in America, 1909–1969* (2005)

Meier, August, and Elliot Rudwick. *Black Detroit and the Rise of the UAW* (1979).

White, Walter. *A Man Called White: The Autobiography of Walter White* (1948).

DONALD YACOVONE

Curry, George Edward (23 Feb. 1947–), journalist, editor, and commentator, was born in Tuscaloosa, Alabama, the eldest of four children and the only son of Martha Brownlee Curry, a domestic worker, and Homer Lee Curry, an automobile mechanic. Curry's parents divorced when he was a boy, and he and his sisters were raised in public housing by their stepfather, William Henry Polk, a dumptruck driver. Polk, an avid reader of black newspapers with a deep interest in current events beyond the South, was a major influence in Curry's life. Other important influences were his neighbors, including Miss Bessie and Miss Dot, and his high school principal McDonald Hughes, who encouraged children to pursue higher education and to overcome the hardships of segregation. Curry was also inspired by the civil rights leaders Dr. MARTIN LUTHER KING JR., JESSE LOUIS JACKSON SR., RALPH ABERNATHY, CORDY TINDELL (C.T.) VIVIAN, and FRED LEE SHUTTLESWORTH and northerners, including the comedian DICK GREGORY, "who came to my little home town to help us end segregation, putting their lives on the line" (Bernstein, 22).

Curry attended segregated schools. As a boy he was keenly aware of the humiliation of blacks forced to ride in the back of buses, drink from "colored" water fountains, attend inferior schools, and work at dead-end jobs. His hatred of injustice fueled a determination to blaze a trail to a better life for himself and his sisters. In the eighth grade he decided to be a journalist. "When I read newspapers," he recalled, "African Americans were portrayed as athletes, entertainers, and crime suspects. It wasn't my world." He said his stepfather's subscription to the black *Pittsburgh Courier* "opened the world to me, as I read about J. A. ROGERS and W. E. B. DuBois. There was a story other papers weren't telling about the black experience, and who better to tell it than me?" (Bernstein, 6).

In 1965 he graduated from Druid High School, where he had played football and wrote for the school newspaper. Curry attended Knoxville College in Tennessee, played quarterback, and edited the college newspaper. In 1966–1967 he dropped out for lack of money and went to live with a cousin in New York to earn enough to return. As a mail clerk at *Life* magazine, he told Bill Trent, a black personnel assistant, "One day I want to come back here and be a reporter" (Bernstein, 6).

Returning to college in 1968–1969 he received summer scholarships to Harvard and Yale, and another to intern at *Sports Illustrated* magazine. In 1970 Curry married Jacqueline Smith, an operations analyst with the Social Security Administration; together they had a son, Edward. They divorced in 1997.

In 1970 he graduated from Knoxville College with a B.A. in History and was hired as a reporter for *Sports Illustrated* in New York (1970–1972), reporting on football, track, and basketball. He was the second African American writer to work for the magazine. The journalist and Curry's mentor Ernest Holsendolph encouraged Curry to get newspaper experience, and he landed a job at the *St. Louis Post-Dispatch* as a news and investigative reporter (1972–1983). There he pursued stories in inner-city neighborhoods and housing projects, walking the streets and covering subjects neglected at that time—gang-related violence, drugs in the white community, corrupt management in St. Louis housing projects. His front-page stories—twenty-five in the first year—earned awards for the newspaper and for Curry, including the National Urban Coalition's 1982 journalism award.

In 1977 Curry published his first book, about Florida A&M's legendary black football coach and Hall of Famer with a record of 85 percent wins and no losing seasons, *Jake Gaither: American's Most Famous Black Coach*. In that year Curry also founded the St. Louis Minority Journalism Workshop, and opened a branch in Washington, D.C., where he moved in 1984. The workshop trained young people for newspaper and publishing careers, and assisted with job placement.

From 1984 until 1993 Curry served as New York bureau chief and Washington correspondent for the *Chicago Tribune*, traveling widely, covering politics, crime, social justice, and education, and interviewing public figures from presidents to schoolteachers. He became an authority on, and advocate for, affirmative action—policies meant to remedy racial inequality in education, employment, and housing through various measures, including quotas in college admissions—writing and appearing in the 1986 PBS *Frontline* documentary, "Assault on Affirmative Action."

From 1993 until 2000 he was editor in chief of *Emerge*, published by Black Entertainment Television (BET)—the only black in-depth news magazine. Under Curry, the magazine became a staple of information, historical analysis, and critical discussion of issues important to the black community, including its achievements. A hallmark of Curry's leadership was the racial diversity of editorial and artistic directors and contributing writers—people of many backgrounds, famous and unknown, on both sides of the issues. *Emerge* reached a circulation of 170,000 and won more than forty national magazine awards. In 2000 Curry became the first African American elected president of the American Society of Magazine Editors, and appeared frequently on BET's *Lead Story*.

Drawing from *Emerge*, Curry edited two anthologies: *Affirmative Action Debate* (1996), detailing how discrimination in all aspects of life affected not only African Americans but also Latinos, Asian Americans, and others; and *The Best of Emerge* (2003), articles representing the magazine's scope and literary excellence.

A world traveler and public speaker, Curry appeared frequently on television news and panels. In 2003 he became editor in chief of the National Newspaper Publishers Association News Service (NNPA) and BlackPressUSA.com, and was named Journalist of the Year by the National Association of Black Journalists. His weekly column of reportage and commentary began syndication in more than 200 African-American newspapers and on GeorgeCurry.com.

FURTHER READING

Bernstein, Alice. Unpublished interview with George Curry for the oral history project, "The Force of Ethics in Civil Rights," Washington, D.C. (15 Dec. 2005).

Contemporary Authors Online (2007), Document #H1000022450, available online at http://galenet.galegroup.com/servlet/BioRC. *Contemporary Black Biography, Vol. 23* (1999).

Mosley, Walter, et al., eds. *Black Genius: African American Solutions to African American Problems* (1999).

ALICE BERNSTEIN

Curtis, Austin Maurice (15 Jan. 1868–13 July 1939), physician and surgeon, was born in Raleigh, North Carolina, the son of Alexander Curtis and Eleanora Patilla Smith. One of nine children, Curtis attended the Raleigh public schools and went north to college, graduating from Lincoln University in Pennsylvania in 1888. He received his medical degree from Northwestern University in 1891 and became the first intern hired by Chicago's fledgling Provident Hospital. The first voluntary black hospital, Provident opened the doors of its two-story frame building a few months before Curtis started his internship. Provident Hospital boasted an interracial medical staff as well as the first training school for black nurses. There Curtis formed alliances with two individuals who would influence the rest of his life. The first was DANIEL HALE WILLIAMS, a renowned black physician and one of the founders of Provident Hospital, who hired Curtis for the Provident internship. The second was seventeen-year-old Namahyoke "Nama" Sockum, whom Curtis married in either 1888 or 1891. They would go on to have four children and would become one of the most prominent and active couples in black society of their time.

After his one-year internship at Provident, Curtis opened a private general surgical practice in Chicago. His wife continued her volunteer activities; for example, she helped organize Colored American Day at the 1893 World's Columbian Exposition in Chicago and became active with the National Republican Committee. Within three years of opening his medical practice, Curtis had made a name for himself among Chicago physicians and in the community. In one case, the 1895 *Chicago Journal and Evening Press* carried a report of a man who suffered a blow to his head by an irate cook wielding a butcher's cleaver. Curtis was called to the hospital to save the man's life and on arriving discovered that he had treated this patient twice in the past, once repairing damage done to the man's head by a pitchfork and another time patching wounds from a blow with a beer bottle. Despite the extensive injuries caused by the cleaver attack, Curtis managed to perform the delicate operation necessary to save the patient's life.

Curtis also participated in a number of charity endeavors and belonged to the Chicago Society Baseball League. He helped found the city's Civic League, as he said, not only to "help worthy colored people attain to a higher mode of life, but to suppress crime."

When the city commission decided in 1895 that it was time to appoint a black man to the medical staff of Cook County Hospital, Curtis's name was among the first considered. At the time no black man had ever been asked to join the staff of a nonsegregated hospital. But that year Theodore W. Jones, himself a black man, had been elected to the post of city commissioner. Among the many duties of the city commissioner was filling positions on the medical and surgical staff of Cook County Hospital. Jones convened a committee of twelve local physicians to select the newest addition to the hospital's surgical staff, and the group agreed that the time had come to integrate the staff. A tight battle ensued, with the group nearly equally divided between Curtis and another physician, but they finally chose Curtis.

Curtis maintained that job, along with his growing private surgical practice, until 1898 when his old mentor Williams stepped down from the post of surgeon in chief of Freedmen's Hospital in Washington, D.C. Among those suggested for the job was Curtis. At first it did not look as though Curtis would win the much-coveted position. He finished second in the civil service examination required for all applicants, and many black newspapers throughout the country lobbied ardently for a different candidate. Nevertheless, Curtis was eventually offered the post, an offer that some speculated owed more to his wife's political connections than to his qualifications.

However, once Curtis moved to Washington and assumed the post, the rumors and controversy quieted. Curtis was acutely aware of the role that the hospital, founded in the midst of the Civil War, played in the minds of the country's black population. He defended the institution in a report he wrote in 1899 to the secretary of the interior, whose office oversaw its operations and who, in an earlier report, had made staffing and regulation suggestions. "To the negro race especially Freedman's Hospital means a great deal more, both from a philanthropic and scientific standpoint, than can be made to appear in such a brief statement as this necessarily is," Curtis wrote. He helped usher the hospital into the twentieth century, overseeing the installation of a modern telephone system, a new children's ward, and the expansion of the nurses'

home. In the four years he served as surgeon in chief, 428 surgeries were performed, among which there were only 5 deaths.

Although Curtis resigned from the post of surgeon in chief in 1902, he remained on the surgical faculty of Freedman's Hospital until 1938. From 1911 to 1912 Curtis served as president of the National Medical Association, the professional association for black physicians. He was known among the students at Howard University Medical School, with which Freedman's Hospital was affiliated, for his careful and extensive explanations in the surgical theater and his powers of observation. He drilled into these students his favorite surgical saying, "Diagnosis must depend upon the preponderance of symptoms." Howard students were not the only ones to enjoy the benefit of his teachings. He offered frequent demonstration clinics in West Virginia and elsewhere throughout the South. Among his favorite students were his three sons, all of whom became doctors and trained at Howard University. To distinguish him from his second son, who bore his name, Curtis's colleagues gave him the nickname "Pop." Curtis remained close to all his sons and opened a private surgical hospital in Washington with the eldest, Arthur Leo.

Over the years Nama continued to follow her activist instincts. During the Spanish-American War she played an instrumental role in helping the military recruit African American nurses who had already had yellow fever to join the ranks of those caring for ill soldiers in Cuba and throughout the United States. She traveled to Louisiana, Alabama, and Florida and persuaded more than thirty immune black nurses to sign up. Although she herself was not a trained nurse, she volunteered with the American Red Cross after floods had devastated Galveston, Texas, and in 1906 she journeyed to San Francisco to lend a hand with the earthquake relief project. In recognition of her wartime service, she was buried in Arlington National Cemetery when she died in 1935. Curtis died in Washington, D.C.

FURTHER READING

Cobb, William Montague. "Medical History" section, *Journal of the National Medical Association* 46 (1954): 294–98.

Logan, Rayford. *Howard University: The First Hundred Years, 1867–1967* (1969).

This entry is taken from the *American National Biography* and is published here with the permission of the American Council of Learned Societies.

SHARI RUDAVSKY

Curtis, King (7 Feb. 1934–13 Aug. 1971), saxophonist, was born Curtis Ousley in Fort Worth, Texas, and was adopted by William Ousley, a guitarist, and Ethel (maiden name unknown) of Mansfield, Texas. He began playing saxophone at about the age of twelve, initially playing alto saxophone but later switching to tenor, which remained his principal instrument. He performed in the school band at I.M. Terrell High School, where he also learned baritone saxophone. Around the age of fifteen he began leading his own group, playing at the Paradise Inn in Fort Worth and becoming a protégé of its proprietor, Aaron Watkins. In 1952, on a visit to an uncle in New York City, Curtis won the amateur contest at the Harlem Apollo Theater twice. On this visit he also made his first issued recordings with the Doc Pomus All Stars, including Mickey Baker, and the Doc Kent Band.

Curtis subsequently toured with a band that included LESTER YOUNG, then he returned to Texas to continue his education. He had offers of scholarships from Bishop College and Wyley College. He made further records in Fort Worth, most of which feature the vocalist Melvin Daniels, and performed with a band led by Red Connor, which also included ORNETTE COLEMAN and David "Fathead" Newman. In 1953 he joined LIONEL HAMPTON's orchestra when it passed through Fort Worth, staying with it for several months and leaving in New York City, where he had arranged to study saxophone with the jazz musician Garvin Bushell.

In New York City, Curtis worked a variety of musical jobs, including engagements with the society bands of Art Mooney and Lester Lanin as well as many jazz and rhythm and blues dates with Doc Pomus and the guitarist Mickey Baker at Snooky's in Manhattan. Curtis formed his own trio, initially with the pianist HORACE SILVER and the drummer Osie Johnson, later replaced by Earl Knight and Lenny McBrowne, respectively. As a result of this exposure, Curtis embarked on a career as a session musician, which began on 14 December 1955 when he recorded with "Mr. Bear" (Teddy McRae) for RCA's Groove subsidiary.

For the remainder of his life Curtis was in constant demand as an accompanist and recorded for many record companies with hundreds of performers. They included jazz, blues, and rhythm and blues artists, such as Sammy Price, BIG JOE TURNER, RUTH BROWN, LAVERN BAKER, and Mickey and Sylvia (Mickey Baker and Sylvia Vanderpool); popular vocalists, among them Buddy Holly and later John Lennon; and vocal groups, including the Isley Brothers, the Drifters, and the Coasters. He even worked occasionally behind country and western performers, including Lester Flatt and Earl Scruggs on a CBS TV special in 1961. He is featured on numerous pop hits, of which the Coasters' "Yakety Yak" (1958) is perhaps the best known.

Away from the studios, Curtis led a quintet that held residencies at the Club Baby Grand in Brooklyn and Small's Paradise in Harlem. He also became involved in the development of rock and roll, appearing in Alan Freed's show at the Brooklyn Paramount from 30 August to 8 September 1957. At Small's Paradise he was heard by the record producer Bobby Robinson, under whose direction he began to achieve popular hits under his own name, such as "Soul Twist" (1962). On some of these records he also sang. In the wake of this success, Curtis's groups appeared regularly during the 1960s at prestigious New York City venues, such as the Harlem Apollo, Birdland, and the Village Gate. In 1965 Curtis and his orchestra were chosen to be the feature attraction supporting the British pop group the Beatles on their American tour that began at Shea Stadium in Flushing, New York, on 15 August.

In the 1960s Curtis's session work was mainly for Atlantic Records, and he accompanied many of its star blues, soul, and popular singers, including FREDDIE KING, WILSON PICKETT, ROBERTA FLACK, and ARETHA FRANKLIN. His own band recorded extensively as King Curtis and the Kingpins after a brief incarnation as the Noble Knights. In this period he began doubling on the saxello, a variant of the soprano saxophone.

In 1971 Curtis became Franklin's musical director and accompanied her on a European tour in June, during which he also played and recorded at the Montreux Jazz Festival in Switzerland. Curtis returned to the United States the following month, and at the time of his death he was musical director of the Channel 13 TV show *Soul*, for which he wrote the musical theme "Soulful 13." He died in New York City of stab wounds received during a fight that developed when he tried to drive off two drug addicts who were blocking access to a building he owned at 50 West Eighty-Sixth Street. He was survived by his wife, Ethelynn, from whom he had been estranged for seven years, and a son.

Curtis belonged to the group of jazz tenor saxophonists often referred to as the southwestern school and played in an intense, full-toned, muscular style related to that of Arnett Cobb and ILLINOIS JACQUET. His musical reputation suffered in his lifetime from his extensive involvement with commercial and novelty music, but his best recorded work, much of which is in his accompaniments to blues singers such as ROOSEVELT SYKES, Sunnyland Slim, and Champion Jack Dupree, shows him a worthy and inspired representative of the style. He is also regarded as one of the most significant instrumentalists in the rock and roll and soul idioms.

FURTHER READING

Obituaries: *New York Times*, 15 Aug. 1971; *Fort Worth Telegram*, 19 Aug. 1971.

DISCOGRAPHY

Simonds, Roy. *King Curtis: A Discography* (1984).
This entry is taken from the *American National Biography* and is published here with the permission of the American Council of Learned Societies.

HOWARD RYE

Curtis, Namahyoke Sockum (1861–25 Nov. 1935), nurse, was born Namahyoke Gertrude Sockum in California as the first of seven children. Her maternal grandmother was German, and her maternal grandfather was African American. Her mother, whose name is unknown, married Hamilton Sockum, a Native American of the Acoma Pueblo tribe of New Mexico. Raised by an aunt, Curtis attended grade school in San Francisco. She furthered her education by graduating from Snell Seminary in Oakland in 1888. After graduation Curtis went to Philadelphia, Pennsylvania, to visit relatives. There she met AUSTIN MAURICE CURTIS and eloped with him on 5 May 1888. After the marriage she returned to California while her husband attended Northwestern University Medical School. When the Sockum family learned of the marriage, they sent their daughter to rejoin her husband in Chicago.

While living in Chicago, Curtis became absorbed in efforts to uplift the black community. She played an instrumental role, with Dr. DANIEL HALE WILLIAMS and the Reverend Jenkins Jones, in the establishment of Provident Hospital in 1891. At this time the few hospitals that admitted African American patients typically provided substandard care to them. In response, black families usually cared for loved ones at home. A hospital for blacks offered both the promise of better care and the lifting of a burden from the family members of the sick and dying. Additionally, black men and women who wanted to pursue medical or nursing careers were often blocked by racial segregation from attending school. The Provident Hospital soon gained a reputation for providing a high standard of medical care and became a training facility for black nurses and physicians, including Austin Curtis. Upon completing his residency he acted as the first physician in training, or chief resident, at Provident from 1897 to 1898.

A Republican like many blacks of her day, Namahyoke Curtis served in politics at every level. She supported William McKinley's presidential campaign in 1896 and held various political posts in Chicago. In 1898 Austin Curtis accepted a position as the surgeon in chief and administrator of Freedmen's Hospital in Washington, D.C., which later became the medical school at Howard University, and the Curtises relocated. Austin Curtis remained at the institution for forty years as a professor of surgery.

In May 1898 the United States declared war on Spain. Many of the troops that went to Cuba to fight were felled by yellow fever. Namahyoke Curtis had been bitten by the yellow fever mosquito at some point in her life and as a result was presumed to possess immunity to the disease. She was asked by Dr. Anita Newcomb McGee, a public health physician, to organize and lead a group of immune nurses. These women were to assist in the care of American troops who had become ill with yellow fever and other tropical diseases. On 13 July 1898 Curtis began searching states like Louisiana, Florida, and Alabama—states known to have been especially hard-hit by yellow fever outbreaks—for nurses. She recruited thirty-two African American nurses who accepted pay of thirty dollars a month plus a daily food ration. Ultimately, eighty black women served during the war. They were not official members of any military branch but instead were commissioned by the War Department as contract nurses. Curtis received high official commendation for recruiting and leading the nurses, as well as for the nursing care that she provided. At the conclusion of the war Curtis applied for and received a lifetime government pension for her work with the army. Her efforts helped pave the way for the acceptance of women as nurses in the armed forces, although full acceptance would take decades.

In subsequent years Curtis continued nursing and public service work, specializing in offering aid during public disasters. When a great flood leveled Galveston, Texas, in 1900, she worked under the direction of Clara Barton as a Red Cross volunteer.

When an earthquake and the resulting fires destroyed most of San Francisco in 1906, Curtis received a commission from Secretary of War William Howard Taft to provide assistance to victims. She also continued to work on behalf of African Americans and during World War I helped obtain military approval for a black officers' training camp at Fort Des Moines in Iowa. As Curtis recognized, military service helped demonstrate that African Americans deserved all the rights of full citizenship. Upon her death in 1935, Curtis was eulogized at her home in Washington, D.C., for her patriotism and lifelong activism on behalf of African Americans. She is buried at Arlington National Cemetery in recognition of her services to the troops.

FURTHER READING

Carnegie, Mary Elizabeth. *The Path We Tread: Blacks in Nursing, 1854–1984* (1986).

Hine, Darlene Clark. *Black Women in White: Racial Conflict and Cooperation in the Nursing Profession, 1890–1950* (1989).

CARYN E. NEUMANN

Custer, Frank Andrew (4 Dec. 1878–28 May 1954), an experienced cattle butcher, was elected as a floor committeeman of the Stockyards Labor Council (SLC)—organized by the Chicago Federation of Labor and the Amalgamated Meatcutters union—in 1917. Custer served a multiracial local at the Wilson Packing Company plant, along with ROBERT BEDFORD, another northern African American, and William Bremer, the American-born son of German immigrants.

The historical video drama *The Killing Floor*, produced by Elsa Rassbach and directed by Bill Duke, characterizes Custer as representative of sharecroppers migrating from Mississippi and Arkansas to seek work in the stockyards, but census and military draft records strongly suggest that he was born Frank Andrew Custer in Springfield, Ohio, to Maggie Custer, born in Indiana, and a father born in Kentucky. His maternal grandfather had been born in Virginia, his maternal grandmother in Ohio. He had an older sister Jessie, born in 1874; younger brothers, James, born in 1882, Noah, in 1886, and Earl, born in 1890; and sisters Fannie, born in 1880, and Aura, born in 1893. The name of their father has yet to be identified, but it appears that his union with Maggie Custer lasted for twenty years or more, and ended before 1900—whether by death, divorce, or separation (Census, 1900, 1920).

Sometime in his early twenties, Custer moved to the Cincinnati area, which at the time rivaled Chicago as a center for butchering and meatpacking. It is likely he obtained his butchering skills there. Starting around June 1916, he began working intermittently at the Wilson and Company meatpacking plant in Chicago, where he had steady employment during 1918 and most of 1919 (Records of the Federal Mediation and Conciliation Service [FMCS], 259). By 1918 he married Helen Custer, born in 1899, who worked as a clerk in a mail-order house. Helen Custer's father was born in Louisiana, and her mother in Omaha, Nebraska, as was Helen herself, suggesting a close connection with the meatpacking industry. The Custers resided in 1918 at 3731 Forest Avenue in Chicago, and in 1920 in a multifamily building at 3142 Calumet (WWI Draft Registration; Census 1920).

Custer was elected floor committeeman in April or May 1919 by a racially mixed local representing Wilson employees (FMCS, 259). He had held that position for a month or so when he was called to testify at a Federal Mediation and Conciliation Service hearing concerning tensions between union and nonunion workers. Samuel Alschuler, a federal district judge serving as mediator, noted that the union members were three-quarters "white" but the elected grievance committee were "one white man and two black men." Custer responded, "The white man is scared to be on a committee on that floor. There have been three white men, and they all withdrew because they were scared of their lives."

Custer and his fellow committeemen had to contend with black workers, led by Austin "Heavy" Williams, fiercely agitating against the union. Custer told Alschuler that "the men are naturally working in fear on that floor, and the only way to get out of that fear is to get these agitators out of there" (FMCS, 293). Pointing out that the killing floor was too small to butcher the 150 cattle per hour Wilson's demanded, Custer added that with men working in a crowded space with sharp knives, and tension over the union "the knives are sharp as a razor, and if they happen to touch you, you are cut, you are apt to get blood poison, that is your life" (FMCS, 291). The company men and nonunion men, he added, abuse those who complain or object. Others testified that anti-union agitators Joe Hodges and John Wells carried guns and threw bricks at union men.

Custer described Williams as underhanded, but "one of the most popular colored men on the floor," and despite their persistent confrontations about the union, he said, "I like Heavy, but I don't trust him as if I would like him, because he is against my bread and butter" (FMCS, 266). Alschuler was perplexed by "the mad mixture of love and fear," particularly after Custer asserted, "We are all good friends on that floor judge. We all love each other. Heavy can tell you the same thing" (FMCS, 298).

While trying to explain the urgency of getting anti-union agitators off the killing room floor, Custer expressed the conflicting pressures of racial identity. The management of the meatpacking companies, he said "are not only making agitators on that floor, but they are making them all over Chicago. Supposing race trouble starts, I am a colored man, and love my family tree, and I ain't going to stand for no white man to come imposing on my color. If he imposes on my race, there is going to be a fight.... I don't care if the colored man wears a [union] button or not. He has that love in his heart for one another, that is, if he is a man."

Advocating interracial solidarity against the owners of the major packing houses, Custer had to contend with forces within "white" and "black" communities that drove people to identify on racial lines. Most families arriving from Mississippi and Arkansas during this period were used to staying apart from anyone classified as "white," and had no experience with unions. Some of those who did observed, "Unions ain't no good for a colored man," because "I've seen too much of what they don't do for him" (Halpern, 52). The Chicago Urban League and the "colored" Wabash Avenue YMCA, anxious to place new arrivals in jobs, advocated "plant loyalty."

Custer lamented that "if our people is so weak minded as to let the packers use them against their own race, and to keep their own race down, they are dirty enough and low enough and weak enough to kill you if the packers tell them to do so." He also had his successes, describing a fellow who approached him to join the union because "the only way us poor colored people have to get together is to get into this union, and plan our methods and make white men take notice of us, and perhaps they will help us along after they see we are men enough to help ourselves" (FMCS, 281).

Like many of the rank-and-file leadership within the Stockyards Labor Council, Custer disappeared from the historical record by the mid-1920s. After a debilitating power struggle between national Amalgamated Meatcutters leadership and the Stockyards Labor Council in 1919, followed by

a disastrous strike in 1921–1922, active union representatives were widely blacklisted. He was not in Chicago for the resurgence of organizing that developed the Packinghouse Workers Organizing Committee (PWOC) beginning in 1937.

In 1942 he was settled in Springfield, Ohio, living at 337 Baltimore Place with the family of his sister, Fannie, who had married Walter J. Lowry between 1900 and 1910. Custer worked at the Heaume Hotel (WWII Draft Registration Card; Census 1910, 1930). When he died in 1954, the Springfield *Daily News* described him as "a life long resident of the city," living at 1879 Michigan Avenue, most recently employed as a janitor at the National Supply Co. plant. He had been ill for a year, and was survived by Mrs. Lowry, and her daughter, Mrs. Ruby Porter. His mother preceded him in death 19 December 1941, recorded as "Maggie Custard" by the Ohio Department of Health.

FURTHER READING

Barrett, James R. *Work and Community in the Jungle: Chicago's Packinghouse Workers 1894–1922* (1987).

Halpern, Rick. *Down on the Killing Floor: Black and White Workers in Chicago's Packinghouses, 1904–54* (1997).

Halpern, Rick, and Roger Horowitz. *Meatpackers: An Oral History of Black Packinghouse Workers and Their Struggle for Racial and Economic Equality* (1996).

Trotter, Joe William, Earl Lewis, and Tera W. Hunter. *African American Urban Experience: Perspectives from the Colonial Period to the Present* (2004).

Records of the Federal Mediation and Conciliation Service (FMCS), "Violation of Agreement by Employers," Honorable Samuel Alschuler, Arbitrator, 20 June 1919. National Archives, College Park, M.D., RG 280, Case 33/864, Box 42.

CHARLES ROSENBERG

Custis, Lemuel Rodney (4 June 1915–24 Feb. 2005), first black police officer in Hartford, Connecticut; Tuskegee Airman; and government worker, was born in New York City to Mary and Charles Custis. Very little is known about his life as a child, except that he was the youngest child in his family. Custis attended Hartford Public Schools and graduated from Howard University. In 1939, he joined the Hartford Police Department in Connecticut, becoming the first black police officer in Hartford.

When World War II broke out, having heard of the program at Tuskegee to train black pilots, Custis joined the Army Air Corps as an Aviation

Cadet and because of his outstanding background and qualifications was admitted to the first class-42-C and graduated in 1942. Custis flew ninety-two combat missions and received the Distinguished Flying Cross for his effort in the war. After Custis left Hartford, he was missed for several months until his picture appeared on the *Pittsburg Courier,* one of the most widely read black newspapers; it was then the Hartford community learned that the modest Custis was serving his country. The image showed Custis, a second lieutenant, with four other pilots, all showing their Army Air Corps wings. Afterward, he was assigned to the all-black 99th Fighter Squadron, also known as the "Red Tails," and was located to North Africa, Sicily, and Italy from April 1943 to July of 1944. He had his first successful shoot down of a German Bf-109 in 1944. By then, the 99th Fighter Squadron was flying as the 332nd Fighter Group, an all-black, elite group of fighter pilots. The 332nd Fighter Group was composed of four all-black fighter squadrons: the 99th Fighter Squadron, 100th Fighter Squadron, 301st Fighter Squadron, and 302nd Fighter Squadron. Although they lost no bombers, the Airmen still had indignities and challenges to overcome at the airbases. These challenges included racial discrimination and no rotations between home and the war zone for many months.

After World War II ended, Custis returned to Tuskegee Airfield as an Advanced Flight Instructor, where he stayed for two years. Afterward, he left the military in 1946 at the rank of major. He returned to Connecticut and became active in the state government as the Chief Examiner of Sales Tax Division until his retirement in 1980. He was also on the Board of Directors at the New England Air Museum in Windsor Locks, Connecticut. Custis was active with Tuskegee Airmen, Inc., serving as a member of the East Coast Chapter located in Washington, DC.

Custis was described by his friends as a gentleman and as a positive role model. Custis did not discuss his military accomplishments until the last few years of his life, when he spoke about his treatment in the military. "After our success at Anzio and Salerno…we had an inkling that perhaps we had made a real contribution," Custis said during an interview in April 2000. "And then, of course, as the years went by, and you got older and you had a better perspective of history and so forth, we could realize that we had really done something from a historical standpoint" (Owens, p. B1).

Custis died on 24 February 2005 at the age of eighty-nine, one day short of the sixty-third anniversary of his graduation as a fighter pilot. He and his wife Ione Custis had no children. He was buried with full military honors with a missing man flyover of USAF A-10 Warthogs. As the first black police officer in Connecticut's capital city and as a government Tax Examiner, Custis made community history; furthermore, he demonstrated the ability to excel at aerial training, and with his fellow Tuskegee Airmen, left an indelible mark on military and national history.

FURTHER READING

Death Record retrieved from Social Security Death Index, Number 577-12-0398; Issue State District of Columbia; Issue Date Before 1951.

Fifteenth Census of the United States (1930). Hartford, CT, Roll 263; Page 16.A; Enumeration District No. 34; Image 985.0.

Owens, David. *Hartford Courant,* 2 Mar. 2005.

U.S. World War II Army Enlistment Records, (1938–1946).

Obituary: *Hartford Courant,* 2 Mar. 2005.

J'VAUGHN JOSEPH
VINCE J. MACK

Cuthbert, Marion Vera (15 Mar. 1896–5 May 1989), educator, administrator, writer, and activist, was born in Saint Paul, Minnesota, the daughter of Thomas Cornelius Cuthbert and Victoria Means. She attended grammar and secondary school in her hometown and studied at the University of Minnesota before transferring to Boston University, where she completed her B.A. in 1920.

Following her graduation, Cuthbert moved to Florence, Alabama, and became an English teacher and assistant principal at Burrell Normal School. Promoted to principal in 1925, she began to lead students and faculty in bold new perspectives on gender equality and interracial harmony.

In 1927 Cuthbert left Burrell to become one of the first deans of Talladega College in Talladega, Alabama. In her essay "The Dean of Women at Work," published in the *Journal of the National Association of College Women* (Apr. 1928), she articulated her belief that covert sexism at the administrative level of black colleges limited their effectiveness. As dean, Cuthbert strengthened her academic credentials by completing a master's degree in psychology at Columbia University in 1931, after taking a sabbatical from Talladega during the 1930–1931 academic year to focus on her studies.

Following three years of administrative service, Cuthbert left Talladega College in 1932 to begin a twelve-year affiliation with the Young Women's Christian Association (YWCA) as one of the first African Americans hired in the leadership division of the national office in New York City. In this capacity she was responsible for staff development and education, particularly that of black employees. Among her early professional contributions was the creation of the YWCA Summer Training Institutes, which began at Oberlin College in 1938 as four-week training sessions designed to enhance the effectiveness of the YWCA and public agencies in general. She also traveled abroad to conduct similar workshops on interracial relations, volunteer education, student development, and administration. Cuthbert's influence as an executive at the YWCA's National Negro Leadership Conference held at West Virginia State College (20–23 June 1942) led to a motion to endorse a "national human relations conference, interracial in character, with common problems emphasized rather than differences." This endorsement reflected her commitment to interracial work and to the promotion of conferences that precluded separate black constituencies, an issue for many national organizations during that era.

Cuthbert completed her Ph.D. at Columbia University in 1942 and resumed her academic career in 1944 by joining Brooklyn College's Department of Personnel Services. Two years later she became the first black faculty member in the College's Department of Sociology and Anthropology. In addition to her academic work, Cuthbert retained her affiliation with the YWCA and rose to prominence in a wide range of national and international groups. She was a member of the board of directors and a vice president of the NAACP, and she served as a counselor for the United Board of Christian Colleges in China and as an adviser to several other local and national organizations, including the Federal Council of Churches and the United Council of Church Women. She held memberships in the American Association of University Women, the American Association of University Professors, Pi Lambda Theta, Alpha Kappa Theta, and the American Sociology Society. She was also a fellow of the National Council on Religion in Higher Education.

Cuthbert's written work, published throughout her career, reflects her commitment to education, interracial harmony, and the well-being of African Americans. She frequently published articles in the *Woman's Press*—the YWCA's official publication from 1918 to 1953—and the *YWCA Magazine*, and she collaborated on numerous pamphlets and conference proceedings. She also authored four books, including *Juliette Derricotte* (1933), a short biography of a black YWCA activist; *We Sing America* (1936), a children's book highlighting the achievements of African Americans; *April Grasses* (1936), a collection of poetry; and *Songs of Creation* (1949), a book of inspirational verse. Perhaps most significant among her published scholarly works was her doctoral dissertation, *Education and Marginality: A Study of the Negro Woman College Graduate* (1942), a work that affirms the reality of black women's oppression, especially in relation to that of black men and white women, and documents the effect of college education on their personal, social, and professional lives.

In 1961 Cuthbert retired from Brooklyn College as an associate professor and moved to Plainfield, New Hampshire, where she continued to use her gifts as an educator and administrator to serve the community. She spoke widely to various groups on social issues and literary concerns and remained active with the YWCA as an honorary national board member and a participant in international training projects. She held membership in the Plain-Meri Homemakers Group, the College Club of Windsor, and the Mothers and Daughters Club, and she attended the Plainfield Community Baptist Church. Additionally, she served as Plainfield Library trustee and incorporator of the Sullivan County Mental Health Association.

In 1968 she moved several times for health reasons between Concord, New Hampshire; Windsor, Vermont; and Claremont, New Hampshire, where she died. Her ashes were scattered from the top of Mount Ascutney in Vermont, symbolizing how much of the land and its people she had touched by her activism in the areas of education and race relations.

FURTHER READING

Cuthbert's personal papers, which include data on the YWCA Summer Training Institutes and YWCA annual reports (1932–1980), are located in the Spelman College Archives in Atlanta, Georgia.

Roses, Lorraine Elena, and Ruth Elizabeth Randolph. *Harlem Renaissance and Beyond* (1990).

Smith, Jessie Carney, ed. *Notable Black American Women* (1992).

This entry is taken from the *American National Biography* and is published here with the permission of the American Council of Learned Societies.

MARILYN BUTTON

Cuyjet, Marion Helene Durham (29 July 1920–22 Oct. 1996), dance educator and business owner, was born in Philadelphia, Pennsylvania, the youngest of three children of Alonzo Durham, a navy yard worker, and Frances Henrietta Morgan, a housewife. Cuyjet's parents hailed from a small community in Cheswold, Delaware, referred to as Delaware Moors. The family had moved to Philadelphia in the early 1900s in search of a better standard of living and educational opportunities for Cuyjet and her older brothers. Cuyjet attended Landreth Elementary School, Barratt Junior High School, and graduated from South Philadelphia High School.

The family settled in the Point Breeze section of South Philadelphia, an area densely populated by African Americans. Cuyjet grew up during the Great Migration, during which Philadelphia's black population increased rapidly. Between 1917 and 1930 thousands of blacks had left the south for the urban north in search of employment opportunities. The fusion of southern and northern cultures created a modern black Philadelphia with a rich tradition in the arts, literature, and sports.

The popular Alma Polk Kiddie Revue, a once-a-year event in black Philadelphia, served as Cuyjet's initial introduction to dance. The performers were children, rehearsals ran usually six weeks, and the shows were held at the local Elks Club. Between 1930–1932 Cuyjet performed in the revues, including a song and dance routine with then teenagers HAROLD and FAYARD NICHOLAS, who later became renowned tap dancers on the Broadway stage and in Hollywood musicals.

Her formal introduction to dance training began in 1934, when she was fourteen years old, with the dance education pioneer and socialite Essie Marie Dorsey. Dorsey's lavish recitals became popular events in black Philadelphia, usually running three consecutive nights. She joined her Sunday school friends at Dorsey's dance studio open house and was invited to enroll in the school on scholarship.

The emphasis at the Dorsey school was ballet, a first for black Philadelphia. The training was intense, and Dorsey was an exacting teacher. Sydney King was Dorsey's leading dancer when Cuyjet began her studies at the studio. She and Cuyjet became close friends and often coached each other between classes. They excelled in their dance studies and Dorsey promoted them to student-teacher status. They were responsible for teaching children's ballet classes at the school. Cuyjet was a diligent student and novice teacher but her technical proficiency was average. Dorsey, however, encouraged Cuyjet to become a teacher.

Cuyjet had discontinued her studies and teaching with Dorsey when she renewed her interest in dance. In 1944 she married Stephen Cuyjet, a postal worker, who supported her desire to open a dance studio. She began offering classes in her home in 1945, and in 1946 entered a brief partnership with childhood friend Sydney King. They operated the Sydney-Marion School of Dance for two years.

In 1948 Cuyjet began her solo teaching career and founded the Judimar School of Dance. The studio was a family affair with Cuyjet and her husband affectionately known as Miss Marion and Mr. Steve. Stephen Cuyjet served as its business manager, children Judy and Mark took classes and taught on occasion during their teen years, and Stephen Jr. assisted with facilities and recitals. Cuyjet's initial goal was to nurture the first black ballerina in the United States, but her vision expanded to include ballet, tap, Caribbean, and modern dance as a means to enhance social, educational, recreational, and cultural development.

Striving to become an advanced-level ballet teacher, Cuyjet began studying privately with the Philadelphia dance educator Thomas Cannon in 1948. Between 1950 to 1957 she and her advanced students traveled to New York City to study at the KATHERINE DUNHAM School of Theatre Arts, and the Ballet Arts dance studio at Carnegie Hall. Since Philadelphia dance studios were off limits to African Americans until the 1960s, many black dancers had relocated to New York City beginning in the mid-1940s. Cuyjet, herself, building up her school during the post–World War II era, when the struggle for equality for black American was beginning to gain momentum, groomed ballerinas at a time when black dancers were making small strides in the mainstream dance world. The success of African American dancers JANET COLLINS, CARMEN DE LAVALLADE, ALVIN AILEY, and Mary Hinkson inspired her work.

Cuyjet transformed herself into a "master teacher" (an official distinction) of ballet and the Judimar School emerged as a symbol of excellence and artistic integrity. Her ability to produce dancers who gained professional status and prominence bolstered her reputation. The school closed in 1971 but her legacy continued in the work of former students such as Judith Jamison (Alvin Ailey American Dance Theatre), Delores Browne Ableson

(New York Negro Ballet Company), Donna Lowe Warren (Philadelphia Grand Opera Company), China White (Dance Theatre of Harlem), John Jones (Harkness Ballet), Arthur Hall (Arthur Hall Afro-American Dance Ensemble), and Elmer Ball (Katherine Dunham Dance Company).

In the 1980s Cuyjet taught company ballet classes for the Philadelphia Dance Company (Philadanco) and its performing studio was renamed in her honor. The company founder and Cuyjet protégée Joan Myers Brown established the Marion D. Cuyjet Scholarship in 1997. Between 1986 and 1996 she was honored for her contributions to dance education by the Philadelphia Urban League, the Women's Way of Philadelphia, and the New York Public Library for the Performing Arts exhibit "Classic Black."

Known as a "gutsy" lady with a determined spirit, Cuyjet was revered as a visionary of dance education in black Philadelphia and remained active in the Philadelphia dance community until her death in 1996.

FURTHER READING

Ballard, Allen B. *One More Day's Journey* (1984).

Jamison, Judith. *Dancing Spirit: An Autobiography* (1993).

Maynard, Olga. *Judith Jamison: Aspects of a Dancer* (1982).

White Dixon, Melanye. "Black Women in Concert Dance: The Philadelphia Divas," in *Black Women in America*, ed. Kim Marie Vaz (1995).

Obituary: *Philadelphia Inquirer*, 26 Oct. 1996.

MELANYE WHITE DIXON

Da Costa, Mathieu (?–1607), interpreter, was probably born in the sixteenth century in the region of West Africa under Portuguese influence. What is known of his career comes from legal cases and documents carried out in the Dutch Republic and France from 1607 to 1619. Da Costa's African Portuguese origin can be surmised from his Portuguese name, and the fact that a community of interpreters, some of African descent and some of mixed African and Portuguese descent, had formed in West Africa in the fifteenth and sixteenth centuries. That Da Costa appeared to his European contemporaries as black can be shown from the use of the word *naigre* to refer to him. However, his particular point of origin is not certain, nor is the way in which Da Costa's skills as an interpreter transferred from the African coast to that of North America.

Da Costa first appears in the historical record in 1607, when a French colonial trader named Pierre Dugua de Monts complained in Amsterdam about the Dutch seizing some of his trading vessels near Tadoussac, and among other things enticing Da Costa from Dugua de Monts's service to the Dutch. The next year Da Costa signed a contract with Dugua de Monts, agreeing to serve as an interpreter on his voyages to Canada and Acadia. Da Costa's service was supposed to extend beyond a single voyage, an indication of the respect held for his skills as a trader and interpreter and strongly suggesting that Da Costa had built a record of competence on North American trade expeditions. The contract was meant to begin in January 1609 and last for three years at a handsome price of sixty crowns a year. However, the relationship between Da Costa

and Dugua de Monts was less than completely successful. In late 1609 Da Costa was in jail in the French town of Le Havre for "insolences." This is the last appearance of Da Costa himself in the historical record, although a legal case dragged out until 1619 between Dugua de Monts and a Rouen merchant, Nicholas de Bauquemare, over the responsibility for paying for getting Da Costa out of the clutches of the Dutch and paying his living expenses. The time and place of Da Costa's death are unknown.

The skills Da Costa possessed as an interpreter would have included extensive knowledge of languages. In addition to Portuguese and whatever African languages he knew, Da Costa would have had ability in French, Dutch, and the trading languages developed between North American Native communities and European traders. These "pidgins," like the pidgins used in communications between West Africans and European traders, were constructed from Native American and European vocabularies. The most common pidgins along the North Atlantic coast of Canada in the early seventeenth century blended the languages of the Native American Micmac and Montagnais with that of European Basques, who had a long history in the region as cod fishers and whalers.

Da Costa's story was forgotten for over three hundred years. He did not make his first appearance in a printed text until 1939, in William Inglis Morse's *Pierre de Gua, Sieur de Monts Records: Colonial and Saintongeois.* By the late twentieth century, however, the interpreter had become an iconic figure for African Canadians and Canadian multiculturalists. The Department of Canadian Heritage launched a "Mathieu da Costa Challenge" in 1996 as part of Canada's Black History Month. This was an essay competition that focused on Aboriginal, African, and other ethnocultural people and their contributions to Canadian society. In 2004 a bill to establish 1 February as "Mathieu da Costa Day" was introduced in the Canadian Parliament.

FURTHER READING

Morse, William Inglis. *Pierre du Gua, Sieur de Monts, Records: Colonial and Saintongeois* (1939).

WILLIAM E. BURNS

Dabney, Austin (c. 1760–1830), Revolutionary War veteran, was born a slave in Wake County, North Carolina. Not much is known about Dabney's life before the war. Several factors made both slavery and freedom for African Americans especially peculiar institutions in the environment of Revolutionary War–era Georgia, from which Dabney emerged. Slaves were initially prohibited when the colony was founded in 1733. Ethnic groups such as the Continental Protestants at Ebenezer, known as Salzburgers, and the Highland Scots at Darien supported this prohibition until Georgia's trustees, under extreme public pressure, finally allowed slavery in 1749. The Quakers at Wrightsborough never allowed slavery among their membership. The supporters of the American Revolution in Darien issued a declaration against slavery as late as 1775, although this effort was not continued after the war. The War of Independence created unusual circumstances for African Americans, both those who were free and those who were slaves. Georgia's state military had no qualms about enlisting free persons of color from outside the state. One such person, Nathan Fry, would draw a federal pension for his service first in the Georgia State Minutemen and later in the Georgia Continentals. He served under the Georgia general Lachlan McIntosh at Valley Forge and later at Yorktown. Another free black man, Joseph Scipio, was a private in the Fourth Georgia Continental Battalion. At least one of the Georgia Continentals killed at the Battle of Thomas Creek, Florida, in 1777 was black. Both slaves and freemen served on Georgia's continental galleys.

Efforts by the Continental Congress to encourage Georgia and South Carolina to enlist slaves as soldiers, however, came to nothing. Although no offer of freedom was made to slaves as an inducement to enlist, the state of Georgia would eventually grant freedom to a slave named Harry for picking up a musket during an Indian attack against Sherrill's Fort in 1773. Harry inspired the white defenders not to give up, and he shot one of the Indian leaders in the eye. Another slave, David Monday, was granted his freedom for his services as a drummer and lived in Savannah, Georgia, after the war, where he performed at city functions.

Opportunities for emancipation were hardly greater in the British camp. Blacks were reported among the followers of Loyalist partisans, but only in the last days of the Revolution did the British in Georgia create a special unit of African American loyalists, known as the King of England's Soldiers. They were left behind when the British evacuated Georgia in 1782. These black loyalists formed a colony in the swamps of Effingham County that was destroyed in 1787 after several battles with the Georgia militia. Similar colonies of escaped slaves would be broken up in the years that followed, including in 1816 the "Negro Fort" on the Apalachicola River. Some slaves, however, were emancipated from the British camps. The Tory leader Henry Sharp of Burke County emancipated his slave GEORGE LIELE on 12 August 1777. Liele founded the first black Baptist congregations, in Georgia if not everywhere, and would evacuate Georgia with the British army to take his ministry to Jamaica. Disciples of Liele made this movement even more international.

Austin Dabney was a true product of these times, although that fact has only been fully appreciated by modern scholars of the Revolutionary War. Dabney, who appears in the historical record as a "mulatto" belonging to Richard Aycock, was wounded and permanently disabled while fighting under the patriots Captain Barber and Colonel Elijah Clarke in Augusta, Georgia, on 25 May 1782. With Clarke's support, the state of Georgia purchased Dabney and emancipated him. The state also granted him land in 1784 and 1821 as well as a state pension. The U.S. government later took over the disability pension. Dabney attached himself to Giles Harris and later to Giles's son William in Wilkes, Elbert, Oglethorpe, and Madison counties. He supported himself as a small farmer, slave owner, racehorse owner, and businessman before his death in September 1830 in Pike County.

The story of Austin Dabney became notable, however, not because of his success as a freedman decades before the Civil War but because of attitudes in the antebellum era. For many years, Dabney's life was presented erroneously by former Georgia governor George Rockingham Gilmer, who filled his memoirs with often unreliable tales and gossip he had heard during his long public career. In Gilmer's version of Dabney's life, first given in 1851, Dabney received his wounds at the legendary Revolutionary War battle of Kettle Creek on 14 February 1779. Also, in Gilmer's 1850s parables, Dabney appears as a subservient member of the household and a model for a patriotic, humble, grateful inferior who recognizes the obvious superiority of his white hosts. (Dabney, however, actually supported the Harris family as least as much as they patronized him and even Gilmer mentioned Dabney's financing William Harris's training as an attorney.) The former governor did write that Dabney became such a popular figure that he had a respectful fellowship with such legendary Georgia white leaders as Governor James Jackson and Judge John Mitchell Dooly, but unlike many of the white heroic figures made public in Gilmer's book, Austin Dabney never had a town or county named for him. However, Gilmer's patronizing version of the white ideal of a loyal black man who still knew his "place" in the South's slave society would be repeated in numerous works of Georgia history unchallenged until the serious documentary research by Kenneth H. Thomas Jr. in the 1970s revealed a credible historical Austin Dabney.

FURTHER READING

The story of Austin Dabney as person and legend must be pieced together from the Wilkes County court and deed records used in conjunction with the following publications.

Austin Dabney File, File II Names, Georgia Division of Archives and History.

Final Revolutionary War Pension Payment Vouchers: Georgia (National Archives microfilm M1746, roll 2).

Gilmer, George R. *Georgians: Sketches of Some of the First Settlers of Upper Georgia, of the Cherokees, and the Author* (1855).

Mitchell, Lizzie R. *History of Pike County, Georgia* (1932).

Thomas, Kenneth H., Jr. "Georgia Family Lines: Harris," *Georgia Life Magazine* 2 (Winter 1975–1976).

ROBERT SCOTT DAVIS

Dabney, Ford (15 Mar. 1883–21 June 1958), songwriter and bandleader, was born Ford Thompson Dabney in Washington, D.C., to a musical family. Both his father and an uncle, the renowned WENDELL PHILLIPS DABNEY, were professional musicians. Dabney studied first with his father, then with

Charles Donch, William Waldecker, and Samuel Fabian. In 1904 he traveled to Haiti where he was retained as court pianist to President Noro Alexis, remaining in that post until 1907. On his return to the United States he resettled in Washington where he became the proprietor of a vaudeville and motion picture theater. He also organized touring companies, including Ford Dabney's Ginger Girls, which toured in African American vaudeville. Two members of this troupe, Lottie Gee and Effie King, became well-known entertainers in their own right.

The precise beginnings of Dabney's work as a composer are difficult to pin down with any precision. His catalog of original works is small, and he generally worked as half of a team with another composer. Dabney co-wrote "That Minor Strain" in 1910 with CECIL MACK. His other works included "Oh You Devil" and "Porto Rico" (both instrumentals). However, his major composition during these years was "(That's Why They Call Me) Shine" (1910, with lyrics by Cecil Mack and Lew Brown), a remarkable comic song that became a standard. Among the many fine performances of the song in later years was one by the vaudevillian JOHN BUBBLES (real name John Sublett) in the film *Cabin in the Sky*.

Dabney's original material is probably what first brought him to the attention of JAMES REESE EUROPE, and he was featured in Clef Club concerts from the outset of that illustrious organization's history in 1910. In 1913 Dabney moved permanently to New York City, where he soon became associated with the Tempo Club, the rival to the Clef Club. In this venture Dabney worked very closely with Europe, who had resigned from the Clef Club in a schism at the end of 1913. Together Europe and Dabney soon dominated dance music in New York through their close association with Vernon and Irene Castle, who revolutionized social dance in New York, the United States at large, and even London and Paris. Europe and Dabney wrote much of their dance repertoire, at least eight numbers of which were published. These included "The Castle Walk," "Castle Maxixe," "Castle Perfect Trot," "Castles' Half and Half," "The Castle Combination," "Castle Innovation Tango," "Castle Lame Duck Waltz," and "Enticement: An Argentine Idyll." As a joke, and to provide a bit of variety, the sheet music for this last number named the composers as "Eporue and Yenbad." All of these pieces appeared in the spring of 1914, published by the New York firm of Joseph Stern. Dabney, Europe, and the Castles were now at the very pinnacle of the entertainment world.

World War I broke up this highly productive aggregation. Vernon Castle enlisted in order to aid his British homeland in the war effort and was killed on a training flight in 1917. Europe led a highly acclaimed military band in France and returned to America in triumph in 1919, but he was murdered shortly thereafter. Dabney played a featured role among the musicians in Europe's funeral procession. During the Tempo Club years he had found a niche as a bandleader in Times Square. He organized a dance band to play the "midnight frolics" at the roof garden of Florenz Ziegfeld's New Amsterdam Theater, a job he held for eight years, ending only in the 1920s. The personnel of this band was highly stable, and it included some of the finest talent of the period in which ragtime gradually gave way to the new strains of jazz. Among these performers were the renowned cornetist "Cricket" Smith and a number of the other musicians featured in the bands of James Reese Europe. For several summers this ensemble played at the Palais Royale in Atlantic City during the hot summer months.

Ford Dabney recorded all of his known sides from 1917 to 1922, most of them for the Aeolion Vocalion label. In addition to the dance band recordings (in a prejazz ragtime style) Dabney recorded a number of sides with a standard military band, and with that aggregation his work was further still from the incipient jazz ideal. However, there are interesting modern touches in the dance band recordings, which feature some of the leading African American soloists of the World War I era, such as the cornetist Smith. The best of these players were veterans of Dabney's long-term residency as the New Amsterdam Theater roof garden. Apart from Smith and Dabney himself (on piano), the capable personnel included Allie Ross, an important Harlem player in both classical and popular music for several decades, on violin. Dabney claimed in an interview some years later that the band personnel consisted of cornet, trombone, clarinet, saxophone, piano, bass (doubling tuba), and drums. However, on listening to these recordings it is evident that there are additional brass players on many tracks and also one or more flutes (doubling piccolo), multiple violins, banjo(s), and possibly sometimes mandolin.

The repertoire on the Dabney recordings closely follows the records of his better-known contemporaries, such as James Reese Europe and the white vaudeville bands of the period. Pieces like SHELTON BROOKS's "Darktown Strutters' Ball" are featured. Among the medleys is "How You Gonna Keep 'Em Down on the Farm" (also recorded by Europe), in which the title tune is merely the opening and closing strain on a recording that diverges in the middle to include a diverse range of alternate material including "My Bonnie Lies over the Ocean." This mix-and-match format was facilitated by Vocalion's innovative "close groove" technology for cutting 78-rpm records, which made for longer playing time.

In the latter part of his career, after 1923, Dabney was less active as a composer than as a performer and entrepreneur. He ran an entertainment bureau, booking the acts of other performers, and also continued to perform himself, usually in resorts beyond the confines of New York City: Newport, Rhode Island, in summer, and Palm Beach and Miami, Florida, in winter. In 1927 the F. E. Miller and Aubrey Lyles show *Rang Tang* featured a number of songs by Dabney (music) and Jo Trent (words). In addition to the title song, these included "Brown," "Harlem," "Jungle Rose," "Monkey Land," "Sambo's Banjo," "Sammy and Topsy," "Summer Nights," and "Zulu Fifth Avenue." None of these songs became standards of the jazz age. However, Ford Dabney had played a crucial role in African American music in the first two decades of the twentieth century, as both a composer and a bandleader. He was a resident of Harlem at the time of his death in 1958 at the age of seventy-five.

FURTHER READING

ASCAP Biographical Dictionary of Composers, Authors, and Publishers (1952).

Badger, Reid. *A Life in Ragtime* (1995).

Brooks, Tim. *Lost Sounds: Blacks and the Birth of the Recording Industry, 1890–1919* (2004).

Obituary: *New York Times*, 23 June 1958.

ELLIOTT S. HURWITT

Dabney, Wendell Phillips (4 Nov. 1865–5 June 1952), composer, journalist, musician, political activist, and publisher, was born in Richmond, Virginia, the son of John Dabney and Elizabeth Foster, both former slaves. John Dabney later became a caterer. Young Wendell completed his elementary and middle school education in Richmond and became influenced by the religious beliefs and political views of his father. John Dabney, who taught himself to read and write at a young age, instilled in his children the ability to use Christianity to combat the harsh effects of racism. He also embedded in his sons the belief that only the Republican Party would support African Americans. As a teenager, during the school year, Dabney spent most afternoons selling newspapers, while his evenings consisted of homework and playing the guitar with his older brother. In the summer months Dabney waited tables at a local restaurant, where he learned to disdain whites for their belief in the inferiority of African Americans.

During his senior year at Richmond High School, Dabney led a student protest against the school's administration when it was discovered that the graduation ceremony for its African American students would be held at local church, instead of at the school's theater where the white graduation exercise would take place. In the end, after several days of open demonstrations, the school relented and agreed to allow the African American senior class to graduate at the local high school. In 1883 Dabney entered the Preparatory Department at Oberlin College in Ohio. At Oberlin he became a first violinist at the Oberlin Opera House and a member of the Cademian Literary Society. These accomplishments, along with his earlier success as a political organizer back at Richmond High School, increased his self-confidence. More importantly, Dabney began to believe that regardless of the negative views and attitudes of white Americans, if given equal opportunities, African Americans could become successful citizens. In 1884, at the age of twenty, Dabney finished his freshman year at Oberlin, returned home to Richmond, and again acquired a job as a waiter. However, within several months he quit and obtained a teaching position at a local elementary school in Louisa County, Virginia. At the same time, he taught several guitar classes. Six years later Dabney left the region to open a school in Boston for both amateur and professional musicians. Then in 1894 he moved to Cincinnati, Ohio, to manage the Dumas Hotel, a facility his mother had inherited from her aunt, Serena Webb. Built during the early 1840s the Dumas was at one time Ohio's only black-owned hotel and before the Civil War had been a stop on the Underground Railroad. To generate more money for the hotel Dabney converted one part of the building into a gymnasium, while another section was used as a banquet and meeting hall.

Dabney decided to make Cincinnati his permanent home and in August 1897 he married Nellie Foster Jackson. Though their only son died in 1898, Dabney adopted Jackson's two sons from a previous relationship. In need of more income to support his new family, he began offering private music lessons to various family members of Cincinnati's white elites. He also wrote and sold several songs to the George Jaberg and Wurlitzer music companies. However, his passion for politics slowly brought his musical career to an end. In 1895 Dabney became the city's first African American license clerk. From 1898 to 1923 he served as the assistant and eventually head paymaster of the Cincinnati Department of Treasury. He also established a local political organization, named in honor of FREDERICK DOUGLASS, to help improve race relations and expand the educational opportunities for Cincinnati blacks. In 1915 Dabney became the first president of the Cincinnati NAACP chapter. Under his leadership the local NAACP branch organized several demonstrations and fought against the continued use of segregated housing throughout the city.

Dabney also published a variety of books and articles on the experiences of African Americans in Cincinnati. In general, these works proclaimed that despite numerous obstacles and against seemingly impossible odds, black Cincinnatians developed a vibrant and relatively unified community. His most influential book was *Cincinnati Colored Citizens* (1926), but he also authored several other studies on the broader topics of race relations, discrimination, segregation, and urbanization, such as *The Wolf and the Lamb* (1923), *Maggie L. Walker: The Woman and Her Work* (1927), *Chisum's Pilgrimage and Others* (1927), and "Slave Risings and Race Riots," that appeared in *A Negro Anthology* (1934). Dabney is best remembered, however, for starting the daily newspaper, the *Union*. Established on 13 February 1907 the newspaper had as its motto "No people can become great without being united, for in union there is strength." Until its final editions in 1952 the *Union* published many articles, editorials, and essays on the condition of black Cincinnatians, covering society, education, and politics.

On 4 November 1949, on Dabney's eighty-fourth birthday, more than 400 people attended a surprise birthday celebration to honor one of the city's leading black citizens. The next year, the National Convention of Negro Publishers honored him for his many decades of excellence in journalism. Two years later Wendell Phillips Dabney passed away at the age of eighty-seven.

FURTHER READING

The few surviving Dabney papers and several issues of the *Union* are housed at the Cincinnati Historical Society.

Dabney, Wendell Phillips. *Cincinnati's Colored Citizens* (1926).

Beaver, Joseph T. *I Want You to Know Wendell Phillips Dabney* (1958).

Berry, Gail Estelle. *Wendell Phillips Dabney: Leader of the Negro Protest*. M.A. thesis, University of Cincinnati (1965).

Horstman, Barry M. *100 Who Made a Difference: Greater Cincinnatians Who Made a Mark on the 20th Century* (1999).

Obituary: *Cincinnati Post*, 5 June 1952.

ERIC R. JACKSON

Daddy Grace. *See* Grace, Charles Emmanuel.

Dafora, Asadata (4 Aug. 1890–4 Mar. 1965), singer, dancer, and choreographer, was born John Warner Dafora Horton in Freetown, Sierra Leone. Little is known of his parents, but both were part of the prominent black elite in colonial society. Dafora's great-great-grandfather was the first black man to be knighted by Queen Victoria and the first black mayor of Sierra Leone. Dafora's parents, moreover, met in England, while his father was studying at Oxford and his mother studying the piano. Dafora received a British education at the local Wesleyan School in Freetown and went on to study music and dance in Italy and Germany.

Dafora's career took off after he moved to New York City in 1929, traveling with a troupe of African dancers. His first years in New York were rather unremarkable, however, and there is little evidence of Dafora's influence on the theatrical scene during this period. But that soon changed with Dafora's production of *Kykunkor* (Witch Woman) in 1934, the theatrical event of the season. The show had languished until it received critical notice in the *New York Times* from John Martin, the dance critic, on 9 May 1934. After Martin's glowing account, 425 people appeared at the theater that evening, 200 of whom had to be turned away. The large crowds continued, forcing the show to move to a bigger theater at City College and eventually reopen in other venues around town as the show sold out from May to August, almost all of its unplanned run.

Kykunkor told the story of a wedding ritual in West Africa in which a jealous rival of the groom employs Kykunkor to cast a death spell on the groom, who is eventually saved by a witch doctor. Full of drama and celebration, the conventional story of love and jealousy gained its allure from witches, spells, and elaborate ceremonies. The story also served as a showpiece for vibrant group dances and pantomime solos, all accompanied by vigorous drumming and singing. Eighteen men and women, some African, some African American, in colorful costumes, dancing to live music, created quite a visual feast.

Many audience members viewed the production as a concert direct from the jungle. Leading artists and intellectuals of the time, including George Gershwin, Sherwood Anderson, Theodore Dreiser, and Carl Van Vechten, populated the audience, seeking an authentic experience of "primitive" Africa. The souvenir program following the production went so far as to claim that *Kykunkor* impressed even scientists and explorers as a rare, truthful vision of Africa. James Chapin, curator of the American Museum of Natural History, declared, "Never outside of Africa have I ever seen or heard anything so typically Ethiopian. ... The drum rhythms and most of the singing rang so true as to carry me back to the dark continent."

Leading African Americans also praised the authenticity of *Kykunkor*. Premiering during the final years of the Harlem Renaissance, the production received the praise of the stringent critic ALAIN LOCKE. An influential promoter of the Harlem Renaissance, Locke saw in Dafora's *Kykunkor* true African art transplanted to America. He extolled its stylistic purity and its artistry, devoid of the baseness and vulgarity that he often criticized in the cultural forms of African Americans. According to Locke, this was "primitive" art at its best, undiluted and inspirational.

Much of the stamp of authenticity came from the prominence of African dancing in the production. Vastly different from the linear and tightly held backbones of ballet and even modern dance at this time, African dance featured flat-footed stomping, isolated actions of the hips, torso, and shoulders in rhythmic patterns, and bodies bent forward from the waist on deeply bowed legs with protruding buttocks. Since many observers considered the barefoot dancing and pounding drums to be innately racial, *Kykunkor* in some sense reinforced common stereotypes of dark-skinned peoples as being close to nature, animals, and the basic functions of living, including sex.

Dafora worked within these conceptions and excelled partly because of them. *Kykunkor* established him as the prime exponent of authentic African dance. He went on to work on the Negro Theatre Unit of the Works Progress Administration's Federal Theatre Project, choreographing Orson Welles's direction of a Haitian version of *Macbeth* in 1936. He then left the Federal Theatre Project to work on his next production, *Zunguru* (1938). *Zunguru* was similar to *Kykunkor* in its use of African ritual, music, and dance, but it never achieved the success of its predecessor. In 1939 Dafora choreographed dances for PAUL ROBESON's revival of *Emperor Jones*.

Much of Dafora's reputation rested on the spectacular success of *Kykunkor*, and he was never able to re-create that achievement on stage. In the early 1940s, however, he became a noted spokesperson for the African Academy of Arts and Research, founded in 1943. The academy's purpose was to foster interest in and support of African culture, and Dafora was one of its stars. He and his troupe played a prominent role in the successful African festivals sponsored by the academy beginning in 1943. The first two festivals, in 1943 and 1945, even attracted the attendance of the First Lady Eleanor Roosevelt, who was eager to show her support of cultural events promoting racial understanding.

Dafora went on tour around the United States with his troupe in 1946–1947. Appearing at all the leading African American colleges, he carried through with his lifelong attempt to promote African culture. He had less and less opportunity to do so as he grew older, facing competition from younger dancers and choreographers such as PEARL PRIMUS and KATHERINE DUNHAM, who creatively combined African and Caribbean rituals with American theatrics. Dafora's African "authenticity" eventually led him to make an appearance at the Great Apes House at the New York Zoological Society in June 1949, an outward indication that his trademark authenticity had become a kind of cage, restricting his creativity and narrowly marking his talents.

In 1947 Dafora created *Batanga*, another dance-drama in the tradition of *Kykunkor*, but it received little praise. He languished in the 1950s, retreating from public view. Fed up with the United States, he went back to Sierra Leone in May 1960, returning only briefly to the United States in 1962 for health reasons. The following year he returned again to Sierra Leone. He died in Harlem, New York.

FURTHER READING

Dafora's papers are at the New York Public Library's Schomburg Center for Research in Black Culture.

Emery, Lynne Fauley. *Black Dance from 1619 to Today*, rev. ed. (1988).

Long, Richard. *The Black Tradition in American Dance* (1989).

Thorpe, Edward. *Black Dance* (1989).

This entry is taken from the *American National Biography* and is published here with the permission of the American Council of Learned Societies.

JULIA L. FOULKES

Dahmer, Vernon Ferdinand (10 Mar. 1908–10 Jan. 1966), civil rights activist, was born in Hattiesburg, Mississippi, the eighth of twelve children of a white father, George Dahmer, and a mother of mixed racial heritage, Ellen Kelly. Vernon Dahmer's complex heritage derived from both sides of the family. Born the illegitimate son of a German immigrant and a white American mother, George Dahmer had been raised with eight younger black siblings, the result of his mother's later marriage to a former slave. Ellen Kelly was the daughter of a white planter father, who gave Ellen and George Dahmer part of his land near Hattiesburg, Kelly Settlement. The Dahmer children looked white and three of Vernon's five brothers migrated to the North, where they married white women and passed as white. Some members of the family on both sides of the color divide were ignorant of the existence of relatives on the other. In adulthood, Vernon Dahmer had to navigate these difficult circumstances, facilitating contacts among the knowing without alerting the unknowing, and sometimes allowing ties gradually to wither.

His skills as a farmer, as well as the migration of three brothers out of the region, helped Dahmer inherit Kelly Settlement. Dahmer's first marriage produced three sons who, like their father, looked white. His second marriage brought another three sons, who were dark in complexion. In 1952 Dahmer married a third time to Ellie Jewell Davis, with whom he had two dark-skinned children. When Dahmer travelled with his eldest children, the family could pass as white. But when he did so with other family members, he could obtain service from white establishments only by leaving his family outside. Occasionally, when they encountered the Dahmers, unfamiliar whites assumed that Vernon Dahmer had servants with him and made racist comments to him about his family.

Dahmer became a successful commercial farmer and businessman with a sawmill and a grocery store. The Dahmers' relative wealth and deportment seemed to have earned them acceptance from many local whites, although Vernon Dahmer's success produced bitterness among others.

Dahmer joined the Forrest County branch of the NAACP on 9 October 1946, one month after its charter by the national NAACP. He became president of the county NAACP in 1956, served two terms, and recruited his neighbor Clyde Kennard to head the branch's Youth Council.

In 1958 Kennard applied for admission to the all-white University of Southern Mississippi in Hattiesburg. After meeting with William D. McCain, the university's president, and Zack Van Landingham of the Mississippi State Sovereignty Commission about his application in September 1959, Kennard was arrested for reckless driving and liquor possession. With NAACP support, Kennard beat the charge, only to be framed in 1960 for stealing chicken feed. While Kennard began a seven-year sentence and developed terminal cancer, Dahmer assisted with Kennard's chicken farm and worked for his release, which came in 1963.

In tribute to Kennard, Dahmer proposed that his church, Shady Grove Baptist, built on land donated by Dahmer, host a voter registration meeting. Since he had taken office in 1959, the county registrar, Theron Lynd, had refused to register black voter applicants and thereby kept black voter registration in double figures. Dahmer helped identify witnesses for a U.S. Justice Department suit against Lynd. Although Dahmer made a powerful appeal to his church, its pastor argued that the church should abstain from politics and prevailed on the congregation to expel Dahmer, his supporters, and their families.

At a meeting of NAACP branch presidents in spring 1962, Dahmer agreed to house Hollis Watkins and Curtis Hayes, two activists with the Student Nonviolent Coordinating Committee (SNCC), while they undertook a voter registration effort. During the campaign, Dahmer and his sons responded to a threatening nighttime phone call by rushing outside and firing warning shots. Although because of Lynd's defiance of federal court rulings SNCC's nine-month effort added only seven blacks to the voting rolls, it did succeed in widening local black participation in the civil rights movement, extending it beyond the local NAACP branch, which had initially opposed the registration effort, much to Dahmer's frustration.

In 1963 Dahmer allowed his grocery store to act as a polling place in a statewide mock election that sought to demonstrate black aspirations for political inclusion. Dahmer did not join civil rights demonstrations, but when civil rights groups began a major voter registration campaign in Hattiesburg in 1964 he fed and housed visiting white clergy participants. Dahmer worked closely with the National Council of Churches' Delta Ministry, which operated a project in Hattiesburg as part of its effort to aid Mississippi's civil rights movement. The Delta Ministry's local office occupied part of Dahmer's property in the city, and he allowed the ministry to operate a clothing distribution center from his farmland. Dahmer's activities brought the cancellation of all of his insurance.

Following the passage of the Voting Rights Act of 1965, Dahmer registered to vote. However, Mississippi registrants were still required to pay a poll tax, pending a federal constitutional amendment that would soon outlaw the practice. In January 1966 Dahmer announced on local radio that he would collect the poll tax for registrants at his store and pay it for those who could not afford to.

At 2 A.M. on 10 January, Ku Klux Klansmen burned Dahmer's store, fired into his house, and set it ablaze. Emerging from the back room where he and his family had been sleeping, Dahmer shot back to enable his family to escape before joining them. He died in hospital from burns later that afternoon.

In 1968 state charges resulted in the murder convictions of three men and hung juries for two others, including the Klan leader Sam Bowers, and one arson conviction. A year later a federal jury convicted one man but freed ten others accused of voting rights violations. In August 1998 new evidence at last brought Bowers's conviction and life sentence for murder. Ellie Dahmer, who had pressed for the case to be reopened, and her daughter testified at the trial. The Dahmer family were present in court for the reading of the verdict.

FURTHER READING

Branch, Taylor. *Pillar of Fire: America in the King Years, 1963–65* (1998).

Dittmer, John. *Local People: The Struggle for Civil Rights in Mississippi* (1994).

Newman, Mark. *Divine Agitators: The Delta Ministry and Civil Rights in Mississippi* (2004).

MARK NEWMAN

Dailey, London (c. 1748–8 June 1832), Revolutionary War soldier and civic leader, is a man about whom few early personal details are known. Probably a former slave he was a free man and resident of New Hampshire when he joined the Continental army in July 1779 from the town of Gilmanton.

Dailey's service in the Revolutionary War mirrored that of many other blacks in New England, both slaves and free men, including such soldiers as

Lambert Latham, OLIVER CROMWELL (1752–1853), and his fellow New Hampshire resident PRINCE WHIPPLE. Whether or not Dailey was a free man before he joined the army is an open question. He may have already been a free man, or he could have used the bounty money he received for enlisting to purchase his own freedom, a method by which many slaves throughout New England gained their freedom during the war.

Once he joined the Continental army, London Dailey served alongside his fellow soldiers without any formal racial distinction, a relatively common occurrence in those times. He wore the same uniform, slept in the same tent or barracks, ate the same food, performed the same duties, and was paid the same pay as his white counterparts. New England was well known for its employment of black troops to fill their regiments, much to the dismay and distaste of the southern colonies. Even General George Washington, the leader of the Continental army, was uncertain as to the employment of blacks as soldiers in the first year of the war. However, the need for troops to fill New England's quota of regiments would soon take precedence, allowing men like Dailey to join the army. New Hampshire, despite laws to the contrary that forbade blacks from serving, suffered no political repercussions from the use of black troops, unlike other New England states.

By the time London Dailey joined the renowned Second New Hampshire Regiment it had seen more than its share of fighting and was now stationed at West Point, New York. This is where Dailey spent most of his service, and he did not take part in any major battles. While Dailey was on furlough from the army in 1781 he returned to New Hampshire, marrying his first wife, Margaret, on 11 March 1781 in Exeter, the state's Revolutionary War capital. London and Margaret would have a sizable family, including four boys, before her death sometime around 1819.

London Dailey continued his service as a soldier for New Hampshire until his discharge on 7 June 1783. He had served for four years, and was recognized for his duty when he was presented with the Badge of Merit. Dailey's discharge certificate, which attested to his faithful service, was signed personally by General Washington. Whatever initial qualms the general may have had about using black troops, the service of men like Dailey surely proved their worth.

After the war Dailey returned to New Hampshire to live in Exeter. Here he and Margaret became fixtures in both black society and white society. The Dailey home was described in an 1879 edition of the *Exeter News-Letter* as "quite a comfortable cottage" and its interior "a pattern of neatness." Margaret Dailey was well known for the fine cake and ale she served to the students of Phillips Academy, while London was known as a skilled gardener. Exeter also had one of New Hampshire's largest black populations and London was one of its leaders. However, the Daileys did not always enjoy financial security; London was sued by his fellow black veteran Prince Light in 1811 for failing to pay for goods he had taken from him, including thirty pounds of feathers and four loads of manure that he either used on his own fields or in his gardening work for others. Later in life, in October 1820, London Dailey was arrested and imprisoned for a debt he could not repay to a fellow citizen who was white.

Dailey no doubt symbolized the sad plight of the free black man, if not in all of New England, then certainly in New Hampshire, where the economic times after the Revolutionary War were difficult and some free blacks were forced to become indentured servants or to return to work for their former masters. Free blacks, moreover, were seldom viewed by most towns as desirable citizens, and were often treated as vagrants—whatever their character or means—and warned to depart. In 1817, perhaps spurred on by his own experiences, Dailey decided that it was time for "The people of *colour* throughout the state" to form a society "beneficial to said people" (*Exeter Watchman*, 22 July 1817). He called for a meeting to be held at his home in Exeter on 13 August 1817 with the intent of forming such an organization. Following the meeting, it was noted that "an Oration will be pronounced" (*Exeter Watchman*, 22 July 1817). Dailey was the lead organizer and likely orator of this event, while Rufus Cutler, the son of the black veteran Tobias Cutler, was his secretary.

Not long after Dailey proposed his statewide organization, his wife Margaret died. London married a second time, this time to Nancy Barhew, in 1820. Together they would have at least one child. Dailey soon moved from Exeter to nearby Deerfield and subsequently to Epsom, New Hampshire, where he would live for the remainder of his life.

Though we know little about Dailey's organization and its subsequent history, his activities clearly demonstrate that he was a man with a vision of the future. Perhaps emboldened by his dedicated service during the Revolutionary War, he eagerly sought to extend the ideals of freedom and equality to members of his own race. London Dailey's statewide organization, the first of its kind for African Americans in New Hampshire, was an early and noteworthy addition to the growing ranks of black rights and anti-slavery societies that would become increasingly common throughout the century.

FURTHER READING

Kaplan, Sidney, and Emma Nogrady Kaplan. *The Black Presence in the Era of the American Revolution* (1989).

Knoblock, Glenn A. *Strong and Brave Fellows: New Hampshire's Black Soldiers and Sailors of the American Revolution, 1775–1784* (2003).

Quarles, Benjamin. *The Negro in the American Revolution* (1961).

GLENN ALLEN KNOBLOCK

Dailey, Ulysses Grant (3 Aug. 1885–22 Apr. 1961), surgeon, was born in Donaldsonville, Louisiana, the son of Tony Hanna Dailey, a bartender, and Missouri Johnson, a teacher. His parents were then living in Fort Worth, Texas; Mrs. Dailey had returned to her mother's home to give birth. The Daileys visited Chicago, Illinois, several times, and Grant (as he preferred to be called) had some of his early schooling there. He was also educated in Donaldsonville, in the preparatory academy at Straight College (later Dillard University) in New Orleans, and at the Fort Worth High School. Brought up by his mother (the couple separated after a few years) in an atmosphere of books and music, Grant became a piano player.

As a student in Fort Worth, Dailey became the office assistant for Ernest L. Stephens, a white physician and professor of materia medica in the medical department of Fort Worth University. Impressed by Dailey's seriousness, Stephens encouraged the young man to read widely. When a typhoid epidemic struck the city, Stephens dispatched Dailey to visit his homebound patients to take temperatures and perform similar tasks. As his experience in medicine deepened, Dailey decided to pursue this profession rather than music.

Dailey was accepted by the Northwestern University Medical School after several conversations with the dean and enrolled there in the fall of 1902. Despite being the youngest of the 150 students in his class and having to work to pay his way, he did well. The director of the anatomical laboratory hired him as an assistant and instructor for two years. Dailey received an M.D. in June 1906.

Dailey was then denied the opportunity, on the basis of his race, to spend two weeks at Mercy Hospital in Chicago to do obstetrics in the charity ward. Allen Kanavel, professor of clinical surgery at Northwestern University Medical School, wanted to take Dailey on as an assistant but could not do so for the same reason. In 1907 Provident Hospital, a black-run Chicago hospital, appointed Dailey gynecologist to its dispensary. In 1910 he became an associate surgeon, and from 1912 to 1926 he held the title of attending surgeon.

The major turning point in Dailey's medical career came in 1908 when Dr. DANIEL HALE WILLIAMS of Provident Hospital invited Dailey to be his surgical assistant. Remaining in this capacity until 1912, Dailey learned much in the way of surgical technique. From 1916 to 1918 he also served as an instructor in clinical surgery at Northwestern, and from 1920 to 1926 he was an attending surgeon at Fort Dearborn Hospital. In 1912 and 1925 Dailey took two trips of several months each to Europe for postgraduate studies on surgical subjects.

In February 1916 Dailey married Eleanor Curtis, sister of Dr. AUSTIN M. CURTIS of Washington, D.C. Shortly after, Dailey suffered a nearly fatal attack of tuberculosis and was ill for several months. The couple adopted five-year-old twins in 1924.

In 1926 Dailey purchased two large houses at Michigan Boulevard and Thirty-Seventh Street and had them remodeled into the Dailey Hospital and Sanitarium, free from racial restrictions. Unhappily, one of his patients there was Williams, to whom Dailey had to deliver a terminal diagnosis. The economic Depression forced Dailey to close this institution in 1932. During its existence the hospital provided affiliations for young black specialists and good care for black patients.

From Williams, Dailey had learned the importance of surgical clinics and educational lectures for black surgeons in the South. He frequently organized and took part in such endeavors at Meharry Medical College in Nashville, Tennessee, the John A. Andrew Clinical Society in Tuskegee, Alabama, and in other locations throughout the South as well as in Washington, D.C., and New York.

In 1945 the American College of Surgeons elected Dailey a member (along with three other black surgeons). The only previous African American members had been Dailey's mentor, Williams, a charter member in 1913, and LOUIS TOMPKINS WRIGHT in 1943.

Dailey joined the National Medical Association (the black counterpart of the American Medical Association) in 1908 and remained a member for fifty-three years. Active at the annual meetings as a speaker and discussant, Dailey served as chairman of the Surgical Section in 1914 and gave the Oration in Surgery in 1940. In 1928 he began a four-year stint as chairman of the National Program Committee, and in 1932 he presented one of the association's first scientific exhibits, on sixty operations for goiter. As president of the association in 1915–1916, Dailey was the youngest president up to that time and the first from Chicago. However, his primary activity was with the *Journal of the National Medical Association*, on which he served as a member of the editorial board (1910–1943), associate editor (1943–1948), and editor (1948–1950). In 1950 he was named consulting editor. He also wrote several columns for the journal in which he alternated reviews of the literature with reports of his own work. The association honored him with its Distinguished Service Award in 1949.

In 1935 Dailey became a charter member of the International College of Surgeons. He served on the board of trustees, the editorial board, and as associate editor for the *Journal of the National Medical Association*. His major efforts for the college consisted of several extended trips to Pakistan, India, Japan, and other countries, during which he gave frequent surgical lectures and clinics and promoted local efforts for undergraduate and graduate medical education. A high point of his travels was a five-day visit with Albert Schweitzer in 1953 at Schweitzer's Forest Hospital in Lambaréné, Gabon.

Dailey's major surgical interests were the treatment of peptic ulcer (for which he initiated the technique of phrenic nerve crush in 1950) and the treatment of the thyroid. He spoke and wrote often on these and other topics both in the United States and abroad, and some sixty of his articles were published.

In 1952 Dailey retired from his position as chief of the surgical staff at Provident Hospital, and four years later he retired from active practice. He and his wife had purchased a house near Port-au-Prince in Haiti, a country they had often visited and enjoyed and for which he had served as honorary consul in Chicago for several years. However, after a few months on the island worsening health forced Dailey to sell his home and return to Chicago, where he died.

FURTHER READING

Beatty, William K. "Ulysses Grant Dailey: Surgeon, Teacher, and Ambassador," *Proceedings of the Institute of Medicine of Chicago* 38 (1982).

Preston, Donald. *The Scholar and the Scalpel* (1966).

Obituaries: *Chicago Daily Defender*, 24 Apr. 1961; *Chicago Tribune, Chicago Sun Times, Chicago American*, and *New York Times*, 23 Apr. 1961.
This entry is taken from the *American National Biography* and is published here with the permission of the American Council of Learned Societies.

WILLIAM K. BEATTY

Daly, James A. (6 Dec. 1947–13 Dec. 1998), Vietnam War veteran and conscientious objector, was born in Brooklyn, New York, to James and Mary, a city employee, and raised in the Bedford-Stuyvesant neighborhood. Although his father abandoned the family, his mother was a positive and loving influence, and Daly remained close to his older sister Phyllis, and younger siblings Pamela, Dennis, Ralph, Martin, and Elaine. Daly graduated from Franklin K. Lane High School in June 1966. He was a thoughtful youth, tall and awkward, with an interest in cooking and baking. Raised a Baptist, Daly became interested in the Jehovah's Witnesses at the age of eleven. Although he accepted their beliefs and hoped to become a minister, he never officially converted.

Daly thought he would escape military service in Vietnam; "because of my religious beliefs—because I was totally against killing, in any war—I was confident that I would be given conscientious objector status and would not be drafted" (Daly and Bergman, *A Hero's Welcome*, 1). He checked with the local Selective Service office and was astounded to learn that, not being a minister, he was not even eligible to apply for conscientious objector (CO) status. Discouraged, Daly naively consulted with an army recruiting sergeant (who was also black) about his options and was advised to enlist. The recruiter deceived Daly into believing that he would be given noncombatant status and would be guaranteed a job as either a cook or a clerk after he completed basic training. Despite a vaguely uneasy feeling, he accepted the recruiting sergeant's advice and enlisted in the army. On 17 January 1967 he was officially a soldier in the U.S. Army, thus setting in motion a tragic chain of personal events that mirrored the impact of the Vietnam War on America's political and social psyche.

Even in basic training, Daly continually emphasized his beliefs against killing in a polite but persistent way to his superior officers and tried to gain CO status. Nevertheless, he did his best to fit in to regulated army life and never disobeyed orders. After completing basic training, Daly was sent to infantryman's training school, not cooking school as originally promised, where once again he emphasized his beliefs, yet faithfully followed orders. A base chaplain advised him to "Go home on leave—and stay home! Let the MPs pick you up. You'll be charged with AWOL, but you'll get attention and be able to plead your case" (Daly and Bergman, *A Hero's Welcome*, 36). While on leave, Daly briefly considered leaving the country, but he could not leave his family. He considered the chaplain's advice about going AWOL (absent without leave) but was advised by a Jehovah's Witness overseer that breaking the law was not acceptable. Instead, Daly returned to duty and was subsequently sent to Vietnam on 29 September 1967 as a private first class in Company A, Third Battalion, Twenty-first Infantry, 196th Light Infantry Brigade.

Daly held firm in his convictions against killing and continued to ask for CO status while in Vietnam. But his company officers continued to send him on patrol, even with the knowledge that Daly refused to load and fire his rifle as a combatant. He largely kept his personal thoughts to himself and was by no means an antiwar agitator in his unit. The historian Jeff Loeb states that Daly was "absolutely consistent in his ethical strategy" (Daly and Bergman, *Black POW*, 28) and never wavered in his beliefs. On 8 January 1968 Daly and his fellow soldiers in Company "Alpha" were moved to the deceptively named "Happy Valley" in Quang Tin province in support of "Charlie" and "Delta" companies that had sustained heavy losses in previous days. Daly arrived on the scene and "I just stood there for a full minute, looking at all those ripped-up pieces of bodies that only the day before had been living men ... it made me understand like I never had just how horrible war really is" (Daly and Bergman, *A Hero's Welcome*, 71). The following morning, Delta and Alpha companies moved out to continue their search for missing soldiers from Charlie Company. Spread out in a long line while crossing an open rice paddy, the men were ambushed by a large force of North Vietnamese troops and quickly overwhelmed. Four members of Alpha Company and Daly were wounded and subsequently captured. Daly would spend the next five years as a prisoner of war (POW).

For the first three years of his captivity, Daly was held in the south in primitive camps where malnutrition and disease were all too common and medical treatment almost nonexistent, resulting in deaths among fellow prisoners. Although subject to continuous "reeducation" during his imprisonment, Daly never signed any letters his captors crafted protesting U.S. action in Vietnam, as he was frequently asked to do. Although conditions were brutal, Daly and his fellow prisoners were never subjected to torture, though beatings were administered to those who tried to escape. In early 1971 he was transferred to North Vietnam and imprisoned at Plantation Gardens in Hanoi. For Daly, the transition was "like going from hell to heaven" (Daly and Bergman, *A Hero's Welcome*, 174). Plantation Gardens consisted of prison cells with electricity, clean clothes, blankets, and a supply of personal hygiene items. Daly remained firm in his moral convictions throughout his imprisonment, and despite the squalid conditions in which he was held, he retained some empathy for his captors. He was particularly struck by how the war affected Vietnamese civilians, especially women and children, and was distressed when he learned that the United States was deliberately poisoning Vietnamese rice paddies. By Christmas 1971 Daly had joined the Peace Committee at Plantation Gardens, a prisoner group that had signed letters opposing the war. Ironically, while the Vietnam War was widely denounced in the United States, Daly and the other members of the Peace Committee would later be branded as traitors. He was finally released from captivity on 16 March 1973 in the second major release of U.S. POWs and returned to the United States. Some of his fellow POWs, led by air force colonel Theodore Guy, would soon accuse Daly and other members of the Peace Committee of failing to adhere to the Code of Conduct for POWs. When these charges were dropped, additional charges of mutiny—specifically, failure to obey an officer's orders while a prisoner—were also brought against Daly. This charge was also quickly dropped.

In April 1974 Daly married Ira Jean Worthy, a South Carolina native, and he would remain with her for the rest of his life. Even before his service was over, Daly was contacted by the author and writer Lee Bergman about the possibility of writing a book about his Vietnam experiences. As Bergman recalled, "I read about his story in the *New York Times* and the charges brought against him and it seemed to me this was an important story of the Vietnam War from the perspective of an American POW who was moved ultimately to speak out against it. I contacted him through his lawyer and he was agreeable to the idea. In the months to follow I taped his account and hours were spent editing the tapes before writing the book. Daly was a complex person, very open ... he felt strongly about everything he said, and enjoyed telling his story" (Bergman, phone interview, 13 May 2007). The resulting book, *A Hero's Welcome: The Conscience of Sergeant James Daly vs. the United States Army*, received good reviews but quickly faded from the public eye at a time when most Americans wanted to forget the Vietnam War. Daly's account remained an important one, however, and one of the few books published by a black soldier who served in Vietnam.

Because of his actions in Vietnam, Daly was shunned by the POW community and remained a controversial figure. True to his humanist morals, however, Daly dared to put a human face on his captors and strove to dispel the notion that the Vietnamese were evil. His civilian life was quiet. Jane Fonda asked him to accompany her on a speaking tour, but this never came about. He was interviewed by Walter Cronkite but broke down and could not finish the interview, so only a portion was later broadcast. James and Jean Daly opened a laundromat in New Jersey, and he also worked as a postal carrier in Teaneck, and later Willingboro, New Jersey. He retired due to a diabetic condition in 1993, and suffered the amputation of both his legs shortly before dying at his home in 1998. His legacy, like that of the Vietnam War era, is a controversial one, but Daly deserves to be remembered as a man of unwavering conviction who served his country under the most difficult of circumstances.

FURTHER READING

Interviews about James Daly were conducted with Jean Daly, the widow of James Daly, in a telephone interview on 16 June 2007 and subsequent follow-up discussions, as well as Lee Bergman and Jeff Loeb, who provided personal insights into the character of James Daly.

Daly, James A., and Lee Bergman. *Black POW: A Conscientious Objector's Vietnam Memoir*, with foreword and commentary by Jeff Loeb (2000).

Daly, James A. *A Hero's Welcome: The Conscience of Sergeant James Daly vs. the United States Army* (1975).

GLENN ALLEN KNOBLOCK

Daly, Marie Maynard (16 Apr. 1921–28 Oct. 2003), biochemist, was born in Corona, Queens, New York, one of three children of Ivan C. Daly and Helen Page. Her father emigrated from the West Indies and received a scholarship from Cornell University to study chemistry; however, he had to drop out because he could not pay his room and board. Forced to abandon his dream, he became a postal worker. Daly's interest in science came from her father's encouragement and the desire to live his dream. Her maternal grandfather had an extensive library, and her mother spent many hours reading to the children. Daly found books about science and scientists, like Paul D. Kruif's *Microbe Hunters*, most interesting. She graduated from Hunter College High School, a competitive, all-girls public school in Manhattan. Her science teachers encouraged her to study chemistry at the college level.

After graduating, Daly attended Queens College in Flushing, New York, and graduated magna cum laude in 1942 with a bachelor of science in Chemistry. The chemistry department offered her a part-time job as a laboratory assistant, and she received a fellowship to study for a master's degree in Chemistry at New York University, where she received her degree in 1943. She continued to work for a year at Queens College in order to earn money to pursue a doctorate in Chemistry. Because of the heightened need for scientists during World War II, Daly was able to secure a fellowship from Columbia University to study for a Ph.D. with Mary L. Caldwell. In 1947 she received her Ph.D. in Chemistry from Columbia University, becoming the first African American woman to receive this degree from any American university. The title of her dissertation was "A Study of the Products Formed by the Action of Pancreatic Amylase on Corn Starch."

Daly wanted to begin her career doing cancer research with A. E. Mirsky at the Rockefeller Institute, but she had to independently fund her research. She applied for funding from the American Cancer Society, but as this was not immediately forthcoming she went to work at Howard University as an instructor of physical science under the noted black physicist HERMAN R. BRANSON. In 1948 she received the grant from the American Cancer Society and left Howard for the Rockefeller Institute, where she was the only black scientist. With scientific luminaries like Francis Crick, Rosalind Franklin, Linus Pauling, and James Watson working on the structure of DNA, this was an exciting moment in biochemistry. Daly worked on the research team with A. E. Mirsky and V. G. Allfrey, focusing on cancer research at the DNA level. The work of Allfrey, Daly, and Mirsky would be cited by Watson in his Nobel Award address.

Daly worked at the Rockefeller Institute for seven years before taking a position, in 1955, at the College of Physicians and Surgeons at Columbia University, where she taught biochemistry. She also became a research associate at Goldwater

Memorial Hospital working with Dr. Quentin B. Deming. There she would study the underlying causes of heart attacks. Her early research examined the metabolism of the arterial wall and how this process is affected by aging, hypertension, and arteriosclerosis. She discovered the role that cholesterol plays in heart problems and the effects of sugar and smoking on the heart.

In 1960 Daly and Deming moved their research team to Yeshiva University's Albert Einstein College of Medicine, where Daly became an assistant professor of biochemistry. The following year, Daly married Vincent Clark. In 1971 she was promoted to associate professor, a position she held until her retirement in 1986. At Albert Einstein, Daly taught both medical and graduate students. She was instrumental in recruiting, training, and mentoring minority students at the school. To that end, Daly served on the faculty committee that ran the MARTIN LUTHER KING–Robert F. Kennedy Program for Special Studies, established in 1968. This program prepared select African American students for admission to the college of medicine. In her last years at Einstein her research focused on understanding the uptake of creatine by muscle cells by the in vitro synthesis of radiolabeled creatine.

Daly was a member of the National Organization for the Professional Advancement of Black Chemists and Chemical Engineers. On 3 May 1980 she moderated the important session on "Black Women in Chemistry, Biochemistry and Chemical Engineering: Confronting the Professional Challenges." In addition, Daly was a member or fellow of several professional organizations, including the American Chemical Society, New York Academy of Science, American Association for the Advancement of Science, New York Academy of Science, Harvey Society, American Biological Society, Council on Arteriosclerosis and the American Heart Association, NAACP, National Association of Negro Business and Professional Women, and Sigma Xi.

Daly retired in 1986. In 1988 she established a scholarship for African American chemistry and physics majors at Queens College in memory of her father. She died of cancer.

FURTHER READING

Cattell, Jaques. *American Men and Women of Science: Physical and Biological Sciences*, 15th ed. (1971).

Grinstein, Louise S., Rose K. Rose, and Miriam H. Rafailovich, eds. *Women in Chemistry and Physics: A Bibliographic Sourcebook* (1993).

Sammons, Vivian Ovelton. *Blacks in Science and Medicine* (1990).

Seifter, Samuel. "In Memoriam," *Einstein* (Winter 2005).

Warren, Wini. *Black Women Scientists in the United States* (1999).

Who's Who among Black Americans (1985): 199.

Who's Who among Black Americans (1996–1997): 353.

JEANNETTE ELIZABETH BROWN

Dameron, Tad (21 Feb. 1917–8 Mar. 1965), arranger, bandleader, and composer, was born Tadley Ewing Peake Dameron in Cleveland, Ohio. Information on his parents is not available. Dameron attended Oberlin College and took premed courses before deciding to become a musician. His career began rather inauspiciously as a singer in 1938 with Freddy Webster's band. It then continued with several lesser-known groups that included Zach Whyte, BLANCHE CALLOWAY (CAB CALLOWAY's sister), and Vido Musso (Benny Goodman's former saxophonist). At the age of twenty-three, Dameron was hired by HARLAN LEONARD, an alumnus of BENNIE MOTEN's band who was then leading a band formed from the former Thamon Hayes Rockets. The Harlan Leonard Rockets thrived in Kansas City from the mid-1930s to the mid-1940s, along with the bands of COUNT BASIE and JAY MCSHANN. The Rockets' style was permeated with the blues and consisted of a swinging rhythm section and strong soloists. Dameron contributed several compositions that featured dense orchestrations, chromatic harmonies, unison lines, and strong swing concepts, including "A la Bridges" and "Dameron Stomp," both recorded by Leonard in 1940.

Dameron's arranging skills led to his writing "If You Could See Me Now" for SARAH VAUGHAN (1946). This was one of the first bebop ballads, developed from a DIZZY GILLESPIE cadenza performed on "Groovin' High." The composition became a featured tune for both Dameron and Vaughan, who was then a pianist and vocalist for the BILLY ECKSTINE band. Dameron composed the title song for COLEMAN HAWKINS on *Half-Step Down, Please* (1947). Dameron also wrote songs for JIMMIE LUNCEFORD, George Auld, and Dizzy Gillespie, including "Good Bait," "Our Delight," and "Soulphony," which Gillespie's bebop big band premiered at Carnegie Hall in 1948. Dameron's ability to harmonize, orchestrate, and expand the small-band bebop format into a creative vehicle for a progressive big band is especially evident on the singles "Good Bait" (1947) and "Our Delight"

(1947). He appeared as a sideman on Gillespie's 1945 recording of "Hot House," one of several compositions that became jazz standards.

Dameron made his performance debut as a bandleader with BABS GONZALES's Three Bips and a Bop in 1946–1947 at Minton's Playhouse in New York. Some of his compositions are based on contrafactum, a common practice of bebop composers; for example, "Hot House" was a new bop melody fitted to the chords of Cole Porter's song "What Is This Thing Called Love?" Other pieces, however, such as "Lady Bird," feature atypical chord changes and harmonic rhythm.

In addition to being an arranger and composer of real talent, Dameron was considered a capable pianist. He served as the leader of groups featuring some of the finest jazz musicians of his day. In September 1947 one of his bands featured FATS NAVARRO as its principal soloist. At the Royal Roost in 1948 Dameron played with Navarro, Allan Eager, Curley Russell, and KENNY CLARKE. That year WARDELL GRAY also joined the Royal Roost group. This band recorded several of Dameron's compositions that became standards, including "The Chase," "The Squirrel," "Our Delight," and "Dameronia" (all 1947); and "Jahbero," "Lady Bird," and "Symphonette" (all 1948).

In May 1949 Dameron went with MILES DAVIS to the Paris Jazz Festival and the two were involved in several unsuccessful American groups. Dameron lived in England for a while, scoring occasionally for Ted Heath's big band. When Dameron returned to the United States, he found work as a pianist and the director of Bull Moose Jackson's rhythm and blues band from 1951 to 1952. In 1953 Dameron formed a band of his own, which included the trumpeter CLIFFORD BROWN. He featured Brown (muted solo) on "Theme of No Repeat" on the *Arranger's Touch* album as well as on a short three-movement composition titled "Fontainebleau" (1956). Dameron's drug addiction grew out of control, however, and led to his imprisonment in 1958. After three years he was released, but he did not become active again as a composer and musician. Dameron died of cancer in New York City.

Dameron is considered one of the most important composers and arrangers of the bebop era. Although he played "arranger's piano" (a la Gil Evans and Carla Bley), he was important nonetheless as a performer with his groups featuring Navarro, which made some of the finest recordings from the late 1940s. "Hot House" and "Lady Bird" in particular remain cornerstones of the bebop repertoire. Through his writing, Dameron posthumously became a key figure in the revival of bebop that began to flourish under WYNTON MARSALIS and others in the 1980s.

FURTHER READING
Burns, J. "Tadd Dameron," *Jazz Journal* 20, no. 8 (1967).
Chambers, Jack. *Milestones.* Vol. 1, *The Music and Times of Miles Davis to 1960* (1983).
This entry is taken from the *American National Biography* and is published here with the permission of the American Council of Learned Societies.

EDDIE S. MEADOWS

Dance, Daryl Cumber (17 Jan. 1938–), folklorist, writer, and educator, was born Daryl Cumber in Richmond, Virginia, the only child of Allen Whitfield Cumber, a proprietor of a restaurant and tavern, and Veronica Bell, a teacher. Raised in Charles City, Virginia, she earned her B.A. degree in English in 1957 from Virginia State College (now known as Virginia State University), a historically black institution located just outside of Richmond in Petersburg, Virginia. In 1958 she married Warren Dance and had three children, two sons and one daughter. She continued to pursue her English studies at Virginia State College and earned her M.A. in English there in 1963.

Dance taught at both Virginia Union and Armstrong High School of Richmond before earning her Ph.D. in English in 1971 at the University of Virginia, which was by then an integrated institution. Although Dance and her family had deep roots in Virginia, she was both influenced by and would have influence on the world beyond. Her interest in documenting and preserving the folktales and legends of African Americans and Afro-Caribbean people illustrates her ability to connect and expand the scope of the narratives of America. In her first book, *Shuckin' and Jivin': Folklore from Contemporary Black Americans* (1978), she assembles stories, songs, and jokes that showcase African American humor, wit, and resilience. This anthology established her voice and her broader project of documenting the stories of African American life that are shared at the kitchen table, at the barber shop, and in pews at church.

From 1972 to 1992, Dance rose through the professional ranks at Virginia Commonwealth University in Richmond. She received tenure as a full professor while also serving as the coordinator of Afro-American Studies in 1983–1984. Her research in Caribbean studies acts as a bridge for African Americans to connect their experiences to the larger black diaspora and explore the similarities and differences of each culture. Her second book, *Folklore from Contemporary Jamaicans* (1985), is a comprehensive selection of folktales, myths, and songs accompanied by maps, drawings, and photographs.

Dance's expertise in connecting to the common folk through tales of triumph and laughter is reminiscent of the Federal Writers' Project of the Works Progress Administration (WPA) in the 1930s. During President Roosevelt's administration this project was commissioned to send out writers and teachers to collect the narratives, legends, and folktales of surviving ex-slaves. The interviews produced a wealth of history, stories, and language that show how African Americans can be inspired by their ancestors' abilities to overcome tremendous odds. In an interview with *Richmond Alumni Magazine* in 2004 she credits "her inspiration from elders on the front porch passing on family and community legends, and reciting African proverbs." Underlying much of her work is the idea that laughter and lessons can be derived from any situation.

It is often that legends are derived from real life incidents and people. Dance is able to weave the creativity of fiction in with the stark sketches of fact and history. Her book *Long Gone: The Mecklenburg Six and the Theme of Escape in Black Folklore* (1987) memorializes the prison escape of six condemned men from the Mecklenburg Correctional Center in Boydton, Virginia, in 1984. Their story of escape is just as enthralling as stories of slaves' escapes, and "the magnitude and audacity of their escape evokes memories of outlaws on the run in [b]lack folktales and [b]lack music" (*Long Gone*, p. xv). By following the tales of another Virginia legend, Dance draws on her own family tree by cataloging the historical achievements of the Cumber family in her self-published work, *The Lineage of Abraham: The Biography of a Free Black Family in Charles City, Virginia* (1998). Dance's family has had a long, rich history in Charles City, Virginia, dating back to a free black man named Abraham Brown, who was a successful eighteenth-century landowner. In this work she pays homage by detailing her relatives' contributions to Virginia and to American history as a whole.

Dance joined the Department of English at the University of Richmond in 1993 and has served on various international and local boards such as the Association of Caribbean Studies and Richmond's Black History Museum and Cultural Center, Inc. Her 2002 book *From My People: 400 Years of African American Folklore* won several prestigious awards such as the 2004 Storytelling World Award and was selected as one of the Top 10 African American Nonfiction books reviewed by *Booklist* between February 2001 and February 2002. Her alma mater, Virginia State University, honored her with the Legacy Award in 2008. A brief memoir, "A Birth and a Death, or Everything Important Happens on Monday," is included in the collection *Shaping Memories: Reflections of African American Women Writers* (2009).

FURTHER READING

Cudjoe, Selwyn. *Caribbean Women Writers: Essays from the First International Conference* (1990).

Lohmann, Bill. "From Her People: Daryl Dance's Research Inspired by African American Folklore." *Richmond Alumni Magazine*, Fall 2004. http://magazine.richmond.edu/fall2004/features/feature2.html.

TIFFANY BOYD ADAMS

Dancy, John Campbell (8 May 1857–13 Apr. 1920), editor and public official, was born in Tarboro, North Carolina, the younger son and third child of John C. Dancy and Eliza Dancy, slaves owned by John S. Dancy, a local planter. After the Civil War, John C. Dancy became a prosperous carpenter and contractor, and was later elected as an Edgecombe County commissioner. John Campbell Dancy was educated in the common schools in Tarboro, where he worked briefly as a newspaper typesetter before entering the normal department at Howard University in Washington, DC.

After his father's death, John Dancy interrupted his studies to return to Tarboro, where he became a schoolteacher and principal of the public school for African American children. U.S. Congressman JOHN ADAMS HYMAN (R-NC) secured an appointment for Dancy at the U.S. Treasury Department in 1876, and Dancy briefly returned to Washington. By 1880 he was again teaching in Tarboro, where he was now politically active in the Republican Party. Beginning in 1880, he served five times as chief secretary of the state Republican convention, and that same year, was elected to the first of two terms as Edgecombe County's register of deeds.

Dancy had also become active in the African Methodist Episcopal Zion Church and the North Carolina Independent Order of Good Templars, whose international convention he attended in

London in 1879. Committed to the cause of temperance, he was elected president of a black state convention of temperance activists in 1882, and soon began editing the *North Carolina Sentinel* in Tarboro. After his defeat for reelection as registrar of deeds in 1884, Dancy was offered the editorship of the A.M.E. Zion newspaper, the *Star of Zion*. In 1885, he moved his family to Salisbury, North Carolina, where he also became a trustee of the church-run Livingstone College.

Dancy remained active in Republican politics, serving as a state delegate to the 1884 and 1888 national party conventions. In 1887 he was secretary of the State Convention of Colored Men. Four years later, President Benjamin Harrison appointed Dancy as collector of the port of Wilmington, North Carolina, the state's most lucrative federal patronage position, which he held until after Grover Cleveland's inauguration in 1893. While there he also edited the *A.M.E. Zion Quarterly Almanac*.

Dancy was married twice. His first wife, Laura G. Coleman of Morganton, died in December 1890, after bearing four children, of whom two lived to adulthood: JOHN C. DANCY JR., and a daughter, Lillian G. Dancy. In 1893 Dancy married Florence V. Stephenson of Pennsylvania, a music teacher; they had one son, Joseph.

In 1897 Dancy was among several African Americans considered for the influential post of recorder of deeds of the District of Columbia by President William McKinley. McKinley selected the former congressman HENRY P. CHEATHAM (R-NC), but reappointed Dancy to his previous post as port collector in Wilmington, a position he held until January 1902. He was living in Wilmington during that city's racial violence of November 1898, in which at least seven black citizens were killed by armed whites who overthrew the elected Republican government. Dancy and his family briefly fled the city, but he was one of the few black Republicans allowed to return afterward.

In September 1898 Dancy was elected as first vice president of the new National Afro-American Council, a civil rights organization formed in Rochester, New York, with A.M.E. Zion Bishop ALEXANDER WALTERS of New Jersey as president. For several years, Dancy was also a member of the council's national executive committee. In January 1902 President Theodore Roosevelt selected Dancy to succeed Cheatham as the recorder of deeds of the District of Columbia, the highest federal appointment in the municipal structure. After his confirmation by the U.S. Senate, Dancy served

as recorder of deeds until 1910, and remained in Washington, DC, after his retirement.

In October 1906 Dancy was a featured speaker at the National Afro-American Council's annual meeting in New York City, attempting to calm angry members upset by the deadly Atlanta riots of the previous week. According to the *New York Times* (10 Oct. 1906), Dancy declared that "it was the purpose of the Council to call men back to their reason, not to go down and blow up the South."

His son John C. Dancy Jr. (1886–1968), a graduate of the University of Pennsylvania, later served as head of the National Urban League chapter in Detroit, Michigan; he recalled his father and his childhood in his 1966 autobiography, *Sands against the Wind*.

John Dancy died in Washington, DC, in 1920.

FURTHER READING

Dancy, John C., Jr. *Sands against the Wind* (1966).
Krieger, Marvin. "John Campbell Dancy Jr." in *Dictionary of North Carolina Biography, Volume 2 D–G* (1986).

BENJAMIN R. JUSTESEN

Dancy, John Campbell, Jr. (13 Apr. 1888–10 Sept. 1968), Detroit Urban League executive director, was born in Salisbury, North Carolina, the son of John C. Dancy, a public official, and Laura Coleman. Brought up with three siblings in a comfortable, educated, southern family, he embraced his father's commitment to the African Methodist Episcopal Zion church and BOOKER T. WASHINGTON's accommodationism. His father was a successful typesetter, schoolteacher, newspaper editor, county politician, collector of customs in Wilmington, North Carolina, and recorder of deeds in Washington, D.C. Young Dancy attended Livingstone College (grade school), Phillips Exeter Academy (prep school), and the University of Pennsylvania. He studied sociology and graduated in 1910 but shied from the Republican Party politics that benefited his father. He wed Maude Bulkley in 1917, and after her death in 1931, he married Malinda Wells, who died in 1964. He had no children.

Initially, Dancy became principal of Smallwood Institute in Claremont, Virginia, and secretary of a Young Men's Christian Association (YMCA) in Norfolk, both black institutions. In 1916 he moved to New York City to become secretary of the Big Brother Program, later remembering his assistance to a very young COUNTÉE CULLEN, the Harlem Renaissance poet. There he also came in contact with Eugene K. Jones, executive secretary of the National Urban League, who influenced him to serve as industrial secretary of the metropolitan area. Two years later Dancy took the helm of the Detroit Urban League, succeeding Forrester B. Washington, and concentrating on job opportunities for black city dwellers. He brought workers and employees together through a personal diplomacy that turned on accommodationism and an anti-union position, producing mostly unskilled jobs in a racist climate and boom-bust economy. He also managed to place some blacks in skilled industrial and white-collar positions, often breaking the color line in Detroit's private and public sectors. During World War II Dancy shelved his antiunion position when the United Automobile Workers began enrolling black members and permitting them leadership roles in some locals and in the international.

Defense production needs reduced the league's role as an employment agent. Long before that occurred, however, Dancy pushed the league into travelers' aid, recreation, education, health, and housing. He provided southern migrants entering Detroit with temporary lodging and employment possibilities. Beyond sponsoring community dances and athletic contests for school-age children year round, he conceived of the Green Pastures Camp for poor and working-class youngsters. He established a baby clinic and promoted National Negro Health Week throughout Detroit's black neighborhoods. He furthered scholarship assistance to promising students and supported construction of the Brewster Homes, the first government-funded units for black Detroiters. Dancy also emphasized social etiquette and cultural programs, opening community centers in east side and northwest areas. In all of these endeavors, he appealed to corporate sponsorship or, in the case of the clinics and housing project, municipal and federal support, respectively.

From 1918 through World War II, Dancy sought equal, albeit oftimes separate treatment for black residents. Each of his programs addressed an area in which blacks, particularly new arrivals, were excluded from vital opportunities and services. Like his father, who owed his most important federal appointments to Booker T. Washington, he endeavored to work through existing structures with philanthropic-minded and, in some cases, segregation-minded whites. Hence Dancy's temperament, conservatism, allies, and United Community Services–funding from individuals and influential businesses required a low profile in legal and militant protests, lest he risk the loss of income necessary

to operate the Detroit Urban League (DUL). In the OSSIAN H. SWEET case (1925), which was litigated by the National Association for the Advancement of Colored People (NAACP), he helped raise defense funds for the noted black physician accused of shooting white rioters who had opposed his move into their neighborhood; Dancy testified at Sweet's trial as an expert on housing conditions in Detroit. But Dancy acted as an individual, not as a DUL official. More often he stood well beyond conflict, as in the Sojourner Truth Housing controversy (1942), which turned bloody before black defense workers and their families—under armed guard—occupied the federally funded units that whites had opposed being located in their neighborhood.

In the face of changing racial attitudes and increased black militancy, Dancy and the DUL still played an important, though less prominent, role in postwar race relations. Less protest-minded than most black and union leaders of the period, he maintained contact with entrepreneurs, philanthropists, and politicians, now openly embracing unionism and integration as each became increasingly acceptable to black workers and white benefactors, respectively. He continued to enlighten many white leaders on racial issues and to administer a larger, more bureaucratic league facing new socioeconomic and demographic realities created by an expanding black population.

For forty-two years Dancy assisted hundreds of blacks, migrants and residents alike, and articulated the aspirations of thousands more. He also aided and inspired the development of numerous individuals, including the surgeon Remus Robinson, the social worker Geraldine Bledsoe, and the artist HUGHIE LEE SMITH. He served as black Detroit's advocate and conduit, often as its only voice or one of its very few voices on various official and private bodies such as the Detroit House of Correction and the American Red Cross, and he facilitated similar appointments of other prominent blacks. An elitist, Dancy practiced "moral guardianship" (Levine, 122); an architect, he advanced "community building strategies" (Thomas, 63).

In his autobiography, *Sand against the Wind* (1966), Dancy advocated developing "a climate of good human relations" as the key to racial progress. He stressed persuasion over provocation and civility over confrontation; he seemed every bit a member of W. E. B. DuBois's talented tenth, yet he embraced Booker T. Washington's gradualism and deference, altering his accommodation—as did Washingtonians elsewhere in the North—to meet changing urban conditions and Urban League principles. Dancy's leadership style was soft-spoken and dignified. Sincere and accomplished, though limited by his own class bias and cultural distance from rank-and-file blacks, he symbolized an era in race relations that had ended long before his death in Detroit but that had benefited from his life. He presented one of many black viewpoints, helped build a community, bolstered its working and middle classes, and cultivated its white allies, which collectively assisted the civil rights movement of another generation.

FURTHER READING

Dancy's personal papers are scant, while those of the Detroit Urban League are extensive; both collections are a part of the Michigan Historical Collections, Bentley Historical Library, University of Michigan.

Dancy, John Campbell, Jr. *Sand against the Wind* (1966).

Meier, August, and Elliott Rudwick. *Black Detroit and the Rise of the UAW* (1979).

Thomas, Richard W. *Life for Us Is What We Make It* (1992).

Obituary: *Chronicle*, 21 Sept. 1968.

This entry is taken from the *American National Biography* and is published here with the permission of the American Council of Learned Societies.

DOMINIC J. CAPECI

Dandridge, Dorothy (9 Nov. 1922–8 Sept. 1965), movie actress and singer, was born Dorothy Jean Dandridge in Cleveland, Ohio, the daughter of Cyril Dandridge, a Baptist minister, and Ruby Jean Butler, a movie and radio comedian. Dorothy, a child entertainer, was in and out of school while her mother directed and choreographed her two children in a sister vaudeville act. The "Wonder Kids" performed in Cleveland's black Baptist churches and toured throughout the South for five years.

In the early 1930s Ruby, whose husband had left her just before Dorothy's birth, moved her family to the Watts section of Los Angeles, California, to further their careers in show business. The Wonder Kids recruited another girl, ETTA JONES, and formed a singing group called the Dandridge Sisters. In 1937 the act was sold to Warner Bros. for a movie called *A Day at the Races*. The Dandridge Sisters also made appearances at the Cotton Club in Harlem, New York, and toured with DUKE ELLINGTON, CAB CALLOWAY, and JIMMIE LUNCEFORD.

The outbreak of World War II interrupted the Dandridge Sisters' international tour and initiated their demise. Around this time Dorothy Dandridge met HAROLD NICHOLAS, who was one of the famous dancing Nicholas Brothers, and in 1942 they were married. In 1945 Dandridge's only child was born, and Harold immediately deserted his family because their child was severely brain damaged. In later years Dandridge joined with both Rose Kennedy and Jacqueline Kennedy Onassis in an effort to help the mentally challenged under the auspices of the Joseph P. Kennedy Jr. Foundation.

Dandridge's first important film role was Queen of the Jungle in Columbia Pictures' *Tarzan's Peril* (1951). Dore Schary of MGM then hired Dandridge to play a compassionate black schoolteacher in *Bright Road*, costarring HARRY BELAFONTE. During this time, Dandridge began her nightclub and concert engagements. In 1951 the bandleader Desi Arnaz agreed to temporarily employ Dandridge in his act at the Hollywood Mocombo. This appearance compelled Maurice Winnick, a British theatrical impresario, to offer Dandridge an engagement at the Cafe de Paris in London. The next year the Chase Hotel in St. Louis, Missouri, which had never employed a black performer to entertain in its dining room, booked her for an engagement. Dandridge informed the management that she would not perform unless blacks were allowed to obtain reservations and be permitted to use the main entrance. These conditions were agreed upon by the hotel management, and a table was reserved for black members of the National Association for the Advancement of Colored People on opening night. The most memorable and award-winning screen performance for Dandridge was in the title role of *Carmen Jones* (1954) produced by Otto Preminger in association with Twentieth Century–Fox. *Carmen Jones* costarred PEARL BAILEY and Belafonte. In 1955 Dandridge became the first black actor to be nominated for an Oscar in a starring role and the first black woman to take part in the Academy Awards show, presenting the Oscar for film editing. Dandridge also won a Golden Globe Award of Merit for Outstanding Achievement for the best performance by an actress in 1959. Dandridge's international acclaim led Twentieth Century–Fox to offer her a three-year contract that was the first and most ambitious offer given to a black performer by that studio. During the same year, Dandridge became the first black headliner to appear at the Waldorf-Astoria Hotel in New York City.

antidepressant Tofranil, at her apartment in West Hollywood, California.

A retrospective article in the *Los Angeles Herald Examiner* lamented that Dandridge's passing meant "the ceasing of exquisite music … she walked in beauty … regal as a queen." In her lifetime Dandridge was named by a committee of photographers as one of the five most beautiful women in the world. She was an international celebrity who believed in breaking down barriers to achieve racial equality. Dandridge realized that a black male could become a big star without romantic roles, but a sexy black actress like her was limited because the American public was not ready for interracial romance on the screen. On 20 February 1977 Dandridge, the first black leading lady, was posthumously inducted into the Black Filmmakers Hall of Fame at the annual OSCAR MICHEAUX Awards presentation in Oakland, California. VIVIAN DANDRIDGE, her sister, accepted the award. In December 1983 Belafonte, Poitier, and others petitioned to secure a star on the Hollywood Walk of Fame for Dandridge, a trailblazer for blacks in the American film industry.

FURTHER READING

There is a clippings file on Dorothy Dandridge in the Billy Rose Theatre Collection, New York Public Library for the Performing Arts, Lincoln Center.

Dandridge, Dorothy, with Earl Conrad. *Everything and Nothing: The Dorothy Dandridge Tragedy* (1970).

Agan, Patrick. *The Decline and Fall of the Love Goddesses* (1979).

Bogle, Donald. *Dorothy Dandridge: A Biography* (1999)

Mills, Earl. *Dorothy Dandridge* (1999).

Obituary: *New York Times*, 8 Sept. 1965.

This entry is taken from the *American National Biography* and is published here with the permission of the American Council of Learned Societies.

SAMUEL CHRISTIAN

Dorothy Dandridge, actress and singer, swooping up the fifty-yard skirt of a halter-necked pink tulle dress, fastened with a jeweled belt, 21 June 1953. (AP Images.)

During the 1950s Dandridge starred in several films for Twentieth Century–Fox, Columbia Pictures, and foreign film companies. *Island in the Sun* (1957), with James Mason, Joan Fontaine, and Belafonte, was Hollywood's first major interracial film and was a box office success. In *Tamango* (1959), Dandridge portrayed an African slave in love with a white ship captain, played by the Austrian actor Curt Jurgens. She costarred with SIDNEY POITIER in *Porgy and Bess* (1959). In addition to her film credits, Dandridge appeared on several television shows during the 1950s including *The Mike Douglas Show*, *The Steve Allen Show*, and *The Ed Sullivan Show*. In November 1954 she also appeared on the cover of *Life* magazine, making history as the first black to do so.

In 1959 Dandridge married Jack Dennison (or Denison), a white restaurateur and nightclub owner; the marriage ended in divorce in 1962. In 1961 Dandridge costarred in a film with Trevor Howard, titled *Malaga*. Dandridge's last concert appearances included engagements in Puerto Rico and Tokyo. Her death was reported as the result of acute drug intoxication, an ingestion of the

Dandridge, Ray (31 Aug. 1913–12 Feb. 1994), baseball player, was born Raymond Emmitt Dandridge in Richmond, Virginia, the son of Archie Dandridge, a cigarette factory worker, and Alberta Thompson. The family moved to Buffalo, New York, when Ray was ten years of age. There he participated in various sports, including Golden Glove boxing and high school football. The latter sport led to a knee injury that plagued him in his later career. At age twenty he played for the Richmond Paramount Giants against the Detroit Stars of the Negro National League. The Paramount Giants gave his father $25, and Ray, packing a straw suitcase, boarded the bus to play against the Stars. He hit only .211 as a rookie in the Negro National League, and at season's end, he said, the team had to pawn its bus to raise the money to send him home.

Moving to the Newark Dodgers in 1934, Dandridge concentrated on hitting line drives instead of home runs. As a result he blossomed offensively, batting .436. Meantime, veteran players such as Jud Wilson and Dick Lundy taught the bowlegged youngster how to charge ground balls. "Dandridge had plenty of guts," one old-time pitcher said. "Guys used to fake bunts to draw the third baseman in. Some wouldn't come in too close. Dandridge would." Laughed another old-timer: "You could drive a freight train between his legs, but you couldn't drive a baseball through them." Nicknamed "Hooks," "because he had a great pair of hands," Dandridge grew into one of the best infielders of all time as well as a good line-drive hitter. Those who saw him play have compared him to the Hall of Fame third baseman Brooks Robinson, who later played with the Baltimore Orioles.

The *Baseball Encyclopedia*, based on exhaustive research of newspaper box scores, credits Dandridge with a .369 batting average in 1935. As a result of this performance, he was selected to play in the East-West All-Star game and in Puerto Rico over the winter, on a black all-star team matched against white major leaguers.

The Newark Dodgers changed their name to the Eagles in 1936, and Dandridge batted .301 and .354 for the next two years. In 1937 GEORGE MULE SUTTLES, the all-time Negro League home-run champion, joined the Eagles at first base. With WILLIE "Devil" WELLS at shortstop, DICK SEAY at second base, and Dandridge at third base, the Eagles boasted "a million-dollar infield." Clark Griffith, owner of the white Washington Senators of the American League, considered Dandridge and Wells to be better than any two infielders in the major leagues at that time. "Nothing could get through that little hole between us," Dandridge beamed.

Dandridge had one of his best years at bat in 1938, hitting .375. That year the *New York Daily News* columnist Jimmy Powers urged the New York Giants to sign him and several other black stars, but integration was still nearly a decade away. In 1939, with Negro League payrolls depressed, Dandridge signed with Veracruz in the Mexican League and batted .346 and .367 the next two years, teaming with Wells and the home-run champion

JOSH GIBSON to win the pennant. The president of Mexico presented him with a trophy inscribed, "He came, he conquered."

From 1942 through 1944 Dandridge batted .310, .354, and .370. The wealthy Mexican baseball magnate Jorge Pascual named Dandridge player-manager of the Mexico City Reds in 1945; that season the Reds won the league pennant, while Dandridge batted .366 and hit in 29 consecutive games.

After JACKIE ROBINSON joined the Dodgers in 1947, the Negro Leagues began folding. However, Mexican teams started to bid for both white and black stars, and several major leaguers accepted the offers. Against four former big league pitchers, Dandridge batted .455. Upset that the white players generally were paid more than he was, Dandridge decided to leave Mexico. But Pascual sent police to stop him, offer him $10,000, and bring him back in a limousine. He also bought Dandridge a new house in Newark. The reconciled player rewarded the magnate by batting .373 in 1948 to lead the league.

Later in 1948 Cleveland Indians owner Bill Veeck wanted to sign Dandridge for the pennant drive. But because Veeck refused to pay a bonus, Dandridge chose to stay in Mexico for another year. When future Yankees pitcher Whitey Ford played in Mexico, Dandridge "hit him like he owned him," one player laughed. Years later Dandridge would reminisce on the TV show *Good Morning America*, "I know Whitey Ford had one of the best curve balls. But I had one of the best bats!"

In 1949, while Dandridge was player-manager of the New York Cubans, a black team, the major league New York Giants saw him play at their stadium, the Polo Grounds. Impressed, the Giants signed him to a minor league contract and sent him to their top farm team in Minneapolis. "I was 35," Dandridge said, "but I told them I was 30."

Dandridge was a hit both with the fans and with his teammates. He stayed in white hotels everywhere but Louisville, Kentucky, and Kansas City, Missouri, where he boarded with black families. At first Dandridge played second base, then was shifted to third, where he made some spectacular plays. He also batted .362 and just missed winning the American Association batting title. Although Dandridge led Minneapolis to the league pennant that season, the Giants still did not promote him to the major leagues.

The next year, 1950, Dandridge batted .311 and was voted his league's most valuable player. Yet the Giants still refused to promote him, believing he was too old. Sal Maglie, who had known Dandridge in the Mexican League, was then a Giant pitcher. He reacted to the decision angrily, saying, "I know damn well we'd have won the pennant with Dandridge." Meantime, a rookie named WILLIE MAYS reported to Minneapolis, and Dandridge took charge of him. "He was like a father to me," Mays said later. When the Giants needed help in their 1951 pennant drive, it was Mays who got the call, not Dandridge.

Dandridge played winter ball in Cuba from 1937 to 1952. In 1953 he was on the Sacramento and Oakland teams of the Pacific Coast League, batting .268. He ended his career at Bismarck, South Dakota, in 1955.

When Dandridge retired, his career batting averages were .326 in the Negro Leagues, .318 at Minneapolis, and .347 against barnstorming big leaguers. In 1987 he was elected to the National Baseball Hall of Fame by the Veterans' Committee.

After his playing days were over, Dandridge scouted briefly for the Giants, tended bar in Newark, and supervised a city recreation center. He died in Palm Bay, Florida.

FURTHER READING

Holway, John B. *Blackball Stars* (1988).
Overmayer, James. *Effa Manley and the Newark Eagles* (1994).
Peterson, Robert. *Only the Ball Was White* (1970).
Riley, James. *Dandy, Day and the Devil* (1987).
Obituary: *New York Times*, 14 Feb. 1994.
This entry is taken from the *American National Biography* and is published here with the permission of the American Council of Learned Societies.

JOHN B. HOLWAY

Dandridge, Vivian (22 Apr. 1921–26 Oct. 1991), actress, singer, and dancer, was born Vivian Alferetta Dandridge in Cleveland, Ohio. Affectionately called "Vivi" by her family, she was the oldest daughter of the minister and mechanic Cyril and the actress Ruby Jean Butler Dandridge. She is perhaps best known for being the sister of the accomplished actress DOROTHY DANDRIDGE, the first black woman to be nominated for an Academy Award for Best Lead Actress; however, Vivian was an accomplished performer in her own right. Her mother separated from her father a year after she was born, leaving the family home on East 103rd Street in Cleveland. With little contact with their father, the girls were raised by Ruby and her friend Geneva Williams, also known as "Neva." Although Cyril expressed an interest in

his daughters' lives, Ruby apparently sought to distance Cyril from Vivian and Dorothy (Bogle, 44).

Though she was a screen and radio actress in her own right, Vivian's mother cleaned houses to support herself and her daughters. Ruby had a strong passion for the arts, and in 1927 she began to instruct her daughters to sing songs, recite poetry, and perform acrobatic ballet in various local churches, schools, and theater groups.

The foursome later left Cleveland to find more theatrical work in Nashville, where Neva had studied music at Fisk University. Shortly thereafter they dubbed their act "the Wonder Children," and signed to tour with the National Baptist Convention to provide entertainment by singing, dancing, and reciting poetry. The onset of the Great Depression three years later brought an end to a subsequent tour. Seeking stardom, the foursome packed up again and moved to Hollywood in 1934. Once there, Vivian and Dorothy enrolled in middle school at the Hooper Street School, where she also took more dance lessons. This was a pivotal time for the two sisters, for this was where they met ETTA JAMES, who became the third member of their singing group. With James's participation and the direction of the agent Ben Carter, the group now became known as the Dandridge Sisters. This group would become one of the many popular female trios of the time and made an appearance on the television series *Amos 'n' Andy*. In 1935 the Dandridge Sisters made a cameo appearance in *The Big Broadcast of 1936*. A big break came for the trio when they appeared in the Marx Brothers' film *A Day at the Races* in 1937. The same year they also shot a crime drama titled *It Can't Last Forever*. When Vivian turned seventeen, both she and Dorothy dropped out of Jefferson High School and left Los Angeles with Neva. Their mother stayed behind to advance her own career. The Dandridge Sisters, with Neva in tow, moved to New York to play the Cotton Club with the legendary DUKE ELLINGTON, CAB CALLOWAY, W. C. HANDY, and BILL "Bojangles" ROBINSON. The girls' father visited them in New York. It was the first time he had seen his daughters since they had become young adults. The Dandridge Sisters also began to play the chitlin circuit, appearing in predominantly African American venues in the southeastern United States.

In 1938 the group appeared in the movies *Going Places* with LOUIS ARMSTRONG and MAXINE SULLIVAN, and *Snow Gets in Your Eyes*. Soon after these film appearances, they received an offer to tour in Europe. Although they embarked on the

Vivian Dandridge, singer and member of the Dandridge Sisters, 1955. (Library of Congress/New York World-Telegram & Sun Collection.)

tour, it was cut short by the beginning of World War II. When they returned to the United States in 1940, Dorothy wanted to try her luck with a solo career and the group broke up. Her career would eventually soar; Etta James would become a respected jazz singer. As a black performer trying to succeed in the early to mid-twentieth century, Vivian Dandridge, like other African American performers, struggled with the pervasive stereotypical roles she was asked to play, including the ignorant pickaninny, the tragic mulatto, the oversexed vixen, and other subservient roles, many of which went uncredited. She appeared in *Irene* with her sister and in 1943 she made an uncredited appearance as Melisse in the horror film *I Walked with a Zombie*. Her voice was again used without credit as "So White" in the animated cartoon *Coal Black and De Sebben Dwarfs*. From 1945 to 1954 she and her sister provided radio voiceovers for the *Beulah Show*, in which their mother had a role as Oriole. Vivian made another uncredited appearance as Miss Nelson in *Bright Road* in 1953, opposite her sister and HARRY BELAFONTE. During this time she also continued to perform as a blues and jazz singer at venues all over the West Coast.

Dandridge went through a series of marriages. Her first, in 1942, was to a welder named Jack Montgomery—a seemingly impetuous decision to assert her independence and that only lasted six months. After ending her marriage with Montgomery in 1943, she met Emmett "Babe" Wallace on the set of *Stormy Weather*. Although she never officially married the Brooklyn-born actor, the relationship produced a son, Michael Wallace. Following this relationship, in 1946, she wed the musician-cum-physician Ralph Bledsoe. This was another short-lived partnership that lasted a little over a year and ended in 1947 because of the couple's financial difficulties.

Dandridge attended the Academy Awards ceremony with her sister in 1955 when Dorothy was nominated for Best Leading Actress for her role in *Carmen Jones*. Afterward, Vivian's relationship with her sister soured and, struggling to find work, she left Los Angeles once again for New York where she resided on the Upper West Side. She remained out of contact with her sister throughout the late 1950s, except to send her a telegram that she was marrying Gustav Friedrich in April 1958. During the late 1950s, Dandridge assumed the stage name Marina Rozell and packed her bags for Europe. She began studies in psychology, and periodically made ends meet as a hairdresser. In 1963 she ended her marriage to Friedrich. She also returned to singing in nightclubs after a six-year hiatus. Dandridge proved a skilled performer who sang in French, German, Hebrew, and English throughout saloons and nightclubs in New York, Canada, and Europe.

In the 1970s she returned to Los Angeles from Europe, but became disheartened by the rampant racial and sexual harassment she faced. Despite the turmoil she encountered, her friend Howard Farley said, "She was the ultimate professional. When she stepped up she owned the stage, whether it was a small room or a 100 feet wide. Her opening number for most shows was 'This Could Be the Start of Something Big.'" In her later years, Dandridge spent a short time in Detroit and subsequently relocated to Seattle, Washington, in 1983. There she lived in a small apartment in Ross Manor in the Pike Place Market with a view of Elliott Bay. She occasionally performed at local open-mic venues. Fellow performer Patricia Croghan remembered, "She was color-blind with people. She saw through to the essence of people." She would also use her voiceover skills to present puppet shows to children at a daycare center in Post Alley near her apartment.

She even made a cameo appearance in the Public Broadcasting Service television miniseries *Brown Sugar* in 1986.

Her mother died of Alzheimer's in a Los Angeles nursing home in 1987, but she left her only surviving child, Vivian, nothing in her will. This appeared to be reflective of the dynamics that characterized her family life. Her father, Cyril, died two years later. Dandridge lived in relative obscurity in Seattle until her death from a stroke in 1991, leaving unfinished a book about herself and her sister. She was buried at Lake View Cemetery on Capitol Hill in Seattle. Dandridge was survived by her son, Michael Wallace, and her granddaughters, Lisa and Nayo Wallace, of Detroit.

FURTHER READING

Bogle, Donald. *Dorothy Dandridge: A Biography* (1997)

Conrad, Earl. *Everything & Nothing: The Dorothy Dandridge Tragedy* (1970).

Mills, Earl. *Dorothy Dandridge* (1970).

Simmons, Sheila. "Dorothy Gets to Oz," *Cleveland Plain Dealer* (Oct. 1997).

Obituary: *Seattle Times*, Nov. 1991.

MELINDA BOND SHREVE

Daniel, Everard Washington (22 Feb. 1879–6 Sept. 1939), the rector of Detroit's St. Matthew's Protestant Episcopal Church and anti-union labor recruiter for Ford Motor Company, was born in St.-Thomas, Danish Virgin Islands, of middle-class parents, about whom little is known. His father was a Danish-speaking white man and his mother, Clementina, a black woman from the British colony of St. Kitts. Daniel was bilingual and considered Danish his first language. St. Thomas had a tradition of liberal education of slaves and free blacks and Daniel, considered a brilliant student, would benefit from the educational policies of the colony. He emigrated from St. Thomas in 1892 to New York to complete his education and his mother followed a year later. Daniel became an American citizen in 1901, twenty-six years before the United States purchased the Danish Virgin Islands.

Daniel attended St. Augustine College in Raleigh, North Carolina, where he received his B.A. and then moved to New York, where he received an M.A. from New York University. He then attended the Union Theological Seminary in New York and earned a doctorate in divinity. He was ordained in the Protestant Episcopal Church in 1902 and became curate of the wealthy and prestigious St. Philip's Episcopal Church in New York City, a position he held for seventeen years. He married his wife, Marcelline, in 1903. The couple's only child, a son named Langton, was born the same year they wed. Marcelline's father, like Daniel, was Danish-speaking and from St. Croix in the Virgin Islands. Her mother was born in Pennsylvania, while Marcelline was born in New Jersey about 1880 and moved to New York where she earned a living giving piano lessons.

In 1921 Daniel left New York for Detroit to become the rector of St. Matthew's. At the time, the city's black population was increasing exponentially as southern migrants poured in, seeking jobs in the automotive industry. St. Matthew's is the third-oldest black church in Detroit, with professionals, business owners, and skilled workers making up its comparatively small, elite congregation. A significant portion of the congregation, like Daniel, was of West Indian extraction. In accordance with the social service agenda of the Protestant Episcopal Church, he founded the Dorcas Society, an organization to distribute food and clothing to the poor. Daniel encouraged his parishioners, many of whom had emigrated from the West Indies, to become American citizens and purchase homes. Early in his pastorate he established a benefit society to provide financial assistance to members of his congregation. His major endeavor entailed finding them employment.

In 1914 Ford Motor Company began recruiting and hiring black men for employment at its plant in Highland Park and later in the huge Rouge plant in Dearborn, Michigan. The company preferred to hire married men, whom Ford viewed as more deserving and in greater need of the high wages he paid. Ford viewed the churches as ideal locations to recruit steady, industrious, and sober workers. In spite of brutal work conditions in the hot and dangerous foundry where most blacks were employed, the company became the largest employer of black men in Detroit and one of the only firms where black men could earn enough to support their families. In 1921 Ford's head of production, Charles Sorensen, approached Robert Bradby, the pastor of the oldest and largest of Detroit's black churches, Second Baptist, about employing members of his church at the company. In 1923 Sorensen made a similar arrangement with Daniel and an intense rivalry developed between the two pastors. Each wanted influence in securing employment for his parishioners, but Daniel's congregation was perceived as more polished than Bradby and the southern migrants of Second Baptist. The rivalry increased and continued throughout the 1920s and into the next decade. They frequently denounced each other from their pulpits and at parochial meetings. One member of Second Baptist warned Bradby that Daniel and Marshall were conspiring to employ only West Indians from St. Matthew's at Ford. Unionists reviled Daniel and Marshall for their control of black workers and the methods they used to discourage unionization.

By the mid-1920s Daniel had become the favorite of Ford executives because of his urbane manner and loyalty to Henry Ford, making him the most influential leader in Detroit's black community in the period between the two world wars. With only six of the city's black pastors having attended college, Daniel commanded respect as the most educated. Daniel and Sorensen, both Danish speakers, developed a close relationship and Henry Ford would annually attend services at St. Matthew's. To directly oversee the performance of black workers in the Rouge plant, Ford hired one of the parishioners at St. Matthew's, a former Detroit policeman named Donald J. Marshall, known for his violent methods of keeping black workers in line.

Because Ford endorsed Republican Party candidates, Daniel and Marshall were expected to deliver the votes of the members of the congregation and black men employed with the company. When workers in the church chose to vote for Democratic candidates, they received reprimands from the pair and some Ford workers lost their jobs as punishment for their political choices.

Daniel and Marshall vehemently denounced labor unions as their association with Ford, a notorious anti-union company in an open-shop city, dictated. Because of his close relationship to the company, Daniel had to adhere to its conservative and often repressive policies. He regarded the National Association for the Advancement of Colored People (NAACP) as a foe because of its pro-union stance and threatened to boycott the organization's national meeting held in Detroit in 1937.

Daniel's influence in Detroit had mixed results. For over fifteen years he secured relatively high-wage employment for black men. But the jobs they received with Daniel's recommendation often entailed working in the foundry, where the most dangerous and unsanitary conditions of the plant existed. Daniel's elitism led him to favor middle-class West Indian immigrants over poor black migrants from the South, and fueled his pragmatic subservience to Ford's corporate and personal philosophy, which promoted a decidedly conservative

agenda, ultimately hindering black workers. He carried these activities and views into the Depression.

In April 1939, Daniel became ill and Marshall took over many of the duties at St. Matthews. Daniel died of an undisclosed illness in that year. His funeral was attended by many officials of the Episcopal Church, and he was buried in Detroit's historic Elmwood Cemetery. With his death, the labor movement lost one of its foremost opponents, and the UAW would begin organizing at Ford in 1941.

FURTHER READING

The papers of St. Matthew's Protestant Episcopal Church are held in the Bentley Historical Library at the University of Michigan.

Lewis, David. "History of Negro Employment in Detroit Area Plants of Ford Motor Company, 1914–1941," Seminar Paper, University of Detroit (1954).

Maloney, Thomas N., and Warren C. Whatley. "Making the Effort: The Contours of Racial Discrimination in Detroit's Labor Markets, 1920–1940," *Journal of Economic History* (1995).

Thomas, Richard. *Life for Us Is What We Make It: Building Black Community in Detroit, 1915–1945* (1992).

KATHRYN L. BEARD

Danticat, Edwidge (19 Jan. 1969–), writer, was born in Port-au-Prince, Haiti, the eldest child of André Danticat and Rose Danticat. Her father, unable to find work in Haiti, immigrated to the United States when his daughter was two. There he worked at a glass factory and a carwash before becoming a taxi driver. Danticat's mother immigrated two years later, becoming a textile worker. She left her daughter and younger son, Eliab, in the care of their father's brother, a minister, and his wife, in Bel Air, a poor section of Port-au-Prince. Though Danticat came to love the couple as a second set of parents, she would later recall having to be physically separated from her mother when she realized her mother was to leave Haiti without her.

As a child Danticat was fascinated with the ritual of storytelling practiced by her aunts and grandmothers. "Krik?" the women called out. Children ready to listen to the promised stories responded "Krak!" She also became an author at a young age, rewriting the popular *Madeline* children's books to include a Haitian heroine. Her first short story involved a group of women who visit another woman at night. This story would later be incorporated into "Between the Pool and the Gardenias," part of *Krik? Krak!*, a collection of short stories published in 1995.

When she was twelve years old Danticat joined her parents in a predominantly Haitian American neighborhood in Brooklyn, New York. There she met two younger brothers who had been born in the United States. Danticat did not speak English and was teased for her accent. Her Haitian education had been in French, she spoke French Creole at home, yet she wrote fluently in neither language. Feeling between languages and already shy, Danticat withdrew into books. She first read Maya Angelou's *I Know Why the Caged Bird Sings*, which stunned her with its honesty and taught her that such candor could be a part of writing. She kept journals and learned to compose in English, assembling ideas first in fragmented English, Creole, and French. Though language felt like a barrier when she was first in New York, it was this blend of languages that would become such an integral element in Danticat's own storytelling as a writer.

Taught that success-minded immigrants went into medicine, law, or engineering, Danticat originally planned to pursue nursing, but a scholarship enabled her to earn a B.A. in French literature from Barnard College (1990) and then an MFA at Brown University (1993). She had already published her first piece of writing at fourteen. In high school she had used her vivid memories from the Duvaliers' dictatorships to write an article for a teen magazine about her own departure from Haiti. At Brown she expanded the article into her thesis, *Breath, Eyes, Memory*, which was published as a novel in 1994. The story, about four generations of women overcoming their powerlessness, centered on a twelve-year-old Haitian girl who, like Danticat herself, was reunited with her mother in New York, but its use of Haitian history and cultural practice emphasized how the past both grounds and impairs the present. The piece drew complaints from some in the Haitian American community for its frank discussion of the process of "testing" daughters to confirm their virginity. The novel's fragmented presentation, like that in *Krik? Krak!*, reflected the immigrant's discomfort with a new language. In addition, women's confidence and identity is strengthened in both works through the recognition of the many generations of women who have come before them, spirits that remain vibrant in memory and can be evoked for both counsel and courage.

Many of Danticat's stories are set in contemporary Haiti, but one event, the 1937 murders of Haitian citizens by soldiers from the Dominican Republic (an estimated 15,000 to 20,000 Haitian were killed at the Massacre River dividing the two countries) often remains fundamental in her characters' psyches, never more so than in *The Farming of Bones* (1998). Here she offered a frank portrayal of the starting point of Haiti's political realities by relating narratively how political upheaval affects ordinary people, in this case the lives of Amabelle and her lover Sebastian. Danticat strove to depict Haitian people as individuals rather than as an indefinable political mass.

Not one to discriminate when presenting Haitian views, Danticat gave voice to a *ton ton Macoute* (literally translated as "bogeyman" in Haitian Creole, but in this context a name for the dictator Francois Duvalier's secret police who were given license to torture and kill Duvalier's opponents) in *The Dew Breaker* (2004). This unnamed "dew breaker"—a torturer who would collect his victims at dawn—remains haunted by his participation in multiple murders. Many years later both he and his victims' family members have no choice but to reinvent themselves.

Though she was regarded by many as a contemporary literary voice of and for Haiti, Danticat did not view herself as a representative of Haitian Americans, feeling that to perceive her as such would silence all other Haitian voices. Danticat's works centered on the themes of migration, separation, gender, sexuality, power (or lack of it), and female unity, but her literary wish was to give voice to the lost. Each of her works suggests one should be a witness within any community. Moreover, her writing demonstrated that the definition of multiculturalism changes each time a new wave of immigrants enters American society.

Equally interested in portraying Haitian pride as well as its suffering, Danticat served as associate producer of a documentary made by Jonathan Demme, *Courage and Pain* (1996), about Haitian torture survivors. She maintained that Haiti, one of the most underrepresented countries in the world, is in fact one of the strongest countries on earth because of its people. Danticat's 2007 memoir, *Brother I'm Dying*, won the National Book Critics Circle Award and was nominated for the National Book Award. In 2011 she was the recipient of a MacArthur Fellows Program "Genius" Award.

FURTHER READING

Anglesey, Zoë. "The Voice of the Storytellers: An Interview with Edwidge Danticat," *MultiCultural Review* 7.3 (1998).

Lyons, Bonnie. "An Interview with Edwidge Danticat," *Contemporary Literature* 44.2 (2003).

Shea, Renée H. "The Dangerous Job of Edwidge Danticat: An Interview," *Callaloo* 19.2 (1996).

LISA MUIR

Darby, Dorothy (b. 1909?), parachutist and pilot, was born in Cleveland, Ohio. Nothing is known about her parents, childhood, or education. She was attracted to flying by the career of BESSIE COLEMAN, aviation's first African American female licensed pilot and an inspiration to many blacks and women who dreamed of pursuing a career in aviation, even after her untimely death in 1926. Darby, along with WILLIE SUICIDE JONES, was one of the few blacks to make a living as a barnstorming daredevil. In 1932 Darby took flying lessons at the Curtiss-Wright Aeronautical University in Chicago, a flight school and aeronautical engineering training ground named after American aviation pioneers, Glenn Curtiss and the Wright brothers. She made her first parachute jump in the summer of 1932 and quickly embraced the activity, performing exhibition jumps. One such jump in October of 1932 in St. Louis, Missouri, ended badly when she broke both ankles and suffered significant internal injuries. After her recovery she found herself in demand at air shows all over the Midwest, where she performed daredevil jumps to thrill the crowds. In 1935 she performed a notable publicity jump, parachuting into the boxer JOE LOUIS's training camp as he was preparing for an upcoming heavyweight fight against Max Baer.

Although Darby's first flying lessons were in 1932, she did not earn her pilot's license until 1938, when she completed flight training at the Pontiac Municipal Airport in Michigan. She continued to attract attention through a series of publicity events, including a flight in 1938 on Memorial Day in which she was commissioned by black Chicago-area aviators to drop a wreath of flowers on Bessie Coleman's grave as part of a tribute celebrating the aviation pioneer. On 21 June 1938 she again visited a Joe Louis training camp, this time flying in with over 50,000 signatures on board from fans in Detroit and surrounding Michigan towns, offering support for the "Brown Bomber of Detroit" in his rematch with the German boxer Max Schmeling.

FURTHER READING

Gubert, Betty Kaplan, Miriam Sawyer, and Caroline M. Fannin. *Distinguished African Americans in Aviation and Space Science* (2002).

DOUGLAS FLEMING ROOSA

Darden, Christine Voncile Mann (10 Sept. 1942–), aeronautical engineer at NASA, was born Christine Voncile Mann in Monroe, North Carolina, the youngest of five children born to two schoolteachers, Noah Horace Mann, Sr. (a former Latin teacher who later became an insurance salesman), and Desma Chaney Mann. Darden credits her success and her early interest in science to her parents' emphasis on their children's education. She recalls that when she was just three years old her mother began taking Darden and her siblings to classes she taught at the two-room schoolhouse across the street from the family home. Darden began doing the schoolwork that the other children did and was soon working two grades ahead in school. Her father also encouraged his daughter's interest in auto mechanics and fixing things around the house, early training for an engineer. Because she was younger than her classmates and therefore socially vulnerable, her parents sent her to a Methodist college preparatory boarding school for African American girls, where Darden developed an interest in mathematics.

Her parents expected their children to attend college, as all of Darden's older siblings did, and so Darden enrolled at the Hampton Institute in Virginia in the late 1950s. Neither the all-black parochial high school nor Hampton were subject to the battles over integration and civil rights demonstrations at public schools throughout the South in those years, so Darden was able to focus on her studies, and her interests in math and science were nurtured by teachers. She graduated from Hampton in 1962 with a degree in physics and minor in mathematics, as well as a teaching certificate because her parents wanted to make sure she was prepared for an occupation. Soon after graduation she married William Darden, Jr., a middle school science teacher, and taught junior high and high school math for several years while also starting a family. She applied for and received an assistantship to pursue graduate studies at Virginia State College, completing her master's degree in applied mathematics in 1967 and immediately securing a position as a data analyst or "computer" at the NASA Langley Research Center in Virginia.

The computers were a nearly all-female staff who performed mathematical calculations for the engineers. Even though she used her math background in this position, Darden became bored and requested a position in the engineering group. She initially met resistance to this idea since women, even those with comparable skills and experience as the male engineers, were generally confined to jobs in the computing pool. In 1973 Darden was finally promoted to engineer and decided to pursue a Ph.D. at George Washington University (GWU) in Washington, D.C., in order to advance her career to the next level. At GWU she was often the only woman and the only African American in her classes. At this time, there were very few women of any race in university engineering programs, much less employed in high-level positions.

Darden received her Ph.D. in mechanical engineering in 1983. At this time only 13.1 percent of the scientists and engineers employed at NASA were women and approximately 8.7 percent were black. Still, this was greater representation than throughout industry at large, where, in 1984, 12 percent of scientists and engineers were women, but only 2 percent were black. Two decades later absolutely no progress had been made, as women and African Americans continue to be underrepresented in these fields. According to National Science Foundation statistics for 2003, still only 2 percent of engineers were black and only 9.2 percent were women, actually a drop from twenty years earlier. The actual numbers of black women in engineering are even more dismal. Out of 93,400 employed doctoral-level engineers accounted for by the NSF in 2003, only 200 of these were black women, all of which makes Darden's long and prominent career in a specialized sub-field, that of aerospace engineering, even more remarkable. By the time Darden was pursuing her Ph.D. she was also raising three children and, like most professional women, found it difficult to juggle her own career and educational goals with the demands of a young family. She always felt, however, that she received support and encouragement from her colleagues and supervisors at NASA to continue in her career.

At NASA in the 1970s and 1980s Darden became recognized as an expert on the effects of sonic booms. She created a computer software program for simulating and testing sonic booms in wind tunnels. Her program, aspects of which are still in use today, was a less expensive and more efficient replacement of earlier methods that relied upon building and testing actual aircraft models. She eventually became leader of the sonic boom research team and later worked on redesigning the wings and nose cone of the supersonic transport airplane to minimize the sonic boom when flying over populated areas. Her team also researched the environmental and atmospheric effects of supersonic aircraft.

After 1999 Darden had a more administrative than research-based role at NASA. She was director of the Aero Performing Center and has authored or coauthored more than fifty technical publications. As an administrator, she has been an important advisor on programs and budgets at NASA. Her service and research have been recognized with numerous awards and honors, including the A.T. Weathers Technical Achievement Award of the National Technical Association (1985), the Candace Award for Science and Technology of the National Coalition of 100 Black Women (1987), and NASA Certificates of Outstanding Performance (1989, 1991, and 1992). In 1988 she was named Black Engineer of the Year in Government by the corporate and academic partner-publishers of *Black Engineer* magazine. Darden has also been active in her church community and was ordained as an elder in the Presbyterian church in 1980. She has been a role model and path breaker for women and African Americans, not only at NASA, but in the field of engineering in general.

FURTHER READING
Warren, Wini. *Black Women Scientists in the United States* (1999).

TIFFANY K. WAYNE

Dart, Isom (1848–3 Oct. 1900), black cowboy and rustler, also known as Ned Huddleston, was born in Arkansas. Dart's early life is an enigma. Biographical accounts give a lively Wild West picture of an itinerant cowboy and occasional gang member based on legend and folklore. What is known is that sometime in the mid-1880s Dart settled in Brown's Hole, an isolated area where the borders of Colorado, Wyoming, and Utah meet. He worked initially for the Middlesex Land and Cattle Company but later found gainful employment on the Bassett Ranch.

Dart was adept at many practical trades, but his true calling was as a cowboy. His skill in handling horses and in the use of the rope soon distinguished him as one of the best cowhands in the region. Dart's congeniality also helped him gain acceptance in social circles. He became an adopted member of the Bassett family. In time he became quite knowledgeable about the people with whom he worked or who worked in the area, both honest and dishonest. Although a sociable man, he never married.

Dart's notoriety as a rustler mirrored his cultural surroundings. Brown's Hole was well known as an outlaws' hangout because of its rugged terrain and its distance from law-enforcement centers. Even some resident ranchers, such as Elizabeth Bassett for whom Dart worked, were suspected of rustling the livestock of their neighbors.

Many remember Dart as but another resident cowboy who supplemented his income by rustling livestock and was very good at it. To his credit, Dart tried to establish a legitimate ranch of his own. His personal property was always meager compared with that of the large landowners, but he had some business savvy. Though some people did not believe that all his stock had been acquired legally, public records reveal only a few concerted efforts to bring him to justice. From 1888 to 1890 Dart appeared in district court only five times in Sweetwater County, Wyoming, and in Routt County, Colorado, on the charges of larceny, destruction of personal property, stealing horses, and illegally branding neat cattle. Unable to find either any credible evidence to the contrary or any witnesses to testify against Dart, the Sweetwater County attorney dismissed all the charges.

An often-reported story portrays Dart as an honest and, through inference, forgiving man. In 1888 the Sweetwater County deputy sheriff Elroy Philbrick sought out and arrested Dart. At one point during the long ride to Green River the buckboard slipped off the road, and Philbrick was seriously injured. Dart came to his aid, took Philbrick to the hospital, and then turned himself over to the sheriff. At Dart's trial Philbrick told the jury what Dart had done. As the story goes, the jury was so impressed by Dart's honesty and generosity that it ignored the evidence against him and rendered a verdict of not guilty.

In reality, after his cases were dismissed, Dart sued Philbrick for $5,000 in personal damages. At issue was Philbrick's authority to arrest Dart. Dart argued that he was in Routt County, Colorado, at the time of his apprehension and that Philbrick's warrant from Wyoming Territory was thus not applicable in Colorado. Only extradition proceedings could legally bring Dart to Sweetwater County from Colorado. Philbrick countered that he, Philbrick, may have been in Colorado, but he had a valid warrant for Dart's arrest anyway. Philbrick was found innocent. Dart's lawyer asked for a new trial, but none was held.

In Routt County, Dart was charged along with two other men with theft and destruction of property. Dart was taken into custody and stood trial. Although found guilty, he apparently eluded punishment by escaping from jail.

By 1900 vigilante justice had come to the Brown's Hole area. Fed up with the continuing problem of rustlers, wealthy cattlemen hired Tom Horn, a notorious stock detective, to do their bidding. Horn mailed anonymous warnings to his intended victims, instructing them to leave the area or face the consequences. Horn's threats did not deter anyone. That summer Horn killed two of Dart's neighbors, Matt Rash and James McKnight. Ten years had passed since Dart's last court appearance, but he was still under suspicion for rustling livestock. While walking outside his cabin, Dart was shot and died immediately. No one was charged with Dart's death, but most historians believe that Tom Horn killed Dart.

Isom Dart was well known for being a skilled cowboy, and by all accounts he relished that lifestyle. More important, Dart's presence as a black cowboy was part of the cultural diversity characteristic of the American West, and his fate was but another example of how prominent cattlemen once brandished their influence.

FURTHER READING

Civil and criminal case files involving Isom Dart are at the Wyoming State Archives and at the Colorado State Archives.

McClure, Grace. *The Bassett Women* (1985).

Tittsworth, W. G. *Outskirt Episodes* (1927).

Stiff, Cary. "Isom Dart," *Empire Magazine* (13 July 1969): 10–16.

Wilson, Sandy. "Horse Thief: Cattle Rustling and Legitimate Wrangling," *Wild West*, Feb. 1985, 10–12 and 16.

Obituary: *Craig Courier*, 13 Oct. 1900.

This entry is taken from the *American National Biography* and is published here with the permission of the American Council of Learned Societies.

CARL V. HALLBERG

Dash, Julie (22 Oct. 1952–), screenwriter, director, producer, and novelist, was born in Long Island City, New York. Although Dash grew up in New York City, she often visited the South Carolina Sea Islands. Her father and his family were raised in the Gullah culture, and Dash ate Gullah cooking and heard the Gullah language spoken among them. She was inspired by her uncle, St. Julian Bennett Dash—a tenor saxophone player who introduced Dash to his Bolex and the camera equipment he used to document his tours with his band—to make films. The young Dash explored the equipment and began to experiment with photography.

Dash's film career got an early start when she enrolled in a film production workshop at the

Studio Museum of Harlem in 1968. At first, she thought she had enrolled in a course in photojournalism, but she soon learned that it was a motion picture workshop. She had, accidentally, found her niche. She went on to attend the City College of New York (CCNY), where she majored in film production. Dash was awarded a bachelor's degree from CCNY in 1974, at which point she had already made a short documentary, *Working Models of Success* (1973), for the New York Urban Coalition.

In 1975 Dash was awarded a fellowship to study at the American Film Institute (AFI), and she moved to Los Angeles to study, first at the AFI and then at the University of California, Los Angeles (UCLA), where she pursued a graduate education in film. At UCLA, Dash was able to "explore film as both a political tool and [an] expressive medium" (Harris, 17). In the 1970s, during her time at UCLA, Dash also became part of what was known alternately as the "L.A. Rebellion" or the "L.A. School of Filmmakers," a movement in black independent film that sought to create new images of black men and women in both film and television. This group of black independent filmmakers included people like Haile Gerima, CHARLES BURNETT, and Billy Woodberry.

During her time at the AFI and at UCLA in the 1970s and 1980s, Dash produced *Diary of an African Nun*, which was adapted from a short story by ALICE WALKER in 1977, and subsequently Dash won a Director's Guild Award in 1977; *Four Women* (1978), a choreopoem; and, one of her most famous works, *Illusions* (1982), a short film about a black female film industry executive who passes for white in Hollywood during World War II. *Illusions* earned a number of awards, including the 1989 Jury Prize for Best Film of the Decade by the Black Filmmakers Foundation. Dash was awarded an MFA in Motion Picture and Television Production from UCLA in 1986. Dash's highly acclaimed *Daughters of the Dust* (1992) was the first theatrical-release feature film produced by an African American woman and "one of the best, and certainly one of the most important films to have emerged from the African Diaspora" (Michael Dembrow, 1). Dash had to raise money for six years in order to finish *Daughters*, which takes place in 1902 and tells the story of the Peazants, a Gullah family living on the Sea Islands off the coast of South Carolina but who are preparing to move north. Many distributors turned Dash down, claiming that there was no market for such a film, and she did not receive any financial support from the Hollywood studios. However, on the basis of footage she shot, Dash was able to secure funding in 1988 from the PBS series *American Playhouse* and began work on the film at that time.

Daughters of the Dust is a nonlinear film that focuses on the Gullah people, direct descendants of slaves who worked on rice plantations in Georgia, South Carolina, and the surrounding area. The film is most well known for its images of beautiful and diverse black women, its use of vivid color (the cinematography was by ARTHUR JAFA), its inclusion of West African traditions in the characters' culture and day-to-day routines, and of its acknowledgement of the continuing effects of the Atlantic slave trade on the Sea Islands. In 1992, at the time of its release, it was considered groundbreaking for African American film generally, and for the ways in which it offered alternative characterizations of African American women in particular.

The film and its director went on to win a number of awards and salutations. In 1999, for example, the Newark Black Film Festival honored Dash and called *Daughters of the Dust* one of "the most important cinematic achievements in Black Cinema in the 20th century." In 2004, *O, The Oprah Magazine* touted *Daughters* as one of its "50 Greatest Chick Flicks." In the same year, the Library of Congress placed *Daughters of the Dust* in the National Film Registry, where it joined 400 other American films that have been preserved as national treasures.

Despite the success of *Daughters of the Dust*, Dash had to find most of the financial backing for her films in television rather than in Hollywood. In 1997, for example, she directed the short "Sax Cantor Riff" for HBO's *Subway Stories: Tales from the Underground*, a compilation of short films about New York by different directors. In 1999 Dash directed *Funny Valentines* and *Incognito* for Black Entertainment Television. The following year she directed *Love Song* for MTV. During this time she also directed a number of music videos for artists ranging from Tony! Toni! Toné! to Tracy Chapman.

Dash again helmed a made-for-television film when she agreed to direct *The Rosa Parks Story* in 2002, at the request of ANGELA BASSETT, the film's star. The CBS television movie was awarded the NAACP Image Award, the Family Television Award, and the New York Christopher Award, and at the Fifty-fifth Annual Directors Guild Awards, Dash was nominated for Outstanding Directorial Achievement for her work on the film. Following this, Dash directed *Brothers of the Borderland* (2004), a short film for the National Underground Railroad Freedom Center Museum in Ohio.

Dash had one daughter, Nzinga, with the cinematographer, videomaker, and cultural critic Arthur Jafa. Her original vision and outstanding talents helped make her a major contributor to African American film and a prominent voice in the national dialogue about race and representation.

FURTHER READING

Dash, Julie. *Daughters of the Dust: The Making of an African American Woman's Film* (1992).

Dembrow, Michael. Notes Taken From the Cascade Festival of African Films #15. Available at http://spot.pcc.edu/~mdembrow/daughtersprogram.htm.

Foster, Gwendolyn Audrey. *Women Filmmakers of the African and Asian Diaspora: Decolonizing the Gaze, Locating Subjectivity* (1997).

Harris, Kwasi. "New Images: An Interview with Julie Dash and Alile Sharon Larkin," *Independent* (Dec. 1986).

NATASHA BAAFI

Dash, Leon Decosta, Jr. (16 Mar. 1944–), Pulitzer Prize–winning journalist and author, was born Leon DeCosta Dash Jr. in New Bedford, Massachusetts, the son of Leon Dash Sr. and Ruth Dash. His father worked as a postal clerk (and eventually a supervisor) and his mother was employed as an administrator for New York City's Health Department. Dash was raised in the Bronx and Harlem, New York, and originally aspired to become a lawyer. His interest shifted to journalism while he worked as an editor of the school newspaper at Lincoln University, a historically black college in Pennsylvania. He studied at Lincoln for two and a half years before transferring to Howard University in Washington, D.C., in the 1960s. He found work steam-cleaning building exteriors, but in winter the work was too challenging for him, so in 1965 he started working indoors at the *Washington Post* as a copy person. He worked the lobster shift—an overnight shift that began at 6:30 P.M. and ended at 2:30 A.M.—and in 1966 he was hired as a journalism intern and rookie reporter. Dash graduated from Howard University two years later and joined the U.S. Peace Corps.

From 1968 until 1970, Dash taught in Kenya, before he returned to the United States to resume working as a journalist at the *Post* in 1971. His love of social justice and the recently enacted civil rights laws inspired his interest in journalism. But his youthful idealism faded a bit early in his career. In 1997 he told Guy Friddell, a *Virginian-Pilot* reporter, "Within a decade I started doing the same stories over, particularly on the dilapidated conditions of public housing in Washington.... And those conditions had not changed. And up to this day it hasn't changed." Despite his reservations about his ability to effect change as a journalist, Dash continued to succeed as a writer. He went on to write three books, beginning with *The Shame of the Prisons*, coauthored by Ben Bagdikian, in 1972. Several years later, he became the West African bureau chief for the *Washington Post*, between 1979 and 1984. He had two children: Destiny Kloi Dash and Darla Dash.

He wrote not only about teenage pregnancy, murder, and prison guards' drug addictions, but he also reported from Angola (where he walked 2,100 miles in the company of guerrillas to cover the war there), Trinidad and Tobago, Barbados, Guadeloupe, Martinique, and St. Thomas.

During the next decade Dash came into his own as an investigative reporter and began to focus on the growing concerns about teenage parenthood. The problem was nationwide, but had assumed particular resonance in African American communities. The solution to the problem vexed critics both on the right and the left of the political spectrum. The stories he wrote about the issue led to his second book, published in 1989, *When Children Want Children: The Urban Crisis of Teenage Childbearing*. The book received a PEN/Martha Albrand Nonfiction special citation, which was one of many prestigious awards his work earned him. In 1986 he was awarded a general news award by the National Association of Black Journalists, an organization that Dash helped found, along with forty-three others. The following year, he received a first-place award from the Investigative Reporters and Editors Organization.

In the years that followed, he spent four years following and writing about the life of Rosa Lee Cunningham, a heroin addict born in 1936 who had borne eight children by six different fathers, and had been jailed repeatedly for dealing drugs and theft by the time Dash met her. The series appeared in the *Post* in 1994, and in 1995 it won the Pulitzer Prize for explanatory journalism and first prize for print journalism of the Robert F. Kennedy Book and Journalism Awards. The reportage that appeared in the series appeared in book form as *Rosa Lee: A Mother and Her Family in Urban America* (1996). Rosa Lee had become his friend, he told a reporter, and when she died from complications associated with HIV he not only missed her but he told the London *Observer* reporter Nicci Gerrard, "witnessing her life made me unable to judge any longer. After all, I am black. It could have been me."

In 1998 Dash retired from the *Washington Post* and took a professorship at University of Illinois at Urbana-Champaign, where he taught journalism and African American studies at the College of Media. He has also been a visiting professor at the University of California, San Diego, and a Media Fellow of the Henry J. Kaiser Family Foundation. He was awarded an honorary Doctor of Humane Letters degree from Lincoln University in Pennsylvania in 1996.

FURTHER READING

Dash, Leon. *Rosa Lee: A Mother and Her Family in Urban America* (1996).

JOSHUNDA SANDERS

Dave the Potter (also known as David Drake, Dave of the *Hive*, and Dave Pottery) (c.1800–?), typesetter, potter, and poet, was born and lived his entire life in and around Edgefield, South Carolina, an important center for pottery production in the nineteenth century. Dave's parents were slaves belonging to Samuel Landrum, a Scottish immigrant who had moved his family and slaves to Edgefield, South Carolina, in 1773. The outlines of Dave's life story can be traced through the business activities and legal papers of his various owners, oral history from Edgefield, and Dave's own pottery upon which he inscribed sayings, verses, and dates.

After moving to Edgefield the Landrum family became involved in the making of pottery and other entrepreneurial enterprises. Amos and Abner Landrum, sons of Samuel, became partners with a third man, Harvey Drake, in a pottery concern. Dave first appears in the legal record in a 13 June 1818 mortgage agreement between Harvey Drake and Eldrid Simkins, both pottery factory owners in Edgefield. In this document, Dave, "a boy about 17 years old country born," and a female slave were mortgaged to Simkins. Four months later Amos Landrum settled the debt and Dave was back under the ownership of the Landrums and Harvey Drake. Dave next appears listed as an asset in a 1 July 1830 partnership agreement between Harvey and Reuben Drake.

In addition to being a partner with Harvey Drake in the pottery business and co-owner of Dave, Abner Landrum was also the publisher of two newspapers, the *South Carolina Republican*, a pro-Union paper, and later the *Hive*, an anti-nullification paper. Abner Landrum may have allowed, or even helped, Dave to learn to read and write so that Dave could work as a typesetter for his papers. Regardless of how Dave learned to read, Landrum apparently did not just tolerate but even exploited Dave's skills to his advantage. An editorial in the *Edgefield Advertiser* dated 1 April 1863 described "Dave Pottery" as an older man who was "once connected with a paper known as the *Edgefield Hive*." Abner Landrum's pro-Union views, not popular in Edgefield in the years of the nullification crisis, led him to cease publication of his newspapers and move to Columbia, South Carolina, in 1832.

Dave remained behind in Edgefield, where he next appears in court records after the death of Harvey Drake. Drake's estate inventory from 31 January 1833 lists "1 Negro man named Dave," sold to Reuben Drake and Jasper Gibbs. Reuben and Harvey Drake had been partners in a pottery operation before Harvey's death; after his death, Reuben Drake and Jasper Gibbs became partners.

Exactly when Dave began to turn pots is unknown, but the first surviving vessels that can be firmly attributed to him date to 1834, a year after the formation of Drake & Gibbs. Dave's first signed pottery is dated 12 July 1834 and is inscribed with the verse: "Put every bit all between/surely this jar will hold 14." Two jars dated 1836, and two dated 1840 are inscribed with short poems composed and signed by the artist. On 31 July 1840 Dave inscribed a pot with the lines "Dave belongs to Mr. Miles/wher [sic] the oven bakes & the pot biles [sic]," a verse that indicates that by 1840, he had been transferred from Drake & Gibbs to Miles, who was Abner Landrum's son-in-law. The exact history of his legal ownership in the 1840s and 1850s is difficult to trace. Nevertheless it is certain that he continued to turn pots for the Edgefield pottery owners Lewis Miles, B. F. Landrum, and John Landrum during these years. Several "Dave" jars dated in the 1840s are marked "Lm," indicating they were made for Lewis Miles's factory. In the *Edgefield Advertiser* of 17 February 1846 an advertisement for the sale of John Landrum's estate lists Dave among the "properties" to be sold as "an excellent Stone Ware Turner." That Dave continued to belong in some capacity to the Landrum family is suggested by a pot of 14 April 1859, which says "When Noble Dr. [Abner] Landrum is dead/May Guardian Angels visit his bed."

Almost nothing is known of Dave's personal life and family. One clue appears on a pot dated 16 August 1857, which proclaims, "I wonder where is all my relations/Friendship to all—and every nation." Whether he was married or had children is not known for certain, but one interpretation of the poignant 1857 verse suggests that Dave's family had been sold away from him, an all too common misfortune common for enslaved families.

Dave continued to throw pots, some of enormous size, until at least 1864, when his last signed and dated piece is known. After Emancipation, Dave took the surname of his former owner Harvey Drake. How long David Drake continued to produce pottery after 1864 is unknown. Toward the end of his production years he began turning with an assistant potter, and his jars decreased in size. Both of these facts suggest that Dave began to find it more difficult to manage the pottery wheel as he aged. David Drake last appears in the federal census of 1870, in which he is listed as seventy years old. He does not appear in the 1880 federal census for Edgefield. The exact date of his death is unknown.

Dave's pottery is remarkable on several fronts. His largest pots, with a capacity of twenty-five gallons or more, remain among the largest thrown pottery ever created in the United States. Such large jars require both great physical strength and tremendous technical mastery of throwing, coiling, glazing, and firing techniques. Oral tradition from Edgefield asserts that Dave suffered the loss of one leg as a young man in an accident on the railroad tracks. The exact identification of Dave the Potter as the one-legged Dave of Edgefield is not entirely certain, but seems likely. To throw pots as large as Dave's is physically as well as artistically and technically demanding, and to have done so with one leg makes his large jars all the more remarkable.

In addition to his outstanding skills as a master craftsman Dave is remembered for his verses. A total of twenty-nine surviving pots by Dave contain verse inscriptions, and more than a hundred surviving jars are signed and dated. The subjects of his poetry range from meditations upon Bible scripture and general moral lessons, to instructions for using (and proud descriptions of) his pots, to observations about society and his position as a slave, to tributes to various members of the Edgefield community, to flirtatious overtures and innuendoes. His verses are marked by a sophisticated use of language and evince familiarity with poetic forms as well as biblical scripture and record a rare first-hand voice from within the institution of slavery.

By 1834 it had become illegal in South Carolina for slaves to learn to read. That Dave was able to learn to read and write in this climate is a remarkable feat. That he sometimes visibly flouted the law prohibiting slaves from becoming literate by inscribing pottery with his verses is also a testament to his courage. Gaps between inscribed vessels,

sometimes of several years, may simply mean that some of Dave's pottery has not survived; however it has been suggested that in the repressive climate of the late antebellum years Dave's "silence" may indicate that there were times when he chose to remain silent to avoid bringing any dangerous attention to his illegal accomplishment.

In the years of Dave's most prolific production, he created both the largest and greatest number of pots thrown by an Edgefield potter. Facing formidable social, legal, and physical obstacles, Dave nevertheless became the area's most accomplished turner, and is still considered one of America's true master potters. His jars are esteemed for their beauty, the technical prowess of their maker, and their extraordinary poetic inscriptions. Dave Drake's inscribed jars are held in the collections of several major museums, including the Smithsonian Institution, the Charleston Museum, the Atlanta History Center, and the McKissick Museum at the University of South Carolina.

FURTHER READING

DeGroft, Aaron. "Eloquent Vessels/Poetics of Power: The Heroic Stoneware of 'Dave the Potter,'" *Winterthur Portfolio* 33.4 (1998).

Koverman, Jill Beute, ed. *I Made This Jar ... Dave: The Life and Works of the Enslaved African-American Potter, Dave* (1998).

ELIZABETH KUEBLER-WOLF

Davenport, Charles Edward "Cow Cow" (23 Apr. 1894–3 Dec. 1955), pianist, singer, and composer, was born Charles Edward Davenport in Anniston, Alabama, one of eight children of Queen Victoria Jacobs, a church organist, and Clement Davenport, a minister. He showed an interest in music early in childhood, teaching himself organ and briefly taking piano lessons at age twelve. At his father's urging he attended Alabama Theological Seminary (1910–1911) to train as a minister, but was later expelled for playing a march in ragtime style at a social event. Moving to Birmingham, he worked as a pianist at various venues including a club on Eighteenth Street. He then toured widely in towns in Alabama and Georgia. In 1917 he was discovered by the pianist Bob Davies and was invited to join his touring company, the "Barkroot Carnival." Working for the carnival gave Davenport a valuable range of musical and theatrical experience, including solo singing and playing, accompanying singers, and working as a comedian. Under Davies's mentorship Davenport considerably broadened his piano skills.

For several years thereafter he worked as a solo act and an accompanist in vaudeville and other types of entertainment including Haeg's Circus in Macon, Georgia, where he worked for an extended period as a blackface minstrel. Around 1917 he found a job as a brothel pianist in the Storyville section of New Orleans.

Davenport married Helen Rivers in 1921, but the union was short-lived. By 1922 he had teamed with the singer Dora Carr, and the pair toured extensively on the so-called Theater Owners' Booking Association (TOBA) and other vaudeville circuits. Initially playing in the South, by 1924 they were performing at major venues in the North such as the Lincoln Theater in New York. The same year Davenport made his first recordings, two sides for Okeh of vocal duets with Carr accompanied by CLARENCE WILLIAMS on piano. These were successful, and in the following two years Okeh released eight more sides featuring the duo, most of them blues-based vaudeville-style duets in the manner of other black comedy teams of the period such as Butterbeans and Susie. Between 1925 and 1927 Davenport recorded a series of piano rolls for Vocalstyle, US Music, and QRS. Although less well known than his disc recordings, his piano rolls are an integral part of his legacy and widely admired by connoisseurs.

Davenport's partnership with Carr ended probably in 1926 when she left him for another man. By the end of the year he had formed a new partnership with the singer Ivy (or Iva) Smith, with whom he toured on the TOBA as "Davenport & Smith's Chicago Steppers." The duo recorded for the Paramount, Vocalion, and Gennett labels between 1927 and 1930. Over the same period Davenport recorded important solo sides for these labels as well as accompanying a number of singers, including the vaudevillian Hound Head Henry and the minstrel Jim Towel. A major discovery was the singer Sam Theard, whom Davenport found in Chicago and with whom he made an important series of recordings, mainly for Brunswick, during 1929–1930.

Nearly all Davenport's most important recordings were made between 1925 and 1930. Although he has often been characterized as a boogie-woogie pianist, his basic style is a potent brew of folk blues and ragtime best described as "barrelhouse." Despite its earthy origins his playing never sounds crude, but instead his style combines technical sophistication with creativity and a depth of blues feeling matched by few other pianists. An example

is "Texas Shout" (Vocalion, 1929) an up-tempo, strident blues combining twelve-bar and sixteen-bar sections and featuring lightning-fast split octaves in the bass. No less impressive is Davenport's ability to sustain a slow blues. An outstanding instance is "My Own Man Blues" (Paramount, 1927) with Ivy Smith on vocal and Leroy Pickett on violin. Taken at an extremely slow, almost static, tempo, the track achieves an astonishing emotional intensity with a great economy of musical material.

A fine composer with a gift of adapting folk-based materials in a most creative manner, Davenport composed most of his important recordings. Perhaps his best known composition is "Cow Cow Blues," a rollicking barrelhouse number recorded by Davenport no less than eight times, including three times on piano roll. Originally titled "Railroad Blues," the song was later recycled as "Cow Cow Boogie," in which form it became, in 1942, a major swing-era hit (as Davenport was not credited for its composition, he sued for copyright infringement but was persuaded to settle out of court for just $500). No less important is "Mama Don't Allow," which became a jazz standard. Davenport also claimed authorship of the well-known "(I'll Be Glad When You're Dead) You Rascal You."

During the Depression Davenport organized a new act with Ivy Smith. The show toured extensively in the South; but after a promising start the show ran into trouble in Mobile. Unable to meet his costs by legitimate means, Davenport ended up in prison for six months. After his release Davenport, now broke and without work, rejoined Haeg's Circus as a minstrel and then, dispirited, went to Cleveland to live with his sister Martha. Cleveland was to become his permanent base. It was there he met his third wife, the dancer and singer Peggy Taylor. Their marriage was to last the rest of his life (his second marriage was to Iva France in the 1930s).

Davenport's career never regained its momentum after the Depression. His piano playing was compromised first by an illness in the 1930s, which Davenport described as pneumonia, then by a severe stroke in 1938, and finally by arthritis. He recorded little: just five sides for Decca in 1938 as a vocalist. For the rest of his life he performed only intermittently at New York nightspots like the Onyx Club (c. 1942) and the Stuyvesant Casino (1948), along with venues in Cleveland and elsewhere. He was for a time an editor of the magazine *Jazz Record*. He became an ASCAP member in 1946, which provided him with a small but steady income. He recorded sixteen piano sides made in

1945–1946 for the Comet, Circle, and Jazz Record labels, only eight of which were released. Around 1947 Davenport, semiretired from music, worked for the rest of his life at a Cleveland defense plant called Thomson Products. He died at his home from hardening of the arteries. Davenport's recordings from the 1920s show him as one of the finest early blues pianists, combining originality and depth of expression. It is regrettable that ill health compromised his playing at such a relatively early age.

FURTHER READING

Davenport, Cow Cow. "Mama Don't Low No Music," in *Selections from the Gutter: Jazz Portraits from The Jazz Record*, ed. Art Hodes (1977).

Evans, David. *Cow Cow Davenport Vol. 3: The Unissued 1940s Acetate Recordings*, Document DOCD-5586.

Harris, Sheldon. "Cow Cow Davenport," in *Blues Who's Who: A Biographical Dictionary of Blues Singers* (1979).

Silvester, Peter. *A Left Hand Like God: The Story of Boogie-Woogie* (1988).

PETER MUIR

David, Charles Walter, Jr. (20 June 1917–5 Feb. 1943), World War II coastguardsman and medal winner, was born and raised in New York, possibly in the borough of Manhattan. Nothing is known of David's early life.

While it is uncertain whether Charles David Jr. joined the coast guard prior to the war, or after the attack on Pearl Harbor, his rating at the time of his death suggests that he voluntarily enlisted late in 1941 or early 1942. By late 1942 David had joined the crew of the coast guard cutter *Comanche*, a 165-foot-long vessel that carried a crew of about six officers and sixty enlisted men. As an African American, David was assigned the only rating that blacks were allowed to hold at the time, that of steward's mate (with promotion available to steward). It was the job of the stewards and stewards' mates to serve the ship's officers, help to prepare and serve their meals, clean their quarters, and perform other affiliated duties. While general ratings (non-steward) for African Americans in the coast guard would eventually become available, opportunities were limited and usually restricted to those duty stations and ships outside of combat zones. However, that does not mean that black men like Charles David were not a part of the fighting coast guard; like any man aboard ship, in addition to their regular duties, he was also assigned general quarters stations when combat situations arose. In

this case, David and others like him could serve in a variety of capacities, perhaps as ammunition passers, stretcher bearers, or as a member of a gun crew. While it is unclear what Charles David's general quarters assignment was aboard *Comanche*, it is thought that sometime in 1942 he received training as a rescue swimmer. It was while serving in that capacity that David would be decorated for his heroism and sacrifice.

While little is known regarding the extent and duration of Charles David's rescue training, he surely showed acumen in learning endurance swimming, line and small raft handling, and perhaps some first-aid basics. This new "rescue retriever" type of technique practiced by David and others was one devised by the coast guard out of sheer necessity. With the ever-increasing number of Allied ships and men lost to German U-boats in the North Atlantic in 1942 and early 1943, new methods had to be used to save lives, and African American coastguardsmen would be a small but vital part of the solution.

On 29 January 1943 Steward's Mate First Class Charles Walter David Jr. was aboard the *Comanche* at St. John's, Newfoundland, and heading out to sea for convoy duty. Along with several other cutters, David's ship would be escorting two merchant vessels and the armed transport *Dorchester* to Greenland as part of convoy SG-19. The armed transport was a large and valuable ship, carrying nearly 1,000 sailors and soldiers; in the early morning hours of 3 February the *Dorchester* fell victim to a German U-boat attack, hit by five torpedoes from the U-223. The cutter *Comanche* was just 2,500 yards away and quickly manned its battle stations, but it was too late. Just twenty minutes after the attack, the *Dorchester* sank by the stern, taking down with it over 650 souls. This incident would soon gain international renown, not only because of the huge loss of life but also because of the heroism of four army chaplains who sacrificed their lives so that others might live. The chaplains aboard the *Dorchester*, one Catholic, one Jewish, one Methodist, and one Dutch Reformed, helped the ship's passengers and crew into lifeboats and gave up their own life jackets to needy passengers, as well as offering encouragement and spiritual support. Their deeds would be commemorated in memorials, songs, and a postage stamp. However, there were other heroes born out of the *Dorchester* incident that have been all but forgotten; the African American coastguardsmen and rescue swimmers Charles David Jr. and WARREN DEYAMPERT.

Once the area of the sinking was determined to be clear of enemy submarines, the cutter *Comanche* moved in to assist in the rescue efforts. The cutter rescued ninety-seven men utilizing the rescue-retriever method, of which Charles David was one of the main participants. Spending several hours in the frigid waters David repeatedly dove overboard to save a number of men, and even saved the life of the *Comanche's* executive officer, Lieutenant Langford Anderson, who could not pull himself out of the water owing to exposure and exhaustion after participating in rescue efforts. However, David would pay the ultimate price for his heroism; two days later he died from the effects of hypothermia suffered during the rescue operations.

For his courage David was posthumously awarded the Navy and Marine Corps Medal. David's final resting place is unknown; he may have been buried at sea, or in Greenland, where his ship made port to land *Dorchester* survivors. If the latter were the case, he may have been re-interred at a private cemetery in his native New York after the war. Whether owing to a clerical error or simply because he was given a private burial, David is not listed on any World War II soldier or sailor memorials. However, David deserves to be remembered as an exemplar of African American service in the coast guard during the war, and one whose courage and sacrifice helped to pave the way for future generations of black coast guard men and women who would serve and be judged based on their individual qualities, not on the color of their skin.

FURTHER READING

Knoblock, Glenn A. *Forgotten Sacrifice: African American Naval, Coast Guard, and Merchant Marine Casualties in World War II* (forthcoming 2008).

United States Coast Guard. *Comanche, 1934 (WPG-76)*. Available from http://www.uscg.mil/history/webcutters/Cutters_W_PG_76.html.

United States Coast Guard. *Negroes Died WW II* (undated handwritten list in the Coast Guard Historian's Office, n.d., c. 1947).

GLENN ALLEN KNOBLOCK

Davidson, Shelby J. (10 May 1868–2 Aug. 1930), inventor, was born to Shelby Jeames and Amelia Scott Davidson in Lexington, Kentucky. He attended public school in his hometown of Lexington and then attended college in Louisville to study education. This school's program did not challenge Davidson or adequately prepare him for a career. So

in the fall of 1887 he enrolled at Howard University in Washington, D.C. However, his previous academic training was not sufficient to gain admission to Howard University's college department. He spent his first two years completing the preparatory program and finally received a degree in 1896. That same year he began to study law, and by June 1896 he had completed standard readings in the law curriculum under the direction of William A. Cook.

In 1893, while Davidson completed his education, he found employment as an unclassified laborer for the Treasury Department, making $600 per year. He secured this position through the help of William C.-P. Breckenridge—a congressman from Kentucky's Seventh District. After a few years, Davidson began to rise through the governmental ranks. The Treasury Department eventually transferred Davidson to the office of the auditor for the Post Office Department. He was soon promoted to an assistant messenger position on 4 February 1897, and then to a class C money order assorter on 1 May 1898. The year 1899 saw his rapid rise within the Treasury Department, and he was also admitted to the bars of Kentucky and the District of Columbia.

Davidson's success at obtaining federal employment directly resulted from the aid of supporters such as Breckenridge and Congressman Walter Evans, from Kentucky. On 16 August 1899 a "friend" within the Treasury Department informed Davidson of an impending appointment. How Davidson was able to cultivate such important and influential friends is uncertain, but his series of swift promotions implies a judicious use of contacts. By mid-September his promotion won approval, and by January of 1900 he was promoted to the one-thousand-dollar salary grade. Early in the twentieth century, the Post Office Division of the Treasury Department began testing the feasibility of using adding machines. It was at this time that Davidson became intrigued and captivated by these highly complex devices. By 1901 the post office was using about a dozen adding machines, but their performance proved disappointing. At one point, five of the twelve machines required repair. John B. Sleman, the head of the division, desperately searched for a solution to the growing problem. Word made its way back to Sleman that Davidson seemed to have quite a command of the workings of adding machines. He asked, or more likely persuaded, Davidson to fix the machines, and in a short time Davidson was unofficially designated the chief clerk in charge of "repairs, care and maintenance of adding machines" (letter from Shelby J. Davidson to WILLIAM HENRY LEWIS,

27 Jan. 1912, Shelby J. Davidson Collection, Howard University). He performed well enough to merit promotions in 1903, 1906, and 1909, by which time he was making $1,600 annually.

On 1 February 1894 Davidson married the enterprising Leonora Coates. She was a beauty culturist and chiropodist and taught these subjects at the National Institute for Women and Girls in Washington, D.C. For a short period she even marketed her own lineaments and owned and managed a cafeteria business in Washington. As his work for the Treasury Department blossomed, the Davidsons also became integral members of the black elite in Washington, D.C. By the middle of the twentieth century's first decade, Davidson had become a key member of Washington's most prestigious clubs. On 4 March 1905 the Pen and Pencil Club of Washington commissioned him as a colonel. Davidson was also member of the more exclusive Mu-So-Lit Club, which catered exclusively to the finest of Washington's black male population. In May 1905 the Bethel Literary and Historical Association (BLHA) elected Davidson president.

As Davidson's social standing solidified, his inventing career began to simultaneously emerge. In March 1906 Davidson filed his first patent application for an adding machine device. By this time, Davidson was solely in charge of his division's adding machines and witnessed the impact they were having on the work environment. Davidson had designed an advanced system for auditing data. Below is a list of innovations and accomplishments that he had, by his own estimation, been responsible for:

- Clamp-board for holding money-orders.
- Plan of voucher audit submitted to auditor Timme (1906).
- "Rewind Device" for saving paper, patented.
- Synopsis of plan resulting in present machine audit.
- Planned and secured the repair shop.
- Suggested and supervised test of placing transcripts on machine.
- Supervised the successful test of auditing certificates deposits.
- Standardized, through Board of Supplies, ribbons for machines.
- Suggested and planned style of table used for machines.
- Suggested and secured typewriter chairs for operators.
- Suggested and successfully tested using adding machines to carrying out accounting.
- Invented metal adjustable [money order] holder.

- Invented "Automatic Fee Device," patent pending.

Davidson had technical success, but as government space began to segregate he would eventually lose all of his power and authority in the division. Davidson, in a letter to the Honorable William H. Lewis, assistant attorney general of the United States, on 27 January 1912, would cogently explain his situation:

> [b]ecause I am a colored man and this is the crux of the whole situation, I believe the whole situation of relieving me of the supervisory work on [adding] machines was for this reason and I, the only negro [sic] in this Bureau who had worked up from a laborer to such a place.... Every other man in a supervisory capacity on this division, except one has come on the work since I did and record to record have done no more than I by way of effort and the success of work assigned to me.... Had I been white instead of colored I do not doubt at all that I would have been chief of one of the divisions instead of now being on trial, hounded, persecuted and expected to make another record in order to maintain my present rating and this under the most adverse and painful conditions.... Bluntly put I have obeyed the mandate of the service.... I have earned recognition, as long as I was quiet and content to so remain, all was well, as soon as I contended for what I had earned and had reason to expect, I am side-tracked and by shifting am [sic] expected to llose [sic] my rating, the whole situation is anomalous, unjust; it is just this that is enervating the service and causing reproach to government.

Although Davidson had been able to avoid the racial constraints of previous years, he was now fully in their grasp. He seemed to be fighting for all exploited and undervalued black government workers. No matter how hard Davidson worked to invent an environment for the Treasury Department's Post Office Division, American racial discrimination would not allow him to succeed. Davidson resigned from government service in 1912.

Davidson had smartly positioned himself to leave the comfortable confines of government service. He would not have quit such a well-paying (albeit mundane) job if he did not have an alternate plan. That alternative plan was to make use of his legal education. The entire time Davidson worked for the Treasury Department's Post Office Division he was bolstering his legal credentials. In 1903 the D.C. Court of Appeals admitted him to practice law. Then in 1912 the United States Supreme Court admitted Davidson to practice law before the high court. Law was not the only thing Davidson engaged himself with when he vacated his post. He had founded a real estate business around 1909. The House of Davidson specialized in the management of "desirable properties for colored clients." Socially he continued to command a position of esteem among black elites. The General Alumni Association of Howard University elected him president in 1916 and 1917. He also became more politically active and strengthened his relationship with the NAACP. In addition to being appointed a colonel in 1921, he also became the executive secretary and chairman of the membership committee of the District of Columbia's NAACP in the early 1920s. Davidson had built a very comfortable life for himself by the time he passed away in 1930.

FURTHER READING

Fouché, Rayvon. *Black Inventors in the Age of Segregation* (2005).

RAYVON FOUCHÉ

Davis, Alexander K. (fl. 1869–1877), lieutenant governor of Mississippi, was probably the most obscure of the African American politicians to reach high state office during Reconstruction. In 1871 Davis testified before a select committee of the U.S. Congress that he had moved from Shelby County, Tennessee, to Noxubee County in eastern Mississippi in June 1869, but he did not state how old he was or whether he had been a slave or free before the end of the Civil War. If he was born a slave it would be significant since all but one of the eighteen blacks elected to statewide office in the South during Reconstruction were born free, many of them in northern states. Although Davis testified before Congress that he had been admitted to the bar, he did not mention in which state he earned this qualification, though it was almost certainly not Mississippi. IRVIN C. MOLLISON's extensive history of early black lawyers in Mississippi indicates that no African Americans were admitted to the bar in Mississippi prior to 1873 and makes no mention at all of Davis in his study. It is possible, though, that like many early southern black lawyers he had studied law in Canada or a northern state.

Whatever his legal qualifications, Davis must have impressed the local Republican Party and the voters of Noxubee County who elected him to the Mississippi House of Representatives in November 1869, only five months after he arrived from Tennessee. Two other African Americans were elected to the house from Noxubee County, the population of which at that time was around 80 percent black. Almost immediately the white minority in Noxubee began to challenge the new political order. Shortly after the 1869 elections the county's leading white newspaper changed its masthead to read, "All the Time in Opposition to Negro Suffrage." The Ku Klux Klan and other white supremacist groups also grew in strength in the county, lynching between fifteen and twenty blacks in 1870 and 1871 and whipping or beating many others, including women and children. Davis testified to Congress in 1871 that many whites opposed being taxed to pay for the new public school system as well as that masked whites had burned down both black and white schools. He also noted the success of the Klan in intimidating witnesses and preventing any of the perpetrators of these crimes from being prosecuted in the court. In spite of similar efforts to intimidate black voters in the 1871 elections, Noxubee County returned Davis to the Mississippi House for a second term.

In the 1873 elections Davis was one of several black Republican legislators to seek statewide office. Historians of Reconstruction in Mississippi have generally agreed, however, that he was probably the least accomplished of the candidates for lieutenant governor and that most African Americans in the legislature supported Hannibal C. Carter for that post. For reasons that are not entirely clear, however, Adelbert Ames, the Republican Party's nominee for governor chose Davis and not Carter as his running mate. Following the election of Ames and Davis in November 1873, many observers expected that Ames would use his position as governor to secure a seat in the U.S. Senate, leaving Alexander K. Davis as Mississippi's first African American governor and as only the second black governor in the nation, after P. B. S. PINCHBACK.

Davis's tenure in office proved highly controversial. By attempting to work with the Democratic minority to reduce taxes, he fell afoul of many of his fellow black Republicans. He also courted controversy in May 1874 when, as acting governor while Ames was visiting New Orleans, he removed several of the governor's appointees, replacing them with friends of his own, as well as pardoning several felons. Ames promptly restored many of his appointees when he returned to the state, but Democrats gleefully attempted to use the conflict between the governor and Davis to weaken the Republican Party prior to the 1875 elections. When, after a campaign of violence and intimidation, the Democrats regained the Mississippi legislature, they immediately launched impeachment proceedings against both Ames and Davis, though they impeached

Davis first, so as to prevent him from succeeding Ames as governor, even for a short period. Although Davis attempted to resign before he was impeached, Governor Ames refused to accept it. On 13 March 1876 the Mississippi Senate voted by a large majority to remove Alexander Davis from office on five charges of misconduct, including bribery. Although he was later cleared of the bribery charge in criminal court, Davis played no further role in Mississippi politics. It is unknown when or where he died.

FURTHER READING

For Alexander K. Davis's testimony about Ku Klux Klan activities in Noxubee County, see *Testimony Taken by the Joint Select Committee to Inquire into the Condition of Affairs in the Late Insurrectionary States. Mississippi. Volume I* (1872).

Harris, William C. *The Day of the Carpetbagger: Republican Reconstruction in Mississippi* (1979)

Wharton, Vernon Lane. *The Negro in Mississippi, 1865–1890* (1947).

STEVEN J. NIVEN

Davis, Allison (14 Oct. 1902–21 Nov. 1983), social anthropologist, psychologist, and educator, was born William Allison Davis in Washington, D.C., the son of John Abraham Davis, a federal employee, and Gabrielle Dorothy Beale, a homemaker. His younger brother JOHN AUBREY DAVIS became a civil rights activist and educator. He also had a sister, Dorothy. Davis enrolled at Williams College in Massachusetts, where segregationist policies prevented him from living on campus. He earned a B.A. in English and was the valedictorian of the class of 1924. From 1925 to 1932 he taught English literature at Hampton Institute, an historically black school in Virginia. One of his students at Hampton was the sociologist ST. CLAIR DRAKE JR., who later collaborated with Davis and Gunnar Myrdal on *The Negro Church and Associations in the Lower South: Research Memorandum [and] The Negro Church and Associations in Chicago* (1940).

Davis earned an M.A. in Comparative Literature in 1925 and an M.A. in Anthropology in 1932 from Harvard University then conducted field research for the social anthropologist W. Lloyd Warner from 1932 to 1935. In 1929 Davis married Alice Elizabeth Stubbs. He was a professor of anthropology at Dillard University in New Orleans from 1935 to 1938 and was a research associate at Yale University's Institute of Human Relations in 1938–1939. In that latter year he was given a three-year faculty appointment at the University of Chicago underwritten by the Rosenwald Fund, becoming arguably the first African American to hold a tenure-track teaching position at a major, northern, predominantly white institution. He and ABRAM LINCOLN HARRIS were the first two African Americans to be granted tenure at the University of Chicago.

Davis earned his Ph.D. from the University of Chicago in 1942. As the recipient of a prestigious Julius Rosenwald Fund Fellowship he studied anthropology at the London School of Economics in 1933. The Rosenwald Fellowship allowed Davis and his wife to move to London, where he studied with noted the British anthropologists Bronislaw Malinowski and Lancelot Hogben. Davis held visiting appointments at Columbia University, the University of Michigan, Smith College, the University of Pittsburgh, and the University of California at Berkeley. He also won MacArthur Foundation "genius" grants in 1982 and 1983 that allowed him to further his work on the life and career of MARTIN LUTHER KING JR. The end result of this study was his last book, *Leadership, Love, and Aggression: How the Twig Is Bent* (1983), a psychological profile of King, W. E. B. DuBois, RICHARD WRIGHT, and FREDERICK DOUGLASS coauthored with Robert J. Havighurst. In 1988 he established the Allison Davis Lecture Series at the University of Chicago, which annually brought to campus a distinguished African American scholar for a lecture and short residency.

Davis was a member of the American Academy of Arts and Sciences (and its first fellow elected from the field of education), the American Psychiatric Association, and the Center for Advanced Study in the Behavioral Sciences, where he was also a fellow from 1959 until 1960. Davis was the first recipient of the John Dewey Distinguished Service Professor at University of Chicago, in 1970, and earned the Teachers College Distinguished Service (in education) Medal from Columbia University, and the SOLOMON CARTER FULLER award from the American Psychiatric Association in 1977. From 1978 to 1980 and again in 1981 and 1982 he won grants from the Spencer Foundation.

Davis retired as professor emeritus from the University of Chicago in 1978. He served on the President's Commission on Civil Rights from 1966 to 1967, during the administration of Lyndon B. Johnson, and was vice-chair of the Commission on Manpower Retraining for the U. S. Department of Labor from 1968 to 1972, under President Richard M. Nixon. He was also a member of the Conference to Ensure Civil Rights in 1965 and the White House Task Force on the Gifted in 1968.

Among other works, his books include *Children of Bondage: The Personality Development of Negro Youth in the Urban South* (1940), coauthored with John Dollard and published by the American Council on Education. He also coauthored *Deep South: A Social Anthropological Study of Caste and Class* (1941) with the researchers Burleigh B. Gardner and Mary R. Gardner. A study of the cotton plantation system and color caste system in Natchez, Mississippi, and surroundings, *Deep South* was the first work to apply anthropological techniques to a critical analysis of race. It was a risky collaboration between the Gardners, a white couple who interviewed the whites in the study, and Davis and his first wife, Elizabeth Stubbs Davis, who interviewed the blacks (after Elizabeth's death in 1966, Davis married Lois Mason in 1969). Both books continue to be among the most consulted research on American blacks.

Davis's other publications include *Social-Class Influences upon Learning* (1948), which pointed out the cultural and class biases of IQ tests against children from economically disadvantaged backgrounds, and *Compensatory Education for Cultural Deprivation*, which he wrote with Benjamin S. Bloom and Robert Hess in 1964. His investigation into test bias spurred the development of early childhood learning programs such as Head Start. Davis and Kenneth Walter Eells also developed the *Davis-Eells Test of General Intelligence or Problem-Solving Ability* in 1953. Davis died a month after unsuccessful heart surgery in Chicago.

Davis's investigation of the relationship between culture, social class, and race and the nature of intelligence contributed to the theoretical foundations later attributed to the multicultural education movement of the 1960s. He was the first to systematically challenge the validity of standardized testing and to suggest that IQ tests were culturally biased against lower socioeconomic and minority children. His research directly fostered pedagogical changes in the teaching of socially and economically disadvantaged children.

FURTHER READING

Davis's papers are at the University of Chicago Library Special Collections Research Center.

Hillis, Michael R. "Allison Davis and the Study of Race, Social Class, and Schooling," *Journal of Negro Education* 64 (1995).

Obituaries: *Chicago Tribune*, 24 Nov. 1983; *Newsweek*, 5 Dec. 1983.

JAYNE R. BEILKE

Davis, Angela Yvonne (26 Jan. 1944–), radical activist, scholar, and prison abolitionist, was born in Birmingham, Alabama, to Frank and Sally Davis. Her father, a former teacher, owned a service station, and her mother was a schoolteacher. Both had ties to the NAACP and friends in numerous radical groups, including the Communist Party. When Angela was four years old, her family moved from a housing project to a white neighborhood across town. The experience of being the only African Americans surrounded by hostile whites taught Davis at a young age the ravages of racism. Indeed, during the mid- to late 1940s, as more black families began moving into the area, white residents responded with violence, and the neighborhood took on the unenviable nickname "Dynamite Hill." Davis's racial consciousness was further sharpened by attending the city's vastly inferior segregated public schools. As a junior at Birmingham's Parker High School, at the age of fourteen, Davis applied to two programs that could get her out of Alabama: early entrance to Fisk University, where she wanted to pursue a degree in medicine, and a program sponsored by the American Friends Service Committee to attend an integrated high school in the North. After much deliberation and with the encouragement of her parents, she opted for the latter, and in 1959 she moved to New York City. Davis lived with a leftist Episcopalian priest and his wife in Brooklyn and each day went to the Elisabeth Irwin High School on the edge of Greenwich Village. Stimulated intellectually and politically, she read the *Communist Manifesto* for the first time and later recalled that it hit her "like a bolt of lightning" (Davis, 109). During this time Davis also began going to meetings of an organization called Advance, a Marxist-Leninist student group affiliated with the Communist Party, as well as attending the lectures of the historian Herbert Aptheker at the American Institute for Marxist Studies.

Although her interest in radical theory did not wane during her college years at Brandeis University in Waltham, Massachusetts, it was tempered by what she viewed as the complacency of the student body there. One of only three African Americans in her freshman class in the fall of 1961, Davis often felt alienated and alone, but she eventually befriended a handful of international students. In the midst of white middle- and upper-class political apathy, she forged ahead in her own pursuit of knowledge and experience outside the confines of Brandeis. During the summer of 1962 she traveled to Helsinki, Finland, to participate in the Eighth World Festival for Youth and Students. She spent 1963–1964, her junior year, in France and, upon her return, began an intense intellectual relationship with the German-born Marxist philosopher Herbert Marcuse.

After receiving a B.A. in French Literature in 1965, Davis entered the University of Frankfurt in West Germany to pursue a Ph.D. in Philosophy. During her two years there, she followed a pattern that marked her entire career, combining intensive study with political activism. In Frankfurt, Davis joined numerous socialist student groups and regularly participated in protests and demonstrations. But as she watched, from across the Atlantic, the civil rights movement in the United States take a dramatic turn away from nonviolence and toward black power and black nationalism, she yearned to be involved in what she referred to in her autobiography as the Black Liberation Movement. Davis left West Germany for the University of California, San Diego, where Marcuse was teaching. There she worked with the Black Panther Political Party (which was not affiliated with the Black Panther Party for Self-Defense, led by ELDRIDGE CLEAVER, BOBBY SEALE, and HUEY NEWTON) and a fledgling Los Angeles branch of the Student Nonviolent Coordinating Committee (SNCC). In 1969, however, she left both groups after being frustrated by their ideological infighting, sexism, and anticommunism and officially joined the Communist Party. She became a member of a cell in Los Angeles known as the Che-Lumumba Club (named after Che Guevara, the Latin American revolutionary, and Patrice Lumumba, the radical Congolese independence leader).

Davis's activism made her well known among southern Californian leftists, but she did not achieve national or international attention until the late 1960s, when two events catapulted her into the spotlight. Indeed, they would secure for Davis the near mythic status, depending on one's political perspective, of an iconic hero or the country's most dangerous subversive. The first episode occurred in 1969, when the Board of Regents of the University of California, supported by Governor Ronald Reagan, fired Davis from her teaching position at University of California at Los Angeles, where she had received a non-tenure-track appointment in the philosophy department while completing her Ph.D. They cited a 1949 law prohibiting the hiring of Communists in the state university system. After months of legal wrangling, the board finally voted in June 1970 not to extend her

Angela Davis, civil rights activist, at her home in East Oakland, California, 9 September 1974. She wears two chains representing her commitment to struggle. One is the hammer and sickle of the Communist Party. The other is an ivory dragon, an ancient symbol of strength. (AP Images.)

appointment to a second year. Davis filed an appeal, but the controversy was soon overshadowed by the defining moment in her life as a political activist, the Soledad Brothers case.

In February 1970 GEORGE JACKSON, John Clutchette, and Fleeta Drumgo, three African American inmates at the Soledad prison in north-central California, had been indicted for the murder of a white prison guard. The lack of evidence or witnesses to the crime, which had occurred during a melee inside prison walls, led many to believe that this was yet another example of the entrenched racism within the justice system, a perversion of the very system that was designed to protect American citizens, and a frame-up. Angela Davis quickly became a leader in the Soledad Brothers Defense Committee and soon developed a close relationship with Jackson, the most visible of the three, whose letters from prison would be published in 1971. On 7 August 1970, Jackson's younger brother Jonathan entered a courtroom in Marin County, pulled out a machine gun, and allegedly demanded the release of the Soledad Brothers. With the help of three San Quentin inmates who were present in the courtroom, Jackson took the judge and four other people hostage. Before they could get away, guards opened fire; in the ensuing gun battle Jonathan Jackson, two prisoners, and the judge were killed.

Less than ten days later a Marin County judge issued a warrant for the arrest of Angela Davis on one count of murder and five counts of kidnapping. According to the warrant, two of the guns used in the escape attempt were registered to Davis, which made her an accomplice. Thus began a high-profile manhunt, which included Davis's appearance on the FBI's Ten Most Wanted list and a cavalcade of press coverage, in which she was nearly universally described as a "black militant," "black radical," or "militant black Communist." She was finally caught in a Manhattan Howard Johnson's on 13 October 1970 and imprisoned in a Greenwich Village jail for women. Davis was soon extradited to California, where her trial began in January 1971. Eighteen months later, during which time an international movement to "Free Angela Davis" flourished, she was acquitted on all charges.

Although Angela Davis would never again reach this level of notoriety, she was instantly enshrined in the pantheon of legendary African American freedom fighters, and she continued to wage a political and intellectual battle against all forms of inequality for decades after her imprisonment. In the classroom, as a professor at San Francisco State and, beginning in 1991, the University of California, Santa Cruz; on the campaign trail, as a candidate for vice president on the Communist Party ticket in 1980 and 1984; and on the lecture circuit, as an outspoken critic of the U.S. prison system and its basis and role in the institutional perpetuation of racial and economic inequality, Davis remained a vibrant and vital voice on the political left during a period of ascendancy of conservatism in the United States.

Davis published numerous books and articles, including her own autobiography in 1974 and a study of the interconnectedness of gender, racial, and economic oppression, *Women, Race, & Class*, in 1981. During the 1990s she appeared at rallies and demonstrations across the country, on issues ranging from the Million Man March, to the campaign to free MUMIA ABU-JAMAL from prison, to the ballot initiative against affirmative action in California. By the early years of the twenty-first century Angela Davis was leading the fight against what she termed the "prison industrial complex," calling for the abolition, rather than merely the reform, of prisons in the United States. Ever a lightning rod for controversy and a voice of true radicalism, this struggle was no less compelling for its unpopularity—something to which Davis had long been accustomed.

FURTHER READING

Davis, Angela. *Angela Davis: An Autobiography* (1974)

Aptheker, Bettina. *Morning Breaks: The Trial of Angela Davis* (1975).

Gates, Henry Louis, Jr. ed. *Bearing Witness: Selections from African American Autobiography in the Twentieth Century* (1991).

STACY BRAUKMAN

Davis, Anthony Curtis (20 Feb. 1951–), pianist and composer, was born in Paterson, New Jersey, son of Charles Davis and Jeanne C. Davis. The family lived in New York City until Anthony was five and then moved to Pennsylvania, where his father, an English professor, founded the African American studies program at Penn State University. Anthony grew up around college communities and began to study music with Penn State faculty members when he was in junior high school. He focused at first on classical piano but became interested in jazz after listening to THELONIOUS MONK, and he began to explore improvisation when he was around fifteen. Davis studied English, philosophy, and music at Yale, where he received a B.A. in Music in 1975. Yale provided little support for his interest in jazz, however, so his training there was largely in European classical music. To pursue his growing interest in non-Western music he studied with the South Indian drummer Amrad Raghavan at Wesleyan University.

Davis's early influences were the great jazz modernists—Monk, DUKE ELLINGTON, BUD POWELL, and CECIL PERCIVAL TAYLOR—but he was also drawn to the playing and philosophy of the Association for the Advancement of Creative Musicians (AACM) in Chicago, whose influence encouraged him to explore the widest possible expression of the African American musical tradition. While still a student at Yale he formed the group Advent, a free jazz quintet, with trombonist GEORGE LEWIS and percussionist Gerry Hemingway. From 1974 to 1977 he was a member of the New Dalta Ahkri Band, a group led by trumpeter Leo Smith, Davis's first important mentor and leader of a New Haven cooperative group that drew its inspiration from the AACM. Davis formed a second group, a quartet that included vibraphonist Jay Hoggard, bassist Mark Helias, and drummer ED BLACKWELL, and in 1975 he toured Europe both as a soloist and as part of a trio with violinist Leroy Jenkins and flutist James Newton. Davis moved to New York City in 1977, a relatively late entry to the center of the jazz world that gave him a chance to avoid the powerfully conformist pressures of the music community. He developed close associations with a small group of equally adventurous musicians—the trombonist Lewis, pianists MUHAL

RICHARD ABRAMS and Amina Claudine Myers, and tenor saxophonists Frank Lowe and Ricky Ford. Davis was a member of the violinist Jenkins's trio from 1977 to 1980, and from 1978 to 1980 he led a duo and quartet with flutist James Newton. He recorded his first album as a leader in 1978, a Monk-influenced solo effort called *Past Lives*. The same year he recorded *Of Blues and Dreams*, with solo piano pieces, a three-part suite for quartet, and another piece for quartet. His solo effort *Lady of the Mirrors* (1980) reflected his growing interest in the Balinese gamelan and in Wayang, the Indonesian shadow-puppet theater; it included the piece "Wayang IV." The later, orchestrated version of this piece appeared on 1980's *Under the Double Moon* and showed a composer tightly controlling improvisation in an essentially tonal piece pervaded with Asian and African influences.

Hidden Voices (1979), a quintet effort that included Lewis, Newton, and drummer Pheeroan akLaff, was an interesting mixture of free and melodic playing, but in retrospect it seems preparatory to the formation of the group Episteme in 1981. That group served as an outlet for Davis's growing interest in the role of composition in a predominantly improvisational art form; the influence of Ellington in particular is evident. He began to use more notation in his compositions, and in his own words, "The improviser is required to work his way through the composition to find moments of personal expression" (Gramavision). The subsequent octet album, *Episteme*, was an initial exploration of these ideas; the compositions are characterized by a lyrical minimalism driven by a powerful rhythmic pulse. The next three albums continued in the same direction. *Variations in Dreamtime* (1982) is filled with complex melodic lines, propulsive rhythms, and unusual time signatures, and *I've Known Rivers* (1982), a trio with cellist Abdul Wadud and Newton, continues to explore the mixture of jazz rhythm and classical form. *Hemispheres* (1983) is a dance suite for a ten-member ensemble of winds, percussion, and strings in five movements, written with the dancer/choreographer Molissa Fenley and premiered as part of Brooklyn Academy of Music's Next Wave Festival. The piece is a musical depiction of Esu-Elegbara, a Pan-African trickster figure, filled with the rhythmic density that characterizes Davis's music in this period. By the mid-1980s Davis had grown restless with the constraints of the mainstream jazz tradition. In 1982 the New York Philharmonic performed his first piece for orchestra, "Still Waters." But it was the stage that

Davis eventually settled on. He began to develop his first opera, *X: The Life and Times of* MALCOLM X in workshops at the American Music Theater Festival. His brother Christopher first suggested the topic, and his cousin, the poet THULANI DAVIS, wrote the libretto. *X* received its initial performance in Philadelphia in 1985, and was officially premiered by the New York City Opera in 1986. The opera was recorded in 1992 and nominated for a Grammy Award for Best Contemporary Classical Composition in 1993. The framework for the opera is firmly Germanic, in the European modernist tradition of Richard Wagner and Alban Berg, but the orchestra includes Episteme as an improvising core within the larger score. The musical styles evolve with the plot: act I, big band swing; act II, bebop; and act III, JOHN WILLIAM COLTRANE modality; critics have also heard echoes of CHARLES MINGUS JR., Philip Glass, and Steve Reich. But the synthesis is true and unique. The opera's positive reception affirmed Davis's compositional skills and reinforced his personal affinities. As he noted, "I love opera, I love writing for the voice, and I love telling stories with music."

Davis's second opera was *Under the Double Moon*, a science fiction piece that was commissioned by the Opera Theatre of St. Louis. His third was *Tania*, based on the kidnapping of Patricia Hearst. The American Theater Music Festival premiered *Tania* in 1992, and a recording was released in 2001. The libretto by Michael John LaChiusa reflects the influence of musical theater; the piece has a strong comic element and is, by Davis's own account, the most obviously jazz-influenced of his operas. It evokes styles ranging from BILLIE HOLIDAY to Motown to Stephen Sondheim. The Chicago Lyric Opera premiered *Amistad*, Davis's fourth opera, in 1997, again with a libretto written by his cousin Thulani Davis. This work originated in a choral piece commissioned by several groups (including pianist Ursula Oppens) that Davis wrote in 1991, "Voyage through Death to Life upon These Shores," based on a ROBERT EARL HAYDEN poem that describes the Middle Passage. A fifth opera, *Ghost Factory*, was inspired by a painting done by his nine-year-old son Timothy; the libretto tells the story of a factory that removes the bones from bodies after death and turns them into ghosts.

By the early 1990s Davis devoted his attention almost entirely to composition. His classical pieces include a violin sonata (1991) commissioned by Carnegie Hall; "Maps" (1988), a violin concerto, commissioned by the Kansas City Symphony, and "Wayang 5," for piano and orchestra, both issued on a 1988 Gramavision recording, *The Ghost Factory*; "Notes from the Underground" (1988), commissioned by the American Composers' Orchestra; "Happy Valley Blues," commissioned by the jazz group the String Trio of New York and included on the 1997 String Trio/Davis Album, *Ellington, Monk, Mingus, Davis*; and "Pale Grass and Blue, Then Red" (1995), for the Jose Limon Dance Company. He has also completed a trilogy: "Esu Variations," commissioned by the Cultural Olympiad for the Atlanta Symphony and premiered in 1995; "Jacob's Ladder," commissioned by the Kansas City Symphony Orchestra and premiered in 1997; and "Tales (Tails) of a Signifying Monkey," commissioned by the Pittsburgh Symphony and premiered in 1998. In 1993 he composed the music for Tony Kushner's Broadway play *Angels in America*.

Davis did not completely abandon jazz composing and performance. In 1989 he recorded *Trio2* with Newton and Wadud, and in 1995 he toured with the David Wadud quintet. In 1981 and 1982 he taught at Yale, where he was also visiting composer in 1990, 1993, and 1996. He was a senior fellow in the Society for the Humanities at Cornell University in 1987, and he taught at Harvard from 1992 to 1996 as professor of music in the department of Afro-American studies. In 1998 he was appointed to the faculty of the University of California, San Diego. Davis was married to the soprano Cynthia Aaronson-Davis; the couple had a son, Jonah, and Davis had a son, Timothy, from a previous marriage.

Anthony Davis won widespread critical acclaim throughout his career and was accorded numerous honors, including an Academy Award (1996) and grants from the National Endowment of the Arts and the Lila Wallace Fund/Meet the Composer Fund for Jazz and Opera in America, the Ford Foundation, the National Institute for Musical Theater, and the Kitchen Center for Video, Music, Dance, Performance, and Film. He forged his own synthesis of European classical, African American jazz, and non-Western musical styles, and he creatively explored the fruitful, tension-filled relationship between notation and improvisation that has become central to modern jazz composition. Davis's view, expressed in a 1982 interview, is that "I would like to write orchestral works which would involve improvisation, but *scored* improvisation, so those works could be played by improvisers and non-improvisers alike" (Davis, 7). And as a composer, he

notes: "I feel free to draw from any influence, Black, Brown, or Beige, Asian, European, or African. In a sense, this freedom can only be realized through the composition, through the Musical Idea" (Tirro, 462).

FURTHER READING

Tirro, Frank. *Jazz: A History*, 2d ed. (1993).

Van Trikt, Ludwig. "Anthony Davis: Interview," *Cadence* 12 (Oct. 1986); *Coda* 272 (1997).

RONALD P. DUFOUR

Davis, Arthur Paul (21 Nov. 1904–21 Apr. 1996), scholar, professor, and cultural critic, was born in Hampton, Virginia, the youngest of nine siblings in one of Hampton's most socially prominent black families. His father, Andrew Davis, born a slave, was an 1872 graduate of Hampton Institute and was the "leading plasterer and plastering contractor in Hampton" (*Negro History Bulletin*, Jan. 1950). He and his wife, Frances S. Nash, were strict disciplinarians who taught their children to refuse any form of charity during the difficult Depression era and to refuse menial job offers from whites. Davis's parents also taught him high standards of decorum, including not eating watermelon, not shelling peas on the front porch, and avoiding "emotional excesses" (for example, "shouting" in church and talking loudly), he recalled in a 1944 essay called "When I Was in Knee Pants" (47).

Davis's parents sent him to the privately funded Whittier Elementary School, which employed the stern educational traditions of New England and had a well-stocked library funded by the town of Norwich, Connecticut. In the South of 1912 a grammar school library was rare. The well-known philanthropists Francis Greenwood Peabody, George Foster Peabody, Andrew Carnegie, and BOOKER T. WASHINGTON visited Whittier on yearly tours of black schools. Other notables, including former president William Howard Taft, spoke at the school and during their visits interacted with students, events Davis recounted in his essay "I Go to Whittier School." Davis graduated from Hampton Institute in 1922. He attended Howard University for the 1922–1923 academic year in order to meet language requirements for Columbia University, which had awarded him a scholarship. From Columbia University he received a B.A. degree in Philosophy and election to Phi Beta Kappa in 1927, an M.A. in 1929, and a Ph.D. in 1942.

Davis was the second black student to be elected to Phi Beta Kappa at Columbia University, and he attributed his high academic achievements to his concern that any "failure" meant disappointing his entire race (*Obsidian*, Winter 1978, quoted in *New Directions*, July 1980, 9). The photographer for the *New York Times* front-page article erroneously proclaimed him to be the first black Phi Beta Kappa and declined to photograph Davis upon seeing that he was too light-skinned to look like an African American in a photograph. In spite of his academic accomplishments, Davis was not offered an assistantship or teaching position during his graduate studies at Columbia University, a slight he attributed to racism. He supported himself by working outside the university as waiter, elevator operator, settlement house worker, and summer manager of a "Negro" motel, a position from which Davis often remarked that his "real" education came. As a resident of Harlem during the flourishing of the New Negro Renaissance, he met "Negroes of all kinds and classes" and socialized with celebrated writers, artists, and intellectuals, including LANGSTON HUGHES, COUNTÉE CULLEN, WALLACE THURMAN, and ALAIN LOCKE, editor of the ground-breaking anthology *The New Negro: An Interpretation* (1925).

Davis began his teaching career as an instructor of English from 1927 to 1928 at North Carolina College in Durham. He was a professor of English at Virginia Union University in Richmond from 1929 to 1944 and a professor of graduate English for Hampton Institute Summer School from 1943 to 1949. At Howard University he was a professor of English from 1944 to 1969 and a university professor from 1969 to 1980. From 1964 until his retirement in 1980, Davis taught the nation's first graduate course in black literature at Howard University. Teachers, graduate students, and postdoctoral scholars from across the nation took the two-semester survey course, which was offered during the regular academic year and in summer sessions to meet the needs of public school teachers.

A prolific writer of essays, scholarly articles, and newspaper columns, Davis's writing career began when his valedictorian address, "The Contribution of the Individual," was published in the *Southern Workman*'s August 1922 issue. He wrote for the *Norfolk Journal and Guide* a weekly newspaper column titled "Cross Currents," later named "With a Grain of Salt," from 1933 through 1950. Davis's first major academic publication, *Isaac Watts: His Life and Works* (1943), was self-published as a requirement of earning a Ph.D. from Columbia. However, in 1948 the biography was published in London in

recognition of Watts's bicentenary and received high critical acclaim there from the *Times' Literary Supplement*, which praised its "careful scholarship" and its unprecedented achievement of placing Watts "so well in historical perspective" (*London Times*, 27 Nov. 1948).

Davis's *The Negro Caravan* (1941), coedited with STERLING A. BROWN and ULYSSES LEE, received wide critical acclaim as a landmark anthology of black literature. Davis coedited *Cavalcade: Negro American Writing from 1760 to the Present* (1971) with J. SAUNDERS REDDING. This became a leading textbook in African American literature. He coedited with Joyce Ann Joyce *The New Cavalcade: African American Writing from 1760 to the Present*, Vols. I (1991) and II (1992). The second volume included an unprecedented number of black women poets. He also coedited with Michael Peplow *The New Negro Renaissance: An Anthology* and created *Ebony Harvest*, a series of twenty-six forty-five-minute radio lectures broadcast from American University radio station WAMU-FM in 1972 and 1973 and aired by approximately one-hundred public radio stations. Between 1922 and 1979 he published at least twenty-two cultural commentaries and essays for *The Crisis*, *Journal of Negro Education*, *Negro Digest*, *Common Ground*, and others; twenty-seven book reviews for *Opportunity*, *CLA Journal*, *Midwest Journal*, the *Washington Post*, and the *Journal of Negro History*; and thirty-five scholarly articles and essays in *Phylon*, the *CLA Journal*, and the few other venues interested in articles on black literature. His only published short story, "How John Boscoe Outsung the Devil," was published in several anthologies. While a university professor he also wrote speeches for John Cheek, at the time the president of Howard University. The recipient of numerous national and local awards, recognitions, and tributes, Davis died in Washington, D.C.

FURTHER READING

At Howard University, Washington, D.C., the Moorland-Spingarn Research Center's Reading Room contains a vertical file and card catalog entries for Davis, and the Moorland-Spingarn Manuscript Collection has several cataloged boxes of correspondence, manuscripts, and other materials by Davis.

Davis, Arthur Paul. "I Go to Whittier School," *Phylon* 21 (Summer 1960).

Davis, Arthur Paul. *Selected Black American, African, and Caribbean Authors: A Bio-Bibliography*, comps. James A. Page and Jae Min Roh (1985).

Davis, Arthur Paul. "When I Was in Knee Pants,"
Common Ground (Winter 1944).
Obituary: *Washington Post*, 23 Apr. 1996.

BEVERLY LANIER SKINNER

Davis, Artur (9 Oct. 1967–), U.S. congressman,
was born Artur Genestre Davis in Montgomery,
Alabama, and raised in a religious home by his
grandmother (name unknown) and mother
(name unknown), the latter an employee of the
Montgomery County school system for thirty
years. Davis lived a humble life on the lower-in-
come west side of Montgomery. Upon graduating
from Jefferson Davis High School with honors, he
left his hometown to attend Harvard University in
Cambridge, Massachusetts.

In 1990 he graduated magna cum laude with a
bachelor's degree in government from Harvard and
then began graduate studies at Harvard University
Law School. During his tenure at Harvard he made
the acquaintance of Barack Obama, the future president of the United States. Obama, then attending
Harvard Law School and president of the *Harvard
Law Review*, delivered a speech to students that
made a lasting impression on Davis; the two men
soon became friends. As a student, Davis served as
intern to Alabama Democratic U.S. Senator, Howell
Heflin, and earned the "Best Oralist Award" in the
Ames Moot Court Competition at Harvard Law.
He graduated cum laude with a Juris Doctorate
from Harvard Law School in 1993.

As a newly minted attorney Davis found himself
in demand. Despite offers to work at elite law firms
in the North, he had aspirations to effect positive
change and growth in his home state. Davis returned
to Montgomery, Alabama, and assumed an internship with the Southern Poverty Law Center, a legal
organization founded in 1971 to confront racism
and social injustices and once headed by the civil
rights leader JULIAN BOND. Later that same year
he began to clerk for Judge Myron H. Thompson,
who had been the first African American assistant attorney general for Alabama and the second
African American federal judge in the state. In 1994
Davis began work as an assistant U.S. attorney.
Having a near 100 percent conviction rate, he prevailed in numerous high-profile cases against drug
dealers and white-collar criminals. In 1998 Davis
entered private practice as a litigator and in 2000
ran against Congressman Earl F. Hilliard, who had
been a congressman for eight years and state politician in Alabama for thirty years, in the Democratic
Party primary. He lost the 2000 election, drawing

only 34 percent of the vote compared to Hilliard's
58 percent; however, he was determined to serve his
state and country as a member of the U.S. House of
Representatives and ran again in 2002. Hilliard won
the primary by a narrow 3 percent margin, neces-
sitating a runoff in June. Davis defeated Hilliard in
the runoff with 56 percent to his opponent's 44 percent and assumed office January 2003 as the representative for Alabama's 7th Congressional District.
The 7th Congressional District spans twelve counties from Birmingham and Tuscaloosa to the Black
Belt. In a 2004 primary Davis won 88 percent of the
vote over his opponent, Albert Turner Jr., whose
father was a leader of the "Bloody Sunday" march
in Selma, Alabama. In 2008 Davis ran unopposed
for the House seat.

In 2007 Davis became the first congressman outside of Illinois to publicly support Senator Obama's
candidacy for president. His seconding speech
at the 2008 Democratic National Convention in
Denver, Colorado, formally placed Barack Obama's
name for nomination. That same year, Davis worked
tirelessly as Obama's trusted campaign manager in
Alabama.

Davis has served the Committee on the Judiciary
subcommittees on Immigration, Citizenship,
Refugees, Border Security, and International Law
and on Crime, Terrorism, and Homeland Security,
as well as the Committee on Ways and Means
subcommittees on Social Security and on Income
Security and Family Support. He has served as a
member of the Congressional Black Caucus and
as vice chairman of the Democratic Congressional
Campaign Committee and the House New
Democratic Coalition. Davis was appointed Southern
regional co-chair for the Democratic Congressional
Campaign Committee and to the senior whip team
for the Democratic Caucus of the 109th Congress.
He is an unapologetic conservative democrat and
voted to have Congressman Charles B. Rangel,
member and co-founder of the Congressional Black
Caucus since 1971, removed as chairman of the
House Ways and Means Committee under allegations of ethical violations and failures to follow tax
laws. During the 111th Congress, Davis voted with the
Democratic Party 94.9 percent of the time. However,
in November 2009 he voted against the H.R. 3962
Affordable Health Care for America Act passed in
the Democrat-controlled House of Representatives,
making him the only member of the Congressional
Black Caucus to oppose the bill.

On 1 January 2009 forty-one-year-old Davis
married Tara Johnson of Montgomery, Alabama.

On 6 February 2009 Davis announced his highly anticipated candidacy for governor of Alabama. At the time of his announcement, Alabama had yet to nominate an African American on a major party ticket for governor; he could be the first. A win for Davis would make him the first African American governor of Alabama and one among a very short list of African American governors in U.S. history through 2009, including P. B. S. PINCHBACK of Louisiana, DOUGLAS WILDER of Virginia, DEVAL PATRICK of Massachusetts, and David Paterson of New York. However, Davis's opposition to President Obama's health care legislation proved his undoing in the 2010 Democratic Party primary, where his white opponent supported the law, and won the majority of African American votes. Davis later retired from Congress in 2010. By 2012 Davis had joined the Republican Party, and spoke at that year's Republican National Convention in support of GOP presidential candidate, Mitt Romney.

FURTHER READING

Davidson, Roger H., Walter J. Oleszek, and Frances E. Lee. *Congress and Its Members* (2007).

Fineman, Howard. "Part of Something Larger," *Newsweek*, 25 Feb. 2008.

Ifill, Gwen. *The Breakthrough: Politics and Race in the Age of Obama* (2009).

Wolffe, Richard. *Renegade: The Making of a President* (2009).

SAFIYA DALILAH HOSKINS

Davis, Belle (26 Apr. 1872–after 1938), dancer, singer, choreographer, and director, is a person whose origins are the subject of some question. According to the English-born black entertainer Gordon Stretton, Belle Davis "was a mezzo-soprano; tall black girl, native from New Orleans, very beautiful," but on a 1938 ship passenger list Davis signed in as a Chicagoan born in 1874. On a 1904 emergency passport issued in London she swore, "I was born at Houston, in the State of Texas" in 1872. (Besides this confusion in geography, over the years Davis apparently became younger, on other documents indicating her year of birth as 1873.) Her father was George Davis; the name of her mother is unknown. After an apprenticeship in American minstrelsy, she spent most of her professional career touring Europe from 1901 until 1938. Not only had she performed in front of a movie camera at least three times during the early years of the twentieth century but she also began recording "coon songs" in 1902. She became the second black woman in his-

tory to make a recording, preceded only by May C. Hyers, who recorded on cylinders in 1898.

By age seventeen, Belle Davis was a member of Sam T. Jack's Creole Company (1891), alongside Charles Johnson, DORA DEAN, Mattie Wilkes, BOB COLE, and other performers who were to become famous. The advance man—the man who traveled ahead to arrange the details of scheduling, publicity, accommodation, and other matters connected with a traveling show—was JOHN W. ISHAM, who organized his own Royal Octoroons Company in 1895, with Davis in the original cast. By 1897 this company had become so popular that Isham put out two additional companies of Octoroons. During 1896 to 1897 the cast included Mattie Wilkes, Inez Clough, J. ROSAMOND JOHNSON, Strut Payne, and the HYERS Sisters. The *Washington Morning Times* reported the following on 9 November 1896: "Among the many features of the great show were … the maids of the Oriental Huzzars, led by Miss Belle Davis … Miss Belle Davis gave a pleasing imitation of May Irwin in 'I Want You, Ma Honey' and other popular songs." The irony of this report is that Davis was praised for imitating a white singer, who imitated blacks as portrayed by white songwriters.

In the 1890s her performance style gradually took on a more decorous manner, in which prancing children—who combined suppleness with comedy—provided the amusement. She directed their stage act, and with two (and sometimes three or four) black children the vigorous act made for popular entertainment in British and Continental theaters. Davis's European and African ancestry sometimes got her billed as a "Creole," and in the United States, it was not uncommon for booking agents to encourage Miss Davis to "darken down," that is, to blacken her face. In the United States she was known as the "Queen of the ragtime singers," and the important music publisher E. B. Marks remembered her as a "coon shouter."

After the director John W. Isham's retirement, the last Octoroons company continued under the management of Will H. Isham (previously the company's acting manager), starring BILLY KERSANDS in a farcical vaudeville comedy titled *King Rastus*, with the Mallory Brothers (Edward and Frank), Mazie Brooks, and the team of Walter Smart and George. Davis owned the show's scenery and later foreclosed on the company and closed the show after the Octoroons failed to pay for the scenery's use. It was unusual for a performer like Davis to own the scenery, which suggests that her role went beyond that of a regular member.

Belle first toured Britain in a show called *Oriental America* in 1897–1898. By 1899 she had returned to the States and also toured on her own and appeared at the New York Venetian Terrace. In the 1900 program of the Octoroon company's *Seven-Eleven-Seventy-Seven*, she concluded the performance of "Thirty Minutes around the Opera" with "Oh, Listen to the Band." However, the black music critic Alex Rogers reviewed the program and pointed out Miss Davis's inability to deliver. He found her singing quite unsatisfactory and the opera scenes "butchered" (*Howard's American Magazine* [1900]; quoted in Arthur LaBrew, *Afro-American Music Review* [Jan.–June 1985]).

Davis's future career, however, would flourish mainly on European shores. She returned to Europe in 1901 when she was twenty-seven years old. She could already look back on a long and varied professional career. For her European adventure in 1901 she selected nine-year-old Irving "Sneeze" Williams and seven-year-old Fernandes "Sonny" Jones, both of whom would continue their careers as jazz musicians in 1920s Europe, as members of the International Five. The children would tap-dance and play harmonica. In later years her troupe included Walter Humphrey, LOUIS DOUGLAS, Archie Ware, Ralph Grayson, Lewis Hardcastle and presumably also Harry Fleming (sometimes spelled Flemming). Davis's troupe appeared on the reputable Empire Theatre circuit in late 1901, recorded in London in 1902 (including one of the earliest syncopated songs, "The Honey-Suckle and the Bee"), continued touring London and the provinces in 1903, and ventured to the Continent. Dozens of other African Americans were entertaining the British at this time, and on 9 June 1904 Davis married one of the more successful, HENRY TROY, in London.

In Vienna in 1904 Davis toured with three juveniles. Around late 1906 she was filmed for commercial distribution: Although the three versions of her silent movies were advertised as *Die schöne Davis und ihre drei Neger* (Belle Davis and her three Negroes), only two youngsters can be seen cavorting about. A fourth child joined the troupe in 1909. When the boys grew too large she recruited younger boys from America. The Empire circuit continued to employ the group, as did other leading theaters. In addition to their shows in England, the group presented their ten-minute stage act in Ireland, Scotland, and Wales between May 1906 and August 1909, and appeared in Berlin, the Hague, Paris, Vienna, St. Petersburg, and Brussels during the same period. By 1913 Belle Davis was widowed, but it is unknown as to when her first husband, Henry Troy, passed away. That year, Davis married her second husband, Edward Peter "Eddie" Whaley (a theatrical artist from Alabama). Her act had been seen by hundreds of thousands of Britons by 1914, but from 1914 to 1918 World War I prevented continental touring, and even more British audiences were exposed to Belle Davis (sometimes spelled Davies) and "Her Cracker Jacks," which were her youthful colleagues.

Although Davis remained in England during the war, in 1919 she moved to Paris, which became her new permanent home. During the 1920s she became choreographer for the world-famous Casino de Paris. She was responsible for the dance routines of revues such as *Paris en fleurs* (1925–1926), *Paris qui chante* and *Paris* (both 1926–1927), *Paris–New York* (1927), and *Tout Paris* (1928–1929). In 1929, now in her mid-fifties, she once again went on tour with a show of her own. In June, at the Hamburg Alcazar, she presented *Wunderland der Liebe—Tropische Leidenschaft*, a revue set in the South Seas. Her all-black cast included Hester Harvey, Bobby Vincent, and Annie and Willy Robbins (the latter, the only male in the troupe, appeared in blackface). She probably retired soon after. In 1938 she boarded the *Queen Mary* in Southampton to return to Chicago.

In Europe, Davis's well-dressed director's elegance was praised and is evidenced by surviving promotional material and her portrait on sheet music covers. The mercurial entertainment business could boast few acts that top theaters employed for the length of time she worked in Europe. Her qualities as a singer and dance director, combined with her professionalism while travelling from town to town and country to country, were solid. Davis enjoyed success at her chosen profession for three decades.

FURTHER READING

Abbott, Lynn, and Doug Seroff. *Ragged but Right: Black Travelling Shows, "Coon Songs," and the Dark Pathway to Blues and Jazz* (2007).

Lotz, Rainer E. *Black People: Entertainers of African Descent in Europe and Germany* (1997).

Marks, Edward Bennet. *They All Sang: From Tony Pastor to Rudy Vallee. As Told to Abbott J. Liebling* (1935).

RAINER E. LOTZ

Davis, Belva (13 Oct. 1932–), television journalist, was born Belvagene Davis in Monroe, Louisiana, to Florence Howard Mays and John Melton, a lumber worker. She grew up in Berkeley and Oakland, California, with her mother's family. As a child, Belva lived in housing projects, all eleven family members cramped into two small rooms. In 1951 she graduated from Berkeley High School in Berkeley, California. Although her grades were exceptional and she was accepted into San Francisco State University, she could not afford the tuition. Instead she began work in a clerical position with Oakland's Naval Supply Center.

In 1950 she married her boyfriend and next-door neighbor, Frank Davis Jr. and they moved to Washington, D.C., where Frank was stationed in the air force. Belva Davis took a job with the Office of Wage Stabilization. The couple's first child, Steven, was born in 1953. Frank's next station was Hawaii, but after two years the couple returned to Oakland. Davis's marriage dissolved not long after her second child, Darolyn, was born in 1959.

Without formal training, Davis learned the journalism trade by freelancing for *Jet* magazine and several weekly black newspapers, including the *Bay Area Independent* and the San Francisco *Sun-Reporter*. While working at the *Bay Area Independent* during a period of intense racial strife, she served as interpreter for MALCOLM X. At the time, Malcolm and the Black Muslims considered whites to be devils and refused to speak to them. Davis would repeat her white co-workers' interview questions so that, coming from a black person, Malcolm X would acknowledge the questions and reply.

In her first broadcasting job at Oakland radio station KSAN, Davis was the first black female at the station. She left KSAN to work at radio station KDIA, where her two-hour show included studio interviews, music, and political coverage. In 1963 she married the photographer William Moore.

In 1966 Davis joined KPIX-TV, San Francisco's CBS affiliate, replacing the television news anchor Nancy Reynolds and becoming the first female African American television reporter on the West Coast. Davis also hosted and helped to create *All Together Now*, one of the country's first primetime public affairs programs to focus on ethnic communities. In 1977 Davis moved to KQED, the PBS affiliate in San Francisco, where she anchored *A Closer Look* and the nightly news *Evening Edition* from 1977 to 1981.

For nearly two decades, starting in 1981, Davis was the news anchor and urban affairs specialist for KRON-TV, the NBC affiliate station in the San Francisco Bay Area. She covered topics ranging from political issues and fiscal concerns to city planning visions. She co-hosted the Sunday morning news and the public affairs program *California This Week*, where she remained for

eighteen years. In 1999 she became a special projects reporter for KRON-TV. As a features reporter, Davis interviewed political and community leaders on NewsCenter 4 *Daybreak Sunday Morning* and *Close-Up with Belva Davis*. In her *Bay Area Close-Up* reports, she profiled local people, organizations, and institutions that had a positive effect on their communities. In 1993 Davis went on to host KQED's Friday night current affairs program *This Week in Northern California*.

Davis retired from KRON in 1999 but kept working at KQED. For more than three decades she was instrumental in covering urban affairs and the needs of ethnic communities in the San Francisco Bay Area. For years Davis felt insecure because she lacked a college degree; however, she was inspired by the numerous politicians, celebrities, and activists she interviewed, among them the civil rights leader MARTIN LUTHER KING JR., the former U.S. attorney general Robert Kennedy, the migrant rights crusader Cesar Chavez, five U.S. presidents, the Cuban president Fidel Castro, and the former heavyweight boxing champion of the world MUHAMMAD ALI.

Davis was awarded three honorary doctorates for her television work and community service, the first from John F. Kennedy University in Pleasant Hill, California, the second from Golden Gate University in San Francisco, and the third from California State University at Sonoma. She won lifetime achievement awards from the International Women's Media Foundation, the National Association of Black Journalists, the Peralta Community College District, and her alma mater Berkeley High School. In 1996 she received the Governor's Award, the Northern California Chapter of National Academy of Television Arts and Sciences' highest lifetime achievement award. Earning six local Emmy's for her reporting, Davis received numerous other awards for her journalism, including national recognition from the Corporation for Public Broadcasting, Ohio State University, San Francisco State University, and the National Education Writers Association. She also won a Certificate of Excellence from the California Associated Press Television and Radio Association.

In 2004 the CORO Foundation presented Davis with its highest recognition, the Eagle Award; and the Legacy Foundation of Women's Forum West published Davis's oral history as a book and DVD, distributing it to colleges across the country. She was most proud of the International Women's Media Foundation's Lifetime Achievement Award, which recognized pioneering women journalists who paved the way for younger women.

Also well known for her labor activism, Davis served many years as a national vice president of the American Federation of Television and Radio Artists (AFTRA) and was the national chairperson of the union's Equal Employment Opportunities Committee. As the National Equal Employment Opportunities chair of AFTRA, she spent countless hours advocating for women, minorities, and those with disabilities. In 2002 Davis spoke at Federal Communication Commission hearings on setting new equal employment opportunity rules. She was a longtime activist for minority access and equality in the broadcast industry.

Davis received numerous community service awards for her volunteer work on behalf of a wide variety of causes. Active in the San Francisco Bay Area community, she served as trustee of the Fine Arts Museums of San Francisco, the Fort Mason Foundation, and the Glide Church Foundation. She sat on the Advisory Council of the International Museum of Women and was president of the San Francisco Museum of the African Diaspora, which opened in 2005. Davis helped shape the vision and content of the museum, which is dedicated to the idea that all of humanity is part of a vast extended family connected by Africa.

FURTHER READING

"Honoring a Media Icon." *Jet* 106.11 (13 Sept. 2004).

Stein, M. L. *Blacks in Communications, Journalism, Public Relations, and Advertising* (1972).

MARILYN L. GEARY

Davis, Benjamin Jefferson (27 May 1870–28 Oct. 1945), publisher and political figure, was born in Dawson, Georgia, the son of Mike Davis (who changed his name from Mike Haynes in 1868 or 1869) and Katherine Davis, farmers and former slaves. Benjamin's formal education ended after the sixth grade, and he worked as a bricklayer and teacher before becoming a printer. He learned the trade while working for Tom W. Loyless, a white Dawson publisher and printer, and then opened his own printing business. He soon became a moderately wealthy man, living in a two-story, fifteen-room house while his siblings eked out their livings as sharecroppers. In 1898 he married Jimmie Willard Porter, a Dawson native who had been educated at Hampton and Tuskegee institutes; they had a son and daughter.

In 1903 Davis began publishing the *Independent*, a black weekly newspaper that was sold throughout Georgia and that within a year reported a circulation of 100,000. Although the paper consisted mostly of club, social, and church news, as well as feature stories on new black-owned businesses, its scathing editorials condemning lynching, convict labor, and disenfranchisement made Davis "the idol of the backwoods poor Negro farmers." Banned in many Georgia towns because of its militancy, the *Independent* thrived on the advertising dollars that it attracted from Atlanta businesses and financial institutions, both white and black, after Davis relocated to that city in 1909.

Davis was a strong supporter of BOOKER T. WASHINGTON, who often contributed articles to the paper, and a detractor of MARCUS GARVEY and W. E. B. DuBOIS, although all three men felt the sting of Davis's barbs when he felt that they deserved them. As DuBois noted, Davis was "a fearless and forceful man." In 1919, when a bundle of papers was returned from a small Georgia town with a threatening note attached to it, Davis drove to the town and personally handed out the papers while about two hundred armed blacks and whites watched.

In Atlanta, Davis became a leader of the District Grand United Order of Odd Fellows, a black fraternal organization. Largely because of Davis's influence, the Odd Fellows grew to 33,000 members by 1912 and became the wealthiest black fraternity in the South. In 1912 he helped oversee the development of the Odd Fellows Block in downtown Atlanta. The block formed the center of the city's black commercial and professional community, and the Odd Fellows Building, which housed the *Independent*'s new offices, was the fraternity's crown jewel.

Davis was one of the wealthiest men in Atlanta; he owned three automobiles when most whites owned none, and he hired white people to buy his family's clothes in white stores so that his wife would not have to confront Jim Crow. Davis once received the president of Liberia at his mansion, the site of many a lavish party. His wealth and status as a businessman propelled him into partisan politics, and he soon became a force in the Republican Party. He attended every GOP national convention as a delegate from 1908 until his death.

In 1916 Davis appeared before the Platform Committee to advocate decreasing southern representation in Congress in direct proportion to black disenfranchisement. He served as secretary of the Georgia Republican Party for eighteen years and in 1925 became a member of the Republican National Committee. As a national committeeman during Calvin Coolidge's administration, Davis dispensed patronage, and appointments to all federal posts in

Georgia required his personal approval. His son "used to view with sardonic pleasure the small-time [white] postmasters beating a path to my father's door ... seeking favors of a Negro political boss."

Davis paid a high price for such power. Twice the Ku Klux Klan burned crosses on his lawn in protest of his political clout, and unknown assailants frequently threw rocks through his windows and slashed his cars' tires. After his inauguration in 1928, Herbert Hoover set out to purge powerful blacks like Davis from positions of importance in the state Republican organizations of the South, particularly in Georgia, South Carolina, and Mississippi, in an effort to make the GOP more attractive to southern white voters. Rumors began circulating that Davis had sold federal positions to the highest bidder and that he had humiliated white applicants for such jobs.

In 1928 Davis was called before a U.S. Senate special committee investigating campaign expenditures. He was grilled for a week, primarily by Senator Walter George (a democrat from Georgia), who got Davis to admit receiving $2,000 from Hoover to cover campaign expenses. When Davis could neither recall how he had spent the money nor produce any records or receipts, Hoover forced him to resign from the national committee.

Despite this embarrassment, Davis retained a great deal of influence in the state party organization. He was very successful at recruiting black voters for the GOP, an important fact in Atlanta, where blacks could vote in municipal elections. He also served as president of the Young Men's Republican Club of Georgia at the age of seventy-three. But in 1944 Davis showed signs of abandoning the GOP, as so many other blacks had done following their effective removal from positions of importance in the state organizations. The national convention attempted to unseat Davis's "black and tan" delegation (comprising both black and white members) in favor of an all-white one. Davis, whose son, BENJAMIN JEFFERSON DAVIS JR., had just won election to the New York City Council as a Communist, made reference to that election when addressing the convention and threatened to lead the GOP's few remaining blacks into the Communist Party if his delegation was not seated.

Davis stopped publishing the *Independent* in 1932, when its circulation had dropped to 27,000. Instead he devoted himself to political, fraternal, and community work through the Odd Fellows, the Young Men's Christian Association, the Atlanta Community Chest, the Masons, the Elks, and the Knights of Pythias. He became president of the Baptist Layman's League of Georgia and at the time of his death was editor of the *National Baptist Review*. He also assisted his son's political career despite their obvious philosophical differences. Davis died in Harlem during a visit with his children.

FURTHER READING

Horne, Gerald. *Black Liberation/Red Scare: Ben Davis [Jr.] and the Communist Party* (1993).

Walton, Hanes. *Black Republicans: The Politics of the Black and Tans* (1975).

Obituary: *New York Times*, 29 Oct. 1945.

This entry is taken from the *American National Biography* and is published here with the permission of the American Council of Learned Societies.

CHARLES W. CAREY JR.

Davis, Benjamin Jefferson (8 Sept. 1903–22 Aug. 1964), Communist Party leader, was born in Dawson, Georgia, the son of BENJAMIN JEFFERSON DAVIS SR., a publisher and businessman, and Willa Porter. Davis was educated as a secondary-school student at Morehouse College in Atlanta. He entered Amherst College in 1922 and graduated in 1925. At Amherst he starred on the football team and pursued lifelong interests in tennis and the violin. He then attended Harvard Law School, from which he graduated in 1928. He was a rarity—an African American from an affluent family in the Deep South; however, his wealth did not spare him the indignities of racial segregation. While still a student at Amherst, he was arrested in Atlanta for sitting in the white section of a trolley car. Only the intervention of his influential father prevented his being jailed. As he noted subsequently, it was the horror of Jim Crow—the complex of racial segregation, lynchings, and police brutality—that pushed him toward the political left.

After graduating from Harvard, Davis was well on his way to becoming a member of the black bourgeoisie. He worked for a period at a black-owned newspaper, the *Baltimore Afro-American*, and in Chicago with W. B. Ziff, who arranged advertising for the black press. He then returned to Georgia, where he passed the bar examination and opened a law practice.

At this point an incident occurred that led to Davis's joining the Communist Party (CP). ANGELO HERNDON, a young Communist in Georgia, was arrested under a slave insurrection statute after leading a militant demonstration demanding relief for the poor. WILLIAM PATTERSON, a black lawyer and Communist who led the International Labor

Defense, recruited Davis to handle Herndon's case. Through discussions with his client, Davis decided to join the party in 1933.

As Davis was joining the Communist Party, those African Americans who could vote were in the process of making a transition from voting for Republicans to voting for the Democratic party of Franklin D. Roosevelt. The GOP—particularly in the South, where Davis's father was a Republican leader—was pursuing a "lily-white" strategy that involved distancing itself from African Americans, who had been one of its staunchest bases of support; simultaneously, Roosevelt's "New Deal" promised relief from the ravages of the Great Depression.

Davis did not favor the Democrats, because in the South they continued to lift the banner of Jim Crow. His joining the CP was not unusual, given the times: many prominent African American intellectuals of that era—LANGSTON HUGHES and PAUL ROBESON, for example—worked closely with the Communists, not least because theirs was one of the few political parties that stood firmly in favor of racial equality. Moreover, the Soviet Union and the Communist International, which it sponsored—unlike the United States and its European allies—stood firmly in favor of the decolonization of Africa. Davis felt that capitalism was inextricably tied to the slave trade, slavery, and racism itself, and that socialism was the true path to equality.

Davis handled the trial of Herndon, and after the case went to the U.S. Supreme Court, with another lawyer dealing with the appeal, his client was freed. Davis went on to serve as one of the lawyers for the SCOTTSBORO BOYS, African American youths charged falsely with the rape of two white women. They too were eventually freed because of decisions by the high court—after many years and many appeals—but Alabama then retried and convicted them.

Threats on Davis's life and the CP's desire to provide a more prominent role for him led to his moving to New York City in the mid-1930s. There he worked as journalist and editor with a succession of Communist journals, including the *Harlem Liberator*, the *Negro Liberator*, and the *Daily Worker*. At that last paper, he worked closely with the budding novelist RICHARD WRIGHT, with whom he shared a party cell; in this Communist organizational unit, Davis had the opportunity to comment on and shape some of Wright's earliest writings.

At its zenith during the 1930s, the Communist Party in New York State had about twenty-seven thousand members, of whom about two thousand were African Americans. Davis played a key role in the founding of the National Negro Congress, which had been initiated by the Communists; for a while the NNC included leading members of the National Association for the Advancement of Colored People (NAACP), the labor leader A. PHILIP RANDOLPH, and the Reverend ADAM CLAYTON POWELL JR.

Davis developed a close political relationship with Powell, a New York City councilman. When Powell moved on to represent Harlem in the U.S. House of Representatives, he anointed Davis as his successor. Davis was duly elected in 1943 and received a broad range of support, particularly from noted black artists and athletes such as BILLIE HOLIDAY, LENA HORNE, JOE LOUIS, TEDDY WILSON, and COUNT BASIE. He received such support for a number of reasons. There were his qualifications—lawyer, journalist, powerful orator, and organizer. There was also the fact that at this time both the Democrats—who were influenced heavily by white southerners hostile to desegregation—and the Republicans were not attractive alternatives for African Americans. Moreover, in 1943 the United States was allied with the Soviet Union, which had led to a decline in anticommunism, a tendency that in any event was never strong among African Americans.

On the city council Davis fought for rent control, keeping transit fares low, and raising pay for teachers, among other measures. He received substantial support not only from African Americans but also from many Jewish Americans, who appreciated his support for the formation of the state of Israel and for trade unions. In 1945 he was reelected by an even larger margin of victory. By the time he ran for reelection in 1949, however, the political climate had changed dramatically. The wartime alliance with the USSR had ended, and in its place there was a cold war internationally and a "Red Scare" domestically. Supporting a Communist now carried a heavy political price; simultaneously, many of Davis's African American supporters were now being wooed by the Democratic administration of President Harry Truman.

During his race for the presidency in 1948, Truman was challenged from the left by Henry Wallace, nominated by the Progressive Party. Because Wallace received the support of such African American luminaries as Paul Robeson and W. E. B. DuBois, there was fear among some Democrats that Truman's support from black voters would be eroded; in a close race this could mean victory for Republican candidate Thomas Dewey. Furthermore, Truman found it difficult to portray his nation as a paragon of human rights in its cold war struggle with the Soviet Union when blacks were treated like third-class citizens. Those pressures led Truman to put forward a civil rights platform in 1948 that outstripped the efforts of his predecessors in the White House. The Democrats succeeded in helping to undermine electoral support for Wallace and for Davis. Not only was Davis defeated in his race for reelection to the city council in 1949; he was also tried and convicted, along with ten other Communist leaders, of violating the Smith Act, which made the teaching or propagation of Marxism-Leninism a crime. After the U.S. Supreme Court in 1951 upheld these convictions in *Dennis v. United States*, Davis was jailed in federal prison in Terre Haute, Indiana, from 1951 to 1955. While there, he filed suit against prison segregation; *Davis v. Brownell*, coming in the wake of the 1954 High Court decision invalidating racial segregation in schools (*Brown v. Board of Education*), led directly to the curbing of segregation in federal prisons. After his release from prison, Davis married Nina Stamler, who also had ties to the organized left; they had one child, a daughter.

Davis's final years with the CP were filled with tumult. In 1956, in the wake of the Soviet intervention in Hungary, the revelations about Stalin's brutal rule aired at the Twentieth Congress of the Soviet Communist Party, and the Suez War, turmoil erupted in the U.S. party. Davis was a leader of the "hardline" faction that resisted moves toward radical change spearheaded by "reformers." Some among the latter faction wanted the Communists to merge with other leftist parties and entities and become a "social democratic" organization, akin to the Socialist Party of France; others did not want the Party to be identified so closely with Moscow. There were those who disagreed with Davis's opposition to the actions of Israel, Britain, and France during the Suez War. Some felt that Davis's acceptance of the indictment of Stalin was not sufficiently enthusiastic; still others thought that Davis and his ideological allies should not have backed the Soviet intervention in Hungary. These internal party squabbles were exacerbated by the counterintelligence program of the Federal Bureau of Investigation that was designed, in part, to disrupt the party and ensure that it would play no role in the nascent civil rights movement.

When MARTIN LUTHER KING JR., the Atlanta minister and civil rights activist, was stabbed by a crazed assailant in New York City in 1958, Davis rushed to the hospital and provided blood for him. The Davis-King tie led J. Edgar Hoover to increase the FBI's surveillance of the civil rights movement. But as the civil rights movement was blooming, the Communist Party was weakening. Nevertheless, during the last years of his life Davis became a significant and frequent presence on college campuses, as students resisted bans on Communist speakers by inviting him to lecture. The struggle to invite Communists to speak on campus was a significant factor in generating the student activism of the 1960s, from the City College of New York to the University of California at Berkeley.

By the time Davis died in New York City, the Party was a shadow of its former self. His life showed, however, that African Americans denied equality ineluctably would opt for more radical solutions, and this in turn helped to spur civil rights reforms. African slaves had been an early form of capital and a factor in the evolution of capitalism; that a descendant of African slaves became such a staunch opponent of capitalism was, in that sense, the closing of a historical circle.

FURTHER READING

Davis's papers, including the unexpurgated version of his memoir, are at the Schomburg Center for Research in Black Culture of the New York Public Library.

Davis, Benjamin Jefferson. *Communist Councilman from Harlem: Autobiographical Notes Written in a Federal Penitentiary* (1969).

Foster, William Z. *History of the Communist Party of the United States* (1968).

Herndon, Angelo. *Let Me Live* (1937).

Horne, Gerald. *Black Liberation/Red Scare: Ben Davis and the Communist Party* (1994).

Obituaries: *New York Times*, 24 Aug. 1967; *Worker*, 1 Sept. 1967.

This entry is taken from the *American National Biography* and is published here with the permission of the American Council of Learned Societies.

GERALD HORNE

Davis, Benjamin O., Jr. (18 Dec. 1912–4 July 2002), was born Benjamin Oliver Davis Jr. in Washington, D.C., the son of the U.S. army's first black general, BENJAMIN O. DAVIS SR., and his wife, Elnora Dickerson. Davis spent most of his childhood living on different military bases. By the time he entered high school, his family had settled in Cleveland, Ohio, where he attended a predominantly white school. At his high school, he began to prove his leadership ability, winning elections for class president. After high school, he enrolled in Cleveland's Case Western Reserve University and later the University of Chicago, before he was accepted in 1932, through the influence of the congressman OSCAR DEPRIEST, into the United States Military Academy at West Point.

At West Point, which discouraged black cadets from applying at the time, Davis faced a hostile environment and routine exclusion by his peers. His classmates shunned him and only talked to him when it was absolutely necessary. No one roomed with him, and he ate all of his meals in silence. Although he faced less humiliation, perhaps, than the black West Point cadets before him, such as the academy's first black graduate, HENRY O. FLIPPER, Davis remembered his four difficult years at West Point as a time of solitude and loneliness that, in spite of its struggle, prepared him for life in and outside of the military. The anonymously written statement about Davis in the 1936 *Howitzer*, the West Point yearbook, alludes obliquely and evocatively to his experience and presages his later success, "The courage, tenacity, and intelligence with which he conquered a problem incomparably more difficult than Plebe year won for him the sincere admiration of his classmates, and his singleminded determination to continue in his chosen career cannot fail to inspire respect wherever fortune may lead him." His endurance and subsequent success in the military permanently opened the doors of the prestigious military academy to African Americans. Davis graduated in the top 15 percent of his class, becoming one of the two African American line officers in the U.S. Army. The other was his father. Shortly after his graduation from West Point, Davis married Agatha Scott. Davis was commissioned as a second lieutenant upon graduation and, because of his high class standing, should have been able to choose which branch of the military he wanted to join. But when he applied to be an officer in the Army Air Corps, he was denied. The military was not ready to send a black officer to lead an all-white squadron. Instead, he was assigned to the all-black Twenty-fourth Infantry Regiment at the segregated Fort Benning Army Base and charged with a variety of inconsequential duties. He was even barred from the officers club at Fort Benning, an insult he later described as one of the worst he suffered during his service in the military.

In 1940, as the U.S. prepared for World War II, there was growing public support for increased

Benjamin O. Davis Jr. in flight gear, standing next to an airplane at the air base in Ramitelli, Italy, March 1945. (Library of Congress.)

African American participation in the war. In an effort to address those concerns and simultaneously reach out to African American citizens as he prepared for the upcoming election, President Roosevelt promoted Benjamin O. Davis Sr. to brigadier general, the highest post ever held by any African American in the U.S. Army. He also established a training program for black pilots at Tuskegee Institute (now Tuskegee University) in Alabama that prepared African Americans to join the Air Corps on an experimental basis. Davis entered this program with eleven other officers, a group that later attracted national attention and became known in history as the Tuskegee Airmen. During the program, Davis became the first black officer to fly solo in an army aircraft, and he received his wings in March 1942. About a year later, with the rank of lieutenant colonel, Davis was charged with leading the first African American regiment of pilots, the Ninety-ninth Pursuit Squadron. Although he and the unit he commanded felt prepared to advance to the frontlines of battle, some senior military officers discouraged the idea of blacks fighting in the war, believing their tactical and judgmental abilities were inferior, and the Ninety-ninth was assigned routine non-combat missions in North Africa. In Washington hearings, Davis fiercely defended his men before both Pentagon and War Department authorities.

Near the end of 1943, Davis was promoted to colonel and assigned to a larger black unit, the 332nd Fighter Group, commonly called the Red Tails. With the 332nd, Davis arrived in Ramitelli, Italy, in January

1944, where his unit set out to disprove the widely accepted notion that blacks were inferior soldiers and airmen. Upgraded from the P-40 War Hawk aircraft the unit had flown in North Africa to the highly sophisticated P-47 Thunderbolt and P-41 Mustang fighter planes, on 9 June 1944, the unit accomplished its most noted military mission. Escorting B-24 bombers to targets in Munich, Germany, Davis led thirty-nine Thunderbolts in a battle with one hundred German Luftwaffe planes that resulted in the downing of six German planes. Following this action, Davis was awarded the Distinguished Flying Cross for leadership and bravery.

Under the command of Colonel Davis, his squadron carried out more than 15,000 missions, shot down 111 enemy aircraft, and destroyed another 150 on the ground, losing only 66 aircraft of their own. More remarkably, Davis's unit carried out 200 successful escort missions without a single casualty. In a highly classified report issued shortly after the war, U.S. General George Marshall declared that black soldiers were just as capable of fighting, and equally entitled to serve their country, as white soldiers.

After the war, President Truman, impressed and influenced by the shining performance of Davis and his unit, issued Executive Order 9981 requiring the integration of the armed forces. Davis was appointed to posts at the Pentagon and served again as Chief of Staff in the Korean War, when he led an integrated unit. In 1954 he was promoted to brigadier general and in 1965 earned the three stars of lieutenant general. Davis was the first African American in any branch of the military to climb to that rank. He later served in the Philippines as commander of the Thirteenth Air Force, followed by a position as commander of the United States Strike Command in Florida. He retired in 1970 after leading the Thirteenth Air Force unit in Vietnam. Other military decorations include the Silver Star, Legion of Merit with two oak leaf clusters, the Air Medal with four oak leaf clusters, the Air Force Commendation Medal with two oak leaf clusters, and the Philippine Legion of Honor.

After his retirement from the military, Davis became director of public safety in Cleveland under that city's first black mayor, CARL STOKES, though Davis soon quit because he could not abide the deal-making that occurred in municipal government and his by-the-book military style clashed with Stokes's tolerance for civil disobedience exhibited by some black extremist groups. He later accepted a position with the Department of Transportation as Assistant Secretary of Transportation for Environment and Safety, where he directed the bureau's anti-hijacking and anti-theft initiatives. He was instrumental in passing the 55 miles per hour speed limit set to save lives and gas. In 1998 President Clinton promoted Davis to full general.

Benjamin O. Davis Jr.'s rise to prominence followed in the remarkable path of his father's career accomplishments. But his clear sense of purpose, evidenced by a record of professional advances in spite of blatant racism and legalized segregation, tell the story of a soldier not only inspired by his father's career but also determined to triumph on his own over all the odds stacked against him. Davis became one of the earliest notably honored African American military officers, breaking down racial barriers with honor, discipline, and an unflinching will.

FURTHER READING

Davis, Benjamin O., Jr. *Benjamin O. Davis, Jr. American: An Autobiography* (2000).

Marvis, B., and Nathan I. Huggins, eds., *Benjamin Davis, Sr. and Benjamin Davis, Jr.: Military Leaders.* (1996).

Obituary: *New York Times,* 7 July 2002.

TANU T. HENRY

Davis, Benjamin O., Sr. (28 May 1880–26 Nov. 1970), U.S. Army officer, was born Benjamin Oliver Davis in Washington, D.C., the youngest of three children of Louis Patrick Henry Davis, a messenger for the U.S. Department of the Interior, and Henrietta Stewart, a nurse. Benjamin attended the Lucretia Mott School, one of Washington's few integrated schools, and then the segregated M Street High School. Impressed in his interactions with Civil War veterans and black cavalrymen, Benjamin joined the M Street Cadet Corps, earning a commission in the all-black unit of the National Guard for his senior year.

Although he had taken courses at Howard University during his senior year of high school, and despite his parent's objections, Davis chose a military career over college. He enlisted during the Spanish-American War in 1898 and joined the all-black Eighth U.S. Volunteer Infantry in Chickamauga, Georgia. A year later Davis reenlisted in the regular army. He served with the all-black Ninth Cavalry in Fort Duchesne, Utah, and quickly advanced to sergeant major, the highest rank for an enlisted soldier. In 1901 he underwent two weeks of officers' exams, becoming, along with John E. Green, one of two black candidates to earn a commission at a time when CHARLES YOUNG

(West Point class of 1889) was the only African American officer in the U.S. armed forces. Other than Young, West Point's only other black graduates, HENRY O. FLIPPER (class of 1877) and John Alexander (class of 1887), were, respectively, dishonorably discharged and dead. The next African American to graduate from West Point was Davis's son, in 1936.

Davis's first service as a commissioned officer was with the Ninth Cavalry in the Philippines, after which he was transferred to the Tenth Cavalry in Fort Washakie, Wyoming. He returned to Washington in 1902 to marry his childhood friend Elnora Dickerson. In 1905, following the birth of the couple's first child, Olive, and his promotion to first lieutenant, Davis was made professor of military science and tactics at Wilberforce College in Ohio. After serving as military attaché to Liberia from 1909 to 1911, Davis was reassigned to the Ninth Cavalry at Fort D. A. Russell, Wyoming. Davis's next detail, patrolling the United States–Mexican border in Arizona, necessitated sending his family to Washington within a year of the birth of his son, BENJAMIN O. DAVIS JR., in 1912. Following his promotion to captain in 1915, Davis returned to Wilberforce and to family life. The reunion, however, was short-lived; Elnora died in 1916 several days after the birth of their third child, Elnora.

When Davis was assigned the command of a supply troop in the Philippines in 1917, he sent his children to live with his parents in Washington. Two years later he married Sadie Overton, a Wilberforce teacher. After World War I, Davis, now a lieutenant colonel, taught at Tuskegee Institute in Alabama from 1920 to 1924. His next assignment was as instructor of the 372nd Infantry of the Ohio National Guard, a newly reorganized all-black unit. After four years, he was again transferred to Wilberforce for a year.

Davis became increasingly frustrated with teaching posts that undervalued his expertise and with assignments incommensurate with his rank. While the army routinely promoted Davis, he was assigned to noncombat positions, where he would not be in command of white personnel. He had spent World War I far away from the action and was repeatedly denied opportunities for more active duty. "I am getting to the point where I am beginning to believe that I've been kept as far in the background as possible," Davis wrote to Sadie in 1920 (Fletcher, 54). Adding to his dissatisfaction was the social ostracism the Davises encountered

from other military families. Davis was certainly aware that, in 1920 alone, more than seventy black World War I veterans had been lynched.

In 1930 Davis was promoted to colonel, becoming not only the highest ranking African American soldier in U.S. history, but—because John Green had retired in 1929—the *only* black officer in the U.S. Army. Despite repeated efforts to land a leadership position, Davis was reassigned to the Tuskegee classroom from 1930 to 1937. Davis's first high-profile appointment as colonel—escorting mothers and widows of slain World War I soldiers to European cemeteries in the summers of 1930 through 1933—was the result of self-promotion. "Let a colored officer," he successfully lobbied, "look after colored gold star mothers.... As you know I have traveled over the battlefields. I have a speaking knowledge of French" (Fletcher, 71). After another brief transfer to Wilberforce, Davis was finally put in charge of troops in 1938, when he was appointed regimental commander and instructor of the all-black 369th National Guard Infantry in New York City. Davis spearheaded the conversion of this service unit to an antiaircraft regiment, a move received by the black community as an indication that blacks could and should serve in all branches of the military.

In October 1940 Davis was promoted to brigadier general, becoming the first African American general. The timing of Davis's appointment, by President Franklin D. Roosevelt, just days before the 1940 presidential election, reflects pressure from African American leaders. When Davis's name did not appear on the list of proposed promotions circulated in September, the African American press responded—"Pres. Appoints 84 Generals, Ignores Col Davis" headlined the *New York Age*.

Roosevelt had signed the Selective Training and Service Act (1940), establishing the first peacetime draft in U.S. history, and although it included an antidiscrimination clause and the potential for expanded roles for African American soldiers, the legislation maintained segregation. Agitation by African American leaders, especially A. PHILIP RANDOLPH, helped secure Davis's promotion and other changes, including the establishment of a flight training program at Tuskegee (launched in January 1941), the appointment of Judge WILLIAM HENRY HASTIE as civilian aide to the Secretary of War, and the inclusion of an African American on the Selective Service board.

Davis retired in June 1941 but was immediately recalled to active duty and assigned to the Office of the Inspector General in Washington, D.C., as

Benjamin O. Davis, Sr., brigadier general, watches a Signal Corps crew erecting poles, 8 August 1944, France. (Library of Congress.)

an adviser on racial matters. As was often the case, racial discrimination began close to home. Davis arrived at his new office to find two colonels refusing to make room for his desk. Because there were no facilities open to blacks at the state department, Davis ate lunch at his desk while he worked to support the promotion and improve the morale of black soldiers. Davis investigated complaints of racial discrimination, including the assignment of inferior officers to black units, the banning of black soldiers from army base facilities, and incidents of racial violence. Although appointed a member of the War Department's Advisory Committee on Negro Troop Policies in 1942, Davis's recommendations—which included assigning African American officers to command black troops, discontinuing the policy of segregating blood and plasma, gradually removing black soldiers from southern posts, better supervision and racial integration of military police, desegregating base entertainment facilities, and instituting a mandatory course on racial relations and black history—were routinely omitted from final committee reports.

At the end of 1944, in response to a severe shortage of combat soldiers, Davis, then adviser to General Dwight D. Eisenhower, drafted a plan using black soldiers as replacements in all-white units. Although Eisenhower refused Davis's suggestion of assigning soldiers based on "need not color," he allowed black soldiers to be grouped into replacement platoons for white companies. Davis's job included the production of public relations and educational materials related to issues of race, the most significant of which, *The Negro Soldier* (1944), was produced by the U.S. Army film unit run by Frank Capra. This film, which includes references to the history of African American soldiers and prominent blacks, was shown to all incoming soldiers. Davis was instrumental in arranging for the film to be released to the general public and for the production of a sequel, *Teamwork* (1946).

The longer he lived abroad, the more vocal became Davis's opposition to the army's segregationist policies. In a memo dated 9 November 1943, he lamented the difficulties facing the black soldier "in a community that offers him nothing but humiliation and mistreatment.... The Army, by its directives and by actions of commanding officers, has introduced the attitudes of the 'Governors of the six Southern states' in many of the 42 states" (Redstone Arsenal Historical Information papers). Davis was clear in his testimony before a 1945 congressional committee: "Segregation fosters intolerance, suspicion, and friction" (Fletcher, 147). Davis's unprecedented visibility—there was even a story about both Benjamin Sr. and Jr. in *True Comics* in 1945—drew fire from those who criticized what they considered Davis's accommodationist approach to combating discrimination within the army.

In 1945 Davis was awarded the Distinguished Service Medal for his work "on matters pertaining to Negro troops." A year later he was reassigned to the Office of Inspector General and focused on the army's postwar policy regarding black soldiers. The results of integrating the replacement program were encouraging; of the 250 white soldiers queried, 77 percent answered "Yes, have become more favorable towards colored soldiers since having served in the same unit with them" (U.S. Army report, 3 July 1945).

At a ceremony presided over by President Harry S. Truman in the White House Rose Garden, Davis retired on 14 July 1948 after fifty years of service. Twelve days later, President Truman issued Executive Order 9981, which established "equality of treatment and opportunity for all persons in the armed services without regard to race, color, religion or national origin." The last racially segregated unit was abolished in 1954. Davis, who died of leukemia, is buried in Arlington National Cemetery.

In 1997 a commemorative U.S. postage stamp was issued in his honor.

FURTHER READING
The papers of Benjamin Oliver Davis Sr. are held by Mrs. James McLendon of Chicago.
Fletcher, Marvin E. *America's First Black General* (1989).

LISA E. RIVO

Davis, Blind John (7 Dec. 1913–12 Oct. 1985), blues pianist, was born John Henry Davis in Hattiesburg, Mississippi, the son of a speakeasy owner. Davis was blinded from a tetanus infection at the age of nine. Later the young man moved with his family to Chicago, where as a teenager he began playing the piano professionally for his father, who owned several speakeasies in the city. Though his playing was based in the blues, Davis incorporated various American musical forms, including ragtime, New Orleans jazz, swing, and boogie-woogie. Throughout the Chicago blues scene he became known for his versatility and for his clear, relaxed style.

In the 1930s and 1940s Davis earned a living as a regular session player for Lester Melrose's Blue Bird Records Label, the most popular blues label of the period. He recorded with many of Chicago's most prominent blues musicians, including TAMPA RED, "BIG BILL" BROONZY, and JOHN LEE "SONNY BOY" WILLIAMSON. Davis performed on such classic recordings as Tampa Red's "It Hurts Me, Too," Williamson's "Whoo Doo," "Sloppy Drunk Blues," and "Western Union Man," and Broonzy's "I Feel So Good."

While working for Blue Bird, Davis also led his own six-piece and seven-piece bands, which played in nightclubs, dance halls, and hotels, both in Chicago and across the United States. Davis's groups reflected the pianist's broad tastes, playing popular standards and swing jazz as well as traditional blues. Though best known as an accompanist and bandleader, in 1938 and 1939 Davis made several solo recordings on the Vocalian label.

In 1952 Davis joined Broonzy on a tour of Europe, the first ever by blues musicians. Over the next twenty years Davis returned many times to Europe, where he developed a more loyal following than he could have had in the United States. During that period, when he was not touring, Davis often performed with the drummer Judge Riley in Chicago nightclubs.

Davis released three LPs during his career, *Stomping on a Saturday Night* (Alligator Records), an album recorded in 1977 at Club Popular in Bonn, West Germany; *You Better Cut That Out*, which was released by Red Beans Records in 1985; and *Blind John Davis*, a collection of his 1938 and 1939 Vocalian recordings, which was released by Story of Blues.

Though not generally known for his work as a solo performer, Davis is nonetheless considered one of the most consistent, versatile, and skillful piano accompanists in the blues music industry of the twentieth century. His performances in Europe in the 1950s opened a new and vigorous market for blues musicians at a time when interest in the music was waning in the United States. Davis died in Chicago.

FURTHER READING
Santelli, Robert. *The Big Book of Blues: A Biographical Encyclopedia* (1993).
Hess, Norbert. "In Memoriam," *Blues Forum*, no. 19 (Feb. 1986), 18–21.
Obituary: *Living Blues*, no. 70 (1986), 45.
This entry is taken from the *American National Biography* and is published here with the permission of the American Council of Learned Societies.

THADDEUS RUSSELL

Davis, Corneal Aaron (28 Aug. 1900–17 Apr. 1995), minister and politician, served thirty-six years (1943 to 1979) in the Illinois State House of Representatives for the 22nd District and acted as associate pastor at Chicago's Quinn African Methodist Episcopal (AME) Church. Corneal was born on a farm near Vicksburg, Mississippi, to a white landowner and an African American former slave named Pearl Darden. After attending primary school at Sisters of the Holy Ghost, a Roman Catholic School, Davis graduated from Magnolia Public High School. At Magnolia there had been one teacher who taught all the subjects.

Davis attended Tougaloo College, a historically black institution near Jackson, Mississippi. Established in 1869 by the Home Missionary Society of the Disciples of Christ, Tougaloo offered a first-class liberal education to African Americans. At Tougaloo he read the newspaper almost every day and participated in the debate society, which would help his oratory skills in his later life as a politician.

In 1917 after attending Tougaloo College, Davis enlisted in the U.S. Army along with several football teammates who shared his motivation to get out of Mississippi—away from the lynching, burnings, and poll taxes that kept African Americans from voting—and earn a living to support his mother.

In the army, Davis's education got him placed into the medical corps. During World War I, he served in France and experienced combat on the front lines during the Meuse-Argonne offensive. He later cited black troops as a key component of success in World War I.

After returning to Vicksburg, Mississippi, in 1919 Davis and his mother moved to Chicago to avoid racial violence. They hoped to find the promised land of Lincoln and freedom, but instead they moved to the city during the "red summer" of 1919, when Chicago experienced one of the worst race riots in history. After arriving in Chicago, Davis found fewer economic opportunities than he expected. Unable to secure a job after writing "colored" as the racial designation on his applications, Davis switched to designating his race as "American"; consequently, he attained his first job, working as a shipping clerk.

He turned to politics after working under the Republican leadership of Second Ward Alderman Louis Anderson and OSCAR DEPRIEST, who at the time was alderman of the city's Third Ward. Acting as Anderson's driver, Davis accompanied the alderman around the precincts and then advanced to researching, speechwriting, and door-to-door campaigning. He also supported WILLIAM L. DAWSON's bid for Congress by making public speeches around the city and making such statements as, "This is the only district north of the Mason-Dixon line where a black man can be elected to Congress and you ought to elect him." Dawson lost the election and then became a Democrat. Davis followed suit, gaining inspiration to run for the Illinois House of Representatives also as a Democrat. When Davis arrived in the capital city of Springfield for the first time after being elected to the Illinois House of Representatives in 1943, he was not allowed to stay in the Abraham Lincoln Hotel because he was African American. He walked to several other hotels in the area but none of them would let him stay; so he spent his first night in Springfield sleeping on a bench at the Gulf, Mobile, and Ohio gas station. As State Senator Margaret Smith (D-Illinois) recounts: "The new state representative spent his first night in Springfield sleeping near a train station and the rest of his Springfield days fighting discrimination in that town."

Davis's political career aimed at achieving racial justice, beginning with a movement to end discrimination at the University of Illinois Medical School by threatening to withhold state funds in the early 1940s.

In 1944 Davis filed a suit in the federal court at Cairo, Illinois, on behalf of black teachers who were being paid half as much as their white counterparts. He worked with the attorney THURGOOD MARSHALL, who later became a Supreme Court Justice. They received a judicial consent decree to examine the public records of teacher salaries to reveal the payment inequalities, which helped them win the case.

Davis was elected eighteen times to the Illinois House of Representatives and served in the General Assembly for thirty-six years between 1943 and 1979. He also served on the University of Illinois Appropriations Committee from 1949 to 1958 and used his position on the committee to assist in the integration of public schools. He was the first African American appointed chairman of the Public Aid and Public Health Committee in 1961. While in the Illinois legislature, one of Davis's greatest achievements was helping to pass the state's Fair Employment Practices Commission Bill in 1962. He was also appointed chairman of the Illinois Emancipation Proclamation Commission in 1963. In 1964 he attended the Democratic National Convention as an Illinois delegate. In 1967 he amended the bill to provide public funds for private development to spur low-income housing (and between 1968 and 1971 the bill was amended to include women). The mayor of Springfield at the time presented Davis with a key to the city for all of his contributions to the state of Illinois.

In addition to his political career, he was an associate pastor at the Quinn AME church on Chicago's South Side and people referred to him as the "Deacon" because he led the statehouse in prayer when the official chaplain was absent. He was the first African American scoutmaster in Chicago for the Boy Scouts of America, and he and his wife, Elma, helped to raise funds for Jane Addams's Hull-House. He was also a member of the National Association for the Advancement of Colored People, the Omega Psi Phi fraternity, and the Free and Accepted Masons. Davis worked closely with Chicago political legends (including Mayor HAROLD WASHINGTON), and he was recognized by President Gerald Ford at the Sixty-fourth National Urban League Convention in San Francisco. He was also the first African American to serve in the leadership of the House when he was appointed as assistant minority leader in 1971.

Davis retired from the Illinois General Assembly in 1979 later served as a Board of Elections

Commissioner from 1979 through 1986. He died in a Chicago nursing home on 17 April 1995.

FURTHER READING

Black, Timuel D., Jr. *Bridges of Memory: Chicago's First Wave of Black Migration* (2003).

Davis, Corneal. "Corneal A. Davis (Illinois General Assembly Oral History Program)," Legislative Studies Center of Sangamon State University (1984).

Smith, Margaret. "State Sen. Smith Remembers Corneal A. Davis," *Chicago Weekend*, 7 May 1995.

Obituary: *Chicago Sun-Times*, 19 Apr. 1995.

ALEXIS CEPEDA MAULE

Davis, Danny K. (6 Sept. 1941–), U.S. Congressman, educator, and public administrator, was born in rural Parkdale, Ashley County, Arkansas, to low-income sharecroppers Hezekiah "H. D." Davis and Mazzie L. Glass Davis, who had four other sons and seven daughters. Danny Davis grew up in and remained in the Missionary Baptist Church. Although known in adulthood for his distinctive, eloquent orator's voice, as a child he stuttered. His teachers, especially Mrs. Beadie King, and his family elders encouraged his enjoyment of reading and learning. Danny Davis attended segregated public schools and graduated from Parkdale's Savage High School in 1957.

Majoring in history and minoring in education, he earned a B.A. from Arkansas Agricultural, Mechanical, & Normal College (later the University of Arkansas at Pine Bluff) in 1961. In college, he found inspiration in the student activities of the African American civil rights movement. Davis and six of his siblings attended Arkansas AM&N, followed by several cousins, three nephews, and a niece.

After graduation, he moved to Chicago and worked as a postal clerk (1961–1965) and as a teacher at Ferdinand Magellan, a public school (1962–1968). In 1968 he achieved an M.S. in school guidance from Chicago State University. Davis and his wife, Vera, decided that they would live with their two children, Jonathan and Stacey, on Chicago's majority-black, low-income West Side. He worked as executive director, Greater Lawndale Conservation Commission, (1969); director of training, Martin Luther King Jr. Neighborhood Health Center (1969–1971); manpower consultant (1971–1972) and executive director, Westside Health Planning Organization (1972–1981); and special assistant to the president, Mile Square Community Health Center (1976–1981). He earned a Ph.D. in public administration from Union Institute, Cincinnati, Ohio (1977). As an adjunct faculty member, Davis taught courses at the Illinois Benedictine College, University of Illinois School of Public Health, Malcolm X College, National College of Education, and Roosevelt University.

Davis was first elected alderman of Chicago's 29th Ward in 1979 as an independent, although he later affiliated with the Democratic Party. In 1984, he became the ward's committeeman. His years as an alderman included the infamous "Council Wars" era (1983–1986). This era was characterized by the election of HAROLD WASHINGTON as the first black mayor of Chicago and the subsequent intense conflict between Washington's multiracial group of allies, including Davis and a predominantly "white ethnic" bloc of aldermen. The conflict ended in stalemate. Harold Washington's supporters faced another setback following the mayor's sudden death from a heart attack in 1987, just after his reelection to a second term.

Davis remained on the city council until 1990, when he resigned to serve six continuous years on the Cook County Board of Commissioners. He ran for the U.S. Congress but lost twice (1984, 1986). He also ran unsuccessfully for Chicago mayor (1991). Representing the 7th District of Illinois, which encompassed poor, black, inner-city neighborhoods in Chicago as well as majority-white, prosperous suburbs, Davis was finally elected to the 105th U.S. Congress. Succeeding CARDISS COLLINS, he was sworn in on 3 January 1997. As of mid-2009, he had been elected to seven consecutive terms.

Danny Davis established himself in the House as a reliable champion of progressive Democratic policies, including single-payer health care and same-sex marriage. A member of the Democratic Socialists of America, he received a 2008 rating of 80% from Americans for Democratic Action, and a lifetime rating of 2.92% from the American Conservative Union. Along with the Congressional Black Caucus, whose secretary he became in 2005, in 1997 Davis joined and remained active in the following Congressional caucuses: Art, Asian Pacific American, Cancer, Children's, Community Health Centers, Heart and Stroke, Hellenic Issues, Labor and Working Families, Mental Health, Progressive, Rural Health, and Steel. He also joined the Iraq Fallen Heroes caucus and chaired the Postal caucus. He has been a frequent public speaker, particularly on behalf of the National Federation for the Blind.

From 1997 to at least mid-2009, from the 105th at least through the 111th Congress, Davis served on the Government Reform and Oversight Committee. In late 2008 he was awarded one of the most prestigious

House appointments, a membership on the Ways and Means Committee. He joined its subcommittees on Oversight and on Income Security and Family Support. Danny Davis also belonged to the Education and the Workforce Committee (2003–2007).

Davis's time in Congress has not been free of controversy. He was among the few to vote against the 2002 authorization of the Iraq War, and he also forcefully questioned the results of the disputed 2004 presidential election. In 2004, he was severely criticized for taking part in a ceremony that honored Sun-Myung Moon, the controversial head of the Unification Church. He was also challenged about a 2005 trip to Sri Lanka. Although Davis claimed he did not know the whole story when he took the trip, it was funded by the Tamil Tigers, a group the U.S. government identified as a terrorist organization.

In 2008, however, Danny Davis escaped (as of this writing) the notorious political corruption scandal surrounding then-Illinois governor Rod Blagojevich. When BARACK OBAMA was elected President, Blagojevich tried to exchange his vacated U.S. Senate seat for money. When Blagojevich offered the seat to Davis, he turned it down. Before he was ousted from office, Blagojevich appointed another veteran Black Chicago politician, ROLAND BURRIS, to the seat.

In the *Congressional Record* of 17 September 2008, Danny Davis reflected on his own life story as he explained his advocacy for Historically Black Colleges and Universities (HBCUs). "It was an HBCU that started me on my path to become the person that I am today.... If it were not for the University of Arkansas at Pine Bluff, I strongly believe that my family members and I would not have been able to attend college. Many African American members of Congress and many of our nation's leaders have attended HBCUs—JESSE JACKSON, JR., JESSE JACKSON, SR., ALCEE HASTINGS, DR. MARTIN LUTHER KING, W. E. B. DuBOIS, and THURGOOD MARSHALL, just to name a few. The continued support and funding of HBCUs is essential to create more opportunities for people of color to thrive in education and become leaders of tomorrow."

FURTHER READING

Black Americans in Congress. Available online at http://baic.house.gov/.

"BuzzFlash Interview, Congressman Danny Davis." Apr. 2001. Available online at http://www.buzzflash.com/interviews/2001/04/Danny_Davis_042901.html.

Crowe, Larry. "Biographical Note: The HistoryMakers Video Oral History Interview with Danny K. Davis," 15 Dec. 2003. Available online at http://www.thehistorymakers.com.

"Danny K. Davis." In *Biographical Directory of the United States Congress*. Available online at http://bioguide.congress.gov.

"Extended Biographical Sketch: Congressman Danny K. Davis, Ph.D. (IL-07)." Available online at http://www.davis.house.gov/index.php.

"Representative Danny K. Davis." Project Vote Smart. Available online at http://www.votesmart.org/bio.php?can_id=233.

Sweet, Lynn. "Davis Said Thanks, But No Thanks," *Chicago Sun-Times*, 31 Dec. 2008.

MARY KRANE DERR

Davis, Eddie "Lockjaw" (2 Mar. 1922–3 Nov. 1986), tenor saxophonist, was born in New York City, the son of Eleanor (maiden name unknown). His father (name unknown) worked menial jobs and saw little of his family. Davis dated his admiration for musicians to a time when his older brother was a bouncer at the Savoy Ballroom and would let Eddie and his twin brother in for free. He decided drummers and saxophonists had the greatest fame and finest women. The drums being cumbersome, he bought a saxophone. Self-taught, he was playing at Monroe's Uptown House eight months later. He married Beatrice (maiden name unknown) around 1941. They had one daughter.

With the aim of eventually getting into the New York musicians' union via a transfer, Davis moved to Philadelphia, Pennsylvania, where he joined the local union and Jimmy Gorham's Kentuckians, a big band, in 1940 or 1941. In the summer of 1942 Gorham's band was at the Club Harlem in Atlantic City. That same year COOTIE WILLIAMS heard Davis and BUD POWELL in a group at the Club Caravan and hired them, along with three other sidemen, for his big band. They worked at the Savoy Ballroom in New York City before embarking on a six-month tour on the RKO theater circuit. In 1944 Davis quit Williams's orchestra in Los Angeles and returned to New York. He joined the big bands of LUCKY MILLINDER, in 1944; LOUIS ARMSTRONG, for four months around 1945; and ANDY KIRK, from 1945 to 1946. In the meantime Davis began working with small modern jazz groups, initially in a quartet including THELONIOUS MONK. Davis disliked Monk's idiosyncratic piano accompaniments and he later maintained a firm intolerance for anything remotely connected to avant-garde jazz performance.

At Davis's first session as a leader in May 1946, the Savoy record producer Bod Shad named one of the performances *Lockjaw*, hence his nickname and the subsequent affectionate abbreviations "Lock" and "Jaws." He also was known as the Fox, for his shrewdness and wisdom. During a long stay at Minton's Playhouse from around 1947 to 1952, he led informal sessions. In addition to performing, he acted as the "policeman" on the bandstand, asking unqualified musicians not to play and asking fine musicians to stop, if they hogged the stage for too long. He took three- to four-week breaks from Minton's for other jobs and in 1951 toured for sixteen weeks with George Shearing and the All American All Stars.

In the summer of 1951 Davis made his first tenor saxophone and Hammond organ recordings with the organist Bill Doggett, the bassist OSCAR PETTIFORD, and the drummer SHADOW WILSON. He joined COUNT BASIE's big band in May 1952, staying to the end of July 1953, when he was replaced by Frank Foster. He said that he left because, under the producer John Hammond's influence, Basie was featuring PAUL QUINICHETTE (imitating LESTER YOUNG) as the tenor saxophone soloist. Returning to the sax and organ combination, Davis worked with the organist Doc Bagby from 1954 to 1955 and then led a trio with the organist SHIRLEY SCOTT, beginning in February 1955. He rejoined Basie late in September 1957, touring Europe in the fall and then leaving at the New Year. He reactivated the trio, which was resident at Count Basie's club in Harlem from 4 February 1958 to 1 February 1959, and then toured. From this period came his (and Scott's) greatest series of albums, collectively called *The Eddie "Lockjaw" Davis Cookbook*.

Tiring of the sax and organ combination, Davis became co-leader of a quintet with the saxophonist Johnny Griffin in 1960, recording the album *Tough Tenors* in November and a session at Minton's Playhouse in January 1961 (issued under various *Live* titles). Albums apart from Griffin included *Trane Whistle* (1960), which placed Davis's improvising in a big band setting, and *Afro-Jaws* (1961), a Latin jazz collection. After two successful years the group began to lose money. Griffin immigrated to Europe in 1963 because of tax difficulties. Davis saw too many musicians growing old and still having to endure long hours and difficult travel to survive. Seeking an alternative, he withdrew from performance in June 1963 to act as a booking agent with Shaw Artists Corporation. In July 1964 he temporarily replaced Foster in Basie's group, pending the arrival of Sal Nistico. He briefly resumed his job as a booking agent but then became road manager for Basie in November 1964 and a few weeks later took a second salary as tenor saxophonist, replacing Nistico. John Shaw described Davis as "warm, outgoing: ... a highly articulate conversationalist."

For the next decade Davis was in and out of Basie's band. Among his leaves of absence were an expansion of the two-tenor idea, in a tour of England with the tenor saxophonists Ben Webster, Bud Freeman, Eddie Miller, and Alex Welsh in the spring of 1967; a period with Tommy Flanagan's trio in Los Angeles in November of that year; and work alongside Basie's orchestra as a member of the Jazz at the Philharmonic All Stars in June 1972. To take advantage of a lower tax rate, Davis made his home in Las Vegas, Nevada, from 1973 or 1974, although he was on the road performing most of the year. He toured internationally as a leader for another decade. Among his albums were *Swingin' Till the Girls Come Home* (1976), *Straight Ahead* (1976), and *The Heavy Hitter* (1979). He also co-led a group with Harry "Sweets" Edison from about 1975 to 1979. Their albums included *Edison's Lights* (1976). In 1984 Davis was stricken by stomach cancer, and in his last year he performed only occasionally. He died in Culver City, California.

In a review of *The Heavy Hitter*, Shirley Klett wrote that "Jaws could be likened to Humphrey Bogart—a rough exterior with unexpected depths" (*Cadence* 6, no. 2, Feb. 1980, p. 17). His playing epitomized the "tough tenor" style. Equally founded in swing, bop, gospel, and rhythm and blues, it combined gutsy timbres, hard driving rhythms, and emotive rhetorical gestures, with instrumental virtuosity, harmonic subtlety, and a sophisticated sense of melodic design.

FURTHER READING

Murray, Albert. *Good Morning Blues: The Autobiography of Count Basie* (1985).

Shaw, John. "Lockjaw Davis: A Musician Who Matters," *Jazz Journal* 23, no. 9 (Sept. 1970).

Wilmer, Valerie. *Jazz People* (1970).

Obituary: *San Francisco Examiner*, 5 Nov. 1986.

This entry is taken from the *American National Biography* and is published here with the permission of the American Council of Learned Societies.

BARRY KERNFELD

Davis, Ernie (14 Dec. 1939–18 May 1963), football player, was born in New Salem, Pennsylvania, a coal mining district. The names and occupations of his parents cannot be ascertained. He never knew his father, who left the family soon after his son's birth and subsequently died in an accident. His mother moved to Elmira, New York, leaving one-year-old Ernie with his grandparents in nearby Uniontown, Pennsylvania. Ten years later Davis rejoined his mother in Elmira.

Davis's athletic career began at the Elmira Free Academy, where he starred in both basketball and football. He was named a *Scholastic Coach* magazine high school All-American in both sports in 1957–1958 but was recruited to play football by more than thirty-five schools, including Notre Dame. He chose to go to Syracuse University because of its nearness to Elmira and the intercession of an Elmira attorney and a Syracuse alumnus.

Davis led his freshman football team to an undefeated season in 1958. He then played three years of varsity football at Syracuse, during which time the team achieved a record of twenty wins and five losses. They beat Texas in the 1960 Cotton Bowl and Miami in the 1961 Liberty Bowl; the team had won the national championship in 1959. Davis, the leading rusher all three seasons, led the team in pass receiving in 1961, gained 3,414 all-purpose yards, and averaged 6.6 yards per carry in his career. His 15.7 yards per carry in one game against West Virginia in 1959 and his seasonal average of 7.8 yards per carry remained Syracuse records as of 2007. In the 1960–1961 seasons he gained more than 100 yards per game eleven times. Davis was chosen the outstanding player in both the Cotton and Liberty bowls.

Davis made All-American in 1960 and was chosen again in 1961 unanimously. His numerous honors included the 1961 Heisman Trophy, awarded annually to an outstanding college football player. Davis was the first African American to earn the Heisman, winning it in close balloting over fullback Bob Ferguson of Ohio State and his old boyhood friend from Uniontown, Sandy Stephens, who had gone on to star at the University of Minnesota.

Syracuse used the "winged T" formation with an unbalanced line. Davis would run from either the tailback or wingback position. At six feet two inches and 205 pounds he possessed, in the words of his coach Ben Schwartzwalder, that "rare combination of power and speed." Davis ran effectively off tackle, on reverses, and on power sweeps around end and proved to be an effective blocker and a sure-handed pass receiver. He had the ability to break open games with long gains, including his eighty-seven-yard run with a pass against Texas in

the 1960 Cotton Bowl. Playing before the free substitution rule was introduced, Davis was an effective defensive back. He was often compared with JIM BROWN, the 1956 Syracuse All-American who had become a star in the National Football League (NFL) with the Cleveland Browns. Davis, in fact, broke ten of Brown's intercollegiate records. During his junior year, 1960–1961, Davis also played varsity basketball. He graduated from Syracuse in 1962 with a bachelor's degree in business administration and was honored by his classmates as a senior marshall at the commencement. Davis was a deeply religious man and a member of the Baptist church.

In 1962 Davis played in the East-West Shrine game, in an all-star game in June, and later that summer in the college all-star game against the Green Bay Packers. The first player chosen in that year's professional football draft, he was the focus of an intense bidding war between the NFL's Washington Redskins, the Buffalo Bills of the rival American Football League, and the Canadian Football League. Washington subsequently traded his NFL rights to the Cleveland Browns, which in December 1961 signed him to an $80,000 three-year contract.

Davis became ill with acute monocytic leukemia during practice for the college all-star game in 1962. He participated in preseason practice with the Browns and worked briefly as a sales trainee for the Pepsi-Cola Company, but he was too disabled to play professional football. His condition deteriorated that fall, and after one last visit to a Syracuse spring practice game in April he reentered a Cleveland hospital, where he died. Davis was buried in Elmira.

Although subjected to racial taunting from the earliest days of his career, Davis said after the racially charged Cotton Bowl game against Texas in 1960 that he never gave much thought to such issues. This response stood in sharp contrast to the militancy of some of his fellow African American athletes later in that decade. In 1979 Davis was elected posthumously to the National Football Foundation College Hall of Fame.

FURTHER READING

Brown, Paul, with Jack Clary. *PB: The Paul Brown Story* (1979).

Clark, Steven. *Fight against Time: Five Athletes—A Legacy of Courage* (1979).

Gallagher, Robert C. *Ernie Davis: The Elmira Express* (1983).

Obituaries: *New York Times,* 19, 22, and 23 May 1963; *Syracuse Herald Journal,* 18 May 1963; *Syracuse Post Standard,* 19 May 1963.

This entry is taken from the *American National Biography* and is published here with the permission of the American Council of Learned Societies.

DANIEL R. GILBERT

Davis, Frances Elliott (28 Apr. 1882–2 May 1965), nurse, educator, and community advocate, was born in Shelby, North Carolina, the daughter of an unlawful interracial marriage between Darryl Elliott, a part African American Cherokee sharecropper, and Emma (maiden name unknown), the daughter of a plantation owner and Methodist minister. Darryl Elliott fled the state early in Davis's life, leaving her to be raised by her mother. Both parents had died by 1887, after which Davis was raised in a succession of foster homes. At the age of twelve she was sent to Pittsburgh, Pennsylvania, where she lived under the guardianship of the Reverend Vickers. In the Vickers household she was regarded more as a domestic helper than a ward; consequently her early formal education was pursued on a sporadic basis. Determined to succeed, she possessed the intrepidity to improve her reading skills on her own.

In 1896, at the age of fourteen, Davis was granted permission by the Vickers family to seek outside employment and had the good fortune to have her services retained by the Joseph Allison Reed household. Taking an interest in Davis, the Reeds assumed the role of patrons and helped her to flee to Knoxville, Tennessee, two years later when the Vickerses demanded she resign her position. The Reeds continued their sponsorship by financing her education to the end of normal school. By 1905 she had secured the prerequisites for normal school training at Knoxville College, from which she graduated in 1907 at the age of twenty-five, and, on the advice of Mrs. Reed, she undertook a teaching career to maintain her subsidized education.

Pursuing her early dream "to be a nurse and help little children," Davis worked for a year at a hospital at Knoxville College until poor health forced her to resign. Temporarily, she assumed a teaching post in Henderson, North Carolina, instructing third and fourth graders at the Henderson Normal Institute. Having saved enough money for the training program, Davis applied in 1910 to the Freedmen's Hospital Training School for Nurses in Washington, D.C. Anxious that her application not be denied on the basis of age, she changed her birth date from 1882 to 1889 and started her training at the age of twenty-seven years.

In 1913 the District of Columbia administered exams to the graduating students on the basis of their race, with the exam for the white nurses considered the most rigorous. Davis demanded a chance to take the test for whites and became the first African American in the district to pass the exam.

From 1913 to 1916 Davis held various positions, first as a private duty nurse, then in 1914 she accepted the position of nursing supervisor at Provident Hospital, an all-black hospital in Baltimore, Maryland. During the summers of 1916 and 1920 she acted as a camp nurse for a community-based camp for needy mothers and young children in the Washington, D.C., area. While at Provident, Davis made an application to the American Red Cross, where, under the tutelage of M. Adelaide Nutting, head of the nursing department, she became the first African American to attend its approved program at Teachers College, Columbia University. To compensate for her inexperience in the areas of public and rural health, she took a field placement in July 1917 at Lillian Wald's Henry Street Settlement House in New York City.

Having completed her training, Davis was assigned by the American Red Cross Town and Country Nursing Service to Jackson, Tennessee, which had specifically requested the services of an African American nurse. In addition to using her midwifery skills, she conducted preventive medicine classes in basic sanitation and prenatal care.

In April 1917, when the United States entered World War I, Davis's race precluded her from joining the Army Nurse Corps, which refused African American applicants until after the war. While her white colleagues were automatically awarded their American Red Cross pins, allowing them to transfer to the corps, Davis's pin did not arrive until 2 July 1918 and was inscribed with a "1A." The letter A designated the wearer as "Negro," indicating that she was the first African American Red Cross nurse. The A system remained in effect until 1949. Davis's involvement with the war effort was indirect in that she nursed soldiers in training at Chickamauga, Tennessee. Unfortunately that same year Davis succumbed to an influenza epidemic that left her heart permanently damaged.

Davis's talents as an educator, community-based nurse, and administrator were recognized, and for the remainder of her career her services were in constant demand. In 1919 while serving as director of nurses training at John A. Andrew Memorial Hospital in Tuskegee, Alabama, she accepted a proposal from Dunbar Hospital in Detroit, Michigan, that she be responsible for organizing the first training school for African American nurses in Michigan.

The following year she also accepted a staff position with the Detroit Visiting Nurses Association, an affiliation that she would maintain for many years.

In 1921 Davis took a leave of absence to marry William A. Davis of Detroit, a professional musician who performed in a band as well as offering private lessons. Their only child was stillborn in 1922, and in 1923 Davis resumed her career. She returned to Dunbar determined to upgrade the training program for nurses. Although she was able to garner funding from Senator James Couzens, a Michigan philanthropist, hospital physicians refused to accept monies that would only benefit nurses. Disgusted with their tactics Davis resigned her position in March 1927. She left Dunbar to accept a position with the Child Welfare Division of the Detroit Health Department, where she directed prenatal, maternal, and child health clinics.

In 1929 Davis was awarded a Julius Rosenwald Fellowship for pursuit of a B.S. in nursing at her alma mater, Teachers College; however, she was forced to withdraw from the program as a result of ill health. When she and her husband returned to Michigan, they moved to Inkster, a predominantly African American community outside of Detroit.

During the height of the Depression Davis devoted her time to running a commissary at the Ford Motor plant that distributed food to the inhabitants of Inkster. She had also petitioned Henry Ford to act as a patron, in which capacity he paid the utility bills, provided clothing, and supplied the means for repairing homes. In return recipients were able to earn a wage by helping to improve the physical appearance of Inkster. She also organized projects that qualified youths for National Youth Administration grants, which also created a wage mechanism. In 1932 Davis resigned her position with the Detroit Health Department to devote her time to the commissary.

In 1935 Davis returned to work for the Visiting Nurses Association, where she remained for five years, while at the same time serving as a member on the Inkster school board. After leaving the VNA she established a day nursery in Inkster. This nursery was such a success that it attracted the attention of Eleanor Roosevelt, who demonstrated her support by soliciting funds for the center. In 1940 Davis left the day nursery center to assume a position at Eloise Hospital in Wayne County, Michigan, where she remained until 1951, when illness forced her to take a leave of absence. Once recuperated, she chose to remain at home to nurse her husband, who died in 1959.

Scheduled to be honored at the American Red Cross convention on 11 May 1965, Davis died on May 2 in Mount Clemens, Michigan. Her Red Cross pin was presented to the convention officials to be entered into their historical collection.

FURTHER READING
Bullough, Vern L., et al. *American Nursing: A Biographical Dictionary* (1988).
Carnegie, M. Elizabeth. *The Path We Tread: Blacks in Nursing Worldwide, 1854–1944* (1995).
Hine, Darlene Clark. *Black Women in White: Racial Conflict and Cooperation in the Nursing Profession, 1890–1950* (1989).
This entry is taken from the *American National Biography* and is published here with the permission of the American Council of Learned Societies.

DALYCE NEWBY

Davis, Frank Marshall (31 Dec. 1905–26 July 1987), radical journalist and poet, was born in Arkansas City, Kansas, to parents about whom little is known except that they separated only a year after his birth. During his childhood Davis became familiar with the horrors of Jim Crow violence. Arkansas City had a contradictory policy on segregation that allowed discrimination against African Americans while, at the same time, tolerating racially integrated schools. Davis attended Arkansas City High School and then Friends University in Wichita. He was also able to receive formal education in journalism, studying at Kansas State Agricultural College (later Kansas State University) from 1924 to 1926 and from 1929 to 1930. During his college years Davis also started writing poetry, which provided him with an alternative way of writing about the social and racial injustices he had seen and faced.

Between his two periods at Kansas State, Davis worked in Chicago, where he started to earn his long-lasting reputation as a controversial journalist willing to confront racial discrimination without pandering to whites. After graduating in 1930 he moved to Atlanta, where he edited the *Atlanta Daily World*. Davis confirmed his reputation as an outspoken author who openly confronted the problem of lynching, racial discrimination, and class oppression. As Davis recollected in his posthumously published autobiography *Livin' the Blues: Memoirs of a Black Journalist and Poet* (1992), he was particularly versatile in his assignments: "I served not only as straight news reporter but as rewrite man, editor, editorial writer, political commentator, theatrical and jazz columnist, sports writer and occasionally news photographer" (231). As a journalist Davis exploited the whole range of topics he wrote about to expose racial segregation and to promote journalism as a tool for social change.

From 1935 to 1947 Davis was again in Chicago working as executive editor for the Associated Negro Press. During these years, his politics became more radical and Davis increasingly came into contact with left-wing circles and personalities. He was an active member of the League of American Writers, also serving as the treasurer of its Chicago chapter, and he lectured on jazz at the Abraham Lincoln School, which was organized by the Communist Party. While attending the Conference of the National Negro Congress held in Chicago in 1936, Davis met RICHARD WRIGHT, as well as other prominent African American writers and thinkers on the left such as LANGSTON HUGHES, ARNA BONTEMPS, COUNTÉE CULLEN, PAUL ROBESON, A. PHILIP RANDOLPH, and MARGARET WALKER. With them, Davis gave lectures, chaired meetings, and participated in New Deal programs linked to the WPA Writer's Project. He also cooperated closely with the American Youth for Democracy (the former Young Communist League) and wrote for the left-wing literary magazine *New Masses*. His political engagement culminated with his joining the Communist Party in the middle of World War II. His egalitarian ideas, together with his participation in the collective pamphlet "Writers Take Sides," put Davis under scrutiny by both the FBI and the House Un-American Activities Committee, something he took as a compliment: "I was positive that by now I had attracted the special attention of the House Un-American Committee. If so, I would accept any resultant citation as an honor for it would indicate I was beginning to upset the white power structure" (*Livin' the Blues*, 279).

Davis's newspaper articles and essays played a key role in the establishment of jazz criticism and in linking it to political activism. In the jazz column he wrote for the ANP, Davis celebrated jazz as a black working-class achievement that could undermine the cultural hegemony of whites. Davis described jazz as an important weapon in the hands of African Americans, a way to resist the Euro-American cultural paradigm.

Davis's Chicago years were also his most productive poetically, witnessing the publication of four collections: *Black Man's Verse* (1935), *I Am the American Negro* (1937), *Through Sepia Eyes* (1938), and *47th Street: Poems* (1948). In his poems

Davis confronted the same themes as in his prose pieces and contributed to the radicalization of the Harlem Renaissance poetic legacy. Davis experimented with literary form and themes, employing experimental versification to express political dissent and racial consciousness. In "Tenement Room," Davis describes the precarious environment where the black urban experience unfolds: "—A crippled table, gray from greasy water; / Two drooping chairs, spiritless as wounded soldiers / shoved into a prison hole; / A cringing bed, age-weary; / Corseted with wire squats a flabby stove." However, Davis's poems are not only concerned with black poverty and despair. They also celebrate the poetic power of jazz. Free versification is often employed with sound patterns, onomatopoeia, and alliterations to reproduce the improvisation of jazz rhythms in poetry: "Play that thing, you jazz mad fools! / Boil a skyscraper with a jungle / Dish it to 'em sweet and hot— / Ahhhhhhhh / Rip it open then sew it up, jazz band!" ("Jazz Band").

Critical of the Hitler-Stalin pact and of Earl Browder's party leadership during the war years, Davis started to collaborate closely again with the Communist Party after the end of the world conflict. In 1948, however, with the rising anticommunist hysteria of McCarthyism, Davis decided to turn a vacation to Hawaii into a permanent residence. He became a regular columnist for the *Honolulu Record* and started a wholesale paper business. During the cold war years, Davis's work fell into critical disrespect, a fate Davis shared with many writers on the left whose writings were considered too dogmatic and propagandistic by critics. His voice was silenced by the cultural politics of the cold war until his books were rediscovered by Black Arts Movement figures such as the poet DUDLEY RANDALL and the critic Stephen E. Henderson, who celebrated Davis as one of poetry's pioneering figures. His return to the continental United States was marked by a series of readings across the country in 1973 and, in 1978, he published his final volume, *Awakening, and Other Poems*. The volumes *Livin' the Blues: Memoirs of a Black Journalist and Poet* (1992) and *Black Moods: Collected Poems* (2002) were published after Davis's death.

Like many other African American intellectuals involved in left-wing and popular front politics, Frank Marshall Davis deserves to be reinscribed in the canon of African American and American culture. His journalistic and poetic writings represent a bold challenge to a world where segregation and racial discrimination were legally sanctioned.

FURTHER READING

Barnes, D. "I'd Rather Be a Lamppost in Chicago: Richard Wright and the Chicago Renaissance of African American Literature," *Langston Hughes Review* 14 (1996).

Gennari, J. "'A Weapon of Integration': Frank Marshall Davis and the Politics of Jazz," *Langston Hughes Review* 14 (1996).

Rodgers, L. R. "Richard Wright, Frank Marshall Davis and the Chicago Renaissance," *Langston Hughes Review* 14 (1996).

Takara, K. W. "Frank Marshall Davis: A Forgotten Voice in the Chicago Black Renaissance," *Western Journal of Black Studies* 26 (2002).

Tidwell, J. E. "'I was a weaver of jagged words': Social Function in the Poetry of Frank Marshall Davis," *Langston Hughes Review* 14 (1996).

LUCA PRONO

Davis, Gary D. (30 Apr. 1896–5 May 1972), guitarist and religious singer, was born in Laurens County, South Carolina (south of Spartanburg), the son of John Davis and Evelina (maiden name unknown), farmers. One of eight children, he grew up on a farm he later described as being so far out in the country "you couldn't hear a train whistle blow unless it was on a cloudy day." Partially blinded as a baby, Davis was placed in the care of his grandmother. He showed an aptitude for music as a boy, first playing harmonica and later, with his grandmother's help, constructing a guitar. When he was between the ages of seven and ten his mother gave him a guitar, and over the next several years he became proficient, possibly learning from a local musician, Craig Fowler, and an uncle. By age ten he was singing in a Baptist church and playing for local dances. In his teens Davis began adding blues to a repertoire that already included country dance tunes and religious songs.

Around 1910 Davis began working in Greenville with a local string band that included the guitarist Willie Walker, a blind musician he greatly admired. In 1914 Davis entered the South Carolina School for the Deaf and the Blind but left after six months because he did not like the food—an example of the willful independence that characterized his life. Returning to Greenville, he resumed working with the string band, and in 1919 he married Mary Hendrix, a woman five years his senior. By 1926, when he showed up in Durham, North Carolina, he was single again, supposedly because Mary had jilted him for another blind musician, Joe Walker, Willie Walker's brother.

After working as a street musician for several years, Davis, now completely blind, became increasingly focused on his religious convictions. He went to Washington, North Carolina, where he was ordained in the Free Baptist Connection Church, and he began traveling as a singing preacher on the religious revival circuit. Around 1933 he returned to work as a street singer in Durham, where he began playing with guitarist BLIND BOY FULLER and George Washington, a guitar and washboard player also known as "Bull City Red," who doubled as Fuller's "lead boy." Through Fuller, Davis met James Baxter "J. B." Long, manager of the Durham United Dollar Store and a scout for American Record Company. When Long took Fuller to New York to make records in the summer of 1935, he took Davis and Bull City Red along. On 23 July, under the name "Blind Gary," Davis recorded two solo blues, "I'm Throwin' Up My Hand" and "Cross and Evil Woman Blues," the only early examples of his blues repertoire. Several days later he recorded thirteen religious sides, twelve of which were issued. Paid a flat fifty dollars for the session, Davis later concluded that Long had shortchanged him, and tension between the two men precluded any further recording activity.

Throughout the 1930s and into 1940 Davis was listed on Durham welfare rolls, hiding his street singing to retain eligibility. Davis told suspicious caseworkers he was seldom home because he was preaching and was interested only in saving souls.

Always aware of his vulnerability to larceny, Davis routinely carried weapons, among them a large pocketknife. According to legend, an acquaintance once tried to snatch away a dollar bill that had just been placed in Davis's hand by a passerby. It was supposed to be a prank, but Davis instantly seized the prankster and stabbed him repeatedly until he collapsed, all the while thanking the Lord for delivering a thief and sinner into his hands.

In the late 1930s or early 1940s Davis married Annie Bell Wright, a woman from Wake County, North Carolina. He moved from Durham to Raleigh and in about 1940 moved to New York. He remained in the New York City and New Jersey areas for the rest of his life. In New York he was ordained again, becoming a minister of the Missionary Baptist Connection Church. Over the next two decades he became a familiar figure in Harlem, preaching and singing on the streets.

During the 1940s Davis reunited with the harmonica player SONNY TERRY and the guitarist BROWNIE McGHEE, with whom he had played in

Durham. He also taught for a time at McGhee's Home of the Blues Music School in Harlem. Possibly through his friendship with Terry and McGhee, Davis came to the attention of the nascent folk revival movement in the 1950s. A flurry of New York recordings for Stinson in 1954, Riverside in 1956, and Folk Lyric in 1957 established his folk credentials, and in the 1960s Davis became a fixture on the coffeehouse and folk festival circuits. He excited audiences with his instrumental skills on guitar, banjo, and harmonica and even consented to perform secular material along with his large repertoire of religious songs. He recorded for Prestige, Folkways, Biograph, and other documentary labels up to 1971 and toured England several times to critical acclaim. Davis was also featured in several short films and in the 1970 documentary *Black Roots*.

Despite his revival fame, Davis remained close to his roots in the church, serving as an assistant pastor in the True Heart Baptist Church in the Bronx and retaining ties with other Baptist congregations and groups. He continued to tour as a folk musician in the early 1970s and suffered a fatal heart attack in Hammonton, New Jersey, on the way to a concert.

A Piedmont-style guitarist, Davis employed only two fingers (the thumb and index finger) in his picking technique but was nevertheless able to generate formidable speed and complexity. To complement his picking, he had great command of chord positions. As one fellow Durham area guitarist, Willie Trice, told interviewer Bill Phillips, "While you were playing one chord, Davis would play five."

Although Davis had the repertoire of a songster, he much preferred material with spiritual meaning. Critics dubbed his music "holy blues" because it blended sacred content with secular vocal and guitar stylings. While many traditional African American artists performed blues-tinged religious songs—indeed, blues and gospel share a common heritage—Davis was singular for the complexity of his instrumental technique. Among the artists and followers of the folk revival, he was lionized for his instrumental pyrotechnics and his authenticity—a living street singer who had known legends such as Blind Boy Fuller and Willie Walker. Davis also influenced other guitar technicians, including Ry Cooder and Stefan Grossman, and his songs have been reprised by artists ranging from Peter, Paul, and Mary to TAJ MAHAL to John Cephas.

FURTHER READING

Bastin, Bruce. *Red River Blues: The Blues Tradition in the Southeast* (1986)

Charters, Samuel. *The Blues Makers* (1991).

Phillips, Bill. "Piedmont Country Blues," *Southern Exposure* 2.1 (Spring–Summer, 1974), 56–62.

Obituary: "Rev. Gary D. Davis," *Living Blues* 8 (Spring, 1972), 6.

This entry is taken from the *American National Biography* and is published here with the permission of the American Council of Learned Societies.

BILL MCCULLOCH AND
BARRY LEE PEARSON

Davis, Griffith Jerome (18 Apr. 1923–Aug. 1993), photographer, journalist, and diplomat, was born on the campus of Atlanta University (later Clark Atlanta University), in Atlanta, Georgia. He attended Oglethorpe Laboratory Elementary School, a practice school on the campus. Davis's professional career began in high school and continued until his retirement in 1985. He was first introduced to photography by William (Bill) Brown, an instructor at the Atlanta University Laboratory High School where Davis was a student. Throughout high school and later as a student at Morehouse, Davis supported himself through photography assignments from local newspapers and public relations firms.

Davis's college education was suspended in 1944 when he joined the armed forces during World War II and fought with the Ninety-second Infantry Division in Italy. After his tour, Griffith returned to Atlanta in 1946 and continued his college studies. He befriended writer and professor LANGSTON HUGHES and civil rights activist and classmate MARTIN LUTHER KING JR. Griffith and Hughes, who became his lifelong friend, sometimes collaborated on stories. Throughout his studies at Morehouse, he photographed and wrote for a number of publications, including *Time*, *Ebony*, and the *Atlanta Daily World*. His "big break" was an *Ebony* assignment to prepare a photo essay on the Palmer Memorial Institute, a boarding school in North Carolina. His accomplishments attracted the attention of esteemed Morehouse president Dr. BENJAMIN E. MAYS, who became a mentor, providing professional and personal guidance. He graduated in 1947 with a B.A. in Photography.

After graduation Davis was hired as a roving editor for *Ebony*, the first person to hold such a position at the magazine. It provided him the freedom to write articles and photograph subjects that interested him. After one year with the magazine, he enrolled in the Columbia Graduate School of Journalism and rented a room in Hughes's Harlem brownstone. In 1949 he earned his M.A. in Journalism and was hired by the Black Star Publishing Company as a freelance photojournalist. Affectionately referred to as "Grif" by his friends, he called himself "an observer of life." The struggle for independence taking place in a number of former African colonies captured his attention, and in 1949 he traveled to Liberia, West Africa, on the first of several trips to photograph and write about the impending changes. His final trip was in 1952, the year he left Black Star. His photographs are vital to the study of Liberia before the coup of 1980. His work appeared in *Ebony*, *Fortune*, *Time*, *Modern Photography*, and other magazines.

During his professional career, he also traveled elsewhere in Africa recording historic transformations with his camera. In 1952 Davis joined a pioneer wing of the U.S. Foreign Service that was the forerunner of the U.S. Agency for International Aid (USAID). Between 1949 and 1974, during his years with both the Black Star Publishing Company and USAID, Davis traveled to twenty-five African countries, including Liberia, Nigeria, and Tunisia. At the completion of this travels he assumed the position of director of the Information, Education and Communications branch of the Office of Population at USAID. In 1977 he was appointed adviser on International Affairs to the mayor of Atlanta, MAYNARD JACKSON, who was the first African American to serve as mayor of a major southern city. Davis retired from the USAID in 1985 after thirty-three years of service.

Davis's photographs comprise a rich visual resource of the leaders and events that propelled the political changes in West Africa during the mid-twentieth century and their impact on the cultural and physical environment. Images of African leaders such as Emperor Haile Selassie of Ethiopia, Ghanaian President Kwame Nkrumah, and President William V. S. Tubman of Liberia accompany photographs of missionaries, including Dr. Albert Schweitzer, Dr. George Harley, and Howard University president MORDECAI WYATT JOHNSON. Images of industry, technology, and everyday life document each country's social and economic development. His work has been on display at various sites, including Howard University, Duke University, and the Smithsonian's Museum of Natural History. His work is published in journals and books, such as in DEBORAH WILLIS-

THOMAS's *An Illustrated Bio-Bibliography of Black Photographers*. In 1993 his alma mater in Atlanta awarded him the Bennie Trailblazer Award (named after Benjamin E. Mays) for personal and professional achievements.

FURTHER READING

Griffith Davis Collection, Moorland-Spingarn Research Center, Howard University.

Mason, Herman "Skip," Jr. *Hidden Treasures: African American Photographers in Atlanta, 1870–1970* (1991).

Thomas, Deborah. *Reflections in Black: A History of Black Photographers, 1840 to the Present* (2000).

DONNA M. WELLS

Davis, Harry E. (26 Dec. 1882–4 Feb. 1955), attorney, politician, and author, was born in Cleveland, Ohio, the eldest son of Jacob Henry and Rosalie Davis. When he was eighteen years old he enlisted in the army, advancing to first lieutenant of Company D, Ninth Battalion, Ohio National Guard. In 1904 he attended Hiram College in Hiram, Ohio, but later transferred to Western Reserve University in Cleveland, where he graduated with a law degree in 1908. In 1909, utilizing an 1896 Ohio civil rights law, Davis brought racial discrimination charges against a Burrows store merchant who refused to sell to him. The merchant was found guilty, and though the jury denied Davis damages, he considered this a small victory for the civil rights movement.

Davis spent his entire life in Cleveland, working as an attorney. Realizing his love of history, in 1910 Davis joined a Masonic lodge through which he conducted historical research on the foundation of African American Masonry in America. He would continue this work for more than twenty-five years. In 1946 he published *A History of Freemasonry among Negroes in America*. Considered an authority on the matter of Prince Hall Masonry, he was frequently called upon to speak, and he was said to be able to talk all night on the subject. In 1935 Davis was commissioned as special deputy of foreign relations and became an advocate of racial understanding within freemasonry by meeting with white and black supreme councils. He received the Northern Supreme Council Gold Medal for Achievement in 1951.

Davis was one of the early members of the Cleveland branch of the NAACP and served as a committee member for several years. His local service in the NAACP led to his selection as a director of the national organization in 1919, a position he held until his death. In 1920 Davis and JAMES WELDON JOHNSON lobbied Republican presidential candidate Warren Harding, but they failed to persuade him to endorse several civil rights proposals. Three years later Davis was a member of the delegation representing the state of Ohio at the funeral in Arlington Cemetery of Colonel CHARLES YOUNG, who had been the highest ranking African American officer in the U.S. Army in World War I and the first to ever reach that rank.

Davis was a devoted member of the Republican Party all his life, serving in the Ohio General Assembly as an elected representative for Cuyahoga County in 1921. He held the position for three terms and was soon elected service commissioner by the Cleveland City Council. After holding the position for six years, he was elected as a member of the Cuyahoga County Charter Commission in 1934, where he served under Harold H. Burton, later an associate justice of the U.S. Supreme Court. From 1947 to 1949 he served as a state senator, in an office that had never been filled by an African American. For his service, Davis was characterized by journalists as "the best legislator in the state" and "the most able member in a quarter century."

In addition to politics, Davis was also active in promoting social welfare in Cleveland. In 1926 he was appointed the first African American member of the trustee board of the Karamu House, a well-known settlement house established to challenge interracial conflict through cultural arts. He served this organization until his death. He was a trustee of the Euclid Avenue Christian Church, which he attended for more than sixty years.

Davis devoted most of his spare time to researching the history of blacks in Cleveland. By the time of his death he had completed a lengthy manuscript on the topic. This work was reorganized and updated by his brother, Russell H. Davis, and published in 1972 as *Black Americans in Cleveland*. His knowledge of Masonry led him to write and publish many articles on the subject. Among them were "The Cathedral," a historical sketch published as a pamphlet in December 1940; "The Prince Hall Sodality," a series of ten articles on Prince Hall Masonry published in the *Pittsburgh Courier*; "Documents Relating to Negro Masonry" (Apr. 1935); "Prince Hall Masonry" (*Opportunity*, 1935); "St. John's Lodge No. 350 of Pennsylvania," an excerpt from *The Prince Hall Sodality*; and "Prince Saunders," a biographical sketch of an early African American mason (May 1940).

Perhaps best known for his outspokenness in the field of masonry and civil rights matters, Harry E. Davis changed the way African Americans were seen in Cleveland and all over the United States. When he died he was buried in the Lakeview Cemetery in Cleveland. Davis was married to Louise Wormley of Washington, D.C., who died in 1946. The two were married for twenty-nine years and had no children.

FURTHER READING

Many of Davis's materials can be found in the departmental clipping file (on microfiche cards) in the Cleveland Public Library in Cleveland, Ohio. Information on Harry Davis can also be found in Russell Davis's personal papers, housed at the Western Reserve Society.

Coyle, William. *Ohio Authors and Their Books* (1962).

Davis, Russell H. *Memorable Negroes in Cleveland's Past* (1969).

CHESYA BURKE

Davis, Henrietta Vinton (Aug. 1860–23 Nov. 1941) actress, activist, and elocutionist, was born in Baltimore, Maryland, to Mansfield Vinton Davis, a musician, and Mary Ann (Johnson) Davis. Davis's talents as an actress and elocutionist were apparently inherited from her father, while her inclination toward activism came from her stepfather, George A. Hackett, who was a recognized leader within the African American community in Baltimore. Both Mansfield Davis and George Hackett died while she was still young. After her stepfather's death, Davis and her mother moved to Washington, D.C., where she had the advantage of attending the best schools, and with her fondness for books, made rapid progress in her studies. At the age of fifteen she passed the necessary exams to become a teacher and began teaching in the Maryland school district. During this time she was recruited by the Louisiana State Board of Education, "who tendered her for a higher position to teach" (Majors, 103) and received a certificate for her commitment to teaching. She remained with the Louisiana board of education until her mother became ill and she returned to Washington.

After returning to Washington in 1878, she began working as a copyist in the Office of the Recorder of Deeds under George A. Sheridan and later FREDERICK DOUGLASS. Like her teacher Miss Mary Bozeman, who recognized her student's talents and encouraged Davis to study elocution, Frederick Douglass also encouraged her to study acting. On 25 April 1883 at Marine Hall in Washington, D.C., Davis made her debut as an elocutionist—a dramatic reader—and was introduced by Douglass. The critical reviews of her performance were mixed. The *Washington Bee* (1883) stated "our lady readers has [sic] found fault with Miss Davis' readings"; while the *People's Advocate* (1883) noted that if more blacks had been in attendance "they could have provided her with moral support." At the same time the *Bee's* reporter wrote, "There are none in Washington who can equal her in dramatic art." John E. Bruce supported this: "I can recall the wild enthusiasm of the audience" (as quoted in Searlie, 8). She was described as "the first lady of her race to publicly essay ... a debut of Shakespeare and other legitimate characters" (Errol Hill, 65).

Following her debut, Davis performed to great acclaim in New York City, New Haven, Hartford, and Boston. Her tour ended with an appearance at the Colored National Convention in the fall of 1883, in Washington, D.C.

After her appearance at the Colored National Convention, Davis left her job at the Office of Recorder of Deeds in 1884 to study for the dramatic stage under Marguerite E. Saxon, with whom she began working in 1880. In 1883 she began to study with other teachers, including Edwin Lawrence of New York City and Rachel Noah of Boston, and she attended the Boston School of Oratory.

In 1884 Thomas T. Symmons, whom she later married, became her manager. Davis and Symmons were married from 1884 to 1893 when they divorced and dissolved their business relationship. As her manager, he booked tours for her not only in the United States but also in the West Indies and Central and South America. She performed works by PAUL LAURENCE DUNBAR and other African American writers, as well as Shakespeare, Mark Twain, and others.

Even with her popular and critical success it was difficult for Davis to obtain a sponsor or to join any of the legitimate dramatic companies that were under white management and did not hire African American performers. Unlike many of her colleagues who eventually became vaudeville performers, she was committed to the legitimate theater. T. THOMAS FORTUNE, one of her supporters and the editor of the *New York Age*, stated that she "could achieve fame and fortune on the regular stage ... if [she] ... [had] a manager with plenty of money behind him" (quoted in Searlie, 8). Fortune believed that this was true not only for Davis but also for other African American performers. Despite not having a backer, Davis started her own dramatic company in Chicago in 1893. The company performed William

Edgar Easton's *Dessalines* and Ignatius Donnelly's *Doctor Huguet*, along with *Our Old Kentucky Home* and *Christophe: A Tragedy*.

During her career as an elocutionist, Davis was admired by African American leaders such as Douglass, Bishop HENRY M. TURNER, BOOKER T. WASHINGTON, and I. F. Aldridge. Their endorsements were instrumental in her appearing at churches where she assisted ministers in their fund-raising campaigns. In his endorsement of Davis, Frederick Douglass stated that "she commands attention and sympathy; and when her deep, fine voice is heard, her audience at once give themselves up to the pleasure of hearing her" (Majors, 105). It was her voice, her style, and her presence that drew many out to hear her read. Along with this Davis was known as "a lover of God's Zion, and is always willing to help it first, and herself last.... Her terms are easy, her work laborious" (Majors, 105). Therefore, churches were able to raise more money for their campaigns while offering Davis a reasonable fee for her performances. In her work as a performer, Davis was concerned with providing African Americans with exposure to the works of African American writers as well as those of white writers.

In 1912 Davis and Nonie Hardy, a contralto singer, toured Jamaica. There she was befriended by John E. and Florence Bruce, supporters of MARCUS GARVEY. Garvey had been born in Jamaica, studied at several colleges, was influenced by Booker T. Washington, founded the Universal Negro Improvement Association (UNIA) in May 1914 in Jamaica, and embraced the philosophy of having pride in one's heritage and ancestry and determining for oneself how to live and contribute to society. Davis introduced the Loyal Knights and Ladies of Malachite, an African American benevolent society, to Jamaicans and assisted in establishing a local chapter. Taking a break from the tour, Davis briefly managed Kingston's Covent Garden Theater and held fund-raisers to build schools. In early 1913, after completing their tour in Central America, Davis and Hardy returned to the United States.

From watching her father, George A. Hackett, to hearing Garvey's message on race love, self-determination, and the redemption of Africa, Davis was always an activist. She believed it was her responsibility "to serve my race and humanity" (Searlie, 9) whether as a performer, a member of UNIA, or as a citizen of the world. This was evident when she contacted Ignatius Donnelly, the Populist Party candidate for president in 1892. In a letter she informed him that she would be willing to deliver speeches "in any part of the country where I could do the most good among my brothers" (Searlie, 9). Along with doing "the most good," she also recognized the lack of cohesiveness among African Americans and strove to overcome it.

It was her unique oratorical skills, her eloquent yet simple statements, her ability to attract a wide audience, and the similarities of their beliefs that attracted Marcus Garvey to Davis. It is not clear when Garvey and Davis met. She noted that they first saw each other in Jamaica and again in 1919 when Garvey invited her to speak at the Harlem Palace Casino. It was immediately after her performance that she joined Garvey and became one of the thirteen original members of Universal Negro Improvement Association (UNIA), New York. Leaving the stage was a difficult decision, but using her talents on behalf of her race, she believed, was more important.

In June 1919 she was appointed international organizer of UNIA and director of the Black Star Shipping Company, and second vice president of the Black Star Corporation, both of which were enterprises of UNIA. Over the next twelve years, she served as first and fourth assistant president general of UNIA, as delegate to Liberia, and as secretary general, and she was an organizer of the Black Cross Navigation and Trading Co. and the Universal African Legion and Black Cross Nurses. In addition she was one of the signers of the Declaration of Rights of the Negro People of the World (August 1920), which consisted of fifty-four resolutions which, among other items, stated that the colors red, black, and green were the colors of the African people; demanded that the word "Negro" be written with a capital "N"; called for self-determination of all people; and for the right to unlimited and unprejudiced education (Hill et al.).

As an international organizer for UNIA, Davis traveled across the United States, Cuba, and Central and South America, building support and advocating black unity and nationalism. Using her oratorical skills, she made eloquent yet simple speeches encouraging her audiences to support Garvey, "to migrate to Africa; to fight for African freedom from colonization; to take pride in using 'Negro' instead of 'colored' as the race designation; to fight segregation and never bow to suppression; and to teach their children to love their race, their blackness, and their African heritage" (Collier-Thomas, 256).

Garvey, along with members and leadership of UNIA, were supportive of the contributions Davis was making to the organization. She was honored with the Lady Commander of the Sublime Order of the Nile at the August 1921 UNIA convention. At the 1920 Convention, when the new officers were inaugurated, Garvey announced that the new officers would receive an annual salary to assist with the work they were doing for the race. The salaries ranged from $3,000 to $12,000, with Garvey receiving an annual salary of $10,000 and Davis an annual salary of $6,000.

Throughout the 1920s Davis continued to encourage UNIA members and those who came to hear her to share and support Garvey's greatness. In her speeches, she described Garvey as "the Solomon of the present day" (Hill et al.); urged audiences to know the man who was divinely sent and champion of all African people; informed them of his courage, intelligence, and sacrifices; and urged them to understand that he was "the new negro ... a man, a full fledged man, asking, demanding his right of the powers that be" (Hill et al., 500). Davis sought to make sure that others would know his purpose, ambition, and hope for African people. This was especially true during the period of his arrest and trial and eventual deportation to Jamaica in 1927. In 1922 Garvey had been arrested and convicted for mail fraud and served a two-year sentence. During this period she was appointed fourth assistant president-general. In her acceptance speech, she stated her loyalty to Garvey: "I have sworn that should he go up, I will go up, and should he fall, I shall fall by his side" (Searlie, 14). As fourth assistant president-general, she worked with the women within the organization to make sure that women's rights were protected and that they could function without restrictions from the men. Garvey supported this ideal, for he recognized that half of his membership were women and the backbone of the movement, serving as officers on both the local and national level, and that they were loyal and offered unconditional support. Garvey idealized women in his speeches, editorials, songs and poems, and praised women like MAGGIE LENA WALKER, MADAME C. J. WALKER, and ANNIE TURNBO MALONE. Women of the UNIA recognized and challenged their secondary status, yet continued to support Garvey, stand by their men, and bolster the ideal of strong black manhood.

In her efforts to keep the organization intact, conflicts arose between Davis and Garvey. The conflict began when Garvey refused to pay Davis's salary effective June 1923, later accusing her of "doing nothing to give new life to the organization" (Garvey, 170), and then slighting her at the 1929 convention where she was elected secretary-general of the UNIA of the World. Despite the conflict, Davis initially remained loyal to Garvey and the organization. But by 1932 Davis and Garvey had drifted apart, and she left UNIA of the World and became first a member, then first assistant president-general, later acting president, and finally in 1934 president of UNIA, Inc. The separation between the UNIAs began in 1926 when members held their own convention, without Garvey's approval, and elected George Weston as president; in addition, this group held the UNIA incorporation papers and title to Liberty Hall. The new organization became known as UNIA, Inc. The UNIA of the World was headquartered in Jamaica with Garvey as president and Davis as secretary-general. The goal of the UNIA of the World was to continue the work put forth by the original principles of the UNIA and to continue to establish chapters throughout the world.

With the UNIA, Inc., Davis continued to uphold Garvey's principles and organized a national employment exchange. The national employment exchange was created to inform blacks about available jobs throughout the nation and to offer them job training. This was one of her last major efforts to provide for her race. Even as a member and leader in UNIA, Inc., she remained loyal to Marcus Garvey.

Once known as the "modern day Joan of Arc" and "the jewel of the Negro" (Hill et. al., 311, 653), Henrietta Vinton Davis died unnoticed in Washington, D.C., in 1941.

FURTHER READING

Bair, Barbara. "Henrietta Vinton Davis," in *Black Women in America: A Historical Encyclopedia*, eds. Darlene Clark Hines et al. (1993).

Collier-Thomas, Bettye "Henrietta Vinton Davis," in *Notable Black American Women*, ed. Jessye C. Smith (1993).

Garvey, Amy J. *Garvey & Garveyism* (1970).

Gyant, LaVerne, "Amy Jacques Garvey and Henrietta Vinton Davis of the Universal Negro Improvement Association," in *Black American Intellectualism and Culture: A Social Study of African American Political Thought*, ed. James L. Conyers (1999).

Hill, Errol. *Shakespeare in Sable* (1984).

Hill, Robert, et al. (eds) *Marcus Garvey and the Universal Negro Improvement Association Papers* (1983–1989).

Majors, M. A. *Noted Negro Women* (1893, repr. 1971).

Matthew, Mark D. "Our Women and What They Think, Amy Jacques Garvey and the Negro World," *Black Scholar* (May–June 1979).

Searlie, William. "Henrietta Vinton Davis and the Garvey Movement," in *Afro-Americans in New York Life & History* (1983).

LAVERNE GYANT

Davis, John (?–25 Dec. 1812), sailor during the War of 1812, was a crewman on the privateer *Governor Tompkins*, a fourteen-gun schooner owned by principals from Baltimore, Maryland. Nothing is known of his early life or place of origin. The schooner departed New York in July 1812 under Captain Nathaniel Shaler. Among his crew were two black men, Davis and JOHN JOHNSON (?–1812). While little information is known about either man, it is likely that they were free men and skilled sailors. Given the fact that the *Governor Tompkins* sailed from New York, it may be reasonably inferred that Davis and many of the crew, if not from that city, had previously been employed there.

Once out into the Atlantic, Captain Shaler and his crew cruised in search of British merchantmen to capture. This was the purpose of a privateer; to hit the enemy where it hurt by capturing valuable merchant cargoes that were then brought to American ports to be sold at great profit. As for those Americans serving in a privateer, they too profited greatly; though the lion's share of the prize money went to the ship's owners and its captain, even the smallest of prize shares earned by such men as John Davis far exceeded what could be earned by serving in the regular U.S. Navy, with the added benefit that discipline in privateers was far less harsh than that aboard regular men of war. Because of such opportunities, thousands of black men like John Davis served as seamen in the War of 1812. Indeed, their contribution in manning private ships of war was invaluable and a natural extension of the pivotal role they had played in manning merchant vessels in times of peace since well before the American Revolution.

The action in which Davis gained renown began on the Christmas morning of 1812 when Captain Shaler and his crew discovered three ships at sunrise. Believing one of the ships to be a large and potentially valuable transport, the men of the *Governor Tomkins* worked their ship closer to their intended prey. At 3 P.M. a sudden squall struck, driving the enemy ship closer yet to Captain Shaler's vessel, upon which the captain discovered that his intended victim was not a transport at all, but rather the forty-four-gun frigate *Laurel*, one of the newest frigates in the British Navy, and reputed to be the fastest. The fighting began at 3:30

P.M., as Shaler continued to tack his vessel. The first broadside from the *Laurel* struck the hardy schooner and wrought havoc among its crew, but caused no mortal damage to the ship. The battle continued for half an hour, but further enemy fire missed the *Governor Tompkins* and by 5:30 P.M. the battle was over. As Shaler would relate in a letter to his agent a week later regarding his casualties, "John Davis … fell near me, and several times requested he be thrown overboard, saying he was only in the way of the others. While America has such sailors, she has little to fear from the tyrants of the ocean" (Coggeshall, 143).

FURTHER READING

Brown, William Wells. *The Negro in the American Rebellion: His Heroism and His Fidelity* (1866, rpt. 1971).

Coggeshall, George. *History of the American Privateers and Letters-of-Marque, During Our War with England in the Years 1812, '13 and '14* (1861).

GLENN ALLEN KNOBLOCK

Davis, John (July 1853–19 Aug. 1903), sailor and Medal of Honor recipient, was a native of Kingston, Jamaica, who immigrated to America prior to 1877. Little is known of his life before his naval service, except that he resided in Virginia, was there married to his wife, Maria, a native of Virginia, in 1877, and that his daughter Emily was subsequently born in 1879.

Like so much else about the life of John Davis, just when he enlisted in the U.S. Navy is uncertain. Though Davis was aboard the screw steamer U.S.S. *Trenton* when he earned the Medal of Honor in 1881, he was not aboard that ship, the flagship of the navy's European Station, when it departed New York for France in March 1877. John Davis likely enlisted in the navy in Virginia in 1877, about the time he was married, and was subsequently assigned duty on a vessel that departed for the European Station from Hampton Roads, Virginia. Once overseas, Davis was assigned to the *Trenton* at an unknown time by early 1881. His rating of ordinary seaman while aboard the *Trenton* is a general indicator of his beginner status in the navy; below him in the navy's rating system were those men rated as a landsman, men without any seafaring experience, while above him were those men who were rated as able-bodied seamen and were fully proficient in their sailor skills. No matter when John Davis entered the navy, and what his experiences may have been, he put what skills

he had to good use on the *Trenton*. On or about 17 February 1881 while the ship was at Toulon, France, he was working topside along with fellow sailor Alexander Turvelin, a Russian immigrant, when another crewman, Coxswain Augustus Ohlensen, fell overboard and was close to drowning because he could not swim. However, John Davis and Turvelin quickly responded by diving overboard to save Ohlensen. The heroism performed by Davis and Turvelin, though it occurred in foreign waters, did not go unnoticed stateside and was reported on soon after by the *New York Times* based on information received from the *Trenton*'s captain, Commander Francis Ramsay. It was undoubtedly Ramsay, though details are lacking, who recommended Davis for the Medal of Honor, probably upon his returning stateside in late 1881.

The naval service of men like John Davis, JOHN JOHNSON, and DANIEL ATKINS is important in several regards. First and foremost, they were members of a unique, but largely forgotten group of men who earned their nation's highest military decoration under peacetime circumstances; indeed, the eight African American sailors that are a part of this group are the only black sailors ever to be awarded the Medal of Honor. Further, the service of these men, and the recognition accorded them for their heroic deeds, is indicative overall of the equality and diversity generally found among the men serving in the enlisted ranks of the U.S. Navy during the years prior to 1900. After this time the Jim Crow policies of the navy slowly but surely restricted blacks to a segregated and subservient role that was not reversed until 1948.

Following his Medal of Honor heroics in February 1881, the specifics of John Davis's naval career are uncertain. It is likely that he continued to serve on the *Trenton* during the remaining time it spent on the European Station before returning to Hampton Roads, Virginia, on 12 October 1881. Whether Davis saw subsequent shore duty in Virginia, or served aboard another vessel is unknown, but he was still an ordinary seaman in October 1884, when he was finally awarded the Medal of Honor. After leaving the navy at an unknown date, John Davis resided in the Wythe district of Hampton, Virginia, for the remainder of his life. In addition to his wife, Maria, and daughter Emily, his family included another daughter, Amelia (born 1884), and his son, Robert (born 1886). John Davis subsequently worked as a pile driver in his civilian life. At his death at the age of fifty, he was buried in the Hampton National

Cemetery in Hampton, Virginia, where a Medal of Honor headstone marks his final resting place.

FURTHER READING

Hanna, Charles W. *African American Recipients of the Medal of Honor* (2002).

"National Capital Topics—Naval Intelligence," *New York Times*, 9 Mar. 1881.

GLENN ALLEN KNOBLOCK

Davis, John Aubrey (10 May 1912–16 Dec. 2002), educator, civil rights activist, and government official, was born in Washington, D.C., the son of John Abraham Davis, a federal employee, and Gabrielle Beale, a homemaker. John's older brother (William) Allison Davis later became a noted psychologist and educator. He also had a sister, Dorothy.

Davis earned a B.A. degree (summa cum laude) in English from Williams College in Williamstown, Massachusetts, in 1933 and a master's degree in political science from the University of Wisconsin, Madison, in 1934, where he was a university fellow. He married Mavis E. Wormley in 1935. Davis received a prestigious two-year Julius Rosenwald Fellowship, from 1938 to 1940 (renewed in 1940), to study toward his doctorate at Columbia University. Although he was initially interested in studying the role of blacks in politics in New York, he was persuaded by the Rosenwald Committee to instead focus his dissertation on the regional organization of the Social Security Board. He earned a Ph.D. in Political Science from Columbia in 1949. He lectured at Howard University in Washington, D.C., during 1935–1936 and was assistant professor and professor of political science at Lincoln University in Pennsylvania from 1936 to 1953. He was a visiting lecturer at Ohio State University from 1950 to 1951. He joined the City College of New York as associate professor of political science in 1953, served as professor and department chair from 1961 to 1980, and was named professor emeritus in 1980.

Davis's lifelong interest in fair employment practice stemmed from an incident that occurred upon his return to Washington, D.C., during the summer of 1933. He discovered that the white owners of the Hamburger Grill in a black neighborhood had fired three black employees in order to give jobs to three white men. As a key organizer of the New Negro Alliance, which exhorted blacks to "buy where you can work," Davis organized a boycott of the Hamburger Grill, which subsequently closed. One of the earliest civil rights protests in Washington, D.C., it laid the foundation for establishing the legality of economic boycotts to fight employment discrimination.

In 1933 Davis was the founder and first executive director of the New Negro Alliance, an organization that organized pickets and boycotts to protest the employment practices of dozens of Washington, D.C., business establishments. While many of the protests were halted by court order, a 1938 case involving Safeway (then known as the Sanitary Grocery Company, Incorporated) reached the U.S. Supreme Court, which upheld the right of the protesters to "peacefully persuade others" to act against racial discrimination in employment. Davis began working for the federal government as a research assistant for the Department of Labor in 1934–1936. His federal governmental employment also included the Office of Emergency Management, the President's Commission on Fair Employment Practice, and executive director of the commission's Division of Review and Analysis from 1943 to 1946. In 1942 Davis authored *How Management Can Integrate Negroes in War Industries* for the New York State Commission on Discrimination in Employment. In 1944 he published "The Employment of Negroes in the Local Transit Industry" in *Opportunity* magazine.

At the state level Davis served as assistant director of New York State's Committee against Discrimination in Employment, the first organization of its kind in the nation, in 1942, and head of the commission from 1957 to 1961. During 1956–1957 he was a consultant to the governor of New York on the administration of a proposed law against age discrimination in employment.

As the director of non-legal research for the NAACP in the case *Brown vs. Board of Education of Topeka* in 1953 and 1954, Davis directed research on questions from the U.S. Supreme Court relating to the intentions of the framers of the Fourteenth Constitutional Amendment (which deals with equal protection and due process) with regard to segregation in education, as well as queries regarding the amendment's legal history and sociology. From 1963 to 1975 Davis served as a board member and executive committee member of the NAACP Legal Defense and Education Fund.

Over the years Davis worked with many organizations. He sat on the Faculty Fellowship Board of the United Negro College Fund from 1959 to 1961 and was chief of the U.S. Delegation to the World Conference of Black Writers in Paris in 1956. He was the founder, executive director from 1957 to 1962, and president from 1962 to 1966 of the American Society of African Culture. He served on the board of editors of the *Presidential Studies Quarterly* from 1974 to 2002 and the board of directors of the Library of U.S.

Presidential Papers from 1966 to 1970, the Seminar on Africa from 1967 to 1968, and the Council on Foreign Relations from 1964 to 2002. He served in key posts with the American Political Science Association. He was a member of the Advisory Committee of the Democratic National Committee from 1957 to 1960, and member of President Lyndon B. Johnson's Committee on Domestic Affairs from 1964 to 1966.

The recipient of numerous awards including the Chevalier of the Republique Federale du Cameroun in 1964 and the Commandeur de l'Ordre National from the Republic of Senegal in 1966, Davis authored or edited several works on Africa, including *Southern Africa in Transition* and "The Influence of Africans on American Culture." He was the editor of *Africa Seen by American Negro Scholars*, produced by Presence Africaine in 1963 and the author of *Regional Organization of the Social Security Administration: A Case Study* in 1968. Davis died of pneumonia at an assisted living facility in Scottsdale, Arizona, at the age of ninety.

FURTHER READING

MacGregor, Morris J. *The Emergence of a Black Catholic Community: St. Augustine's in Washington* (1999).

Obituaries: *New York Times* and *Washington Post*, 21 Dec. 2002.

JAYNE R. BEILKE

Davis, John Preston (19 Jan. 1905–11 Sept. 1973), lawyer, journalist, director of the National Negro Congress, publisher of *Our World* magazine, was born in Washington, DC, the son of Dr. William Henry Davis and Julia Hubbard Davis, who had moved to the capital in 1899 from Louisville, Kentucky. The elder Davis worked in several occupations; in addition to obtaining a doctorate of Pharmacology from Howard University, he developed a successful business school, became official stenographer for the National Negro Business League, and during World War I served as special assistant to Dr. Emmett Scott, special assistant to the United States secretary of war.

In 1922 the younger Davis graduated from Dunbar High School, in Washington, DC, and entered Bates College in Lewiston, Maine. He was selected as editor in chief of the campus newspaper *The Bates Student* in 1925, served as president of the debating fraternity, Delta Sigma Rho, and represented Bates in an international debate with Oxford University, then was chosen to go to England with the Bates team for debates at Oxford and Cambridge.

Drawn to Harlem, Davis wrote for *Fire!*, a magazine introduced in November 1926 by the Harlem Renaissance icon WALLACE THURMAN. Devoted to "Younger Negro Artists," it represented something of a revolt against the "talented tenth" championed by DR. W. E. B. DuBois. For a time, Davis was the magazine's business manager. From 1926 to 1927, he earned a masters degree in Journalism from Harvard University, then accepted a position as director of publicity at Fisk University, Nashville, Tennessee, 1927–1928.

In 1932 Davis married Marguerite DeMond, the Iowa-born daughter of a Baptist minister, and researcher at the Association for the Study of Negro Life and History. They had four children: Michael DeMond Davis, Miriam Judith Davis Nason, Marguerite Davis, and John Preston Davis Jr. In 1933 Davis returned to Harvard, earning an LLB degree from the law school the same year. There he connected with ROBERT C. WEAVER, who was his roommate, and WILLIAM HASTIE, both fellow alumni of Dunbar, and RALPH BUNCHE, working on his doctorate in Political Science.

Davis and Weaver developed a common concern that none of the major national Negro organizations appeared to be doing much about black participation in the New Deal. They established the Negro Industrial League, privately naming Davis the "Negro" while Weaver was the "Industrial League." In office space donated by a man named Robert Pelham, and with enough money to hire a secretary, the two began to appear at hearings of the National Recovery Administration (NRA). Davis was the primary spokesperson as they appeared at hearing after hearing concerning minimum wage codes.

During cotton textile hearings in July 1933, Davis protested that fourteen thousand Negro cleaners and other nonskilled mill help had been excluded from the textile code's minimum wage class. At the time, 70 percent of wage workers in the United States were employed by manufacturers of steel, textiles, oil products, automobiles, and coal. (*Time*, 10 July 1933, p. 11). After observing that price supports were ruining black farmers— particularly tenants evicted in blatant violation of the Agricultural Adjustment Act—and that the Social Security Act excluded millions of black and white domestic and farm workers, Davis once quipped that NRA—the acronym for President Franklin D. Roosevelt's National Recovery Act— stood for "Negroes Robbed Again." Twenty-six organizations, including the YWCA, National Urban League, and the NAACP, soon joined to form the Joint Committee on Economic Recovery, which employed Davis as executive secretary and legislative lobbyist until 1936.

Between 1934 and 1938, Davis, along with THURGOOD MARSHALL and CHARLES H. HOUSTON, undertook investigations into the Tennessee Valley Authority's racially discriminatory practices for the NAACP. Congress did not act on their reports, which unsurprisingly showed that the TVA reflected the biases of its southern environment in hiring and administration, nor did the press pay much attention. In 1935, Davis authored "A Black Inventory of the New Deal" published in *The Crisis*, May 1935 (Vol. 42, pp. 141–142, 154).

An author of the pamphlet *Let Us Build a National Negro Congress* in May 1935 and an original sponsor of the NNC's founding convention in February 1936, Davis served as executive secretary until 1942. Formed by 817 delegates representing 585 organizations, and with the support of the Communist Party (of which NNC cofounder JAMES FORD was a member), NNC built seventy local organizations across the United States, initiating campaigns concerning police brutality, housing, and employment. Many of the active participants in the civil rights actions of the mid to late 1950s got their first experience in mass petition drives, rent strikes, antilynching protests, and picketing retail stores, as NNC volunteers.

During the Spanish Civil War, Davis reported from Spain for the *Pittsburgh Courier*, also visiting France and Russia during the late 1930s. In 1938, he participated in founding the Southern Conference on Human Welfare in Birmingham, Alabama, together with Clark Foreman, MARY MCLEOD BETHUNE, Joseph Gelders, Lucy Randolph Mason, Virginia Durr, and Eleanor Roosevelt. The founding group was threatened with arrest by police commissioner Eugene "Bull" Connor, who still held that position in 1963, when he turned police dogs and fire hoses on volunteers for the Southern Christian Leadership Conference.

Davis authored *The National Negro Congress Reports to the People* in 1940, the only such report in NNC history. That same year, at NNC's third convention, Randolph denounced the Soviet Union as a dictatorship, while Davis responded that he had seen "its many nations and people busy and working in amity, collaboration and peace" (*New York Times*, 28 Apr. 1940, p. 9). The NNC lost credibility and significance in the mid-1940s, as Communist Party members sought to make it a propaganda organ for party resolutions rather than the effective mass organization it had originally been; Davis

resigned in early 1943. That year, he filed a lawsuit challenging segregated schools in Washington, DC, after the principal of Noyes elementary school refused to admit his son, Michael.

The first issue of *Our World*, a magazine which Davis founded and published in New York City, hit newsstands in April 1946 and featured the singer LENA HORNE on the cover. Written and marketed primarily for African American readers, it covered sports, entertainment, health, fashion, politics, and what was then known as "Negro history." In the first few years, *Our World* attracted major advertisers, including Liggett & Myers, Calvert, Seagram, Quaker Oats, Pabst Blue Ribbon, Carnation, Pet Milk, Philco, and Admiral, as corporate managers recognized that African Americans were earning four times as much in 1950 as they had in 1940.

In 1948 Davis was hired by the Democratic National Committee as an assistant director of publicity for the Truman-Barkley campaign. Working with William Hastie, he kept the majority of black voters supportive of Truman, rather than Progressive Party candidate Henry Wallace. As a result, Truman's margin of 70 percent of African American voters in key cities such as Chicago, Cleveland, and Los Angeles was larger than his statewide plurality in Illinois, Ohio, and California; the loss of any of those states, even if he had kept a nationwide lead in the popular vote, could have tipped the electoral college to the Republican candidate Thomas Dewey.

Although Davis himself was harassed by Senator Joseph McCarthy for associating with known communists during the 1930s, he stepped forward to testify on behalf of Dr. Ralph Bunche (by then a United Nations official and recipient of the Nobel Peace Prize) before the Senate Internal Security Subcommittee 10 March 1953. *Our World* ceased publication in 1957 due to loss of advertising; John H. Johnson, founder and publisher of *Ebony*, later recalled that there were not enough readers or advertisers for both magazines, and one or the other had to win.

From 1958 to 1961, Davis worked as a fund-raiser for the Lincoln Center for the Performing Arts in New York City. He was invited to a private, informal dinner at the White House in April 1958 by President Dwight D. Eisenhower. Hired as editor of special publications for the Phelps-Stokes fund in 1963, Davis created the first *American Negro Reference Book*, published by Prentice-Hall in 1966, and retired due to ill health in 1968. Davis died in New York, survived by his wife and children, and his sister, Sara Louise Davis Taylor, of Washington,

DC. Marguerite DeMond Davis died in 1978 in San Diego, California, at the age of seventy.

FURTHER READING

Egerton, John. *Speak Now against the Day: The Generation before the Civil Rights Movement in the South* (1995).

Jensen, Hilmar, III. "The Rise of an African American Left: John P. Davis and the National Negro Congress." Unpublished Ph.D. dissertation, Cornell University (1997).

Nelson, Bruce. *Divided We Stand: American Workers and the Struggle for Black Equality* (2001).

Weaver, Robert C. "Blending Scholarship with Public Service," in *Against the Odds: Scholars Who Challenged Racism in the Twentieth Century* (2004).

CHARLES ROSENBERG

Davis, John Warren (11 Feb. 1888–12 July 1980), educator, administrator, and civil rights pioneer, was born in Milledgeville, Georgia. At the age of five, Davis was sent to live with distant relatives, Mr. and Mrs. Sylvannus Carter, in Americus, Georgia. An itinerant preacher, Carter instilled both moral values and a deep appreciation for education in the young Davis. Davis attended secondary school and college at the Atlanta Baptist College (Morehouse College), and worked summers in the Chicago stockyards of Swift & Company to raise money to pay for his education. He graduated from Morehouse College with a bachelor's degree in 1911. Encouraged and aided by John Hope, the president of Morehouse College, Davis enrolled as a graduate student in chemistry and physics at the University of Chicago. He then returned to Morehouse College in 1914, where he taught those subjects, served as the registrar, and was a part-time football assistant.

In 1917 Davis left Atlanta to serve as the executive secretary of the Twelfth Street branch of the Young Men's Christian Association (YMCA) in Washington, D.C., where he aided in the integration of the organization. Davis told the leadership that if they wanted to segregate facilities, then they would have to remove the word "Christian" from the association's title.

After a personal recommendation by the educator CARTER G. WOODSON, Davis became the president of the West Virginia Collegiate Institute (later West Virginia State College, WVSC) on 1 September 1919. Under his direction for the next thirty-four years, the institute grew from twenty-seven college-level students to more than two thousand. Davis wanted it to be a state college, and in 1927 he saw the institute accredited with the North Central Association for Colleges and Secondary Schools, making it the first black institution with a black president and a completely black faculty to be accredited by a regional association.

Throughout the 1920s, as blacks pressed for higher education and whites resisted the change from a vocational to an academic curriculum, Davis developed the school through protest, negotiation, political action, and litigation. He instituted a building program, expanded the curriculum, created influential alliances, and strategically outmaneuvered politicians and the state board of control. Using a personal approach, Davis gained publicity and support, persuading some of the best black educators in the nation to teach at the college, including Carter G. Woodson, who served as academic dean. The college soon became a nationally recognized educational institution for blacks in both academics and athletics. In the process Davis laid the foundation for WVSC to become the most integrated college in the United States.

The school soon became a crucial center for black West Virginians, serving as the home for public institutions like the black agricultural extension program. Davis also began integrating the faculty and students at WVSC in the late 1930s and early 1940s. In September of 1939 Davis gained approval for the establishment of a civilian pilot training program at WVSC from the Civilian Aeronautics Authority in Washington, D.C., making WVSC the first African American college to participate in that program. In 1940 WVSC became the first black college to enroll white trainees into its flight program, a preliminary step toward the integration of the U.S. armed forces in 1948. Among the black enrollees were George Spencer Roberts, the first African American appointed to the U.S. Army Air Corps, and Rose Agnes Rolls Cousins, the first black woman solo pilot in the program.

Following the attack on Pearl Harbor in 1941, Davis placed WVSC on a war footing by adjusting the curriculum to meet military needs, urging complete integration among faculty and students, and encouraging cooperation, academic freedom, creativity, and debate. Receptions were often held in the Davis home, and there was no racial segregation at cultural affairs held at WVSC. After submitting applications for nineteen years, in 1942 WVSC became the first African American college to obtain authorization for a Reserved Officers Training Corps (ROTC), affording blacks the opportunity to serve as officers.

In 1952 Davis announced that he would retire as president of WVSC the following year. President Harry S. Truman immediately appointed Davis as the U.S. director of the Technical Cooperative Administration in Liberia. Given a leave of absence from the college, Davis served as director from 1952 to 1954. Elected to serve on the board of directors of the NAACP Legal Defense and Education Fund at its beginning in 1939, the director THURGOOD MARSHALL asked Davis to serve as the fund's director of education in 1954. Davis served the fund until his death in 1980.

Davis participated in numerous organizations throughout his illustrious career. He was the first African American member of the Committee on Institutions of Higher Education in the North Central Association of College and Secondary Schools and was a member of the National Land-Grant College Survey staff, the National Advisory Committee on the Education of Negroes, the National Education Association, the Association of School Administrators, the Society for the Advancement of Education, the American Academy of Political Science, the Association of State College Presidents, the National Freedom Day Association, the National Urban League, and the American Society of African Culture. He served as president of the National Association of Teachers in Colored Schools (American Teacher's Association), the first African American chairperson of a National Education Association (NEA) commission, president of the Conference of Presidents of Negro Land Grant Colleges, and president of the West Virginia Council of State Colleges and Universities.

President Herbert Hoover appointed Davis to the Organization of Unemployed Relief, and President Truman appointed him to the first board of directors of the National Science Foundation. Davis founded the Herbert Lehman Educational Fund to provide scholarships for black youth and the Earl Warren Legal Training Program to provide funds for African Americans to attend law school. In 1980 the National Education Association awarded Davis the Trenholm Award for his outstanding contributions to education. Davis served on the board of directors and board of trustees of numerous organizations and obtained fourteen honorary degrees, including those from Morehouse College, State College at Orangeburg, South Carolina, Wilberforce University, and Howard University. He was the author of many articles, including "Land Grant Colleges of Negroes," "Problems in the Collegiate

Education of Negroes," "Negro Education vs. the Education of the Negro," "Minority Report National Advisory Committee on Education," and "Wilberforce University as a Cause."

Davis and his first wife, Bessie Rucker, had two daughters, Constance (born in 1918) and Dorothy (born in 1919). Bessie Davis died shortly after Davis became president of the West Virginia Collegiate Institute. Davis married his second wife, Ethel McGhee Davis, the dean of women at Spelman College, on 2 September 1932. He was a member of the Prince Hall Masonic Grand Lodge, Sigma Pi Phi, and Boule. Davis later lived in Englewood, New Jersey, where he died at the age of ninety-two.

FURTHER READING

The papers of John W. Davis are housed in the Moorland-Spingarn Research Center at Howard University.

Duran, Elizabeth Chidester, and James A. Duran Jr. "Integration in Reverse at WVSC," *West Virginia History* 45 (1984).

Harlan, John C. *History of West Virginia State College, 1891–1965* (1968).

Obituaries: *New York Times* and *Charleston Gazette*, 15 July 1980.

CONNIE PARK RICE

Davis, Lelia Foley (7 Nov. 1941–), the first black woman mayor in the United States, was born Lelia Kasenia Smith in Taft, Oklahoma, the youngest daughter of Willie Smith, a sharecropper, and Canzaty Smith, a midwife. The Smiths were a large family and although very poor, they were generous at heart. Canzaty Smith often accepted food in the place of her $15 fee for delivering a baby, and she and her husband once took in a homeless family, which impressed upon her daughter the importance of caring for community and having respect for all people.

Lelia Smith, a graduate of Moton High School, became a single mother at the age of twenty. By 1967 she had five children and was receiving public assistance to support herself and her children. She later married, becoming Lelia Foley, but she was soon divorced. In a candid 1973 interview with *Essence* magazine, Foley discussed the struggles of being an unwed, single mother, and revealed that she was always unhappy on welfare, and endured continual harassment from social workers. She was employed for a short time as a teacher's aide, and in 1969 she became staff assistant and later director of Taft's Office of Economic Opportunity community action center. Budget cuts forced Foley out of her job in 1972, and she found herself unemployed again. In January 1973 Foley entered the world of politics, launching an unsuccessful campaign for the local school board. But inspired by a book, *The Making of a Black Mayor*, she decided to continue in public service and ran for mayor of Taft, Oklahoma. She campaigned door-to-door with her children in tow, pledging to clean up Taft and attract new businesses to the area. In 1973, she was elected by the city council of Taft to serve as mayor, marking the first time a black woman was elected mayor in the United States. Being mayor of the small town of 600 did not ensure financial security. Her mayoral salary was only $100 per year, and as it was her full time work, Foley continued to draw unemployment.

One of only a handful of black townships still in existence in Oklahoma, Taft was founded in 1904 by former slaves and freedmen who moved west after the Civil War. Once prosperous, the town had slid into decline in the mid twentieth century. As mayor, Foley created a volunteer fire department, oversaw the construction of affordable housing in the area, and brought better water service to Taft, but her tenure was not without trials.

In August 1974 Foley invited the comedian REDD FOXX to serve as Taft's chief of police. Foxx had adopted the town of Taft as his own and consistently said this would not be a symbolic position. He pledged $10,000 for a new public pool and community center, and promised several new police vehicles. But within a year, Foley believed that Foxx would not deliver, and she worked to have him removed from office. Her efforts angered fellow council members, and in the 1975 election, although she carried the popular vote for city council (which historically meant she should be voted mayor by the city council), she was voted out of the mayor's seat by her colleagues. Soon after, Foley was accused of embezzling the $10,000 donated by Foxx. Unable to afford a lawyer and finding no support from the National Council of Black Mayors, Foley faced tough times on the city council and in town. She later recalled this experience as one of the toughest in her life, as she received death threats and watched helplessly as her children were harassed.

Foley attempted to move on and ran unsuccessfully for state senate in 1976. She also attended junior college in 1977 with aspirations of majoring in political science, but she withdrew when her mother fell ill. By July 1978 Foley had been cleared of all embezzlement charges by a grand jury after investigations revealed the $10,000 in question was removed from the bank by someone claiming to represent Foxx. On 22 November 1978 Foley married Earl Davis, a stonemason, and went on to add four stepchildren, twenty-four grandchildren, and thirteen step-grandchildren to her family.

Lelia Foley Davis was reappointed to a four-year term as mayor in April 1979 and returned to the work of improving Taft. She served until 1989 when she resigned because of political infighting. Of particular concern for Davis was the removal of Taft's schools, a move that she believed would drain the future from Taft. Davis's growing discontent with the direction of Taft kept her involved in politics. In the 1990s Davis was re-elected to the town council and returned to the office of mayor in 1999, seeking to curb the flow of human resources out of Taft. The removal of Taft's schools was one of many factors forcing people out of the Taft area; the only major source of revenue for the community was now two new correctional facilities, an unsatisfactory substitution according to Davis. Davis served two more years, focusing on the issues of local education, employment, and nursing home care for the elderly.

In 2000 and 2004 Davis campaigned unsuccessfully for state representative and for state senate. In 2005 Davis remained active on the Taft city council. Davis's legacy and example challenges those who believe someone of her size, race, gender, and education should not be in public office. When she ran for state senate in 1976, Davis said, "I wanted to prove to women, especially Black women, that we are somebody" (*Essence*, 43). Lelia Foley Davis provides a significant role model for black women and should be remembered as an integral part of African American political history.

FURTHER READING

"Lelia Foley Davis," *Essence* (May 1980).

Chenault, Julie. "Her Honor, the Mayor," *Essence* (July 1983).

Dunnigan, Alice A. "Essence Woman: Lelia Foley," *Essence* (1973).

Smith, Ronn. "Lelia Foley Davis," *Muskogee Daily Phoenix and Times-Democrat*, 24 Feb. 2004.

Walton, Rod. "A Leader of Strong Determination," *Tulsa World*, 8 May 1999.

MONIKA R. ALSTON

Davis, Madison (27 Sept. 1833–20 Aug. 1902), wheelwright, politician, and postmaster, was born a slave in Athens, Georgia, to parents whose names have not been recorded. Little is known about the first three decades of his life, other than that he worked as a wheelwright for his master, a carriage maker. Davis learned to read and write while still a slave, skills that helped propel him to the forefront of black political leadership in Reconstruction-era Athens, alongside the tailor, WILLIAM FINCH.

Davis attended one of Georgia's earliest freedmen's conventions in Augusta in January 1866 and rose to prominence as captain of Athens's first black fire company. His reported "coolness and energy" in dealing with a major fire in Athens in 1866 was probably a factor in his election as one of Clarke County's two black delegates to Georgia's constitutional convention, which sat from 1867 to 1868. In the first elections under that new constitution—and under the protection of armed federal troops—Clarke County voters sent Davis and Alfred Richardson, a black carpenter, to the Georgia house of representatives. One local white-owned newspaper declared the result "heart-sickening and disgusting beyond anything we have ever conceived of before" (Hester). In all, twenty-seven blacks entered the legislature that year, the most notable of whom were HENRY M. TURNER, TUNIS G. CAMPBELL, and AARON A. BRADLEY. Unlike that triumvirate, who had either been born or spent much of their lives in the North, Davis was fairly typical of the first generation of Georgia lawmakers in that he was born a southern slave but had never worked in the fields; was literate but had received no formal academic training; and owned some property and real estate but not much. In 1870 his real estate holdings were valued at $700, slightly higher than those of the average black Reconstruction legislator, though his personal property, valued at $100, was lower than the average.

The main difference between Davis and his colleagues was his light skin color, which enabled him to remain in the state legislature after Democrats and conservative Republicans expelled twenty-six African American legislators in September 1868. Davis, along with Edwin Belcher, another light-skinned representative, simply denied that they were black in order to remain in the House. The gambit worked, even though whites in Clarke County knew that Davis had been a slave and viewed him as black. Black Republican members of Clarke County's Union League immediately denounced Davis, however, "for treason to his color," though that did not prevent him from securing re-election to the Georgia House in December 1870, with strong African American support (cited in Drago, 70). Davis was one of only a handful of black Republicans elected to that overwhelmingly Democratic legislature. Less charismatic than his colleagues Turner and Bradley he nonetheless worked diligently to serve his constituents, black and white. Only two of the five bills he introduced during the 1870–1872 session were passed. One of these was to provide relief for a prominent white Athens widow, who had fallen on hard times. Although he persuaded several Clarke County blacks to invest in Georgia Railroad stock, Davis's bill to authorize a new railroad line through Athens was defeated.

Davis's moderation earned him the support of some Democrats and conservative whites who praised him for "always being on the side of law and order" (cited in Drago, 89). The real problems in establishing law and order, however, lay on the conservative side. In September 1868 whites killed seven blacks and injured many others in the southwestern Georgia town of Camilla; in addition to brutally murdering several black politicians the Ku Klux Klan also attempted to kill Davis's fellow Clarke County representative Alfred Richardson twice, in 1870 and 1871. The intensification of racial violence and the restoration of a poll tax that greatly reduced the black electorate probably persuaded Davis not to seek re-election in 1872.

On leaving the state legislature in 1873 Davis returned to Athens, where he became a merchant and remained active in the much-weakened Clarke County Republican Party, serving as chairman until 1882, when his open support for an independent white Congressman led to his dismissal. That same year President James A. Garfield appointed Davis as postmaster of Athens, one of the few federal patronage jobs still available to African Americans. He served in that post with distinction until 1886 and again from 1890 to 1893, but failed to secure a reappointment when President William McKinley appointed Monroe "Pink" Morton, also a prominent Athens Republican, as postmaster. There was some mild opposition among Athens whites to these federal appointments, though nothing on the scale of the violence and intimidation faced by MINNIE COX as postmaster of Indianola, Mississippi, in 1902.

When Davis died of a stroke in Athens, both the black and white local newspapers praised his contribution to civic affairs in Clarke County.

FURTHER READING
Drago, Edmund L. *Black Politicians and Reconstruction in Georgia: A Splendid Failure* (1982).

Hester, Conoly. "*Clarke's First Black Legislators Set an Inspiring Example*," Athens *Banner-Herald*, 2 Sept. 2001.

Thurmond, Michael. *A Story Untold: Black Men and Women in Athens History* (1978)

STEVEN J. NIVEN

Davis, Miles (26 May 1926–28 Sept. 1991), trumpeter, bandleader, and composer, was born Miles Dewey Davis III in Alton, Illinois, the son of Miles Davis II, a dentist, and Cleota H. Henry, both from Arkansas. When Miles was one year old, his family moved to a multiracial neighborhood in East St. Louis, Illinois, where his father prospered, buying a farm in nearby Millstadt. Young Miles first studied trumpet with Elwood C. Buchanan and Joseph Gustat, the principal trumpeter with the St. Louis Symphony Orchestra, and he soon found work in local dance bands.

Caught up in the new music called bebop, Davis left for New York City after graduation and enrolled in the Juilliard School of Music, where he was exposed to the music of such composers as Hindemith and Stravinsky, and where he studied trumpet with William Vacchiano, principal trumpeter with the New York Philharmonic. Davis's nights were spent in the clubs on Fifty-second Street, where he first saw his heroes, CHARLIE PARKER, BILLIE HOLIDAY, EDDIE DAVIS, and COLEMAN HAWKINS, and soon began to perform with them. At a time when other trumpet players were emulating DIZZY GILLESPIE's bravura runs into the upper register and high-speed improvising, Davis cultivated an elegant soft tone and a deliberative approach. His solos were filled with space—pauses and phrasing that let the rhythm section be heard—and he abandoned the fast vibrato that most trumpet players favored. Such a spare approach led some to hear what he was attempting as amateurish, the efforts of a second-rate musician, but many of his contemporaries appreciated his individuality. In 1945 Irene Cawthorn, Davis's high school sweetheart, was pregnant with their first child, and she joined him in New York during his second semester at Juilliard. He left school the next fall to join Charlie Parker's quintet, and played and recorded with them off and on for the next few years. When Parker and Dizzy Gillespie left for the West Coast in 1946, Davis followed them and joined the Benny Carter Orchestra, then went back East with the BILLY ECKSTINE Orchestra, a large bebop band filled with the music's finest players. It was while in the Eckstine Orchestra that Davis first began to use cocaine and heroin.

Now recognized as an innovator in bebop, Davis began to explore other ways of playing, and he made musical change his defining feature. In 1948, with the help of arranger and composer Gil Evans, he withdrew from the heat of bebop to develop the chamber-like music of a nine-piece group. Later dubbed the "Birth of the Cool" band, the group was, paradoxically, modeled on the somber, understated Claude Thornhill Orchestra, a white dance band. Almost immediately afterward, Davis formed a quintet that abandoned the aesthetics of cool and formulated what some call "hard bop," a music that intensified elements of bebop. Almost single-handedly, Davis had set into motion two warring styles that have been the subject of critical debate ever since.

After a trip to Paris in 1949, where he met the writers and avant-gardists Boris Vian and Jean-Paul Sartre, and fell in love with Juliette Greco, doyenne of the French bohemian world, Davis began making a number of important records in the 1950s with younger innovators such as SONNY ROLLINS and ART BLAKEY. In 1955 Davis put together a quintet with the innovative saxophonist JOHN COLTRANE, the drummer PHILLY JOE JONES, the bassist PAUL CHAMBERS, and the pianist RED GARLAND. This popular group produced a series of recordings for Prestige Records, including *Relaxin'* (1956) and *Steamin'* (1956). The quintet's stylish mix of bebop lines and show tunes came to define jazz in the 1950s and in years to come. In a move that paid off handsomely, Davis recorded with this band for Columbia Records while still on contract at Prestige. Columbia released *'Round About Midnight* (1956) as soon as his contract with Prestige had expired.

Columbia had big plans for Davis and promoted him as both a bebopper who had played with Charlie Parker and as a romantic figure who could play for a larger audience. After a few experimental recordings that blended classical and jazz music, released as *The Birth of the Third Stream* (1956), Davis followed with a series of albums that caught the public's fancy. *Miles Ahead* (1957) paired him again with arranger Gil Evans, and extended the Birth of the Cool idea into a larger instrumental setting. *Porgy and Bess* (1958) was next, with Evans's lush settings providing Davis the popular platform he had been seeking. For *Sketches of Spain* (1959–1960), Evans turned to compositions by Joaquim Rodrigo, Manuel de Falla, and Spanish folk melodies, allowing Davis to display the dramatic elements of his playing, and producing a jazz record that simultaneously gestured toward classical, world, and mood music. When the French film director Louis Malle asked Davis to improvise the score for his film *Ascenseur pour l'échafaud* in 1957, the results were so successful that Davis undertook additional film music work, scoring music for *Siesta* (1987), *The Hot Spot* (1990), and most notably *A Tribute to Jack Johnson* (1970).

Outside these side projects and recordings with large groups, Davis continued to work nightly with his quintet. In 1958 he added the alto saxophonist Julian "Cannonball" Adderley and the pianist Bill Evans to the group, and in 1959 they recorded *Kind of Blue*, a largely improvised album of pieces based on modes rather than chord progressions. This turned out to be Davis's most popular record, and possibly the best-selling jazz record of all time.

Just as Davis had disregarded the conventional wisdom on what jazz should sound like, he also rejected nostalgia, adulation, and the cultivation of fans. Dressed in designer suits, Davis left his *Playboy*-inspired house on New York's Upper West Side and drove to gigs in his Ferrari. Once on the bandstand, he refused to announce songs or introduce musicians, ignored applause, and when not playing, either turned away from the audience or left the stage. By refusing even a smile, Davis gained a certain magisterial distance, an air of nobility that reversed a century of performance haunted by the obsequiousness of minstrelsy. He would soon insist that the white female models who routinely adorned jazz album covers in the 1950s be replaced by black models, and more often than not it was his own face staring emotionless into the camera.

All this was part of what drew crowds to Davis's performances. He gained a sympathetic following among beats and hipsters. His persona and his onstage naturalism made him an exemplar for Method actors like James Dean, Dennis Hopper, and Marlon Brando. The Davis enigma was compounded by his silence about his work, both to the public and to his musicians, whom he seldom rehearsed or instructed about playing. On the rare occasions when Davis did speak, contradictions abounded. He might declare his allegiance to African American culture, and denounce white music, and then hire white musicians or proudly declare that he had learned to phrase on trumpet from listening to Frank Sinatra and Orson Welles. He would praise popular black performers like Sly and the Family Stone (SEE SLY STONE) and JIMI HENDRIX, but just as quickly announce that he was studying the works of the Polish classical composer

Miles Davis, jazz virtuoso, in concert in the old Roman Amphitheater in Caesarea, Israel, on 1 June 1987. (AP Images.)

Krzysztof Penderecki and planning to record an instrumental version of Puccini's *Tosca*. His political views were complex and contradictory. Too much the hipster to espouse causes in depth, Davis nonetheless sometimes played for leftist political rallies, and often spoke forcefully on the subject of white control of the entertainment business.

Davis's stylish dress and modish lifestyle gave him a visibility that other jazz musicians never achieved, and made him popular in the world of show business. He traveled widely, made a great deal of money, and married or lived with a number of women, most of whom were in show business, including the dancer Frances Taylor and the actress CICELY TYSON. In addition to music, Davis had a number of interests that endlessly fascinated his audience. A friend of the welterweight champion Johnny Bratton, Davis trained as a boxer, and he raised horses, which he entered into competitions. He appeared on screen in the television series *Miami Vice* (1984) and in such films as *Dingo* (1991), and late in life he took up painting, working collaboratively with another painter, in effect improvising collectively.

There were times when the facts of Davis's social life threatened to overwhelm his music. Although he overcame heroin, other addictions plagued him for most of his life and contributed to his ongoing illnesses and physical ailments, including recurring nodes on the larynx (that led to his distinctive growl), diabetes, sickle-cell anemia, heart attacks and strokes, a degenerative hip, gallstones and ulcers, and what was rumored to be AIDS. In 1959 Davis's picture—his head bandaged, blood streaming down his tailored khaki jacket, a policeman leading him by handcuffs—appeared in newspapers. After refusing a policeman's order to move along from in front of New York City's Birdland club, Davis had been beaten over the head with a nightstick. Charges against Davis were ultimately dropped, but the message of the event was clear to many—the beatings received by civil rights demonstrators in the Deep South were also a danger in the North, even for the most famous of black Americans.

In the 1960s Davis tried various new combinations of musicians, eventually putting together an exceptional quintet composed of WAYNE SHORTER on saxophone, HERBIE HANCOCK on piano, Ron Carter on bass, and TONY WILLIAMS on drums. This group was abstract and earthy, traditional and free at the same time, and intensely rhythmic and full of melodic invention. Records such as *E.S.P.* (1965), *Miles Smiles* (1966), and *Nefertiti* (1967) redefined what jazz was capable of becoming.

Davis had always forced his audience to catch up with him, but now he went even further, adding electric piano and hinting at rock rhythms and tone color on *Filles de Kilimanjaro* (1968). He followed with *In a Silent Way* (1969), another shift in thinking. *In a Silent Way* was a surprisingly long, soft, and dreamlike work, closer to Ravel than to post-bop or rock, a purely textual piece, more sonic than improvisational. Davis now counted on the editing of producer Teo Macero to shape his work, and the two next recorded *Bitches Brew* (1969–1970), an album whose sound, production methods, cover art, and two-LP length signaled that Miles Davis—and jazz—were in motion again. Most critics and fans heard this music as Davis's foray into a new hybrid jazz-rock, although he saw it as a new way of thinking about improvisation and the role of the studio. Recordings Davis made in the mid-1970s, including *On the Corner* (1972) and *Dark Magus* (1974), were so richly textured with electronics and underpinned by funk rhythms that they became even harder to categorize—Psychedelic jazz? Free rock?

Davis's illnesses and addictions led to a breakdown in 1975, and he withdrew into the darkness of his house for the next four years. With the help of friends and lovers, he began to recover and play again, and in 1979 he formed a series of rock-inflected groups that made a series of uneven records, such as *Star People* (1982–1983) and *You're Under Arrest* (1984–1985). Breaking with Evans and Macero in 1986, Davis began to record the synthesizer-driven albums, like *Tutu* (1986–1987) and *Amandla* (1988–1989), that made him an international superstar. Although these studio recordings show Davis as restrained and often being led through the paces by producers, his live recordings from this period, such as *Live Around the World* (1988–91), were spirited reinventions. His final recordings, including *Miles and Quincy Live at Montreux* (1991), which he recorded with QUINCY JONES, were a return to his old style. An effort at hip-hop (*Doo-Bop*) was not completed before his death in Santa Monica, California, in 1991.

FURTHER READING

Davis, Miles, with Quincy Troupe. *Miles: The Autobiography* (1989).

Carr, Ian. *Miles Davis: The Definitive Biography* (1998).

Chambers, Jack. *Milestones: The Music and Times of Miles Davis* (1998).

Szwed, John. *So What: The Life of Miles Davis* (2002)

Tingen, Paul. *Miles Beyond: The Electric Explorations of Miles Davis, 1967–1991* (2001).

Obituary: *New York Times*, 6 Oct. 1991.

DISCOGRAPHY

Lohmann, Jan. *The Sound of Miles Davis: The Discography* (1992).

JOHN SZWED

Davis, Noah (Mar. 1804–?), slave, shoemaker, and pastor, was born in Madison County, Virginia, to John and Jane Davis, slaves belonging to Robert Patten, a wealthy merchant and mill owner. Both of Davis's parents were devout Baptists who instilled in Davis a strong relationship to the church.

By Davis's account, Patten was a comparatively fair master who valued his slaves and who accorded John Davis many privileges, among them the ability to raise livestock and to keep his children with him until they were old enough to go into trade. John Davis was the head miller at Patten's merchant mill located on Crooked Run, a stream between

Madison and Culpeper County. He was able to read and figure, but he could not write.

When Noah Davis was about twelve, Patten sold his mill and emancipated Davis's mother and father. Davis's family moved to one of Patten's farms near Stevensburg. In 1818, at the age of fourteen, Davis was apprenticed to Thomas Wright, a boot- and shoemaker who lived in Fredericksburg, about fifty miles from Davis's home. Davis's older brother was also apprenticed to Wright, and his presence helped assuage some of Davis's homesickness.

For the first year of his apprenticeship, Davis helped Mrs. Wright in the house and kitchen, as was required of black apprentices. In his second year Davis entered the shop. He picked up drinking from the other shoemakers but was an honest and hard worker who enjoyed the esteem of both Mr. and Mrs. Wright.

In addition to learning the shoemaking business, Davis learned how to write. He had already learned the alphabet from his father and now began to copy the names of customers written on the lining of boots and shoes. Davis also became increasingly religious. He had what he described as a conversion experience and was baptized at the Baptist church in Fredericksburg on 19 September 1831. He was subsequently elected a deacon of the church and married another recently converted slave, with whom he eventually had nine children.

In an attempt to pursue his religious calling, Davis approached Patten to purchase his freedom. Patten agreed, fixing a price of five hundred dollars. In July 1845, Davis traveled to Boston, New York, Philadelphia, and other northern cities to raise his purchase price. After four months he returned to Fredericksburg with only one hundred fifty dollars. Discouraged, Davis returned to shoemaking but was then unexpectedly invited to Baltimore to serve as a Baptist missionary to the African American community. Leaving his wife and seven small children, Davis accepted the offer and, with the help of his white Baptist friends, secured an appointment as missionary of the Domestic Board of the Southern Baptist Convention.

While in Baltimore, Davis raised, through subscriptions and loans, the money to purchase his wife and two of his children. He worked steadily to increase the city's small Baptist population, establishing a church and a Sunday school. In 1855 the church moved to a new building and was christened the Saratoga Street African Baptist Church.

Despite the increased financial burden of his church's new facilities, Davis managed to purchase the freedom of two more of his children. To help raise the money to free his last three children, Davis traveled to Baptist churches in Providence and New York to plead his case in front of their congregations. In 1859 he also published a slave narrative titled *A Narrative of the Life of Rev. Noah Davis, a Colored Man, Written by Himself, at the Age of Fifty-Four*. In its conclusion Davis voiced his hope that by "making a book" he may not only raise the funds to free his children but also to discharge the heavy debt incurred by his church. Appended to the end of the narrative was one of Davis's sermons.

Davis's narrative is similar to that of MOSES GRANDY in its function as a fund-raising device to purchase enslaved family members. Unlike other slave narratives, however, Davis's work is unusual for its conspicuous absence of scenes of violence. Robert Patten and the Wrights are good masters, and Davis does not appear to endure or even witness whippings or starvation. The presence of the concluding sermon also suggests the narrative's function as religious document, in keeping with Davis's position as a Baptist missionary. It has been noted that Davis's account of his conversion experience is reminiscent of Bunyan's *Pilgrim's Progress*. As such, his work is a notable example of the intersection between spiritual autobiography and the slave narrative.

FURTHER READING

Davis, Noah. *A Narrative of the Life of Rev. Noah Davis, a Colored Man, Written by Himself, at the Age of Fifty-Four* (1859).

Andrews, William L. *To Tell a Free Story: The First Century of Afro-American Autobiography 1760–1865* (1986).

Foster, Frances Smith. *Witnessing Slavery: The Development of Ante-bellum Slave Narratives* (1979).

Starling, Marion. *The Slave Narrative: Its Place in American History* (1982).

JULIA SUN-JOO LEE

Davis, Ossie (18 Dec. 1917–4 Feb. 2005), writer, actor, and director, was born in Cogdell, Georgia, the oldest of four children of Kince Charles Davis, an herb doctor and Bible scholar, and Laura Cooper. Ossie's mother intended to name him "R.C.," after his paternal grandfather, Raiford Chatman Davis, but when the clerk at Clinch County courthouse thought she said "Ossie," Laura did not argue with him, because he was white.

Ossie was attacked and humiliated while in high school by two white policemen, who took him to their precinct and doused him with cane syrup.

Laughing, they gave the teenager several hunks of peanut brittle and released him. He never reported the incident but its memory contributed to his sensibilities and politics. In 1934 Ossie graduated from Center High School in Waycross, Georgia, and even though he received scholarships to attend Savannah State College and Tuskegee Institute he did not have the minimal financial resources to take advantage of them. Instead, he spent a year clerking at his father's pharmacy in Valdosta, Georgia, before hitchhiking to Howard University, in Washington, D.C. Ossie spent the next four years at Howard, but he did not receive a degree, as he had taken only the classes that appealed to him. However, at Howard, Ossie met the poet and scholar STERLING BROWN, who introduced him to the work of LANGSTON HUGHES and COUNTÉE CULLEN. Brown, Ossie later wrote, showed him that the "interest of my people was at stake, and I could only be a hero by serving their urgent cause. The Struggle opened a new chapter in my imagination" (Davis and Dee, 74–75). ALAIN LOCKE, his Howard theater teacher, began by introducing him to the world of black drama and ended up, according to Ossie, "giving me my life."

Another early influence on Ossie was Eldon Stuart Medas, leader of a West Indian student bull-session group at Howard, who showed Ossie how to love English poets and playwrights and how to use them to win political arguments. As Ossie was preparing to leave Howard in 1939, he attended the 16 April concert given by MARIAN ANDERSON on the steps of the Lincoln Memorial. This event, he later reflected, "married in my mind forever the performing arts as a weapon in the struggle for freedom…. It reminded me that whatever I said and whatever I did as an artist was an integral part of my people's struggle to be free" (Davis and Dee, 86–87). Davis moved to Harlem at the suggestion of Locke, who recommended that the budding playwright apprentice himself to Dick Campbell, founder and artistic director of the Rose McClendon Players (RMP). At the RMP, Davis learned the fundamentals of acting and stagecraft and appeared in four plays between 1939 and 1941, including *Booker T. Washington*, a play by William Ashley starring Dooley Wilson. Davis later said of the RMP that "it cultivated and serviced the Harlem Community with high-grade entertainment that gave Negroes a chance to see their own lives … [and gave] Negro actors, stage managers, set designers, and assorted technicians, a chance to learn and practice their craft under the best instruction" (Davis, "The Flight from Broadway," 15).

In 1942 Davis's career was interrupted when he was drafted during World War II; he served as a medic in Liberia until 1945, after which he returned to New York, where the director Herman Shumlin cast him as the lead in Robert Ardrey's play *Jeb*. The drama, the story of a returning African American veteran who faces down the Ku Klux Klan to marry his girlfriend, costarred RUBY DEE. Davis and Dee appeared together again later that year in the national tour of *Anna Lucasta* and in 1948 at the Lyceum Theater in *The Smile of the World*. The couple married in 1948 and had three children: Nora, Guy, and Hasna.

Although Davis performed in fifteen plays between 1948 and 1957—including Marc Connelly's *Green Pastures* (1951) and *Jamaica* (1958) opposite LENA HORNE on Broadway, for which he received a Tony Award nomination—he thought of himself principally as a playwright. Since 1939, however, he had been struggling to complete "Leonidas Is Fallen," the story of a slave hero—modeled after the slave revolt leaders GABRIEL, DENMARK VESEY, and NAT TURNER—who dies fighting for his freedom. Davis hoped to create a "new kind of drama," different from contemporary black musical comedies and adaptations. During this period, Davis attended meetings of the Young Communist League in Harlem, paying close attention to the political speakers but also to the writers, from whom he hoped to find literary, as well as political, solutions. Davis never became a Communist, but he eventually became a playwright, with help from a playwriting class at Columbia University in 1947.

When Davis replaced SIDNEY POITIER opposite Dee in *A Raisin in the Sun*, it encouraged him to finish his play, *Purlie Victorious* (1961), which Davis described as the "adventures of Negro manhood in search of itself in a world for white folks only," that revealed "a world that emasculated me, as it does all Negro men … and taught me to gleefully accept that emasculation as the highest honor America could bestow" (Davis, "Purlie Told Me!" 155–156). In 1963 Davis adapted the play into a film, *Gone Are the Days*, in which he and Dee starred. In 1970 he retooled the play as a musical for Broadway, *Purlie*, which was nominated for a Tony Award for Best Musical.

Davis's film and television work began in 1950 with the film *No Way Out*, in which he starred with Dee. Over the next fifty years, working with many of America's best filmmakers and performers, he appeared in more than one hundred film and television projects, including *The Joe Louis Story* (1953);

The Cardinal (1963), directed by Otto Preminger; *The Hill* (1965), directed by Sidney Lumet; *A Man Called Adam* (1966), featuring SAMMY DAVIS JR., CICELY TYSON, and LOUIS ARMSTRONG; *The Scalphunters* (1968), directed by Sidney Pollack; *Let's Do It Again* (1975), directed by Sidney Poitier and starring Poitier and BILL COSBY; *Harry and Son* (1984), directed by Paul Newman; and *I'm Not Rappaport* (1996), costarring Walter Matthau. Davis maintained a particularly rich creative relationship with the filmmaker SPIKE LEE, appearing in *School Daze* (1988), *Do the Right Thing* (1989), *Jungle Fever* (1991), *Malcolm X* (1992), and *Get on the Bus* (1996).

In addition to his many television guest appearances, Davis had recurring roles in a number of television series, including the detective drama *The Outsider* (1967); *B. L. Stryker* (1989–1990), opposite Burt Reynolds; *Evening Shade* (1990–1994); and *The Promised Land* (1996). He starred in numerous television dramas and miniseries, including many African American–themed works, such as *Roots* (1979), which also featured Dee; *Don't Look Back: The Story of Leroy "Satchel" Paige* (1981); and *King* (1978), in which he played MARTIN LUTHER KING SR. Davis's writing credits include *For Us the Living: The Medgar Evers Story* (1983), which he cowrote with MYRLIE EVERS-WILLIAMS for *American Playhouse*, and three children's books: *Just like Martin* (1992) about MARTIN Luther KING JR.; *Escape to Freedom: A Play about Young Frederick Douglass* (1978), winner of the Jane Addams Children's Book Award and the American Library Association's CORETTA SCOTT KING Award; and *Langston, a Play* (1982).

In 1970 Davis directed his first film, *Cotton Comes to Harlem* (1970), an adaptation of CHESTER HIMES's detective novel about an armed robbery at a Back-to-Africa rally in Harlem. The commercial success of *Cotton*, for which Davis also wrote the screenplay and several songs, paved the way for what became known as the "blaxploitation" films of the 1970s. Although he was wary of many of the blaxploitation films, Davis agreed with the critic Clayton Riley that they constituted "part of a stage of development for a number of people" (Riley, "On the Film Critic," *Black Creation*, 1972, 15), and he agreed to direct the film adaptation of J. E. Franklin's play *Black Girl* in 1972. Davis chose the project—about a high school dropout who dreams of becoming a ballet dancer but settles for dancing in a bar—in order to demonstrate to Hollywood and to black filmmakers, in particular, that black film could be both entertaining and reflective of the

Ossie Davis, playwright and actor, as Gabriel in *The Green Pastures*, 12 April 1951. (Library of Congress/Carl Van Vechten, photographer.)

lives of real African Americans. In the early 1970s Davis directed *Kongi's Harvest* (1971), *Gordon's War* (1973), and *Countdown at Kusini* (1976), which he also wrote, and he established the Third World Cinema Corporation, a New York–based production company that trained African Americans and Latinos for film and television production jobs.

In 1980 Davis and Dee founded their own production company, Emmalyn II Productions Company. Together they produced and hosted three seasons of the critically acclaimed PBS television series *With Ossie and Ruby* and three years of the *Ossie Davis and Ruby Dee Story Hour*, a radio broadcast for the National Black Network. The couple has participated, separately and together, in the creation of numerous documentary and nonfiction projects, including *Martin Luther King: The Dream and the Drum*; *Mississippi, America*; and *A Walk through the 20th Century with Bill Moyers* for PBS. In 1998 they cowrote an autobiography, *With Ossie and Ruby: In This Life Together*. In 2002 Davis completed a new play, *A Last Dance for Sybil*, which ran in New York starring Dee.

Davis and Dee's commitment to civil rights and humanitarian causes was central to their life and work. They labored to introduce staged productions and readings into schools, unions, community centers, and, especially, black churches, because they were repositories "of all we thought precious and worthy to be passed on to our children" (Davis and Dee, 253). In the 1950s they risked their careers by stridently resisting Senator Joseph McCarthy's black-listing activities. Highly active and visible during the civil rights movement, they served as masters of ceremonies for the 1963 March on Washington, and in 1964 they helped establish Artists for Freedom, which donated money to civil rights organizations in the name of the four little girls killed in Birmingham, Alabama. Davis's stirring eulogy at the 1965 funeral of Malcolm X flawlessly articulated black America's loss: "Malcolm had stopped being a 'Negro' years ago. It had become too small, too puny, too weak a word for him. Malcolm was bigger than that. Malcolm had become an Afro-American and he wanted—so desperately—that we, that all his people, would become Afro-Americans too.... Malcolm was our manhood, our living, black manhood! This was his meaning to his people. And, in honoring him, we honor the best in ourselves." Davis and Dee's political work continued unabated over the next decades.

In addition to their many individual honors, Davis and Dee jointly received the Actors' Equity Association PAUL ROBESON Award (1975), the Academy of Television Arts and Sciences Silver Circle Award (1994), and induction into the NAACP Image Awards Hall of Fame (1989). In 1995 they were awarded the National Medal of Arts by President Bill Clinton, and in 2000 they received the Screen Actors Guild's highest honor, the Life Achievement Award.

Davis was found dead of natural causes in a hotel room in Miami, where he was working on a film titled *Retirement*. His last role was on the groundbreaking Showtime series *The L Word*, where he played a dying character struggling to accept his daughter's sexuality. Ruby Dee was present during the filming of his death scene, which aired shortly after his own death on 4 February 2005.

FURTHER READING

Davis, Ossie. "The Flight from Broadway," *Negro Digest* (April 1966).

Davis, Ossie. "Purlie Told Me!" *Freedomways* (Spring 1962).

Davis, Ossie, and Ruby Dee. *With Ossie and Ruby: In This Life Together* (1998).

SAMUEL A. HAY

Davis, Piper (3 July 1917–22 May 1997), baseball player-manager, was born Lorenzo Davis. The only child of John, a coal miner, and Georgia, a housewife, Lorenzo earned the nickname "Piper" after his hometown of Piper, Alabama. Although he would never make it to the major leagues, which did not accept blacks until 1947, his is one of the premier names in the annals of Negro League baseball history.

Gifted scholastically, Davis often claimed that he should have been valedictorian at all-black Fairfield Industrial High School but that administrators passed him over in favor of a pregnant student. The truth of that claim is unknown. The coal miner turned athlete did, however, earn a partial basketball scholarship to Alabama State University in Montgomery. Forced to quit after a year for financial reasons, he found employment in the Birmingham steel mills. In 1938 he married Laura Perry and had a son, Lorenzo, Jr., the same year. By 1939 he began playing with ACIPCO (American Cast Iron Pipe Company), the mill's all-black team in the Birmingham City League.

In 1942, while Davis was making $3.36 a day working in the mill, Winfield Welch, manager of the Birmingham Black Barons, offered to pay Davis $5 per game and $7.50 per double header as a part-time player. Davis, now with a growing family to support, after the birth of his daughter Faye in 1940, jumped at the offer. The following year, his pay was upped to $10 per game and $15 for a double header.

For the next seven seasons Davis's prodigious talent would be a key ingredient in the Birmingham Black Baron lineup. Versatile in his ability to play first and second base, the lanky, smooth fielding infielder excelled at turning double plays with lightning precision.

In his first full season (1943) the six foot three inch, right-handed batsman exploded onto the scene, hitting a career best .386 average, which led the Black Barons to the first of two consecutive Negro American League pennants. Davis suffered a "sophomore jinx," plunging to a disappointing .150 average in 1944. But he bounced back with consistently strong outings in his remaining years with the Black Barons, with averages of .313, .273, .360, .353, .378, and .383.

A seven-time All Star, he missed his first outing in 1945 after being suspended for having a physical altercation with an umpire. His replacement was Kansas City Monarchs' rookie JACKIE ROBINSON. In subsequent All Star appearances, Davis redeemed himself by racking up an overall average of .308.

In 1948 Davis had a league leading sixty-nine runs batted in (RBIs) and took over the reins as player-manager. As skipper, he guided the Black Barons to its third Negro American League championship, only to be defeated by the Homestead Gray in the Negro World Series. That season he also signed a young sixteen-year-old prospect named WILLIE MAYS.

A two-sport athlete, Davis spent two seasons playing basketball with the Harlem Globetrotters (1943–1944). Once again encouraged by his mentor, Welch (also the Globetrotters head coach), Davis joined the high-jinks basketball team during baseball's off season. He also served as road manager and bus driver.

Always looking to improve his game, Davis played eight winter seasons in several Latin American countries including Venezuela, Puerto Rico, Mexico, and the Dominican Republic.

On 17 July 1947 Davis nearly made history along with his All Star game sub Jackie Robinson when the St. Louis Browns acquired his contract. Opting out of the deal, the Browns passed over Davis in favor of Kansas City Monarchs' outfielders Hank Thompson and Willard Brown, offering Davis a minor league contract instead. Focused on the Majors, Davis declined. He returned to the Negro Leagues for three more seasons and continued in his role as player-manager. At the end of the 1950 season Davis became the first black player signed by the Boston Red Sox's organization and was assigned to its Scranton, Pennsylvania, Class A affiliate.

After reporting to spring training camp in Cocoa, Florida, Davis was subjected to racism not only from teammates who would not speak to him, but also from fans who taunted him with slurs and threats. Furthermore, Southern Jim Crowism barred him from dressing, living, or eating with his teammates.

Although the baseball veteran was leading the farm team in home runs, RBIs, and stolen bases and had a .333 batting average, the Red Sox released Davis from his contract, citing "economical reasons," just two days before they were obligated to pay the second half of his $15,000 purchase price. Davis later said that he knew his dismissal was "a joke because [Red Sox owner] Tom Yawkey was one of the richest men in the East." The Red Sox would be the last major league team to integrate.

Having to pay his own train fare home, the dejected slugger got another chance at the big leagues the following year when he joined the Oakland Oaks of the Pacific Coast League. For six seasons he enjoyed great success on the West Coast, having his best outing in 1953, batting .288, with thirteen home runs, ninety-seven RBIs, and ninety runs scored.

In 1956 the Dodger's Hollywood, California, AAA farm team signed Davis, where he hit .316 in his debut season. The following year, with the aging veteran's performance waning, he was sent down to the AA Texas League (Fort Worth team). At age forty-two, with still no time on the big league stage, Davis sent an unsigned contract back to the Dodgers for the 1959 season and retired from baseball. But he was not one to go out quietly. In his final Texas league game, Davis showed off his versatility by playing all nine positions.

After retiring, Davis played, albeit briefly, with the Globetrotters. For over a decade he scouted for several big league teams including the St. Louis Cardinals, Detroit Tigers, and Montreal Expos. He also worked as a night auditor for A. G. Gaston Enterprises and prided himself for having the prettiest lawn on the block.

Piper Davis was the only former Negro League player named to Alabama's All-Time Sports Team in a 1987 *Birmingham News* poll. In 1993 he was inducted into the Alabama Sports Hall of Fame. He died of a heart attack in Birmingham, Alabama.

FURTHER READING
Fullerton, Christopher. *Every Other Sunday* (1999).
Kilma, John. *Willie's Boys: The 1948 Birmingham Black Barons, the Last Negro League World Series, and the Making of a Baseball Legend* (2009).
Lester, Larry. *Black Baseball's National Showcase* (2001).
Loverro, Thom. *The Encyclopedia of Negro League Baseball* (2003).
Riley, James A. *The Biographical Encyclopedia of The Negro Baseball Leagues* (1994).

BYRON MOTLEY

Davis, Richard L. (24 Dec. 1864–25? Jan. 1900), coal miner and officer of the United Mine Workers of America (UMWA), was born in Roanoke, Virginia. Little is known about his family life, including the names of his parents and the size of his family. He obtained his early education in the Roanoke schools, which he attended during the winter months. At eight years of age he took a job in a local tobacco factory. After spending nine years in the tobacco industry, Davis became increasingly disgusted with the very low wages and unfavorable conditions on the job. In 1881 he migrated to southern West Virginia and took his first job as a coal miner in the newly opened Kanawha and New River coalfields. The following year he moved to Rendville, Ohio, a small mining town in the Hocking Valley region, southeast of Columbus. In Rendville, Davis married, supported a family, and worked until he died from lung failure. Upon his death the UMWA paid special tribute to Davis, lamenting that the organization had lost a "staunch advocate" of the rights of workers.

Davis's coal mining career is well documented in the columns of the *United Mine Workers' Journal* (*UMWJ*) and the *National Labor Tribune* (*NLT*), a labor paper published in Pittsburgh, Pennsylvania. In 1891 Davis was elected to the executive board of the UMWA District Six (Ohio). He held the Ohio post for six years, and in 1896 and again in 1897 he was elected to the national executive board, the highest position held by an African American in the UMWA. Davis's influence was felt at the local, regional, and national levels. In 1892, for example, when owners sought to segregate one mine in Rendville by using black laborers exclusively, paying those workers lower wages, and forcing them to work under poorer conditions than had been the case in integrated mines, Davis rallied black and white workers against the company's effort to divide workers along racial lines. In another instance Davis opposed the development of segregationist policies in Congo, Ohio. After calling attention to segregated housing, he observed a similar pattern in the mines and urged an end to such racial stratification.

He also used the labor press to strengthen the cause of labor solidarity across ethnic and racial lines. In numerous articles in the *UMWJ* and the *NLT*, he not only attacked the unjust policies of coal companies but also criticized rank-and-file white miners and their leaders for perpetuating racially discriminatory policies in the mines and unions. Although he consistently encouraged blacks to join the union (and at times severely criticized them for their reluctance), he placed their grievances squarely before white workers. He opposed exclusionary hiring practices, advocated the election of blacks to leadership positions in the union, and protested white miners' discriminatory attitudes and behavior toward black workers. On one occasion Davis rebuked his white counterparts for referring to black men as "big buck niggers." "I assure anyone that I have more respect for a scab than I have for a person who refers to the negro in such way, and God knows the scab I utterly despise." Davis urged white workers not to play into the hands of operators by discriminating against blacks, exhorting them instead to organize against corporate exploitation and confront those who gained unequal benefits from the "sweat and blood" of fellow workers.

Although change occurred slowly, Davis was a tireless organizer and defender of workers' rights through the 1890s. He helped to establish new locals, strengthen existing ones, and advise miners during bitter industrial disputes in West Virginia, western Pennsylvania, and Alabama as well as Ohio. During his organizing efforts in West Virginia and Alabama, Davis faced threats on his life and had to flee. At some point, as a result of his organizing activities, Davis lost his job; his family faced deprivation, and he found it exceedingly difficult to push forward. In 1898, for example, operators refused to hire him, and for its part the UMWA rejected his bid for employment as a paid organizer. Davis nearly despaired: "I have been sandbagged; I have been stoned, and last of all deprived of the right to earn a livelihood for myself and family.... It makes me almost crazy to think of it." African American miners decried Davis's treatment. As one black miner stated, "If he was a white man he would not be where he is—mark that—but being a negro he does not get the recognition he should have.... Such treatment will not tend to advance the interest of our union, but will retard its progress and cause colored men to look with suspicion upon it."

Despite the debilitating effect of racial injustice from within and from without the union, Davis retained his commitment to organized labor and influenced the U.S. labor movement at a pivotal moment in its history. Although blacks constituted less than 15 percent of the nation's 400,000 coal miners in 1900, thanks in part to the organizing activities of black miners like Davis, they made up 24 percent of the union's membership in the bituminous mines.

At a time when African Americans faced increasing restrictions on their civil rights, witnessed the meteoric rise of BOOKER T. WASHINGTON, and turned increasingly toward the ideology of racial solidarity and self-help, black and white workers joined the UMWA, an interracial union within the American Federation of Labor. Davis's life symbolized this complicated intertwining of workers' class and racial identities at the turn of the twentieth century. It also suggests how some Americans regarded their position in the political economy, how they used their union to foster working-class solidarity, and how they articulated an alternative ideology in the industrial age. In many ways Davis's work prefigured the legendary unionizing activities of A. PHILIP RANDOLPH.

FURTHER READING

Foner, Philip. *Organized Labor and the Black Worker, 1619–1973* (1974).

Gutman, Herbert. "The Negro and the United Mine Workers of America: The Career and Letters of Richard L. Davis and Something of Their Meaning, 1890–1900," in *Work, Culture, and Society in*

Industrializing America, ed. Herbert Gutman
(1977).

Lewis, Ronald L. *Black Coal Miners in America: Race
Class and Communist Conflict 1780-1980* (1987).

Trotter, Joe W., Jr. *Coal, Class, and Color: Blacks in
Southern West Virginia, 1915-32* (1990).

This entry is taken from the *American National
Biography* and is published here with the permission of
the American Council of Learned Societies.

JOE W. TROTTER

Davis, Rodney Maxwell (7 Apr. 1942–6 Sept. 1967),
Medal of Honor recipient, was born in Macon,
Georgia, the son of Mr. and Mrs. Gordon N. Davis.
Always an active youth Davis enjoyed outdoor
activities, fishing in particular. Later, at Macon's
Peter G. Appling High School, he played basket-
ball and football, was a member of the school
band, and played the clarinet. He graduated on 29
May 1961.

Davis enlisted in the U.S. Marine Corps
on 31 August 1961. He reported to U.S. Marine
Corps Recruit Training Depot, Parris Island,
South Carolina, where he was a member of the
First Recruit Training Battalion. Upon graduation Davis attended Individual Combat Training
at Camp Lejeune, North Carolina, as a member
of the Second Battalion, First Infantry Training
Regiment. He completed Individual Combat
Training in February 1962. Davis continued his
tenure at Camp Lejeune and joined Company K,
Third Battalion, Second Marines, Second Marine
Division, Fleet Marine Force. During the interven-
ing time at Camp Lejeune, Davis was promoted to
private first class on 1 April 1962 and lance corporal on 1 January 1964. He served as a rifleman until
May 1964.

Ordered to London, England, Davis spent a
three-year tour of duty as a guard with the U.S.
Marine Detachment, Naval Activities. Davis's
London sojourn was professionally fruitful as he
was promoted to corporal on 1 January 1966 and
sergeant on December 1 of the same year.

Upon completion of his London tour, Davis
was ordered to Vietnam in August 1967 during the
midst of the U.S. military's escalating involvement in
Southeast Asia. Assigned as a Platoon Guide with B
Company, First Battalion, Fifth Marines, First Marine
Division, he willingly sacrificed his life to protect his
fellow Marines by throwing himself on a hand grenade while engaged in vicious combat with North
Vietnamese Army regulars in Quang Nam Province.
Rodney Maxwell Davis died on 6 September 1967 as
a result of his injuries and was subsequently awarded
the Congressional Medal of Honor, the United States
of America's premier military decoration awarded
only for conspicuous gallantry.

Rodney M. Davis was survived by his wife, Judy,
his parents, and his daughters Nochola and Samantha.
He was the second African American to be awarded
the Medal of Honor in Vietnam after Private
JAMES ANDERSON COOPER JR. Davis also received
the Purple Heart, the Good Conduct Medal, the
National Defense Service Medal, the Armed Forces
Expeditionary medal, the Vietnam Service Medal, the
Military Merit Medal, the Gallantry Cross with Palm,
and the Republic of Vietnam Campaign Medal.

FURTHER READING

All information featured in this biographical sketch
was obtained courtesy of the U.S. Marine Corps
History and Museums Division through the
primary source documents present in Rodney M.
Davis's personal file. Documents were provided by
the historian Annette Amerman as per the author's
request of 3 Oct. 2006.

CHARLES EDWARD WILES, IV

Davis, Sammy, Jr. (8 Dec. 1925–16 May 1990), singer,
dancer, and actor, was born in Harlem, New York,
the first of two children of Sammy Davis Sr., an
African American vaudeville entertainer, and Elvera
Sanchez, a Puerto Rican chorus dancer. Sammy's
paternal grandmother, "Mama Rosa," raised him
until he was three years old, when his father, who
had separated from Elvera, took his son with him
on the road. Within a few years, the child's role grew
from that of a silent prop to that of a show-stealing
singer and dancer, the youngest member of the Will
Mastin Trio, featuring Sammy Davis Jr.

Fellow performers were the only family Sammy
knew, and the world of the theater was the only
school he ever attended. He was billed as "Silent
Sam, the Dancing Midget" to hide him from tru-
ant officers and child labor investigators. After a
period during which the group could not find work
or shelter, Davis's father thought about returning
the boy to his grandmother, only to discover that
the young ham had already become addicted to the
stage, the spotlight, and the adulation of approv-
ing audiences. In retrospect, Davis said he had "no
chance to be bricklayer or dentist, dockworker or
preacher" (Early, 4). By age seven he had made his
film debut in the comedy *Rufus Jones for President*
(1933), in which he played the title role of a little
boy who falls asleep in the lap of his mother, played

by Ethel Waters, and dreams that he is elected president of the United States.

During the Depression, Davis traveled on the "Chitlin' Circuit," a network of clubs that hired black acts to fill the time between performances by white headliners. Black entertainers had only a few minutes on stage and were prohibited from speaking directly to the audience; therefore, they often used a rapid variety of singing, dancing, and joking to hold the audience's attention. This eclectic quality came to define Davis's career. He believed it made him a superior entertainer; some critics believe he might have done better to focus on singing or dancing. Thus while Davis mastered several vocal and dance styles, nailed a number of impersonations, and played the drums, trumpet, vibes, and other instruments, he never developed his own style. Bill "Bojangles" Robinson, Stepin Fetchit, Moms Mabley, and Redd Foxx were among Davis's early influences, but he made the transition from vaudeville to Vegas, from burlesque to Broadway more easily than any of his predecessors and became one of the first "crossover" African American celebrities in the United States.

Groucho Marx saw Davis perform at the Hillcrest Country Club and said, "This kid's the greatest entertainer," and then turned to Al Jolson, who was seated at his table, and remarked "and this goes for you, too" (Levy, 49). Davis's big break, however, occurred in 1941, when the Will Mastin Trio was performing in Detroit as an opening act for Frank Sinatra. Sinatra was so impressed by the fifteen-year-old entertainer that he used his growing fame to help Davis get some of the recognition and respect he deserved. Later Sinatra, too, would say that Davis was the greatest performer he had ever seen, because he could "do anything except cook spaghetti" (*Boston Globe*, 17 May 1990).

Davis's promising career was briefly interrupted when he was drafted into the U.S. Army, serving from 1943 to 1945. Although his unit at Fort Warren, Wyoming, was integrated, Davis suffered racial discrimination and beatings. After basic training, Davis was placed in Special Services, where he entertained enlisted men along with George M. Cohan. Throughout his life, Davis was determined to use his talent to make audiences love him even if they hated him. For him, performance was not only a way of transcending racial barriers, it was a means of gaining acceptance and distinguishing himself. As he wrote, "If God ever took away my talent I would be a nigger again" (Early, 20–21). Yet he realized that his success was Pyrrhic, that "being a star

Sammy Davis, Jr., laughing with Rev. Dr. Martin Luther King, Jr. in Davis's dressing room after his performance in *Golden Boy* at New York's Majestic Theatre, 4 March 1965. (AP Images.)

has made it possible for me to get insulted in places where the average Negro could never hope to go and get insulted" (Curt Schleir, "The Public Acclaim and Private Pain of Sammy Davis Jr.," *Biography*, 4.2 [Feb. 2000], 88).

After leaving the army, Davis made his first recording with Capitol Records and was named Most Outstanding New Personality of 1946 by *Metronome* magazine. The Will Mastin Trio regrouped and began opening for Mickey Rooney in Las Vegas in 1947 and the following year for Frank Sinatra in New York. These engagements led to television appearances on Eddie Cantor's *Colgate Comedy Hour* and the *Ed Sullivan Show*. By the early 1950s Davis had enough clout to force the integration of many of the hotels at which he performed. In 1954 his career could have ended when his car smashed into another vehicle while driving from Las Vegas to California. Davis lost his left eye in the accident, but within ten months he was back on stage performing with an eye patch—and, because of the publicity, he was bigger than ever.

In 1956 Davis played the lead in the Broadway musical *Mr. Wonderful*, in 1958 he appeared opposite Eartha Kitt in the film *Anna Lucasta*, and in 1959 he played Sporting Life in the film version of George Gershwin's *Porgy and Bess*. Beginning with *Ocean's Eleven* (1960), Davis made six films as part of a group of jet-setting actors dubbed the "Rat Pack," including Frank Sinatra, Tony Curtis, Dean Martin, Peter Lawford, and Joey Bishop. During this period, Davis's flashy jewelry, ostentatious dress, and characteristic jive talk made him the epitome of "hip" and, along with MILES DAVIS, the king of the "Cool Cats."

Controversy was an inseparable part of Davis's popularity. In an effort to quell rumors about his relationships with white women, Davis rushed into a marriage with Loray White, an African American dancer, in 1958. The marriage lasted only a few months. His highly publicized conversion to Judaism, which began sincerely with Rabbi Max Nussbaum after his accident and was based on an affinity he felt with the Jewish people, was suspected by some of being an indication of his desire to escape his blackness by assimilating into another culture. His relationship with the black community became more problematic after his 1960 marriage to the Swedish actress May Britt, with whom he had one child, Tracey, and adopted two, Mark and Jeff. Despite the fact that Davis was a strong supporter of the civil rights movement and a generous contributor to black charities—qualities that helped him earn the NAACP's Spingarn Award in 1969—his lifestyle was an easy target for the militants of the 1960s, and his embrace of Republican President Richard M. Nixon in 1972 brought his loyalties into question. Drinking, drug use, and his associations with people in the adult film industry and in satanic cults gave Davis a reputation that he both flaunted and regretted.

Davis was a top draw as a nightclub performer, earning $15,000 for a single performance and as much as $3 million a year, yet he always spent more than he earned. When his accountant expressed concern about his profligate spending, Davis bought him a gold watch with the inscription, "Thanks for the advice." Although he had become a solo act by the 1960s, he continued to share his salary with his father and Will Mastin for many years thereafter. In 1965 he was nominated for a Tony Award for his performance in *Golden Boy*, and in 1966 he briefly hosted his own television program, the *Sammy Davis Jr. Show*. He also appeared as a guest star on such popular shows as *Lawman* (1961), *Batman* (1966), *I Dream of Jeannie* (1967), and *The Mod Squad* (1969–1970). His appearance on *All in the Family* (1972) set a Nielsen ratings record, and on several occasions he was a substitute host on *The Tonight Show*.

In 1970, two years after his divorce from May Britt, Davis married the African American dancer Altovise Gore and adopted another son, Manny. His recording "Candyman" hit the top of the chart in 1972, and other hits, such as "Mr. Bojangles," "That Old Black Magic," and "Birth of the Blues," kept him in constant demand. His activities slowed during the 1980s as Davis struggled with various kidney and liver ailments and a hip replacement. President Ronald Reagan presented him the Gold Medal for Lifetime Achievement from the Kennedy Center for the Performing Arts in 1987.

Davis played his final role, as an aging dancer, in the movie *Tap* (1989), with his protégé Gregory Hines. He died the following year of throat cancer. He left three autobiographies, twenty-three films, and two dozen recordings to entertain future generations.

FURTHER READING

Davis, Sammy, Jr. *Hollywood in a Suitcase* (1980).

Davis, Sammy, Jr. *Why Me?* (1989).

Davis, Sammy, Jr. *Yes I Can* (1965).

Early, Gerald. *The Sammy Davis, Jr., Reader* (2001).

Haygood, Wil. *In Black and White: The Life of Sammy Davis, Jr.* (2003).

Levy, Shawn. *Rat Pack Confidential* (1998).

Obituaries: *New York Times*, 17 May 1990; *Rolling Stone*, 28 June 1990; *Ebony*, July 1990.

SHOLOMO B. LEVY

Davis, Thulani (22 May 1948–), writer, performer, and teacher, was born Barbara Davis in Hampton, Virginia, the youngest of four children of Willie Louise Barbour and Collis H. Davis. Her parents were educators at Hampton University, the traditionally black college once attended by BOOKER T. WASHINGTON. Her mother died in 1955, when Davis was only seven years old. Davis graduated from the Putney School in Vermont in 1966, received her bachelor's degree from Barnard College in 1970, and did graduate work at both Columbia University and the University of Pennsylvania.

By the age of twenty Davis was publishing and performing her poetry. While living in San Francisco in the mid-1970s, she wrote and performed with NTOZAKE SHANGE, Jessica Hagedorn, and other spoken word artists, all members of a group called the Third World Artists Collective. During this time she also worked as a reporter for the San Francisco *Sun-Reporter*, covering the ANGELA DAVIS case and interviewing figures such as George Jackson and HUEY NEWTON. She moved back to New York City in the late 1970s and worked at the *Village Voice* as a proofreader, writer, and editor from 1979 to 1990.

Davis continued writing and performing in New York, working again with Shange and Hagedorn on several plays, including *Where the Mississippi Meets the Amazon* at the New York Shakespeare Festival in 1977 and *Shadow & Veil* at the New Heritage Theatre in 1982. She also wrote and performed a one-woman show, *Sweet Talk and Stray Desires*, at the Chelsea Westside Theatre in 1979. In addition to several staged readings of her plays, Davis adapted Bertolt Brecht's *The Caucasian Chalk Circle* for the New York Shakespeare Festival, directed by GEORGE C. WOLFE, in 1990. The festival also produced her play *Everybody's Ruby: Story of a Murder in Florida* in 1999, and she adapted W. E. B. DuBois's *The Souls of Black Folk* in a performance for five actors for the National Black Arts Festival in 2003.

Moving comfortably between genres was Davis's hallmark as a writer, and she began composing lyrics in the 1980s, collaborating with her cousin, the composer ANTHONY CURTIS DAVIS, on several works, including the librettos for the full-length works *X, The Life and Times of Malcolm X* at the New York City Opera in 1986 and *Amistad* at the Lyric Opera of Chicago in 1997. She also collaborated with her husband, the musician Joseph Jarman, on several works, such as *Steppin' Other Shores* at The Kitchen in 1983. In 1998 Davis wrote the text for a multimedia documentary oratoria, *Dark Passages*, produced at the Asian Art Museum in San Francisco, exploring the internment of Japanese Americans during World War II.

Practicing Buddhist priests, Jarman and Davis founded the Brooklyn Buddhist Association in the 1980s. They continued their musical collaborations through their Buddhist practice, and Davis led several Buddhist meditation groups in response to the terrorist attacks of 11 September 2001. She taught writing at Barnard College and New York University and regularly published book reviews, interviews with artists such as TONI MORRISON and Helen Elaine Lee, and longer essays. Her coverage of the 1986 Howard Beach incident in Queens, New York, in which three African American men were assaulted, one killed by a motorist while trying to flee, grew into a documentary film, *Thulani Davis Asks, Why Howard Beach?* in 1987. Davis's other work in documentary included film and radio work for PBS, Mode Records, National Public Radio, and other producers. She wrote the screenplays for the films *Paid in Full* for Miramax (2002) and *Maker of Saints* for DCI Productions (2006), based on her 1996 novel of the same name.

Maker of Saints, her second novel, explored creativity and identity struggles faced by African American artists through the unraveling of a murder mystery. *1959*, Davis's first novel (1992), examined the lives of African Americans in the midst of the civil rights period through the eyes of Willie Tarrant, the twelve-year-old daughter of a widowed father, set beside the story of her great-aunt, whose diary Willie reads in secret. Davis drew on her own family history in the creation of this novel, and in embarking on what she thought would be another novel, Davis continued researching her family tree, full of ancestors named Tarrant, Campbell, and Curry. The project culminated instead in a non-fiction work, *My Confederate Kinfolk: A Twenty-First Century Freedwoman Confronts Her Roots* (2006), in which Davis told the story of her African American great-grandmother, Chloe Curry, a freed slave, and her southern white great-grandfather, William Argyle Campbell, as well as many more of her white Confederate ancestors. Davis believed that the relationship between Chloe and Will, as she called them, was consensual and indeed loving, since it lasted more than twenty years, and their only child, Davis's grandmother, characterized it as such in her unpublished writings. Davis also confronted the fact that the Campbells, whom she resembled, had family members involved in the brutal lynching of a black congressman in 1875 and the massacre of nearly 200 African American soldiers during the Civil War. Ironically, *My Confederate Kinfolk* appeared on reading lists at more than one white supremacist Web site; Davis enjoyed crossing this surprising boundary and employing language unexpected from an African American writer in her claim of kin to white Confederates.

Her poetry collection, *All the Renegade Ghosts Rise* (1978), is back in print, and she wrote the text for *Malcolm X: The Great Photographs* (1993). She won a Grammy Award for her liner notes on ARETHA FRANKLIN's *The Atlantic Recordings* in 1993, and was nominated for a Grammy for her opera *X*. Other honors include induction into the Black Writers Hall of Fame (1998) and a Charles H. Revson fellowship on the Future of the City of New York at Columbia University (2003–2004). Davis returned to the *Village Voice* as a senior editor in 2001, where she developed a mentoring program for young writers of color. In 2004 she was laid off in what appeared to be a purging of employees of color, though she continued to write occasional articles and reviews for the

Voice. Through her Buddhist practice, her teaching, and her writing, Davis demonstrated her commitment to peace and justice, uncovering the hidden truths of African American life, and the complicated experience of race for those who benefit from racial privilege and those who do not.

FURTHER READING

Davis, Thulani. *My Confederate Kinfolk* (2006).

Prince, Richard. "Losing Voices of Color: Village Voice Lays Off Thulani Davis, Tate Cuts Back," *Journal-Isms, An Online Column* (9 Aug. 2004).

ALICE KNOX EATON

Davis, Willie (24 July 1934–), NFL football player and entrepreneur, was born William Delford Davis in rural Lisbon, Louisiana, to David Davis, a laborer, and Nodie Bell Davis. The family struggled in the poverty of the Depression and Davis's parents instilled in him a strong work ethic. He attended Booker T. Washington High School in Texarkana, Texas, where he played football for coach Nathan Jones. As Davis grew tall and athletic, Jones emphasized that a big, strong man could also be intelligent and could transcend commonly held misconceptions about athletes.

Willie was the first member of his family to go to college, entering Grambling University on a football scholarship and playing for the legendary coach EDDIE ROBINSON. Majoring in industrial arts with minors in mathematics and physical education, he excelled in both sports and academics, serving as team captain and making the dean's list in both his junior and senior years.

Davis was talented enough to play professional football, but at that time Grambling was little scouted by the NFL. He was selected by the Cleveland Browns in the seventeenth round of the 1956 draft, but the Army also drafted him and he served for two years before reporting to the Browns in the summer of 1958. Davis made an immediate impact in Cleveland, starting as a rookie and playing both offense and defense in three games that season (the last Cleveland Brown to do so). His main position under the regime of coach Paul Brown was defensive tackle, but Brown remained unsure of where to best use him.

In the off-season following his rookie year, Davis worked as a substitute math and industrial arts teacher in Cleveland secondary schools and took courses in education at Case Western Reserve University. In 1959 he married Ann McCollum, with whom he would raise a son and daughter; Ann McCollum Davis passed away in 1997. In the same year of his marriage, Paul Brown traded Davis to Green Bay, a vote of no confidence never to be forgotten by Davis. He briefly considered leaving the game, but his first meeting with Packers coach Vince Lombardi in 1960 changed his mind. Lombardi had taken over the moribund Packers franchise one year earlier and had immediately begun to instill a winning attitude in a group of athletes that had suffered many losing seasons. Lombardi recognized Davis's worth, characterizing him as "a hell of a young man…. In Willie Davis we got a great one."

Green Bay, Wisconsin, in 1960 was not a bastion of racial diversity; only 128 African Americans lived in all of Brown County. Davis was one of just four black players on the team that year, but he prospered under the leadership of Lombardi, who cared only about a player's ability and threatened to cut any Packer who uttered a racial slur. Davis's ebullient personality quickly won over his teammates, who nicknamed him "Dr. Feelgood." He wore number 87 and was moved to defensive end, where he played for eight seasons under Lombardi and a total of ten for the Packers. At six feet, three inches tall and 245 pounds, Davis was not exceptionally large even for that era, but he possessed formidable speed for a lineman.

The Packers built a dynasty during Davis's career, winning five championships in seven years and an unparalleled three consecutive titles from 1965 to 1967. Davis was a favorite player and a sometime confidant of the fiery Lombardi, but he and the coach regularly clashed—to his teammates' amusement—during Davis's contract negotiations. Davis was captain of the defense from 1966 until his retirement, and he never missed a game, playing in 162 straight contests including 138 consecutive regular season games, 6 NFL championship games, and the first two Super Bowls (both won by the Packers). A five-time All-Pro with twenty-one career fumble recoveries, Davis was honored with five Pro Bowl appearances. He is a member of the Packer Hall of Fame and was elected to the Pro Football Hall of Fame in 1981.

Early in his NFL career, Davis began to prepare for life after football. In 1964 he began an MBA program at the University of Chicago. He received his degree in 1968, an accomplishment all the more remarkable because the start of his winter classes was often disrupted by postseason football. During his last few seasons as a Packer he worked for the Schlitz Brewing Company, and in 1969 he risked his life savings to purchase a Los Angeles Schlitz distributorship. His zest for hard work led to immediate success in his business career, and he was one of the first African Americans named to Schlitz's board of directors.

Davis's business career took a new direction in Los Angeles in 1977 when, at the suggestion of sports announcer Curt Gowdy, he purchased a failing radio station in Watts. While building it into the highly successful KACE-FM, Davis formed All-Pro Broadcasting and proceeded to buy two stations in Milwaukee, one in Houston, and one in Seattle. At its peak, All-Pro controlled eleven radio stations, but seven were later sold off. Adopting Vince Lombardi's winning philosophies in training his employees, Davis became one of the nation's leading African American entrepreneurs.

Former U.S. Secretary of State George Shultz has said, "In whatever setting you place Willie Davis, he will be a leader. People pay attention to him." He has done a great deal of charitable work and has been honored by the NAACP. Davis has served on the boards of directors of Mattel, the Fireman's Fund, Alliance Bank, MGM/UA, K-Mart, Wisconsin Energy, Bassett Furniture Industries, Checkers Drive-In Restaurants, Dow Chemical Company, Fidelity National Information Systems, Johnson Controls, MGM Grand, Manpower, Metro-Goldwyn-Mayer, Sara Lee Corporation, and Strong Capital Management. He is a Director of the Green Bay Packers and has served as a Trustee of the University of Chicago and Marquette University, a Member of the Grambling College Foundation, and a member of the Ewing Marion Kauffman Center for Entrepreneurial Leadership Development Committee.

FURTHER READING

Kramer, Jerry, with Dick Schaap. *Distant Replay* (1985).

Maraniss, David. *When Pride Still Mattered: A Life of Vince Lombardi* (1999).

Schaap, Dick. *Green Bay Replay: The Packers' Return to Glory* (1997).

DAVID BORSVOLD

Davis Trussell, Elizabeth Bishop (26 Apr. 1920–1 Feb. 2010), physician, professor, mental health activist, and Harlem community leader, was born Elizabeth Bishop in Pittsburgh, Pennsylvania, the eldest of the three children of Shelton Hale Bishop and Eloise Carey. Her mother's father, Archibald James Carey Sr., was an influential African Methodist Episcopal (AME) clergyman in Chicago. Her father's father, Hutchens C. Bishop, was the first black graduate of General Theological Seminary in New York City, the oldest seminary of the Episcopal Church. He was also the fourth rector of the important and influential Saint Philip's Episcopal Church in Harlem. Bishop's parents continued their families' tradition of public service. Her father, who received a B.A. and a doctorate of divinity from Columbia University, succeeded his own father as the fifth rector of Saint Philip's. Her mother was a teacher.

Elizabeth Bishop's interest in psychiatry can be traced to the work of her father. He was an important early advocate of adequate mental health care for African Americans and helped found the La Fargue Clinic, the first mental health treatment facility in Harlem. In honor of his work in this area, his successor as rector of Saint Philip's, M. Moran Weston, created the Bishop House, which provides independent living facilities for the mentally handicapped.

However, even before watching her father's work in advocating for mental health care in Harlem, Bishop, as a youngster sitting near her father's office and overhearing discussions between her father and various parishioners seeking advice, became aware that there were some people her father could not help, people who needed the care of a professional mental health expert but had only the services of their rector available to them. This early realization of the causal relationship between poverty and mental illness became the cornerstone of much of her work. Later in life Bishop argued that as a result of racial segregation and poverty in America black people were more likely to be poor and thus were more likely to be exposed to psychologically damaging experiences.

Bishop attended Barnard College and, a member of Phi Beta Kappa, graduated in 1941 with a major in psychology. The day after her graduation she married Charles Davis. Two years later she entered Columbia University's College of Physicians and Surgeons (P&S), graduating in 1949 as a member of Alpha Omega Alpha, the medical honor society.

After medical school Davis did residencies at the New York State Psychiatric Institute as well as at the Columbia University Center for Psychoanalytic Training and Research, from which she received a certificate in psychoanalysis in 1955. Because she wished to work in Harlem after completing her residency, Davis went to work at Harlem Hospital under Dr. Harold Ellis, who headed the outpatient mental health clinic there. It was the only medically affiliated psychiatric clinic available in Harlem, but it was quite inadequate. Because it was exclusively outpatient the physicians could not hospitalize patients but could only refer them to other hospitals. The clinic also was terribly underfunded and understaffed. Davis became so frustrated by the city's lack of interest in the people of Harlem that she left to run the clinic at New York Presbyterian Hospital, where she felt that she could help the people of Harlem more once they were referred there.

By the early 1960s Davis had received a junior faculty appointment at P&S, divorced Charles Davis, and married Judge Andrew Tyler, a respected legal figure from Harlem. In 1962 she received the job offer of a lifetime when she was appointed director of the newly created department of psychiatry at Harlem Hospital. In the early 1960s Ray E. Trussell, then the Commissioner of Hospitals for New York City, saw that the public hospital system was in terrible shape. In order to revitalize the system he decided to create affiliations between the public hospitals and their neighboring medical teaching institutions and matched Columbia University with Harlem Hospital. This decision allowed for the creation of a comprehensive department of psychiatry at Harlem Hospital for the first time in its history. Davis was appointed the department's first director on the recommendation of P&S, becoming the first woman director of a medical department at the hospital.

An example of Davis's work while at Harlem Hospital involved a controversy over the dispensation of birth control early in her tenure there. The controversy began when Ray Trussell wanted to introduce birth control in all the city hospitals. Davis, having seen the negative effect that unwanted pregnancies had had on the mental health of her poor black female patients, supported the measure fully. But the plan came under heavy opposition from the Catholic diocese. However, after some negotiation Ray Trussell was able to get a statement approved saying that reproductive health services were necessary for the physical and social health of women and must be available at all hospitals. With that go-ahead Davis set up a birth-control consultation service for women that included sterilization consultation for women who were prone to postpartum depression. Davis's program was a success. Offering family planning consultations and voluntary sterilization to women reduced the birthrate and the incidence of postpartum depression at Harlem Hospital.

Davis remained director of the Harlem Hospital psychiatry department and a clinical professor of psychiatry at Columbia's P&S until 1978, when she and her third husband, Ray Trussell, whom she had married in 1968, decided to retire from their professional positions. They spent thirty-one years together until his death in 1999. Davis Trussell had one daughter, Liberty Rashad (by her first husband,

Charles Davis), and three grandsons. She received many awards for her work from institutions such as Barnard College (Medal of Distinction), Columbia P&S (Distinguished Service), and the New York State Office of Mental Health (Lifetime Achievement). She died in New York City at the age of 89.

FURTHER READING

The personal papers of Elizabeth Bishop Davis Trussell are held at the Columbia Health Sciences Library Archives and Special Collections.
Hutson, Jean Blackwell. Interview with Dr. Elizabeth Bishop Davis (1983).

ELVITA DOMINIQUE

Davy, Gloria (29 Mar. 1931–), opera singer and university professor, was born in Brooklyn, New York, one of four children of Lucy Chick Davy, a housewife, and George Davy, a civil servant. Gloria's parents were West Indians who had moved to New York from Saint Vincent in the Windward Islands.

Gloria was recommended by a music teacher at her elementary school for matriculation at the New York High School of Music and Art. Her acceptance into the highly specialized and competitive program came with the distinction of being the first student to study there from Public School 129. Gloria's high school experiences provided a foundation for her to build upon musically, intellectually, and socially.

After graduation Davy went to the Juilliard School of Music, where she was a student of Belle Julie Soudant's, and from which she graduated in 1954 with a bachelor of science degree. Davy remained at Juilliard after graduation for a year of special study in opera with Frederic Cohen, Frederick Kiesler, and Frederic Walden, who held various directorships with the Juilliard Opera Theater. This time of matriculation at Juilliard led to her winning the role of the Countess in the U.S. premiere of Richard Strauss's *Capriccio* in 1954. Other notable teachers and coaches with whom Davy worked include Muriel Landecker, Victor de Sabata, Rosetta Ely, and Maussia le Marc Hadour.

Davy's first performance love was the recital stage. The turn toward opera came in 1954 when she was chosen to replace LEONTYNE PRICE in a touring company of Gershwin's *Porgy and Bess*. Playing the score's heroine, she performed throughout the United States, Canada, and Europe. It was within this setting that she learned the craft of acting.

On 12 February 1958, with Fausto Cleva on the podium, Davy became the first African American soprano at the Metropolitan Opera to be cast in the title role of Verdi's *Aïda*. At the Metropolitan she also performed the roles of Pamina in Mozart's *Magic Flute* (1958), Nedda in Leoncavallo's *Pagliacci* (1959), and Leonora in Verdi's *Il Trovatore* (1961). Her last of fifteen Metropolitan performances was on 4 April 1961.

Davy's Metropolitan career did not benefit from the social and political awareness that was then rising within the nation. The civil rights movement was in its infancy, she was not well cast (a result that could have been rooted in and perpetuated by the hue of her skin), and the powers that be were not yet ready to move beyond tokenism. When the Breen-Davis Production company with which Davy performed Gershwin's heroine Bess returned to America, she stayed behind and settled in Milan, Italy, where she felt she would find greater opportunity than was available in the United States. Afterward Davy called Europe home, and it was in Europe that her career developed, propelled, and sustained. Even during Davy's time as a professor at Indiana University School of Music, from 1985 until 1993 (at which time she was named professor emeritus), she maintained her residence in Geneva, Switzerland.

In Milan, Davy became a regular at La Scala, where between 1957 and 1964 she performed to great acclaim the title role in Puccini's *Madama Butterfly*, Nedda in Leoncavallo's *Pagliacci*, both Donna Anna and Donna Elvira in Mozart's *Don Giovanni*, and the principal role in Kurt Weill's *Rise and Fall of the City of Mahagonny*. Davy was also acclaimed in Europe for her portrayal of Aida in Nice, France, at the Theatre de l'opera with an Italian company from Milan (1957), at Covent Garden in London (1960), at the Vienna State Opera at the invitation of Herbert von Karajan (sung in German; 1959), and at the Deutsch Oper (also sung in German) under the direction of Wieland Wagner (under guest contract; 1961–1969). In Brussels she performed Pamina in Mozart's *Magic Flute* (1961–1962).

Davy was also acclaimed as a recitalist and as an exponent of the concert literature. At La Scala she performed, in Russian, the Italian premiere of Shostakovich's *Vocal and Instrumental Suite* (1978). At the Donaueschingen Festival of Contemporary Music in 1957 she introduced Werner Henze's song cycle *Nachtstücke und Arien*, for which she won great acclaim. Davy created and extensively performed two Karlheinz Stockhausen works: *Momente*, premiered in 1972 (later recorded) at Beethoven Hall in Bonn, and *Vortrag über HU*, premiered in 1974 at the Donaueschingen Festival.

Gloria Davy, opera singer, as Aida, 22 February 1958. (Library of Congress/Carl Van Vechten, photographer.)

Davy's legacy is her contribution and involvement as a pioneer in making the Metropolitan Opera more accessible to African American women. Davy married and later divorced the German businessman Herman Penningsfeld; she was the mother of a son, Jean-Marc Penningsfeld.

FURTHER READING
Abdul, Raoul. *Blacks in Classical Music* (1977).
Cheatham, Wallace McClain. "African American Women Singers at the Metropolitan Opera before Leontyne Price," *Journal of Negro History* 84 (Spring 1999).
Dunbar, Ernest. *The Black Expatriates* (1968).
Gray, John. *Blacks in Classical Music* (1988).
WALLACE MCCLAIN CHEATHAM

Dawes, Kwame Senu Neville (28 July 1962–), writer, was born in Accra, Ghana, to Neville Dawes, a Jamaican writer, teacher, and political worker, and Sophie Dawes, a Ghanaian artist and social worker. Dawes was the fourth of five children born to his parents (he also had a half-sister, born to his father); Neville had moved to Ghana in the 1950s to be part of the independence movement and work on his writing. Growing up with an avowed Marxist and author as a father, Dawes was no stranger to an environment of artists and revolutionaries in his home during the evening. As Ghana become more unstable during the 1960s, the family moved back to Neville's home country of Jamaica in 1971, where he began work for the Institute of Jamaica.

Following his graduation from Jamaica College secondary school, Dawes attended the University of the West Indies in Mona. Despite his father's proclivity and the numerous writers who frequented his house, he had no thought of becoming a writer—he believed he would be a lawyer or historian—until entering UWI, where he found entry into the literary world through theater. Along with an intense extracurricular life in which he was a star batsman on the cricket team and performed in a steel drum band, Dawes began writing for the drama organization and became heavily involved in a large Christian affiliation. After graduating from UWI in 1983 with a B.A. in English, Dawes continued to explore these last two interests: his graduate thesis in 1984 explored Christianity in a 1971 major Caribbean play, and he joined Jamaica's Christian Graduate Theater Company as both an actor and playwright.

As an emerging writer, Dawes was made an Honorary Fellow as part of the University of Iowa's writing program in 1986, and was invited to America as part of an International Writers Program, where he wrote, taught, and gave lectures. Dawes continued his studies at the University of New Brunswick, where he not only pursued his exploration of writing and theater, but also started singing in a reggae band. He married his wife, Lorna, in 1990, and shortly before receiving his Ph.D. from the university, had his first of three children. In the fall of 1992, Dawes began teaching in the English department at the University of South Carolina in Sumter.

Though Dawes started as a playwright—along with producing, directing, and acting in his works—he moved to poetry and short stories throughout the 1990s. In 1994, his debut poetry collection, *Progeny of Air*, won the United Kingdom's prestigious Forward Poetry Prize for Best First Collection. Since that debut work, he published more than a dozen poetry collections; in 2001, he won the small-press-oriented Pushcart Prize for his oeuvre. Dawes's more autobiographical works, including *A Far Cry from Plymouth Rock*, a memoir and reflections about his time in Ghana and Jamaica, examined the condition of being an immigrant, and the tenuousness of national—and black—identity.

As Dawes put it, reflecting on his Ghanaian birth, and upbringing in Jamaica with brief visits in London and America, "I have described myself as being seen by critics and reviewers as a Jamaican writer. But since I was not born in Jamaica, defining what Jamaica means to me is always complicated" (*A Far Cry from Plymouth Rock*, p. 65).

Dawes expanded his repertoire into critical writing, publishing reviews domestically and internationally, including pieces in the *London Review of Books* and the *Washington Post*—on literature and cultural identity. Along with articles and books on reggae poetry, Dawes published a dense, analytical study of the reggae-master and fellow countryman Bob Marley's lyrics in *Lyrical Genius*.

Dawes served as head of the MFA writing program in Creative Writing at the University of South Carolina, and in 1996 was named associate fellow at the University of Warwick's Center for Caribbean Studies. In 2001, Dawes cofounded the Calabash International Literary Festival, an annual three-day event held in St. Elizabeth, Jamaica. In 2007, Dawes received an Emmy for his journalistic work on the multimedia and multidiscipline website LiveHopeLove, a project funded by the Pulitzer Center that explored the AIDS crisis in Jamaica.

Dawes married his wife, Lorna, a media specialist, in 1990 in Canada; their first child, Sena, was born in Canada; their first son (Kekeli) and second daughter (Akua) were both born in the United States.

FURTHER READING

Collins, Walter P. "An Interview with Kwame Dawes," *Obsidian III*, Fall, 2007.

Dawes, Kwame. *A Far Cry from Plymouth Rock* (2006).

ADAM W. GREEN

Dawkins, Darryl (11 Jan. 1957–), professional basketball player, was born in Orlando, Florida, and was raised by his mother, Harriet, and grandmother, Amanda Jones. He attended Maynard Evans High School and led the basketball team to the 1975 state championship. Dawkins was tall and talented, but he never played college basketball. After high school, Dawkins applied for the 1975 National Basketball Association (NBA) draft as a hardship case—an exception allowing players who had not yet completed college to play in the NBA if they could prove economic hardship. A year earlier the Utah Stars of the American Basketball Association had drafted a highschooler named Moses Malone, and Dawkins looked to follow Malone's pro path. The Philadelphia 76ers drafted Dawkins with the fifth choice.

Dawkins was a man-child, almost seven feet tall but a raw player who was drafted on potential alone. In time he would match his potential but his first year in the NBA was hardly spectacular—he averaged about 5 minutes and 2 points a game in thirty-seven games and did not appear in Philadelphia's three playoff games. The next year his games and minutes played increased, and by the 1977 playoffs Dawkins was a solid contributor as the 76ers fell to Portland in a memorable six game finals. For the next five years, although not a starter, Dawkins averaged double digit points. Philadelphia lost in the finals twice more during his stay with the team. In August 1982 he was traded to New Jersey, where he was a starter for two years but injuries curtailed his playing after 1984. He also played sparingly for Utah and Detroit, but 1989 was his last year in the NBA. For his career Dawkins averaged twelve points and six rebounds a game, never reaching his full potential. He played briefly with the Globetrotters and in the Continental Basketball Association and coached in professional basketball's minor leagues. In 2009 Dawkins was named the head basketball coach at Lehigh Carbon Community College in Pennsylvania.

Dawkins was one of the NBA's most popular players, combining a powerful style with a flair for crowd pleasing dunks. In November 1979, in a game against Kansas City, he shattered a backboard with a powerful dunk and did it again in a December game. (These dunks eventually led to the collapsible rim and backboards in arenas today.) But the flamboyant Dawkins continued his crowd pleasing style and began to name his dunks, thus leading to his nickname, "Chocolate Thunder." Off the court Dawkins grew in popularity, often claiming he was from the planet Lovetron. His lifestyle reflected his spectacular play, all recounted in his 2003 autobiography (with Charley Rosen), *Chocolate Thunder: The Uncensored Life and Times of Darryl Dawkins.* True to his caricature, Dawkins the entertainer related tales of drugs, sex, and racism in a tell-all book that left readers laughing and shocked. Involved in charitable events and children's and community activities, Dawkins was also active in a blood pressure awareness campaign by NBA players and is a frequent talk show guest. In 2001 Dawkins married Janice, his fourth wife. He has four children.

FURTHER READING

Dawkins, Darryl, with Charles Rosen. *Chocolate Thunder: The Uncensored Life and Times of the NBA's Original Showman* (2003).

Dawkins, Darryl, with George Wirt. *Chocolate Thunder: The In-Your-Face, All-Over-the Place, Death-Defyin', Mesmerizin', Slam-Jam Adventures of Double D* (1986).

BOYD CHILDRESS

Dawson, Andre Nolan (10 July 1954–), baseball player, was born in Miami, Florida, the eldest son of Mattie Brown, a homemaker and part-time baker, and Floyd Dawson. Born to his mother when she was fifteen years old and an absent father who went to college and then the army, Dawson and his seven siblings were primarily raised by his mother and maternal grandmother, Eunice Taylor.

Dawson became enamored of baseball early, using rocks and a mop handle to play as a young boy. When the city denied financial assistance for a Little League in a segregated part of Miami, his maternal uncles organized one for Dawson and his friends. As a nine year old sharing the field with older players, he received a nickname that would stay with him for his adult life—"The Hawk"—for his intense focus.

Dawson was a star athlete at Miami's Southwest High School, but while playing safety on his football team he incurred an injury to his left knee that would haunt him throughout his baseball career. Though the Kansas City Royals expressed interest in him at a summer tryout, Dawson ended up enrolling at Florida A&M, a black college popular with athletes, including his uncle Theodore Taylor, who had played minor league baseball.

In July 1975, Dawson was selected in the eleventh round of the Major League amateur draft by the Montreal Expos. Dawson received a $2000 signing bonus and was assigned to the Pioneer (Rookie) League in Lethbridge, Alberta. Dawson led the league in hits and home runs that summer and won the Player of the Year award.

Promoted quickly through the system, Dawson made his debut with the Expos in September 1976 and later recorded his first career hit off future Hall-of-Fame pitcher Steve Carlton. Dawson won the starting centerfield job for the Expos the following spring training and with nineteen home runs and twenty-one stolen bases was named Rookie of the Year.

Following the season, Dawson attended an opening night at a Miami theater and invited a friend of his sisters', Vanessa Turner; engaged two months later, they married following the 1978 season and would have two children: Darius DeAndre and Amber Chanelle.

By 1981, Dawson had established himself as a bonafide star: that season he was selected to his first of eight All-Star teams, finished second in the MVP voting, and was named *The Sporting News's* Player of the Year. Dawson also established himself with his teammates, forming a rapport with fellow Floridian outfielders Warren Cromartie and Tim Raines. As testament to his character, Dawson was credited with helping Raines seek counseling for cocaine addiction following the 1982 season.

In 1982, Dawson was the victim of racial profiling in Montreal, when he was frisked in a department store by police officers who mistook him for a suspected black shoplifter. Though Dawson sought a public apology through the Expos' front office, none came. However, it was a more physical malady that lessened Dawson's love affair with the franchise: the synthetic turf of Montreal's Olympic Stadium wrought havoc on Dawson's knees.

Following the 1986 season, Dawson turned down a contract with a sizable pay cut from the Expos. Eager for the opportunity to play on grass, Dawson gave the Chicago Cubs' general manager Dallas Green a literal blank check for his services at a private meeting. Green offered Dawson a one-year, $500,000 contract, less than half of what he earned with Montreal. As would be revealed, Dawson was a victim of collusion between Major League owners, who had agreed not to bid exorbitantly for other teams' free agents. Five years later, he was awarded over $2 million from a grievance ruling.

Despite the paltry contract, Dawson had a career year in 1987, posting 49 home runs and 137 runs batted in, becoming the first MVP for a last-place team. Dawson reemerged as a National League force and was elected to the All-Star game for five years in a row with Chicago.

When his tenure with the Cubs ended in 1992, Dawson signed a two-year contract with the Red Sox and then a similar deal with the Marlins as a bench player before announcing his retirement halfway through the 1996 season.

Despite undergoing numerous knee surgeries throughout his twenty-one-year career, Dawson was primarily considered a threat on the basepaths. When he retired, he was one of just two Major League ballplayers to tally 400 home runs and 300 stolen bases, the other being Willie Mays. Mays himself, when asked about the young Dawson in 1983, acknowledged his blend of speed, power, and fielding prowess, calling him "the most complete player in the game today."

Dawson joined the front office of the Florida Marlins in 2000 as a special assistant and received a World Series ring for the team's 2003 victory. After nine years on the ballot, Dawson was voted into the Major League Baseball Hall of Fame in January 2010.

FURTHER READING
Bradley, John Ed. "Whatever It Takes, Dawson Will Do It," *Washington Post*, 5 July 1983.
Dawson, Andre, and Tom Bird. *Hawk* (1994).
Fimrite, Ron. "Don't Knock the Rock," *Sports Illustrated*, 25 June 1984.

ADAM W. GREEN

Dawson, William Levi (26 Apr. 1886–9 Nov. 1970), congressman, was born in Albany, Georgia, the son of Levi Dawson, a barber, and Rebecca Kendrick. Dawson received his early education in Albany, then attended Fisk University in Nashville, Tennessee, and received a bachelor's degree in 1909.

In 1912 Dawson joined thousands of other African Americans migrating to Chicago. Hoping to become one of the few black professionals in the city, he enrolled at the Kent School of Law. In 1917 he interrupted his law studies to volunteer for military service in World War I. He served as a first lieutenant with the 365th Infantry in France, where he was wounded in the shoulder and gassed during the Meuse-Argonne campaign.

After the war Dawson resumed his legal studies at Northwestern Law School and was admitted to the Illinois bar in 1920. Two years later he married Nellie Brown, with whom he had two children. He practiced law until 1928, when he waged an unsuccessful campaign in the Republican primary against the incumbent white congressman, Martin Madden, who represented the largely African American First Congressional District in Chicago.

In 1933 Dawson campaigned successfully for a seat on the Chicago City Council. Five years later, at a time when most African Americans were switching their party allegiances to the Democrats, Dawson was nominated by the Republican Party to run against the Democrat Arthur Mitchell for the congressional seat for the First District. Dawson ran on an anti–New Deal platform and lost. A year later he also lost his city council seat to a Democrat. Following Dawson's city council defeat, he was approached by Chicago Mayor Edward J. Kelly, a Democrat who was eager for an African American to lead the party in the city's largely black

Second Ward. Dawson accepted Kelly's offer to be Democratic committeeman and soon established himself as Chicago's preeminent black Democratic leader, a position he held for the rest of his life.

Dawson quickly won favor with the Chicago Democratic organization by building an effective vote-producing machine in African American neighborhoods. In 1942 he was elected to Congress from Chicago's First Congressional District, defeating first EARL DICKERSON in the Democratic primary and then the Republican candidate, William King, in the general election. When Dawson took his seat in 1943, he was the only African American member of the House of Representatives.

As a member of Congress, Dawson sought to advance a limited civil rights agenda while maintaining that the United States was the best place "in all the world for our people." He called for an end to discrimination in defense industries, voted against regressive income tax measures, and testified before the House Judiciary Committee against the poll tax. In 1948 Dawson was selected to chair the Negro Division of the Democratic National Committee. Based on seniority, Dawson gained the chair of the House Committee on Governmental Operations (later renamed Government Operations) in 1949, becoming the first African American chairman of a congressional committee.

A loyal Democrat, Dawson toed the party line on foreign policy, faithfully supporting measures to contain communism even during the Vietnam War, a turbulent period during which many black Democratic leaders broke with the administration of President Lyndon B. Johnson. Throughout his congressional career Dawson continued to control political patronage on Chicago's South Side and was the leading black member of the city's Democratic machine. He delivered huge blocks of votes for Democrats in municipal, state, and national elections. In 1955, for example, Dawson's four wards accounted for 40 percent of Richard J. Daley's winning margin in the Chicago mayoral election. Criticized by some civil rights activists for "selling out" his black constituency to a party that failed to challenge Jim Crow laws in the South or de facto segregation in the North, Dawson replied, "Where else but in the Democratic organization could a black man, whose ancestors were slaves, rise so high?"

During the 1960s Dawson came under increasing attack from civil rights activists, in part for his unwillingness to criticize the Democratic Party for acting too slowly against segregation and for his hostility toward civil rights leaders. When

William Dawson, Democratic representative from Chicago, c. 1945. (Library of Congress/Congressional Portrait Collection.)

the Reverend MARTIN LUTHER KING JR. initiated a campaign in Chicago in 1966 to challenge racial discrimination and poverty among the city's African American population, Dawson denounced King as an "outside agent."

Dawson fell ill while campaigning in 1962 and never fully recovered his health. He died in Chicago.

FURTHER READING

Christopher, Maurine. *America's Black Congressmen* (1971).

Clay, William L. *Just Permanent Interests: Black Americans in Congress, 1870–1991* (1992).

Stone, Chuck. *Black Political Power in America*, rev. ed. (1970).

Obituary: *New York Times*, 10 Nov. 1970.

This entry is taken from the *American National Biography* and is published here with the permission of the American Council of Learned Societies.

THADDEUS RUSSELL

Dawson, William Levi (26 Sept. 1899–2 May 1990), composer, conductor, and educator, was born in Anniston, Alabama, the oldest of the seven children of George W. Dawson, an illiterate day laborer and former slave, and Eliza Starkey. A precocious and self-determined child William Dawson developed an affinity for music at an early age, delighting in the band concerts and traveling musical shows that passed through his hometown. Encouraged by his mother, who had come from an educated family, he began taking music lessons from S. W. Gresham, a former bandmaster at the Tuskegee Institute. Dawson aspired to attend the institute headed by BOOKER T. WASHINGTON. His parents had no money for his education but Dawson, determined to play in the Tuskegee Band, boarded a train at the age of thirteen and headed for Tuskegee, Alabama. Paying his tuition by working in the fields surrounding Tuskegee, Dawson participated in every musical activity he could, joining the choir, playing trombone in the band, and traveling with the famous Tuskegee Singers before graduating in 1921.

Following graduation Dawson moved to Kansas, where he taught band at Kansas Vocational College for a year. He then moved to Kansas City, Missouri, where he joined the Blackman's Concert Band. Hoping to attend Ithaca Conservatory the next year, Dawson sold his first composition, "Forever Thine," door-to-door to earn tuition money. Financial problems, however, ended that dream, and he accepted a job with Lincoln High School in Kansas City, Missouri, in 1922. His choir became well known for its performances of African American spirituals, which Dawson arranged, leading to the publication of "King Jesus Is A-Listening" in 1925 by H. T. FitzSimmons of Chicago. By year's end Dawson was also supervising the instrumental music program for all the African American schools in the city.

Although Dawson was now teaching full-time he did not abandon his dreams of higher education. He enrolled in the bachelor of music program at the Horner Institute of Fine Arts in Kansas City, privately studying with professors at night because of segregationist policies at the school. At his graduation ceremonies in 1925 the Kansas City Orchestra played his trio for violin, cello, and piano, but Dawson was unable to acknowledge the audience's applause because he sat not with his classmates but in the balcony reserved for African Americans.

In 1927 Dawson left Kansas City for the thriving musical scene in Chicago, where he soon became the first chair trombonist and the only black member of the Civic Orchestra of Chicago. He also played in Charlie "Doc" Cook's dance band, Doctors of Syncopation. Dawson continued his musical studies at the Chicago Musical College and the American Conservatory of Music, earning his master of music in composition in 1927 under the guidance of Adolph Weidig. He also worked at Gamble-Hinged Music and H. T. FitzSimmons, arranging and editing music for both publishing houses. That same year he married Cornella Lampton, daughter of an African Methodist Episcopal (AME) bishop and a musician in her own right. Sadly, she died less than a year later.

While Dawson was living in Chicago he began work on a symphony. Inspired by Antonin Dvorak's *New World Symphony*, he wanted to produce a piece that reflected his heritage. "It is an attempt to develop Negro music," Dawson explained in an interview in the *New York Times* in 1933, "something they have said again and again couldn't be developed. I never doubted the possibilities of our music, for I feel that buried in the South is a music that somebody, someday, will discover." To ensure there would be no doubt that the symphony was based in African American folk idioms, he titled his work the *Negro Folk Symphony*. On 20 November 1934 Leopold Stokowski led the Philadelphia Orchestra in its first performance of the *Negro Folk Symphony* in Carnegie Hall in New York City.

Although Dawson continued to compose he remained committed to education. In 1930 Dawson returned to his alma mater to organize and conduct its school of music. By 1925 Tuskegee Institute had transformed from a secondary to a collegiate level institution, and Dawson established a program that reflected both Tuskegee's heritage as a vocational school and its future as a center for higher learning, hiring faculty members with impressive credentials, yet remaining committed to a strong music education program. Shortly thereafter, on 21 September 1935, he married Cecile Demae Nicholson in Atlanta, Georgia, in the home of the artist HALE WOODRUFF.

Under Dawson's masterful direction the Tuskegee Institute Choir became one of the most popular of its generation. The one hundred voice choir appeared at the opening of Radio City Music Hall in New York in 1932, sang for presidents Herbert Hoover and Franklin D. Roosevelt, and was the first African American performing organization to appear at Constitution Hall in Washington, D.C., in 1946, breaking a long-standing race barrier. During his tenure as the director of the Tuskegee Choir

Dawson also composed a number of arrangements of African American spirituals such as "There Is a Balm in Gilead" and "Ezekiel Saw de Wheel." These beloved arrangements have become permanent fixtures in the choral repertoire and remain perennial favorites of audiences and choirs around the world.

Despite the busy touring schedule of the Tuskegee Institute Choir, Dawson frequently traveled internationally. In 1952 he took a yearlong sabbatical to West Africa, visiting Sierra Leone, Liberia, the Gold Coast (later Ghana), Nigeria, Senegal, and Dahomey (later Benin). He carried one of the first battery-operated reel-to-reel tape recorders and recorded African performing groups and tribal dances. In 1956 the United States State Department invited Dawson to tour Spain to train local choirs in the African American spiritual tradition. That same year he retired from the Tuskegee Institute, after twenty-five years of leadership in the music department.

Despite his official retirement William Levi Dawson continued to publish and conduct. Committed to educating audiences and students about African American music he led seminars and guest conducted high school and college choirs. He also established his own music publishing business, printing his arrangements under the imprint Music Press. William Levi Dawson died in Montgomery, Alabama, at the age of ninety.

FURTHER READING

Dawson's papers are housed in the Manuscript, Archives, and Rare Book Library, Emory University, Atlanta, Georgia.

Dawson, William L. "Interpretation of the Religious Folk Song of the American Negro," *Etude Magazine* (Mar. 1955).

Haberlen, John B. "William Dawson and the Copyright Act," *Choral Journal* 23.7 (Mar. 1983).

Spady, James G., ed. *William Dawson: A Umum Tribute and a Marvelous Journey* (1981).

ELIZABETH A. RUSSEY

Day, Caroline Stewart Bond (18 Nov. 1889–5 May 1948), anthropologist, writer, and educator, was born in Montgomery, Alabama, the daughter of Georgia Fagain and Moses Stewart. Day was of African American, Indian, and European descent. The Stewart family lived several years in Boston, Massachusetts, where Caroline attended public schools. After her father's death, Caroline and her mother moved to Tuskegee, Alabama, where Georgia Stewart taught school and married John Percy Bond, a life insurance executive. The couple had two children, and Caroline adopted Bond's name. She attended Tuskegee Institute and in 1912 earned a bachelor of arts degree from Atlanta University. She taught English at Alabama State College in Montgomery for a year and then worked for the Young Women's Christian Association (YWCA) in Montclair, New Jersey. In 1916 she began studying English and classical literature at Radcliffe College of Harvard University, earning a second bachelor's degree in 1919. At Radcliffe she impressed her anthropology professor, Earnest A. Hooton, who encouraged her to begin collecting the physiological and sociological data on the "almost inaccessible class of educated persons of mixed Negro and White descent" that eventually led to her graduate studies.

After World War I Caroline Bond took a semester off and worked in New York City as executive secretary of the Circle for Negro War Relief under the leadership of W. E. B. DuBois. She also served as student secretary of the National Board of the YWCA. After graduating, she moved to Waco, Texas, and taught English at Paul Quinn College, where she served as dean of women, and then at Prairie View State College, where she was head of the English department. There she met and married Aaron Day, a chemistry teacher, in March 1920. He then became a salesman for the National Benefit Life Insurance Company, where his wife's stepfather also worked. From 1922 to 1929 Caroline Day taught English and drama at Atlanta University. Her essays, short stories, plays, children's stories, and poetry, published in magazines and anthologies, reflect her interest in the life and problems of blacks and those of mixed race. An article in the *Crisis* (Sept. 1925) discusses plays suitable for black student actors, and her autobiographical story "The Pink Hat" in *Opportunity* (Dec. 1926) describes a young woman's experience "passing" in white society.

In 1927 Earnest Hooton, Day's former teacher, received a grant from the Bureau of International Research of Harvard University and Radcliffe College, which allowed Day to continue her research. Although her work was interrupted by a rheumatic heart condition, she entered Harvard's graduate school of anthropology and earned a master of arts in 1930. The Harvard African Studies series *Varia Africana* published her master's thesis, *A Study of Some Negro-White Families in the United States* (1932, republished in 1970). This study of mixed race families was the first of its kind in anthropology, treating sociological, genealogical, and physiological aspects of "Negro-White crosses."

In 1930 the Days moved to Washington, D.C. Unable to have children because of her weak heart, Caroline Day befriended and informally adopted a teenage boy. She taught English at Howard University, worked as a social worker and director of a D.C. settlement house in 1934, and was appointed general secretary of the Phillis Wheatley "Colored" YWCA in 1937. In 1935 Aaron Day was promoted to the head office of the North Carolina Mutual Life Insurance Company, and in 1939 the family joined him in Durham, North Carolina. There Caroline Day began teaching English and drama at North Carolina College for Negroes (later North Carolina Central University). Poor health continued to limit her career, and except for occasional teaching and some unpublished writings, she spent the rest of her life with her family—gardening, reading, and attending club activities. She died in Durham from complications of her chronic heart condition.

Day came to her study of mixed-blood crosses from her experience as a person of mixed race. Proud of her heritage, she also understood the handicaps facing blacks and the temptation to "pass for white" in a race-biased society. Her study involved people who, she said, were not "the types with which the public is familiar" nor "those used as literary material by the novelists and playwrights" of her day (*A Study of Some Negro-White Families in the United States*, 3); rather she presented a "real cross-section of life among colored people of mixed blood in this country" (*Inventory*, 3). In reviewing her work in the *Crisis* (Mar. 1930), Day noted that intermarriage was a problem rarely written about because "few popular writers have dared attempt the subject and few scientists have had sufficient material at their disposal to warrant venturing conclusions" (81). Focusing on the racial categories "Negro, Indian, and White," she documented not only the physiological characteristics—skin color, physical measurements, hair samples, and appearance—of 346 families (including 1,347 living individuals of a total of 2,537) but she also collected photographs, family stories, and information relating to their homes, occupations, salaries, religion, education, political connections, and sometimes their "passing" into white society. Collecting data was difficult because of what Day recognized as the "mystery and humiliation of illegitimacy" and the "fear of exposure" of families in the white community (*Study*, 4–5). Hooton qualified the anthropometric conclusions of Day's study because of her limited sample, and others have criticized her methodology as unsophisticated; nevertheless, Day's findings

and sociological observations are valuable to biographers, historians, genealogists, and anthropologists. Her data challenged stereotypes and refuted theories that miscegenation produced inferior types. Her stories of hardship and achievement demonstrate the strength and resiliency of black and mixed-race individuals. In dealing with the question of whether blacks should be absorbed into the white population, Day contended, "The grim joke of the whole matter is that for 150 years and more he has been absorbed and his descendants are constantly rubbing elbows in daily life with some of the very ones who are discussing them" (*Study*, 11).

FURTHER READING

Day's papers are held at the Peabody Museum, Harvard University, Cambridge, Massachusetts. The collection is catalogued in *Inventory of the Papers of Caroline Bond Day* (rev. 1996).

Sollers, Werner, et al. *Blacks at Harvard: A Documentary History of African-American Experience at Harvard and Radcliffe* (1993).

Obituary: *Durham Morning Herald*, 7 May 1948.

This entry is taken from the *American National Biography* and is published here with the permission of the American Council of Learned Societies.

CAROL BAKER SAPORA

Day, John, Jr. (18 Feb. 1797–15 Feb. 1859), missionary and founding father of the state of Liberia, was born in Hicksford, Greensville County, Virginia, the elder son of John Day Sr., an affluent furniture maker, farmer, and landowner, and Mourning Stewart Day. The Days were free African Americans, and Day's father, as early as the 1789 election, was accorded voting status.

In an era when formal education for African Americans was rare, Day reaped the benefits of being the offspring of two prominent families. His father arranged for him to board in Edward Whitehorne's home, and Day, along with the Whitehorne children, attended Jonathan Bailey's school. While residing with the family, Day received some level of religious instruction from Whitehorne. In 1807 Day's father, who had been residing in Dinwiddie County, Virginia, purchased a plantation in Sussex County, Virginia, near the Whitehorne residence, and Day then attended William Northcross's school.

At the age of nineteen, Day attended a four-day evangelical meeting in Sussex County, at the outset of the Second Great Awakening, and it was there that his spiritual awakening began. One year later, in 1817, Day's father, apparently plagued by personal and financial problems, sold his plantation, returned to Dinwiddie County, and then moved to Warren County, North Carolina. Day remained in Virginia, opened a furniture-making shop in Scottsville, and paid off his father's debts before moving his business to another location in Scottsville.

Day labored successfully as a furniture maker until his establishment was set afire by an intoxicated man, leaving Day destitute. After refusing his neighbors' offer to rebuild and accepting only a hat and coat from a friend, Day walked to Warren County. He obtained his father's woodworking tools, borrowed some money, and moved to Milton, a town in Caswell County, North Carolina, and opened a furniture-making shop in the early 1820s. His brother, Thomas, joined him. The Day brothers were successful, yet John Day, who was baptized in 1820 and licensed to preach in 1821, was not content. To the Reverend Abner Clopton, pastor of a Baptist church in Milton and superintendent of the Milton Female Academy, he expressed a desire to do missionary work in Africa. Clopton, who had earned a master's degree from the University of North Carolina and studied at the Medical School of the University of Pennsylvania, encouraged Day to pursue his goal, and directed his studies. However, Day's initial attempts to go to Africa failed.

In 1824 Day decided to do missionary work in Haiti, and in 1825, after selling his house and property in Milton, he left North Carolina. However, Day's missionary plans were deferred for five years when for a reason that is not known he instead returned to Virginia, residing in Sussex and then Hicksford. Meanwhile, Thomas Day remained in Milton, and his enterprise eventually became one of North Carolina's largest furniture businesses.

In 1830 Day, Polly Wickham Day (whom he had married in 1821), and their four children traveled to Liberia, arriving in Monrovia on 4 December 1830. There Day took work as a preacher and a furniture maker. However, misfortune followed. Of those who had traveled to Liberia with the Days, some 107 passengers, 61 had died within a year. Among the deceased, in 1831, were Day's wife, three daughters, and his son. Day rejected the requests of family and friends to return to America.

As pastor for several Liberian churches and as a schoolteacher, Day was a missionary for the American Baptists from 1836 to 1846. After 1846 and until the time of his death, Day was a missionary for the Southern Baptist Foreign Mission Board. He was appointed superintendent of the missions in Liberia and Sierra Leone. Day was also active in the founding of the state of Liberia. He was one of twelve signers of Liberia's Declaration of Independence, dated 16 July 1847. Day was one of the four signers from Bassa County, Liberia, and the Bassa County's flag commemorates Day and the three other men with a stripe on the flag for each signer. In addition, Day served as Liberia's second chief justice of the Supreme Court. He eventually remarried, and he and his wife were the parents of two sons, William and Thomas, as well as an infant daughter. However, Day's wife and daughter died in 1851. Eight years later, Day's own health was in serious decline. On Sunday, 6 February 1859, Day walked to church, but as he stood before the congregation, intending to begin his sermon, illness overcame him, and he was unable to continue and required assistance in order to return to his residence. About a week later he died; he was survived by his third wife, Catherine, and his sons, William and Thomas.

Day's early years in Virginia and North Carolina as a free black who successfully pursued his educational, entrepreneurial, and religious goals provide insight into life in America during the eighteenth and nineteenth centuries. In addition, insight into nineteenth-century life in Africa is gleaned from Day's years in Liberia as a religious leader and founding father. Throughout his life, John Day remained steadfast in his desire to do God's work and help others.

FURTHER READING
Barfield, Rodney D. "Thomas and John Day and the Journey to North Carolina," *North Carolina Historical Review* 78.1 (Jan. 2001): 1–31.
Carter, Janie Leigh. "John Day: A Founder of the Republic of Liberia and the Southern Baptist Liberian Missionary Movement in the 19th Century," master's thesis, Wake Forest University, 1998.

LINDA M. CARTER

Day, Leon (30 Oct. 1916–13 Mar. 1995), baseball player, was born in Alexandria, Virginia, the son of Ellis Day, a glass factory worker, and Hattie Leet. Leon grew up in the Mount Winans district of Baltimore and finished the tenth grade before dropping out of school. As a youth, he was a fan of the Baltimore Black Sox of the Eastern Colored League, where he met his idol and future teacher, the pitcher Lamon Yokeley. Day's baseball career began in 1934 with the local semipro Silver Moons. A right-handed pitcher, he used a deceptive no-windup delivery to fire off sneaky fastballs and roundhouse curves. He became known as an excellent fielding pitcher and an above-average hitter, and he sometimes played the field so that his bat would remain in the lineup. He quickly caught the attention of the Baltimore Black Sox player-manager Herbert "Rap" Dixon and finished the season with the team, earning $60 a month.

The following season Dixon jumped to the Brooklyn Eagles of the Negro National League and took Day with him. Named by the Eagles manager Ben Taylor as his top pitcher, Day led the Eagles' staff in wins with a 9–2 record, which included a one-hitter, earning him his first selection to the prestigious East-West All-Star game in Chicago, Illinois. In 1936 the Eagles were sold to Abe Manley and relocated to Newark, New Jersey. The next season Day enjoyed one of his finest campaigns, compiling a perfect 13–0 record and batting .320 with eight home runs. On 17 July 1939 Day married Helene Johnson; they had no children.

Except for missing most of the 1938 season due to a sore arm, from 1936 to 1943 Day was the undisputed staff ace. In 1942 he established a league record with 18 strikeouts in a game against the Baltimore Elite Giants, including the future Hall of Fame catcher ROY CAMPANELLA three times. In the East-West All-Star game that year in Chicago, Day struck out five of the first seven batters he faced, en route to a win. Overall, in his nine all-star pitching appearances, Day recorded 16 strikeouts in 21⅓ innings. That year the *Pittsburgh Courier* named him "Best Pitcher" in the Negro Leagues.

In 1944 and 1945 Day fulfilled his military commitment as a corporal in the 818th Amphibian Battalion that landed in Normandy on Utah Beach during the Allied invasion on D-day. After the victory celebration, Day pitched his service team to a win over a major league all-star team led by the Cincinnati Reds pitcher Ewell Blackwell. In Munich, Germany, he pitched a one-hitter in the "GI World Series" before a reported crowd of 100,000 fans. Returning from the service in 1946, Day pitched the only Opening Day no-hitter in Negro League history, against the Philadelphia Stars. He finished the season with a 13–4 record and led the league in strikeouts, innings pitched, and shutouts, while batting a lofty .353. The Eagles, managed by BIZ MACKEY and paced by the power hitting of the youngsters LARRY DOBY and MONTE IRVIN, defeated the powerful Kansas City Monarchs in the Negro League World Series, four games to three, with Day pitching in two games. That season Day was paid a reported $450 dollars a month,

his Negro League career high. Contracts available from earlier years show that he had received $210 per month in 1941 and was given a raise of $15 per month the following year.

The five foot nine inch, 170-pound Day played many winters in the Cuban (1937–1938, 1947–1948), Puerto Rican (1939–1942, 1949–1950), Mexican, and Venezuelan leagues. During the 1941–1942 winter season, with the Aquadilla Sharks in the Puerto Rican League, he struck out a record 19 batters in an 18-inning marathon game. In three seasons with the Aquadilla team he hit .307, .330, and .351, while compiling a pitching record of 34–26. The three Puerto Rican campaigns saw 186, 149, and 168 batters strike out on Day deliveries. Day played in the Mexican Leagues for the Mexico City Reds in 1947 and 1948, before returning to the Negro National League in 1949 to help the Baltimore Elite Giants win the pennant. The following year Day joined manager WILLIE WELLS's Winnipeg Buffaloes in the independent semipro Manitoba-Dakota (Man-Dak) League, where he hit .324 and compiled a 4–2 pitching record.

In 1951, at the age of thirty-four, four years after JACKIE ROBINSON integrated the formerly segregated world of "organized" baseball, Day joined the Toronto Maple Leafs (AAA) of the International League. The following season he played with the Scranton Miners of the Eastern League, compiling a 13-9 record and batting .314. He finished his brilliant career with the Edmonton Eskimos of the Western International League (1953) and the Brandon Greys of the Man-Dak League (1954).

Upon retiring from baseball, Day was employed by Tragfer Bakery, Revere Brass and Copper, and the Liberty Security Companies as a security guard in Newark, New Jersey. He later worked as a substitute mail carrier for the Conmar Zipper Company and served as a part-time bartender for his former Eagle teammate Leonard Pearson's sports bar Lennie's Lounge. He eventually returned to Baltimore's Harlem Avenue. After the death of his first wife, he married Geraldine "Jerry" Ingram from Wallace, North Carolina, in November 1980.

Day's former teammate Larry Doby said, "I don't see anybody in the major leagues that was better than Leon Day. If you want to compare him with BOB GIBSON, stuff wise, Day had just as good of stuff. Tremendous curve ball, and a fast ball at least 90–95 miles an hour. You talk about Satchel [SATCHEL PAIGE]—I didn't see any [pitcher] better than Day." Another teammate, Monte Irvin, confirmed this view: "People don't know what a great pitcher Leon Day was. He was as good or better than Bob Gibson. He was a better fielder, a better hitter, could run like a deer. When he pitched against Satchel, Satchel didn't have an edge. You thought Don Newcombe could pitch. You should have seen Day! One of the best complete athletes I've ever seen."

On 31 January 1992 Day was honored by Baltimore mayor KURT L. SCHMOKE with a proclamation by the city for Leon Day Day. He was also honored for his contributions to baseball by President George H. W. Bush in the White House on 19 February 1992 and by Maryland governor William Donald Schaefer on 18 May 1992. In 1993 he was elected to the Puerto Rican Hall of Fame. Day's final tribute came on 7 March 1995, when he received news of his election to the National Baseball Hall of Fame. Day died six days later in Baltimore.

On 30 July 1995 Day's wife, Geraldine, revealed something of Day's quiet, unassuming character by speaking at his induction in Cooperstown, New York. She noted that Day was "a kind, gentle and humble man, and a wonderful athlete. He never bragged about his many accomplishments. He was always quick to praise others, and deserving of this great honor."

FURTHER READING

Clark, Dick, and Larry Lester. *The Negro Leagues Book* (1994).

Holway, John B. *Black Ball Stars: Negro League Pioneers* (1988).

Peterson, Robert. *Only the Ball Was White* (1970).

Riley, James. *Dandy, Day and the Devil* (1987).

Obituary: *Baltimore Sun*, 14 Mar. 1995.

This entry is taken from the *American National Biography* and is published here with the permission of the American Council of Learned Societies.

LARRY LESTER

Day, Thomas (1801?–1861), furniture maker and entrepreneur, was born in Dinwiddie County, Virginia, to free landowning parents, John Day and Mourning Stewart. John Day was a furniture maker and plantation owner, whose periodic financial difficulties may have been exacerbated by struggles with alcohol and gambling.

According to JOHN DAY JR., Thomas's older brother, their father was the son of a white South Carolina plantation owner and her black coachman. After becoming pregnant, she was sent to a Quaker community with which she left the newborn when she returned to her family. On several occasions when John Sr. met financial failures and briefly abandoned his family, John Jr. was left to cover his father's debts. Thomas Day's mother, Mourning Stewart of Dinwiddie County, Virginia, was the descendant of mixed-raced landowners and the daughter of "Dr." Thomas Stewart, owner of an eight-hundred-acre plantation and as many as nineteen slaves. Day and Stewart were married in 1795 or 1796 and their first child, John Jr., was born in 1797 in Hicksford, Virginia. Although a web of laws restricted the education of African Americans, Thomas and John Jr. were highly educated, attending predominantly white schools in Sussex County, Virginia. There John Jr., and presumably Thomas, boarded with a white family, the Edward Whitehornes, whose children were their classmates at the Jonathan Bailey School. Thomas Day's business records and private letters reveal a highly literate and thoughtful correspondent.

In 1817 the Day family moved near Nutbush Township in Warren County, North Carolina, a village of free blacks just south of the Virginia border. At the time North Carolina was the poorest and least populated state in the South, with close to one half of its population unable to read or write. It was slightly more hospitable to free blacks than were the other southern states, being generally slower to enact laws against blacks. For instance, North Carolina did not adopt laws forbidding the migration of free blacks into the state until 1826.

Around 1823, following several years as a cabinetmaker in Orange County, North Carolina, Thomas joined his brother John Jr., who had opened a furniture-making business in Milton, a town in Caswell County, North Carolina, less than one mile from the Virginia border. The Day brothers worked together for a year or two until John left Milton and returned to Virginia. In 1830 John, who had undergone a religious conversion in 1816, moved with his wife and children to Liberia, where he became a Baptist missionary and one of twelve signatories of Liberia's declaration of independence in 1847. Thomas, meanwhile, built up his furniture-making business, buying a storefront on Main Street for $550 in 1827, just four years after arriving in Milton. Day expanded the property in 1828 and again in 1836. In a surviving advertisement from the 1 March 1827 *Milton Gazette*, Day appealed directly to his customers, revealing an amiable marketing approach found throughout his business correspondence:

THOMAS DAY, CABINET MAKER. Returns his thanks for the patronage he had received, and wishes to inform his friends and the public that he has on hand, and intends on keeping, a handsome supply of Mahogoney, Walnut and Stained FURNITURE, the most fashionable and common BEDSTEADS, & which he would be glad to sell very low.

Day's decision to marry Aquilla Wilson, a free black from Halifax County, Virginia, in 1829, tested his relationship with his white neighbors. To bring his new wife into North Carolina, Day needed an exception from the 1826 state law that barred free blacks from migrating to the state. Day's successful petition to the state legislature was supported by Romulus Saunders, the state's attorney general and former U.S. congressman, and sixty-one white North Carolina businessmen. Identifying Day as "a first rate workman, a remarkably sober, steady and industrious man, a high minded, good and valuable citizen, possessing a valuable property in this town," the petition specifically noted that Day was the owner of slaves, as well as of property and land.

As Day's furniture business flourished he branched out, investing in the State Bank and local real estate. At one point he owned three properties, including a 270-acre tobacco plantation outside of town. The Days were established members of the Milton community and prominent members of the local Presbyterian church, where they sat in the first-floor pews generally reserved for white congregants. Day himself built the walnut, yellow poplar, and pine pews.

The Days educated their three children, Mary Ann, Devereaux, and Thomas Jr., at Wesleyan Academy in Wilbraham, Massachusetts. In 1848 Day purchased the Union Tavern (sometimes called the Yellow Tavern), the largest building on Main Street, for $1,050. He added a large workshop to the back of the building and converted the upstairs into a residence and the first floor into a showroom. Together the property had five chimneys and twelve fireplaces. By 1850 he was running one of the largest furniture businesses in North Carolina. The shop employed a large workforce of free black and white laborers as well as slave and white apprentices. Day mechanized his shop in the mid-1850s, introducing steam-powered machinery before most of his competitors. Throughout the 1850s Day maintained a credit rating with R. G. Dun and Company of Boston, which estimated his worth in 1855 at $40,000.

In his shop Day carried a standard line of furniture that he sold both to retailers and directly to customers. He became known, however, for his custom-designed and custom-built furniture, especially his expert handling of fine woods and veneer, which he cut unusually thin, down to one-sixteenth of an inch. Day produced pieces, including sofas, sideboards, tables, washstands, beds, and secretaries, in the high urban styles of the period, initially Federal and Empire, and later in the revivalist styles, primarily Gothic and Rococo.

In addition to his furniture Day was commissioned to design interior architectural millwork for grander houses. Many of the moldings, staircases, newel posts, and mantels that he installed still exist in homes in North Carolina and Virginia. Day often included unique elements and combinations of different styles in his designs, prompting some later collectors to suggest an African influence on particular pieces and, more generally, on his improvisational style. More likely, however, Day's approach reflected a working style common to regional artisans, who felt freer to introduce eclectic combinations and folk and vernacular traditions into their designs. His workshop drew customers from throughout the South, including David S. Reid, governor of North Carolina from 1851 to 1854, who bought forty-seven pieces of furniture from Day in 1855, and the University of North Carolina, which commissioned Day to design and build furniture for the Philanthropic and Dialectic Societies' debating hall.

By the end of the 1850s increased legal restrictions against African Americans, escalating racial tensions, growing competition, and a poor economy brought on by the financial panic of 1857 had profoundly eroded Day's business. In 1858, only a few short years after the height of his professional success, Day was forced to sell his property and put his business under trusteeship. In 1859 Thomas Jr.—like his uncle before him—took over his father's debts and purchased the furniture-making business with loans from white Milton businessmen. Thomas Jr. ran the shop through the Civil War and Reconstruction. Following his financial collapse, Thomas Day Sr. succumbed to rapidly declining health and died in 1861.

Though the life of Thomas Day reflects elements of the experience of antebellum free blacks, particularly those of mixed race, his uncommon financial, professional, and social achievements establish him as an exceptional figure. Day's prominence brought him unusual opportunities to massage and even circumvent the complex legal sanctions against free blacks in pre–Civil War southern states. Day was part of the dramatic increase in the population of free blacks in the Upper South, which grew by 90 percent between 1790 and 1800 and by 65 percent between 1800 and 1810, making free blacks the fastest growing population in the South during this period. By 1818 one out of every twelve African Americans in the South was free.

Day, of course, was not the only successful black entrepreneur, skilled artisan, or property owner in first half of the nineteenth century. The Day family, highly educated and skilled beyond the average white southerner, benefited from their status as free blacks, mixed race, landowners, and slave owners. The 1850 census shows that Thomas Day, whose parents and maternal and paternal grandparents had all owned slaves, owned fourteen slaves whom he worked in his shop and on his farm. African American slave ownership was not as rare as was once believed. In 1830 in Day's home state of North Carolina there were two hundred free black slave owners. In all of the slave states combined, blacks owned more than fourteen thousand slaves in 1830. As late as 1860 blacks owned more than a million dollars in personal real estate and property, some of which included slaves.

Several, partially fanciful, biographical accounts of Thomas Day written in the 1920s established him as a folk hero whose success—and eventual bankruptcy—both met and challenged depictions of the Old South. Later interest in Day and his work resulted in museum exhibitions, a children's book, and the establishment of the Thomas Day Education Project, which works to improve the teaching of African American history and culture. In 1997 the Andy Warhol Foundation funded an inventory of North Carolina buildings featuring Day's millwork, and in 1975 the Union Tavern/Thomas Day House in Milton was designated a national historic landmark. A 1989 fire badly damaged the building, which subsequently received $40,000 from the North Carolina state legislature and a $250,000 Save America's Treasures federal matching grant toward the restoration of the property.

Examples of Day's furniture survive in the collection of a number of private collectors, foundations, and museums, including the North Carolina Museum of History, which owns twenty pieces.

FURTHER READING

Barfield, Rodney. *Introduction to Thomas Day, Cabinetmaker: An Exhibition at the North Carolina Museum of History* (1975).

Barfield, Rodney. "Thomas and John Day and the Journey to North Carolina," *North Carolina Historical Review* (Jan. 2001).

Marshall, Patricia Phillips. "The Legendary Thomas Day: Debunking the Popular Mythology of an African American Craftsman," *North Carolina Historical Review* (Jan. 2001).

LISA E. RIVO

Day, William Howard (16 Oct. 1825–2 Dec. 1900), educator and editor, was born in New York City, the son of John Day, a sailmaker, and Eliza Dixon, a seamstress. J. P. Williston, an inkmaker from Northampton, Massachusetts, first met Day during a visit to a school for black children in New York City. Williston was so impressed with the young student that he persuaded Day's mother to allow him, a white man, to adopt her son. Day spent five years in Northampton, where he attended school and was apprenticed as a printer at the *Hampshire Herald*. Refused admission to Williams College because of his race, Day enrolled at Oberlin College in Ohio (1843–1847). Soon after graduating, he was hired by the *Cleveland True Democrat* as a reporter, compositor, and local editor. He later published and edited the *Aliened American* (1853–1854), which aimed to promote education and defend the rights of African Americans. It was also the mouthpiece of the state's Negro Convention Movement, in which Day was a leading figure. Day married fellow student Lucy Stanton in 1852; one child was born to the marriage.

Five years out of college, Day organized a meeting in Cleveland to honor surviving black veterans of the Revolutionary War and the War of 1812. It was in part a memorial to his father, a sailor in the War of 1812 who had died tragically in 1829, and also partly an expression of Day's conviction that such valor in the defense of the nation was grounds enough to be recognized as citizens. "We ask for liberty; liberty here—liberty on Chalmette Plains—liberty wherever floats the American flag," Day wrote. "We demand for the sons of the men who fought for you, equal privileges" (*Cleveland True Democrat*, 9 Sept. 1852). The struggle for equal rights dominated Day's life.

The failure of his newspaper and increasing discrimination prompted Day and his family to join the growing number of African Americans immigrating to Canada. There he became involved in John Brown's preparations for the 1859 attack on Harpers Ferry, printing Brown's constitution in an isolated shack outside St. Catharines. Day was in Britain raising money for the fugitive slave settlement at Buxton, Ontario, when the attack occurred. He spent the next four years in Britain lecturing against slavery and working with the African Aid Society, an organization formed to support the efforts of MARTIN R. DELANY, HENRY HIGHLAND GARNET, Robert Campbell, and other advocates of African American immigration to the west coast of Africa. By the time of his return to the United States in 1863, Day's marriage had fallen apart because of what he considered to be irreconcilable differences. It is difficult to determine what these differences were, but it is clear that Day's long absences from home must have been a contributing factor. William and Lucy Day were finally divorced in 1872, after years of wrangling. A few months later Day married Georgie Bell of Washington, D.C.; he had no children with his second wife.

After returning to the United States, Day settled in New York City, devoting most of his time to working with the American Freedmen's Friend Society, a black-led freedmen's aid organization, and as lay editor of the *Zion Herald*, the organ of the African Methodist Episcopal Zion Church. In 1867 he was named by the Freedmen's Bureau as superintendent of schools for the freedmen of Maryland and Delaware. Day used this office to promote education, to support the construction of schools, and to work with local associations to increase educational opportunities for the freedmen. In spite of local and state opposition, Day reported significant growth in schools built and in attendance. Day lost his job in 1869 when the Freedmen's Bureau reorganized its local offices.

In 1872 Day moved to Harrisburg, Pennsylvania, after purchasing a local newspaper, *Progress of Liberty*, and changing its name to *Our National Progress*. Published simultaneously in Harrisburg and Philadelphia; Wilmington, Delaware; Camden, New Jersey; and New York City, Day saw the paper as both a regional and a national mouthpiece of African Americans. Despite its wide circulation, the paper ceased publication in 1875 largely on account of difficulties brought on by the economic depression of 1873. Day ran unsuccessfully for the Harrisburg School Board in 1873; five years later he became the first African American to be elected to the board. He remained a member for the rest of the century with the exception of brief periods in the 1880s when he refused renomination. In 1891 the board unanimously elected Day its president, a position he held until 1895. He finally retired from the board in 1899, ending an involvement in education lasting more than fifty years.

Day was a prominent force in central Pennsylvania Republican circles. His active involvement in the 1872 campaign led to his appointment to a clerkship in the state auditor general's office. But frustration with token appointments and the continued corruption of the state Republican machine under Simon Cameron led Day to break with the party in 1878. He temporarily threw his support to the Democrats but was back in the Republican fold in 1881. Although he remained an active supporter of the party, Day never again regained his place of prominence, nor was he, or any other black Pennsylvanian during Day's lifetime, ever nominated to significant office.

After his return from Britain in 1863, Day had become actively involved in the AME Zion Church. His parents' home had served as a meeting place for the fledgling denomination in the 1820s, and Day had been baptized by JAMES VARICK, the first bishop of the church. By 1870 Day was unquestionably the most prominent member of the denomination in Pennsylvania. He was named secretary-general of the national body in 1876 and presiding elder of the Philadelphia and Baltimore Conference in 1885. As elder he supervised a district that included Washington, D.C., and parts of Pennsylvania, Maryland, and Delaware. He was later appointed secretary of the board of bishops.

Day, a contemporary observed, was "one of the grandest and most refined men of this country regardless of race" (*Harrisburg Telegraph*, 14 Apr. 1898). It was a fitting tribute to a man who had spent all of his adult life promoting the cause of freedom and equality in the United States. Day died in Harrisburg as a result of a series of strokes.

FURTHER READING

A few letters from or about Day can be found at the American Missionary Association Papers, Amistad Research Center, New Orleans; the Anti-Slavery Collection, Cornell University Library; Bureau of Refugees, Freedmen and Abandoned Lands, National Archives; the Leon Gardiner Collection, Pennsylvania Historical Society; the Gerrit Smith Papers, Syracuse University Library; and in *Black Abolitionists Papers, 1830–1865*, microfilm edition, reel 11.

Blackett, R. J. M. *Beating against the Barriers: Biographical Essays in Nineteenth-Century Afro-American History* (1986).

Simmons, William J. *Men of Mark: Eminent, Progressive and Rising* (1887).

Stutler, Boyd B. "John Brown's Constitution," *Lincoln Herald* 50–51 (1948).

Wheeler, B. F. *Cullings from Zion's Poets* (1907).

Obituary: *Harrisburg Telegraph*, 3 Dec. 1900.

This entry is taken from the *American National Biography* and is published here with the permission of the American Council of Learned Societies.

R. J. M. BLACKETT

Daylie, Holmes "Daddy-O" (15 May 1920–6 Feb. 2003), television personality and disc jockey, was born in Covington, Tennessee, into a family of twelve children. His mother died during his birth and his father passed away when Holmes was five, so his older brother Clinton and his wife raised Holmes on the South Side of Chicago. Daylie attended John D. Shoop Elementary School. He was an excellent athlete at Morgan Park High School, and after graduation he played basketball in the professional Negro League for the Harlem Yankees and the Globetrotters. After a few years of touring with the teams, Daylie wanted to settle in one place. He joined the Beige Room staff tending bar at the Pershing Hotel in Chicago in the 1940s and quickly developed a loyal clientele that enjoyed the verbal patter he used while he worked.

Daylie became known as "Daddy-O" while tending bar at various bars in Chicago. He was well-known for his jive talk and for his performance of bartending acrobatics with bottles and glasses at Club Kuttawa at 117th and Vincennes in Morgan Park, the DuSable Lounge on Oakwood Boulevard, and the El Grotto Supper Club and Beige Room at the Pershing Hotel on 64th Street. Daylie tossed ice cubes into the air while rhyming and juggled bottles while mixing drinks. Many jazz musicians visited the bars and gambling rooms where Daylie worked, and he became quite knowledgeable about jazz and musicians (both local artists and international stars). In the 1940s he became close friends with the jazz music greats DUKE ELLINGTON and LOUIS ARMSTRONG, both of whom he met at the DuSable Lounge.

Daylie's radio career was encouraged by the radio personality and disc jockey Dave Garroway, who after watching Daylie in action at the El Grotto Supper Club in 1948 suggested that he attend broadcasting school. That same year Daylie was hired by WAIT to spin records for his own forty-five-minute program called *Daddy-O's Jazz Patio*. The show became popular with many Chicagoans, who enjoyed Daddy-O's mix of jazz, blues, and swing.

Daylie remained at WAIT until 1956, at which time he left to host a late-night contemporary jazz and commentary show. Daylie, sponsored by the Anheuser-Busch Brewing Company, was the first African American to host a regular show on Chicago's network-owned and -operated stations. His best-known radio slogans were, "For those who live it, those who love it, and those who make a living of it," and "I'm the musical host who loves you the most." During the 1950s and 1960s,

Daylie wrote album liner notes for such jazz greats as WES MONTGOMERY and Jimmy Smith. The trumpeter MILES DAVIS and the alto-saxophone player JULIAN "CANNONBALL" ADDERLEY recorded "One for Daddy-O" in 1958 on the legendary jazz album *Somthin' Else*. The song was written by NAT ADDERLEY, Julian's brother, for Daylie. CLARK TERRY's album *Daylight Express Featuring Paul Gonsalves* (recorded late in the 1950s but remastered and released in 1998) and *Out on a Limb with Terry Clark* (1957) were produced by Daylie and feature two songs dedicated to him, "Blues for Daddy-O's Jazz Patio" and "Daddy-O's Patio."

Over the course of his career Daylie was involved in a number of charitable causes. One of Daddy-O Daylie's earliest charities (in the 1950s) was the Hine Veterans Administration Hospital. Operation Christmas Basket was one of Daylie's favorite personal charities, and each year he would urge his listeners to contribute food for Chicagoans who would otherwise go hungry over the holidays. He hosted the *Daddy-O Daylie Fun Leagues* that sponsored a number of community bowling events during the year to assist the city's needy.

Daylie, along with the Chicago banker Jacoby Dickens, bought the Starlight Bowl on East 87th Street in Chicago in the early 1970s and continued to operate the bowling alley when many other neighborhood merchants had closed because of gang activity. On his radio shows Daylie spoke about the gang situation and stressed the importance of the community coming together to stop the violence. He purchased two local gasoline stations when national chains sold their businesses owing to problems with crime, and he regularly hired neighborhood youth to work at the bowling alley and gas stations. Daylie worked with the Reverend Curtis Burrell, director of the Kenwood-Oakland Community Organization (KOCO), and applied for job training grants for programs to recruit gang members who wanted to leave the life and gain job skills. The men were successful in receiving grants from the U.S. Office of Economic Opportunity (OEO), the Sears Foundation, and the YMCA, but they were only marginally successful in decreasing local gang violence. When Burrell and Daylie organized local residents in marches against violence, their own lives were threatened and both had to be placed under police protection against gang assassins.

In 1968, even as he continued to work at his radio show, Daylie was approached by a local Chicago television station about creating a special public affairs program with the noted journalist and news anchor Warner Saunders. Management selected Daylie based on the amount of respect he held in the local African American community. Using a format borrowed from popular shows in other cities, the two men co-hosted *For Blacks Only* every week for more than a decade.

During the rioting in Chicago that followed the 1968 assassination of the Reverend Dr. MARTIN LUTHER KING JR., Daylie was approached by federal authorities and city leaders to broadcast a message of nonviolence to the city's black community.

Daylie worked as the late morning disc jockey on the Chicago all-jazz radio station WAAF (950 AM) and stayed there when its name changed in 1967 to WGRT, "Great Radio." Later the Johnson Publishing Company, publishers of *Ebony* and *Jet*, purchased the station and renamed it WJPC. Despite changes in ownership, Daylie remained on the air, finally retiring from radio in 1988. He died in Chicago at the age of eighty-two after suffering a stroke.

FURTHER READING

The papers for stations WAAF and WMAQ are located in the Library of American Broadcasting, University of Maryland.

Travis, Dempsey J. *An Autobiography of Black Jazz* (1983).

Obituary: *Chicago Sun-Times*, 11 Feb. 2003.

PAMELA LEE GRAY

De Baptiste, Richard (11 Nov. 1831–21 Apr. 1901), Baptist leader and race advocate, was born in Fredericksburg, Virginia, to free parents, Eliza (maiden name unknown) and William De Baptiste. Born in a slave state at a time when individuals were fined and incarcerated for teaching blacks, enslaved or free, Richard was fortunate to have parents who earnestly sought to educate their children and some relatives in their home, despite the law and heavy surveillance. In 1846 his family moved to Detroit, Michigan. Richard received additional education and for a time attended classes at the University of Chicago. Once the leading building and manufacturing contractor in Fredericksburg, William De Baptiste, following an unsuccessful partnership in a grocery enterprise, returned to the construction business. Richard became a partner in the business before his twenty-first birthday and served for some years as its manager. From 1858 to about 1861 he also taught black youth in the public schools of Mount Pleasant, Hamilton County, Ohio.

De Baptiste was married three times. In 1855 he wed Georgiana Brischo of Cincinnati, Ohio; at the time of her death in 1872 they had at least three children. The death of his second wife, Mary, ended a marriage of only eight months. Finally, in 1890 he married Nellie Williams of Galesburg, Illinois.

Conversion at a revival meeting in 1852 in the Second Baptist Church of Detroit and affiliation with that church impressed De Baptiste with a call to the ministry, though he did not make this known until he had served for some time in a number of church positions. Licensed to preach by the church upon his departure to Ohio in 1858, De Baptiste continued his preaching in Mount Pleasant and organized a Sunday school. In 1860 he was ordained as an elder, and three years later he assumed the pastorate of Olivet Baptist Church in Chicago, a post he held until 1882. His work there was effective in terms of church construction and reconstruction after the 1874 Chicago Fire, providing refuge and educational opportunities for African Americans as well as evangelistic outreach. Olivet became the city's largest assembly of African Americans. Despite the desire of the congregation that he remain, De Baptiste resigned in 1881 because of his children's poor health and reduction in church membership. He continued pastoral work in smaller Illinois congregations.

While De Baptiste maintained a fervent commitment to the ministry, he made great contributions in the organization and consolidation of Baptist groups among African Americans, especially in the Midwest and South. He was a popular official in various Baptist groups, winning frequent reelection. He played a major role in establishing and maintaining black denominations independent of white churches, though he himself had interracial church involvements. He served Baptist conventions as statistician, corresponding secretary, and president. De Baptiste was involved in the Wood River Baptist Association; the Northwestern and Southern Baptist Convention from its inception in 1865; the Consolidated American Baptist Missionary Convention, where he held the office of president from its organization in 1867 to 1871 and from 1872 to 1877; the American Baptist Free Mission Society, a biracial organization fiercely opposed to slavery, of which he was elected president in 1870; the Baptist General Association of Western States and Territories, of which he served as corresponding secretary; and the American National Baptist Convention from its organization in 1886, when he was elected corresponding secretary. De Baptiste also served as statistician of the American National Baptist Convention, demonstrating that black Baptist membership numbered more than a million, contrary to earlier counts by white Baptists who placed the number at 800,000. Finally, De Baptiste's strong emphasis on racial independence led him to support vigorously the founding of the National Baptist Convention (NBC) in 1895, the first permanent national organization of African American Baptists. He also worked for the establishment of the NBC's publishing board and the active support of African missions work through the NBC and earlier black Baptist conventions.

De Baptiste, a prolific writer for both religious and secular news organs, edited a number of newspapers: the *Conservator,* the first black newspaper in Chicago, which he coedited with another minister; the *Western Herald,* during the period 1884 to 1885 the sole black Baptist news organ in the midwestern states and territories; the *St. Louis Monitor* and *Baptist Herald* (Keokuk, Iowa), for which he served as corresponding secretary; and the *National Monitor,* sponsored by the Consolidated American Baptist Missionary Convention and based in New York, for which he served on the editorial staff. As a pastor and denominational leader, race spokesperson and advocate, and journalist, De Baptiste was an outstanding religious leader of the nineteenth century.

FURTHER READING

Martin, Sandy D. *Black Baptists and African Missions* (1989).

Pegues, Albert W. *Our Baptist Ministers and Schools* (1892).

Simmons, William J. *Men of Mark: Eminent, Progressive and Rising* (1887; repr., 1968).

Washington, James M. *Frustrated Fellowship: The Black Baptist Quest for Social Power* (1986).

This entry is taken from the *American National Biography* and is published here with the permission of the American Council of Learned Societies.

SANDY DWAYNE MARTIN

De Lavallade, Carmen (6 Mar. 1931–), dancer, chorographer, and teacher, was born in New Orleans, Louisiana, and raised by her aunt Adele, who owned the Hugh Gordon Book Shop, one of the most prominent African American book stores in the city. She was influenced by the success of her cousin, JANET COLLINS, who was the first black dancer to perform with the Metropolitan Opera Ballet company.

At the age of sixteen de Lavallade received a scholarship to study at the Lester Horton Dance Theater in Los Angeles. After her initial studies in modern dance, ballet, and various other dance forms, she joined Lester Horton's Dance Theater in 1949 and danced the lead from 1950 to 1954, taking over the roles previously danced by the legendary dance pioneer Bella Lewitzky before Lewitzky's departure from the company. Horton then created chorography especially for de Lavallade, including the role of Salome in *The Face of Violence.* She made her New York debut in 1953.

After Horton died in 1953, ALVIN AILEY took over the role of choreographer for the company, with de Lavallade contributing to the choreography. By the early 1960s de Lavallade had become a principal member of Ailey's company, going to Europe as part of the company's first tour in 1962. She also worked with Donald McKayle in 1964 and appeared as a guest artist in the American Ballet Theater productions of *The Four Marys* and *The Frail Quarry,* choreographed by Agnes de Mille in 1965.

The actor and dancer LENA HORNE mentored de Lavallade and arranged for her to study with the Italian ballerina Carmelita Maracci. Additionally, de Lavallade studied acting with Stella Adler as part of her training at Horton's studio, and she began working in film at seventeen years of age when she contracted with Twentieth Century–Fox Studios in 1952. She appeared in four films in three years, the best known being *Carmen Jones* (1954). The film director Herbert Ross was impressed with de Lavallade's work with Alvin Ailey in *Carmen Jones* and recruited them both to work for him on the musical *House of Flowers* on Broadway. It was on this production that she met her future husband—the artist, chorographer, and dancer GEOFFREY HOLDER. They were married in a Haitian-style wedding on 26 June 1955. Their only child, Leo, was born in 1957.

In 1956 the Metropolitan Opera hired de Lavallade as a lead dancer, where she followed in the footsteps of her cousin Janet Collins. Collins, who had danced with KATHERINE DUNHAM and TALLEY BEATTY, was one of de Lavallade's mentors. At the same time, de Lavallade was the principal in John Butler's dance company and made her television dance debut in 1956 in Butler's ballet *Flight.* Her television and film work continued in the late 1950s with *A Drum Is a Woman,* a television production of DUKE ELLINGTON's work. She also appeared in *Odds against Tomorrow* in 1959, opposite HARRY BELAFONTE. Her dance performance created tension on *The Ed Sullivan Show* in 1961, when the sponsor refused to allow her to be partnered with the white dancer Glen Tetley, insisting that Claude Thompson, a black member of the Ailey company, be substituted for Tetley. By the time she began teaching movement for actors at Yale University in 1966, she had danced with Louis Johnson, Donald McKayle, and JOSEPHINE BAKER, and with numerous troupes, including the Dance Theater of Harlem, the Joyce Trisler Danscompany, and the New York City Opera, taking parts in many of her husband's choreographed works. She taught dance from 1977 at Adelphi University in Long Island and directed the dance department at the school for three years in the late 1990s. De Lavallade joined the Yale School of Drama as performer-in-residence and choreographer in 1970, becoming a full professor and a member of the Repertory Theater. Her students included the actors Henry Winkler, Meryl Streep, and Sigourney Weaver. De Lavallade left Yale in the 1980s and expanded her teaching and lecturing as well as her own performance schedule. She appeared with the BILL T. JONES/Arnie Zane Dance Companies at the Joyce Theater in New York City and choreographed Otto Schenk's productions of Wagner's *Die Meistersinger von Nürnberg* (1992) and Dvořák's *Rusalka* (1993) at the Metropolitan Opera. Her vision for movement—which has been variously described as "dance verismo," expanded gesture, or dance movement as part of total theater—was inspired by her early training with Horton. Horton's students were trained not only in dance but also in costuming, set design, painting, sculpture, music, and lighting.

In 1983 de Lavallade danced with her husband, Geoffrey Holder, for the *Kennedy Center Honors: A Celebration of the Performing Arts.* Her later film roles include appearances in *Lone Star* (1996) and *The Hours* (2002). She made guest television appearances on *The Cosby Show* and *Another World.* Throughout her career de Lavallade supported the work of others to research and document the lives of pioneering American blacks in the field of dance, including taking part in the documentary of the black singer and actor DOROTHY DANDRIDGE, televised in 2003. She and Holder appeared in *Carmen and Geoffrey*, a 2005 film about their careers, directed by Linda Atkinson and Nick Doob.

De Lavallade was an advocate of using older dancers. Arvin Brown, staging *Porgy and Bess* at the Metropolitan Opera in 1990, found that de Lavallade would accept his invitation to choreograph Gershwin's opera only on the condition that

Carmen de Lavallade, dancer, choreographer, and actress, 3 March 1955. (Library of Congress/Carl Van Vechten, photographer.)

she would be allowed to use some older dancers. Beginning in the 1990s she developed a form of exercise for seniors that included coordination of imagination and movement. The basics of the program involved use of props and hand-eye coordination, with movements influenced by de Lavallade's early training with dance innovator Horton.

De Lavallade's honors include the Clarence Bayfield Award from Actors Equity for Outstanding Classical Performance Off Broadway, a 1966 award from *Dance Magazine* for her contributions to dance, the Balasaraswati/ Joy Ann Dewey Beinecke Endowed Chair for Distinguished Teaching at the American Dance Festival in 2003 for her role in shaping modern dance and passing on traditions, and the 56th Capezio Dance Award in 2007 for her role in bringing respect, stature, and distinction to dance. She was awarded an honorary doctorate of fine arts from the Boston Conservatory of Music and an honorary doctorate of arts from Adelphi in 2003, and her fiftieth year in dance was celebrated in June 1999 with a tribute event at the Hudson Theater. De Lavallade last danced in the Paradigm trio with

Gus Solomons Jr. and Dudley Williams, but she also worked with other companies, including the Alvin Ailey American Dance Theater, for which she resurrected John Butler's often forgotten portrait of BILLIE HOLIDAY, *Portrait of Billie* (originally created for de Lavallade in 1959). The Carmen de Lavallade award is presented each year for lifetime achievement in dance by the New York Dance Festival.

FURTHER READING

Emery, Lynne Fauley. *Black Dance from 1619 to Today* (1988).

Foulkes, Julia L. *Modern Bodies: Dance and American Modernism from Martha Graham to Alvin Ailey* (2002).

Long, Richard A. *The Black Tradition in American Dance* (1989).

PAMELA LEE GRAY

De Mortie, Mark Réné and Louise De Mortie (8 May 1829–3 Sept. 1914) and (1833–10 Oct. 1867). Mark Réné De Mortie, abolitionist, politician, and businessman, and his sister, Louise De Mortie, dramatic reader, singer, and philanthropist, were born in Norfolk, Virginia, perhaps to Mark Anthony De Mortier and his wife Francis De Mortier. Census records provide conflicting information about the siblings' parents, describing the father as born either in Virginia or France and the mother as French-born. All printed sources describe the two as free-born in Norfolk and local records reveal that as early as 1822 a free Haitian family named "Demortier" lived in Norfolk.

In 1870, however, the Washington *Evening Star* charged that Mark had been a slave and recent genealogical research may have turned up evidence in Norfolk borough court records that Louise had been freed in the early 1850s. The fact that the two turned up in Boston after passage of the 1850 Fugitive Slave Law may speak to their uncertain status in Virginia or, more likely, to the brother's underground railroad work.

Beginning at age eighteen, Mark met a mysterious "Dr." Harry Lundy, evidently a free black who smuggled slaves out of Norfolk and needed De Mortie to write letters to his contacts, especially in Philadelphia, to arrange for the care of fugitives. De Mortie also recruited cooperative sea captains willing to stow escapees aboard their vessels for a fee and take them north. De Mortie himself traveled to Boston in 1851, where he met LEWIS HAYDEN, and afterward returned to Norfolk to continue his labors. He worked closely with Hayden and for a time directed many fugitives to the seacoast black community in New Bedford, which possessed one of the commonwealth's most active underground railroad networks. De Mortie then opened a shoe store in partnership with William Dunn, the brother of Sally Jackson, whom he had helped escape from Virginia. De Mortie decided to remain in Boston after a letter arranging the escape of Jackson (then known as Sally Waller) was intercepted by her owner. Fearing for his safety, De Mortie sought advice from prominent white leaders, including future governors John A. Andrew and Benjamin F. Butler, who advised him to buy a gun and keep it near his store's cash box. If he feared arrest by southern agents, Butler told De Mortie, he should prefer standing trial for murder in Massachusetts than face charges for stealing slaves in Virginia.

De Mortie benefited considerably from Hayden's numerous political connections and quickly assumed a leadership position in the city. In 1853, the year that his sister settled in Boston, De Mortie joined the Free Soil Party and allied with the Know-Nothings the next year, along with LEONARD A. GRIMES, JOHN STEWART ROCK, JOSHUA BOWEN SMITH, and Hayden. The Massachusetts Know Nothings took in antislavery elements of the Whig party (until the rise of the Republicans), and joined with temperance forces and the anti-Catholic (anti-Irish) contingent to offer Bay State blacks a party that mimicked Freemasonry and advanced reform. De Mortie and other black leaders offered their support to state political leaders James M. Stone, Charles W. Slack, and John L. Swift (known as the "three S's"), who returned the favor in 1855 by orchestrating the end of segregated schooling in the commonwealth. The previous year, De Mortie had participated in the ill-fated attempt to liberate the fugitive slave ANTHONY BURNS from the Boston Court House. De Mortie joined Hayden, his future father-in-law GEORGE THOMAS DOWNING, and a host of other black and white abolitionists, and raided the court house, killing a marshal in their unsuccessful bid to save Burns from slavery. De Mortie continued agitating for black rights thereafter, joining with BENJAMIN FRANKLIN ROBERTS to help blacks seek city jobs, and became a Republican stalwart, increasing his circle of contacts among prominent state political leaders.

During the 1860 election, De Mortie worked with JOHN P. COBURN and Hayden to organize the West Boston Colored Wide Awakes, a large body of uniformed marchers who supported Abraham Lincoln. At the outset of the war, De Mortie served with Robert Morris, Sr. and WILLIAM COOPER NELL on a committee to draft resolutions in support of the

Union—despite the Lincoln administration's refusal to recruit black troops—that were adopted at a meeting held in the Twelfth Baptist Church. In recognition of his standing in the community, De Mortie was assigned to help organize and then officially convene the 1 January 1863 Emancipation Proclamation celebration at Tremont Temple. At the insistence of the city's black leadership, Governor Andrew in 1863 appointed him as the official sutler of the famed Fifty-fourth Massachusetts Regiment. He traveled with the unit to South Carolina and supported the eighteen-month campaign to win equal pay by accepting credit from the men during the pay strike. De Mortie, who had entered into the venture with Joseph Paul Winfield, a black from Buffalo, New York, loaned the regiment's soldiers about $14,000, "which they paid like men" at the war's end (Dworkin, 366). De Mortie then returned to Boston where he invested his profits in a successful tailoring business.

At the same time, his sister Louise used her increasing fame as a dramatic reader and singer to support the freedmen. After arriving in Boston in 1853, she married the free black carpenter and future American Missionary Association (AMA) missionary John Oliver who had moved to Boston from Petersburg, Virginia, sometime before March 1851. Although Oliver received the endorsement of the *Liberator* as "a neat and capable workman, accomplishing much in a short time," he probably could not secure enough work and sought his fortune in California goldfields, which caused De Mortie to divorce him (*Liberator*, 16 Oct. 1851). Beginning in 1862, she began a career as a dramatic reader which continued throughout the Civil War. Her "eloquent rendering of the poets, pleasing manner, and good sense gained for her a host of admiring friends, among whom were some of the leading men and women of the country" (Brown, 496). Her good looks caught the attention of many, especially the black abolitionist WILLIAM WELLS BROWN, who clearly admired her "Grecian cast of countenance, eyes dark and sparkling, lips swelling, forehead high, [and] refined manners." Indeed, De Mortie came to embody ideal black womanhood for black male intellectuals from Brown to W. E. B. DuBois. She performed readings around New England and in New York, focusing on the works of John Greenleaf Whittier, Henry Wadsworth Longfellow, Grace Greenwood, and others, clearly appealing to white and black audiences. By 1862 she had become known as "Madame De Mortie" (*Christian Recorder*, 27 Dec. 1862), with commentators inevitably focusing on her good looks,

wonderful voice, ability to pack an audience, and her mixed racial heritage.

As early as March 1865, Louise De Mortie had ventured to New Orleans to assist the city's orphaned black children. She organized fairs and continued her performances to secure funds for the girls' orphan asylum she had established in June at the mansion previously owned by Pierre Soulè, a French-born U.S. Senator and diplomat. Her activities, including fund-raising trips throughout the North, raised "considerable sums," a necessity since the Freedmen's Bureau limited its support to two other orphanages in the city (*Liberator*, 19 May 1865). Her work for the orphaned girls received much publicity in the city and throughout the North and by 1867 she had raised enough money, including one astonishing gift of $10,000 from an unidentified Frenchman, to erect a new building. Her sudden death from yellow fever in the fall of 1867, shortly after completion of the new facility, instantly turned De Mortie into a martyr. Edmonia Highgate, a teacher and AMA missionary, praised her as a "brilliant flash of lightning and as fully charged with magnetism … [who] electrified the land with her rare powers." She was, to Highgate, "one of the noblest representatives of American higher civilization" (*Christian Recorder*, 16 Nov. 1867).

In 1868, Mark De Mortie attended the Soldiers' National Convention in Chicago and formed a real estate partnership with JOHN JONES, one of the city's most successful black businessmen. He also began a sassafras oil business in Nottoway, Virginia, southeast of Richmond. Another successful business venture, the oil company became an exhibitor at the 1878 Universal Exposition in Paris. He also renewed his political aspirations and in 1877 became a Congressional candidate for Virginia's Fourth District and won the election, only to be swindled out of his seat by whites. As consolation, Republicans made him deputy collector of internal revenue and sent him as an alternate representative to the 1880 National Convention in Chicago.

In May 1870, in a ceremony that symbolized post-war black aspirations, De Mortie married Cordelia Downing, the daughter of former black abolitionist and now wealthy businessman George T. Downing. The wedding received press coverage across the nation, including in the *New York Times*, as representing "the elite of colored fashion and high life" (Sterling, 221–223). The *New Era*, managed by Frederick Douglass's sons, described the elaborate ceremony, attire, and gifts that few Americans, white or black, could match. The couple visited Chicago one last time, only to be ejected from a restaurant because of their "slight tinge of negro blood" amid cheers from the white patrons (*Boston Daily Advertiser*, 16 Feb. 1871). De Mortie brought suit against the owner for $5,000 in damages and won, but the court awarded him only one cent. The *Chicago Tribune* reminded its readers that while blacks may have won their political rights, they could not depend upon the government to guarantee their "social rights" and indeed had no inherent right to be patrons at any "private" facility (19 Feb. 1871).

De Mortie's marriage proved fruitful; the couple produced three children (Louise J., Cordelia, and Irene). The family also took in his wife's sister Georgianna, and possessed sufficient wealth to employ a live-in female servant. The 1880 Census showed that the De Mortie's home in the Haytokah section of Nottoway County lay on the exact dividing line between black and white communities, reflecting the family's light color and uncertain status between the separate worlds of black and white America.

De Mortie unsuccessfully ran again for Congress in 1882, promoted black education, and prospered in the sassafras oil business. But misfortune struck in 1887 when his facility, valued at $6,000, burned to the ground. Without insurance, he sold his land holdings and returned to Boston and the more humble tailoring and clothes-cleaning business. He resumed his influential role in Boston politics and raised funds to establish scholarships at Harvard and Tufts Universities in honor of Wendell Phillips. He also worked with his father-in-law to agitate against lynching and move Congress to adopt anti-lynching legislation, most notably the unsuccessful Moody Bill of December 1901. By 1910 De Mortie and his wife left Boston and moved to Newport, Rhode Island, where he had briefly resided in 1860, and where his son-in-law, the physician and x-ray promoter Marcus F. Wheatland, and other Downing relatives lived. Mark De Mortie died in Newport after suffering for years from a form of paralysis.

FURTHER READING

Blassingame, John. *Black New Orleans, 1860–1880* (1973).

Bogger, Tommy L. *Free Blacks in Norfolk, Virginia, 1790–1860* (1997).

Brown, William Wells. *The Rising Son; or The Antecedents and Advancement of the Colored Race* (1874).

Dworkin, Ira, ed. *Daughter of the Revolution: The Major Nonfiction Works of Pauline E. Hopkins* (2007).

Ferris, William H. *The African American Abroad; or His Evolution in Western Civilization*. 2 vols. (1913).

Sterling, Dorothy, ed. *The Trouble They Seen: The Story of Reconstruction in the Words of African Americans* (1994).

DONALD YACOVONE

De Moss, Elwood (5 Sept. 1889–26 Jan. 1965), baseball player and manager, was born in Topeka, Kansas. His parents' full names and occupations are unknown and little is known about his childhood, though according to a 1910 census, De Moss was living at home with his mother, Eley, a widow. In 1905 he began his baseball career as a shortstop with the Topeka Giants. Although his speed allowed him to cover extensive ground, an injured arm that year from a brief outing as a pitcher caused him to switch to second base. He is generally recognized as the best second baseman in black baseball prior to the formation of the Negro National League in 1920.

De Moss made appearances with strong independent teams such as the Kansas City (Kansas) Giants from 1910 to 1912, the French Lick (Ind.) Plutos from 1913 to 1914, the Saint Louis Giants in 1913, the West Baden (Ind.) Sprudels from 1912 to 1914, and the Chicago Giants in 1913. In 1915 he joined the Indianapolis ABCs, owned by Tom Bowser and managed by the legendary C. I. TAYLOR. He excelled at every phase of the game, exhibiting quickness and agility in the field and proving to be an offensive threat with the bat. Considered by baseball historians a "scientific" hitter, the right-handed De Moss hit the ball to all fields, depending on the pitcher's delivery. The players called him "Bingo," because, it was said, wherever he wanted to hit the ball, bingo, it would go there. An excellent bunter, master of the hit-and-run, and seldom a strikeout victim, he proved to be a valuable weapon in a team's batting order.

In his first year at Indianapolis, De Moss batted .316 and stole thirty-four bases in fifty games. In 1915 the ABCs lost to RUBE FOSTER's Chicago American Giants in the playoffs. The American Giants won the first and third games, with the ABCs winning the second. A rematch occurred in September of the following year; the American Giants won three out of four games with scores of 3–1, 4–2, and 5–2, with their only loss by a 7–4 score. The ABCs, with De Moss, the future Hall of Famer OSCAR McKINLEY CHARLESTON, and the submarine pitcher William

"Dizzy" Dismukes, then met the American Giants in October for a twelve-game series. Foster's Giants went down to defeat five games to four, with three games unplayed, and De Moss and his teammates claimed unofficial title to the world's black baseball championship.

In 1917 De Moss joined Foster's American Giants, who exhibited a more up-tempo, aggressive, and daring style of play that was better suited to De Moss's offensive skills. After World War I De Moss replaced PETE HILL, an outstanding hitter and outfielder, as captain of the team and held the position for the next six years. During this period the American Giants won the Negro National League, which was organized in 1920, pennants in 1920, 1921, and 1922, before relinquishing the title to the Kansas City Monarchs in 1923. During the 1923 and 1924 seasons the league was raided by the newly formed Eastern Colored League, weakening some of its original teams. The league commissioner Rube Foster sent DeMoss and George Dixon to the Indianapolis ABCs, after the 1925 season in an attempt to balance power within the league.

De Moss was called by the Homestead Grays owner CUM POSEY "the king-pin of keystoners." The Chicago American Giants manager Dave Malarcher said that De Moss "had the courage, confidence and ability written all over his face and posture. He was the smartest, the coolest, the most errorless ball player I've ever seen."

De Moss spent one season with the Indianapolis ABCs before the team folded. He joined the Detroit Stars in 1927 and was manger for the next four seasons. Although the Stars never captured first place, they compiled an impressive 195–158 won-lost record, a .545 percentage during De Moss's tenure. De Moss retired after the 1930 season, only to reemerge in 1942 as manager of a semiprofessional team called the Chicago Brown Bombers, capitalizing on the boxer JOE LOUIS's moniker. The next year the Brown Bombers folded and De Moss went back into retirement.

In 1945 Branch Rickey started an experimental league, the United States Baseball League, to develop black ballplayers for possible integration into the major leagues. Rickey said he hoped the league would become a model for all leagues to follow and would eventually make the black players eligible to be drafted by major league clubs. One of six teams formed was the Chicago Brown Bombers, with De Moss named as manager. The new team with an old name played their games at Wrigley Field when the Chicago Cubs were out of town. De Moss won 57 percent of his games as manager of the Brown Bombers, which later became associated members in 1946, the last year of Rickey's provisional league.

After 1946 De Moss vanished from the baseball scene and lived a quiet life in Chicago until his death there. There is no record of him after 1946. League standings and game results were never published, and little information was available on the United States League. Little is known of his personal life, although he was survived by his wife, Maranda (maiden name unknown), and two daughters. A brilliant manager and an excellent ballplayer, De Moss's contribution to baseball history has remained virtually unknown.

FURTHER READING
Holway, John. *Voices from the Great Black Baseball Leagues* (1975).
Peterson, Robert. *Only the Ball Was White* (1970).
Riley, James. *All-Time All-Stars of Black Baseball* (1983).
This entry is taken from the *American National Biography* and is published here with the permission of the American Council of Learned Societies.

LARRY LESTER

De Paris, Sidney (30 May 1905–13 Sept. 1967), jazz trumpeter, was born in Crawfordsville, Indiana, the son of Sidney De Paris, a trombonist, music teacher, and leader of the De Paris Family Band. De Paris's mother (name unknown) played alto horn, and his older brother, WILBUR DE PARIS, played trombone and later led a successful jazz band. De Paris received cornet lessons from his father, and starting in 1916 he toured the South with the band, playing at carnivals, tent shows, and vaudeville theaters. In 1924 he left the group to work in Washington, D.C., with the pianist Sam Taylor, and the following year, moving to Harlem, he joined Andy Preer's Cotton Club Orchestra, making his first recordings with that band in November 1925. Starting in 1926 he worked on and off with Charlie Johnson's jazz orchestra at Small's Paradise, chiefly as a substitute for JABBO SMITH. In early 1927 he left New York to join his brother's band at the Pearl Theater in Philadelphia, Pennsylvania, but after about a year he rejoined Johnson as Smith's permanent replacement.

De Paris's blues-based growl style was first showcased on Johnson's Victor recordings of September 1928, "The Boy in the Boat" and "Walk That Thing," and on "Harlem Drag" and "Hot Bones and Rice" from May 1929. Throughout the late 1920s he was considered one of the best hot trumpeters on the Harlem scene, his facility with mutes and his mastery of the growl technique popularized by BUBBER MILEY being especially influential on such other young trumpeters as REX STEWART, Bobby Stark, and COOTIE WILLIAMS. The superior quality of his heated, heartfelt blues playing at the time, on both muted and open horn, can best be heard on the Johnson records and the November 1929 recordings of "Miss Hannah," "Peggy," and "Wherever There's a Will There's a Way" by McKinney's Cotton Pickers, a highly rated midwestern band then led by DON REDMAN. After leaving Johnson in 1931, De Paris briefly led his own group and played for a time in Benny Carter's orchestra, but in early 1932 he joined Redman's new big band, with which he remained through mid-1936.

After a short trip to Cleveland with NOBLE SISSLE, whose orchestra was then sparked by the soprano saxophonist SIDNEY BECHET, De Paris spent 1937 and 1938 in Willie Bryant's and Charlie Johnson's bands as well as participating in Mezz Mezzrow's inspired but ill-fated attempt to launch a racially mixed big band. During its brief existence late in 1937, Mezzrow's fourteen Disciples of Swing played at the Harlem Uproar House and the Savoy Ballroom, but racial pressures and lack of public support worked against the group's success. Beginning in October 1938 De Paris spent several months in Allie Ross's theater pit band for the *Blackbirds* show; he then returned to Redman briefly before forming his own eight-piece band for a job in Baltimore.

In September 1939 De Paris played alongside Bechet, ALBERT NICHOLAS, and ZUTTY SINGLETON on two JELLY ROLL MORTON recording dates for Bluebird, and from December through June 1940 he frequently augmented Singleton's trio at Nick's in Greenwich Village. At times during this residency, Singleton enlarged his trio, with Nicholas on clarinet, to a sextet, adding De Paris and others to fill out the ensemble sound of a traditional New Orleans jazz band. Bechet used him on a June 1940 record date with his own New Orleans Feetwarmers as well as engaging him for later jobs. After some occasional work, he again joined Carter's big band for a ten-month stay ending in September 1941, when he rejoined Singleton and spent a few weeks in the trumpet section of Charlie Barnet's popular swing band. In 1942, while working in the pianist Art Hodes's combo, De Paris and Singleton appeared on a widely praised recording session for Decca. With solid connections such as Bechet, Singleton, Eddie Condon, and Hodes, De Paris became part of the New York small band jazz scene, while remaining active in big bands.

In the spring of 1943 the De Paris brothers, with Wilbur as leader, took their own sextet into Jimmy Ryan's on Fifty-second Street, and in February 1944 they received their first joint billing as leaders on the Commodore label. De Paris also had his own first date in June for Blue Note with an exceptional seven-piece group featuring the clarinetist EDMOND HALL, the trombonist VIC DICKENSON, and the pianist JAMES P. JOHNSON; one of the four numbers recorded, "The Call of the Blues," became his most memorable achievement. De Paris worked the summer months touring with ROY ELDRIDGE's orchestra. From late 1943 until 1945 De Paris recorded as a sideman on dates led by Hall, Johnson, Eldridge, Bechet, Cliff Jackson, and J. C. HIGGINBOTHAM; however, he did not record again as a leader until June 1951, when he assembled a New Orleans-styled sextet including the clarinetist OMER SIMEON, the trombonist JIMMY ARCHEY, and the bassist POPS FOSTER for another Blue Note session. His most prolific period began in 1952, when as a featured member of his brother's Rampart Street Paraders he appeared on thirteen albums before the end of 1961.

In 1946 De Paris made several USO tours with CLAUDE HOPKINS's band, and in 1947 he rejoined his brother for engagements at Jimmy Ryan's, Child's Paramount, and the Palladium Ballroom. In the winter of 1950 the De Paris brothers were hired by Bechet's young disciple, Bob Wilber, for a stay at Storyville in Boston, during which time Wilbur De Paris decided to form another band—this one modeled on the style and organizational structure of Morton's late 1920s' Red Hot Peppers. In September 1951 the De Paris brothers opened at Ryan's for what would prove to be the longest-lasting run of any jazz band on Fifty-second Street. Not wishing to travel, De Paris led his own group at Ryan's when Wilbur De Paris took the band on a State Department–sponsored tour of Africa during the spring of 1957. However, De Paris resumed his role as sideman upon his brother's return. De Paris's health had been failing for some time before the early 1960s, and increasingly the trumpeter DOC CHEATHAM was called on to provide relief. But even at these times De Paris doubled on cornet, flugelhorn, and tuba. He played infrequently in his last years and came to depend on his brother's daily care. He died in New York City.

FURTHER READING
McCarthy, Albert. *Big Band Jazz* (1974).
Schuller, Gunther. *Early Jazz* (1968).

Schuller, Gunther. *The Swing Era: The Development of Jazz, 1930–1945* (1989).

DISCOGRAPHY

The Complete Edmond Hall/James P. Johnson/Sidney De Paris/Vic Dickenson Blue Note Sessions (Mosaic MD4-109).

Bruyninckx, Walter. *Swing Discography, 1920–1988* (12 vols.).

Bruyninckx, Walter. *Traditional Jazz Discography, 1897–1988* (6 vols.).

Rust, Brian. *Jazz Records, 1897–1942* (1982).

This entry is taken from the *American National Biography* and is published here with the permission of the American Council of Learned Societies.

JACK SOHMER

De Paris, Wilbur (11 Jan. 1900–3 Jan. 1973), jazz trombonist, was born in Crawfordsville, Indiana, the son of Sidney De Paris, a trombonist, music teacher, and bandleader. Nothing is known of his mother except that she played alto horn. In 1907 Wilbur also started playing the alto horn, and by 1916 he was playing baritone horn in his father's band. His younger brother SIDNEY DE PARIS also had been added to the band on cornet. Throughout the 1910s the De Paris Family Band toured in carnivals and tent shows and played on the Theater Owners' Booking Association (TOBA) vaudeville circuit. After Wilbur had switched to trombone, sometime between 1919 and 1922, he joined Billy and Mary Mack's Merrymakers and traveled with them to New Orleans, where he sat in with the trumpeter LOUIS ARMSTRONG at Tom Anderson's Cabaret and worked with ARMAND PIRON's orchestra. In 1925 he led a band in Philadelphia, Pennsylvania, and later played in Harlem at Connie's Inn with LeRoy Smith and in Atlantic City with Bobby Lee's Cotton Pickers. In 1927 he led a big band at the Pearl Theater in Philadelphia, and from early 1928 through late 1937 he worked and recorded with Smith, CLARENCE WILLIAMS, EDITH WILSON, JELLY ROLL MORTON, BUBBER MILEY, Dave Nelson, Benny Carter, Spike Hughes, NOBLE SISSLE, the Mills Blue Rhythm Band, Edgar Hayes, and Teddy Hill, almost always as a utilitarian sectionman (he could play any part, whether lead, solo, or harmony). In that capacity, between November 1937 and September 1940 he worked with the Louis Armstrong Orchestra and, following a brief stay with ELLA FITZGERALD, toured with ROY ELDRIDGE's big band.

In the spring of 1943 De Paris and his brother Sidney took a jazz sextet into Jimmy Ryan's on Fifty-second Street in New York City, and in 1944 he appeared on record dates led by Eldridge, Cliff Jackson, Eddie Condon, and George Wettling and recorded under the name of the De Paris Brothers for the first time. Resolved to become part of the burgeoning small-band jazz scene in New York, on 26 December 1944 De Paris organized a jam session concert at Greenwich Village's Pied Piper that featured SIDNEY BECHET, BILL COLEMAN, HANK DUNCAN, MARY LOU WILLIAMS, and others. In late 1945 he was hired on with DUKE ELLINGTON, in whose orchestra he remained until the spring of 1947, when he re-formed his sextet and played engagements at Jimmy Ryan's, Child's Paramount, and the Palladium Ballroom. Featuring his brother Sidney (who doubled on trumpet and sometimes played tuba), the clarinetist EDMOND HALL, and the drummer COZY COLE, this was essentially a swing-style unit that, like the similarly manned group he had led in 1944, also played traditional jazz numbers. In early March 1949, along with Bechet and BUSTER BAILEY, De Paris played opposite the saxophonist CHARLIE PARKER's all-star bebop group in a "Battle of the Bands" concert at the Waldorf-Astoria, and in April 1950 he participated in Bechet's recording date for Commodore. The next winter he and his brother joined the band of Bechet's disciple, Bob Wilber, at the Storyville Club in Boston, a job that was to lead directly to the most fruitful engagement of his career.

Convinced that the time was ripe for a band dedicated to the principles of organized New Orleans–style jazz as exemplified by Jelly Roll Morton's Red Hot Peppers, De Paris formed the Rampart Street Paraders. In September 1951, with a personnel including his brother, the famed New Orleans clarinetist OMER SIMEON, the pianist Don Kirkpatrick, the New Orleans banjoist and the guitarist Danny Barker, and the drummer Freddie Moore, the De Paris band opened at Ryan's for a residency that would last until early 1962, when the club was razed to make room for the new block-long CBS building. During this period De Paris was absent only twice, first in 1957 when he embarked on a fifteen-week State Department tour of Africa, during which time Sidney took over at Ryan's, and then in 1960 when the band appeared at the Cannes Jazz Festival in Antibes, France. In addition to being a major tourist attraction, the band also recorded thirteen successful albums and was showcased on radio and television. His film credits include *The Pirate*, a 1948 musical with Judy Garland and Gene Kelly, and *Windjammer*, a 1958 travelogue.

Considering its lengthy run the De Paris band maintained fairly constant personnel over the years, the major flux being in the rhythm section. When Simeon died in September 1959, his place was taken permanently by the versatile Garvin Bushell, who was not only a skilled clarinetist but also an expert jazz bassoonist. An earlier but less noticeable change took place in December 1954 when Sonny White replaced Kirkpatrick. Barker left in early 1952 and was replaced first by Eddie Gibbs and then by Lee Blair and John Smith. The succession of bass players went from Harold Jackson through Nat Woodley, Wendell Marshall, and BENNIE MOTEN before De Paris finally settled on Hayes Alvis in early 1958. Moore was succeeded by ZUTTY SINGLETON in 1953, by George Foster in 1955, and from 1956 on by Wilbert Kirk, who also doubled on harmonica. On occasion the trumpeter DOC CHEATHAM was added to the group, and as Sidney's health worsened in the early 1960s, Cheatham was relied on even more frequently.

Compared to the best jazz trombonists of his time—Jack Teagarden, Jimmy Harrison, Tricky Sam Nanton, BENNY MORTON, J. C. HIGGINBOTHAM, DICKY WELLS, and VIC DICKENSON—Wilbur De Paris was a dependable but bland player. For the major part of his career he was employed as a sectionman in big bands, and it was not until the mid-1940s, with the renewed popularity of older styles of jazz, that he even considered forming a small band of his own. In March 1930 he had participated as a minor functionary on three successive recordings with Jelly Roll Morton, and these experiences with the dynamic leader so impressed him that when the opportunity came to him twenty years later he adopted the Morton format rather than return to the swing combo approach of his 1944 sextet. Accordingly, he enlisted the aid of Simeon, a ten-year veteran of the Orchestra and the clarinetist on most of Morton's best recordings. A devoted scholar of jazz history, De Paris developed a wide repertoire of compositions that went back to early ragtime cakewalks and previously overlooked songs of the 1920s, including a considerable number of Morton tunes and other jazz classics. To these he added several stylistically related, exotic compositions of his own. An astute bandleader, De Paris realized his own limitations as an improviser and gave most of the solos to others in the group, but his hand in the structure of his band's performances is always recognizable. A sincere lover of historic jazz and one of the rare analysts and intellectuals in the field of traditional jazz, De Paris was always ready to discuss the interweaving connections among the many ingredients that went into the making of jazz, from its seminal roots in African rhythms and polyphonic singing through its Creole and Caribbean influences to its flowering in late nineteenth-century New Orleans.

After the demise of Ryan's the band worked at the Broken Drum and the Room at the Bottom in Greenwich Village and in the summer of 1965 in a Mardi Gras Show at Jones Beach. De Paris never married. Relatively inactive after his brother's death in 1967, Wilbur De Paris opened a rehearsal studio in 1971, led another short-lived band, and then died at home in New York City.

FURTHER READING

Chilton, John. *Sidney Bechet: The Wizard of Jazz* (1987).
Shaw, Arnold. *52nd St.: The Street of Jazz* (1971).
Obituary: *New York Times*, 6 Jan. 1973.

DISCOGRAPHY

Bruyninckx, Walter. *Swing Discography, 1920–1988* (12 vols., 1985–1989).
Bruyninckx, Walter. *Traditional Jazz Discography, 1897–1988* (6 vols., 1985–1989).
Rust, Brian. *Jazz Records, 1897–1942* (1982).
This entry is taken from the *American National Biography* and is published here with the permission of the American Council of Learned Societies.

JACK SOHMER

de Passe, Suzanne Celeste (1 July 1947?–), music executive, television and film producer, and screenwriter, was born in New York, New York. Her father worked for Seagram's and her mother was a schoolteacher. Her paternal grandfather was a physician in Harlem.

Her parents divorced when she was three but managed to maintain a supportive environment for their daughter. She spent the week with her mother and the weekend with her father. He remarried when de Passe was nine, and the three adults formed a supportive alliance that continued to nurture de Passe.

She lived the elite life of prominent black families in New York. She summered on Martha's Vineyard; attended the private, progressive, and integrated New Lincoln School; graduated from Manhattan High School; and entered Syracuse University in 1964. She found the university and its extremely small African American student body not to her liking, so transferred to Manhattan Community College to major in English.

Suzanne de Passe poses with actor Samuel L. Jackson in Los Angeles on 22 March 2002. [AP Images.]

While she had a dream of being a writer, according to a feature in *Essence*, de Passe spent much time at Cheetah, the city's "number one get-down disco" at the time. While there she freely let managers know her opinion of acts booked. That led to de Passe becoming part of the group who evaluated talent auditions at the club, which resulted in a full-time position as talent coordinator for Cheetah. De Passe then quit school to pursue a career in the entertainment industry. De Passe recalled that her father responded by going "flako berserko when I told him I was quitting school" (Allen, p. 92).

While working as talent coordinator for Cheetah in 1967, she first met BERRY GORDY JR., founder of Motown. The two were introduced by her friend Cindy Birdsong, who later became a member of the Supremes.

De Passe offered Gordy a ride in her limousine. The next time de Passe met Gordy, she was working as a talent consultant for the Howard Stein firm, which was having trouble booking Motown talent. According to one feature, de Passe took the opportunity to tell Gordy "something was terribly wrong with his company. If Motown had been organized, they wouldn't have needed to hire me" (Allen, p. 92). He invited her to Detroit for an interview in 1968 and ultimately hired her as his creative assistant. One of her first assignments was to critique a WILLIAM SMOKEY ROBINSON performance in New Jersey. Eventually, De Passe did "everything but type" (Allen, p. 92). She was one of the first Motown executives to move to Los Angeles, when Motown moved there in 1970, and held titles of director of West Coast creative division and vice president of Motown Industries before becoming president of Motown Productions in 1980.

Between 1970 and 1972 de Passe went back to her original dream of being a writer and wrote "Diana," DIANA ROSS's solo television special, served as head writer for "Goin' Back to Indiana," a Jackson Five special. She also coauthored with Chris Clark the screenplay for *Lady Sings the Blues*, a biopic starring Ross as BILLIE HOLIDAY, for which she received an Oscar (Academy Award) nomination in 1972.

She married actor Paul Le Mat in 1978.

On becoming president of Motown Productions, de Passe was given a $10 million budget to develop better movie, theater, and television projects. The position and budget gave her a very high profile as a female executive in Hollywood. Although many observers made the stereotypical assumption that her relationship with Gordy was more than just a business partnership, de Passe denied it, claiming that she "would never have had to work so hard if I were Berry Gordy's old lady" (Ingham and Feldman, p. 193).

She produced successful television specials such as "Motown 25—Yesterday, Today, and Forever," which won de Passe the Peabody Award and Emmy for producing the best music/variety special of the year. In 1985 she was the executive producer of "Motown Returns to the Apollo" and won her second Emmy. She also backed several unsuccessful projects such as *The Last Dragon*, a 1985 film.

That same year she optioned Larry McMurtry's Pulitzer Prize–winning book *Lonesome Dove*, and in 1989 coproduced the highly successful television miniseries. It not only won de Passe another Emmy, but also brought $10 million in profits to Motown Industries and won Peabody and Golden Globe awards.

De Passe left Motown in 1988 and began her own production company, de Passe Entertainment, where she has produced award winning specials for all the major television networks, including "Small Sacrifices," an award winning four-hour miniseries; "Motown 30: What's Going On!"; "The Jacksons: An American Dream," another four hour miniseries; a sequel to "Lonesome Dove," "Return to Lonesome Dove"; and the comedy series *Sister, Sister*, which ran on ABC (1994–1995); and *The WB* (1995–1999).

FURTHER READING

Allen, Bonnie. "Suzanne de Passe: Motown's $10 Million Boss Lady." *Essence* 12 (September 1981): 89–92; 141–144.

Elias, Jaan. *Suzanne de Passe and Motown Productions* (1996).

Ingham, John N., and Feldman, Lynn B. *African-American Business Leaders: A Biographical Dictionary* (1994).

CLARANNE PERKINS

De Priest, Oscar Stanton (9 Mar. 1871–12 May 1951), politician, was born in Florence, Alabama, the son of Martha Karsner, a part-time laundress, and Neander R. De Priest, a teamster and farmer. His father, a former slave, joined the Republican Party. After a neighbor's lynching, the family moved to Salina, Kansas, in 1878. Young Oscar had sandy hair, blue eyes, and a light complexion and often fought over racial slurs made in his presence. After two years at Salina Normal School, he left home at seventeen, settling in Chicago. He apprenticed as a house painter and by 1905 had a successful contracting and real estate business. In 1898 he married Jessie L. Williams; they had one child.

De Priest was elected Cook County commissioner in 1904 and 1906 because he delivered a bloc of African American voters from the city's Second and Third wards for the Republican Party. He educated his constituency about city and county relief resources but lost the 1908 nomination over a dispute with the First District congressman Martin B. Madden. For the next few years he maneuvered among various factions, sometimes supporting Democrats over Republicans. He reconciled with Madden and backed white Republican candidates for alderman against African Americans running as independents in 1912 and 1914.

In 1915 the growing African American community united to elect De Priest to the city council. Significant support came from women, who had won the municipal ballot in 1913. As alderman, he introduced a civil rights ordinance and fought against job discrimination. Indicted in 1917 on charges of taking a bribe from a gambling establishment, De Priest claimed the money as a campaign contribution. He was successfully defended by Clarence Darrow but was persuaded not to run again. He campaigned as an independent in 1918 and 1919 but lost to black Republican nominees. In the 1919 race riots, his reputation was revived when, armed with pistols, he drove twice a day to the stockyards to supply his community with meat.

The riots helped De Priest renew ties to the Republican mayor, William Hale Thompson, and he was a delegate to the 1920 Republican National Convention. In 1924 he was elected Third Ward committeeman. His help in Thompson's 1927 election won De Priest an appointment as assistant

Illinois commerce commissioner. In the 1928 election he again ran successfully for Republican delegate and Third Ward committeeman. That same year he supported the renomination of Congressman Madden, who died shortly after the primary, and used his influence with the Thompson faction of the Republican party to win the nomination for Madden's seat. After he was nominated, he was indicted for alleged gambling connections and vote fraud, charges that his supporters maintained were politically motivated. De Priest refused to withdraw and won the election to represent the predominantly black First District. The case against him was subsequently dismissed for insufficient evidence.

De Priest became the first African American to serve in the U.S. Congress in twenty-eight years and the first from a northern state. He considered himself "congressman-at-large" for the nation's 12 million black Americans and promised to place a black cadet in West Point, fight for enforcement of the Fourteenth and Fifteenth Amendments, and secure work relief for the unemployed. But he vowed to "represent all people, both black and white."

While denying that he sought "social equality," De Priest used his position to secure the rights of citizenship for African Americans. When his wife's attendance at First Lady Lou Hoover's traditional tea for congressional wives in 1929 created controversy, De Priest used the publicity to promote a fund-raiser for the National Association for the Advancement of Colored People (NAACP). He was much in demand as a speaker, urging audiences to organize and to vote, even in the South, where threats were made against his life. Although the Great Depression, which began shortly after his arrival in Congress, lured his constituents toward the Democrats, he won reelection in 1930 and 1932. He opposed federal relief, preferring state and local measures.

De Priest sponsored a number of bills to benefit his constituents, including pensions for surviving former slaves and appropriations for African American schools in the District of Columbia. His most important legislative victory was an amendment to the 1933 bill creating the Civilian Conservation Corps barring discrimination based on race, color, or creed. After the infamous 1931 SCOTTSBORO BOYS case in which nine young African American men were sentenced to death after being convicted on questionable evidence by an all-white jury of raping two white women, De Priest called for a law to enable a trial to be transferred to another jurisdiction if the defendant was deemed not likely to get a fair trial. Warning that the country would suffer if one-tenth of its population were denied justice, he said, "If we had a right to exercise our franchise … as the constitution provides, I would not be the only Negro on this floor." The bill died in the Judiciary Committee, as did his proposal for an antilynching bill. He also fought unsuccessfully to integrate the House of Representatives restaurant, where he was served, but his staff was not.

By 1934 De Priest faced charges that his party was doing little to help African Americans hard hit by the Depression, and he lost to ARTHUR W. MITCHELL, the first African American Democrat elected to Congress. De Priest was vice chairman of the Cook County Republican Central Committee from 1932 to 1934, a delegate to the Republican National Convention in 1936, and alderman from the Third Ward in 1943–1947. He lost the 1947 election for alderman, partly because of charges of cooperating with the Democratic mayor. He continued in the real estate business with his son Oscar De Priest Jr. and died at his home in Chicago.

Skillful at organizing a coalition of black voters and using this bloc to pressure the dominant white political machine, De Priest was the forerunner of many local African American politicians in the latter part of the twentieth century. His six years in Congress enabled him to raise black political consciousness. Kenneth Eugene Mann, writing in the *Negro History Bulletin* in October 1972, noted that De Priest "took advantage of his opportunities and frequently created them."

FURTHER READING

The Arthur W. Mitchell Papers at the Chicago Historical Society have material on De Priest. For De Priest's speeches and resolutions in Congress, see the *Congressional Record*, 71st to 73rd Congresses.

Christopher, Maurine. *Black Americans in Congress* (1971; repr. 1976).

Grossman, James R. *Land of Hope: Chicago, Black Southerners, and the Great Migration* (1989).

Ragsdale, Bruce A., and Joel D. Treese. *Black Americans in Congress 1870–1989* (1990).

Obituaries: *New York Times* and *Chicago Tribune*, 13 May 1951; *Chicago Defender*, 19 May 1951.

This entry is taken from the *American National Biography* and is published here with the permission of the American Council of Learned Societies.

KRISTIE MILLER

Deal, Borden (12 Oct. 1922–22 Jan. 1985), journalist and fiction writer, was born in Pontotoc, Mississippi, the youngest of three children of Jimmie Anne (Smith) Deal and Borden Lee Deal, a black farmer who owned his own land. Originally named Loyse Youth Deal, the author Borden Deal grew up in Union County, Mississippi, near New Albany. His family struggled during the Depression, when his parents lost the family farm after the collapse of cotton as a commodity crop. One of President Franklin D. Roosevelt's economic rehabilitation programs helped the Deal family cope with their predicament by providing them with rental housing and work at a government-sponsored farming project in Enterprise, Mississippi. The family later moved to a similar community in Darden, Mississippi. Deal attended Macedonia Consolidated High School, located near Myrtle, Mississippi. In 1938, after his father's accidental death, Deal left his family to find work in various temporary jobs, including seasonal agriculture, millwork, and forest-fire fighting in the Pacific Northwest with the Civilian Conservation Corps. He also spent time working as a circus roustabout.

After a stint as an auditor for the U.S. Department of Labor from 1941 to 1942, Deal served from 1942 to 1945 in the U.S. Navy as an aviator cadet and (after a bout of pneumonia curtailed his future as a pilot) as a radar instructor, based in Ft. Lauderdale, Florida. After the war Borden enrolled in the University of Alabama at Tuscaloosa, majoring in English and studying creative writing with Hudson Strode. Deal also studied the psychological theories of Carl Jung, which would heavily influence his fiction. Deal's first publication came in 1948, when his short story "Exodus" was awarded first prize in *Tomorrow* magazine's national college writer's contest and was selected for the annual anthology *Best American Short Stories of 1949*. Receiving a B.A. at the University of Alabama in 1949, Deal pursued graduate study in 1950 at Mexico City College while also working as a freelance journalist. While in Mexico, Deal married Lillian Slobtotosky. The marriage soon ended in divorce, having yielded one child. In 1952 Deal married fellow writer Babs Hodges, and the couple eventually had three children. The Deals would divorce in 1975.

After returning from Mexico, Deal worked in a variety of temporary occupations: as a correspondent for Association Films in New York City, a skip tracer for a Birmingham, Alabama, auto finance company, a telephone solicitor for a New Orleans newspaper, and a copywriter for radio stations in Mobile,

Alabama. By 1954 Deal was writing full time, and in 1956 his first novel, *Walk through the Valley*, was published; it received an honorable mention in the American Library Association Liberty and Justice Awards contest. The next year saw the publication of his best-known novel, *Dunbar's Cove*, which explored the Tennessee Valley Authority's effect on the lives of small farmers in the South; the book was subsequently republished by *Reader's Digest* in a condensed version. Also in 1957 Deal was awarded a Guggenheim Fellowship for creative writing.

Other significant Deal novels soon followed: *The Insolent Breed* (1959), which concerned the music-making of rural white southerners; *Dragon's Wine* (1960), which explored the mythic nature of the interrelationships within a small southern community; *A Long Way to Go* (1965), a symbolic portrayal of several children's coming of age; *The Tobacco Men* (1965), which was based upon notes originally made by the novelist Theodore Dreiser and which portrayed the struggles over tobacco between landowners and "nightriders" in late-nineteenth- and early-twentieth-century Kentucky; and *Interstate* (1970), a fictional account of conflicts between environmentalists and developers over the plight of a swamp hosting the last surviving population of ivory-billed woodpeckers. Deal also produced a trilogy of novels—*The Loser* (1964), *The Advocate* (1968), and *The Winner* (1973)—that examined the contrast between traditional and modern value systems in the New South. Forming another trilogy (which Deal called the "Olden Times" series) were three other novels—*The Least One* (1967), *The Other Room* (1974), and the overtly autobiographical *There Were Also Strangers* (1985)—that focused on Deal's own youthful experience of growing up in a Deep South farming community during the Depression era. Deal also wrote novels under the pseudonyms Loyse Borden, Lee Borden, and Leigh Borden, as well as erotica under the pseudonym Her, Him, and Us.

Deal's short stories were published in many magazines and literary journals, including *Saturday Evening Post*, *McCall's*, *Collier's*, *Good Housekeeping*, and *Southwest Review*; in high school and college textbooks; and in such compilations as *Best American Short Stories of 1962*, *Best Detective Stories of the Year*, and *The Wonderful World of Dogs*. One of his most often anthologized short stories was "Antaeus," which reflects Deal's belief in the healing power of nature and the importance of the urban poor remaining in contact with nature. Additional writings by Deal—poems and reviews—appeared in various periodicals, including the *New York Times Book Review* and the *Saturday Review*.

Deal's fiction was translated into more than twenty languages. In 1963 he received the Alabama Library Association Literary Award, and in 1981 the University of Alabama designated Deal as a Sesquicentennial Scholar during that school's 150th anniversary celebration. Deal attended the MacDowell Colony and was a member of the Authors Guild, the PEN American Center, the Tennessee Squire Association, and the Sarasota Writers' Roundtable. Deal's work was adapted for the stage and for the entertainment media (radio, film, and television). For example, *The Insolent Breed* was an inspiration for the 1966 Broadway musical *A Joyful Noise*, while *Dunbar's Cove* was cited by the film director Elia Kazan as a major influence on the screenplay for Kazan's 1960 movie *Wild River*.

During his writing career, Borden Deal lived in Scottsboro and Tuscaloosa, Alabama, and in Osprey, Venice, and Sarasota, Florida. He died in Sarasota of a heart attack. His manuscripts and other literary materials are housed at Boston University.

Deal was a prolific author who wrote approximately twenty novels and one hundred short stories, most of which are set in the American South. Several critics have commented that Deal chronicled the twentieth-century history of the southeastern United States as thoroughly and insightfully as many more acclaimed southern authors. Deal himself believed that the enduring value of his work lay in the fact that it represents "the progressive panorama of the 'real' South (not the 'Gothic' South so beloved by the literary critics).... If someone two hundred years from now wants to know about the *real* South, of people working and living, they'll have to go to my books."

The critic John C. Calhoun, summarizing the literary achievement of Borden Deal, stated that Deal produced "carefully crafted regional novels that treat real-life social problems ... through a combination of believable character portraiture and absorbing local color."

FURTHER READING

Deal, Borden. "Storytelling as Symbolism," *Southwest Review* 53 (1968.)

Calhoun, John C. "Borden Deal: Mississippi Novelist," in *Notes on Mississippi Writers* (1976).

Hitchcock, Bert. "Borden Deal," in *Lives of Mississippi Authors, 1817–1967*, ed. James B. Lloyd (1981).

TED OLSON

Dean, Dora (1872–13 Dec. 1949), dancer and vaudevillian was born in Covington, Kentucky, in 1872. According to her husband, Charles E. Johnson, Dean was born Dora Babbige, and her brother, Clarence Babbige, served as a judge in Kentucky during the Reconstruction period. By the mid-1880s her family moved to Indiana, and Dean found employment as a nursemaid in nearby Ohio.

Dean entered show business as a "statue girl" in *The Creole Show*, a popular touring production staged by Sam T. Jack. Dean possessed a striking figure, a pleasing smile, and a quality of warmth and personal charm that she was able to project from the stage; billed as "The Black Venus," she struck dramatic poses during musical numbers and made a hit with the audience. Paired with talented soft-shoe dancer Charles E. Johnson, Dean also became known for her performance of the cakewalk, a dance developed by blacks in the antebellum South, but virtually unknown elsewhere. Johnson and Dean's rendition of the cakewalk made them the stars of *The Creole Show*, and as the show traveled, the team played an instrumental role in igniting the cakewalk craze that swept the country at the turn of the century. Johnson and Dean married during the 1893 World's Fair in Chicago. The same year they left the Dean's Creole Company and entered vaudeville with their own act.

By 1897 the team was one of the few black acts booked on the Orpheum circuit, the most prestigious and highly remunerative chain of theaters in the western half of the country. Johnson and Dean were billed as a "song and dance" act, but their version of song and dance differed sharply from vaudeville convention. Most African American song and dance teams comprised two men, often former minstrel players, who dressed in ragged clothes and performed material steeped in self-mocking racial stereotypes. Johnson and Dean by contrast cultivated an image of genteel elegance and dignity. Billed as "The King and Queen of Colored Aristocracy," they created a sensation by being the first vaudevillians, black or white, to appear in full formal evening wear. Dean's tailor-made gowns were the stuff of theatrical news, as were estimates of their cost (ranging from several hundred to a thousand dollars). Charles Johnson sported top hat and tails, wore gloves and a monocle, and carried a cane. The team's innovative costuming sparked a trend in vaudeville, particularly among the leading ladies.

In 1897 Johnson was among the first to use steel taps in his shoes, and in 1901, the team added another surprise to their act: a strobe light. The fluttering illumination underscored the artful nature of their performance, as the light seemed to capture the dancers in a rapid sequence of graceful poses. The overall appeal of the act was based in fact on its artfulness, a product of Johnson and Dean's powerful stage presence, genteel image, and use of innovative theatrical devices. Neither actually sang. Instead, they "talked" their songs, interspersing the verses with Johnson's dance turns. Dean posed, as she had in her days as a statue girl.

By the conclusion of their first Orpheum tour, Johnson and Dean had established themselves as stars. In the summer of 1897, they were the first black act to headline at Tony Pastor's, the most prestigious independent vaudeville house in the country. At around the same time, Dean's picture appeared, captioned as "The Sweet Caporal Girl," in a cigarette advertisement, and BERT WILLIAMS and GEORGE WALKER included a paean to Dean in their act:

Say have you ever seen Miss Dora Dean
She is the finest girl you've ever seen
I'm a-goin' to try and make this gal my queen,
Next Sunday morning I'm goin' to marry Dora
Dean.

In 1901, having established themselves on the American stage, Johnson and Dean made their first tour of Europe, where they received an enthusiastic reception. In Berlin, artist Ernest Hellman paid Dean a week's salary to pose for him and painted a life-sized canvas of her performing a cakewalk strut. The portrait was displayed to appreciative crowds at the Paris Expo in 1902. Johnson deemed it a faithful likeness and kept a reproduction of it until his death.

After further American appearances, the team returned to Europe in 1903. Here they were such a success that until 1914, they rarely returned to the United States. Highlights of their career in Europe include two months as headliners at the Palace Theatre in London beginning on 15 January 1904, followed by annual two-month bookings; repeated engagements in the major cities of Germany, France, Austria, and Hungary; and in May of 1907, performances in St. Petersburg, where the runaway success of the African American Russian dance specialist Ida Forsyne was making the city a magnet for black performers. Johnson and Dean also spent six months touring Australia. The team made occasional appearances in the United States, with bookings at prestigious New York venues. However, while the black press continued to praise the act, comments from white reviewers (always hostile to Europeans, and increasingly hostile to blacks) took on a critical edge because they did not think the duo was "black" enough. On 2 October 1909 *Variety* encouraged Dean to "forget about the European adulation" and drop a new Hungarian number from the act.

Johnson and Dean embarked on their last Continental tour in 1913. The act now included one of the first jazz bands to play in Europe (featuring Peggie Holland on drums and Kid Coles at the piano) and the comedy dance team of Rufus Greenlee and Teddy Drayton. The formation of the Johnson and Dean Company was a significant departure for its principals, who for a decade had not shared the stage or billing with other performers. The expanded, substantially modernized act made a success of its initial fourteen-country tour. According to Rufus Greenlee, however, the genteel lady and gentleman of the stage did not enjoy an amicable private life. In 1914, when World War I compelled Johnson and Dean to return to the United States, they terminated their professional and personal relationship.

Dean, now in her forties, embarked on the second phase of her career. Beginning in 1914, she headed a "pick" (short for the offensive term "pickaninny") act; Dean, the featured adult performer, was accompanied by three African American girls. Although a number of black women (May Whitman, for example) had performed with "picks," this type of act was usually headed by a white woman, making Dean's choice a novelty. For two years, Dora Dean and Company (later, Dora Dean and her Fancy Phantoms) played the Loew, a respectable circuit, but a far cry from her headline appearances with Johnson. Dean then accepted a chorus role in the musical production *Darktown Follies of 1916*, and in 1922, she starred in the Lafayette Theater's production of Flournoy Miller's *Going White*, a play about a family of mixed racial extraction. Neither of these later ventures was particularly successful (in fact, *Darktown Follies* was a flop). Nor did Dean become involved with any of the black musicals that abounded on Broadway in the 1920s.

In 1930 Dean went to the West Coast to take a supporting role in the film *Georgia Rose* (1930). While in Hollywood, Dean reunited with Charles Johnson and returned with him to his hometown of Minneapolis, where he had made a modest second career in real estate. In 1936 Johnson and Dean made a handful of comeback appearances at Connie's Inn in Harlem. Vaudeville was on the wane, however, and Dean's health was weakening.

She stopped performing before a leg injury forced Johnson from the stage in 1942. Dora Dean Johnson died in Hennepin, Minnesota, in 1949.

Dean's stylish, dignified manner of self-presentation exerted a powerful influence on younger African American women on the stage, most notably AIDA OVERTON WALKER. Johnson and Dean's example also served as inspiration to Rufus Greenlee and Teddy Drayton, pioneers of the "class act" jazz dance style, which emphasizes a smooth, seemingly effortless elegance in both dress and movement. Remembered less as a singer and dancer than as a captivating stage presence, Dean brought a new, refined image of African American womanhood to the stage.

FURTHER READING

Sampson, Henry T. *Blacks in Black and White* (1995).

Sampson, Henry T. "Cakewalk King," *Ebony* (February 1953).

Sampson, Henry T. *The Ghost Walks: A Chronological History of Blacks in Show Business, 1865–1910* (1988).

Stearns, Marshall, and Jean Stearns. *Jazz Dance: The Story of American Vernacular Dance* (1968).

JOANNA WOOL

Dean, Harry Foster (20 Nov. 1864–1935), adventurer, mariner, and African emigrationist, was born to Susan Cuffe and John Dean in Philadelphia, Pennsylvania. Harry Foster Dean followed the family profession when he decided to become a seafarer. By the age of thirteen he was on an around-the-world cruise captained by his Uncle Silas. A decade later he had made his way to Southampton, England, where he was mentored by a Captain Forbes. He later reported that he won his captain's license in that port, beginning a new phase in his life. According to Dean, his mother, Susan, was a granddaughter of the black Yankee PAUL CUFFE. As the progeny of the Cuffe family, Dean considered himself a black aristocrat. Since Cuffe was a merchant and back-to-Africa advocate, Dean dreamed of reversing the effects and trajectories of the Middle Passage and removing himself to his ancestral continent of origin. Much of what is known about his career, whether factual or fanciful, revolves around this ambition and his proselytizing it.

By 1900 discussion of the immigration of New World and European blacks to West Africa was more than a century old. In that year, Dean purchased a Norwegian merchant ship called the *Pedro Gorino*, which he sailed into Cape Town toward the end of 1900. In a series of adventures captured in his subsequent narrative of the same name, Dean went into business in Cape Town. Even as the Anglo-Boer War raged on, Dean was partaking in Capetonian commerce and scouting for lands hospitable for resettlement by American and European blacks. Using a crew made up of African and African Antillean men, Captain Dean plied the seas of Delagoa Bay in Lourenço Marques port in nearby Mozambique. Landing there he had conversations with local inhabitants and British consular officials, fueling his ambitions.

Next on his itinerary was a visit to the Pondoland region of South Africa's Eastern Cape. Replying to a request issued by the African Methodist Episcopal (AME) Church bishop LEVI JENKINS COPPIN, a recent arrival to South Africa, Dean was enlisted along with the Reverend Metinso, a local Xhosa-speaking minister, to construct schools and churches in the Pondoland area. Support for the endeavor was initially forthcoming from Pondo paramount Sigcawu until the enterprise was curtailed by the internecine conflict between Pondo and Mpondomise.

In 1901 Dean joined an effort initiated by Coppin and the Sierra Leonean émigré journalist F. Z. Peregrino, editor of the local *South African Spectator*, to promote unity among rival local communities in the face of the dual threats of colonization and competition. Despite the men's best efforts, however, it proved unavailing. Though he was able to secure a concession from Basutoland (Lesotho) paramount Lerothodi, who had a great desire to see learning institutions erected, Dean was defeated by circumstances and then by his competitors who ultimately forced him to sell his property and quit Southern Africa altogether. Returning to the United States from Liberia, Dean made several attempts to get back into the Africa trade business, but was prevented from realizing his fervent hope of returning. He lived in Illinois and California before finally settling in Chicago in 1928. It was there that the University of Chicago social scientist George H. Mead interceded on Dean's behalf by asking the Wisconsin-born graduate student Sterling North to help him assemble and write of his life, dictated from his recollections.

FURTHER READING

Harry Dean's diaries are held by the DuSable Museum, Museum of African American History, Chicago.

Dean, Harry Foster. *The Pedro Gorino, the Adventures of a Negro Sea-Captain in Africa and on the Seven Seas in His Attempts to Found an Ethiopian Empire* (1929).

Burger, John S. "Captain Harry Dean: Pan-Negro-Nationalist in South Africa," *International Journal of African Historical Studies* 9.1 (1976): 83–90.

Cobley, Alan Gregor. "'Far from Home': The Origins and Significance of the Afro-Caribbean Community in South Africa to 1930," *Journal of Southern African Studies* 18.2 (June 1992): 349–370.

"Trader Dean." *Time*, 10 June 1929.

DAVID H. ANTHONY III

Dean, Jennie (1852–3 May 1913), educator, was born enslaved in Prince William County, Virginia, the eldest of four children of Charles and Annie Dean. She was named Jane Serepta but was called Jennie by her family and Miss Jennie by those on whose behalf she labored. It is probable that her only formal education was obtained in a school established by the Freedmen's Bureau when the Civil War ended.

Dean's father was a literate and ambitious man who, immediately after the end of the Civil War, contracted to buy a farm. Within a short time he died, and Dean assumed responsibility for the support of the family. She found employment as a domestic in Washington, D.C., and by living frugally, amassed the funds to pay off the mortgage. She also provided tuition for her siblings, at least one of whom became a teacher.

Dean became an active member of the 19th Street Baptist Church, the oldest black Baptist church in the nation's capital. Concerned about the paucity of religious institutions in the area where she spent her childhood, she also played a major role in the establishment of four black churches in Prince William County. These churches were used to provide elementary reading and writing classes as well as cooking and sewing lessons for children in the area. Out of this effort, in which Dean assisted, her vision of establishing a school was born.

Virginia's public schools for blacks were inadequately funded, the semesters were less than six months long, the teachers poorly educated, the physical plants unsound, and books and other necessary items were in short supply. In the counties surrounding Prince William, there were approximately twelve-thousand school-aged children whose educational needs were not satisfactorily addressed. Disturbed by these conditions but encouraged by the work of BOOKER T. WASHINGTON at Tuskegee Institute, Dean envisioned a residential facility that would provide instruction for blacks in northern Virginia. With the assistance and encouragement of black ministers, in 1888 Dean began her decade-long fund-raising efforts.

Dean, who was by no means wealthy, used much of her meager earnings to purchase land and equipment for the school. With only $60 of her savings and $40 in donations, she contracted to purchase land that cost $2,650. Her first fundraiser, a countywide picnic, raised $75. Additional monies were acquired as a result of Dean's speaking in churches, before women's groups and fraternal organizations, and at suffrage meetings. One of the largest donations Dean received was $12,000 from the women's rights activist Susan B. Anthony. Other whites with whom she had formed positive relationships also contributed; however, much of the money was supplied by struggling African Americans who wanted a better life for their children. Blacks with no money to donate gave their time, farm produce, and their labor, clearing the land and constructing buildings.

The Manassas Industrial School was chartered by the state on 7 October 1893. The first building on the campus, Howland Hall, was named for Emily Howland, a northerner active in the suffrage movement, who donated $2,500. FREDERICK DOUGLASS was the featured speaker at the dedication service held on 3 September 1894. The school was to be a residential facility for children over the age of fourteen, offering both industrial and academic course work. Many black educators of the era, cognizant that most philanthropic whites believed that industrial education was the only suitable model for blacks, did not outwardly admit that academic courses were being taught. Dean's institution, however, offered mathematics, science, geography, physiology, music, literature, and English, in addition to carpentry, blacksmithing, shoemaking, cooking, sewing, and other trades. Dean wanted her students to be self-sufficient, and for that reason some classes were not restricted by gender; girls were allowed to study carpentry, and boys, cooking.

Dean opened her school with six students. For the first year the staff, three teachers and a principal, received room and board but no salary. In less than a year there were 75 students, and more than 150 were enrolled by 1900. While most public schools for blacks were open between three and six months of the year, the Manassas Industrial School's semester was from October through May. As was the case at Hampton and Tuskegee, poor students could work on campus in lieu of tuition payments.

From the inception of her dream until her death, Dean never wavered in her devotion to the education of northern Virginia blacks. With missionary zeal, she devoted all of her efforts and resources to the establishment and maintenance of the Manassas Industrial School. On more than one occasion, fire destroyed essential buildings on campus, leading Dean to intensify her fund-raising efforts. Dean traveled to northern states, where she worked as a domestic and solicited funds from wealthy whites. The school survived as a private institution for twenty-five years after Dean's death and educated more than sixty-five hundred students from Virginia, Washington, D.C., and other states. It evolved into an accredited high school, funded and operated by the state of Virginia. A museum was later established on the site of the original school, and an elementary school was named in honor of Dean.

The word *educate* has its roots in a Latin word meaning to raise or lift up. Jennie Dean, an unmarried childless woman, died in 1913, apparently never having taught in a classroom. At Manassas Industrial School she worked as a matron in the girls' dormitory, served on the board of trustees, and was the primary fund-raiser for the school. For her Herculean efforts she deserves the title of educator.

FURTHER READING

Koman, Rita G. "Legacy for Learning: Jennie Dean and the Manassas Industrial School," *OAH Magazine of History* 7 (Summer 1993).

Koman, Rita G. "Two Tales of Southern Success: Diversity Helps Chart a Community," *OAH Magazine of History* 16 (Winter 2002).

Lewis, Stephen Johnson. *Undaunted Faith—The Life Story of Jennie Dean: Missionary, Teacher, Crusader, Builder: Founder of the Manassas Industrial School* (1942).

Workers of the Writers' Program of the Works Progress Administration in the State of Virginia. *The Negro in Virginia* (1994).

DONNA TYLER HOLLIE

Dean, Lillian Harris "Pig Foot Mary" (1870–1929),

entrepreneur in the food service and real estate arenas, was born Lillian Harris in the Mississippi Delta. She made a small fortune selling pigs' feet and other southern culinary delicacies on the streets of Harlem, first out of an old baby carriage, later out of a steam table attached to a newsstand owned by John Dean, who became her husband. She multiplied this small fortune through shrewd real estate investments and retired comfortably in California, where she died in 1929. According to the journalist ROI OTTLEY, she arrived in New York in 1901 and first worked as a domestic. She soon began selling pigs' feet in the San Juan Hill section of Manhattan, which was then a large African American neighborhood (before Harlem gained prominence) and later became the site of the Lincoln Center for the Performing Arts. DUKE ELLINGTON immortalized the rough and tumble San Juan Hill neighborhood in a lively, blues-inflected composition of the same name.

Ottley claims Harris moved her business to Harlem around 1917, setting up shop on the corner of Lenox Avenue (later MALCOLM X Boulevard, though commonly known by both names) and West 135th Street, where Dean had his newsstand. This corner was important for cultural and civic reasons, as it was the home to both Harlem Hospital and the Schomburg Center for Research in Black Culture. The historic Harlem YMCA was nearby on 135th Street. (The corner also had an important culinary history, from Dean's pigs' feet cart up through Pan Pan's, a long-established and famous soul food lunch counter that burned down in 2004.) The New York City Department of City Planning devoted a Web page on its "Virtual Tour of Malcolm X Boulevard" to "Pig Foot Mary's," the "tiny feed stand where she sold her famous boiled pigs' feet." The virtual tour goes on to call her "one of Harlem's shrewdest entrepreneurs."

A traditional southern dish thought by some African American traditions to be good luck when eaten on New Years' Day, pigs' feet was not the only dish Dean sold. According to JAMES WELDON JOHNSON in his 1925 article "The Making of Harlem," Mary Dean, whom "everybody who knows the corner ... knows," later also sold fried chicken and hot corn at her stand, and many pedestrians were "tempted by the smell" (637). Johnson, the great poet, memoirist, novelist, journalist, and activist, also wrote about Dean in *Black Manhattan* (1930), where he described the rush of post–World War I Harlem real estate transactions, which effectively amounted to the ethnic transfer of most of Harlem from white to black: "All classes bought. It was not an unknown thing for a colored washerwoman to walk into a real-estate office and lay down several thousand dollars on a house. There was Mrs. Mary Dean, known as 'Pig Foot Mary'.... She paid $42,000 for a five-story apartment house ... which was sold later to a colored undertaker for $72,000" (154). The purchase and sale took place in 1917 and 1923, respectively. Presumably there were a few similar deals.

According to Ottley, Dean retired with a fortune of $375,000 (worth approximately $4 million in 2005, adjusted for inflation). Though Dean was apparently a great cook who was also shrewd and charismatic, the role of her husband in her success has not been commented on in most of the anecdotes about her, which tend to emphasize her skill in business. John Dean, who already owned a newsstand on the important Harlem corner when she arrived, certainly must have played some role, and Ottley notes that John Dean encouraged his wife's investments. Lillian Dean, described by Ottley as being physically large with a deep voice, was perhaps an inspiration for the formidable character of Mary Rambo, a strong and independent African American woman who rescues the narrator in RALPH ELLISON's *Invisible Man* (1952). The character as originally written in a section published a few years after the novel seems to have more in common with Pig Foot Mary (more fire and gusto) than does the somewhat milder sketch of the character published in the novel. Pig Foot Mary also was a minor character in the 1997 historical gangster film *Hoodlum*, a major Hollywood production and respectable box office success (starring LAURENCE FISHBURNE and Tim Roth). Pig Foot Mary was played by Loretta Devine, a highly regarded actress of the late twentieth century.

FURTHER READING

Johnson, James Weldon. *Black Manhattan* (1930).

Johnson, James Weldon. "The Making of Harlem," *The Survey Graphic* (Mar 1925).

New York City Department of City Planning. "Malcolm X. Boulevard: Virtual Tour of Living Landmarks and Lenox Shadows." Available at www.nyc.gov/html/dcp/html/mxb/mxsite47.shtml.

Ottley, Roi. *New World A-Coming* (1943)

PAUL DEVLIN

Deas, Edmund H. (10 June 1855–1 Aug. 1915), politician and public official, was born in Georgetown, South Carolina, the son of a slave mother owned by the white planter E. H. Deas of Charleston, where the youth lived in 1860. Little is known of his childhood or early education in the small Sumter County town of Stateburg, where Edmund Deas moved after the Civil War and lived until the early 1870s.

By 1874, Deas had moved to Darlington, South Carolina, where he became active in Republican Party politics. Though not yet able to vote, he served as precinct chairman and campaign worker that year for the black Republican U.S. congressman JOSEPH H. RAINEY, seeking reelection in the 2nd district, and by 1876, had become a federal constable in South

Carolina. In 1878 he became chairman of his party's congressional district committee, serving for eight years, and in 1880 he was elected both Darlington County chairman and member of the state executive committee. During this period he held a number of local offices: county supervisor, deputy marshal, and deputy county treasurer. He appears to have been nominated by President Chester Arthur as postmaster of Florence, South Carolina, in early 1883, but never assumed the office.

In 1883 Deas left Darlington to attend Howard University's law department at Washington, DC. While a student during the following year, he was employed as a clerk at the Interior Department's Pension Bureau, at an annual salary of $1,000. In 1884 Deas left Howard to return to South Carolina, campaigning as the Republican nominee for Congress against the incumbent Democrat George William Dargan in the 6th congressional district. Deas lost overwhelmingly, drawing 3,628 votes to Dargan's 10,814. When Dargan retired in 1890, Deas ran as the Republican nominee a second time, losing to the Democrat Eli Thomas Stackhouse.

Deas served as Darlington County's Republican party chairman for two decades and, as his influence increased, he became known as the "Duke of Darlington." The chronicler J. J. Pipkin, in a brief sketch (p. 60), describes Deas as "the most active and aggressive Republican in the state." A delegate to every national convention from 1884 to 1908, Deas generally represented the 6th congressional district, serving as an at-large state delegate in 1892 and 1908. In 1892 he was among a handful of black delegates chosen to notify President Harrison of his renomination; in 1896 and again in 1900, he traveled to Canton, Ohio, to notify William McKinley, the Republican nominee. Three times he was a candidate for state presidential elector. In 1902 he was elected South Carolina state party chairman, defeating the challenger John R. Tolbert to win reelection in 1906.

Deas and his wife, Beulah Anna, were married in 1906. They had one daughter, Julia, born in 1914.

As a powerful figure in Republican circles, Deas was appointed twice as U.S. deputy collector of internal revenue for South Carolina, first serving under President Harrison (1889–1894). In 1897 Deas was reappointed deputy collector by President William McKinley, and held that position until after McKinley's death in 1901.

Deas was also able to shepherd appointments of black Republicans during both the Harrison and McKinley administrations. One of the men whose names he proposed in 1892 was the schoolteacher

Frazier B. Baker, who was appointed and served for a year as postmaster at his hometown of Effingham, in Darlington County. In 1897 Deas again proposed Baker as postmaster, but this time at all-white Lake City; despite strong opposition from local citizens and Democratic leaders, Baker began work in the fall of 1897. Citizens responded by boycotting the post office, which was burned in January 1898.

Despite death threats and several shooting incidents, Deas encouraged Baker to remain in Lake City, where postal inspectors helped open a temporary post office in a converted schoolhouse, which also housed Baker's family. On 22 February 1898, as the family slept, the post office building was set afire by a band of armed men, who shot Baker and his infant daughter to death when he tried to escape, and wounded Baker's wife and three other children.

Deas and other South Carolina officials visited President McKinley soon after Baker's murder to press for a federal investigation. Eleven men from Lake City were tried in Charleston 1899 on federal charges of conspiracy in Baker's death, but none were convicted. No state charges were ever brought.

Deas died at age sixty at his home in Darlington. The home he purchased in 1905 still stands; it was added to the National Register of Historic Places in 1989.

FURTHER READING

Gatewood, Willard B., Jr. *Theodore Roosevelt and the Art of Controversy* (1970).

Pipkin, J. J. *The Story of a Rising Race: The Negro in Revelation* (1902).

BENJAMIN R. JUSTESEN

DeBaptiste, George (1814?–22 Feb. 1875), abolitionist and businessman, was born in Fredericksburg, Virginia, the son of John DeBaptiste, a businessman, and Frances "Franky" (maiden name unknown). Although the details of DeBaptiste's early life are uncertain, he appears to have traveled to Richmond, Virginia, as a youth, where he learned to barber and where, perhaps in 1829, as a free black he first helped a slave escape. While still in Virginia, he married his first wife, Maria Lucinda Lee, a slave, and bought her freedom. DeBaptiste subsequently remarried and had two children; his second wife's name is unknown. As a young man he demonstrated strong loyalty to his family, who remained in Fredericksburg. On two separate occasions in the 1820s he financially secured the property of two sisters when they faced significant debt.

Between 1836 and 1838 DeBaptiste moved to Madison, Indiana, where he barbered, engaged in a number of other business enterprises, and served as a conductor for the Underground Railroad. Although the number of slaves he directly assisted is unknown, DeBaptiste gained a reputation as an abolitionist and conductor by crossing the Ohio River into Kentucky and escorting fugitive slaves into Indiana and Ohio. From there they would go to Michigan and eventually Canada. His reputation as a conductor drew the ire of local whites. Probably as a result of his notoriety, the state of Indiana prosecuted DeBaptiste for residing in the state without paying the bond required of free blacks. He was saved from expulsion and possible sale into slavery by Stephen C. Stevens, a former member of the Indiana Supreme Court and prominent white attorney who opposed slavery. Stevens argued against the order expelling DeBaptiste, claiming that it was unconstitutional and did not specify his state of origin (where he was to be returned) as the law required. The court agreed only that the order was defective and allowed DeBaptiste to remain a resident.

While trading goods between Madison and Cincinnati, DeBaptiste met General William Henry Harrison and became Harrison's personal servant during the 1840 presidential campaign. After the inauguration of President Harrison, DeBaptiste was a White House steward, attending the president until his death in 1841. He then returned to Madison and worked as a barber for seven years until he found the atmosphere too hostile and moved farther north to Detroit, Michigan.

In Detroit DeBaptiste quickly became a leader in the black community. He bought an interest in a local barbershop and accepted a position as the chief clerk and salesman for a wholesale clothier. While living in Detroit he belonged to a secret society against slavery variously called the Order of the Men of Oppression, African-American Mysteries, and the Order of Emancipation. He also served as president of the black Union League and continued to participate in Underground Railroad operations. A letter to FREDERICK DOUGLASS, dated 4 November 1854, demonstrates his commitment: "all the good news I have, is that the Underground Railroad Company is doing a very large business at this time…. We have had, within the last ten or fifteen days, fifty-three first class passengers landed at this point, by the Express train from the South" (*Black Abolitionist Papers*, frame 0230).

DeBaptiste also tried many different business pursuits while living in Detroit. After Robert Banks closed his clothing store in 1850, DeBaptiste purchased William Lee's bakery and ran it for a number of years. His next venture after selling the bakery was buying a steamboat, *T. Whitney*. DeBaptiste employed a white captain because Michigan law did not allow a black man to hold a steamboat license. After selling the steamer, he went into the catering business. During the Civil War he and John D. Richards helped raise a black regiment for Michigan. DeBaptiste and Richards served in the regiment as sutlers, spending six months of 1864 in South Carolina. DeBaptiste returned to Detroit and to catering, later opening a restaurant, an ice-cream parlor, and finally, in 1874, a country house restaurant in Hamtramck. In 1867 his realty holdings in Detroit were valued at $10,000.

In addition to his business ventures, DeBaptiste stayed active in community affairs, using his business success to help those less fortunate. He served as a temporary agent for the Freedmen's Association after the war, gathering supplies for freedmen's schools in Louisiana. His obituary in the *Detroit Advertiser and Tribune* credits him with working to have black children receive the same education as whites and to have them admitted to the public schools. He also helped organize a large celebration of the passage of the Fifteenth Amendment in Detroit's black community. DeBaptiste died in Detroit.

A prominent member of the black community in Detroit, DeBaptiste was counted among its most wealthy figures. Throughout a variety of jobs and business ventures including being a hack, barbering, working as a personal servant, catering, and clerking, DeBaptiste remained an active abolitionist and assisted fugitive slaves in their flight northward.

FURTHER READING

Fitzgerald, Ruth Coder. *A Different Story* (1979).
Hayden, Robert. *History of the Negro in Michigan* (1957)
Katzman, David M. *Before the Ghetto* (1973).
Thornbrough, Emma Lou. *The Negro in Indiana* (1957).
Obituary: *Detroit Advertiser and Tribune*, 23 Feb. 1875.
This entry is taken from the *American National Biography* and is published here with the permission of the American Council of Learned Societies.

DAVID F. HERR

DeBaptiste, John (1740–3 Sept. 1804), soldier, sailor, and shipbuilder during the War of Independence, was born free in the British colony of St. Kitts of mixed race parentage. Little is known about his early life. Prior to adulthood he became literate, fluent in French and English, and he trained as a skilled craftsman in building dwellings and ships. As a free person of color in one of the older sugar colonies, he would have benefited from an increasing emigration of whites and, by 1745, a plantation system characterized by a high level of absenteeism by white landowners. These factors contributed to the growth of a small colored elite, financed largely by credit given by white relatives but still facing legal and de facto discrimination. For example, until 1830 the laws of St. Kitts prohibited free people of color from attending the colony's few public schools, although they paid taxes to fund them.

As a sailor DeBaptiste earned a steady income, an accomplishment many free people of color failed to attain. Free black mariners were vital to stable households and free black communities. Their wages allowed them to contribute to the schools, churches, benevolent societies, and fraternal orders that emerged as the cornerstones of black society. Furthermore, black seamen fashioned an intricate network of communication that linked the communities constituting the African diaspora. His maritime vocation provided wages, an expanded worldview, and a means to disperse his knowledge of the wider world among others.

DeBaptiste emigrated from St. Kitts to Virginia around 1766, near the time the two British plantation colonies established a trade relationship. The implementation of trade between the colonies as well as the date of his arrival in this North American British colony probably corresponded to the economic and social upheavals associated with the end of the Seven Years' War, when the colony saw a marked decrease in the population of whites while that of free blacks increased.

Records of the war mention a ship's captain named "Baptist," one of the several renderings of the family name. Though it is not certain whether DeBaptiste served in any maritime capacity, he had to have had some firsthand experience with the war in its Caribbean theater. The war's end resulted in tightening legal restrictions for free people of color in St. Kitts who competed economically with working-class whites, which may have contributed to his decision to emigrate.

Settling in the free black community of Fredericksburg, Virginia, DeBaptiste became one of its well-known residents, noted for the construction of many of the city's buildings. When the War of Independence began, DeBaptiste used his skills as a shipbuilder and sailor to support the colonists' pursuit of independence. In 1776 he assisted in the construction of the American warship *Dragon* and served as part of the ship's crew as it patrolled the Rappahannock River and fought battles in the Chesapeake Bay. Approximately 140 black men served in Virginia's navy during the war to defend the strategically significant region. DeBaptiste served in the Continental Army as well and received a pension for his military service at the end of the war.

DeBaptiste's service on the side of the American colonists during the war may be explained by his early life in St. Kitts. The year prior to his migration from the colony, the residents of the island engaged in riotous behavior in reaction to the Stamp Act. The vehement rejection of the Stamp Act by the island's residents made St. Kitts one of the few British possessions the American colonies did not boycott. DeBaptiste was exposed to colonial protests against the Crown prior to his arrival in Virginia and exposure to the rhetoric of its patriots. DeBaptiste's service in the military would have been enhanced by his command of both French and English. He certainly would have had the ability to communicate with the sailors of the French fleet accompanying Admiral François de Grasse at the battle of Yorktown. Also he had firsthand information crucial to the voyages of the ships supplying the war effort, many of which sailed from Virginia to the Dutch island of St. Eustatius as well as to St. Kitts.

After the war DeBaptiste raised a family and established several business concerns in Fredericksburg. He married a local freeborn woman of mixed race, Francis Campbell, who was known as Franky. The couple had at least seven children: Benjamin, John, William, Edward, George, Frances, and Polly. There is evidence that suggests that DeBaptiste and Campbell had a highly tempestuous marriage (Fitzgerald, 1979). Campbell seems to have left him frequently for the company of another man, although they later reconciled. Much of the storminess of their marriage was recorded in the newspaper advertisements DeBaptiste placed in local papers, rejecting any responsibility for bills Campbell or her paramours accrued during her absences. DeBaptiste would write at least one public apology to Campbell for even suspecting her of unfaithfulness.

In spite of the apparently unsettled nature of his home life, DeBaptiste would become one of the most prominent businessmen of any race in Fredericksburg. In 1787 he rented land along the Rappahannock River. By 1796 he had purchased the land where he built a pier that continues to be called "French John's Wharf." DeBaptiste acquired the funds necessary for his land purchases and construction projects by means of an entrepreneurial endeavor he began in 1792. He successfully made a bid to the state assembly to acquire an annual contract to operate a ferry from the nearby town of Falmouth. DeBaptiste called his vessel the "Free Ferry," and this may allude to a role in assisting runaway slaves in their escape, an activity for which his grandson, GEORGE DeBAPTISTE, became well known.

After DeBaptiste's death, his eldest son, Benjamin, managed and expanded the family's shipping interests. They were the most successful entrepreneurs in Fredericksburg until the 1840s, when members migrated from the state to educate their children. In 1998, DeBaptiste was inducted into the Sons of the American Revolution, and the Culpeper, Virginia, chapter of the organization placed a plaque on his grave in Falmouth.

FURTHER READING

Information concerning the DeBaptiste family can be found in the Ronald Palmer Papers, Howard University, Moorland Spingarn Research Center.

Bolster, W. Jeffrey. *Black Jacks: African American Seamen in the Age of Sail* (1997).

Fitzgerald, Ruth Coder. *A Different Story: A Black History of Fredericksburg, Stafford, and Spotsylvania, Virginia* (1979).

O'shaughnessy, Andrew Jackson. *An Empire Divided: The American Revolution and the British Caribbean* (2000).

Quarles, Benjamin. *The Negro in the American Revolution* (1996).

KATHRYN L. BEARD

DeBerry, William Nelson (29 Aug. 1870–20 Jan. 1948), Congregational clergyman and social service worker, was born in Nashville, Tennessee, the son of Caswell DeBerry and Charlotte Mayfield, former slaves. His father was a railroad shop worker and a lay preacher in a local Baptist church; his mother's occupation is unknown. DeBerry was educated in Nashville and entered Fisk University in 1886, graduating ten years later with a B.S. degree. DeBerry then went to Oberlin College in Ohio where he received a Bachelor of Divinity degree in 1899. That same year he was ordained in the Congregational ministry, became the pastor of St. John's Congregational Church in Springfield, Massachusetts, and married Amanda McKissack of Pulaski, Tennessee; they had two children. After the death of his first wife (date unknown), DeBerry married Louise Scott in 1943.

DeBerry served as pastor of St. John's Congregational Church until 31 December 1930, during which time the church grew from approximately 100 members to about 500 members. In 1911 DeBerry launched St. John's Institutional Activities as the church's social outreach to the city's black population. Eventually, it offered boys' and girls' clubs, classes in cooking and sewing, an employment bureau, a music program, a playground, and a summer camp. In 1917 it became affiliated with the National Urban League. DeBerry was widely recognized for the work of St. John's Institutional Activities, the first systematic effort in Springfield to meet the social needs of its growing African American community. In 1913 he was appointed to the Governor's Committee on Religious and Interracial Understanding, and a year later Lincoln University awarded him an honorary Doctor of Divinity degree. In 1915 he became the first alumnus to serve as a trustee of Fisk University. DeBerry was elected Second Assistant Moderator of the National Council of Congregational Churches in 1919, and in 1925 he was elected Recording Secretary of the American Missionary Association. In 1927 DeBerry received the Harmon Foundation's first award "for distinguished service in religion among Negroes of the United States," and the following year he was given the William Pynchon medal from the city of Springfield for "distinguished public service."

DeBerry directed a sociological survey of black Springfield in 1921, published in 1922, that studied the population growth and industrial opportunity for Springfield's black community during World War I. In a follow-up study two decades later, DeBerry edited and published *Sociological Survey of the Negro Population of Springfield, Mass.* (1940), which discovered that the Depression decade had caused a slight population decline and diminished black employment opportunities. DeBerry resigned from his pastorate in 1930 to devote his full attention to social work among blacks in Springfield. He became the executive director of the Dunbar Community League, an agency that absorbed St. John's Institutional Activities, and in 1935 DeBerry was appointed to the Springfield Board of Public Welfare. Although he retired from the league in 1947, he continued to direct Camp Atwater, a summer camp for black children that he had founded in East Brookfield, Massachusetts. He died in a Springfield hospital after a long illness.

William Nelson DeBerry was among a small group of early twentieth-century African American clergymen who saw the necessity of specialized attention to the secular needs of an urban African American community. Through St. John's Institutional Activities, his ministry enriched and gave texture to the cultural, recreational, and social lives of Springfield's African American community and pioneered the way for the social activism of black churches in the civil rights era and beyond. When he died, the *Journal of Negro History* remembered him as "one of the greatest churchmen of his time."

FURTHER READING

Hammond, Lily Hardy. *In the Vanguard of a Race* (1922).

Mather, Frank Lincoln, ed. *Who's Who of the Colored Race* (1915).

Obituaries: *New York Times* and the *Springfield Union*, 21 Jan. 1948.

This entry is taken from the *American National Biography* and is published here with the permission of the American Council of Learned Societies.

RALPH E. LUKER

DeCarava, Roy (9 Dec. 1919–27 Oct. 2009), photographer, artist, and educator, was born in Harlem, New York City, the only child of Andrew DeCarava and Elfreda Ferguson.

DeCarava never knew his father; his mother worked as a clerical worker for the Works Progress Administration.

Elfreda DeCarava arrived in New York from Jamaica as the Great Migration of African Americans from the South to the North was transforming Harlem into a predominantly African American community. She tried to foster her son's creativity as a single mother when he was a boy by getting him a violin and an expensive velvet short suit, in which he said he used to run through Harlem to get to practice. While DeCarava never became a violinist, he became actively interested in and a part of a wide range of artistic endeavors from sketching to movies.

As an eight-year-old boy, he used chalk or pieces of Plaster of Paris to sketch large murals of cowboys along 105th Street. He wrote that he enjoyed playing "street games" like skelly that emphasized the creativity of children who didn't have a lot of money to buy toys. DeCarava also spent most of his free afternoons at movie matinees, which he has said was a huge influence on him and piqued his interest in photography.

DeCarava was raised in Harlem as it became a well-known hub of creativity among blacks. As he came of age, Harlem would be home to the best known black artistic movement of the twentieth Century, the Harlem Renaissance. The combination of an influence of well-known artistic mentors and guides—from poet and writer LANGSTON HUGHES to the artist CHARLES WHITE—and his working-class roots certainly influenced his aesthetic.

His photography is notable for its darkness and its emphasis on people who are not necessarily well-known. His trademark style is one that includes very little light or light that is judiciously used. He also insisted on photographing people who were not necessarily well-known so that the roots of human life could be seen by looking at the common black person. He would go on to chronicle the civil rights movement and jazz musicians, in addition to common folk.

As a teenager, DeCarava worked odd jobs—from selling bags at the supermarket to selling newspapers on the subway—even before he was in high school. Eventually, when he worked in a variety of fields as an adult—from printmaking and sign-painting to working in advertising—he became a man of collective action by organizing unions and was dedicated to the plight of the average worker.

He was a student at the Harlem annex of the Textile High School, where he soon learned he received an inferior education to the students at the main, predominantly white campus in Manhattan. With the encouragement of persistent teachers, DeCarava and another student transferred to the Manhattan campus, though they were the only African Americans in the student body. There DeCarava was exposed to the works of well-known artists like Leonardo da Vinci and Vincent Van Gogh. When he graduated in 1938, he found work painting signs for the Works Progress Administration, a federally funded program created by President Franklin D. Roosevelt's New Deal legislation to curb unemployment during the Great Depression. Elfreda passed along her clerical position with the WPA to her son.

A graphic-design scholarship allowed DeCarava to attend Cooper Union, an art and engineering college near Greenwich Village in downtown Manhattan. Producing work as a painter and designer in an environment hostile to blacks took its toll on him and he left after two years to attend the

Roy DeCarava, known for highly personal images of his beloved New York, poses at his Brooklyn home on 6 May 1991. [AP Images.]

Harlem Community Art Center, where actor and orator PAUL ROBESON, poet LANGSTON HUGHES and artists ROMARE BEARDEN and JACOB LAWRENCE had offices. He spent roughly six or seven months in the Army, which was so traumatic he was hospitalized in the psychiatric ward, which, he noted, was the only place in the army that wasn't segregated at the time.

DeCarava also attended the George Washington Carver Art School, where he studied with Charles White between 1944 and 1945. His initial interest in photography was really to record images that he enjoyed painting, he said. Later, he made photographs as a way of gathering material for his prints and by the end of the 1940s, DeCarava had dedicated himself to photography. He married Sherry Turner in June 1947, and they eventually raised three daughters.

DeCarava became one of the most acclaimed African American photographers and teachers of his era by rendering residents of his native Harlem artfully in elegant black and white photographs. His work was heavily influenced by the Frenchman Henri Cartier-Bresson, who viewed the ordinary man on the street as the embodiment of human values. Art critics have deemed DeCarava a pioneer in serious devotion to a black aesthetic and in an artful attentiveness to the black experience in America.

His first solo show was held in 1950. Two years later, he was the first African American photographer to be awarded a Guggenheim Fellowship. He summed up his perspective on photography in his Guggenheim proposal this way: "I want to show the strength, the wisdom, the dignity of the Negro People. Not the famous and the well known, but the unknown and the unnamed, thus revealing the roots from which spring the greatness of all human beings...."

His best known book is *The Sweet Flypaper of Life* (1955) a series of 140 DeCarava photographs combined with a monologue written by Langston Hughes. DeCarava also took hundreds of photographs of jazz musicians like JOHN COLTRANE, MILES DAVIS, and BILLIE HOLIDAY, some of which were included in his 2001 book, *The Sound I Saw: Improvisation on a Jazz Theme* which had been shelved for decades. In 1956, DeCarava opened the first commercial gallery in New York City to open in half a century, A Photographer's Gallery, but it closed two years later.

Throughout his career, DeCarava was a committed arts organizer and participated not only in the Committee for the Negro in the Arts, but also the Ad Hoc Emergency Cultural Coalition. He went on to earn a living for nearly two decades as a freelance photographer, and he joined the faculty at Hunter College in 1975 where he taught for more than thirty years. In 2006, he was a recipient of a National Medal of Arts from the National Endowment of Arts. DeCarava passed away in New York City in 2009 at the age of 89.

FURTHER READING

Alinder, James (ed.). *Roy DeCarava, Photographs* (1981).

The Museum of Modern Art, New York. *Roy DeCarava: A Retrospective* (1996). Available at http://www.artic.edu/museumstudies/ms242/portfolio16.shtml.

Robinson, Fern. "Masterful American Photographer Roy DeCarava." *American Visions* (2009, Jun 29). Available at http://findarticles.com/p/articles/mi_m1546/is_6_14/ai_58509275/.

JOSHUNDA SANDERS

Dédé, Edmond (20 Nov. 1827, sometimes listed as 23 Apr. 1829–1901, sometimes listed as 1903), composer, violinist, and conductor, was born in New Orleans to parents who were free Creoles of color. His father and mother were originally from the French West Indies but immigrated to the United States in approximately 1809 as part of the mass political exile during that period. His father was a professional musician who worked as a bandmaster for a local military unit. As a child, Dédé studied the clarinet and then began playing the violin. His teachers were Ludovico Gabici and Constantin Debergue. Debergue was director of the Philharmonic Society established by the free Creoles of color in the area; he was also a violinist, which may account for Dédé's particular affection for that instrument. Gabici, an Italian, was one of the earliest music publishers in New Orleans and the director of the Saint Charles Theater orchestra. Dédé was schooled in music by many French musicians in the city, including Eugène Prévost (a winner of the French Prix de Rome Award), with whom he studied harmony and counterpoint, and the free black musician Charles Richard Lambert, who was conductor of the Philharmonic Society.

The New Orleans Philharmonic Society was a non-theatrical, mixed-race orchestra composed of over one hundred musicians. During Dédé's youth, musicians were experiencing labor disputes over salaries and the number of full-time, paid musical seats available. The labor disputes were not unique to New

Orleans. What was unique was the interracial nature of the Philharmonic's roster and the tensions such a composition created. Whites demanded additional positions in the orchestra and took over seats from black players. Accounts vary as to the reasons for Dédé's departure from New Orleans to study music in Mexico in 1848. Some music historians claim his father wanted him to study in that country, while others state that he left owing to the ethnic tensions in the orchestral world of the city. After studying in Mexico, he returned to New Orleans briefly to take a job making cigars. While so employed, Dédé also played with the city's various symphony orchestras and became a well-recognized artist.

Dédé then left New Orleans for Europe. His route of travel is undocumented, but there is evidence that he visited England and Belgium. He then went to France to study at the famous Paris Conservatoire de Musique (Paris Conservatory of Music) under Jacques-François Halévy in 1857. The music historian Arthur La Brew maintains that Dédé was the first black to study music and compose an opera at the Conservatoire. Dédé also took lessons from Jean-Delphin Alard, a famous French violinist. His compositions and conducting ability earned him work in Paris, and he soon abandoned thoughts of returning to the United States, instead remaining in France to direct the Théâtre de l'Alcazar of Bordeaux, a position that he held for more than twenty-five years. He also conducted at the Folies Bordelaises. While holding both positions, he composed ballets, operettas, and chamber music, as well as popular songs. Dédé married a French woman named Sylvie Leflet in 1864 and their son was born in the same year. Dédé's most recognized piece is *Le Palmier* Overture. Dédé traveled in Europe and Africa and composed *Le Sermente de l'Arabe* while on a visit in 1865 to Algeria. W. E. B. DuBois noted in his history of New Orleans society that Dédé conducted one of the leading French symphony orchestras. He was elected to membership in the French Society of Authors and Editors of Music.

Dédé's compositions were performed in New Orleans in 1865 in a concert conducted by Samuel Snaer Jr. His "Quasimodo" Symphony was given its premiere on that program. Historical accounts are unclear as to how often Dédé returned to the United States, but most scholars agree that he returned in 1893. The yearlong U.S. tour that he undertook was a critical success but not a personal one, since he lost his favorite violin, "the Cremona," when his ship was wrecked during the October 1893 crossing to the United States. Everything else he brought with him for the tour was also lost in that disaster except for another violin and a silk hat. He was able to continue his tour only after the black community in Galveston, Texas, organized a benefit on his behalf. While in the United States he performed his own composition *Patriotisme*, which was based on a poem by the African American historian Rodolphe Lucien Desdunes and dealt with the problem of prejudice. It was on this visit that Dédé was given full membership in the Société des Jeunes-Amis, a social club for Creoles of color. His son, Eugène Arcade Dédé, also became a composer and musician; the elder Dédé orchestrated several of his son's compositions.

Before his death in Paris in 1901, Dédé had been working on several compositions, including one titled *Le Sultan d'Ispahan*. Some of Dédé's compositions and papers are still scattered throughout Europe, but the majority of his known papers and scores are located in the archives at the Bibliothèque Nationale in Paris. Dédé held membership in the French Society of Dramatic Authors and Composers from 1894 until his death.

Dédé and his music had been forgotten in the United States until 2000, when the conductor Richard Rosenberg, researching in the archives at the Bibliothèque Nationale in Paris, discovered a large body of Dédé's compositions and papers. He prepared performable versions of a handful of pieces and conducted *Chicago, Francoise, et Tortillard, Mon Sous Off!*, and other works at the Hot Springs Music Festival in Arkansas. Dédé's *Mon Pauvre Coeur* (1852), the oldest surviving sheet music for a composition by a New Orleans Creole of color, also was performed at the festival. Recordings of several works were released on a compact disc in 2000. The remainder of Dédé's compositions awaits editing for performance by the modern orchestra. There is also a need for scholars to translate Dédé's papers to develop a more complete history of his life and contributions to the music of France.

FURTHER READING

Bell, Caryn Cosse. *Revolution, Romanticism, and the Afro-Creole Protest Tradition in Louisiana, 1718–1868* (1997).

Hirsch, Arnold R. *Creole New Orleans: Race and Americanization* (1992).

La Brew, Arthur R. "Edmond Dede, 1827–1901," *Afro-American Music Review* (1984).

Wyatt, Lucius R. "Six Composers of Nineteenth-Century New Orleans," *Black Music Research Journal* (1990).

PAMELA LEE GRAY

Dee, Ruby (27 Oct. 1924–), actress and writer, was born Ruby Ann Wallace in Cleveland, Ohio, the third of four children of teenage parents, Gladys Hightower and Edward Nathaniel Wallace, a Pullman car porter. After Gladys ran off to follow a preacher, the couple divorced in 1924, and Edward married Emma Amelia Benson, a former schoolteacher, who lived in New York City. Emma, whom Ruby called "Mother," reared the Wallace children in Harlem, New York, where family lessons included picketing white-owned Harlem businesses that refused to hire African Americans.

Ruby graduated from Hunter College High School in 1939 and entered Hunter College, in New York City. Her professional theater career began in 1940 during her sophomore year, when the writer and director Abram Hill cast her in his social satire, *On Strivers Row* (1940) at the American Negro Theater (ANT), which he had cofounded with FREDERICK DOUGLASS O'NEAL and Austin Briggs-Hall earlier that year. Over the next few years Ruby appeared in five other ANT plays, including Hill's powerful indictment of white racism and exploitation, *Walk Hard* (1944). In 1941 she married Frankie Dee Brown, a midget and well-off liquor salesman, whom she divorced in 1945 because of his obsessive jealousy. Dee's busy personal and professional life took its toll on her academic work. After flunking out of school, she was reinstated and graduated from Hunter in 1944. Dee made her Broadway debut in the original production of *South Pacific* in 1943 and replaced ALICE CHILDRESS in the Broadway production of *Anna Lucasta* the next year. In 1945 Dee played the female lead in Robert Ardrey's play *Jeb*, the story of a returning African American veteran who faces down the Ku Klux Klan to marry his girlfriend; the part of Jeb was played by OSSIE DAVIS. Davis and Dee appeared together again later that year in the national tour of *Anna Lucasta* and in 1948 at the Lyceum Theater in *The Smile of the World*. The couple married in 1948 and had three children: Nora, Guy, and Hasna.

In 1959 Dee opened in the original cast of LORRAINE HANSBERRY's Broadway play *A Raisin in the Sun*, first opposite SIDNEY POITIER and later opposite her husband. Despite her reservations about the role—"It seemed that I'd been playing that same character, more or less, in almost everything I'd done" (Davis and Dee, 281)—Dee received great notices. In the mid-1960s, when she starred as Kate in *Taming of the Shrew* and Cordelia in *King Lear*, Dee became the first African American woman to play lead roles

Ruby Dee, writer, director, actor, and activist, 25 September 1962. (Library of Congress/Carl Van Vechten.)

at the American Shakespeare Festival. During her illustrious theater career, Dee won an Obie Award for playing Lena opposite JAMES EARL JONES in Athol Fugard's Off-Broadway play *Boesman and Lena* (1970) and a Drama Desk Award for *Wedding Band* (1973), a play by Alice Childress. Other theatrical highlights include her starring role in the 1988 Broadway comedy *Checkmates* opposite PAUL WINFIELD and the role of Laura in *The Glass Menagerie* at the Arena Stage in Washington, D.C., in 1989.

Like her husband, Dee was committed to increasing the black presence among television and film crews. She had found it particularly ironic that 1950's *No Way Out*, the story of a wounded racist robber who does not want to be treated by a black intern, "deliberately barred [blacks] from participation in this image-making business" (Davis and Dee, 199). In addition to her stage work, Dee began appearing in film in the late 1940s, including *The Fight Never Ends* (1949), with JOE LOUIS playing himself; *The Jackie Robinson Story* (1950), in which she played Rachel Robinson opposite Jackie Robinson playing himself; *Edge of the City* (1957); *St. Louis Blues* (1958), with NAT KING COLE, EARTHA KITT, CAB CALLOWAY, and ELLA FITZGERALD; *A Raisin in the Sun* (1961), reprising her role as Ruth; *The Balcony* (1963); *The Incident* (1967); *Up Tight* (1968), set in a Cleveland slum after the death of MARTIN LUTHER KING JR.; *Buck and the Preacher* (1972), directed by Poitier and costarring HARRY BELAFONTE; *Go Tell It on the Mountain* (1985), based on the book by JAMES BALDWIN; and two SPIKE LEE films, *Do the Right Thing* (1989) and *Jungle Fever* (1991).

For her work on television, Dee has been nominated for an Emmy Award seven times. She won an Emmy for *Decoration Day* (1990) and a Cable ACE Award for her performance in *Long Day's Journey into Night*. She played recurring characters on both *Guiding Light* (1967) and *Peyton Place* (1968–1969) on television and has appeared in such television dramas as *I Know Why the Caged Bird Sings* (1979), adapted from MAYA ANGELOU's memoir; *To Be Young, Gifted, and Black* (1981); *The James Mink Story* (1996); *The Court Martial of Jackie Robinson* (1990); *Zora Is My Name*, about ZORA NEALE HURSTON, which she cowrote; and *Having Our Say: The Delany Sisters' First Hundred Years* (1999), in which she appeared as BESSIE DELANY. Dee has written several books, including *Glowchild and Other Poems* (1972); *My One Good Nerve* (1999), which she turned into a one-woman show; and two children's books, *Two Ways to Count to Ten* (1988), winner of a Literary Guild Award; and *Tower to Heaven* (1991).

Davis and Dee worked together—on stage, film, and television as performers, writers, and producers—for almost sixty years. In 1980 they founded their own production company, Emmalyn II Productions Company, and over the years produced both a television and a radio series, as well as numerous documentary and nonfiction projects. The couple also worked together in civil rights and humanitarian causes, on the small and large scales. In the 1950s they risked their careers by stridently resisting Senator Joseph McCarthy's blacklisting activities. Their roles came to national attention when they served as masters of ceremonies for the 1963 March on Washington. The following year they helped establish Artists for Freedom, which donated money to civil rights organizations in the name of the four little girls killed in Birmingham, Alabama. Dee helped organize a summit of "prominent black leaders in the Struggle … [so that they] could meet in an informal atmosphere, talk, map strategy without press participation, without cameras" (Davis

and Dee, 307). Dee often worked behind the scenes, helping establish Concerned Mothers, which raised money for BETTY SHABAZZ and her children after the death of Shabazz's husband, MALCOLM X. She and Davis were active in supporting the NAACP Legal Defense Fund and sickle-cell-disease research. They also campaigned for the release of MUMIA ABU-JAMAL, on death row since 1982 for killing a Philadelphia policeman, and protested civil rights abuses, including the killing of Amadou Diallo by New York police. On 4 February, 2005 Davis died.

In addition to their many individual honors, Davis and Dee have jointly received the Actors' Equity Association PAUL ROBESON Award (1975), the Academy of Television Arts and Sciences Silver Circle Award (1994), a Grammy for the spoken word version of their memoir (2007), and induction into the NAACP Image Awards Hall of Fame (1989). In 1995 they were awarded the National Medal of Arts by President Bill Clinton, and in 2000 they received the Screen Actors Guild's highest honor, the Life Achievement Award.

For her role as Mama Lucas, mother of gangster Frank Lucas (played by DENZEL WASHINGTON) in *American Gangster* (2007), Dee received her first Academy Award nomination, in 2008. Later that year the NAACP awarded Dee its highest honor, the Spingarn Medal.

FURTHER READING

Davis, Ossie, and Ruby Dee. *With Ossie and Ruby: In This Life Together* (1998).

SAMUEL A. HAY

Dees, Clement (c.1837–?), Civil War sailor and Medal of Honor nominee, was born in San Antonio, Cape Verde Islands, off the coast of Africa. Nothing is known of Dees's family background or life, except that he was practicing the trade of a sailor when he arrived in the United States at Eastport, Maine.

Dees enlisted in the U.S. Navy in Eastport, Maine, on 6 June 1864, joining the crew of the newly commissioned U.S.S. *Pontoosuc*, a side-wheel gunboat built in Portland, Maine. Dees, who enlisted for a term of two years, was one of a dozen men who enlisted at Eastport, and was credited to the town's draft quota. While serving aboard the *Pontoosuc* in the first months of its service, Dees saw service in Southern waters as the ship performed blockade duties, and then in Northern waters, as far as Halifax, Nova Scotia, during its pursuit of the Confederate raider C.S.S. *Tallahassee*. In December 1864 the *Pontoosuc* and its crew returned to Southern waters, and was stationed off Wilmington, North Carolina, as part of a blockading squadron. It was here, during the attack on the Confederate Fort Fisher, that Dees and his fellow crewmen would take part in one of the largest naval actions of the Civil War.

Though little is known about Dees's individual service during the Civil War, by virtue of his maritime background he was very likely an experienced sailor, as many young men from his native island nation were, and was surely a valued addition to the *Pontoosuc*'s crew. Though standing but five feet four inches in height, the diminutive seaman well knew how to handle the ship's ropes and other gear. However, as with any crew member serving on a naval vessel during the war, Dees might also have been required to handle a weapon and serve as a fighting sailor should the need arise. The need would inexorably arise at Fort Fisher.

The siege and subsequent capture of Fort Fisher by Union forces was a complicated and large affair, involving the close cooperation between the army and navy that lasted from early December 1864 until the fort's final capitulation on 15 January 1865. Among the forces deployed for the final assault on the fort was a naval brigade of sixteen hundred sailors and four hundred marines armed with swords and revolvers. Landed on the sands before Fort Fisher early on the afternoon of 15 January, these mariners, Clement Dees among them, led an attack on the fort that was considered by the Confederate troops to be the main assault. Despite their offensive, the naval brigade took heavy casualties and failed to capture the fort. The assault, however, was a vital diversion: a subsequent attack by Union soldiers successfully caught the Confederates off guard, and by the evening hours Fort Fisher had capitulated to Union hands.

Seaman Clement Dees was subsequently commended for his "gallantry, skill, and coolness in action" (Hanna, p. 28) and was recommended for the Medal of Honor. The award was subsequently approved on 22 June 1865, but Dees never received his medal. After the battle for Fort Fisher and the subsequent end of the Civil War in April, Dees was transferred to the receiving ship U.S.S. *Ohio*, where he awaited his final discharge from the navy. Perhaps anxious to return to civilian life, Dees subsequently deserted from the navy at Boston, Massachusetts, on 22 July 1865. Because he had deserted, the award was rescinded. It's likely that Dees never knew of his commendation.

Interestingly, Dees's desertion from the navy was not unusual. Many sailors and soldiers, both white and black, deserted from Union forces after the war had ended instead of waiting for their formal discharge. With his desertion, and subsequent forfeiture of the Medal of Honor, Clement Dees disappeared from history, and nothing further of his life is known. However, Dees is nonetheless deserving of remembrance not only for his actions that made him worthy of a Medal of Honor award, but also because he is representative of the approximately eighteen thousand African American sailors, men like JOHN LAWSON and ROBERT BLAKE, who served ably and honorably during the Civil War.

FURTHER READING

Hanna, Charles W. *African American Recipients of the Medal of Honor* (2002).

Reidy, Joseph P. "Black Men in Navy Blue during the Civil War." http://www.archives.gov/publications/prologue/2001/fall/black-sailors-1.html.

GLENN ALLEN KNOBLOCK

DeFrantz, Anita L. (4 Oct. 1952–), Olympic rower and administrator, was born in Philadelphia, Pennsylvania, to Robert David DeFrantz, a social worker, YMCA administrator, and local school board member, and Anita Page, a speech pathologist and university professor. When DeFrantz was eighteen months old, her family moved to Indiana, living first in Bloomington and then Indianapolis.

DeFrantz was greatly influenced by her family's history of social and political activism. Her grandfather, FABURN EDWARD DEFRANTZ, was executive director of the Senate Avenue YMCA in Indianapolis from 1916 until 1952. Under his leadership, the Senate Avenue Y's "Monster Meetings" became an important forum over a span of several decades for the examination of issues affecting African Americans. They were public educational gatherings that brought to town such African American luminaries as W. E. B. DuBois, LANGSTON HUGHES, PAUL ROBESON, A. PHILIP RANDOLPH, JACKIE ROBINSON, ROY WILKINS, and THURGOOD MARSHALL. DeFrantz's parents met in the late 1940s as students at Indiana University. Her father was president of the campus NAACP chapter. Her mother was among the first group of African Americans to integrate student housing at the university. DeFrantz's early athletic accomplishments were modest. As an elementary school student, she swam at Indianapolis's Frederick Douglass Public Park Pool and participated in local competitions. She attended Shortridge High School in Indianapolis. Although active in several extracurricular activities such as madrigal, band, orchestra, Quill and Scroll, and thespians, she did not play a sport.

A high school friend who graduated a year before DeFrantz and went to Connecticut College encouraged DeFrantz to apply to the college. She did so and was accepted. DeFrantz played basketball during her freshman year. In the fall of her sophomore year, she discovered rowing. One day on campus, she spotted a strange-looking boat in front of the student union. When DeFrantz, who was nearly six feet tall, asked what it was, the college rowing coach told her it was for rowing, adding, "You'd be perfect for it" (Thomas, 1).

After graduating from college with honors in 1974, DeFrantz enrolled in law school at the University of Pennsylvania. She chose to attend the university primarily because the Vesper Boat Club, a training center for elite rowers, was located in Philadelphia. While in law school, DeFrantz trained for rowing three times a day and held a part-time job working from 10:00 P.M. to 6:00 A.M. at Philadelphia police headquarters interviewing defendants before their bail hearings.

Training under the tutelage of coaches at Vesper, she made her first national rowing team in 1975. That year she competed in the world championships, in the four-oared shell, at Nottingham, England, finishing fifth. The following year, 1976, was the first year that women competed in Olympic rowing. DeFrantz made the United States team as a member of the women's eight-oared shell. The team won a bronze medal at the Montreal Olympic Games.

After the Olympic Games, DeFrantz spent the fall of 1976 working at the Center for Law and Social Policy, in Washington, D.C. She completed law school in 1977 and was admitted to the Pennsylvania Bar later that year.

She continued rowing with the goal of winning a gold medal at the 1980 Moscow Olympic Games. DeFrantz was a member of every United States national team between 1975 and 1980. She won a silver medal at the 1978 world championships, competed in world championship finals four times, and won six national titles. She supported herself financially by working as a staff attorney for the Juvenile Law Center of Philadelphia from 1977 to 1979, and then from 1979 to 1981 as a pre-law adviser and director of the Third World Center at Princeton University.

The 1970s also marked the beginning of DeFrantz's involvement in sports governance. Fellow athletes elected her to the United States Olympic Committee Athletes Advisory Council in

Anita DeFrantz, (right), Olympic rower, announces an athletes' suit against the U.S. Olympic Committee for depriving Americans the opportunity to compete in the Moscow Games at a news conference in New York City, 24 April 1980. Ira Glasser, the executive director of the **TK** (AP Images.)

1976, a position she held until 1984. She become a member of the United States Olympic Committee (USOC) board of directors in 1976 and joined the committee's executive board in 1977.

President Jimmy Carter's call for an American boycott of the 1980 Moscow Olympic Games in response to the Soviet Union's 1979 invasion of Afghanistan proved to be a pivotal event in DeFrantz's life. In April 1980 the USOC, under strong pressure from the Carter administration, voted against sending a team to Moscow. The decision outraged DeFrantz, who was considered a leading contender for the 1980 Olympic team. She argued that the federal government had never provided any financial support for athletes' training and that individual athletes should have the right to decide for themselves whether to compete in Moscow. She led a group of eighteen other athletes, one coach, and one administrator who filed a suit in United States District Court in April 1980 seeking to overturn the USOC decision. The suit failed, but it caught the attention of the International Olympic Committee (IOC), which in July 1980 awarded DeFrantz the Bronze Medal of the Olympic Order for her stand.

DeFrantz's defense of athletes' rights also attracted the attention of Peter Ueberroth, the president of the Los Angeles Olympic Organizing Committee. Ueberroth offered her a job developing the plan for the three Olympic villages used at the 1984 Games. She began at the committee in 1981, became the committee's vice president for Olympic Villages, and ran the day-to-day operations of the Olympic Village at the University of Southern California during the Games.

The 1984 Games generated a surplus of $223 million. Approximately $93 million of the surplus was used to establish the Amateur Athletic Foundation (AAF) of Los Angeles, a nonprofit corporation devoted to developing youth sports in Southern California. DeFrantz joined the foundation staff in 1985. In 1987 the board of directors elected her president. Under DeFrantz's leadership, the AAF invested more than $100 million in youth sports through grant making and self-initiated programs designed primarily to meet the needs of young people historically underserved by private and public sports programming.

While still a staff member of the AAF in 1986, DeFrantz was elected to the IOC. She became the first African American and only the fifth woman elected to the organization. In 1992 the IOC elected DeFrantz to its executive board. Two years later she became the first woman elected vice president in the committee's 103-year history. DeFrantz, however, was unsuccessful in her attempt in 2001 to win the IOC presidency.

Throughout her tenure on the IOC, DeFrantz has been a leading advocate of expanding the Olympic program to include more female athletes and more events for women. She became chair of the newly formed IOC Working Group on Women and Sport in 1995. The influence of DeFrantz and other advocates of gender equity in international sports was reflected in the changing composition of the Olympic Games. At the 1984 Los Angeles Games, two years before DeFrantz's election, women competed in sixty-two events and composed comprised 23 percent of all athletes. At the 2000 Sydney Games, there were 132 events for women, who made up 38.2 percent of all athletes.

Membership in the IOC provided DeFrantz entry to a variety of other international sports posts from the 1990s forward. She was vice president of the International Rowing Federation, a member of the executive committee of the Atlanta Committee for the Olympic Games, a member of the Board of Trustees for the Salt Lake Olympic Organizing Committee, and an arbitrator for the Court of Arbitration for Sport.

DeFrantz occupies an unusual, if not unique, position as an administrator of two distinctly different types of sports organizations. She is a member of several elite national and international sports governing bodies. At the same time, DeFrantz runs a foundation committed to youth sports. She is best known as an Olympic leader, a role she fulfills on a volunteer basis. Her actual vocation, however, is the development of community-based sports programs for children and teenagers. This dual identity, combined with her reputation as an advocate of women's sports and her visibility as an African American woman in sports administration, an arena dominated by white men, has earned DeFrantz a variety of awards and recognitions. These include the *Ladies Home Journal* 100 Most Important Women in America, 1988; NAACP Legal Defense and Educational Fund's Black Woman of Achievement Award, 1988; Women's Sports Foundation's Billie Jean King Contribution Award, 1996; *The Australian Magazine* 100 Most Powerful Women in the World, 1997; and *The Sporting News* 100 Most Powerful People in Sports, 1991–1999.

FURTHER READING

The most detailed account of Anita L. DeFrantz's life is an oral history transcript available at the Amateur Athletic Foundation sports library in Los Angeles.

Harvey, Randy. "Is She the Most Powerful Woman in Sports?" *Los Angeles Times Magazine*, 30 June 1996.

Jones, Charisse. "She Offers a Sporting Proposal," *Los Angeles Times*, 17 Dec. 1989.

Moore, Kenny. "An Advocate for Athletes," *Sports Illustrated* (29 Aug. 1988).

Thomas, Emory, Jr. "Inside Moves: Former U.S. Medalist Emerges as Quiet Force in the Olympic Arena," *Wall Street Journal*, 28 June 1996.

WAYNE WILSON

DeFrantz, Faburn (9 Feb. 1885–24 Sept. 1964), Executive Secretary of Indianapolis's Senate Avenue Young Men's Christian Association (YMCA), was born in Topeka, Kansas, to Samella (Sina in some censuses) and Alonzo DeFrantz. Alonzo, a barber by trade, had helped lead the Exodusters, thousands of former slaves fleeing the post-Reconstruction South to the relative freedom of Kansas. He instilled in his son a deep Christian faith, an independent streak, and a commitment to work aggressively for African American civil rights.

DeFrantz studied medicine at Washburn College in Topeka, the University of Kansas, and Kansas Medical College. But his older brother Robert secured jobs for him at the Kansas Avenue Y in Topeka and then the Twelfth Street Y in Washington, D.C., and DeFrantz was soon converted to their mission. Created in the nineteenth century to help rural

African American migrants adjust to their new lives in northern and southern cities, the YMCA, like the church, became a pillar of urban African American communities, providing recreation and respite as well as social services, education, and occupational support.

DeFrantz took the job of physical director of Indianapolis's Senate Avenue YMCA in 1913. Three years later, on 1 August 1916, he became the association's first African American director. His young charges tagged DeFrantz, who stood well over six feet, with broad shoulders and an imposing, upright carriage, with the nickname "Chief." The moniker was picked up quickly by the rest of Indianapolis's African American population as DeFrantz transformed the Senate Avenue Y from a handful of elite members attending Boy Scouts, Bible classes, and swim lessons into the heart of the community and the largest black YMCA in the country.

DeFrantz insisted his branch serve the widest possible needs and interests of local African Americans. Under his direction the Y offered more clubs, camps, and classes than many colleges, as well as a dormitory, job placement services, relief programs, college counseling, and legal aid. Within two years of DeFrantz's appointment as Executive Director, membership in the Senate Avenue Y grew almost ten-fold, to 3300. Within a decade over 5000 men and boys subscribed, with many fathers buying memberships for their sons as soon as they were born. Each year over 100,000 people used the Y, an average of 300 a day, every day.

The Y's most prominent program was its annual lecture series, the Monster Meetings—the name parodying the segregated Central Y's Big Meetings—that were held Monday nights from November through March. DeFrantz developed the Monster Meetings from a pulpit for local preachers into a forum showcasing a "who's who" of African Americans—including everyone from W. E. B DuBois to Martin Luther King, Jr., and from Alain Locke to Jackie Robinson—and the best-attended and oldest consecutive lecture series in the country. Monster Meetings served as a sounding board and rallying point for African Americans in Indianapolis, with hundreds of African American men, a few white men, and, on special occasion, women of both races attending and audiences regularly spilling out of the Y's two-story gym into the lobby, where they listened on loudspeakers.

At a time when the local NAACP had devolved into backbiting squabbles, DeFrantz and Senate Avenue YMCA members and employees took leading roles in every civil rights effort in the city and state. Developing from the Monster Meetings the Citizen's Committee of One Hundred investigated pending legislation and any other regional activity likely to negatively impact African Americans, often reporting directly to Monster Meeting audiences. The Anti-Hate Bill, which passed the 1949 Indiana legislature, was written in DeFrantz's office. This bill dealt with desegregating public schools though the nativist, anti-Semitic, racist sentiments that had spawned it remained. DeFrantz lent personnel and funds to fight the segregation of Indianapolis public schools in 1928. Indeed, the Senate Avenue Y under DeFrantz would play a leading role in the integration of Indiana University, downtown Indianapolis theaters, the Indiana High School Athletic Association, city administration jobs, and, ultimately all Indiana public schools.

DeFrantz never involved the Y in an effort he wouldn't take on himself. In the 1920s, when the Ku Klux Klan was at the height of its power nationally and headquartered in Indiana, he told the Indianapolis mayor he would cause "real trouble" if robed Klansmen marched through the city's African American neighborhood. They marched, but unmasked and under DeFrantz's withering stare. When three black teens were lynched in Marion, Indiana, in August 1930 (the last known lynching in the North), DeFrantz drove through the night to protest the horror. He loudly refused segregated accommodations at area cafeterias and restaurants and threw cigar butts at opposing fans yelling racial epithets at Indiana University's African American football players. According to his obituary, he often told friends and reporters, "They say that DeFrantz is too aggressive, but as long as I stay in this town I shall see to it that the Negro is in the picture of what is going on."

DeFrantz's aggressiveness was tempered by his personal charm, charisma, and keen political sense. He cultivated relationships with the state's most powerful whites such as governors, pharmaceutical tycoon Eli Lilly, and Indiana University president Herman Wells, with whom he worked to integrate the university dormitories, cafeterias, administration, and varsity basketball team. He involved them in fund-raising campaigns and often had them to dinner at the house he shared with his wife, Myrtle, an Indianapolis native, and two sons, Fay Jr. and Robert. He understood well the power of closed-door negotiations and use of political pressure in Indiana, and he used both to great effect in school and workforce integration.

DeFrantz's activism made him unpopular with officials at the white Central Y, of which the Senate Avenue Y was a branch, and they forced him to retire upon turning sixty-five although he was a few months short of qualifying for Social Security. He remained on the boards of the Madam C. J. Walker Manufacturing Company and Howard University, which provided an income until his death in 1964. Without DeFrantz's direction, and with integration diffusing the African American community around it, the Senate Avenue Y closed in 1959. The Monster Meetings were transplanted to another Indianapolis Y, where they continued into the 1970s.

FURTHER READING
Faburn DeFrantz's unpublished autobiography is in the possession of his family.
Graham, Tom, and Rachel Graham Cody. *Getting Open: The Unknown Story of Bill Garrett and the Integration of College Basketball* (2006).
Warren, Stanley. "The Monster Meetings at the Negro YMCA in Indianapolis," *Indiana Magazine of History* 90 (March 1995).
Warren, Stanley. *The Senate Avenue YMCA: For African American Men and Boys, Indianapolis, Indiana, 1913–1959* (2005).
Obituary: *Indianapolis Star*, 25 September 1964.

RACHEL CODY

DeGrasse, John Van Surly (June 1825–1868), physician, was born in New York City, the son of George DeGrasse, a prosperous landowner, and Maria Van Surly. After obtaining his early education in both public and private schools in New York City, he entered Oneida Institute in Whitesboro (near Utica), New York in 1840. Oneida was one of the first colleges to admit African Americans, nurturing a strong antislavery stance. In addition to welcoming black students to its campus, the institute invited abolitionists as lecturers and provided both a manual arts and an academic program.

In 1843 DeGrasse attended Aubuk College in Paris, France. Returning to New York City in 1845, he started medical training through an apprenticeship with Dr. Samuel R. Childs. After two years of clinical work and study under Childs, DeGrasse was admitted into the medical studies program at Bowdoin College in Brunswick, Maine, in 1847. Finishing his medical studies with honors in two years, he received an M.D. in May 1849. His admission to Bowdoin's medical course had been aided and sponsored by those Americans (organized as the American Colonization Society) who wanted to create colonies of free blacks and former slaves in Africa. Their intent was to promote social equality by preparing black professionals who would then immigrate to Liberia in West Africa. This plan did not materialize. Instead, with a medical degree in hand, DeGrasse returned to Europe and worked in hospitals in Paris and London. He continued his professional development as an assistant surgeon to the French surgeon Velpeau.

In 1853 DeGrasse crossed the Atlantic again, this time as a surgeon on the ship *Samuel Fox*, as he returned to New York City. Prompted by the frequent capture of blacks under the Fugitive Slave Law of 1850, DeGrasse became a founding member of Vigilante Committee of Thirteen, formed by free blacks to give protection to fugitive slaves.

After practicing medicine in his home city for about two years, DeGrasse moved to Boston, Massachusetts, where he continued his medical career. There he was quickly recognized as a talented and skillful surgeon, and on 24 August 1854 he was admitted into membership in the Massachusetts Medical Society, in what is believed to be the first admission of an African American to a professional medical association in the United States. A Boston newspaper, the *Liberator* (24 Aug. 1854), reported of DeGrasse, "Earning a good reputation here by his diligence and skill, he was admitted a member," and observed that "others of his class may be stimulated to seek an elevation which has hitherto been supposed unattainable by men of color.... Many of our most respectable physicians visit and advise with him whenever counsel is required. The Boston medical profession, it must be acknowledged has done itself honor in thus discarding the law of caste, and generously acknowledging real merit, without regard to the hue of the skin." DeGrasse was viewed as one of "the most accomplished" of the African American medical pioneers in the pre–Civil War era.

An active abolitionist in Boston, DeGrasse helped organize vigilante groups to intercept slave hunters on the streets of Boston during the enforcement of the 1850 Fugitive Slave Law. In 1863 he volunteered to serve as a medical officer in the Union army in the Civil War. One of eight African American physicians appointed to the Army Medical Corps, he served as an assistant surgeon. His meritorious service was celebrated when Governor John A. Andrews of Massachusetts presented him with a gold-hilted sword from the Commonwealth of Massachusetts.

One of several free African Americans who were formally trained in and who practiced medicine in the North before the Civil War, DeGrasse continued as an active physician until his death and was a recognized leader in the African American community in Massachusetts.

FURTHER READING

Johnson, Leonard, Jr. "History of the Education of Negro Physicians," *Journal of Medical Education* 42 (1967): 439–46.

Nell, William C. *The Colored Patriots of the American Revolution* (1855).

Williams, George Washington. *History of the Negro Race in America* (1883; repr., 1968).

This entry is taken from the *American National Biography* and is published here with the permission of the American Council of Learned Societies.

ROBERT C. HAYDEN

DeJohnette, Jack (9 August 1942–), jazz drummer, was born in Chicago. His mother Eva Jeanette Johnson, a poet, and his uncle, Roy L. Wood, Sr. (a popular jazz radio announcer on the South Side), helped foster in him a love of music, as did his grandmother Rosalie Wood, who bought him his first piano. DeJohnette's earliest musical involvement was on the piano, on which he took lessons from age four to fourteen, and not the drums for which he later became famous. In his teens he became immersed in jazz, blues, classical, and every kind of popular and commercial music. DeJohnette did not begin to take up the drums until high school, when he played with the concert band. He continued piano studies at the American Conservatory of Music in Chicago, from which he later graduated.

DeJohnette's early influences as a drummer included ART BLAKEY, ROY HAYNES, ELVIN JONES, MAX ROACH, PHILLY JOE JONES, Art Taylor, RASHIED ALI, Paul Motian, TONY WILLIAMS, and Andrew Cyrelle. At an early age he sought to be completely eclectic in style and musical direction. In his late teens he began to lead his own groups, playing both piano and drums and becoming proficient in Bop and avant-garde jazz. At the Association for the Advancement of Creative Musicians, based in Chicago, he came into contact with MUHAL RICHARD ABRAMS, Roscoe Mitchell and Joseph Jarman. At twenty-four he was playing with the JOHN COLTRANE Quintet, and in 1966 he moved to New York City, where he played with giants of jazz, including Bill Evans, THELONIOUS MONK, Stan Getz, JACKIE MCLEAN, and Freddie Hubbard. As a member of the well-known Charles

Lloyd Quartet for two years, DeJohnette played alongside a brilliant young pianist, Keith Jarrett, who would mean a great deal to his career.

In 1968 DeJohnette made his first record, *The DeJohnette Complex*, for the Milestone label. The following year, he had a rite of passage common to so many top young players of that era when he joined MILES DAVIS's band (soon followed by Jarrett). With Davis he recorded *Bitches Brew*, the landmark album that created the genre of "fusion" between jazz and rock. In Miles's orbit DeJohnette also encountered other cutting-edge musicians such as Chick Corea, Dave Holland, and John McLaughlin.

In 1971 DeJohnette began a fruitful association with record producer Manfred Eicher when he made his first recording with Jarrett, *Ruta and Daitya* (released 1973), for Eicher's ECM label. The following year, DeJohnette left Miles Davis's group. The community of artists in the ECM stable that freely interchanged roles of leader and sideman through the 1970s and 1980s included Jan Garbarek, Pat Metheny, Gary Peacock, Bennie Maupin, Stanley Cowell, Miroslav Vitous, Eddie Gomez, Alex Foster, Peter Warren, David Murray, Rufus Reid, Chico Freeman, John Purcell, John Abercrombie, Dave Holland, Alex Foster, Warren Bernhardt, Mike Richmond, and ARTHUR BLYTHE. DeJohnette would also work with trumpeter LESTER BOWIE, a friend from Chicago, from time to time until Bowie passed away in 1999.

From the 1970s onward, DeJohnette lived the jazz musician's dream: moving from project to project in an always-stimulating rotation of club bookings, tours, and recordings. Like many of his peers, DeJohnette joined groups that worked together only sporadically. He also formed three successful bands of his own. With guitarist John Abercrombie, bassist Mike Richmond, and saxophonist Alex Foster, he formed Directions to play progressive fusion. Later on, bassist Eddie Gomez replaced Richmond and Lester Bowie took over for Foster, in a new incarnation called New Directions—but each version of the band continued to exist and make recordings. In 1979, DeJohnette formed an acoustic free jazz unit called Special Edition, with saxophone players David Murray and Arthur Blythe. Later on, electric guitars and keyboards were added to Special Edition, which frequently rotated its front line personnel (including many musicians already mentioned, as well as newcomers Greg Osby, Michael Cain, Lonnie Plaxico, and Gary Thomas) as it morphed toward electrified pop.

Other bands of which DeJohnette has been a member are Gateway, a trio with John Abercrombie and Dave Holland, and Keith Jarrett's very popular Standards Trio, with Gary Peacock. In between these recurring collaborations, DeJohnette has performed and recorded in every imaginable combination: *Parallel Realities* with keyboardist HERBIE HANCOCK and guitarist Pat Metheny; *Music for the Fifth World*, a CD inspired by study with a Seneca Indian elder; or his three albums of completely improvised music with Keith Jarrett. Other musicians with whom he has worked include ORNETTE COLEMAN, SONNY ROLLINS, SUN RA, Chet Baker, George Benson, STANLEY TURRENTINE, RON CARTER, LEE MORGAN, JOE HENDERSON, Freddie Hubbard, ABBEY LINCOLN, BETTY CARTER, EDDIE HARRIS, John Scofield, Larry Goldings, BOBBY MCFERRIN, Don Byron, Danilo Perez, Bennie Maupin, Stanley Cowell, and Gonzalo Rubalcaba.

DeJohnette has composed several scores for TV and video. With percussionist Don Alias, he released a documentary video called *Talking Drummers*. DeJohnette also appeared briefly as a member of the Alligator Blues Band in the movie *Blues Brothers 2000*.

Stylistically, DeJohnette is noted for complete versatility, a wide-ranging approach to tonal colors and sounds, and pinpoint control. He is renowned for his impeccable sense of time and also inventiveness within that time. He has received numerous awards and honors, including the 1979 French Grand Prix du Disque; two Album of the Year awards from *Downbeat* magazine readers and one in the *Downbeat* annual critics' poll; two albums of the year in Japan; and innumerable drumming awards in *Downbeat* and other publications. DeJohnette was awarded an Honorary Doctorate of Music from Berklee College of Music in Boston in 1991. He has designed "Resonating Bells" instruments for the cymbal manufacturer Sabian, and launched a record label called Golden Beams Productions. His wife, Lydia, is a massage and healing specialist. They have a daughter, Minya, and live in an A-frame cabin outside of Woodstock, New York.

FURTHER READING

DeJohnette, Jack, with Charlie Perry. *The Art of Modern Jazz Drumming: Multi-directional Technique* Vols. I–II–III (1979).

Mattingly, Rick. *The Drummer's Time: Conversations with the Great Drummers of Jazz* (1998).

DAVID BORSVOLD

DeLaine, Joseph Armstrong (2 Jul. 1898–3 Aug. 1974), minister, schoolteacher, and civil rights leader, was born in Manning, Clarendon County, South Carolina, the seventh of thirteen children of Tisbia Gamble DeLaine and Henry Charles DeLaine, a pastor at Liberty Hill African Methodist Episcopal (AME) Church.

The family owned farmland, which they worked to keep food on the table, and the children walked miles to a rundown segregated school. When he was fourteen, while walking to school, DeLaine shoved a white boy who had accosted his sister. After this incident was reported to his school's principal, DeLaine ran away to escape punishment of twenty-five lashes, which a school authority was compelled to administer. He spent four years in Georgia and Michigan working as a laborer and attending night school, returning to Manning in 1916. DeLaine worked his way through college and in 1931 earned a B.A. from Allen University in Columbia, South Carolina, where he became a minister in the AME Church and began a teaching career of seventeen years in black schools.

On 12 November 1931 he married Mattie Belton, a schoolteacher, and they had three children: Joseph Jr., Ophelia, and Brumit. Both DeLaines were hired as teachers in Jamison, South Carolina, where they stayed for two years.

In 1932 DeLaine became principal of the Macedonia School, a black boarding school in Blackville, where his wife also taught. In 1934 they moved to Clarendon County, where DeLaine pastored at Spring Hill Church until 1940, at which time he was transferred to a church circuit and moved to Summerton. He taught at Liberty Hill Elementary School while Mattie DeLaine taught at Scott's Branch School. In 1942 DeLaine chartered the Clarendon County branch of the NAACP—an organization obliged to be secret in the racist South. His role as a leader grew including as adviser on federal programs for agricultural development. In 1945 he earned his bachelor's of theology from Allen University.

The AME Church considered social activism for equality to be a duty of the church. A tenet of the church was action in behalf of what is right—emphasizing life on earth, not the hereafter—something DeLaine pursued with dedication and courage. His belief in justice as fundamental to democracy and true religious commitment was reflected in the title of his earliest biography, Julie Lochbaum's *The Word Made Flesh* (1999)—the *Word* being both the U.S. Constitution and the Bible. In sermons titled "You Rascal" and "Go Forward," DeLaine wrote, "Jesus Christ invites us to …

treat this life as a time of sacred opportunity … in three directions:

1. Cultivation of our own nature;
2. The service of mankind;
3. The worship of God and work in his broad field.…

The enemy may even use the dogs; prodding rods; dynamite; burn your home; … But die with the staff in your hand going forward" (Lochbaum, 38, 30).

In 1947 DeLaine was inspired by hearing the Reverend James Hinton, head of the state NAACP, attack the doctrine of "separate but equal" black and white public schools. Black schools were anything but equal as the county spent $179 per white child and $43 per black child in a school year. The NAACP sought a community willing to file a lawsuit challenging unequal school buses—black children had none. When called upon by his neighbors to lead them, DeLaine accepted with the proviso that they be prepared to go all the way to the Supreme Court, and perhaps even be killed. In 1948 Levi Pearson, a farmer whose children walked nine miles to school, courageously filed a lawsuit to secure a school bus, *Levi Pearson v. County Board of Education*, but his case was thrown out on a technicality. After years of court dismissals and stonewalling, a petition by twenty Clarendon County parents, *Briggs v. Elliott*, was filed—not for a school bus alone, but for equal schools. While they lost this case with two of the three white presiding judges voting for segregation, federal Judge J. Waites Waring dissented, stating that "[segregation] is *per se* inequality" (quoted in Tinsley Yarbrough, *A Passion for Justice* [2001]: 196).

Reprisals against Harry and Eliza Briggs and the others were fast and brutal—they lost their jobs and credit. Since many were renting or sharecropping, they were evicted from their homes. Justice Waring himself, ostracized and threatened, was forced to leave the South.

Nevertheless, *Briggs v. Elliott* was re-filed and later merged with lawsuits in Delaware, the District of Columbia, Virginia, and Kansas as *Brown v. Board of Education*. Argued before the Supreme Court by the NAACP chief counsel THURGOOD MARSHALL, the result was the momentous 1954 decision outlawing segregation in public schools.

In 1955 DeLaine received an unsigned letter telling him to get out of town or die, and Ku Klux Klan nightriders fired shots into his house. The police advised DeLaine to shoot back if the nightriders returned, to mark the car. It was a frame-up. Soon his church was burned down, and when the Klan again fired into his home, DeLaine fired back. The state issued a warrant

for his arrest, alleging that he wounded two people. Friends and neighbors sheltered Mrs. DeLaine while helping the Reverend DeLaine to flee the state—his wife following soon after.

DeLaine went to Buffalo, New York, where he was joined by his family, and in 1956 chartered the DeLaine-Waring AME Church, named to honor Judge Waring. He remained in exile, spending several years pastoring a church in Brooklyn, New York, and traveling on behalf of African Methodism to Africa, Europe, the Middle East, Mexico, the West Indies, and Canada. He received many awards for outstanding service to the church and for civil rights. In 1972 DeLaine was stricken with cancer. Heartbroken that he could not return to South Carolina because the warrant remained in effect, he moved to Charlotte, North Carolina, where he died. Forty-five years after the shoot-out and thirty years after his death, in 2000 the warrant was finally dropped, clearing DeLaine's name.

In 2003 Congress issued gold medals to honor DeLaine, Harry and Eliza Briggs, and Levi Pearson for their contributions leading to *Brown*. In 1955 OSSIE DAVIS wrote a play with DeLaine as the central character, *The People of Clarendon County*, celebrating their role in the Supreme Court ruling. This inspired other dramas about *Briggs v. Elliott*: Loften Mitchell's *A Land Beyond the River* (1957), and Julian Wiles's *The Seat of Justice* (2004). DeLaine was also a character in the 2004 film about *Brown* directed by Peter Gilbert, *With All Deliberate Speed*.

FURTHER READING
Joseph Armstrong DeLaine papers (c. 1918–2000) are housed at the University of South Carolina, South Carolina Library, Columbia.
DuBose, Sonny. *The Road to Brown: The Leadership of a Soldier of the Cross, Reverend J. A. DeLaine* (2002).
Kluger, Richard. *Simple Justice* (2004).
Lochbaum, Julie Magruder. *The Word Made Flesh: The Desegregation Leadership of the Rev. J. A. DeLaine* (1999).
Williams, Cecil J. *Out-of-the-Box in Dixie—Cecil Williams' Photography of the South Carolina Events That Changed America* (2007).

ALICE BERNSTEIN

Delaney, Beauford (30 Dec. 1901–26 Mar. 1979), painter, was born in Knoxville, Tennessee, the eighth of ten children, to Delia Johnson, a domestic worker, and John Samuel Delaney, a Methodist minister. Beauford attended the segregated Knoxville Colored High School, from which he graduated with honors. As a teenager, he met a local artist,

Lloyd Branson, who painted impressionist-style landscapes and portraits. For several years Beauford worked for Branson as a porter in exchange for art lessons and began creating representational landscapes and portraits of local Knoxville blacks. Recognizing the young artist's talent, Branson pushed him to pursue formal art studies in Boston and helped finance his education.

In September 1923 Delaney left Knoxville for Boston, where he attended the Massachusetts Normal Art School (now Massachusetts College of Art), studying portraiture and academic traditions. He took classes at the Copley Society, the South Boston School of Art, and the Lowell Institute, and he copied original works of art at the Museum of Fine Arts, the Isabella Stewart Gardner Museum, and the Fogg Art Museum in Cambridge, refining his skills as a draftsman. Gradually, Delaney became fascinated by more modern work, especially that of the impressionist painter Claude Monet, which he saw in a retrospective mounted just after the artist's death in 1926. Monet's late water lily paintings provided an important example of abstract brushwork, light, and color that would prove critical to Delaney's later expressionistic painting.

Delaney arrived in New York City in November 1929 during the height of the Harlem Renaissance and settled in Greenwich Village, where he lived in several different apartments during his twenty-three-year stay. During the early 1930s Delaney supported himself doing traditional pastel and charcoal portraits of dancers and society. He also began producing more experimental works, sketching and painting people in the streets of Greenwich Village and Harlem, using erratic line and bright color. Delaney credited this stylistic shift to his New York environment. "I never drew a decent thing until I felt the rhythm of New York," he explained. "New York has a rhythm as distinct as the beating of a human heart. And I'm trying to put it on canvas.... I paint people. People—and in their faces I hope to discover that odd, mysterious rhythm" (*New York Telegraph*, 27 Mar. 1930).

Newspaper critics increasingly recognized Delaney's work, and in February 1930 the Whitney Studio Gallery included three of his oil portraits and nine pastel drawings in a group exhibition. The Whitney offered him work as a caretaker, gallery guard, and doorman, and in return he received a studio in the basement for two years. Delaney continued his studies with the Ashcan school artist John Sloan and the American regionalist artist Thomas Hart Benton at the Art Students' League

in New York. In late 1930 he began a series of pastel and charcoal drawings of famous African American jazz musicians, including DUKE ELLINGTON, ETHEL WATERS, and LOUIS ARMSTRONG.

During the Works Progress Administration era, Delaney worked as an assistant to CHARLES ALSTON on his Harlem Hospital mural project but found himself drawn to European modernists, such as Cézanne, Gauguin, Van Gogh, and the fauves. He also loved the American modernists, including John Marin, Alfred Stieglitz, Arthur Dove, Georgia O'Keeffe, and Stuart Davis, and saw their work often at Stieglitz's gallery, An American Place. As art sales were slow during the Depression, Delaney earned money teaching art classes at various Greenwich Village schools and at an adult education project in Brooklyn.

In addition to experiencing the racial injustices of the time, Delaney also struggled with his homosexuality. Moreover, he began to suffer long bouts of depression and paranoia aggravated by alcoholism, and these illnesses plagued him throughout the remainder of his life.

In 1934 Delaney began exhibiting in the Washington Square Outdoor Exhibit, and his work became increasingly expressionistic, using distortion, heightened color, and manipulated perspective to create psychologically and spiritually charged paintings. During 1938 Delaney had two solo exhibitions of portraits, at the Eighth Street Playhouse in New York and Gallery C in Washington, D.C., and in October 1938 *Life* magazine featured him as "one of the most talented Negro painters." Delaney became a close friend of the writer JAMES BALDWIN in the early 1940s, and this pivotal friendship lasted throughout Delaney's life, providing companionship and intellectual camaraderie. Over the years Delaney painted roughly twelve portraits of Baldwin, including *Dark Rapture* (1941) and *James Baldwin* (1965).

During the 1940s Delaney's psychological problems and economic circumstances worsened, and, according to many of his notes, his paintings became a kind of salvation, a means of escaping the difficult realities of his daily life. Delaney's commitment to modernism and abstraction intensified, and the influence of European artists, particularly the post-impressionists and the fauves, can be seen in many works of this period, including *Can Fire in the Park* (1946), *Green Street* (1946), and *Washington Square* (1949). By the late 1940s Delaney had become an established expressionist painter in the New York art scene. He received positive reviews when he showed in two group exhibitions at Roko Gallery in 1949, and the following year he was given a solo exhibition there.

In 1950 Delaney won a two-month fall fellowship at the Yaddo writers and artists' community in Saratoga Springs, New York. While there, he read extensively and began thinking seriously about traveling to Paris, where many African American artists were working and living in exile. He returned to Yaddo in November 1951 and, after dispersing his paintings, sailed for Paris on 28 August 1953. Delaney settled in the Montparnasse section of Paris, going to many galleries, and frequenting the Musée d'Art Moderne, the Orangérie, and the city's many galleries. In Paris he found a circle of expatriate artists that included his dear friend James Baldwin, the painters Larry Calcagno, Larry Potter, and Bob Thompson, and the photographer ED CLARK.

While some of his paintings during this time were purely abstract, such as *Abstraction* (1954), others reflect Delaney's travels in Europe. In 1954 he exhibited at the Salon des Réalités Nouvelles in the Musée d'Art Moderne and the Ninth Salon at the Musée des Beaux Arts. By the fall of 1955 he had left Montparnasse for the suburb of Clamart. Still supporting himself through sporadic painting sales and generous contributions from friends, Delaney could not afford psychiatric treatment and suffered ongoing bouts of depression and paranoia that affected his ability to work. When he could concentrate, he vacillated between large-scale abstraction and figuration. In *Composition 16* (1954), Delaney's canvas glows with thick, swirling, intensely colored green, red, and yellow impasto surrounding a central glowing yellow light. *Self-Portrait* (1961) demonstrates the same fascination with light and gestural brushwork, integrated with an expressive likeness of the artist. The most important works to come out of his Paris years, however, were the allover abstractions, both the oil-on-canvas paintings and a series of gouache works on paper, which he showed in three important solo exhibitions at Galerie Paul Facchetti in 1960, the Galerie Lambert in 1964, and the Galerie Darthea Speyer in 1973.

In the summer of 1961 Delaney traveled to Greece. During the trip he was plagued by taunting, threatening voices that eventually led to his hospitalization, a subsequent suicide attempt, and then temporary institutionalization. His patron, Darthea Speyer, the cultural attaché at the American Embassy in Paris, arranged for his return to Paris. Eventually, Delaney's friends began to urge him to get professional psychological help, and he briefly rested at La Maison du Santé de Nogent sur Marne outside Paris. Afterward he stayed with Madame du Closel, a French art collector, and her husband. Delaney soon came under the care of a psychiatrist, Dr. Ferdiere, who specialized in depression and who diagnosed Delaney with acute paranoia. During this period Delaney created a series of quickly executed gouache works on paper that he called Rorschach tests, some done at his doctor's request. Delaney's final years in Paris were spent in a studio at rue Vercingetorix, where he was supported mainly by the du Closels. Despite his doctor's warnings, he drank sporadically, nullifying the effects of his antipsychotic medication. Delaney spent his final years institutionalized in St. Anne's Hospital for the Insane in Montparnasse, where he died in 1979.

FURTHER READING

Leeming, David. *Amazing Grace: A Life of Beauford Delaney* (1998).

Leeming, David, and Robert Rosenfeld Gallery. *Beauford Delaney Liquid Light: Paris Abstractions, 1954–1970* (1999).

Long, Richard, and Studio Museum of Harlem. *Beauford Delaney: A Retrospective* (1978).

Obituaries: *New York Times*, 1 Apr. 1979; *Le Monde*, 5 Apr. 1979; *International Herald Tribune*, 6 Apr. 1979.

LISA D. FREIMAN

Delaney, Emma B. (18 Jan. 1871–7 Oct. 1922), nurse, foreign missionary, and school founder, was born to Anna L. Delaney and Daniel Sharpe Delaney in Fernandina Beach, Florida. Emma Beard Delaney came of age in the postbellum generation that witnessed the collapse of Reconstruction and the fading of the early promise of African American emancipation. Against the rising tide of segregation and racial violence, however, Delaney's family managed to sustain a measure of economic security and educational advancement. Her father, Daniel, held the distinction of being the only African American helmsman commissioned for service on the Revenue Cutter *Boutwell*, a federal ship that patrolled the ports of Savannah, Georgia; Jacksonville, Florida; and Charleston, South Carolina, as a forerunner of the U.S. Coast Guard. The unique benefits of her father's government employment enabled the Delaney family to support an expansive education for Emma and her sister, Annie. In 1889, shortly after completing secondary classes in a convent school in Fernandina Beach, Emma and Annie traveled nearly four hundred miles northwest of their Florida home to begin professional training at Spelman Seminary in Atlanta, Georgia.

When Delaney and her sister arrived in Atlanta, Spelman Seminary's experiment in the exclusive education of African American women and girls was almost a decade old. In 1881 African American Baptists in Georgia joined in a cooperative venture with Sophia Packard and Harriet Giles, representatives of the predominantly white and Boston-based Woman's American Baptist Home Mission Society, to found a freedmen's school that would address the limited opportunities for southern African American women's evangelical education. At the close of its first decade, Spelman Seminary, the school that emerged from the interracial and cross-regional partnership, expanded its early literacy classes and Bible studies to offer professional courses that enabled African American women to assume more expansive leadership roles within southern African American communities. Delaney enrolled in Spelman's newly organized nurse training department and soon became a distinguished student in the seminary's higher education curriculum. After earning a gold medal diploma from the nursing program in 1892, Delaney began professional teacher training in Spelman's academic department. Delaney graduated from the teachers' program in 1894 and enrolled in a third course of study at Spelman. In 1892 the seminary introduced a missionary training department that prepared its graduates to serve as ministers' assistants and missionary teachers for domestic missions to African American and Native American communities in the United States and for foreign missions to colonial Africa. Delaney entered the third class of Spelman's missionary training department. From 1894 through her graduation in 1896 she studied international methods in missiology during the seminary's fall and winter terms, and when Spelman recessed for the summer Delaney completed missionary fieldwork in Gainesville, Macon, and Athens, Georgia.

The lay ministry cultivated in Delaney's missionary studies confirmed what she came to identify as the calling of her life's work. As a child in Fernandina Beach Delaney had attended a church meeting led by an African American missionary returned from Africa and became captivated by the work of Christian missions in the African continent. Although Delaney's family believed her interest in Africa and foreign missionary service was a childhood fancy, her studies in Spelman's missionary training department strengthened the evangelical convictions she experienced as a child. After graduating from Spelman's missionary training department in 1896 Delaney campaigned for a foreign missionary appointment to Africa. As she explained to her classmates and teachers at Spelman, Delaney realized that the post-Reconstruction United States offered a wide and immediate field for Christian witness and reconciliation, but she believed that the more profound fulfillment of Christianity's Great Commission, to go forth and preach the Gospel, called her to undertake the foreign evangelical work that most U.S. Protestants were reluctant to assume. Identifying SOJOURNER TRUTH and the Old Testament Ruth as her evangelical foremothers, Delaney vowed "to leave home, friends, and native land" to carry a message of Christian salvation to the "uttermost parts" of un-Christian Africa (*Spelman Messenger*, Feb. 1902: 5).

Delaney's missionary quest had a number of obstacles to overcome. Her family objected to her trans-Atlantic venture, and as an unmarried African American woman her missionary candidacy troubled the prevailing presumption that the wives of male missionaries were most suited for missionary service. Delaney's foreign commission was not forthcoming, and she accepted a teaching appointment at the Florida Baptist Institute in Live Oak, Florida, instead. Delaney's work at the Florida Baptist Institute brought her to the attention of the African American women's board of Florida's black Baptist state convention. In 1899 the women's board nominated Delaney as a foreign missionary for the National Baptist Convention (NBC), the assembly of African American Baptist state conventions founded in 1895. Delaney's nomination drew the enthusiastic support of the national Woman's Convention of the NBC, and with that organization's pledged support, the Foreign Mission Board of the NBC appointed Delaney as an assistant missionary to the NBC-sponsored Providence Industrial Mission in Chiradzulu, Nyasaland (present-day alawi).

On 15 January 1902 Delaney boarded a New York-docked steamer to begin her two-month journey to the foothills of Central East Africa. From the turn of the nineteenth century through World War I, roughly one hundred African American men, their wives, and a smaller number of unmarried African American women departed the United States as missionaries to Africa. Delaney was the first single black woman appointed by the NBC, and when she arrived in Chiradzulu in the spring of 1902, she became the second African American Baptist to serve within the British Protectorate in Nyasaland. From 1902 to 1905 Delaney worked alongside Rev. Landon Cheek, a black Baptist missionary from Mississippi, and Rev. John Chilembwe, the African evangelist who led the first anticolonial uprising against British governance in Nyasaland in 1915. With the assistance of her young interpreter, an African child christened Daniel Malekebu, Delaney taught sewing, singing, and Bible classes at the Providence Industrial Mission, while attending to the wounds of the African men, women, and children who arrived at the mission station seeking refuge from the violence and political instability in the region.

Delaney returned to the United States in 1905 to recover from a lingering illness she had caught in Chiradzulu. With photographs taken at the Providence Industrial Mission, she began a lecture tour that introduced assemblies of African American Baptists to ethnologies of African life and customs and outlined the needs for a future black Christian union in Africa. Delaney also campaigned for a second missionary appointment to the African continent and in 1912 the New Jersey state convention of black Baptists sponsored her NBC commission to Liberia. Shortly after arriving in the capital of Monrovia in the summer of 1912, Delaney petitioned the Liberian government for a plot of land to build a mission station that would extend the black Christian cooperative modeled at the Providence Industrial Mission. With the government's permission and through a series a negotiations with Golah and Mandingo chiefs, Delaney purchased twenty-five acres of land in Suehn, Liberia, nearly thirty miles inland of Monrovia. Enlisting the labor of West African men living in the region, Delaney founded the Suehn Industrial Mission, an amalgam of church, boarding school, and farm that became the first sustainable black Baptist mission within an interior settlement of Liberia. From 1912 through 1921 the Suehn Industrial Mission expanded to 225 acres that included a rubber tree plantation, palm oil production, and dormitories for the sixty Vey, Bassa, Pessy, Mandingo, Kroo, Congo, Mohammedan, and Americo-Liberian children who arrived at the mission station to learn a common language and unifying system of religious belief.

Delaney departed Liberia in 1921 and arrived at Spelman Seminary to lecture on her experiences directing the Suehn Industrial Mission during the First World War. In 1922 Delaney returned to her family in Fernandina Beach, where she succumbed to the illness that recurred throughout her years in Africa. In the decades that followed her passing, the international and anticolonial politics of the modern civil rights movement largely criticized the Christian bias and imperial overtones that informed foreign missions to colonial Africa. Although Delaney's evangelical project fell out of favor, the mission stations she served at the turn of the twentieth century continued to provide a staging ground for the alliance of African and African American Protestants. In 1926 Daniel Malekebu, the young interpreter Delaney adopted in Nyasaland and sponsored for education in the United States, returned to Chiradzulu to resume the Providence Industrial Mission destroyed in John Chilembwe's thwarted 1915 uprising and laid the foundation for the National Baptist Convention (NBC) of Africa. Despite financial hardship and political instability, the Suehn Industrial Mission, often under the direction of African American Baptist women, continued to convene its interethnic classes until the mission station was destroyed in Liberia's civil wars in the 1990s.

FURTHER READING

Across the first decades of the twentieth century, Emma Beard Delaney's correspondence and missionary reports from Nyasaland and Liberia were regularly republished in her alma mater's *Spelman Messenger* and the National Baptist Convention Foreign Mission Board's *Mission Herald.*

Ashley, Willie Mae Hardy. *Far From Home: A Biography of Emma B. Delaney, Missionary to Africa, 1902–1922* (1987).

Martin, Sandy D. *Black Baptists and African Missions: The Origins of a Movement, 1880–1915* (1989).

Read, Florence M. *The Story of Spelman College* (1961).

BRANDI HUGHES

Delaney, Joseph (1904–21 Nov. 1991), portraitist and American scene painter, was born in Knoxville, Tennessee, the son of a Methodist minister, John Samuel Delaney, and his wife, the former Delia Johnson, who supplemented the family income as an itinerant domestic. Joseph was the ninth of ten children in a family that produced another visual artist of rare ability, his older brother, the noted abstractionist BEAUFORD DELANEY, who was three years Joseph's senior. The Delaneys' early interest in art developed at least in part as a result of drawing on Sunday school cards during their father's regular church services. In an essay written for a catalog of his brother's works in 1978, Joseph Delaney wrote:

Those early years which Beauford and I enjoyed together I am sure shaped the direction of our lives as artists. We were constantly doing something with our hands—modeling with the very red Tennessee clay, also copying pictures…. Beauford and I were complete opposites: me an introvert and Beauford the extrovert.

Joseph Delaney attended the segregated public schools of Knoxville through the ninth grade. Following the death of his father in 1919, Delaney withdrew from Knoxville Colored High School and embarked upon a career of odd jobs in his hometown; he also sought work in Cincinnati and Detroit and found employment as a caddy and bellhop. He went to Chicago in 1924 and returned to Knoxville in 1929.

In 1930 Joseph Delaney left Knoxville once again, this time for New York City, where he joined his older brother Beauford and enrolled at the Art Students League. There he soon came under the influence of the American regionalist painter Thomas Hart Benton and was introduced into a milieu that became the basis of the so-called New York School of the avant-garde, including Delaney's classmates Jackson Pollock, Henry Stair, and Bruce Mitchell.

In 1932 Delaney exhibited in the first Washington Square Outdoor Art Show and continued to work as a sketch artist at this venue for the next forty years; he drew celebrities and society figures such as Eleanor Roosevelt and the actors Tallulah Bankhead, Arlene Francis, and EARTHA KITT. Delaney had a particular talent for capturing the vitality and pulse of urban life, and he indulged his passion for the streets of the city in various images over the years, depicting New York neighborhoods in midtown, uptown, and downtown. In 1934— during the throes of the Depression—the Works Progress Administration (WPA) commissioned Delaney for a variety of projects, including work on murals for Pier 72 and the New York Public Library mural on *The Story of the Recorded Word*.

During this period Delaney began to teach in Harlem and Brooklyn and at the Art Students League while working and socializing with such noted American artists as Reginald Marsh, Pollock, Norman Lewis, ERNEST CRICHLOW, and others. A striking work from this period, a self-portrait dated 3 July 1932 and drawn in graphite (in the collection of Aaron Galleries), shows a sensitive, pensive young man with a haunting gaze of penetrating intelligence, rendered in the best tradition of classical realism. Such a work is quite different from the more mannered, heavily expressionist influenced, and profoundly agitated figurative style that became the hallmark of Delaney's later works.

A Julius Rosenwald Fellowship awarded in 1942 permitted Delaney to travel along the Eastern Seaboard, and he spent his time sketching the region's scenery. Noted particularly for his images of famous personalities, Delaney was influenced by Benton's style. Both artists represented the human figure with a volatile, animated quality of line. Although Delaney remained a representational, figurative artist, the restless surface qualities of his works owe some debt to abstract expressionism. Indeed, Delaney was at least socially linked to the New York School, for Pollock was among his Art Students League associates.

In 1964 Delaney worked as a sketch artist for the New Orleans exhibition of the New York World's Fair and was also employed in a similar capacity for the Ghana exhibition at the same venue. The University of Tennessee recognized Delaney's contributions to American scene painting in 1970 through an exhibition of his works; it purchased his well-known painting *V-J Day, Times Square* (1961), a large, chaotic composition depicting New Yorkers' jubilation at the end of World War II. The work combines critical elements of social realism: Its intrinsic cultural commentary is interpreted in an expressionistic line, and a pulsating, almost overwhelming, sensual vitality comes from in its exaggerated and grotesque forms.

The Comprehensive Employment and Training Act engaged Delaney's services as an artist-in-residence at the Henry Street Settlement from 1978 to 1980. In 1979 his brother Beauford Delaney died in Paris in the asylum of Saint Anne's Hospital. Beauford, who had achieved greater renown as an artist than Joseph, died destitute, and Joseph Delaney was obliged to pay more than six thousand dollars to the French government to recover and transport Beauford's accumulated paintings and personal effects to the United States.

The exhibition Joseph Delaney: A Retrospective, held at the University of Tennessee's Ewing Gallery in 1986, may have prompted his longtime friend, the author ALEX HALEY, to suggest that Delaney serve as the university's artist-in-residence. Delaney was subsequently appointed to the position and lived in a house on Twenty-second Street in Knoxville, close to the university campus, until his death in his native Tennessee in 1991.

FURTHER READING
Delaney, Joseph. "Beauford Delaney, My Brother," in *Beauford Delaney: A Retrospective* (1978).

Bearden, Romare, and Harry Henderson. "Joseph Delaney," in *A History of African-American Artists From 1792 to the Present* (1993): 287–292.

Honig-Fine, Elsa. "Joseph Delaney," in *The Afro-American Artist: A Search for Identity* (1973): 134–136.

Lewis, Samella. "Joseph Delaney," in *Art: African American* (1978): 97.

FRANK MARTIN

Delaney, Lucy Ann Berry (1830?–1890?), autobiographer and religious leader, was born Lucy Ann Berry in St. Louis, Missouri, to Polly Crocket Berry, who was born free in Illinois, but was kidnapped and enslaved as a child. She and her husband, whose name is not known, were enslaved by Major Taylor Berry of St. Louis and had two children, Lucy and Nancy. Delaney's early childhood was relatively happy; she was not aware of her position as a slave nor was she expected to perform any labor for her owners. Lucy Delaney's peaceful childhood was interrupted when Major Berry, who had paradoxically been both a master and a friend to her father, was killed in a duel. After Berry's death, his widow remarried, and Delaney's father was sold south, contrary to the Major's will. This traumatic separation only increased Polly Berry's determination to escape with her daughters to freedom; she reminded them frequently that she was a free woman, and promised that they would not die as slaves.

Berry, using the knowledge she had gained growing up in the free state of Illinois, choreographed Nancy's escape to Canada. With Nancy in safety, both Lucy and Polly remained ever-watchful for their own opportunity of escape. After an argument with Mrs. Mary Cox, Major Berry's daughter and her new mistress, Polly Berry was sold south for daring to speak independently. Three weeks later Polly escaped, finding kind support despite the enactment of the Fugitive Slave Law. Caught up by slave-catchers in Chicago, Polly was surrounded by hundreds of indignant supporters, but finally gave herself up and returned to St. Louis for fear that Mr. Cox would revenge her loss by harming Lucy. Polly hired a lawyer and sued for her freedom; abundant testimony supported her claim that she had been kidnapped, so the jury ruled in her favor and her free papers were issued.

Though her mother was now at liberty, Lucy herself struggled under the burden of domestic labor in the service of another of the Major's daughters, a Mrs. Mitchell. Unaccustomed to performing household labor, Lucy was now expected to perform the arduous chores of laundry and ironing. Her failure at the task—she unwittingly stained the clothes with the muddy Mississippi water available for the job—prompted an angry confrontation with her mistress. Lucy successfully repelled her mistress's attacks with shovel, broomstick, and other instruments at hand. Mitchell, uncomfortable with the violence Lucy's presence elicited in his wife and unwilling to whip Lucy himself as Mrs. Mitchell urged, suggested selling the girl. Lucy was no less anxious to be sold than to be whipped. She ran away, hoping to take shelter at her mother's home nearby; though Polly was away working, a white neighbor woman was able to help the child open her mother's door. Late that night, after her return, Polly took Lucy to a friend's house for concealment.

On 8 September 1842 Polly Berry sued Mitchell for possession of her daughter, claiming that Delaney's status as the daughter of a freedwoman made her enslavement illegal. Delaney spent seventeen months in jail awaiting her trial. Berry, on the advice of friends, approached Judge Edward Bates and asked him to plead the case. Bates, an abolitionist of Quaker descent who identified with the Free Labor party in Missouri during the Missouri Compromise and lost to Abraham Lincoln at the 1860 National Republican Convention, though he later became Lincoln's Attorney General, agreed, taking Berry's lack of funds into consideration and requiring only money to cover his expenses. At the trial Bates's stirring testimony, which recounted Berry's attempts to gain her freedom as well as her devotion to her daughter, enthralled his listeners. Despite the bitter arguments of Mitchell's lawyer, Thomas Hutchinson, the judge granted Delaney her freedom and her release prompted an intensely joyful reunion between mother and daughter.

Finally able to live in freedom, the two began to ply their talents, Delaney as a seamstress and Berry as a laundress, in hopes of funding a trip to Canada to visit her sister Nancy. Berry enjoyed a reunion with Nancy, now married to a successful farmer, and her children. In 1845 Delaney married a steamboat hand named Frederick Turner and moved with him to Quincy, Illinois, but shortly thereafter Turner was killed by an explosion aboard the steamboat *Edward Bates*, connecting Delaney's first great joy—freedom—with her first great sorrow. Four years later, she married Zachariah Delaney of Cincinnati. Though the couple bore four children, two died as infants and two others died in their early twenties. Polly Berry continued to live with Lucy until her death. Delaney kept up a continual search for her father and was eventually rewarded with a reunion forty-five years after their initial separation. However, his hard labor on a plantation near Vicksburg had marked him heavily, and he felt out of place in his old home, preferring to return to Vicksburg rather than stay with his daughter. Delaney's later years were devoted to the religious, social, and relief activities of the Methodist Episcopal Church, which she joined in 1855. She held numerous leadership positions, serving as president of the Female Union, the "first colored society" for women, as well as the Daughters of Zion (Delaney, 62). The date and circumstances of Lucy Delaney's death are unknown.

FURTHER READING

Delaney, Lucy. "From the Darkness Cometh the Light, or Struggles for Freedom," in *Six Women's Slave Narratives* (1988).

SARA KAKAZU

Delaney, Sarah Peterson (Sadie Delaney) (26 Feb. 1889–4 May 1958), librarian and bibliotherapist, was born in Rochester, New York, the third of seven children born to Julia Frances (Hawkins) and James Johnson. Delaney's father, who worked as a valet in Poughkeepsie, New York, was a direct descendant of a woman who had escaped from slavery on the Underground Railroad. Born Sara Marie Johnson, Sadie graduated from high school and went on to attend Miss McGovern's School of Social Work, the City College of New York, and the New York Public Library's library school. She was married to Edward Louis Peterson from 1906 to 1921 and together they had one daughter, Grace Peterson Hooks, born in 1907. In 1928, she married Rudicel A. Delaney of Virginia.

In 1920 Delaney began her career as a librarian at the 135th Street Branch of the New York Public Library in Harlem, where she was to become acquainted with many figures of the burgeoning Harlem Renaissance. Delaney and her library played host to many of the movement's premier writers and artists during weekly forums, programs, and exhibits. During her tenure at the Harlem library Delaney also worked with several specialized groups of library users, developing an interest and expertise in youth library services and in services to the blind and handicapped. She even learned Braille to better serve her special needs library clientele. Her energy, creativity, and professionalism touched many and she consistently received commendations and recognition from her colleagues and from the Harlem community.

Perhaps Delaney's greatest contribution to the field of librarianship was her groundbreaking work in the development of the library specialty of bibliotherapy, which she promoted beginning in 1924 when she left the New York Public Library to become the founding chief librarian of the United States Veterans Administration (VA) Hospital in Tuskegee, Alabama. Opening the brand new library in January 1924 with limited space and supplies she enlivened her library with plants, maps, and photographs in an effort to make the library welcoming and mentally stimulating. As the library began to grow Delaney added various types of reading materials and even began a small collection of books and journals for use by the hospital staff. The library also offered cultural programs and discussion groups, not unlike Delaney's program offerings in New York.

Delaney defined bibliotherapy as "the treatment of a patient through selected reading" (Bethel, 262). Bibliotherapy, as used in consultation with the hospital's medical staff, became an effective tool through which to help black veterans fight and reduce anxiety, depression, loneliness, aggression, guilt, boredom, and other emotional ailments. Books, other reading materials, and the library's auxiliary programs and events became an escape and source of great pleasure for the hospital's patients, to whom Delaney introduced all manner of literature and many different genres of reading. Perhaps it is no surprise that the black veterans favored the literature of the Harlem Renaissance and any and all reading materials concerning African American life. The literature provided comfort and enlightenment, and enabled the veterans to reconnect with their culture and the society they had left.

To the VA hospital Delaney also brought her knowledge of Braille and her interest in the blind and handicapped; she equipped her library with the essential instruments and talking books, expanding her library services and bibliotherapy efforts. To be sure, Delaney did not create bibliotherapy, but she did greatly enhance the practice and raise the bar for future practitioners. Bibliotherapy remained a useful tool in the medical, counseling, teaching, and library communities as a method of reaching various population groups, including those with emotional and mental disorders, and children and young adults in need of coping skills.

During her thirty-four years at the VA hospital Delaney made strides inside the library and in the professional library community; her work with bibliotherapy made her a sought-after speaker and teacher, and her experiences and methods were shared on an international level. Many bibliotherapy programs were created and modeled on Delaney's work. Delaney belonged to numerous professional library organizations, including the American Library Association's Hospital Library Division and the International Hospital Library Guild, and many other cultural organizations such as the National Council of Colored Women, the NAACP, and the Friendship League of America. Outside of her professional interests, Delaney collected stamps and coins and she was a refined connoisseur of antiques and art objects, such as glass works and rare porcelain.

Before her death of a heart attack Delaney received over fifty commendations for her bibliotherapy, volunteer, and cultural endeavors. Her accolades came from the library and medical fields and from many different cultural organizations, including the National Urban League. Most notably Delaney received an honorary doctorate from Atlanta University in 1950. For her contributions to the library profession and to the African American community Delaney remains revered as a pioneer.

FURTHER READING

Bethel, Kathleen. "Librarianship," in *Black Women in America*, 2nd edition, ed. Darlene Clark Hine (2005).

Dawson, Alma. "Celebrating African-American Librarians and Librarianship," *Library Trends* 49.1 (2000).

Gubert, Betty K. "Sadie Peterson Delaney: Pioneer Bibliotherapist," *American Libraries* 24.2 (1993).

Gubert, Betty K. "Sara 'Sadie' P. Delaney," in *Notable Black American Women*, vol. 1, ed. Jessie Carney Smith (1992).

NICOLE A. COOKE

Delany, Bessie and Sadie Delany (3 Sept. 1891–25 Sept. 1995) and (19 Sept. 1889–25 Jan. 1999), were born Annie Elizabeth Delany and Sarah Louise Delany in Raleigh, North Carolina, the daughters of Henry Beard Delany, an educator and Episcopal bishop, and Nanny James Logan. Bessie was to become a dentist, and Sadie a schoolteacher; late in life, they gained fame for their published reminiscences. Descended from a mix of black, American Indian, and white lineages, the sisters grew up in a family of ten children in Raleigh on the campus of St. Augustine's, the African American school where their father, a former slave, served as priest and vice principal. The sisters graduated from St. Augustine's

(Sadie in 1910 and Bessie in 1911) at a time when few Americans, black or white, were educated beyond grammar school. "We had everything you could want except money," recalled Bessie. "We had a good home, wonderful parents, plenty of love, faith in the Lord, educational opportunities—oh, we had a privileged childhood for colored children of the time" (*Smithsonian*, Oct. 1993, 150).

After completing their studies at St. Augustine's, both Sadie and Bessie went on to teaching jobs in North Carolina. Their father had strongly urged his daughters to teach, since he was unable to finance further education at a four-year college. He also advised them to make their own way, warning them against accepting scholarships that would obligate them to benefactors. Bessie took a job in the mill town of Boardman, while Sadie became the domestic science supervisor for all of the black schools in Wake County. Although she received no extra salary, Sadie also assumed the duties of supervisor of black schools in the county. Both sisters were shocked by the conditions their students lived in. Bessie later said in the sisters' joint memoir, *Having Our Say: The Delany Sisters' First 100 Years* (1993), that she found the families in Boardman "poor and ignorant" (89). Sadie remarked that her students' families in Wake County were "in bad shape" and that they "needed help with the basics" and "didn't know how to cook, clean, eat properly, or anything" (81). She therefore concentrated her efforts on teaching sanitation, hygiene, and food preparation. She also convinced many of her charges to continue their education.

In 1916 Sadie moved to Harlem in New York City and enrolled at Pratt Institute, then a two-year college. After graduating in 1918 she enrolled at Columbia University, where she earned a B.S. in 1920. She returned to North Carolina briefly with the intention of helping her people but, discouraged by the pervasive Jim Crow system, soon returned to Harlem. She encountered racism in New York but concluded that the North "was an improvement over the South" (107). She began teaching in an elementary school in Harlem in 1920, and for several years she also ran a candy business. In 1925 she received her master's degree in education from Columbia. Beginning in 1930, she taught at Theodore Roosevelt High School, a white school in the Bronx. Having skipped the interview because she feared her color would cost her the job, Sadie stunned school officials on the first day of school; but as she later observed, "Once I was in, they couldn't figure out how to get rid of me" (120). With her appointment, Sadie became the first African American in New York City to teach domestic science at the high school level.

In 1918, after teaching for a short time in Brunswick, Georgia, and taking science courses at Shaw University in Raleigh, Bessie joined her sister in New York, where she enrolled the following year in the dentistry program at Columbia University. She completed her DDS in 1923 and became only the second black female dentist licensed in the state of New York, with a practice in Harlem. She was well known there as "Dr. Bessie" and her office was a meeting place for black leaders, including JAMES WELDON JOHNSON and E. FRANKLIN FRAZIER. During the Depression of the 1930s she found herself twice evicted from her office, but she persisted in her work.

During their childhood the Delany sisters had encountered the segregation and the discrimination of the Jim Crow South and the threat of violence that underlay the system. Bessie remembered the first time she faced segregation when, as a child in the mid-1890s, she found she could no longer go to the park that she had previously played in, and she also recalled experimenting with drinking the water from a "whites only" fountain and discerning no difference in its taste. Yet, like her sister, she found that in the North, too, restrictions and dangers hemmed her in. Bessie's closest brush with the Ku Klux Klan came not in the South, however, but on Long Island.

Neither Bessie nor Sadie ever married. Nanny Delany had urged her daughters to decide whether they were going to marry and raise families or have careers. As Bessie said years later, it never occurred to anyone that a woman could have both a family and a profession, and the sisters decided on careers. Bessie and Sadie lived together for nearly eight decades in New York City and then in nearby Mount Vernon, and they were surrounded by family members. All but one of their siblings settled in Harlem, and after their father's death in 1928 their mother lived with them. The sisters were devoted to their mother, and it was largely to please her that after World War II they left Harlem and moved to a cottage in the north Bronx. In 1950 Bessie gave up her dental practice to care for their mother full time. After their mother's death in 1956, the sisters moved to Mount Vernon, where they purchased a house in an all-white neighborhood. Sadie retired in 1960. Sadie was amiable by nature, having broken the color barrier in the New York City public schools through craft instead of confrontation. By contrast,

Bessie was feisty and contentious, accustomed to speaking her mind. "We loved our country," she observed, "even though it didn't love us back" (60). Asked her impression of the Statue of Liberty when she first entered New York harbor, she replied that it was important as a symbol to white immigrants but meant nothing to her. Regarding her experience at Columbia University, she noted: "I suppose I should be grateful to Columbia, that at that time they let in colored people. Well, I'm not. They let me in but they beat me down for being there! I don't know how I got through that place, except when I was young nothing could hold me back" (115).

The Delany sisters might have escaped notice by the wider world had they not in 1993 coauthored a best-selling memoir with the assistance of Amy Hill Hearth. *Having Our Say: The Delany Sisters' First 100 Years* had its origins in an essay that Hearth had written for the *New York Times* on the occasion of Bessie's one-hundredth birthday. So enthusiastic were readers' responses to the article that Hearth continued her interviews and produced the book. Published when Bessie was 102 and Sadie was 104, *Having Our Say* offered a perceptive, witty review of the sisters' lives through the previous century. As Hearth observed in her introduction to the book, it was meant less as a study of black history or of women's history than of American history, but the sisters' age, race, and gender combined to provide a tart perspective on the past. These two black women spoke of their strong family, the racism and sexism that could have thwarted them, and their triumphs. They spoke of their experiences as teachers in the segregated South, their participation in the mass migration of African Americans from the South to the urban North, and—although more briefly—their recollections of the Harlem Renaissance in the 1920s and the Great Depression of the 1930s. *Having Our Say* remained on the *New York Times* best-seller list—first in hardback and then as a paperback—for seventy-seven weeks.

By the time Bessie Delany died at age 104 at her Mount Vernon home in 1995, *Having Our Say* had sold nearly a million copies in hardback or paper and had been translated into four foreign languages. Reviewers were generally enthusiastic about the book, but an unsigned commentary in the *Women's Review of Books* in January 1994 questioned the role of Amy Hill Hearth as a white woman selectively pulling together the recollections of two elderly black women. Such criticism did not, however, diminish the popular appeal of the sisters' story, which was adapted as a Broadway play in 1995 and as a television movie in 1999, starring DIAHANN CARROLL as Sadie and RUBY DEE as Bessie. That same year Sadie Delany died in Mount Vernon, at age 109.

FURTHER READING

The Delany family papers are at St. Augustine's College, Raleigh, North Carolina.

Delany, Sarah L., and A. Elizabeth Delany, with Amy Hill Hearth. *The Delany Sisters' Book of Everyday Wisdom* (1994).

Delany, Sarah L., and A. Elizabeth Delany, with Amy Hill Hearth. *Having Our Say: The Delany Sisters' First 100 Years* (1993).

Delany, Sarah L., with Amy Hill Hearth. *On My Own at 107: Reflections on Life without Bessie* (1997).

Obituaries: Bessie Delany: *New York Times* and *Washington Post*, 26 Sept. 1995; Sadie Delany: *New York Times*, 26 Jan. 1999.

This entry is taken from the *American National Biography* and is published here with the permission of the American Council of Learned Societies.

RICHARD HARMOND AND
PETER WALLENSTEIN

Delany, Clarissa Scott (1901–1927), poet, essayist, educator, and social worker, was born Clarissa Mae Scott in Tuskegee, Alabama, the third of five children born to EMMETT JAY SCOTT and Elenor Baker Scott. Her father served as secretary to BOOKER T. WASHINGTON, the founder of Tuskegee Institute; secretary-treasurer at Howard University; and special adviser on African American Affairs to President Woodrow Wilson. Scott spent her early years in Tuskegee, where she had access to intellectual, social, and cultural activities available to students, faculty, and staff at Tuskegee Institute; she was educated in New England, entering Bradford Academy in 1916, then Wellesley College in 1919.

At Wellesley, Scott was an active, competitive student, who earned scholarship honors, participated on the debate team, and earned a letter in field hockey. She was also a talented singer and pianist, and held memberships in various social groups and religious organizations. Delany attended meetings of Boston's Literary Guild and is identified as one who contributed to the writing of poetry by African American Bostonians, an activity that provided her entry into the cultural activities of the Harlem Renaissance. The era was characterized by the production of copious amounts of literature, increased racial consciousness; there were outpourings of

music, painting, and dancing as well as social and political involvement. Scott graduated from Wellesley with Phi Beta Kappa honors in 1923, which led to an article about her in the June 1923 issue of *The Crisis* with her photograph on the cover.

Scott traveled to France and Germany and after returning to the United States, she accepted a teaching position at Dunbar High School in Washington, D.C., where she chose to remain only three years. During this period, she started her brief writing and publishing career. Scott was further immersed in the atmosphere of the Harlem Renaissance through her participation in the Saturday Nighters Club in Washington, D.C., where GEORGIA DOUGLAS JOHNSON hosted the literary gatherings in her home. In this setting, the younger and the more established writers discussed their works, exchanged ideas, and received encouragement and inspiration from each other. Guests included such well-known figures of the period as William Waring Cuney, STERLING BROWN, ANGELINA WELD GRIMKÉ, Richard Bruce Nugent, LANGSTON HUGHES, JEAN TOOMER, ALICE DUNBAR-NELSON, JAMES WELDON JOHNSON, W. E. B. DuBois, JESSIE FAUSET, ALAIN LOCKE, and GWENDOLYN BENNETT.

After her marriage to HUBERT T. DELANY in the fall of 1926, the couple moved to New York City, where she was employed as a social worker. She became director of the Joint Committee on the Negro Child Study. In a venture with the National Urban League and the Women's City Club of New York, Delany gathered information and published a study regarding delinquency and neglect of New York City black children. Hubert Delany, a successful attorney, earned prestigious positions, including that of a court justice.

Because of patterns of exclusion, it was customary for many women writers of the early twentieth century to have their works published in anthologies and literary periodicals. Lyric poetry was widely considered a proper genre for women. Delany's four published poems illustrated her talents. "Solace" tied for fourth place in a 1925 poetry contest sponsored by *Opportunity: A Journal of Negro Life*. In 1926, "Joy" appeared in *Opportunity* and "The Mask" in *Palms*. In 1927 COUNTÉE CULLEN published these three poems and "Interim" in *Caroling Dusk: An Anthology of Verse by Negro Poets*. "The Mask" makes use of a common theme in African American literature, reflecting the practice of African Americans to hide their thoughts and feelings as a form of protection. The narrator states, "I turned aside until the mask was slipped once more in place." Both "Joy," and "Interim," make use of figurative language and present descriptions of nature with references to "roistering wind," "stalwart pines," sun, and rain. The tone of these poems is solemn and introspective.

In an essay titled "A Golden Afternoon in Germany," published in *Opportunity*, Delany described her experiences touring Europe. She also wrote several reviews, which were also published in *Opportunity*. Her contemporaries, W. E. B. DuBois among them, praised her poetry. Angelina Weld Grimké eulogized her in a poem, "To Clarissa Scott Delany," which was published in CHARLES S. JOHNSON's *Ebony and Topaz* in 1927. Illustrating the strength, relevance, and timelessness of her lyrics, JOHNNETTA COLE selected Delany's "Interim" for inclusion in her inaugural address as president of Spelman College in 1988. The actor DANNY GLOVER included lines from "Interim" in his address celebrating Spelman's 121st commencement. He charged the graduates to not be afraid to venture out, quoting the closing lines of Delany's poem, "Another day will find me brave/ And not afraid to dare."

In 1927 Delany returned to her parents' home in Washington, D.C., where she died. Her death, as noted on her death certificate, was caused by kidney disease, possibly a reaction to streptococcal infection that she had endured over a six-month period. It was also speculated that she died of a lung infection, probably tuberculosis. In 1931 her family established YWCA Camp Clarissa Scott on land they donated on Chesapeake Bay.

FURTHER READING

Hatch, Shari, and Michael R. Strickland, eds. "Delany, Clarissa (nee Scott)," *African-American Writers: A Dictionary* (2000).

Roses, Lorraine, and Ruth Randolph. "Delany, Clarissa M. Scott (1901–1927)," *Harlem Renaissance and Beyond: Literary Biographies of 100 Black Women Writers 1900–1945* (1990).

Smith, Jessie Carney. "Clarissa Scott Delany," *Notable Black American Women* (1992).

GWENDOLYN S. JONES

Delany, Hubert T. (11 May 1901–28 Dec. 1990), lawyer, judge, politician, and civil rights advocate, was born Hubert Thomas Delany in Raleigh, North Carolina, the eighth of ten children of Nanny Logan Delany and the Episcopal Suffragan Bishop Henry Beard Delany.

Until he was fourteen years old Delany assumed that he would follow his father into the priesthood of the Episcopal Church. But in 1915 Delany visited Christ Church on Capitol Square in Raleigh to hear a choir that accompanied a prominent bishop from New York. Much to his surprise he was guided into the gallery by an usher who asked the young man why he did not attend Saint Ambrose, the colored Episcopal church.

Having grown up on the campus of historically black Saint Augustine's College where his parents taught, Hubert Delany had, until that moment, been protected from the rigid system of racial segregation that gripped North Carolina in the early twentieth century. Disappointed in his church, Delany turned his future toward the law.

Completing the high school program at Saint Augustine's in 1919 Delany soon followed his older siblings to Harlem. Working his way through college as a Red Cap at Penn Station, Delany graduated from City College in 1923, and taught at P.S. 80 in Harlem while studying law at night at New York University, graduating in 1926. That same year Delany married Clarissa Scott, a Phi Beta Kappa graduate of Wellesley and a promising poet who taught at Washington's elite black Dunbar High School. Born in Tuskegee, Alabama, Clarissa was the daughter of EMMETT JAY SCOTT, the former personal secretary to BOOKER T. WASHINGTON and secretary-treasurer at Howard University. Within the year, CLARISSA SCOTT DELANY died of kidney disease.

Delany set up his law practice in an office shared with James S. Watson at 240 Broadway. An active Democratic politician Watson was patriarch of a prominent Harlem family of Jamaican origins. Through his wife Delany became acquainted with the luminaries of the Harlem Renaissance and many of them remained his friends and clients throughout his life, including LANGSTON HUGHES and PAUL ROBESON. In 1927 Delany was appointed assistant U.S. attorney for the southern district of New York. Two years later he received the Republican nomination to fill Greater Harlem's 21st District congressional seat. Delany was advised not to campaign in Washington Heights in hopes that Irish Americans would assume, based on his name, that he was one of them. He campaigned there and lost the election. Fellow Republican Fiorello La Guardia was running for reelection in a nearby district and the two men became friends. When La Guardia was elected mayor of New York in 1933, he appointed Delany to the City Tax Commission.

In that same year, 1933, Delany became the only black partner in a law firm made up of former assistants in the U.S. Attorney's office, the second black member of the Bar Association of New York City, and was admitted to practice before the U.S. Supreme Court.

After the Harlem Riot of 1935 Mayor La Guardia appointed Delany and others, including E. FRANKLIN FRAZIER, COUNTÉE CULLEN, and A. PHILIP RANDOLPH, to the investigatory commission that found that the riot was caused not by communist agitators but by economic deprivation, racial discrimination, and an unresponsive city government.

Hubert Delany was an early member of the Council on African Affairs, founded in 1937 by Paul Robeson and MAX YERGAN. In 1947 the attorney general of the United States included the council on his list of subversive "communist-front" organizations. The next year Delany and several other members of the council, including the educator MARY MCLEOD BETHUNE and the Harlem pastor and politician ADAM CLAYTON POWELL JR., resigned, possibly in response to cold war pressures and a growing schism between Robeson and Yergan.

By the late 1930s Delany was serving on the executive boards of the National Lawyers Guild and the National Association for the Advancement of Colored People. At the NAACP he was initially among the strongest supporters of the *Crisis* editor W. E. B. DuBois, whose political philosophy was becoming increasingly separatist. However, in 1948, Delany supported DuBois's termination. Ten years later, however, when DuBois celebrated his ninetieth birthday, Delany was one of the principal speakers.

Among Delany's many clients was the classical contralto MARIAN ANDERSON. After the Daughters of the American Revolution refused to allow Anderson to perform in Constitution Hall in Washington, D.C., in 1939 Delany introduced the resolution to the executive board of the NAACP that led to her performing instead on the steps of the Lincoln Memorial.

Delany married the former Willetta Smith in the 1940s. A native of Yonkers, New York, and an alumna of Howard University, she had served as Delany's secretary at the Tax Commission. This second marriage made Hubert Delany the father of a daughter, Madelon, who became a professor at City College, and a son, Harry, who became one of New York's leading surgeons.

Mayor Fiorello La Guardia appointed Delany to the Domestic Relations Court in New York in 1942, where he served until 1955 when Mayor Robert F. Wagner refused to reappoint him because of his "left-wing views." Wagner refused to elaborate on his objections to Delany's politics and his action prompted a storm of protest from black organizations and individuals. Writing in the *New York Post*, TED POSTON described Wagner's action as a victory for the Democratic Manhattan borough president Hulan Jack. In late 1959, as MARTIN LUTHER KING JR. left Montgomery's Dexter Avenue Baptist to return to his father's church, Ebenezer Baptist in Atlanta, Alabama, authorities charged King with failure to pay income tax. At the historic moment when lunch counter sit-ins were spreading across the South, Hubert Delany, leading King's legal team, won a "not guilty" verdict from an all-white Alabama jury.

Hubert Delany died of heart disease in New York City.

FURTHER READINGS

Almost nothing has been written about Hubert Delany, although he is mentioned in passing in a number of books about the Harlem Renaissance, New York politics, and the civil rights movement. He corresponded with most of the leading figures of African American culture and politics in the twentieth century and his letters can be found in several collections in the Beinecke Library at Yale, the Library of Congress, and the Moorland-Spingarn Collection at Howard University.

ROBERT HINTON

Delany, Martin Robison (6 May 1812–24 Jan. 1885), political activist, doctor, newspaper editor, and author, was born in Charles Town, Virginia (now West Virginia), son of Samuel Delany, a slave, and Pati Peace, the free daughter of free and African-born Graci Peace. In 1822 Pati fled with her children to Chambersburg, Pennsylvania; Samuel joined her in 1823 after purchasing his freedom.

In 1831 in Pittsburgh, Delany studied history, geography, literature, and political economy, informally, with Lewis Woodson and Molliston M. Clark. Here Delany began his restless, wide-ranging advocacy of African American political rights, cultural self-reliance, and independent enterprise. Opposed to physical and "servile" work, Delany apprenticed himself to a white doctor in 1833. During his time in Pittsburgh he joined or helped found several African American antislavery, temperance, historical, literary, and moral reform societies. When Pennsylvania rescinded black suffrage in 1839,

Delany explored Mexican Texas, where slavery was illegal and blacks could become citizens. However, usurping American slaveholders were moving in, and Delany returned to Pittsburgh, ending his first attempt to find or found a nation for himself and his people. In 1843, by now an established "cupper and leecher" (a person who drew blood for medicinal purposes), Delany married Catherine A. Richards, daughter of a once-wealthy mixed-race businessman. Unusually, they named their six surviving sons after prominent black heroes; their daughter, symbolically, Halle Amelia Ethiopia.

In August 1843, Delany launched the *Mystery*, a weekly newspaper that argued against slavery and for equality between the races. In 1847, now a recognized leader and an officer in his Freemason's Lodge, Delany impressed the abolitionists William Lloyd Garrison and FREDERICK DOUGLASS. Garrison wrote to his wife (16 Aug. 1847) that Delany was "Black as jet, ... a fine fellow of great energy and spirit." Promised a wider editorial field, Delany joined the staff at Douglass's forthcoming *North Star*. For a year and a half he promoted the newspaper, lectured, attended meetings, described and criticized the conditions and attitudes of black people from Detroit to Delaware, and wrote editorials on black political possibilities from Canada to Cuba. But by July 1849, his domestic reports turned pessimistic and he resigned a poor man from the financially strapped *North Star* and returned again to Pittsburgh.

Concluding that the Fugitive Slave Law section of the Compromise of 1850, which commanded Americans to return slaves fleeing to the North, also threatened to reenslave free blacks, Delany was moved to bolder assertions of his rights. Delany took recommendations from seventeen doctors to Harvard Medical School, where he was allowed to study for one term before a majority of white students petitioned that he be expelled. Delany made his way home by lecturing to black audiences on the physiological superiority of blacks to whites. Back in Pittsburgh, Delany moved his family to a section called Hayti, practiced medicine, and also served as principal of the Colored School.

Delany began to travel further afield. The 1851 North American Convention of Colored Freemen in Toronto, which resolved to encourage American slaves to come to Canada instead of going to Africa, took him to Canada. Then in April 1852 a settlement of free blacks in Nicaragua elected Delany "Mayor of Greytown ..., civil governor of the Mosquito Reservation and commander in chief of the military forces of the province" (Ullman,

139). A lack of funds stranded him in New York City, but there he hurriedly cobbled together the first book-length, antisentimental, sociopolitical report on "free" African Americans: *The Condition, Elevation, Emigration, and Destiny of the Colored People of the United States, Politically Considered* (1852). Sketches of contributions to the nation from 104 blacks were surrounded by reminders of white repression, condescension, and black dependence, leading to bold anticolonizationist, black-nationalist, pro-black–led emigrationist arguments and conclusions. Appearing, however, only a month after Harriet Beecher Stowe's *Uncle Tom's Cabin*, Delany's book received little attention.

Almost a year later, Delany criticized Douglass for commending Stowe's efforts while neglecting Delany's attempts to reshape black political discourse. By 1853 Delany was well along in composing his long fiction, *Blake*, but before its appearance, he published his "Origin and Objects of Ancient Freemasonry," a pamphlet claiming that Africans were the founders of the order and demanding white acceptance or rejection. He organized the National Emigration Convention in Cleveland, Ohio, in opposition to Douglass's often-praised "We will fight it out here" Colored National Convention in Rochester, New York, in 1853. Delany's keynote address at the Cleveland convention sharpened the emigrationist arguments he had introduced in *Condition*.

Despite being honored in Pittsburgh for his efforts in an 1854 cholera epidemic, Delany moved his family to largely black Chatham, Canada, in 1856. Two years later, he arranged a meeting between African Americans and the militant white abolitionist John Brown, while also attempting to raise money to explore Africa. The U.S. Supreme Court's 1857 DRED SCOTT decision denied African Americans full citizenship rights and stated that, even in the North or in the new free territories, blacks were "beings of an inferior order" with "no rights which the white man was bound to respect." The ruling led several prominent black leaders to contemplate leaving the United States, as Delany had done, and encouraged some African Americans to plan immigration to Canada, Haiti, Central America, and Africa.

Delany's fiction found a publisher in January 1859, when the new monthly *Anglo-African Magazine* began printing twenty-six chapters of *Blake, or the Huts of America: A Tale of the Mississippi Valley, the Southern United States, and Cuba*. The work deliberately challenged earlier representations of slaves and free blacks. Not a novel, its freer form sampled several genres and offered a wide-ranging, conversational, song-and-verse-infused mix of imagined and real-world situations, characters, and observations. Its daring but careful hero prepared blacks to revolt against their oppressors from Texas to Dahomey in Africa. In July, the tale's printing was suspended because its author was in Africa. Delany explored Liberia before going on to present-day Nigeria, where he and his fellow explorer, Robert Campbell, negotiated an agreement with several chiefs allowing African American emigrants the right to settle on arable land.

Delany subsequently spent seven months in England, where he raised interest in and money for his African emigration project. He returned to Canada on the eve of the American Civil War and published American and English versions of his *Official Report of the Niger Valley Exploring Party* (1861). Although he continued to encourage American blacks to consider emigration, he discovered in 1862 that white British missionaries and colonialists had undermined his African plans. Stymied again, Delany returned to writing. He simplified *Blake's* dialect transcriptions and a complete version appeared in the *Weekly Anglo-African* newspaper between November 1861 and June 1862. Unfortunately, the May 1862 issues have been lost, and only seventy-four of the promised eighty chapters survive. The last available words portentously warn: "'Woe be unto those devils of whites, I say!'" (*WAA*, 26 Apr. 1862).

The Emancipation Proclamation of January 1863 opened up the prospect of full citizenship for African Americans, and immediately Delany began recruiting for black regiments across the North. Around that time he moved his family to a new home near Wilberforce College in Ohio. In February 1865 he became the first black major to be assigned a field command when he was commissioned as a major in the 104th United States Colored Troops. Although the war was soon over, Delany continued to serve the unionist and abolitionist cause by taking a position with the Freedmen's Bureau.

For three years, Delany lectured and encouraged blacks in South Carolina, where African Americans were in the majority, to gain education, land, and a level of self-respect and political power that had been impossible under slavery—or even in the antebellum North. He brokered formal and informal contracts between blacks and whites, poor landholders, even-poorer workers, and racially prejudiced northerners and southerners. In 1868

he was a delegate to the democratically innovative South Carolina State Constitutional Convention.

Delany also continued to write. From war's end through 1871, he wrote essays on the failures of southern political leadership during the war, the economic hopes for freedmen, and the racist neglect of a once glorious African culture in Egypt. His writings also examined the rights and duties of citizenship, and ways in which northern capital, southern land, and black workers might make a better United States.

During these busy years, Delany worked with FRANCES ROLLIN on *Life and Public Services of Martin R. Delany* (1868, reprinted in 1883), one of the few nineteenth-century biographies of an African American. However, the book's optimistic prediction of improved circumstances for Delany and other blacks did not materialize. Stubbornly, he persistently sought to establish for himself a respectable position, but was unsuccessful in his campaign to serve as U.S. Consul to Liberia. In 1870 he worked for the South Carolina Bureau of Agricultural Statistics, and the following year he opened a real estate agency. From 1870 to 1872 Delany worked tirelessly, yet unprofitably, for the Republican Party as an honorary state militia member, before resigning because he had discovered rising corruption within that organization.

In 1873 and 1874, Delany, then a poorly paid federal customs clerk, courted southern whites while seeking a law requiring fair political representation of both races. He ran for lieutenant-governor of South Carolina as an independent Republican, but lost in a close election. Behind local pressure, the state's last Republican governor appointed Delany as a trial justice (justice of the peace) in 1875. A year later, Delany supported a white Democrat, Wade Hampton, for governor and was reappointed as a trial justice through 1878. By then, Reconstruction, and the possibility of full black citizenship, had nearly ended. Late in 1877 Delany became involved with the Liberian Exodus Joint Stock Steam Ship Company, whose emigration ventures soon failed. Defeated there and in South Carolina, he headed north.

In 1879, Philadelphia's Harper & Brothers published Delany's *Principia of Ethnology: The Origin of Races and Color*, a biblically inspired swan song asserting the eternal and essential differences between blacks and whites. From 1880 through 1883 Delany worked at various civil service jobs around Washington, D.C., and in 1884 he joined a Boston firm with offices in Central America. Falling ill, he returned to Ohio and died in the home of his self-reliant, much-respected wife.

FURTHER READING

Levine, Robert S. *Martin Delany, Frederick Douglass, and the Politics of Representative Identity* (1997).

Ullman, Victor. *Martin R. Delany: The Beginnings of Black Nationalism* (1971).

ALLAN D. AUSTIN

Delany, Samuel R. (1 Apr. 1942–), writer, literary critic, and professor, was born in New York City to Samuel R. Delany and Margaret Carey Boyd Delany, funeral parlor owners. Delany spent his childhood in Harlem. Thanks to his wealthy family background, he was able from an early age to cultivate his many cultural interests. He first attended the Bronx High School of Science and then went on to City College, but dropped out after only one semester. Although he later came out as gay, Delany married and fathered a child with the Jewish poet Marilyn Hacker in 1961 (the couple divorced in 1980).

In 1962, when he was only twenty years old, Delany published his first novel, *The Jewels of Aptor*, the first in a long series of science fiction books. After his literary debut, he gained a reputation as a prodigy in science fiction and enjoyed his renown, taking an active part in the social and sexual experimentation of New York's East Village. He produced almost a book a year during the 1960s: *Captives of the Flame* (1963), *The Towers of Toron* (1964), *City of a Thousand Suns* (1965), *The Ballad of Beta-2* (1965), *Empire Star* (1966), *Babel-17* (1966), *Einstein Intersection* (1967), and *Nova* (1968). Delany's early fiction explores the intersecting identities of being black and gay. As Delany recalls in his autobiography *The Motion of Light in Water: Sex and Science Fiction Writing in the East Village: 1957–65* (1988):

> I was a young black man, light-skinned enough so that four out of five people who met me, of whatever race, assumed I was white…. I was a homosexual who now knew he could function heterosexually. And I was a young writer whose early attempts had already gotten him a handful of prizes…. So, I thought, you are neither black nor white. You are neither male nor female. And you are that most ambiguous of citizens, the writer. (52)

The author's struggle to come to terms with his own multiple identities is paralleled by his protagonists' quests to reconstruct their pasts and their cultural heritage. To Delany, science fiction was not merely a narration of spaceship battles but also entailed sophisticated literary sensitivity and

knowledge of mythology. He used the genre to challenge sexual roles, racial stereotypes, morality, and received standards of narration.

The plot of these early novels was often structured around a quest or a fantastic voyage undertaken by physically and psychologically scarred heroes or heroines. Several early novels also focused on problems of communication and linguistics, which became fundamental in later novels. *Babel-17*, winner of the prestigious Nebula Award in 1966, features a female poet hero and spaceship captain who has to decipher a new language that has the power of transforming its speakers into political traitors. The novel was strongly influenced by the Sapir-Whorf hypothesis that language forms thought. Delany's interest both in existing myths and in the ways new ones are produced also was central. In *The Ballad of Beta-2* a student anthropologist explores the facts behind a folk song from a primitive earth culture. *The Einstein Intersection*, which earned the author his second Nebula Award in 1967, constructs a collage of ancient and modern myths. In their struggle to adapt to the human world and its history, the aliens who have come to a deserted earth in ruin find themselves forced to re-create powerful human myths such as that of Orpheus. *Nova* combines the myths of Prometheus and the quest for the Holy Grail.

With his short story "Aye, and Gomorrah …" (1967), Delany won his third Nebula, and the novelette *Time Considered as a Helix of Semi-Precious Stones* won him another Nebula and the Hugo Award. By the end of the 1960s his reputation as one of the major authors in the genre's New Wave, which privileged cultural and philosophical speculations over technological details and space adventures, was fully established. Delany's use of science fiction was instrumental to his challenge to social and sexual conventions. His books call into question compulsory heterosexuality, exploring homoeroticism and sadomasochism. This exploration was also carried out in Delany's two pornographic volumes, *The Tides of Lust* (1973) and *Hogg*, which was written in the early 1970s but published only in 2004. In the 1970s Delany also started his academic career, accepting teaching positions as a visiting writer at Wesleyan University's Center for the Humanities in 1972, and visiting Butler Chair Professor at the State University of New York (SUNY) at Buffalo in 1975. In 1977 he was a senior fellow at the Center for Twentieth Century Studies at the University of Wisconsin, and in 1978 he was writer in residence at SUNY at Albany. He also penned two semiotic and structuralist studies, *The*

Jewel-Hinged Jaw: Notes on the Language of Science Fiction (1977) and *The American Shore: Meditations on a Tale of Science Fiction by Thomas M. Disch-Angouleme* (1978). Delany's novels of the 1970s were *Dhalgren* (1975) and *Triton* (1975). The former became a best-seller, despite its mixed critical reception, and constitutes a meditation on writing and the status of being a writer. *Triton* further developed his reflections on sexual roles and orientations, presenting a series of future societies differentiated mainly along sexual lines. It charted the transformation of its male protagonist who, at the beginning, is an insensitive male chauvinist but ultimately chooses to become a woman.

The four books in the Nevèrÿon series, *Tales of Nevèrÿon* (1978), *Neveryóna* (1983), *Flight from Nevèrÿon* (1985), and *The Bridge of Lost Desire* (1987; also known as *Return to Nevèrÿon*), masqueraded important contemporary issues under the genre of sword and sorcery fantasy. Part three of *Flight from Nevèrÿon*, for example, "The Tale of Plagues and Carnivals," paralleled observations on the AIDS crisis in New York in the early 1980s with the narration of a similar plague in the fantasy realm.

In 1988 Delany accepted a position of professor of comparative literature at the University of Massachusetts, Amherst, where he remained for eleven years. He subsequently taught at SUNY/Buffalo and in 2001 began teaching English and creative writing at Temple University. His fictional production was complemented by academic and deconstructive studies such as *Starboard Wine: More Notes on the Language of Science Fiction* (1984), *Wagner/Artaud: A Play of 19th and 20th Century Critical Fictions* (1988), *The Straits of Messina* (1989), *Longer Views: Extended Essays* (1996), and *Shorter Views: Queer Thoughts and the Politics of the Paraliterary* (2000).

Delany's *The Mad Man* (1994), *Bread and Wine: An Erotic Tale of New York* (1999), *1984* (2000), and *Phallos* (2004) confirmed his interest in homoerotic narratives and the depiction of a variety of cultures that aim at making morality and ethics more relative, inclusive, and pluralistic.

FURTHER READING

Jackson, Earl. *Strategies of Deviance: Studies in Gay Male Representation* (1995).

McEvoy, Seth. *Samuel R. Delany* (1984).

Sallis, James, ed. *Ash of Stars: On the Writing of Samuel R. Delany* (1996).

Tucker, Jeffrey Allen. *A Sense of Wonder: Samuel R. Delany, Race, Identity, and Difference* (2004).

LUCA PRONO

DeLarge, Robert Carlos (15 Mar. 1842–14 Feb. 1874), politician, was born in Aiken, South Carolina. His father was a free black tailor, and his mother was a cloak maker of Haitian descent; their names are unknown. Though several records claim that DeLarge was born into slavery, it is more likely that his parents were free blacks who owned slaves. This peculiar and paradoxical designation surely inspired the dual sensibilities that later characterized his political and social life as both an advocate for universal black enfranchisement and a member of South Carolina's propertied, often exclusionist, light-skinned elite. Fortunate to receive the benefits of the prewar education available to free black children, DeLarge attended primary school in North Carolina and Wood High School in Charleston. For a short time he was employed as a tailor and farmer, and some sources indicate that he was also a part-time barber. During the Civil War, he amassed some money as an employee of the Confederate navy, a curious affiliation in light of his Republican activities during Reconstruction. He later donated most of his Civil War earnings to the state Republican Party. By the time he became active in Reconstruction politics, DeLarge was a citizen of considerable standing in Charleston, as indicated both by his net worth of $6,650 in the 1870 census and his membership in the Brown Fellowship Society, an elite fraternal and charitable association founded in 1870.

DeLarge's active political career began in 1865. Widely considered a "politician by inclination," he attended every political gathering he could get to and "talked continually at all of them" (Lamson, 37). An agent for the Freedmen's Bureau, he was named chairman of the Credentials Committee of the September 1865 Colored People's Convention in Charleston, where he mesmerized evening crowds with passionate speeches. Prompted by the lack of civil and educational rights for blacks in South Carolina following the Civil War, DeLarge and 102 colleagues drafted a petition to the state legislature calling for stronger civil rights provisions. The 1865 convention adopted DeLarge's resolution demanding the establishment of a universal public school system. Though he openly supported barring "ignorant" whites and blacks from voting, he also signed a petition asking for impartial male suffrage regardless of "race, color or previous condition." In November 1865 DeLarge attended the state black convention, and he chaired the Platform Committee of the 1867 South Carolina Republican Convention, where he was instrumental in advocating for public schools, the abolition of capital punishment, universal male suffrage with literacy restrictions, tax reform, welfare assistance to the poor of both races, funds for internal improvements like canals and railroads, and land distribution efforts. Despite DeLarge's earlier activities, at the 1868 constitutional convention he emerged as an effective, though at times overly loquacious, leader. Described unimpressively as "a short man with brush sideburns and a receding hairline," he had a tendency to be stubborn and overbearing. His colleague ROBERT BROWN ELLIOTT referred to him as "a pigmy who is trying to play the part of a giant, elocutionizing himself into a perspiration which stood out upon his skin like warts." Nonetheless, DeLarge had considerable influence as a member of three standing committees. He supported the cessation of "further confiscation of lands and disfranchisement for political offenses" of ex-Confederates and former planters, which measure was ultimately defeated. Though he opposed laws to make school attendance compulsory, he argued successfully for a state-funded public school system. He advocated radical land redistribution initiatives, and the convention passed his resolution to ask Congress for a $1 million grant to purchase lands that would then be sold to the state's white and black poor. The petition was later denied at the federal level.

Elected to the state house of representatives following the convention, DeLarge served from 1868 to 1870 as chairman of the Ways and Means Committee and sponsored important railroad legislation. Also active as a civic leader, he cofounded the Enterprise Railroad Company, was a member of the Sinking Fund Commission and the board of regents of the state lunatic asylum, and served as a delegate to the 1869 state labor convention.

In April 1870, while still a member of the state legislature, DeLarge was appointed as C. P. Leslie's successor to head the troubled South Carolina Land Commission. According to DeLarge, the land monopolies that still existed in the postbellum South made "the rich richer and the poor poorer," and as head of the land commission he promised to heed "the voice of the impoverished people of the state." In March 1871 he reported that nearly two thousand small tracts had been sold or would soon be taken over by homeowners who would have eight years to pay for them. Shortly thereafter, however, it became clear that DeLarge's public promises to facilitate the state's radical land experiment belied a series of unscrupulous private transactions at the expense of the commission. His tenure at the land

Robert Carlos DeLarge, African American legislator from South Carolina, between 1860 and 1875. (Library of Congress/Brady-Handy Photograph Collection.)

commission was marked by fraud and mismanagement. The widespread opinion was that Governor Robert Scott, a Republican, had manufactured the appointment so that DeLarge could steal enough money from the coffers of the land commission to unseat Christopher C. Bowen, a white congressman. DeLarge subsequently defeated Bowen by fewer than a thousand votes in the election of 1870. DeLarge was involved in some unauthorized and highly questionable exchanges of money, and when he resigned from the commission in March 1871, his successor, Secretary of State FRANCIS L. CARDOZO, discovered that DeLarge had kept no written records of the commission's operations or financial transactions.

DeLarge seized his victory over Bowen in the hotly contested congressional election as an opportunity to "demand for my race an equal share everywhere." As a member of Congress, he criticized the lawlessness of blacks and whites in both political parties and supported the Fourteenth Amendment and the quick readmission of former Confederates to political life. Despite his moderate successes as a statesman, he spent most of his short congressional career mired in controversy. In a speech during the 1870 campaign he said, "I hold that my race has always been Republican for necessity only." Consequently he was accused of advocating the creation of a "black man's party" as a challenge to the Republicans. Though he denied harboring such sentiments, DeLarge's occasional tendency to ally himself publicly with black nationalists like MARTIN R. DELANY did not bolster his cause with white Republicans and more integrationist black leaders. Furthermore, during the second half of his term in Congress, DeLarge was largely preoccupied with trying to prove his right to keep his seat. On 24 January 1873, before his term expired, the House accepted a Committee on Election report that concluded that fraud and "other irregularities" were so common during the 1870 campaign between Bowen and DeLarge that neither candidate deserved a congressional seat. Shortly thereafter DeLarge was unseated and returned to Charleston, where he was quickly appointed a city magistrate by Governor Scott. DeLarge enjoyed considerable influence until his death from consumption in Charleston. The date of his marriage and the name of his wife are not known. He had one daughter.

DeLarge's life and career constitute something of a tragedy. A political figure committed at once to self-promotion and social justice, he was revered by the people of Charleston and yet unsuccessful in the halls of legislative power. DeLarge's social conservatism was often challenged during Reconstruction by his associations with more radical black peers. Nonetheless, on the day of his funeral city magistrates closed their offices to observe a day of mourning for the loss of their popular young colleague.

FURTHER READING

Aptheker, Herbert. "South Carolina Negro Conventions, 1865," *Journal of Negro History* 31 (1946).

Foner, Eric. *Reconstruction: America's Unfinished Revolution, 1863–1877* (1988).

Hine, William C. "Black Politicians in Reconstruction Charleston, South Carolina," *Journal of Southern History* 49 (1983).

Lamson, Peggy. *The Glorious Failure: Black Congressman Robert Brown Elliott and the Reconstruction of South Carolina* (1973).

This entry is taken from the *American National Biography* and is published here with the permission of the American Council of Learned Societies.

TIMOTHY P. MCCARTHY

Delia (1886–25 Dec. 1900), woman whose murder is described in the ballad "Delia," also known as "Delia('s) Gone" and "One More Rounder Gone,"
was born Delia Green in Savannah, Georgia. Nothing is known about her early life except that in 1900 she lived with her mother at 113 Ann Street. Moses "Cooney" (or "Mose") Houston (pronounced "HOUSE-tun") was also born in 1886. In 1900 he lived with his mother at 123 Farm Street, five blocks west of Delia's home. Two blocks southeast of her home was 509 Harrison Street, where Delia worked for Emma West. These addresses are all in Yamacraw, a famed African American neighborhood in Savannah.

By Christmas Eve 1900 Cooney and Delia had been seeing each other for about four months. Around 7 P.M. Cooney went to the West house looking for Delia. Emma's husband, Willie, sent Cooney out to get beer and whiskey and to pick up a pistol from a gun repairman. On his return Cooney put the pistol under a napkin. Everyone in the house had been drinking. When another boy, Eddie Cohen, picked up the pistol and started playing with it, he and Cooney "in fun … kind of struggled for it" (Statement of Defendant, Brief of Evidence, *State vs. Mose Houston*, Murder, in Chatham Superior Court, March Term 1901, 7). Cooney won the struggle, but the gun discharged and the bullet hit Delia in the left groin. She was taken home and seen by a doctor, but she died at about 3 A.M. on Christmas morning.

That is the story, supported by other witnesses, that Cooney told at his trial. Willie Mills, who was brought from jail to testify, said that he had seen the tussle for the gun and its accidental discharge. Further, "he was in a crowd of men and women drinking…. There were a crowd of women in the room … as many as twenty in the same room." The gunsmith testified that Willie West had left the pistol with him and that Cooney had picked it up (Testimony of Willie Mills, Brief of Evidence, *State vs. Mose Houston*, Murder, in Chatham Superior Court, March Term 1901, 8).

The Wests and others told a different story. Willie West denied that he had left the pistol for repair, that it was his, and that there was a struggle for it. Neither Willie Mills nor Eddie Cohen was at his house. There was no crowd, and there was no drinking. Only six or seven people were present, all sober. At about 11 P.M. they were gathered around the organ on the first floor singing hymns. According to this account of events, Delia and Cooney argued something as follows:

Delia: Stop, Cooney! Don't put your hands on me!
Cooney: You don't know how I love you.

Delia: You have been going with me for four months. You know I am a lady.

Cooney: That is a damn lie! You know I have had you as many times as I have fingers and toes. You have been calling me "husband."

Delia: You lie! You son of a bitch! (Conversation reconstructed from testimonies of Rosella West and Emma West, Brief of Evidence, *State vs. Mose Houston,* Murder, in Chatham Superior Court, March Term 1901, 2–4)

After Willie West admonished him to behave, Cooney went outside for a while. When he came back, he sat on a trunk near Delia, who was sitting on a bed. As the party was breaking up and they were starting for the door, Cooney suddenly shot Delia. She fell back on the bed. Cooney left the house, but Willie West caught up with him and turned him over to a policeman, J. T. Williams. Williams testified that Cooney told him that "he shot her because she called him a son of a bitch … [H]e would do it again" (Testimony of J. T. Williams, Brief of Evidence, *State vs. Mose Houston,* Murder, in Chatham Superior Court, March Term 1901, 6–7).

Contradictions and inconsistencies in the testimony make it impossible to be confident of a detailed scenario, but it seems that Cooney had drunk too much, perhaps for the first time in his life. When his loosened tongue claimed intimacies with Delia, she reacted angrily with an insult that hurt him deeply. He shot her in a fit of uncontrolled fury.

Perhaps that's all there is to it, but certain aspects of the situation and testimony suggest more. Prostitution was widespread in Savannah. At Cooney's trial S. Thomas was not allowed to testify as to the exact nature of the West house, but Raiford Falligant, the young lawyer who defended Cooney, later called it a "rough house" (Raiford Falligant, Petitioner's Attorney, the Petition of Mose Houston, c. 1912, 1). Both Cooney and Willie Mills referred to the "Emma West house," rather than the "Willie West house." This would have been natural if Emma West had been the madam of a brothel, which is consistent with Willie Mills's testimony that there had been "as many as twenty" women in the room. A musical instrument on the first floor is a typical feature of a "parlor house." Shortly before she was shot, Delia had been upstairs, perhaps with a customer. Being a prostitute could account for the ballad tag line, "One more rounder gone." Cooney's dismay at her prostitution could have fueled their argument. Several versions of "Delia" contain lines that suggest that she had other men.

In any case Cooney was convicted of murder. When he was sentenced to life in prison at hard labor, he thanked the judge, because he could have been sentenced to death. In 1913 he was paroled by the Georgia governor John M. Slaton. Cooney is said to have moved to New York and died there before 1927.

Stanzas from various versions of the ballad reflect some of these details:

Coonie told Delia on a Christmas Eve night,
If you tell me 'bout my mama, I'm sho going to take your life.
She's dead. She's dead and gone.
(P. Bordelon, *Go Gator and Muddy the Water* [1999], 73)

Now Delia cursed Tony, 'twas on one Saturday night,
And she cursed him such a wicked curse that he swear to take her life.
Delia's gone! One more round, Delia's gone!
(Blind Blake in M. Paterson and S. Heyward, *Calypso Folk Sing* [1963], 26)

Delie, Delie, why didn't yo' run?
When yo' seen dat coon a-comin' wid his forty-fo' caliber gun?
All I done had done gone.
(N. I. White, *American Negro Folk-Songs* [1928], 215)

Cooney's in the basement drinking from a silver cup,
Delia's in the graveyard never come back up.
Well, that's one more rounder gone.
(Blind Willie McTell, Library of Congress recording, 1940)

So Tony was locked up, the judge refused to set bail,
For such a crime, he should do time, say, 99 years in-jail.
Delia gone, one more round, Delia gone!
Then Tony said "Thank you, your honor treated me fine."
He knew the judge could well have said: Nine hundred ninety-nine.
Delia gone, one more round, Delia gone!
(Arthur Bayas and Lipton Nemser, *Best Bluegrass Songbook—Yet!* 1978)

During and after the Civil War Savannah did considerable business with Nassau. Certainly by 1927 "Delia('s) Gone" was traditional in the Bahamas. This title and the tag line, "Delia('s) gone! One more round, Delia('s) gone!," are not found in American versions prior to 1952, when a recording by the Bahamian "Blind Blake" Alphonso Higgs was released in the United States. "One more round, Delia('s) gone" may be a mutation of the American line, "One more rounder gone." A hit recording of "Delia Gone" by the Bahamian artist Stevie S. was released in 2003.

From the 1950s on, many Americans have recorded "Delia" or "Delia('s) Gone." During the 1990s hit recordings were released by Bob Dylan ("Delia") and Johnny Cash ("Delia's Gone," a rewrite).

"Delia" is said to have been sung in the Savannah area by the spring of 1901. President William McKinley was assassinated in the fall of that year, and shortly thereafter a ballad about the assassination arose. "McKinley," or "White House Blues," used the same tune as "Delia" and included similar verses.

Roosevelt in the White House, drinkin' out a
    silver cup,
McKinley in the graveyard, he'll never wake up.
He's gone a long old time.
(Alan Lomax, *The Folk Songs of North America*
    [1960], 275)

Thus, a poor African American girl, who never had much of a chance in her short life, has colored our memory of a president. Her ballad may have made Delia Green Savannah's most widely known citizen. According to her death certificate she is buried, apparently in an unmarked grave, in Laurel Grove South Cemetery.

FURTHER READING

Materials relating to the murder and ballad of Delia Green can been found in the Robert Winslow Gordon Collections in the Library of Congress American Folklife Center's Archive of Folk Culture, and in Gordon's Notes on American folklore, folk songs, and ballads, and personal papers, 1909–1934, in the Special Collections and University Archives, University of Oregon. The Georgia Archives in Morrow, Georgia, include the Mose Houston Clemency File.

Ayers, Edward L. *Vengeance & Justice* (1984).

Garst, John. "Delia," *Blues & Rhythm*, No. 189 (May 2004).

Savannah Morning News, 26 Dec. 1900; 14–15 Mar. 1901.

Savannah Press, 26 Dec. 1900; 14 Mar. 1901.

Wilentz, Sean. "The Sad Song of Delia Green and Cooney Houston," in *The Rose & the Briar*, eds. Sean Wilentz and Griel Marcus (2005).

JOHN GARST

Delille, Henriette (11 Mar. 1813–16 Nov. 1862), Roman Catholic nun and founder of a religious order, was born in New Orleans, the daughter of Marie Josephe Diaz, a free woman of color, and Jean Baptiste Delille-Sarpy, a wealthy white aristocrat. Legally categorized as a person of mixed race, Delille attended a school for free children of color under the direction of Catholic sisters in New Orleans. Her father did not support the family in any measurable fashion, and her mother suffered from mental illness, all of which required that Delille and her two surviving siblings support themselves at a young age. As a teenager, she began to identify less with the aristocratic society of free people of color and more with the religious lives of Catholic sisters. She became a catechist to free people of color and a lay leader in Catholic confraternities. Legal and social standards, however, limited the extent to which she was able to teach enslaved persons and join a Catholic religious order composed of white women.

In 1836 Delille organized a group of free women of color into a confraternity, or a voluntary lay group under the authority of the church, called the Congregation of the Sisters of the Presentation of the Blessed Virgin Mary. Members of the confraternity pledged to nurture their own spirituality, to support their religious community, and to care for the needs of the sick, infirm, and poor. The bishop of New Orleans asked the Catholic Church in Rome to associate the Congregation of the Presentation with the prestigious and international Sodality of the Blessed Virgin Mary, which allowed Delille and the others to receive the indulgences of the larger sodality and to garner further support from the Diocese of New Orleans for full recognition as a religious order.

The Congregation of the Presentation, under the leadership of Delille, became a religious order on 21 November 1842. The sisters of the Presentation, however, did not take formal vows of poverty, chastity, or obedience because of the restrictions imposed upon organizations of free people of color. The designation of a black community as a religious order did not yet fit into the Louisiana legal system and Catholic ecclesiastical regulations. In 1847, after the community gained further respect from the diocese, Delille oversaw the incorporation of her small order into the Society of the Holy Family. She organized charitable services for free people of color in New Orleans and participated in the baptism of many enslaved persons, but she rarely promoted such activities on a public level.

In 1850 Delille joined the Sisters of the Sacred Heart in Convent, Louisiana, as a novice with an interest in learning the rules of religious life so as to implement them in the Society of the Holy Family. She returned to New Orleans and took her first vows in 1852, after which she continued to lead the Society of the Holy Family in teaching enslaved and free children of color and caring for the elderly. Yet despite the all-black student body, many mothers of free children of color complained that their children were associating with the children of enslaved mothers. Priests from various churches supported the sisters with monthly donations that allowed them to maintain several residences and charitable activities. Tension often developed, however, between the Sisters of the Holy Family and other, white religious orders in the city.

The success of the Society of the Holy Family relied on the financial support of free people of color and the Diocese of New Orleans, as well as on the inconsistent tolerance of the increasingly racist white population of New Orleans. Delille, as a result, made difficult decisions about the work of the religious order based on the issue of race. As the primary author of the rules of the order, Delille believed that only free women of color and higher standing should be admitted to the sisterhood for the purpose of avoiding legal and ecclesiastical problems. Such a rule provided the best chance of success as a religious order in New Orleans. Laws against the education of enslaved persons without the consent of slaveholders also inhibited the mission of the sisters to care for the religious and practical needs of enslaved persons in the area. Delille, in fact, came from a family of slaveholders, and she herself was the owner of a woman named Betsy. She kept Betsy as a slave largely because of the legal restrictions against manumission in Louisiana. It was not until after the Civil War that the sisters of the Society of the Holy Family were able to align themselves more closely with the radical black Creoles of New Orleans, who often opposed the racist standards of the church and the government.

In 1862 Delille died of tuberculosis in New Orleans. The Catholic newspaper of New Orleans included an obituary that referred to the deceased leader as "the humble servant of slaves." However, the public recognition of her contribution to the communities of free and enslaved blacks was not widespread at the time. The sisters of the Society of the Holy Family came under considerable stress after the death of their founder and superior, which resulted in the departure of nearly half of the sisters from the order. The Society of the Holy Family, nevertheless, survived the tumult of the Civil War, Reconstruction, and Jim Crow. As the founder of one of only two religious orders accepting free women of color before the Civil War, Delille provided a religious and practical service to the black population of New Orleans, a service that did not always receive significant attention from other religious and civic leaders.

Since the 1990s the Archdiocese of New Orleans has been making the case for the canonization of Delille. Other citizens of New Orleans, many of whom refer to themselves as Creoles of mixed race, have been more interested in the debate over the identification of Delille as a representative of the African American community or the Creole community.

FURTHER READING

Davis, Cyprian, O.S.B. *Henriette Delille: Servant of Slaves, Witness to the Poor* (2004).

Deggs, Sister Mary Bernard, with Virginia Meacham Gould, and Charles E. Nolan. *No Cross, No Crown: Black Nuns in Nineteenth-Century New Orleans* (2001).

Detiege, Sister Audrey Marie. *Henriette Delille: Free Woman of Color* (1976).

Fessenden, Tracy. "The Sisters of the Holy Family and the Veil of Race," *Religion and American Culture* 10 (2000).

MICHAEL PASQUIER

Dellums, C. L. (3 Jan. 1900–6 Dec. 1989), labor and civil rights leader, was born Cottrell Laurence Dellums in Corsicana, Texas, to Emma Dellums. He was raised by his mother and his stepfather, William H. Dellums, a barbershop owner. Frustrated by racial discrimination in his Texas hometown, Dellums moved to Oakland, California, in 1925 in hopes of finding better opportunities. What he found, however, was that there were only three ways an African American could make a living in Oakland: "on the trains, on ships, and by doing something illegal" (Michael Harris, *San Francisco Chronicle*, 8 Aug. 1977). Dellums chose the trains, going to work as a porter on a Pullman Company sleeping car operating out of Oakland. It was a marginal and humiliating experience, one that perfectly epitomized the gap between black and white in American society. In 1928 he married Walter Lee Allen; they had one daughter.

Porters were rightfully proud of their work, but they knew that no matter how well they performed, they would never be promoted. They could never be conductors. Those jobs were reserved for white men. And it was white employers and white passengers who decided what the porters must do and what their compensation would be. The need for unionization was obvious. Porters commonly worked twelve or more hours a day—fetching drinks, shining shoes, making beds, emptying and cleaning cuspidors, and running errands. They earned only $72.50 per month, out of which they had to pay for their meals, uniforms, even the polish they used on passengers' shoes.

Dellums quickly discovered the lack of rights for blacks. Soon after going to work for Pullman, he was fired for joining A. PHILIP RANDOLPH in trying to organize the company's workers. Randolph's style was "to resist with quiet and indomitable will" (Anderson, 212). But though warm and gentle to friends, Dellums's style was "to blast away at his enemies … with his fists, if necessary, like the 'roughneck' he liked to call himself…. He could look—when he wanted—as truculent as a clenched fist" (Anderson, 212).

Dellums's fellow workers offered to pay his rent for three months after his firing if he agreed to stay with the union. He managed to stay on, thanks to those donations, his wife's earnings as a maid, and donations made later at monthly rent parties in his modest West Oakland bungalow that became the lifelong home for him and his wife. Dellums was not the only union activist to suffer. Pullman dismissed ninety porters in Oakland after they joined the union.

The organizing drive, begun in 1925, led to the founding of the Brotherhood of Sleeping Car Porters (BSCP) in New York three years later, the first union organized by African Americans. Finally in 1935 Congress passed the Wagner Act at the urging of President Franklin D. Roosevelt, granting workers the legal right to unionize. That same year the BSCP, representing fifteen thousand porters and other Pullman employees, became the first African American union chartered by the American Federation of Labor (AFL). Randolph was the union's president and Dellums one of its vice presidents.

In 1937 the BSCP won a contract with the Pullman Company, paving the way for the granting of equal rights to millions of other black workers. The contract was signed precisely twelve years after Randolph called his first organizing meeting, but the long struggle was well worth it. The contract pulled the porters out of poverty. It brought them pay at least equal to that of unionized white workers in many other fields, a standard work week, a full range of fringe benefits, and the right to continue bargaining collectively with their employers on those and other vital matters. Above all the contract brought the porters dignity and respect and set important precedents for black workers in general. Dellums also struggled hard and long against racism inside the labor movement, most particularly against the practice of unions setting up separate locals for black and white members.

The porters' union joined with the NAACP, in which Dellums was also a leader, to serve as the major political vehicle of African Americans from the late 1930s through the 1950s. The two organizations led the drives in those years against racial discrimination in employment, housing, education, and other areas that laid the groundwork for the civil rights movement of the 1950s and 1960s.

Dellums also was a key figure in the campaign that pressured President Roosevelt into creating a Fair Employment Practices Commission (FEPC) during World War II with the aim of combating racial discrimination in housing as well as employment. Because he could not afford to alienate voters in the South, Roosevelt resisted repeated demands for creation of such a body but abruptly reversed his position after Randolph threatened to lead a march on Washington by 100,000 black workers and others who were demanding federal action against discrimination. The 1941 march was cancelled after Roosevelt issued Executive Order 8802, prohibiting racial discrimination in defense contractor and other federal employment.

Congress later abolished the commission, but its creation led to the establishment of several state commissions. The most important was established in California after fourteen years of intense lobbying by Dellums in his dual role as western regional director of the NAACP and regional vice president of the porters' union. He held the NAACP post from 1948 until 1967 and was a union vice president from 1929 until succeeding Randolph as president in 1968, when he also was elected a vice president of the AFL-CIO. Dellums served on California's FEPC from its inception in 1959 until 1985, seven years after he retired as union president.

In 1978 the porters' union merged with the much larger Brotherhood of Airline and Railway Clerks (later renamed the Transportation and Communications International Union). But before the union disappeared, it achieved the goals that Dellums had devoted his life to achieving—goals as important as any ever sought by an American union or organization of any kind.

FURTHER READING

Anderson, Jervis. *A. Philip Randolph: A Biographical Portrait* (1987).

Tye, Larry. *Rising from the Rails: Pullman Porters and the Making of the Black Middle Class* (2004).

DICK MEISTER

Dellums, Ronald (24 Nov. 1935–), Congressman, author, and educator, was born Ronald Vernie Dellums in Oakland, California, the son of Vernie Dellums, a longshoreman, and Willa, a beautician and government clerk. Ronald's father had moved from Texas to California with the hopes of attending college and becoming a journalist. He first found work as a Pullman porter with his brother C. L. DELLUMS, a close associate of A. PHILIP RANDOLPH in the Brotherhood of Sleeping Car Porters. C. L. was Ronald's childhood idol and even as a young man, Ronald admired his uncle's courage and fiery oratory when Governor Ronald Reagan appointed him to California's Fair Employment Commission. Though he never became a journalist, Vernie went on to become a union organizer among the dockworkers, and his voracious reading habits and work as a labor activist greatly influenced the trajectory of his son's life.

Ronald's parents were Protestants, but they sent Ronald and his sister to St. Patrick's Catholic School, where they believed the educational standards were higher than in the public schools. When Ronald was twelve his parents separated and the family resources diminished, but by using a relative's address they managed to send Ronald to Westlake Junior High School, where he and another student were the only black males. During the 1950s so-called white flight turned West Oakland, which had been a poor but integrated town, into a black ghetto. After Ronald was sent to the predominantly black McClymonds High School, his mother intervened once again to get him admitted to Oakland Technical High School.

In 1954 Dellums, still uncertain about a career path, enlisted in the U.S. Marine Corps. He benefited from the discipline and physical training, and his superior scores on aptitude tests—and an error that listed him as caucasian—got him an interview for officer's training, although he was subsequently rejected when his interrogators saw him in person. During his military service he married his first wife, Arthurine, with whom he had a daughter before their two-year marriage ended in divorce. After receiving an honorable discharge in 1958 Dellums used the G.I. Bill to earn an associate's degree from Oakland City College. He then enrolled at San Francisco State College and was awarded a bachelor's degree in 1960. Finally in 1962 he received a master's degree in Social Work from the University of California at Berkeley. In that year he married Leola Roscoe Higgs, a lawyer, with whom he had three children.

From 1962 to 1964 Dellums worked with psychiatric patients for the California Department of Mental Hygiene. He then assumed a managerial position as program director for the Bayview Community Center in San Francisco before becoming the director of the Hunters Point Youth Opportunity Council from 1965 to 1966. In these positions he discovered that he was an effective leader who loved to work with young people. These interests led him to accept positions from 1968 to 1970 as a lecturer at San Francisco State College and the University of California's School of Social Work. Just as Dellums was leaning toward pursuing a Ph.D. at Brandeis University in preparation for a career as a professor, he won a seat on the Berkeley City Council (from 1967 to 1971) that drew him into the world of electoral politics for the next three decades.

A confluence of three factors led to Dellum's meteoric rise to power: his articulate and stately bearing appealed to the white, affluent liberals who made up 70 percent of his congressional district; his advocacy of civil rights—as demonstrated by his bold support of the Black Panther HUEY P. NEWTON—endeared him to poor black voters; and his emergence as an antiwar candidate at a time when opposition to the war in Vietnam was gaining momentum made him broadly appealing to younger voters and those who had grown weary of the long conflict in Southeast Asia. With the help of CORETTA SCOTT KING and Cesar Chavez, Dellums was able to unite these constituencies and unseat his Democratic opponent, Jeffrey Cohelan, in the 1970 election. When he arrived in Washington, Republican president Richard Nixon controlled the White House and Democrats controlled the Congress. His first act in that august body, where freshmen are expected to be silent and deferential, was to nominate JOHN CONYERS, a black colleague from Michigan, to be Speaker of the House. His temerity signaled that he was going to be the most radical black congressman since ADAM CLAYTON POWELL JR. Undeterred by critics who labeled him a Communist, Dellums accepted the vice presidency of the Democratic Socialists Organizing Committee (later the Democratic Socialists of America). Because of his controversial positions, his office and telephones were bugged under COINTELPRO, a clandestine government counterintelligence program.

As the first African American to serve on the powerful and influential Armed Services Committee Dellums made reform of the military a centerpiece of his legislative career. He began by holding hearings examining allegations of discrimination in the military. He then fought to check the growth of the military industrial complex which encouraged American militarism abroad and diverted resources from vital domestic programs at home, arguing, "The budget defines the values, the principles, and the priorities of a nation" (Dellums, 107). In foreign policy Dellums took the legislative lead against apartheid in 1973 as the first lawmaker to introduce a bill to impose a complete economic embargo against South Africa. To the consternation of many of his Jewish supporters, in 1973 he also voted against sending military aid to Israel during the Yom Kippur War. In 1974, along with the civil rights activists MARY FRANCES BERRY, RANDALL ROBINSON, and many others, he was arrested while protesting at the South African embassy.

In 1979 he was part of the delegation that went to the former Soviet Union to negotiate treaties to slow the proliferation of nuclear weapons. In 1980 Dellums became chair of the subcommittee and vigorously opposed President Ronald Reagan's defense buildup—particularly weapon systems such as the Pershing II and Minuteman Missiles, the B-1 Bomber, and the "Star Wars" anti–ballistic missile technology. He was on the cutting edge of the Iran-Contra investigation, he filed suit to block the sending of military advisors to El Salvador, and he led a fact-finding mission to Grenada that debunked the premise for its invasion. His views about the military became the subject of his book, *Defense Sense: The Search for a Rational Military Policy* (1983). In 1986 a more moderate sanctions bill introduced by congressman WILLIAM H. GRAY III became law. Dellums successfully fought to restore Haitian President Jean-Bertrand Aristide to power after he was deposed in a military coup. Dellums also attempted to normalize U.S. relations with Cuba and was in the vanguard of those interested in increasing trade with Africa and relieving the AIDS epidemic on that continent. In late 1990 Dellums, with fifty-two other members of Congress and one senator, presented a lawsuit, *Dellums v. Bush*, which invoked the War Powers Act and proved instrumental in forcing President George H. W. Bush to obtain congressional approval before beginning the Gulf War in 1991. During the Bill Clinton presidency, Dellums urged lifting all bans against gays in the military, instead of the "don't ask, don't tell" compromise instituted in 1993.

On the domestic front Dellums was a tireless proponent of establishing a national health care system, he was a strong defender of women's rights—particularly reproductive freedom, and he favored decriminalizing the use of marijuana. A progressive and social reformer, he once defined "niggers" as people of any race who are politically marginalized and downtrodden. In looking at the causes of social strife he wrote, "Peace has remained stalled by the absence of justice" (Dellums, 79). Dellums pursued policies that attempted to redress the inequities between rich and poor, and as chair of the House Committee on the District of Columbia, he repeatedly introduced bills for D.C. statehood. Dellums retired from Congress in 1998, and in 1999 the University of California honored his career as "one of America's leading voices for peace and human rights" by establishing the Ronald V. Dellums Chair in Peace and Conflict Studies. While many black politicians have been influenced by the example of Dr. MARTIN LUTHER KING JR. Dellums was most struck by King's willingness to break with the Democratic Party and other civil rights leaders when matters of principle were at stake. This quality, more than any other, defined Dellums as a political maverick.

FURTHER READING

Dellums, Ronald. *Lying Down with the Lions: A Public Life from the Streets of Oakland to the Halls of Power* (2000).

Clay, William L. *Just Permanent Interests: Black Americans in Congress* (1992).

Swain, Carol M. *Black Faces, Black Interests: The Representation of African-Americans in Congress* (1993).

SHOLOMO B. LEVY

Demby, Edward T. (13 Feb. 1869–14 Oct. 1957), the first African American Episcopal bishop elected to serve in the United States, was born Edward Thomas Demby V and raised in Wilmington, Delaware, the eldest child of freeborn parents, Edward T. Demby IV and Mary Anderson Tippett. Young Edward was tutored by his uncle, "Professor" Eddy Anderson, for the majority of his primary and secondary school years. Anderson was the headmaster of a private high school located behind Ezion (Northern) Methodist Episcopal Church, a hub of Wilmington's black community.

After leaving Wilmington, Demby embarked on an educational odyssey that encompassed Philadelphia's prestigious Institute for Colored Youth, followed by Centenary Bible Institute (now

Morgan State University) in Baltimore, Howard University in Washington, D.C., Wilberforce University in Ohio, and National University in Chicago. He usually taught in some capacity to support himself through college and operated more than one private academy in the course of his studies. By 1894 he was an ordained African Methodist Episcopal clergyman teaching theology at Paul Quinn College in Waco, Texas.

In 1895, while serving as dean of Paul Quinn, Demby converted to the predominantly white Episcopal Church and immediately began a process leading to the priesthood. He was first a catechist, or lay reader, responsible for churches in Denver and rural West Tennessee, then a deacon in West Tennessee, and finally a priest in West Tennessee. When he was examined for the priesthood, he caused a sensation. The examiners were flabbergasted at Demby's command of sacred languages and overall intellectual prowess. Afterward, they felt compelled to admit that "no one" could have done better on certain parts of the examination. As for Demby, he was already mindful of the possibility of one day becoming a bishop, and he did not want it said that he was given any shortcuts by reason of his color. Demby credited himself for being the first African American to operate a school that offered correspondence courses in sacred languages.

After the death of his first wife, Polly Alston Sherrill, Demby transferred to St. Augustine's, Kansas City, where in 1902 he married Antoinette Martina Ricks, a graduate of the first nursing class of Freedmen's Hospital, Howard University, and the head nurse at Freedman's Hospital in Kansas City.

Over the next five years, Demby served as a priest to churches in Cairo, Illinois, and Key West, Florida. In both cases he strove to reach large migrant populations via the parochial school adjacent to each church. At St. Michael's in Cairo, he discovered that Polly's Tuskegee background was especially effective in drawing attention to the school. However, while he served at St. Peter's in Key West, Demby no longer identified with Tuskegee. In 1907, at the zenith of the debate between W. E. B. DuBois and Booker T. Washington over the direction of African American education, Demby publicly condemned Washington's philosophy of industrial education. He said it was not in the best interests of African Americans and personally attacked Washington for being overly manipulative toward blacks and overly servile toward whites.

Simultaneously, Demby published letters regarding the election of black bishops to serve in the United States, a volatile issue confronting the 1907 General Convention of the Episcopal Church. It was a choice between two plans. The first, named the missionary district plan, called for the organization of black churches into missionary districts that would, in turn, elect black representatives to general conventions and be represented by black bishops in the national House of Bishops. Black missionary bishops and their delegates would enjoy political equality in exchange for wholesale segregation of the church, especially in the South. The second plan, called the suffragan bishop plan, would not have written segregation into church law, but would have allowed each diocese to elect suffragan (assistant) bishops to supervise black ministries in the same diocese. Suffragans would be under the authority of white bishops. They would have rights to the floor, but no vote in the House of Bishops. Like the Conference of Church Workers among the Colored People, the primary black advocacy group in the Episcopal Church, Demby preferred the missionary district plan for its autonomy and the vestige of equality it guaranteed. Ultimately, the general convention passed the suffragan plan into law.

Also in 1907, Demby moved back to Tennessee. His chief calling was Emmanuel Church in Memphis, but he served in many locations. He organized and supervised black missions in the Memphis area, served as dean and archdeacon of Tennessee's black Episcopalians, and supervised the establishment of Hoffman–St. Mary's Industrial Institute, the flagship of black education in Episcopal Tennessee. He was a leader in several religious, civic, and charitable groups in Memphis and considered himself an emissary to the white community.

In 1917 the dioceses in Arkansas, Texas, New Mexico, Oklahoma, Missouri, and Kansas elected Demby the nation's first black bishop. Although he was appointed to the Diocese of Arkansas, the bishops of the Province of the Southwest intended that Demby supervise black ministries throughout the region. However, by the time he was consecrated in 1918, dissenting black churches and their bishops had effectively reduced his jurisdiction to a mere handful of small churches in Arkansas. In addition, he had no official residence and no salary. Thus began a ministry Demby described as "making bricks without straw."

From 1918 to 1931 Demby confined his administrative duties primarily to Arkansas as he struggled for funds and credibility. As of 1922 the national church began appropriating additional funds for his operating expenses, and it finally began paying him a meager salary. However, these appropriations enabled Demby to establish Christ Church Parochial and Industrial School in Forrest City, Arkansas, and recruit teachers to staff it. Likewise, he was able to recruit priests to fill pulpits in Arkansas and Oklahoma. The self-sufficient black church became his creed, and in 1930 he announced a ten-year plan to transform Arkansas's five black churches into independent parishes. Meanwhile, the 1925 General Convention, realizing that Demby's jurisdiction had been heavily compromised at the outset, contemplated relocating him or reducing his appropriations. Inspired, or perhaps shamed, by these developments, the bishops of the Southwest made greater use of his ministry. Likewise, the church's black clergy, who had never been reconciled to Demby's second-class bishop status, began, nonetheless, to rally to his defense and grant him greater recognition. As for Demby, he toured the Southwest, as well as the rest of the country, preaching, marrying, and burying, and otherwise promoting black Episcopal missions. He found soliciting especially difficult, as he was by nature not a fund-raiser; rather, he believed that viable ministries engendered their own support. Nevertheless, he pressed on with nationwide canvasses in 1921 and 1927, and the situation was much improved in Arkansas by the end of the decade.

Demby's ministry in Arkansas and the Southwest was never the evangelical success he expected, and after 1932 it was even less so. The cause, aside from the general economic decline of the Great Depression, was the Newport incident of May 1932, when the annual convention of the Episcopal Diocese of Arkansas elected a bishop at Newport, Arkansas. In August, Demby and his white allies protested the racist conduct of that convention, and especially the election. As a result, the House of Bishops overturned the Arkansas election. The protest, however, inspired retaliatory acts by the offended parties, acts that had negative repercussions for Demby's ministry. By 1934 his situation was very ambiguous.

As Demby became more of a bishop in name only, he turned his energies upon the national church and the greater issue of black ministries in general. He was appointed a member of the church's Joint Commission on Negro Work, and, as such, influenced the General Convention of 1940, which made several landmark decisions with regard to the status of African Americans in the Episcopal Church. Most importantly, Demby made the keynote speech, defeating yet another attempt to enact the missionary district plan. This event signaled the end of the plan and the demise of segregation as acceptable church policy. Diocese by diocese, institution by institution, the Episcopal Church desegregated itself over the next fifteen years.

Demby retired from his post in 1938 and spent the remainder of his life serving individual churches in Kansas, Pittsburgh, and Cleveland. He also traveled the country and spoke at events with a biracial theme. He died in Cleveland in 1957 and was eulogized as someone who could eradicate racism by sheer good example, if that were possible.

FURTHER READING

The Demby Family Papers can be found at the Schomburg Center for Research in Black Culture, New York Public Library.

Beary, Michael J. *Black Bishop: Edward T. Demby and the Struggle for Racial Equality in the Episcopal Church* (2001).

Lewis, Harold T. *Yet with a Steady Beat: The African American Struggle for Recognition in the Episcopal Church* (1996).

Shattuck, Gardiner H., Jr. *Episcopalians and Race: Civil War to Civil Rights* (2000).

MICHAEL J. BEARY

Denby, Charles (Matthew Ward Denby) (1908–1983), writer and union activist, was born in rural Alabama. As a youth Denby endured the hardships of farm labor. During the 1920s he joined the Great Migration of African American workers who migrated to the northern industrial centers in search of employment. Denby ended up in Detroit, where he found work as an auto assembler on the production lines.

The 1930s were a period of militant mobilization and organization among workers in the auto industry, and Denby became a leading participant in the wildcat strikes that swept through the industry in the 1930s and 1940s—crucial struggles in the development of the United Auto Workers (UAW). His involvement in these organizing campaigns both reinforced his view that struggles over race and class were intricately enmeshed and convinced him that working-class gains could not be made unless unions were prepared to attack systemic racism, a perspective that was not always maintained within the union leadership.

Part of the difficulty, especially following the success of the union recognition campaigns of the 1930s, which led to formal legal status for unions, was the emergence and consolidation of an institutional bureaucracy within unions, at local and national levels. This bureaucracy, which held legal status as the official bargaining agent for the union's membership, adopted an approach that favored conciliation and compromise with employers rather than one that sought broader social or systemic change. This was evident with the auto unions as they, under UAW president Walter Reuther, quickly moved to purge militants and Communists from its ranks.

But it was Denby's contributions as a writer that would be best remembered. Denby recognized very early in the process of union institutionalization that growing divisions existed between the rank-and-file autoworkers and the union bureaucracies. Much of his writing during the 1940s and 1950s addressed this very issue, including the element of racism. His autobiography, *Indignant Heart: A Black Worker's Journal,* was a powerful and significant example of rank-and-file literature. The book consisted of two volumes, the first being written in 1952. Unlike many radical members, who sought to change the unions by forming oppositional caucuses and running for leadership positions, Denby asserted that the problem the unions faced, in terms of growing conservatism, was structural— the bureaucracy itself. It would not be addressed by getting leftists or reformers into positions of authority within existing union structures. Denby, who refused throughout his life to become a part of the formal union leadership, instead sought to develop rank-and-file militancy and strength within the union and the workplace. This was, in many ways, a slower and more difficult path, and one that meant addressing head-on the divisions that existed within the union membership, especially in terms of racism.

The internal racism that split the union movement in its struggles against bosses also fatally undermined the capacity of rank-and-file workers to challenge the union leadership. In order to address union racism, Denby advocated patient dialogue between white and black workers so that shared class interests might be made more obvious. At the same time, he actively organized black caucuses within the union so that the specific concerns of black workers could be raised in a collective manner in the face of an often recalcitrant union bureaucracy.

Unfortunately, Denby found that racism, despite rhetoric to the contrary, was a regular feature of the radical parties of the left, even the Trotskyist movement to which he belonged. Denby spoke out against racism in his own Socialist Workers' Party (SWP), which had branches that opposed interracial marriage as well as sexual relations between black and white members.

During the 1950s Denby became involved with the small group of libertarian Marxists, the Johnson-Forest Tendency, former Trotskyists, associated most notably with its leading figures C. L. R. James and Raya Dunayevskaya. When James and Dunayevskaya eventually split in 1955, Denby chose to remain with Dunayevskaya. Among the points of disagreement between James and Denby had been the need for a modern revolutionary organization to redevelop dialectical thought in relation to contemporary struggles, a matter that Denby viewed as a crucial task for Socialists in the twentieth century. Along with Dunayevskaya, Denby would contribute to the development of a Marxist humanism that sought to express a holistic theory of revolution emphasizing Hegel's thinking on the dialectic and Marx's writings on alienation.

Within this Marxist humanism the organizational focus was shifted away from the strategic and tactical considerations and vanguardist approaches to these questions that characterized much of the Socialist left. Denby and Dunayevskaya advocated a return to what they saw as the humanist kernel of Marx's thought, emphasizing visions of a society centered on human needs and capacities rather than the pragmatism or political expediency of authoritarian forms of Socialism. In 1955 Denby and Dunayevskaya founded the Marxist newspaper *News & Letters;* Denby served as editor. Denby also took part in such historic events as the Montgomery Bus Boycott in 1955–1956 and the Detroit uprising of 1967. The second volume of his autobiography was written in 1978; it not only documented Denby's struggles, from his youth in the rural South to his adult life in the auto plants, but also integrated this narrative with a straightforward expression of his philosophical beliefs. His front-page column "Worker's Journal" appeared in every issue until his death in 1983.

FURTHER READING

Alan, John. "Dialectics of Black Freedom Struggles,"
    News & Letters (2003).
Dunayevskaya, Raya. "American Civilization on Trial,"
    News & Letters (1963).

JEFF SHANTZ

Dennis, Lawrence (25 Dec. 1893?–20 Aug. 1977), diplomat, preacher, and author, was born in Atlanta, Georgia, the son of Sallie Montgomery. Nothing is known of his biological father. His mother, however, was an African American, and Dennis was of mixed race parentage. In 1897 he was adopted by Green Dennis, a contractor, and Cornelia Walker. During his youth Dennis was known as the "mulatto child evangelist," and he preached to church congregations in the African American community of Atlanta before he was five years old. By the age of fifteen he had toured churches throughout the United States and England and addressed hundreds of thousands of people.

Despite his success as an evangelist Dennis had ambitions to move beyond this evangelical milieu. In 1913, unschooled but unquestionably bright, he applied to Phillips Exeter Academy and gained admission. He graduated within two years and in 1915 entered Harvard.

Dennis's decisions to attend these schools signaled both a departure from his evangelical career and a shift in his racial identity. Born into the African American world of the South, he now "passed" into white America and constructed a new racial identity for himself. By becoming "white" he opened up opportunities previously beyond his reach. Although many former acquaintances knew his secret, and subsequent ones suspected, as a recent biographer, Gerald Horne, has written, there was a widespread "don't ask, don't tell" policy. In later years, despite keeping company with white supremacists, he distanced himself from their views, and opposed segregation.

Dennis availed himself of these new opportunities almost immediately. As a student he received military training and during World War I served as a first lieutenant in France. After the war he graduated from Harvard and in 1921 entered the U.S. Foreign Service. He served in Haiti, Romania, Honduras, and Nicaragua. His most notable assignment was in 1926 as chargé d'affaires in Nicaragua, where he presided over a peace conference between warring liberals and conservatives. Dennis resigned his position in 1927 and joined J. W. Seligman and Company, a banking firm, to be its representative in Peru.

In 1930, as the Depression deepened, Dennis left the world of international finance and was soon writing articles and commenting in public forums on American foreign and economic policy. His earliest articles criticized American interventionism in Latin America. In his first book, *Is Capitalism Doomed?* (1932), he broadened his scope to analyze the sustainability of the American economy. He criticized businesspeople as incapable of providing the spiritual leadership needed to reinvigorate a now moribund capitalism, and he called on the state to find a solution to unemployment.

While the election of Franklin Roosevelt in 1932 mollified many Americans, Dennis condemned what he called the "planless Roosevelt revolution." In 1933 he became associate editor of the *Awakener*, a right-wing semimonthly publication, and entered the camp of far-right critics of the New Deal. By 1936, with the publication of his book *The Coming American Fascism*, Dennis made his reputation as a theorist of "fascism," or what he called an "authoritarian executive state." He believed that Americans would either descend into chaos with the Depression or select some form of "totalitarian" system, such as communism or fascism. Liberalism had failed and fascism was the only likely and desirable choice for Americans. In 1933 Dennis married Eleanor Simson; they had two daughters before divorcing in 1957.

Dennis left the *Awakener* in 1935 and joined E. A. Pierce and Company, a New York brokerage firm, as an economist. Along with a partner in the firm, he traveled to Europe, where he met Adolf Hitler and Benito Mussolini. He then traveled around the United States for the company, speaking on political and financial issues to groups of businesspeople, where he established a reputation as an expert on these matters. He left his position in 1938 to publish his own subscription newsletter, the *Weekly Foreign Letter*.

In his newsletter Dennis combined investment advice with analysis and opinion on global political developments. Although Dennis rejected the most explicitly racist aspects of Nazi ideology, he argued that it was inevitable that America would have to adopt fascist ideas in response to the continuing economic crisis. Walking a fine line between explanation and affiliation, Dennis would later claim his writings were based purely on an objective assessment of the times. Though anti-Semitic, this did not constitute an important part of his writings and his views were widely shared among contemporary American elites. He did, however, fight against American involvement in Europe. He denounced intervention as part of a "religious" war waged for an ideology of "internationalism." An outspoken isolationist, he found himself censured in 1941 by Secretary of the Interior Harold Ickes as an appeaser and "the brains of American fascism."

Dennis published his most ambitious book, *The Dynamics of War and Revolution*, in 1940. No longer using the controversial term "Fascist," he now argued that a "Socialist" world revolution was occurring and that democracies suffering from historical stagnation would "go Socialist." This would happen in the United States, he suggested, in the process of fighting a futile war against Germany, Italy, and Japan.

Dennis achieved a new level of intellectual respectability with this book, which was widely reviewed in political and academic journals. Yet with the outbreak of war, Dennis found that his reputation as an advocate for fascism and isolationism created serious legal problems. The army denied him a commission and considered removing him from the East Coast for security reasons. The postmaster general banned *The Dynamics of War and Revolution* from the mail, and in early 1944 the Justice Department charged Dennis and twenty-nine codefendants with sedition.

The charge against Dennis, conspiring with the Nazis to cause insubordination in the military, could not be sustained by the prosecution. The so-called Mass Sedition Trial ended after seven months, when the presiding judge died of a heart attack, and by 1947 the indictments were dismissed. In 1946 Dennis coauthored a scathing account of the episode, *A Trial on Trial: The Great Sedition Trial of 1944*.

The trial and Dennis's identification as "America's Number One Fascist" made him a political pariah. After World War II he retired to his Becket, Massachusetts, farm, where he resumed publication of his newsletter, renamed the *Appeal to Reason*. Though he was outspokenly hostile to communism, Dennis continued to endorse isolationism. He opposed cold war confrontations in Korea and Vietnam and condemned political persecution in the guise of McCarthyism. In 1959 or 1960 he married Dora Shuser Burton; they had no children. Dennis published one last book, *Operational Thinking for Survival*, in 1968 and continued to publish the *Appeal* until 1972.

Though Dennis died in obscurity in Spring Valley, New York, he made his mark in the interwar years as a critic of liberalism and an outspoken isolationist. His criticism of liberal capitalism was often incisive. His advocacy of authoritarianism, however, made him an object of political derision and repression. He ended his life a political outcast.

FURTHER READING

Dennis's papers are held by the Hoover Institution.
His oral history, "The Reminiscences of Lawrence Dennis" (1967), is available on microfiche in the Oral History Research Office, Columbia University.
Dennis, Lawrence. *Life-Story of the Child Evangelist Lonnie Lawrence Dennis* (n.d.).
Doenecke, Justus. "Lawrence Dennis: Revisionist of the Cold War," *Wisconsin Magazine of History* (Summer 1972): 275–86.
Horne, Gerald. *The Color of Fascism: Lawrence Dennis, Racial Passing, and the Rise of Right-Wing Extremism in the United States* (1996).
Radosh, Ronald. *Prophets on the Right* (1975).
Ribuffo, Leo. *The Old Christian Right: The Protestant Far Right from the Great Depression to the Cold War* (1983).
Schlesinger, Arthur M., Jr. *The Politics of Upheaval* (1960).
Obituary: *New York Times*, 21 Aug. 1977.
This entry is taken from the *American National Biography* and is published here with the permission of the American Council of Learned Societies.

STEVEN LEIKIN

Dennis, Walter Decoster (23 Aug. 1932–30 Mar. 2003), Episcopal bishop, was born Walter Decoster Dennis in Washington, D.C., the son of Walter Decoster Dennis and Helen Louise (maiden name unknown). At an early age the Dennises moved to Petersburg, Virginia, where Walter attended the segregated public schools.

Bishop Dennis began his career at the Cathedral of Saint John the Divine as a curate following his graduation from General Theological Seminary in New York City. During his first tenure at the Cathedral, the then Reverend Dennis was noted for his conferences on civil rights, concern for the urban communities of New York City, and his keen interest in constitutional law and history. During this period he became friendly with THURGOOD MARSHALL, at that time a civil rights attorney and a champion of the *Brown v. Board of Education* Supreme Court decision in 1954; then, during his second tenure, he provided the eulogy at Supreme Court Justice Marshall's funeral in the Cathedral in January of 1993. Though having been ordained by Bishop Horace Donegan, he was best known for his association with the controversial dean of Saint John the Divine, James Pike, who later became the bishop of California.

In 1960 Bishop Dennis assumed the position of vicar of Saint Cyprian's Church in Hampton, Virginia, and adjunct professor of constitutional law and American history at Hampton Institute (later Hampton University). During his tenure there, Bishop Dennis was actively involved in the support of the civil rights movement, making Saint Cyprian's a hospitable place for the northern liberals who wished to have a firsthand experience with the student movement of that period. He also opened Saint Cyprian's to the Freedom Riders of the Congress of Racial Equality in 1961 and provided important pastoral support to the various college student leaders engaged in the 1960s civil rights movement. In the spring of these years he held Religious Emphasis Week at the college in coordination with the college chaplain. He invited to the college notable speakers who raised the bar for students inquiring about spiritual and social change, among them the Reverend William Sloane Coffin and the Reverend Malcolm Boyd. He opened his home to other personalities, such as Margaret Mead, who could challenge and inspire the student's intellectual pursuits. While serving as chaplain to the Episcopal students, he offered summer programs for seminarians to work in the community and enlarged their horizons with regard to the black religious experience.

Returning to New York in 1965, once again to serve as priest, and later invested as the canon residentiary, Bishop Dennis was active in his pastoral responsibilities in the diocese and became recognized as an authority on both canonical and constitutional law. Having helped form the Guild of Saint Ives, whose purpose was to give legal assistance with a pastoral dimension in areas of canon and civil law, Bishop Dennis pursued those interests in postgraduate studies at New York University.

Another important aspect of his ministry was his authorship of several articles on Puerto Rican, Mexican American, and Asian communities in New York and his support of programs to enhance the urban ministry of the diocese. He served as the suffragan, or assistant bishop, in the Diocese of New York from 1976 to 1998, having been consecrated on 6 October of that former year. He was the second African American to serve in that position. Prior to his election Bishop Dennis was canon residentiary of the Cathedral of Saint John the Divine in New York City. During his tenure in that position Bishop Dennis was a leader in social policy reform, civil rights, and social justice.

Upon the election of Bishop Paul Moore as the diocesan and following his own election as bishop, he often provided an Episcopal presence in the northern part of the diocese, in the Poughkeepsie region. He thus showed his own ministerial dexterity, being equally comfortable in both the rural and urban sections of the Diocese of New York. Wherever he was located, Bishop Dennis was always outspoken on the issues of the day, prodding both church and society to confront the gap between its profession of equality of opportunity and its performance. He continued his penchant for sponsoring conferences on important topics and was a much sought after counselor and mentor.

In 1992 he was appointed by the presiding bishop to chair the church's Standing Commission on Constitution and Canons, and served with distinction on that important body until 1994. He also served as the chair of the Episcopal Black Ministries Commission and was one of the founding members of the Union of Black Episcopalians. Never forgetting his roots in the segregated South, Bishop Dennis helped formulate a comprehensive plan for the recruitment, training, and deployment of black clergy and was instrumental in assisting in the formation of the Organization of Black Episcopal Seminarians, all under the auspices of the Commission on Black Ministry. He was frequently invited to preach in predominantly black churches, often at the ordinations of black clergy.

He also served on the board of Planned Parenthood, the Episcopal Society for Cultural and Racial Unity (ESCRU), the Society of Juvenile Justice, and the Board of the National Association for the Study for the Reform of Marijuana Laws. Although a graduate of General Theological Seminary, he was instrumental in recruiting black lay and clergy persons for the boards of other seminaries and the various committees and commissions of the Episcopal Church, in addition to his equally strong commitment of involving persons of color in civic and social change organizations. He was well respected in the House of Bishops of the Episcopal Church for his keen mind and sharp wit. He was also quite knowledgeable regarding parliamentary procedure and always provided orientation on these matters to the pre–General Convention Caucus of Black Bishops and Deputies.

Bishop Dennis was best known for his triennial articles, in the *Sewanee Theological Review* of the University of the South, on major issues confronting the church prior to its General Convention. These articles were eagerly awaited by those who followed the politics of the Episcopal Church and those who wished to have an understanding of what to look for at these often pivotal gatherings. In these articles Bishop Dennis was unafraid to speak candidly about the controversial issues, make clear the complicated ones, and champion reform of the church's policies and practices with regard to people of color, women, and gays. As a result he was a much sought after speaker and commentator regarding the effects of the actions taken at General Convention. This was particularly true in regard to the significant changes that were made at that time in the canons affecting disciplinary actions against bishops and clergy for misconduct.

Respected as a teacher, by his students at Hampton Institute, by black seminarians, and by the clergy and laity of the Diocese of New York, Bishop Dennis was constantly speaking to the "teachable moment." Renowned as a preacher for his insightful and often caustic sermons that were designed to comfort the afflicted and afflict the comfortable, he stood in a long line of black clergy and lay preachers who frequently served as the conscience of the church. Celebrated as an important mentor for many successful clergy, Bishop Dennis left an impressive legacy of faithfulness, prophetic ministry, and abiding pastoral care to the people of the Diocese of New York and to Afro-Anglicans throughout the world. He died in Hampton, Virginia, following a long illness. Bishop Dennis was ranked number 734 in the succession of Episcopal bishops in the United States.

EDWARD RODMAN

Denny, John (1848?–28 Nov. 1901), Buffalo Soldier, was born in Big Flats, New York, along the banks of the Chemung River, not far from the town of Elmira. Nothing is known about Denny's family aside from the fact that he had a sister. Denny's career as a Buffalo Soldier in the Ninth Cavalry spanned thirty years, during which time he earned the nation's highest military honor, the Medal of Honor. Denny enlisted in the U.S. Army on 13 June 1867, one year after President Andrew Johnson signed legislation establishing two cavalry and four infantry regiments composed of African American men. All of these units were sent to the western frontier to defend settlers from Indian tribes, rustlers, thieves, and bandits.

Denny was assigned to Company C, Ninth Cavalry, stationed at Fort Davis, Texas, near the Mexican border. Its orders were to protect stage and mail routes between El Paso and San Antonio, patrol borderlands between the United States and Mexico, and defend settlers. Though the Ninth had received little training at its camp in Louisiana before being sent to the frontier, the regiment overcame its inexperience through ongoing skirmishes and battles that turned the men into well-organized and disciplined troopers. By the time the army transferred the Ninth Cavalry to the district of New

Mexico in the winter of 1875–1876, the unit's commander Colonel Edwin Hatch had a regiment with a reputation as one of the toughest military fighting forces on the frontier.

During the 1870s the federal government tried to confine American Indians to tribal reservations that it had created. As tribes throughout the arid West found themselves shunted onto lands with insufficient food, water, wood, and pasturage for their everyday needs, younger warriors decided to drive the unwanted interlopers out of the region. Shortly after Denny's regiment arrived in New Mexico Territory, the Ninth began patrolling the unfamiliar territory in search of elusive bands of renegades led by skilled Apache warriors like Geronimo, Victorio, Sinya, and Nana. In an incident in January 1877 that involved Denny's company, Lieutenant Henry H. Wright, six Company C troops, and three Navajo scouts left Fort Bayard to track a group of Chiricahua Apache that had attacked the Sixth Cavalry in Arizona and escaped eastward. Along the trail Wright's group suddenly found itself surrounded by a force of thirty to forty warriors. Outnumbered, Wright attempted to talk the warriors into surrender. Failing this, Wright ordered his men to leave. A fight broke out at close quarters, and the Buffalo Soldiers fought with such vengeance that the Indians fled. Denny's Company C and a contingent of men from Company A mounted a pursuit. The troops located and attacked a camp of about twenty-five warriors who also fled, leaving behind all their equipment and supplies.

The January 1877 skirmish was just the beginning. In September, Chief Victorio, considered one of the most fierce and dangerous of the Apache warriors, left the San Carlos Apache reservation in Arizona with three hundred warriors and headed east into New Mexico. For the next three years both Colonel Hatch's Ninth Cavalry and Colonel Benjamin Grierson's Tenth Cavalry pursued the rebellious Apache in attempts to return them to the reservation. It was during a battle on 18 September 1879 that Acting Sergeant Denny took the actions that led to his Medal of Honor nomination.

Victorio's warriors had trapped the Ninth Cavalry Companies B and E in a box canyon of the Las Animas Canyon area. Victorio's men knew the area well and had stationed themselves along the vertical upper canyon walls. The sounds of an intense battle reached nearby Companies C and G, and the men hurried into the canyon to join the fight. Soon after they arrived Denny saw a badly wounded soldier in the open, unable to move

John Denny, sergeant, c. 1900. (Library of Congress/ Collection of W. E. B. DuBois.)

the incident, and in 1894 Captain C. W. Taylor nominated Denny for the Medal of Honor, recalling that Denny had picked up Private Freeland, a "heavy man," and carried him to shelter under a hill.

Following six difficult years in New Mexico Territory, capped by the pursuit of another Apache warrior named Nana into Mexico, the army transferred Ninth Cavalry headquarters to Fort Riley, Kansas, with troops stationed at Forts Elliot (Texas), Hays (Kansas), Sill (Nevada), and Supply (Indian Territory). In 1885 Fort McKinney in Wyoming became regimental headquarters for the Ninth, with men stationed at Forts Robinson and Niobrara in Nebraska and Fort DuChesne in Utah. John Denny was among the troops stationed at Fort Robinson, where he ended his thirty-year career, retiring prior to the Ninth Cavalry's departure for Cuba during the war with Spain.

Denny lived in nearby Crawford, Nebraska, and reportedly worked periodically at the Fort Robinson post exchange. Denny's career spanned the entire period of the Indian wars, and he fought in numerous engagements with dedication and courage. He died in Washington, D.C., and is buried at the U.S. Soldiers' and Airmen's Home National Cemetery there. A monument in Denny's honor stands in Wisner Park, Elmira, New York.

FURTHER READING

Leckie, William H. *The Buffalo Solders: A Narrative of the Negro Cavalry in the West* (1967).

Schubert, Frank N. *Black Valor: Buffalo Soldiers and the Medal of Honor* (1997).

Schubert, Frank N. *Buffalo Soldiers, the Braves, and the Brass: The Story of Fort Robinson, Nebraska* (1993).

MOYA B. HANSEN

himself to safety. Denny asked his commanding officer, Captain C. D. Beyer, for cover while he rescued the private, but Beyer ordered Denny to remain sheltered. Sergeant Denny disobeyed Beyer with the knowledge that if he survived, he could be court-martialed. Denny ran approximately one hundred yards under heavy fire to the wounded man and carried him to cover on his back.

Later that same day First Lieutenant Robert T. Emmet of Company G asked for volunteers to execute a move that might allow the Buffalo Soldiers to escape the canyon. The highly risky plan called for the soldiers to climb one side of the cliffs and displace the Apache. Not until Denny stepped forward did four other soldiers and two Navajo scouts volunteer to go. The group could not reach the top of the cliff because of heavy Apache fire, but neither could the Apache warriors fire on the cavalry with the volunteers strategically placed in the middle. When the troops below had escaped, the small band fought its way down. A Navajo scout was wounded, and Denny again carried a wounded man to safety on his back. Denny was not court-martialed after

Dent, Tom (20 March 1932–6 June 1998), journalist, poet, playwright, and community arts activist, was born Thomas Covington Dent in New Orleans to Dr. Albert Walter Dent, the president of Dillard University, and Ernestine Jessie Covington Dent, an Oberlin- and Juilliard-educated pianist and a dedicated humanitarian.

Dent pursued his interest in writing and community engagement throughout his formal education. In 1947 he graduated from Gilbert Academy, a college preparatory school for black students in New Orleans. He then matriculated at Morehouse College, where he served as editor in chief of the student newspaper *The Maroon Tiger* and graduated with a B.A. in Political Science in 1952. Until 1956 he completed doctoral coursework at Syracuse University's School of International Studies, leaving without completing the degree, and in 1974 he earned an MFA in Creative Writing from Goddard College. Dent also served in the U.S. Army from 1957 to 1959.

In an interview published in 1993 Dent reflects critically on his formal education:

I grew up here in New Orleans as a reading child, and began to do some kind of writing early. In a more developed society—in terms of literature or say, literacy—I would have been encouraged to write seriously. But at that time there was no nurturing ground.... even at Morehouse College I didn't get any sense of direction.... The whole module of Black success we were programmed toward was doctor, lawyer, preacher, teacher— that was it. There was just no concept of doing anything else (ya Salaam, 328).

In this interview Dent goes on to talk about three significant experiences to which he attributes his early development as a writer. First, he describes reading black newspapers as a child. Second, he mentions taking a correspondence course from *Writer's Digest* while in the army. And third, he credits his enrollment in a New York writing workshop as an important introduction to other beginning black writers (329).

Dent's real maturation as a writer and arts activist began when he moved to New York City in 1959. Through his job at *New York Age*, a black newspaper, he began to meet other people who "wanted to do more creative work than a newspaper would allow" and to attend readings by young black poets (Dent, "Umbra Days," 105). He worked as the public information director for the NAACP Legal Defense Fund from 1961 to 1963, assisting THURGOOD MARSHALL, and became a member of On Guard for Freedom, a group of young black intellectuals that included Nora and Calvin Hicks, Rosa Guy, HAROLD CRUSE, ARCHIE SHEPP, AMIRI BARAKA, MAX ROACH, and ABBY LINCOLN. When On Guard dissolved in 1962, a number of writers affiliated with the group decided to form the Umbra Writers Workshop. Regular members included Dent, CALVIN HERNTON, DAVID HENDERSON, Askia Muhammed Touré, LORENZO THOMAS, ISHMAEL REED, and many others. The Umbra group played a vital role in the cultural life of New York's Lower East Side, throwing fund-raising parties, publishing *Umbra* magazine, and giving public readings, and its importance as a gathering of black writers would be far-reaching. As Dent suggests, "The members of Umbra and other N.Y. black writers (like Amiri Baraka) can be seen as representing an intermediary, transitional stage between the naturalistic protest writing of RICHARD WRIGHT and what was in a few years to become a separatist, community-oriented, African-flavored Black Arts Movement" (Dent, "Umbra Days," 107–108).

Dent's experience with Umbra would shape the rest of his career in the arts. In his words:

If Umbra has any lingering meaning/importance for younger black writers it is in the example of black artists working together to produce something. How important this is, because if we don't turn to and develop our own cultural institutions we'll have nowhere to go but the white establishment.... This doesn't mean all black artists, even within a group, have to agree.... But it does mean that we have to have a sense of our role beyond our individual visions (Dent, "Umbra Days," 108).

After moving home to New Orleans in 1965, Dent became associate director of the community-based Free Southern Theater (FST) and the founder of the FST Writing Workshop, BLKARTSOUTH, and the journal *Nkombo*, all dedicated to supporting the work of emerging southern black writers. He also founded the New Orleans–based Congo Square Writer's Union and *The Black River Journal*, and participated in the founding of *Callaloo*, still a vital organ for the dissemination of African diaspora literature and literary criticism.

In the 1970s and 1980s Dent published two books of poetry, *Magnolia Street* (1976) and *Blue Lights and River Songs* (1982), and a number of plays, including *Ritual Murder* (1976). During this time he also conducted oral histories of Mississippi civil rights workers and New Orleans musicians, taught at the University of New Orleans (1979–1981), worked as a writer on ANDREW YOUNG's autobiography (1984–1986), and served as executive director of the New Orleans Jazz and Heritage Foundation (1987–1990). He spent the 1990s traveling in the United States, Africa, and the Caribbean to gather data for various book projects. Although Dent died of a heart attack in 1998 in New Orleans before seeing these projects through, in 1997 he published *Southern Journey: A Return to the Civil Rights Movement*, a book based on interviews he conducted throughout the South in 1991, in which he talked with people about their memories of the 1960s and asked them what changes the civil rights movement had wrought.

Tom Dent committed his life to the creation of art and institutions to support it, to the invigoration of African American communities through the arts, and to individuals' words. It is fitting that the annual Tom Dent Literary Festival, sponsored by the African American Resource Center of the New Orleans Public Library, has been created to honor him and to celebrate African American writing and reading.

FURTHER READING

The Will W. Alexander Library, Dillard University, houses the Dent Family Collection. The Amistad Research Center in New Orleans holds Dent's oral histories.

Dent, Tom. "Lower East Side Coda," *African American Review* 27:4 (December 1993).

Dent, Tom. "Umbra Days," *Black American Literature Forum* 14:3 (Autumn 1980).

"In Memoriam: Thomas Covington Dent, 1932–1998," *Mississippi Quarterly* 52:2 (Spring 1999).

"Thomas Covington Dent," *Contemporary Authors Online* (2000).

Thomas, Lorenzo. "Tom Dent," *Dictionary of Literary Biography Online* (1985).

ya Salaam, Kalamu. "Enriching the Paper Trail: An Interview with Tom Dent," *African American Review* 27:2 (Summer 1993).

JENNIFER DRAKE

DePreist, James (21 Nov. 1936–), symphonic conductor, composer, and poet, was born in Philadelphia, Pennsylvania, to James Henry DePreist and Ethel Anderson. Ethel's sister, James's aunt, was the distinguished singer MARIAN ANDERSON, a contralto who became the first African American to appear with the New York Metropolitan Opera. In Philadelphia, DePreist attended Central High School, the second-oldest high school in the country. One of the best college preparatory schools in the country, it is also a public magnet school renowned for its strong music department. During high school DePreist played percussion and timpani in the all-Philadelphia high school band and orchestra. The orchestra's director, Louis Werson, became a significant musical influence on DePreist and used his musical background to help his student start the Jimmy DePreist Quintet, a jazz band.

In 1958 DePreist received a bachelor's degree as a pre-law student at the Wharton School of the University of Pennsylvania, followed by a master's degree in 1961 from the same school. Uncertain about his future, DePreist was sure of one thing: He would not pursue a career in law. After graduating from the University of Pennsylvania, he studied musical history and the theory of harmony and orchestration at the Philadelphia Conservatory of Music. The tutelage of the famed American composer Vincent Persichetti helped DePreist to begin viewing himself as a composer and to continue to explore job opportunities in music.

In 1962 the State Department invited DePreist to participate in its American Specialist Program playing drums in the king of Thailand's band. This was the start of his professional musical career. DePreist contracted polio while in Thailand, which became a chronic health condition throughout his adult life. During his time in Thailand, he was introduced to Leonard Bernstein, a friend of his aunt Marian, who advised him to take risks. DePreist paid attention, and when he returned to the United States he entered the Dimitri Mitropoulos Conducting Competition in 1963. He was not expected to do well both because an American had never won the competition before and because he appeared with crutches because of his polio, yet he became a semifinalist. DePreist went back to Thailand for most of the next year, conducting and playing music, so that he felt more prepared when he entered the Mitropoulos again the following year. His top finish in 1964 made him the first American ever to win first prize, which garnered him praise from the *New York Times* as well as the Mitropoulos judge Antal Dorati.

For the 1965–1966 season, Bernstein selected DePreist as an assistant conductor of the New York Philharmonic. Though this brought DePreist increased publicity, he was still unable to find work. Seeing more musical opportunities in Europe, he moved to Holland in 1966. He met with a disappointing lack of invitations and focused himself almost solely on learning and growing as a musical artist. Finally, DePreist made his debut in Europe at a Rotterdam Philharmonic Promenades concert in 1969. This appearance in turn led to invitations to substitute and perform in concerts around Europe in Stockholm, Amsterdam, Berlin, and various Italian cities. Two years after DePreist's European debut in Holland, Dorati asked him to become associate conductor of the National Symphony in Washington, D.C.

In 1976 DePreist accepted his first leadership role with a major symphony as music director for the Quebec Symphony Orchestra in Canada. While living in Quebec, he met his future wife, Ginette, who was the co-producer of a CBC radio program. DePreist spent seven years as conductor of the Quebec Symphony, which he left in 1983. For the 1980–1981 season he signed with the Oregon Symphony, where he not only became an inspirational force to the orchestra but also was a community leader, contributing to positive cultural and social changes in Portland. DePreist used his artistic taste to take what was a small town orchestra and make it nationally recognized. He emphasized the works of American composers, but DePreist evaluated music on musical and aesthetic terms, not social or political terms, and therefore chose a wide variety of music. He became a figure in the social and cultural life in Portland and so was able to shed light on the value of the symphony and strengthen its image in Portland and later the nation as a whole.

Despite the early career struggles DePreist faced, his perseverance and effort culminated in many years of conducting around the globe and numerous honors and awards. In addition to conducting almost every major orchestra in North America, he conducted in Europe, Asia, and Australia. DePreist received thirteen honorary doctorates, the Insignia of Commander of the Order of the Lion of Finland, and the Officer of the Order of Cultural Merit of Monaco. He was an elected fellow of both the American Academy of Arts and Sciences and the Royal Swedish Academy of Music. With more than fifty recordings, fifteen with the Oregon Symphony, he earned a reputation as one of America's most accomplished conductors.

In addition to his musical endeavors, DePreist published two collections of poems, *This Precipice Garden* (1987) and *The Distant Siren* (1989), both of which met with critical acclaim. Though he declared that he would like to be a poet, he never expected a published career but rather viewed poetry as another passionate form of artistic expression.

After twenty-three years as music director of the Oregon Symphony, DePreist stepped down in 2003 and became the orchestra's laureate music director. In 2004 he became the director of conducting and orchestral studies at the Juilliard School in New York, an institution which had awarded him an honorary doctorate in 1993. In the early 2000s he appeared frequently at the Aspen Music Festival, with the Boston Symphony at Tanglewood, and with the Philadelphia Orchestra at the Mann Music Center. He also served as principal artistic adviser to the Phoenix Symphony. In 2005 he accepted a position as music director and permanent conductor of the Tokyo Metropolitan Symphony Orchestra.

DePreist made his mark in American and musical history as the first African American to conduct a major symphony. He embodied the universal nature of music, crossed musical genres, and helped integrate and expand a field that was once exclusively white.

FURTHER READING

Oregon Symphony. "James DePreist: Oregon Symphony Laureate Music Director," http://www.orsymphony.org/orchestra/conductors/depreist.aspx (2007).

DISCOGRAPHY

Oregon Symphony. Discography, http://www.orsymphony. org/discography/ (2007).

HARMONY A. TEITSWORTH

DeRamus, Lawrence DePriest, Sr. (8 Jul. 1929– 9 Mar. 2002), educator, community leader, and business leader, was the ninth child born to John Archie Bradson DeRamus and Sadie Mae Goodson DeRamus, a farming couple, in Joffre Community, Prattville, Alabama. He was given the name DePriest in honor of Oscar DePriest, the first African American elected to Congress in the twentieth century. Educated in the segregated Autauga County School System in Autauga County, Alabama, he finished high school in 1947. He received his B.S. Degree in Elementary Education from Alabama State University in 1955. He later married Vernetta Clarke, a teacher, and settled in Enterprise, Alabama. They had one son, Lawrence DeRamus Jr.

Lawrence DeRamus enlisted in the army and served in the Korean Conflict, receiving the Korean Service Medal, Good Conduct Medal, three bronze stars, and the Distinguished Unit Citation and Occupational Medal. Returning from military service, DeRamus finished his degree and began his teaching career in Enterprise, Alabama. He taught fifth grade at Enterprise Academy School. While there, he also served as a counselor, attendance officer, janitor, and basketball coach. Answering the call for leadership, he raised funds to install a hardwood floor in the gymnasium, served as the coordinator for the A.G. Gaston Spelling Bee, and organized a Boy Scout troop. In 1966, DeRamus established a Head Start program for the children of Coffee County. He also established the first summer recreational program for black youth in the city and served as director of the program, supervising five employees from 1955 to 1967.

Concerned with the economic plight of teachers, DeRamus spearheaded the effort to establish the first and only Federal Credit Union for Education Employees in the Coffee and Geneva County area. Employees of the city of Enterprise were organized and chartered in 1959. In the early

1970s, he also laid the groundwork for teachers to receive payroll deduction. He served as Chairman of the Board for this credit union from 1959 to 1975, when payroll deduction was assured by the Board of Education. The credit union is now a multimillion dollar business that has made loans of more than $12 million.

Mr. DeRamus harbored a great concern about the dire poverty he witnessed in the blackbelt counties of Alabama. In the 1960s, the blackbelt region of Alabama was one of the poorest areas in the United States. In an effort to assist impoverished families, after twelve years, he left teaching to become Deputy Director in Charge of Program Writing and Budgeting for the Organized Community Action Program (OCAP) in 1966. The Organized Community Action Program is the title given to the program established in Troy, Alabama, under Title II, Section 201, of the Economic Opportunity Act (EOA) of 1964, which provided funding to community action programs across the country. These programs were charged with uplifting impoverished rural and urban communities by providing housing, food, clothing, health care, job placement, and other vital services.

As Deputy Director for OCAP, Mr. DeRamus wrote one of the first funded proposals for an Equal Opportunity Officer in the state of Alabama. He also wrote a funded proposal for one of three Adult Education Programs funded through the National Research Mental Health Program for Head Start Children in 1965. He served as Head Teacher for the Adult Education program in 1965 and 1966. In 1967, after the NAACP was legalized in the state of Alabama, Mr. DeRamus was instrumental in establishing the NAACP charter for Coffee County, Alabama. In 2002, for his service, the NAACP honored him with a Lifetime Achievement Award.

When OCAP was chartered in the blackbelt region in 1966, it had an initial budget of $16,000. DeRamus wrote program proposals that increased the initial funding of $16,000 to millions of dollars that flowed directly into the economies of Coffee, Pike, Bullock, Crenshaw, and Butler counties. Under the direction of Mr. DeRamus, these programs greatly decreased the poverty level in all five counties and improved the quality of life in the region by providing jobs, sufficient quality housing, and health care. In 1972, DeRamus left OCAP for two and a half years to become executive director of the Southeast Alabama Community Development Corporation, an incorporated nonprofit organization charged with stimulating economic growth in the region. The objective of the program was to assist individuals and groups in establishing businesses. These businesses in return pumped millions of dollars back into the local communities.

In 1975, DeRamus returned to Community Action as director of the Five County Head Start program in the blackbelt region. As director, he secured a center for the Head Start Program and expanded the program to cover more than eight counties in the blackbelt region of Alabama with a budget of nearly $5 million. He also served as consultant on evaluation, budgeting, and administration of Head Start Programs for the State of Alabama and the Regional Office in Atlanta, Georgia. In honor of his service and dedication to the children of the blackbelt region, the Men's Progressive Club honored DeRamus by renaming the building housing the Coffee County Headstart Program the DeRamus Head Start Center.

In the 1980s, DeRamus was recruited to serve as Equal Employment Specialist at Fort Rucker in Troy, Alabama. His duties there were to monitor the Consent Decree regarding Affirmative Action at Fort Rucker. He later became complaints manager as well as manager of the Blacks in Government (BIG) organization. He was later appointed by two governors to serve as a Jury Commissioner in Coffee County. Throughout his career, Mr. DeRamus received many honors including the Office of Equal Opportunity (OEO) Rural Service Award for his service and dedication to alleviating the problems for poor and rural Americans, Past President Award of the Federal Credit Union, and the Progressive Men's Club Community Service Award. At his death, the DeRamus family received a Letter of Condolence from Governor Don Siegelman of Alabama.

In 2001, DeRamus was diagnosed with colon cancer. After several difficult months, he succumbed to the disease on 9 March 2002. Lawrence DeRamus was a community leader whose greatest interest was in his community and the welfare of those around him. Through his work with OCAP and the Southeast Alabama Community Development Program, millions of dollars flowed into the blackbelt region of Alabama providing economic growth for one of the nation's poorest areas.

FURTHER READING

Brunson, Marion Bailey. *Pea River Reflections: Intimate Glimpses at Area Life during Two Centuries.* 3d Edition (1984).

BRANDON K. WALLACE

Derricotte, Juliette Aline (1 Apr. 1897–7 Nov. 1931), educator, was born in Athens, Georgia, the daughter of a cobbler, Isaac Derricotte, and a seamstress, Laura (Hardwick) Derricotte. The Derricottes created a healthy home for their nine children, of which Juliette was the middle child.

A spirited and perceptive child, Juliette Derricotte recognized early the peculiarities of southern society in the 1900s. She wondered why her family was not granted attention until white families were attended in stores, and why her color prohibited her enrollment in the Lucy Cobb Institute—a school located in a suburban section of town. Experiences like these were the seeds of Derricotte's commitment to stand against discrimination.

Derricotte completed her secondary education in Atlanta, and then with the help of recruiters she convinced her parents to allow her to attend Talladega College in Alabama at fifteen dollars a month for tuition, room, and board. Although she welcomed the campus's spatial environment of tall trees and beautiful buildings, she resisted the reality that the faculty at this African American college was all white. Derricotte remained at Talladega and became popular among students, faculty, and administrators for her warm personality, obvious potential, self-confidence in public speaking, leadership on the debate team and YWCA, and diplomacy in resolving conflicts between students and faculty.

Upon earning her degree in 1918 from Talladega College, Derricotte accepted a position with the YWCA as National Student Council secretary. Through this appointment she traveled to colleges, building leadership and blazing the trail for an interracial structure. As a result of her demonstrated commitment, Derricotte was one of two African American delegates sent to England to represent American college students at the 1924 World Student Christian Federation. As the 1928 delegate she traveled to Mysore, India, and remained in Asia for several weeks, traveling to Burma and Ceylon (Sri Lanka), then to China and Japan, where she met with students who shared various forms of oppression endured in their respective nations.

Derricotte earned her master's degree in religious education in 1927 at Columbia University, and from 1929 to 1931 she served as the only female trustee of her alma mater, Talladega College. In 1929 Derricotte accepted a position at Fisk University as dean of women. At the time of her arrival students were embroiled in conflict with administrators regarding the strictly monitored and enforced rules for women living on campus. As dean of women, Derricotte used her skills at negotiation to assist the women students with adjustments to the restrictive policies, creating a more liberating environment in which students could exercise adult freedoms.

In 1931, beloved by her students, Derricotte met with an untimely, ironic, and tragic death. Accompanied by three students from Georgia, Derricotte set out on a road trip to visit her mother. Their vehicle was involved in an auto accident just outside of Dalton, Georgia. She and one of the students sustained serious injuries and received emergency care in the offices of white doctors in Dalton. The local hospital did not admit African Americans. The student died overnight. Derricotte was taken by ambulance to Walden Hospital in Chattanooga, Tennessee, where she died the following day. Her death was met with national outrage. A series of investigations was undertaken, including inquiries by the NAACP and the Commission of Interracial Cooperation of Atlanta on behalf of Fisk. Services in her honor and memory were held across the nation. She was eulogized in Athens, Georgia, by the famed theologian HOWARD THURMAN. Her words from the conference in Mysore, India, anchored the message:

> With all the entanglements of international attitudes and policies, with all the bitterness and prejudice and hatred that are true between any two or more of these countries, you are here friends working, playing, living together in the finest sort of fellowship, fulfilling the dream of the World's Student Christian Federation "That All May Be One" (Derricotte, 282).

FURTHER READING

Derricotte, Juliette. "The Student Conference at Mysore, India," *Crisis* 36 (August 1929): 282.

MARCELLA L. MCCOY

Derricotte, Toi (12 Apr. 1941–), poet and educator, was born Toinette Webster in Hamtramck, Michigan, the daughter of Benjamin Webster, a mortician, and Antonia Banquet Webster, a systems analyst. Derricotte was raised as part of the black middle class in Hamtramck, a Detroit suburb. As her poetry indicates, she was conscious of the importance of separating herself from those less fortunate with the veil of respectability to which the black middle class clung. As she remembers, "Most of the people who lived in the neighborhood I grew up in had just escaped the ghettoes of the city and the sense of the absolute vulnerability of the poor was more than a memory, it was palpable"

(Derricotte, 53). Although her extended family was a "rainbow" of colors, Derricotte's immediate family, particularly her matrilineal family, was light enough to pass for white, which she occasionally did with her grandmother when shopping in downtown Detroit. Her poem "Weakness," in *Captivity*, describes the fear she felt entering department stores where even the elevator operators were white.

Derricotte attended Wayne State University in Detroit, where she first majored in psychology then switched to special education after the birth of her son, Anthony. Despite this early pregnancy and a failed first marriage, she earned a B.A. in 1965 and taught for five years in the Michigan school system. She remarried in 1967 and moved to New Jersey with her second husband, Clarence Bruce Derricotte, a banker, and son. Derricotte, who began writing poetry and journal entries at the age of ten, first shared her work with an older cousin when she was fifteen, but after he pronounced it "morbid," she kept her work private until she began attending poetry workshops at age twenty-seven. Once she did, however, she was soon recognized as a promising poet. In 1974 the New Jersey State Council on the Arts selected her as a poet-in-residence for the Poets-in-the-Schools program, and she continued in this program until 1988, becoming a master teacher in 1984.

Derricotte received a Pen and Brush Award for an unpublished manuscript in 1973 and an Academy of American Poets prize in 1974 for "Unburying the Bird." Her first major fellowship for poetry came from the National Endowment for the Arts in 1985, and she received the award again in 1990. She received numerous prizes and awards for her work, including the Folger Shakespeare Library Poetry Book Award in 1990, Pushcart Prizes in 1989 and 1998, and a Guggenheim Fellowship in 2004. She earned an M.A. in English Literature and Creative Writing from New York University in 1984 and in 1991 became a professor in the Department of English at the University of Pittsburgh.

Derricotte's poetry is often autobiographical but avoids impenetrable allusions and repetition. She published four collections of poetry and a prose book that defies generic categorization. Her first collection, *The Empress of the Death House*, was published by Lotus Press in 1978. It is dedicated to her paternal grandmother, the figure of the collection's title, and Derricotte described the collection as moving "from death to resurrection." The text ends with "unburying the bird," which could apply to Derricotte's own "unburying" of her talent, as her second collection, *Natural Birth* (1983), indicates. This second collection chronicles the birth of her son in a home for unwed mothers, an event she revealed to him seventeen years later by writing *Natural Birth*. This work was reprinted in 2000 with a new introduction by Derricotte, providing more background on her birthing experience.

Captivity (1989) was perhaps her most acclaimed collection of poetry. The poetry gathered in this text treats subjects as varied as the poet's mother dressing for Christmas Eve, a nun's testimony while on trial for infanticide, and a bookstore clerk refusing Allen Ginsberg's request to use the bathroom. The diverse subject matter testifies to the different, and unexpected, forms of imprisonment we create for ourselves and others. Derricotte continued her probing of painful subjects with *Tender* (1997). It opens with the title poem, a short six lines that she designates as the "hub" for the following seven sections of poetry. Although the various forms of violence in the volume are to be read as circular, *Tender* ends on a positive note with "Clitoris," which itself ends on the word "tenderness." Also published in 1997, *The Black Notebooks: An Interior Journey* is a twenty-five year journal of Derricotte's writings on race, color, and class privilege. She began the journal when she moved into an all-white neighborhood in Upper Montclair, New Jersey. The book combines poetry and prose and contains expanded descriptions of some of the incidents that inspired her poetry.

In 1996, with her fellow poet Cornelius Eady, Derricotte founded Cave Canem, a learning space for African American poets. The program expanded from a summer retreat to include workshops, prizes, publications, and events. Her work with young poets in Cave Canem and other workshops was indicative of her particular blend of poet and educator. In a 2004 interview, two high school poets asked Derricotte, "What is one thing you really love?" Derricotte responded, "You young writers! Because I know you're going to be great. I know you're going to change the world" (*hArtworks*, 34).

FURTHER READING

Derricotte, Toi. *The Empress of the Death House* (1978)

hArtworks. "*hArtworks* Presents Guest Poet Toi Derricotte" (2004).

Love, Monifa. "Toi Derricotte," in *Contemporary American Women Poets* (2002).

Rowell, Charles H. "Beyond Our Lives: An Interview with Toi Derricotte," *Callaloo* 14.3 (1991).

KELLY BAKER JOSEPHS

Desdunes, Rodolphe Lucien (15 Nov. 1849–14 Aug. 1928), author, advocate for the civil rights of African Americans in Louisiana, an organizer of the Citizen's Committee that launched the *Plessy v. Ferguson* legal challenge to racial segregation in public transportation, was the son of Jeremie Desdunes and Henriette Gaillard Desdunes.

Rodolphe Desdunes's grandson, Theodore Frere, recalled in 1971 that Jeremie Desdunes was Haitian and Henriette from Cuba; the couple reported in the 1880 census that both were born in Louisiana, Jeremie's mother was born in Cuba, and Henriette's father in France. All the Desdunes's sons consistently reported that their parents were both born in Louisiana (Census 1880, 1900, 1920). The Desdunes family was part of New Orleans's large community of *gens de couleur libre*—free people of color, primarily French-speaking. The 1840 census lists a Jeremie Des Dunes in the Third District of New Orleans, whose household included five free colored males and nine free colored females, seven under the age of twenty-four.

The Desdunes family had a cigar manufacturing business; there is an oft-repeated account that they owned a tobacco plantation, but family circumstances do not reflect great wealth. Jeremie Desdunes was also a wheelwright, and in 1880, was listed in the census as a blacksmith. In 1850, when Rodolphe Desdunes was less than a year old, he and his older brother, Aristide, lived in the home of Beliser Fernandez, a mason. Another resident in the household was twenty-year-old Henriette Guillard, most likely their mother. Residents of the neighborhood were generally skilled craftsmen, listed as mulatto (Census, 1850).

In the late 1860s Desdunes married Mathilde Chaval; their children included Daniel, Agnes, Louise, Wendel, Coritza, Lucille, and Jeanne. His wife's mother, born in Pennsylvania, lived with their growing family. Desdunes obtained a job in 1879 as a messenger with United States Customs Service, and the following year was promoted to clerk. He lost this job in 1885, probably as a result of the election of Democrat Grover Cleveland as president, which cost the Republican Party patronage in federal jobs. In the meantime, he graduated in 1882 from Straight University, a multiracial institution, with a law degree.

Desdunes was a vigorous opponent of Louisiana Governor P. B. S. Pinchback, who repeatedly supported separate institutions for the state's black population. Desdunes argued against establishment of Southern University in 1881 as a campus specifically for students of African descent. He later derided Pinchback's assertion that racially separate rail passenger cars would guarantee citizens of African descent first-class treatment from the state's railroads. Desdunes insisted that "every honorable person knows that the law was passed to discriminate against the colored people so as to degrade them" (Medley, p. 116).

He appears to have taken up the family cigar business for a time, being listed in 1890–1891 at his parent's former address with cigars as his occupation, but resumed employment with the customs service in 1891 under the Republican president Benjamin Harrison. He kept the position until 1894, the second year of Cleveland's second term.

Desdunes served on the board of directors, and as a teacher, of the Bernard Couvent School, founded by Madame Bernard Couvent for free persons of color, named for her husband, a free man of color and a carpenter, who died in 1829. Occasional sources infer that Desdunes himself was a student there; the school included a coeducational, nonsectarian day school, with separate classes for boys and girls, as well as an orphanage. However, in writing about Madame Couvent and the school, Desdunes never mentions having attended classes there. The school declined during the 1860s and 1870s, and was revived in 1884, the period when Desdunes became directly involved.

Desdunes was a contributing writer to *The Crusader*, a newspaper published by Louis Andre Martinet, from 1889 to 1898. In 1891, Desdunes was a founding member of the *Comité des Citoyens* to test the constitutionality of Louisiana's Separate Car Law. The Citizens Committee was formed at the suggestion of Aristide Mary, one of the wealthiest Creoles in New Orleans, with Martinet as unofficial leader; Arthur Esteves, born in Haiti, as president; and the former lieutenant governor Caesar Carpentier Antoine as vice president. Desdunes wrote critically that the majority of the African American community "believed it was better to suffer in silence than to attract attention to their misfortunate and weakness," whereas in his view "the obligation of the people is resistance to oppression" (Lobel, p. 105).

Desdunes's son Daniel attempted to create the first test case, purchasing a first-class ticket from New Orleans to Mobile, Alabama. This did not result in the head-on challenge to Louisiana's law that the *Comité* sought, because the Louisiana Supreme Court ruled that the state law applied only to intrastate travel. Desdunes's friend Homer

Rodolphe Lucien Desdunes, c. 1911. (Louisiana Division/City Archives, New Orleans Public Library.)

ADOLPH PLESSY tested the law by riding in a "white's only" coach to a destination within Louisiana, for which he was arrested. This resulted in the 1896 case that bears his name, after he appeared initially in the court of Judge J. H. Ferguson.

In March 1907, Desdunes published *A Few Words to Dr. DuBois 'With Malice Toward None,'* taking exception to DR. W. E. B. DuBOIS's general characterization that the southern Negro lacked book learning and industrial skills. "The Negroes of the South do not deserve to stand under the indictment which the first part of that declaration conveys" observed the well-educated southern man of color (Desdunes, p. xvii). Desdunes, however, indulged his own stereotypes, distinguishing in the same pamphlet the "Latin Negro" from the "American Negro." He wrote, "One hopes, the other doubts. Thus we often perceived that one makes every effort to acquire merits, the other to gain advantages. One aspires to equality, the other to identity. One will forget that he is a Negro in order to think that he is a man; the other will forget that he is a man to think that he is a Negro" (Cox,

Robert S., *Body and Soul: A Sympathetic History of American Spiritualism*, p. 171).

Desdunes resumed customs work in New Orleans, as assistant weigher, in 1899. In 1900, his household included his married daughter Coritza Mora, with her sons Octave Mora Jr. and Daniel; his married daughter Agnes, her husband George Frere, and their daughter Inez; Desdunes's son Wendel; as well as two younger daughters, Lucille and Jenny (Census, 1900). He retired in 1912, as a result of being blinded, in 1911, by dust blown from a load of granite in a ship he was inspecting. In 1908, Desdunes completed *Nos hommes et notre histoire*, an account of the *gens de couleur libre*, published in 1911, which in 1973 was translated into English and published as *Our People and Our History: Fifty Creole Portraits*.

Sometime before 1920, Desdunes moved to Omaha, Nebraska, where he lived with his son Wendel (Census, 1920). Another son, Daniel, also lived in Omaha, teaching music at Boys Town. Desdunes died in Omaha from cancer of the larynx, survived by his wife and several children. His body was returned to New Orleans for burial in his family's tomb in St. Louis Cemetery.

FURTHER READING

Bell, Caryn Cossé. *Revolution, Romanticism, and the Afro-Creole Protest Tradition in Louisiana* (2004).

Desdunes, Rodolphe Lucien. *Our People and Our History: Fifty Creole Portraits.* Translated by Dorothea Olga McCants (2001).

Kein, Sybil. *Creole: The History and Legacy of Louisiana's Free People of Color* (2000).

Lobel, Jules. "Plessy v. Ferguson," in *Success without Victory: Lost Legal Battles and the Long Road to Justice in America* (2003).

Medley, Keith Weldon. *We as Freemen: Plessy v. Ferguson* (2003).

Scott, Rebecca Jarvis. *Degrees of Freedom: Louisiana and Cuba after Slavery* (2005).

CHARLES ROSENBERG

Deslandes (Deslondes), Charles (1780–15 Jan. 1811), leader of the largest slave revolt in U.S. history, has largely evaded the scrutiny of historians. Most studies have suggested that he was a free man of color born in Saint-Domingue who was part of the large 1809 immigration to Louisiana from that colony. An as yet unpublished work by the scholar Gwendolyn Midlo Hall suggests however that Deslondes (sometimes spelled Deslandes) was a Louisiana-born slave.

Whatever his origins, it is clear that in 1811, Charles Deslondes was the leader of the revolt known as the German Coast Uprising or the Deslondes Uprising, which occurred along the eastern bank of the Mississippi River in Louisiana. On the evening of 8 January 1811, at the age of thirty-one, Deslondes led a band of rebels downriver on River Road. They began in modern-day Norco and continued through the parishes of St. Charles and St. John the Baptist in Louisiana, approximately forty miles from the city of New Orleans. At the beginning of the nineteenth century, the region was part of the larger Territory of Orleans. In 1804 the Territory of Orleans was all of the land in the Louisiana Purchase south of the 33rd parallel. Because of its initial settlement by a small enclave of Germans, locals dubbed the province "the German Coast." The historian Eugene D. Genovese estimated that Deslondes, inspired by the Haitian Revolution (1791–1804), led between three hundred and five hundred slaves in the rebellion.

Participants in subsequent hearings described Charles Deslondes as a "mulatto" from Saint-Domingue. Details of his childhood or experience during the Haitian Revolution are currently unknown. At the time of the rebellion in 1811, we know that Deslondes was a privileged slave driver at the Woodland Plantation, owned by Manuel Andry, in east-bank St. John Parish, Louisiana. Although the record does not state what provoked Deslondes to initiate the revolt on the 8 January, witnesses later stated that he organized the slaves on the Andry plantation, along with runaways who had formed a maroon society in the nearby swamps. It is also of note that the rebellion took place at the end of the harvest, when masters often granted slaves some free time, and were themselves involved in balls and other social galas. This brief period of relative autonomy for slaves and outside distractions for masters may have provided Deslondes with an opportunity to strike. Whatever the circumstances and motivation, it is known that Andry was wounded with an ax when the slaves began to rebel. Andry's son and his head planter, Jean Francois Trepagnier, died when confronting the mob. Deslondes then instructed the rebelling slaves to pillage all valuable resources from the plantation including horses, ammunition, and liquor.

Although the slaves under Deslondes's leadership possessed very few firearms, they engaged in combat with the local militia led by General Wade Hampton (1752–1835), a plantation owner, three days after the rebellion began. Hampton had responded to a call from William C. C. Claiborne, the governor of the Territory of Orleans, to suppress the revolt. A second brigade from Baton Rouge, under the command of Major Homer Virgil Milton, was also roused to combat the slaves. The two militias merged the following morning, 11 January 1811, near Francois Bernard Bernoudi's plantation. The slaves fought with pikes, hoes, and axes. They carried banners, marched to the beat of drums, and were broken into subunits that each had individual leaders on horseback. The slaves wreaked havoc on the region, set plantations on fire as they marched toward New Orleans, and recruited additional slaves, while white residents fled to the city of New Orleans or the backwoods nearer their plantations. At the end of two days' fighting the militias had largely quelled the rebellion and captured Deslondes and other rebels. Some estimates from white officials and journalists at the time claimed that sixty-six rebels were killed, with a further sixteen arrested and seventeen missing, though that number may have been higher.

Beginning on 13 January 1811, a two-day tribunal was held at the Destrehan Plantation under the jurisdiction of St. Charles Parish judge Pierre Bauchet St. Martin to determine what should be done with the remaining slaves. As the slave rebels were not equipped with firearms, the militia had killed at least sixty of them, and wounded many more. The tribunal sentenced sixteen of the rebellion leaders for execution. The tribunal also decapitated them and displayed their heads along the river.

Deslondes was executed on 15 January. His body was mutilated, dismembered, and put on public display as a warning against other attempts at slave uprising. Such an aggressive display of retribution by the Louisiana authorities may have been directed at the more than nine thousand recent refugees from Saint-Domingue who were living in Louisiana, and whom Cuba had expelled in 1809. The substantial number of former and current slaves who witnessed the success of the Saint-Domingue slave revolt undoubtedly posed a constant threat to the region. Newspapers across the country chronicled the event in gory details. However, the national historical memory of Charles Deslondes and the German Coast Uprising pales in comparison to the much smaller revolt known as NAT TURNER's Rebellion that took place in Virginia in 1831. This is most likely because Louisiana, at the time, was a very recent annexation into the United States and therefore still seen as untamed territory where violence and lawlessness could be anticipated.

FURTHER READING

Dormon, John H. "The Persistent Specter: Slave Rebellion in Territorial Louisiana." *Louisiana History* 18 (1977): 389–404.

Kendall, John S. "Shadow over the City." *Louisiana Historical Quarterly* 22 (1939): 142–144.

Sternberg, Mary Ann. *Along the River Road: Past and Present on Louisiana's Historic Byway* (1996).

Thompson, Thomas Marshall. "National Newspaper and Legislative Reactions to Louisiana's Deslondes Slave Revolt of 1811." *Louisiana History: The Journal of the Louisiana Historical Association* 33, no. 1 (Winter 1992): 5–29.

RHAE LYNN BARNES

Destiné, Jean-Léon (26 Mar. 1928–), dancer and choreographer, was born in St. Marc, Haiti, to an upper-class family about whom little is now known. Unlike many of his fellow elite, however, who shunned the rituals of Haiti's poor, Destiné chose to plunge into Vodou and other aspects of national popular culture. In the process he became one of the most influential figures to bring these expressions of Haitian life to the stage and around the world.

Destiné began his training as a teen in Haiti with Lina-Mathon Blanchet, whose group performed folklore-based dance. Later he studied at the Institute d'Ethnologie in Port-au-Prince, where he had the opportunity to analyze Vodou as well as many other local dance styles as performed by practitioners from throughout the nation.

In 1941 he traveled to Washington, D.C., with Blanchet's company to dance at the National Folk Festival, where the group performed to acclaim. Soon after, Destiné returned to the United States for an extended stay. Although he continued to nurture his interest in dance, he also took the opportunity to study both journalism and graphics at Howard University and, later, at Columbia University, thanks to a Rockefeller scholarship. While working as a journalist he began taking classes with the legendary anthropologist, dancer, and choreographer KATHERINE DUNHAM, herself a devotee of Vodou and a translator of its dance forms to theater and film. Destiné joined Dunham's company in 1946, dancing lead roles in such works as *Shango*, in which he played a boy possessed by a snake, and *Bal Négre*, in which he not only danced but also sang a Carnival meringue. Three years later he left Dunham to create his own group. That summer, the Destiné Afro-Haitian Dance Company performed at the Jacob's Pillow Dance Festival in what would be the first of ten appearances at this major institution.

At the request of the Haitian government Destiné returned to Port au Prince in 1949 to establish a new company. The group was intended to be a major attraction at the International Exposition that celebrated the capital city's 200th anniversary. After conducting extensive auditions he drew the performers for the first *Troupe Folklorique Nationale* from the very community that actually practiced Vodou and other social dances. As the dance scholar Kate Ramsey has stressed, this was a time when the powers-that-be in the Haitian government (with a nod of approval and an assist from the United States) looked to folklore to attract tourists—and Vodou rituals, especially in their "safe" secular and theatrical version, proved especially popular (Ramsey, 356–358, 369).

The magnitude of Destiné's accomplishments, and the obstacles he had to overcome to achieve his success with Vodou-related choreography, cannot be overestimated. Criminalized from 1915 until 1934 (during which time the United States occupied Haiti), and depicted in movies worldwide and in popular literature as a religion of horror and superstition, Vodou provoked fear in foreigners and distaste in upper-class Haitian society. As Ramsey observes, however, hatred for the American occupation led many intellectuals (like Destiné himself) to turn to Vodou and other indigenous forms as way to assert their opposition to American tactics and to affirm national pride (Ramsey, 349–350). Yet the ambivalence remained: The choreographer and dancer Ted Shawn, who journeyed to Haiti in 1950 to watch the Troupe Folklorique Nationale perform at the Exposition, saw firsthand the reaction of many of Destiné's countrymen. Recalling that Destiné, at the start of his career, had been "ostracized by society and excommunicated by the church," Shawn noted that even though with "fame and success, he has been taken back into both folds, the elite audience is somewhat embarrassed seeing voodoo [*sic*] dancing turned into an art form … their applause is restrained and polite" (Shawn, 34).

In addition to the negative and exoticized reactions stirred up by Vodou, Destiné had to cope with the larger issues faced by all black choreographers working on the concert stage at that time. Not only were their opportunities fewer but also even the positive reactions sometimes came for the wrong reasons. Many dance historians—including Susan Manning, Brenda Dixon Gottschild, and John O. Perpener III—have discussed the way white audiences frequently regarded the work of African American and African diasporan choreographers as a result of "natural" abilities rather than conscious artistic decision, skill, and talent. A January 1952 review in *Dance Observer* magazine by one "B.G." provides a glimpse of this perspective and how widespread it was even among otherwise astute observers. While reviewing the renowned critic Walter Terry's workshop on "primitive" dance, in which Destiné appeared, he summed up Terry's views thusly: "there exist two kinds of primitive in dance: the ethnic, which comes from the usage of uncivilized and hence genuinely primitive people, and the primitive techniques of modern dance, in which there is an attempt to return to what is basic, or 'primary' in human movement" (12). Clearly, for Terry, and for *Dance Observer*'s reviewer, Destiné (and the Haitians whose work he represented) fell into the former category. This despite the fact that, as Shawn approvingly noted, recasting a work for the stage in which none of the performers had professional experience, and whose movement and patterns normally emerged from the impulse of the gods rather than by the strategies of the choreographer, was a remarkable achievement. Yet even Shawn, when taken by Destiné to an actual Vodou ceremony, could not help but couch his descriptions in the overheated language of the exotic, such as the "maddening" rhythms of the drums. This stereotypical reaction would repeat itself through Destiné's career.

Destiné's choreography remained firmly grounded in his experience of the performances of non-professionals from throughout Haiti. Kate Ramsey stresses that he "chose dancers who 'specialized' in particular regional traditions." His concern for authenticity, and respect for those local differences, set him apart from many other choreographers who placed Vodou dance in a theatrical setting (Ramsey, 363). His major works include *Slave Dance*, *Creole Mazurka*, and *Witch Doctor*, the latter of which won prizes at both the Venice and the Edinburgh International Film Festivals in 1952. A marvelous dancer Destiné earned consistent critical praise from reviewers; Jack Anderson admired the "sheer force of his gestures" in a live performance of *Witch Doctor*, and extolled his piece *The Chosen One* for "depict[ing] states of spiritual possession with remarkable conviction" (*New York Times*, 5 Nov. 1979).

Over the course of his career Destiné became one the most respected and sought-after teachers of Haitian dance. He served as a guest artist in the ALVIN AILEY Dance Center from 1960 until 1968, lectured extensively at such places as the Museum of Natural History in New York and the Caribbean Cultural Center, and was a pioneering member of the National Museum of Dance. In 1960 the U.S. government appointed Destiné cultural attaché for Haiti. While in New York carrying out those duties he also began to teach at the New Dance Group Studio—an arts center established in 1932, in the midst of the Great Depression, dedicated to social action through dance—as well as at NYU and other dance schools in the United States and abroad.

FURTHER READING

Emery, Lynne Fauley. *Black Dance from 1619 to Today* (1988).
Ramsey, Kate. "Vodou, Nationalism, and Performance: The Staging of Folklore in Mid-Twentieth Century Haiti," in *Meaning in Motion: New Cultural Studies of Dance*, ed. Jane Desmond (1997).
Shawn, Ted. "Black Christmas: Pages from the Journey of a Haitian Odyssey by the Noted Dancer," in *Dance Magazine* (May 1950).

KAREN BACKSTEIN

Dett, R. Nathaniel (11 Oct. 1882–2 Oct. 1943), composer and educator, was born Robert Nathaniel Dett in Drummondsville (later Niagara Falls), Ontario, Canada, the son of Robert Tue Dett, a musician and music teacher, and Charlotte Johnson, a musician. The Detts were a highly literate and musically active family, especially interested in European concert traditions. For young Dett, the classical traditions formed his musical roots, and he would never lose touch with them.

Dett initially pursued formal musical study at Oberlin College in Ohio, where he graduated in 1908. Thereafter Dett intermittently studied on the graduate level at Columbia University in New York City, the University of Pennsylvania, the American Conservatory of Music in Chicago, and at Harvard University in Massachusetts, where he won prizes for both literature and music. He also studied advanced composition in Paris in 1929 with the renowned teacher Nadia Boulanger. For much of his professional life, from 1913 to 1931, Dett served as director of music at the Hampton Institute in Virginia. Throughout these years he also devoted himself to musical composition. In 1916 he married Helen Elise Smith, with whom he had two children.

Both in his compositions and in his teaching at Hampton, Dett displayed ambivalence toward the issue of racial identification in art. During the early and mid-twentieth century, artists and critics discussed at length the roles and obligations of African American artists. As was the case with writers and painters, a key issue for composers was whether one should strive to be a consciously African American composer or else a composer who happened to be African American. Historians, journalists, and other commentators have tended to sympathize with the former position and, if only by implication, have criticized those who have chosen the latter course as having somehow sidestepped the center of cultural ferment. While the strengths and weaknesses of this perspective continue to be debated, Dett's career brings context to this question.

Dett undoubtedly saw himself as a composer who happened to be African American. At Hampton he insisted that his music students engross themselves in the classical traditions of Europe. When he took the Hampton Choir on tour he rarely performed spirituals or gospel music, though audiences in America and Europe eagerly hoped he would. Instead, Dett preferred the mainstream choral literature. To Dett the question of a recognizable racial identity was best regarded as a kind of final layer, a cultural epidermis, which if given excessive attention could easily become distracting, obscuring the rest of the cultural body. In this regard he felt that many of the popular music forms such as ragtime, blues, and jazz had lost their artistic integrity, falling into titillation and pandering. In a letter Dett wrote:

We have this wonderful folk music, ... but this store will be of no value unless we treat it in such a manner that it can be presented in choral form, in lyric and operatic works, in concertos and suites and salon music, unless our musical architects take the loose timbre of Negro themes and fashion from it music which will prove that we too have national feelings and characteristics.

As with the contemporary novelist William Faulkner, the ideal for Dett was to create art that was rooted in history and geography but that would resonate among those unacquainted with that history and locale. The quotable hymn or folk fragment was not nearly enough; artful interpretations and settings were critical.

In 1926 Carl Engel, chief of the music division at the Library of Congress, asked Dett to write a quartet for piano, violin, saxophone, and banjo. Engel was seeking a piece that would merge African American traditions with those of Western Europe. Dett politely declined the offer, stating that "any effort from the outside to lay down rather strict lines along which art should develop can only result in self-consciousness and consequently in inartistic and insincere results."

Dett's compositions generally employed the harmonies and forms of traditional nineteenth-century symphonic and choral writing. But unlike many of the romantics, Dett rarely sought to incorporate identifiable idioms into his music. Like the writers of his day who led the Harlem Renaissance, Dett chose to define himself in relation to established classical traditions; but, unlike them, he preferred no identification with any cultural movement. He wrote some well-regarded grand oratorios and several suites for solo piano. His most famous work is one of his piano pieces, *In the Bottoms Suite* (1913). It contains thematic, geographic, and dance references. Here Dett revealed his convictions about how the soul can be properly displayed. The work shows his brilliant command of setting and form, with head and heart in gentle harmony.

Dett's compositions remain known in the world of American concert music, particularly among lovers of choral and piano music, but his refinement may have limited his music's broader appeal. Artists like Dett, who considered their race to be incidental, seem destined to be ignored as long as most enthusiasts of African American arts seek racial consciousness from the artists they wish to promote. Ironically, this political priority limits the visibility of many great African Americans of the past. R. Nathaniel Dett deserves the attention he sought—as a mainstream American composer. Dett died in Battle Creek, Michigan.

FURTHER READING
Dett's papers are at the library of Hampton University in Virginia.

Gray, Arlene. *Listen to the Lambs* (1984).
McBrier, Vivian Flagg. *R. Nathaniel Dett, His Life and Works* (1977).
This entry is taken from the *American National Biography* and is published here with the permission of the American Council of Learned Societies.

ALAN LEVY

Detter, Thomas (c. 1829–June or July 1891), writer, activist, minister, doctor, and businessman, was born in Washington, D.C., or nearby Maryland, probably to Thomas Detro (or Detrow), a stonemason, and his wife, Eleanor. Detter was educated in Washington, D.C., and was apprenticed to a shoemaker. Little is known of his early years. In 1852 he traveled aboard the steamer *John L. Stephens* to San Francisco, where he worked as a barber before moving to Sacramento. He quickly became active in northern California's black community and was Sacramento's delegate to the state Colored Conventions of 1855, 1856, and 1857; the 1855 Convention named him to the Executive Board.

Apparently frustrated by the lack of civil rights progress in California, he left the state in late 1857. Over the next decade he traveled throughout Idaho, Washington, and Oregon, spending extended periods in areas around Boise, Walla Walla, Idaho City, and Silver City. He returned to California occasionally, and married his first wife, Caroline (sometimes listed as Carolina), a Maryland-born resident of San Francisco, in 1860. The couple had a son, Robert, in about 1865. Detter remained in touch with the California black community through some three-dozen letters to San Francisco's two black newspapers, the *Pacific Appeal* and the *Elevator*, both published between 1863 and 1874. Those letters, which ranged from cutting analyses of racism to satiric treatments of Democrats, helped develop Detter's reputation as a keen thinker on the politics of race.

Detter found a more permanent home in Nevada at the end of the 1860s, settling in Elko with his wife and son in February 1869 and then moving to nearby Eureka in 1872. He continued to work as a barber and sold a hair restorative that he had developed and begun marketing in 1866. He achieved notable economic success: Detter and his wife were listed with over $2,000 in personal property in the 1870 Census. He quickly became a leader among black Nevadans, and according to the 15 April 1870 San Francisco *Elevator*, he gave one of two keynote addresses at Elko's 1870 celebration of the Fifteenth Amendment—urging his fellows to "go forth in the great battle field of life, and with your ballot, guard well your liberties." This kind of activist stance led Detter to work for equal schools for Nevada's black children and some renewed emphasis on aiding black educational and religious efforts. On 4 March 1871 Detter was granted a license to preach by Bishop Thomas M. D. Ward of the African Methodist Episcopal (AME) Church—in part in recognition of his work with Sacramento's AME Church (which began at least as early as 1860) and his work as a part-time minister in the Idaho territory in the early 1860s.

In 1871 Detter published *Nellie Brown or the Jealous Wife, with Other Sketches*. This collection, a novelette, a pair of short stories, and six essays, was the first book of fiction published by an African American in the West. Though Detter asserted that his work was "perfectly chaste and moral in every particular," he also noted in his preface that *Nellie Brown* specifically studied how a family was "rent in

twain by … malignant characters." Indeed, two of the three pieces of fiction in the volume treat divorce, one story—"The Octoroon Slave of Cuba"—considers the complex status of mixed race characters, and the book's essays offer challenging statements on race in the West (and the United States generally). Though the title tale is a bit clumsy in both characterization and plotting, San Francisco black newspapers promoted *Nellie Brown*, and the book achieved a modest level of success before disappearing from view.

If the early 1870s offered great hope for Detter, such was short-lived. His wife was forced to travel to San Francisco in September 1873 for medical treatment, and she died there on 10 February 1874. His young son Robert died barely three months later on 19 May 1874. And though Detter returned to San Francisco in April 1875 to give a major address at a celebration of the anniversary of the Fifteenth Amendment, western African Americans' hopes born from early Reconstruction advances were fast failing. After 1875 Detter seems to have withdrawn somewhat from writing and speaking and focused on his business—which now included a "cough tonic." Still, he prepared a report presented to the AME California Conference's July 1876 meeting and, on 2 November 1876, married Virginia-born San Francisco resident Emily Brinson. The character and duration of the marriage remain unknown; the 1880 Census does not list Emily with Detter.

Detter lived in Nevada until at least 1884, when local papers reported that BLANCHE K. BRUCE had named him Honorary Commissioner for Nevada at the World's Cotton Exhibition. At some point later in the decade, he moved to Louisiana. In the summer of 1889 he was at Patterson, Louisiana, where he served as physician to the dying AME clergyman Rev. Elijah Richardson. He lived for a time in New Orleans, and seems to have moved from creating various tonics to doctoring and occasional preaching. Later, he moved to the Tangipahoa Parish in northern Louisiana; the AME minister Charles Malone, who conducted Detter's funeral services, wrote in a letter published in the 16 July 1891 *Christian Recorder* of his death after a short illness—and of his final words: "Where I fall bury me beneath the cross to show that a soldier fell in battle for the Lord." As an author and activist Thomas Detter made important contributions to the nineteenth-century African American West. Though now largely forgotten, at the time of his death Detter's old California friend the Reverend James H. Hubbard recalled in a 6 August 1891 *Recorder* letter that, while Detter "had a nervous, restless disposition," he was "a man to be observed and admired" and a "willing hand" in struggles for civil rights. Where "sturdy blows were to be struck for God and humanity," Hubbard wrote, "Thomas Detter was there."

FURTHER READING

Foster, Frances Smith. "Introduction." *Nellie Brown or the Jealous Wife, with Other Sketches* by Thomas Detter (1996).

Rusco, Elmer. *Good Time Coming? Black Nevadans in the Nineteenth Century* (1975).

Rusco, Elmer. "Thomas Detter: Nevada Black Writer and Advocate for Human Rights," *Nevada Historical Society Quarterly* 47.3 (2004).

Obituaries: *Christian Recorder*, 16 July and 6 Aug. 1891.

ERIC GARDNER

Deveaux, John H. (1848–9 June 1909), politician and editor, was born free, probably in Savannah, Georgia. The names of his parents are unknown, but he had at least one older brother, James, who helped found the Georgia Republican Party. John H. Deveaux first appears in the historical record in 1864, when Savannah's Register of Free Persons of Color listed him as residing with a woman named Rosa Deveaux, who may have been his mother. More likely she was a sister or aunt, since the register lists a Dr. Richard D. Arnold as John Deveaux's guardian. As part of Savannah's free-born elite Deveaux was literate and gained at least an elementary school education prior to the Civil War.

In 1870, the same year his brother James B. Deveaux was elected to the Georgia state senate, John Deveaux was appointed a clerk at the U.S. customs house in Savannah, the first of several federal patronage posts he would hold over the next three decades. John Deveaux was less successful in his attempt to enter local politics in Savannah, however, losing a race for clerk of the Superior Court of Chatham County in 1874. His loss was hardly surprising given the brevity of the Reconstruction experiment in Georgia, which lasted only until 1872, at which point the Democratic Party's imposition of a poll tax greatly reduced the number of African Americans eligible to vote.

Although the end of Reconstruction greatly weakened black political power in Georgia, wealthy black Savannahians like the Deveaux brothers remained politically active. Alongside his brother James—also defeated in the 1874 state senate elections—John H. Deveaux responded to black Georgians' narrowed political opportunities by founding a newspaper, the *Savannah Tribune*, in late 1875. The *Tribune* quickly became the most influential African American newspaper in the region, in part because of Deveaux's front-page editorials. Deveaux's political views lay somewhere between the Reconstruction-era radicalism of Georgia Republicans like TUNIS CAMPBELL and HENRY M. TURNER and the late-nineteenth-century accommodationism of BOOKER T. WASHINGTON. Like Washington, Deveaux preached the importance of good relations with whites and the importance of encouraging black-owned businesses and institutions. Like Henry Turner, by then a bishop in the African Methodist Episcopal (AME) Church, Deveaux advocated full citizenship rights for blacks as well as an end to segregated public transportation in Savannah, though he opposed Turner's plans for a mass exodus of American blacks to Liberia. The *Tribune*'s pages also served as a social register for Savannah's colored elite.

In the fifteen years he served as editor of the *Tribune*, Deveaux continued to be active in the Georgia Republican Party and to serve in Savannah's federal customs court, at least in those years when Republicans sat in the White House. In 1876 he was famously the only customs official to remain on duty in Savannah during a major yellow fever epidemic. President Benjamin Harrison appointed Deveaux collector of customs in Broughton, Georgia, in 1889, and President William McKinley appointed him to the same post in Savannah in 1897. White merchants of the Savannah Cotton Exchange actively opposed his nomination, claiming that a person of color in charge of customs at Georgia's busiest port would harm business and discourage immigration. The U.S. Senate approved Deveaux's nomination in 1897, nonetheless, and he remained collector of customs for Savannah, the highest federal post in Georgia, until his death twelve years later.

Beginning in 1878 Deveaux was also prominent in the state's segregated militia, eventually attaining the rank of lieutenant colonel and commanding officer of the First Battalion Georgia State Troops (Colored). An ardent patriot and loyal Republican, the fifty-year-old Deveaux volunteered his battalion's services to President McKinley following the outbreak of the Spanish American War in 1898, but the proposal was vetoed by the Georgia governor William Atkinson. A reorganization of the state militia the following year left Deveaux in command of all black militia companies in Georgia, but demoted him to the rank of major. Public pressure later persuaded the General Assembly to restore Deveaux's former rank, the highest for black officers in the segregated militia, but the legislature was also at pains to point out that he only held that position by special privilege of the Georgia Assembly. Upon his death there were to be no more black lieutenant colonels in the state militia. Despite these slights, and the chronic problem of underfunding of the separate and far from equal black militia companies, Deveaux assured the adjutant general of the Georgia State Volunteers in 1903 that he and his colored troops remained "ever ready" to serve the state (Diamond, 312). Two years later white concerns about the training and arming of African Americans led to the abolition of the black militia unit; in 1908, a year before Deveaux's death, the state militia was officially reorganized to include able-bodied white men only.

At the time of his death in 1909 John Deveaux was one of the wealthiest and most powerful African Americans in Savannah. In addition to his federal patronage post and leadership of the Republican Party and state colored militia, he was a director of a savings and loan, a prominent black mason, and a leading lay figure in Savannah's St. Stephen's Protestant Episcopal Church. Because of the restrictions of Jim Crow Georgia, however, Deveaux's achievements, power, and wealth were considerably less than his talents merited.

FURTHER READING

Diamond, B. I., and J. O. Baylen. "The Demise of the Georgia Colored Guard, 1868–1914," *Phylon* 45.4 (1984).

Dittmer, John. *Black Georgia in the Progressive Era, 1900–1920* (1977).

Perdue, Robert. *The Negro in Savannah* (1973).

STEVEN J. NIVEN

Devine, Annie Belle Robinson (1912?–22 Aug. 2000), civil rights activist, was born in Mobile, Alabama, and relocated to Canton, Mississippi, as a child, where she was raised by her mother's sister. Annie Devine grew up in Canton, and after two years of education at Tougaloo Southern Christian College (later Tougaloo College) she graduated and went on to teach elementary school in Flora, Mississippi. She later returned to Canton where she married and had four children, but eventually divorced after ten years of marriage. By the 1960s she had obtained work as a debit manager for the black-owned Security Life Insurance Company.

During the civil rights movement, women's activism was strongest on the local level, where women extended their roles within church, community, and secular organizations to work for political change. Within the community of Canton, Devine was a highly respected church worker, which earned her an invitation to become a member of the Congress of Racial Equality (CORE). As a part of CORE, Devine organized voter registration drives in Canton and the surrounding Madison County, where fewer than 100 of the county's estimated 10,000 black adults were registered.

Although Mississippi had a higher proportion of black residents than did any other state, structural barriers to black voting systematically disenfranchised them. Some of these restrictions dated back to the post-Reconstruction era's revision of the state constitution, including a literacy requirement as a prerequisite to registering to vote. Thanks largely to Devine's efforts, blacks began to show up at the county courthouse almost daily, demanding to register.

In April 1964, along with FANNIE LOU HAMER, a volunteer and victim of voter registration violence in Mississippi, and Victoria Gray, an organizer of voter registration drives in Mississippi, Devine founded the Mississippi Freedom Democratic Party (MFDP). The party was developed to contest the Mississippi delegation to the Democratic National Convention held at Atlantic City, New Jersey. The all-white delegation excluded black delegates and openly embraced segregation. Both the leadership and rank-and-file of the MFDP were working class, a departure from traditional black leadership in the civil rights movement. Over 800 delegates attended the MFDP's state convention in Jackson, Mississippi, on 6 August 1964, electing sixty-eight delegates and national representatives. Among them were Victoria Gray as national committeewoman, Fannie Lou Hamer as vice-chair of the delegation, and Annie Devine as secretary.

Seasoned civil rights activists by August 1964, Devine, Gray, and Hamer attended the Democratic National Convention in Atlantic City with an objective to unseat their state's all-white delegation. The first step in doing so entailed an appearance before the Credential Committee. The MFDP presented compelling evidence of disenfranchisement and violence against black Mississippians. Testifying on behalf of the MFDP were national civil rights leaders, including Dr. MARTIN LUTHER KING JR. However, it was Fannie Lou Hamer's heart-wrenching account of the black experience in Mississippi that garnered national attention. So moving was her testimony that President Lyndon Baines Johnson, fearing that recognition of the MFDP would cost him southern votes, pre-empted her and announced an emergency televised news conference.

Ultimately the MFDP challenge ended in a compromise proposed by national Democratic leaders, who offered two at-large seats to the MFDP in addition to the seating of the regular delegation at the convention. A faction of the MFDP led by Devine, Hamer, and Gray rejected the compromise declaring that it gave the MFDP no leverage at all and was nothing more than an empty offer. The efforts of the MFDP were not totally disregarded as the rules for selection of the 1968 Democratic delegation were changed to adopt a nondiscrimination clause, in turn making the future of the convention more racially inclusive.

Devine and the MFDP did not easily accept defeat. Upon their return to Mississippi they began the "Mississippi Challenge," a protest against the state representatives to the U.S. Congress convening in January 1965. The MFDP argued that the five Mississippi representatives had been illegally elected due to black voter disenfranchisement. Annie Devine, Fannie Lou Hamer, and Victoria Gray were chosen to challenge the congressional representatives from their districts. With the commencement of congress in January 1965 the women traveled to Washington, D.C., to make their case. It was eight months before they were granted a hearing date. On 17 September 1965 Devine, Hamer, and Gray became the first black women in the United States to be seated on the floor of the U.S. House of Representatives as they offered testimony and presented over 15,000 pages of sworn testimony documenting the harassment and violence aimed at black voters as evidence to challenge the regular white Mississippi congressmen.

Ultimately these women and the MFDP were defeated, yet they can be credited with changing the face of Mississippi politics. In succeeding years black candidates ran successfully for a number of local offices, with ROBERT CLARK elected as Mississippi's first black representative to U.S. Congress since Reconstruction, in 1967. In addition, because of the Mississippi Challenge, the MFDP led a nationwide lobbying drive by the Mississippi Freedom Democrats and influenced calls for a congressional investigation into voting practices in Mississippi. In essence, Annie Devine and her contemporaries were trailblazers of the Voting Rights Act of 1965.

Devine's community service reached beyond the realm of civil rights. In the 1960s she helped found the Child Development Group of Mississippi. With its support she was a longtime volunteer in the Head Start program, the goal of which was to increase the school readiness of young children in low-income families.

Annie Bell Robinson Devine died at the age of eighty-eight in Ridgeland, Mississippi. Though her efforts as a member of the MFDP were unsuccessful in unseating the National Democratic Delegation and state representatives, Devine is a significant symbol of the civil rights movement. As a grassroots organizer Devine gave a voice to the silenced, the poor, the working class, and women involved in civil rights, those normally eclipsed by iconic leaders of the movement. Annie Devine is an example of a leader elected for the people and by the people, who dedicated her life to fighting for not only her own but also her race's liberties.

FURTHER READING

Collier-Thomas, Bettye, and V. P. Franklin. *Sisters in the Struggle: African American Women in the Civil Rights–Black Power Movement* (2001).

Hine, Darlene Clark. *Black Women in America* (2005).

Lee, Chana Kai. *For Freedom's Sake: The Life of Fannie Lou Hamer* (1999).

Obituary: *New York Times,* 2 Sept. 2000.

LISA M. PENN

Dexter, James Oronoko (fl. 1782–1798), activist, was named Oronoco (variously spelled *Oronoke, Oranque,* or *Oronogue*) in the earliest documents that record his early life as a Philadelphia, Pennsylvania, slave. In 1749 he was inherited upon the death of his master, Henry Dexter, by Dexter's son, James. When James died in debt in 1767, the trustees of the estate freed Oronoco for the price of £100. In his manumission papers he is identified as "Oronoko royal Slave," presumably an allusion to the African prince in Aphra Behn's novella *Oroonoko, or The Royal Slave* (1688) or in Thomas Southerne's dramatic transformation of the story titled *Oroonoko, a Tragedy* (1696), which remained one of the most popular dramas staged in Britain throughout the eighteenth century. If he was indeed born into African royalty, Oronoco nevertheless changed his name upon gaining his freedom, and he is usually noted in public records thereafter as James Oronoko Dexter or just James O. Dexter.

While enslaved, Oronoco was hired out to work at the tavern named the "Three Tun," and about that time he met the woman he wished to marry—a young slave named Priss. William Jones, her owner, demanded a high price for her, and only after Dexter was freed was the cost lowered to permit him to purchase her manumission for £50. Dexter had saved £30 and borrowed another £20, but he managed to repay the debt before his marriage. Unfortunately, no details of Dexter and Priss's marital life are known; their children, if any, are lost to history. However, a washerwoman named Sarah Dexter, who lived, by 1801, in Hoffman's Alley (located directly behind Dexter's house at 84 North Fifth Street) may have been Dexter's daughter or, conceivably, his second wife (and widow). Perhaps Richard Dexter, a shoemaker, who lived elsewhere in Philadelphia, was his son.

During the 1780s Dexter worked for the influential Quaker merchant and preacher John Pemberton, possibly as a coach driver. When Pemberton died in Germany in 1794, he bequeathed to Dexter a legacy amounting to £50 a year, with an additional bequest, jointly with ABSALOM JONES, in trust for the "Society of Black People for the support of the poor." This title may refer to the Free African Society, a benevolent and religious group promoting temperance, morality, and freedom, which Jones, RICHARD ALLEN, and other prominent Philadelphians established in 1787. Dexter was deeply committed to the Free African Society by the time the members decided to establish their own church, and he may have been involved from its inception. Along with Cyrus Bustill, John Black, Samuel Saviel, Cuff Douglass, Aram Prymus, and William Gray, Dexter took his first-known public action by petitioning the state government in 1782. The petition requested that a portion of South East Square, which then served as the city's potter's field (the burial ground of the poor), be fenced off so that African Americans might rent the plot and lay claim to their own cemetery. The next step in advancing the autonomy of free African Americans was a census conducted by the Free African Society; the committee determined that one thousand African Americans lived in the immediate vicinity (which included the city, Southwark, and Northern Liberties), and, since there existed a pool of potential supporters and the society experienced difficulty in finding rooms for worship, by 1792 plans were under way to build an African American place of worship. The members purchased lots at the intersection of Adelphi and

Fifth streets and drew up a plan of church government as well as articles of faith and practice.

The Free African Society essentially came to a close with the new project, and several members withdrew their support. During this initial phase Dexter appears to have been an elder in the organization and a prominent member of the planning and construction committee assigned the specific task of acquiring the stones needed for construction. Most recorded meetings of the elders, deacons, and trustees included Dexter, and several meetings were held in his home. The African Episcopal Church of Saint Thomas opened for worship on 17 July 1794, and Samuel Magaw's inaugurating sermon reminded the African American congregation to be mindful of their debt to their Quaker benefactors, to the Pennsylvania Abolition Society, and to the citizens of Philadelphia who had assisted the enterprise by donations and loans. The church was incorporated in 1796 as an institution for the sole use of African Americans. At that time Dexter was elected to the vestry, an office concerned with the day-to-day management of the church, while Absalom Jones was nominated as a candidate for Orders and, though a layman, permitted to perform the duties of a minister.

Dexter's labors on behalf of the church may have continued until 1807 when balances on his account and those of other building-material suppliers were finally settled. During the years 1795 and 1796 his name appears regularly in the church's accounts. Whether the amounts alongside his name represent construction debts and payments, or, as one church historian has suggested, a record of the donations he collected and the commissions he earned, is not clear. After 1796 his name appears only once in church records, on April 9, 1807, but it remains to be seen whether he remained alive, and an active participant in church affairs, until that time, or if the account simply remained open until all construction accounts were settled.

Shortly after the church was incorporated, Dexter disappeared from the historical record. From about 1790 he had lived in a Quaker and black community on North Fifth Street, next door to Ebenezer Robinson, a Quaker abolitionist by vocation and a brush maker by trade, who had built and insured Dexter's house. Presumably Dexter worked for Robinson as his coach driver. The historian Anna Coxe Toogood speculates that, with his inheritance from John Pemberton, Dexter chose to go into business for himself in 1799. Indeed, a fruiterer named James Dexter opened a business at 34 North

Fifth Street, just a half block south of Dexter's old residence, and was listed for two years in the local trade directory. Nevertheless, Dexter's date of death remains unknown.

The testimonials of Pemberton's relatives attest to Dexter's benevolent and trustworthy character, while the African Episcopal Church of Saint Thomas serves as a monument to his concern for the material and spiritual welfare of his African American neighbors. Undoubtedly, he facilitated the emergence of an autonomous black community in Philadelphia. Archaeological excavations in the vicinity of Dexter's house, historians' ongoing research into the archives of the Pennsylvania Abolition Society, and their future researches into the records of Saint Thomas's Church will no doubt contribute to a more complete picture of this man, his family, and his purposeful journey from slavery into public service.

FURTHER READING
The collection consisting of copies of historical records and articles on Dexter and the excavation of his home, which was compiled by Anna Coxe Toogood (National Historical Park Service) and Daniel Rolph (Historical Society of Pennsylvania), is housed at the Independence National Historical Park, Philadelphia, Pennsylvania, while the archives of the African Episcopal Church of Saint Thomas (1792–1996), once opened to public scrutiny, will doubtless provide further biographical information about James Oronoko Dexter.

Iwanisziw, Susan B., ed. *Troping Oroonoko from Behn to Bandele* (2004).

Nash, Gary B. *Forging Freedom: The Formation of Philadelphia's Black Community, 1720–1840* (1988).

Toogood, Coxey. "James Dexter, a Biographical Sketch." *Independence National Historic Park: Historic Research Study (Appendix F),* http://www.cr.nps.gov/history/online_books/inde/hrs/hrsaf.htm.

SUSAN B. IWANISZIW

DeYampert, Warren Traveous (10 July 1922–13 June 1943), World War II coastguardsman and medal award winner, is a man about whom little personal information is known. A native of Attalla, Alabama, he entered the coast guard at Baltimore, Maryland, on 12 July 1941. Like all African Americans who joined the coast guard at this time DeYampert was assigned the rating of mess attendant (a designation changed during the early war years to steward's mate and steward), which meant that his job was to serve a ship's officers their meals and to take care of their quarters and other personal chores. Demeaning as such work might be, the steward's rating was at the time DeYampert's only available option. By the end of World War II things would change, but only to a small degree; of the just over five thousand African Americans who served in the coast guard during the war years, 63 percent served as stewards.

DeYampert's specific ship assignments in his first year and a half with the coast guard are unknown, though records list the locales in which he served as Baltimore and Pittsburgh, Pennsylvania. Despite his race-restricted regular duties DeYampert's personal qualities and strengths were recognized at some point in 1942 and he received training in a newly conceived coast guard program as a rescue swimmer. Though the specific details of his training are unknown, DeYampert gained the needed skills in endurance swimming, diving, line and raft handling, and other techniques vital to helping sailors and seamen stranded in the ocean after their ships had been torpedoed. DeYampert joined the crew of the cutter *Escanaba* sometime after January 1942 when that ship was transferred from duty on the Great Lakes to wartime Atlantic convoy duty operating out of Boston. It was on the *Escanaba* that Warren DeYampert would distinguish himself as a true coast guard hero.

On 23 January 1943 *Escanaba*, with DeYampert aboard, and the cutters *Tampa* and *Comanche*, were assigned to escort three ships, the U.S.A.T. *Dorchester*, SS *Lutz*, and SS *Biscaya*, from St. John's, Nova Scotia, to Greenland. Convoy duty in the frigid waters of the North Atlantic was both arduous and dangerous. Attacks by German U-boats were so common that the area was nicknamed "Torpedo Junction" and many Allied ships were lost. The most important ship in the convoy was undoubtedly the armed transport *Dorchester*; it carried over nine hundred soldiers and sailors on the voyage, manpower destined for service in Greenland and beyond. At just after 1 A.M. on 3 February 1943 the *Dorchester* was hit by enemy torpedoes; the ship immediately began to sink by the stern and all was chaos. Among those who helped to get men off the *Dorchester* before it sank just twenty minutes later were four army chaplains who sacrificed their lives by giving their life jackets and spiritual comfort to men in need. After the incident, in which nearly seven hundred men perished, the four chaplains gained fame for their heroic actions. However, forgotten in the sinking of the *Dorchester* were the equally heroic actions of Warren DeYampert and his fellow steward turned rescue swimmer on the *Comanche*, CHARLES WALTER DAVID JR.

Upon the sinking of the *Dorchester*, the cutter *Escanaba* raced to the scene to pick up survivors, and its rescue swimmers went over the side into the frigid waters. The most prominent of these men were Warren DeYampert and the ship's white cook, Forrest Rednour. While Rednour worked the longest hours of all, DeYampert was almost as hardworking; he toiled nearly four hours in the water and the darkness, pulling rafts close to his ship, and securing lines to survivors so they could be hauled aboard *Escanaba*. The danger was great and both he and Rednour were in constant danger of being crushed to death as they approached the side of their ship. DeYampert's most heroic deed came in rescuing a single survivor, whom he kept afloat at the stern of the ship and clear of the ship's propeller until he could be brought aboard.

In all, the rescue swimmers on the *Escanaba* and *Comanche*, including the two African American stewards, white enlisted men, and officers, performed heroically and made the best of a bad situation, rescuing 230 men. For his heroism that day Warren T. DeYampert was later posthumously awarded the Navy and Marine Corps Medal, the nation's fourth-highest award for valor. Unfortunately, while the four chaplains went on to gain fame immemorial (and rightly so) for their heroism, and even had a postage stamp issued in their honor, Warren DeYampert and Charles Walter David Jr. have been all but forgotten. Such has often been the case with African American military heroes, whose deeds usually only gain due recognition on a level approaching that of their white counterparts after the passing of many years.

Following the *Dorchester* sinking, Warren DeYampert continued his service on the cutter *Escanaba* for the next sixteen months. On 13 June 1943 the ship was part of convoy GS-24 escorting ships from Narsarssuak, Greenland, to St. John's, Nova Scotia, when it was wracked by an explosion at approximately 5 A.M. while passing near an ice field. The *Escanaba* and nearly its entire crew, DeYampert included, were lost, the cutter sinking so quickly that there was no time to send out a distress signal. Though the cause for the loss remains inconclusive, it is thought that the *Escanaba* was sunk by either a German U-boat or a mine explosion. Warren T. DeYampert, through his heroic service and ultimate loss, stands as a shining example of the many African Americans who served honorably in the coast guard during World War II. He and his fellow shipmates on the *Escanaba*, all Purple Heart winners, are memorialized at the East Coast Sailors Memorial at New York.

FURTHER READING

DeYampert, Warren T. Coast Guard Service Record, serial number 234126. Obtained from the National Personnel Records Center under the Freedom of Information Act.

Knoblock, Glenn A. *Forgotten Sacrifice: African American Naval, Coast Guard, and Merchant Marine Casualties in World War II* (Forthcoming 2008).

United States Coast Guard. *Escanaba* (WPG-77), 1932. Available at http://www.uscg.mil/history/webcutters/Escanaba_WPG_77.html.

United States Coast Guard. "Negroes Died World War II" (n.d., c. 1947), a handwritten list in the possession of the Coast Guard Historian's office.

GLENN ALLEN KNOBLOCK

Dial, Thornton, Sr. (10 Sept. 1928–), artist, was born to Mattie Bell, an unmarried, teenage sharecropper in Emelle, Alabama. Dial was the second of Bell's twelve children and was named simply "Buck" at birth. He did not have a formal surname and grew up uncertain of the identity of his biological father. Mattie Bell married a man named Dan Pratt shortly after the birth of her third son, and the couple went on to have nine more children. His mother's new and growing family proved to be a difficult adjustment for Buck, and he was sent to live with his great-grandmother, Had Dial, on the nearby farm of Bell's older cousin, Buddy Jake Dial. The Dials, who were of African and Native American descent, raised and cared for Thornton; they put him to work on the farm, and gave him the last name of Dial.

Dial's artistic sensibilities, in part, developed out of the rural Black Belt region of Alabama, an area with a long history of racial oppression compounded by the trials of the Great Depression. The landscapes Dial saw were littered with handmade architectural structures, such as toolsheds and garages, as well as devotional sculptures, and other vernacular art forms created by neighbors and family members in Emelle and surrounding communities. Made with found, recycled, and scrap materials touched with brightly colored paint, this unique aesthetic had been passed down from enslaved African ancestors. Routine encounters with such creations would have a lasting impact on the artistic methodologies that would become a focus of Dial's art later in life.

Dial's childhood was marked by hard labor with minimal formal education. As was typical of African American families in the area, the Dials faced financial hardships. "They were sharecropping, picking cotton," the artist had said of his family's struggles. "They kept on farming and didn't ever come out of debt. The Man advance people from one end of the year to the other end. Every year the Man always say, 'You just about come out of debt this time but didn't quite make it'" (Arnett et al., 275). From the time he could walk, this harsh reality kept Dial working in the fields and out of the schoolroom. From such oppression he developed a deep cynicism and personal distrust of white American culture that would later emerge as underlying themes in his artwork. In 1940, with the prospect of better job opportunities, a twelve-year-old Dial joined his half brother Arthur in the segregated and industrialized Birmingham suburb of Bessemer.

There, the rumblings of World War II were met with the development of new factories and an increase in the production of iron and steel in the ore-rich lands of Birmingham and its vicinity. They lived with their maternal great-aunt, Sarah Dial, and her husband, Dave Lockett, who quickly became a father figure to Thornton. He remained in Bessemer, later marrying longtime acquaintance and neighbor Clara Mae Sardis on 15 July 1951. Over the next ten years they had five children, several of whom went on to become notable artists themselves, often exhibiting their work alongside their father's.

During his early years in Bessemer, Dial attempted to attend school, but soon left to earn money primarily as a laborer. He was employed by the waterworks department and other local businesses before taking a job as a welder's assistant with the Pullman-Standard boxcar factory in 1953. At the start of Dial's employment, Pullman-Standard was segregated, imposing the Jim Crow laws that were strictly enforced until the Civil Rights Act was passed in 1964. During his more than thirty years of service, Dial was affected by many unfair company practices that favored white employees. For example, several of Dial's suggestions for better productivity were quickly implemented by the company, but they never acknowledged Dial's contribution. During his tenure at Pullman-Standard, however, he learned the techniques and process of metal design. And when the company ceased operations in 1983, he started a home-based outdoor furniture business with his three sons, Richard, Dan, and Thornton Dial Jr., who were also left jobless by the factory's closing. The business, Dial Metal Patterns, featured furniture that was shaped, welded, and painted by hand.

Dial had been constructing artistic objects from the time he was young, but the Dial Metal Patterns venture marked the first time he devoted a significant amount of time to the creative process. It also led to a renewed focus on the production of his signature assemblage-style paintings. Using scrap metals, carpet remnants, pieces of plastic, wood, and paint, Dial built up detritus layers with intense social and political underpinnings that also reflected his life experiences. With large-scale formats often ranging from three to nine feet, Dial's works have a presentation similar to murals, with subjects that are difficult to ignore. Although he had been creating this type of artwork for years, it was not something he shared openly. He would often hide, destroy, or bury his creations on his property, recycling their parts when more materials were needed. Like many of the vernacular artists in the communities of Dial's upbringing, he never considered himself an artist. A chance meeting in 1987 with an artist named Lonnie Holley would lead to a change in Dial's perception of himself and his work. Holley introduced Dial to art collector William Arnett, who would become Dial's first patron and help alter the course of his life. Arnett recognized the traditional and vernacular qualities of Dial's work, and appreciated how its fluidity and emotional charge set him apart from others producing similar forms.

As Arnett and others worked to get Dial recognition in the art world, his work became more sophisticated and his output more prolific. Through his art, he continued to address contemporary issues of race, status, and culture. In 1994 Dial was granted a solo exhibition hosted by two major New York City venues: the Museum of American Folk Art and the New Museum of Contemporary Art. The exhibition, Thornton Dial: Image of the Tiger, met with much critical acclaim and drew attention to the so-called self-taught (or outsider) artists of the South. His work so impressed viewers that it sparked debate about the language critics used to describe his work. According to some, Dial's pieces were just as accomplished as works created by formally trained artists, deeming the terms "self-taught" and "outsider" irrelevant. The exposure Dial garnered from this first New York show marked the beginning of his exhibition career.

Thornton Dial overcame many obstacles, brought attention to a previously disregarded art form, and forged new paths for black artists. Among the relevant topics addressed in his work were the 1992 Los Angeles riots, the quiet workings of the Gee's Bend quilt makers, the 2001 attacks on the World Trade Center, and the elite social order of the art world.

"Black folks know what they got to do to live, and they will do it, they will work hard as they know how, as hard as the next man, by the sweat of their own brow. They want to have their own strategy for working, to use their own energy and spirit the way it come to them to do it—not do something because someone else make you do it. That's freedom.... My art is the evidence of my freedom" (Arnett et al., 291).

FURTHER READING

Arnett, William, John Beardsley, Alvia J. Wardlaw, and Jane Livingston. *Thornton Dial: In the 21st Century* (2005).

Rosenberg, Willa S. *Thornton Dial: Strategy of the World* (1990).

Whelchel, Harriet, and Margaret Donovan, eds. *Thornton Dial: Image of the Tiger* (1993).

CANDACE L. LECLAIRE

Dibble, Eugene Heriot, Jr. (14 Aug. 1893–1 June 1968), physician, was born in Camden, South Carolina, the son of Eugene Heriot Dibble and Sally Lee. He graduated from Atlanta University in 1915 and earned his medical degree at Howard University Medical College four years later. After a one-year internship at the Freedmen's Hospital in Washington, D.C., Dibble accepted a surgical residency at the John A. Andrew Memorial Hospital in Tuskegee, Alabama.

At that time, medical care for southern blacks was limited and often inferior. Dibble realized the urgent need for more black physicians to provide adequate health care. As assistant medical director of the John A. Andrew Memorial Hospital, he helped organize the first postgraduate course in surgery for southern black physicians.

By 1923 Dibble had become the chief of the surgical section of the newly established Veterans' Administration hospital in Tuskegee. The large number of black World War I veterans created an acute medical demand and necessitated a solution to the problem of providing care and treatment for all who needed it. The Veterans' Bureau selected Tuskegee as the site for a hospital to rehabilitate disabled veterans. Community hostility toward black medical professionals resulted in violence, but eventually black physicians replaced white personnel.

The Tuskegee Veterans' Hospital supported six hundred patients, half suffering from neuropsychiatric disorders and half from tuberculosis. The latter patients were transferred to other facilities, and Dibble and his staff focused on veterans sick from manic depression, dementia, spinal cord injuries, and brain diseases. He modified traditional treatments for veterans, taking into account genetic, environmental, and socioeconomic factors; many veterans, white and black, lacked immunities to diseases such as syphilis, and physicians carefully evaluated viral vaccines to combat infections and prevent illnesses. Dibble also oversaw occupational therapy to assist veterans returning to their homes and employment.

In 1925 Dibble completed postgraduate work at Harvard University and returned as medical director of the John A. Andrew Memorial Hospital. In 1926 he married Helen A. Taylor; they had five children. During the early 1930s he became involved in a controversial public health experiment. Officials representing the Venereal Disease Program, Division of Special Health Services of the U.S. Public Health Service, wanted to study untreated syphilis. They approached Dibble in 1932, and he secured the approval of Dr. ROBERT R. MOTON, the Tuskegee Institute's president.

Dibble emphasized that the research would be of "world wide significance" and give "added standing" to the hospital. He also stressed the "educational advantages," explaining that the work would provide training and employment for black nurses and interns. He had helped improve Tuskegee's nursing program and was discouraged that graduates were unable to secure work because of the Depression and racism. Dibble also viewed the experiment as a way for black physicians, himself included, to acquire professional acceptance. He agreed to provide staff and facilities for examinations supervised by Dr. Raymond Vonderlehr, the Public Health Service officer in charge. Dibble also convinced county health officials and physicians to cooperate.

Local black men suffering from syphilis were promised hot meals and their burial costs paid in exchange for examinations, including lumbar punctures. Most residents were too impoverished to consult physicians and believed that they would receive treatment for syphilis and other health problems. One patient recalled that Dibble assured him that medicine was in his injection, which in fact was a spinal tap.

Appointed in 1933 as a special consultant in the U.S. Public Health Service, Dibble eagerly sought prestige and recognition for his "crucial role." He autopsied patients to determine the results of untreated syphilis, sending the brain tissues, spinal cord, and organs to the National Institutes of Health. Seeking the approval of his white colleagues,

Dibble wrote Vonderlehr, "Please let me tell you how much both Doctor [Jerome J.] Peters and myself enjoyed the autopsy." In the 1970s details of the Tuskegee Syphilis Experiment were revealed, and medical ethics and individual morality were questioned. The public was outraged because only black patients were examined and were misled to think that they were being treated with potent medicine.

From 1936 to 1946 Dibble acted as manager and medical director of the Veterans' Administration hospital. During the next decade, the veterans' hospital reorganized and constructed more buildings, increasing bed space "to care for and to rehabilitate, where possible, the lame, halt, and diseased defenders of our Country" (Morais, 239). Prominent visitors, including Franklin Roosevelt and Eleanor Roosevelt, military officers, and Hollywood stars, visited the hospital. In a 1943 speech, "Care and Treatment of Negro Veterans at Tuskegee," Dibble told how the hospital acquired modern equipment and his staff learned new scientific advancements and pharmaceutical treatments. During World War II, a cadet nurses program, which Dibble monitored, was established at Tuskegee. Owing to the shortage of army doctors, Dibble joined the military as colonel, the military position given to all veterans' hospital managers, and he was the first black medical officer to hold this rank. He was discharged from the U.S. Army Medical Corps in June 1946 and resigned from the veterans' hospital the following month.

After World War II Dibble assumed the medical directorship of the John A. Andrew Memorial Hospital. Throughout his career Dibble sought to improve the professional status of black physicians and enhance medical care for the African American community. He focused on eradicating diseases afflicting impoverished residents and was especially concerned with the high mortality rates of mothers and children. "Everything at the hospital is intended to impress unconsciously upon the student the fundamental laws of health," he stressed (Dibble, "Hospital Symposium," 138). He utilized the John A. Andrew Clinical Society, of which he was secretary, to achieve his goals.

From 1925 to 1965 Dibble developed this society as a means of postgraduate education of the "science and art" of medicine for black doctors. Although the profession was segregated, he arranged for talented white and black doctors, from rural and urban practices, to collaborate during seminars, lectures, and operations. Physicians were able to learn the most recent techniques and share ideas with distinguished colleagues with whom they would not have had contact otherwise. They focused on diseases prevalent in the South and concentrated on alleviating suffering.

Dibble hoped that participants, ranging from specialists to general practitioners, would learn skills so that they "may be better able to fulfill their life's work." Dibble "poured immeasurable creative energy" into the clinical society, serving as the "prime moving spirit" promoting "work, study, and service." The clinics "tremendously promoted professional interracial understanding and good will." Hoping to encourage racial harmony, Dibble invited Billy Graham and civil rights leaders to speak to clinic participants, city officials, and college students and faculty. He established clinic lectures named in honor of other black physicians to memorialize them. Dibble also used the clinics to mentor young minority doctors and then secured employment for them.

In 1958 Dibble joined a medical mission to the Far East and Africa sponsored by the Baptist World Alliance. He also served on the editorial board of the *Journal of the National Medical Association*, preparing special issues on the Tuskegee hospitals and revising papers presented at the clinical society. Dibble served on the board of trustees of Meharry Medical College. He was a member of the Medical Advisory Committee to the Children's Bureau, Department of Health, Education and Welfare; Dibble also helped establish the Macon County Medical Care Program, cooperating with the Alabama State Board of Health and Children's Bureau in counties surrounding Tuskegee.

The John A. Andrew Clinical Society presented Dibble the C. V. Roman Distinguished Service Medal in 1943. He received the National Medical Association's Distinguished Service Medal by unanimous vote in 1962, honoring his "career-long selfless dedication to the improvement of health care for the people he has served and the eminent success he has achieved as an organizer, administrator and promoter of activities for professional advancement." Howard University gave him an Alumni Distinguished Service Medal, and he was named an honorary member of Alpha Omega Alpha.

Dibble retired in 1965. His family worshiped at St. Andrews Episcopal Church. Dibble was active in the U.S. Army Reserve, Alpha Phi Alpha, and the Masonic order. Diagnosed with bronchogenic carcinoma, he decided not to undergo therapy, which he feared would interfere with his medical duties. He worked until shortly before he died at home in

Tuskegee and was buried in the Tuskegee Institute Cemetery on campus.

FURTHER READING

Dibble's correspondence is held in the Tuskegee University Archives and in the Public Health Service records at the National Archives.

Collier, Fred C. "Eugene Heriot Dibble, M.D., 1893–1968," *Journal of the National Medical Association* 60 (Sept. 1968): 446.

Jones, James H. *Bad Blood: The Tuskegee Syphilis Experiment*, rev. eds. (1993).

Morais, Herbert M. *The History of the Afro-American in Medicine* (1976).

Yancey, Asa G., Sr. "Tuskegee Veterans Administration Medical Center: Genesis and Opportunities It Provided in Surgery," in *A Century of Black Surgeons: The U.S.A. Experience*, eds. Claude H. Organ and Margaret M. Kosiba (1987).

This entry is taken from the *American National Biography* and is published here with the permission of the American Council of Learned Societies.

ELIZABETH D. SCHAFER

Dickens, Dorothy Lee (10 Nov. 1908–30 Apr. 1993), housekeeper, nurse's aide, and writer, was born in New York City, the oldest of the three daughters of James Lee Dickens, a barber and night watchman, and Laura Breckinridge Paige Dickens Potter, a housekeeper and cook. The household also included extended family members, Ethel and Edna Paige (Dorothy's older half-sisters), whose father was deceased. They attended Abyssinian Baptist Church in Harlem during some of the years in which ADAM CLAYTON POWELL SR. (who was Laura Dickens's first cousin) was the head pastor. The family moved from Harlem to Mamaroneck, New York, when Dorothy was young, on the recommendation of the family doctor who suggested a more favorable location to cure her case of rickets. Her younger sisters, Evelyn and Irene, were born in Mamaroneck, and all three of the Dickens girls attended local schools in that city. The three Dickens sisters shared the measles and chicken pox and rheumatic fever, which seems to have contributed to the heart conditions that would develop later in their lives.

The Dickens sisters shared similar experiences as other African American girls of their time. They frequented nearby Rye Beach and Playland (an amusement park), and attended Barry Avenue African American Episcopal (AME) Zion Church in Mamaroneck, where they sang in the choir and went to Sunday school picnics. Dickens recited poems in church on Christmas and Easter, and wrote plays.

James Lee Dickens died when Dorothy was in the ninth grade, forcing the sisters to take jobs to help with household expenses. Dorothy worked as a housekeeper in private homes and as a secretary, and later trained as a nurse's aide and worked at United Hospital in Port Chester, New York. She wrote at night and on her days off, particularly about people she would see while sitting in Central Park in New York City.

The only available sources about Dickens's life and works are the introduction and the book jacket of *Black on the Rainbow*, her 1952 novel, some poems published in poetry anthologies, and her obituary. Later interviews with her sister, Evelyn Yizar, and her daughter, Marlene High—executor of Dickens's estate—provided vital information and identified her as someone who had been active in the Harlem Renaissance. Between 1944 and 1952 Dickens worked as an aide at the New Rochelle Hospital and as a registered Red Cross Volunteer Aide. She also belonged to the HARRIET TUBMAN Club, the Girl's Cooperative Club, and the Artists' and Entertainers Guild, which she organized. Dickens was well known in Westchester, and in Harlem at the 135th Street Branch of the New York Public Library, for her readings. She read from her book, *The Black Rose and Other Poems*, that includes patriotic, historical, lyrical, and devotional narratives. Dickens also read poems of hers that were published in anthologies such as *Rhyme an' Rhythm*, *Important American Writers*, and *Poets of the Empire State*. Other poems appeared in *Talent: Songwriters and Poets of Tomorrow*, another anthology.

Dickens was hurt in a train and car accident in Port Chester, New York, as she was coming home from Harrison, New York, one day in 1943. As Dickens descended from the train, a car driven by a drunk driver struck her and knocked her under the train. Dickens was taken to United Hospital in Port Chester, where a steel plate was put in her right leg. Her right knee was re-centered, twice, and she was able to walk without a cane. With money she received from a settlement following the accident, she was able to publish her first novel, *Black on the Rainbow*, through a vanity publisher. The book was inspired by a trip to North Carolina with her younger sister, Irene, and her husband, Woodrow McMillian, who was a North Carolina native.

Hilda Ann Parker, a woman of mixed race and a native of Columbus, Georgia, is the protagonist of

Black on the Rainbow. She makes her way to New York City, where she passes as a white woman and becomes a successful dancer. Hilda Ann is engaged to a prominent white man when her secret is discovered. She leaves New York, her life changes for the worse, and her face is later disfigured by a jealous lover. The protagonist is given a second chance when she meets her lost sister, a nun, on a ship during a return trip from Lisbon, Portugal, to the United States in 1931. An explosion in the boiler room causes the ship to sink, and Hilda Ann loses her sister, Violet Ava, and her longtime white friend, Dorothy Paerman. Before the accident, Hilda Ann promised Violet Ava that she would seek God immediately, and she does so, rededicating herself to a Christian life and leaving behind her unsavory past life. Hilda Ann returns to her family in Georgia, and learns the truth about the sisters' biological parents, their separation, and their adoptions. Finding a direction in race uplift work, Hilda Ann once again begins to lead a rewarding life. She marries a childhood friend, a minister, and works with him and various civic organizations to improve the lives of African Americans through education and industriousness.

Dickens's work is didactic: faith serves as the vehicle for a better life and a more understanding attitude toward others. Science, religion, and education are advocated as subjects through which racial prejudice will be reduced, tolerance increased, and individual intellect encouraged. The plot of *Black on the Rainbow* bears a resemblance to a number of so called "tragic mulatto" works, but Hilda Ann Parker Marshall is not dead, nor even in dire circumstances at the end of her tale. She knows and embraces her heritage. The novel ends with the final words of "The Lord's Prayer."

Dickens continued to write after the publication of *Black on the Rainbow*. Her poems appeared in *New Voices in American Poetry* in 1976 and in the *Anthology of International Poets*. She also worked as a housekeeper for some influential families in the Harrison area. Around 1983 Dickens used some of the settlement from her accident to purchase a home in Otisville, New York. She was a former member of the National Writers Club, and a member of the International Platform Association. Later in her life Dickens was working on another novel and a collection of poems. She died in Otisville, New York, of congestive heart failure, cardiorespiratory arrest, arterial sclerotic heart disease, and coronary insufficiency—possibly caused by her childhood bout of rheumatic fever.

FURTHER READING

Zackodnik, Teresa C. *The Mulatta and the Politics of Race* (2004).

LOU-ANN CROUTHER

Dickenson, Vic (6 Aug. 1906–16 Nov. 1984), jazz trombonist, was born Albert Victor Dickenson in Xenia, Ohio, the son of Robert Clarke Dickenson, a plastering contractor and amateur violinist. His mother's name is unknown. Using his brother Carlos's instrument he began to play trombone in high school. In 1921 he played with the Elite Serenaders while also working days for his father as a plasterer, but after suffering a severe back injury as a result of a fall from a ladder, he decided to concentrate on music exclusively. Around 1922 his family moved to Columbus, where he and his brother, now a saxophonist, started working with local bands. In 1925 he played his first professional job with Don Phillips in Madison, Wisconsin, and after returning home he heard and was influenced by the trombonists Claude Jones and DICKY WELLS. He was particularly impressed by their smooth tones and deceptively easy techniques, virtues that he had already admired on records by Miff Mole, Charlie Green, BENNY MORTON, and Jimmy Harrison.

In May 1927 Dickenson joined Willie Jones's band in South Bend, Indiana, and in November made his first records with that group, later working with the bands of Bill Broadhus, Wesley Helvey, and Leonard Gay. Dickenson stayed with Gay through a summer 1929 residency in Madison and then joined the Toledo-based Speed Webb band for about a year. In December 1930 he went with Zack Whyte's Chocolate Beau Brummels to work at the Savoy Ballroom in New York City and on a five-band tour, but he left in early 1932 and moved to Kansas City, where he played in a BENNIE MOTEN spin-off band, led by the trombonist Thamon Hayes, that also included COUNT BASIE, HOT LIPS PAGE, and BUCK CLAYTON. Also in 1932 Dickenson married Otealia Foye; the couple had no children. With the exception of a brief job in Ohio with Clarence Paige's Royal Syncopators, he remained with Hayes into 1933. From the summer of 1933 through early 1936 Dickenson toured the theater and ballroom circuit with the singer Blanche Calloway's band, after which he spent three years in CLAUDE HOPKINS's orchestra, most often in residence at the Roseland Ballroom in New York City. In the spring of 1939 he joined Benny Carter for extended stays at the Savoy, where he met the pianist EDDIE HEYWOOD, an important transitional figure in his career.

In January 1940 Dickenson replaced one of his longtime friends, Benny Morton, in Count Basie's band, but because almost all of the trombone solos fell to another early mentor, Dicky Wells, he left in January 1941, rejoining Carter in February for a job at Nick's in Greenwich Village and a midwestern tour. That summer he played with SIDNEY BECHET at a summer resort in upstate New York and then returned to Manhattan to work with the trumpeter FRANKIE NEWTON.

Later in 1941 Dickenson went to Chicago with Page and in 1942 resumed working with Newton, first in Boston and then at New York's Café Society Downtown. The Newton group played opposite the Eddie Heywood Trio, and when Newton left to take another job, Heywood enlarged his trio to a sextet, using Dickenson as his first choice for the three-horn front line. From September 1943 through October 1946, with the exception of a brief layoff because of illness in early 1946, Dickenson remained with the Heywood group, playing long residencies in both New York and Los Angeles and making himself known to the larger community through a remarkably diverse and prolific series of record dates with other jazzmen.

After a lengthy period of freelancing in Los Angeles between 1947 and 1948, during which time he led his own group at Billy Berg's, in the spring of 1949 Dickenson settled in Boston, where he worked primarily in EDMOND HALL's band at George Wein's Savoy Café and Storyville Club. During this time he also appeared at various New York jazz concerts and worked with Bechet in New York and Philadelphia. During 1951 he played with Bobby Hackett and in October 1953 reunited once again with Bechet at Storyville, and in 1956 he played with Hackett in several venues. In early 1958 he moved to New York permanently and began working in RED ALLEN's band at the Metropole. That July he played with Bechet on a European tour, and in the summer of 1959 he led his own group at the Arpeggio in New York. Between 1961 and 1963 Dickenson worked with Wild Bill Davison and for five years starting in 1963 co-led the Saints and Sinners with the pianist Red Richards.

Throughout the 1960s he toured with Wein's Newport Jazz Festival All-Stars and also worked occasionally at Eddie Condon's in New York City. In March 1964 he toured Australia, New Zealand, and Japan with a Condon band that included BUCK CLAYTON, Pee Wee Russell, Bud Freeman, and JIMMY RUSHING. The next year he embarked on a solo tour of England and Europe, while stateside

he continued to work with his own Saints and Sinners. Dickenson co-led a popular quintet with Hackett between 1968 and the spring of 1970, when they enjoyed a successful residency at Manhattan's prestigious Roosevelt Grill. At this same time he also began a lengthy association with the World's Greatest Jazz Band, an all-star group that, during Dickenson's tenure from 1970 to 1974, included, among others, Yank Lawson, Billy Butterfield, Hackett, Lou McGarity, Morton, Bob Wilber, and Freeman. In 1973 he worked regularly with Hackett and also appeared with Jimmy McPartland. In March 1975 he worked at the new Eddie Condon's Club and spent the remainder of the decade free-lancing and traveling, appearing at the Newport, Nice, and other jazz festivals. He died at his home in New York City.

During his career, Vic Dickenson participated in close to 300 recording sessions, from his first date with Willie Jones in 1927 through a blinding array of big-name associations that ended with Wilber in 1982. In the early period he played almost exclusively in larger bands, but a few recorded solos stand out, such as "Catch On" (1934) and "I Need Some Lovin'" (1935) with BLANCHE CALLOWAY; "Twinkle Dinkle," "Ja Da," and "Walkin' the Dog" (1937) with Claude Hopkins; "My Favorite Blues" (1941) with Benny Carter; and "I Never Knew," "Louisiana," "Let Me See," "Blow Top," "The World Is Mad," and "Rockin' the Blues" (1940–1941) with Count Basie. Standouts from his first small band dates include "Blues in the Air" and "The Mooche" in 1940 and "After You've Gone," "Bugle Call Rag," and "St. Louis Blues" in 1943 with Sidney Bechet. From 1944 on, though, Dickenson recorded much and in many different settings, most frequently with LOUIS ARMSTRONG (1946–1947), Count Basie (1956, 1977), Ruby Braff (1954–1981), Buck Clayton (1957–1976), Bobby Hackett (1969–1970), Edmond Hall (1943–1958), Eddie Heywood (1944–1946), Art Hodes (1944, 1959), Jimmy McPartland (1950–1977), Pee Wee-Russell (1946–1959), Saints and Sinners (1960–1968), George Wein (1954–1974), and the World's Greatest Jazz Band (1970–1974). He also recorded in groups such as Big Eighteen (1958), Dixieland All Stars (1959), Dixieland at Carnegie Hall (1958), Jazz at Storyville (1951), Jazz from a Swinging Era (1967), Jazz Giants (1956), Manassas Jazz Festival (1969), New York Jazz Repertory Company (1974), Tribute to Louis Armstrong (1974), and Tribute to Bobby Hackett (1980).

Though his style is not easily categorized, it is convenient to think of Dickenson as a Dicky Wells disciple who also had the flexibility to fit in with a variety of mainstream approaches, from so-called Dixieland through modern swing. That he could improvise just as convincingly in relatively traditional settings with such diversely talented giants as Sidney Bechet, Edmond Hall, Pee Wee Russell, and Bobby Hackett as he could in more modern environs with ROY ELDRIDGE, COLEMAN HAWKINS, and LESTER YOUNG speaks eloquently enough for his adaptability. That does not, however, explain the essence of his style, a basic element of which lay in Dickenson's personality. Humor was never very far from the surface in his playing, and to this purpose he used his gruff, sly, insinuating tone, sardonic growls, patented single-note triplets, and invariably imaginative, well-structured lines to advance his agenda of "storytelling." Indeed, where the growl technique of Tricky Sam Nanton was used to marvelously somber and thrilling effect, in Dickenson's hands it took on a wholly different, irreverent, self-parodic character. When he growls, smears, or bends his already shaggy pitch, the listener is frequently compelled to smile, a reaction rarely prompted by other jazz trombonists.

FURTHER READING

Balliett, Whitney. *American Musicians: 56 Portraits in Jazz* (1986).
Dance, Stanley. *The World of Swing* (1974).
McCarthy, Albert. *Big Band Jazz* (1974).
Obituary: *New York Times,* 18 Nov. 1984.

DISCOGRAPHY

Bruyninckx, Walter. *Traditional Jazz Discography, 1897–1988* (6 vols.).
Hilbert, Robert. *Pee Wee Speaks: A Discography of Pee Wee Russell* (1992).
Rust, Brian. *Jazz Records, 1897–1942* (1982).
Selchow, Manfred. *Profoundly Blue: A Bio-Discographical Scrapbook on Edmond Hall* (1988).
This entry is taken from the *American National Biography* and is published here with the permission of the American Council of Learned Societies.

JACK SOHMER

Dickerson, Addie Whiteman (1878–31 May 1940), reformer, businessperson, politician, author, clubwoman, and peace activist, was born Addie Whiteman into one of the best-known families in Wilmington, North Carolina. The sixth child of John H. Whiteman, a drayman, and Hester Leonard Whiteman, she was educated at Gregory Institute and Scotia Seminary (later Barber Scotia College) in Concord, North Carolina. Before moving to Pennsylvania, she taught grammar school in North Carolina. In Philadelphia she attended classes at Temple University and the University of Pennsylvania. In 1908 Whiteman married G. Edward Dickerson, a prominent African American Philadelphia attorney. Their thirty-four-year partnership was active and prosperous. They collaborated on business pursuits, Republican politics, and a variety of civil rights efforts. They had one son, Edmund Whiteman Dickerson, who was born in 1914 but died in infancy.

Building on her time as a teacher, Dickerson actively supported education. She was a cofounder of the Philadelphia Young Woman's Christian Association (YWCA) and often spoke to a range of educational organizations. She served on the advisory boards of many educational institutions, including the Alice Palmer Memorial Institute in Sedalia, North Carolina, and Bethune-Cookman College in Daytona Beach, Florida. She was also a trustee for the FREDERICK DOUGLASS Home in Washington, D.C. Dickerson wrote a number of articles for the *Philadelphia Tribune* on the 1937 National Youth Conference in Washington, D.C. (where she was a delegate), social reform, and African American womanhood, and was the author of "Anti-Slavery Women," and "Status of Negro Women in America."

Keenly interested in social reform, Dickerson was one of the founders of the Federated Women's Club movement in Philadelphia. On the national level she was a prominent member of the National Association of Colored Women (NACW) and was elected auditor and statistician of the organization during the 1920s and 1930s. She was one of the original members of the National Council of Negro Women (NCNW), founded by MARY McLEOD BETHUNE in 1935, and was elected treasurer in 1936. In 1938 Dickerson was part of an NCNW delegation that was invited to the White House to discuss social welfare issues with First Lady Eleanor Roosevelt and the heads of several bureaus, and was one of six women called upon to provide greater insight into the needs of the African American community. As a member of Philadelphia's Central Presbyterian Church, she was also chairperson of the International Council of Church Women.

Dickerson is best known, however, for her involvement in the international peace movement. Using her prominence in Philadelphia society to draw large audiences for discussions on foreign relations, she spoke on behalf of the Women's International League of Peace and Freedom (WILPF) and the American Interracial Peace Committee. She helped found the International Council of Women of the Darker Races (ICWDR), with MARGARET MURRAY WASHINGTON and other prominent NACW women, in 1922 to organize women of color worldwide to focus on three main goals: education, political affairs, and social uplift. At the first meeting, Dickerson was elected Foreign Relations Committee Chair, later called the Committee on International Relations, and was sent to represent the ICWDR as a delegate to the Fourth Pan-African conference in New York City in August 1927. She was elected president of the ICWDR in 1928, a post she held until her death in 1940. In 1929 Dickerson traveled with the clubwoman ADDIE HUNTON to Prague, Czechoslovakia, where they served as delegates to the Congress of the Women's International League of Peace and Freedom. In 1933 she served as part of a WILPF delegation meeting with State Department representatives to protest U.S. military intervention in Liberia.

Less well known are Dickerson's extensive political activities. A lifelong Republican, she was a sought-after speaker on both the local and national levels. In 1930 Dickerson mounted an unsuccessful campaign for the Pennsylvania House of Representatives, advocating old age pensions, equal educational opportunities for every child, equal pay for equal work regardless of race or sex, a civil rights bill, and equal political recognition for African American women. As chair of the Philadelphia Republican Council of Colored Women, she was often on the program of political rallies and shared the rostrum with such noted speakers as OSCAR DE PRIEST, the African American congressman from Chicago, and ROBERT L. VANN, editor of the *Pittsburgh Courier*. During the 1932 presidential campaign Dickerson was tapped to discuss the Republican platform on a CBS national radio program with Mary Emma Woolley, president of Mount Holyoke College. In 1936 she met with the leaders of the Eastern Colored Voters Division of the GOP to plan strategy and was designated a member of the "Flying Squadron"—a group of four female African American women appointed to provide Republican speeches throughout the Mid-Atlantic region. Illness severely curtailed her activities from 1939 until her death a year later.

Addie Dickerson had been a successful real estate broker (and the first female African American notary public in Pennsylvania), specializing in mortgages and real estate transactions in Atlantic City, New Jersey, and in Philadelphia, where she was a member of the Philadelphia Chamber of Commerce. The Dickerson estate, probated upon the death of G. Edward (who passed away four months after his wife), included twenty-seven houses and additional investments valued at forty thousand dollars. The value of the real estate was used to establish the G. Edward and Addie W. Dickerson Foundation, a trust fund designed to aid worthy African American students. Outspoken and steadfast in her beliefs, Dickerson was a leader of Philadelphia's African American political women and her success as a businesswoman afforded her the opportunity to become an advocate for her race and specifically for woman and children. Her activism and influence reached well beyond the boundaries of Philadelphia and included leadership in national organizations and participation at international conferences on peace and social reform.

FURTHER READING

Clift-Pellow, Arlene. "Addie Whiteman Dickerson," in *Notable Black American Women, Book II*, ed. Jessie Carney Smith (1996).

Davis, Elizabeth Lindsay. *Lifting as They Climb* (1933).

Rief, Michelle. "'Banded Close Together': An Afrocentric Study of African American Women's International Activism, 1850–1940, and the International Council of Women of the Darker Races." Ph.D. diss., Temple University, 2003.

Who's Who in Colored America, 5th ed. (1940).

Obituary: *Philadelphia Tribune*, 6 June 1940.

JENNIFER REED FRY

Dickerson, Carroll (1895–Oct. 1957), was a jazz and popular bandleader and violinist. His birthplace, family, and upbringing are unknown. Through the 1920s Dickerson led jazz bands in Chicago, including residencies at the Entertainers' Café in 1921, and Sunset Café from 1922 to 1924, where the cornetist GEORGE MITCHELL and the clarinetist BUSTER BAILEY were among his sidemen, playing for a revue that featured the singer Frankie "Half-Pint" Jaxon. The trombonist HONORE DUTREY and the pianist EARL HINES joined Dickerson's orchestra at the Entertainers' and remained with him when, after the club closed, Dickerson made a forty-two-week tour of the Pantages theater circuit, taking the band to the West Coast and Canada in 1926.

The success of the tour earned Dickerson an engagement in Chicago at the Sunset, where the trumpeter LOUIS ARMSTRONG joined the orchestra. Dickerson sidemen such as Hines and the drummer ZUTTY SINGLETON later participated in Armstrong's Hot Five and Savoy Ballroom Five sessions, which are among the most important recordings in jazz history. Dickerson's excessive drinking led to his firing in February 1927; Armstrong was made nominal leader and Hines the music director. By February 1928 Dickerson had become violinist and conductor in the pianist Clarence M. Jones's band at the Metropolitan Theater, playing alongside Armstrong and Singleton. Jones moved over to the Vendome Theater and then in April, under Dickerson's leadership, the bulk of the group began a residency at Chicago's new Savoy Ballroom. The following month Dickerson's group "tore the roof off the Congress Hotel," according to a review in the *Chicago Defender* (quoted in Collier, 165).

In the spring of 1929 the orchestra left Chicago for New York, with Armstrong as its leader and Dickerson as conductor. Initially it presented the musical revue *Hot Feet*, created by FATS WALLER, Harvey Brooks, and ANDY RAZAF. Beginning in June, Armstrong sprinted nightly between these performances uptown with Dickerson to those at the downtown location for the show at the Hudson Theater, where it acquired its better-known title, *Hot Chocolates*. This show introduced the hit song "Ain't Misbehavin." Dickerson's group also accompanied Armstrong for a week at the Lafayette Theater late in June and the following week recorded "Symphonic Raps" and "Savoyagers' Stomp" under Dickerson's name, with Armstrong and Hines as the featured soloists (replacing the trumpeter Willie Hightower and the pianist Gene Anderson). From the late summer of 1929 Dickerson's group supported Armstrong at Connie's Inn in Harlem for Waller and Razaf's show *Loads of Coal*, a spin-off of *Hot Chocolates* that introduced a new hit, "Honeysuckle Rose."

Armstrong broke away from Dickerson at the end of 1929, and the band quickly unraveled without its star. Dickerson played briefly with the Mills Blues Rhythm Band. Having recorded with KING OLIVER during the first part of 1930, he served as Oliver's manager, conductor, and violinist while they toured with little success through the midwestern and south-central states that spring and summer. He then returned to Chicago, where he led lesser-known bands. In 1934 and 1935 Dickerson's band filled in at the Grand Terrace while the resident group, Earl Hines's big band, was on tour. In this capacity they participated in the 1934 debut of *Rhythm for Sale*, a musical revue created by

the English composer Paul Denniker and the lyricist Razaf. The number of well-respected jazzmen playing with Dickerson during this period—the trumpeters Guy Kelly and Zilner T. Randolph, the trombonists Preston Jackson and Al Wynn, the reed player Franz Jackson, the pianists Charlie Beal and Zinky Cohn, the drummer Zutty Singleton—suggests that this was a fine band, but it never recorded. In 1937 Dickerson temporarily ceased full-time playing. He resumed early in 1939, and during the 1940s he held a long residency at Chicago's Rhumboogie Club. He died in Chicago.

Dickerson was comfortable in styles as different as hot jazz and light classics. According to Hines, Dickerson "was a very strict guy so far as playing instruments was concerned. He wanted everything to be just right." Audiences "had never seen tap dancing and comedy like we had" at the Sunset, Hines said. "For beautiful picture numbers, the producer would find very hard music, like *Black Forest Overture*, *Poet and Peasant Overture* and *Rhapsody in Blue*" (Dance, 40–41, 46). Dickerson's orchestra was prominent in Chicago's nightlife of the 1920s, but it left scarcely any recorded legacy and few published accounts. Hence lasting memories of Dickerson are not for what he did in his own right but for his having nurtured Armstrong and those sidemen who made great music with Armstrong, independent of Dickerson.

FURTHER READING
Dance, Stanley. *The World of Earl Hines* (1977, 1983).
McCarthy, Albert. *Big Band Jazz* (1974).
This entry is taken from the *American National Biography* and is published here with the permission of the American Council of Learned Societies.

BARRY KERNFELD

Dickerson, Earl Burrus (22 June 1891–1 Sept. 1986), lawyer, businessman, civil rights leader, and Chicago alderman, was born in Canton, Mississippi, to Edward Dickerson and Emma Garrett Fielding. Earl Dickerson's maternal grandfather, Benjamin Franklin Garrett, bought his freedom in the 1850s and owned a livery stable as well as several other properties in Canton. His business was destroyed during the Civil War, however, and by the time Earl was born the family lived in relative poverty. Edward Dickerson, who worked away from home as an upholsterer, died when Earl was five and he was raised by his mother, who did laundry for local whites, his paternal half-sister, and his maternal grandmother, who ran a small boarding house in Canton.

In 1906 Dickerson was sent to live with relatives in New Orleans, where he attended the preparatory school of New Orleans University. Unfortunately, family finances forced him to return to Canton in the spring of 1907. Through the efforts of one of his teachers who recognized his potential, he was given the rare opportunity to attend the University of Chicago's Laboratory School that fall. Once again, however, the Dickersons ran out of money after the first year, but this time a series of fortuitous events led to a meeting with the principal of Northwestern University's Evanston Academy, who arranged for Earl to finish high school there. After graduation in 1909 Dickerson worked briefly on Pullman cars out of Chicago and later attended Northwestern University. In 1911 he transferred to the University of Illinois at Champaign-Urbana, but in 1913 broke off his studies to take a job teaching at the Tuskegee Institute led by BOOKER T. WASHINGTON. After a year he returned to Champaign to finish his degree, and in 1915 he accepted a position as the principal of a segregated school in Vincennes, Indiana. The school was badly understaffed and undersupplied, with few textbooks or educational materials. Dickerson was appalled by the substandard conditions under which his students were expected to work. At the end of the term, frustrated by the lack of response to his complaints, he decided to attend law school at the University of Chicago.

During his second year of law school the United States entered World War I, and Dickerson was accepted to a segregated officer's candidate school at Fort Sheridan, Illinois. Dickerson, who reached the rank of lieutenant, served in France as an interpreter and later saw action in the Argonne Forest with the Ninety-second Division. Like many returning African American soldiers, he was acutely aware of the respectful way the French treated him in contrast to his experience of racism in America. When he returned to Chicago and his studies at law school he was a changed man—angry about the lack of opportunity for African Americans and committed to fighting racism.

In the spring of 1919 Dickerson attended the founding congress of the American Legion, in St. Louis, and was instrumental in fighting the proposed segregation of African American posts. Dickerson received his law degree from the University of Chicago in 1920, but, although he was a top student, he was unable to find a job with any of the law firms in Chicago, and was forced to open his own office. In 1920 he was hired as legal counsel for the newly formed Supreme Liberty Life Insurance Company, the first African American legal reserve life insurance company in the North. Dickerson remained with Supreme Liberty throughout his professional career and later became its president and CEO. Dickerson was appointed to the board of the Chicago Urban League in 1925 and became chairman of the NAACP's legal redress committee in 1926. In 1933 he was appointed as an assistant attorney general for the state of Illinois and argued several cases before the Illinois Supreme Court.

In 1931 Dickerson ran as the Democratic candidate for alderman of Chicago's Second Ward against William E. King. This was a period when the African American vote was beginning to swing away from the Republican Party, and Dickerson was instrumental in this shift when he became the first Democratic alderman of the predominantly black ward and the first black Democratic alderman in Chicago. In that post Dickerson proved himself to be a hardnosed activist whose primary concerns were jobs, housing, and education for black Chicagoans at a time when the African American population of the city was growing at an exceptional rate and when the effects of racism and segregation were intensifying poverty and overcrowding. Money for New Deal programs was slow to reach the black population in Chicago and Dickerson fought tirelessly to meet the needs of an increasingly desperate African American community. Unfortunately Dickerson's unswerving activism and his distaste for compromising with party bosses led to his losing reelection in 1943. In 1942 Dickerson had run in the primary for a U.S. congressional seat against WILLIAM LEVI DAWSON (1886–1970); Dickerson lost, largely for the same reasons. These events effectively marked the end of Dickerson's political career in Chicago.

In 1941 the United States entered World War II, and Dickerson was appointed to President Roosevelt's first Fair Employment Practice Committee (FEPC), which sought to guarantee minority participation in the economic boom generated by the war effort. Once again Dickerson proved himself to be an outspoken activist who found it impossible to compromise with racist, exclusionary practices. As a member of the FEPC Dickerson participated in hearings with industrial leaders and union bosses around the country, during which he never hesitated to point out discriminatory policies and demand that they be eradicated from all government contract jobs immediately, without any regard for political finesse. He made a particular stir in June 1942 in Birmingham, Alabama, where, as a black man representing the federal government, his aggressive cross-examination of white industrialists and union leaders was unprecedented. Dickerson was not subsequently reappointed to the second FEPC in 1943.

Dickerson is perhaps best known for having argued and won *Hansberry v. Lee* before the U.S. Supreme Court in 1940. This groundbreaking case challenged a racially restrictive covenant in Chicago, which prevented African Americans from buying property in the predominantly white Woodlawn neighborhood. Carl Hansberry arranged with Dickerson, who, as legal counsel for the Supreme Liberty Life Insurance Company, secured a mortgage from the company for Hansberry to purchase property in the restricted area knowing that this would lead to a lawsuit. After losing in the lower courts the case was heard before the U.S. Supreme Court, which on 12 November 1940 decided in Hansberry's favor. Although the *Hansberry v. Lee* case was won on a technical point of law and did not eradicate racially restrictive covenants in principle, it was still an important victory and set the stage for the 1948 *Shelley v. Kraemer* case, which effectively put an end to all such discriminatory contracts by making them non-actionable. Carl Hansberry was the father of LORRAINE HANSBERRY, whose play *A Raisin in the Sun* gives a highly-fictionalized account of these events.

In the long run Dickerson's most important accomplishments may well have been with the Supreme Liberty Life Insurance Company. Dickerson was elected president and CEO of Supreme Liberty on 4 October 1955 after serving the company for over thirty-five years. In Dickerson's view, full social, legal, and political equality for African Americans could never be won without accompanying economic stability, and this could only be achieved when black-owned businesses could compete in the mainstream of American economic life. Dickerson always stressed that Supreme Liberty's mission was to help achieve this end by supplying capital to the black community through policies, loans, and mortgages that would produce long-term economic opportunity. In this way Dickerson hoped to point the way for other successful black-owned companies. Dickerson was an outspoken civil rights activist and a friend to such illustrious black leftists as W. E. B. DuBois and PAUL ROBESON, but he was also a committed capitalist who believed firmly that without concrete economic prospects the African American community would remain excluded from real opportunity and a reasonable hope for prosperity.

In 1944, twenty-four years after he earned his law degree, Dickerson was called before the board of the Chicago Bar Association after he applied—as a manner of protest—for membership in the then-segregated organization. Because of his civil rights activism and his association with the political left, the question was posed "Are you a communist?" Dickerson replied:

> As I understand communists, particularly in Russia, they don't mind being dominated by a few men at the top. Also the communist state takes over all private property. The test is this: In practicing law I have accumulated a few funds and pieces of property; if any one of you were to undertake to deprive me of that property, you would find out whether I am a communist. (Earl Dickerson's recollection from a taped interview with Robert Blakely in 1983.)

FURTHER READING

Dickerson's papers are housed at the Chicago Historical Society, Chicago, Illinois.

Blakely, Robert J., with Marcus A. Shepard. *Earl B. Dickerson: A Voice for Freedom and Equality* (2005).

Finkelman, Paul, ed. *African Americans and the Legal Profession in Historical Perspective* (1992).

Grimshaw, William J. *Bitter Fruit: Black Politics and the Chicago Machine 1931–1991* (1992).

MARCUS SHEPARD

Dickerson, Eric Demetric (2 Sept. 1960–), football player, was born in Sealy, Texas, to Richard Seal and Helen Johnson, both high school sophomores. With his biological parents just sixteen years old at the time of his birth, Dickerson was adopted and raised by the two people he would consider his parents: Kary Dickerson, a railroad track worker, and Helen's great-aunt, Viola. Dickerson was fourteen years old when he learned that Helen, whom he had believed was his sister, was actually his mother. Dickerson showed a propensity for athletics at an early age, starring in football, basketball, and track at Sealy High School. Though he won the state championship for the 100-yard dash in track his senior year, it was his football exploits that garnered him national attention: *Parade* magazine named him America's top high school running back his senior year in 1978, and he helped lead his high school team to the state division title. College coaches looking to recruit Dickerson were a constant presence in the small town, and he often stayed at friends' houses to avoid the pressure. With numerous scholarship offers pouring in, Dickerson initially preferred the University of Oklahoma, but